THE OXFORD HA

THE SOCIAL SCIENCE OF POVERTY

THE OXFORD HANDBOOK OF

THE SOCIAL SCIENCE OF POVERTY

Edited by

DAVID BRADY

and

LINDA M. BURTON

OXFORD

UNIVERSITY PRESS

OXFORD
UNIVERSITY PRESS

Oxford University Press is a department of the University of Oxford. It furthers
the University's objective of excellence in research, scholarship, and education
by publishing worldwide.Oxford is a registered trade mark of Oxford University
Press in the UK and certain other countries.

Published in the United States of America by Oxford University Press
198 Madison Avenue, New York, NY 10016, United States of America.

© Oxford University Press 2016

First Edition published in 2016

First issued as an Oxford University Press paperback, 2019

Library of Congress Cataloging-in-Publication Data
Names: Brady, David, 1972– editor. | Burton, Linda, 1954– editor.
Title: The Oxford handbook of the social science of poverty / edited by David Brady and Linda M. Burton.
Description: New York, NY: Oxford University Press, [2016] | Includes bibliographical references and index.
Identifiers: LCCN 2015019762 | ISBN 978–0–19–991405–0 (hardcover: alk. paper) |
ISBN 978–0–19–094736–1 (paperback: alk. paper)
Subjects: LCSH: Poverty. | Poverty—Social aspects. | Social justice.
Classification: LCC HC79.P6 O974 2016 | DDC 305.5/69—dc23 LC record available at
http://lccn.loc.gov/2015019762

Contents

SECTION I CONCEPTS, THEORIES, AND ORIENTING QUESTIONS

SECTION II CLASSIC DEBATES

SECTION III PLACE AND CONTEXT

SECTION IV CAUSES AND THE
REPRODUCTION OF POVERTY

SECTION V CONSEQUENCES

SECTION VI POLICIES, SOLUTIONS, AND RESPONSES

FOREWORD: THOSE LEFT BEHIND

CAROL B. STACK

MIDWINTER, back in the late 1990s, I was sitting with a group of graduate students from the University of Naples, Federico, one of the world's oldest universities. The young sociologists leaning together over a venerable round table at a cafe near the corner of Piazza Plebiscito had been studying racism and the sociology of poverty in the United States. Over endless cappuccinos they did not hesitate to fault America's lack of universal healthcare and the absence of a commitment to the social welfare of its citizens. Yet, these students asked me during their indictment of the United States and with a turn to uncertainty and somehow expecting me to have an answer: "Why did Italy endure centuries of persistent poverty in the Naples ghetto and elsewhere in the country? Apart from the surge of global immigrants to Naples, centuries of Italian families faced persistent poverty, and as Edmondo, one of the students, told me, "We do not have racism to blame."

I did not have an answer to their query. Poverty lingers, even in rich countries and is holding steady or getting more severe among countries that provide substantial assistance within a welfare state. Even with the aid of the welfare state, most poor families remain poor. These structural factors remain a constant reminder of how important this interdisciplinary and comparative collection of chapters authored by global scholars is to poverty research. This *Handbook* provides a basis for a global discourse on poverty. These scholars ask questions beyond the local and beyond the urban that challenge us to scrutinize new frames of analysis. They ask us to observe poverty through the lenses of time and space and across generations. They follow population movements and particular social experiments and policy assumptions through a global hologram. And, they demand that we pay attention to social policies and practices that shape and are shaped by many actors, and policies that require us to ponder intractable social forces that create greater equality in some nation states and not in others.

Many of the authors in this volume chose to focus on the structural violence of poverty from the time they were young scholars, and over the decades they continued to pay attention amid the tensions of evolving time and space. We learn as we read through this volume that the ideologies about the poor and what they need, and how they need to change, but have not changed much despite the tenacity and vigilance of scholars who have entered into the fray and never left the scene. At the same time that the scholars who penned these pages have broadened their lenses and advocated globally for greater attention to poverty, they have often found themselves as public intellectuals occasionally trapped within some of the same stifling and paradoxical language and structures they critiqued in the early days of their careers. Yet these authors persist as the consequences of poverty deepen, as many of the same old debates grow new teeth, and in the face of the global context of racial and ethnic disparities, immigration, deportation, refugees, early morbidity and mortality, asylum, hunger, gender inequities, and criminalization. With intelligence, and for some, with decades of dedication, the authors in this *Handbook* collectively and individually are making some headway, bringing new and compelling questions into the conversation. Their contributions insist on interdisciplinarity and together they are building a conversation across countries and disciplines that unearths the commonality and complementarity of the scholarship of poverty in the United States, other rich democracies, and developing countries.

Back to Edmondo and his colleagues at the cafe in Naples. During a month of conversations he began to teach me as he taught himself that the ghetto poor in Naples had worked and served at the bottom rung of society for centuries for a pittance, and the niche they occupied slowly had quickly disappeared, like quicksand, with new immigrant workers who lacked a voice, who lacked citizenship, and did the "dirty work" in their place. This worldwide phenomenon has framed a new narrative on poverty. But the old narrative and the people left behind by staying in place still lack a permanent solution.

LIST OF CONTRIBUTORS

Ronald J. Angel, Professor of Sociology, University of Texas, Austin.

Christopher Barrett, Stephen B. and Janice G. Ashley Professor of Applied Economics and Management; and David J. Nolan Director of the Charles H. Dyson School of Applied Economics and Management, Cornell University.

Max Besbris, PhD Student in Sociology, New York University.

Sambit Bhattacharyya, Senior Lecturer in Economics, University of Sussex.

Agnes Blome, Research Fellow in the Inequality and Social Policy Department, WZB Berlin Social Science Center.

Natascia Boeri, PhD Student in Sociology, Graduate Center, City University of New York.

Francois Bonnet, Assistant Research Professor, National Center for Scientific Research (CNRS) France.

David Brady, Professor of Public Policy and Director of the Blum Initiative on Global and Regional Poverty, University of California-Riverside; and Fellow at the WZB Berlin Social Science Center.

Heather E. Bullock, Professor and Chair of Psychology, University of California-Santa Cruz.

Tania Burchardt, Deputy Director of CASE and Senior Lecturer of Social Policy, London School of Economics and Political Science.

Linda M. Burton, Dean of Social Sciences and James B. Duke Professor of Sociology, Duke University.

Sandra K. Danziger, Professor of Social Work; and Research Professor of Public Policy, University of Michigan.

Paul Farmer, Kolokotrones University Professor of Global Health and Social Medicine, Harvard University.

Simon Feeny, Associate Professor of Economics, RMIT University.

Liana Fox, Postdoctoral Fellow, Swedish Institute for Social Research (SOFI), University of Stockholm.

Michael Friedson, Postdoctoral Fellow, New York University.

Jérôme Gautié, Professor of Economics, University of Paris.

Christina M. Gibson-Davis, Associate Professor of Public Policy, Psychology and Neuroscience, and Sociology, Duke University.

Janet C. Gornick, Director of Luxembourg Income Study Center; and Professor of Political Science and Sociology, Graduate Center, City University of New York.

Emily Hannum, Associate Professor of Sociology and Education, University of Pennsylvania.

Rod Hick, Lecturer in Social Policy, University of Cardiff.

Matthew O. Hunt, Professor and Chair of Sociology, Northeastern University.

Markus Jäntti, Professor of Economics, Swedish Institute for Social Research (SOFI), Stockholm University.

Rosanne M. Jocson, PhD Student in Psychology, University of Michigan.

Peter A. Kemp, Vice Dean for Academic Affairs, and Professor of Public Policy, University of Oxford.

Hanna Kleider, Assistant Professor of Political Science, University of Georgia.

Inhoe Ku, Professor of Social Welfare, Seoul National University.

Elyse Kovalsky, Ph.D. Student in Sociology, Northwestern University.

Anirudh Krishna, Edgar T. Thompson Professor of Public Policy, Duke University.

Basak Kus, Assistant Professor of Sociology, Wesleyan University.

Jennifer Laird, PhD Student in Sociology, University of Washington.

Cheol-Sung Lee, Associate Professor for Sociology, University of Chicago.

Laura Lein, Katherine Reebel Collegiate Professor of Social Work; Dean and Professor of Social Work; and Professor of Anthropology, University of Michigan.

Daniel T. Lichter, Director of Cornell Population Center; Ferris Family Professor of Life Course Studies; Professor of Policy Analysis and Management; and Professor of Sociology, Cornell University.

Erin C. Lentz, Assistant Professor of Public Affairs, LBJ School of Public Affairs, University of Texas, Austin.

Philip Mader, Researcher in Sociology, University of Basel.

Douglas S. Massey, Henry G. Bryant Professor of Sociology and Public Affairs, Princeton University.

Mark McGillivray, Research Professor in International Development, Deakin University.

Vonnie C. McLoyd, Ewart A. C. Thomas Collegiate Professor of Psychology, University of Michigan.

Lorraine C. Minnite, Assistant Professor of Public Policy and Administration, Rutgers University.

Brian Nolan, Professor of Social Policy, and Director of Employment, Equity, and Growth Programme, University of Oxford.

Alice O'Connor, Professor of History, University of California-Santa Barbara.

Mary Pattillo, Harold Washington Professor of Sociology and African American Studies, Northwestern University.

Frances Fox Piven, Distinguished Professor of Political Science, Graduate Center, City University of New York.

Sophie Ponthieux, Senior Researcher, INSEE, Crest, University of Paris.

Mark R. Rank, Herbert S. Hadley Professor of Social Welfare, Washington University-St. Louis.

John N. Robinson III, PhD Student in Sociology, Northwestern University.

Jake Rosenfeld, Associate Professor of Sociology, Washington University-St. Louis.

Barbara Rylko-Bauer, Adjunct Associate Professor of Anthropology, Michigan State University.

Kai A. Schafft, Associate Professor of Education and Director of the Penn State Center on Rural Education and Communities, The Pennsylvania State University.

Sandra Susan Smith, Associate Professor of Sociology, University of California, Berkeley.

H. Luke Shaefer, Associate Professor of Social Work, University of Michigan.

Patrick Sharkey, Associate Professor of Sociology, New York University.

Timothy M. Smeeding, Arts and Sciences Distinguished Professor of Public Affairs and Economics, University of Wisconsin, Madison.

Carol B. Stack, Professor Emeritus, Education, Women's Studies, and Anthropology, University of California, Berkeley.

Jessi Streib, Assistant Professor of Sociology, Duke University.

Amanda Tillotson, PhD Student in Social Work, University of Michigan.

Florencia Torche, Associate Professor of Sociology, New York University.

Guillermo Trejo, Associate Professor Political Science, University of Notre Dame and Faculty Fellow at the Kellogg Institute for International Studies.

Sudhir Venkatesh, Williams B. Ransford Professor of Sociology, Columbia University.

SaunJuhi Verma, Assistant Professor in School of Management and Labor Relations, Rutgers University.

Robert H. Wade, Professor of Political Economy and Development, London School of Economics and Political Science.

Jane Waldfogel, Compton Foundation Centennial Professor of Social Work for the Prevention of Children's and Youth Problems; and Professor of Public Affairs, Columbia University.

Celeste Watkins-Hayes, Associate Professor of Sociology and African American Studies, Northwestern University.

Whitney Welsh, Research Scientist, The Social Science Research Institute, Duke University.

Christopher T. Whelan, Emeritus Professor of Sociology and Senior Fellow at the Geary Institute for Public Policy, University College Dublin.

Abigail B. Williams, PhD Student in Psychology, University of Michigan.

William Julius Wilson, Lewis P. and Linda L. Geyser University Professor of Public Policy and Sociology, Harvard University.

Yu Xie, Bert G. Kerstetter '66 University Professor of Sociology and the Princeton Institute for International and Regional Studies (PIIRS) and Director of the Center on Contemporary China, Princeton University.

CHAPTER 1

....

INTRODUCTION

....

DAVID BRADY AND LINDA M. BURTON

It almost goes without saying that poverty is one of the world's most persistent and unresolved social problems. Poverty's history is mired in paradoxes and puzzles, failures, complex social changes, and unsettling individual and group behaviors. Politicians and policymakers often apply meek partial solutions to address poverty while simultaneously positioning themselves to claim absolution when their solutions fail (Edelman 2013). The stewards of humanitarianism, through their work in non-profit, philanthropic, and religious organizations, stridently seek to meet the needs of the poor but are frequently constrained in what they can accomplish by inhospitable or indifferent political economic contexts. Meanwhile, public sentiments often take form as adversarial dialogues about the deserving and underdeserving poor (Gans 1994). While many publically admonish poverty, they often implicitly engage in a variety of generic social behaviors that reproduce socioeconomic disadvantage among specific populations across space, time, race, and generations (Schwalbe et al. 2000).

Scholars are also not exempt from contributing to unresolved issues regarding poverty. For far too long, the social science of poverty has been fractured and fragmented. There is a rich tradition of research on urban poverty in the United States, however this literature rarely engages with research on rural poverty even within the United States (Burton et al. 2013; Lichter and Schafft this volume). Poverty research on the United States broadly neglects the study of poverty in other rich democracies (Brady 2009). The literature on poverty across rich democracies rarely engages with the study of poverty in developing countries. At the same time, scholars of poverty in developing countries seem to exist as a separate community from scholars studying poverty in the United States or Europe.

The segregation across disciplines is perhaps even more striking. Political scientists and sociologists often complain that economists fail to cite (or even read) their research. There is some basis for this critique as economists studying poverty often operate without connection to other disciplines. However, sociologists often neglect poverty researchers in the fields of social work and anthropology. Psychologists, anthropologists, and social work scholars rarely fully incorporate the structural and institutional contexts that many sociologists emphasize. Compared to the other social sciences, political scientists simply do not study poverty as much (especially in comparison to their interest in studying inequality more broadly). The entire field of poverty studies has not sufficiently incorporated the insights of historians.

Across disciplines, there are often parallel perspectives and concepts that do not share comparable nomenclature. As a result, poverty research is segmented into academic silos that rarely engage in conversations with each other. Advances in one segment of the poverty literature go unnoticed by other segments. Other times, disciplines take contrasting positions from each other without being aware they are doing so. Worse still, many proceed as if other highly relevant fields have made no contributions to understanding poverty at all. As a result, the field revisits and rehashes debates with insufficient progress from, or even awareness of, prior debates (Katz 1989; O'Connor 2001). Questions are framed as new in one field, even though the same questions have been thoroughly addressed in another field. Provocative arguments are routinely made even though extensive research in other areas contradicts their claims or even premises. Case studies are often not contextualized relative to the meso- or macro-level institutions and structures in which they are embedded. Consequently, scholars do not seem to be reflexive as to what generalizations they can or cannot make. Cross-national comparisons often lack an appreciation of meaning and place, and therefore conclusions reached from these studies feel disconnected from people on the ground. Like many other fields, and with some notable exceptions, qualitative and quantitative researchers often fail to genuinely engage each other.

Progress in methods, data, and theory in one country are not taken up by scholars in other countries. Even if economists ignore sociologists, it is equally problematic that American sociologists often act as if the United States is the only country in the world. Sociologists of poverty routinely fail to acknowledge their research is U.S.-specific and typically do not build on scholarship from other countries. The United States is not a universal case, and lessons from the United States may not apply to other countries (Brady and Burroway 2012). Indeed, as Henrich and colleagues (2010:74) write in their masterful review of ethnocentrism in behavioral science samples, "Americans are, on average, the most individualistic people in the world." It is equally plausible that poverty scholarship based on rich democracies might not be generalizable to the majority of the world's population. Henrich and colleagues (2010:61) even conclude that rich democracies provide "among the least representative populations one could find for generalizing about humans." Partly because of biases from concentrating solely on the United States, U.S. scholars often speak of the "intractability" and "persistence" of poverty.[1] The problem is that they neglect the clear progress other rich democracies have actually made in reducing poverty. Brady and Destro (2014) refer to this bias as the "fallacy of intractability." The lack of international integration in poverty research is so apparent that Michael Katz (1989:238) wrote in his classic *The Undeserving Poor*, "Indeed, European scholars often find American approaches to poverty, including those of the most respected social scientists, bizarre."[2]

At the end of the day, the siloing of these various approaches to studying poverty does not make sense. We argue that such fragmentation is counterproductive for understanding poverty. In many ways, and with so much potential human capital invested, it is unfortunate that despite more than a century of rigorous social science research on poverty, there is a demonstrative lack of integration and accumulation.

This volume intends to counter these prevailing tendencies toward segregation and fragmentation in poverty scholarship. We aim to integrate the social sciences of poverty and to advance genuine interdisciplinary and international dialogue in poverty research. We seek common ground in the study of poverty, and a broader awareness of the distinctive valuable contributions of different types of poverty research. We do so by having collected a diverse set of chapters penned by an even more diverse set of scholars. The chapters provide a state-of-the-art compilation of salient debates across the social sciences of poverty. We incorporate influential theories and concepts regarding poverty worldwide, and summarize and review contemporary social science on many central topics in poverty research. We view this handbook as representing the expertise and knowledge of diverse communities of scholars. Therefore, we aim for the volume to serve as a foundation for a comprehensive social science of poverty.

Henceforth, we summarize the themes of the volume and contents of the chapters. Before doing so, we situate our volume relative to the prior literature. In particular, we discuss precisely how our volume integrates the diverse field of poverty research. We also discuss how the prior literature has not fully accomplished such integration.

THE CASE FOR INTERNATIONAL INTERDISCIPLINARITY IN THE SOCIAL SCIENCES OF POVERTY

We do not believe there should or ever could be one social science of poverty. We also understand the caution and skepticism against strong programs of unification. There is a possible danger that unifying all the social sciences of poverty will have a homogenizing and dulling effect that constrains and weakens the field. We also agree that the diversity of poverty scholarship is a strength and that the heterogeneity of theory, method, and perspective is a valuable asset. Therefore, we seek to make clear that we do not believe all the social sciences of poverty should look the same.

Instead, this volume was designed following the premise that greater strides could occur if the social sciences of poverty were more integrated in their thinking, more aware of one another, and more engaged in reciprocal dialogue. As editors, our experience of putting this volume together has clearly broadened and deepened our knowledge of poverty through identifying and recruiting diverse authors and by jointly reading and reviewing each chapter. Perhaps, if we had known when we launched this project how diverse the poverty literature actually was, we might have never pursued this ambition. Nonetheless, our experience confirms that poverty scholars in different areas can learn a great deal by reading the various strands of knowledge integrated in the chapters in this volume. We now know this to be a truism rather than conjecture: Poverty research can advance considerably if scholars genuinely engage with other disciplines and with scholars in other countries.

Our conviction for interdisciplinary research on poverty is strengthened by the fact that there have been some previous successful efforts of integration in poverty research. For example, in the 1990s, a few rich interdisciplinary literatures on poverty emerged. One genuinely interdisciplinary body of work focused on neighborhood poverty (e.g. Duncan et al. 1997; Jencks and Peterson 1991). Another focused on the consequences of child poverty and included the contributions of psychologists, economists, sociologists, human development scholars, education researchers, and other fields of inquiry (e.g., Duncan and Brooks-Gunn 1997; Huston 1991). Unfortunately, these literatures were predominantly focused on the United States, and these debates tended not to include international research. Nevertheless, simply by being interdisciplinary, considerable intellectual progress resulted.

Another area where poverty research has been fairly international, interdisciplinary, and incorporated rich and poor countries is poverty measurement. This partly reflects the efforts of international organizations, like the World Bank, European Commission, and the Organization for Economic Cooperation and Development (OECD), which have convened scholars and practitioners and put the social sciences to work monitoring poverty. Equally important have been the data infrastructure efforts of international organizations like the Luxembourg Income Study (LIS) (Rainwater and Smeeding 2004). Perhaps as much as any other organization in the world, the LIS has advanced the internationalization of poverty research. To be sure, much of poverty measurement, especially in the United States, lags behind European scholarship in this area and uses provincial or problematic measures (see chapter by Smeeding in this volume; Brady 2009). Nonetheless, serious scholars of poverty measurement have moved in the right direction. As one example, the Spring 2010 issue of the *Journal of Policy Analysis and Management* was a special issue on international poverty measurement (Couch and Pirog 2010). Included were chapters on the distributional impact of in-kind public benefits in Europe; asset-based measures with the cross-national Luxembourg Wealth Study (by our volume author Smeeding); social exclusion in global context; material deprivation in Europe (by our volume authors Nolan and Whelan); the regressive consequences of indirect taxes in Europe; and poverty dynamics in India and other countries (by our volume author Krishna). This special issue is an encouraging signal of what can be accomplished if poverty scholars cross national and disciplinary boundaries.

Indeed, the value of diversity in the social science of poverty is exemplified by the outstanding collection of authors featured in this volume. Our authors include a wide variety of disciplines: African American studies, anthropology, child development, demography, development studies, education, economics, global health, history, international development, management and labor relations, medicine, political science, psychology, public policy, social policy, social work, sociology, statistics, and women's studies. Though there are a considerable number of sociologists in the volume, and both editors are sociologists, nonsociologists are present in more than half the chapters. Economists are also present in nearly half the chapters. What is more, we were able to enlist authors working in or originating from a large number of different countries, including Australia, Chile, China, Finland, France, Germany, India, Ireland, Mexico, the Netherlands, the Philippines, South Korea, Sweden, Switzerland, the UK, and the United States. About half the chapters have at least one author from outside the United States, and about one-third include an expert on developing countries. Of course, we do not cover every possible salient question or theory on poverty, nor do we have representatives from every country in the world. Nevertheless, we have had the good fortune of including a truly heterogeneous group of scholars from many different countries and representing the remarkable diversity of the social sciences of poverty.

We charged this set of authors with three common criteria. We required every chapter to (1) be interdisciplinary, (2) be international, and (3) integrate scholarship on rich countries and countries in the developing world. Admittedly, not every single chapter perfectly fulfills all criteria. Some chapters do focus disproportionately on the United States, and some chapters do lean toward one discipline. Every chapter, however, accomplishes these three criteria on some level. Moreover, the majority of the chapters do come quite close to genuinely addressing and balancing all three criteria. In addition, the volume holistically integrates the social science of poverty by covering many different topics and areas. Thus, while a given chapter might concentrate most on developing countries, other chapters devote greater attention to rich democracies. While some chapters use economics as a baseline, others are motivated by fields quite distinct from economics. Therefore, the volume is designed to achieve these three criteria through the cumulative and interacting contributions of all chapters. We expect the whole is greater than the sum of the individual parts.

Returning to the issue of fragmentation raised at the outset of this chapter, we stress that international and interdisciplinary integration has not yet been fully realized in the poverty literature.[3] To the best of our knowledge, no volume integrates the international social sciences of poverty in the way we do. By that, we mean that there are very few handbooks of poverty research with a truly interdisciplinary and international approach, and with attention to both rich and developing countries. Therefore, this handbook addresses a noteworthy lacuna in the field.

To demonstrate this point, consider several of the most influential recent edited volumes on poverty. Among the volumes that seek to study poverty comprehensively, Jefferson's (2012) *The Oxford Handbook of the Economics of Poverty* assembles an impressive group of scholars. This volume, however, focuses mostly on the United States and does not address the international literature systematically. As is clear from its title, it concentrates only on the discipline of economics, and the vast majority of authors are economists. Crane and Heaton's (2008) *Handbook of Families and Poverty* is interdisciplinary and analyzes poverty in diverse populations. However, the predominant approach used is family demography, and the focus is on contemporary U.S. families. Bannerjee and colleagues (2006) produced a rich and important volume, which is quite international and has some similar goals to our volume (also Bebbington et al. 2008). Nonetheless, their volume concentrates on poverty in developing countries, and all the authors appear to be economists. Some recent and more focused volumes also deserve mention. For example, Grusky and Kanbur's (2006) *Poverty and Inequality* includes state-of-the-art literature reviews and is international. However, the volume achieves interdisciplinarity by contrasting the perspectives solely of economists and sociologists. Similarly, Devine and Waters' (2004) *Social Inequalities in Comparative Perspective* collects essays and empirical pieces on social inequality in different countries, but each chapter focuses on one country rather than on broader themes across countries. Although both volumes include eminent scholars discussing central themes in poverty research, these anthologies do not have the scope of our volume.

Perhaps most visible are a series of volumes linked to the Institute of Research on Poverty at the University of Wisconsin. The volumes represent a collection of state-of-the-art science on poverty. The most recent example is *Changing Poverty, Changing Policies*, edited by Cancian and Danziger (2009). This series is consistently rigorous and provides an excellent set of scholarly resources. Yet, these volumes focus almost exclusively on the contemporary United States, neglect other rich democracies, and have no discussion of developing countries. For example, Danziger and colleagues' (1994) collection contains no chapters explicitly focused on or comparing non-U.S. countries. Only 1 of 15 chapters in Danziger and Haveman (2001) places U.S. poverty in comparative perspective. In that chapter, Smeeding (one of our volume authors) and his colleagues (2001) stress that U.S. poverty research "rests on an inherently parochial foundation, for it is based on the experiences of only one nation" (p. 162). In Cancian and Danziger (2009), only 2 of 14 chapters devote any attention to non-U.S. countries. One chapter by our volume author Markus Jäntti (2009) compares U.S. mobility patterns to other rich democracies. Another chapter, by Meyer and Wallace (2009) analyzes trends in U.S. poverty and spends about 15 percent of its space comparing those trends to other countries. In addition, these volumes include only a marginal presence of disciplines besides economics and public policy. At most, one psychologist or social work scholar is included, but all the remaining contributors are from economics and public policy.[4]

If there is one volume that has previously accomplished most of the goals we set out to achieve, it may be McFate and colleagues' 1995 volume *Poverty, Inequality, and the Future of Social Policy*. Their volume is interdisciplinary, including economists, sociologists, political scientists, demographers, and ethnographers, among others. The volume also incorporates many countries, and almost every chapter is international and comparative. The chapters that are not comparative predominantly focus on countries outside the United States. The volume, however, does not incorporate less developed countries and only examines the "Western" countries of North America and Europe. In addition, even though the volume was a major contribution, it has been 20 years since it was published and about 25 since many of the chapters were written.

In sum, the prior literature has not fully realized our goal of a volume that genuinely integrates the international social sciences of poverty. Though fine volumes have been edited by others, most are confined to one discipline, and most focus either on the United States or developing countries. There is a tangible absence of integration across national boundaries, between rich and poor countries, and across the social sciences. This volume aims to address that need.

THEMES OF THE VOLUME

Our volume is organized into six sections: (1) concepts, theories, and orienting questions; (2) classic debates; (3) place and context; (4) causes and the reproduction of poverty; (5) consequences; and, (6) policies, solutions, and responses. The first section focuses on the big picture questions, leading explanations and definitions of poverty, and how people, including the poor, understand poverty. The second comprises chapters about the enduring concerns, recurring paradoxes, and long-standing discussions that have oriented the field. The third analyzes how geography, spatial context, and location shape the nature, causes, and consequences of poverty. The fourth considers the social forces generating poverty and how those forces are often themselves reciprocally reinforced by poverty. The fifth examines how poverty shapes, harms, and constrains people's lives and life chances. And, the sixth section reviews how poverty has been addressed, and what has worked and could work to alleviate poverty and its consequences. Every chapter includes a state-of-the-art review of the literature. In addition, chapters narrate the evolution of the field and point readers toward where the field is headed. Each chapter raises questions, identifies problems and gaps in the literature, and evaluates what has been learned and what needs to be learned.

SUMMARY OF CHAPTERS

Section I: Concepts, Theories, and Orienting Questions

In Chapter 2, Smeeding discusses the measurement of poverty. Smeeding convincingly demonstrates that measurement is an essential first step in the study of poverty. He defines poverty as having too few resources to participate fully in society. He discusses the origins and contemporary practices of poverty measurement across different countries and disciplines. Smeeding considers measures based on a various economic resources (e.g., income or wealth) and assesses absolute, relative, and anchored measures. He then displays patterns and trends in poverty with different measures across a variety of countries. Smeeding provides a definitive guide for how different poverty measures perform and informs social scientists for how best to measure poverty.

Rylko-Bauer and Farmer present the theory of structural violence in Chapter 3. This theory emerges from the fields of anthropology and medicine and has been highly influential in the international social sciences. Structural violence entails the consequences of unequal and unjust social structures that work in combination to marginalize and undermine the disadvantaged. In contrast to individualistic accounts, they emphasize structures that "violently" lead to death, harm, and suffering for groups experiencing common forms of oppression. Tracing structural violence's history and application in different disciplines, they place importance on history and context and the interdependence of structural factors.

Hick and Burchardt's Chapter 4 focuses on the concept of capability deprivation. This approach was initially developed by Amartya Sen as a way to conceptualize and measure poverty. Critiquing income-centric understandings of poverty, capability deprivation focuses not just be on what people *have* but also on what they can *do* and *be*. The authors present and assess the key concepts that comprise the capability approach—functionings and capabilities—and discuss what the approach means for concepts of well-being. They also review empirical applications inspired by the capability approach and assess the central questions for employing the capability approach.

In Chapter 5, Hunt and Bullock examine what people believe about the causes of poverty. Their analysis revisits and builds on Kluegel and Smith's classic essay on ideology and beliefs about social stratification. Like Kluegel and Smith, they focus on four topics: (1) what people believe about poverty, (2) selected social psychological processes governing the *intra*personal organization of poverty beliefs, (3) various factors shaping patterns of belief, and (4) selected consequences that beliefs about poverty hold for the person and for politics.

Chapter 6, by Brady, Blome, and Kleider, presents the political and institutional sources of poverty. They argue that poverty is fundamentally shaped by the combination of power resources (mobilized class-based collective political actors) and institutions (formal rules, regulations, and arrangements). Within each of power resources and institutions, they explain core arguments and key concepts, and review recent empirical research. They contend state policy plays a key mediating role between politics/institutions and poverty, and catalog a set of six generic mechanisms for how state policies matter to poverty. They also diagnose the challenges facing power resources and institutional explanations, and outline broader methodological issues for research on the political and institutional sources of poverty.

Human development and the life course are the topics of McLoyd, Jocson and Williams' Chapter 7. Building on the research agenda evolving from the United States in the 1980s, scholars have studied the effects of the duration, timing, and context of childhood poverty, and documented the mediating processes of these effects. This literature coalesced around three perspectives—social causation, social selection, and an interactionist perspective implicating both causation and selection. Although studies

on child poverty in developing countries have given less attention to mediating processes, that literature shares several common themes with the U.S.-based literature. The
authors explain how leading models may be applicable in a variety of national contexts,
and how those models could be improved by incorporating context-specific variables.

Section II: Classic Debates

In Chapter 8, O'Connor reviews the historical origins and evolution of poverty research
from its roots in Progressive Era social investigation through the post–World War II
emergence of the multidisciplinary field, to the present increasingly globalized field of
inquiry. After tracing the rise of the field of poverty research, O'Connor demonstrates
how poverty knowledge was shaped by various transformations associated with the rise
of neoliberalism. She also shows how that framework remains dominant today. In the
process, her essay provides a crucial historical context for many developments in policies, scholarship, and debates about poverty.

Watkins-Hayes and Kovalsky's Chapter 9 reviews the concept and discourse of
deservingness. They show that many countries deploy this concept to frame debates
about poverty and argue this frame emphasizes the behavior of the poor and deempha-
sizes the role of structural causes. They link the frame of deservingness to race, gender, class, and other categories of difference. They narrate the history of deservingness
with special attention to cash assistance and health care in the United States. Further,
they show how deservingneess has been used to justify regulation, stratification, moral
judgment, and the withholding of resources.

Chapter 10, by Gornick and Boeri, assesses the link between gender and poverty. The
authors highlight the role of gender in various theoretical perspectives informing poverty research and discuss the often-cited and controversial concept of the feminization
of poverty. They review the empirical literature on poverty and gender, focusing on
interdisciplinary studies that define poverty via economic resources. The authors then
present select results from a group of 26 high- and middle-income countries based on
data from the LIS Database. These figures illustrate some of the key factors regarding
gendered poverty. The authors also discuss the challenges of assessing the link between
gender and poverty.

Streib, Verma, Welsh, and Burton's Chapter 11 examines the rise, fall, and seeming
resurrection of cultural explanations of poverty. They devote particular and critical
attention to one recurring and prominent cultural explanation: the culture of poverty
thesis. They argue that four routine scholarly practices inadvertently prop up the culture of poverty thesis: (1) missing and false comparison groups; (2) the selection of one-
sided research agendas; (3) biased interpretations of research findings; and (4) limited
theoretical alternatives. They ultimately explain how culture-based scholarship on poverty can avoid these trappings and make valuable contributions to the field.

In Chapter 12, Bhattacharyya explores the causal relationships between historical factors (e.g., geography, disease, colonial history, and technology) and poverty in

developing countries. The author unifies existing theories into a novel framework for explaining historical and contemporary patterns of development and global inequality. The essay applies this framework to the question of why Africa, Latin America, and Russia fell behind. The central argument is that Western Europe benefited from favorable geography, which led to highly productive agriculture, food surpluses, and institutions conducive to development. In contrast, Africa continues to suffer from unfavorable geography and disease. Also, institutional weaknesses in Latin America and Russia explain their relatively weak long-term economic performance.

Krishna's Chapter 13 examines the essentially dynamic nature of poverty. The author points out that many diverse studies show that there is tremendous variation in the inter- and intragenerational mobility and reproduction of poverty. The essay explains how there are different causes of descents into and escapes from poverty, and how this inhibits uniform policies to reduce poverty. The author frames this as a "cycle of poverty" that leads to simultaneous growth and reduction in poverty. Further, he argues that combining "preventative" (curbing descents) and "promotional" (enhancing escapes) policies is the best strategy. The essay explains that longer periods in poverty undermine capacities to escape and health care is a paramount social policy to prevent poverty.

Section III: Place and Context

The third section begins with Chapter 14 authored by Lichter and Schafft. The chapter explains how rural contexts and rurality shape poverty. The authors discuss the inherent difficulties of measuring poverty and deprivation among rural people and places. They highlight six key features of contemporary rural poverty that distinguish it from inner city poverty. These dimensions of rural poverty also are evaluated within a broader comparative assessment of theory, measurement, and rural policy in the United States, the European Union, and developing countries. An overarching goal of the chapter is to highlight the unique issues faced by rural people and places and to call greater attention to disadvantaged rural populations.

In Chapter 15, Patillo and Robinson stress the spatial manifestations of poverty at the neighborhood level. The authors push the literature forward in at least two ways. First, they argue for a broader metropolitan-level perspective on neighborhood poverty. Second, they argue that research on neighborhood poverty must integrate the political economy of place, the economic causes of concentrated poverty, and household mobility patterns. The essay then discusses the lived reality in poor neighborhoods by reviewing qualitative literature that emphasizes the disadvantages of, assets and resilience within, and heterogeneity of poor neighborhoods. They also discuss the effects of poor neighborhoods on residents and what this means for policy debates.

In Chapter 16, Massey focuses on residential segregation. He traces the emergence of segregation to the formation of cities and shows that it was limited until the rise of industrialization. Industrial cities segregated groups on the basis of economic and occupational status through market mechanisms, but nonmarket mechanisms of systematic exclusion and discrimination were also invoked against out-groups. In the United States, residential segregation has been identified as the "linchpin" of racial stratification, as it was similarly in South Africa under apartheid. With mass immigration in the late twentieth century, racial-ethnic segregation has become a component of stratification in developed nations throughout the world.

Wilson's Chapter 17 provides an overview of the relationship between urban poverty, race, and space. The author concentrates on the emergence and persistence of concentrated African American poverty in inner cities, while drawing comparisons to other countries. As causes of concentrated black poverty, the author stresses the combined roles of: (1) both explicitly racial political forces and ostensibly nonracial political forces; (2) impersonal economic forces; and (3) two types of cultural forces (racial beliefs systems and cultural traits). The chapter also includes an examination of the recent rise, and surprising positive impacts, of immigration on areas of concentrated urban poverty. The author concludes with a multipronged policy agenda.

Section IV: Causes and the Reproduction of Poverty

Gibson-Davis focuses on the role of marriage and nonmarital fertility for poverty in Chapter 18. Nonmarital families, which are families that consist of children who reside with a single mother or with cohabiting parents, have increased in prevalence worldwide and reflect the growing separation between marriage and childbearing. Despite being associated with poverty at the individual level, nonmarital family structures account for relatively little of the cross-national variation in poverty. Nevertheless, children growing up in poor households are disproportionately likely to be poor as adults, and this has contributed to economic inequality. At the same time, strategies to promote marriage have not been effective in addressing poverty. A far more effective strategy for poverty among nonmarital families is private and public transfers.

In Chapter 19, Smith investigates how social ties and networks shape job-finding among the poor. The author addresses the pertinent questions and reviews theories of network and organizational embeddedness, network theories of social capital, and theories of social capital activation and mobilization. While some have recently critiqued the prevailing view that social ties have causal effects on the job-matching process, she contends that such critiques are premature. The essay contends that social ties do matter, in complex and nuanced ways, to poverty and job-finding among the poor.

Hannum and Xie's Chapter 20 provides an overview of research across the social sciences on the links between poverty and education. They begin by discussing conceptual definitions of poverty and education and the ways these concepts have been operationalized in the literature. They then review literatures related to two broad themes: how poverty shapes educational outcomes, and how education affects chances of living in poverty. Within each theme, the authors draw on a remarkably cross-national base of evidence, while also devoting considerable attention to the United States and China. They also stress the value of studying education and poverty at the national, subnational, household, and individual levels.

Chapter 21 authored by Gautié and Ponthieux examines employment and the working poor. The authors demonstrate that the bulk of the working poor reside in developing countries. Surprisingly, however, it is only in rich countries that working poverty has truly been framed as a significant social issue. This reflects that, in rich countries, working poverty is considered as a paradox: those who work (enough) should be able to avoid poverty. The authors explain that while employment certainly reduces the odds of poverty, overwhelming evidence reveals that work is not sufficient to avoid poverty. They also explore the conceptual and measurement challenges in measuring working poverty. Additionally, they consider the level of analysis of the study of working poverty and the role of public policy.

In Chapter 22, Wade analyzes how the world economy has performed in improving human well-being. In the process, he examines economic development and inequality on a global scale. He describes the key patterns and trends in global poverty and income inequality, economic development, and economic growth. Based on these trends, he critically examines neoliberal economic theory, which has been prominent in global public policy since the 1980s. The author concludes that he is not very confident in the good news and finds much of the bad news credible. The author argues accumulating evidence undermines the neoliberal paradigm.

In Chapter 23, Fox, Waldfogel, and Torche review the theoretical and methodological approaches to measuring intergenerational mobility. Drawing on research in economics and sociology, the chapter evaluates the evidence on the degree of intergenerational mobility overall and among the poor. The authors also assess the arguments and evidence for possible underlying mechanisms. The chapter concludes with an international comparison of mobility in wealthy and developing countries, as well as directions for future research.

Chapter 24, by Brady and Jäntti, reviews the literature on how economic performance and the business cycle influence poverty in rich countries. They concentrate on the effects of economic growth, unemployment rates, economic development, and labor market structure. Considerable attention is devoted to the statistical models used in this literature and the particular challenges and (often strong) assumptions of such models. They review studies on economic performance's effects on poverty, while also incorporating literature on income inequality and the welfare state. They also distinguish between studies analyzing variation within countries versus studies comparing between countries.

Section V: Consequences

The fifth section begins with Kus, Whelan, and Nolan's Chapter 25 on material deprivation and consumption. The authors point out that much research on poverty in rich countries relies on income data. They explain the limitations of income as the sole means of measuring poverty and advocate for a multidimensional approach. While acknowledging the obstacles to this approach, they review research on material deprivation, poverty, and social exclusion. The essay displays data on material deprivation in the European Union, which suggests some mismatch between income poverty and deprivation. They then focus on recently developed multidimensional poverty measures than can be decomposed by dimension.

Chapter 26 authored by Barrett and Lentz examines hunger and food security. The authors explain how the relationship between poverty and food insecurity is complex and bidirectional and that there are multiple causes of food insecurity (including some unrelated to household poverty). Food insecurity results from a complex combination of availability, access, and/or utilization failures. Multiple measures of food insecurity exist, each with strengths and weaknesses, and some of which are inconsistent with one another. The authors conclude that domestic private food production and distribution systems matter more to food security than do national public food-assistance policies and programs, which in turn matter more than international food aid.

Crime is the topic in Chapter 27, authored by Sharkey, Besbris, and Friedson. The authors explain how the literature has shown a consistent association between poverty and crime at both the individual- and community-level. However, they emphasize that it is less clear whether this association is causal, spurious, or mediated by other factors. The authors argue for moving beyond the assumption that more poor people translates directly into more crime. They adopt a situational perspective, focusing on what makes an incident of crime more or less likely. This entails a shift from "who is likely to commit a crime" toward a focus on "when, where, and why crime is likely to occur."

In Chapter 28, Bonnet and Venkatesh investigate informal economic activity. The authors critically examine different definitions and conceptual frameworks about informal economies, including the dualist or development perspective, the legalist or neoliberal perspective, and the structuralist or neo-Marxist perspective. They also discuss different types of mediation, dispute resolution, and regulation that emerge out of informal economic transactions. The authors argue that informal economic activities reward specific skills that are not valued in the formal labor market. Finally, the essay considers methodological challenges involved in studying informal economies.

In Chapter 29, Angel documents the health consequences of poverty. He details how health is very unequally distributed, within and between countries. This inequality in health reflects differential access to health care, as well as other social, political, and economic factors, all of which are equally as important as purely biological factors. He considers the challenges in identifying the mechanisms between poverty and health. The chapter utilizes the concepts "social capital" and "the new morbidity" to provide insight into the sources of differential heath vulnerabilities. Angel demonstrates how poverty is clearly bad for one's health, and how poverty interacts with race to worsen health inequalities.

Section VI: Policies, Solutions, and Responses

Feeny and McGillivray begin the final section of the handbook by discussing foreign aid in Chapter 30. They acknowledge that the effect of aid on poverty is a highly controversial topic. Proponents see it as a beneficial transfer that pulls many out of poverty. Opponents assert poverty would be lower in the absence of aid and the problems that come with it. Investigating the impact of aid on poverty reduction, the authors conclude that income poverty would most likely be higher in the absence of aid. They concede that it remains unclear exactly how much aid reduces poverty.

In Chapter 31, Lee and Koo review how the welfare state shapes poverty in developed and developing countries. The authors first discuss how well typologies of welfare and production regimes account for variations in poverty in rich democracies. Then, they review several central debates about the welfare state and poverty: the ineffectiveness of targeting; the impact of growing aging populations; the unexpectedly worsening poverty in universal welfare states; and the increasing poverty gap between labor market insiders and outsiders. The authors conclude the essay with a focus on the roles of democracy, partisan politics, and social policies in increasing or decreasing poverty in developing societies.

Lein, Danziger, Shaefer, and Tillotson's Chapter 32 focuses on social policies, transfers, programs, and assistance. The authors categorize and classify the major transfers and services that governments provide. They contrast U.S. programs with other developed and developing countries, highlighting differing national approaches in the context of the turn toward neoliberalism and the Great Recession. The authors stress the complexity of various benefits, noting the salience of national and state differences in factors like eligibility, conditionality, rules, and implementation.

Piven and Minnite discuss poor people's politics in Chapter 33. The essay argues that in the context of electoral and institutional instability, political action by poor people critically influences public policy. The essay critiques prevailing theories of the welfare state for neglecting the political agency of the poor. The authors review the "dissensus politics" perspective that stresses the significance of what they call the "interdependent" power of poor people. The authors compare and contrast the rise of the U.S. welfare state against other rich democracies and emerging democracies of the developing world. The authors conclude by discussing how globalization and neoliberalism are producing divergent trends for poverty in rich and developing countries.

In Chapter 34 Trejo analyzes collective action—especially peaceful protest, armed insurgency, and civil war—among rural peasants in the developing world. He examines the causes that drive peasants to seek to overcome their conditions of destitution by means of direct political action. He explores both microlevel motivations for action and organizational vehicles that have facilitated mobilization. He explains that religious networks have been a powerful vehicle for the mobilization of the rural poor and emphasizes how state repression/reform are decisive for whether rural resistance is peaceful or violent. Finally, he discusses the long-term impact of rural collective action.

Rosenfeld and Laird focus on labor unions in Chapter 35. They emphasize that labor unions clearly curtail poverty even though union members are unlikely to be poor. They review the evidence on the antipoverty effectiveness of unions and consider what institutional arrangements facilitate this effectiveness. The authors note the relative lack of literature on unions and poverty in the developing world. They distinguish between indirect or direct linkages between organized labor and poverty. They also explain the need for a better understanding of mechanisms and demonstrate how historical research is useful in that regard.

Chapter 36 written by Kemp examines housing programs. Although studies of income poverty often lack scrutiny of housing expenditures and programs, housing is one of the most expensive necessities. The author examines how "housing problems" have been conceived and contested, and the implications of this for how programs are designed and how programs influence inequality. The essay explains that housing programs for the poor are often politicized or portrayed in negative ways and how this differs from more universal welfare programs. Nevertheless, both types of programs have made very substantial contributions to improving the housing and lives of the poor.

In Chapter 37, Mader examines microfinance, which is currently considered one of the most important tools for international development and poverty alleviation. Mader critically assesses the actual effectiveness of microfinance for poverty and various other relevant outcomes. He identifies the historical precursors to microfinance and traces its rise and evolution. The chapter also discusses the problems induced by microfinance, including a series of crises and strong critiques levied against it.

In the conclusion, Rank draws on the volume's chapters to articulate a new paradigm for understanding poverty. His proposed paradigm represents a break with traditional ways of viewing poverty. Within his paradigm are the following claims: the recognition that poverty is largely the result of structural failings; the understanding of poverty as a conditional state that individuals move in and out of; the acknowledgment of poverty as deprivation; the recognition that the moral ground on which to view poverty is one of social injustice; and a realization that poverty affects us all. Rank asks us to view poverty within a wider context of an interconnected environment rather than our traditional individualistic way of viewing poverty.

Taken together, the chapters in this volume cover: (1) concepts, theories, and orienting questions; (2) classic debates; (3) place and context; (4) causes and the reproduction of poverty; (5) consequences; and, (6) policies, solutions, and responses. As we explained earlier, this edited collection aims to fuel interdisciplinary integration in the social science of poverty. Moreover, the volume builds bridges across the international field of poverty research, including among rich democracies, and between rich and poor countries. The collective contributions of the authors' chapters have the potential to substantially advance the social science of poverty. Our hope is that ongoing and future research on poverty will be enhanced by the dialogue and cross-fertilization that this volume initiates. Each of the social sciences has much to learn from other fields, just as the United States can learn from the experiences of other countries and their scholars. This volume is one small step toward advancing a genuinely international and interdisciplinary social science of poverty.

It is the appropriate time for a comprehensive volume on the international social sciences of poverty. Poverty is the subject of lively debate in nearly every polity and across many academic disciplines. Economics, sociology, political science, history, anthropology, psychology, and several other disciplines contribute theoretical and empirical knowledge on the meaning, causes, and consequences of poverty. Despite remarkable economic advances in many societies during the latter half of the twentieth century, poverty remains an enduring social concern. There are vast cross-national and historical differences in poverty. Yet, every society in the world continues to have some segment of its population that is poor. Poverty remains a prominent part of the wealthiest countries in the world while dominating the landscape of many less developed countries. Poverty shapes a remarkable variety of aspects of life including identity and behavior, health and life chances, social relations, and collectivities ranging from families to social movements. Indeed, it is not an overstatement to say that understanding the forces, processes, and outcomes of poverty is critical for interpreting variations in many aspects of the social world.

NOTES

1. This can be attributed to a story the political scientist and sociologist John Stephens tells about conversations he has had with at least one relatively famous American poverty scholar.

2. Katz (1989:238) also quotes the eminent Swedish sociologist and political scientist Walter Korpi at length in a passage worth reproducing: "In American controversies about social policy, notes Swedish social scientist Walter Korpi, 'the European observer finds lively debates on issues that he or she has previously met only in the more or less dusty pages of historical accounts of the development of social policy at home.' In his comparison of national American and European poverty research, Korpi points out how American poverty researchers, he adds, neglect both unemployment and politics. American poverty research lacks theories that accord economic resources and political power a central role or that explain inequality as the outcome of 'conflicts over distribution.' To Korpi, this silence about politics remains 'striking,' given the 'high degree of conflict in American society.'" This summarizes Korpi's (1980) underappreciated essay.

3. It is important to acknowledge that we are not the only scholars calling for international and interdisciplinary integration. Hulme and Toye (2007), for example, make a convincing case for cross-disciplinary social science research on poverty, inequality, and well-being in the development literature.

4. It is worth noting that the concentration of economists in these Institute of Research on Poverty volumes was not historically preordained (Katz 1989; O'Connor 2001). Earlier volumes with similar goals were more interdisciplinary, and these volumes could have followed the precedent set by such earlier volumes. For example, a predecessor and likely influence on these volumes was Moynihan's (1968) *On Understanding Poverty*.

Moynihan's volume included sociologists like Duncan, Gans, S. M. Miller, Moynihan, Rainwater, an anthropologist in Lewis, and a historian in Thernstrom, alongside economists like Rosenthal and then director of the Institute Research on Poverty Watts.

REFERENCES

Bannerjee, Abhijit Vinayak, Roland Benabou, and Dilip Mookherjee. 2006. *Understanding Poverty*. New York: Oxford University Press.

Bebbington, Anthony J., Anis A. Dani, Arjan de Haan, and Michael Walton. 2008. *Institutional Pathways to Equity: Addressing Inequality Traps* Washington, DC: World Bank.

Brady, David. 2009. *Rich Democracies, Poor People: How Politics Explain Poverty*. New York: Oxford University Press.

Brady, David and Rebekah Burroway. 2012. "Targeting, Universalism, and Single Mother Poverty: A Multilevel Analysis across 18 Affluent Democracies." *Demography* 49:719–46.

Brady, David and Lane M. Destro. 2014. "Poverty." Pp. 585–602 in *The Oxford Handbook of U.S. Social Policy*, edited by D. Béland, C. Howard, and K. J. Morgan. New York: Oxford University Press.

Burton, Linda M., Daniel T. Lichter, Regina S. Baker, and John M. Eason. 2013. "Inequality, Family Processes, and Health in the 'New' Rural America." *American Behavioral Scientist* 57:1128–51.

Cancian, Maria and Sheldon H. Danziger. 2009. *Changing Poverty, Changing Policies*. New York: Russell Sage Foundation.

Couch, Kenneth A. and Maureen A. Pirog. 2010. "Poverty Measurement in the U.S., Europe, and Developing Countries." *Journal of Policy Analysis and Management* 29:217–26.

Crane, D. Russell and Tim B. Heaton. 2008. *Handbook of Families and Poverty*. Thousand Oaks, CA: Sage.

Danziger, Sheldon and Robert Haveman. 2001. *Understanding Poverty*. Cambridge, MA. and New York: Harvard University Press and Russell Sage Foundation.

Danziger, Sheldon, Gary D. Sandefur, and Daniel H. Weinberg. 1994. *Confronting Poverty* Cambridge, MA and New York: Harvard University Press and Russell Sage Foundation.

Devine, Fiona and Mary Waters. 2003. *Social Inequalities in Comparative Perspective*. New York: Wiley-Blackwell.

Duncan, Greg and Jeanne Brooks-Gunn. 1997. *Consequences of Growing Up Poor*. New York: Russell Sage Foundation.

Duncan, Greg, Jeanne Brooks-Gunn, and J. Lawrence Aber. 1997. *Neighborhood Poverty* New York: Russell Sage Foundation.

Edelman, Peter. 2013. *So Rich, So Poor*. New York: New Press.

Gans, Herbert J. 1994. "Positive Functions of the Undeserving Poor: Uses of the Underclass in America." *Politics & Society* 22:269–83.

Grusky, David B. and Ravi Kanbur. 2006. *Poverty and Inequality*. Stanford, CA: Stanford University Press.

Henrich, Joseph, Steven J. Heine, and Aara Norenzayan. 2010. "The Weirdest People in the World." *Behavioral and Brain Sciences* 33:61–135.

Hulme, David and John Toye. 2007. "The Case for Cross-Disciplinary Social Science Research on Poverty, Inequality and Well-Being." *Journal of Development Studies* 42:1085–1107.

Huston, Aletha. 1991. *Children in Poverty*. New York: Cambridge University Press.

Jäntti, Markus. 2009. "Mobility in the United States in Comparative Perspective." Pp. 180–200 in *Changing Poverty, Changing Places*, edited by M. Cancian and S. Danziger. New York: Russell Sage Foundation.

Jefferson, Philip N. 2012. *The Oxford Handbook of the Economics of Poverty*. New York: Oxford University Press.

Jencks, Christopher and Paul E. Peterson. 1991. *The Urban Underclass*. Washington, DC: Brookings Institution.

Katz, Michael. 1989. *The Undeserving Poor*. New York: Pantheon.

Korpi, Walter. 1980. "Approaches to the Study of Poverty in the United States: Critical Notes from a European Perspective." Pp. 287–314 in *Poverty and Public Policy*, edited by V. T. Costello. Cambridge: Shenkman.

McFate, Katherine, Roger Lawson, and William Julius Wilson. 1995. *Poverty, Inequality and the Future of Social Policy*. New York: Russell Sage Foundation.

Meyer, Daniel R. and Geoffrey L. Wallace. 2009. "Poverty Levels and Trends in Comparative Perspective." Pp. 35–62 in *Changing Poverty, Changing Places*, edited by M. Cancian and S. Danziger. New York: Russell Sage Foundation.

Moynihan, Daniel P. 1968. *On Understanding Poverty*. New York: Basic Books.

O'Connor, Alice. 2001. *Poverty Knowledge*. Princeton, NJ: Princeton University Press.

Rainwater, Lee and Timothy M. Smeeding. 2004. *Poor Kids in a Rich Country*. New York: Russell Sage Foundation.

Schwalbe, Michael, Sandra Godwin, Daphne Holden, Douglas Schrock, Shealy Thompson, and Michele Wolkomir. 2000. "Generic Social Processes in the Reproduction of Inequality: An Interactionist Analysis." *Social Forces* 79:419–52.

Smeeding, Timothy M., Lee Rainwater, and Gary Burtless. 2001. "U.S. Poverty in Cross-National Context." Pp. 162–89 in *Understanding Poverty*, edited by S. Danziger and R. Haveman. Cambridge, MA and New York: Harvard University Press and Russell Sage Foundation.

SECTION I

CONCEPTS, THEORIES, AND ORIENTING QUESTIONS

CHAPTER 2

POVERTY MEASUREMENT

TIMOTHY M. SMEEDING

In this chapter, I examine the complexities and idiosyncrasies of poverty measurement from its origins to current practice. I begin with the various concepts of poverty and their measurement and how economists, social statisticians, public policy scholars, sociologists, and other social scientists have contributed to this literature. I then turn to a few empirical estimates of poverty across and within nations. I rely mainly on Luxembourg Income Study (LIS) and Organisation for Economic Cooperation and Development (OECD) data to provide some data on levels and trends in overall poverty, though I refer also to the World Bank's measures of global absolute poverty. In the empirical examinations, I look at rich and middle-income countries and some developing nations, comparisons of trends in relative poverty over different time periods, and comparisons of relative and anchored poverty across the Great Recession (GR). Due to space and other limitations, I cannot delve into the vast literature on child and elder poverty (with one exception), gendered poverty, central city versus rural poverty, or other similar issues.

CONCEPTS, ORIGINS, AND DEVELOPMENT OF POVERTY MEASUREMENT

The fundamental concept of poverty concerns itself with having too few resources or capabilities to participate fully in a society. As Blank (2008:387) reminds us, "poverty is an inherently vague concept and developing a poverty measure involves a number of relatively arbitrary assumptions." Ultimately, social scientists need to first establish the breadth and depth of the social phenomenon called "poverty" before they can meaningfully explore its ultimate causes and remedies. Thus, I turn to measures and comparisons of poverty employed by social scientists within and across nations.

Poverty Measurement: Some History

Social science has traditionally been more interested in the explanation of poverty than in its measurement, though almost all scientists believe that poverty statistics are meaningful social indicators of basic needs (Piachaud 1987; Townsend 1979; Ringen 1985; Brady 2003). Some interests in poverty center on the ideas of the "culture" of poverty and the effects of "place" on poverty which are often measured differently and consequently hard to compare. The urban/central city/ghetto aspects of this issue are well-treated in the work of Wilson (1987), Massey and Denton (1993), and Massey (1996). Harrington's classic work, *The Other America*, covers rural deprivation as well (Harrington 1981). Most economists and social statisticians prefer strictly quantitative measures of poverty as a social indicator, with some nuanced discussion of why poverty is as it is, be it health and structural factors that limit earnings, or about how the bad "choices" that poor people make might result in poverty. I will have much more to say about these measures in this chapter.

Roles of culture, power, social structure, and other factors largely out of an individual's control are the main forces that sociologists and social workers use to explain poverty. In general, this school of thought is critical of the economist's perspective of choice models whereby individuals control their own destiny and are therefore the cause of their own poverty (Piachaud 1987). In addition some sociologists have argued that poverty has a functional role to play in capitalist society (e.g., Gans 1972).

The basic working hypothesis for the cultural window on poverty is that individuals are strongly influenced by the physical and cultural context in which they live. "Neighborhood" exerts a strong influence on behavior and concentrated poverty in central city ghettos and therefore has a strong negative effect on future life chances and long-run deprivation. Indeed, in the United States, this discourse has spawned interest in the so-called underclass that goes beyond poverty alone to include all persons with "dysfunctional behaviors" living in "bad" neighborhoods (Mincy, Sawhill, and Wolf 1990). The European term for a similarly disaffected population is "social exclusion," which is also beyond the narrow bounds of poverty measurement per se (Room 1999; Hills 1999; Glennerster et al. 1999). Recently, several social scientists have tried to separate neighborhood from local school effects, while at the same time noting the increased social and economic segregation within cites and across schools and school districts (Sharkey 2013; Reardon 2011; Katz 2014).

Concepts of Poverty

My discussion is framed by Figure 2.1, which reviews most of the possibilities of poverty concepts and measures. The conceptual underpinnings of poverty measures are anchored in economics (Lampman 1964), sociology (Grusky and Kanbur 2006), social statistics (Orshansky 1965), and social policy (Rowntree 1901; Booth 1903). Here,

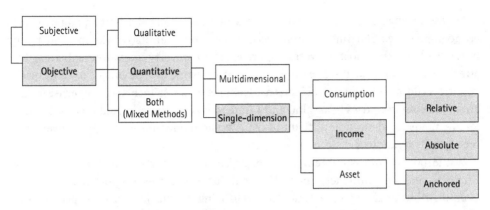

FIGURE 2.1 Concepts and Measures of Poverty

Source: Adapted from Dhongde (2013).

I am mostly interested in the concept of objective poverty measures according to some standard definitions of means versus resources. I am also mostly interested in objective and quantitative poverty measurement using a single dimension of "resources," income, and several notions of "needs" standards: those that are relative, absolute, and—closely related—"anchored" poverty lines. I chose income poverty because of its domination in modern (post-1960s) poverty studies and because of its linkages to the income inequality and social mobility literatures that often closely follow from poverty measures. Other measures and concepts of poverty are also discussed but not empirically investigated.

Income or living-standards poverty measurement began in the Anglo-Saxon countries and dates back at least to Rowntree (1901), who was the first to employ the concept of a poverty line in his empirical work on York, England. And thanks to his enterprise, and that of Booth (1903) who invented the idea of a poverty line for London, the field has a meaningful social indicator of basic needs (see for instance, Townsend 1979, 1993; Piachaud 1987; Ringen 1985; Ravallion 2014a). I also note that official poverty measurement began as an Anglo-American social indicator. But since then, "official" measures of poverty (or measures of "low income") now exist in over 100 countries and for Europe as a whole (Eurostat 2005). The United States (DeNavas-Walt et al. 2012) and the United Kingdom (Department for Work and Pensions 2012) have long-standing "official" poverty series. Statistics Canada publishes the number of households with incomes below a "low-income cutoff" on an irregular basis, as does the Australian government with those below the "Henderson line." In northern Europe and Scandinavia the debate centers instead on the level of income at which minimum benefits for social programs should be set. In other words, their concept of insufficient "low income" is directly fed into programmatic responses to social needs (Björklund and Freeman 1997; Marx and Nelson 2013; Ravallion 2014a).[1] Recent years have also seen the development of global poverty measures and global poverty-reduction targets whereby a combination of microdata and other assumptions allows the World Bank and others to estimate world poverty.

Figure 2.1 suggests that objective studies of poverty can be both qualitative (or ethnographic, see Harrington 1981; Liebow 1967) or quantitative (as focused upon here). Perhaps the most powerful approaches to poverty measurement are situations where both qualitative and quantitative work is combined in both rich countries (Edin and Lein 1997; Halpern-Meekin et al. 2014; Tach and Halpern-Meekin 2013) and poor countries (Carvalho and White 1997). But these "mixed methods" studies are almost by definition difficult to compare across nations or to repeat over time on a fixed (say, annual) scale.

While poverty measurement is an exercise that is particularly popular in the English-speaking countries, most rich nations share the Anglo-Saxon concern over distributional outcomes and the well-being of the low-income population. There is no international consensus on guidelines for measuring poverty, but international bodies such as the United Nations Children's Fund (UNICEF 2000), the United Nations Development Programme (UNDP 1999), the Organisation for Economic Cooperation and Development (OECD 2008, 2013), and the European Statistical Office (Eurostat 1998, 2005) have published several cross-national studies of the incidence of poverty in rich countries. A majority of these studies have been based on the LIS database, which can be accessed at www.lisdatacenter.org. Some examples of these studies include Brady (2003, 2005, 2009); Brady et al. (2010); Förster (1993); Jäntti and Danziger (2000); Smeeding, Rainwater, and Burtless (2000); Kenworthy (1998); Smeeding, O'Higgins, and Rainwater (1990); Rainwater and Smeeding (2003); and Smeeding (2006). More recently, the European Union (2005) and the OECD have regularized measurement of poverty but use different standards and data sources.

Today, one can find poverty measures in over 100 countries and some harmonized measures from the World Bank that use both secondary (published) data and micro data-based measures of consumption and income to determine those living below some particular amount of income per person day (Ravallion and Chen 2011; Chen and Ravallion 2012). Much of their work centers on an absolute poverty line of $1.25 per person per day (Chen and Ravallion 2010, 2013; Ferriera and Ravallion 2009). Global poverty estimates involve two sets of data: national income and consumption surveys (collated in the World Bank's PovcalNet), and international data about prices around the world, using the International Comparison Program (ICP), which compares what people buy and at what local currency price they buy those things; this makes up the "purchasing power parity" (or PPP) exchange rate that is designed to equalize the power of, say, a renminbi to buy what Chinese buy with the power of a dollar to buy what an American buys.

One important issue here is the use of PPPs. Indeed in May 2014, a new set of PPPs was released by the ICP (2014) that appears to have halved the number of people living on $1.25 per day, falling from 18.9 percent to between 8.9 and 11.2 percent! (Dykstra et al. 2014). This result is largely because the PPPs for China and India rose dramatically, meaning that the same amount of local currency could buy much more than previously estimated. For instance, India's 2011 PPP per capita from the World

Bank World Development Indicators was $3,677; but, by the new ICP PPPs, it has risen to $4,735, cutting Indian poverty from almost 400 million persons to just over 100 million persons. Clearly the sensitivity of the results to PPPs is central to this argument. But surely we have made vast progress in the fight against world poverty as well (Chen and Ravallion 2013; Ravallion 2014b).

Measuring Poverty

Most broadly, the measurement of poverty in rich, poor, and middle-income nations involves the comparison of some index of household well-being with household needs. When command over economic resources falls short of needs, a household (or person or family) is classified as poor. Here I consider well-being as economic, referring to the material resources available to a household. The concern with these resources among most social scientists is generally not with material consumption alone but also with the capabilities such resources give to household members so they can participate fully in society (Sen 1983, 1992; Brandolini, Magri, and Smeeding 2010). These capabilities are inputs to social activities, and participation in social activities in return gives rise to a particular level of well-being (Rainwater 1990; Coleman and Rainwater 1978). Methods for measuring a person's or household's capabilities differ according to the context in which one assesses them: over time, across nations, or among subpopulations within a nation, for example, rural versus urban India.

All advanced societies are highly stratified and, hence, some individuals have more resources than others. The opportunities for social participation are affected by the resources that a household disposes. These resources, the "family income package" (Rainwater and Smeeding 2003) come from personal effort (earnings), family efforts, and others outside the household, principally governments but also other third parties like nonprofits. Money income is therefore a crucial resource, as are "near-cash" benefits in kind that are close substitutes for money, for instance housing allowances or food vouchers. Of course, there are other important kinds of resources, such as social capital, wealth, noncash benefits, primary education, and access to basic health care, all of which add to human capabilities (Coleman 1988). These resources may be available more or less equally to all people in some societies, regardless of their money incomes. But there are also many forces in rich societies that reduce well-being by limiting capabilities for full participation in society, including inadequacies in neighborhoods where people live, racial and ethnic discrimination, neighborhood violence, low-quality public schools and other social services, lack of good jobs, and job instability, all of which increase economic insecurity, reduce human capabilities, and increase poverty, as dozens of analysts, including those mentioned earlier, have established.

Because there is no single commonly accepted way to measure poverty among social scientists, there is a desire to go beyond the popularly used income poverty definition employed in this article. And so there exists a wide variety of additional poverty measures that substitute for or complement the preponderance of income-based measures used by quantitative sociologists and economists (e.g., see Haveman 2009; Ruggles 1990; Boltvinik 2000). In principle, poverty is a multidimensional concept and should reflect several aspects of personal well-being as shown in Figure 2.1. Forms of deprivation other than economic hardship can certainly be relevant to poverty measurement and to antipoverty policymaking. A number of authors have suggested that separate measures of needs ought to be developed for different goods and services (Aaron 1985). Housing and health care are often mentioned in this context, although the latter is particularly of interest in medically unequal nations such as the United States, while the former is of much greater interest in the United Kingdom (U.K. 1993).

The concept of multidimensional poverty is also flourishing in sociology and economics. Official measures of social exclusion, material deprivation, and material hardship exist mainly in Europe and are beyond the empirical bounds of this chapter. Europe adopted the official Laeken set of social indicators in 1995, including the at-risk-of-poverty indicator, with an explicit objective of reducing poverty and social exclusion (Marlier et al. 2007). Indeed, indicators of material deprivation now form part of the Europe 2020 target of poverty reduction (Atkinson and Marlier 2010: Chapter 6).

Both consumption poverty and asset poverty have been proposed as an alternative to income poverty in rich nations (Meyer and Sullivan 2012a, 2012b; Brandolini et al. 2010). And, in a few nations, asset and income poverty can be combined into a joint measure (Gornick et al. 2009) as can consumption and income poverty (Meyer and Sullivan 2012a, 2012b). But consumption and asset poverty measures are not yet ready for widespread use on a cross-national basis, despite their usefulness for some types of poverty measurement (e.g., many income-poor elderly consume more than their income due to savings and spending from assets). Definitions of consumption vary widely across and within nations, and most consumption databases actually are constructed to measure weights for the Consumer Price Index, and hence measure expenditures, not actual consumption. This leaves one with the problem of how to value durables consumption, so-called imputed rent where one consumes housing services for below average prices, and so on (Fisher, Johnson, and Smeeding 2014). There has been little work on cross-nationally harmonized consumption measures, making such comparisons difficult. Asset poverty creates similar challenges, as liquidity is an issue, and while cash on hand is a good measure of ability to withstand a negative shock to income, how to value less-liquid assets, like housing, are not yet resolved (Gornick et al. 2009). But here at least there have been some attempts at cross-nationally comparable databases (e.g., the Luxembourg Wealth Study, at http://www.lisdatacenter.org/our-data/lws-database/).

Likewise, the study of time poverty has not yet reached prominence, though its importance is denied by no social scientist (Vickrey 1977). These studies mainly point to those who work long and hard hours but then have little time for leisure, child rearing, or other pursuits, in both rich (Heggeness et al. 2013) and poor countries (Bardasi and Wodon 2009).

In summary, following the shaded boxes in Figure 2.1, I am interested primarily in objective, quantitative, comparative cross-national poverty measured in income terms. Not only because income-based poverty measures are more comparable across nations, but also because income-based poverty allows us to connect our empirical work and poverty measurement to overall inequality. As mentioned, income is generally a better measure of resources than consumption in rich countries. In the rapidly growing middle-income countries, the differences in living standards between rural and urban populations cause the most angst over consumption versus income poverty. In poor nations, most find it easier to measure consumption, largely because of food produced for (or bartered for) own consumption and informal work. And indeed, the most inclusive concept of income and consumption derives from the suggestions of Haig and Simons. Haig (1921) stated that income was "the money value of the net accretion to one's economic power between two points of time" and Simons (1938) defined personal income as "the algebraic sum of (1) the market value of rights exercised in consumption and (2) the change in the value of the store of property rights between the beginning and end of the period in question." Hence income and consumption differ only by net wealth or debt, which is less a problem for the poor than other income groups.

But the richer the country, the more income becomes a better and more comparable measure. At the frontier of such comparisons, LIS work on "production for own consumption" and "informal labor" income help ease the comparisons across diverse areas within nations and bring expanded income much closer to consumption as a poverty measure for middle-income countries like China and Brazil.

Absolute, Relative, and Anchored Poverty in Rich and Selected Middle-Income Countries

An absolute poverty standard is defined in terms of a level of purchasing power that is sufficient to buy a fixed bundle of basic necessities at a specific point in time. A relative standard, on the other hand, is defined relative to the typical income or consumption level in the wider society. The purchasing power of a relative poverty standard will change over time as society-wide income or consumption levels change, while an absolute poverty standard will change only with the prices of commodities it can buy and, as seen earlier, with the currency exchange mechanism (PPP) to convert one currency's buying power into another. Most cross-national comparisons use the relative definition of poverty, especially since purchasing power parities to convert any absolute measure to country currency are subject to fluctuation and sometimes severe measurement error (Jäntti and Danziger 2000; Dykstra et al. 2014).

And, in the broadest sense, all measures of poverty or economic need are relative, because context is important to the definition of even "absolute" needs. The World Bank uses poverty measures of $1.25 to $2 per person per day (in 2005 dollars)—or $1,095 to $2,190 per year for a family of three—for the developing nations of Africa,

Central Asia, or Latin America (Chen and Ravallion 2012). The measures may make little sense for a rich country today but might have as a post–Civil War poverty line set in the late 1860s. The concept of "extreme" poverty, living on less than $2 in cash per day or less than 50 percent of the U.S. absolute poverty line, has recently been studied in the United States by Shaefer and Edin (2013). But of course living rent-free with others or adding food stamps and other income in kind can radically change the real level of living in such cases.

In contrast, the 2011 U.S. "absolute" poverty threshold was about $18,000 for a family of three—8 to 17 times the World Bank's poverty line (depending on family size). And absolute and relative measures may also differ substantially within and across nations. One-half of median income, the preferred relative poverty standard in the United States, is another 25–30 percent above the official U.S. poverty line or 10 to 21 times the poverty standard in poor countries. Moreover, as economic inequality has increased in most rich societies over the past 20 years, the study of relative deprivation and poverty has taken on a new life (Gottschalk and Smeeding 2000; Gornick and Jäntti 2013; OECD 2011, 2013).

Cross-national comparisons of poverty in rich countries therefore rely heavily on openly and directly relative concepts of poverty, which are a reflection of the fact that a poverty standard or a minimum-income standard ought to reflect the overall standard of living in society. One early source of this formalization (Abel-Smith and Townsend 1965) came about in arguing that the officially defined minimum level of income in the United Kingdom, as represented by the National Assistance scale, should increase with the rising standard of living and not just with consumer prices. It was Townsend's work in the early 1960s, culminating in his famous 1979 book. that really launched the relative-poverty approach on a much wider scale. Townsend (1979:31) wrote:

> Individuals, families and groups in the population can be said to be in poverty when they lack the resources to obtain the type of diet, participate in the activities and have the living conditions and the amenities which are customary, or at least widely encouraged or approved in the societies to which they belong.

The measurement of relative poverty has more recently been generally operationalized with a definition of the poverty line as a fraction of median income. Cross-national studies typically compare the percentage of persons living with income below some fraction of the family-size-adjusted national median income.

Measurement of relative poverty in the United States also began in the 1960s and was pioneered by Fuchs (1967) who followed the thinking of Townsend and Abel-Smith and linked relative and absolute income poverty measurement. When Fuchs began his study, the absolute poverty measure in the United States begun by Lampman (1964) and then Orshansky (1965) was based on a poverty line of about $3,000 for four persons. Fuchs pointed out that this was half the median income at that time and that one could think differently about relative poverty compared to absolute poverty (Gilbert 2008:136).[2]

A relative poverty measure comparison is also consistent with a well-established theoretical perspective on poverty (Sen 1983, 1992; and, again, Townsend 1979). However, the fraction of income at which the poverty line ought to be set is open to debate. Most cross-national studies (LIS, OECD) focus on half the median income, following Fuchs and others. But many poverty scholars argue that a 50-percent-of-median standard is too low. It implies a poverty cut-off well below half the mean in unequal societies,[3] and it also affects the country rankings.[4] The European Statistical Office Working Group on Poverty Measurement has employed 60 percent of the national median income as the common poverty threshold for European community poverty studies in the new millennium (Eurostat 2005).

A fully relative measure of poverty changes in lockstep with median income, while an absolute measure changes only with prices. The income elasticity of the poverty line is therefore between zero for the absolute measure and one for the fully relative measure. In some countries, such as the United States, the measure of poverty has become "semi-relative" or "quasi-relative" as the poverty line advances only with the living standards of the bottom part of the distribution and not the whole distribution. Ravallion and Chen (2011) refer to these as "weakly relative measures" which have the feature that the poverty line will not rise proportionately to the median or mean but will have income elasticity less than unity. These are also called "quasi-relative" poverty standards in the new "Supplemental Poverty Measure" for the United States, which varies by considering expenses on basic needs for a low-income family and how they change over time (Short 2012). That is, the poverty line changes with low-income persons' expenses for food, clothing, and shelter. While these do rise and fall with median income in the United States, they change by less than median income itself (see Johnson and Smeeding 2012).

In my opinion, it is worthwhile to consider both absolute *and* relative poverty measures because they tell different things about living standards as well as deprivation. Increasingly, the idea of "anchored" poverty measures has become important as they can be employed to indicate both relative (or weakly relative) and absolute poverty trends within a given nation.[5] Anchored poverty measures begin with the same fully or weakly relative measure in one year (t) and then compare relative poverty in some future year (say year $t + 10$) to poverty measures against a poverty line that has been changed only for prices between year t and year $t + 10$. These measures are especially useful in periods of rapid expansion *or* contraction in an economy, where relative poverty may not change by a lot, but where absolute poverty does change due to economic growth or contraction (see Atkinson et al. 2002; Smeeding 2006; Brady 2009; Johnson and Smeeding 2012; Wimer et al. 2013; OECD 2013). Any absolute poverty line is also therefore an anchored poverty line. The difference is that an anchored poverty line can be updated to any period that is policy relevant, given the analysis. As suggested earlier, the absolute (or anchored) U.S.-Orshansky poverty line for the 1960s was about the same as a fully relative half median income measure at that time. The United States has anchored its "official" poverty measure at this same point since that date. Now 50 years later, the U.S. poverty line is only at about 30 percent of median income—not the 50 percent at its inception (Smeeding 2006). Hence, analysts prefer to anchor their U.S. poverty studies at a semi-relative line (Johnson and Smeeding 2012).

Here, for simplicity and breadth, I focus exclusively on the "headcount" measure of poverty, the share of people who fall below some definable point that indexes poverty. This approach does not measure the depth of economic need, the poverty gap, or the severity of poverty. People who are poor could become richer or poorer, with no change in a headcount measure of poverty. A pragmatic reason for using the poverty gap is that the headcount may be quite sensitive where there are spikes in the distribution, due to the payment of flat-rate social transfers such as minimum social retirement level (or changes to the minimum wage).[6] Others, see especially Sen (1976) and Foster, Greer, and Thorbecke (1984), focus on poverty measures that examine the distribution of poverty among the poor, taking account of both the depth of poverty and its severity. Because headcount measures are more easily understood, compared, and implemented than other, more complex measures, we rely on them below.

The data we use are taken from LIS and the OECD and are limited mainly to rich and middle-income countries. The OECD includes a large number of rich nations, but also Chile, Mexico, and Turkey. Both LIS and OECD have been interested in the BRICS countries (Brazil, Russia, India, China, and South Africa). LIS has also expanded to include other Latin American nations and Mexico. But, to establish trends in income poverty, one must have at least a decade or two of data, and here the number of middle-income countries we can examine is severely limited.[7]

The Unit of Account Adjustments for Household Size and Periodicity and Persistence

Measurement of poverty also requires that one consider the unit of account where income or consumption is shared; how needs can be adjusted to take account of the size of the relevant unit; and the periodicity of poverty measurement as well as the length of time one is poor, or persistence. While the United States focuses on families (those related by blood, marriage, or adoption) and unrelated individuals (wherever they may live), this leaves couples living together outside marriage (cohabiting couples) to be treated as two unrelated individuals, thus ignoring any resource sharing amongst them. The new Supplemental Poverty Measure treats cohabiters (including those with children) as married couples and in so doing reduces measured poverty by 2 or more percentage points in the United States (Short 2012). Internationally, the preferred unit of account is the household—all those sharing one set of living quarters. The assumption is that while not all resources need be shared equally, the economies of scale for living together are large enough to make the household unit the most relevant for determination of poverty. Indeed, even if food and clothing budgets are fully individualized, the act of sharing a common structure (heat, lighting, and living spaces) is such that the economies of scale increase the consumption of each unit enough to help them overcome poverty if sufficient total resources are available to the household.

The issue of how much economies of scale are available to households is called the equivalence scale issue. The basic point is that two can live more cheaply together than apart, because of shared resources, and then four more cheaply than two. The question is how do "needs" for food, clothing, and shelter vary as household size (and composition) changes. One of the most common scales is the single-parameter constant-elasticity equivalence scale reviewed by Buhmann et al. (1988) and Ruggles (1990), which is used most often in international comparisons of poverty (Rainwater and Smeeding 2003). In general, the constant-elasticity scales are given by (family size) ^{e}, in which ^{e} is the scale elasticity. Notice that if the elasticity equals one, then the scale equals family size, there are no assumed economies of scale in living arrangements, and the equivalent resources are simply the per-capita resources. The World Bank is often criticized because their poverty line is in terms of a given number of dollars a day per person and hence allows for no economies of scale—the poverty line for a household of eight is just eight times the individual poverty line. Alternatively, if the elasticity equals zero then there is no adjustment for family size, there are complete economies of scale in living, and the marginal cost of another person is zero. Following the suggestions by Ruggles (1990) and Buhmann et al. (1988), much research uses an elasticity of 0.5. This scale indicates that the resources for a two-person family must be 41 percent more than that of a single-person family for the two-person family to have the same standard of living as the single-person family.

Some scales adjust for more than just the number of adults and children in the family. For instance, the scales implicit in the poverty thresholds adjust for the age of the household head. And the new the three-parameter scale (see Betson 1996; Short et al. 1999) used in the Census's Supplemental Poverty measure provides more economies of scale between singles and childless couples, which are more similar to those in the poverty scale.

The choice of equivalence scale can impact the level and trend in poverty. Coulter, Cowell, and Jenkins (1992) demonstrate that the constant elasticity equivalence scale yields a U-shape relationship between poverty and the scale parameter, ^{e}. Johnson (2004) compares alternative scales and shows that the choice of scale has a dramatic effect on the relative standard of living of different families. A lower equivalence scale implies that the family's resources will be adjusted upward, hence increasing their equivalent resources. For example, single adults will have a higher standard of living relative to the reference group under the three-parameter scales (compared to the poverty scales).

But in all cases of poverty measurement, except for the World Bank, everyone agrees that a household-size adjustment is necessary. Once an equivalence scale is adopted, one can either vary the poverty line by household size or mix, or adjust income for the equivalence factor and compare it to one single poverty line, be it a relative, absolute, or anchored line.

Finally, periodicity and persistence are aspects that must be mentioned. The period used by most analysts is the calendar year. That period may in fact be too long for poverty measurement, as many low-income households live month to month or even week to week. However the survey vehicles that gather data for measurement are almost all based on the calendar year, both within and especially across countries. And so we use annual data in this chapter.

The introduction of panel data has allowed analysts to measure poverty across several periods, say years, to see how persistent poverty is, and to assess the events that led to persons moving into a spell of poverty, and then the event associated with moving out. Some of the best studies to date on this topic include those in the United States (Bane and Ellwood 1986; Stevens 1999, 2011; Blank and Card 2008; Cellini, McKernan, and Ratcliffe 2008), Great Britain (Jenkins 2011), and Europe (Layte and 2003; Vandecasteel 2010). The topic deserves more study.

MEASURING THE LEVEL AND TREND
IN POVERTY

I examine the level and trends in poverty in a set of graphs and one table, all based on the LIS key figures data set, plus some special tabulations to determine the level of anchored poverty using both LIS and OECD data. The percentage of persons living below the half-median poverty line can now be examined for 38 nations using the LIS data (Figure 2.2). The 28 light-shaded bars are the richest Anglo-Saxon, EU, and OECD nations; the 10 darker bars are the MICS: the BRICS nations and several South American nations.[8] The measure of resources we use is "adjusted disposable income." Disposable income includes earnings and capital income, net of direct (income and payroll) tax and gross of net transfers (both cash and near-cash benefits), and this definition of disposable income is further adjusted by an equivalence scale. This income measure is the current widely accepted income measure, endorsed by the Canberra reports (2001, 2011) on income-distribution statistics. The only difference is that the OECD and LIS use slightly different equivalence scales to adjust for household size and composition. But the same scales are used for all nations within each group of studies.

Levels. If a "less poor" country is one with a "single digit" poverty rate (where between 5 and 10 percent of its population are poor), 17 countries have hit that target in the mid- to late-2000s, as shown in Figure 2.2. The Scandinavian and Nordic nations are generally lowest, along with a number of "middle" western, central, and eastern European nations who have joined the EU 27 (from Belgium and the Netherlands west to Luxembourg, Germany, France, Austria, plus Switzerland, the Czech Republic, Slovakia, Hungary, Slovenia, and Romania). This pattern has been more or less the same since the first LIS measures appeared 20 to 25 years ago

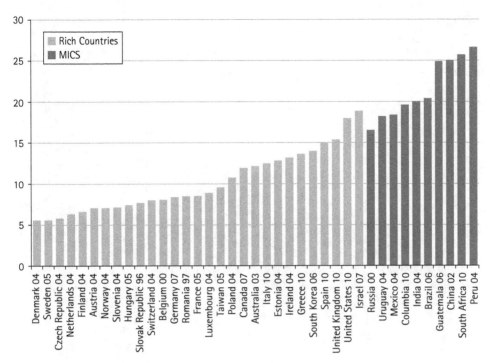

FIGURE 2.2 Relative Poverty Rates for Total Population (mid- to late-2000s using LIS data)

Note: Poverty is measured by the percent of persons living in households with family-size-adjusted income below half the median national income.

(Smeeding et al. 1990; Atkinson, Rainwater, and Smeeding 1995), though the number of nations has now expanded considerably. Taiwan weighs in with the 17th lowest poverty rate—about 9.5 percent. Another nine nations have relative poverty rates from 10 to 15 percent, including Italy, Spain, Greece, Poland, Estonia, Canada, Australia, Ireland, and South Korea. Three rich nations are between 15 and 19 percent: the United Kingdom (15), the United States (18), and Israel (19). Moving to the MICs, six countries overlap the three rich nations in the 15 to 20 percent range, with Russia having a poverty rate below the United States and Israel, and Uruguay and Mexico more or less even with the United States. Finally, Colombia, India, and Brazil were all at 20 percent poverty. Poverty rates are 25 percent and above in Guatemala, China, South Africa, and Peru. In short, the range of comparable relative poverty rates from the most comparable cross-national data source varies by a factor of five.

The OECD data in Figure 2.3 provides essentially the same picture, but with all nations measured in 2010, compared to 2002 to 2010 in Figure 2.2. The OECD data is not actually harmonized but collected for country experts using a common formula. In general, they are closer to the LIS "gold standard" rates. The OECD data also adds a few nations (Iceland, Chile, and Turkey) to those in Figure 2.2 and also presents some data on 15-year trends in poverty, where available. Here Israel leads the league in the table of poverty, with headcount rates surpassing 20 percent. The advantage of the OECD data

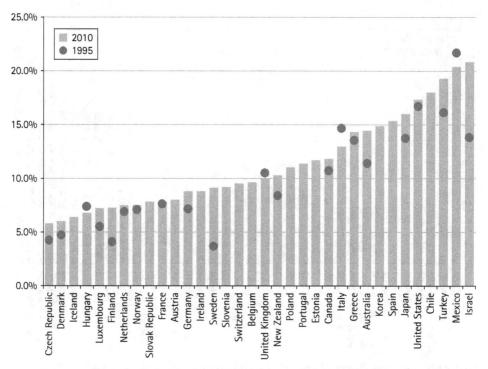

FIGURE 2.3 Levels and Trends in Relative Poverty in OECD Nations: 1995–2010

Note: Poverty is measured by the percent of persons living in households with family-size-adjusted income below half the median national income.

Source: OECD Income Distribution Database (via www.oecd.org/social/income-distribution-database.htm).

is its rapidity of observation with 15-year trends up through 2010 and beyond. Because it is clear that relative poverty rates may change substantially over short periods of time, and especially since 2005, such timely observations are very useful.

Poverty in LIS (and in OECD) data is typically somewhat higher among children (Figure 2.4).[9] Poverty averaged 13.5 percent among the countries for the total population but 16.5 for children. The correlation between child poverty and poverty in the total population is, however, quite high at .91, as reflected in Figure 2.4. The slope of the regression line in Figure 2.4 is 1.32, suggesting that child poverty rises about one-third faster than does overall poverty in these nations. The same sets of countries that are "high," "middle," and "low" poverty countries in Figures 2.2 and 2.3 also fall in the same relative positions for child poverty, but in some nations, like Uruguay and Brazil, child poverty is disproportionately higher than overall poverty. In South Korea, child poverty is substantially lower than overall poverty. In the others, child poverty and overall poverty track each other closely. In general, poverty among the elderly is both lower and falling compared to that among children, which is higher and rising in most nations (LIS Key Figures; OECD 2013: Figure 8).

Trends. Relative poverty trends using these same measures can be evaluated using the same data. The various time series allows us to break the countries into several

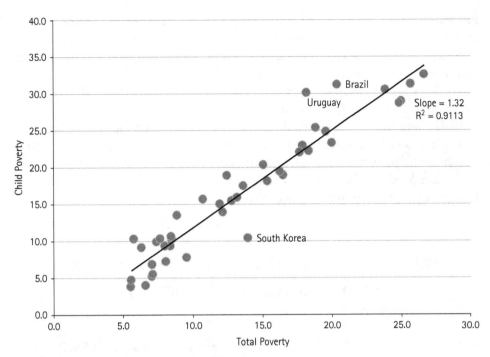

FIGURE 2.4 Correlation between Total Population Poverty (horizontal) and Child Poverty (vertical) in 38 Rich and Middle-Income Countries (late 2000s using LIS data)

Note: Poverty is measured by the percent of persons living in households with family-size-adjusted income below half the median national income.

different groups based on the range of years over which data are available and geographic/institutional comparability. The LIS data allows trends for 14 different countries since 1979.[10] Shorter term trends from 1995 to 2010 are best illustrated using the OECD data in Figure 2.3, where we have such data for 21 nations, but the longer term LIS trends (not shown here) are also interesting.

In analyzing trends in poverty, I am interested in both the direction of change and its magnitude. One finding from the LIS data series is that none of the 12 rich countries with the longest series of data back to 1979 have poverty that is appreciably (3 percentage points) lower in the most recent year than in the initial year of data from the late 1970s or early 1980s.[11] The shorter term trend data from the OECD (1995 to 2010 in Figure 2.3) suggests that relative poverty fell only in Italy and Mexico over that period, but both by less than 3 percentage points.

Each of the other rich countries with long trends has seen poverty rise or remain flat. Two countries stand out for particularly large increases: Israel and the United Kingdom each had poverty rates more than 6 points above their 1979 origins by the late 2000s. Poverty also rose steadily in the United States and Germany, increasing by about 3 percentage points in each, and by 4 points in Taiwan and more than 3 points in Belgium from 1979 until the late 2000s. The rest generally stayed within plus or minus 3 percentage point bands from the origin rate until the final year. The Nordic countries stand out as a cluster for seeing very little change in relative poverty according to the LIS data. In contrast, the OECD data in Figure 2.3 shows a massive increase in Swedish poverty, coming mostly after 2005, and almost no change from 1995 to 2010 in the United Kingdom. While relative poverty more than doubled in Sweden, appreciable increases can also be found in Australia, Finland, Israel, and Turkey over the 1995 to 2010 period (Figure 2.3).

While lessons can be drawn about the importance of the start and end dates in term of volatility, as well as differences across data sources, these trends suggest that progress against relative poverty was uneven and rare in rich nations over the past 20 to 30 years. Other than Mexico, relative poverty rates were not consistently falling over the past 25 years in any of the nations examined here.[12]

RELATIVE VERSUS ANCHORED POVERTY AND THE GREAT RECESSION

A different way to examine progress against poverty is to take a set of OECD nations and examine changes in both relative and anchored poverty in 12 nations over an 8- to 15-year period using LIS (Table 2.1) or across the shorter period of the Great Recession (GR) from 2005 or 2007 to 2010 (Figure 2.5). On average, relative poverty did not change much in the LIS between the mid-1990s and the mid- to late 2000s, but anchored poverty fell by about a third from 11.7 to 8.0 percent as shown in Table 2.1, suggesting that rising living standards amongst those near the poverty line, for people with incomes that would have been considered poor in the initial period are now higher than in the original period. Indeed, anchored poverty fell in every nation, reflecting rising living standards in Europe and elsewhere in the rich and MIC world, up until the Great Recession. In contrast, the changes in relative poverty over this same period were small on average in the LIS data but ranged from an increase of 4.6 percentage points in the United Kingdom to a fall of 2.5 percentage points in Hungary and Mexico. All other relative poverty rates changed by less than 2 percentage points over this period.

The effects of the GR are included in the four LIS data sets in bold for the United States, United Kingdom, Italy, and Greece in Table 2.1. In each nation a data point is also available for 2007 (or 2008, for Italy only) but is not shown in Table 2.1. In each nation, relative poverty rose by .2 to 2.2 percentage points through 2010, suggesting greater relative income losses for the poor than the rich in each nation during the GR. And despite the overall downward trends in each nation, anchored poverty *rose* between 2007/08 and 2010 in each of these four nations. Over the GR period, it increased by 1.2 points in the United States, 1.9 points in Italy, 2.6 points in Greece, and by 3.0 percentage points in the United Kingdom. Hence, in each nation, despite the

Table 2.1 Trends in Relative and Anchored Poverty

		Poverty Rates			Percentage Point Change from Initial Year	
		Initial Year	End Year			
	Years	Relative	Relative	Anchored	Relative	Anchored
Czech Republic	1996–2004	5.1	5.8	3.4	0.7	−1.7
Germany	1994–2007	7.7	8.4	7.3	0.7	−0.4
France	1994–2005	8.0	8.5	7.2	0.5	−0.8
The Netherlands	1993–2004	8.1	6.3	4.4	−1.8	−3.7
Hungary	1994–2005	9.9	7.4	4.8	−2.5	−5.1
United Kingdom	1994–2010	10.8	15.4	7.2	4.6	−3.6
Canada	1994–2007	11.3	11.9	7.6	0.6	−3.7
Australia	1995–2003	11.4	12.2	7.8	0.8	−3.6
Italy	1995–2010	14.1	12.5	9.5	−1.6	−4.6
Greece	1995–2010	15.4	13.6	6.4	−1.8	−9.0
United States	1994–2010	17.6	17.9	14.5	0.3	−3.1
Mexico	1994–2004	20.8	18.3	16.5	−2.5	−4.3
Average		11.7	11.5	8.0	−0.2	−3.6

Note: Poverty is measured by the percent of persons living in households with family-size adjusted income below half the median national income.

Source: Author's calculations from LIS data.

overall reductions in anchored poverty over the 10–15 year period shown in Table 2.1, the poor lost ground in both relative and real terms over the course of the GR.

The OECD data (Figure 2.5) suggest much the same pattern in these four nations but add many others as well. Iceland, Mexico, Spain, Estonia, and Ireland join the list above, where living standards fell during the GR and anchored poverty rose much faster than relative poverty. Indeed, relative poverty did not increase much at all during the GR except in Spain (and even fell by 2 percentage points in five years in Portugal and Ireland). In Belgium and Germany, anchored poverty fell but relative poverty did not change as much. In Portugal and Chile, both anchored and relative poverty fell during the GR. The changes in other nations were less.

In summary, I conclude that there was little progress in reducing relative poverty in almost all the rich nations examined here over the past two or three decades. Anchored poverty did decline in almost all rich nations from the 1990s up until the Great Recession in 2007. But since the onset of the GR, anchored poverty trends have been upward, with increases in anchored poverty in a majority of nations reducing some of the progress in real living standards for low-income households over the past 20 years, especially in the nations hardest hit by the GR. Relative poverty rates changed much less during the GR.

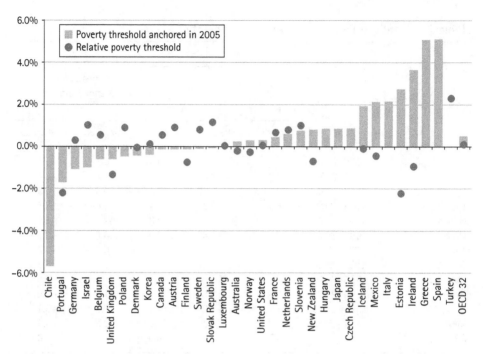

FIGURE 2.5 Anchored Poverty in OECD Countries: 2005–2010

Note: Poverty is measured by the percent of persons living in households with family-size-adjusted income below half the median national income.

SUMMARY AND CONCLUSIONS

This chapter is devoted to the intricacies of measuring poverty using objective quantitative, income-based measures, as is common in the vast majority of the published data in high- and middle-income and developing countries. Additional poverty concepts and measurement techniques abound. But the vast majority of poverty measures that are comparable across nations and across time are based on household-size adjusted disposable income (or some combination of consumption and income for global poverty measures).

Three main ways of setting a poverty line have emerged: absolute, relative, and anchored poverty measures. In many nations, poverty lines are set in some absolute way and perpetuated over time with change only for the cost of purchasing a given bundle of goods. But cross-national comparisons then demand translation of the same basket of goods across many nations, despite the fact that these baskets may differ substantially. The recent changes in the number of persons living below $1.25 per capita in 2005 dollars due to the change in PPPs makes one wary of the stability of such widespread price adjustments. Progress in reducing poverty means an increase in the real standard of living for those who cross the line and the opposite when real incomes fall, as in many nations during the Great Recession. Relative measures of poverty are most often used in cross-national comparisons, as they are easily administered and represent the idea that the poverty line varies with the living standards of other households in a given nation, so poverty ought to be measured relative to the median or middle person in a society, whether the median income is rising or falling. Both absolute and relative measures tell us something about changes in living standards for low-income people. In order to measure both relative and absolute progress in countries where one has a long and consistent measure of income, analysts increasingly use the idea of anchored poverty, whereby one fixes a poverty line within a country at the relative value in a given year and prices that forward to the most recent year. In this way falling or rising anchored poverty is similar to absolute poverty in terms of what it tells you about how standards of living are changing at the bottom of the income distribution.

When one uses these concepts across a range of nations, one can trace both changes in real or absolute living standards for low-income people and relative progress or regress compared to the middle person in a society. When we do so, we find that some of the progress against absolute poverty in rich countries between 1980 or 1990 and 2005 was undone by the GR, whose effects in most nations stretches beyond the 2010 period that we observed in this chapter. Longer term periods of rising inequality met with shorter term stagnant or falling real incomes in many nations over the course of the GR. These trends bear watching as we try to ensure adequate real standards of living for the poor in the face of rising economic inequality in most rich nations.

Notes

1. In addition to these objective poverty measures, several economists have used subjective measures of poverty and well-being, including income sufficiency (Clark and D'Ambrosio 2014; Groedart et al. 1977; van Praag 1968; Ravallion 2014b).

2. Lampman's chapter "The Problem of Poverty in America" (Council of Economic Advisors 1964) preceded President Johnson's declaration of the War on Poverty in his 1964 State of the Union address. But while Lampman used $3,000 of money income for his measure, it was not adjusted for family size. Orshansky (1965) produced a measure that had a similar poverty count, and a similar poverty line for a four-person family, but which differed by family size. In the late 1960s, Orshansky's measure became the official U.S. poverty measure.

3. Most relative poverty or deprivation measures rely on the median not the mean income, especially in cross-national studies, because the latter may be affected by sampling and nonsampling error in different surveys. Moreover the reference to the standard of living enjoyed by the middle or average family means the median family. See Smeeding et al. (1990).

4. See LIS key figures for country poverty rates at 40, 50, and 60 percent of the median, at http://www.lisdatacenter.org/data-access/key-figures/search/ and compare rankings there with European community rates from Eurostat (2012).

5. The idea of an anchored poverty line was developed by Atkinson et al. for the European Union in 2002 and Smeeding for a wider range of countries (2006). While on some occasions, it produces difficult to explain results (Brady 2009), it does offer a glimpse at how

a society is progressing compared to a given absolute living standard which is more time-wise proximate to a fully relative measure.

6. A pragmatic reason for not using the poverty gap, especially in cross-national studies, is that underreporting of incomes, the definition of incomes, and editing for item nonresponse may differentially affect the lowest incomes and overstate the poverty gap.

7. Indeed, we do not use the Eurostat (2012) poverty measures for two reasons. First, both the LIS and OECD measures rely on the same European Union Survey of Income and Living Conditions (EU-SILC) data for most of the European Union Nations and, second, because the EU-SILC data are very recent, starting only in 2005.

8. The Eurostat (2005) produces poverty measures for all 27 EU nations, including some which are not captured in either OECD or LIS data, and measures of poverty depth and severity as well. But their figures are at the 60 percent of poverty level and are not comparable to the half-median figures in LIS and OECD.

9. Here we look only at LIS data in Figure 2.4. For more on other OECD nations, see OECD (2008, 2013).

10. These 14 are the four Anglo-Saxon nations: the United States, the United Kingdom, Canada, and Australia; five central European nations: Belgium, Germany, France, Netherlands and Switzerland; two Nordic nations, Norway and Sweden; and three other nations: Israel, Mexico, and Taiwan.

11. Appreciably here means a more than 3 percentage point change. Atkinson and Marlier (2010) discuss the definition of a salient change in the poverty percentage, explaining that there are both supply (sampling error and other design elements) and demand considerations (use of the figures). They end up applying a 2 percentage point change criterion. The period examined here is a much longer one, so we choose 3 percentage points as the cutoff. The lines in Figure 2.5 show the 3 percentage point bounds in each panel.

12. Ferreira de Souza (2012) also suggests that both poverty and inequality fell in Brazil during the 1995–2009 period.

References

Aaron, Henry J. 1985. "Comment: The Evaluation of Census Bureau Procedures for the Measurement of Noncash Benefits and the Incidence of Poverty." Pp. 57–62 in *Proceedings of the Bureau of the Census Conference on the Measurement of Noncash Benefits*. Washington, DC: U.S. Department of Commerce.

Abel-Smith, Brian and Peter Townsend. 1965. "The Poor and the Poorest." Occasional Papers in Social Administration 17, London: Bell.

Atkinson, Anthony B., Bea Cantillon, Eric Marlier, and Brian Nolan. 2002. *Social Indicators: The EU and Social Inclusion*. Oxford: Oxford University Press.

Atkinson, Anthony B. and Eric Marlier. 2010. *Income and Living Conditions in Europe*, Eurostat (http://epp.eurostat.ec.europa.eu/cache/ITY_OFFPUB/KS-31-10-555/EN/KS-31-10-555-EN.PDF).

Atkinson, Anthony B., Lee Rainwater, and Timothy M. Smeeding. 1995. *Income Distribution in OECD Countries: The Evidence from the Luxembourg Income Study (LIS)*. Paris: OECD.

Bane, Mary Jo and David Ellwood. 1986. "Slipping Into and Out of Poverty: The Dynamics of Spells." *Journal of Human Resources* 21(1):1–23.

Bardasi, Elena and Quentin Wodon. 2009. "Working Long Hours and Having No Choice."
    Policy Research Working Paper No. 4961. World Bank Poverty Reduction and Economic
    Management Network Gender Group and Human Development Network, June.

Björklund, Anders and Richard Freeman. 1997. "Generating Equality and Eliminating
    Poverty—The Swedish Way." Pp. 33–78 in *The Welfare State in Transition: Reforming the
    Swedish Model*, edited by R. B. Freeman, R. Topel, and B. Swedenborg. Chicago: University
    of Chicago Press.

Blank, Rebecca. 2008. "How to Improve Poverty Measurement in the United States." *Journal
    of Public Analysis and Management* 27(2):233–54.

Blank, Rebecca and David Card. 2008. "The Changing Incidence and Severity of Poverty
    Spells Among Single Mothers" *American Economic Review* 98(2):387–91.

Boltvinik, Julio. 2000. *Poverty Measurement and Trends*. UN Development Programme,
    SEPED Series on Poverty Reduction. New York: United Nations (www.undp.org/poverty/
    publications/pov_red).

Brady, David. 2003. "Rethinking the Sociological Measurement of Poverty." *Social Forces*
    3(81):715–52.

Brady, David. 2005. "The Welfare State and Relative Poverty in Affluent Western Democracies,
    1967–1997." *Social Forces* 83:1329–64.

Brady, David. 2009. *Rich Democracies, Poor People: How Politics Explain Poverty*.
    New York: Oxford University Press.

Brady, David, Andrew Fullerton, and Jennifer Moren Cross. 2010. "More Than Just Nickels
    and Dimes: A Cross-National Analysis of Working Poverty in 18 Affluent Democracies."
    Social Problems 57:559–85.

Brandolini, Andrea, Silvia Magri, and Timothy M. Smeeding. 2010. "Asset-Based Measurement
    of Poverty." *Journal of Policy Analysis and Management* 29(2):267–84.

Buhmann, B., L. Rainwater, G. Schmauss, and T. M. Smeeding. 1988. "Equivalence Scales,
    Well-being, Inequality, and Poverty: Sensitivity Estimates across Ten Countries Using the
    Luxembourg Income Study Database." *Review of Income and Wealth* 34:115–42.

Booth, Charles. 1903. *Life and Labour of the People of London*. Second Series, Industry, Vol. 5.
    London: Macmillan.

Canberra Group. 2001. *Final Report and Recommendations of the Canberra Expert Group on
    Household Income Statistics*. Ottawa, Canada.

Canberra Group. 2011. *Canberra Group Handbook on Household Income Statistics*. 2nd. ed.
    Geneva   (http://www.unece.org/fileadmin/DAM/stats/groups/cgh/Canbera_Handbook_
    2011_WEB.pdf).

Carvalho, Soniya and Howard White. 1997. *Combining the Quantitative and Qualitative
    Approaches to Poverty Measurement and Analysis: The Practice and the Potential*.
    Washington, DC: World Bank.

Chen, Shaohua and Martin Ravallion. 2013. "More Relatively Poor People in a Less Absolutely
    Poor World." *Review of Income and Wealth* 59:1–28.

Chen, Shaohua and Martin Ravallion. 2010. "The Developing World Is Poorer Than
    We Thought, but No Less Successful in the Fight against Poverty." *Quarterly Journal of
    Economics* 125:1577–1625.

Chen, Shaohua and Martin Ravallion. 2012. "Absolute Poverty Measures for the Developing
    World." Chapter 20 in *Measuring the Real Size of the World Economy*. Washington,
    DC: World Bank.

Cellini, Stephanie, R. Signe-Mary McKernan, and Caroline Ratcliffe, 2008. "The Dynamics of Poverty in the United States: A Review of Data, Methods, and Findings." *Journal of Policy Analysis and Management* 27:577–605.

Clark, Andrew and Conchita d'Ambrosio. 2014. "Attitudes to Income Inequality: Experimental and Survey Evidence." Chapter 14 in *Handbook of Income Distribution*, edited by A. B. Atkinson and F. Bourguignon. New York: Elsevier-North-Holland.

Coleman, James. 1988. "Social Capital in the Creation of Human Capital." *American Journal of Sociology* 94:S95–S120.

Coleman, Richard P. and Lee Rainwater. 1978. *Social Standing in America: New Dimensions of Class.* New York: Basic Books.

DeNavas-Walt, Carmen, Bernadette D. Proctor, and Jessica C. Smith. 2012. *Income, Poverty, and Health Insurance: 2011.* Current Population Reports, P60-243, U.S. Census Bureau (http://www.census.gov/prod/2012pubs/p60-243.pdf).

Department for Work and Pensions (UK). 2012. *Households below Average Income* (http://research.dwp.gov.uk/asd/index.php?page=hbai).

Dhongde, Shatakshee. 2013. "Measuring Multidimensional Poverty in the U.S." Presentation at the Institute for Research on Poverty, University of Wisconsin–Madison, March 20.

Dykstra, Sarah, Charles Kenny, and Justin Sandefur. 2014. "Global Absolute Poverty Fell by Almost Half on Tuesday." Center for Global Development. May 2 (http://www.cgdev.org/blog/global-absolute-poverty-fell-almost-half-tuesday).

Edin, Kathy and Laura Lien. 1997. *Making Ends Meet: How Single Mothers Survive Welfare and Low-Wage Work.* New York: Russell Sage.

Eurostat. 1998. *Recommendations of the Task Force on Statistics on Social Exclusion and Poverty.* Luxembourg: European Statistical Office.

Eurostat. 2005. *Income Poverty and Social Exclusion in the EU25.* Statistics in Focus. Luxembourg: Official Publications of the European Communities.

Ferreira, F. H. G. and M. Ravallion. 2009. "Poverty and Inequality: The Global Context." Pp. 599–638 in *The Oxford Handbook of Economic Inequality*, edited by W. Salverda, B. Nolan, and T. Smeeding. Oxford: Oxford University Press.

Fisher, Jonathan, David Johnson, and Timothy Smeeding. 2014. "Inequality of Income and Consumption in the US: Measuring the Trends in Inequality from 1984–2011 for the Same Individuals." *Review of Income and Wealth.* July 2, 2014, DOI: 10.1111/roiw.12129.

Förster, Michael. 1993. "Comparing Poverty in 13 OECD Countries: Traditional and Synthetic Approaches." *Studies in Social Policy 10*, Paris: OECD.

Foster, James, Joel Greer, and Erik Thorbecke. 1984. "A Class of Decomposable Poverty Measures." *Econometrica* 3(52):761–66.

Fuchs, Victor R. 1967. "Redefining Poverty and Redistributing Income." *Public Interest* 8:88–95.

Gans, Herbert J. 1972. "The Positive Functions of Poverty." *American Journal of Sociology* 78(2) (September): 275–89.

Gilbert, Geoffrey. 2008. *Rich and Poor in America: A Reference Handbook.* New York: ABC-CLIO Press.

Glennerster, Howard, Ruth Lupton, Philip Noden, and Anne Power. 1999. "Poverty, Social Exclusion and Neighborhood: Studying the Area Bases of Social Exclusion." CASE paper 22, Centre for the Analysis of Social Exclusion. London: London School of Economics.

Gornick, Janet C. and Markus Jäntti. 2013. *Inequality and the Status of the Middle Class.* Cambridge, MA: Cambridge University Press.

Gornick, Janet C., Eva Sierminska, and Timothy M. Smeeding. 2009. "The Income and Wealth Packages of Older Women in Cross-National Perspective." *Journals of Gerontology: Psychological Sciences* 64B(3):402–14.

Gottschalk, Peter and Timothy Smeeding. 2000. "Empirical Evidence on Income Inequality in Industrialized Countries." Pp. 261–308 in *Handbook of Income Distribution,* edited by A. B. Atkinson and F. Bourgignon. New York: Elsevier-North Holland.

Grusky, David B. and Ravi Kanbur. 2006. "Introduction: The Conceptual Foundations of Poverty and Inequality Measurement." Pp. 1–29 in *Poverty and Inequality,* edited by D. Grusky and R. Kanbur. Studies in Social Inequality. Stanford, CA: Stanford University Press.

Hagenaars, Aldi J. M. and Bernard M. S. van Praag. 1985. "A Synthesis of Poverty Line Definitions." *Review of Income and Wealth* 31(2):139–54.

Haig, R. M. 1921. "The Concept of Income—Economic and Legal Aspects." Pp. 1–28 in *The Federal Income Tax,* edited by R. M. Haig. New York: Columbia University Press.

Halpern-Meekin, Sarah, Kathryn Edin, Laura Tach, and Jennifer Sykes McLaughlin. 2014. *It's Not Like I'm Poor: The Financial Lives of the Working Poor.* Berkeley: University of California Press.

Harrington, Michael. 1981. *The Other America: Poverty in the United States.* 2nd expanded ed. Harmondsworth, Middlesex: Penguin.

Haveman, Robert. 2009. "What Does It Mean to Be Poor in a Rich Society?" Pp. 387–408 in *Changing Poverty, Changing Policies,* edited by M. Cancian and S. Danziger. New York: Russell Sage Foundation.

Heggeness, Misty L., Sarah Flood, and José D. Pacas. 2013. "Defining Poverty in Terms of Time and Income: Understanding Parental Time." Paper Presented at Population Association of America, April 12.

Hills, John. 1999. "Social Exclusion, Income Dynamics, and Public Policy." Annual Sir Charles Carter Lecture, Northern Ireland Economic Council, Report No. 129, Belfast, NIEC.

International Comparison Program. 2014. *Purchasing Power Parities and Real Expenditures of World Economies: Summary of Results and Findings of the 2011 International Comparison Program.* World Bank Group (http://siteresources.worldbank.org/ICPINT/Resources/270056-1183395201801/Summary-of-Results-and-Findings-of-the-2011-International-Comparison-Program.pdf).

Jäntti, Markus and Sheldon Danziger. 2000. "Income Poverty in Advanced Countries." Pp. 309–78 in *Handbook of Income Distribution,* edited by A. B. Atkinson and F. Bourguignon. North-Holland, Amsterdam.

Jenkins, S. P. 2011. *Changing Fortunes: Income Mobility and Poverty Dynamics in Britain.* Oxford: Oxford University Press.

Johnson, David S. and Timothy M. Smeeding. 2012. "A Consumer's Guide to Interpreting Various U.S. Poverty Measures." *Fast Focus* 14-2012. Madison, WI: Institute for Research on Poverty (http://www.irp.wisc.edu/publications/fastfocus.htm).

Katz, Lawrence. 2014. "Neighborhoods vs. Schools." Robert Lampman Memorial Lecture. Institute for Research on Poverty, Madison, WI. April 23 (http://www.irp.wisc.edu/newsevents/other/lampman/media/2014/LampmanVideo2014.htm).

Kenworthy, Lane. 1998. "Do Social-Welfare Policies Reduce Poverty? A Cross-National Assessment." Luxembourg Income Study Working Paper No. 188, Center for Policy Research, Syracuse University, New York, September (http://lissy.ceps.lu/wpapersd.htm).

Lampman, Robert. 1964. "The Problem of Poverty in America." Pp. 55–79, in *Economic Report of the President, 1964*. Washington, DC: GPO.

Liibow, Elliot. 1967. *Tally's Corner: A Study of Negro Streetcorner Men*. New York City: Rowman and Littlefield.

Marlier, Erik, Anthony B. Atkinson, Bea Cantillon, and Brian Nolan. (2007). "The EU and Social Inclusion: Facing the Challenges." *Journal of Common Market Studies* 45(2):518–33.

Marx, Ive and Kenneth Nelson. 2013. *Minimum Income Protection in Flux*. Basingstoke: Palgrave Macmillan.

Massey, Douglas. 1996. "The Age of Extremes: Concentrated Poverty and Affluence in the 21st Century." *Demography* 33(4):395–412.

Massey, Douglas and Nancy Denton. 1993. *American Apartheid: Segregation and the Making of the Underclass*. Cambridge, MA: Harvard University Press.

Meyer, Bruce D. and James X. Sullivan. 2012a. "Identifying the Disadvantaged: Official Poverty, Consumption Poverty, and the New Supplemental Poverty Measure." *Journal of Economic Perspectives* 26(3):111–36.

Meyer, Bruce D. and James X. Sullivan, 2012b. "Winning the War: Poverty from the Great Society to the Great Recession." Brookings Papers on Economic Activity, Economic Studies Program, the Brookings Institution, 45(2) (Fall):133–200.

Mincy, Ronald, Isabel Sawhill, and Douglas Wolf. 1990. "The Underclass: Definition and Measurement." *Science* 248:450–53.

OECD. 2000. *Trends and Driving Factors in Income Distribution and Poverty in the OECD Area*. Social Policies Studies Division Occasional Paper No. 42, August. Paris: OECD.

OECD. 2008. *Growing Unequal? Income Distribution and Poverty in OECD Countries*. Paris: OECD.

OECD. 2011. *Divided We Stand: Why Inequality Keeps Rising*. Paris: OECD.

OECD. 2013. *Crisis Squeezes Income Puts Pressure on Inequality and Poverty*. Paris: OECD.

Orshansky, Molly. 1965. "Counting the Poor: Another Look at the Poverty Profile." *Social Security Bulletin* 28(1):3–29.

Piachaud, David. 1987. "Problems in the Definition and Measurement of Poverty." *Journal of Social Policy* 16(2):147–64.

Rainwater, Lee. 1990. "Poverty and Equivalence as Social Constructions." Luxembourg Income Study Working Paper No. 91, Center for Policy Research, the Maxwell School. Syracuse, NY.

Rainwater, Lee and Timothy Smeeding. 2003. *Poor Children in Rich Country*. New York: Russell Sage Foundation.

Ravallion, Martin. 2014a. "The Idea of Antipoverty Policy." In *Handbook of Income Distribution*, edited by A. B. Atkinson and F. Bourguignon. New York: Elsevier-North-Holland.

Ravallion, Martin. 2014b. "Income Inequality in the Developing World." *Science* 344(6186):851–55.

Ravallion, Martin and Shaohua Chen. 2011. "Developing World is Poorer Than We Thought, but No Less Successful in the Fight Against Poverty." *Quarterly Journal of Economics* 125(4):1577–1625.

Reardon, Sean F. 2011. "The Widening Academic Achievement Gap between the Rich and the Poor: New Evidence and Possible Explanations." Pp. 91–116 in *Whither Opportunity? Rising Inequality, Schools, and Children's Life Chances*, edited by Greg J. Duncan and Richard J. Murnane. New York: Russell Sage.

Ringen, Stein. 1985. "Toward a Third Stage in the Measurement of Poverty." *Acta Sociologica* 28:99–113.

Room, Graham J. 1999. "Social Exclusion, Solidarity and the Challenge of Globalization." *Inter Social Welfare* 8:166–74.

Rowntree, Benjamin Seebohm. 1901. *Poverty: A Study of Town Life*. London: Macmillan.

Ruggles, Patricia. 1990. *Drawing the Line: Alternative Poverty Measures and Their Implications for Public Policy*. Washington, DC: Urban Institute Press.

Sen, Amarta. 1976. Poverty: An Ordinal Approach to Measurement." *Econometrica* 46:437–46.

Sen, Amartya. 1983. "Poor, Relatively Speaking." Oxford Economic Papers 35:153–69.

Sen, Amartya. 1992. *Inequality Reexamined*. Cambridge, MA: Harvard University Press.

Shaefer, H. Luke and Kathryn Edin. 2013. "Rising Extreme Poverty in the United States and the Response of Federal Means-Tested Transfer Programs." National Poverty Center Working Paper No. 13-06. May (http://npc.umich.edu/publications/u/2013-06-npc-working-paper.pdf).

Sharkey, Patrick. 2013. *Urban Neighborhoods and the End of Progress toward Racial Equality*. Chicago: University of Chicago Press.

Short, Kathleen. 2012. *The Research Supplemental Poverty Measure: 2011*. Current Population Reports: P60-244, Washington, DC: U.S. Census Bureau, November (http://www.census.gov/prod/2012pubs/p60-244.pdf).

Simons, H. 1938. *Personal Income Taxation: The Definition of Income as a Problem of Fiscal Policy*. Chicago: University of Chicago Press.

Smeeding, Timothy M. 2006. "Poor People in Rich Nations: The United States in Comparative Perspective." *Journal of Economic Perspectives* 20:69–90.

Smeeding, Timothy M., Michael O'Higgins, and Lee Rainwater. 1990. *Poverty, Inequality and the Distribution of Income in an International Context: Initial Research from the Luxembourg Income Study (LIS) Project*. London: Wheatsheaf Books; Washington, DC: Urban Institute Press.

Smeeding, Timothy M., Lee Rainwater, and Gary Burtless. 2000. "United States Poverty in a Cross-National Context." Mimeo, Center for Policy Research, Syracuse University, NY, August.

de Souza, P. H. G. Ferreira. 2012. "Poverty, Inequality, and Social Policies in Brazil, 1995–2009." Working Paper No.87, International Policy Centre for Inclusive Growth UNDP, February.

Stevens, Ann Huff. 1999. "Climbing Out of Poverty, Falling Back In: Measuring the Persistence of Poverty over Multiple Spells." *Journal of Human Resources* 34(3):557–88.

Stevens, Ann Huff. 2011. "Poverty Transitions." Center for Poverty Studies, University of California, Davis, June.

Tach, Laura and Sarah Halpern-Meekin. 2013. "Tax Code Knowledge and Behavioral Responses among EITC Recipients: Policy Insights from Qualitative Data." *Journal of Policy Analysis and Management*. Retrieved June 3, 2014 (http://onlinelibrary.wiley.com/doi/10.1002/pam.21739/pdf).

Townsend, Peter. 1979. *Poverty in the United Kingdom*. Harmondsworth, UK: Penguin.

Townsend, Peter. 1993. *The International Analysis of Poverty*. London: Harvester Wheatsheaf.

UNICEF Innocenti Research Centre. 2000. "A League Table of Child Poverty in Rich Nations." *Innocenti Report Card 1*, UNICEF, Florence, June (http:///www.unicef-icdc.org).

United Kingdom Department of Social Security. 1993. *Households below Average Income*. London: Government Statistical Service.

United Nations Development Programme (UNDP). 1999. *Human Development Report*. July. New York: United Nations.

Vandecasteel, L. 2010. "Poverty Trajectories after Risky Life Events in Different European Welfare Regimes." *European Societies* 12 (2):257–78.

van Praag, Bernard. 1968. *Individual Welfare Functions and Consumer Behavior*. Amsterdam: North-Holland.

Vickrey, Clair. 1977. "The Time Poor: A New Look at Poverty." *Journal of Human Resources*. 12(1):27–48.

Wilson, William Julius. 1987. *The Truly Disadvantaged: The Inner City, the Underclass and Public Policy*. Chicago: University of Chicago Press.

Wimer, Christopher, Liana Fox, Irv Garfinkel, Neeraj Kaushal, and Jane Waldfogel. 2013. "Trends in Poverty with an Anchored Supplemental Poverty Measure." Institute for Research on Poverty Discussion Paper No. 1416-13 (http://www.irp.wisc.edu/publications/dps/pdfs/dp141613.pdf).

CHAPTER 3

....

STRUCTURAL VIOLENCE, POVERTY, AND SOCIAL SUFFERING

....

BARBARA RYLKO-BAUER AND PAUL FARMER

STRUCTURAL violence is the violence of injustice and inequity—"embedded in ubiquitous social structures [and] normalized by stable institutions and regular experience" (Winter and Leighton 2001:99). By structures we mean social relations and arrangements—economic, political, legal, religious, or cultural—that shape how individuals and groups interact within a social system. These include broad-scale cultural and political-economic structures such as caste, patriarchy, slavery, apartheid, colonialism, and neoliberalism, as well as poverty and discrimination by race, ethnicity, gender, sexual orientation, and migrant/refugee status. These structures are violent because they result in avoidable deaths, illness, and injury; and they reproduce violence by marginalizing people and communities, constraining their capabilities and agency, assaulting their dignity, and sustaining inequalities.

While these outcomes are "experienced individually, structural violence targets classes of people and subjects them to common forms of lived oppression. Hence, the experience of structural violence and the pain it produces has been called 'social suffering'" (Singer and Erickson 2011b:1). Like structural violence, this concept defies neat categorization, since it "results from what political, economic, and institutional power does to people, and reciprocally, from how these forms of power themselves influence responses to social problems" (Kleinman, Das, and Lock 1997:ix). Social suffering captures the lived experience of distress and injustice, while exposing the "often close linkage of personal problems with societal problems," thereby challenging the problematic tendency in the social, health, and policy sciences to focus mainly on the individual and ignore broader determinants (Kleinman et al. 1997:ix).

Structural violence focuses attention on the social machinery of exploitation and oppression—"the ways in which epic poverty and inequality, with their deep histories, become embodied and experienced as violence" (Farmer 2010:293). We have yet to find a better phrase to convey these harmful and often fatal processes. We begin with a vignette from the poorest country in the Western Hemisphere that vividly illustrates such processes and puts a face on structural violence. We then discuss the historical roots and characteristic features of this concept, explore its relationship to other types of violence, and survey how it has been applied across various disciplines to enhance our understanding of social problems linked to profound poverty and social suffering. We conclude with an overall assessment of the utility and relevance of structural violence to social analysis.

The Face of Structural Violence

Mirebalais is a busy market town in the middle of Haiti's Central Plateau. It appears on maps from the colonial era, when French slaveholders extracted great bounty from their most productive colony until a slave revolt that began in 1791 brought at least this form of exploitation to a bloody end. Through the first century of Haiti's independence, Mirebalais was a small agricultural hub where peasant farmers—the descendants of the victorious rebel slaves—gathered on Saturdays to buy and sell their wares.

In the 1920s, the Central Plateau was the site of skirmishes between the United States' Marine Corps, who were then occupying Haiti, and the armed resistance that ensued. The remainder of the twentieth century was not particularly kind to Mirebalais either. While its population grew, the town enjoyed very little in the way of modern infrastructure development. A few paved roads crossed the town square, and a single bridge spanned the Latem River. This relative modernity may have accounted for the decision in 2004 to site the regional hub of the UN's peacekeeping mission there.

In 2008, four hurricanes hit Haiti in less than two months. During the third of these, a tributary of the Latem rose in fury through the peacekeepers' camp, manned largely by Nepali troops, sweeping white containers emblazoned with the UN logo first into the river and then against the bridge, which collapsed. The bridge over the Latem has never been repaired; only a cement ford connects the Central Plateau to Haiti's western coast.

The hurricanes, powerful though their impact was, did not change life in Haiti as radically as the 2010 earthquake that killed over a quarter-million people and displaced over three million more, including 500,000 to the Central Plateau. One consequence was the nation's first recorded cholera epidemic. The lack of clean water in Haiti had been earlier identified as a predisposing risk factor for epidemic illness, including cholera (Varma et al. 2008). With few sources of water for drinking and cleaning other than the local rivers, the stage was set for the introduction of waterborne pathogens and their rapid spread throughout the country. Among the most vulnerable were those living with both poverty and mental illness (Ivers and Walton 2012).

From the age of 12, Pierre (a pseudonym) and his family knew that something was wrong. Pierre "heard things," and his auditory hallucinations evolved into frank paranoia and grossly disorganized thought. He left his family and took to wandering the streets of Mirebalais, often naked, sometimes taunted by local children and pass-ersby, but mostly left alone as *moun fou* (crazy person). He regularly bathed and drank directly from the Latem River, living a fragile, often miserable existence on the city's streets.

On October 12, 2010, Pierre, now in his 30s, suffered a violent onset of profuse watery diarrhea. He returned home but quickly died before his family could seek medi-cal attention. They contacted a funeral home in Mirebalais, where Pierre was bathed, dressed, and laid out for a classic Haitian wake. When two of the helpers who had prepared Pierre's body for burial fell ill with similar explosive diarrhea, suspicions of communicable disease were raised. By October 20, less than two weeks after Pierre's attack of sickness, there were scores of cases of profuse diarrhea in Mirebalais and in the villages connected to it by the Latem and its tributaries. The epidemic raced west along Haiti's largest river, reaching the coastal cities of Gonaïves and Saint-Marc. By October 22, the Haitian authorities, working with international authorities, announced that for the first time in recorded history, cholera had reached Haiti—likely brought there by Nepali UN forces and introduced into the river system through faulty sanitary practices at the UN base camp at Mirebalais.

In reporting on this first case, Ivers and Walton (2012:37–38) conclude: "This patient's case illustrates the relationship between an infectious disease epidemic, mental health, and globalization. It highlights the fact that to provide and maintain health in circum-stances of destitute poverty where many factors are at play . . . attempts to address indi-vidual pieces of health without consideration of the whole are as the Haitian proverb goes, 'like washing your hands and drying them in the dirt.'"

Understanding Structural Violence

Historical Roots

The term "structural violence" was introduced in a 1969 essay by Norwegian soci-ologist Johan Galtung, the main founder of peace and conflict studies and of the *Journal of Peace Research*. He defined peace as the absence of not only direct physical violence—ranging from interpersonal to collective violence—but also indirect struc-tural violence, caused by forces such as poverty, marginalization, and exploitation.[1] According to Weigert (1999:432), the notion of peace as more than the absence of war originates with Quincy Wright (1942:1305), who in *A Study of War* wrote that "the positive aspect of peace—justice—cannot be separated from the negative aspect—elimination of violence." Galtung (1969:183) further conceptualized "positive peace" as the "absence of structural violence" and explicitly linked structural violence to unequal power, especially "the power to decide over the distribution of resources," which results in "unequal life chances" (1969:171). He claimed that structural vio-lence led to more death and suffering than physical violence, an observation later confirmed by Köhler and Alcock (1976), who estimated that the fatal consequences of structural violence globally for 1965 were about 130 times greater than for direct violence (Gilligan 1999).

Galtung illustrated the idea of structural violence as avoidable harm by noting that deaths from tuberculosis in the eighteenth century were unavoidable, "but if [a person] dies from it today, despite all the medical resources in the world, then violence is present," and he similarly argued that "differential social impact" from earthquakes is preventable (Galtung 1969:168, 186). Since then, others have linked the structural violence of poverty and environmental destruction to the increased risks and consequences of "so-called natural disasters, where conscious policies have made populations vulnerable and unprepared for predictable harms triggered by dramatic weather events" (Demenchonok and Peterson 2009:53; Kagawa 2005).

The tragic aftermath of the 2010 Haitian earthquake, for example, included immediate fatalities and injuries as well as subsequent deaths and disease that were due to largely avoidable circumstances—lack of clean water, inadequate shelter, insufficient food, and poor access to medical care. It brutally exposed the pervasive, deeply rooted, and multifaceted structural violence that has plagued Haiti for decades (Farmer 2011a). The earthquake was, to use a term from clinical medicine, an "acute-on-chronic" event—direct violence on layers of structural violence. "It was devastating because a history of adverse social conditions and extreme ecological fragility primed Port-au-Prince for massive loss of life and destruction when the ground began shaking on January 12" (Farmer 2011b:3).

Johan Galtung expanded on structural violence in later writings, suggesting ways of measuring its impact (Galtung and Høivik 1971), examining "social science as structural violence" (1975:264), and exploring how all types of violence are legitimized (1990). There were even attempts to compute an "index of structural violence" (Høivik 1977) that focused on differential outcomes, such as life expectancy, death rates, or loss of life years.

Other scholars and advocates of social justice have explored the relationship of violence and injustice. Martin Luther King Jr. (1966) referred to "the violence of poverty" (see also Lee 1996; Gilligan 1997), and others have written about the violence of racism (Geiger 1997) and of hunger in the midst of plenty (Brown 1989). Newton Garver characterized violence as the violation of fundamental human rights, illustrated through examples from inner city ghetto life. His category of covert institutional violence that "operates when people are deprived of choices in a systematic way by the very manner in which transactions normally take place" is similar to Galtung's structural violence (Garver 1973:265). The feminist movement also played a role "in opening up the definitions of violence to include a range of behaviours including . . . physical, emotional and psychological abuse" (Morgan and Björkert 2006:442).

Around the same time, Latin American liberation theologians, such as Gustavo Gutiérrez (1973, 1983) and Dom Helder Camara (1971) were applying tools of social analysis to understand violence in that part of the world. Social structures such as profound poverty and racism, in conjunction with pervasive political oppression, were causing great suffering. Brazilian philosopher Paulo Freire (2004:118) wrote in 1977 that violence "refers not only to direct, physical violence, but also to . . . violence and hunger, violence and the economic interests of superpowers, violence and religion, violence and politics, violence and racism, violence and sexism, violence and social classes"—in other words, structural violence.

STRUCTURAL VIOLENCE: A VIEW FROM BELOW

For the last three decades, considerable effort has been devoted to critically examining and analyzing the epidemiology, political economy, and sociocultural nature of two deadly but treatable infectious diseases of global proportions: AIDS and tuberculosis—both the "centuries-old" TB and the "new" TB in its multi-drug-resistant forms (see Farmer 1992, 1997a, 1999, 2003, 2010). The aim of this work was to use theory and knowledge to advance praxis—to improve prevention and treatment for those *most at risk* of acquiring these diseases and dying from them. AIDS and TB serve as perfect laboratories for the study of structural violence (Farmer 1997b; Farmer et al. 2006), and are best understood as biosocial phenomena shaped by history, geography, and political economy, as well as the biological and social context of individuals and their communities (Farmer 2004). Both diseases disproportionately target populations living in great poverty. And such poverty is closely linked with gender inequality, racism, lack of access to the basic necessities of life, and lack of access to resources that maintain well-being, such as healthcare, education, jobs, and security (Farmer 2003; Mukherjee 2007).

All diseases that affect primarily the poor are, by definition, neglected diseases, and cholera offers an object lesson. One hundred fifty years after John Snow took the handle off the Broad Street pump, more than a century after his suspicions of bacterial origin were confirmed, 60 years after antibiotic therapy was discovered, and 30 years after a safe and effective oral vaccine was developed, cholera remains—among the world's poorest—a leading infectious killer.

The cholera epidemic in Haiti, an island nation of 10 million, is the world's largest in recent history. In its first year, cholera claimed some 6,500 lives and caused half a million cases (Farmer and Ivers 2012). These official numbers are undoubtedly low because there is little reporting capacity in rural areas, where the disease struck first and hardest.

If we know so much about cholera and its pathophysiology, epidemiology, treatment, and prevention, how did it become the leading infectious killer of young adults in Haiti during the international humanitarian response to the January 2010 earthquake? The short answer is that expectations are lowered for diseases that disproportionately afflict poor people. Investment in long-term public-sector water and sanitation systems, the bulwark against cholera and other waterborne diseases, have stalled or failed to keep up with demand. Safe, effective, and affordable oral vaccines exist, and yet remain largely unavailable in Haiti, and the same is true for timely diagnosis and care. We have the knowledge and tools for prevention and treatment; what we lack is an equity plan linked to a delivery system (Farmer and Ivers 2012).

The Haitian epidemic also demonstrates why structural violence is so often hard to describe. It is *distant*. In our postmodern world of global connections and instant images, "being a spectator of calamities taking place in another country is a quintessential modern experience" (Sontag 2003:18). Nevertheless, while the suffering of individuals whose lives and struggles recall our own tends to move us, the anonymous suffering of those more remote, geographically, culturally, or socially is often less affecting (Farmer 2006a).

It is largely *invisible*. Physical violence shows, whereas "structural violence is silent . . . [and] may be seen as about as natural as the air around us" (Galtung 1969:173). Many structural inequities are long-standing; they seem a natural part of the social order. But as anthropologist Nancy Scheper-Hughes reminds us (1996:889), "invisible" does not mean "secreted away and hidden from view, but quite the reverse. . . . [T]he things that are hardest to perceive are often those which are right before our eyes and therefore simply taken for granted." Haiti's extreme poverty and underdevelopment has certainly been visible for decades (Farmer 1997a; 2006b). Another factor is the preoccupation of politicians and the media with dramatic forms of violence. "Injustice—in either deed or word—is never linked to violence but rather interpreted in an economic, symbolic, or psychologist register. . . . [P]hysical violence . . . is never related to that other violence—of exclusion, discrimination, and humiliation" (Fassin 2009:117).

It is *massive*. The sheer weight and enormity of suffering is not easily or effectively conveyed by statistics or graphs. Economist Amartya Sen (1998:2) has argued for moving beyond "cold and often inarticulate statistics of low incomes" to look in detail at the various ways in which agency—"the capabilities of each person"—is constrained. In other words, we need individual case studies that are embedded in the larger matrix of culture, history, and political economy.

While no single axis of inequality—gender, race, ethnicity, immigrant status, sexual orientation, class—can fully define extreme human suffering, we argue for the primacy of poverty, which is often linked with other structures of inequity. "Today, the world's poor are the chief victims of structural violence—a violence that has thus far defied the analysis of many who seek to understand the nature and distribution of extreme suffering" (Farmer 2003:50).

Typologies and Intersections of Violence

In an effort to address violence as a global public health problem, the World Health Organization (WHO), developed a typology (Krug et al. 2002) that focuses on a "minimalist" notion of violence as direct and physical force, with no mention of structural violence despite recognizing poverty as an important risk factor in all kinds of violence (Bufacchi 2007:23; Perry 2009:377). As this example illustrates, typologies of violence, while useful (Rutherford et al. 2007), can lead to narrow conceptualizations of social issues. In addition, within real-life contexts, such categories are fluid and not so easily delineated. For example, in their discussion of how interpersonal physical violence becomes a routine part of everyday urban life for vulnerable and marginalized groups, Singer and Erickson (2011a) identify the subsets of "street violence" and "private violence," subcategories that often overlap or merge.

Rape, especially gang rape, can be a form of street violence but most often (certainly in the United States) occurs out of public view. In both instances it is often linked to structural factors, such as poverty and gender inequality, and to sociocultural meanings ascribed to women and their bodies. Rape can also be political violence when used systematically as a weapon of aggression or war (Stark and Wessells 2012), and its consequences often lead to increased structural violence. The global distribution of the AIDS epidemic, for example, is determined to a large degree by structural violence and "rape is a major factor driving the AIDS epidemic" (Mukherjee 2007:117). In such circumstances, rape encompasses several kinds of violence, with roots well established in "peacetime meanings of sexuality" (Olujic 1998b:33). Similarly, in the context of refugee and IDP (internally displaced persons) camps, rape may have all of these connotations and be a manifestation of structural violence, since it goes largely unreported and is often dismissed by humanitarian organizations and their staff as an "unfortunate" part of the refugee context (Whiteford 2009).

This complex relationship between direct and structural violence was noted over 150 years ago by German physician and anthropologist Rudoph Virchow, who wrote that "war, plague and famine condition each other" (cited in Rather 1985:115). There is ample evidence that war and political violence have grave impacts on the health and well-being of individuals, communities, and nations—beyond the immediacy of conflict-induced injury and death (Geneva Declaration Secretariat 2008; Levy and Sidel 2008; Pedersen 2002; Taipale et al. 2002).

Anthropologists, in particular, have shown that war and conflict not only affect infrastructures supporting local health care, education, markets, and farming activities, but also disrupt families and community support systems, damage the environment, interrupt means of livelihood, and displace populations (Leatherman and Thomas 2008; Rylko-Bauer and Singer 2010; Rylko-Bauer, Whiteford, and Farmer 2009; Singer and Hodge 2010). These impacts are often mediated by preexisting forms of structural violence which, in the aftermath of conflict, contribute to even greater levels of poverty, political marginalization, and racism (Fassin 2009; Miller and Rasmussen 2010; Nordstrom 2004; Panter-Brick 2010; Quesada 2009). Moreover, these consequences often have a long half-life (Becker, Beyene, and Ken 2000; Das 2007; Johnston 2007, 2011; Johnston and Barker 2008). Women are especially victimized by multiple forms of violence, which often interact and are shaped by both gendered dimensions of conflict and preexisting gender discrimination (Annan and Brier 2010). And children are particularly vulnerable, but the "costs [they] pay for the actions of war and its devastating aftermath ... are often neglected" (Quesada 1998:64–65; see also Kent 2006; McEvoy-Levy 2001; Nordstrom 2009; Olujic 1998a).

Structural violence, in turn, contributes in complex ways to the preconditions for explosive direct violence (Bonnefoy, Burgat, and Menoret 2011; Rylko-Bauer and Singer 2010; Rylko-Bauer et al. 2009; Singer and Hodge 2010). Armed conflict is more likely in low to middle-income countries with slower economic growth, greater gaps in income and resource distribution, and high rates of poverty, hunger, and poor health (Krug et al. 2002; Pinstrup-Andersen and Shimokawa 2008; Stewart 2002). Structural violence has even been examined as a form of genocide (Ahmed 2007; Lewy 2007). Rwanda is a compelling example. Decades of colonial and imperialist exploitation, coupled with the construction of ethnic difference, laid the groundwork for the explosive violence of 1994 (Farmer 2009). Western development aid ignored structural inequities and human rights violations, thus contributing to already existing poverty, unequal distribution of land and resources, social exclusion, and class divisions—so that by "the 1990s, the interaction between structural violence and racism created the conditions for genocidal manipulation by the elites" (Uvin 1999:54).

Several models have been proposed for exploring how both direct and indirect violence serve as precursors to collective physical violence (De Jong 2010). One example is the notion of a continuum of violence (Scheper-Hughes 1996, 2007; Scheper-Hughes and Bourgois 2004), based on the recognition that social tolerance of "everyday" structural violence, and the humiliation that accompanies it, sets the stage for normalization of more overt and visible forms, from police brutality and state-directed political violence to massacres and genocides (Scheper-Hughes 1996; Uvin 1999).

This is particularly applicable to Latin America where there has been a shift from the brutal political violence of the latter twentieth century to the more recent growth in criminal and interpersonal violence (Briceño-León and Zubillaga 2002; Sanchez 2006). These rates correlate with lower levels of development and higher income inequality within the region (Bliss 2010; United Nations Office on Drugs and Crime 2011). While conventional analyses link these trends to drug trafficking, gang membership, readily available firearms, and a weak criminal justice system (World Bank 2011), a number of anthropologists see a deeper link with the past (Bourgois 2001; Heggenhougen 2009; Manz 2009; Metz, Mariano, and García 2010), a "continuum of violence spanning the civil war years to the present ... [the] outcome of a history of structural violence, gender norms, and political repression" as well as racism directed against indigenous populations (Bourgois 2009:36).

Layered upon this legacy of political violence is the more recent "structural violence [of] rampant economic inequality, social exclusion, and persistent poverty arising from the imposition of neoliberal economic policies," namely structural adjustment programs linked to development aid and unfair international trade agreements (Sanchez 2006:179; Quesada 2009). Similar processes in other parts of the Global South have exacerbated the poverty, dislocation, and lack of jobs in the formal economy that serve "as a trigger" for growing rates of "reactive" social and criminal violence (Winton 2004:166–67).

Understanding Invisible Violence

Structural violence is only one among several forms of less visible violence that are interconnected in complex ways. Anthropologist Philippe Bourgois (2009) has proposed a conceptual framework for critically examining how the invisible processes of structural, as well as symbolic, and normalized violence are linked across time and space to various kinds of direct violence. A central element in all three concepts is the normalization of unequal power relations.

Symbolic violence is associated with sociologist Pierre Bourdieu (2000) and refers to sociocultural mechanisms and relations of unequal power and domination that exist within interpersonal relationships and in other spheres of life. It is embedded in ordinary daily life, manifested through language, symbolism, and actions that are perceived by both perpetrator and victim as normal or deserved, a legitimate and inevitable part of the natural social order. "Symbolic violence is . . . so powerful precisely because it is *unrecognizable* for what it is." Its power "rests precisely in its lack of visibility—in the fact that for those exposed to it the doubts and the fear engendered by it cause them to question themselves" (Morgan and Björkert 2006:448). A classic example is that of intimate partner violence, where women blame themselves and are blamed by others for the violence perpetrated against them.

Symbolic violence harms both psychologically and emotionally and is often used to justify everyday interpersonal and structural violence, as Simić and Rhodes (2009) demonstrate in their study of street sex workers in Serbia. Similarly, in his research of Puerto Rican crack dealers in New York's East Harlem, Bourgois (2003) shows how structural and symbolic violence interact and set conditions for the everyday interpersonal conflicts "that the socially vulnerable inflict mainly onto themselves (via substance abuse), onto their kin and friends (through domestic violence and adolescent gang rape), and onto their neighbors and community" (Bourgois 2001:11).

The *normalized violence* that Bourgois (2001, 2009) refers to is an adaptation of the concept of *everyday violence* initially developed by Scheper-Hughes (1992) to highlight the extreme poverty and high infant and child mortality that characterized life in Brazilian shantytowns. She later applied this concept to life circumstances affecting other socially marginalized people, such as Brazilian and South African street youth or the elderly in U.S. nursing homes (Scheper-Hughes 1996, 2007).

The concept of normalized violence recognizes the indifference in broader society and identifies mechanisms by which violence becomes an inevitable part of daily life for its victims. For example, in his life history of a street drug addict named Tony, Merrill Singer (2006:72) observes that "the threat of violence—emotional and physical—daily preparation for violence on the street, and enduring the agony of violence-inflicted pain were all commonplace to [Tony] as an integral part of the world of street drug use and sales. He had come to accept violence as he had bad weather, harsh but unavoidable." Some scholars have called for more detailed and nuanced analysis. For example, in examining the "routinization of political violence as a social violence of the everyday" in communist China, Kleinman (2000:235) concludes that we should pay closer attention to the "multiplicity of violences of everyday life" across classes of people and social contexts, each with "different histories, sustained by different social dynamics," and varied "outcome[s] in trauma and suffering."

APPLYING STRUCTURAL VIOLENCE IN SOCIAL ANALYSIS

Recent social science reviews call for multidisciplinary perspectives on violence (Bufacchi 2009; Krause 2009; Panter-Brick 2010) that counter the tendency to compartmentalize, with "few links among different . . . approaches" (McIlwaine 1999:455). We decided to examine the potential of structural violence as a unifying cross-disciplinary concept by surveying the literature in social science, social medicine, and public health from the last 15 years (1997–2012). We focused on published articles and limited the search to structural violence per se. The articles covered a broad range of topics, varied methodologies, and often appeared in cross-disciplinary journals, which made it difficult at times to assign articles to one particular discipline.[2] We begin with general remarks on how this concept has been used and then provide a more disciplinary-focused assessment.

Structural violence has definitely become part of the social science and public health lexicon. It seems to be used most often by scholars who take a critical materialist or political economy approach to social problems and issues. The majority reference Galtung's classic 1969 essay, and others refer to Farmer and his colleague's elaboration of this concept.[3]

The nature of structures of violence and the harms they inflict are context specific, which may explain the variability we found in how authors define structural violence. Many definitions are quite general: "violence inherent in the social order" (Eckermann 1998:304); "institutionalized injustice" (Nevins 2009:915); or "political and economic inequality" (Shannon et al. 2008:914). More detailed definitions tend to stress specific elements, such as exclusion, unequal distribution of resources, avoidable harm, or historically rooted, large-scale forces: "the systematic exclusion of a group from the resources needed to develop their full human potential" (Mukherjee et al. 2011:593); "processes historically rooted in . . . institutions that differentially enrich or deprive individuals of resources based on the individual's membership in a specific group" (Kohrt and Worthman 2009:239); and "social arrangements that systematically bring subordinated and disadvantaged groups into harm's way and put them at risk for various forms of suffering" (Benson 2008:590).

Authors refer to structural violence variously as a lens, frame, rubric, model, the-ory, or perspective, but in most cases, it seems to primarily serve as a conceptual framework that broadens levels of analysis. Many note its utility in countering tradi-tional explanatory models that narrowly focus on individual-level proximate causes relating to biology, behavior, attitudes, and cultural values of vulnerable persons or groups (e.g., Banerjee et al. 2012; Chakrapani et al. 2007; Huffman et al. 2012; Parker 2012; Sinha 1999; Towle and Lende 2008) or that assume agency, choice, and individ-ual control over behavior and circumstance (Adimora et al. 2009; Mukherjee 2007; Shannon et al. 2008).[4]

A structural violence framework shifts attention to "what puts people *at risk of risks*" (Link and Phelan 1995:80); it moves "beyond identifying health disparities to a clear understanding of the inequalities that shape inequalities" and the power relations that structure and sustain them (Leatherman and Goodman 2011:33); and it gets at cumula-tive root causes (Peña 2011) by addressing historical forces and social, economic, and political processes that shape risk and local reality. This has important implications for the kinds of measures chosen to restore social stability, security, and peace in the after-math of violence (Sanchez 2006).

Critiques of the concept urge greater attention to how structural violence is under-stood locally, by examining emotions, perceptions, and meanings within studies of how those affected by poverty, exclusion, and discrimination respond against or adapt to these assaults (Biehl and Moran-Thomas 2009; Bourgois and Scheper-Hughes 2004). This includes assessing how poverty, racism, and exclusion create contexts of shame, stigma, humiliation, loss of respect, and violation of self-integrity, which in turn affect health, well-being, and interpersonal relations, and sometimes lead to self-destructive behavior, extralegal activities, and physical—even collective—violence (Benson 2008; Bourgois 2003; Bufacchi 2007; Gilligan 1997; Metz et al. 2010; Uvin 1999).

Many of the articles we looked at can be classified as reviews or analytic essays, but there were also a number of largely qualitative empirical studies, They focus on var-ied sets of structural factors, depending on the topic being analyzed, but only a few attempt to operationalize and measure dimensions of structural violence (James et al. 2003; Kohrt and Worthman 2009). Variables chosen as proxies for structural violence are often not readily applicable to other research problems or contexts. For example, one study identified childhood malnutrition and diarrhea as the dependent variable and operationalized structural violence along dimensions such as development and gender inequality, measured by country and individual-level indices (Burroway 2011). Another multilevel study identified the closing of supermarkets in poor urban neigh-borhoods of Syracuse, New York, as an outcome of the structural violence of poverty and racism. The resulting poor access to food variety was associated with statistically significant increased risk for intrauterine growth restriction, a premature condition linked to low birth weight and other subsequent health problems (Lane et al. 2008). The most detailed example of operationalization is the *National Index of Violence and Harm*, developed to measure trends in the United States by explicitly quantifying both direct violence and the harm "done through negligence" or "the structuring of society overall" (Brumbaugh-Smith et al. 2008:352). The Societal subindex is divided into two domains: *institutional* and *structural*. Variables of structural harm include *social negligence* in addressing "basic human needs" relating to food, housing, health care, and education; *infant mortality and life expectancy*, as general indicators of quality of life; *hate crimes*, as reflections of prejudice; *employment discrimination; poverty disparity*, examined along lines of class, race, gender, and age; and *gang membership*, as a measure of disenfranchisement (Brumbaugh-Smith et al. 2008:355–57).

Some studies explicitly examine the interaction of a select group of such factors by incorporating multiple levels of analysis (Annan and Brier 2010; Shannon et al. 2008), modeling how structural violence relates to other kinds of violence (James et al. 2003), or developing a heuristic framework that includes facets of structural violence along with other factors that operate at different ecological levels—in one case, to understand the social epidemiology of HIV/AIDS (Poundstone, Strathdee, and Celentano 2004). Other studies diagram how structural violence within family, community, legal, and health care systems leads to interpersonal violence, discrimination, stigmatization, and increased HIV vulnerability (Chakrapani et al. 2007); model the interactions of factors—within employment, legal, and health care contexts—that increase vulnerability to tuberculosis and reduce treatment access for poor Uzbek labor migrants in Kazakhstan (Huffman et al. 2012); and identify ecological pathways for how macrolevel risk factors interact to increase HIV vulnerability for women of color (Lane et al. 2004b).

Structural violence clearly covers a long list of structures and harms. This has been a point of critique by some (Nichter 2008:148–49) who argue that it conflates different kinds of violence (Wacquant 2004) or labels all inequality as violent (Boulding 1977), critiques that both Galtung (1987) and Farmer (2004) have responded to. We believe that this flexibility is a positive feature of structural violence, making it applicable to a wide range of problems and issues which can be characterized as unjust, historically and socially determined, insidious, widespread, and causing avoidable social suffering.

USE OF STRUCTURAL VIOLENCE
ACROSS DISCIPLINES

The largest number of sources was distributed across political science and peace studies, public health and social medicine, and anthropology, but our survey starts with *philosophy*. Vittorio Bufacchi (2007, 2009) broadly defines violence as violation of a person's physical and psychological integrity and proposes a theory of violence that incorporates social justice without requiring a separate concept. While acknowledging that structural violence focuses needed attention on victims and the harm and humiliation they suffer from forces such as poverty and oppression, he critiques it for overlapping with the notion of social injustice. Others concerned with the ethics of peace have looked at the relationship between the globalization of violence and the structural violence of globalization (Demenchonok and Peterson 2009).

Critical geographers, in turn, have used the concept as an analytic tool to examine the geographies of disease (Hunter 2007); the shift in postsocialist Poland from intentional structural violence of the state, as in expulsions of minorities, to the indirect structural violence of the market (Fleming 2012); the geopolitics of militarization, disease, and humanitarianism (Loyd 2009); the relationship of increased violence and crime to unequal development in the aftermath of political repression in different parts of the world (McIlwaine 1999; Winton 2004); and negative impacts of postcolonial imperialism that have stymied justice and reparations for wrongs perpetuated during Indonesia's invasion and occupation of East Timor (Nevins 2009). These studies affirm that geography matters in the global distribution of injustice.

Articles with *sociological analyses* focus largely on issues of gender inequality and sexuality in relation to poverty and health. Several studies demonstrate the links between gendered structural violence and intimate partner violence (Morgan and Björkert 2006); disenfranchising economic policies that force poor women into sex work (Hudgins 2005); exploitative working conditions that result in poor quality of elder care and increased risk of physical violence against female caretakers (Banerjee et al. 2012); and the feminization of poverty due to neoliberal policies in sub-Saharan Africa (Ezeonu and Koku 2008). Others focus attention on the less studied topic of children as victims of structural violence, millions of whom are condemned to die from easily preventable and treatable diseases (Kent 2006). For example, structural factors relating to economic development and women's status, such as maternal education, control over reproduction, and political participation, were found to predict variation in childhood malnutrition and diarrhea across a sample of developing countries (Burroway 2011). Clearly, addressing gendered structural violence and improving the status of women are critical to continued progress in children's well-being and broader global health and development (Mukherjee 2011).

Galtung's influence is especially evident in *peace psychology*, which is concerned with "theories and practices aimed at the prevention and mitigation of direct and structural violence," and focuses on the devastating impact of social forces and structures such as moral exclusion, patriarchy, militarism, globalization, and human rights violations (Christie, Wagner, and Winter 2001:7). *Social psychology* has also been increasingly concerned with the causes and psychological antecedents of both direct and structural violence, especially regarding racism and discrimination against ethnic minorities (Vollhardt and Bilali 2008), and this is reflected in articles on gender, poverty, and violence (James et al. 2003); the consequences of historical racism and assimilation policy for Aboriginal Australian children (Bretherton and Mellor 2006); and the importance of historically determined poverty in understanding domestic violence within African American communities (Conwill 2007). Psychiatrist James Gilligan (1997:192), who incorporates structural violence into his key work on the root causes of violence, argues for shifting attention "from a clinical or psychological perspective, which looks at one individual at a time, to the epidemiological perspective of public health and preventive medicine."

Examples from *peace and conflict studies* or *political science* include critiques or expansions of Galtung's notion of structural violence (Barnett 2008; Parsons 2007); how structural inequalities shape peace-building efforts (McEvoy-Levy 2001); attempts to conceptualize and measure different facets of institutional and structural violence (Brumbaugh-Smith et al. 2008); explorations of how violent activism in the Persian Gulf region (Bonnefoy et al. 2011) or interpersonal violence in Latin America (Sanchez 2006) are shaped by historically rooted contexts of structural and everyday violence; assessment of the role of gendered inequality in predicting intrastate conflict (Caprioli 2005); and analyses of historic and contemporary global economic policies, such as transatlantic slavery, colonization and imperialism, artificial famines, and neoliberalism (Ahmed 2007; Prontzos 2004). Many of these studies crossover into development economics since they deal with the harmful consequences of global economic policies (Briceño-León and Zubillaga 2002; Uvin 1999).

The frequency of articles from *public health, social epidemiology, and social medicine* reflects, in part, the influence of those who have helped redefine notions of epidemiological risk by shifting attention from individual to sociocultural, political-economic, and environmental factors that constrain or shape behavior (Janes and Corbett 2011:139; Krieger 1994, 2005; Marmot and Wilkinson 2005). Many studies are cross-disciplinary and often focus on how poverty, racism, and gender inequity become embodied or expressed as disease and illness, in contrast with the "predominant public health approach to ... health disparities" that targets health promotion and has "each person take responsibility for his/her own health" (Lane et al. 2008:417). A fair number examine how structural violence shapes increased risk for HIV infection or decreased access to prevention and treatment among vulnerable and disadvantaged populations, such as poor women, male and female sex workers, and ethnic minorities (Adimora, Schoenbach, and Floris-Moore 2009; Cameron 2011; Chakrapani et al. 2007; Lane et al. 2004b; Renwick 2002; Shannon et al. 2008; Simić and Rhodes 2009).

Several qualitative empirical studies link these broader social and structural contexts to individual experiences, perceptions of self, or cultural norms and prejudices that determine the reality of those at risk or living with HIV/AIDS. For example, Towle and Lende (2008) demonstrate how cultural constraints on women's decision-making and roles in childbearing, childrearing, and health-care seeking intersect with poverty and women's disenfranchisement to negatively impact effective prevention of mother-to-child HIV transmission. They support the assertions that "structural violence ... is the shadow in which the AIDS virus lurks" (Mukherjee 2007:116) and that AIDS is "a symptom of 'structural violence'" (Hunter 2007:691).

Others look more specifically at how stigma and prejudice based on HIV/AIDS status and other health conditions, or sexual orientation, or immigrant/migrant laborer status, lead to discrimination and structural barriers to care, resulting in poor outcomes for health and well-being (Abadía-Barrero and Castro 2006;

Chakrapani et al. 2007; Huffman et al. 2012; Larchanché 2012; Parker 2012). For example, stigmatization, coupled with poverty, homelessness, and disproportionate incarceration, adversely influence the presentation, management, and outcome of mental illness and limit the role and voice of the mentally ill in civic and social life (Kelly 2005), which translates into "a lack of emphasis on mental health issues on social and political agendas" and inadequate services for the mentally ill (Kelly 2006:2121). Gender inequality, poverty, and marginalization also play a role in explaining women's experiences and risk for depression and anxiety in parts of India and Nepal (Kohrt and Worthman 2009; Rao, Horton, and Raguram 2012).

Expanding Structural Violence: Anthropology's Perspective

Structural violence was introduced to anthropology primarily through the work of Farmer (2003, 2004) and colleagues (Farmer, Connors, and Simmons 1996), whose understanding of the concept includes the importance of global connections, historical processes, and social context in shaping local realities; the embodiment of these inequalities as disease and social suffering; the interaction of biology with culture and political economy; and the limits of resistance and agency. Other anthropologists have expanded on this in creative ways (many have been cited throughout this chapter), some of whom have focused their ethnographic attention specifically on those forces that constrain agency and create suffering (Vine 2009). For example, one case study of environmental degradation and labor safety in Ciudad Juárez, Mexico, incorporated the previously mentioned elements of structural violence in a multifactorial analysis of health risks associated with a foreign-owned chemical plant and their consequences to well-being for nearby residents and workers (Morales et al. 2012). Another example is Akhil Gupta's (2012) multilayered ethnography of bureaucracy and poverty in India, which highlights key mechanisms of structural violence enacted by the state: corruption, the use of written records in a context where the poor are largely illiterate, and the expansion of bureaucratization. These result in the normalization of high poverty rates and avoidable deaths, despite large state investment in less-than-successful programs aimed at improving the lives of the poor.

Biological anthropologists, who take a critical biocultural approach, have found the concept useful in understanding how history and political economy help explain "the causes of malnutrition, disease, and other *biological outcomes of social processes*," such as poverty and racism (Leatherman and Goodman 2011:40) and in analyzing the origins and impact of conflicts (Leatherman and Thomas 2008; Martin 2008). Critical archaeologists have used a structural violence framework to address academic inequities (Bernbeck 2008); expand analyses of the slave trade and African diaspora

(Eiselt 2009:139); and examine the misuse of archaeology in revising national histories, reinforcing nationalism and state control, and appropriating land and cultural heritage within the Israeli-Palestinian context (Hole 2010; Starzmann 2010).

The widest application of structural violence has been in medical anthropology, especially among proponents of critical medical anthropology, some of whom have used this framework in much of their research (e.g., Lane and Rubinstein 2008; Lane et al. 2004a, 2004b, 2008; Leatherman and Thomas 2008; Leatherman 2011; Singer 2009a). Linda Whiteford, for example, highlights how particular groups are systematically excluded from basic resources—the poor from health care access in the Dominican Republic, volcano-relocated families from access to their lands and livelihoods, indigenous peoples in highland Ecuador from clean water and sewage disposal, and refugee women from reproductive health care—resulting in increased disease, illness, and social suffering (Whiteford 2000, 2005, 2009; Whiteford and Tobin 2004). Others have integrated structural violence with an environmental justice perspective (Johnston 2011; Morales et al. 2012; Peña 2011) or with critiques of unhealthy public policies, shaped by racism and political-economic interests, that increase vulnerability to harm, prevent access to care, deny human rights, and sustain poverty and other inequalities (Benson 2008; Castro and Singer 2004; Holmes 2013; Quesada, Hart, and Bourgois 2011; Rylko-Bauer and Farmer 2002).

Medical anthropologists have called for refining structural violence "as a theoretical frame, a method of inquiry, and a moral/ethical imperative" by paying attention to "the complexity and the contradictions of the lives of the poor" (Green 2004:319–20); by documenting how structural violence "operates in real lives" (Bourgois and Scheper-Hughes 2004:318) and how it is expressed "physically and psychically in everyday social suffering" (Walter, Bourgois, and Loinaz 2004:1167); by analyzing how past and present oppression and discrimination are inscribed in public policy and discourse, and on bodies and biographies (Fassin 2007, 2009); and by fleshing out the subjective aspects—emotions, meanings, perceptions—of social suffering and exploring the interconnections of structure and agency (Biehl and Moran-Thomas 2009), as well as examining how structural forces are mediated by cultural understandings.

Building upon Leatherman's (2005) notion of a "space of vulnerability," Quesada and colleagues have proposed extending "the economic, material, and political insights of structural violence to encompass . . . cultural and idiosyncratic sources of physical and psychodynamic distress" through the concept of *structural vulnerability* (Quesada et al. 2011:341), which they apply to their analysis of the living and working conditions of Latino immigrants in the United States. (Cartwright 2011; Holmes 2011). Others have noted the cumulative nature of structural vulnerabilities (Huffman et al. 2012; Ribera and Hausmann-Muela 2011).

Finally, *syndemics* offers another means of refining the concept of structural violence. Developed initially by Merrill Singer (1996) to describe the complex interaction between substance abuse, violence, and AIDS among inner city poor, syndemics is "the concentration and deleterious interaction of two or more diseases or other health conditions in a population, especially as a consequence of social inequality and the unjust exercise of power" (Singer 2009b:xv). It underscores the synergistic "adverse health effects arising from connections among epidemic disease clustering, disease interaction, and health and social disparities" (Singer 2009b:18), and has been applied to a wide variety of cases (Cartwright 2011; Ribera and Hausmann-Muela 2011; Singer 2009a; Singer et al. 2011). Using this perspective, Singer (2009b:140–53) notes that the impact of structural violence on health and well-being can be direct via factors such as poverty and racism that often have a cumulative effect, or it can be mediated through mechanisms such as stress, environmental conditions, diet, and self-destructive strategies for coping with the social suffering that structural violence inflicts.

CONCLUSION: THE RELEVANCE AND UTILITY OF STRUCTURAL VIOLENCE

As the chapters in this *Handbook* demonstrate, poverty is a complex phenomenon linked to other forms of social, political, and economic inequities and often rooted in long-standing, historically determined social structures. The analytic framework of structural violence focuses attention on mechanisms that support poverty and other forms of inequity, highlights the interdependence of these structural factors and their relationship to other forms of violence, and identifies the ways by which they cause unequal distribution of harm.

We have described how structural violence redefines the notion of risk by expanding the analytic gaze from individual characteristics or interpersonal relations to a nested series of broader social contexts and structural forces. Many authors argue that the understandings gained from such an approach, grounded in the real-life experiences of vulnerable populations, can lead to more effective local interventions, better social policy, and social change that addresses the roots of poverty, inequality, and social suffering (e.g., Abadia-Barrero and Castro 2006; Adimora et al. 2009; Towle and Lende 2008; Whiteford and Whiteford 2005).

Structural violence is a morally weighted term, not only because "structures of violence" clearly carry a negative social valence, but also because it is firmly linked to the notion of social and economic human rights (Lykes 2001). The "violence" part of the concept lends "the needed sense of both brutality and intent" (Mukherjee et al. 2011:593) and focuses attention on "the premature and untimely deaths of people. Violence here is not so much the violation of the everyday but the reduction to bare life" (Gupta 2012:21). The emphasis on *avoidable* harm is at the heart of structural violence and raises issues of social responsibility, redefines global ethics, and challenges the prevailing social change paradigm that is guided by utilitarian economics, where basic human needs like food, clean water, housing, and health— all too often denied to the poor—are viewed dispassionately as variables in global economic development.

Finally, structural violence challenges the notion of a purely descriptive and objective social science. It demands that we look at the world through the eyes of those least able to change it and that our research be linked in some way to advocacy and action. The end result will be a more engaged social science with a better chance of making a difference in alleviating poverty and addressing other pressing social issues of our time.

NOTES

1. Galtung (1969:170, 171) used "personal" instead of "physical" to emphasize that such direct violence involved some actor, be it an individual, a group, an army, or the state, in contrast to structural violence, "where there is no such actor . . . the violence is built into the [social] structure."
2. Four search engines were used: Google Scholar, JSTOR, PubMed, and Web of Science. Commentaries, book reviews, and gray literature were not included. We were greatly assisted in this task by Gretchen Williams Pierce (n.d.).
3. One study (James et al. 2003) draws its understanding of structural violence from Bulhan's (1985) work on Frantz Fanon and several cite Amartya Sen's (1999) theory of "development as freedom" and notion of "capabilities and needs."
4. See the following for discussions of this point within epidemiology (Heggenhougen 2005; Link and Phelan 1995), public health and medicine (Farmer 2010; Farmer et al. 2006; Quesada et al. 2011), environmental health (Peña 2011), and psychology (Christie et al. 2001).

REFERENCES

Abadía-Barrero, César and Arachu Castro. 2006. "Experiences of Stigma and Access to HAART in Children and Adolescents Living with HIV/AIDS in Brazil." *Social Science and Medicine* 62:1219–28.

Adimora, Adaora A., Victor J. Schoenbach, and Michelle A. Floris-Moore. 2009. "Ending the Epidemic of Heterosexual HIV Transmission Among African Americans." *American Journal of Preventive Medicine* 37(5):468–71.

Ahmed, Nafeez Mosaddeq. 2007. "Structural Violence as a Form of Genocide: The Impact of the International Economic Order." *Entelequia. Revista Interdisciplinar* 5:3–41.

Annan, Jeannie and Moriah Brier. 2010. "The Risk of Return: Intimate Partner Violence in Northern Uganda's Armed Conflict." *Social Science and Medicine* 70:152–59.

Banerjee, Albert, Tamara Daly, Pat Armstrong, Marta Szebehely, Hugh Armstrong, and Stirling Lafrance. 2012. "Structural Violence in Long-term, Residential Care for Older People: Comparing Canada and Scandinavia." *Social Science & Medicine* 74:390–98.

Barnett, Jon. 2008. "Peace and Development: Towards a New Synthesis." *Journal of Peace Research* 45(1):75–89.

Becker, Gay, Yewoubdar Beyene, and Pauline Ken. 2000. "Memory, Trauma, and Embodied Distress: The Management of Disruption in the Stories of Cambodians in Exile." *Ethos* 28(3):320–45.

Benson, Peter. 2008. "El Campo: Faciality and Structural Violence in Farm Labor Camps." *Cultural Anthropology* 23(4):589–629.

Bernbeck, Reinhard. 2008. "Structural Violence in Archeology." *Archaeologies: Journal of the World Archeological Congress.* 4(3):390–413.

Biehl, João and Amy Moran-Thomas. 2009. "Symptom: Subjectivities, Social Ills, Technologies." *Annual Review of Anthropology* 38:267–88.

Bliss, Katherine. 2010. "Gender Based Violence in Latin America." Blog, November 3. Washington, DC: Center for Strategic and International Studies. Retrieved July 23, 2012 (http://www.smartglobalhealth.org/blog/entry/gender-based-violence-in-latin-america/).

Bonnefoy, Laurent, François Burgat, and Pascal Menoret. 2011. "Introduction." Special issue, "From Structural Violence to Violent Activism around the Persian Gulf." *The Muslim World* 101:125–29.

Boulding, Kenneth E. 1977. "Twelve Friendly Quarrels with Johan Galtung. *Journal of Peace Research* 14(1):75–86.

Bourdieu, Pierre. [1997] 2000. *Pascalian Meditations.* Translated by Richard Nice. Stanford CA: Stanford University Press.

Bourgois, Philippe. 2001. "The Power of Violence in War and Peace: Post–Cold War Lessons from El Salvador." *Ethnography* 2(1):5–34.

Bourgois, Philippe. 2003. *In Search of Respect: Selling Crack in El Barrio.* 2nd ed. New York: Cambridge University Press.

Bourgois, Philippe. 2009. "Recognizing Invisible Violence: A Thirty-Year Ethnographic Retrospective." Pp. 17–40, in *Global Health in Times of Violence,* edited by Barbara Rylko-Bauer, Linda Whiteford, and Paul Farmer. Santa Fe: School for Advanced Research Press.

Bourgois, Philippe and Nancy Scheper-Hughes. 2004. "Commentary on an Anthropology of Structural Violence." *Current Anthropology* 45(3):317–18.

Bretherton, Di and David Mellor. 2006. "Reconciliation between Aboriginal and Other Australians: The 'Stolen Generations.'" *Journal of Social Issues* 62(1):81–98.

Briceño-León, Roberto and Verónica Zubillaga. 2002. "Violence and Globalization in Latin America." *Current Sociology* 50:19–37.

Brown, J. Larry. 1989. "When Violence Has a Benevolent Face: The Paradox of Hunger in the World's Wealthiest Democracy." *International Journal of Health Services* 19(2):257–77.

Brumbaugh-Smith, Heidi Gross, Neil Wollman, and Bradley Yoder. 2008. "NIVAH: A Composite Index Measuring Violence and Harm in the U.S." *Social Indicators Research* 85(3):351–87.

Bufacchi, Vittorio. 2007. *Violence and Social Justice.* New York: Palgrave Macmillan.

Bufacchi, Vittorio. 2009. "Rethinking Violence." *Global Crime* 10(4):293–97.

Bulhan, Hussien Abdilahi. 1985. *Frantz Fanon and the Psychology of Oppression.* New York: Plenum.

Burroway, Rebekah. 2011. "Structural Violence and Child Health: A Multi-Level Analysis of Development, Gender Inequality, and Democracy in Developing Countries." PhD dissertation, Department of Sociology, Duke University, Durham, NC.

Camara, Helder. 1971. *Spiral of Violence.* London: Sheed and Ward.

Cameron, Drew. 2011. "The Consequences of Rationing Antiretroviral Treatment in Sub-Saharan Africa." *Journal of International Service* 20(1):1–18.

Caprioli, M. 2005. "Primed for Violence: The Role of Gender Inequality in Predicting Internal Conflict." *International Studies Quarterly* 49:161–78.

Cartwright, Elizabeth. 2011. "Immigrant Dreams: Legal Pathologies and Structural Vulnerabilities Along the Immigrant Continuum." *Medical Anthropology* 30(5):475–95.

Castro, Arachu and Merrill Singer, eds. 2004. *Unhealthy Health Policy: A Critical Anthropological Examination*. Walnut Creek, CA: AltaMira.

Chakrapani, Venkatesan, Peter A. Newman, Murali Shunmugam, Alan McLuckie, and Fredrick Melwin. 2007. "Structural Violence Against *Kothi*-Identified Men Who Have Sex with Men in Chennai, India: A Qualitative Investigation." *AIDS Education and Prevention* 19(4):346–64.

Christie, Daniel J., Richard V. Wagner, and Deborah Du Nann Winter. 2001. *Peace, Conflict, and Violence: Peace Psychology for the 21st Century*. Upper Saddle River, NJ: Prentice Hall.

Conwill, William L. 2007. "Neoliberal Policy as Structural Violence: Its Links to Domestic Violence in Black Communities in the United States." Pp. 127–46 in *The Gender of Globalization*, edited by Nandini Gunewardena and Ann Kingsolver. Santa Fe: School for Advanced Research.

Das, Veena. 2007. *Life and Words: Violence and the Descent into the Ordinary*. Berkeley: University of California Press.

De Jong, Joop T. V. M. 2010. "A Public Health Framework to Translate Risk Factors Related to Political Violence and War into Multi-level Preventive Interventions." *Social Science and Medicine* 70:71–79.

Demenchonok, Edward and Richard Peterson. 2009. "Globalization and Violence: The Challenge to Ethics." *American Journal of Economics and Sociology* 68(1):51–76.

Eckermann, A.-K. 1998. "The Economics of Aboriginal Education." *International Journal of Social Economics* 25(2):302–13.

Eiselt, B. Sunday. 2009. "Americanist Archaeologies: 2008 in Review." *American Anthropologist* 111(2):137–45.

Ezeonu, Ifeanyi and Emmanuel Koku. 2008. "Crimes of Globalization: The Feminization of HIV Pandemic in Sub-Saharan Africa." *The Global South* 2(2):112–29.

Farmer, Paul. 1992. *AIDS and Accusation: Haiti and the Geography of Blame*. Berkeley: University of California Press.

Farmer, Paul. 1997a. "On Suffering and Structural Violence: A View From Below." Pp. 261–83 in *Social Suffering*, edited by Arthur Kleinman, Veena Das, and Margaret Lock. Berkeley: University of California Press.

Farmer, Paul. 1997b. "Social Scientists and the New Tuberculosis." *Social Science and Medicine* 44(3):347–58.

Farmer, Paul. 1999. *Infections and Inequalities: The Modern Plagues*. Berkeley: University of California Press.

Farmer, Paul. 2003. *Pathologies of Power: Health, Human Rights, and the New War on the Poor*. Berkeley: University of California Press.

Farmer, Paul. 2004. "An Anthropology of Structural Violence." *Current Anthropology* 45(3):305–25.

Farmer, Paul. 2006a. "Never Again? Reflections on Human Values and Human Rights." Pp. 137–88 in *The Tanner Lectures on Human Values*. Vol. 26, edited by Grethe B. Peterson. Salt Lake City: University of Utah Press.

Farmer, Paul. 2006b. *The Uses of Haiti*. 3rd ed. Monroe, ME: Common Courage Press.

Farmer, Paul. 2009. "'Landmine Boy' and the Tomorrow of Violence." Pp. 41–62 in *Global Health in Times of Violence*, edited by Barbara Rylko-Bauer, Linda Whiteford, and Paul Farmer. Santa Fe: School for Advanced Research Press.

Farmer, Paul. 2010. *Partner to the Poor: A Paul Farmer Reader*, edited by Haun Saussy. Berkeley: University of California Press.

Farmer, Paul. 2011a. *Haiti after the Earthquake*, edited by Abbey Gardner and Cassia Van Der Hoof Holstein. New York: PublicAffairs.

Farmer, Paul. 2011b. "Writing about Suffering." Pp. 1–245 in *Haiti After the Earthquake*, edited by Abbey Gardner and Cassia Van Der Hoof Holstein. New York: Public Affairs.

Farmer, Paul E., Margaret Connors, and Janie Simmons, eds. 1996. *Women, Poverty, and AIDS: Sex, Drugs, and Structural Violence*. Monroe, ME: Common Courage Press.

Farmer, Paul E., and Louise C. Ivers. 2012. "Cholera in Haiti: The Equity Agenda and the Future of Tropical Medicine." *American Journal of Tropical Medicine and Hygiene* 86(1):7–8.

Farmer, Paul E., Bruce Nizeye, Sara Stulac, and Salmaan Keshavjee. 2006. "Structural Violence and Clinical Medicine." *PLoS Medicine* 3(10):1686–91.

Fassin, Didier. 2007. *When Bodies Remember: Experiences and Politics of AIDS in South Africa*. Translated by Amy Jacobs and Gabrielle Varro. Berkeley: University of California Press.

Fassin, Didier. 2009. "A Violence of History: Accounting for AIDS in Post-apartheid South Africa." Pp. 113–35 in *Global Health in Times of Violence*, edited by Barbara Rylko-Bauer, Linda Whiteford, and Paul Farmer. Santa Fe: School for Advanced Research Press.

Fleming, Michael. 2012. "The Regime of Violence in Socialist and Postsocialist Poland." *Annals of the Association of American Geographers* 102(2):482–98.

Freire, Paulo. 2004. *Pedagogy of Indignation*. Boulder, CO: Paradigm.

Galtung, Johan. 1969. "Violence, Peace, and Peace Research." *Journal of Peace Research* 6(3):167–91.

Galtung, Johan. 1975. "Is Peaceful Research Possible: On the Methodology of Peace Research." Pp. 263–79 in *Peace, Research, Education, Action: Essays in Peace Research*. Vol. 1, edited by Johan Galtung. Copenhagen: Christian Ejlers.

Galtung, Johan. 1987. "Only One Quarrel with Kenneth Boulding." *Journal of Peace Research* 24(2):199–203.

Galtung, Johan. 1990. "Cultural Violence." *Journal of Peace Research* 27(3):291–305.

Galtung, Johan and Tord Høivik. 1971. "Structural and Direct Violence: A Note on Operationalization." *Journal of Peace Research* 8(1):73–76.

Garver, Newton. 1973. "What Violence Is." Pp. 256–66 in *Philosophy for a New Generation*. 2nd ed., edited by A. K. Bierman and James A. Gould. New York: Macmillan.

Geiger, H. Jack. 1997. "Inequity as Violence: Race, Health and Human Rights in the United States." *Health and Human Rights* 2(3):7–13.

Geneva Declaration Secretariat. 2008. *Global Burden of Armed Violence*. Geneva, Switzerland: Geneva Declaration Secretariat.

Gilligan, James. 1997. *Violence: Reflections on a National Epidemic*. New York: Vintage Books.

Gilligan, James. 1999. "Structural Violence." Pp. 229–33, in *Violence in America: An Encyclopedia*, edited by Ronald Gottesman. New York: Charles Scribner and Sons.

Green, Linda. 2004. "Commentary on an Anthropology of Structural Violence." *Current Anthropology* 45(3):319–20.

Gupta, Akhil. 2012. *Red Tape: Bureaucracy, Structural Violence, and Poverty in India*. Durham, NC: Duke University Press.

Gutiérrez, Gustavo. 1973. *A Theology of Liberation*. Edited and translated by Sister Caridad Inda and John Eagleson. Maryknoll, NY: Orbis Books.

Gutiérrez, Gustavo. 1983. *The Power of the Poor in History*. Translated by Robert R. Barr. Maryknoll, NY: Orbis Books.

Heggenhougen, H. K. 2005. "The Epidemiology of Inequity: Will Research Make a Difference?" *Norsk Epidemiologi* 15(2):127–32.

Heggenhougen, H. K. 2009. "Planting 'Seeds of Health' in the Fields of Structural Violence." Pp. 181–99, in *Global Health in Times of Violence*, edited by Barbara Rylko-Bauer, Linda Whiteford, and Paul Farmer. Santa Fe: School for Advanced Research Press.

Hole, Brian. 2010. "Overcoming Structural Violence: The WAC Inter-Congress in Ramallah, August 2009." *Public Archaeology* 9(1):48–57.

Holmes, Seth M. 2011 "Structural Vulnerability and Hierarchies of Ethnicity and Citizenship on the Farm." *Medical Anthropology* 30(4):425–49.

Holmes, Seth M. 2013. *Fresh Fruit, Broken Bodies: Migrant Farmworkers in the United States.* Berkeley: University of California Press.

Høivik, Tord. 1977. "The Demography of Structural Violence." *Journal of Peace Research* 14(1):59–73.

Hudgins, Anastasia. 2005. "NGO Policy, Sex Workers and Structural Violence: Looking Beyond the Brothel Village." *Voices* 7(1):9–12.

Huffman, Samantha A., Jaap Veen, Monique M. Hennink, and Deborah A. McFarland. 2012. "Exploitation, Vulnerability to Tuberculosis, and Access to Treatment among Uzbek Labor Migrants in Kazakhstan." *Social Science and Medicine* 74:864–72.

Hunter, Mark. 2007. "The Changing Political Economy of Sex in South Africa: The Significance of Unemployment and Inequalities to the Scale of the AIDS Pandemic." *Social Science and Medicine* 64:689–700.

Ivers, Louise C. and David A. Walton. 2012. "The 'First' Case of Cholera in Haiti: Lessons for Global Health." *American Journal of Tropical Medicine and Hygiene* 86(1):36–38.

James, Susan E., Janice Johnson, Chitra Raghavan, Tessa Lemos, Michele Barakett, and Diana Woolis. 2003. "The Violent Matrix: A Study of Structural, Interpersonal, and Intrapersonal Violence Among a Sample of Poor Women." *American Journal of Community Psychology* 31(1/2):129–41.

Janes, Craig R. and Kitty K. Corbett. 2011. "Global Health." Pp. 135–57 in *A Companion to Medical Anthropology*, edited by Merrill Singer and Pamela I. Erickson. Malden, MA: Wiley-Blackwell.

Johnston, Barbara Rose, ed. 2007. *Half-Lives & Half-Truths: Confronting the Radioactive Legacies of the Cold War.* Santa Fe, NM: School for Advanced Research Press.

Johnston, Barbara Rose, ed. 2011. *Life and Death Matters: Human Rights, Environment, and Social Justice.* 2nd ed. Walnut Creek, CA: Left Coast Press.

Johnston, Barbara Rose and Holly M. .Barker. 2008. *Consequential Damages of Nuclear War: The Rongelap Report.* Walnut Creek, CA: Left Coast Press.

Kagawa, Fumiyo. 2005. "Emergency Education: A Critical Review of the Field." *Comparative Education* 41(4):487–503.

Kelly, Brendan D. 2005. "Structural Violence and Schizophrenia." *Social Science and Medicine* 61:721–30.

Kelly, Brendan D. 2006. "The Power Gap: Freedom, Power and Mental Illness." *Social Science and Medicine* 63:2118–28.

Kent, George. 2006. "Children as Victims of Structural Violence." *Societies without Borders* 1:53–67.

King, Martin Luther Jr. 1966. "The Violence of Poverty." *New York Amsterdam News*, January 1, p. 6.

Kleinman, Arthur. 2000. "The Violences of Everyday Life: The Multiple Forms and Dynamics of Social Violence." Pp. 226–41 in *Violence and Subjectivity*, edited by Veena Das, Arthur Kleinman, Mamphela Ramphele, and Pamela Reynolds. Berkeley: University of California Press.

Kleinman, Arthur, Veena Das, and Margaret Lock, eds. 1997. *Social Suffering*. Berkeley: University of California Press.

Köhler, Gernot and Norman Alcock. 1976. "An Empirical Table of Structural Violence." *Journal of Peace Research* 13(4):343–56.

Kohrt, Brandon A. and Carol M. Worthman. 2009. "Gender and Anxiety in Nepal: The Role of Social Support, Stressful Life Events, and Structural Violence." *CNS Neuroscience and Therapeutics* 15:237–48.

Krause, Keith. 2009. "Beyond Definition: Violence in Global Perspective." *Global Crime* 10(4):337–55.

Krieger, Nancy. 1994. Epidemiology and the Web of Causation: Has Anyone Seen the Spider? *Social Science and Medicine* 39(7):887–903.

Krieger, Nancy. 2004. *Embodying Inequality: Epidemiologic Perspectives*. Amityville, NY: Baywood.

Krug, Etienne G., Linda L. Dahlberg, James A. Mercy, Anthony B. Zwi, and Rafael Lozano, eds. 2002. *World Report of Violence and Health*. Geneva: World Health Organization.

Lane, Sandra D. and Robert A. Rubinstein. 2008. "Collaborating to Confront Health Disparities in Syracuse, New York." *Society for Applied Anthropology Newsletter* 19(1):19–20.

Lane, Sandra D., Robert H. Keefe, Robert A. Rubinstein, Brooke A. Levandowski, Michael Freedman, Alan Rosenthal, Donald A. Cibula, and Maria Czerwinski. 2004a. "Marriage Promotion and Missing Men: African American Women in a Demographic Double Bind." *Medical Anthropology Quarterly* 18(4):405–28.

Lane, Sandra D., Robert A. Rubinstein, Robert H. Keefe, Noah Webster, Donald A. Cibula, Alan Rosenthal, and Jesse Dowdell. 2004b. "Structural Violence and Racial Disparity in HIV Transmission." *Journal of Health Care for the Poor and Underserved* 15:319–35.

Lane, Sandra D., Robert H. Keefe, Robert Rubinstein, Brooke A. Levandowski, Noah Webster, Donald A. Cibula, Adwoa K. Boahene, Olabisi Dele-Michael, Darlene Carter, Tanika Jones, Martha Wojtowycz, and Jessica Brill. 2008. "Structural Violence, Urban Retail Food Markets, and Low Birth Weight." *Health & Place* 14:415–23.

Larchanché, Stéphanie. 2012. "Intangible Obstacles: Health Implications of Stigmatization, Structural Violence, and Fear among Undocumented Immigrants in France." *Social Science and Medicine* 74:858–63.

Leatherman, Thomas. 2005. "A Space of Vulnerability in Poverty and Health: Political-Economy and Biocultural Analysis." *Ethos* 33(1):46–70.

Leatherman, Thomas. 2011. "Health, Human Rights, and War: Structural Violence, Armed Conflict, and Human Health in the Andes." Pp. 333–48, in *Life and Death Matters: Human Rights, Environment, and Social Justice*, 2nd ed., edited by Barbara Rose Johnston. Walnut Creek, CA: Left Coast Press.

Leatherman, Thomas and Alan H. Goodman. 2011. "Critical Biocultural Approaches in Medical Anthropology." Pp. 29–47 in *A Companion to Medical Anthropology*, edited by Merrill Singer and Pamela I. Erickson. Malden, MA: Wiley-Blackwell.

Leatherman, Thomas and R. Brooke Thomas. 2008. "Structural Violence, Political Violence and the Health Costs of Civil Conflict: A Case Study from Peru." Pp. 196–220 in *Anthropology and Public Health: Bridging Differences in Culture and Society*. 2nd ed. Oxford: Oxford University Press.

Lee, Steven. 1996. "Poverty and Violence." *Social Theory and Practice*. 22(1):67–82.

Levy, Barry S. and Victor W. Sidel, eds. 2008. *War and Public Health*. 2nd ed. New York: Oxford University Press.

Lewy, Guenter. 2007. "Can There Be Genocide Without the Intent to Commit Genocide?" *Journal of Genocide Research* 9(4):661–74.

Link, Bruce G. and Jo Phelan. 1995. "Social Conditions as Fundamental Causes of Disease." *Journal of Health and Social Behavior*. Extra Issue: 80–94.

Loyd, Jenna M. 2009. "A Microscopic Insurgent": Militarization, Health, and Critical Geographies of Violence." *Annals of the Association of American Geographers* 99(5):863–73.

Lykes, M. Brinton. 2001. "Human Rights Violations as Structural Violence." Pp. 158–67 in *Peace, Conflict, and Violence: Peace Psychology for the 21st Century*, edited by Daniel J. Christie, Richard V. Wagner, and Deborah Du Nann Winter. Upper Saddle River, NJ: Prentice Hall.

Manz, Beatriz. 2009. "The Continuum of Violence in Post-War Guatemala." Pp. 151–64 in *The Anthropology of War: Views from the Frontline*, edited by Alisse Waterston. New York: Berghahn Books.

Marmot, Michael and Richard G. Wilkinson. 2005. *Social Determinants of Health*, 2nd ed. Oxford: Oxford University Press.

Martin, Debra L. 2008. "Ripped Flesh and Torn Souls: Evidence for Slavery in the Prehistoric Southwest, AD 800–1500." Pp. 159–80 in *Invisible Citizens: Slavery in Ancient Pre-State Societies*, edited by Catherine M. Cameron. Salt Lake City: University of Utah Press.

McEvoy-Levy, Siobhan. 2001. "Youth, Violence and Conflict Transformation." *Peace Review* 13(1):89–96.

McIlwaine, Cathy. 1999. "Geography and Development: Violence and Crime as Development Issues. *Progress in Human Geography* 23(3):453–63.

Metz, Brent, Lorenzo Mariano, and Julián López García. 2010. "The Violence After 'La Violencia' in the Ch'orti' Region of Eastern Guatemala." *Journal of Latin American and Caribbean Anthropology* 15(10):16–41.

Miller, Kenneth E. and Andrew Rasmussen. 2010. "War Exposure, Daily Stressors, and Mental Health in Conflict and Post-conflict Settings: Bridging the Divide between Trauma-focused and Psychosocial Frameworks." *Social Science and Medicine* 70:7–16.

Morales, Oscar, Jr., Sara E. Grineski, and Timothy W. Collins. 2012. "Structural Violence and Environmental Injustice: The Case of a US-Mexico Border Chemical Plant." *Local Environment* 17(1):1–21.

Morgan, Karen and Suruchi Thapar Björkert. 2006. "'I'd Rather You'd Lay Me on the Floor and Start Kicking Me': Understanding Symbolic Violence in Everyday Life." *Women's Studies International Forum* 29:441–52.

Mukherjee, Joia. 2007. "Structural Violence, Poverty and the AIDS Pandemic." *Development* 50(2):115–21.

Mukherjee, Joia S., Donna J. Barry, Hind Satti, Maxi Raymonville, Sarah Marsh, and Mary Kay Smith-Fawzi. 2011. "Structural Violence: A Barrier to Achieving the Millennium Development Goals for Women." *Journal of Women's Health* 20(4):593–97.

Nevins, Joseph. 2009. "Embedded Empire: Structural Violence and the Pursuit of Justice in East Timor." *Annals of the Association of American Geographers* 99(5):914–21.

Nichter, Mark. 2008. *Global Health: Why Cultural Perceptions, Social Representations, and Biopolitics Matter*. Tucson: University of Arizona Press.

Nordstrom, Carolyn. 2004. *Shadows of War: Violence, Power, and International Profiteering in the Twenty-First Century*. Berkeley: University of California Press.

Nordstrom, Carolyn. 2009. "Fault Lines." Pp. 63–87 in *Global Health in Times of Violence*, edited by Barbara Rylko-Bauer, Linda Whiteford, and Paul Farmer. Santa Fe: School for Advanced Research Press.

Olujic, Maria B. 1998a. "Children in Extremely Difficult Circumstances: War and Its Aftermath in Croatia." Pp. 318–30, in *Small Wars: The Cultural Politics of Childhood*, edited by Nancy Scheper-Hughes and Carolyn Sargent. Berkeley: University of California Press.

Olujic, Maria B. 1998b. "Embodiment of Terror: Gendered Violence in Peacetime and Wartime in Croatia and Bosnia-Herzegovina." *Medical Anthropology Quarterly* 12(1):31–50.

Panter-Brick, Catherine. 2010. "Conflict, Violence, and Health: Setting a New Interdisciplinary Agenda." *Social Science and Medicine* 70(1):1–6.

Parker, Richard. 2012. "Stigma, Prejudice and Discrimination in Global Public Health." *Cadernos de Saúde Pública* [Reports in Public Health] 28(1):164–69.

Parsons, Kenneth A. 2007. "Structural Violence and Power." *Peace Review: A Journal of Social Justice* 19(2):173–81.

Pedersen, Duncan. 2002. "Political Violence, Ethnic Conflict, and Contemporary Wars: Broad Implications for Health and Social Well-Being." *Social Science and Medicine* 55:175–90.

Peña, Devon G. 2011. "Structural Violence, Historical Trauma, and Public Health: The Environmental Justice Critique of Contemporary Risk Science and Practice." Pp. 203–18 in *Communities, Neighborhoods, and Health: Expanding the Boundaries of Place*, edited by Linda M. Burton, Susan P. Kemp, ManChui Leung, Stephen A. Matthews, and David T. Takeuchi. New York: Springer.

Perry, Ivan. 2009. "Violence: A Public Health Perspective." *Global Crime* 10(4):368–95.

Pierce, Gretchen Williams. n.d. "Structural Violence: A Review of the Literature." Unpublished ms.

Pinstrup-Andersen, Per and Satoru Shimokawa. 2008. "Do Poverty and Poor Health and Nutrition Increase the Risk of Armed Conflict Onset?" *Food Policy* 33:513–20.

Poundstone, K. E., S. A. Strathdee, and D. D. Celentano. 2004. "The Social Epidemiology of Human Immunodeficiency Virus/Acquired Immunodeficiency Syndrome." *Epidemiologic Reviews* 26:22–35.

Prontzos, Peter G. 2004. "Collateral Damage: The Human Cost of Structural Violence." Pp. 299–324 in *Genocide, War Crimes and the West: History and Complicity*, edited by Adam Jones. London: Zed Books.

Quesada, James. 1998. "Suffering Child: An Embodiment of War and Its Aftermath in Post-Sandinista Nicaragua." *Medical Anthropology Quarterly* 12(1):51–73.

Quesada, James. 2009. "The Vicissitudes of Structural Violence: Nicaragua at the Turn of the Twenty-First Century." Pp. 157–80 in *Global Health in Times of Violence*, edited by Barbara Rylko-Bauer, Linda Whiteford, and Paul Farmer. Santa Fe: School for Advanced Research Press.

Quesada, James, Laurie Kain Hart, and Philippe Bourgois. 2011. "Structural Vulnerability and Health: Latino Migrant Laborers in the United States." *Medical Anthropology* 30(4):339–62.

Rao, Deepa, Randall Horton, and R. Raguram. 2012. "Gender Inequality and Structural Violence among Depressed Women in South India." *Social Psychiatry, and Psychiatric Epidemiology*, online publication, 5 April. Retrieved August 26, 2012 (http://www.springer-link.com.proxy1.cl.msu.edu/content/n862l327897516q3/fulltext.pdf).

Rather, L. J., ed. 1985. *Rudolf Virchow: Collected Essays on Public Health and Epidemiology.* Boston: Science History.

Renwick, Neil. 2002. "The 'Nameless Fever': The HIV/AIDS Pandemic and China's Women." *Third World Quarterly* 23(2):377–93.

Ribera, Joan Muela and Susanna Hausmann-Muela. 2011. "The Straw That Breaks the Camel's Back: Redirecting Health-Seeking Behavior Studies on Malaria and Vulnerability." *Medical Anthropology Quarterly* 25(10):103–21.

Rutherford, Alison, Anthony B. Zwi, Natalie J. Grove, and Alexander Butchart. 2007. "Violence: A Glossary." *Journal of Epidemiology and Community Health* 61:676–780.

Rylko-Bauer, Barbara and Paul Farmer. 2002. "Managed Care or Managed Inequality? A Call for Critiques of Market-Based Medicine." *Medical Anthropology Quarterly* 16(4):476–502.

Rylko-Bauer, Barbara, and Merrill Singer. 2010. "Political Violence, War, and Medical Anthropology." Pp. 219–49, in *A Companion to Medical Anthropology*, edited by Merrill Singer and Pamela I. Erickson. Malden, MA: Wiley-Blackwell.

Rylko-Bauer, Linda Whiteford, and Paul Farmer. 2009. "Prologue: Coming to Terms with Global Violence and Health." Pp. 3–16, in *Global Health in Times of Violence*, edited by Barbara Rylko-Bauer, Linda Whiteford, and Paul Farmer. Santa Fe: School for Advanced Research Press.

Sanchez, Magaly. 2006. "Insecurity and Violence as a New Power Relation in Latin America." *Annals of the American Academy of Political and Social Science* 606:178–95.

Scheper-Hughes, Nancy. 1992. *Death without Weeping: The Violence of Everyday Life in Brazil.* Berkeley: University of California Press.

Scheper-Hughes, Nancy. 1996. "Small Wars and Invisible Genocides." *Social Science and Medicine* 43:889–900.

Scheper-Hughes, Nancy. 2007. "The Gray Zone: Small Wars, Peacetime Crimes, and Invisible Genocides." Pp. 159–84 in *The Shadow Side of Fieldwork: Exploring the Blurred Borders between Ethnography and Life*, edited by Athena McLean and Annette Leibing. Malden, MA: Blackwell.

Scheper-Hughes, Nancy and Philippe Bourgois. 2004. "Introduction: Making Sense of Violence." Pp. 1–31 in *Violence in War and Peace: An Anthology*, edited by Nancy Scheper-Hughes and Philippe Bourgois. Malden, MA: Blackwell.

Sen, Amartya. 1998. "Mortality as an Indicator of Economic Success and Failure." (Text of the Innocenti Lecture of UNICEF, Florence, Italy, March 1995.) *Economic Journal* 108(446):1–25.

Sen, Amartya. 1999. *Development as Freedom.* New York: Knopf.

Shannon, Kate, Thomas Kerr, Shari Allinott, Jill Chettiar, Jean Shoveller, and Mark W. Tyndall. 2008. "Social and Structural Violence and Power Relations in Mitigating HIV Risk of Drug-Using Women in Survival Sex Work." *Social Science and Medicine* 66:911–21.

Simić, Milena and Tim Rhodes. 2009. "Violence, Dignity and HIV Vulnerability: Street Sex Work in Serbia." *Sociology of Health and Illness* 31(1):1–16.

Singer, Merrill. 1996. "A Dose of Drugs, a Touch of Violence, a Case of AIDS: Conceptualizing the SAVA Syndemic." *Free Inquiry in Creative Sociology* 24:99–110.

Singer, Merrill. 2006. *The Face of Social Suffering: The Life History of a Street Drug Addict.* Long Grove, IL: Waveland Press.

Singer, Merrill. 2009a. "Desperate Measures: A Syndemic Approach to the Anthropology of Health in a Violent City." Pp. 137–56 in *Global Health in Times of Violence*, edited by

Barbara Rylko-Bauer, Linda Whiteford, and Paul Farmer. Santa Fe: School for Advanced Research Press.

Singer, Merrill. 2009b. *Introduction to Syndemics: A Systems Approach to Public and Community Health.* San Francisco: Jossey-Bass.

Singer, Merrill and Hans Baer. 1995. *Critical Medical Anthropology.* Amityville, NY: Baywood.

Singer, Merrill and Pamela I. Erickson. 2011a. "As the Future Explodes into the Present: Emergent Issues and the Tomorrow of Medical Anthropology." Pp. 515–32, in *A Companion to Medical Anthropology*, edited by Merrill Singer and Pamela I. Erickson. Malden, MA: Wiley-Blackwell.

Singer, Merrill and Pamela I. Erickson. 2011b. "Introduction." Pp. 1–5 in *A Companion to Medical Anthropology*, edited by Merrill Singer and Pamela I. Erickson. Malden, MA: Wiley-Blackwell.

Singer, Merrill, D. Ann Herring, Judith Littleton, and Melanie Rock. 2011. "Syndemics in Global Health." Pp. 159–79 in *A Companion to Medical Anthropology*, edited by Merrill Singer and Pamela I. Erickson. Malden, MA: Wiley-Blackwell.

Singer, Merrill and G. Derrick Hodge, eds. 2010. *The War Machine and Global Health.* Lanham, MD: AltaMira.

Sinha, Murli M. 1999. "Sex, Structural Violence, and AIDS: Case Studies of Indian Prostitutes." *Women's Studies Quarterly* 27(1/2):65–72.

Sontag, Susan. 2003. *Regarding the Pain of Others.* New York: Farrar, Straus and Giroux.

Stark, Lindsay and Mike Wessells. 2012. "Sexual Violence as a Weapon of War." *JAMA* 308(7):677–78.

Starzmann, Maria Theresia. 2010. "Structural Violence as Political Experience in Palestine: An Archaeology of the Past in the Present." *Present Pasts* 2, August. Retrieved September 2, 2012 (http://www.presentpasts.info/article/view/ pp. 29/51).

Stewart, Frances. 2002. "Root Causes of Violence Conflict in Developing Countries." *British Medical Journal* 324:342–45.

Taipale, Ilkka, with P. Helena Mäkelä, Kati Juva, Vappu Taipale, Sergei Kolesnikov, Raj Mutalik, and Michael Christ, eds. 2002. *War or Health? A Reader.* London: Zed Books and Helsinki: Physicians for Social Responsibility.

Towle, Megan and Daniel H. Lende. 2008. "Community Approaches to Preventing Mother-to-Child HIV Transmission: Perspectives from Rural Lesotho." *African Journal of AIDS Research* 7(2):219–28.

United Nations Office on Drugs and Crime. 2011. *Global Study on Homicide.* Vienna: UN Office on Drugs and Crime. Retrieved July 18, 2012 (http://www.unodc.org/documents/ data-and-analysis/statistics/Homicide/Globa_study_on_homicide_2011_web.pdf).

Uvin, Peter. 1999. "Development Aid and Structural Violence: The Case of Rwanda." *Development* 42(3):49–56.

Varma, Monika Kalra, Margaret L. Satterthwaite, Amanda M. Klasing, Tammy Shoranick, Jude Jean, Donna J. Barry, Mary C. Smith Fawzi, James McKeever, and Evan Lyon. 2008. "Wòch Nan Soley: The Denial of the Right to Water in Haiti." *Health and Human Rights* 10(2):67–89.

Vine, David. 2009. *The Secret History of the U.S. Military Base on Diego Garcia.* Princeton, NJ: Princeton University Press.

Vollhardt, Johanna K. and Rezarta Bilali. 2008. "Social Psychology's Contribution to the Psychological Study of Peace: A Review." *Social Psychology* 39(1):12–25.

Wacquant, Loïc. 2004. "Commentary on an Anthropology of Structural Violence." *Current Anthropology* 45(3):322.

Walter, Nicholas, Philippe Bourgois, and H. Margarita Loinaz. 2004. "Masculinity and Undocumented Labor Migration: Injured Latino Day Laborers in San Francisco." *Social Science and Medicine* 59:1159–68.

Weigert, Kathleen Maas. 1999. "Structural Violence." Pp. 431–40 in *Encyclopedia of Violence, Peace, and Conflict*. Vol. 3, edited by Lester Kurtz. San Diego, CA: Academic Press.

Whiteford, Linda M. 2000. "Local Identity, Globalization, and Health in Cuba and the Dominican Republic." Pp. 57–78, in *Global Health Policy, Local Realities: The Fallacy of the Level Playing Field*, edited by Linda M. Whiteford and Lenore Manderson. Boulder, CO: Lynne Rienner.

Whiteford, Linda. 2005. "Casualties in the Globalization of Water: A Moral Economy of Health Perspective." Pp. 25–44, in *Globalization, Water, & Health*, edited Linda Whiteford and Scott Whiteford. Santa Fe, CA: School of American Research Press.

Whiteford, Linda. 2009. "Failure to Protect, Failure to Provide: Refugee Reproductive Rights." Pp. 89–112, in *Global Health in Times of Violence*, edited by Barbara Rylko-Bauer, Linda Whiteford, and Paul Farmer. Santa Fe, CA: School for Advanced Research Press.

Whiteford, Linda M. and Graham A. Tobin. 2004. "Saving Lives, Destroying Livelihoods: Emergency Evacuation and Resettlement Policies." Pp. 189–202 in *Unhealthy Health Policies: A Critical Anthropological Examination*, edited by Arachu Castro and Merrill Singer. Walnut Creek, CA: AltaMira.

Whiteford, Linda and Scott Whiteford. 2005. "Paradigm Change." Pp. 3–15 in *Globalization, Water, & Health*, edited by Linda Whiteford and Scott Whiteford. Santa Fe, CA: School of American Research.

Winter, Deborah Du Nann and Dana C. Leighton. 2001. "Structural Violence: Introduction." Pp. 99–101, in *Peace, Conflict, and Violence: Peace Psychology for the 21st Century*, edited by Daniel J. Christie, Richard V. Wagner, and Deborah Du Nann Winter. Upper Saddle River, NJ: Prentice Hall.

Winton, Ailsa. 2004. "Urban Violence: A Guide to the Literature." *Environment and Urbanization* 16(2):165–84.

World Bank. 2011. *Crime and Violence in Central America: A Development Challenge*. Washington, DC: World Bank. Retrieved July 18, 2012 (http://siteresources.worldbank.org/INTLAC/Resources/FINAL_VOLUME_I_ENGLISH_CrimeAndViolence.pdf).

Wright, Quincy. 1942. *A Study of War*. Vol. 2. Chicago: University of Chicago Press. Available through the Internet Archive. Retrieved July 13, 2012 (http://archive.org/details/studyofwarvol11001580mbp).

CHAPTER 4

CAPABILITY DEPRIVATION

ROD HICK AND TANIA BURCHARDT

INTRODUCTION

IN focusing on capability deprivation as the basis for analyzing poverty, the capability approach makes a break from the dominant income-centric tradition of poverty analysis. Developed initially by the economist and philosopher Amartya Sen, the capability approach questions the "informational space" on which considerations of poverty, inequality, justice, and so forth, should be based—encapsulated in the title of the 1979 Tanner lecture in which Sen first outlined the approach: *Equality of What?* (Sen 1982).

The appropriate "space" for analyzing poverty, according to the capability approach, is not what people *have*, nor how they *feel*, but what they can *do* and *be*. The capability approach requires us to ask: What, in understanding poverty, is our ultimate concern? Sen argues that while people's incomes (or, more broadly, their resource holdings) are important, they are only of *instrumental* importance: important because of what they allow a person to do or be. In contrast, what a person can do or be is *intrinsically* important (e.g., Sen 2009)—our ultimate concern when analyzing poverty.

Nothing of great import turns on this distinction as long as a person's resources are a good measure of what they can do and be. But the capability approach holds that this is unlikely to be the case because people have different needs, which means that they may require different amounts of resources in order to achieve the same beings and doings (Sen calls these variations "conversion factors") and because some important ends (such as the ability to avoid discrimination, for example) may not respond sensitively to differences in resources at all. The existence of conversion factors and the nonmonetary nature of some dimensions of well-being offer two reasons for making a shift away from income-centric analysis.

The capability approach offers a flexible framework for social assessment, and one which can be applied in a range of fields—that is, analyzing poverty is just one of its possible applications (as we will see when we turn to empirical applications). Nonetheless, its potential relevance for analyzing poverty is considerable because of the continued dominance of income-centric analysis—whether this is in terms of the World Bank's "dollar a day" approach in developing countries (e.g., Ravallion, Chen and Sangraula 2009), or the use of relative income poverty lines of, say, 60 percent of median income within European poverty analysis (see Nolan and Whelan 2011 for a discussion).

The contribution of the capability approach lies in its insistence that we consider what it is about the problem of poverty that should command our attention; in pointing to some important deficiencies of standard income-centric approaches; and in offering an alternative way of understanding poverty that focuses on impoverished lives and not just depleted wallets (Sen 2000).

In this chapter, we present the concepts that comprise the capability approach, discuss some key questions within the literature regarding the nature of the approach, and provide an overview of some prominent empirical applications that have been inspired by the capability approach. These themes form the basis of the three sections that follow. The chapter closes with a discussion about the current state-of-the-art literature on the capability approach, which identifies some issues for future research.

THEORY

According to Sen, there are various "spaces" in which well-being may be considered. One option is to focus on a person's *resources*. Alternatively, we may wish to consider what people *can do* with the resources at their disposal. Or, we may decide that the relevant "space" is the *utility they derive* from what they do. The first option corresponds to the metric of "primary goods" as outlined in John Rawls's (1971) *Theory of Justice*, which Rawls defines as "rights and liberties, opportunities and powers, income and wealth" (1971:92), but which, for the most part, Sen interprets as income and wealth. The third space reflects the philosophical tradition of utilitarianism, the foundations of which date back centuries (e.g., Bentham 1948), but which is in the midst of a resurgence in recent years (e.g., Layard 2006).

The primary concepts of the capability approach are functionings and capabilities. A "functioning" is something a person succeeds in "doing or being" (Sen 1999:75), such as participating in the life of society, being healthy, being happy, and so forth; while a person's "capability" refers to the "alternative combinations of functionings the person can achieve, and from which he or she can choose one collection" (Sen 1993:31). Conceived this way, a person's capability comprises both the outcomes that actually occur (i.e., a person's actual functionings) and the alternative outcomes that *could* have been achieved given different choices. The distinction between functionings and capability is thus between "achievements on the one hand, and freedoms or valuable options from which one can choose on the other" (Robeyns 2005a:95).

To understand *why* Sen claims we should focus on functionings and capabilities, we return to the comparison with resources and with utility. The primary advantages of focusing on people's resources are that they provide a clear and common metric in which to evaluate advantage and disadvantage, and that a resource-centric perspective allows analysts to remain neutral toward the diverse conceptions of the good life that people hold (see especially Rawls 1971). There is a great variation in people's conception of the good life, argued Rawls, but whatever their ends, primary goods are the relevant means (1971:92). Thus, by focusing on *means*, one can avoid the necessity of specifying the good life prior to social assessment.

However, Sen argues that resource-centric approaches neglect another important source of variation—namely the variation *between means and ends*, or what Sen has labeled "conversion factors." He claims that "the relationship between resources and poverty is both variable and deeply contingent on the characteristics of the respective people and the environment in which they live—both natural and social" (Sen 2009:254). For example, someone with a disability might need *more* income in order to achieve the *same functioning* as a nondisabled person (2009:256), and such variation is, Sen argues, likely to be extremely pervasive. In essence, conversion factors reflect the differing needs that people have, and they are problematic from an evaluative point of view because they mean that we do not know what a person *can do* or *be* with the resources at their disposal. Furthermore, since some capabilities are not "purchased" or related to resources in any straightforward way, it may not be possible to draw inferences about them based on a person's resources at all. And since people's capabilities and functionings are *intrinsically* important, while their resources are only *instrumentally* important—indeed, the importance of resources is as a means to functionings and capabilities and is thus both instrumental and contingent (Sen 2009:233)—this implies we cannot rely on standard resource-based approaches to analysis, argues Sen. These arguments have particular relevance for poverty analysis given the continued dominance income-centric approaches to understanding poverty.

Turning to utility, Sen argues that this too is the wrong metric with which to engage in interpersonal evaluation because of its sheer *adaptability*, particularly in the face of adverse conditions. In an oft-quoted passage, Sen (1987:11) noted that

> the fulfilment of a person's desires may or may not be indicative of a high level of well-being or of standard of living. The battered slave, the broken unemployed, the hopeless destitute, the tamed housewife, may have the courage to desire little, but the fulfilment of those disciplined desires is not a sign of great success and cannot be treated in the same way as the fulfilment of the confident and demanding desires of the better placed.

On many occasions, adapting one's desires to feasible possibilities can be a sensible psychological mechanism (Burchardt 2009), but for the analyst it must call into question the extent to which utility can, on its own, provide an evaluative measure for poverty and well-being. The point here is not that happiness does not matter at all, but rather that it is not the only thing that matters, and that it is not suitable as an overall measure.

The capability approach, then, focuses on each person's capabilities and functionings, and Sen views the process of development as a process of expanding the real freedoms that people enjoy (1999:36). In conceptualizing capability as a set of the alternative combinations of functionings a person is able to achieve, Sen's concept is analogous to an opportunity set in the field of social choice theory. To expand a person's capability set is to expand their real opportunity to achieve a variety of functionings. The capability set thus provides a measure of real opportunity (to achieve alternative forms of living) *without* retreating from ends to means (Robeyns and van der Veen 2007). It offers a way to respect the plurality of ends that people hold while also accounting for the variation in converting resources (or means) into functionings (or ends). Sen notes, "A person's advantage in terms of opportunities is judged to be lower than that of another if she has less capability—less real opportunity—to achieve those things that she has reason to value" (Sen 2009:231). Such a conception places value not only on the outcomes that do, in fact, occur but also on the *extent of choice* for people to live in various ways.

In addition to the concept of capability, which is intended to capture the "opportunity" aspect of freedom, Sen also discusses the "process" aspect of a person's freedom. Whereas the concepts of capabilities and functionings focus respectively on what a person can do and does do (irrespective of how these opportunities came about), the process aspect of freedom is likened to "having the levers of control in one's own hands (no matter whether this enhances the actual opportunities of achieving our objectives" (1993b:522). This process aspect of freedom focuses on the extent of one's autonomy and immunity from the interference of others (e.g., Sen 1993b) and is thus related to the "negative" tradition of liberty.

In a practical sense, then, the opportunity and process aspects of freedom can be used to distinguish between opportunities which may be "given" to a person, and other opportunities where people themselves have been central to choosing particular options (for example, through a deliberative or participative process). By extending the focus of freedom to include process freedoms, the capability approach can assess the conditions under which people's capabilities come about and are exercised—whether the person was consulted, was passive, discriminated against, part of a collective decision-making process, and so forth.

However, while the primary concepts of the capability approach are each reasonably clear, there are a number of ambiguities about how they should be applied, as we will see in the next section. These ambiguities reflect the fact that Sen's articulation of the approach is "deliberately incomplete"; certain aspects of the approach have not been determined by Sen, and their specific form is likely to be influenced by the particular context of application. These ambiguities have resulted in particular debates within the capability literature regarding a number of "key questions," which we discuss in the next section.

The deliberately incomplete nature of the capability approach ensures that it is a flexible framework for social assessment and can be applied in a range of fields and disciplines. Sen's background is as an economist and philosopher, and this is reflected in his use of the approach to discuss comparative quality of life assessment. Other authors have drawn on the approach for different purposes. Another prominent capability theorist, Martha Nussbaum, intends her capabilities approach to form the basis of a partial theory of justice—to identify a set of constitutional guarantees that all people, she argues, have a right to demand from their governments (2000a; 2006). Nussbaum offers a "thicker" conception than Sen, adopting a distinct—and in many cases more specific—position regarding some of the important debates within the capability literature. Thus, while the core concepts of the approach are relatively clear, there remain a number of important questions about how these concepts work together, and how they should be employed and operationalized in practice.

Key Questions in the Capability Literature

Sen's decision to leave the capability approach "deliberately incomplete" has meant that further conceptual work is required before it can be adequately applied. It has also resulted in a number of debates within the capability literature and something of a bifurcation between conceptual papers that treat the approach as problematic and in need of supplementation, and empirical (particularly quantitative) papers that attempt to apply the approach, which are often relatively silent on these challenges. Three key questions that feature prominently within this literature will be discussed here. These are the question of whether to focus on functionings or capabilities, the question of a capability list, and the question of aggregation.

The Question of Functioning and/or Capabilities

The first question concerns the relative weight we should give to the concepts of functionings and capabilities, and contributions to this debate address both conceptual and practical considerations. The purpose of the concept of capability, we have noted, is to provide a measure of *opportunity* in a way that overcomes the problems associated with conversion factors. As such, a focus on capabilities, which reflect opportunities, rather than on functionings, or outcomes, would be consistent with recognizing that our ethical focus in assessment should be on the *constraints* that people face and not on the particular choices they make. Martha Nussbaum, for example, is unambiguous in her preference for the capability concept, arguing that it respects the conceptions of the good that people hold and thus avoids the charge of paternalism (Nussbaum 2000a:87–88; see also Robeyns 2005a:101). One comparison frequently invoked by Sen in justifying the priority of capabilities over functionings is between a person who starves and another who fasts—Gandhi is sometimes identified as the latter. While both may share the same (lack of) functioning, the person who fasts possesses the *capability* to be well-nourished, while the person who starves does not.

However, normative arguments have also been put forward for focusing on people's functionings. Gandjour (2008) has argued that, in a dynamic perspective, "some functionings are not only the result of capabilities, but also their prerequisite" (Gandjour 2008:345), claiming that there is a mutual dependency and reinforcement between functionings and capabilities. Gandjour's point is that it may be problematic to confine our normative attention solely to capabilities when we know that actual achievement of certain functionings (in terms of mental and physical health, and education) may be required in order to guarantee capability formation in the future.

Other, more practical reasons have also been offered for focusing on a person's functionings: most notably because of the difficulty in actually capturing a capability set in operational terms (Kuklys and Robeyns 2005; Basu 1987). Indeed, some authors have questioned whether capabilities can be measured directly at all (Comim 2008; Krishnakumar 2007) due to the inclusion of nonchosen functioning vectors within the capability set, which the approach deems constitutive of an individual's well-being. This helps explain why empirical applications focus overwhelmingly on functionings (for a review, see Kuklys 2005; but also Arndt and Volkert 2007)—and this includes Sen's own empirical applications of the approach (e.g., Drèze and Sen 1989, 2002).

Sen (1992:112) has suggested that in some cases it may be possible to use information about a person's functionings to draw inferences about their capabilities, since, at least for relatively basic functionings, such as avoiding starvation, for example, lacking the relevant functioning is usually indicative of lacking the relevant capability.

It may be argued that, where such inferences are drawn, one should be explicit that this is the case and defend the assumptions which such inferences rely on. Burchardt (2006:13–14) has suggested a tricotomy of (1) situations in which all differences in outcomes might reasonably be attributed to differences in capabilities (such as where a person is assaulted); (2) situations where differences in preferences *may* result in differences in outcomes, but where for the purposes of public policy it may be possible to assume that any differences are a result of differing levels of capabilities; and (3) situations in which additional evidence may be needed in order to determine whether differences in outcomes are genuinely a result of differences in capability.

Others, however, have criticized this practice of drawing inferences about a person's capability from data on their functionings. Comim (2008:174) argues that focusing on functionings while at the same time stressing the ethical importance of capabilities "seems to frustrate theoretical arguments about the importance of capabilities vis-à-vis functionings (Sen 1981:209). If at the end of the day we are pushed into using functionings when applying the CA, then the idea of capability seems to have less practical relevance."

One alternative to choosing between capabilities and functionings is to rely on what Sen has called "refined" functionings, or "a functioning which takes note of the available alternatives" (Robeyns 2006:354; see also Sen 2009:237) For example, we might focus on whether a person does, in fact, participate in certain social activities (i.e., their functioning in this domain) but *also* look at the extent of choice they had in whether to participate.

There is, thus, some flexibility in terms of whether one focuses on functionings, "refined" functionings, capabilities, or even some combination of these (e.g., Sen 2009:236; Vizard and Burchardt 2007; Robeyns 2006), and the precise context of application is likely to influence the balance between these concepts (Sen 2009:232). It is important to recognize, however, that it is the concept of capability which attracts ethical attention, and the arguments in favor of a focus on functionings are either entirely practical (in terms of aiding empirical application) or are dependent on the concept of capability in some way (e.g., a lack of functioning now may restrict one's future capability; a lack of functioning is indicative of a lack of capability; a refined functioning takes account of the available alternatives, and so forth).

The Question of a Capability List

The second key question in the capability literature is that of *which* dimensions we are interested in. The fact that something may be formulated as a capability does not mean that we should devote much concern to it (Sen 1993:44–46): some capabilities are trivial, such as the capability to use a particular kind of washing powder (Sen 1992:44); others are manifestly bad, such as the capability for cruelty (Nussbaum 2011:25). Thus, there is an inescapable question of *valuation*, although there is no agreement on *how* valuation should occur or *who* should conduct the valuation.

Sen himself has neither provided a list of capabilities and their respective weightings nor suggested the method by which this might occur, save that the choices involved should be explicit and should be subject to public participation and scrutiny. Indeed, he has been critical of the idea of a capability list, arguing that "to have such a fixed list, emanating from pure theory, is to deny the possibility of fruitful public participation on what should be included and why" (Sen 2006:362) and that "pure theory cannot 'freeze' a list of capabilities for all societies for all time to come, irrespective of what the citizens come to understand and value" (Sen 2006:363).

In the UK, Burchardt and Vizard (2011) adopted a deliberative approach in constructing their capability-based framework for monitoring equality and human rights in England, Scotland, and Wales. They drew on a "minimum core" of dimensions from existing human rights frameworks and subsequently engaged in deliberative consultation with the general public and with groups at risk of discrimination and disadvantage in order to refine and expand on this core.

The desirability of adopting a purely participatory approach has been questioned, however, because the selection of capabilities in participatory deliberation may be subject to adaption (Gasper 2007; Clark 2005), because those involved—and particularly people living in poverty—may lack the necessary knowledge to consider potential alternative lifestyles (Clark 2005), and because participation may become dominated by the "organised poor" (Arndt and Volkert 2009:17). It is for these reasons that Burchardt and

Vizard (2011:92–93) prioritize preexisting international human rights standards over participative process, noting that participatory deliberations are often "'imperfect' due to resource and time constraints and/or are 'non-ideal' in terms of their underlying democratic conditions and representation" (Burchardt and Vizard 2011:100).

Not all authors have pursued a deliberative approach, however. In her work establishing basic constitutional guarantees, Martha Nussbaum has put forward a list of 10 central human capabilities which, she claims, citizens of any nation can legitimately demand from their governments "as a bare minimum of what respect for human dignity requires" (2000b:222, see also 2011, 2006, 2000a). These capabilities are life; bodily health; bodily integrity; senses, imagination, and thought; emotions; practical reason; affiliation; other species; play; and control over one's environment. These 10 capabilities are philosophically derived, based on "years of cross-cultural discussion" (2000b:231), and the list itself remains open and contested, subject to change and revision in the future (2006:75–77). While there is not an explicit role for participatory processes, there is, nonetheless, an appeal to impartiality—the idea that people with diverse religious or metaphysical convictions can achieve an "overlapping consensus" about the importance of the capabilities she specifies (Nussbaum 2006:6). Nussbaum's approach has been criticized by Robeyns, however, for lacking democratic legitimacy (2006), who has also questioned whether, in practice, an overlapping consensus to support Nussbaum's list of central human capabilities can be attained (Robeyns 2005b: 206–7).

Robeyns (2005b:205–6; 2006:356) has put forward "procedural criteria" for the selection of capabilities: (1) providing a clear list of capabilities, the selection of which is justified (explicit formulation); (2) proving clarity about the method that has generated the list, so that this can be scrutinized by others (methodological justification); (3) where the capability list is nonideal, for example due to data constraints, providing both ideal and nonideal capability lists (different levels of generality); and (4) all important capabilities should be included (exhaustion and nonreduction). These criteria have been described by Burchardt and Vizard (2011:111) as "good practice" guidelines.

For some, the lack of a capability list raises yet more questions about whether the approach can be properly operationalized. Sugden, for example, notes that "[g]iven the rich array of functionings that Sen takes to be relevant, given the extent of disagreement among reasonable people about the nature of the good life, and given the unresolved problem of how to value sets, it is natural to ask how far Sen's framework is operational" (1993:1953; a question that Sen acknowledges is relevant, see Sen 2005a:vii).

The lack of an agreed capability list presents an acute problem for applied analysis. In practice, the selection of functioning dimensions is frequently performed in an ad-hoc manner and in accordance with the preferences of the analyst (Kuklys 2005), particularly in quantitative applications, where the selection is likely to be influenced by the limitations of secondary data (Robeyns 2006). In his own empirical work, Sen has restricted himself to a focus on certain basic capabilities that, he argues, would be included in any reasonable list of valued capabilities (Sen 2005b:159; Drèze and Sen 1989, 2002).

Finally, though it is often claimed that the *context* of application will have an important role to play in determining the relevant dimensions, it is nonetheless the case that many "lists" of dimensions of well-being, capability inspired and otherwise, have been shown to display a considerable degree of overlap *despite* the rather distinct contexts in which they were created. As Alkire notes, "natural areas of consensus seem to emerge" (2010:19, 2002) when dimensions of well-being are selected. On the one hand, this perhaps suggests that the context dependence of particular lists should not be overestimated; on the other, the identification of a shared component to many lists, created in different countries and for different purposes, arguably adds to the normative force that there are certain dimensions that are constitutive of human well-being.

The Question of Aggregation

In addition to the question of *what* the relevant dimensions are, there remain further questions: Should the valued dimensions be aggregated into an overall measure, and if so, how? Some authors have stressed the *inherent plurality* of human capabilities. In her capabilities approach, Martha Nussbaum adopts this position, arguing that her capability list is one of distinct, individual capabilities and that a trade-off between them cannot occur (2000a:81). In a similar vein, Burchardt and Vizard (2011:106, see also Burchardt 2009, 2006:15) preserve the multidimensional structure of their Equality Measurement Framework in order to reflect "the intrinsic value and importance of each domain."

If these arguments in favor of retaining multidimensionality are theoretical, others are practical: Ravallion (2011), for example, has likened multidimensional poverty indices to replacing the dials on a car dashboard with a single dial that would summarize all information—and in the process create total confusion (slow down or get fuel?). Sen (1999:103) himself has noted that a "constructed aggregate may often be far less interesting for policy analysis than the substantive pattern of diverse performances." But Jenkins (2011:28) notes that while "[d]isaggregated information is useful in some circumstances, . . . there is a high demand for aggregate summaries," arguing that the problems inherent in aggregating multidimensional information offers one reason to prefer income-centric over multidimensional poverty analysis.

Indeed, one of the motivations for developing the Human Development Index, an aggregated measure of economic and social development (see discussion below), was recognition of the need to produce a simple, aggregated, people-centered measure that could rival GDP per capita. In poverty analysis more broadly, there has been something of a trend toward multidimensionality (e.g., Nolan and Whelan 2011:5), and this has included a greater focus on the creation of new multidimensional *measures* (see e.g., Alkire and Foster 2011).

If multidimensional information is to be aggregated, then this raises the question of how to determine the relevant weights for the various capabilities and, again, there have been a number of alternative approaches suggested and employed. Sen (2006) has emphasized the role of participation and public reasoning in determining the weights. In practice, most empirical analyses employ one of two methods when aggregating information across dimensions: in the first, the analyst specifies the weights, if only to assign them an equal weighing (e.g., UNDP 2010; Kuklys 2005); in the second, the data itself is used to construct the weights (e.g., Krishnakumar 2007). Ultimately, the idea of aggregation rests, in turn, on that of substitutability; that is, that well-being in one area can be sensibly traded off against that in another, and on this there are divergent views.

Conclusion of Section

These three questions are prominent issues within the capability literature; of these, at least the first two (the question of functionings or capabilities; the question of a capability list) raise questions about whether the approach can be fully operationalized at all, while the third is relevant in considering the merits and demerits of multidimensional approaches vis-à-vis income-centric analysis. And yet, while the issues discussed here remain important in applying the capability approach, it is important to recognize that they are not unique to that approach. At a minimum, the question of the capability list (which reflects questions of dimensionality) and the question of aggregation are questions for *any* multidimensional approach, a topic we return to in the concluding discussion.

APPLICATIONS

Doubts about the whether the approach can be operationalized at all have, perhaps, been eased by the emergence of actual applications inspired by the approach. Indeed, two recent applications—employing the capability approach to understand the use of mobile phones in the agricultural sector in Indonesia (Wahid and Furuholt 2012) and teacher performance in Tanzania (Tao 2013)—demonstrate the ability of the approach to support empirical analysis in a diverse range of fields.

Perhaps the most prominent of all applications is that of the UN Human Development Index (hereafter HDI), which has formed the basis of the UNDP's Human Development Reports since their inception in 1990. The HDI is an aggregated measure of income, life expectancy, and education and was proposed by the Pakistani economist Mahbub ul Haq to shift attention from *economic* development (as encapsulated by GDP per capita) to *human development* (which would be partially captured in HDI rankings) (see also Sen 2000b).

In focusing on income, life expectancy, and education, the HDI falls far short of the richness that the capability approach can provide. Indeed, Sen harbored significant reservations about the project initially; it was ul Haq who argued that only an index that resembled the simplicity of GDP per capita was capable of shifting the focus away from that measure of economic progress (Fukuda-Parr 2003). The HDI is thus a highly reductive form of the capability approach, as Sen has noted: "These are useful indicators in rough and ready work, but the real merit of the human development approach lies in the plural attention it brings to bear on development evaluation" (Sen 2000b:22).

Nonetheless, even this simple measure demonstrates the distinctiveness of an approaches focusing on income alone to one which incorporates information about people's education and life expectancy. Ranking countries in terms of their Gross National Income (GNI), on the one hand, and their Human Development Index, on the other, produces many similarities. But there are also important differences. For example, in the 2013 *Human Development Report*, New Zealand, Cuba, and Madagascar are all placed substantially higher in terms of HDI rankings compared to their GNI rankings (+25 positions or more), while the United Arab Emirates, Botswana, and Bhutan are all ranked substantially lower (−25 positions of more) than their incomes would suggest (2013:144–6).

Developed-World Applications

The approach has also inspired a number of high-profile monitoring frameworks in developed countries. In the UK, Burchardt and Vizard's (2011) capability-based framework for monitoring equality and human rights in England, Scotland, and Wales focuses on the dimensions of life; physical security; health; education and learning; standard of living; productive and valued activities; participation, influence, and voice; individual, family, and social life; identity, expression, self-respect; and legal security.

Burchardt and Vizard (2011) argue the capability approach requires a focus not only on functionings (what people actually do and be) but also on treatment ("immunity from arbitrary interference, discrimination and other forms of detrimental treatment, such as lack of dignity and respect") and autonomy ("empowerment, choice and control in relation to critical decisions that affect a person's life"). Their framework thus includes a focus on both "process" and "opportunity" freedoms in its measurement approach.

The capability approach has provided the basis for the German government's Poverty and Wealth Reports since 2005 (Arndt and Volkert 2011). These reports focus on "high and low incomes, financial wealth and debts, education, health, housing, employment, political and social participation" (2011:320), with a particular focus on the performance of families, immigrants, disabled people, and other vulnerable groups.

Robeyns and van der Veen (2007) used the capability approach to create an index of quality of life that also takes account of sustainability. They selected dimensions that were considered to unequivocally contribute to quality of life and which were within the remit of government action, although they emphasized that their list is open and tentative. These dimensions are physical health; mental health; knowledge and intellectual development; labor; care; social relations; recreation; shelter; living environment; mobility; security; nondiscrimination and respect for diversity; and political participation.

Beyond these monitoring frameworks, a number of developed-world applications also serve to demonstrate the ability of the approach to motivate a concern with a range of monetary and nonmonetary capabilities. For example, Brandolini and d'Alessio (1998) used the approach to support a multidimensional poverty analysis focusing on health, education, employment, housing, social relationships, and economic resources. Bonvin and Dif-Pradalier (2010) have emphasized the importance of the capability for work and the capability for voice. Anand and colleagues have attempted to operationalize Nussbaum's list of capabilities by fielding their own UK-based survey (e.g., Anand et al. 2009), which, they suggest, demonstrates the "feasibility although non-triviality" of using the capability approach to support empirical analysis. The range of dimensions considered in these monitoring frameworks and empirical applications gives a sense of the richness of the approach in terms of the dimensionality which may be considered.

Developing-World Applications

Applications of the capability approach have in no way been limited to the developed world, however. Two recent developing-world applications point to the ability of the approach to focus on nonmonetary constraints to well-being. In the first, Kerstenetzky and Santos (2009) use the approach to understand how living in one of Rio de Janeiro's *favelas* systematically reduces levels of well-being, *both above and below typical income poverty lines*. These authors claim that "living in a favela by itself imposes a sizable discount" on what people can do and be, with the violence associated with favelas proving to be a particular inhibitor of people's functionings in terms of their housing, health, work and schooling, trust in the police, respect and self-esteem, job opportunities, and collective action (2009:209). In the second, Biggeri Trani, and Mauro (2011) examine the nature and extent of child poverty in Afghanistan and find, demonstrating the "pattern" of disadvantages that can flow from a multidimensional perspective, that while boys and girls perform similarly on some dimensions (health; social inclusion; care, etc.), on others—in particular, education—girls displayed elevated rates of disadvantage.

In taking a broad view of the constraints that limit human lives, the capability approach is open about the policy responses which may be required to tackle capability deprivation—improving people's material resources is just one of the possible policy solutions. The point is, of course, not to suggest that people's incomes are not important; simply that the nature of an antipoverty response is not predetermined by the analytic framework. Antipoverty initiatives, in this perspective, may require increasing people's incomes, but they may also require the provision of public housing; the introduction of a vaccination program, and so forth.

Between Developing and Developed Worlds

The real challenge is not simply to compare rates of poverty within the developing and developed worlds, however, but also *between* them. Here there are noticeably fewer studies, though the UN Human Development Report provides a useful starting point.

Any framework that seeks to compare the prevalence of poverty between nations must identify a common metric which will be used in order to make like-for-like comparisons. The income-centric approach, for example, seeks to account for differences in prices between countries by computing adjustments to income values so that they are expressed in a comparable terms—typically, U.S. dollar purchasing power parity (PPP) (for a recent example, see Milanovic 2011).

Adopting a capability perspective, on the other hand, would entail comparing capabilities directly. Again, the multidimensional perspective that results can provide evidence of diverse performance in terms of poverty and deprivation. It may be that some of the dimensions are particularly relevant for poorer nations—for example, in terms of premature mortality and illiteracy—in a way that they may be less relevant for developed nations. But adopting a capability perspective also allows us to compare—in quite a tangible way—the ways in which people in poverty in rich nations may, in fact, have *lower* living standards than many in poorer countries, at least on some dimensions.

For example, in *Development as Freedom*, Sen shows how U.S. African American men have a lower "chance of reaching advanced ages than do people in the immensely poorer economies of China or the Indian state of Kerala (or in Sri Lanka, Jamaica or Costa Rica)" (Sen 1999:21). By focusing on capability deprivation *directly*, instead of relying on income proxies, we can potentially arrive at quite a different pattern of deprivation both within and between nations than if an income perspective is adopted.

Concluding Section

This review of some empirical applications of the capability approach points to some of its defining characteristics—its multidimensionality, and its focus on both monetary and nonmonetary dimensions and constraints. These existing applications present at least something of a challenge to those who have suggested that the approach might not be suited to empirical application. Nonetheless, such applications do not imply in any sense that significant challenges do not remain, and, in the final section, we attempt to take stock of the current state-of-the-art literature and offer some final reflections.

CONCLUDING DISCUSSION

The capability approach provides the basis for a framework for poverty analysis that adopts a multidimensional perspective and which focuses on both monetary and nonmonetary dimensions and constraints. The approach provides a strong critique of income-centric analysis and thus adopts a distinct position to much existing poverty analysis. It suggests that poverty analysis should focus on impoverished lives and not just depleted wallets (Sen 2000). As we have sought to demonstrate, the capability approach has been applied by authors working in a very wide range of fields and disciplines.

The capability approach has, since its inception, transcended disciplinary boundaries, and the variety of applications that now exist only serve to reinforce its multidisciplinary nature. However, there is a need to continue to reach out and engage with other fields and disciplines in terms of understanding the themes, problems, and questions that are shared with other researchers, including those who do not themselves adopt a capability perspective. There are important parallels between the concerns of the capability approach and other, non-capability-inspired analyses, and these need to be more clearly understood. To offer just one example—namely, the relationship between the capability approach and the field of social policy—the emphasis on *constraints* as being central to the concept of poverty, which is reflected in the focus on people's capabilities, has also been a feature of poverty analysis within the field of social policy where indicators of material deprivation have been employed (on this see Piachaud 1981; Hick 2012 for a discussion; and Chapter 25 of this volume, "Material Deprivation and Consumption"). Similarly, Sen's distinction between means and ends bears some resemblance to Ringen's (1988) distinction between "indirect" (i.e., low income) and "direct" (i.e., low living standards) approaches to understanding poverty. Thus, one of the tasks required of those working with the capability approach is to more clearly locate that approach with respect to other, non-capability-inspired analyses in order to identify common problems and perhaps even shared solutions.

Questions about whether the capability approach can support empirical applications at all have perhaps lost some of their force given the emergence of actual empirical applications. But other questions regarding the ability to operationalize the approach remain; for example, what is the "distance" between what is measured and the ideal conceptual framework to which particular applications are supposed to relate? Thus, the emergence of actual capability applications does not silence questions about operationalization, but rather changes the nature of these questions and shifts their attention to whether empirical applications do justice to the conceptual aspirations of the capability approach.

The demanding nature of the capability approach means that there is typically some distance between actual applications of the capability approach and the ideal to which they aspire. This is likely to be a particular issue when the analysis relies on secondary data sets (Robeyns and van der Veen 2007) and undoubtedly constitutes a disadvantage of employing a capability-based framework. However, it is important to recognize that the problem of data availability is one for all multidimensional approaches, capability inspired or not, and given the current trend toward a multidimensional understanding of poverty (Nolan and Whelan 2011), enhancing the breadth of data collected in social surveys is likely to constitute an important program of work for poverty analysis in the future.

The capability approach offers the basis for understanding poverty as inherently multidimensional, focusing on what people can do and be, and not just on what they have, or how they feel. The capability approach is undoubtedly a more complex and informationally demanding approach than the income-centric approach. However, if the income-centric perspective fails to identify those individuals who experience capability deprivation; if it fails to capture the richness and breadth of the deprivations that people face; and if it fails to point toward the relevant policy solutions to remedy deprivations in what people can do and be, then this complexity can, it is argued, be justified, and the capability approach can be used in order to understand the problem of poverty.

ACKNOWLEDGEMENTS

We would like to thank the editors for their constructive feedback on this chapter. The remaining errors are, of course, ours alone. Some of the material presented here is based on work supported by the Economic and Social Research Council (grant number ES/G01808X/1).

REFERENCES

Alkire, Sabina. 2002. *Valuing Freedoms: Sen's Capability Approach and Poverty Reduction.* Oxford: Oxford University Press.

Alkire, Sabina. 2010. "Human Development: Definitions, Critiques and Related Concepts: Background Paper for the 2010 Human Development Report." Oxford: Oxford Poverty and Human Development Initiative.

Alkire, Sabina and James Foster. 2011. "Counting and Multidimensional Poverty Measurement." *Journal of Public Economics* 7–8:476–87.

Anand, Paul, Graham Hunter, Ian Carter, Keith Dowding, Franscesco Guala, and Martin van Hees. 2009. "The Development of Capability Indicators." *Journal of Human Development and Capabilities* 10(1):125–52.

Arndt, C. and J. Volkert. 2007. "A Capability Approach for Official Poverty and Wealth Reports: Conceptual Background and First Results." Tübingen: Institut für Angewandte Wirtschaftsforschung.

Arndt, Christian and Jürgen Volkert. 2009. "Poverty and Wealth Reporting of the Germent Government: Approach, Lessons and Critique." Tübingen: Institut für Angewandte Wirtschaftsforschung.

Arndt, Christian and Jürgen Volkert. 2011. "The Capability Approach: A Framework for Official German Poverty and Wealth Reports." *Journal of Human Development and Capabilities* 12(3):311–37.

Basu, Kaushik. 1987. "Achievements, Capabilities and the Concept of Well-Being: A Review of *Commodities and Capabilities* by Amartya Sen." *Social Choice and Welfare* 4 (1):69–76.

Bentham, Jeremy. 1948. *A Fragment on Government with an Introduction to the Principles of Morals and Legislation.* Oxford: Basil Blackwell.

Biggeri, Mario, Jean-Francois Trani, and Vincenzo Mauro. 2011. *Child Poverty Measurement: the Case of Afghanistan.* Working Papers Series. Firenze: Universita'degli Studi di Firenze, Dipartimento di Scienze Economiche.

Bonvin, Jean-Michael and M. Dif-Pradalier 2010. "Implementing the Capability Approach in the Field of Education and Welfare: Conceptual Insights and Practical Consequences." Pp. 93–111 in *Final Comparative Report: "A blue-print of capabilities for work and education",* edited by Otto, Hans-Uwe and Ziegler, Holger. Retrieved August 10, 2015 (http://workable-eu.org/images/stories/publications/2_2_final_report_wp2_workable_2010.pdf) .

Brandolini, Aandrea and Giovanni D'Alessio. 1998. "Measuring Well-being in the Functioning Space." Rome, Banco d'Italia Research Department.

Burchardt, T. 2006. "Foundations for Measuring Equality: A Discussion Paper for the Equalities Review." *CASEpaper 111,* London: London School of Economics.

Burchardt, Tania. 2009. "Agency Goals, Adaptation and Capability Sets." *Journal of Human Development and Capabilities* 10(1):3–19.

Burchardt, Tania and Polly Vizard. 2007. "Developing a Capability List: Final Recommendations on the Equalities Review Steering Group on Measurement." *CASEpaper 121.* London: London School of Economics.

Burchardt, Tania and Polly Vizard. 2011. '"Operationalising' the Capability Approach as a Basis for Equality and Human Rights Monitoring in Twenty-first Century Britain." *Journal of Human Development and Capabilities* 12(1):91–119.

Clark, David A. 2005. "Sen's Capability Approach and the Many Spaces of Human Well-being." *Journal of Development Studies* 41(8):1339–68.

Comim, Flavio. 2008. "Measuring Capabilities." Pp. 159–200 in *The Capability Approach: Concepts, Measures and Applications,* edited by F. Comim, M. Qizilbash and S. Alkire. Cambridge: Cambridge University Press.

Drèze, Jean and Amartya Sen. 1989. *Hunger and Public Action.* Oxford: Oxford University Press.

Drèze, Jean and Amartya Sen. 2002. *India: Development and Participation.* New Delhi: Oxford University Press.

Fukuda-Parr, Sakkiko. 2003. "The Human Development Paradigm: Operationalising Sen's Ideas on Capabilities." *Feminist Economics,* 9 (2/3):301–17.

Gandjour, Afshin. 2008. "Mutual Dependency between Capabilities and Functionings in Amartya Sen's Capability Approach." *Social Choice and Welfare* 31:345–50.

Gasper, Des. 2007. "What Is the Capability Approach? Its Core, Rationale, Partners and Dangers." *Journal of Socio-Economics* 36:335–59.

Hick, Rod. 2012. "The Capability Approach: Insights for a New Poverty Focus." *Journal of Social Policy* 41(2):291–308.

Jenkins, Stephen P. 2011. *Changing Fortunes: Income Mobility and Poverty Dynamics in Britain.* Oxford: Oxford University Press.

Kerstenetzky, Celia Lessa and Santos, Larissa. 2009. "Poverty as Deprivation of Freedom: The Case of Vidigal Shantytown in Rio de Janeiro." *Journal of Human Development and Capabilities* 10(2):189–211.

Krishnakumar, Jaya. 2007. "Going Beyond Functionings to Capabilities: An Econometric Model to Explain and Estimate Capabilities." *Journal of Human Development* 8(1):39–63.

Kuklys, Wiebke. 2005. *Amartya Sen's Capability Approach: Theoretical Insights and Empirical Applications.* Berlin: Springer.

Kuklys, Wiebke and Ingrid Robeyns. 2005. "Sen's Capability Approach to Welfare Economics." Pp. 9–30 in *Amartya Sen's Capability Approach: Theoretical Insights and Empirical Applications,* edited by W. Kuklys. Berlin: Springer.

Layard, Richard. 2006. *Happiness: Lessons from a New Science.* London: Penguin.

Lelli, Sara. 2008. "Operationalising Sen's Capability Approach: The Influence of the Selected Technique." In *The Capability Approach: Concepts, Measures and Applications,* edited by F. Comim, M. Qizilbash and S. Alkire. Cambridge: Cambridge University Press.

Milanovic, Branko. 2011. *The Haves and the Have Nots: A Brief and Idiosyncratic History of Global Inequality.* New York: Basic Books.

Nolan, Brian and Chrsitopher T. Whelan. 2011. *Poverty and Deprivation in Europe.* Oxford: Oxford University Press.

Nussbaum, Martha C. 2000a. *Women and Human Development: The Capabilities Approach.* Cambridge: Cambridge University Press.

Nussbaum, Martha C. 2000b. "Women's Capabilities and Social Justice." *Journal of Human Development* 1(2):219–47.

Nussbaum, Martha C. 2006. *Frontiers of Justice: The Tanner Lectures on Human Values.* Cambridge, MA: Harvard University Press.

Nussbaum, Martha C. 2011. "Capabilities, Entitlements, Rights: Supplementation and Critique." *Journal of Human Development and Capabilities* 12(1):23–37.

Piachaud, David. 1981. "Peter Townsend and the Holy Grail." *New Society,* 10:418–20.

Ravallion, Martin. 2011. "On Multidimensional Indices of Poverty." World Bank Policy Research Working Paper No. 5580. Washington, DC, World Bank.

Ravallion, Martin, Shaohua Chen, and Prem Sangraula. 2009. "Dollar a Day Revisited." *World Bank Economic Review* 23(2):163–84.

Rawls, John. 1971. *A Theory of Justice.* Cambridge, MA: Harvard University Press.

Ringen, Stein. 1988. "Direct and indirect measures of poverty." *Journal of Social Policy* 17(3):351–65.

Robeyns, Ingrid. 2005a. "The Capability Approach: A Theoretical Survey." *Journal of Human Development* 6(1):63–117.

Robeyns, Ingrid. 2005b. "Selecting Capabilities for Quality of Life Measurement." *Social Indicators Research* 74:191–215.

Robeyns, Ingrid. 2006. "The Capability Approach in Practice." *Journal of Political Philosophy* 14(3):351–76.

Robeyns, Ingrid and Robert J. van der Veen. 2007. "Sustainable Quality of Life: Conceptual Analysis for a Policy-Relevant Empirical Specification." Amsterdam: Netherlands Environmental Assessment Agency/University of Amsterdam.

Sen, Amartya. 1982. "Equality of What?" In *Choice, Welfare and Measurement.* New Delhi: Oxford University Press.

Sen, Amartya. 1987. "The Standard of Living: Lecture I: Concepts and Critiques." In *The Standard of Living*, edited by in G. Hawthorne. Cambridge: Cambridge University Press.

Sen, Amartya. 1992. *Inequality Re-examined*. Cambridge, MA: Harvard University Press.

Sen, Amartya. 1993. "Capability and Well-Being." in *The Quality of Life*, edited by M. C. Nussbaum and A. Sen. Oxford: Oxford University Press.

Sen, Amartya. 1999b. "Markets and Freedoms: Achievements and Limitations of the Market Mechanism in Promoting Individual Freedoms." *Oxford Economic Papers* 45(4):519–41.

Sen, Amartya. 1999. *Development as Freedom*. Oxford: Oxford University Press.

Sen, Amartya. 2000. "Social Exclusion: Concept, Application, and Scrutiny." *Social Development Papers*, No. 1. Manila: Asian Development.

Sen, Amartya. 2000b. "A Decade of Human Development." *Journal of Human Development* 1 (1):17–23.

Sen, Amartya. 2005a. "Preface." In *Amartya Sen's Capability Approach: Theoretical Insights and Empirical Applications*, edited by W. Kuklys. Berlin: Springer.

Sen, Amartya. 2005b. "Human Rights and Capabilities." *Journal of Human Development* 6(2):151–66.

Sen, Amartya. 2006. "Capabilities, Lists and Public Reason: Continuing the Conversation." In *Capabilities, Freedom and Equality*, edited by B. Agarwal, J. Humphries, and I. Robeyns. New Delhi: Oxford University Press.

Sen, Amartya. 2009. *The Idea of Justice*. London: Allen Lane.

Sen, Amartya. 2012. "Values and Justice." *Journal of Economic Methodology* 19(2):101–108.

Sugden, Robert. 1993. "Welfare, Resource and Capabilities: A Review of *Inequality Re-examined* by Amartya Sen." *Journal of Economic Literature* 31(4):1947–62.

Tao, Sharon. 2013. "Why Are Teachers Absent? Utilising the Capability Approach and Critical Realism to Explain Teacher Performance in Tanzania." *International Journal of Educational Development* 33(1):2–14.

UNDP. 2010. *The Real Wealth of Nations: Pathways to Human Development. Human Development Report 2010*. New York: UNDP.

UNDP. 2013. *The Rise of the South: Human Progress in a Diverse World. Human Development Report 2013*. New York: UNDP.

Vizard, Polly and Tania Burchardt. 2007. "Developing a Capability List: Final Recommendations of the Equalities Review Steering Group on Measurement." London: London School of Economics.

Wahid, Fathul and Bjorn R. Furuholt. 2012. "Understanding the Use of Mobile Phones in the Agricultural Sector in Rural Indonesia: Using the Capability Approach as Lens." *International Journal of Information and Communication Technology* 4(2):165–78.

CHAPTER 5

IDEOLOGIES AND BELIEFS ABOUT POVERTY

MATTHEW O. HUNT AND HEATHER E. BULLOCK

INTRODUCTION

JUST over 30 years ago, Kluegel and Smith (1981) provided the first comprehensive summary and critique of scholarly research on beliefs about social stratification. In their *Annual Review of Sociology* article, Kluegel and Smith defined the "stratification beliefs" domain as the study of "what people believe about who gets what and why" (p. 30). Focusing primarily on the United States and Great Britain, these authors reviewed research on public beliefs in three primary areas: opportunity, the distributive process, and social class. In so doing, they identified four key questions that continue to define research in this area: (1) What is believed about social inequality? (2) What principles organize thought around social inequality? (3) What determines what is believed? (4) What are the consequences of these beliefs?[1]

In framing their review around those four questions, Kluegel and Smith focused primary attention on: (1) describing what Americans (and to a lesser extent, the British) perceive and believe about social inequality;[2] (2) explicating the nature of ideologies and other social psychological processes governing the *intra*personal organization of beliefs; (3) exploring selected factors that shape patterns of belief (e.g., socio-demographic variables); and (4) identifying selected consequences that stratification beliefs hold for the person and for politics. We have organized the current chapter around these same four overarching questions and provide an update of research in one focal area: *beliefs about the causes of poverty*.[3] Like Kluegel and Smith, we focus primary attention on Americans' beliefs, though we also attend to noteworthy developments in this literature outside the United States. Before embarking on the main tasks of our review, we briefly discuss the origins and development of the poverty-beliefs research area.

Background

Systematic empirical research into what Americans believe about the causes of poverty is traceable to a 1969 national survey investigation by sociologist Joe Feagin (1972, 1975), who identified three types of beliefs: individualistic, structuralist, and fatalistic. Individualistic beliefs focus on aspects of poor persons themselves as an explanation for poverty (e.g., "lack of thrift," "lack of effort," "loose morals"). Structuralist beliefs focus on aspects of the social and economic system in which poor people reside (e.g., "failure of society to provide enough good schools," "low wages," "failure of private industry to provide enough jobs"). Fatalistic beliefs focus on supraindividual but *non-social structural* factors (e.g., "sickness and physical handicaps," "bad luck") when explaining why some people are poor. Most research using Feagin's items has focused on the first two belief types because of the relative unpopularity of fatalistic explanations in the United States, and because the fatalism items have typically failed to form a statistically reliable subscale.

Since Feagin's seminal work, two additional national U.S. survey investigations have utilized some or all of his original 11 survey items. First, Kluegel and Smith (1986), in their 1980 Stratification Beliefs Survey, used the same set of items (with minor wording changes). And, more recently, the National Opinion Research Center included four items—two individualistic ("lack of effort," "loose morals,") and two structuralist ("failure of society to provide good schools," and "failure of private industry to provide enough good jobs") in the 1990 wave of their General Social Survey (GSS) (NORC 2010). Taken together, these three investigations provide the primary means of assessing Americans' beliefs about poverty (and possible trends therein) using nationally representative data sources.

That said, numerous other studies shed important light on Americans' beliefs about poverty, including (1) nationally representative studies using *other* sets of survey items (e.g., Nilson 1981); (2) regionally limited surveys using Feagin's (Hunt 1996) and/or supplemental sets of items (e.g., Smith and Stone 1989); (3) surveys using convenience samples of college undergraduates (e.g., Cozzarelli et al. 2001); and (4) investigations into beliefs about the causes of specific aspects of poverty such as homelessness (e.g., Lee et al. 1990). Additionally, there are now many more studies from outside the United States (and Britain) than when Kluegel and Smith (1981) published their review (e.g., Lepianka et al. 2009).[4]

What Is Believed?

Regarding descriptive facets of what people believe about the causes of poverty, Kluegel and Smith (1981) reported that existing research demonstrated a decidedly

negative view of the poor in the United States, in the sense that the poor were consistently blamed "partially or totally for their poverty" (p. 31). That is, individualistic
attributions received significantly more support than structuralist and fatalistic ones
in American public opinion. For instance, in Feagin's 1969 data, the four individualistic items were the four most popular reasons cited (as indexed by the percentage of
respondents citing these reasons as "very important") (Feagin 1972, 1975). Analysis
of other nationally representative data sources using these same items suggests that
individualistic beliefs continued to predominate among Americans in the decades
following Feagin's work (Kluegel and Smith 1986; W. Wilson 1996). Specifically, in
1980, the *same* four individualistic items that were most popular in Feagin's data
were also four of the five most strongly endorsed reasons (with the structuralist
item focusing on "schools" ranking fourth) in Kluegel and Smith's survey. And, in
the more limited 1990 GSS data collection, the two individualistic items ranked first
and second.

Structuralist (and especially fatalistic) reasons were less popular in the United States
at each time period. In 1969, structuralist items ranked sixth through tenth in popularity, in 1980 they ranked fourth, and then seventh through ninth; and, in 1990, the two
offered structuralist reasons ranked third and fourth. By far the least popular item in
both 1969 and 1980 was the "just bad luck" fatalistic explanation (rated "very important" by only 8 and 12 percent of respondents respectively). The other fatalistic item—
sickness and handicaps—ranked fifth in 1969 and sixth in 1980. We turn next to a set
of studies that are more regionally limited and/or that use different sets of questions to
gauge Americans' beliefs. This research introduces some nuance and complexity to the
picture regarding the predominance of individualistic accounts across time, place, and
different aspects of poverty.

Regional and Temporal Variation

Despite evidence from national studies suggesting that Americans are decidedly individualistic, regionally specific evidence suggests that structuralist views of poverty may
predominate under certain circumstances (e.g., Hunt 1996). For example, using data
from a 1993 survey of southern Californians that included the same basic set of items
used by Feagin (1972) and Kluegel and Smith (1986), Hunt observed that structuralist beliefs were more popular than individualistic beliefs about poverty. This pattern
was interpreted as consistent with Kluegel and Smith's (1986) argument that during
times of unusual social and/or economic strain structuralist beliefs may temporarily
come to the fore and challenge the "dominant ideology" of individualism. In addition, using data from a 1990 sample of Nashville residents, Lee et al. (1990) examined
public beliefs about the causes of homelessness, also observing that structuralist (and
fatalistic) reasons were favored over individualistic ones. Whether this finding provides
further evidence of regional and/or temporal variation in the relative popularity of different belief-types or is the result of the stimulus—that is, homelessness may elicit more

public sympathy than the issue of "poverty" more generally—is unknown, though some subsequent research (reviewed later in this chapter) supports the latter interpretation.

Explaining Different Types of Poverty

Most surveys of public beliefs about the causes of poverty are based on a generic "poverty" or "the poor" stimulus. However, building on Lee at al.'s (1990) study of beliefs about homelessness, research has documented that Americans do, in fact, distinguish among different types or aspects of poverty (G. Wilson 1996). Drawing on a survey sample of Baltimore residents, Wilson asked respondents about the causes of poverty among three different groups: welfare recipients, migrant laborers, and the homeless. Respondents explained the existence of the homeless in primarily structural terms, welfare recipients in predominantly individualistic ways, and migrant laborers with a mix of structuralist and individualistic attributions—patterns that Wilson argues may stem from differential racialization (e.g., welfare recipients as black) and media coverage of each group (i.e., greater structuralist accounting of homelessness) in ways that reflect the "deserving/undeserving" poor distinction in American culture (Gans 1995; Gilens 1999).

Additionally, the growth of research in the developing world has spurred novel attempts to assess poverty beliefs in ways that are more attuned to such settings. For example, Harper et al. (1990) factor analyzed 18 survey items from a Causes of Third World Poverty Questionnaire (CTWPQ) and observed four distinct belief clusters: one "dispositional" (blaming the poor themselves), and three "situational" (blaming third world governments, blaming nature, and blaming international exploitation). Consistent with prior work (e.g., Furnham and Gunter 1984), Harper et al. (1990) observed a positive association between dispositional attributions for poverty and a "belief in a just world" (Lerner 1980). Additionally, subsequent research using the CTWPQ found that Brazilians were more likely than Australians to invoke corruption (by third world governments) as a cause of poverty (Carr et al. 1998), while Malawians were more dispositional (and less situational) than Australians in explaining poverty (Carr and Maclachlan 1998).

Untapped Dimensions of Poverty Beliefs?

While nationally representative studies in the United States using Feagin's items have produced a relatively stable pattern of results, research using different sets of items reveal more complexity—casting some doubt on the exhaustiveness and validity of Feagin's three-type scheme (Lepianka et al. 2009). For instance, Nilson (1981) factor analyzed 12 items used in the 1972 National Election Study and found distinct individualistic, structuralist, and what she called "institutional" sets of beliefs, with the latter focusing on "meso-level" factors such as the ways educational systems, corporate seniority systems, and trade unions work to disadvantage the poor. These institutional-level reasons are seen as representing an ideological compromise wherein the adherent does not commit to an either *purely* person-centered or structural account.

Later, Smith and Stone (1989) explored 38 items representing reasons for poverty and wealth corresponding to ideological "meta-theories" they term individualism, cultur-alism, structuralism, and fatalism. Reminiscent of Nilson's "institutional" dimension, Smith and Stone argue that "culturalism" represents a belief-type that "bridges" the individual and structural levels by blending individualism's emphasis on personal fac-tors with various social structural and situational considerations (e.g., items referring to broken families; having too many children). In their words, culturalism represents the view that "personality traits as well as social structures and institutions that mark the wealthy and the poor are mutually reinforcing producers of self-perpetuating, adap-tive ways of life—in social science jargon, subcultures of wealth and poverty" (p. 94). More recently, Cozzarelli et al. (2001) factor analyzed data from a sample of college undergraduates and observed a three-factor solution that they interpret as individual-istic, structuralist, and cultural attributions, with the latter interpreted as a "culture of poverty" set of beliefs.

As Lepianka et al. (2009) have noted, factors such as Nilson's institutional and Cozzarelli et al.'s cultural belief-types positively correlate with structuralist belief scales (while institutional and structuralist beliefs are either uncorrelated, or inversely cor-related, with individualistic beliefs). This suggests "the presence of a category of expla-nations that falls between strictly structural and purely individualistic attributions, yet is still somehow closer to the external reasons for poverty"—a pattern that leads "the public to see the poor as active agents yet entangled in a web of social constraints" (pp. 425–26). The 2001 Poverty in America Survey (PIAS) (National Public Radio 2001) is an underutilized nationally representative data set that could shed useful light on these matters given that it contains items reminiscent of Feagin's individualistic type (e.g., "poor people lacking motivation"); Feagin's structuralist type ("a shortage of jobs"); and a residual set of items that refer to factors such as a "decline in moral values," "the welfare system," and "too many immigrants."[5]

Beyond the United States and Great Britain

Owing to various international social survey programs, such as the Eurobarometer and European Values Study (Lepianka et al. 2009), the International Social Justice Project (Kluegel et al. 1995), and a variety of other single-country and cross-national studies (more details later), we know far more about poverty beliefs outside the United States (and Britain) than in 1981. Single-country studies from the past three decades include those conducted in Canada (Guimond et al. 1989; Love et al. 2006), Germany (Sachweh 2012), India (Furhnam 1982; Pandy et al. 1982), Iran (Hayati and Karami 2005), Israel (Rim 1984; Strier 2005; Weiss and Gal 2007; Weiss-Gal et al. 2009), Lebanon (Abouchedid and Nasser 2001; Nasser 2007), Malaysia (Halik and Webley 2011), Nigeria

(Ige and Nekhwevha 2014), South Africa (Bonn et al. 1999), and Turkey (Morcol 1997). Cross-national research from this same time period includes studies comparing beliefs in Australia and Brazil (Carr et al. 1998); Australia and Malawi (Carr and MacLachlan 1998); Barbados and Dominica (Payne and Furhnam 1985); Canada and the Philippines (Hine and Montiel 1999); Central Asia, Russia, and Ukraine (Habibov 2011); and Lebanon, Portugal, and South Africa (Nasser et al. 2002). In addition, there have been studies comparing 20 (Van Oorschot 2000) and 28 European countries (Lepianka et al. 2010) respectively.

While space limitations preclude an exhaustive summary of the complex findings across these various investigations, a few generalizations are warranted: (1) Several studies confirm the often-cited three-factor belief structure of individualism, structuralism, and fatalism (e.g., Abouchedid and Nasser 2001; Nasser et al. 2002; Habibov 2011; Hayati and Karami 2005; Ige and Nekhwevha 2014); (2) several employ alternative lists of items, in some cases observing more belief types (e.g., Halik and Webley 2011; Love et al. 2006; van Oorschot 2000; Weiss and Gal 2007); and (3) in contrast to the findings of most U.S.-based studies, the majority of these non-U.S. studies document a stronger endorsement of structuralist than individualistic beliefs (e.g., Nasser et al. 2002; Abouchedid and Nasser 2001; Habibov 2001; Hayati and Karami 2005; Love et al. 2006; Morcol 1997; Nasser 2007). This last pattern—observed in contexts such as Lebanon, South Africa, Russia, Iran, and Turkey—is consistent with previous work showing that structuralist beliefs predominate in Western Europe (Lepianka et al. 2009).

Explanations for the U.S.-Western Europe divide on poverty beliefs generally focus on the different political and philosophical traditions characterizing these regions. A more "liberal" tradition (Hartz 1955; Bellah et al. 1985) characterizing the United States (and to a lesser extent Britain) is thought to underlie the more negative, individualistic view of the poor (and the United States' less generous welfare state), while a more "patriarchial" tradition (Kluegel et al. 1995) fosters the stronger structuralism (and more generous welfare states) seen in continental Europe. To what extent such generalizations can help us account for the greater structuralism observed in various non-Western settings is unclear. Further complicating notions of American distinctiveness vis-à-vis individualism is found in Whyte's (2004) study of Chinese stratification beliefs in which respondents were decidedly more individualistic (than structuralist) on the subject of poverty. Clearly, more research is needed to disentangle the often complex relationships between national cultures, paths of socioeconomic development, and popular understandings of poverty.

Methodological Innovations

A final noteworthy development since Kluegel and Smith's 1981 review has been the growth in the number of qualitative and other non-survey-based methodologies in the poverty-beliefs literature. These include the use of semistructured and other qualitative interviewing techniques—either alone (Halik and Webley 2011; Sahweh 2012;

Strier 2005) or in the context of mixed-methods research. For instance, Love et al. (2006) employ both telephone survey methods and qualitative interviewing in their exploration of poverty beliefs in the cities of Toronto and Edmonton. Hirschl, Rank, and Kusi-Appouh (2011) used an innovative focus group design to assess beliefs among three groups with differential poverty risk and poverty-related experiences, affirming the common survey-based observation of a predominance of individualism, but also revealing selected challenges to individualism stemming from respondents' direct experiences with the stigma and hardships associated with poverty. And, Sachweh (2012) used in-depth interviews to show that his German respondents supported the notion of inequality in principle but were also concerned with what they saw as unhealthy deviations—in the form of both wealth and poverty—from an acceptable universal standard of living.

In addition, a growing number of studies employ quasi-experimental methods to test the effects of interpersonal contact with the homeless on beliefs about the causes of homelessness (Knecht and Martinez 2009, 2012), as well as the effects of social studies curricula focusing on poverty and inequality on children's stratification beliefs (Mistry et al. 2012). Finally, several studies using multilevel modeling techniques have emerged in the past decade (e.g., Hopkins 2009; Lepianka et al. 2010; Merolla et al. 2011)—work we discuss in greater detail in the section examining determinants of poverty beliefs.

WHAT PRINCIPLES ORGANIZE THOUGHT?

In 1981, Kluegel and Smith aptly observed that stratification beliefs were typically studied in isolation from one another, with limited exploration of relationships *among* beliefs about different aspects of inequality. They also reviewed several exceptions to this tendency in the form of work highlighting basic principles governing the intrapersonal organization of thought around issues of inequality. These included the "dominant ideology thesis" (Huber and Form 1973) and "attribution theory" (Kelley and Michela, 1980; Jones and Nisbett 1972), both of which we revisit given their continued relevance and centrality to poverty-beliefs research. We then turn to more recent work on what has been termed "dual-" or "split-consciousness" and selected developments from the interdisciplinary field of political psychology (e.g., social dominance theory; system justification theory) that represent important contributions to our knowledge of the intrapersonal dynamics governing how people think about inequality.[6]

Dominant Ideology Thesis

Huber and Form (1973) argue that social stratification in the United States is legitimated via a dominant ideology organized around three key values: equality, success, and democracy. These values are logically interrelated such that (1) people generally believe that *equality* exists in the form of equal chances (i.e., opportunity is readily available); thus, (2) people's *success* or positions in society are seen as an outgrowth of effort, ability, or other individual-level factors (rather than structural forces); and, (3) because Americans believe that their country is a *democracy*, they also tend to believe that social injustices can be (and are) quickly remedied through citizen action. In the words of Huber and Form (1973), people who adhere to this dominant ideology believe that

> because educational opportunity is equal, and because everything depends on how hard a person works, the system is fair to everyone. Should the rewards become unfairly distributed, the system could be adjusted and improved because every man has a vote in a political system devoted to protecting individual achievement. Therefore, individuals get the rewards they earn and people get the government they deserve. (Huber and Form 1973:4)

Thus, for Huber and Form (1973), the dominant ideology operates by *first* shaping beliefs about opportunity, which then structure related perceptions such as the causes of inequality and the legitimacy of such hierarchies.

Attribution Theory

Attribution theory holds that people seek to account for events and other aspects of the social world in causal terms. Most research differentiates between "internal" (i.e., dispositional, personal) and "external" (i.e., situational, environmental) attributions, as well as noting numerous biases and/or tendencies associated with these perceptions. The general preference for individualistic over structural attributions for poverty observed in the United States is consistent with the fundamental attribution error, or "the tendency for attributers to underestimate the impact of situational factors and to overestimate the role of dispositional factors in controlling behavior" (Ross 1977:183). A related corollary, the actor-observer effect, refers to the tendency of individuals to attribute their own behaviors and outcomes to situational factors but the behaviors and outcomes of others to stable personal causes (Jones and Nisbett 1972). This corollary has been used to explain the greater tendency of economically disadvantaged groups (actors) to endorse structural attributions and non-poor groups (observers) to support individualistic causes (see Bullock 1999; Carr 1996). Such cognitive "blind spots" may represent a self-serving bias, shielding more privileged groups from acknowledging the role of structural inequality in causing poverty. That said, selected studies from outside the United States remind us that attribution-styles thought to reflect basic underlying tendencies are, in fact, strongly culturally bound (Al-Zahrani et al. 1993; Carr and McLaughlin 1998).

Dual Consciousness

Despite the intuitive appeal of Huber and Form's (1973) dominant ideology thesis and attribution theory's depiction of an internal *versus* external organization of cognitions, we also know that (1) potent system-challenging alternatives to individualism exist in the United States (Kluegel and Smith 1986; Bobo 1991) and (2) individualistic and structuralist attributions for poverty are not ideological alternatives and are, in fact, commonly combined in peoples' thinking (Kluegel and Smith 1986; Hunt 1996). While early research in the stratification beliefs domain conceptualized individualistic and structuralist beliefs as opposites (with the use of forced-choice survey items reinforcing this view), much research over the past three decades demonstrates that such dichotomies are unwarranted (Kluegel and Smith 1986; Lee et al. 1990). Kluegel and Smith (1986) put the matter bluntly: "individual and structural explanations are not alternatives" (p. 17).

Indeed, a central theme of Kluegel and Smith's 1986 book is that *competing* cultural forces shape Americans' thinking about inequality (and related social policies). Echoing Huber and Form (1973), Kluegel and Smith acknowledge the effects of a stable, dominant ideology emphasizing widespread opportunity and individualistic accounts of poverty. At the same time, however, they emphasize the availability of system-challenging alternatives (under the heading of "social liberalism") that focus on the *unequal* distribution of opportunity (e.g., by race and gender) and thus continued need for egalitarian and redistributive social policies. The pattern of simultaneous endorsement of individualistic and structuralist beliefs has been referred to as "compromise" explanations (Lee, Jones, and Lewis 1990), "dual consciousness" (e.g., Hunt 1996; Bullock and Waugh 2005), and "split consciousness" (e.g., Kluegel et al. 1995; Lepianka et al. 1999).

Kluegel, Smith, and Wegener (2000) demonstrate that these patterns generalize to a variety of national and cultural contexts—for example, their work comparing Western "liberal democratic" and Eastern European "post-communist" states reveals the ideologically mixed nature of most persons' thinking about issues of wealth and poverty. More specifically, their "split consciousness" perspective holds that popular thinking about issues such as poverty is simultaneously shaped by two overarching belief systems: (1) a dominant ideology (e.g., economic individualism) that reflects dominant class interests (e.g., equity norms) via a rationalization and justification of the status quo, and (2) counterideologies that stress social responsibility (Bobo 1991) and/or the structural sources of poverty and inequality (e.g., equality norms)—ideas that stem more from the practical realities of ordinary citizens' lives in class-stratified societies (Mann 1970).

New Insights from Political Psychology

Recent research from the interdisciplinary field of political psychology also offers important insights into ideological processes governing how laypersons think about poverty and other aspects of inequality. Specifically, social dominance theory (SDT) (Sidanius and Pratto 1999) and system justification theory (SJT) (Jost and Major 2001) provide comprehensive perspectives on how economic and other forms of inequality are justified and legitimated in the minds of actors (Hunt 2014). Sidanius and Pratto's (1999) SDT synthesizes work from social psychology, political sociology, political science, and evolutionary psychology to understand the "grammar" of social power that they argue underlies the generation and maintenance of group-based social hierarchy in all societies. The result is "neither strictly a psychological nor a sociological theory, but rather an attempt to connect the worlds of individual personality and attitudes with the domains of institutional behavior and social structure" (p. 31). In so doing, SDT relies heavily on a personality construct—"social dominance orientation" (SDO), defined as the "degree to which individuals desire and support group-based social hierarchy and the domination of 'inferior' groups by 'superior' ones" (p. 48).

While SDO levels represent the *foundation* of persons' orientations toward social hierarchies—the relationship between SDO and support for social inequality is mediated by ideologies, or what Sidanius and Pratto call "legitimizing myths" (LMs). LMs are termed "hierarchy enhancing" (HE) if they justify inequality (e.g., individualistic beliefs) and "hierarchy attenuating" (HA) if they challenge it (e.g., structuralist beliefs). As Pratto et al. (1994:741) explain, "societies minimize group conflict by creating consensus on ideologies that promote the superiority of one group versus another . . . these ideologies must be widely accepted within a society, appearing as self-apparent truths (myths)."

SJT (Jost et al. 2004) also focuses on the role of legitimizing beliefs in maintaining inequality, but it is distinct from SDT in a number of ways, including its primary focus on how the ideological orientations and policy stances of disadvantaged groups commonly run counter to their apparent material self-interests (e.g., "false consciousness" in Marxian terms). Jost et al. (2004) summarize the basic stance of SJT as follows: "(a) there is a general ideological motive to justify the existing social order, (b) this motive is at least partially responsible for the internalization of inferiority among members of disadvantaged groups, (c) it is observed most readily at an implicit, non-conscious level of awareness, and, (d) paradoxically, it is sometimes strongest among those who are most harmed by the status quo" (p. 881). SDT and SJT are but two relatively recent developments that represent important facets of the larger project of developing a truly comprehensive and multilevel social psychology of inequality (Hunt 2014; Jost and Major 2001).

WHAT DETERMINES WHAT IS BELIEVED?

In 1981, Kluegel and Smith noted that we knew considerably more about the antecedents of beliefs about social class than about other dimensions of inequality. Further, at that time, existing research typically only considered a few indicators of persons' objective social positions (e.g., age, occupation, gender) as opposed to a variety of other factors—including "personality characteristics of all sorts" and "cognitive complexity" (p. 41)—that may shape beliefs. And, in 1981, existing research generally observed only weak correlations between sociodemographic variables and stratification beliefs (with the exception of the effects of race). Over the past several decades, there have been important developments in our understanding of the factors shaping beliefs about poverty, including: race/ethnicity, religion, community characteristics, and self-concept.

Race and Ethnicity

While Feagin's (1975) seminal work documented the importance of race as a factor structuring beliefs about poverty (e.g., blacks were much more structuralist than whites), Kluegel and Smith (1986) produced the first comprehensive examination of such differences using multivariate statistical methods. As with Feagin's work, Kluegel and Smith (1986) found that blacks were significantly more structuralist than whites but much more similar to whites with respect to individualistic beliefs. These findings resonate with their view that individualism—as a dominant ideology—is hegemonic and pervades the thinking of all (or nearly all) Americans, while structuralism is more variable and contingent on group membership, personal experiences, and other factors, and is "layered onto" (rather than replacing) an individualistic base. Blacks' greater structuralism is attributable to their history of group-based oppression and their continued disadvantage in U.S. society. However, despite this stronger structuralist consciousness, African Americans retain support for core American values in the form of individualism and "stop short of denying the justice of economic inequality in principle and of dismissing the ideas that the rich and poor as individuals are deserving of their fate" (Kluegel and Smith 1986:290)

Hunt (1996) builds on Kluegel and Smith's findings, observing that—in a 1993 survey of southern Californians—blacks and Latinos were more likely than whites to endorse structuralist *and* individualistic explanations of poverty. Hughes and Tuch (1999) later generalized this observation of greater minority "dual consciousness" to Asian Americans. Hunt interpreted his findings in light of the work of Mann (1970) and Bobo (1991). Specifically, Mann (1970) argues that—rather than resting on societal value consensus, the "social cohesion of liberal democracies" is predicated upon the lack of such consensus, particularly among relatively disadvantaged strata such as the working class and ethno-racial minorities.[7] Thus, for Mann, societal stability is rooted in the *inconsistency* of the belief systems of potentially recalcitrant groups. Bobo (1991) reached a similar conclusion, arguing for the existence of an important "social responsibility" constellation of beliefs in American society that relatively disadvantaged groups disproportionately draw upon to counter the dominant ideology of economic individualism. Thus, individualism retains its appearance as hegemonic *not* because of an absence of system-challenging alternatives but because persons most committed to system-challenging beliefs lack political influence owing to their marginalized status.

Religious Affiliation

Regarding the association between religious affiliation and poverty beliefs, Feagin (1975) reported descriptive statistics suggesting that, in the United States, individualistic beliefs were most popular among white Protestants and white Catholics, somewhat less popular among black Protestants, and least popular among Jews. In contrast, structuralist beliefs were most popular among black Protestants, Jews, and white Protestants and Catholics, in that order. Kluegel and Smith (1986) also examined the effects of religious affiliation, adding the rigor of multiple regression modeling—but only for individualistic beliefs—observing that (relative to persons reporting "no religion," who showed the least support for individualistic beliefs), nonconservative Protestants, conservative Protestants, and Catholics ranked in that order on individualistic beliefs and ranked higher than members of other religions and Jews.

Hunt (2002) further documented the effects of religious affiliation on beliefs about poverty, showing that—after controlling for race and other sociodemographic factors—Protestants and Catholics scored highest on individualistic beliefs, while Jews and followers of other religions scored highest on structuralist beliefs. In addition, Hunt observed that affiliations such as Protestant and Catholic showed significantly different effects on poverty beliefs across race/ethnic lines (e.g., among whites, Protestantism predicted lower structuralism, while among blacks and Latinos, the opposite was observed), further reinforcing the need for social psychological studies that are comparative by race/ethnicity (Hunt et al. 2000, 2013). Finally, Lepianka et al. (2010) bring an important cross-national perspective to our understanding of religion and poverty beliefs, showing that persons living in European countries with a strong Catholic tradition show stronger support for external reasons for poverty (e.g., injustice; unluckiness).

Exposure and Contact Effects

Another important line of work demonstrates that beliefs about poverty depend, in part, on the type and quality of the contacts that people have with the poor (which is consistent with what we know about intergroup contact more generally, e.g., see Allport 1954; Blalock 1984; Pettigrew et al. 2011). Studies of self-reported interpersonal contact by Lee et al. (1990) and G. Wilson (1996) both show that exposure to the poor in ways that reflect relatively equal status (e.g., friendship) and/or intimacy (versus anonymity) fosters sympathetic explanations of poverty and disadvantage. For instance, Lee et al. (1990) find that non-poor persons who had had an informal conversation with a homeless person (about something other than money) were significantly less likely to view homelessness as a function of "personal choice." Additionally, G. Wilson (1996) observes that having a friendship with a poor person significantly predicts support for structuralist beliefs about poverty.

In contrast, however, research also suggests that exposure to the poor in primarily impersonal or anonymous ways can foster unsympathetic explanations of poverty. For instance, both Lee et al. (1990) and G. Wilson (1996) observe that exposure to stigmatized behaviors such as panhandling for money increases individualistic beliefs about poverty. Further, these researchers present evidence that indirect exposure to the issue of poverty—via informal conversations with friends about the subject—either increases the perceived importance of individualistic explanations (G. Wilson 1996) or decreases the perceived importance of structural ones (Lee et al. 1990).

Building on these efforts, Lee et al. (2004) introduced an important methodological innovation: multilevel modeling. Linking individual-level survey data with US Census data on the characteristics of respondents' home communities, Lee et al. found support for contact theory in the form of increased sympathy for homeless persons in areas with larger homeless populations. They argue that *exposure*—by increasing opportunities for various types of contacts—is the key mechanism at play. Hopkins (2009) also used multilevel modeling, analyzing two nationally representative data sets to show that (consistent with theories of racial threat), residents of areas in which the white share of the poor population is greater are less likely to endorse the (individualistic) view that poverty is the result of failings of poor persons themselves. He also observed a place-level effect of partisan composition: areas with a larger percentage of persons who voted Republican in the prior presidential election were significantly less structural and more individualistic in explaining poverty. Most recently, Merolla et al. (2011) employed multilevel models to show that people who live in areas with more concentrated poverty are more likely to endorse both individualistic *and* structuralist beliefs. They argue that this "dual consciousness" pattern likely stems from living in closer proximity to poverty, which exposes persons to social conditions that are reinforcing of both sides of the "deserving/undeserving poor" dichotomy in American public opinion (Gans 1995).

Self-Concept

Self-concept theory and research (Rosenberg 1979; Gecas and Burke 1995; McCall and Simmons 1966) demonstrates that the self "matters" (i.e., is consequential) for social behavior and the organization of society. Building on this insight, and in line with Kluegel and Smith's (1981) suggestion that researchers consider belief influences other people's objective social positions, selected research has examined the relationship between self-concept and poverty beliefs. For instance, Kluegel and Smith (1986) and Heaven (1989) both observed patterns of "attributional consistency" regarding the generalization of explanations for personal outcomes to explanations of poverty (i.e., internal self-explanations lead to individualistic beliefs about the poor, while external self-explanations lead to structuralist beliefs about the poor). Hunt (1996) replicated these patterns among whites but observed *reversals* of the earlier documented patterns for African Americans and Latinos—again, reinforcing the need to incorporate race/ethnicity more fully into our theories and models of social psychological processes (Hunt et al. 2000, 2013).[8]

CONSEQUENCES OF BELIEFS

Stratification beliefs are important in their own right but also because of their impact on and relationship with other beliefs and behaviors. As Kluegel and Smith (1981) note, "beliefs about social inequality as a property of society should influence (a) beliefs about the desirability and necessity of social change, and (b) perceptions of what kind of social change is needed" (p. 49). They also lament, however, that "little research exists on the links between individuals' interpretations of the stratification order and their other behaviors and attitudes" (p. 49).

Over the past few decades, our knowledge of the consequences of stratification beliefs has expanded considerably. For instance, Kluegel and Smith (1986) demonstrate the implications of such beliefs for political behaviors such as voting and social movement participation, for persons' emotional lives (e.g., life satisfaction), and for persons' support of public policies. We focus on the last of these: support for inequality-related social policies (e.g., welfare, affirmative action).

Kluegel and Smith (1986) offer a detailed causal model of the determinants of policy attitudes in which stratification beliefs play an important mediating role. Specifically, they argue that sociodemographic factors shape what they term "general beliefs and affect" which, in turn, shape more specific perceptions (e.g., about inequality) and, ultimately, policy views (see Diagram 1, p. 147). The presumption that perceptions of (and beliefs about) phenomena such as poverty causally precede more concrete policy attitudes rests on the assumption that "perceptions of the existing state of affairs serve as the justification for policies intended to change things" (p. 148). Following this logic, research has demonstrated that (after controlling for the effects of "self-interest" using socioeconomic measures, as well as other social structural factors), dominant ideology beliefs (e.g., individualism) generally decrease support for redistributive policies, while system-challenging beliefs (e.g., structuralism) generally increase support for such initiatives (Robinson and Bell 1978; Hasenfeld and Raftery 1989; Hughes and Tuch 1999; Kluegel and Smith 1986; Kluegel and Bobo 1993). Feagin (1975) and Kluegel and Smith (1986) both document that individualistic beliefs about poverty reduced support for welfare spending, while structuralist beliefs increased such support.

Numerous studies have replicated and expanded on these basic findings. Bobo and Kluegel (1993), for instance, observe that among white GSS respondents (in models testing the competing effects of self-interest, racial attitudes, and stratification beliefs) structuralist beliefs about poverty increased support for both race- and income-targeted redistributive policies. Hughes and Tuch (1999), in an innovative multiethnic analysis (comparing the beliefs of whites, blacks, Hispanics, and Asians), demonstrate similar associations between structuralist beliefs and support for affirmative action.

And, Bullock, Williams, and Limbert (2003) found that progressive welfare policy stances stemmed from structuralist beliefs about poverty (along with dissatisfaction with income inequality and attributing wealth to privilege), while individualistic beliefs about poverty (and wealth) predicted support for restrictive welfare policy.

Researchers have also examined role of the perceived *deservingness* of the poor in shaping antipoverty policy support. For instance, in a study reminiscent of G. Wilson's (1996) work on different types of poverty, Appelbaum (2001) found that widows with children, the physically disabled, and the physically ill were seen as more deserving than teen mothers, single mothers, and able-bodied men, and that respondents were more likely to support liberal policies for target groups seen as more deserving. The issue of perceived deservingness has also been investigated vis-à-vis Americans' beliefs about race (and especially, negative racial stereotypes). For instance, using national survey data, Gilens (1999) finds that Americans support public assistance to the poor as long as they believe the policy targets and benefits the *deserving* poor. Gilens further demonstrates that Americans' opposition to "welfare" stems from a belief that *undeserving* persons (particularly African Americans seen as uncommitted to the work ethic) disproportionately benefit from the program. Indeed, in Gilens' multivariate analyses, the strongest predictors of antiwelfare sentiment were beliefs that "blacks are lazy" and "welfare recipients are undeserving" (with the former significantly shaping the latter as well.[9]

Finally, van Oorschott (2006) explored the issue of deservingness in the European context by gauging public support for various "needy" social groups (the elderly, the sick and disabled, the unemployed, and immigrants). Using data from the 1999–2000 European Values Study survey, he observed an across-country consensus in what he terms a "common and fundamental deservingness culture" (p. 23) wherein the elderly are consistently seen as most deserving, followed by the sick and disabled, the unemployed, and immigrants (in that order).

CONCLUSIONS AND RECOMMENDATIONS

In 1981, Kluegel and Smith concluded their analysis by offering a number of recommendations for future work, some of which have been heeded more successfully than others. Research has certainly improved upon what Kluegel and Smith saw as an over-reliance on "small samples from single communities or narrow geographical areas" (p. 50). Their 1986 book, which is based on a nationally representative U.S. survey sample, represents the largest single step forward in this regard, though other work we have reviewed that is based on nationally representative (e.g., Hopkins 2009; W. Wilson 1996) and/or international data (e.g. Kluegel et al. 1995; Whyte 2004; Lepianka et al. 2010) also represents progress. Kluegel and Smith (1981) also noted the failure of U.S.-based research to "represent adequately the beliefs of key subpopulations" (including "blacks") (p. 50). Research has advanced considerably in this regard, not only incorporating the beliefs of African Americans (Kluegel and Smith 1986) but also other major ethno-racial groups in the United States, such as Latinos (Hunt 1996) and Asian Americans (Hughes and Tuch 1999).

Kluegel and Smith's (1981) key methodological criticisms included the reliance "on analyses of bivariate correlations for testing hypotheses" (50), concerns over measurement consistency, and what they termed the "comparative and longitudinal dimension" (52). The first of these has been consistently addressed via the widespread use of multivariate statistical techniques to analyze both the determinants and consequences of beliefs about poverty and related phenomena (Kluegel and Smith 1986; Lee et al. 1990, 2004; Hunt 1996, 2004). Kluegel and Smith's call to "establish measures with a record of repeated use and with known properties of validity and reliability" (51) has been addressed in the United States via multiple nationally representative (Kluegel and Smith 1986) and regionally specific (Hunt 1996) investigations using the set of items originally developed by Feagin (1972). That said, measurement consistency (in the absence of experimentation with new items) can also represent a fetter to innovation, discovery, and the advancement of knowledge. For instance, the widespread use of Feagin's items may have had the unintended consequence of producing a neglect (or outright ignorance) of other important belief-types (Lepianka et al. 2009).

Kluegel and Smith (1981) also noted that the literature on stratification beliefs "has a comparative dimension but it lacks a longitudinal one," though even the comparative studies of the period were limited "by the use of undersized samples, by differences between countries in the segments of the populations represented, and by a lack of comparability of measures" (p. 52). Research has advanced considerably in this respect, thanks to international survey projects and various other cross-national investigations (Lepianka et al. 2009; Kluegel et al. 1995). The longitudinal dimension, however, remains underdeveloped, and we echo Kluegel and Smith's call for more such research that remains critical to the larger task of developing models of how stratification beliefs change over time (e.g., period vs. cohort effects, etc.).

We close with a set of recommendations for future work corresponding to each of the four domains structuring this review. First, regarding the descriptive matter of *what is believed*, future work should strive to develop and implement a wider set of survey items in an effort to shed further light on untapped and underexamined dimensions of beliefs. One strategy for accomplishing this goal is to combine Feagin's items with the promising and suggestive items from more recent studies (e.g., Nilson's 1981 institutional type; Cozzarelli et al.'s 2001 cultural attribution; and selected items from the 2001 PIAS) in future survey undertakings. Future research should also seek to advance our understanding of public beliefs about different types of poverty and poor subgroups (G. Wilson 1996). For instance, Appelbaum's (2001) findings regarding the differential perceived deservingness of diverse low-income groups could be combined with knowledge from G. Wilson's (1996) three-fold categorization to inform the design of future research. A vignette-based factorial survey design such as those supported by the Time-Sharing Experiments in the Social Sciences (http://www.tessexperiments. org) program could be particularly useful in this regard.

Regarding the *principles organizing thought*, research should seek to employ methodologies to further advance our understanding of the often complex patterns of belief-adherence that conventional methodologies may fail to adequately represent (Lepianka et al. 2009). Use of mixed-methods strategies could be useful in this regard, given the effectiveness of qualitative methods (e.g., in-depth interviews, focus groups, etc.) at probing meanings and uncovering patterns that are difficult to glean from closed-ended survey responses. The richness of qualitative approaches to understanding beliefs about poverty is reflected in research by Godfrey and Wolf (2015) and Seccombe (2011). Also useful could be a "modes of explanation" approach to mapping poverty beliefs.[10] This approach takes as a starting assumption the dual- or split-consciousness perspective outlined earlier and seeks to capture patterns of endorsement *across* sets of survey items representing different types of explanation. In the study of beliefs about racial inequality, for instance, research has differentiated between "purely person centered" accounts (i.e., endorsement of individualistic beliefs with rejection of structuralist ones), "purely structuralist" accounts (the reverse pattern), and various "mixed-modes" (e.g., simultaneous endorsement of individualistic and structuralist beliefs) (Kluegel 1990; Hunt 2007). A comparable research design could be employed with reference to lay explanations of poverty.

Regarding the *antecedents* question, considerable strides have been made since Kluegel and Smith lamented the reliance on a small number of objective status variables (and often in isolation from one another). Building on the important insights of work demonstrating links between "place-level" factors (e.g., racial composition; concentrated poverty) and poverty beliefs (e.g., Hopkins 2009; Merolla et al. 2011), we suggest continued use of multilevel modeling procedures to further examine how various features of neighborhoods and larger communities shape stratification beliefs. This endeavor could be fruitfully combined with the effort to expand our knowledge of different belief-types (as well as of beliefs about different types of poverty). For instance, how does the racial composition of local populations affect beliefs about different categories of the poor that are *themselves* more or less racialized?

We also echo Kluegel and Smith's (1981) call to look beyond objective status predictors, building on research into various self-concept/poverty-beliefs associations previously mentioned (Kluegel and Smith 1986; Heaven 1989; Hunt 1996; 2000). For instance, given that Kluegel and Smith (1981) target "personality characteristics" (p. 41) as predictors warranting more attention, a large-scale survey undertaking that included measures of social dominance orientation (Sidanius and Pratto 1999) and other relevant important personality factors uncovered by political psychologists (Jost et al. 2008) could shed important light on our knowledge of (1) how beliefs about poverty are shaped, and (2) the role of both personality and ideological beliefs as mediators between persons' social locations and their support for inequality-related public policies.[11]

Regarding the *consequences* of beliefs about poverty, in addition to political (e.g., voting; social movement participation) and nonpolitical (e.g. subjective well-being) outcomes highlighted by Kluegel and Smith (1986), we suggest that future survey studies strive to include a larger set of both stratification beliefs and policy-support measures. Such an undertaking would allow for examination of the complex inter-relationships between beliefs about different aspects of inequality and support for various policy interventions (e.g., income- vs. race-targeted; opportunity enhancing vs. more outcome focused, etc.). Finally, we also encourage researchers to look *beyond* the policy-attitudes domain to examine the impact of beliefs about poverty on an array of microlevel intergroup interactions (e.g., hiring decisions, teacher-student relationships, caseworker-client exchanges, etc.) that have implications for the construction and reproduction of structured social inequality (see Bullock 2004; Robinson 2011).

NOTES

1. We thank the editors for their helpful comments on a prior draft of this chapter and Ashley Reichelmann for her research assistance. Direct all correspondence to Matthew Hunt (m.hunt@neu.edu).

2. Following Kluegel and Smith (1981) we use the terms "American" and "British" to refer to residents of the United States and Great Britain respectively.

3. Owing to space limitations, we have been necessarily selective in our review of the literature, focusing on what we see as the most compelling developments over the past three decades. For other useful summaries, see: Furnham's (2003) review of psychologists' contributions to poverty-beliefs research, and Lepianka et al.'s (2009) treatment of "lay poverty attributions." Additionally, McCall (2013) offers an extensive treatment of stratification-beliefs scholarship, though she maintains a "stricter analytical separation between inequality and poverty than is common in the literature" (13) following the assertion that "beliefs about economic inequality are shaped by views about the rich and not the poor (who are more central to beliefs about poverty)" (xi).

4. Lepianka et al. (2009) identify two main poverty-beliefs research traditions: (1) the factor analytic approach, and (2) the forced-choice-question approach. Most US-based research is factor analytic, using the set of survey items originally developed by Feagin (1972) or close variants thereof. The forced-choice-question approach is more prevalent in Europe and asks respondents to indicate which of four statements regarding poverty causation they most support (e.g., Eurobarometer surveys).

5. In one published study using the PIAS, Hopkins (2009) reports that "by performing a factor analysis with two factors and varimax rotation . . . we can isolate the individualism and structuralism inherent in the responses" (752). However, it is unclear what effect forcing a two-factor solution may have had in this instance.

6. We also refer interested readers to chapter 2 of Kluegel and Smith's 1986 book, which remains among the most comprehensive and useful summaries of basic social psychological processes underlying how people think about inequality.

7. Consistent with this view, Bullock and Limbert (2003) observed greater dual consciousness among low-income groups, reinforcing the view that this belief-pattern is linked to multiple facets of marginalization (e.g., race, ethnicity, social class).

8. Hunt (2001) also documents that self-esteem and mastery shape ideological beliefs about the causes of poverty; self-esteem is the more consequential aspect of self-evaluation

shaping support for individualistic beliefs about inequalities, while mastery is the key aspect of self-evaluation shaping system-challenging, structuralist beliefs.

9. Detailed consideration of the complex intersection of racial attitudes, stratification beliefs, and policy attitudes lies beyond the scope of this review. For more background on the racial attitudes domain, see Hunt and Wilson 2011; Schuman et al. 1997; Sears et al. 2000; Tuch and Martin 1999.

10. This method was first used in racial attitudes literature (Apostle et al. 1983), including in studies of beliefs about racial inequality (Hunt 2007; Kluegel 1990), and represents a variant of the "compound belief" measurement strategy that is more typical of European stratification beliefs research (Lepianka et al. 2009).

11. As noted, Sidanius and Pratto (1999) argue that various legitimating myths (LMs) mediate the relationship between SDO and policy attitudes. This is broadly consistent with Kluegel and Smith's (1986) causal model outlined earlier.

REFERENCES

Abouchedid, Kamal and Ramzi Nasser. 2001. "Poverty Attitudes and Their Determinants in Lebanon's Plural Society." *Journal of Economic Psychology* 22:271–82.

Allport, Gordon. 1954. *The Nature of Prejudice.* Cambridge, MA: Addison-Wesley.

Al-Zahrani, Saad Said A. and Stan A. Kaplowitz. 1993. "Attributional Biases in Individualistic and Collectivist Cultures: A Comparison of Americans with Saudis." *Social Psychology Quarterly* 56:223–33.

Apostle, Richard A. Charles Y. Glock, Thomas Piazza, and Marijean Suelzle. 1983. *The Anatomy of Racial Attitudes.* Berkeley: University of California Press.

Appelbaum, Lauren D. 2001. "The Influence of Perceived Deservingness on Policy Decisions Regarding Aid to the Poor." *Political Psychology* 22:419–42.

Bellah, Robert, Richard Madsen, William M. Sullivan, Ann Swidler, and Steven M. Tipton. 1985. *Habits of the Heart: Individualism and Commitment in American Life.* Berkeley: University of California Press.

Blalock, Hubert M. 1984. "Contextual-Effects Models: Theoretical and Methodological Issues." *Annual Review of Sociology* 10:353–72.

Bobo, Lawrence. 1991. "Social Responsibility, Individualism, and Redistributive Policies." *Sociological Forum* 6:71–93.

Bobo, Lawrence and James R. Kluegel. 1993. "Opposition to Race-Targeting: Self-Interest, Stratification Ideology, or Racial Attitudes?" *American Sociological Review* 58:443–64.

Bonn, Marta, Dave C. Earle, Stephen Lea, and Paul Webley. 1999. "South African Children's Views of Wealth, Poverty, Inequality and Unemployment." *Journal of Economic Psychology* 20:593–612.

Bullock, Heather E. 1999. "Attributions for Poverty: A Comparison of Middle-Class and Welfare Recipient Attitudes." *Journal of Applied Social Psychology* 29:2059–82.

Bullock, Heather E. 2004. "From the Front Lines of Welfare Reform: An Analysis of Social Worker and Welfare Recipient Attitudes." *Journal of Social Psychology* 144:571–90.

Bullock, Heather E. and Wendy M. Limbert. 2003. "Scaling the Socioeconomic Ladder: Low-Income Women's Perceptions of Class Status and Opportunity." *Journal of Social Issues* 59:693–709.

Bullock, Heather E. and Irma M. Waugh. 2005. "Beliefs about Poverty and Opportunity Among Mexican Immigrant Farm Workers." *Journal of Applied Social Psychology* 35:1132–49.

Bullock, Heather E., Wendy R. Williams, and Wendy M. Limbert. 2003. "Predicting Support for Welfare Policies: The Impact of Attributions and Beliefs about Inequality." *Journal of Poverty* 7:35–56.

Carr, Stuart C. 1996. "Social Psychology and the Management of Aid." Pp. 103–18 in *Psychology and the Developing World*, edited by S. C. Carr and J. F. Schumaker. Westport, CT: Praeger.

Carr, Stuart C. and Malcolm Maclachlan. 1998. "Actors, Observers, and Attributions for Third World Poverty: Contrasting Perspectives from Malawi and Australia." *Journal of Social Psychology* 138:189–202.

Carr, Stuart C., Hoda Taef, Rosaura De M. S. Ribeiro, and Malcolm MacLachlan. 1998. "Attributions for 'Third World' Poverty: Contextual Factors in Australia and Brazil." *Psychology and Developing Societies* 10:103–14.

Cozzarelli, Catherine, Anna V. Wilkinson, and Michael J. Tagler. 2001. "Attitudes toward the Poor and Attributions for Poverty." *Journal of Social Issues* 57:207–27.

Feagin, Joe. 1972. "When It Comes to Poverty, It's Still, 'God Helps Those Who Help Themselves.'" *Psychology Today* 6:101–29.

Feagin, Joe. 1975. *Subordinating the Poor*. Englewood Cliffs, NJ: Prentice Hall.

Furnham, Adrian. 2003. "Poverty and Wealth." Pp. 163–83 in *Poverty and Psychology: From Global Perspective to Local Practice*, edited by in S. C. Carr, S.C. and T. S. Sloan. New York: Kluwer Academic/Plenum.

Furnham, Adrian F. and Barrie Gunter. 1984. "Just World Beliefs and Attitudes Towards the Poor." *British Journal of Social Psychology* 23:265–69.

Gans, Herbert. 1995. *The War against the Poor: The Underclass and Antipoverty Policy*. New York: Basic Books.

Gecas, Viktor and Peter J. Burke. 1995. "Self and Identity." Pp. 41–67 in *Sociological Perspectives on Social Psychology*, edited by K. S. Cook, G. A. Fine, and J. S. House. Boston: Allyn and Bacon.

Gilens, Martin. 1999. *Why Americans Hate Welfare: Race, Media, and the Politics of Antipoverty Policy*. Chicago: University of Chicago Press.

Godfrey, Erin B. and Sharon Wolf. 2015, April 27. "Developing Critical Consciousness or Justifying the System? A Qualitative Analysis of Attributions for Poverty and Wealth among Low-Income Racial/Ethnic Minority and Immigrant Women." *Cultural Diversity and Ethnic Minority Psychology*. Advance online publication.

Guimond, Serge, Guy Begin, and Douglas L. Palmer. 1989. "Education and Causal Attributions: The Development of 'Person-Blame' and 'System-Blame' Ideology." *Social Psychology Quarterly* 52:126–40.

Habibov, Nazim N. 2011. "Public Beliefs Regarding the Causes of Poverty During Transition: Evidence from the Caucasus, Central Asia, Russia, and Ukraine." *International Journal of Sociology and Social Policy* 31:53–74.

Halik, Murnizam and Paul Webley. 2011. "Adolescents' Understanding of Poverty and the Poor in Rural Malaysia." *Journal of Economic Psychology* 32:231–39.

Harper, David J., Graham F. Wagstaff, Tim J. Newton, and Kevin R. Harrison. 1990. "Lay Causal Perceptions of Third World Poverty and the Just World Theory." *Social Behavior and Personality* 18:235–38.

Hartz, Louis. 1955. *The Liberal Tradition in America: An Interpretation of American Political Thought since the Revolution*. New York: Harcourt, Brace.

Hasenfeld, Yeheskel and Jane A. Rafferty. 1989. "The Determinants of Public Attitudes Toward the Welfare State." *Social Forces* 67:1027–48.

Hayati, Dariush and Ezatollah Karami. 2005. "Typology of Causes of Poverty: The Perception of Iranian Famers." *Journal of Economic Psychology* 26:884–901.

Heaven, Patrick C. L. 1989. "Economic Locus of Control Beliefs and Lay Attributions of Poverty." *Australian Journal of Psychology* 41:315–25.

Hine, Donald W. and Christina J. Montiel. 1999. "Perceived Causes of Third World Poverty: A Cross-Cultural Analysis." *European Journal of Social Psychology* 29:943–59.

Hirschl, Thomas, Mark Rank, and Dela Kusi-Appouh. 2011. "Ideology and the Experience of Poverty Risk: Views about Poverty Within a Focus Group Design." *Journal of Poverty* 15:350–70.

Hopkins, Daniel J. 2009. "Partisan Reinforcement and the Poor: The Impact of Context on Explanations for Poverty." *Social Science Quarterly* 90:744–64.

Huber, Joan and William Form. 1973. *Income and Ideology.* New York: Free Press.

Hughes, Michael and Stephen A. Tuch. 1999. "How Beliefs about Poverty Influence Racial Policy Attitudes: A Study of Whites, African Americans, Hispanics, and Asians in the United States." Pp. 165–90 in *Racialized Politics: The Debate about Racism in America,* edited by D. O. Sears, J. Sidanius, and L. Bobo. Chicago: University of Chicago Press.

Hunt, Matthew O. 1996. "The Individual, Society, or Both? A Comparison of Black, Latino, and White Beliefs about the Causes of Poverty." *Social Forces* 75:293–322.

Hunt, Matthew O. 2001. "Self-evaluation and Stratification Beliefs." Pp. 330–50 in *Extending Self-esteem Theory and Research: Social and Psychological Currents,* edited by T. J. Owens, S. Stryker, and N. Goodman. Cambridge, UK: Cambridge University Press.

Hunt, Matthew O. 2002. "Religion, Race/Ethnicity, and Beliefs about Poverty." *Social Science Quarterly* 83:810–32.

Hunt, Matthew O. 2004. "Race, Ethnicity, and Beliefs about Poverty and Wealth." *Social Science Quarterly,* 85:827–53.

Hunt, Matthew O. 2007. "African American, Hispanic, and White Beliefs about Black/White Inequality 1977–2004." *American Sociological Review* 72:390–415.

Hunt, Matthew O. 2014. "Ideologies." Pp. 325–51 in *Handbook of the Social Psychology of Inequality,* edited by Jane McLeod, Ed Lawler, and Michael Schwalbe. Springer.

Hunt, Matthew O., Brian Powell, Lala C. Steelman, and Pamela B. Jackson. 2000. "Color-Blind: The Treatment of Race and Ethnicity in Social Psychology." *Social Psychology Quarterly* 63:352–64.

Hunt, Matthew O. and George Wilson, eds. 2011. "Race, Racial Attitudes, and Stratification Beliefs: Evolving Directions for Research and Policy." *Annals of the American Academy of Political and Social Science.* Vol. 634.

Hunt, Matthew O., Pamela Braboy Jackson, Samuel H. Kye, Brian Powell, and Lala Carr Steelman. 2013. "Still Color-Blind? The Treatment of Race, Ethnicity, Intersectionality, and Sexuality in Sociological Social Psychology." *Advances in Group Processes* 30:21–45.

Ige, Kehinde E. and Fhulu H. Nekhwevha. 2014. "Causal Attributions for Poverty Among Low-Income Communities of Badia, Nigeria." *Social Science Journal* 38:205–18.

Jones, Edward E. and Richard E. Nisbett. 1972. "The Actor and the Observer: Divergent Perceptions of the Causes of Behavior." Pp. 79–94 in *Attribution: Perceiving the Causes of Behavior,* edited by E. E. Jones, D.E. Kanouse, H. H. Kelley, R. E. Nisbett, S. Valins, and B. Weiner. Morristown, NJ: General Learning Press.

Jost, John T., Mahzarin R. Banaji, and Brian A. Nosek. 2004. "A Decade of System Justification Theory: Accumulated Evidence of Conscious and Unconscious Bolstering of the Status Quo." *Political Psychology* 25:881–919.

Jost, John T. and Brenda Major, eds. 2001. *The Psychology of Legitimacy: Emerging Perspectives on Ideology, Justice, and Intergroup Relations.* New York: Cambridge University Press.

Jost, John T., Brian A. Nosek, and Sameul D. Gosling. 2008. "Ideology: Its Resurgence in Social, Personality, and Political Psychology." *Perspectives on Psychological Science* 3:126–36.

Kelley, Harold H. and John L. Michela. 1980. "Attribution Theory and Research." *Annual Review of Psychology* 31:457–501.

Kluegel, James R. 1990. "Trends in Whites' Explanations of the Black-White Gap in Socioeconomic Status, 1977–1989." *American Sociological Review* 55:512–25.

Kluegel, James R. and Eliot R. Smith. 1981. "Beliefs about Stratification." *Annual Review of Sociology* 7:29–56.

Kluegel, James R., David S. Mason, and Bernd Wegener. 1995. *Social Justice and Political Change—Public Opinion in Capitalist and Post-Communist States.* New York: Aldine de Gruyter.

Kluegel, James R. and Eliot R. Smith. 1986. *Beliefs about Inequality.* New York: Aldine De Gruyter.

Knecht, Tom and Lisa M. Martinez. 2009. "Humanizing the Homeless: Does Contact Erode Stereotypes?" *Social Science Research* 38:521–34.

Knecht, Tom and Lisa M. Martinez. 2012. "Engaging the Reluctant? Service Learning, Interpersonal Contact, and Attitudes toward Homeless Individuals." *PS: Political Science and Politics* 45:106–11.

Lee, Barrett A., Chad R. Farrell, and Bruce Link. 2004. "Revisiting the Contact Hypothesis: The Case of Public Exposure to Homelessness." *American Sociological Review* 69:40–63.

Lee, Barrett A., Sue Hinze Jones, and David W. Lewis. 1990. "Public Beliefs about the Causes of Homelessness." *Social Forces* 69:253–65.

Lepianka, Dorota, Wim Van Oorschot, and John Gelissen. 2009. "Popular Explanations of Poverty: A Critical Discussion of Empirical Research." *Journal of Social Policy* 38:421–38.

Lepianka, Dorota, Wim Van Oorschot, and John Gelissen. 2010. "Popular Explanations of Poverty in Europe: Effects of Contextual and Individual Characteristics across 28 European Countries." *Acta Sociologica* 53:53–72.

Lerner, Melvin. 1980. *The Belief in a Just World: A Fundamental Delusion.* New York: Plenum.

Love, Rhonda, Edward Makwarimba, Susan McMurray, Dennis Raphael, Linda I. Reutter, and Miriam J. Stewart. 2006. "Public Attributions for Poverty in Canada." *Canadian Review of Sociology and Anthropology* 43:1–22.

Mann, Michael. 1970. "The Social Cohesion of Liberal Democracy." *American Sociological Review* 35:423–39.

McCall, George J. and Jerry L. Simmons. 1966. *Identities and Interactions.* New York: Free Press.

McCall, Leslie. 2013. *The Undeserving Rich—American Beliefs about Inequality, Opportunity, and Redistribution.* Cambridge: Cambridge University Press.

Merolla, David M., Matthew O. Hunt, and Richard T. Serpe. 2011. "Concentrated Disadvantage and Beliefs about the Causes of Poverty: A Multi-Level Analysis." *Sociological Perspectives* 54:205–28.

Mistry, Rashmita S., Christia S. Brown, Kirby A. Chow, and Geri S. Collins. 2012. "Increasing the Complexity of Young Adolescents' Beliefs about Poverty and Inequality: Results of an 8th Grade Social Studies Curriculum Intervention." *Journal of Youth and Adolescence* 41:704–16.

Morcol, Goktug. 1997. "Lay Explanations for Poverty in Turkey and Their Determinants." *Journal of Social Psychology* 137:728–38.

Nasser, Ramzi Z. 2007. "Does Subjective Class Predict Causal Attribution for Poverty?" *Journal of Social Sciences* 34:197–201.

Nasser, Ramzi, Kamal Abouchedid, and Hilal Khashan. 2002. "Perceptions of the Causes of Poverty Comparing Three National Groups: Lebanon, Portugal, and South Africa." *Current Research in Social Psychology* 8:101–18.

National Public Radio, Kaiser Family Foundation, and the Kennedy School of Government. 2001. *Poverty in America.* Telephone survey of American households. Retrieved September 6, 2015 (http://www.npr.org/programs/specials/poll/poverty/summary.html).

Nilson, Linda B. 1981. "Reconsidering Ideological Lines: Beliefs about Poverty in America." *Sociological Quarterly* 22:531–48.

National Opinion Research Center (NORC). 2010. *General Social Survey.* Retrieved December 10, 2014 (http://www.norc.org/Research/Projects/Pages/general-social-survey.aspx).

Pandy, Janak, Yogonand Sinha, Anand Prakash, and R. C. Tripathi. 1982. "Right–Left Political Ideologies and Attribution of the Causes of Poverty." *European Journal of Social Psychology* 12:327–31.

Payne, Monica and Adrian Furhnam. 1985. "Explaining the Causes of Poverty in the West Indies: A Cross-Cultural Comparison." *Journal of Economic Psychology*, 6:215–29.

Pettigrew, Thomas F., Linda R. Tropp, Ulrich Wagner, and Oliver Christ. 2011. "Recent Advances in Intergroup Contact Theory." *International Journal of Intercultural Relations* 35:271–80.

Pratto, Felicia, James Sidanius, Lisa M. Stallworth, and Bertram F. Malle. 1994. "Social Dominance Orientation: A Personality Variable Predicting Political and Social Attitudes." *Journal of Personality and Social Psychology* 67:741–63.

Rim, Yeshayahu. 1984. "Explanations for Poverty: Personality Aspects." *Personality and Individual Differences* 5:123–24.

Robinson, Gregg. 2011. "The Contradictions of Caring: Social Workers, Teachers and Attributions for Poverty and Welfare Reform." *Journal of Applied Social Psychology* 41:2374–2404.

Robinson, Robert V. and Wendell Bell. 1978. "Equality, Success, and Social-Justice in England and the United States." *American Sociological Review* 43:125–43.

Rosenberg, Morris. 1979. *Conceiving the Self.* New York: Basic Books.

Ross, Lee. 1977. "The Intuitive Psychologist and His Shortcomings: Distortions in the Attribution Process." *Advances in Experimental Social Psychology* 10:174–221.

Sachweh, Patrick. 2012. "The Moral Economy of Inequality: Popular Views on Income Differentiation, Poverty and Wealth." *Socio-Economic Review* 10:419–45.

Schuman, Howard, Charlotte Steeh, Lawrence Bobo, and Maria Krysan. 1997. *Racial Attitudes in America—Trends and Interpretations.* Rev. ed. Cambridge, MA: Harvard.

Sears, David O., Jim Sidanius, and Lawrence Bobo. 1999. *Racialized Politics: The Debate about Racism in America.* Chicago: University of Chicago.

Seccombe, Karen T. 2011. *"So You Think I Drive a Cadillac?" Welfare Recipients' Perspectives on the System and Its Reform.* 3rd ed. Boston: Allyn and Bacon.

Sidanius, Jim and Felicia Pratto. 1999. *Social Dominance: An Intergroup Theory of Social Hierarchy and Oppression.* New York: Cambridge.

Smith, Kevin B. and Lorene H. Stone. 1989. "Rags, Riches, and Bootstraps: Beliefs about the Causes of Wealth and Poverty." *Sociological Quarterly* 30:93–107.

Strier, Roni. 2005. "Gendered Realities of Poverty: Men and Women's Views of Poverty in Jerusalem." *Social Service Review* 79:344–67.

Tuch, Steven A. and Jack K. Martin, eds. 1997. *Racial Attitudes in the 1990s: Continuity and Change.* Westport, CT: Praeger.

Van Oorschot, Wim and Loek Halman. 2000. "Blame or Fate, Individual or Social? An International Comparison of Popular Explanations of Poverty." *European Societies* 2:1–28.

Van Oorschot, Wim and Loek Halman. 2006. "Making the Difference in Social Europe: Deservingness Perceptions Among Citizens of European Welfare States." *Journal of European Social Policy* 16:23–42.

Weiss, Idit and John Gal. 2007. "Poverty in the Eyes of the Beholder: Social Workers Compared to Other Middle-Class Professionals." *British Journal of Social Work* 37:893–908.

Weiss-Gal, Idit, Yael Benyamini, Karni Ginzburg, Riki Savaya, and Einat Peled. 2009. "Social Workers' and Service Users' Causal Attributions for Poverty." *Social Work* 54:125–33.

Whyte, Martin King. 2010. *Myth of the Social Volcano: Perceptions of Inequality and Distributive Injustice in Contemporary China.* Stanford, CA: Stanford University Press.

Wilson, George. 1996. "Toward a Revised Framework for Examining Beliefs about the Causes of Poverty." *Sociological Quarterly* 37:413–28.

Wilson, William J. 1996. *When Work Disappears: The World of the New Urban Poor.* New York: Vintage.

CHAPTER 6

....

HOW POLITICS AND INSTITUTIONS SHAPE POVERTY AND INEQUALITY

....

DAVID BRADY, AGNES BLOME,
AND HANNA KLEIDER

IN the past 15 to 20 years, considerable progress has been made in understanding how politics and institutions shape poverty. Traditionally, studies of poverty, especially in the United States, neglected institutions and politics. Instead, studies predominantly focused on the demographic risks of poverty or how economic performance shaped poverty in the United States. For example, many poverty researchers demonstrated that single mothers were more likely to be poor, and economists often documented how poverty rose and fell with the business cycle. However, scholars have recently devoted increasing attention to how politics and institutions shape the distribution of economic resources and how this ultimately drives poverty (Brady 2009; Brady and Sosnaud 2010; Rank this volume). At the risk of hyperbole, there has been a marked transition in the social science of poverty such that it is now widely understood that much of the variation in poverty across rich democracies is due to politics and institutions. While previously poverty scholars concentrated on demographics and economic performance, scholars are beginning to emphasize, for example, social policy and labor unions. More scholars are drawing attention to how politics and institutions shape poverty in developing countries as well. Scholars have even shown that the effects of demographic risk factors, like single motherhood, are themselves conditioned by politics and institutions. Indeed, political and institutional explanations of poverty and inequality have never been as prominent as today.

At least two factors have contributed to this progress. First, there have been significant improvements in cross-national survey and administrative data on individual and household income. Perhaps the best example is the Luxembourg Income Study, which has greatly facilitated more rigorous cross-national comparisons of poverty and inequality. This, in turn, has allowed scholars to explore the role of country-level factors like social policies. Such comparisons have also included fine-grained scrutiny of taxes and transfers, which has highlighted how essential taxes and transfers are to household income (Rainwater and Smeeding 2004). Because taxes and transfers are largely determined by governments, the nation-state (henceforth "state") and the politics of the state have risen in importance in poverty and inequality research. The rising prominence of the state in inequality research is well-captured by the enthusiastic debates sparked by Thomas Piketty's (2014) *Capital in the Twenty-First Century*, which called for a global tax on capital as a means to moderate inequality.

Second, though initially slow, there has been a genuine scholarly response to rising inequality. Through the early 2000s, scholars often lamented that sociology and political science had failed to study the increasing inequality occurring in rich democracies (e.g., Morris and Western 1999). Yet, over the past 10 to 15 years, there has been growing interest in the sources of rising inequality, and within this literature, political and institutional explanations have grown in prominence. This is partly because the prevailing economic and demographic explanations have proven limited for explaining many of the prominent trends (Brady and Leicht 2008). Therefore, as such explanations have been unable to account for the most important trends in poverty and inequality, political scientists, sociologists and others have stepped in with political and institutional explanations (see Brady and Sosnaud 2010).

This essay reviews theories and literatures on how politics and institutions shape poverty. In the process, we draw a clearer connection between the poverty literature and the broader conceptual and theoretical literatures on how politics and institutions shape inequality. Animating this essay is the general contention that poverty is shaped by the combination of power resources and institutions. On one hand, scholars in the power resources tradition have emphasized the role of class-based collective political actors for mobilizing "power resources" in the state and economy. On the other hand, institutionalists have highlighted the role of formal rules and regulations.[1] Altogether, political explanations of poverty vary across a continuum from those highlighting the active struggle between collective actors to those highlighting the stable arrangements of rules and regulations.[2] At the same time, contemporary political explanations of poverty often draw on insights across this continuum and eclectically blend power resources and institutions into comprehensive accounts. We also posit state policy as a key mediator between politics/institutions and poverty and explain how this means politics/institutions can have both direct and indirect effects on poverty.

The first section reviews power resources theory. We first explain its theoretical arguments and then discuss the evidence for key power resources (i.e., collective political actors like labor unions and parties). The second section covers institutional explanations. Again, we first explain the key concepts and theories and then review the evidence linking the most salient institutions to poverty. The third section explains the pivotal role of state policy by cataloguing the generic mechanisms of how state policy influences poverty. Finally, we conclude by presenting several challenges for future research. Throughout, we draw on literatures from several disciplines and across several world regions.

POWER RESOURCES THEORY

Concepts and Core Arguments

Power resources theory contends that collective actors bond together and mobilize less advantaged classes of citizens around shared interests. Such groups gain electoral power by forming unions and Left parties, and when in office, these parties expand the welfare state (Brady 2009; Brady, Fullerton, and Cross 2009; Hicks 1999; Huber and Stephens 2001; Korpi 1983; Moller et al. 2003).[3] Power resources theory claims that the mobilization of such groups of less advantaged citizens is pivotal because the default distribution of political power in a capitalist democracy favors elites and business. This default favoring business and elites leads to a default unequal distribution of income. Hence, it is essential for the working class, poor, and others to bond together and attract some of the middle class to gain any real political power.

Beyond simply expanding the welfare state, power resources theory offers a more general model of income distribution (Brady et al. 2009; Korpi 1983). In contrast to Left parties mobilizing in elections, business and elites can mobilize in the labor market and corporate boardrooms to funnel more economic resources in their own direction. Because power resources can be mobilized in both workplaces and polities, power resources' effects might manifest in the distribution of earnings and employment— complementary to but potentially separate from the welfare state. Generalizing even further, it is reasonable to think of power resources as a theory about how collective actors accomplish economic egalitarianism by gaining power, and controlling offices and positions with authority over markets, taxation, social policies, and other distribution processes. Therefore, we suggest power resources theory at least partly informs all research on how collective political actors shape equality.

Traditionally, power resources theory anchored its microlevel mechanisms in the rational self-interest of the poor and working class to expand the welfare state. Korpi (1983) built his explanation by deriving the mobilization of classes from their material interests. Many scholars still attribute a considerable role for material interest, especially among political economists (Mahler 2008). This makes sense as it is in the material interests of the poor and working class to have a larger welfare state and more redistribution.[4] Constituencies of beneficiaries, even among the middle class or affluent, have a rational interest in forming coalitions with the working class and poor to maintain existing social policies (Korpi and Palme 1998). At the same time, others have sought to broaden the reasons why the working class and poor will mobilize. Building on power resources theory, but integrating it with public opinion and path dependency literatures, Brooks and Manza (2007) argue that existing social policies cultivate widely held beliefs and normative expectations that feed back into the politics of welfare state (Brady and Bostic 2015). The powerful cultural expectations that result from social policies then greatly influence how people vote and constrain politicians seeking to retrench welfare states. Hence, power resources could be effectively mobilized for the welfare state because citizens have either or both material interests and cultural values favoring egalitarianism.

Unions and Leftist Parties

Influenced by power resources theory, a rich tradition of scholarship demonstrates the effects of labor unions on economic inequality. Considerable research has shown that unionization is associated with higher earnings for the average worker (Kalleberg et al. 1981), lower compensation for elites (Volscho and Kelley 2012), and less earnings inequality (Kristal 2010; Wallace et al. 1999; Western and Rosenfeld 2011). Particularly relevant to poverty, scholars have shown that unionization reduces the presence of low-paid jobs (Gautie and Schmidt 2009; Zuberi 2006) and boosts the earnings of the less skilled, younger, and contingently employed workers that are vulnerable to poverty (Eren 2009; Maxwell 2007). Unions accomplish greater security and better compensation for workers because they pressure management to raise wages, encourage rules against the use of contingent workers (whose presence would reduce wages), and regulate working conditions. Unions also disseminate egalitarian discourses, influence policy, and shape the regulation and governance of labor markets (Western and Rosenfeld 2011). Regardless of how or why, there is clear and convincing evidence of a strong relationship between unionization and higher earnings, and lower inequality and poverty (Brady et al. 2013; Rosenfeld and Laird this volume).

This research has been particularly influential to the emerging study of working poverty (Gautie and Ponthieux this volume; Lohmann 2009). Compared to joblessness, working poverty has been relatively neglected even though the majority of poor people in most rich democracies reside in households with employed people. However, in the past few years, scholars have devoted increasing attention to working poverty, and this nascent literature has highlighted the role of unions (Brady et al. 2010; Zuberi 2006). In an analysis of the United States 1991–2010, Brady and colleagues (2013) show that state-level unionization reduces the odds of individual-level working poverty. Indeed, they find that a state's level of unionization is more important than the economic performance or social policies of that state. What is more, their multilevel approach allows them to control for a wide variety of individual characteristics predicting poverty and to show that unionization benefits both unionized and nonunionized workers.

Unions also matter to poverty because they are key players in electoral politics. Unions mobilize voters, align and form coalitions with political parties, and influence government administrators. Indeed, unionization has often been utilized to show how the power resources of the working class trigger welfare state development

(Hicks 1999; Huber and Stephens 2001; Korpi 1983). Influenced by this research, many show that unionization explains cross-national differences in poverty and inequality (Bradley et al. 2003; Moller et al. 2003). This literature often demonstrates that in addition to directly affecting the workplace and earnings (or household income before taxes and transfers), unions indirectly influence poverty by encouraging more generous social policies (Brady 2009; Brady et al. 2009). Indeed, Brady and colleagues (2010) show that unionization mostly explains cross-national differences in working poverty through its indirect effects through welfare state generosity.

Unions' relevance to electoral politics and social policy complements the role of political parties. In many accounts, Leftist parties are the actors that actually establish egalitarianism by enacting laws and policies favoring the poor (Allan and Scruggs 2004; Kelly and Witko 2012; Korpi and Palme 2003) and reducing inequality (Bradley et al. 2003; Mahler 2004; Sassoon 1996). As Huber and Stephens (2001) argue, parties serve the "crucial mediating role" in implementing policy. As a result, many show a relationship between Leftist party power and lower poverty (Bradley et al. 2003; Moller et al. 2003). The bulk of the evidence suggests it is actually the cumulative and long-term, rather than the current, power of Left parties that matters (Huber and Stephens 2001; Jensen 2010). For instance, Brady (2009) shows that rich democracies with a cumulative history of Left party power tend to have lower poverty than those traditionally governed by centrist and Right parties. Pribble and colleagues (2009) show that poverty tends to be lower in Latin American countries with a greater cumulative presence of Left parties in the legislature—such as Costa Rica or Uruguay.

Business, Elites, and the Right

Power resources theory traditionally presented the political advantages of business and elites as the default and tended to focus on collective actors representing the poor and the working class. As a result, less research examines how the power and mobilization of elites and business affects poverty specifically. This is unfortunate as it is plausible that the power and mobilization of elites and business is quite relevant. On one hand, some literature illustrates how business sometimes acts in favor of egalitarian social policies. This research has often come out of the varieties of capitalism research program, which sought to identify the institutional differences between coordinated market economies like Germany and liberal market economies like the United States. Such scholars show that business has an interest in welfare state expansion in a coordinated market economy environment featuring wage coordination, vocational education systems, and corporatism (Hall and Soskice 2001; Mares 2003; Martin and Swank 2012; Thelen 2012). On the other hand, others argue Right parties mostly operate as a counterweight to Left parties and unions (Allan and Scruggs 2004; Brady and Leicht 2008; Castles 2004). When in power, Right parties tend to retrench the welfare state and alter the tax distribution such that inequality increases (Allan and Scruggs 2004; Brady and Leicht 2008; Hacker and Pierson 2010). Both literatures view the mobilization of business and elites as variable rather than constant and highlight how business and elites have mobilized in response to the growth of the state and the welfare state that occurred in many countries after World War II and until the 1970s (Harvey 2005). Right power resources also need to be mobilized and, indeed, some demonstrate Right power resources have been more consequential than the Left in recent decades (Brady and Leicht 2008; Allan and Scruggs 2004). Thus, modern power resources theory encompasses a range of class-based organized groups and collective actors acting through and outside parties to influence welfare states.

Broadening Power Resources

Finally, beyond class-based actors like business, labor, and parties, scholars have broadened power resources theory to include the mobilization of other disadvantaged groups. Most prominent in this literature, women's electoral mobilization and presence in government influences the development of the welfare state, which ultimately bears on poverty and inequality (Bolzendahl and Brooks 2007; Huber and Stephens 2001). For power resources research to advance, a better understanding of the entire spectrum of political actors would be valuable (Hacker and Pierson 2010; Volscho and Kelly 2012). In that vein, Thelen (2012) proposes a "coalitional approach" to capture how a variety of actors—parties, organized labor, business—come together (or not) to shape inequality. Perhaps such a theoretical direction has potential for research specifically focused on poverty as well.

INSTITUTIONAL EXPLANATIONS

Concepts and Theories

Institutions can be thought of as stable agreements and historical settlements that channel, constrain, and regulate the behavior of firms, workers, and other actors and hence contribute to inequalities in nation-states (Campbell 2004; Fligstein 2001; Pierson 2004). Institutions include formal and informal rules, laws, and policies that define the range of legitimate actions of market actors. There is no one institutional explanation of poverty, and arguably there is less coherence among institutional explanations than among power resources scholarship.[5] Still, institutional explanations are a family of explanations that stress the salience of institutions for poverty and inequality—above and beyond collective political actors.

Proponents of institutional explanations emphasize the role of established and stable macrolevel contexts to explain differences in poverty and inequality across places (Jepperson 1991). Thus, like power resources scholars, institutionalists contend that the environment determines the odds of poverty. Somewhat unlike power resources theory however, institutional explanations stress that the processes driving inequality are less amenable to manipulation by collective political actors. That is, institutions reproduce and structure potential inequalities. They are not active players like collective actors but are better understood as rules of the game and contours of the arena in which the game is played (Thelen 2012).

Partly for such reasons, the self-sustaining quality of institutions is particularly important in institutional explanations. Institutions tend to continue to affect poverty and inequality without active maintenance. As Jepperson (1991:148) explains in his classic essay on "institutional effects": "Institutions are those social patterns that, when chronically reproduced, owe their survival to relatively self-activating social processes. Their persistence is not dependent, notably, upon recurrent collective mobilization, mobilization repetitively reengineered and reactivated in order to secure the reproduction of a pattern." Thus, institutions are "taken for granted," "naturalized as a stable feature of constraining environment," "routine-reproduced," and "relative fixtures of constraining environments" (Jepperson 1991:148–49).

Institutions reflect the "congealed power" or residue of the power of collective actors (Western 1997). Previous established rules, policies, and practices do not disappear overnight and often only slowly evolve over time. Also, contemporary poverty reflects the political settlements of the past as much as the present power of today's political actors. Conversely, long-ago established institutions with little egalitarian content or intention, often end up, after the evolution of time, having egalitarian consequences. For example, Thelen (2004) shows how the German apprenticeship system began as an exclusive inegalitarian institution but evolved into an institution that enhanced social equality and working-class economic security. Institutions put in place decades ago may still matter to poverty today, and institutions put in place today might not matter until significant time has passed. For instance, even if the Democratic Party controlled the U.S. presidency, both houses of Congress, and most state legislatures, their effects on poverty would still be constrained. It takes a long time to change labor laws that undermine unions, to expand or create new social policies, to implement those policies, and to change normative expectations about egalitarianism. Thus, institutionalists often critique power resources explanations for implying that each election represents an active struggle and pivotal event, and instead stress the noticeable stability of poverty and inequality.

In these ways, institutional effects on poverty and inequality often reflect "path dependency" (Pierson 2004). Path dependency is the idea that previous institutions set states on a trajectory whereby only certain subsequent choices are possible or efficient. That is, current politics and institutions depend on the path a state has taken previously. To understand how institutions shape poverty, scholars therefore need a long-time horizon of cause and a long-time horizon of outcomes (Pierson 2004). As a result, scholars tend to focus on cumulative and long-term effects that steadily build and gradually evolve over time and may only have impacts once a certain threshold has been met (Huber and Stephens 2012).

A strong institutionalism would claim that previously established rules and arrangements dominate over contemporary politics as those rules and arrangements "lock in place" a level of egalitarianism. This lock-in is then difficult to overturn or undermine, and therefore poverty and inequality are almost predetermined by these institutions. A weaker institutionalism proposes that previously established arrangements guide how, when, and why political actors can and do shape poverty (Huber and Stephens 2001; Jensen 2010). Previously established rules and regulations constrain the choices available to actors, the subsequent political behavior of actors, and even the cultural interpretation of inequalities in society. Because institutions shape the expectations guiding and resources available to actors, they also have long and complicated causal chains that ultimately shape poverty (Pierson 2004).

Compared to research on power resources and collective actors, there is perhaps less research on how institutions affect poverty. Therefore, even though institutional theories are highly relevant to and often lurk under the surface in poverty research, it is less common for scholars to explicitly highlight institutions. Still, salient research has been done on democracy, and electoral, labor market and educational institutions.

Democracy and Electoral Institutions

Refining the power resources literature, scholars have shown that the effects of parties on poverty are more pronounced once democracy has become firmly established (Huber and Stephens 2012). This is partly because stable democracies are more responsive and effective at channeling state resources toward reducing income inequality (Jenkins and Scanlan 2001; Lee 2005), partly because parties require significant time to maturely crystallize their positions on economic and social policies (Huber and Stephens 2012; Resnick 2012), and partly because weak or new democracies present few opportunities and channels for the political mobilization of the poor (Heller 2009). Whereas authoritarian regimes can more easily repress the poor and workers, parties need to attract the poor and working class as constituencies in democracies (Rueschemeyer et al. 1992). The result of this is that while democracy might not have a simple and direct effect on poverty (Ross 2006), there is a complicated and historically cumulative influence of democracy through parties, other collective political actors, and mature states (Huber and Stephens 2012). Therefore, democratic regimes ultimately matter to poverty by creating an environment in which power resources are likely to be more consequential.

Beyond the stability of electoral democracy, scholars in the past decade have stressed how particular institutions of electoral democracy matter to poverty and inequality (Malesky et al. 2011). Especially central to the literature, Iversen and Soskice (2006) demonstrate with both a formal model and empirical evidence that proportional representation (PR) systems redistribute more than single-member district systems (see also Persson and Tabellini 2004). They show that electoral systems influence the nature of political parties and the composition of governing coalitions, which then shape how much economic resources are redistributed from rich to poor. They demonstrate that PR systems advantage center-Left governments, while majoritarian systems favor center-Right governments. Based on analyses of rich democracies, they show that electoral systems thus indirectly explain why PR countries in Europe have so much less poverty and inequality than majoritarian countries like the United States (also Brady 2009). More generally, the opposite of PR systems—single-member district plurality systems—are one of many veto points (sometimes called "veto players"). Scholars have shown that such veto points (including e.g., presidential systems, federalism, judicial review, bicameralism, and the frequency of referendums) constrain the expansion of social policy (Immergut 1992) and are positively associated with poverty and inequality (Beramendi 2012; Huber and Stephens 2001).

There has also been research on how electoral institutions shape the political behavior of the poor. For instance, in a study of rich democracies, Anderson and Beramendi (2012) show that higher levels of partisan competition on the Left shape the tendencies of dominant Left parties to mobilize poor voters in response to inequality. They demonstrate that without the presence of several contending Left parties, dominant Left parties have little incentive to encourage poor people to vote. This is relevant because the political behavior of the poor has some bearing on the collective actors shaping poverty, as discussed above. Therefore, electoral institutions like the presence of multiparty competition, which is more likely in a proportional representation system, are likely to indirectly affect poverty through the political behavior of the poor.

Labor Market and Educational Institutions

In terms of labor market institutions, an extensive literature investigates how corporatism and wage coordination affect inequality. This literature has shown that earnings inequality is lower in corporatist labor markets that feature stricter employment protection (e.g., rules constraining the firing of workers), power sharing between management and labor (e.g., works councils), and wage coordination (e.g., centrally negotiated national pay scales) (Blau and Kahn 2002; Carbonaro 2006; Koeniger et al. 2007). As noted above varieties of capitalism scholars refer to such corporatist labor markets as coordinated market economies (Hall and Soskice 2001), as countries typically bundle several labor market institutions into a more or less coherent system. According to this literature, corporatism brings together business and labor into cooperative and long-term-oriented relationships that bring about greater equality (Hicks 1999). This literature has influenced the aforementioned literature on working poverty. Indeed, low-wage work and working poverty appear to be less common in labor markets featuring such institutions (Brady et al. 2010; Gautie and Ponthieux this volume; Gautie and Schmidt 2009). Because low-wage work is so salient to working poverty and therefore poverty overall, it follows that this literature on labor market institutions is relevant to poverty research.

Another feature of coordinated market economies, and often coupled with labor market institutions, are the educational systems that feed individuals into labor markets (Allmendinger 1989). Kerckhoff (1995) calls these institutions "the sorting machines" of stratification because they structure the connections between one's class origin, educational attainment, early labor force placements, and labor market trajectories. One of the pronounced differences in education systems is whether countries have well-developed vocational education/training and apprenticeship programs (Kerckhoff 1995; Thelen 2004). Many of the countries that have extensive labor market institutions like corporatism also tend to have vocational education systems, and scholars have pointed out the strong complementarities between the two (Hall and Soskice 2001). Germany is often held up as the model because it has historically had well-developed bridges between schools, vocational training, and apprenticeships. Such vocational systems have been linked to lower poverty and inequality (Allmendinger and Leibfried 2003; Moller et al. 2003). The reason is that vocational education represents a better pathway to work for those who do not get a college degree. So, while workers with college degrees are advantaged almost everywhere, the penalty for lacking a college degree is lessened if one has vocational training. This is because vocational training enhances one's human capital and because these education systems encourage tighter links between education, apprenticeships, and early labor market placement. As a pathway for young people who do not go to college, scholars in the United Kingdom and the United States have proposed the establishment of such vocational education systems to reduce unemployment, labor market precariousness, and even poverty (Rosenbaum 2001). By contrast, others argue it is more important to reduce educational inequalities in general and to raise education overall rather than develop tracks for different groups of students in order to alleviate poverty (Solga 2014).

International Institutions

Finally, one promising direction for poverty research on institutions is the study of international institutions. International institutions, like the European Union, have been linked with government spending and the welfare state (Brady and Lee 2014; Ferrera 2011) and with income inequality (Beckfield 2006). A few have connected international institutions to poverty (e.g., Bradshaw et al. 1993; Kentikelenis, Stubbs, and King 2015). For example, Easterly (2001) shows that International Monetary Fund and World Bank structural adjustment programs aimed at developing countries reduced the effectiveness of economic growth in reducing poverty. Moreover, international institutions have arguably become more salient in recent decades and may become even more so in the future. Thus, it is plausible that international institutions will be increasingly relevant to poverty.

The Pivotal Role of State Policy

Regardless of where scholars sit on the continuum of power resources and institutions, most agree the state plays a pivotal role in shaping poverty. The conventional approach views the state as a mediating variable, such that power resources and institutions often have indirect effects on poverty through the state. According to this approach, power resources and institutions influence the size, practices, and policies of the state, and the state implements egalitarianism. As we discuss later, much research demonstrates how social policy benefits the poor and reduces poverty (Brady 2009; Brady et al. 2009; Lee and Koo this volume; Lein et al. this volume). Relatively less scholarship highlights how state policies can also be harmful to the poor. However, we propose state policy's relevance to poverty is best understood as a combination of social policy and regulatory activities that shape the distribution of economic resources and life chances (Wilensky 2002).

On some level, one could include the entire fields of public and social policy research as relevant to this essay. Rather than summarizing all scholarship on state policy, we distill the literature into a parsimonious typology of how states matter. We identify a set of generic mechanisms for how state policies matter to poverty. Enumerating these mechanisms should facilitate and guide scholarship on the range of roles that states play, and comprehensively evaluating those roles allows us to better understand how states shape poverty.

First, state policies organize the distribution of resources (Moller et al. 2003; Nelson 2004). Typically, this mechanism is presented as redistribution. However, state policies more realistically organize the distribution of resources by influencing how resources are distributed in the market and after the market (Bradley et al. 2003). Through taxation, transfers, and services, social policies take resources from one part of the population and distribute to others or to the same population at different stages of life. Yet, state policies also shape how much people earn and how much investments return. The obvious example of state policies that shape earnings are minimum wage laws, but household income is contingent on a range of policies states have for coercing private and public actors in markets. States also tax many transfers (Ferrarini and Nelson 2003), opt to eschew taxes as an indirect way to "transfer" resources (Wilensky 2002), and occasionally even disproportionately tax the poor (Newman and O'Brien 2011). Hence, state policies both redistribute and distribute, and a narrow focus on redistribution underappreciates the full set of consequences of state policy.

Second, state policies insure against risks (DiPrete 2002). Many social policies are insurance programs against unexpected (e.g., illness and accidents), somewhat unexpected (e.g., unemployment), and relatively expected events (e.g., having a child or growing old). Because of their size, large budgets, legitimacy, and capacity to mandate participation, states are uniquely positioned to insure or require insurance (O'Brien and Robertson 2015). Moreover, because the private sector is often unlikely to insure all regardless of risk profiles, states often must step in and be the insurance provider. States often go further than just insuring against risks but also are actively involved in preventing risks through regulation. For instance, states can reduce workplace injuries, and this enhances the earning power of workers. Thus, state policies both reduce the likelihood of poverty-inducing events and mitigate the consequences when such events occur (DiPrete 2002).

Third, states invest in capabilities. States educate, train, care for, and keep healthy their residents. States also often feed and house their residents, though it is probably mostly through education, training, care, and health care that states contribute to the well-being and development of their populations. In recent years, this package of programs has received increasing attention under the title of "the social investment welfare state" (Morel et al. 2012). Similarly, this role has long been studied as part of the literature on aid and assistance to developing countries (Feeney and McGillivray this volume).

Fourth, and closely related to the third point, state policies allocate opportunities. In addition to preparing people for jobs and caring for people when they cannot work, states actually create jobs and other opportunities. States are often the largest employers in their countries, and public employment is especially relevant to poverty during economic recessions. Though service obviously comes with great potential costs, the military has also been a key state policy that has been a source of social mobility out of poverty and a basis for economic development for relatively impoverished communities (Sampson and Laub 1996). States also allocate these opportunities in more or less equal ways, and this often has consequences for poverty. For example, the aforementioned investments in capabilities such as education and training are often distributed unevenly, and if they were distributed more equally, less poverty would likely result.

Fifth, state policies socialize expectations (Brady 2009). State policies are clearly shaped by the politics of collective actors and widely held beliefs. However, since at least the early 1990s, scholars have stressed how state policies feed back into public opinion and politics (Brady and Bostic 2015; Fernandez and Jaime-Castillo 2013; Huber and Stephens 2001; Skocpol 1992). By explaining how state policies construct interests, ideologies, and coalitions, compelling research has shown how state policies shape norms, beliefs, and the subsequent politics of state policies (Brooks and Manza 2007; Korpi and Palme 1998; Pierson 2004). If those feedback effects are positive, there will tend to be increasing public support for policies, and when those policies are effective, poverty reduction will be reinforced and social equality becomes more institutionalized. Hence, state policies shape the popular expectations about whether poverty is just or necessary, and these likely shape the amount of poverty in society (Brady 2009).

Sixth, states discipline the poor (Soss et al. 2011; Wacquant 2009). The state punishes, warehouses, polices, monitors, stigmatizes, constrains, undermines and limits the freedom of the poor and certain populations. These many processes fit under the broad banner of disciplining the poor (Soss et al. 2011), which may make poverty more likely or persistent. Though many have made such arguments in recent years, the idea was already present in Piven and Cloward's (1993) classic *Regulating the Poor*. While Piven and Cloward emphasized how welfare was used to control and force the poor to work, states today may emphasize punishment and warehousing more because there is not enough well-paid work to sustain the poor (Wacquant 2009). Further, in Piven and Cloward and recent work like Soss and colleagues (2011), the state has often actively sought to paternalistically manage the fertility, partnering, and parenting behavior of the poor. In the past 10 to 15 years, one of the most popular areas of research on state policies and poverty/inequality has been incarceration. This recent research, especially in the United States, has called attention to the state's criminal justice policies as a key source of racial and class stratification. This literature documents the United States' unusually high rates of incarceration, and how this contributes to myriad economic inequalities. Incarceration worsens poverty through multiple channels (DeFina and Hannon 2013; Western and Muller 2013). Directly, ex-prisoners face substantial disadvantages in the labor market (Western 2006). Indirectly, the families of prisoners face severe strain, and there is evidence that increasing incarceration has concentrated childhood disadvantages (Wildeman 2009) and even increased child homelessness (Wildeman 2014). Though dramatically increasing incarceration has clearly been a significant policy intervention that has worsened inequality, it is important to keep in mind there are many other and less studied ways that states discipline select groups in ways that worsen poverty.

In sum, we have identified at least six generic mechanisms linking state policies and poverty. By creating this typology of mechanisms, we aim to clarify the themes in past research and guide future research on state policy effects on poverty.

CHALLENGES FOR FUTURE RESEARCH AND CONCLUSION

In total, great progress has been made in the study of how politics and institutions shape poverty and inequality. Scholars have advanced sophisticated theoretical arguments, and considerable empirical evidence has been accumulated. More than perhaps at any point in the social science of poverty, political and institutional explanations have proven valuable for understanding poverty. Animated often by power resources and institutional theories, scholars have shown the salient impacts on poverty of labor unions, Left parties, elites and business, democracy, electoral systems, and labor market and educational institutions. Nevertheless, despite the progress in the literature, the literature is presently grappling with several challenges and dilemmas. Some challenges are methodological, others are theoretical, and others are simply the result that the world keeps changing in ways that often defy our accounts.

Power Resources Theory

There are at least two pressing dilemmas for the power resources literature. First, even though the existence of power resources representing the disadvantaged are clearly to the benefit and interests of the disadvantaged, such power resources are struggling to survive. Unions, Left parties, and other Left collective actors face significant challenges of solidarity and mobilization and are experiencing declines in their memberships and affiliations. For instance, even though there continues to be stable differences in unionization across rich democracies, unionization is declining in almost every rich democracy (Pinto and Beckfield 2011). While the United States has had low unionization for decades, it is even more notable that Germany's unionization was above 35 percent in the 1980s and has now has fallen below 20 percent. Even Sweden's unionization has fallen from about 85 percent in the mid-1990s to below 70 percent in recent years (Visser 2013). For political parties and voting, there is also evidence of a weakening loyalty of working-class voters to Left parties (e.g., Bornschier and Kriesi 2013; Brady et al. 2011). Such declines raise the question of why power resources are declining even though they continue to benefit the poor and working class.

One answer is that these power resources face the same coordination and mobilization problems that any group faces. There are always free riders, and perhaps the reality is that successfully mobilizing the poor, working class, or anyone is the exception rather than the rule. In turn, maybe we should consider the sustained effective mobilization of power resources in the post–World War II era as partly the product of a unique historical period. If that era truly was unique, we need to revise power resources theory to better incorporate factors like historical contingency and global political economy. What that would mean for the core ideas of power resources theory remains unclear.

A second answer is that poverty and inequality themselves undermine political mobilization. So, there could be feedback effects whereby rising inequality undermines power resources, and some of the observed relationship between power resources and lower poverty may have been the artifact of reverse causality. Indeed, Solt (2008) shows inequality depresses political interest, the frequency of political discussion, and participation in elections among non-rich citizens (also Schaefer 2012). Anderson and Beramendi (2012) find that the poor are less likely to vote where economic inequality is higher. Solt (2008) points out that such evidence challenges arguments that rational self-interest is sufficient to explain the poor's support for power resources. After all, rising inequality should greatly increase the material interests of the poor and working class in supporting power resources for welfare states and egalitarianism. In contrast to such political-economic models (cf. Meltzer-Richard 1981), scholars have shown that rising inequality is not self-correcting, whereby rising inequality prompts the poor and working class to rise up, push back, and successfully demand redistribution.[6] Instead, rising inequality is self-reinforcing as elites use their greater economic resources to further institutionalize rising inequality (Barth, Finseraas, and Moene 2015; Kelly and Ens 2010). The reality is that the poor have always been known to be less politically active

(Rosenstone 1982). Partly because political action entails costs and requires resources, it is even more difficult to mobilize disadvantaged populations when they face the pressure and seemingly insurmountable constraint of rising inequality. As Pontusson and Rueda (2010) show, it is essential for the poor to remain politically active and mobilized for there to be any possibility that rising inequality motivates the poor and working class to successfully demand redistribution. The outcome of this dilemma is that there is little reason to be optimistic about the present state of power resources representing the poor.

The second dilemma, which is linked to the first, is that there is considerable evidence that Left collective actors have become less efficacious. Beginning around 2000, scholars began to demonstrate that the relationship between power resources and welfare states weakened in the 1980s (Hicks 1999; Huber and Stephens 2001). When decomposing the rich democracies into historical periods of welfare state development and retrenchment (e.g., before/after the 1980s), one finds a clear pattern where power resources significantly increase the welfare state in the earlier period and have little effect in the later period (Brady and Lee 2014). On balance, there is still evidence of party effects on poverty (e.g., Brady 2009; Brady et al. 2009), and welfare states in recent decades (e.g., Allan and Scruggs 2004). However, the prevailing theme in the literature is that power resources have become less effective at least in terms of expanding the welfare state. Unfortunately, the literature has not made great progress in understanding precisely why and how this weakening effectiveness of power resources has occurred. One explanation is that rising inequality, and the ensuing political weakness of the poor, shifts the incentives and platforms of political parties toward middle-class and affluent voters (Anderson and Beramendi 2012; Barth et al. 2015; Pontusson and Rueda 2010). Thus, power resources might matter less to poverty in recent years because Left parties have shifted Right on economic issues, and this has weakened the commitment of Left parties to economic egalitarianism. Hence, an important question for the literature is what other power resources can serve the interests of the poor if, indeed, Left parties no longer maintain that commitment as consistently as in the past (Häusermann et al. 2013).

Institutional Explanations

Shifting to the institutions literature, the most important dilemma may come from the dualization literature (Emmenegger et al. 2011; Rueda 2005). Increasingly, scholars have emphasized that while labor market and educational institutions are generally equality enhancing, there is considerable stratification in the benefits of these institutions. Dualization scholars build on the classic literature on dual labor markets (e.g., Reich et al. 1973). Dual labor market scholars argued the U.S. economy was composed of a primary or core labor market located mainly in large manufacturing firms in which workers were well paid and had opportunities for advancement, and a secondary labor market located in the service sector and small enterprises in which pay and opportunities for advancement were limited. The new dualization literature builds on this classic literature to emphasize how labor market and demographic changes present new challenges to previously egalitarian institutions.

Beginning especially in the late 1990s, many institutions and regulations were reformed by, for example, increasing part-time and temporary work and subsidizing low-wage work to create an increasingly large segment of peripheral workers or outsiders in the labor market. Scholars have argued that the result is a dualization of social policies and labor market institutions, with one set of programs for labor market insiders and one for outsiders (Palier and Thelen 2010). So, instead of massive retrenchment of social policies and liberalization of labor market institutions, reform has often been accomplished by dualization (Thelen 2010). The dualization literature highlights that many workers are stuck in a secondary track of social policies, do not benefit from the traditional egalitarian institutions, and may even have blocked or restricted access to the most generous programs. Importantly, such outsiders are more likely to be women, immigrants, the young, and the less skilled or educated. Because these groups were already more likely to be poor, dualization could be very relevant to poverty in rich democracies. If so, the traditional literatures on power resources, welfare states, and institutions will need revision for explaining poverty (Thelen 2012). Particularly interesting is how dualization is emerging at the same time that countries are becoming more egalitarian in other dimensions. For example, Ferragina and colleagues (2012) show how unemployment protection has dualized in many rich democracies at the same time that family policy has become increasingly socialized. Hence, the emergence of dualization is not an isolated trend, but is one of several changes occurring in the policy and institutional context for poverty.

Another dilemma for research on institutions and poverty is the need for studies of the complementarities, constellations, and combinations between various institutions. The literature has long emphasized that a given institution affects poverty and inequality because of the presence of other complementary institutions and the effectiveness of various institutions interdepends on other institutions (Hall and Soskice 2001; Thelen 2012). Of course, it is clear that there are strong correlations between the presence of labor market institutions, like corporatism, and the presence of vocational education systems, unionization, proportional representation, and other institutions. Thelen (2010) adds that employer mobilization is closely attuned to the environment in which they operate—and the nature of employer political mobilization depends on the strength of unions and employers' level of coordination. So, even power resources like labor and business behave differently depending on the combination of institutions in which they operate. Yet, even though the literature has widely stressed both the essential role of complementarities and the correlations between the presence of various institutions, relatively few studies directly incorporate this into the evaluation of institutional effects on poverty and inequality. For the institutional literature to really demonstrate the theoretical arguments about complementarities and constellations, it would be valuable to more explicitly interrogate interactions between and combinations of institutions.

Methodological Challenges

The last challenge we discuss pertains to the majority of the literatures reviewed in this essay. Despite the progress that has been made in studying how politics and institutions shape poverty and inequality, causality deserves greater scrutiny. While the literature often traditionally focuses on stable differences between countries, the methodological literature on causality increasingly scrutinizes counterfactuals and on identifying exogenous effects. The power resources and institutional literatures have only begun to embrace the shift toward counterfactual causality. Indeed, a key challenge for these literatures is the difficulty of reconciling the theoretical interest in big, long-term processes (e.g., Pierson 2004) and macrocontextual differences (e.g., Brady et al. 2009) with the need to identify causal effects. Indeed, it may be reasonable to perceive a tradeoff between theoretical attention on big, long-term process and macrocomparison and the identification of causal effects.

There are several reasons it is so difficult to identify causal effects while focusing on macrolevel context and cross-national differences. First, power resources and institutions are typically very slow moving and have cumulative effects, and there are very few discontinuities that allow one to exploit a sharp break/increase/decline. Second, power resources and institutions are often bundled with and complementary to other power resources, institutions, and state policies. As a result, it is difficult to untangle complementary and coevolved power resources and institutions and to sort out what effects are due to which precise power resource or institutions. Third, while scholars need macro and historical variation to find variation in power resources and institutions, such macro and historical variation is vulnerable to omitted variable bias. It is always difficult to say one has controlled for all differences between countries or historical periods, and biases due to omitted variables are usually plausible. Fourth, the literature has a desire to study the more fundamental and basic causes that precede complex causal chains and underlie more proximate predictors of poverty. After all, this literature was originally motivated to challenge poverty research's concentration on demographic risks and individual-level characteristics (Brady 2009). Pushing against the individualism of poverty, the literature on politics and institutions has sought to understand contextual differences in poverty across time and place (Brady et al. 2009). The problem emerges because identifying precise, concrete, and observable mechanisms often requires narrowing the distance between cause and effect, and such a narrowing tends to exclude fundamental and basic causes from one's view.

Though these matters have not been fully resolved, scholars are beginning to provide more rigorous causal evidence while maintaining the theoretical foci of power resources and institutional theories. Compared to the past, more studies are analyzing change over time within contexts and controlling for stable differences between contexts. Some have utilized instrumental variables or compared across geographically proximate and similar countries to simulate natural experiments or more carefully compare like with like. The advancing presence of multi-level analyses in this literature has allowed for a consideration of macro-level contexts and micro-level risks in the same models. Even though multi-level approaches also have causality challenges, they have shifted attention away from questions exclusively focused on micro-level individual characteristics and demographic risks, and ensured that power resources and institutions are brought into studies of individual-level poverty (Brady et al. 2009). Finally, scholars are increasingly using research designs that display both variation between places and variation within places over time (e.g., Brady et al. 2013; O'Brien and Robertson 2015).

In the end, the challenges of advancing causal approaches within this literature present an excellent opportunity for future research. The next wave of progress in studying how politics and institutions shape poverty and inequality will likely utilize innovative research designs and clever estimation strategies to provide new and even more rigorous evidence. In addition to encouraging greater scrutiny of causality, we conclude by proposing that all the dilemmas and challenges in this section present a promising agenda for future research. We argued at the outset that politics and institutions have never been as prominent in the social sciences of poverty as they are today. If we are correct, these challenges and dilemmas suggest an exciting emerging literature, and one that has the potential to make politics and institutions even more central to understanding poverty.

Notes

1. In this chapter, we define institutions as stable agreements and historical settlements that channel, constrain, and regulate the behavior of firms, workers, and other actors and hence contribute to inequalities in nation-states.

2. This division between power resources and institutions has been prominent in the literature for some time. In Korpi's (1983) account, he presents power resources in contrast to the institutionalist corporatism theories that were prominent at the time (e.g., Schmitter 1977).

3. To define Left, Right, and other parties, several databases have been built on expert coding of party platforms, transnational connections between national parties, and the historical roots and coalitions underlying parties (see e.g., Brady et al. 2014). The Left includes parties linked to social democratic and socialist ideologies and organizations, labor parties and parties with strong connections to labor unions, and parties advocating more generous social policies and egalitarianism (Sassoon 1996).

4. By "redistribution" we are referring to the broad set of activities (e.g., taxes) that extract economic resources from one group and allocate or transfer those economic resources to another group (or services that require economic resources). In rich democracies, redistribution is typically thought of as transferring money from rich to poor. We acknowledge many societies transfer resources from the poor to the rich, and most societies include redistribution in both directions. Nevertheless, we focus on redistribution from rich to poor.

5. For example, Thelen (2012:142) points out that within the political economy of rich democracies literature there are institutional explanations that carry a "Williamsonian" view of institutions as mechanisms for rational and efficient coordination and cooperation, and a "Durkheimian" view as mechanisms for organic and emergent social cohesion.

6. As is clear, this essay eschews Meltzer and Richard's (1981) well-known theory that governments expand when the median voter's income is below the mean income, premised on the median voter's preference for redistribution. We do so because the overwhelming majority of the evidence contradicts the theory while it continues to receive disproportionate attention. While basically ignored by Meltzer-Richard and much of the political economy literature, there was always convincing evidence against their model. Moreover, the basic trends of rich democracies in the past few decades directly contradict Meltzer-Richard. In most rich democracies, the mean income has grown relative to the median, and the size of government and the amount of redistribution has not grown. Research on politics/institutions and poverty/inequality would probably be better off if Meltzer-Richard (or any theory so impervious to empirical evidence) did not figure so prominently.

References

Allan, James P. and Lyle Scruggs. 2004. "Political Partisanship and Welfare State Reform in Advanced Industrial Societies." *American Journal of Political Science* 48:496–512.

Allmendinger, Jutta. 1989. "Educational Systems and Labor Market Outcomes." *European Sociological Review* 5:231–50.

Allmendinger, Jutta and Stephan Leibfried. 2003. "Education and the Welfare State: The Four Worlds of Competence Production." *Journal of European Social Policy* 13:63–81.

Anderson, Christopher J. and Pablo Beramendi. 2012. "Left Parties, Poor Voters, and Electoral Participation in Advanced Industrial Societies." *Comparative Political Studies* 45:714–46.

Barth, Erling, Henning Finseraas, and Karl O. Moene. 2015. "Political Reinforcement: How Rising Inequality Curbs Manifested Welfare Generosity." *American Journal of Political Science* 59:565–77.

Beckfield, Jason. 2006. "European Integration and Income Inequality." *American Sociological Review* 71:964–85.

Beramendi, Pablo. 2012. *The Political Geography of Inequality*. New York: Cambridge University Press.

Blau, Francine D. and Lawrence M. Kahn. 2002. *At Home and Abroad*. New York: Russell Sage Foundation.

Bolzendahl, Catherine and Clem Brooks. 2007. "Women's Political Resources and Welfare State Spending in 12 Capitalist Democracies." *Social Forces* 85:1509–34.

Bornschier, Simon and Hanspeter Kriesi. 2013. "The Populist Right, the Working Class, and the Changing Face of Class Politics," Pp. 10–29 in *Class Politics and the Radical Right*, edited by J. Rydgren. Abingdon: Routledge.

Bradley, David, Evelyne Huber, Stephanie Moller, Francois Nielsen, and John D. Stephens. 2003. "Distribution and Redistribution in Postindustrial Democracies." *World Politics* 55:193–228.

Bradshaw, York, Rita Noonan, Laura Gash, and Claudia Buchmann Sershen. 1993. "Borrowing Against the Future: Children and Third World Indebtedness." *Social Forces* 71:629–56.

Brady, David. 2009. *Rich Democracies, Poor People: How Politics Explain Poverty*. New York: Oxford University Press.

Brady, David, Regina S. Baker, and Ryan Finnigan. 2013. "When Unionization Disappears: State-Level Unionization and Working Poverty in the United States." *American Sociological Review* 78:872–96.

Brady, David and Amie Bostic. 2015. "Paradoxes of Social Policy: Welfare Transfers, Relative Poverty and Redistribution Preferences." *American Sociological Review* 80:268–98.

Brady, David, Andrew S. Fullerton, and Jennifer Moren Cross. 2009. "Putting Poverty in Political Context: A Multi-Level Analysis of Adult Poverty Across 18 Affluent Western Democracies." *Social Forces* 88:271–300.

Brady, David, Andrew S. Fullerton, and Jennifer Moren Cross. 2010. "More than Just Nickels and Dimes: A Cross-National Analysis of Working Poverty in 18 Affluent Democracies." *Social Problems* 57:559–85.

Brady, David, Evelyne Huber, and John D. Stephens. 2014. *Comparative Welfare States Data Set.* University of North Carolina and WZB Berlin Social Science Center.

Brady, David and Hang Young Lee. 2014. "The Rise and Fall of Government Spending in Affluent Democracies, 1971–2008." *Journal of European Social Policy* 24:56–79.

Brady, David and Kevin Leicht. 2008. "Party to Inequality: Right Party Power and Income Inequality in Rich Western Democracies." *Research in Social Stratification and Mobility* 26:77–106.

Brady, David and Benjamin Sosnaud. 2010. "The Politics of Economic Inequality." Pp. 521–541 in *Handbook of Politics: State and Civil Society in Global Perspective*, edited by Kevin Leicht and Craig Jenkins. New York: Springer.

Brady, David, Benjamin Sosnaud, and Steven Frenk. 2011. "The Shifting and Diverging White Working Class in U.S. Presidential Elections, 1972–2004." *Social Science Research* 38:118–33.

Brooks, Clem and Jeff Manza. 2007. *Why Welfare States Persist.* Chicago: University of Chicago Press.

Campbell, John L. 2004. *Institutional Change and Globalization.* Princeton, NJ: Princeton University Press.

Carbonaro, William. 2006. "Cross-National Differences in the Skills-Earnings Relationship: The Role of Labor Market Institutions." *Social Forces* 84:1819–42.

Castles, Francis G. 2004. *The Future of the Welfare State* New York: Oxford University Press.

DeFina, Robert and Lance Hannon. 2013. "The Impact of Mass Incarceration on Poverty." *Crime and Delinquency* 59:562–86.

DiPrete, Thomas A. 2002. "Life Course Risks, Mobility Regimes, and Mobility Consequences: A Comparison of Sweden, Germany, and the United States." *American Journal of Sociology* 108:267–309.

Easterly, William. 2001. "The Effect of IMF and World Bank Programmes on Poverty." WIDER Discussion Papers//World Institute for Development Economics (UNU-WIDER), No. 2001/102, ISBN 9291900273.

Emmenegger, Patrick, Silja Hausermann, Bruno Palier, and Martin Seeleib-Kaiser. 2011. *The Age of Dualization.* New York: Oxford University Press.

Eren, Ozkan. 2009. "Does Membership Pay Off for Covered Workers? A Distributional Analysis of the Free Rider Problem." *Industrial & Labor Relations Review* 62:367–80.

Fernandez, Juan J. and Antonio M. Jaime-Castillo. 2013. "Positive or Negative Policy Feedbacks? Explaining Popular Attitudes Towards Pragmatic Pension Policy Reforms." *European Sociological Review* 29:803–15.

Ferragina, Emanuele, Martin Seeleib-Kaiser, and Mark Tomlinson. 2013. "Unemployment Protection and Family Policy at the Turn of the 21st Century: A Dynamic Approach to Welfare Regime Theory." *Social Policy & Administration* 47:783–805.

Ferrarini, Tommy and Kenneth Nelson. 2003. "Taxation of Social Insurance and Redistribution: A Comparative Analysis of Ten Welfare States." *Journal of European Social Policy* 13:21–33.

Ferrera, Maurizio. 2011. *The Boundaries of Welfare*. New York: Oxford University Press.

Fligstein, Neil. 2001. *The Architecture of Markets*. Princeton, NJ: Princeton University Press.

Gautie, Jerome and John Schmitt. 2009. *Low-Wage Work in the Wealthy World*. New York: Russell Sage Foundation.

Hacker, Jacob S. and Paul Pierson. 2010. "Winner-Take-All Politics: Public Policy, Political Organization, and the Precipitous Rise of Top Incomes in the United States." *Politics & Society* 38:152–204.

Hall, Peter and David Soskice. 2001. *Varieties of Capitalism*. New York: Oxford University Press.

Harvey, David. 2005. *A Brief History of Neoliberalism*. New York: Oxford University Press.

Häusermann, Silja, Georg Picot, and Dominik Geering. 2013. "Rethinking Party Politics and the Welfare State—Recent Advances in the Literature." *British Journal of Political Science* 43:221–40.

Heller, Patrick. 2009. "Democratic Deepening in India and South Africa." *Journal of Asian and African Studies* 44:123–49.

Hicks, Alexander. 1999. *Social Democracy and Welfare Capitalism*. Ithaca, NY: Cornell University Press.

Huber, Evelyne and John D. Stephens. 2001. *The Development and Crisis of the Welfare State*. Chicago: University of Chicago Press.

Huber, Evelyne and John D. Stephens. 2012. *Democracy and the Left*. Chicago: University of Chicago Press.

Immergut, Ellen M. 1992. *Health Politics* New York: Cambridge University Press.

Iversen, Torben and David Soskice. 2006. "Electoral Institutions and the Politics of Coalitions: Why Some Democracies Redistribute More Than Others." *American Political Science Review* 100:165–81.

Jenkins, J. Craig and Stephen J. Scanlan. 2001. "Food Security in Less Developed Countries, 1970 to 1990." *American Sociological Review* 66:718–44.

Jensen, Carsten. 2010. "Issue Compensation and Right-Wing Government Social Spending." *European Journal of Political Research* 49:282–99.

Jepperson, Ronald L. 1991. "Institutions, Institutional Effects and Institutionalism." Pp. 143–63 in *The New Institutionalism in Organizational Analysis*. Chicago: University of Chicago Press.

Kalleberg, Arne L., Michael Wallace, and Robert P. Althauser. 1981. "Economic Segmentation, Worker Power, and Income Inequality." *American Journal of Sociology* 87:651–83.

Kelly, Nathan J. and Peter K. Enns. 2010. "Inequality and the Dynamics of Public Opinion: The Self-Reinforcing Link between Economic Inequality and Mass Preferences." *American Journal of Political Science* 54:855–70.

Kelly, Nathan J. and Christopher Witko. 2012. "Federalism and American Inequality." *Journal of Politics* 74:414–26.

Kentikelenis, Alexander E., Thomas H Stubbs, and Lawrence P. King. 2015. "Structural Adjustment and Public Spending on Health: Evidence from IMF Programs in Low-Income Countries." *Social Science and Medicine* 126:169–76.

Kerckhoff, Alan C. 1995. "Institutional Arrangements and Stratification Processes in Industrial Societies." *Annual Review of Sociology* 15:323–47.

Koeniger, Winfried, Marco Leonardi, and Luca Nunziata. 2007. "Labor Market Institutions and Wage Inequality." *Industrial & Labor Relations Review* 60:340–56.

Korpi, Walter. 1983. *The Democratic Class Struggle*. Boston: Routledge.

Korpi, Walter, and Joakim Palme. 1998. "The Paradox of Redistribution and Strategies of Equality: Welfare State Institutions, Inequality, and Poverty in the Western Countries." *American Sociological Review* 63:661–87.

Korpi, Walter, and Joakim Palme. 2003. "New Politics and Class Politics in the Context of Austerity and Globalization: Welfare State Regress in 18 Countries, 1975–95." *American Political Science Review* 97:425–46.

Kristal, Tali. 2010. "Good Times, Bad Times: Postwar Labor's Share of National Income in Capitalist Democracies." *American Sociological Review* 75:729–63.

Lee, Cheol-Sung. 2005. "Income Inequality, Democracy, and Public Sector Size." *American Sociological Review* 70:158–81.

Lohmann, Henning. 2009. "Welfare States, Labour Market Institutions and the Working Poor: A Comparative Analysis of 20 European Countries." *European Sociological Review* 25:489–504.

Mahler, Vincent A. 2004. "Economic Globalization, Domestic Politics, and Income Inequality in the Developed Countries." *Comparative Political Studies* 37:1025–53.

Mahler, Vincent A. 2008. "Electoral Turnout and Income Redistribution by the State: A Cross-National Analysis of the Developed Democracies." *European Journal of Political Research* 47:161–83.

Malesky, Edmund; Regina Abrami, and Yu Zheng. 2011. "Institutions and Inequality in Single-Party Regimes: A Comparative Analysis of Vietnam and China." *Comparative Politics,* 43:409–27.

Mares, Isabella. 2003. *The Politics of Social Risk.* New York: Cambridge University Press.

Martin, Cathie Jo and Duane Swank. 2012. *The Political Construction of Business Interests.* New York: Cambridge University Press.

Maxwell, Nan L. 2007. "Wage Differentials, Skills, and Institutions in Low-Skill Jobs." *Industrial & Labor Relations Review* 61:394–409.

Meltzer, Allan H. and Scott F. Richard. 1981. "A Rational Theory of the Size of Government." *Journal of Political Economy* 89:914–27.

Moller, Stephanie, David Bradley, Evelyne Huber, Francois Nielsen, and John D. Stephens. 2003. "Determinants of Relative Poverty in Advanced Capitalist Democracies." *American Sociological Review* 68:22–51.

Morel, Nathalie, Bruno Palier, and Joakim Palme. 2012. *Towards a Social Investment Welfare State?* Bristol, UK: Policy Press.

Morris, Martina and Bruce Western. 1999. "Inequality in Earnings at the Close of the Twentieth Century." *Annual Review of Sociology* 25:623–57.

Nelson, Kenneth. 2004. "Mechanisms of Poverty Alleviation: Anti-Poverty Effects of Non-Means-Tested and Means-Tested Benefits in Five Welfare States." *Journal of European Social Policy* 14:371–90.

Newman, Katherine S. and Rourke L. O'Brien. 2011. *Taxing the Poor.* Berkeley: University of California Press.

O'Brien, Rourke and Cassandra L. Robertson. 2015. "Medicaid and Intergenerational Economic Mobility." Institute for Research on Poverty Discussion Paper No. 1428–1415.

Palier, Bruno and Kathleen Thelen. 2010. "Institutionalizing Dualism: Complementarities and Change in France and Germany." *Politics & Society* 38:119–148.

Persson, Torsten and Guido Tabellini. 2004. "Constitutional Rules and Fiscal Policy Outcomes." *American Economic Review* 94:25–45.

Pierson, Paul. 2004. *Politics in Time.* Princeton, NJ: Princeton University Press.

Piketty, Thomas. 2014. *Capital in the Twenty-First Century* Cambridge, MA: Harvard University Press.

Pinto, Sanjay and Jason Beckfield. 2011. "Organized Labor in Europe, 1960–2006: Persistent Diversity and Shared Decline." *Comparing European Workers Part B: Research in the Sociology of Work* 22:153–79.

Piven, Frances Fox and Richard A. Cloward. 1993. *Regulating the Poor.* New York: Vintage.

Pontusson, Jonas and David Rueda. 2010. "The Politics of Inequality: Voter Mobilization and Left Parties in Advanced Industrial States." *Comparative Political Studies* 43:675–705.

Pribble, Jennifer; Evelyne Huber, and John D. Stephens. 2009. "Politics, Policies, and Poverty in Latin America." *Comparative Politics* 41:387–407.

Rainwater, Lee and Timothy Smeeding. 2004. *Poor Kids in a Rich Country.* New York: Russell Sage Foundation.

Reich, Michael, David M. Gordon, and Richard C. Edwards. 1973. "A Theory of Labor Market Segmentation." *American Economic Review* 63:359–65.

Resnick, Danielle. 2012. "Opposition Parties and the Urban Poor in African Democracies." *Comparative Political Studies* 45:1351–78.

Rosenbaum, James E. 2001. *Beyond College For All* New York: Russell Sage Foundation.

Rosenstone, Steven J. 1982. "Economic Adversity and Voter Turnout." *American Journal of Political Science* 26:25–46.

Ross, Michael. 2006. "Is Democracy Good for the Poor?" *American Journal of Political Science* 50:860–74.

Rueda, David. 2005. "Insider-Outsider Politics in Industrialized Democracies: The Challenge to Social Democratic Parties." *American Political Science Review* 99:61–74.

Rueschemeyer, Dietrich, Evelyne Huber Stephens, and John D. Stephens. 1992. *Capitalist Development and Democracy.* Chicago: University of Chicago Press.

Sampson Robert J. and John H. Laub. 1996. "Socioeconomic Achievement in the Life Course of Disadvantaged Men: Military Service as a Turning Point, Circa 1940–1965." *American Sociological Review* 61:347–67.

Sassoon, Donald. 1996. *One Hundred Years of Socialism.* London: Fontana Press.

Schaefer, Armin. 2012. "Consequences of Social Inequality for Democracy in Western Europe." *Zeitschrift für Vergleichende Politikwissenschaft* 6:23–45.

Schmitter, Philippe C. 1977. "Modes of Interest Intermediation and Models of Societal Change in Western Europe." *Comparative Political Studies* 10:7–38.

Skocpol, Theda. 1992. *Protecting Soldiers and Mothers.* Cambridge, MA: Harvard University Press.

Solga, Heike. 2014. "Education, Economic Inequality and the Promises of the Social Investment State." *Socio-Economic Review* 12:269–97.

Solt, Frederick. 2008. "Economic Inequality and Democratic Political Engagement." *American Journal of Political Science* 52:48–60.

Soss, Joe, Richard C. Fording, and Sanford F. Schram. 2011. *Disciplining the Poor* Chicago: University of Chicago Press.

Thelen, Kathleen. 2012. "Varieties of Capitalism: Trajectories of Liberalization and the Politics of Social Solidarity." *Annual Review of Political Science* 15:137–59.

Thelen, Kathleen. 2010. "Economic Regulation and Social Solidarity: Conceptual and Analytical Innovations in the Study of Advanced Capitalism." *Socio-Economic Review* 8:187–207.

Thelen, Kathleen. 2004. *How Institutions Evolve.* New York: Cambridge University Press.

Visser, Jelle. 2013. *Data Base on Institutional Characteristics of Trade Unions, Wage Setting, State Intervention and Social Pacts, 1960-2011 (ICTWSS), Version 4.0.* Amsterdam Institute for Advanced Labour Studies (AIAS), University of Amsterdam.

Volscho, Thomas W. and Nathan J. Kelly. 2012. "The Rise of the Super-Rich: Power Resources, Taxes, Financial Markets, and the Dynamics of the Top 1 Percent, 1949 to 2008." *American Sociological Review* 77:679-99.

Wacquant, Loic. 2009. *Punishing the Poor.* Durham, NC: Duke University Press.

Wallace, Michael, Kevin T. Leicht and Lawrence E. Raffalovich. 1999. "Unions, Strikes, and Labor's Share of Income: The Distributional Consequences of Worker Organization and Militancy in the United States, 1949-1992." *Social Science Research* 28:265-88.

Western, Bruce. 1997. *Between Class and Market.* Princeton, NJ: Princeton University Press.

Western, Bruce. 2006. *Punishment and Inequality.* New York: Russell Sage Foundation.

Western, Bruce and Christopher Muller. 2013. "Mass Incarceration, Macrosociology and the Poor." *Annals of the American Academy of Political and Social Science* 647:166-89.

Western, Bruce and Jake Rosenfeld. 2011. "Unions, Norms, and the Rise in American Earnings Inequality." *American Sociological Review* 76:513-37.

Wildeman, Christopher. 2009. "Parental Imprisonment, the Prison Boom, and the Concentration of Childhood Disadvantage." *Demography* 46:265-80.

Wildeman, Christopher. 2014. "Parental Incarceration, Child Homelessness, and the Invisible Consequences of Mass Imprisonment." *Annals of the American Academy of Political and Social Science* 651:74-96.

Wilensky, Harold L. 2002. *Rich Democracies.* Berkeley: University of California Press.

Zuberi, Dan. 2006. *Differences That Matter.* Ithaca, NY: Cornell University Press.

CHAPTER 7

....

LINKING POVERTY AND CHILDREN'S DEVELOPMENT

Concepts, Models, and Debates

....

VONNIE C. MCLOYD, ROSANNE M. JOCSON, AND
ABIGAIL B. WILLIAMS

THE study of childhood poverty in the United States has evolved over the past three decades in ways that reflect the influence of findings and concepts rooted in economics, sociology, and psychology. This influence is especially evident in the dimensions of poverty to which scholars have devoted the most attention and the perspectives that have emerged as explanations of the link between poverty and children's development. This chapter presents a brief overview of research on the effects and mediators of childhood poverty, with a particular emphasis on the confluence of forces that gave rise to these foci and perspectives. We also consider the applicability of this research for understanding the nature and effects of childhood poverty in developing countries. We begin with a brief discussion of macroeconomic trends as a context for the study of childhood poverty in the United States. Following this discussion, we highlight developments that directed attention to the dynamics and context of childhood poverty as research topics and briefly summarize the findings that this research generated. We then turn to perspectives that have emerged about processes that mediate links between poverty and children's development. In the final section of the chapter, we consider the applicability of these perspectives for understanding the effects of poverty on children living in developing countries and highlight thematic parallels in the poverty-related research conducted in both contexts.

Macroeconomic Trends as a Context for the Study of Childhood Poverty in the United States

The mid-1970s ushered in a period of national deindustrialization in the United States, accompanied by a decline in the manufacturing sector relative to the service section of the economy, and globalization of economic markets. These macroeconomic changes contributed to sluggish economic growth, precipitating significant loss of low-skill but high-wage jobs, loss of work hours, and widespread displacement of workers into much lower paying trade and service positions (Danziger and Danziger 1993). Collectively, these trends culminated in a severe and historic economic recession in the early 1980s. The peak of the recession occurred in the last two months of 1982, when the nationwide unemployment rate was 10.8 percent, the highest since the Great Depression of the 1930s. In the first quarter of 1983, 30 states had double-digit unemployment rates. The child poverty rate increased sharply between 1979 and 1983, from 16 percent to 22 percent, and for children under six, from 18 percent to 25 percent (Corcoran and Chaudry 1997).

Newspapers serving areas hardest hit by the recession, such as Detroit and Flint, Michigan, published countless articles, replete with gripping vignettes, linking plant closings, layoffs, cutbacks, and other indicators of the economic crisis to increases in depressive symptoms in parents, marital discord and dissolution, parent-child conflict, child abuse, and other unfortunate circumstances. Child-focused research organizations tracked family and childhood poverty rates and indicators of child well-being, and child advocacy organizations warned of the dire consequences of poverty for the long-term well-being of children, families, and the nation itself (Sherman 1994). Levy, an economist, referred to the period between 1973 and 1982 as the "quiet depression," because this decade, distinguished by falling median family income and rising rates of child poverty, marked the first continuous decline in American living standards since the Great Depression (Danziger and Danziger 1993).

An important legacy of this "quiet depression" and persistently high rates of childhood poverty through the late 1990s is a voluminous body of research on the effects and mediators of childhood poverty in the United States. In the sections that follow, we summarize key findings pertaining to these issues and highlight some of the factors that shaped the evolution of this research. The macroeconomic trends previously noted also precipitated extensive research on the effectiveness of anti-poverty programs, but discussion of this work is beyond the scope of the present chapter (see McLoyd 1998; McLoyd, Aiken, and Burton 2006).

STUDY OF THE DYNAMICS AND CONTEXT OF CHILDHOOD POVERTY: ANTECEDENT INFLUENCES AND FINDINGS

Two years after the peak of the recession, Duncan, an economist, and his coauthors, published some new and surprising findings about patterns and dynamics of poverty in their critically important book *Years of Poverty, Years of Plenty* (Duncan et al. 1984). The findings, based on longitudinal data collected through repeated annual interviews with a single, continuing sample of over 5,000 American families—known as the Panel Study of Income Dynamics (PSID)—contradicted much of what had been inferred from cross-sectional survey data about patterns and causes of change in families' economic circumstances. For example, contrary to the then-popular conception of the poor as a homogeneous, stable group, and census surveys showing fairly constant numbers and characteristics for poor families each year, Duncan and colleagues found an astonishing amount of turnover in the poverty population. Only a little over one-half of individuals living in families with cash income below the poverty line in a given year were still poor in the following year, and only about one-third of the poor in a given year were poor for at least 8 of the 10 prior years. Another finding from the PSID that contradicted beliefs held at the time was that most of the children raised in welfare families did not themselves receive welfare benefits after they left home and formed their own households.

Duncan and his colleagues also found that the characteristics of the persistently poor were markedly different from those of the population as a whole and differed from the characteristics of individuals who were poor in a given year. The single most powerful factor that distinguished persistently poor people from the poor in a given year was race. More than three-fifths of the persistently poor were black. Although it had long been known that the incidence of annual poverty was much higher among black families than white families, the PSID data revealed that blacks were even more disproportionately represented among the persistently poor than among the poor in a given year. In a follow-up analysis focusing specifically on childhood poverty, they found that 24 percent of black children, compared to six-tenths of 1 percent of non-black children, were poor for at least 10 of the 15 years examined. Some five percent of black children were poor the entire 15-year period, whereas this was true for none of the non-black children (Duncan and Rodgers 1988).

The research agenda that evolved during the late 1980s and into the 1990s gave high priority to estimating the effects of different dimensions of poverty on children's development (McLoyd 1998; McLoyd and Ceballo 1998). Interest in one of these dimensions—the duration of poverty—stemmed directly from Duncan et al.'s work detailing the dynamics of poverty described earlier. In keeping with Duncan et al.'s approach, research on this and other dimensions of poverty examined absolute poverty, typically defined on the basis of cash income, using the United States federal poverty threshold as a marker. It became standard practice for researchers to compute an income-to-needs ratio (calculated as household income divided by the official poverty threshold) as an indicator of the household's degree of poverty or affluence. This ratio indicates how far below or above an individual or family falls relative to the poverty threshold. An income-to-need ratio of 1.0 indicates that a household's income is equal to the poverty threshold and smaller or larger ratios represent more or less severe poverty (or greater affluence), respectively. Use of income-to-need ratios represented a major departure from the operationalization of poverty in child development research published in the 1960s and 1970s, which tended to conflate poverty and low socioeconomic status and to rely on circumstances associated with poverty (e.g., attendance at schools with high proportions of children eligible for reduced-cost or free school lunch, eligibility for federal or state subsidies to the poor, low maternal education) or researchers' subjective impressions, rather than direct measurement of household or family income.

Persistent poverty has consistently been found to have more adverse effects than transitory poverty on the cognitive development of preschool children, with children experiencing both types of poverty scoring lower than never-poor children (e.g., Duncan, Brooks-Gunn, and Klebanov 1994; Korenman, Miller, and Sjaastad 1995; Smith, Brooks-Gunn, and Klebanov 1997). School achievement, like cognitive functioning during the preschool years, has also been found to decline with increases in the duration of poverty (Korenman et al. 1995; Pagani, Boulerice, and Tremblay 1997; Sherman 1994). Data indicated, for example, that the chance that children will be retained in grade or placed in special education increased by two to three percent for every year children lived in poverty, controlling for low birth weight and parents' education (Sherman 1994). Likewise, internalizing problems (Duncan et al. 1994; Pagani et al. 1997; McLeod and Shanahan 1993) and externalizing symptoms (Duncan et al. 1994; Hanson et al. 1997; Korenman et al. 1995) were found to be more prevalent the longer children had been living in poverty. Work examining developmental trajectories revealed that persistently poor children had more rapid increases in antisocial behavior than transiently poor children or children who had not experienced poverty (McLeod and Shanahan 1996).

Scholars also gave extensive attention to two other dimensions of poverty—the timing of poverty and the context of poverty. The notion of the primacy of early experience has long held sway among scholars in human development. A major cornerstone of Head Start, the notion was popularized during the 1960s by Bloom's (1964) influential treatise in which he argued that the effects of the environment on intelligence and other human characteristics are greatest during the early and most rapid periods of development of the characteristics and intervention to ameliorate the effects of environmental deprivation should occur as early in life as possible. This notion came under attack in later years as it became clear that early childhood education did not inoculate children against the effects of continuing economic disadvantage (Zigler and Berman

1983). Nonetheless, bolstered by research showing that the positive effects of early childhood education endured for two to three years thereafter, belief in the singularly potent influence of early experience prevailed. The notion of the primacy of early experience prompted questions about the effects of the timing of poverty, as did the growing prominence of life-course theory, particularly its tenet that the developmental antecedents and consequences of events, circumstances, and life transitions vary according to their timing in the life course (Elder 1974, 1975).

Studies found no relation between timing of poverty within the preschool period and children's internalizing or externalizing symptoms (Duncan et al. 1994). However, Duncan and his colleagues (Duncan and Brooks-Gunn 1997; Duncan et al. 1998) reported evidence pointing to the preschool years as a period of heightened vulnerability to the negative impacts of poverty and low income on cognitive functioning and school achievement. A major source of the evidence for this conclusion is the replication analyses that Duncan and Brooks-Gunn (1997) coordinated across a diverse set of child development studies. Collating the findings in relation to effect sizes and the developmental stage in which income was measured, they found that poverty and low income status during early and middle childhood had much stronger links to cognitive ability and school achievement than did poverty and low-income status during adolescence.

Guo (1998) raised several important caveats about these analyses. Duncan and Brooks-Gunn's estimates of income effects on early cognitive outcomes were based on numerous measures from a variety of samples, whereas income effects on cognitive outcomes during adolescence were based on fewer measures from fewer samples. Moreover, the estimates were not based on the same set of children across developmental periods. That is, income effects on early outcomes were estimated from one set of children, whereas income effects on later outcomes were estimated from another set of children. Guo pointed out that the observed differences between the two sets of children may not be due to differences in timing alone but to other differences between the two groups.

In contrast to the school of thought emphasizing early childhood as a critical period for cognitive development, a competing school of thought emphasizes environmental influences on learning that become more important to children's educational and cognitive outcomes as they age because of their increased understanding of the broader world around them. For example, the latter may result in disillusionment about the real worth of education, internalization of negative stereotypes about the poor, and a fuller understanding of societal messages that he/she receives from an impoverished environment, all of which can undermine academic effort. This school of thought argues that persistent poverty that continues into adolescence will continue to have a strong and unique effect on older children's educational and cognitive outcomes, but for reasons more related to motivational and opportunity factors than ability (Guo 1998).

Guo distinguished between *cognitive ability* and *school achievement*, arguing that the school of thought emphasizing early childhood as a critical period is speaking more to the question of ability, whereas the competing school of thought is speaking more to the question of school achievement—an outcome influenced by not only ability but motivation and opportunity as well. He predicted that poverty experienced in childhood would be more damaging to cognitive ability than poverty experienced in early adolescence, whereas poverty experienced in early adolescence would have a larger impact on academic achievement than poverty experienced in childhood. Guo found that long-term poverty had substantial influences on both ability and achievement as measured in childhood (5th–8th year of life) and early adolescence (11th–14th year of life), but the time patterns of these influences were distinctly different. As he predicted, long-term poverty during childhood (birth to the 5th–8th year of life) had a much stronger link to cognitive ability than poverty experienced in early adolescence or long-term poverty experienced from birth to early adolescence. This pattern suggested that poverty experienced after early to mid-childhood did not have an additional adverse influence on cognitive ability. In contrast and consistent with the claim that poverty experienced during adolescence is particularly important for achievement, poverty experienced in early adolescence was more strongly associated with achievement than poverty experienced during childhood.

The 1990s also witnessed intense focus on the contexts of development, as a wide swath of researchers endorsed an ecological approach to the study of development that takes account of influences at multiple levels of proximity to children. Keen interest in the effects of the economic character of neighborhoods on children was evoked by Bronfenbrenner's (1986) conceptual work, but especially by Wilson's (1987) analysis of historical changes in the spatial concentration of poverty in inner city African American neighborhoods wrought by structural changes in the economy, and Wilson's speculations about the impact of this trend on children's expectancies, attitudes, norms, and development (Brooks-Gunn, Duncan, Klebanov, and Sealand 1993; Chase-Lansdale and Gordon 1996; Duncan et al. 1994).

Duncan et al. (1994) found that the proportion of poor neighbors was unrelated to children's IQ scores at five years of age but having a larger proportion of affluent neighbors was associated with higher IQ scores. Research also indicated that the socioeconomic mix of the children's neighborhoods was related to completed years of schooling. Adolescents who grew up in affluent neighborhoods or neighborhoods with a higher percentage of affluent families completed more years of school and had lower school dropout rates than adolescents from similar families who grew up in poor neighborhoods or neighborhoods with proportionately fewer affluent families (Brooks-Gunn et al. 1993; Corcoran et al. 1992; Duncan 1994), although race and gender moderated some of these relations. The percentage of affluent neighbors had greater predictive power than the percentage of low-income neighbors, a finding that appeared to endorse the notion that neighborhoods affect children's development through positive collective socialization (e.g., role models who enforce societal norms) and institutional resources (Brooks-Gunn et al. 1993; Duncan 1994). There was also evidence that having more low-income neighbors predicted poorer mental health in children (e.g., anxiety/depression, acting out), controlling for family income, poverty status, and numerous confounding factors, but these relations depended on race/ethnicity, indicators of mental health, and other factors (e.g., Duncan et al. 1994; McLeod and Edwards 1995).

EXPLANATIONS OF THE LINKS BETWEEN POVERTY AND CHILDREN'S DEVELOPMENT

Investigations of the effects of different dimensions of poverty on children's development were accompanied by efforts to document the processes that gave rise to these effects. In this section, we discuss this research, the perspectives that inform this work, and the critiques that have ensued. Over the course of the past three decades, three perspectives have emerged as explanations for links between poverty and children's development. A *social causation* perspective espouses the view that poverty and the conditions strongly linked to poverty lead to variations in children's growth and development (Conger, Conger, and Martin 2010). A great deal of the research guided by a social causation perspective emphasizes familial processes, though it has also informed the study of extra-familial contexts such as schools and neighborhoods. Social causation models also undergird experimental studies testing the efficacy of interventions that aim to raise family income and reduce poverty (e.g., Huston et al. 2005). A *social selection* perspective maintains that traits and dispositions of future parents lead to variation in economic well-being, variation in parent's relationships with their children, and ultimately variation in children's development through the endowments and dispositions that parents pass on to their children. Finally, an *interactionist* perspective contends that the relation between socioeconomic status/poverty and development involves both social selection and social causation processes (Conger et al. 2010). In the sections that follow, we briefly review research evidence relevant to each of these perspectives (see Conger et al. 2010; Huston and Bentley 2010; McLoyd, Mistry, and Hardaway 2014 for more detailed reviews).

SOCIAL CAUSATION PERSPECTIVE

A large body of literature identifies two family-based pathways through which socio-economic status broadly, and poverty more specifically, affect child functioning—*parental investments* and *family stress*. Extant scholarship provides strong support for both perspectives, across families diverse with respect to race/ethnicity, family structure, and nativity status. Further, there is some evidence that parental investments pathways are better able to account for variations in children's cognitive and academically oriented outcomes, whereas family stress pathways appear to matter more for children's socioemotional outcomes.

Parental investments. The parental investment model has its roots in economic and sociological perspectives and emphasizes purchasing power (e.g., Becker and Thomas 1986). This model posits that the linkage between income/socioeconomic status and children's outcomes is through parents' procurement of goods and services that enhance children's economic and educational prospects (Linver, Brooks-Gunn, and Kohen 2002). Higher income parents have both the means and opportunities to provide their children with the material goods and experiences associated with social mobility (Lareau 2003). This includes the provision of learning materials in the home (e.g., books, educational materials) and parents' direct (e.g., reading with child) and indirect (e.g., visits to museums and libraries, tutoring, extracurricular activities) support of learning. These income and class differences have been linked to myriad indicators of children's cognitive functioning, verbal skills, language development, and overall school adjustment and attainment (Gershoff et al. 2007; Hoff 2003; Snow 2006; see McLoyd 1998, for a review of earlier research studies). There is also evidence that increases in family income are intertwined with improvements in the quality of the home learning environment and children's cognitive and academic outcomes in both observational and welfare-to-work experimental studies (Huston and Bentley 2010).

A second pathway emphasized by the parental investment model is parents' attitudes, values, and beliefs, as well as more targeted efforts designed to ensure their child's success at school (Magnuson 2007). A voluminous research literature points to parental attitudes as antecedents of academic outcomes among low-income adolescents and as mediators of the link between family income and academic outcomes among adolescents (e.g., Benner and Mistry 2007; Hango 2007; Hill et al. 2004; Schoon, Parsons, and Sacker 2004). For example, levels of academic achievement are higher among low-income adolescents whose parents have higher educational expectations for them (Schoon et al. 2004; Wood, Kaplan, and McLoyd 2007). Higher educational expectations among low-income parents are also associated with better adjustment to secondary school, which in turn, fosters higher educational attainment (Schoon et al. 2004).

Family Stress

A second set of family-based processes through which SES and poverty are proposed to matter for children's well-being is posited by a *family stress model*. The model derives from Glen Elder's seminal study of the effects of parental job and income loss on family functioning and child development during the Great Depression (Elder 1974; Elder, Nguyen, and Caspi 1985), Conger and Elder's (1994) study of family changes brought about by the United States farming crisis of the 1980s, and McLoyd's (1990) extension of the model to African American families living in poverty. Empirical tests of the family stress model yield robust confirmatory evidence of the pathways by which economic stress affects children socioemotional well-being among diverse families, including rural and urban families and families across multiple cultural communities within and outside the United States (e.g., Benner and Kim 2010; Mistry et al. 2002; Parke et al. 2004; Solantaus, Leinonen, and Punamäki 2004). The family stress model hypothesizes that economic hardship (i.e., income declines or living in poverty) induces economic strain and felt pressure in parents. The strain associated with the daily hassles of making ends meet in turn takes a toll on parents' mental health (e.g., depressive symptoms, anxiety), increases inter-parental conflict and discord, and ultimately interferes with high-quality parenting. Surprisingly, few studies of economic hardship model family income and material deprivation separately in their analyses (Huston and Bentley 2010). Gershoff and colleagues' recent study (Gershoff et al. 2007) provides strong empirical support for modeling indirect effects of family income—through material hardship and parent mental health—on children's cognitive and social-emotional competence. They found that when both income and material hardship were included in a model estimating child outcomes, the influence of income on parent mental health was due almost entirely to a reduction in material hardship. Parent mental health, in turn influenced both parental investments and positive parenting behavior, each of which significantly predicted increases in cognitive skills and social-emotional competence, respectively. These associations were generally consistent for families from diverse socioeconomic and race/ethnic backgrounds (Raver, Gershoff, and Aber 2007).

The family stress model gives attention to objective indicators of income and economic resources as well as parents' perceived financial inadequacy as factors that affect parenting and children's well-being. Mistry and colleagues found that parents' felt pressure to meet not only their family's material needs (e.g., rent, food, utility bills) but also more discretionary modest "extras" (e.g., birthday presents and Christmas gifts for their children) had consequences for their own mental health and parenting behaviors (Mistry and Lowe 2006; Mistry et al.2008). Keeping abreast of monthly bills was associated with feeling "okay," but affording modest extras was associated with feelings of accomplishment and of being a successful provider and parent, and in turn was a stronger predictor of children's social-emotional adjustment than was meeting basic needs. Inclusion of both dimensions of economic pressure provided additional insight into why economic hardship matters for child well-being.

Of all the constructs in the family stress framework, parenting problems are posited as the most proximal link to children's compromised development resulting from economic hardship (Elder 1974; McLoyd 1990). Economic stress reduces parents' ability to interact with children in a nurturing, supportive, and responsive manner; decreases their level of involvement and attentiveness toward their children; and increases reliance on more coercive, inconsistent, and harsher parenting practices (Conger et al. 1994; Elder et al. 1985; McLoyd et al. 1994). The family stress model contends that economic strain, depression, and marital conflict make it difficult for poor parents to engage in positive, child-centered parenting, even if they possess strong parenting skills. Low-income and low-SES parents do not necessarily lack good parenting skills but may simply be too compromised by the effects of poverty-related stress to engage in it.

Critiques of the Focus on Family Processes as Mediators of Poverty Effects

In recent years, scholars who themselves espouse a social causation perspective have criticized the literature's predominant focus on family processes for explaining poverty's impact on children's development. Evans (2004) faults research of this ilk largely on the grounds that it lacks an ecological perspective, a core tenet of which is that development is the result of multiple underlying agents and processes of varying proximity to the child. He asserts that psychologists have largely attended to parenting and home environmental factors, while ignoring the physical settings that poor children inhabit and their cumulative exposure to a daunting array of suboptimal psychosocial and physical environmental risk factors known to impact human development (e.g., proximity to toxic waste dumps, elevated levels of exposure to lead and pesticides, ambient air pollution). In their study of rural, white 8–10 year olds, Evans and English (2002) found that those who were poor were more likely than their middle-class counterparts to experience not only psychosocial stressors (e.g., family turmoil, community violence) but physical stressors (e.g., substandard housing, high levels of noise, crowding) as well. Cumulative exposure to these stressors partially mediated the link between poverty and children's psychosocial adjustment (i.e., anxiety, depression, behavioral conduct problems, low self-worth). Moreover, cumulative stressor exposure was a much more powerful mediator of the link between poverty and children's adjustment than were the individual physical and psychosocial stressors.

Of course, scholars who have tested the parental investments and family stress models and variants of these models are not unaware of the multiple disadvantages that accompany poverty and low income. For example, it is well established that impairment of children's physical health status (e.g., prematurity, prenatal exposure to illegal and legal drugs such as cocaine, nicotine and alcohol, lead poisoning, illness during perinatal period) and diminution of children's access to resources that mitigate these impairments are major pathways by which poverty hinders children's cognitive development (see McLoyd 1998 for a review). More than two decades ago, McLoyd (1990) underscored the complex, multifaceted nature of poverty and its relevance to children's socioemotional functioning. Drawing on a rich body of literature, she pointed out that chronic poverty is distinguished by a high contagion of negative life *events* occurring in the context of adverse *conditions* such as inadequate housing, residence in low-resource and sometimes dangerous neighborhoods, and exposure to aversive physical conditions. For this reason, McLoyd and Wilson (1990:52) cautioned against viewing negative parental behavior as the primary pathway through which poverty undermines children's socioemotional functioning, noting that "the multifaceted nature of poverty, especially if it is chronic, appears to require more complex models of causality." McLoyd (1990:314) also presumed that chronic poverty has direct effects on the child because it is "longstanding and defines the child's immediate environment, almost in its entirety."

Nonetheless, Evans's (2004) criticism is sound because mediational models centered on family processes scarcely reflect the multiple disadvantages that poor children experience in their physical and extra-familial environments. That scholars (mostly psychologists) who have directed focal attention to parenting and home environmental factors as mediators of poverty have not made significant forays into these environments to examine mediators of poverty effects (e.g., schools) can be credited, in part, to limited training and expertise in these domains and the challenges of establishing interdisciplinary collaborations. Conversely, their strong focus on parenting and psychosocial characteristics within the family reflects two key contextual influences: (a) a large contingent of these scholars is in the area of family studies; and (b) the conceptual underpinnings of the family stress model rest to a major extent on Elder's (Elder 1974; Elder et al. 1985) research on economic loss, in which parenting and family processes are central mediating pathways.

The fact that poor children experience multiple stressors and cumulative disadvantages has also prompted reservations about the value of research that privileges poverty over other stressors associated with poverty. Sameroff et al. (2003:367) assert that focusing on a single risk factor such as poverty or negative parenting does not address the reality of most children's lives because children often experience multiple adverse conditions and recurring stressors. In their view, "multiple settings and multiple systems must be examined simultaneously because risk factors tend to cluster in the same individuals."

The standard way of capturing such co-occurrences is to create a multiple or cumulative risk score by totaling the number of risk factors for each family or child (with poverty counted as one risk factor). Sameroff et al. (1998) found no differences in child competence by income level when groups of children with the same number of risk factors were compared. They concluded that income seems to make a major difference in child development not because it is an overarching variable in itself, but because it is strongly associated with a combination of other familial and extra-familial risk factors. For example, in their study of adolescents in almost 500 families in Philadelphia who varied widely in socioeconomic status and racial composition, 39 percent of poor children lived in high-risk families with more than seven risk factors, whereas only seven percent of affluent children did. The cumulative risk measure has been employed in numerous studies with economically diverse samples of children and adolescents. In general, these studies report that as the number of risk factors increases, the number or severity of behavioral and psychological problems increases and level of cognitive functioning decreases (e.g., Ackerman, Brown, and Izard 2004; Mistry et al. 2010).

Scholars who study childhood poverty as a focal or overarching variable do so partly because income poverty both precipitates and thwarts efforts to mitigate adverse conditions and recurring stressors and stands as a distinctly common correlate of these conditions and stressors. Undoubtedly, evidence that chronic poverty is more detrimental to children's development than transitory poverty (Duncan and Brooks-Gunn 1994) is rooted partly in the fact that chronic poverty, compared to transitory poverty, is more strongly linked to a range of adverse conditions, recurring stressors, and risk factors. Another key impetus for the focus on income poverty is that, as noted previously, it is generally easier to design and implement programs that alter family income (e.g., increasing welfare benefits, tax credits, and minimum wage) than programs that modify the many family- and context-related risk factors with which it is correlated (e.g., low parental income, neighborhood poverty) (Duncan et al. 1998). Family income below a certain threshold is a common criterion for participation in many child- and adolescent-focused programs and interventions that aim to prevent or ameliorate some of the behavioral, cognitive, and attitudinal correlates of poverty and life circumstances linked to poverty.

SOCIAL SELECTION PERSPECTIVE

Proponents of social selection perspectives argue that individual-level personality and cognitive traits are major contributors to poverty and that failure to take these individual characteristics into account results in an overestimation of the environmental effects of poverty (e.g., Mayer 1997; Rowe and Rodgers 1997). Mayer used a variety of analytic strategies to estimate what she termed the "true" effect of income on children's development—that is, the effect of income after controlling all parental characteristics, both observed and unobserved, that might influence parents' income and children's outcomes. Her conclusions have been questioned because the estimates do not take into account different stages of childhood, because the strategies are not well suited for estimating the effects of income from different sources at the bottom of the income scale, and because income from sources that Mayer argues are less strongly related to parental traits (e.g., interest or child support payments) tends to be miniscule (Duncan and Brooks-Gunn 2000). Other methods for assessing the environmental effects of poverty favored by advocates of the social selection perspective have also drawn skepticism. For example, Rowe and Rodgers's (1997) position that research only employing behavioral genetics methods can provide valid estimates of the causal effects of poverty has been criticized on the grounds that these methods do not measure environment directly and do not include the contributions of any environmental factors other than the parents' level of the characteristic being measured (Huston, McLoyd, and Garcia Coll 1997).

INTERACTIONIST PERSPECTIVE

Notwithstanding the considerations noted in the previous section, it is reasonable to assume that parents' poverty or affluence is due partly to individual differences in abilities and personality characteristics and that relations between family environments and child outcomes are not exclusively the result of environmental influences. Conger et al. (2010) proposed a conceptual model incorporating both social selection and social causation processes as predictors of adult SES status. A test of this model, based on a three-generational data set involving 271 European American rural families, provided support for this interactionist perspective (Schofield et al. 2011). Consistent with the social selection hypothesis that earlier personal characteristics predict later social circumstances and behaviors, "alpha" personality characteristics (i.e., high levels of agreeableness and conscientiousness, low levels of neuroticism) of future parents (second generation) measured in adolescence (9th and 10th graders) predicted their adulthood SES (indexed by per capita income and educational attainment), level of family stress (e.g., economic pressure, parental psychological distress, marital conflict), and emotional investments in their children (e.g., parental warmth, monitoring, consistent discipline). These relations held even when controlling for the socioeconomic status and emotional investments of their own (first generation) parents. The personality characteristics of future parents in adolescence directly predicted their children's (third generation) secure attachment and indirectly predicted children's academic competence and prosocial behavior via emotional investments, family stress, socioeconomic status, and material investments. Except for secure attachment, however, children's adaptive functioning was not directly predicted by their parents' personality measured in adolescence; rather, the linkages were more indirect.

Consistent with the social causation perspective, after controlling for parents' personality during adolescence, (a) parents' socioeconomic status significantly predicted their material (but not emotional) investments in the child, and (b) family stress and parental investments directly predicted children's adaptive functioning. Although parents' personality predicted family stress and emotional investments, it did not account for the association between parental investments and child functioning. McLeod and Nonnemaker's (2000) longitudinal analysis of the effects of the persistence of poverty on children's emotional and behavioral problems provides another notable example of the influence of both proximal conditions and selection processes. They found that current stresses and strains due to economic hardship were significant predictors of children's problems, but so were the psychological disadvantages that accompanied their mothers into poverty (e.g., delinquency, low self-esteem in early life).

Multigenerational studies of the kind Schofield et al. (2011) conducted represent an important step toward integrative research that incorporates assessment of genetic and biological constructs with a sophisticated view and appraisal of the environment at both the individual and social structural levels. Further, replications of Schofield et al.'s study, but with samples drawn from different racial and ethnic groups, have the potential to yield critical insights about the role of psychological characteristics and familial processes as contributors and mediators of poverty and whether and how these processes interact with race and ethnicity.

Poverty and Children's Development
in the Developing World

Discussion of the highly complex and contentious issues pertaining to the measurement of child poverty in developing countries is beyond the scope of this chapter (Gordon et al. 2003; United Nations 2009). These issues are examined in other chapters in this volume. Suffice it to say that individual-level studies of linkages between poverty/income or socioeconomic status and the development of children living in developing countries have used a range of indicators depending on the ecological context and availability of data (e.g., household income quartile, amount of land, material objects in home, quality of the homestead) and have focused on cognitive and health-related child outcomes (e.g., Baker-Henningham et al. 2003; Sigman et al. 1989). In this section, we offer some observations about how research on childhood poverty in developing countries differs from U.S.-based research, highlight themes in the poverty-related research conducted in developing countries that correspond to themes in the U.S.-based research literature, and consider the applicability of the explanatory models discussed earlier for understanding the effects of poverty on children living in developing countries.

The establishment in 2000 of the United Nations Millennium Development Goal to halve global extreme poverty by 2015 was a significant step toward internationalization of an antipoverty agenda (United Nations 2009). Given the broad range and severity of deprivations that characterize the nature of poverty in the developing world, it is not surprising that empirical studies on childhood poverty in developing countries focus on outcomes that concern children's immediate needs and survival, such as health (e.g., stunting, undernutrition, prenatal risk), disease (e.g., HIV/AIDS, malaria), and cognitive and educational deficiencies (see Grantham-McGregor et al. 2007; Walker et al. 2007 for reviews). Moreover, with the 2015 target date for achieving the Millennium Development Goal fast approaching, international scholars consider it of great importance to monitor the progress of developing countries toward achievement of these goals and to provide recommendations about the most efficient targets of intervention. As such, much of the research has been devoted to (a) documenting the incidence, depth, and severity of child poverty across the globe (e.g., Delamonica and Minujin 2007; Gordon et al. 2003); (b) describing the extent of inequity and deprivation experienced by disadvantaged children (e.g., United Nations Children's Fund 2012; Walker et al. 2011); and (c) assessing the effectiveness of child development intervention programs (Engle et al. 2007; Walker et al. 2007). There is notably little emphasis on testing models of processes and pathways through which poverty exerts its influence on children. However, given the supreme importance of parents and material and social resources to the development of all children, irrespective of geographic location, it is predictable that some of the prominent themes in the research focusing on childhood poverty in developing countries coincide with those found in the U.S.-based research literature and highlighted in the prior sections of the chapter. We briefly discuss some of these themes in the following.

POVERTY AND MATERNAL AND CHILD MENTAL HEALTH

Poverty and socioeconomic disadvantage have been identified as important contributors to mental health disorders in individuals living in developing nations (Patel and Kleinman 2003). Although stronger kinship ties may provide a large social support system in some of these contexts (Das et al. 2007), overcoming mental health problems may be challenging, particularly in settings where the poor are subjected to extreme physical and psychosocial stressors. Poor women in some developing countries are especially vulnerable to violence and discrimination, which may lead to feelings of anxiety, depression, loss of self-esteem, shame, and guilt. For example, Zimbabwean women who migrated to South Africa because of poverty reported feeling highly distressed due to experiences of sexual abuse, prostitution, homelessness, substandard living conditions, exploitation, and stigmatization (Chireshe 2010).

Maternal depression is more prevalent in developing countries than in developed countries, and across both contexts, is a strong correlate of child functioning (Walker et al. 2007). Correlational studies done in South Africa, Bangladesh, Barbados, and India indicate that children of depressed mothers exhibit poorer motor and cognitive function and increased level of behavioral problems (Black et al. 2007; Galler et al. 2000; Richter, Griesel, and Barbarin 2000; Patel, DeSouza, and Rodrigues 2000). Apart from cognitive and behavioral outcomes, maternal depression has been found to be significantly associated with children's health. A meta-analysis of 17 studies examining maternal depression in relation to early childhood growth in different countries (e.g., Bangladesh, Vietnam, Nigeria, Malawi, Brazil) found a higher likelihood of being underweight and stunting among children of depressed mothers (Surkan et al. 2011).

PARENTING PRACTICES AND INVESTMENTS

The mechanisms explaining the link between maternal depression and child development have not been extensively examined in developing countries. However, just as in the United States, a few extant studies based in developing countries have found maternal depression to be associated with less involved and sensitive childrearing and lower stimulation in the home environment (Black et al. 2007, 2009; Cooper et al. 1999). In a special section published in *Child Development*, a set of studies used data from the third round of UNICEF's Multiple Indicator Cluster Survey (MICS3) (United Nations Children's Fund 2006), a large-scale international household survey conducted in over 60 low- and middle-income countries, to examine relations between country-level socioeconomic characteristics and caregiving practices important for child development (see Bornstein et al. 2012). Among other findings, the studies revealed that caregivers in countries with higher scores on indicators of socioeconomic well-being (e.g., education, gross domestic product, life expectancy) reported engaging in higher levels of cognitive and socioemotional parenting activities (Bornstein and Putnick 2012) and reported lower likelihood of their children experiencing psychological aggression or physical violence in the household (Lansford and Deater-Deckard 2012).

These caregiving practices, in turn, may have corresponding implications for children's functioning. For example, studies in rural Bangladesh found that mothers' sensitivity and provision of stimulating activities at home were related to higher mental and psychomotor development scores among infants (Black et al. 2007; Hamadani et al. 2012). Harsh corporal punishment has been linked to poor school performance and behavioral and emotional problems among Yemeni children (Alyahri and Goodman 2008).

Recognition of the role of poverty in limiting parents' ability to provide resources and acquire skills that can enhance children's development is evident in studies that assess the effectiveness of parenting-intervention programs conducted in developing countries. Engle et al. (2011) conducted a review of 15 parenting-intervention studies done in low-income and middle-income countries (e.g., Bangladesh, South Africa, China, Turkey, Ethiopia) and reported positive effects in 14 out of the 15 assessments. These programs involved teaching parents responsive feeding, encouraging cognitive stimulation, and increasing parent-child attachment. They were found to enhance children's socioemotional and cognitive development, parents' knowledge, home stimulation, and parents' engagement in learning activities with children. Walker et al. (2007) likewise reviewed 16 parenting intervention studies conducted in developing countries (e.g., Jamaica, Chile, Colombia, India) and found positive effects in 15 out of the 16 assessments. Compared to controls, children of parents who received the intervention (i.e., cognitive stimulation, caregiver sensitivity and responsiveness) had better scores on a range of outcomes including cognitive functioning, social behaviors, self-confidence, and positive affect.

The importance of parental investments is also suggested in a study that examined the relation of maternal cultural participation and child health status in families living in impoverished neighborhoods in Lebanon. Khawaja, Barazi, and Linos (2006) defined cultural participation as involvement in activities such as watching television and attending movies, musical events, or art exhibitions. Whereas no significant relation was found between sociodemographic factors (e.g., education, income, household structure) and child health status, they found that maternal cultural participation was associated with better health in children. To explain this link, they argued that the "cultural capital" that is acquired from exposure to and participation in sociocultural events may widen mothers' sources of information and enhance their social awareness, competence, and communication skills. Certain knowledge and skills can be considered assets or investments that enable mothers to better manage their children's needs, including health care. However, these mechanisms were not directly tested in the study.

The aforementioned findings suggest the importance of mothers' psychological well-being and parenting behaviors as potential pathways between poverty and child functioning. Although there is some evidence supporting the applicability of parental investment and family stress models, scholars working in developing countries should practice caution when adopting these models for a variety of reasons, not the least of which is the wide variation in cultural norms and values pertaining to parenting and child competencies (Nsamenang 2006), vast differences in the family environments that children experience across the globe, and the fact that tests of these models in the United States typically are based on standardized tests that were developed for use in the U.S. context (e.g., Center for Epidemiologic Studies Depression Scale, the Home Observation for Measurement of the Environment Scale [HOME], and the Bayley Scales of Infant Development; Bayley 1993; Bradley and Caldwell 1977; Radloff 1977). The use of such measures may be problematic because of issues regarding the equivalence and relevance of the items in other cultural contexts. For example, a qualitative study on Haitian immigrant women reported these women's difficulties in understanding the concept of depression, as the closest translation of the word in their local language characterized it as "not a sickness of the mind but rather of the body" (Nicolas and Whitt 2012:210). Standard measures like the HOME and the Bayley Scales might fail to take into account caregiving practices and child competencies that are salient and valued in contexts in developing countries but not in mainstream American or European culture.

For these and other reasons, international scholars should give priority to developing measures that tap context-specific meanings, practices, and competencies and articulating models that capture unique processes operating in different cultural contexts, while also searching for general mediating processes and patterns of development. The MICS3, described previously (United Nationals Children's Fund 2006) is notable for allowing cultural adaptations of the questionnaires in each participating country while maintaining cross-country comparability through standardized questions and administration (Bornstein et al. 2012). Simply transplanting Western theoretical frameworks and constructs will neither advance developmental science nor foster knowledge that lays the foundation for developing programs and policies that effectively address the developmental needs of children in developing countries (Marfo 2011).

CUMULATIVE STRESSORS

Measures reflecting emphasis on the multidimensionality of poverty and developed for use in the developing world (e.g., Multidimensional Poverty Index, Multiple Overlapping Deprivation Analysis) recognize the spectrum of deprivation levels that individuals can experience (i.e., mild, moderate, severe, extreme) (Alkire and Foster 2011; De Neubourg et al. 2012; Gordon et al 2003). An important feature of these measures is that they go beyond mere counting the number of risk factors and emphasize weighting the importance of each dimension and the overlaps between risk factors. These measures appear promising as instruments to identify groups or individuals most in need of intervention. The emphasis on the multidimensionality of children's experiences of poverty and deprivation in developing countries is highly consonant with Sameroff et al.'s (2003) cumulative risk framework. It also comports with research conducted with American samples documenting exposure to cumulative stressors as one pathway through which poverty influences children's psychosocial adjustment and health (e.g., Evans and English 2002).

Nonetheless, very little work has assessed cumulative or multiple risk exposure in relation to poverty and the progress of children living in developing countries. One of the few extant studies examined risk exposure in rural Guatemalan children in relation to achievement test performance in adolescence (Gorman and Pollitt 1996). Eight risk variables were assessed: percentage respiratory illness and percentage diarrheal disease up to three years of age, height at three years of age, home stimulation, maternal education, father occupation, housing quality, and a composite cognitive ability score. A median split was used to categorize children as high or low risk for each of the eight risk factors, with the score of 1 assigned to high-risk cases and a score of 0 assigned to low-risk cases. Consistent with evidence based on United States samples (e.g., Ackerman, Brown, and Izard 2004; Mistry et al. 2010), exposure to a higher number of risk factors in early childhood was associated with lower numerical and achievement scores in adolescence.

CONCLUDING COMMENTS

The studies reviewed in this section, although few and limited in scope, show some evidence that parenting and family contexts are viable targets for intervention to improve the well-being of poor children living in developing countries. Along with survival, physical health, and protection, children are equally entitled to a healthy psychosocial environment, which involves nurturing and stimulating interactions with caregivers (Bornstein et al. 2012). However, because the child environment is shaped in part by locally determined childrearing customs and goals, the findings derived from children and families in developed countries cannot be assumed to be universally applicable (Super et al. 2011). Although some parenting strategies are valued in both developed and developing countries, some show cross-country variability, suggesting the role of culture-specific beliefs, policies, and laws that may contribute to parental attitudes and behaviors in each context (Lansford and Deater-Deckard 2012).

These types of variation in family environment conditions across the globe raise questions—even more serious than those raised in the United States context

(Evans 2004)—about the applicability of the parental investment and the family stress models for understanding the effects of poverty on children. The essence of the parental investment and family stress models may be applicable, but enhancing their explanatory power is likely to require nontrivial modifications and extensions that capture important context-specific variables. Extending these models within a cumulative risk framework incorporating a range of physical and psychosocial stressors or deprivations strikes us as a particularly promising direction for future conceptual and empirical work.

In their introduction to *Child Development's* special issue on child development in developing countries, Bornstein et al. (2012) indicated that only about 10 percent of the child development literature comes from parts of the world that account for more than 90 percent of the global population. The research literature is saturated with studies of North American and European children and meager in its attention to children who constitute the majority of the world's population. The advancement of child development research in the developing world offers the prospect of a fresh and culturally anchored framework. Automatically assuming that frameworks developed for understanding childhood poverty in an affluent country such as America will hinder the development of a strong, context-sensitive, and policy-relevant base of knowledge. Ethnographic and participatory research methods may be especially helpful in enriching the cultural and policy relevance of research in these contexts. Other strategies that may enhance child and family research in developing countries include using a mixture of quantitative household surveys and qualitative interviews, employing culturally validated and pretested measures, and collaborating with experienced researchers who are closely connected to the community and who speak the local language (Camfield, Crivello, and Woodhead 2009).

REFERENCES

Ackerman, Brian P., Eleanor Brown, and Carroll Izard. 2004. "The Relations between Persistent Poverty and contextual Risk and Children's Behavior in Elementary School." *Developmental Psychology* 40(3):367–77.

Alkire, Sabina and James Foster. 2011. "Counting and Multidimensional Poverty Measurement." *Journal of Public Economics* 95(7/8):476–87.

Alyahri, Abdullah and Robert Goodman. 2008. "Harsh Corporal Punishment of Yemeni Children: Occurrence, Type and Associations." *Child Abuse and Neglect* 32:766–73.

Baker-Henningham, H., C. Powell, S. Walker, and S. Grantham-McGregor. 2003. "Mothers of Undernourished Jamaican Children Have Poorer Psychosocial Functioning and This is Associated with Stimulation Provided in the Home." *European Journal of Clinical Nutrition* 57:786–92.

Bayley, Nancy. 1993. *Bayley Scales of Infant Development.* 2nd ed. San Antonio, TX: Psychological Corp.

Becker, Gary S. and Nigel Tomes. 1986. "Human Capital and the Rise and Fall of Families." *Journal of Labor Economics* 4(3):S1–S39.

Benner, Aprile and Rashmita Mistry. 2007. "Congruence of Mother and Teacher Educational Expectations and Low-income Youth's Academic Competence." *Journal of Educational Psychology* 99:140–53.

Benner, Aprile and Su Yeong Kim. 2010. "Understanding Chinese American Adolescents' Developmental Outcomes: Insights from the Family Stress Model." *Journal of Research on Adolescence* 20:1–12.

Black, Maureen M., Abdullah H. Baqui, K. Zaman, Shams El Arifeen, and Robert E. Black. 2009. "Maternal Depressive Symptoms and Infant Growth in Rural Bangladesh." *American Journal of Clinical Nutrition* 89:951S–957S.

Black, Maureen M., Abdullah H. Baqui, K. Zaman, Scot W. McNary, Katherine Le, Shams El Arifeen, Jena D. Hamadani, Monowara Parveen, Md. Yunus, and Robert E. Black. 2007. "Depressive Symptoms among Rural Bangladeshi Mothers: Implications for Infant Development." *Journal of Child Psychology and Psychiatry* 48:764–72.

Bloom, Benjamin S. 1964. *Stability and Change in Human Characteristics*. New York: Wiley.

Bornstein, Marc H. and Diane L. Putnick. 2012. "Cognitive and Socioemotional Caregiving in Developing Countries." *Child Development* 83:46–61.

Bornstein, Marc H., Pia Rebello Britto, Yuko Nonoyama-Tarumi, Yumiko Ota, Oliver Petrovic, and Diane L. Putnick. 2012. "Child Development in Developing Countries: Introduction and Methods." *Child Development* 83:16–31.

Bradley, Robert H. and Bettye M. Caldwell. 1977. "Home Observation Measurement of the Environment: A Validation Study of Screening Efficiency." *American Journal of Mental Deficiency* 81:417–20.

Bronfenbrenner, Urie. 1986. "Ecology of the Family as a Context for Human Development: Research Perspectives." *Developmental Psychology* 22:723–42.

Brooks-Gunn, Jeanne, Greg Duncan, Pamela Klebanov, and Naomi Sealand. 1993. "Do Neighborhoods Influence Child and Adolescent Development?" *American Journal of Sociology* 99:353–95.

Camfield, Laura, Gina Crivello, and Martin Woodhead. 2009. "Well-being Research in Developing Countries: Reviewing the Role of Qualitative Methods." *Social Indicators Research* 90:5–31.

Chase-Lansdale, P. Lindsay and Rachel Gordon. 1996. "Economic Hardship and the Development of 5- and 6-Year-Olds: Neighborhood and Regional Perspectives." *Child Development* 67:3338–67.

Chireshe, Regis. 2010. "The Impact of Poverty on Women's Psychosocial Well-being: Narratives from Zimbabwean Migrant Women in South Africa." *Journal of Psychology in Africa* 20:193–98.

Conger, Rand and Glen Elder. 1994. *Families in Troubled Times*. New York: Aldine de Gruyter.

Conger, Rand, Katherine Conger, and Monica Martin. 2010. "Socioeconomic Status, Family Processes, and Individual Development." *Journal of Marriage and Family* 72:686–705.

Conger, Rand, Xiaojia Ge, Glen Elder, Frederick Lorenz, and Ronald Simons. 1994. "Economic Stress, Coercive Family Processes, and Developmental Problems of Adolescents." *Child Development* 65:541–61.

Cooper, Peter, Mark Tomlinson, Leslie Swartz, Matthew Woolgar, Lynne Murray, and Christopher Molteno. 1999. "Post-partum Depression and the Mother-Infant Relationship in a South African Peri-urban Settlement." *British Journal of Psychiatry* 175:554–58.

Corcoran, Mary and Ajay Chaudry. 1997. "The Dynamics of Childhood Poverty." *Future of Children* 7:40–54.

Corcoran, Mary, Roger Gordon, Deborah Laren, and Gary Solon. 1992. "The Association between Men's Economic Status and Their Family and Community Origins." *Journal of Human Resources* 27:575–601.

Danziger, Sandra and Sheldon Danziger. 1993. "Child Poverty and Public Policy: Toward a Comprehensive Antipoverty Agenda." *Daedalus* 122:57–84.

Das, Jishnu, Quy-Toan Do, Jed Friedman, David McKenzie, and Kinnon Scott. "Mental Health and Poverty in Developing Countries: Revising the Relationship." *Social Science and Medicine* 65:467–80.

Delamonica, Enrique Ernesto and Alberto Minujin. 2007. "Incidence, Depth, and Severity of Children in Poverty." *Social Indicators Research* 82:361–74.

De Neubourg, Chris, Jingqing Chai, Marlous de Milliano, Ilze Plavgo, and Ziru Wei. 2012. "Step-by-step Guidelines to the Multiple Overlapping Deprivation Analysis (MODA)." Working Paper 2012-10. Florence, UNICEF Office of Research.

Duncan, Greg. 1994. "Families and Neighbors as Sources of Disadvantage in the Schooling Decisions of White and Black Adolescents." *American Journal of Education* 103:20–53.

Duncan, Greg and Jeanne Brooks-Gunn, eds. 1997. *Consequences of Growing up Poor.* New York: Russell Sage Foundation.

Duncan, Greg and Jeanne Brooks-Gunn. 2000. "Family Poverty, Welfare Reform, and Child Development." *Child Development* 71:188–96.

Duncan, Greg, Jeanne Brooks-Gunn, and Pamela Klebanov. 1994. "Economic Deprivation and Early Childhood Development." *Child Development* 65:296–318.

Duncan, Greg, Richard Coe, Mary Corcoran, Martha Hill, Saul Hoffman, and James Morgan. 1984. *Years of Poverty, Years of Plenty.* Ann Arbor: Institute for Social Research, University of Michigan.

Duncan, Greg and Willard Rodgers. 1988. "Longitudinal Aspects of Childhood Poverty." *Journal of Marriage and the Family* 50:1007–21.

Duncan, Greg., W. Jean Yeung, Jeanne Brooks-Gunn, and Judith Smith. 1998. "How Much Does Childhood Poverty Affect the Life Chances of Children?" *American Sociological Review* 63 (3):406–23.

Elder, Glen. 1974. *Children of the Great Depression.* Chicago: University of Chicago Press.

Elder, Glen. 1975. "Age Differentiation and the Life Course." *Annual Review of Sociology* 1:165–90.

Engle, Patrice L., Maureen Black, Jere Behrman, Meena Carbral de Mello, Paul Gertler, Lydia Kapiriri, Reynaldo Martorell, Mary Eming Young, and the International Child Development Steering Group. 2007. "Strategies to Avoid the Loss of Developmental Potential in More Than 200 million Children in the Developing World." *Lancet* 369:229–42.

Engle, Patrice L., Lia C. H. Hernald, Harold Alderman, Jere Behrman, Chloe O'Gara, Aisha Yousafzai, Meena Cabral de Mello, Melissa Hidrobo, Nurper Ulkuer, Ilgi Ertem, Selim Iltus, and the Global Child Development Steering Group. 2011. "Strategies for Reducing Inequalities and Improving Developmental Outcomes for Young Children in Low-income and Middle-income Countries." *Lancet* 378:1339–53.

Evans, Gary. 2004. "The Environment of Childhood Poverty." *American Psychologist* 59:77–92.

Evans, Gary and Kimberly English. 2002. "The Environment of Poverty: Multiple Stressor Exposure, Psychophysiological Stress, and Socioemotional Adjustment." *Child Development* 73:1238–48.

Galler, Janina R., Robert H. Harrison, Frank Ramsey, Victor Forde, and Samantha C. Butler. 2000. "Maternal Depressive Symptoms Affect Infant Cognitive Development in Barbados." *Journal of Child Psychology and Psychiatry* 41:747–57.

Gershoff, Elizabeth, Lawrence Aber, Cybele Raver, and Mary Clare Lennon. 2007. "Income Is Not Enough: Incorporating Material Hardship into Models of Income Associations with Parenting and Child Development." *Child Development* 78:70–95.

Gordon, David, Shailen Nandy, Christina Pantazis, Simon Pemberton, and Peter Townsend. 2003. *Child Poverty in the Developing World.* Bristol: Policy Press.

Gorman, Kathleen S. and Ernesto Pollitt. 1996. "Does Schooling Buffer the Effects of Early Risk?" *Child Development* 67:314–26.

Grantham-McGregor, Sally, Yin Bun Cheung, Santiago Cueto, Paul Glewwe, Linda Richter, Barbara Strupp, and the International Child Development Steering Group. 2007. "Developmental Potential in the First 5 Years for Children in Developing Countries." *Lancet* 369:60–70.

Guo, Guang. 1998. "The Timing of the Influences of Cumulative Poverty on Children's Cognitive Ability and Achievement." *Social Forces* 77(1):257–88.

Hamadani, J. D., F. Tofail, A. Hilaly, F. Mehrin, S. Shiraji, S. Banu, and S. N. Huda. 2012. "Association of Postpartum Maternal Morbidities with Children's Mental, Psychomotor, and Language Development in Rural Bangladesh." *Journal of Health, Population and Nutrition* 31:193–204.

Hango, Darcy. 2007. "Parental Investment in Childhood and Educational Qualifications: Can Greater Parental Involvement Mediate the Effects of Socioeconomic Disadvantage?" *Social Science Research* 36:1371–90.

Hanson, Thomas, Sara McLanahan, and Elizabeth Thomson. 1997. "Economic Resources, Parental Practices, and Children's Well-Being." Pp. 190–238 in *Consequences of Growing up Poor,* edited by G. Duncan and J. Brooks-Gunn. New York: Russell Sage.

Hill, Nancy, Domini Castellino, Jennifer Lansford, Patrick Nowlin, Kenneth Dodge, John Bates, and Gregory Pettit. 2004. "Parent Academic Involvement as Related to School Behavior, Achievement, and Aspirations: Demographic Variations across Adolescence." *Child Development* 75:1491–1509.

Hoff, Erika. 2003. "The Specificity of Environmental Influence: Socioeconomic Status affects Early Vocabulary Development via Maternal Speech." *Child Development* 74:1368–78.

Huston, Aletha and Alison Bentley 2010. "Human Development in Societal Context." *Annual Review of Psychology* 61:411–37.

Huston, Aletha, Greg Duncan, Vonnie McLoyd, Danielle Crosby, Marika Ripke, Thomas Weisner, and Carolyn Eldred. 2005. "Impacts on Children of a Policy to Promote Employment and Reduce Poverty for Low-Income Parents: New Hope After 5 Years." *Developmental Psychology* 41:902–18.

Huston, Aletha, Vonnie McLoyd, and Cynthia Garcia Coll. 1997. "Poverty and Behavior: The Case for Multiple Methods and Levels of Analysis." *Developmental Review* 17:376–93.

Khawaja, M., R. Barazi, and N. Linos. 2006. "Maternal Cultural Participation and Child Health Status in a Middle Eastern Context: Evidence from an Urban Health Study." *Child Care, Health and Development* 33:117–25.

Korenman, Sanders, Jane Miller, and John Sjaastad. 1995. "Long-Term Poverty and Child Development in the United States: Results from the NLSY." *Children and Youth Services Review* 17:127–55.

Lansford, Jennifer E. and Kirby Deater-Deckard. 2012. "Childrearing Discipline and Violence in Developing Countries." *Child Development* 83:62–75.

Lareau, A. 2003. *Unequal Childhoods: Race, Class, and Family Life.* Berkeley: University of California Press.

Linver, Miriam, Jeanne Brooks-Gunn, and Dafna Kohen 2002. "Family Processes as Pathways from Income to Young Children's Development." *Developmental Psychology* 38(5):719–34.

Magnuson, Katherine. 2007. "Maternal Education and Children's Academic Achievement during Middle Childhood." *Developmental Psychology* 43:1497–1512.

Marfo, Kofi. 2011. "Envisioning an African Child Development Field." *Child Development Perspectives* 5:140–47.

Mayer, S. 1997. *What Money Can't Buy.* Cambridge, MA: Harvard University Press.

McLeod Jane and James Nonnemaker. 2000. "Poverty and Child Emotional and Behavioral Problems: Racial/Ethnic Differences in Processes and Effects." *Journal of Health and Social Behavior* 41:137–61.

McLeod, Jane and Kevan Edwards. 1995. "Contextual Determinants of Children's Responses to Poverty." *Social Forces* 73:1487–1516.

McLeod, Jane, D. and Michael J. Shanahan. 1993. "Poverty, Parenting, and Children's Mental Health." *American Sociological Review* 58:351–66.

McLeod, Jane D. and Michael J. Shanahan. 1996. "Trajectories of Poverty and Children's Mental Health." *Journal of Health and Social Behavior* 37:207–20.

McLoyd, Vonnie "The Impact of Economic Hardship on Black Families and Children: Psychological Distress, Parenting, and Socioemotional Development." *Child Development* 61:311–46.

McLoyd, Vonnie. 1998. "Socioeconomic Disadvantage and Child Development." *American Psychologist* 53:185–204.

McLoyd, Vonnie, Nikki Aikens, and Linda Burton. 2006. "Childhood Poverty, Policy, and Practice." Pp. 700–775 in *Handbook of Child Psychology: Child Psychology in Practice,* edited by W. Damon, R. Lerner, K. A. Renninger, and I. Sigel. Thousand Oaks, CA: Sage.

McLoyd, Vonnie and Rosario Ceballo. 1998. "Conceptualizing and Assessing Economic Context: Issues in the Study of Race and Child Development." Pp. 251–87 in *Studying Minority Adolescents: Conceptual, Methodological, and Theoretical Issues,* edited by V. C. McLoyd and L. Steinberg. Mahwah. NJ: Erlbaum.

McLoyd, Vonnie, Toby Jayaratne, Rosario Ceballo, and Julio Borquez. 1994. "Unemployment and Work Interruption among African American Single Mothers: Effects on Parenting and Adolescent Socioemotional Functioning." *Child Development* 65:562–89.

McLoyd, Vonnie, Rashmita Mistry, and Cecily Hardaway. 2014. "Poverty and Children's Development: Familial Processes as Mediating Influences." Pp. 109–124 in *Societal Contexts of Child Development: Pathways of Influence and Implications for Practice and Policy,* edited by E. Gershoff, R. Mistry, and D. Crosby. New York: Oxford University Press.

McLoyd, Vonnie and Leon Wilson. 1990. "Maternal Behavior, Social Support, and Economic Conditions as Predictors of Distress in Children." Pp. 49–69 in *New Directions for Child Development:* Vol. 46. *Economic Stress: Effects on Family Life and Child Development,* edited by V. C. McLoyd and C. Flanagan. San Francisco: Jossey-Bass.

Mistry, Rishmita, Aprile Benner, Jeremy Biesanz, Shaunna Clark, and Carollee Howes. 2010. "Family and Social Risk, and Parental Investments during the Early Childhood Years as Predictors of Low-Income Children's School Readiness Outcomes." *Early Childhood Research Quarterly* 25:432–49.

Mistry, Rashmita and Edward Lowe, E. 2006. "What Earnings and Income Buy: The 'Basics,' Plus 'a Little Extra': Implications for Family and Child Well-Being." Pp. 173–205 in *Making It Work: Low-Wage Employment, Family Life, and Child Development*, edited by H. Yoshikawa, T. Weisner, and E. Lowe. New York: Russell Sage.

Mistry, Rashmita, Edward Lowe, Aprile Benner, and Nina Chien. 2008. "Expanding the Family Economic Stress Model: Insights from a Mixed Methods Approach." *Journal of Marriage and Family* 70:196–209.

Mistry, Rashmita, Elizabeth Vandewater, Aletha Huston, and Vonnie McLoyd. 2002. "Economic Well-Being and Children's Social Adjustment: The Role of Family Process in an Ethnically Diverse Low-Income Sample." *Child Development* 73:935–51.

Nicolas, Guerda and Courtney L. Whitt. 2012. "Conducting Qualitative Research with a Black Immigrant Sample: Understanding Depression among Haitian Immigrant Women." Pp. 199–217 in *Qualitative Strategies for Ethnocultural Research*, edited by D. K. Nagata, L. Kohn-Wood, and L. A. Suzuki. Washington, DC: American Psychological Association.

Nsamenang, A. Bame. 2006. "Human Ontogenesis: An Indigenous African View on Development and Intelligence." *International Journal of Psychology* 41(4):293–97.

Pagani, Linda, Bernard Boulerice, and Richard Tremblay. 1997. "The Influence of Poverty on Children's Classroom Placement and Behavior Problems." Pp. 311–39 in *Consequences of Growing up Poor*, edited by G. Duncan and J. Brooks-Gunn. New York: Russell Sage.

Parke, Ross, Scott Coltrane, Sharon Duffy, Raymond Buriel, Jessica Dennis, Justina Powers, Sabine French, and Keith Widaman. 2004. "Economic Stress, Parenting and Child Adjustment in Mexican-American and European American Families." *Child Development* 75(6):1632–56.

Patel, Vikram, Nandita DeSouza, and Merlyn Rodrigues. 2002. "Postnatal Depression and Infant Growth and Development in Low Income Countries: A Cohort Study from Goa, India." *Archives of Disease in Childhood* 88:34–37.

Patel, Vikram and Arthur Kleinman. 2003. "Poverty and Common Mental Disorders in Developing Countries." *Bulletin of the World Health Organization* 81:609–15.

Radloff, Lenore Sawyer. 1977. "The CES-D Scale: A Self-Report Depression Scale for Research in the General Population." *Applied Psychological Measurement* 1:385–401.

Richter, Linda M., R. Dev Griesel, and Oscar Barbarin. 2000. "Behavioural Problems among Preschool Children in South Africa: A Longitudinal Perspective from Birth to Age Five." Pp. 159–82 in *International Perspectives on Child and Adolescent Mental Health*, edited by N. Singh and F. Leung. Amsterdam: Elsevier.

Rowe, David and Joseph Rodgers. 1997. "Poverty and Behavior: Are Environmental Measures Nature and Nurture?" *Developmental Review* 17:358–75.

Sameroff, Arnold, W. Todd Bartko, Alfred Baldwin, Clara Baldwin, and Ronald Seifer 1998. "Family and Social Influences on the Development of Child Competence." Pp. 177–92 in *Families, Risk, and Competence*, edited by M. Lewis and C. Feiring. Mahwah, NJ: Erlbaum.

Sameroff, Arnold, Leslie Gutman, and A., Gutman, L. M., and Stephen Peck 2003. "Adaptation among Youth Facing Multiple Risks: Prospective Research Findings." Pp. 364–91 in *Resilience and Vulnerability: Adaptation in the Context of Childhood Adversities*, edited by S. S. Luthar. New York: Cambridge University Press.

Schofield, Thomas, Monica Martin, Katherine Conger, Tricia Neppl, Brent Donnellan, and Rand Conger. 2011. "Intergenerational Transmission of Adaptive Functioning: A Test of the Interactionist Model of SES and Human Development." *Child Development* 82:33–47.

Schoon, Ingrid, Samantha Parsons, and Amanda Sacker. 2004. "Socioeconomic Adversity, Educational Resilience, and Subsequent Level of Adult Adaptation." *Journal of Adolescent Research* 19:383–404.

Sherman, Arloc. 1994. *Wasting America's Future: The Children's Defense Fund Report on the Costs of Child Poverty.* Boston: Beacon Press.

Sigman, Marian, Charlotte Neumann, Ake A. J. Jansen, and Nimrod Bwibo. 1989. "Cognitive Abilities of Kenyan Children in Relation to Nutrition, Family Characteristics, and Education." *Child Development* 60(6):1463–74.

Smith, Judith, Jeanne Brooks-Gunn, and Pamela Klebanov. 1997. "Consequences of Living in Poverty for Young Children's Cognitive and Verbal Ability and Early School Achievement." Pp. 132–89 in *Consequences of Growing up Poor,* edited by G. Duncan and J. Brooks-Gunn. New York: Russell Sage.

Snow, Catherine. 2006. "What Counts as Literacy in Early Childhood?" Pp. 274–94 in *Handbook of Early Childhood Development,* edited by K. McCartney and D. Phillips. Malden, MA: Blackwell.

Solantaus, Tytti, Jenni Leinonen, and Raija-Leena Punamäki. 2004. "Children's Mental Health in Times of Economic Recession: Replication and Extension of the Family Economic Stress Model in Finland." *Developmental Psychology* 40:412–29.

Super, Charles, M., Sara Harkness, Oumar Barry, and Marian Zeitlin. 2011. "Think Locally, Act Globally: Contributions of African Research to Child Development." *Child Development Perspectives* 5:119–25.

Surkan, Pamela J., Caitlin E. Kennedy, Kristen M. Hurley, and Maureen M. Black. 2011. "Maternal Depression and Early Childhood Growth in Developing Countries: Systematic Review and Meta-analysis." *Bulletin of the World Health Organization* 287:607–15.

United Nations. 2009. *Rethinking Poverty: Report on the World Social Situation 2010.* New York: UN Department of Economic and Social Affairs.

United Nations Children's Fund. 2006. *Multiple Indicator Cluster Survey Manual 2005: Monitoring the Situation of Children and Women.* New York: United Nations Children's Fund.

United Nations Children's Fund. 2012. *Inequities in Early Childhood Development: What the Data Say.* New York: United Nations Children's Fund.

Walker, Susan P., Theodore D. Wachs, Sally Grantham-McGregor, Maureen M. Black, Charles, A. Nelson, Sandra L. Huffman, Helen Baker-Henningham, Susan M. Chang, Jena D. Hamadani, Betsy Lozoff, Julie M. Meeks Gardner, Christine A. Powell, Atif Rahman, and Linda Richter. 2011. "Inequality in Early Childhood: Risk and Protective Factors for Child Development." *Lancet* 378:1325–38.

Walker, Susan, P., Theodore Wachs, Julie Gardner, Betsy Lozoff, Gail Wasserman, Ernesto Pollitt, Julie Carter, and the International Child Development Steering Group. 2007. "Child Development: Risk Factors for Adverse Outcomes in Developing Countries." *Lancet* 369:145–57.

Wilson, William J. 1987. *The Truly Disadvantaged: The Inner City, the Underclass and Public Policy.* Chicago: University of Chicago Press.

Wood, Dana, Rachel Kaplan, and Vonnie McLoyd. 2007. "Gender Differences in the Educational Expectations of Urban, Low-Income African American Youth: The Role of Parents and the School." *Journal of Youth and Adolescence* 36:417–27.

Zigler, Edward and Winnie Berman. 1983. "Discerning the Future of Early Childhood Intervention." *American Psychologist* 33:894–906.

SECTION II

CLASSIC DEBATES

CHAPTER 8

....

POVERTY KNOWLEDGE
AND THE HISTORY
OF POVERTY RESEARCH

....

ALICE O'CONNOR

In 1886 a wealthy British shipping merchant named Charles Booth began an investigation of social conditions in London's deeply impoverished East End slums. Tensions were high in the British capital, where the human costs of exploitative labor practices and overcrowded housing were growing more visible and, to the consternation of reform-minded capitalists like Booth, sending working-class militancy on the rise. Booth's study was one of many that countered the radicalism by embracing the social scientific temper of the times. Following an initial set of papers presented to fellow members of the Royal Statistical Society, the project quickly mushroomed into a far more encompassing citywide social survey—of income and wealth distribution, workplace conditions, and religious influences—that would be the basis of his 17-volume *Life and Labour of the People in London* (1889–1903). It also went on to become a standard-bearer for what was only then emerging as a self-consciously scientific tradition of poverty research, gaining recognition for its extensively documented findings and innovative research techniques, and spawning similar, if smaller-scale, inquiries throughout the Atlantic world. (Himmelfarb 1991; Walkowitz 1992; Bulmer, Bales, and Sklar 1992; O'Connor 2001). Though often conducted by self-described amateurs at the start, these proliferating studies signaled a turn to what would eventually become a more fully professionalized social scientific approach to defining, explaining, and grappling with the problem of poverty in the prosperous industrial democracies of the West.

This essay traces the initial emergence and subsequent evolution of that social scientific turn in the age-old practice of gathering knowledge about the poor, from its roots in Progressive Era social investigation through the later development of the multidisciplinary, increasingly globalized field of academic and applied policy inquiry we associate with poverty research today. It distinguishes between *poverty research*—a set of social scientific practices, protocols, and norms—and *poverty knowledge*—a way of defining and otherwise encountering the social problems presented by overlapping economic, racial, gendered, and ethnic inequalities—and argues that the convergence of the two should be understood as a historically specific development that first began to gain wide currency in the late nineteenth century in response to the vast and increasingly visible disparities of industrial capitalism in Western Europe and the United States. It shows how the tradition of poverty research that became dominant in American—and eventually global—policy circles had its origins in a transatlantic research and reform conversation, only later to become more differentiated across national and disciplinary lines during the post–World War II period of welfare-state building and Cold War politics. My discussion situates poverty research within the politics and social organization of knowledge, while also highlighting the influence of broader contextual factors, such as the experiences of deeply destabilizing economic crises and depressions; the creation, expansion, and subsequent restructuring of welfare states in Western industrial democracies; the geopolitical imperatives of empire, decolonization, and the Cold War; and the official declaration of the War on Poverty in the 1960s. After tracing the rise of an officially designated field of poverty research, rooted in the experience of mass affluence and the assumptions of Cold War liberalism and Keynesian economics, the discussion turns to how poverty knowledge was reshaped by the economic, political, and ideological transformations associated with the rise of neoliberalism, which despite powerful challenges from social scientific research remains the dominant framework in shaping debates about the nature and causes of poverty today.

Poverty Research and Transatlantic Reform

Two things made the publication of Booth's *Life and Labour* an important turning point in the history of poverty research. One was its insistence on treating poverty as a subject for empirical measurement rather than more explicitly moral or abstract political economic inquiry. The other was its association with a more wide-ranging and extended reform conversation that would culminate in the modern welfare state. In the immediate moment, however, what stood out as most novel about *Life and Labour* was the basic reformulation involved in its presentation of the poverty problem: away from the emphasis on preventing pauperism among the able-bodied that had been written into policy since the 1834 Poor Law Reforms in England and the launch of the era of the poorhouse there and in the United States, and toward the often conflicting anxieties embedded in the contemporary "labor question," which concerned itself with preventing the laboring masses from turning into a revolutionary proletariat (Polanyi 1944; Himmelfarb 1984; Katz 1996).

Poverty was deeper and more widespread than even radical critics had charged, Booth concluded, affecting one-third of city households, two-thirds in the East End, and a far vaster swath of the "respectable" working classes than popular stereotypes would allow. Low wages, irregular employment, and degraded work and living conditions were to blame—and not, as others before Booth had concluded, personal profligacy and vice. Booth backed these conclusions with extensive empirical data, culled from census statistics and employers but more distinctively from information provided by local school board officials, policemen, charity workers, and clergy who variously monitored and ministered to the poor. He relied, too, on the observations of an extensive staff of field researchers recruited from London's famed settlement houses. But more than any other single factor, what drew worldwide attention to *Life and Labour* were the minutely detailed, color-coded maps displaying the distribution of household income and class standing (black for the very poorest; gold for the most affluent) block by block and neighborhood by neighborhood throughout the city. The maps were magnified for stand-alone exhibition and emulated in studies of poverty throughout the industrialized Atlantic world. Most notable among the imitators were the *Hull House Maps and Papers* (Kelley [1895] 1970), produced by the residents of Jane Addams's famous settlement house, which displayed the overlapping geographies of work, wages, and ethnicity in Chicago's heavily immigrant and working-class 19th Ward. The Hull House maps helped propel the community-based social survey into American reform circles, which in turn became essential training grounds for a generation of empirical social investigation in the United States (Deegan 1988; Rodgers 1998; O'Connor 2001).

Later generations of poverty researchers have tended to neglect or distance themselves from the early social survey tradition, pointing especially to its failure to engage with or generate a body of theory about the social problems and dynamics under investigation. Equally problematic, from the standpoint of the way academic social science developed, was the explicit commitment to reform embedded in the survey tradition—even if that commitment was confined to raising public awareness through continuous, and artful, displays of empirical data. In reality, though, these early surveys of poverty were not entirely devoid of theoretical influences. They rested on a fairly coherent edifice of shared ideas and assumptions that enabled investigators to challenge long entrenched "laws," doctrines, and ways of thinking about political economy and the poor—and that, along with conventions such as Booth's "line of poverty," have subsequently been absorbed into the norms of modern, social scientific poverty research (Gillie 1996; Fisher 2004).

One was the idea that poverty could and should be quantified and categorized based on empirically observable measures such as household income, expenditures, and the cost of basic necessities, as distinct from the narrower, more explicitly moralized assessments of dependency or pauperism handed down from English Poor Law and associated with the need to distinguish between the deserving and undeserving in doling out poor relief. This idea was to find firmer scientific grounding with American agricultural chemist Wilbur O. Atwater's 1896 "discovery" of the calorie as a unit of measurement for calculating the amount and composition of food required for basic human subsistence—a measure in turn picked up by the British chocolate manufacturer-turned social investigator B. Seebohm Rowntree (1901) as the basis of the poverty line in his social survey of York. Second, and related, was the idea that poverty could no longer be considered an inevitable consequence—of the human condition, of Malthusian scarcity, of somehow immutable market or Darwinian evolutionary forces, or, in the language of Engels and Marx, of the immiseration of the proletarianized working class. Poverty could be reduced through reform and regulation, and various forms of social rehabilitation, without necessarily abandoning society's basic commitments to private property and the market economy. And third was the idea that such intervention was a legitimate function of the state, and an increasingly necessary one at a time when the nostrums of laissez-faire were coming under fire as the politically interested ideology of the rich and powerful within and across nations. No single one of these ideas was necessarily new. They combined elements of Enlightenment thinking, republican ideology, and, in the United States in particular, faith that conditions of exceptional plenty and political freedom (for some) would make it possible to escape the scourge of mass deprivation (Herndon 2001; Rockman 2009). Only later, though, in the late nineteenth and early twentieth centuries, and in the context of what would come to be referred to as progressive or "new liberal" reform, would they come together in the more empirically informed, less fatalistic, and more pragmatically meliorist view of poverty cultivated in transatlantic reform and philanthropic circles, and in the increasingly institutionalized social investigations they pursued (Furner 1993).

This is not to say that the self-consciously objective, empirical approach to studying the causes of poverty—or any poverty research for that matter—was devoid of moral judgment: to be classified in Booth's bottom-most black or dark blue categories was to suffer from more than the "vicissitudes of extreme hardship" or the uncertainties of market competition and depression; it was to be part of a "savage" or morally and mentally incapable element submerged within the much larger working class. Rowntree made a behavioral distinction between "primary" and "secondary" poverty, attributing the former to a lack of income adequate for basic subsistence and the latter to the inability live within what should be adequate means. Nor did the preoccupation with the prevention of pauperism by any means disappear. In a significant reversal of the standard formulation, American social reformer Robert Hunter (1904) dedicated his national-level survey of poverty to documenting the hardships of the impoverished working as distinguished from the small but demoralized "pauper" class and used the prospect of welfare dependency as an argument for higher wages, bans on child labor, expanded public health and workplace safety standards, and many other measures to stem the inequities of industrial capitalism. Even the most insistently empirical research, Hunter and his progressive colleagues understood, did not make these investigations apolitical or value free. Hunter drew on Booth and Rowntree in determining measurement standards, but his conclusion that poverty was rooted in economic "disorders" created by "the present ownership of the means and materials of production" (Hunter 1904:331) showed the influence of the socialist intellectuals he had encountered in his travels to Europe and temporary residence at London's Toynbee Hall—an experience common among American intellectuals and reformers at the time, as well as among a generation of social scientists who routinely took years of graduate training in European and especially in German universities, where they gained exposure to socialist, materialist, and more generally historical ways of thinking that would later be marginalized in the American academy (Furner 1975; Ross 1991:102–140).

Progressive intellectuals were less prepared to recognize the racial and gender ideologies embedded in their research. Despite challenges from an increasingly influential cadre of renegades including sociologist W. E. B. Du Bois and anthropologist Franz Boas, a substantial majority embraced eugenics as legitimate race "science" and treated white racial supremacy as established evolutionary fact (Barkan 1992; Recchiuti 2007). Progressives were also conflicted in their approach to the intertwined questions of women, work, and motherhood, advocating an ambiguous mix of protective labor legislation and maternalist social policy applied unevenly across the lines of class, race, and ethnicity, separating middle-class reformers from the people they aimed to help. Of course, in the hands of W. E. B. Du Bois (1899) and several contributors to the famed Pittsburgh Survey (Butler 1909), social surveys could be, and were, used deliberately to challenge and dispel rather than to reinforce the prejudices and pseudoscientific ideologies behind existing social hierarchies. From the start, then, grappling with ideas about race, gender, class, sexual behavior, and morality would continue to be an ambiguous, often unspoken dimension of scientific poverty research.

Structural Roots and Ongoing Transformations

Viewing social scientific poverty research as an outgrowth of the social survey tradition provides us with a reminder of its deeply moral and socially and politically embedded nature. It also draws attention to the importance of social structural and political developments in shaping the historical trajectory of poverty knowledge. Thus, Booth, Hunter, Du Bois and other Progressive Era investigators were laying the groundwork for modern poverty research in a particular historical moment, at the confluence of several structural, political, and social transformations that were changing the actual experience as well as broader social perceptions of poverty in Western industrial democracies. The relentless expansion of corporate industrial capitalism—itself the latest expression of a seemingly permanent market revolution—was the most visible of these, exposing millions to the harsh conditions of unregulated labor markets and low-paid factory work but also to the insecurities of the recurring financial panics and depressions that plagued the nineteenth-century economy. It is no coincidence that the survey movement got its start when these conditions were coming to unprecedented and visible heights during the especially grueling and long-lasting depression of the 1890s—which would remain unsurpassed in the extent and reach of its devastation until the Great Depression of the 1930s—and as an expression of what land reformer and single tax advocate Henry George called the "enigma" of "increase of want with increase of wealth" in his enormously popular and influential work of political economy *Progress and Poverty* (1879). Also important were the great migrations these disruptive market transformations helped instigate, which brought millions to industrial cities from rural and small-town locales within and across national borders, including the disproportionately Southern and Eastern European migrants who at the time constituted the ethnically other, so-called new immigrants to the United States. Poverty research was also profoundly influenced by the global march of European and, increasingly, of American empire, which brought elites of what would later become known as the Global North into real and imagined contact with a host of colonial "others" and created ongoing demands for knowledge of how various native populations would respond to their "civilizing" missions.

Partly in response to these changes, the historical moment that produced the large-scale social surveys was also one of social structural, political, and institutional transformation in the production of social and economic knowledge. The social surveyors themselves heralded one aspect of this transformation: the emergence of a class of highly educated reform intellectuals, many of them women and many taking somehow unconventional career paths, who embraced social investigation as an essential tool in their own efforts to shift from traditional if newly "scientific" charity, with its emphasis on saving individuals through agency-based casework and "friendly" home visitations, to organized philanthropy, with its emphasis on systematic research, legislation, and social change. There is no better example of this shift, and its role in linking poverty research to the work of reform, than the creation of the Russell Sage Foundation in 1907 by the widow of the notoriously mean-spirited industrialist for whom it was named, with the stated intention of funding research for social betterment. Notably, one of the biggest and most visible projects of the new foundation was the massive Pittsburgh Survey (1909–1914), which used a large and heterodox team of researchers and a highly inventive combination of research techniques to document the way the coming of corporate industrial capitalism was transforming the city, encompassing the home lives and the work lives of its residents as well as the socially stratified, environmentally devastated physical landscape (Crocker 2006; O'Connor 2007).

Ironically, other, contemporaneous aspects of the structural transformation of social knowledge would eventually come to mute the reformist sensibilities and marginalize the more amateur, female, and nonwhite practitioners of poverty research. One was the gradual expansion of the state in the production of knowledge about social and economic problems and conditions beyond what the census could reveal. Though resolutely empirical—statistical—in orientation, in its earliest stages this process was led by a decidedly reformist cadre of labor and race intellectuals employed in federal subagencies such as the Department of Labor's Bureau of Labor Statistics, Women's and Children's Bureaus, and the short-lived Division of Negro Economics. This reform impulse would eventually be overshadowed by growing demands for more neutralized expertise in the postwar state (Fitzpatrick 1990; Furner 1990; Hendrickson 2013).

The reform sensibility in early social science was also marginalized by the professionalization and disciplinary fragmentation of social and economic inquiry within the expanding research universities and corporatist policy think tanks funded by the Rockefeller Foundation and Carnegie Corporation among others, based on an increasingly scientistic ideology that conflated objectivity with academic disengagement and political neutrality. Here again the dynamics behind that distancing were complicated, taking place over the course of several decades and later accelerated by the Cold War era impulse to create a full-blown behavioral science on what were then considered to be the certainties and superior predictive capacities of the physical and natural sciences. In the interim, the idea of a politically engaged social science found a home in any number of New Deal agencies, in nongovernmental organizations from labor unions to the National Urban League, and continued to command at least grudging legitimacy in select academic circles through much of the 1940s. Thus, it was by drawing on a range of established theories and methods—and foundation funding—that Swedish economist Gunnar Myrdal produced *An American Dilemma* (1944) and St. Clair Drake and Horace Cayton *Black Metropolis* (1945), two classics of American social science literature that made profoundly important interventions into the highly charged World War II era discourse about race, poverty, and the future of democracy in the United States.

POSTWAR POVERTY KNOWLEDGE: THE COLD WAR AND THE WELFARE STATE

The influence of this constellation of political, structural, and institutional transformations—in capitalism, global empires, social investigation, and the state—would lead social science in a different, more exclusively professionalized and scientistic direction in the postwar United States. As postwar social science became caught up with the preoccupations of a self-consciously affluent society, "poverty" lost any traction it once might have had as a designated subfield of academic research or target of government intervention. These were critical decades for poverty research nonetheless. Conceptual frameworks that would later be deployed to explain the rediscovered "paradox" of poverty in an affluent society were being developed in research on employment, race, urbanization, and "third world" development. It was also during this period that the differences between European and American poverty knowledge came more fully into view, as transatlantic reform networks were displaced by the imperatives of welfare-state building and Cold War politics. The postwar development project had an enormous impact on social scientific research as well, leading to new subfields, such as development economics, while opening up whole new vistas—and funding streams—for studying poor people and places around the decolonizing world.

The trend toward professionalization in the social sciences could be seen in several lines of inquiry that, although not directly competing with or even in direct conversation with one another, represented increasingly divergent disciplinary ways of thinking about the nature of poverty and its significance. Generally speaking, though, postwar social science treated poverty as a symptom or outcome of more broadly conceived social problems and processes rather than as the more specialized subfield it would eventually become. To the limited extent they studied it at all, economists dealt with poverty as a problem of low wages, unemployment or underemployment, and, reflecting a new fascination, of insufficient human capital. Sociologists debated among themselves about whether a whole host of problems identified as distinctively lower class—such as low school achievement and juvenile delinquency—should be seen as symptoms of internalized social "disorganization" or structured social stratification. An especially influential line of thinking, associated principally with the University of Chicago tradition of urban sociology, treated poverty as part of a naturalized cycle of resettlement and readjustment experienced by successive waves of predominantly rural and small-town migrants to industrial cities. Poverty was a symptom of the socially and institutionally disruptive, or "disorganizing," influences of urban life on the uprooted rural peasantries of Europe and the American South, in the idealized Chicago-school model, and would be a temporary or at most one-generation condition as migrants made their way to a "reorganized" state of assimilation. A growing cadre of development experts conceptualized poverty within the framework of economic and cultural modernization, which rested on a vision of history as an unwaveringly forward moving and universal progression from a traditional, agrarian, hierarchical, communal past to a modern, industrial, democratic, individuated future (Gilman 2004). As a problem of underdevelopment, poverty was endemic to communities and decolonizing third world countries left behind, exploited, or simply without the economic and cultural resources necessary to get and stay on the modernizing path.

In their common emphasis on personal and group attributes, individual choices, and cultural and social psychological processes as explanations for poverty, these otherwise divergent lines of inquiry reflected the influence of the government- and foundation-subsidized behavioral revolution in American social science—and more generally of a Cold War–heightened intolerance for analysis that could be deemed subversive of American free enterprise. Even labor markets, it turns out, could be understood as naturalized wage-setting processes and individual choices linking supply and demand rather than institutionally embedded and politically negotiated practices influenced by laws and policies. In their more general disregard for poverty as a serious problem affecting the United States, the social sciences also reflected the growing ease with which poor people and economic hardship could be rendered invisible in the context of postwar affluence, white middle- and working-class prosperity, and suburbanization. Other scholars, wary of the narrowing of what C. Wright Mills called the "sociological imagination," continued to offer more structural and theoretically critical perspectives and to view poverty as a reflection of the power and wealth disparities embedded in the hierarchies of class, race, patriarchy, and place through which elites maintained their privileges and kept potentially unruly minorities at bay (Mills 1959). Suspect though it may have seemed in the chilled atmosphere of the Cold War university, much of this more structuralist thinking drew directly from European—albeit non-Marxist—social theory: Max Weber for understandings of stratification rooted in social and political status as well as economic class; British structural-functionalists for ideas about racial caste; French sociologist Emile Durkheim's concept of structurally induced social *anomie* for explanations of lower class deviance; and British social policy intellectuals Richard Titmuss and T. H. Marshall for ideas about the role—and obligations—of government in creating and (re)distributing social resources (Merton 1938; Weber 1946; Marshall 1964; Miller and Roby 1970; Brick 2006). Still, while various explanations could be found throughout the social and behavioral sciences, poverty was very much treated as a residual in the affluent society: as a social problem, as a social experience, and as a subject for social and economic research. When it did re-emerge as a public issue, formulated as the lingering "paradox" in the midst of such widespread plenty, even the more structurally inclined analysts became fascinated with the internalized mechanisms through which poor people and places supposedly perpetuated their own oppression and became entrapped in all sorts of behavioral and cultural "cycles" that, in the language current at the time, were becoming more difficult to "break." The great "enigma" Henry George presented in *Progress and Poverty*, in other words, was being presented less and less as a commentary on the skewed distribution of wealth, and more and more as a need to understand the pathologies of the poor.

Thus it was as a field researcher in sites targeted for economic development—in Mexico, India, and Puerto Rico—that anthropologist Oscar Lewis began to gather and eventually create an inventory of the economic and character "traits" that formed the basis of his controversial theory of the "culture of poverty," first fully articulated in 1959 (Lewis 1959; Rigdon 1988; O'Connor 2001). Distilled from progressively more sensationalistic life histories and elaborate—later discredited—batteries of psychological tests, Lewis's inventory came to include a hodgepodge of behaviors, attitudes, values, personal habits, and psychological disorders that he claimed to have found among especially marginalized subgroups of poor people who could not adjust to the demands of modernization and who found themselves at the very bottom of their suddenly class-stratified capitalist societies. Once filtered through the channels of Cold War discourse, Lewis's concept quickly lost any hint of systemic or potentially subversive critique—as it did in the work of Lewis himself, who lavished far more attention on the deviant behavior sanctioned within the culture of poverty than on its structural roots. Even in the hands of socialist critic Michael Harrington, who popularized the concept in his book *The Other America* calling attention to the plight of a socially invisible, psychologically alienated substrata of the poor, the culture of poverty did more to underscore the otherness of poor people than to implicate the failures of democratic capitalism—an outcome Harrington later came to regret (Harrington 1962; Isserman 2000).

Chicago-school sociology would follow a similar pathway in the still-emerging canons of poverty research, in this case from social process to internalized cultural pathology, when it came to explaining why certain already urbanized minorities—African Americans and Puerto Ricans in particular—remained so disproportionately poor decades after they had embarked on great migrations in search of better lives. The early Chicago school had already contributed importantly to the behavioral redirection in social research, by pivoting its explanatory framework around assimilation processes rather than labor market inequities, by diminishing the depth and structural nature of racial barriers facing African Americans and other nonwhite minorities, and by obscuring the degree to which the patterns of segregation and uneven mobility encompassed within its naturalistic theories were rooted in actively discriminatory, officially sanctioned policies and social practices. To be sure, there were important exceptions to what Gunnar Myrdal criticized, caustically, as the "do-nothing (laissez-faire)" bias in Chicago school social ecology (Myrdal 1944:1045). Chicago-trained sociologist Charles S. Johnson, then employed as research director for the Chicago Urban League, used the Chicago-school's cyclical theory of racial conflict in his investigation of the devastating Chicago race riots of 1919, ultimately concluding that competition from migration could not explain the extent, or the deliberately planned, officially sanctioned nature of the racial violence (Chicago Commission 1923). Drake and Cayton (1945) similarly drew on Chicago's assimilationist framework to show that African Americans were not following the trajectory of progress it predicted, and that institutionalized color lines in employment, housing, and social relations were to blame. And yet, by the time Daniel Patrick Moynihan (1965) appropriated one of the most influential ideas ever to emerge from Chicago-school sociology—E. Franklin Frazier's concept of the matriarchal Negro family structure, inherited from slavery and subsequently caught up in the disorganizing pathologies of urban life—he had a substantial trove of social science literature on the psychologically and culturally deviant lower class Negro to back up his sensationalistic claims that the black family had hardened into a self-perpetuating cultural pathology that threatened to send lower class African Americans into permanent poverty and welfare dependency (Frazier 1939; Scott 1997).

Riddled as they were with superficial observations, relentlessly negative stereotypes, and chauvinistic cultural assumptions of their own, it has not been difficult to find resonance between these depictions of cultural pathology and the age-old tradition of denouncing the undeserving poor (Katz 2013; Gans 1995). And indeed, in short order both the Moynihan Report and culture of poverty concept had become part of the conservative and neoconservative arsenal in escalating attacks on the character of poor people—minority youth and single mothers in particular—and on the alleged permissiveness of the liberal welfare state (Banfield 1970; O'Connor 2008). It is important to recognize, though, that these ideas had very deep roots in postwar liberal social science and would continue to be deployed throughout the 1960s in support of remedial cycle-of-poverty-breaking interventions at home and in the developing world. Nor were ideas about cultural deprivation seen to be incompatible with the employment and labor market emphasis adopted by liberal economists who were turning their attention to poverty at the time. While generally eschewing culture and psychology as meaningful frameworks for analysis, they, too, were convinced that explanations for the lingering problem of poverty could be located in the attributes of poor people and households—the absence of a male breadwinner, the lack of marketable skills—that prevented them from getting access to the opportunities and protections that a growing economy could and would provide. Economic growth at full employment remained the sine qua non of poverty prevention in the eyes of the Keynesian economists who assumed positions of influence in the Kennedy and Johnson administrations. Education, job training, and other human capital building and remedial interventions, they thought, would break down most remaining barriers to a more inclusive prosperity. It was in this form, and as part of a discourse that focused narrowly on the character and characteristics of the poor, that the idea of a deviant, self-sabotaging, but ultimately remediable subculture became absorbed into the canon of American poverty research and continues to exert a powerful influence to this day.

Though not necessarily unique to the American discourse, this "othering" tendency in poverty knowledge was only further heightened by the domestic politics of race, which played an especially powerful role in the United States in light of its long and agonizing history of slavery, racial apartheid, race-based restrictions on property ownership, and racially charged immigration policies and practices. It was also built into the structure of the U.S. welfare state, which stood apart from its European counterparts in its preference for means-tested rather than universalistic social provision and the number of politically negotiated categorical exclusions that served to deepen existing racial—as well as class and gender—inequities (Gordon 1990; Quadagno 1994; Lieberman 1998; Katznelson 2005). European and American social scientists were more apt to find common ground in the newly expanded and internationalized venues for research, social experimentation, and policy expertise in the so-called emerging nations of Africa, Asia, and Latin America. Joined in the project of putting highly diverse countries on parallel—if not necessarily singular—pathways to economic growth and political and social democratization, the economists, anthropologists, political sociologists, and demographers who played leading roles in development networks came to view third world poverty as part of a more generalized problem of economic, social, and cultural underdevelopment, or traditionalism—and as such altogether distinct from the more isolated "paradox" of want in the land of plenty. While by no means representing a consensus or even a majority view, American ideas about modernization, and about the combination of technocratic top-down and "indigenous" or community-based interventions that would speed its advance, came to dominate in the immediate postwar decades, thanks in no small part to the funding streams generated by President Harry S. Truman's Point IV program of international aid; American influence in newly created international relief and redevelopment agencies such as the World Health Organization and the World Bank; and the ever-more expansive global ambitions of U.S. foundations, led by Rockefeller, Carnegie, and Ford (Cooper and Packard 1997; Latham 2000; Cullather 2010; Ekbladh 2010; Goldstein 2012). Poverty was not seen as the central issue in the development-as-modernization scheme; more important was to identify and create the conditions for capitalist markets and economic growth (Finnemore 1997; Alacevich 2009).

Poverty "Rediscovered"

Several things came together in the early 1960s to put poverty on the map as a subject for academic and government-sponsored research in the United States. Major foundations, having already made a huge investment in modernization theory and area studies as intellectual underpinnings for international development policy, were drawn to poverty as an overarching and unifying concept for the interventions they were sponsoring worldwide. Poverty also held promise as a unifying concept for hitherto uncoordinated domestic programs—in education, social service delivery, and juvenile delinquency prevention—especially in cities struggling with the impact of industrial job loss, white flight, and fears of unrest in the ghettoized neighborhoods of black and brown working classes (O'Connor 2001; Ferguson 2013). The Kennedy administration was also mounting various lines of "attack" on poverty—first global, then domestic—having made it a theme in the 1960 presidential campaign. John F. Kennedy announced the Peace Corps and the Alliance for Progress (in Latin America) in 1961 as first steps toward fulfilling his pledge to join with the United Nations to make the 1960s the "decade of development" and in a larger effort to expand the arsenal of soft power in the Cold War battle for the allegiances of the third world (Latham 2000). Development would also become a keynote of intervention at home, with the successful passage of the long sought-after Area Redevelopment Act in 1961 and a series of experimental urban social service and systems reform initiatives funded by the National Institute of Mental Health. Meantime, a network of academic-, government-, and advocacy group-affiliated social work and social policy intellectuals, activated earlier in the 1950s out of concern over growing numbers of never-married single mothers seeing assistance, realized important legislative successes in their efforts to make Aid to Dependent Children (aka "welfare") a more rehabilitative system that would provide better services and encourage "independence" through work (Mittelstadt 2005).

Nothing was more important in stimulating the growth and defining the initial parameters of poverty research as a social scientific and applied research field, though, than President Lyndon B. Johnson's declaration of the War on Poverty in his January 1964 State of the Union address. The War on Poverty also heightened and exaggerated certain features that, although to some degree already there, would distinguish American-style poverty research from counterpart approaches in European and Nordic welfare states—beginning with the fact that poverty would become the focus of a specialized, multidisciplinary subfield detached from the broader social scientific study of inequality. It would also be the target of a new agency, the Office of Economic Opportunity (OEO), specifically designated to cut through existing bureaucratic channels to make ending poverty its singular priority. Poverty research, as cultivated within the OEO, would be heavily quantitative, statistical and ostensibly atheoretical in orientation, and defined around a fairly circumscribed set of questions about the characteristics of poor people and the measurable outcomes of antipoverty policies. The study of inequality continued, but poverty research as an official matter became about something else—siphoned off, as it were, as a more narrowly construed study of depri-vation (Katz 2013). Important things changed about the practice of poverty research as well. Economists took it up in earnest, as did policy analysts trained in economic research and techniques. It was more and more conducted in specialized academic and contract-research institutions, and in newly created social policy think tanks seeking to emulate what they viewed as the efficiency, applicability, and cost-beneficial achieve-ments of the RAND Corporation and other elements of the Cold War defense research industry. Research would become part of the arsenal of knowledge in the ambitious sights of the War on Poverty. Once again, poverty would be the site of methodological innovation in social research, this time with an emphasis on demographic and budget-ary modeling, large-scale random assignment social experimentation, and outcomes-based program evaluation. For all the effort to apply seemingly apolitical techniques, poverty research would also be driven by an increasingly volatile and explicitly racial-ized politics of fighting poverty, and of welfare reform.

LBJ's announcement immediately generated a great deal of activity in response to the demand, and political incentives, for the kind of poverty knowledge that would meet the newly expansive imperatives of an official policy strategy that had by no means been thought out. It also paved the way for some immediate, largely political deci-sions that would have long-term consequences for the future of poverty research. One demand was for an official definition of the problem—preferably one that could readily be tied to some measurable indicator that the war was being, and ultimately would be, officially won: poverty had to be defined as something that could be eliminated, as LBJ had pledged. This line of thinking proved especially influential in the decision, after substantial internal debate, to define poverty narrowly as a lack of income adequate to sustain a minimal standard of living. The measure of poverty would be absolute rather than relationally defined to a standard such as median income; it would be an assess-ment of individual and household economic need rather than of the institutions and practices that produced political, economic, and social disenfranchisement, as many—including leading figures in European social research—were advocating from within as well as outside official planning circles at the time (Townsend 1962). Another, related decision was for an official standard for measuring income (in)adequacy that could be used as a yardstick for tracking progress but, equally important at the launch, also for determining target groups and eligibility criteria for the wide range of new programs (including Head Start and Job Corps) being generated within the newly created OEO. This is what led to the adoption in 1965 of what is today known as the Orshansky poverty line.

Few were more aware of the limitations of the Orshansky poverty line—especially as an official measure of economic need—than Mollie Orshansky herself. A career government analyst who had moved from earlier stints in the Children's Bureau and the Department of Agriculture (DOA) to the Social Security Administration's (SSA) research division, Orshansky originally came up with the basic formula while working to revise the SSA's protocols for gathering statistical data on low-income families with children—essential data, of course, for the agency responsible for administering both

Social Security survivors' benefits and the Aid to Families with Dependent Children (AFDC) program. Building on the social survey tradition and her own experience assessing family food budgets while at the DOA, Orshansky developed a series of poverty thresholds for families of varying size and age (elderly/nonelderly) based on mid-1950s survey data showing that families spent one-third of household income on food: her poverty thresholds, eventually adopted by the OEO as the official measure, were based on the cost of the DOA's minimalistic economy food plan, multiplied by three and adjusted for family size. Orshansky was among those who drew attention to the limitations of her measure—which, though an improvement over the arbitrary across-the-board figure ($3,000) in use at the time, she regarded as highly provisional and bare bones as an assessment of need. Others pointed out its failure to account for wide variations in the cost of living across geographic areas, among other problems. These and other criticisms notwithstanding, the OEO adopted Orshansky's thresholds in 1965, largely in response to growing pressure from watchful critics, but also to bring some veneer of scientific precision to officially defined poverty and, by extension, to criteria that would be used in determining program eligibility and making budget projections. Since then, the Orshansky poverty line has found few active defenders and a growing chorus of criticism, especially as the cost of food has shrunk dramatically in comparison to other, unacknowledged expenses such as housing, health care, transportation, and child care. As of 2011, the Census Bureau has officially acknowledged these and other inadequacies, albeit obliquely, by publishing a separate Supplemental Poverty Measure alongside the official poverty-line statistics, based on an approach recommended by a National Academy of Sciences panel in 1995. Still, the approach to "counting the poor" (as Orshansky dubbed her initial project) adopted in 1965 retains pride of place as the official poverty measure, kept there by the same combination of expediency and competing political pressures that led to its adoption 50 years ago.

The War on Poverty shaped agendas in various subfields of social and economic research as well, as social scientific networks (and their foundation sponsors) organized to influence public intervention, to respond to the state's growing demand for "usable" programmatic and policy knowledge, and to vie for newly available funding streams. Early childhood was a major growth area for research, reflecting both the enduring political appeal of saving children and the policy entrepreneurship of an emerging network of child development experts who were positioned to take advantage of the administration's immediate need for ideas about how to make good on LBJ's promise to bring poverty to an end, and, more specifically, to OEO's inchoate commitment to "breaking the cycle of poverty" by targeting cultural deprivation among the poor. The establishment of the high-profile (if persistently underfunded) Head Start program was something of a triumph for a widening but as yet largely untested set of ideas about early childhood—about cognitive capacity as malleable, about psychological development as linked to the holistic health and well-being of the child, about early intervention as having lifelong effects (Vinovskis 2005; Zigler and Styfco 2010). It also marked a major investment in a distinctive if historically familiar idea of social policy development and reform, that to date had been cultivated primarily in foundation and more sporadically in federal agency funded projects, as expert driven, grounded in demonstration research, and managed (or engineered) through replicable interventions designed to yield predictable social outcomes. Youth employment and training, itself an offshoot of the Kennedy-Johnson administration's pre–War on Poverty investments in juvenile delinquency prevention, became the focus of a similarly applied subfield of labor economics, thanks to youth-targeted programs such as the Job Corps. In an ironic twist in the trajectory of postwar overseas development, the War on Poverty created an opening for reimporting concepts and interventions honed in putatively underdeveloped nations to communities—in Appalachia, the American Indian Southwest, the rural South, and, more and more, the deindustrializing Rust Belt—said to be stuck in third world conditions in the midst of American plenty (Goldstein 2012; Ferguson 2013). It also generated an expanding demand for evaluation research, here again reflecting the technocratic faith in applied expertise and engineered social change that had become entrenched in the Great Society welfare state more broadly, but also responding to the administration's deep investment in a cost-benefit decision-making model borrowed from the Defense Department funded RAND Corporation, that called above all for assessing program effectiveness through concrete, quantifiable input and outcome measures (O'Connor 2001).

Much of what was being absorbed into the dominant and rapidly growing canon of official poverty knowledge was subject to criticism from scholars, politicians, social service providers, and from within the rank and file of variously mobilized poor people's movements. Program evaluation was an increasingly volatile area of contention, as service providers questioned the validity of hastily constructed outcomes measures, and resisted the idea of withholding services for the sake of the evaluation research industry "gold standard" of control group experimental design. The immense controversy surrounding the Moynihan Report was but the best known among a wider range of field-shaping debates, over the conceptual vagaries and methodological flaws of the culture of poverty in particular, that would invigorate theoretically critical and otherwise alternative lines of social research. Now-classic works of urban ethnography such as Elliot Liebow's *Tally's Corner* (1967) and Carol Stack's *All Our Kin* (1974) challenged the idea that a pathologically damaged, matriarchal subculture had taken hold of the black family and was permanently emasculating black men—in many ways anticipating critiques later levied by feminist theorists of poverty and the welfare state (Gordon 1990). Others pointed to the limitations of Great Society political economy and economic analysis, noting the administration's failure to acknowledge the structural disadvantages faced by workers displaced by automation, by minorities and women shut out of better jobs, and by women with childcare responsibilities, as well as cities threatened by industrial job loss (Weir 1992; Russell 2003; McKee 2008). In their highly influential book *Regulating the Poor* (1971), political scientist Frances Fox Piven and sociologist Richard Cloward shifted the focus of analysis entirely, to capitalism as a system of unequal political and social relations that revolved around employers' need for an impoverished, politically complacent working class in order to thrive. Each of these varied interventions was influential in its own right, with wider reverberations in research, practice, and, in the case of Piven and Cloward in particular, social movement activism. The concept of cultural pathology—with its multiple variants—continued to cast a long shadow over public debate nevertheless, especially when deployed by conservative intellectuals and politicians in their concerted campaign to dismantle the welfare state.

Few things were more important in influencing the larger course of American poverty research than the overheated politics of welfare reform. Although the specter of "dependency" was never wholly absent from debates about poverty and relief, racial resentments over the ghetto uprisings of the mid-1960s made the specter of an entrenched and entitled class of welfare recipients an especially potent lightening rod for politically mobilized backlash against Great Society liberalism and, in turn, for movement building on the part of the emergent conservative Right. In the hands of newly elected President Richard M. Nixon—here borrowing from his specially appointed urban affairs advisor Daniel Patrick Moynihan—exaggerated claims of a looming welfare "crisis" had direct repercussions for poverty research. This became immediately apparent in the fate of the enormously ambitious guaranteed income experiments launched by the OEO in the late 1960s and subsequently picked up by the research offices of the Department of Health Education and Welfare in the wake of the poverty agency's demise. Designed in the heady days of the War on Poverty—as staff economists were generating budgets projecting an end of poverty in 1976—the experiments became subjects of unwelcome scrutiny and growing controversy once Nixon announced his sweeping Family Assistance Plan to replace categorical assistance with a minimal guaranteed income in 1969 (O'Connor 1998).

Notably, the 1960s did not spur a parallel "rediscovery" of poverty in Europe nor anything like the expansive but narrowly targeted poverty research industry that emerged in the United States. Here again, differences in European/American welfare state development proved key. In wealthy European democracies, where measures of poverty were more likely to be tied to median income and a basic social commitment to ending deprivation were embedded in social welfare policy, concern about poverty emerged in the context of rising unemployment, inflation, and economic restructuring that threatened prosperity during the 1970s and as part of a broader problem of "social exclusion" as traditional channels of incorporation proved inadequate to challenges ranging from long-term unemployment to rising immigration and changing family structure. The discourse of social exclusion has complex origins and over time has evolved along divergent lines—in some iterations coming to resemble a European version of the "underclass" debate. Nevertheless, in its basic orientation—relational, structural and institutional, multidimensional, solidaristic—the concept continues to underscore the differences more than the similarities in European and American poverty knowledges (Silver 1994; Levitas 2000; Silver and Miller 2003).

POVERTY KNOWLEDGE
AND NEOLIBERAL REFORM

Though important in their own right, the political fixation on welfare reform in the United States and the emerging discourse of social exclusion in Europe also stemmed from deeper transformations that would have profound importance for the politics and future direction of poverty research. These transformations were heralded by the electoral victories of Prime Minister Margaret Thatcher in England (1979) and President Ronald Reagan in the United States (1980)—the latter on an aggressively antistatist platform built on the back of a mythical "welfare queen." Equally challenging for the avowedly nonideological poverty research establishment was the fact that the self-proclaimed Reagan-Thatcher "revolution" was accompanied by the quieter, behind the scenes mobilization of a conservative counterestablishment anchored in the explicitly ideological foundations, think tanks, advocacy organizations, legal institutes, and media outlets of the Right. Reagan memorably provided the rhetorical frame for a new era of poverty research, which made ending dependency its central focus and put the existing poverty research establishment on the defensive. "My friends," Reagan said in a quip that drew laughter during his 1988 State of the Union address and has been quoted countless times since, "some years ago the federal government declared war on poverty and poverty won" (Reagan 1988). But it was the foot soldiers of the self-styled conservative counterintelligentsia who marshaled the tools of policy analysis to mount an outright war on welfare and on the Keynesian underpinnings of postwar political economy, with lasting effects. With Charles Murray's *Losing Ground* (1984) serving as something of a template, conservative movement think tanks such as the Heritage Foundation, the American Enterprise Institute, the Manhattan Institute, and the Cato Institute issued a steady barrage of books, reports, and, especially, well-placed policy briefs arguing that government intervention only made things worse—generally by coddling bad behavior, interfering in markets, and making it more profitable to rely on welfare than to work. These missives sent shudders through a poverty research establishment still reeling from the impact of the Reagan administration's budget cuts and efforts to "defund the Left," and led to various efforts to challenge the right-wing think tanks on empirical and methodological grounds. Such challenges would only go so far, though, in debates that had never been driven or resolved with empirical evidence alone and that would increasingly be framed around an artificially conceived ideological consensus that too much welfare and too little self-sufficiency, to paraphrase Ronald Reagan, was the problem, not the cure.

The influence of neoliberal policies and ideology could be seen in research in developing countries as well, with somewhat paradoxical results. Having embraced poverty reduction as an official goal in the late 1960s under the leadership of former Secretary of Defense (and Vietnam War architect) Robert S. McNamara, the World Bank's dramatic turn toward market-friendly structural adjustment practices in the 1980s set the stage for its adoption of an extremely narrow and minimalistic global poverty line ($370 or the now proverbial "dollar a day") starting in 1990. Although some have applauded the measure as an essential step toward the commitment embodied in the subsequently adopted Millennium Development Goal of cutting poverty in half by 2015, others have criticized its narrow focus on income and deliberate avoidance of the rising inequality within and between nations that neoliberal structural adjustment has helped bring about. At the same time, neoliberalism's globalizing thrust also became a focal point for more far-reaching and variegated debates about the nature, roots, and measurement of poverty from within developing countries, including research that stems from Amartya Sen's capabilities and associated human development frameworks, and that has drawn attention to the significance of the status of women as both an indicator and a factor in overall social well-being (Tinker 1990; Sen 1999; Anand, Segal, and Stiglitz 2010).

With the neoliberal turn in policy and politics heralding the "end of welfare as we know it" in the United States, it appeared that poverty research and policy had come full circle, to return to the obsession with preventing pauperism that Charles Booth and other Progressive Era social investigators had set out to combat in 1886. In reality, the impulse to pauperize the poverty problem had never entirely disappeared from either popular or social scientific discourse. Despite being couched in the neutralized language of quantification, newly configured distinctions between short- and long-term welfare recipients reflected age-old concerns about undeservingness and, like the growing tendency to draw a line between welfare recipients and the "working poor," helped naturalize the designation of welfare as a stigmatized, socially undesirable state. Meantime, the fallout from the end of welfare has created ever more ways of categorizing the poor, as evaluations of the welfare-replacing Temporary Assistance for Needy Families (TANF) program distinguish among various groups of welfare "leavers," for example, and between presumably permanent leavers and "recividists" in measuring the program's performance over time (Acs and Loprest 2002; Mueser, Stephens, and Troske 2007). More recently, the notion of "deep" or "extreme" poverty has emerged to highlight the growth in the proportion of poor people—largely as a result of the end of most welfare entitlements and the long-term erosion of the safety net—living at or below half the poverty line, a concept one might also think of as a measure of the shift from poverty to pauperism in policy and research (Edelman 2013).

Pauperism is not the only once-discredited concept to reappear in recent poverty research. Despite its well-known and widely documented flaws, Moynihan's "tangle of pathology" has continually been resurrected as a way of talking about ghettoized urban poverty and African American families, initially in the context of the "underclass" debates of the late 1980s and early 1990s and more recently in a variety of efforts to redeem Moynihan's reputation as a prescient social scientist and cultural analyst (Wilson 1987; Patterson 2010; Gans 2011). Especially striking, in light of the ubiquitous abuses of genetics and "race science" in the not-too-distant past, has been the reintroduction and rapid proliferation of genetic and other forms of biological research in poverty research, as seen in a wide range of studies focused on the consequences of exposure to socioeconomic-related stress on health and cognition among children and youth, and more generally on the interaction between genetic inheritance and environment in determining socioeconomic outcomes (Stern 2005; S. Roberts 2009; D. Roberts 2011; Katz 2013:44–49; Kim et al. 2013; Miller and Chen 2013; Gopnik 2013). Scholars engaged in this research might emphasize that their approach is based on an understanding that human biology is not destiny and indeed is mediated by a number of malleable environmental factors. There is no intent, in other words, to revive the notion that poverty is bred in a lower class gene pool, as Richard Hernstein and Charles Murray argued in their incendiary book *The Bell Curve* (1996). Still, the stakes are high: as researchers put faith in seemingly incontrovertible findings that risk playing into a kind of soft determinism about the trajectory of poor children without access to preventive intervention; in a science that risks regressing into a search for yet another set of markers that distinguish certain groups of poor people from everyone else; and in research technologies that rely on an increased capacity to gather genetic data and track physiological responses—a kind of information gathering widely subject to misinterpretation and abuse.

Driven though it may be by breakthroughs in biological research, the most historically significant fact about the growing fascination with understanding the nexus of biology, culture, and behavior in poverty research is that it is taking place against the backdrop of visibly rising structural inequality—at a time when the fruits of economic growth go overwhelmingly to those at the very top of the income and wealth distribution, when poverty has been experienced by a growing proportion of people with at least a tenuous foothold in the middle or working class, and during which a growing proportion of people in poverty have jobs (Rank 2004; Hacker and Pierson 2010; Edelman 2013). Poverty, then, is ever more visibly a dimension of the insecurity and hardship that come with the kinds of structural and political transformations in capitalism that put "life and labour" at the center of poverty knowledge more than a century ago and that have led a number of contemporary social scientists to challenge the dominant tradition in poverty research today (Schram 2002; Grusky and Kanbur 2006; Brady 2009).

REFERENCES

Acs, Gregory and Pamela Loprest. 2002. "Studies of Welfare Leavers: Data, Methods, and Contributions to the Policy Process." Assistant Secretary for Planning and Evaluation. Washington, DC: U.S. Department of Health and Human Services. Retrieved August 15, 2013 (http://aspe.hhs.gov/hsp/welf-res-data-issues02/12/12.htm).

Alacevich, Michele. 2009. *The Political Economy of the World Bank: The Early Years.* Stanford, CA: Stanford University Press.

Anand, Sudhir, Paul Segal, and Joseph E. Stiglitz, eds. 2010. *Debates on the Measurement of Global Poverty.* New York: Oxford University Press.

Banfield, Edward C. 1970. *The Unheavenly City: The Nature and Future of our Urban Crisis.* Boston: Little, Brown.

Barkan, Elazar. 1992. *The Retreat of Scientific Racism: Changing Concepts of Race in Britain and the United States between the World Wars*. New York: Cambridge University Press.

Booth, Charles. 1889. *Life and Labour of the People in London*. London: MacMillan.

Brady, David. 2009. *Rich Democracies, Poor People: How Politics Explain Poverty*. New York: Oxford University Press.

Brick, Howard. 2006. *Transcending Capitalism: Visions of a New Society in Modern American Thought*. Ithaca, NY: Cornell University Press.

Bulmer, Martin, Kevin Bales, and Kathryn Kish Sklar, eds. 1992. *The Social Survey in Historical Perspective, 1880–1940*. New York: Cambridge University Press.

Butler, Elizabeth Beardsley. 1909. *Women and the Trades*. New York: Russell Sage Foundation.

Cooper, Frederick and Randall Packard, eds. 1997. *International Development and the Social Sciences: Essays on the History and Politics of Knowledge*. Berkeley: University of California Press.

Chicago Commission on Race Relations. 1923. *The Negro in Chicago: A Study of Race Relations and a Race Riot*. Chicago: University of Chicago Press.

Crocker, Ruth. 2006. *Mrs. Russell Sage: Women's Activism and Philanthropy in Gilded Age and Progressive Era America*. Bloomington: Indiana University Press.

Cullather, Nick. 2010. *The Hungry World: America's Cold War Battle against Poverty in Asia*. Cambridge, MA: Harvard University Press.

Deegan, Mary Jo. 1988. *Jane Addams and the Men of the Chicago School*. New York: Transaction.

Drake, St. Clair and Horace R. Cayton. [1945] 1962. *Black Metropolis: A Study of Negro Life in a Northern City*. New York: Harper and Row.

Du Bois, W. E. B. [1899] 1996. *The Philadelphia Negro: A Social Study*. Philadelphia: University of Pennsylvania Press.

Edelman, Peter. 2013. *So Rich, So Poor: Why It's So Hard to End Poverty in America*. New York: New Press.

Ekbladh, David. 2010. *The Great American Mission: Modernization and the Construction of an American World Order*. Princeton, NJ: Princeton University Press.

Ferguson, Karen. 2013. *Top Down: The Ford Foundation, Black Power, and the Reinvention of Racial Liberalism*. Philadelphia, PA: University of Pennsylvania Press.

Finnemore, Martha. 1997. "Redefining Development at the World Bank." Pp. 203–27 in *International Development and the Social Sciences*, edited by Frederick Cooper and Randall Packard. Berkeley: University of California Press.

Fisher, Gordon. 1997. "From Hunter to Orshansky: An Overview of (Unofficial) Poverty Lines in the United States from 1904–1965." Washington, DC: U.S. Bureau of the Census. Retrieved August 15, 2013 (https://www.census.gov/hhes/povmeas/publications/povthres/fisher4.html).

Fitzpatrick, Ellen. 1990. *Endless Crusade: Women Social Scientists and Progressive Reform*. New York: Oxford University Press.

Frazier, E. Franklin. 1939. *The Negro Family in the United States*. Chicago: University of Chicago Press.

Furner, Mary O. 1975. *Advocacy and Objectivity: A Crisis in the Professionalization of American Social Science*. Lexington: University of Kentucky Press.

Furner, Mary O. 1990. "Knowing Capitalism: Public Investigation of the Labor Question in the Long Progressive Era." Pp. 241–86 in *The State and Economic Knowledge: The American and British Experience*, edited by Mary O. Furner and Barry Supple. New York: Cambridge University Press.

Furner, Mary O. 1993. "The Republican Tradition and the New Liberalism: Social Investigation, State Building, and Social Learning in the Gilded Age." Pp. 171–241 in *The State and Social Investigation in Britain and the United States*, edited by Michael J. Lacey and Mary O. Furner. New York: Cambridge University Press.

Gans, Herbert J. 1995. *The War against the Poor: The Underclass and Antipoverty Policy*. New York: Basic Books.

Gans, Herbert. 2011. "The Moynihan Report and Its Aftermaths." *Du Bois Review: Social Science Research on Race* 8(2):315–27.

George, Henry. [1879] 1948. *Progress and Poverty*. New York: Robert Schalkenbach Foundation.

Gillie, Allen. 1996. "The Origin of the Poverty Line." *Economic History Review* 49(4):715–30.

Gilman, Nils. 2004. *Mandarins of the Future: Modernization in Cold War America*. Baltimore, MD: Johns Hopkins University Press.

Goldstein, Alyosha. 2012. *Poverty in Common: The Politics of Community Action during the American Century*. Durham: Duke University Press.

Gopnik, Allison. 2013. "Poverty Can Trump a Winning Hand of Genes." *Wall Street Journal*, September 20. Retrieved April 18, 2014 (http://online.wsj.com/news/articles/SB1000142412 7887324492604579083060346652476).

Gordon, Linda, ed. 1990. *Women, the State, and Welfare*. Madison: University of Wisconsin Press.

Grusky, David M. and S. M. Ravi Kanbur, eds. 2006. *Poverty and Inequality*. Stanford, CA: Stanford University Press.

Hacker, Jacob S. and Paul Pierson. 2010. *Winner Take All Politics: How Washington Made the Rich Richer and Turned its Back on the Middle Class*. New York: Simon & Schuster.

Harrington, Michael. 1962. *The Other America: Poverty in the United States*. New York: Macmillan.

Hendrickson, Mark. 2013. *American Labor and Economic Citizenship: New Capitalism from World War I to the Great Depression*. New York: Cambridge University Press.

Herndon, Ruth. 2001. *Unwelcome Americans: Living on the Margin in Early New England*. Philadelphia: University of Pennsylvania Press.

Hernstein, Richard L. and Charles Murray. 1994. *The Bell Curve: Intelligence and Class Structure in American Life*. New York: Free Press.

Himmelfarb, Gertrude. 1984. *The Idea of Poverty: England in the Industrial Age*. New York: Knopf.

Himmelfarb, Gertrude. 1991. *Poverty and Compassion: The Moral Imagination of the Late Victorians*. New York: Knopf.

Hunter, Robert. 1904. *Poverty*. London: Macmillan.

Isserman, Maurice. 2000. *The Other American: The Life of Michael Harrington*. New York: Public Affairs Press.

Katz, Michael B. 1996. *In the Shadow of the Poorhouse: A Social History of Welfare in America*. New York: Basic Books.

Katz, Michael B. 2013. *The Undeserving Poor: America's Enduring Confrontation with Poverty*. New York: Oxford University Press.

Katznelson, Ira. 2005. *When Affirmative Action Was White: An Untold History of Racial Inequality in America*. New York: W.W. Norton.

Kelley, Florence et al. [1895] 1970. *Hull House Maps and Papers: A Presentation of Nationalities and Wages in a Congested District of Chicago*. New York: Arno Press.

Kim, Piyoung et al. 2013. "Effects of Childhood Poverty and Chronic Stress on Emotion Regulatory Brain Function in Adulthood." *PNAS* 110(46):18341–42. doi:10.1073/iti4613110.

Latham, Michael E. 2000 *Modernization as Ideology: American Social Science and "Nation-building" in the Kennedy Era.* Chapel Hill: University of North Carolina Press.

Levitas, Ruth. 2000. "What Is Social Exclusion?" Pp. 357–84 in *Breadline Europe: The Measure of Poverty,* edited by David Gordon and Peter Townsend. Bristol: Policy Press.

Lewis, Oscar. 1959. *Five Families: Mexican Case Studies in the Culture of Poverty.* New York: Basic Books.

Lieberman, Robert C. 1998. *Shifting the Color Line: Race and the American Welfare State.* Cambridge, MA: Harvard University Press.

Liebow, Elliot. 1967. *Tally's Corner: A Study of Negro Streetcorner Men.* Boston: Little, Brown.

Marshall, T. H. 1964. *Class, Citizenship, and Social Development.* Garden City, NY: Doubleday.

Merton, Robert K. 1938. "Social Structure and Anomie." *American Sociological Review* 3(5):672–82.

McKee, Guian A. 2008. *The Problem of Jobs: Liberalism, Race, and Deindustrialization in Philadelphia.* Chicago: University of Chicago Press.

Miller, Gregory E. and Edith Chen. 2013. "The Biological Residue of Childhood Poverty." *Child Development Perspectives* 7(2):67–73.

Miller, S. M. and Pamela Roby. 1970. "Poverty: Changing Social Stratification." Pp. 124–45 in *The Concept of Poverty,* edited by Peter Townsend. New York: American Elsevier.

Mills, C. Wright. 1959. *The Sociological Imagination.* New York: Oxford University Press.

Mittelstadt, Jennifer. 2005. *From Welfare to Workfare: The Unintended Consequences of Liberal Reform: 1945–1965.* Chapel Hill: University of North Carolina Press.

Moynihan, Daniel Patrick. 1965. *The Negro Family: The Case for National Action [The Moynihan Report].* Office of Policy Planning and Research. Washington DC: U.S. Department of Labor.

Mueser, Peter R., David W. Stevens, and Kenneth R. Troske. 2007. "The Impact of Welfare Reform on Leaver Characteristics, Employment and Recidivism: An Analysis of Maryland and Missouri." Presentation at the University of Kentucky Center for Poverty Research, conference on "Ten Years After: Evaluating the Long-Term Effects of Welfare Reform on Children, Families, Welfare, and Work," Lexington, KY, April 12–13. Retrieved August 15, 2013 (http://economics.missouri.edu/working-papers/2007/wp0720_mueser.pdf).

Murray, Charles. 1984. *Losing Ground: American Social Policy, 1950–1980.* New York: Basic Books.

Myrdal, Gunnar. 1944. *An American Dilemma: The Negro Problem and Modern Democracy.* New York: Harper.

O'Connor, Alice. 1998. "The False Dawn of Poor Law Reform: Nixon, Carter, and the Quest for a Guaranteed Income." *Journal of Policy History* 10(1):99–129.

O'Connor, Alice. 2001. *Poverty Knowledge: Social Science, Social Policy, and the Poor in Twentieth-Century U.S. History.* Princeton, NJ: Princeton University Press.

O'Connor, Alice. 2007. *Social Science for What?: Philanthropy and the Social Question in a World Turned Rightside Up.* New York: Russell Sage Foundation.

O'Connor, Alice. 2008. "The Privatized City: The Manhattan Institute, the Urban Crisis, and the Conservative Counterrevolution in New York." *Journal of Urban History* 34(2):333–53.

Patterson, James T. 2010. *Freedom is Not Enough: The Moynihan Report and America's Struggle over Black Family Life: From LBJ to Obama.* New York: Basic Books.

Piven, Frances Fox and Richard Cloward. 1971. *Regulating the Poor: The Functions of Public Welfare*. New York: Pantheon Books.

Polanyi, Karl. [1944] 1971. *The Great Transformation: The Political and Economic Origin of Our Time*. Boston: Beacon.

Quadagno, Jill. 1994. *The Color of Welfare: How Racism Undermined the War on Poverty*. New York: Oxford University Press.

Rank, Mark Robert. 2004. *One Nation Underprivileged: Why American Poverty Affects Us All*. New York: Oxford University Press.

Reagan, Ronald. 1988. "Address Before a Joint Session of Congress on the State of the Union." The American Presidency Project. Retrieved August 15, 2013 (http://www.presidency.ucsb.edu/ws/index.php?pid=36035).

Recchiuti, John Louis. 2007. *Civic Engagement: Social Science and Progressive-Era Reform in New York City*. Philadelphia: University of Pennsylvania Press.

Rigdon, Susan M. 1988. *The Culture Façade: Art, Science, and Politics in the Work of Oscar Lewis*. Chicago: University of Illinois Press.

Roberts, Dorothy E. 2011. *Fatal Invention: How Science, Politics, and Big Business Re-created Race in the Twenty-First Century*. New York: New Press.

Roberts, Samuel K. 2009. *Infectious Fear: Politics, Disease and Health Effects of Segregation*. Chapel Hill: University of North Carolina Press.

Rockman, Seth. 2009. *Scraping By: Wage Labor, Slavery, and Survival in Early Baltimore*. Baltimore, MD: Johns Hopkins University Press.

Rodgers, Daniel. 1998. *Atlantic Crossings: Social Politics in a Progressive Age*. Cambridge, MA: Harvard University Press.

Ross, Dorothy. 1991. *The Origins of American Social Science*. New York: Cambridge University Press.

Russell Sage Foundation. 1909–1914. *The Pittsburgh Survey: Findings in Six Volumes*. New York: Charities Publication Committee.

Rowntree, B. Seebohm. 1901. *Poverty: A Study of Town Life*. London: MacMillan.

Russell, Judith. 2003. *Economics, Bureaucracy, and Race: How Keynesians Misguided the War on Poverty*. New York: Columbia University Press.

Schram, Sanford. 2002. *Praxis for the Poor: Piven and Cloward and the Future of Social Science in Social Welfare*. New York: New York University Press.

Scott, Daryl. 1997. *Contempt and Pity: Social Policy and the Image of the Damaged Black Psyche, 1880–1996*. Chapel Hill: University of North Carolina Press.

Sen, Amartya. 1999. *Development as Freedom*. New York: Knopf.

Short, Kathleen. *The Research Supplemental Poverty Measure: 2011*. U.S. Census Bureau and Bureau of Labor Statistics. Washington, DC: U.S. Census Bureau. Retrieved August 15, 2013 (www.census.gov/hhes/povmeas/methodology/supplemental/research/Short_Research SPM2011.pdf).

Silver, Hilary. 1994. "Social Exclusion and Social Solidarity: Three Paradigms." *International Labor Review* 13(5–6):531–78.

Silver, Hilary and S. M. Miller. 2003. "Social Exclusion: The European Approach to Social Disadvantage." *Indicators* 2(2):1–17.

Stack, Carol. 1974. *All Our Kin: Strategies for Survival in a Black Community*. New York: Harper & Row.

Stern, Alexandra. 2005. *Eugenic Nation: Faults and Frontiers of Better Breeding in Modern America*. Berkeley: University of California Press.

Tinker, Irene, ed. 1990. *Persistent Inequalities: Women and World Development*. New York: Oxford University Press.

Titmuss, Richard M. 1958. *Essays on the Welfare State*. New Haven, CT: Yale University Press.

Townsend, Peter. 1962. "The Meaning of Poverty." *British Journal of Sociology* 13(3):210–27.

Vinovskis, Maris. 2005. *The Birth of Head Start: Preschool Education Policies in the Kennedy and Johnson Administrations*. Chicago: University of Chicago Press.

Walkowitz, Judith. 1992. *City of Dreadful Delights: Narratives of Sexual Danger in Late-Victorian London*. Chicago: University of Chicago Press.

Weber, Max. 1946. "Class, Status and Power," in *From Max Weber*, edited by H. H. Gerth and C. Wright Mills. New York: Oxford University Press.

Weir, Margaret. 1992. *Politics and Jobs: The Boundaries of Employment Policy in the United States*. Princeton, NJ: Princeton University Press.

Wilson, William Julius. 1987. *The Truly Disadvantaged*. Chicago: University of Chicago Press.

Zigler, Edward and Sally J. Styfco. 2010. *The Hidden History of Head Start*. New York: Oxford University Press.

CHAPTER 9

THE DISCOURSE OF DESERVINGNESS

Morality and the Dilemmas of Poverty Relief in Debate and Practice

CELESTE WATKINS-HAYES AND ELYSE KOVALSKY

INTRODUCTION

POLITICS rely on storytelling. When candidates run for office, citizens vote at the ballot box, and political leaders create public policies, they are investing in a specific narrative about their lives and values, the lives and values of others, and how the public's resources should be directed toward those entities. The politics of the moment are critical, but the stories that individuals tell are built from durable narratives grounded in history and ideology. These stories both constitute and shape public opinion.

In this chapter, we explore the trope of deservingness, one of the most enduring narratives used by government officials, the media, and the larger public to classify the poor.[1] Faced with the multitude of people in need and finite public and private resources, individuals' perceived worthiness for assistance has long served as both a rhetorical device and a determinant of who should receive resources and under what conditions. While the groups characterized as the undeserving poor have changed over time, stories of moral failings consistently undergird the deserving/undeserving distinction. The deserving poor are typically defined as those deemed most worthy of public and private assistance to improve their economic situations. They are thought to be unable to work through no fault of their own and therefore have a legitimate claim to resources. The sick, the disabled, and the elderly have most consistently been defined as the deserving poor, with other groups falling in and out of the category over time. The undeserving poor, in contrast, are believed to be poor due to their own lack of virtue. They have violated mainstream norms and ideals that govern work, family, and personal responsibility. Their life choices fall under public scrutiny, and blemishes are then used to justify withholding resources and subjecting them to punitive and surveillance-based mechanisms designed to control behavior.

In this chapter, we begin by exploring the concept of deservingness and how it fits into popular explanations of poverty and the work of distributing public resources. We consider its political, economic, and social uses both domestically and abroad. We then trace the use of the concept throughout the history of poor relief in the United States, highlighting the ways in which race, gender, and citizenship have been deployed to shape deservingness narratives in two important areas of social provision: cash assistance and health care. Our goal is to explore explicit and implicit uses of this distinction in public rhetoric, policy creation, and policy implementation over time. Finally, we look at recent trends in the deployment of the deserving/undeserving trope, pointing to areas in which more analysis is needed.

THE SOCIAL CONSTRUCTION
OF DESERVINGNESS

The notion of deservingness operates within a broader social context that gives it meaning and determines its consequences. The concept is inextricably linked to common assessments of why people end up on the bottom of the economic ladder, how many people are there, how long they stay, and why certain populations are disproportionately represented. These beliefs are transmitted through everyday discourse, popular culture, and political debate (Brady 2009; Iceland 2013; Rose and Baumgartner 2013; Somers and Block 2005). One school of thought emphasizes the role of social structures and macroeconomic forces in explaining the causes and consequences of poverty. "Structuralists" point to low wages, joblessness, racial discrimination, gender inequality, and the constrained economic choices that these conditions produce (Hoynes, Page, and Stevens 2006; Katz 2013; Rank, Yoon, and Hirschl 2003; Wilson 1987). The use of a deservingness frame is deemed problematic because it obfuscates the systemic factors that drive poverty and presents a flawed criterion through which to distribute aid. Structuralists advocate for economic need to be viewed as the most significant, if not sole, determinant of eligibility for assistance and emphasize targeting structural conditions to reduce poverty.

Another school of thought emphasizes individual explanations for poverty. "Individualists" focus on the lack of human capital, the proliferation of single-parent households, cultural norms that undermine the work ethic, the behavioral choices of the poor, and the generosity of government programs to explain lack of mobility among the poor (Herrnstein and Murray 1994; Mead 1997; Murray 1994). Poverty is viewed as "a problem of persons" rather than an outcome of economic and social conditions, with moral, cultural, biological, or personal deficiencies acting as the drivers (Katz 2013). The trope of deservingness aligns with this school of thought more comfortably. In an effort to disincentivize and ultimately interrupt these behaviors and traits, the trope of undeservingness is used to distance poor individuals from the mainstream, stigmatize and label them as morally lacking, and discipline them through increased surveillance and punitive policies. This approach is viewed as critical for economic prosperity by creating harsh disincentives against fraudulent and exploitative uses of public goods and weak labor force attachment. While structuralists are more likely to argue that the mission of public policy is to provide both resources and opportunities to the poor, individualists are more likely to demand that the poor rely on the free market for survival and to advance policies that seek to reform, contain, or punish those who are unsuccessful or resistant (Brady 2009; Katz 2013).

The American ethos that holds that individuals are responsible for their own life fortunes through hard work, rugged individualism, and personal responsibility produces strong messages about deservingness in the United States. In a survey of 240 individuals, Applebaum (2001) found that liberal assistance policies were more likely to be recommended than conservative policies when the target group was perceived to be deserving rather than undeserving, suggesting that many support distinctions based on deservingness in policymaking decisions. Attribution of responsibility for poverty was the strongest predictor of deservingness: respondents were more likely to recommend more generous aid policies when responsibility for the target's poverty was attributed to societal rather than individual causes.

Skeptics of the deservingness framework critique it from many angles, arguing that it undermines the social fabric by leaving many vulnerable; is deployed as a tool of social control; and shapes and is shaped by gender, racial, and other social inequalities. The language of deservingness suggests a one-sided relationship, with resources flowing from the state or private organizations to individual recipients. This rhetoric pays little attention to what individuals may be contributing in families and workplaces, despite having few resources and limited social protection at the bottom of the economic ladder. What Michael Katz (2013) calls this "asymmetrical concept of obligation" perpetuates an emphasis on what poor people owe society but provides little clarity on what society owes them.

Many who see the classification as a tool of social control point to the neoliberal turn of the last several decades as evidence, which simultaneously advocates a limited role for government and market-based solutions to poverty while expanding state surveillance of the economically and socially disadvantaged (Reid 2013; Scott 1998; Soss, Fording, and Schram 2011; Wacquant 2009). An important driver of policy creation and implementation under this regime is what Somers and Block (2005) term the "perversity thesis," the public discourse that has increasingly embraced perversity rather than poverty as the explanation for the condition of the poor and has been shown to powerfully shape and reinforce promarket regimes as the most legitimate approach to addressing the poor. The persistent surveillance and regulation of the poor are mechanisms by which this thesis is operationalized (Soss et al. 2011; Watkins-Hayes 2009). Chunn and Gavigan (2004) write:

> The form of the state and its social policy has shifted; social programmes designed to ameliorate or redistribute have been eroded, laying bare a heightened state presence which condemns and punishes the poor. . . . The effect of this ideological shift has been a huge expansion in the category of undeserving poor. . . . We are witnessing a profound attack on the "social," indeed the erosion of social responsibility, and in this attack, the authoritarian, neoliberal state is an important player. (pp. 231–32)

Other critics of the deservingness framework emphasize the gendered dimensions of the trope, highlighting the ways in which it structures and reinforces patriarchy in policy discourse and implementation (Gordon 1994; Orloff 1991). Able-bodied men have consistently been viewed as undeserving of poor relief, with poverty assumed to be a product of laziness and an inability or unwillingness to live up to the ideal of the male breadwinner that is the linchpin of the marriage between capitalism and patriarchy (Hartmann 1979). In its earliest years, welfare, or Aid to Dependent Children (ADC, later Aid to Families with Dependent Children, or AFDC), was viewed as a reasonable protection for single mothers. Poor never-married and divorced mothers as well as childless women came to be viewed as less deserving over time, believed to be sexually promiscuous and failing as desirable domestic partners and mothers (Abramovitz 1996; Hays 2003). Children have occupied a liminal status, generally regarded as innocent of moral failing, yet linked to parents who are accused of violating conventional gender norms.

For some, opposition to government assistance for the poor is a function of principled conservatism; more progressive policies that attempt to redress social and economic inequalities through the redistribution of resources are viewed as antithetical to principles of equal treatment and free markets (Sniderman and Piazza 1993). However, empirical evidence undermines this as the sole or even the strongest explanation for support of the deservingness framework. Through a nationally representative survey experiment in which respondents were asked to make recommendations regarding who should receive government assistance, political scientist Christopher DeSante (2013) found that when blacks and whites with similar levels of need are put in direct competition for scarce resources, respondents are more likely to approve support for whites in need. DeSante concludes that racial animus operates as a more powerful factor to explain opposition to social policies than race-neutral principled conservatism, as whites hold different standards for whites and blacks regarding hard work and deservingness of assistance.

The work of DeSante (2013) contributes to a large body of evidence that suggests that evaluations of deservingness are inextricably linked with race and other markers of difference in the public imagination. Social antipathies—including racial, gender, and class biases—intersect, and individuals produce and reify the "undeserving" subject in public discourse, policy debates, and policy implementation. If the engine of the deserving/undeserving construct is a preoccupation with the supposed failure of the poor to function appropriately within a capitalist regime, the fuel is a reliance on stereotypes to reinforce those beliefs and justify castigatory treatment (Gans 1994). Viewed as "outsiders" despite their significant societal contributions, marginalized groups have been framed as undeserving of assistance for centuries. Their economic fortunes have been, and continue to be, shaped by the reluctance to provide them with the kinds of social insurance provided to others (Gilens 1999; Neubeck and Cazenave 2001).

Martin Gilens (1999) has powerfully demonstrated the association between poverty, negative racial stereotypes of blacks, and undeservingness in public discourse and media representations. Antiblack sentiment creates the context for poverty-relief policies such as welfare to be racialized, viewed as undesirable, and perceived to be abused by those who fail to demonstrate a strong work ethic. Whites' perceptions of Latinos also shape antiwelfare views. Using survey data, Cybelle Fox (2004) finds that in areas with few Latinos, the stronger the perceptions among whites about the supposed laziness of Latinos, the less support whites lend to welfare spending. Whites were found to hold a more favorable view of Latinos as hardworking in areas with higher numbers of Latinos. Paradoxically however, this favorable view is associated with less support of welfare. Fox hypothesizes that this latter finding is the product of whites' social comparisons of the perceived work ethics of blacks versus Latinos, in which beliefs about a strong Latino work ethic fuel the view that blacks who use assistance are not working hard enough.

Ange-Marie Hancock (2004) links the foundation for the contentious 1996 welfare reform debate to long-standing beliefs about poor African American mothers and their framing as "welfare queens" who have multiple children with multiple partners and contentedly rely on the government while collecting other resources under the table (Also see Collins 2000). These racial, gender, and class stereotypes perpetuated by the news media, politicians, and the public at large hinder democratic discussion by allowing politically motivated misperceptions and a "politics of disgust" to serve as legitimate tools in policy deliberation (Hancock 2004). This in turn stymies public support for state programs associated with black women (Gilens 1999; Hancock 2004).

These intersectional constructs of deservingness are not reserved solely for women. Black and Latino men have historically been viewed as perhaps the least deserving of assistance in the American imagination, absent in most conversations around social insurance yet hypervisible in discussions that inextricably link men's poverty with criminality to justify heightened surveillance and containment (Alexander 2012; Rasheed 1999; Wacquant 2009). Viewed as absent fathers, hidden boyfriends of welfare-reliant mothers, or the criminal element undermining the safety of families and communities, public policies have aggressively marginalized black and brown men, deeming them "undeserving" of public support. In these cases, racial animus that is both gendered and classed is layered onto anxieties about scarce resources, fueling a public push toward exclusion. Stigmatized groups are deemed undeserving of public and private resources, and when those groups fail to gather the necessary resources to survive, they are further stigmatized.

As Herbert Gans (1994) points out in his seminal article "Positive Functions of the Undeserving Poor: Uses of the Underclass in America," the framework has several social, economic, and cultural uses that have unexpected consequences and even some benefits for the more affluent. Gans theorizes that "both the idea of the undeserving poor and the stigmas with which some poor people are thus labeled may persist in part because they are useful in a variety of ways to the people who are not poor" (p. 279). Displaced frustration, vulnerability, and fear find convenient targets in the undeserving poor. Emphasizing the portion of the citizenry who is deemed undeserving because of demographic characteristics, lifestyles, or other signifiers marks "otherness" and invites any number of social ills to be attributed to the group. It strengthens racial, gender, and class privileges held by the dominant group. It encourages scapegoating, reinforces norms that emphasize the primacy of the free market and two-parent heterosexual households, and fuels a reserve army of labor willing to work for low wages under difficult conditions to avoid the "undeserving" designation (Piven and Cloward 1971). Virtue and success go hand in hand under this logic (Katz 2013). The deserving/undeserving trope can therefore be viewed as a tool of the powerful to buttress a pyramid-shaped labor market with few at the top and many on the bottom and to quell any political resistance that may challenge this arrangement.

In this chapter, we look at the linkages between public discourse, policy debates, and policy implementation because this is where we see some of the starkest manifestations of the deserving/undeserving poor trope. As Ingram and Schneider (2005) highlight, "policy is the dynamic element through which governments anchor, legitimize, or change social constructions" and create, expand, diminish, or delegitimate distinctive populations (p. 5). Deservingness is determined at the population level, based on group hierarchies, as well as at the individual level, based on personal characteristics and group membership. Adjudicating deservingness is done abstractly when legislators and administrators design policies targeting an imagined group, as well as concretely when "street level" bureaucrats implement these policies and make decisions about resource distribution on a case by case basis (Watkins-Hayes 2009). We therefore observe a feedback loop in which public policies reflect debate and public opinion about deservingness, in turn reifying categories through ground-level implementation in ways that reinforce their social relevance.

THE POLITICS OF DESERVINGNESS IN GLOBAL CONTEXT

The United States is not alone in using deservingness as a political construct. Several countries engage in a politics of deservingness to justify austerity measures, strengthen the expansion of neoliberalism, and regulate and surveil new groups who make claims on the state, suggesting the global reach of the construct. The trope is used to categorize, divide, distribute, and withhold among populations across the globe. In South Africa, for example, Everatt (2008) describes how the discourse used by African National Congress

(ANC) leadership has shifted with regard to the poor since it gained power post-apartheid. Despite broad goals of lifting the nation out of poverty, internal tensions and lack of a clear antipoverty strategy have led some within the ANC leadership to employ a discourse in which the poor are universally undeserving and dependent on handouts from the state. The deservingness framework can also be imposed to reinforce existing ethnic classifications. For example, discriminating between the Roma and Magyar in Hungary on the basis of deservingness lends moral authority to disparities in the state's resource provision and overall treatment of these populations (Schwarcz 2012).

More commonly, the deservingness frame is used to distinguish between *categories* of needy people, most notably in the United States, Canada, Australia, and parts of Europe (Castañeda 2012; Chouinard and Crooks 2005; Henman 2004; Redden 2011; Willen 2012). Policymakers, the media, and public discourse divide the poor using both discrete binary categories—those who are deserving and those who are not—and continuums, constructing "hierarchies of deservingness" (Little 1994; van Oorschot 2006). Researchers note similarities across European countries in public perceptions of deservingness, with the elderly, the sick, and the disabled consistently perceived as the most deserving, the unemployed less so, and immigrants as the least deserving group (van Oorschot 2006). Those thought to be less deserving are obligated to do more and are afforded less privacy in exchange for government support (Juska and Pozzuto 2004; Korteweg 2006; Little 1994).

Recently in Great Britain, conservatives have adopted the phrase "broken society" as an explanation for social ills that they believe have roots in a dependency culture and broken families, while left-leaning New Labour Party leaders speak of a distinction between "hardworking families" and other families. Both groups present a strong anti-welfare agenda which suggests that welfare receipt by definition makes one part of the undeserving poor (Mooney 2011). The framework is even used by the poor themselves. Shildrick and MacDonald (2013) demonstrate that poor individuals struggling in deindustrialized Britain engage in "poverty talk," constructing a self-identity in contrast to nameless "others" whose hardship is due to their lack of interest in work, desire to claim benefits illegally, and inability to "manage" due to problematic consumption habits. Poor mothers are the targets of much of this criticism, perceived as unwilling to make sacrifices for their children and unable to maintain standards of respectability.

While scholars note that contemporary politicians and policymakers generally do not use "deservingness" explicitly (Guetzkow 2010), discourse and policies reflect the implicit boundary-drawing processes that parse worthiness. Wilson, Meagher, and Hermes (2012) analyze how the Australian Liberal–National coalition government used rhetoric and policy measures to attempt to shore up middle-class economic stability and political loyalty while simultaneously instigating tough policies aimed at single parents and the unemployed. Analyzing a 1999 address by Prime Minister John Howard, Wilson et al. observe:

> The "deserving" mainstream—families, pensioners, carers and "genuine jobseekers"—was consistently pitted against undeserving "dole bludgers," "welfare cheats,"

"job snobs" and "queue-jumping" asylum seekers. The message was clear: the mainstream would be offered support and choices . . . and the "welfare dependent" would be under increasing obligation to "give something back to society." (2012:328)

Scholars of welfare regimes emphasize how the characteristics of those regimes, especially the degree to which government services are universal or selective, affect public perceptions of deservingness of different groups. Those perceptions in turn contribute to varying levels of support for the welfare state across countries, generating a feedback loop between regime type and public support (Larsen 2008). Liberal welfare states such as the United States, Australia, and the United Kingdom have traditionally embraced a market-driven orientation and limit the size and scope of the public safety net by relying heavily on the private provision of health, education, and social services (Esping-Anderson 1990). We therefore see evidence of "need" being discussed in the context of morality and deservingness much more extensively than in social democratic nations like Sweden and Denmark that provide a basic benefit to all citizens to address unemployment and child-rearing.

The emphasis on deservingness in liberal welfare regimes represents a long-standing tension between the desire to meet the basic needs of the poor and the fear of overextending the role of government. Too much assistance is thought to undermine the work ethic and family values, encourage idleness, and cause free riding. Too little assistance becomes worrisome when confronted by the debilitating poverty faced by individuals and its collateral effects on children, neighborhoods, and society overall. The deserving/undeserving distinction has consequently become an efficient, if imprecise, way for political leaders, service providers, and the public to balance those competing philosophies and adjudicate need in the United States and internationally. The process in turn reifies those categories as legitimate and appropriate for determining resource distribution. However, as we will see in more detail, the groups that fall into each category, the behaviors that place one in a particular category, and the uses of the distinction to implement policy have not been static.

THE POLITICS OF DESERVINGNESS
IN HISTORICAL CONTEXT

How have social insurance programs that offer some of life's basic necessities—financial provisions and health care—made deservingness tangible, with material consequences experienced through policy implementation? The policy histories of cash assistance and health care in the United States, two of the largest components of the social safety net for the poor, reflect how the deservingness distinction has been a persistent feature in public discourse, policy formation, and policy implementation for centuries (Katz 1996). We chose these because of the central positions that they occupy in social welfare debates; however, housing, food assistance, and other services and programs have also been framed around deservingness. These components of the social safety net have formally excluded certain groups, and public discourse has informally parsed belongingness and the legitimacy of claims to these community protections. As we will see, policymakers and implementers take cues from public opinion, media and popular discourse, and existing policies. In response to these inputs, they use dominant language and ideologies to make decisions that have clear consequences for poor families.

History of Deservingness in Cash Assistance

The preoccupation with parsing out distinctions between the deserving and undeserving poor has fueled competing surveillance and support impulses from the inception of poor relief efforts. Both public policies and ground-level implementation practices highlight the evolution and reach of the concept in the political, economic, and social realms (Handler and Hollingsworth 1971; Hasenfeld 2000; Hays 2003). The deservingness construct was regularly used in England prior to being exported to the United States. The Elizabethan Poor Laws of 1601 (and their precursors in 1597 and 1598) tasked each locality with providing poor relief to those who could demonstrate a legal connection to the community. By 1834, poor relief took a more definitive turn toward obligating the poor, linking assistance with not simply residential membership but behavioral standards. William Trattner (1999) writes that the poor laws "defined three major categories of dependents—children, the able-bodied, and the impotent—and directed the authorities to adapt their activities to the needs of each: for needy children, apprenticeship; for the able-bodied, work; and for the incapacitated, helpless, or 'worthy' poor, either home ('outdoor') or institutional ('indoor') relief" (p. 11). The poor were clearly defined in relation to potential labor market participation: only those who had a severe physical or mental impairment were exempt from the expectation of work.

This framework laid the groundwork for a locally financed and administered poor relief structure in the early years of the United States. Throughout the colonial period and into the early nineteenth century, local officials distributed money, food, and clothing to the impoverished based on the distinction between neighbors and strangers (Katz 2013). This "outdoor relief" was briefly replaced in several communities with almshouses and poorhouses during the mid-nineteenth century through the early twentieth century (Katz 1996; Wagner 2005).[2] These institutions provided local officials with the power to determine who should have access to community resources and on what terms. The subjective nature of resource distribution in this institutional context allowed the distinction between deserving and undeserving to gain traction.

Beginning in 1869, the Charity Organization Society ushered in an era of scientific charity in which "friendly visitors" from private religious and charity organizations advocated both aiding and studying the poor in an effort to further establish a link between poverty and behavioral deficits. These more systematic goals turned on the provision of limited financial help that was asymmetric to the extensive personal advice that recipients received, encouraging economic self-reliance, moral discipline, and reduced dependence on government support (Myers-Lipton 2006). Interactions therefore involved screening applicants on the basis of perceived deservingness for resources, keeping detailed records of recipients' family histories, and coupling support with heavy behavioral monitoring. Those physically capable were expected to work and lift themselves out of poverty; those not able to do so were seen as morally weak and therefore undeserving. This institutionalized a model of poor support that emphasized the systematic surveillance and regulation of the impoverished as a condition of benefit receipt, an ethos that has endured throughout various incarnations of antipoverty policy.

Despite increased national debates about poverty's causes and consequences during the Progressive Era, the emphasis on deservingness in poor relief prevailed. Administered between 1911 and 1935 by local governments, mothers' pensions were small stipends that allowed mostly widowed mothers to provide for their families to prevent their children from being forced to work, adopted by other families, or institutionalized in orphanages (Goodwin 1997; Skocpol 1992). The juvenile court system, women's groups, and Progressive Era activists advocated the creation of mothers' pensions, and the program was intended to be more honorable and less demeaning than charity. In fact, it was framed as a way to compensate mothers for their service in raising children (Skocpol 1992). Nevertheless, mothers' pensions had strict behavioral standards for eligibility, so individuals could be denied the protective classification of the deserving poor that the program implied (Katz 1996).

The mothers' pensions program was a precursor to the Aid to Dependent Children program, which was created in 1935 as part of the Social Security Act. It was designated to provide cash assistance for children in need of economic support due to the death, continued absence, or incapacity of the primary wage earner (typically the child's father). Because ADC was originally intended primarily for widows, policymakers framed it as a welfare program for women deemed deserving of public resources. However, when more widows became eligible for their husband's Social Security benefits in 1939, the ADC program became highly unpopular in the public eye. The exodus of widows from the welfare system left the program to mostly single, deserted, and divorced mothers who were viewed as the undeserving poor, morally responsible for their plight (Abramovitz 1996).

Clear expectations for women as wives and mothers were therefore grafted onto equally venerable moral distinctions between the deserving and undeserving poor throughout the twentieth century in the United States. In 1960, Louisiana joined several other states in adopting a "suitable home" provision, which stipulated that welfare caseworkers could end or reduce welfare grants should they determine that their grantees were not supplying morally proper homes for their children (Neubeck and Cazenave 2001). Louisiana purged 6,235 families from the rolls when it implemented this policy, denying some 23,000 children benefits due to restrictions that prevented parents (mostly mothers) from living with a member of the opposite sex who was not a legal spouse and penalized mothers for having children out of wedlock or engaging in any other "promiscuous conduct" (Editorial Note 1961). In theory, caseworkers' latitude to investigate everything from their clients' household partners to the cleanliness and safety of their homes gave them the ability to ensure that the children for whom the state provided assistance were in healthy environments. It was, however, through the enforcement of "suitable home" provisions that workers could exercise the greatest discretion and adjudicate deservingness.

Historically, racial categories have also been inscribed onto definitions of deservingness. In welfare's earliest years, southern congressmen successfully resisted nationally set welfare standards that could provide an alternative to the harsh working conditions and desperately low wages that many of their constituents were offering in a segregated labor market. In addition, these politicians were able to get agricultural and domestic work (two of the largest industries for black employment) excluded from eligibility in the early years of social security or "old age" entitlements, precluding blacks working in these sectors from membership in the deserving poor (Lieberman 1998; Neubeck and Cazenave 2001; Quadagno 1994). Taking their cues from policymakers, welfare workers disproportionately denied or limited access to benefits for mothers of color (including widows whose husbands worked in areas excluded from Social Security benefits), ensuring that deservingness was inextricably linked with race. These maneuvers did not go unchallenged. In response to Louisiana's 1960 suitable home provisions, the National Urban League joined the Child Welfare League of America and the American Civil Liberties Union (ACLU) in legally contesting the new law. A memorandum to the commissioner of Social Security written by the ACLU explicitly addressed the law's racial overtones:

> Any legislation passed in Louisiana as part of a parcel of segregation bills, as was the instant statute, raises the presumption that it is part of the state's militant opposition to any attempt at desegregation. Putting to the side legal niceties concerning legislative motive, it would be fair to conclude—as has been generally concluded publicly—that the Louisiana legislature adopted this measure as a punitive step to deter its Negro citizens from pursuing their goal of equality. (Editorial Note 1961:206)

In the 1960s, the Civil Rights Movement, urban unrest in blighted communities, and growing scholarship on poverty's causes and scope increased public awareness of poverty and challenged the prevailing notion that "deservingness" should be linked with marital status, gender roles, or racial identity (Harrington [1962] 1997). Many political leaders had come to the consensus that in-depth attention was needed to respond to the deprivation plaguing many in American communities excluded or ignored by current programs. President Lyndon Johnson's implementation of the War on Poverty, originally conceptualized by advisors to President John F. Kennedy, created programs designed to improve the health, education, and well-being of families. As such, a welfare system that had viewed many as undeserving, subsequently denying or limiting assistance, recalibrated its definition of deservingness and expanded access to the system.

Nevertheless, despite increased access to services, the assumption remained that the economic struggles of impoverished families could and should be solved through interventions at the individual and family levels rather than through any major economic redistribution efforts.[3] Therefore, the War on Poverty focused on offering access to counseling services and job training, while at the same time continuing to emphasize the importance of the "moral uplift" of the poor. There were teeth to reinforce expectations around morality: welfare workers in many states could initiate court proceedings to remove children from their homes, enforce rules barring men from cohabiting with mothers receiving welfare, and monitor family purchases to prevent welfare fraud. Policymakers and welfare administrations held a clear and ever-present assumption that to prove oneself deserving of aid, one had to surrender the right to privacy. Although more people gained access to the rolls during this period, women's home lives remained highly scrutinized by the state and their obligations to demonstrate respectability and therefore deservingness remained intact.

The contentious politics of welfare offices in the 1960s brought the deservingness debate to the forefront as welfare rights groups challenged the toxic mix of unrelenting scrutiny, ostensibly capricious benefit denials, and what social historian Annelise Orleck (2005) describes as "quick, impersonal, and hostile" encounters between caseworkers and clients that often became highly confrontational (Katz 1996; Kornbluh 2007; Nadasen 2005; Piven and Cloward 1971). Welfare and civil rights activists, often working in tandem and sharing many key players, successfully contested the harsh and often discriminatory practices of welfare administrators and their staffs in ways that challenged the deserving/undeserving dichotomy and resisted attempts to distribute resources on the basis of this distinction. They pressed to expand local access to welfare benefits, educated poor women about their legal rights and entitlements, escorted them on visits to the welfare office to ensure an appropriate level of service, and pushed to curb local offices' surveillance techniques which policed a great deal without offering much support in return (Nadasen 2005; Orleck 2005; Piven and Cloward 1971). Their successful agitation, along with several court cases that challenged restrictive rules, made welfare caseworkers more accountable to implement AFDC as a true entitlement program and restructure its staunch gatekeeping function that attempted to adjudicate deservingness.

As the welfare rolls grew, the debate over deservingness emerged again in the 1970s. This time, the discussion was not confined to battles between low-income women and welfare rights organizations on the one hand and policymakers and service providers on the other. Several external factors drove attacks on welfare in the larger public conversation (Katz 1996). First, economic turmoil—rising inflation, high unemployment, and oil shortages—raised anxiety about downward mobility and challenged the assumption of a permanent abundance of public resources to absorb and resolve social problems. Second, a rise in women's labor force participation raised hard questions about why welfare recipients should be permitted to stay at home with their children while many working- and middle-class mothers were at work. Third, the assumption that voluntarism and the nonprofit sector would replace and improve upon federal government services if public sector resources were reduced fueled the public's increasingly hostile attitudes toward the welfare system. And finally, Ronald Reagan's use of the term "welfare queen" to associate public assistance with fraud and manipulation during the 1976 presidential campaign offered a vivid picture of the new face of the undeserving, and the device became a powerful tool to advance several antiwelfare state policies in the 1980s during his presidency. This debate rendered the working poor invisible and reinforced a false narrative that welfare recipients had almost no attachment to the labor force (Edin and Lein 1997; Newman 1999).

After two decades of administrative reforms and state-by-state experiments to reform the welfare system (Brodkin 1986), the Personal Responsibility and Work Opportunity Reconciliation Act (PRWORA) passed in 1996. During the political debate leading up to the passage of the Act, President Bill Clinton frequently stated the dictum, "If you work, you shouldn't be poor." With this, Clinton advanced an ambitious plan to move the working poor out of poverty and affirmed employment as the ticket to an economically stable life for welfare recipients. Clinton, other policymakers, and many journalists used the handpicked stories of welfare recipients who were working hard to lift themselves up to shape public opinion, implicitly portraying those willing to adhere to the WorkFirst Program as the deserving poor. These individuals were expected to benefit from the massive expansions to employment and training programs, childcare assistance, and the Earned Income Tax Credit (EITC) that accompanied welfare reform. Those who would not or could not comply with the short-term and employment-driven nature of the new welfare system would be subject to a variety of more punitive measures such as time limits, work requirements, family caps denying added benefits following an additional pregnancy, and sanctions, effectively marking their undeserving status through the implementation of policy (Cherlin et al. 2002; Soss et al. 2011). Policy debates fueled the narrative that welfare reform was the best way to wean these individuals from dependency, including controversial animalistic analogies presented on the floor of Congress that compared recipients to alligators and wolves best left to fend for themselves (Congressional Record 1995). Despite the early success of PRWORA in the late 1990s that led to a significant reduction in the welfare rolls during a simultaneous economic boom, the economic downturn that began in 2007 has challenged the ability of even the most "compliant" and "deserving" poor to escape poverty.

Through decades of changes in the creation and implementation of welfare policy, the media has been an active partner in shaping the images of welfare recipients. In a study of 252 articles from 1929 through 1996, Misra, Moller, and Karides (2003) corroborate the argument that images of dependency are dominant in media discourse on poverty and welfare. However, they highlight that alternate frames exist, and shifts in these depictions have taken place over time. During the 1920s and 1930s, most articles did not link welfare and dependency. The dependency frame was used most strongly during the 1960s and 1970s, a period marked by higher rates of divorce and unmarried child-bearing, increased access to welfare programs among black and Latina women, and the proliferation of culture of poverty arguments in academic and political discourse (Abramovitz 1996; O'Connor 2009). Welfare policies were viewed with skepticism and as a potential driver of government dependency as well as undermining families and personal responsibility. Concerns about women's dependency grew over time as unwed mothers increasingly became framed as part of the undeserving poor. During the 1980s and 1990s, by highlighting how the program helped the needy, more nuanced portrayals emerged, offering counterexamples to the notion that welfare was associated with dependency. Recent work on the post-1996 era suggests that news stories after the passage of PRWORA reveal more neutral portrayals of the poor, presenting fewer of the older stereotypes or overt negative attitudes of previous years but offering little discussion on poverty's causes or contextual factors (Bullock, Wyche, and Williams 2001). In short, through the welfare system, policymakers, policy implementers, the media, and the general public have co-constructed the deserving/undeserving distinction in ways that, while creating some nuanced discussions of poverty over time, still reinforce persistent beliefs about the individual-based roots of poverty and how best to address them.

History of Deservingness in Health Care

Echoing the case of income support, distinctions of deservingness have also been part of historical debates on health care, although scholarly attention to deservingness in this context has been more limited (Willen 2012). As health care in the United States is accessed and provided through an increasingly complex set of institutions, the system provides opportunities to distribute health care resources differentially across the hierarchy of deservingness. In the realm of cash assistance, the deservingness trope justifies restrictions on cash aid and invasive surveillance and regulation for recipients. In the realm of health, it justifies variation in health care quality and coverage and subjects individuals to varying protection from risk.

Countries such as Britain, Canada, and Sweden have centralized and universal health care systems which tend to generate broad political support, thereby reducing the relevance of distinctions of deservingness (Hacker 2004; Jordan 2010). In contrast, the United States has maintained a decentralized system, largely reliant on employer-sponsored health insurance, which has left large numbers of people uninsured.[4] In 2010, over 16 percent of people in the United States lacked insurance coverage of any kind, while 55 percent had employer-based coverage and nearly 20 percent relied exclusively on government health insurance (DeNavas-Walt et al. 2011). These disparities in coverage, coupled with the increasing costs of medical care and insurance, ensure that distinctions of deservingness remain salient for poor families seeking health care.

In the United States, health care provision for the indigent, alternatively referred to as charity care or welfare medicine, has had a history of repeated legislative efforts to increase the proportion and categories of people considered deserving of government-supported health care. These goals of coverage expansion compete against enduring political resistance to the ideas that government has a role in ensuring that all people have access to care and that care should be of equal quality. From this perspective, health care is viewed as any other commodity in which those with the most resources should lay claim to the highest quality services, and those without are not necessarily entitled to public access.

The origins of charity care in the United States lie in medieval Europe, where cities, local organizations, and wealthy individuals sponsored such care for those they considered deserving poor, usually those with a community or organizational affiliation. For example, as early as the fifteenth century, local religious groups, craft guilds, and wealthy members of society provided care to targeted groups in Belgian cities (Haemers and Ryckbosch 2010). English localities organized their own hospitals for the poor, which were generally affiliated with religious institutions (Fideler 2006). Later, welfare medicine moved toward a standardized system through the English Poor Laws but continued to be locally administered (Fideler 2006). These efforts formed the beginnings of a patchwork system of private and public health care and represented a first step in spreading the financial risk associated with illness beyond kin networks.

While European nations began to incorporate the poor in their nascent national health plans throughout the nineteenth and early twentieth centuries, the tradition of local responsibility for charity care carried over to the United States. This system was tested as populations became increasingly mobile and urban, breaking the bonds that had served as markers of deservingness. In response, religious, ethnic, and immigrant communities founded private sectarian hospitals in cities across the United States in the 1800s and early 1900s. Episcopalians began this trend, establishing hospitals, such as Massachusetts General, to care for members of their religious communities, and other groups followed suit (Engel 2006; Stevens 1989). These hospitals exercised discretion over who was deserving of their services, and ties to these religious groups played an important role in determining if and where someone would receive medical care.

The first half of the twentieth century saw continued debate about the need for national health insurance in the United States, while local and state governments remained responsible for medical care for the poor. The federal government provided limited funds to states and localities for the blind and elderly poor. A watershed moment arrived in 1965 when Medicare and Medicaid were created as part of the Social Security Act. These national programs have remained the centerpiece of government-supported health insurance (Engel 2006; Stevens and Stevens 1974).

While expanding access to care, Medicare and Medicaid made stark and lasting distinctions within the indigent community in ways that reified a continuum of deservingness. The development of Medicare was driven by concern for the elderly in the United States, who were less likely to have private insurance, risking impoverishment if they paid out of pocket for rising medical care costs that would only further increase with age (Stevens and Stevens 1974). Medicare offered a national health insurance program, allowing all elderly citizens to receive subsidized care from private medical providers.[5] The program identifies the elderly as universally deserving—and deserving of privately provided health care—regardless of income, wealth, work history, parenthood, or other characteristics. As a result, neither the program nor its beneficiaries are stigmatized. The program is funded and administered at the federal level, limiting the role of local and state actors in determining deservingness and access to care for this group. The program has enjoyed a politically protected status largely for two reasons. First, as the elderly live longer with medicine's increasing effectiveness, they have represented a significant and consistent voting population. Second, given that all Americans anticipate receiving Medicare benefits when they reach a certain age, the program has had broad appeal.

Medicaid remains the centerpiece of welfare medicine in the United States for the nonelderly poor, offering health insurance to its beneficiaries as the nation's third-largest antipoverty program (Sommers and Oellerich 2013). Unlike Medicare, Medicaid is similar to TANF in that states disburse federal funds and have the power to determine eligibility criteria and reimbursement rates, beyond federally established minimums. While exact rules vary by state, federally mandated eligibility categories include families receiving TANF, pregnant women, the disabled, and the blind. Historically, single and childless adults and working poor families were often ineligible for Medicaid, greatly limiting access to care for a broad swath of the population, especially poor men (Treadwell and Ro 2003). Like Medicaid, the Children's Health Insurance Program (CHIP) provides state-administered health insurance coverage to children in low-income households, indicating their designation as deserving. However, strong resistance to funding the program during the debates on CHIP reauthorization in 2007 and its strict income limits highlight a stark contrast between children (deserving in some cases) and the universally deserving elderly in policy debates (Covering Uninsured Children 2007; Kaiser Commission 2009).

The Patient Protection and Affordable Care Act of 2010 (ACA) includes an expansion of Medicaid to all low-income people below 133 percent of the federal poverty level, a change designed to reach the working and unemployed poor currently without insurance (Rosenbaum and Westmoreland 2012). State lawmakers' resistance to the expansion suggests that for many politicians, these newly eligible individuals represent the undeserving poor. In Texas, lawmakers arguing against the program's enlargement referred to "over a million new able-bodied adults" that would be covered (Deuell et al. 2012), insinuating that these individuals are not meeting their moral obligation to work or to work in a sector that provides health insurance. Rather than framing a lack of health insurance in its broader economic and political context, these politicians focus on individual traits and construct the uninsured as irresponsible, dependent on government, and undeserving.

In the absence of a national health care system, health insurance is tied to employment for over half of Americans, an arrangement legitimized by the deservingness trope. According to its logic, able-bodied people should be working, and those meeting this moral obligation should have access to health care through their employer. This ignores the realities and complexities of the labor market. Seccombe and Amey (1995) found that the industry in which someone works, union membership, full-time versus part-time work, and the hourly wage explain much of the disparity in health insurance rates between the working poor and nonpoor. The language of deservingness also obscures disparities in the labor market on the basis of race, gender, and education level that affect employment opportunities and subsequent access to insurance (Cutler 2003; Shaefer and Sammons 2009; Stanton and Rutherford 2004).

Beyond variability in protection from risk through health insurance, the quality of health care available also differs based on where one is situated on the hierarchy of deservingness. For example, since the 1980s, a shift to managed care for some Medicaid beneficiaries, especially children, parents and pregnant women, has led to the rationing of care for these groups (Hackey and Whitehouse 1996; Iglehart 2011; Kaiser Commission 2012). Managed care organizations limit patients' choice of doctors and covered medical services. Researchers have voiced concern about the quality of care available to Medicaid beneficiaries receiving care under these arrangements (Landon et al. 2007; Olson 2010; Thompson et al. 2003). Even for those deemed deserving of some protection from risk, determinations of deservingness can mean access to lower quality health care.

As in the case of cash assistance, deservingness can also be adjudicated through the implementation of medical policies and practices. Similar to the role of welfare caseworkers, individual and institutional medical providers have been shown to rely on notions of deservingness in decisions about the care they provide for patients (Castañeda 2012; Chirayath 2007; Horton 2004; Lutfey and Freese 2005). For example, some providers make moral judgments based on factors such as patient spending habits, health behaviors, and apparent motivation, linked to assumptions about race, class, and gender. They use these judgments to determine the prescribed treatment regimen and the kind of care to be received. These determinations of how to mete out health care resources create myriad opportunities for differentiated and unequal care across the population, highlighting the uneven and elaborate boundaries of deservingness.

The state's distinctions in levels of deservingness and the policies that reflect these categorizations have resulted in a multitiered health care system—one that meets the moral obligation to provide medical care to the deserving poor but reinforces class differences in the quality of care available and the constraints placed on patients. Even as policies have incrementally expanded the categories of people deemed deserving of access to health care or to the protection of health insurance, the care to which they are entitled looks increasingly different. Those who receive employer-provided health insurance, who can afford to self-insure, or who are eligible for Medicare have much greater discretion in where and from whom they can access care. Medicaid's deserving poor are entitled to medical care but not necessarily the same discretion over what that care will look like. Finally, a large segment of the public is left to seek care from clinics and hospitals willing to serve them, often enduring long waits and discontinuity of care. These individuals represent the undeserving poor in both public discourse on health care and in exclusionary public policies. They are adults seen as failing to meet their moral obligation to work, or to work in a field that provides access to health insurance. Although the ACA has the potential to decrease the number of uninsured in the

United States and improve the quality of care, the ongoing political and legal opposition mounted against it suggests that the rhetoric of deservingness remains relevant in the domain of health care, and the notion of a universal right to health care has not been fully embraced.

UNDESERVINGNESS IN THE PRESENT DAY: SOCIOLOGICAL LESSONS

The persistence of the undeserving poor trope calls for scholars to analyze its latest incarnations. Future research should explore how certain groups are moving in and out of the categories of deservingness, how this undergirds their encounters with public policies, and how this shapes their economic, social, and political experiences. In this section, we identify several social trends that are likely to reinforce, reshape, or perhaps reduce the use of the distinction in public discourse, policymaking, and policy implementation. All call for further analysis.

First, as the millions of individuals who are part of the working poor become more visible in policy debates, it is unclear how they will be framed vis-à-vis deservingness. As this chapter highlighted, once positioned as deserving in the welfare reform debates of the 1990s and early 2000s, this group experienced a different kind of framing in the last decade as it began to make serious demands through living wage campaigns and Occupy Wall Street demonstrations. Their demands for higher wages seem to be met with age-old accusations of killing jobs and stifling commerce, while laws and programs designed to expand their access to health care are heavily criticized and resisted (Garfield et al. 2014; Hiltzik 2014).

Another recent development in the undeserving poor discourse has been its incorporation into a hypervisible and kinetic popular culture (Kendall 2011). In this era of 24-hour news, viewers see many more images of the so-called underserving poor and use those frames to digest contemporary events. For example, Megan Reid (2013) demonstrates how survivors of Hurricane Katrina, one of the most destructive natural and social disasters in the United States, "were caught between two opposing cultural characterizations of 'deservingness'—'deserving' disaster victims and 'undeserving' welfare cheats" (p. 743; also see Sommers et al. 2006). This liminal position was widely believed to shape both the disturbingly slow government response in the immediate aftermath of the disaster and the methods by which poststorm benefits were allocated in the succeeding months and years. As Reid (2013) goes on to observe, survivors who did not fit into a middle-class model of a singular nuclear family with a personal safety net were made to wait while their rental assistance applications were investigated for fraud, having far-reaching economic consequences for individuals struggling for stability in multigenerational or shared households. Public sentiment was shaped by these associations as well. Johnson and colleagues (2009) found through experiment-based research that whites who were primed with stereotypes about the alleged criminality of black Katrina survivors through exposure to pictures of blacks "looting" after the storm opted to reduce support for policy programs that would assist black survivors.

Through reality television, film, music, and other mediums, cultural consumers can voyeuristically peer into the lives of the "undeserving" poor with a safe remoteness. As Bullock and colleagues (2001) point out, low-income individuals are far more likely to appear on afternoon talk shows, true crime programs, and reality television than as characters on fictional programs. Listeners and viewers live vicariously through the undeserving poor, consuming the group's most pernicious stereotypes such as dysfunctional relationships, promiscuity, propensity toward violence, challenging authority, hedonism, criminal activity, and materialism. These same consumers can simultaneously avoid direct contact with the poor through residential and school choices. This relationship encourages both a fascination with and disdain for the poor, and producers of popular culture often exploit this contradiction for economic gain. To attempt to balance pervasive images of the undeserving poor, other portrayals show the gritty realities of the deserving poor, encouraging consumers to become invested in the stories of these "exceptional" people but only from afar. Face to face but from an even greater social distance, slum tourism in the *favelas* of Brazil and townships of South Africa similarly provide brief glimpses into the lives of the poor, satisfying a traveler's curiosity though often sidestepping the complicated politics of these enterprises (Frenzel, Koens, and Steinbrink 2012). Observers can remove themselves from the visual or aural experience when things become too challenging or the entertainment value has dissipated. One of the most damaging aspects of "poverty porn" is that it "provides a view of poverty, and people experiencing poverty, out of context, with no consideration of the underlying social and economic factors that work to generate and reproduce poverty over time" (Mooney 2011:7).

A third important shift has been the emphasis on defining immigrants as the undeserving poor in an era of expanding migration to the United States and European countries. Immigrants have been long targeted in the deservingness discourse, grounded in fears of a foreign population that will migrate to the United States specifically to gain access to services. However, the increased focus on undocumented immigrants has heightened their visibility as the "new undeserving" in the United States and elsewhere and has generated extensive debate on the public services to which they should be allowed (Editorial: Immigrants 2009; Viladrich 2012; Willen 2012). Welfare regime characteristics, national immigration policy, and the form of immigration lead to different relationships between immigrants and the state (Sainsbury 2006). In Europe, deservingness determinations are bolstered by electronic surveillance of "irregular migrants" in European Union migration databases (Broeders 2007). Measures such as an EU-wide fingerprint database of all asylum seekers, irregular migrants, and illegal aliens found in member states potentially mark individuals as undeserving and create opportunities for exclusion. In the United States, government programs are designed to block access to health care for low-income immigrant women, such as California's Port of Entry Detection program that was launched to deter the fraudulent use of health care (Park 2011). Such programs demonstrate the lengths that policymakers feel they must go to emphasize the undeservingness of this population.

The recent political debates around the Affordable Care Act point to immigrants as the height of undeserving (Editorial: Immigrants 2009). Park (2011:139) notes:

> It is evident that "the immigrant" triggers a fundamental national anxiety regarding access to essential public goods such as health care. The politics of deservingness and social belonging have clearly entered a stridently hostile era and concerns about immigrant dependency and personal responsibility have reached a level of moral panic.

This framing within policy debates has led to undocumented immigrants being excluded entirely from the ACA. Some scholars predict that the Act's implementation will actually reduce access to care for immigrants due to changes in the safety net that will end pockets of existing care and intensify undocumented immigrants' isolation from the large population of newly insured individuals (Galarneau 2011; Warner 2012). Departing from notions of deservingness tied to work or personal responsibility, this group is marked as morally lacking and denied access to government resources based on their physical presence and status as noncitizens.

Finally, looking beyond individual behavior to the behavior of states, we see a discourse of deservingness applied in the realm of international aid. Just as governments providing resources to their own deserving poor regulate and surveil recipients, wealthy nations and international organizations regulate and surveil the behavior of developing countries as part of the distribution of aid. The language of responsibility is inscribed in the discussion and recalls the discourse of welfare programs in the United States: "development works best when poor countries have strong policies on governance and economic reform and take responsibility for reducing poverty and spurring economic growth" (Sperling and Hart 2003:9). The formulas used by organizations like the Millennium Challenge Corporation to make determinations about the flow of aid to different countries can be read as elaborate metrics of deservingness (Millenium Challenge Corporation 2014). States are rewarded for aligning themselves with the "political and strategic considerations" of donor countries such as United Nations voting allegiance and trade relationships (Alesina and Dollar 2000; Hoeffler and Outram 2011), effectively exchanging surveillance and regulation of their behavior for economic assistance.

CONCLUSION

The deservingness dichotomy is conceived and enacted in both national and local contexts, and the categories are strengthened through formal policies as well as informal institutional norms. In the realm of policymaking, the deservingness framework simplifies decisions about the distribution of resources in the face of complicated realities. Policy implementation is structured to attempt to buttress improper claims on the state from the undeserving poor, with the limited assistance that they do receive conditioned on surveillance and regulation. Different groups have fallen in and out of the deserving category over time. Group disparities in wealth and income can partly be attributed to the use of the framework, as some populations have been able to rely on a safety net throughout history while others have not. For example, the creation of Social Security fashioned a safety net for the nation's elderly but generated disparities in economic security through the exclusionary practices that removed most black workers from eligibility in the early decades of the program (Lieberman 1998). The creation of Medicare for the elderly reinforced the deservingness of this population and has led to significant reductions in elderly poverty relative to other populations since the 1960s due to their guaranteed health care coverage (Engelhardt and Gruber 2004; Swartz 2013).

These policy histories and current political discourse highlight how ideas and rhetoric matter. What political leaders and the public believe about the poor shape whether they support a robust social safety net to protect the economically vulnerable or an unbridled free market to encourage the poor to lift themselves up by the bootstraps. The language of deservingness provides a structure upon which these beliefs can rest. However, Michael Katz (2013) warns participants in the poverty debate against mistaking classifications for adequate descriptions of real people and failing to interpret these categories as abstract inventions of ideology and convenience. Despite the reality that categorization often takes place through arbitrary processes, these abstract inventions can have concrete effects (Zerubavel 1991). This chapter has demonstrated how the trope of the deserving/undeserving poor has had material and social consequences for both disadvantaged and advantaged groups in multiple sectors of society. These stories persist because, according to Gans (1994), they are useful to a number of groups in society. They are used to build the professional careers of the caretakers and custodians of the poor; keep wages low; justify hierarchies; and serve all manner of other social, economic, and political functions. While the portraits of those deemed deserving and undeserving have changed over time, the functions and results of these categorizations endure.

NOTES

1. It is not our intention to reify these categories by using the phrase deserving/undeserving poor. Rather, we use this phrase to call attention to its explicit and implicit use and to analyze the social, political, and economic implications of this framework.
2. Staff members within poorhouses were tasked with providing resources and supervision in an effort to "rehabilitate inmates," who were largely thought to be responsible for their own circumstances. Poor conditions inside—overcrowding, uncleanliness, health risks, poor management, inadequate funding, and a lack of both assistance and useful work for their residents—eventually led to a return to a focus on outdoor relief.

3. For more on the role of paternalism in social welfare work, see Stone 1977 and Ryan 1971. Both authors highlight the ways in which social welfare work in street-level bureaucracies is organized in a way that focuses on trying to change clients and help them adjust to their life circumstances rather than seeking to change external factors that may contribute to or even produce their conditions.

4. See Shaefer and Sammons 2009 for a history of the rise of employer-based health insurance and Quadagno 2005 for a historical account of resistance to national health insurance in the United States.

5. In addition, Medicare provides insurance coverage to younger adults with permanent disabilities. See "Medicare: A Primer" (2010) for a detailed description of Medicare's eligible populations.

References

Abramovitz, Mimi. 1996. *Regulating the Lives of Women: Social Welfare Policy from Colonial Times to the Present.* Boston: South End Press.

Alesina, Alberto and David Dollar. 2000. "Who Gives Foreign Aid to Whom and Why?" *Journal of Economic Growth* 5:33–63.

Alexander, Michelle. 2012. *The New Jim Crow: Mass Incarceration in the Age of Colorblindness.* New York: New Press.

Applebaum, Lauren D. 2001. "The Influence of Perceived Deservingness on Policy Decisions Regarding Aid to the Poor." *Political Psychology* 22(3):419–42.

Brady, David. 2009. *Rich Democracies, Poor People: How Politics Explain Poverty.* New York: Oxford University Press.

Brodkin, Evelyn. 1986. *The False Promise of Administrative Reform: Implementing Quality Control in Welfare.* Philadelphia: Temple University Press.

Broeders, Dennis. 2007. "The New Digital Borders of Europe: EU Databases and the Surveillance of Irregular Migrants." *International Sociology* 22:71–92.

Bullock, Heather, Karen Fraser Wyche, and Wendy Williams. 2001. "Media Images of the Poor." *Journal of Social Issues* 57(2):229–46.

Castañeda, Heide. 2012. "'Over-Foreignization' or 'Unused Potential'? A Critical Review of Migrant Health in Germany and Responses Toward Unauthorized Migration." *Social Science & Medicine* 74:830–38.

Cherlin, Andrew J., Karen Bogen, James M. Quane, and Linda Burton. 2002. "Operating within the Rules: Welfare Recipients' Experiences with Sanctions and Case Closings." *Social Service Review* 76:387–05.

Chirayath, Heidi. 2007. "Difficult, Dysfunctional, and Drug-Dependent: Structure and Agency in Physician Perceptions of Indigent Patients." *Social Theory & Health* 5:30–52.

Chouinard, Vera and Valorie A. Crooks. 2005. "'Because They Have All the Power and I Have None': State Restructuring of Income and Employment Supports and Disabled Women's Lives in Ontario, Canada." *Disability & Society* 20:19–32.

Chunn, Dorothy and Shelly Gavigan. 2004. "Welfare Law, Welfare Fraud, and the Moral Regulation of the 'Never Deserving' Poor." *Social and Legal Studies* 13:219–43.

Collins, Patricia Hill. 2000. *Black Feminist Thought: Knowledge, Consciousness, and the Politics of Empowerment.* Revised 10th anniversary ed. New York: Routledge.

Congressional Record. 1995. "Debate on the Floor of the House of Representatives about the Personal Responsibility Act of 1995." March 24. Washington, DC: GPO.

"Covering Uninsured Children: The SCHIP Reauthorization Debate." 2007. *Congressional Digest* 86(8):225.

Cutler, David M. 2003. "Employee Costs and the Decline of Health Insurance Coverage." Pp. 27–54 in *Frontiers in Health Policy Research*, Vol. 6, edited by D. M. Cutler and A. M. Garber. Cambridge, MA: MIT Press.

DeNavas-Walt, Carmen, Bernadette D. Proctor, and Jessica C. Smith. 2011. "Income, Poverty, and Health Insurance Coverage in the United States: 2010." U.S. Census Bureau, Washington, D.C.

DeSante, Christopher. 2013. "Working Twice as Hard to Get Half as Far: Race, Work Ethic, and America's Deserving Poor." *American Journal of Political Science* 57(2):342–56.

Deuell, Bob, Charles Schwertner, Mark Shelton, and John Zerwas. 2012. "Passing on Obamacare Medicaid Expansion is Right Call for Texas." Texas Insider. Retrieved November 22, 2012 (http://www.texasinsider.org/passing-on-obamacare%E2%80%99s-medicaid-expansion-is-the-right-call-for-texas/).

Edin, Kathryn and Laura Lein. 1997. *Making Ends Meet: How Single Mothers Survive Welfare and Low-Wage Work*. New York: Russell Sage Foundation.

"Editorial: Immigrants, Health Care and Lies." 2009. *New York Times*, September 11, p. A26.

Editorial Note. 1961. "The 'Suitable Home' Requirement." *Social Service Review* 35(2):203–6.

Engel, Jonathan. 2006. *Poor People's Medicine: Medicaid and American Charity Care since 1965*. Durham, NC: Duke University Press.

Engelhardt, Gary V. and Jonathan Gruber. 2004. "Social Security and the Evolution of Elderly Poverty." Working Paper No. 10466. Cambridge, MA, National Bureau of Economic Research.

Esping-Andersen, G. 1990. *The Three Worlds of Welfare Capitalism*. Cambridge: Polity Press.

Everatt, David. 2008. "The Undeserving Poor: Poverty and the Politics of Service Delivery in the Poorest Nodes of South Africa." *Politikon: South African Journal of Political Studies* 35:293–319.

Fideler, Paul A. 2006. *Social Welfare in Pre-Industrial England: The Old Poor Law Tradition*. New York: Palgrave Macmillan.

Fox, Cybelle. 2004. "The Changing Color of Welfare? How Whites' Attitudes toward Latinos Influence Support for Welfare." *American Journal of Sociology* 110(3):580–625.

Frenzel, Fabian, Ko Koens, and Malte Steinbrink. 2012. *Slum Tourism: Poverty, Power and Ethics*. London: Routledge.

Galarneau, Charlene. 2011. "Still Missing: Undocumented Immigrants in Health Care Reform." *Journal of Health Care for the Poor and Underserved* 22:422–28.

Gans, Herbert J. 1994. "Positive Functions of the Undeserving Poor: Uses of the Underclass in America." *Politics & Society* 22:269–83.

Garfield, Rachel, Anthony Damico, Jessica Stephens, and Saman Rouhani. 2014. "The Coverage Gap: Uninsured Poor Adults in States That Do Not Expand Medicaid—an Update." Henry J. Kaiser Family Foundation. Retrieved November 22, 2014 (http://kff.org/health-reform/issue-brief/the-coverage-gap-uninsured-poor-adults-in-states-that-do-not-expand-medicaid-an-update/).

Gilens, Martin. 1999. *Why Americans Hate Welfare: Race, Media and the Politics of Anti-Poverty Policy*. Chicago: University of Chicago Press.

Goodwin, Joanne L. 1997. *Gender and the Politics of Welfare Reform: Mothers' Pensions in Chicago, 1911–1929*. Chicago: University of Chicago Press.

Gordon, Linda. 1994. *Pitied But Not Entitled: Single Mothers and the History of Welfare, 1890–1935*. New York: Free Press.

Guetzkow, Joshua. 2010. "Beyond Deservingness: Congressional Discourse on Poverty, 1964–1996." *Annals of the American Academy of Political and Social Science* 629:173–97.

Hacker, Jacob S. 2004. "Dismantling the Health Care State? Political Institutions, Public Policies and the Comparative Politics of Health Reform." *British Journal of Political Science* 34:693–724.

Hackey, R. and P. Whitehouse. 1996. "Managed Care and Medicaid: A Critical Appraisal." *Critical Sociology* 22:3–27.

Haemers, Jelle and Wouter Ryckbosch. 2010. "A Targeted Public: Public Services in Fifteenth-century Ghent." *Journal of Urban History* 37:203–25.

Hancock, Ange-Marie. 2004. *The Politics of Disgust: The Public Identity of the Welfare Queen*. New York: New York University Press.

Handler, Joel and Ellen Hollingsworth. 1971. *The "Deserving Poor:" A Study of Welfare Administration*. Chicago: Markam.

Harrington, Michael. [1962] 1997. *The Other America: Poverty in the United States*. New York: Scribner.

Hartmann, Heidi. 1979. "The Unhappy Marriage of Marxism and Feminism: Towards a More Progressive Union. *Capital & Class* 3(2):1–33.

Hasenfeld, Yeheskel. 2000. "Organizational Forms and Moral Practices: The Case of Welfare Departments." *Social Service Review* 74:329–51.

Hays, Sharon. 2003. *Flat Broke with Children: Women in the Age of Welfare Reform*. New York: Oxford University Press.

Henman, Paul. 2004. "Targeted!: Population Segmentation, Electronic Surveillance and Governing the Unemployed in Australia." *International Sociology* 19:173–91.

Herrnstein, Richard J. and Charles Murray. 1994. *The Bell Curve: Intelligence and Class Structure in American Life*. New York: Free Press.

Hiltzik, Michael. 2014. "Medicaid Expansion Is the Final Battle in War over Obamacare." *Los Angeles Times*, May 2.

Hoeffler, Anke and Verity Outram. 2011. "Need, Merit, or Self-Interest-What Determines the Allocation of Aid?" *Review of Development Economics* 15:237–50.

Horton, Sarah. 2004. "Different Subjects: The Health Care System's Participation in the Differential Construction of the Cultural Citizenship of Cuban Refugees and Mexican Immigrants." *Medical Anthropology Quarterly* 18:472–89.

Hoynes, Hilary W., Marianne E. Page, and Ann Huff Stevens. 2006. "Poverty in America: Trends and Explanations." *Journal of Economic Perspectives* 20(1):47–68.

Iceland, John. 2013. *Poverty in America: A Handbook*. Berkeley: University of California Press.

Iglehart, John K. 2011. "Desperately Seeking Savings: States Shift More Medicaid Enrollees to Managed Care." *Health Affairs* 30:1627–29.

Ingram, Helen M. and Anne L. Schneider. 2005. "Introduction: Public Policy and the Social Construction of Deservedness." Pp. 1–34 in *Deserving and Entitled: Social Constructions and Public Policy*, edited by A. L. Schneider and H. M. Ingram. Albany: State University of New York.

Johnson, James D., Nelgy Olivo, Nathan Gibson, William Reed, and Leslie Ashburn-Nardo. 2009. "Priming Media Stereotypes Reduces Support for Social Welfare Policies: The Mediating Role of Empathy." *Personality and Social Psychology Bulletin* 35(4):463–76.

Jordan, J. 2010. "Institutional Feedback and Support for the Welfare State: The Case of National Health Care." *Comparative Political Studies* 43:862–85.

Juska, Arunas and Richard Pozzuto. 2004. "Work-based Welfare as a Ritual: Understanding Marginalization in Post-Independence Lithuania." *Journal of Sociology & Social Welfare* 31:3–25.

Kaiser Commission on Medicaid and the Uninsured. 2012. "Medicaid Managed Care: Key Data, Trends, and Issues." Henry J. Kaiser Family Foundation. Retrieved November 10, 2012 (http://kff.org/medicaid/issue-brief/medicaid-and-managed-care-key-data-trends/).

Kaiser Commission on Medicaid and the Uninsured. 2009. "State Children's Health Insurance Program (Chip): Reauthorization History." Henry J. Kaiser Family Foundation. Retrieved November 21, 2014 (http://kaiserfamilyfoundation.files.wordpress.com/2013/01/7743-02.pdf).

Katz, Michael. 1996. *In the Shadow of the Poorhouse: A Social History of Welfare in America.* 10th Anniversary ed. New York: Basic Books.

Katz, Michael B. 2013. *The Undeserving Poor: From the War on Poverty to the War on Welfare.* 2nd ed. New York: Pantheon Books.

Kendall, Diana. 2011. *Framing Class: Media Representations of Wealth and Poverty in America.* Lanham, MD: Rowman and Littlefield.

Kornbluh, Felicia Ann. 2007. *The Battle for Welfare Rights: Politics and Poverty in Modern America.* Philadelphia: University of Pennsylvania Press.

Korteweg, Anna C. 2006. "The Construction of Gendered Citizenship at the Welfare Office: An Ethnographic Comparison of Welfare-to Work Workshops in the United States and the Netherlands." *Social Politics.* 13(3):313–40.

Landon, Bruce E., Eric C. Schneider, Sharon-Lise T. Normand, Sarah Hudson Scholle, L. Gregory Pawlson, and Arnold M. Epstein. 2007. "Quality of Care in Medicaid Managed Care and Commercial Health Plans." *JAMA* 298:1674–81.

Larsen, Christian Albrekt. 2008. "The Institutional Logic of Welfare Attitudes: How Welfare Regimes Influence Public Support." *Comparative Political Studies* 41:145–68.

Lieberman, Robert. 1998. *Shifting the Color Line: Race and the American Welfare State.* Cambridge, MA: Harvard University Press.

Little, Margaret Hillyard. 1994. "'Manhunts and Bingo Blabs': The Moral Regulation of Ontario Single Mothers." *Canadian Journal of Sociology* 19:233–47.

Lutfey, Karen and Jeremy Freese. 2005. "Toward Some Fundamentals of Fundamental Causality: Socioeconomic Status and Health in the Routine Clinic Visit for Diabetes." *American Journal of Sociology* 110:1326–72.

Mead, Lawrence. 1997. *The New Paternalism: Supervisory Approaches to Poverty.* Washington, DC: Brookings Institution.

"Medicare: A Primer." 2010. Henry J. Kaiser Family Foundation. Retrieved November 21, 2014 (http://kaiserfamilyfoundation.files.wordpress.com/2013/01/7615-03.pdf).

Millenium Challenge Corporation. 2014, "Guide to the Indicators and the Selection Process, FY 2015." Washington, DC. Retrieved November 5, 2014 (http://www.mcc.gov/pages/docs/doc/report-guide-to-the-indicators-and-the-selection-process-fy-2015).

Misra, Joya, Stephanie Moller, and Marina Karides. 2003. "Envisioning Dependency: Changing Media Depictions of Welfare in the 20th Century." *Social Problems* 50(4):482–504.

Mooney, Gerry. 2011. "Stigmatising Poverty? The 'Broken Society' and Reflections on Anti-Welfarism in the UK Today." Oxfam Discussion Paper. Oxford.

Murray, Charles. 1994. *Losing Ground: American Social Policy, 1950–1980.* 10th Anniversary ed. New York: Basic Books.

Myers-Lipton. Scott. 2006. *Social Solutions to Poverty: America's Struggle to Build a Just Society*. Boulder, CO: Paradigm.

Nadasen, Premilla. 2005. *Welfare Warriors: The Welfare Rights Movement in the United States*. New York: Routledge.

Neubeck, Kenneth J. and Noel A. Cazenave. 2001. *Welfare Racism: Playing the Race Card Against America's Poor*. New York: Routledge.

Newman, Katherine. 1999. *No Shame in My Game: The Working Poor in the Inner City*. New York: Russell Sage/First Vintage.

O'Connor, Alice. 2009. *Poverty Knowledge: Social Science, Social Policy, and the Poor in Twentieth-Century US History*. Princeton, NJ: Princeton University Press.

Olson, Laura Katz. 2010. *The Politics of Medicaid*. New York: Columbia University Press.

Orleck, Annelise. 2005. *Storming Caesars Palace: How Black Mothers Fought Their Own War on Poverty*. Boston: Beacon Press.

Orloff, Ann. 1991. "Gender in Early U.S. Social Policy." *Journal of Policy History* 3(3):249–81.

Park, Lisa Sun-Hee. 2011. *Entitled to Nothing: The Struggle for Immigrant Health Care in the Age of Welfare Reform*. New York: New York University Press.

Piven, Francis Fox and Richard Cloward. 1971. *Regulating the Poor: The Functions of Public Welfare*. New York: Vintage Books.

Quadagno, Jill. 2005. *One Nation, Uninsured: Why the U.S. Has No National Health Insurance*. Oxford: Oxford University Press.

Quadagno, Jill. 1994. *The Color of Welfare: How Racism Undermined the War on Poverty*. New York: Oxford University Press.

Rank, Mark R., Hong-Sik Yoon, and Thomas A. Hirschl. 2003. "American Poverty as a Structural Failing: Evidence and Arguments." *Journal of Sociology & Social Welfare* 30(4):3–29.

Rasheed, Janice. 1999. "Obstacles to the Role of Inner-City, Low-Income, Noncustodial African American Fathers." *Journal of African American Men* 4:9–23.

Redden, Joanna. 2011. "Poverty in the News: A Framing Analysis of Coverage in Canada and the UK." *Information, Communication & Society* 14:820–49.

Reid, Megan. 2013. "Social Policy, 'Deservingness,' and Sociotemporal Marginalization: Katrina Survivors and FEMA." *Sociological Forum* 28:742–63.

Rose, Max and Frank R. Baumgartner. 2013. "Framing the Poor: Media Coverage and U.S. Poverty Policy, 1960–2008." *Policy Studies Journal* 41(1):22–53.

Rosenbaum, Sara and Timothy M. Westmoreland. 2012. "The Supreme Court's Surprising Decision on the Medicaid Expansion: How Will the Federal Government and States Proceed?" *Health Affairs* 31:1663–72.

Ryan, William. 1971. *Blaming the Victim*. New York: Random House.

Sainsbury, Diane. 2006. "Immigrants' Social Rights in Comparative Perspective: Welfare Regimes, Forms in Immigration and Immigration Policy Regimes." *Journal of European Social Policy* 16:229–44.

Schwarcz, Gyöngyi. 2012. "Ethnicizing Poverty through Social Security Provision in Rural Hungary." *Journal of Rural Studies* 28:99–107.

Scott, James C. 1998. *Seeing Like a State: How Certain Schemes to Improve the Human Condition Have Failed*. New Haven, CT: Yale University Press.

Seccombe, Karen and Cheryl Amey. 1995. "Playing by the Rules and Losing: Health Insurance and the Working Poor." *Journal of Health and Social Behavior* 36:168–81.

Shaefer, H. Luke and Elizabeth D. Sammons. 2009. "The Development of an Unequal Social Safety Net: A Case Study of the Employer-based Health Insurance (Non) System." *Journal of Sociology and Social Welfare* 36:179–99.

Shildrick, Tracy and Robert MacDonald. 2013. "Poverty Talk: How People Experiencing Poverty Deny Their Poverty and Why They Blame 'The Poor.'" *Sociological Review* 61:285–303.

Skocpol, Theda. 1992. *Protecting Soldiers and Mothers: The Political Origins of Social Policy in the United States.* Cambridge, MA: Harvard University Press.

Sniderman, Paul M. and Thomas Piazza. 1993. *The Scar of Race.* Cambridge, MA: Harvard University Press.

Somers, Margaret R. and Fred Block. 2005. "From Poverty to Perversity: Ideas, Markets, and Institutions over 200 Years of Welfare Debate." *American Sociological Review* 70:260–87.

Sommers, Benjamin D. and Donald Oellerich. 2013. "The Poverty-Reducing Effect of Medicaid." *Journal of Health Economics* 32(5):816–32.

Sommers, Samuel R., Evan P. Apfelbaum, Kristin N. Dukes, Negin Toosi, and Elise J. Wang. 2006. "Race and Media Coverage of Hurricane Katrina: Analysis, Implications, and Future Research Questions." *Analyses of Social Issues and Public Policy* 6(1):1–17.

Soss, Joe, Richard Fording, and Sanford Schram. 2011. *Disciplining the Poor: Neoliberal Paternalism and the Persistent Power of Race.* Chicago: University of Chicago Press.

Sperling, Gene and Tom Hart. 2003. "A Better Way to Fight Global Poverty: Broadening the Millennium Challenge Account." *Foreign Affairs* 82:9–14.

Stanton, Mark W. and Margaret Rutherford. 2004. "Employer-sponsored Health Insurance: Trends in Cost and Access." Agency for Healthcare Research and Quality. Rockville, Maryland.

Stevens, Rosemary. 1989. *In Sickness and in Wealth: American Hospitals in the Twentieth Century.* New York: Basic Books.

Stevens, Robert and Rosemary Stevens. 1974. *Welfare Medicine in America: A Case Study of Medicaid.* New York: Free Press.

Stone, Clarence. 1977. "Paternalism among Social Agency Employees." *Journal of Politics.* 39(3):794–804.

Swartz, Katherine. 2013. "Medicare and Medicaid." Pp. 268–98 in *Legacies of the War on Poverty,* edited by M. J. Bailey and S. Danziger. New York: Russell Sage Foundation.

Thompson, Joseph W., Kevin W. Ryan, Sathiska D. Pinidiya, and James E. Bost. 2003. "Quality of Care for Children in Commercial and Medicaid Managed Care." *JAMA* 290:1486–93.

Trattner, William. 1999. *From Poor Law to Welfare State: A History of Social Welfare in America.* 6th ed. New York: Free Press.

Treadwell, Henrie M. and Marguerite Ro. 2003. "Poverty, Race, and the Invisible Men." *American Journal of Public Health* 93(5):705–7.

van Oorschot, Wim. 2006. "Making the Difference in Social Europe: Deservingness Perceptions among Citizens of European Welfare States." *Journal of European Social Policy* 16:23–42.

Viladrich, Anahí. 2012. "Beyond Welfare Reform: Reframing Undocumented Immigrants' Entitlement to Health Care in the United States, a Critical Review." *Social Science & Medicine* 74(6):822–29.

Wacquant, Loic. 2009. *Punishing the Poor: The Neoliberal Government of Social Insecurity.* Durham, NC: Duke University Press.

Wagner, David. 2005. *The Poorhouse: America's Forgotten Institution.* New York: Rowman and Littlefield.

Warner, David C. 2012. "Access to Health Services for Immigrants in the USA: From the Great Society to the 2010 Health Reform Act and After." *Ethnic and Racial Studies* 35:40–55.

Watkins-Hayes, Celeste. 2009. *The New Welfare Bureaucrats: Entanglements of Race, Class, and Policy Reform.* Chicago: University of Chicago Press.

Willen, Sarah S. 2012. "Migration, "Illegality," and Health: Mapping Embodied Vulnerability and Debating Health-Related Deservingness." *Social Science & Medicine* 74(6):805–11. doi: http://dx.doi.org/10.1016/j.socscimed.2011.10.041.

Wilson, Shaun, Meagher, Gabrielle, and Kerstin Hermes. 2012. "The Social Division of Welfare Knowledge: Policy Stratification and Perceptions of Welfare Reform in Australia." *Policy & Politics* 40(3):323–46.

Wilson, William Julius. 1987. *The Truly Disadvantaged: The Inner City, the Underclass, & Public Policy.* Chicago: University of Chicago Press.

Zerubavel, Eviatar. 1991. *The Fine Line: Making Distinctions in Everyday Life.* New York: Free Press.

CHAPTER 10

....

GENDER AND POVERTY

....

JANET C. GORNICK AND NATASCIA BOERI

KEY CONCEPTS AND OVERVIEW
OF CHAPTER

....

ASSESSING the links between gender and poverty is an immensely complex task—both conceptually and empirically—for several reasons.

First, poverty is defined and measured in myriad ways. In the vast, interdisciplinary literature on poverty, "poverty" refers to diverse conditions—most often, insufficient economic resources (e.g., income, consumption, earnings), the deprivation of human capabilities, or social exclusion and marginalization. Other scholars focus on material hardship (e.g., hunger, homelessness, lack of health care), economic volatility, or intergenerational immobility. There is no single, universal definition of poverty.

Second, the conditions associated with poverty—however defined—vary dramatically both within and across countries. This renders cross-national poverty studies a thorny endeavor. Clearly, a poor woman in Norway faces substantially different circumstances, in absolute terms, than does a poor woman in Mali. More starkly, a poor woman in Norway may be better off, on multiple dimensions, than an affluent woman in Mali—a fact that must be accounted for in poverty studies that cross national borders.

Third, although gender is an individual (i.e., person-level) attribute, poverty is most often conceptualized as a household condition. That disjuncture presents further theoretical and empirical challenges, because precise information about intrahousehold resource distribution is limited, and because adjusting for within-household economies of scale is not always straightforward. Linked to this is the fact that market involvement (for both women and men) often takes place at the person level, while economic well-being may be more meaningfully determined at the household level. More specifically, there is often a mismatch between labor market earnings, on the one hand, and household income, on the other. Many individuals—especially women—command no or little labor market income, but live in households with sufficient or even ample resources.

Likewise, in many families—most acutely, in those headed by a single parent (the vast majority of whom are women)—the breadwinner's earnings may not fall in the lowest earnings strata, but they may be insufficient to keep the household out of income poverty. Thus, unpacking the relationship between gender, paid work, and household structure is crucial in any assessment of gender and poverty.

Overview of Chapter

In the second section, we highlight selected theoretical perspectives that have informed the study of poverty—focusing on economic insufficiency, capabilities deprivation, and social exclusion—and we assess the often-cited and much-critiqued concept of the feminization of poverty.

We review key contributions to the empirical literature on poverty and gender, in the third section, focusing on interdisciplinary studies that define poverty via economic resources. In the fourth section, we present selected empirical results from a group of 26 high- and middle-income countries, based on data from the LIS Database, a database containing harmonized microdata from over 40 countries[1]. Our results—presented in three descriptive figures—correspond to a point in time, the early-middle 2000s. Specifically, we assess the likelihood that women, and men, live in poor households, and how that likelihood varies by two crucial risk factors: family structure and the strength of their attachment to the labor market. These figures illustrate, and highlight, some of the key factors regarding gendered poverty that we discuss in this chapter.

We return, in the fifth section, to the main findings from our review of the literature and our empirical results, and comment on how these contribute to the challenge of assessing the link between gender and poverty.

THEORETICAL PERSPECTIVES

Conceptualizing Poverty: Economic Resources, Capabilities, and Social Exclusion Perspectives

Poverty research requires that analysts define poverty and select a measurement approach. This is always a challenge, and it is especially complex when studying gender and poverty. Interestingly, scholars of both feminism and development have been at the forefront of critiquing and influencing poverty measurement. Their contributions have enhanced the conceptualization and measurement of poverty in ways that take gender into account. Here, we review three major theoretical frameworks used to study poverty and address their usefulness in studying gendered poverty.

Poverty as Insufficient Economic Resources

The most widely used approach to defining and measuring poverty focuses on the economic well-being of households or persons. Within this economic framework, poverty is most often captured via income, or consumption, or earnings, or some combination of the three. Insufficient economic resources may be defined in absolute terms—that is, relative to a threshold that is independent of the population's distribution—or in relative terms, most often with respect to the population median.

The main critique to studying poverty solely through economic metrics is that it offers a narrow and static account of poverty, whereas poverty should be conceptualized as a multidimensional phenomenon that includes both material and social deprivations (Chant 2003). This critique has particular resonance for research on gender and poverty—especially in the developing world. In lower income countries, critics argue, monetized measures are less meaningful indicators of well-being and, by extension, less useful for assessing gender gaps in well-being (Razavi 2000).

Chant (2010) synthesizes this concern:

> Although issues of gender gaps in earnings, expenditures, and the like remain vitally important elements . . . and there is strong evidence for persistent and ubiquitous gender differences in access to economic resources, major doubts have [arisen] in the feminist literature about whether income should be pre-eminent in gender-sensitive conceptions of wellbeing, and whether tackling income poverty is the most effective strategy for solving women's disadvantage. . . . [I]ncome is probably a less "robust" indicator of women's privation than factors such as access to land, agency in decision-making, legal rights within the family, vulnerability to violence, and (self)-respect and dignity. (P. 3)

Poverty as Capability Deprivation

A powerful alternative approach to poverty measurement is the capabilities approach, most often associated with the work of Amartya Sen (see, e.g., Sen 1999). The capabilities approach has greatly expanded the conceptualizing of deprivation to include constraints on persons' opportunities, and abilities, to generate valuable outcomes—in a sense, the freedom to achieve.

The capabilities approach has also helped poverty studies address the fact that economic poverty is generally measured at the household level while gender is an individual-level trait. Gita Sen (2010:101) observes that "looking within the household uncovers the extraordinary extent to which one's economic experiences can differ depending on whether one is a woman or a man." Jackson and Palmer-Jones (2000) note that gendered scholarship that unveils unequal intrahousehold allocations has led many organizations focused on poorer countries to favor conceptualizing poverty in terms of individuals' capabilities and functionings. This is especially the case when assessing gender gaps in well-being in poorer countries, because assumptions about equal sharing within households are understood to apply less well in poorer countries. Assigning to women and men the well-being of their households, as is common in studies of affluent countries, is less useful when studying low-income countries—and the capabilities approach offers an alternative.

One advantage of the capabilities approach is its flexibility; there is no single, definitive list of capabilities. At the same time, that flexibility has a downside: capabilities—and constraints on capabilities—are difficult to operationalize and measure (Sugden 1993). Nevertheless, there have been innovative attempts to measure capabilities, including in conjunction with the Human Development Index produced by the United Nations Development Programme.

Poverty as Social Exclusion

The concept of social exclusion is another alternative to purely economic approaches to analyzing deprivation. Social exclusion—which emerged in France in the 1960s (see Castel 1991) and took hold across Europe in subsequent years—has most often been used to assess "a situation of multiple disadvantages in terms of labour market marginalization, poverty and social isolation" (Gallie and Paugam 2004:35). While social exclusion is framed in a multitude of ways, drawing on diverse intellectual traditions (see, e.g., Barnes et al. 2002), there are universal themes that crosscut nearly all usages (for a review, see Gornick 2002). First, social exclusion is characterized as a process; it is more than an outcome or a collection of outcomes. Second, exclusion is multidimensional and methodologically plural. Third, exclusion is always relational; that is, an individual or group must be excluded from some larger entity. Fourth, the primary causal factors underlying exclusion are found outside the excluded individual or group; at the same time, inclusion emphasizes reciprocity. Finally, social exclusion generally connotes some degree of permanence; it is a long-term affair.

Jackson (1999) has questioned the usefulness of social exclusion theory for feminist analyses of poverty. Its integration of various forms of disadvantage does offer an alternative method to study poverty beyond one based only on economic resources. However, she argues, social exclusion scholarship has poorly conceptualized gendered elements, most prominently in its failure to address the power relations in the subordination of women specifically. Women's exclusion and marginalization are unlike that of other groups (e.g., racial minorities, the poor); they are driven by features of social relations within these groups. Jackson argues that gender "mediates particular forms of exclusion but does not produce categories of people included or excluded in uniform ways" (1999:130); in short, women are often simultaneously included and excluded. Furthermore, she notes, the concept of social exclusion is problematic—for women *and* men—where the poor are not a marginalized minority but a mass phenomenon, as in many developing countries.

The "Feminization of Poverty"

The conceptual murkiness that surrounds the interplay between gender and poverty has been exacerbated by the multiple meanings associated with the popular term "the feminization of poverty." That widely used term was, by most accounts, introduced in the United States by scholar-activist Diana Pearce in the late 1970s. Chen et al. (2005) report that the concept took hold internationally during the UN Decade for Women (1975–1985): "researchers and advocates drew attention to the disadvantaged position of women economically and socially, especially those in female-headed households, and called for a gender perspective in the whole field of poverty research" (2005:37). Chant (2007) reports that the term "feminization of poverty" was further popularized following the famous Fourth World Conference on Women, held in Beijing in 1995. She highlights the call, in the Beijing Declaration and Platform for Action (BDPA), for eradicating the persistent and increasing burden of poverty on women.

Chant (2007) argues that, while there are many interpretations of the "feminization of poverty" in circulation, it has most often referred to three tenets:

- Women are the majority of the world's poor.
- Women's disproportionate share of poverty is rising relative to men's.
- The changing face of poverty is linked to the feminization of female household headship.

Chant further notes that other claims as well have been associated with the "feminization of poverty," including that women's poverty is deeper and more extreme than men's; that women are more prone than are men to persistent poverty; that women face more severe barriers to overcoming poverty than do men; and that the gendered nature of poverty transmits poverty to children.

Given the diversity of interpretations of the "feminization of poverty," it is not surprising that many scholars, especially feminist scholars, have critiqued the language and the underlying concepts. Chant (2007), focusing on low-income countries, cites several fundamental concerns with this "formulaic nomenclature": the term links poverty to women rather than to gender relations; in practice, it overemphasizes income privation; it conflates gender with household structure; and, perhaps most problematically, it confuses changes in women's poverty (a dynamic condition) with women's disproportionate risk of poverty (an inherently static condition). Goldberg (2010), focusing on high-income countries, levels similar concerns—especially about the confusion between states and trends—and further adds that the emphasis in the "feminization of poverty" literature on single women (both mothers and the elderly) fails to capture the economic vulnerability of married women "and the likelihood that many of them would join the ranks of the poor if they were on their own" (2010:4).

The Dominance of the Economic Approach

Despite the powerful criticisms of the economic approach to poverty analyses—some of which are echoed in the critiques of the "feminization of poverty"—this approach clearly dominates the empirical literature on gender and poverty.

Even its critics acknowledge its strengths. Razavi and Staab, for example, observe: "As the capabilities framework has made clear, an insufficient level of income is a very narrow conceptualization of poverty which does not capture its multiple dimensions" (2010:427). Yet, in their empirical work, they adopt an income framework—after offering three reasons for its usefulness. They argue that the economic approach to assessing gender and poverty:

- highlights the crucial relationship between employment and poverty;
- is most amenable to analyses based on quantitative data; and
- is strengthened by the fact that income poverty is often *correlated* with other dimensions of poverty.

An overwhelming majority of empirical studies on gender and poverty focus on economic resources. Accordingly, in the next sections—our review of existing literature and our empirical portrait using the LIS data—we do as well.

THE GENDERED NATURE OF POVERTY

Overview

Many scholars, studying multiple countries, find that, overall, women are more likely to be poor than are their male counterparts (see, e.g., Casper, McLanahan, and Garfinkel 1994; Wright 1995; Pressman 1998, 2002). In this section, we synthesize the primary, and most consi stent, findings that emerge from this body of research.

Using LIS data,[2] for example, Christopher, a sociologist, compares the poverty rates of mothers and fathers (2002b) and also of mothers and all men (2002c), in a sample of affluent countries. She finds a strong cross-national pattern of heightened poverty risk for mothers compared to all men—everywhere except in Finland and Sweden—and for mothers compared to fathers (when both are custodial parents) in all nine countries that she studied. As in earlier LIS-based research, Christopher finds the largest poverty gender gaps in the English-speaking countries; mothers in the United States are fully 58 percent more likely than fathers to be poor (with respect to post-tax-and-transfer household income).

The causes underlying women's higher risk of economic insecurity are complex, overlapping, and cumulative. The most powerful factor is women's weaker attachment to the labor market. On average, women command lower market income, including wages and occupational pensions, than do men and, as a result, they receive lower employment-related social transfers. In addition, as a group, women still earn lower pay than do men for each hour worked, partly due to their concentration in lower paying occupations and partly due to pay discrimination based on gender. In turn, the main reason that women's connection to paid work is weaker than men's is their disproportionate engagement in caring for family members, especially young children. Largely due to their role as family caregivers, women are less likely to be employed than are similarly situated men and, if employed, they average fewer weekly work hours, including among those in full-time employment. Recent evidence indicates that being an active caregiver (independent of gender) further reduces hourly pay—a pay penalty that disproportionately affects women.

In many countries, substantial numbers of parents are raising their children without partners, and everywhere single parents are overwhelmingly women. Single mothers, as a group, typically report worrisome levels of poverty—not surprisingly, as their (mainly unshared) caregiving responsibilities depress their own labor supply, their gender is associated with lower hourly earnings, and their homes typically lack a second earner. Additionally, women are at much higher risk of elderly poverty than men because of the economic disadvantages that they experience earlier in life. Finally, diverse households—young and old, female-headed and male-headed, with and without children—receive tax benefits and public income transfers. Among lower income households, those transfers can make them less poor or lift them out of poverty altogether. In some countries—the United States is a prime example—social benefits targeted to children are meager compared to those granted to other demographic groups. As a result, families with children, which disproportionately include women, are more likely to be poor than are other family types. In many countries, these factors—both micro and macro—operate independently and interactively to raise women's likelihood of poverty relative to men's.

Social Constructs of Care: Gender and Unpaid Work

One of the strongest factors in women's higher risk of poverty is their weaker attachment to the labor market. That, in turn, is linked to women's disproportionate engagement in the work of caregiving, especially for children. Notably, this influential factor—the association of women with unpaid care work—is widespread throughout both developed and developing countries (Folbre 1994; Benería 2003).

Women's constrained "choices" in the labor market, stemming from entrenched divisions of labor at home, result in women—in all countries—being less likely than their male counterparts to work for pay. Among those who do work for pay, women are more likely to be in part-time employment, in precarious jobs, and/or in the informal economy (Vosko, MacDonald, Campbell 2011; Carr and Chen 2002).

Heintz (2010) argues that women's greater likelihood of being employed in less desirable jobs is largely explained by care-related constraints. Women, for example, are more likely to choose home-based work as way to balance work and care responsibilities, even though home-based work is generally less remunerative and often precarious (Carr and Chen 2002). Caregiving duties are also understood to influence the occupations that women enter, due to factors operating on both the supply side and the demand side; the result is that women are overrepresented, for example, in lower paying service and caregiving jobs. In short, women's unique role in unpaid care work—widely understood to be overwhelmingly socially constructed—weakens their participation in the labor market and thus their access to one of the most decisive factors in reducing the risk of poverty: paid work.

Gender Divisions of Labor: Paid Work and Poverty

When assessing the gendered determinants of poverty, paid work matters everywhere—but it matters in different ways in affluent versus poorer countries. In their 2005 UNIFEM report on women, work, and poverty, Chen and her colleagues (2005) argue that, in both developed and developing countries, women are concentrated in more precarious, and more poorly remunerated, forms of employment. In affluent countries, that employment takes the form of part-time and temporary jobs; in developing countries, however, women's precariousness stems from their disproportionate engagement in informal work.

A number of researchers have examined how the changes to the global economy, most notably the rise in low-wage and informal work, have interacted with the quality and quantity of jobs available to women and how this links with gendered poverty (Vosko et al. 2011; Carr and Chen 2002). Collins and Mayer's (2011) study of welfare reform highlights the rise of women's employment in low-wage jobs in the United States, a country with a high prevalence of working poor. Pearson (2010) points to a number of features in the new global economy that have influenced crucial changes in labor markets, namely, the use of inexpensive labor by transnational corporations, the associated loss of "good jobs," the increase in nonunionized labor, and the economic crisis that has squeezed social assistance.

Undoubtedly, the quality of women's paid work shapes their poverty risk. Pressman (2003) assessed the role that occupational segregation plays in the "gender poverty gap." Using a 10-category occupational breakdown, he concluded that, across a group of 10 LIS countries, the gender poverty gap, based on disposable income, would be nearly three percentage points (or about 20 percent) lower if women household heads were employed in the same occupations as male household heads. Orsini, Büchel, and Mertens (2003) studied the impact of mothers' employment on family poverty risk in seven European countries. They concur with the established finding that there is a strong positive effect of mothers' paid work on family income across countries and family types.

In developing countries, in general, informal employment represents a greater share of women's employment than of men's, and, in many countries, over 60 percent of women workers are in informal employment outside agriculture—and substantially more if agriculture is included (Chen et al. 2005). Development scholars note that the link between women's economic hardship and their concentration in informal work has direct policy implications that are specific to low-income countries; these include strengthening efforts to organize women in informal sectors to increase their economic rewards, while, at the same time, implementing policies aimed at expanding formal employment opportunities.

It is important to acknowledge that informality can pose hazards in wealthier countries as well, especially when considering employment disparities by race or immigration status. Ng (2008), for example, assesses low hourly pay among home-based workers in Canada, underscoring the difficulties of regulating home-based work. Likewise, Collins and Mayer (2011:20) observe that welfare reform in the United States has created "a caste of low-wage workers with attenuated rights at the bottom of the labor market."

Poverty, Gender, and Parenting: Single Mothers

When addressing gendered poverty risks, single-mother households are usually at the forefront of discussions. This is understandable given that female-headed households have grown in prevalence in both wealthy (Klett-Davies 2007) and poorer countries (Chant 2007). Goldberg's (2010) volume on women and poverty in seven industrialized countries establishes that, in her study countries, there has been an overall increase in the share of poor households that are female headed. The shift in family structure, in conjunction with the rising poverty rates among single mothers, has led many researchers of gender and poverty to focus on single mothers.

Several studies from the early 1990s, mostly by sociologists, focused attention on the high risk of poverty (or of low income) among single mothers in high-income countries (Sorensen 1994; Gornick and Pavetti 1990; Wong, Garfinkel, and McLanahan 1993; McLanahan, Casper, and Sorensen 1995). Sorensen (1994) reported that a third of single-mother households in Germany—and over half in the United States—lived in poverty; single-mother households with three or more children had far higher poverty rates. In contrast, Sorensen found, Swedish single mothers' poverty rates were remarkably low (7 percent overall). McLanahan et al. (1995) assessed women's poverty cross-nationally, comparing the likelihood of poverty across various work-family combinations. Virtually everywhere, employed wives without children are the least likely to be poor, and single mothers—especially if not employed—the most likely. A substantial literature addresses child poverty; child poverty is, of course, distinct from women's poverty, but the two are inextricably linked because among the highest risk children are those who live with single mothers (see, e.g., Bradbury and Jäntti 1999; Gornick and Jäntti 2009).

A number of researchers have homed in on the role that employment and earnings play in explaining variation, both within and across countries, in single mothers' poverty risks (Nichols-Casebolt and Krysik 1997; Solera 1998; Morissens 1999; Christopher 2002a). Nichols-Casebolt and Krysik (1997) found that the percent of (never married) single mothers with earnings varied sharply across the four countries they studied, ranging from over 60 percent in France to 53–55 percent in the United States and Canada, to only 34 percent in Australia. They also found that being employed significantly reduced single mothers' poverty odds in all four countries, and that the independent poverty-reducing impact of being employed was greater everywhere than the impact of being a recipient of either child support or public transfers. Solera (1998) reports that variation in single mothers' employment rates explains nearly all the variation in single mothers' economic well-being across Sweden, the United Kingdom, and Italy. In Sweden, in particular, high levels of employment, shored up by strong policy supports, leave Swedish single mothers far less poor than, for example, their counterparts in the United Kingdom. In contrast, the majority of British single mothers have no (or very part-time) labor market attachment and rely instead on social assistance. Christopher (2002a) adds that low wages also matter. In the United States in particular, she reports, it is not low employment rates, but the preponderance of poverty-wage jobs that exacerbates U.S. single mothers' poverty. In fact, Christopher reports, compared to their counterparts elsewhere, U.S. single mothers who work full time are among the least likely to work in jobs that pay wages above the poverty line.

In the last decade, researchers—mainly political scientists and political sociologists—have considered the effects of policies outside the tax-and-transfer arena on single mothers' poverty. Huber et al. (2001) pooled LIS datasets across countries and over time to model the effects of labor market and political variables on a range of gendered outcomes; one of their dependent measures was single mothers' pre–tax-and-transfer poverty rate. They find that both union density and having a Left Cabinet have independent, significant, negative effects on single-mothers' market poverty. While having a Left Cabinet seems to operate at least in part by raising single mothers' employment rates, the causality underlying these institutional effects is not completely clear. Using a similar approach, Brady and Kall (2008) assess associations between women's (and men's) poverty and a range of policy and institutional factors. They conclude that economic growth, manufacturing employment (although, interestingly, not public employment), social security transfers, and public health spending all significantly influence both women's and men's poverty.

Given the propensity of lone mothers living in poverty, analysts often link gendered poverty with lone motherhood. Feminists have questioned, however, whether the two are, in fact, intrinsically linked (Chant 2007; Kabeer 2003). Some have critiqued the suggestion that a household is inevitably poorer without a man, noting that some of the assumptions underlying that claim are questionable. Lone females household heads might not have the material support of a male partner, in addition to facing gender inequalities in the labor market; yet the focus on the "feminization of household heads" tends to overlook the possibility that lone mothers (compared to partnered mothers) may enhance their, and their children's, well-being (Chant 2007). For example, women with live-in male partners may suffer due to intrahousehold inequalities. Brickell's (2010) research on gender and poverty in Cambodia found that some women have to work more (than they might wish to) to compensate for their husband's *lack* of work, while others are pressured to earn less money than they would otherwise because their husbands have laid claim to being the main breadwinner. Furthermore, focusing on single mother's poverty obscures the poverty of partnered women and the dependency of women on their partner's income to stay out of poverty.

Gender and Poverty: Age

Elderly women constitute another demographic group that faces an elevated higher risk of poverty, relative to men, in both wealthy and poorer countries. Elderly women's poverty risk stems from a number of factors. First, women tend to live longer than men. Second, the inequalities women face in the labor market throughout their life course follow them into their older years. Third, many pension systems condition benefits on earlier earnings, placing older women at a disadvantage. In short, women enter their older years with fewer resources than men due to disadvantages that have accumulated over the life course—in factors such as education, property holding, income, and social benefits (Vera-Sanso 2010).

In affluent countries, state transfers play a large role in keeping the elderly out of poverty. Goldberg's (2010) edited volume on women in seven high-income countries established that, while countries that place greater emphasis on employment to reduce poverty, such as the United States, might have lower pre-transfer poverty rates, countries with higher levels of poverty reduction report lower rates of post-transfer poverty among elderly women. In fact, after accounting for transfers, the United States has exceptionally high poverty rates among elderly women (Sandström and Smeeding 2005). Yet, current pension systems are designed such that elderly women, especially those who are divorced, widowed, or never married, are at a much higher risk of poverty than are elderly men (ibid.).

Many researchers have addressed the link between the entitlement structure of pension systems and women's pension protection (Budowsky 2010; Falkingham, Evandrou, and Vlachantoni 2010; Vera-Sanso 2010). Many wealthy countries have earnings-related pension systems that are based on economic contributions over the life course. Women are clearly at a disadvantage in these pension systems, due to their greater likelihood of having breaks in employment or periods of part-time work (Falkingham et al. 2010). In these countries, elderly women often rely on means-tested benefits late in life. In contrast, the universal pension schemes, found in Denmark, Finland, and the Netherlands, offer pension income to the elderly regardless of their work history. Falkingham and her colleagues (2010) suggest that policies should either offer universal pension entitlements, or, if that is not viable, they should account for the caring work performed by women when calculating entitlements. Budowsky (2010) warns that, in the latter case, it is important not to institutionalize gendered divisions of labor in unpaid care work; interventions that ease women's care responsibilities earlier in life (such as childcare facilities, school meals, and housing), have the potential to reduce labor market inequality during prime-age years and, in turn, reduce women's risk of elderly poverty.

In the developing country context, Vera-Sanso (2010) examines gender and ageing in India. While some elderly women receive old-age and/or widowhood benefits, the Indian government tends to disregard the older urban poor, expecting them to rely on filial support and/or on working late in life. These expectations are often based on class and gender biases that overlook the plight of the urban poor in India and especially that of women. For example, the age threshold for entitlement does not take into account the life expectancies of the urban poor, nor the more physically demanding jobs that they hold. Furthermore, because remarriage is stigmatized, widows are often forced into paid work, and they often take low-paying jobs.

Although research on elderly poverty most often focuses on developed countries, elderly poverty is a growing concern in developing countries because populations are aging at a more rapid rate than in wealthier countries. In order to address the gendered aspect of elderly poverty, researchers should be cognizant of the complex interactions between women's labor market outcomes and the characteristics of pension systems, keeping an eye on the gendered disadvantages associated with both.

"Engendering" Poverty Alleviation

Not surprisingly, a major theme cutting across gendered poverty studies concerns the impact on poverty of national conditions—including public policies (especially tax-benefit systems and work-family reconciliation policies), political configurations, and macroeconomics outcomes. Social and economic policies and institutions can contribute greatly to poverty alleviation, with policy variation explaining much cross-country variation in poverty rates.

Poverty-alleviation programs, unfortunately, are often insufficiently responsive to the gendered aspects of poverty risks. This is the case for both welfare state policies in wealthy countries and development agendas in poorer countries. Gita Sen (2000:273) identifies key gendered barriers to poverty alleviation:

- The unequal division of (and access to) resources; unequal divisions of labor within and outside the home; and associated ideologies and behavioral norms.
- Nonrecognition of the "care economy" which shapes the resources, labor, and ideologies that underlie the reproduction of human beings.

Sen discusses these challenges in relation to low- and middle-income countries, yet in general the same hold true for high-income countries.

Low- and Middle-income Countries

There have been two main approaches to poverty eradication in the global development agenda: market-driven and labor-intensive growth (Sen 2000). Neither of these adequately addresses gendered poverty. Market-driven and labor-intensive growth approaches rely on economic growth as a means for mitigating poverty. However, feminist scholars have noted that, when considering multidimensional aspects of poverty, a solely market-based approach typically has negative consequences for women. In some cases, these antipoverty approaches have caused further harm to women in developing countries because they disregard the complex interactions among gender, poverty, and social institutions; rather, they focus on the very institution that has produced so much gender inequality—the market.

While employment is key to overcoming poverty, approaches that focus solely on economic activity disregard other dimensions of poverty that have especially significant effects on women. Many of the jobs created through market-driven or labor-intensive growth are low-quality jobs, often in the informal sector—increasing the chance of women being "invisible" to social policy or to poverty-alleviation programs. Gender-blind economic growth can place additional burdens on women's well-being. Brickell's (2010) study, in Cambodia, revealed problematic consequences in the lives of her subjects, including the additional burden that paid work can place on women's familial responsibilities, worsening their time poverty, the continual wage disparities women face in the labor market, and men's lack of acceptance of women's waged work.

High-income Countries

Scholars and activists, similarly, have highlighted the need for poverty alleviation programs in high-income countries to take into account multidimensional aspects of poverty and to acknowledge that women's inequality is rooted both in the labor market and at home. In recent years, social policies have faced retrenchment pressures, with substantial cutbacks currently resulting from the continuing economic crisis. Postausterity welfare states, in conjunction with the rise of low-wage labor markets, are creating an increasingly precarious position for women already at risk of poverty (Collins and Mayer 2011).

Perrons (2010) argues that concentrated efforts should ensure that policies aimed at poor women are actually reaching them. She points out that, even with economic growth, enduring gender inequalities place women at higher risk of poverty. Despite state supplementation of income to help counter poverty, Perron stresses that transfers usually occur at the household level, ignoring the individual dynamics of poverty and gender, as well as the instability of partnerships and households. Perrons highlights the need to address gender inequality and women's likelihood of earning low wages in particular.

A Portrait of Gender and Poverty across 26 High- and Middle-Income Countries

In designing the empirical results presented here, we draw on lessons from this prior literature, by incorporating the main risk factors that have been found to matter—especially women's family structure and their employment status.[3]

Social Policy Regimes

To place the variation across these 26 countries into institutional context, our study countries are grouped into six country clusters. In the text and figures, we refer to these groupings by their geographic/regional or linguistic characteristics. We classify Australia, Canada, Ireland, the United Kingdom, and the United States as *Anglophone* countries;[4] Austria, Belgium, Germany, France, Luxembourg, and the Netherlands as *Continental European* countries; Denmark, Finland, Norway, and Sweden as *Nordic European* countries; Hungary and Slovenia as *Eastern European* countries; Greece, Italy, and Spain as *Southern European* countries; and Brazil, Colombia, Guatemala, Mexico, Peru, and Uruguay as *Latin American* countries.[5] Of course, ultimately it is not geography, region, or language that makes these groupings meaningful for our analyses of gender and poverty across countries. These clusters are meaningful because of their well-established institutional commonalties. Substantial within-cluster variability is undoubtedly evident in all of these groups, but overall they are clearly characterized by common features.

This cluster framework is rooted largely in the theoretical and empirical work of Danish sociologist Gosta Esping-Andersen, as presented in his 1990 book *The Three Worlds of Welfare Capitalism*. Esping-Andersen classified the major welfare states of the industrialized West into three clusters, each characterized by shared principles of social welfare entitlement and relatively homogeneous outcomes. Subsequent cross-national research extended "the three worlds" to characterize other country groupings as well.

While comparative welfare-state research, especially with a European focus, generally excludes Latin America, social policy in these countries also displays some characteristic features. Although Latin America has a long history of social policy development, income benefits have typically been extended only to formal workers, mainly in urban labor markets, and informal and/or rural workers have generally been excluded. One result is that Latin America is characterized by extremely high levels of income inequality, and post-transfer inequality is often greater than pre-transfer inequality. In recent years, new antipoverty programs known as Conditional Cash Transfers (CCT) provide money targeted to poor families, conditional on their adherence to specified behavioral rules (such as attending school or getting medical care). Three countries included in our empirical work, Brazil, Colombia, and Mexico, now have CCT programs—although only the former two were operating at the time that these microdata were collected.

We make use of country clusters in this chapter because they bring into relief the importance of policy configurations for poverty reduction, and because they help us identify empirical patterns across our comparison countries. Working with these well-known groupings will also allow comparative scholars to situate our findings into the larger literature on the nature and consequences of social policy variation across countries.

Data, Methods, and Analytic Strategy

The results reported here are based on data from the LIS Database, a public-access microdatabase, now containing data from over 40 countries. The LIS staff collects datasets (mostly based on household-income surveys), harmonizes them into a common template, and makes them available to registered researchers via remote access. The LIS Database includes repeated cross-sections from participating countries, with datasets available for up to eight points in time, depending on the country. The LIS datasets include income, labor market, and demographic indicators. The microdata are available at the household- and person-level, and records can be linked between levels.[6] This analysis uses datasets from the early and mid-2000s.

Unit of Analysis

Measuring differentials in women's and men's likelihood, or intensity, of poverty is never a simple exercise. As we noted earlier, it is complicated because large numbers of women, especially prime-age women, share their homes with men. Designating "her" and "his" income, for the most part, is not feasible. First, many sources of income, both taxes and transfers, are received at the household level. Second, even if some or all income sources could be disaggregated, doing so has limited meaning, as individuals who live together (especially partners) generally pool their income, so "her" well-being is clearly shaped by "his" income as well as her own. (As a result of these complexities, most research on gender gaps in economic well-being focus on market earnings.[7]) In this study, the approach taken considers individuals poor if they live in poor *households*—an approach that, of course, produces relatively small gender gaps among adults who are partnered.

Poverty Measures

In Figure 10.1, we report poverty outcomes based on income (from earnings, capital, and private transfers), after taxes, but before public transfers are taken into account; this is labeled "pre-transfer income." We compare these to poverty outcomes based on income after both taxes and public transfers (including social insurance and social assistance) have been accounted for; this is labeled "post-transfer income." Figures 10.2 and 10.3 report poverty based on this latter measure, post-tax–post-transfer income.

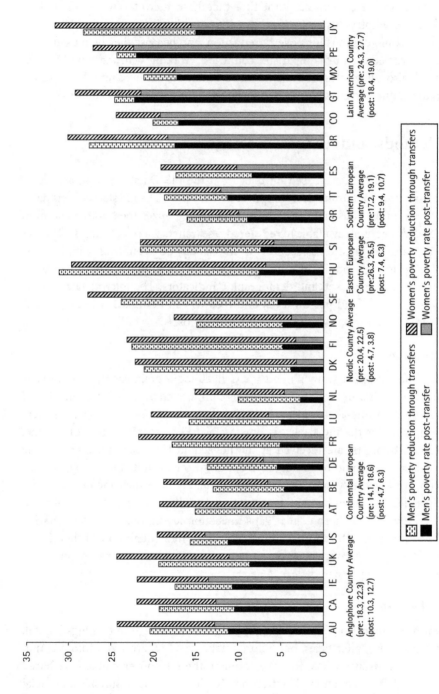

FIGURE 10.1 Poverty Rates by Gender: Pre-transfer Income (early-middle)

Note: All incomes in post-tax. Country group averages are unweighted. Poverty rates are based on relative poverty measures. The total height of the bars represent men's and women's poverty rates, pre-transfer.

Legend:
- Men's poverty reduction through transfers
- Men's poverty rate post-transfer
- Women's poverty reduction through transfers
- Women's poverty rate post-transfer

Anglophone Country Average
(pre: 18.3, 22.3)
(post: 10.3, 12.7)

Continental European
Country Average
(pre: 14.1, 18.6)
(post: 4.7, 6.3)

Nordic Country Average
(pre: 20.4, 22.5)
(post: 4.7, 3.8)

Eastern European
Country Average
(pre: 26.3, 25.5)
(post: 7.4, 6.3)

Southern European
Country Average
(pre: 17.2, 19.1)
(post: 9.4, 10.7)

Latin American Country
Average (pre: 24.3, 27.7)
(post: 18.4, 19.0)

Country axis labels: AU CA IE UK US AT BE DE FR LU NL DK FI NO SE HU SI GR IT ES BR CO GT MX PE UY

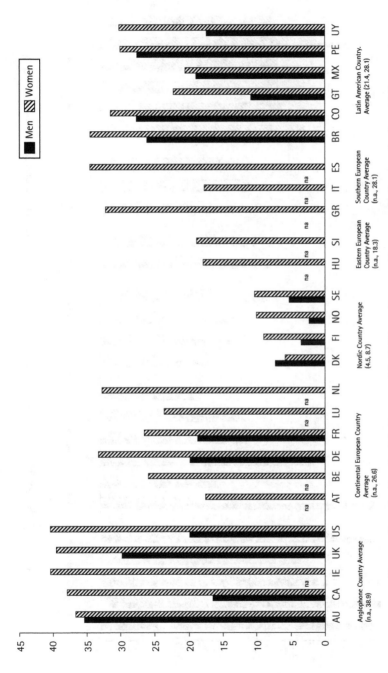

FIGURE 10.2 Poverty Rates by Gender: No Partner with Children, Post-tax–Post-transfer Income (early-middle 2000s)

Note: Country group averages are unweighted. Cell sizes that are too small for reporting are marked "n.a."

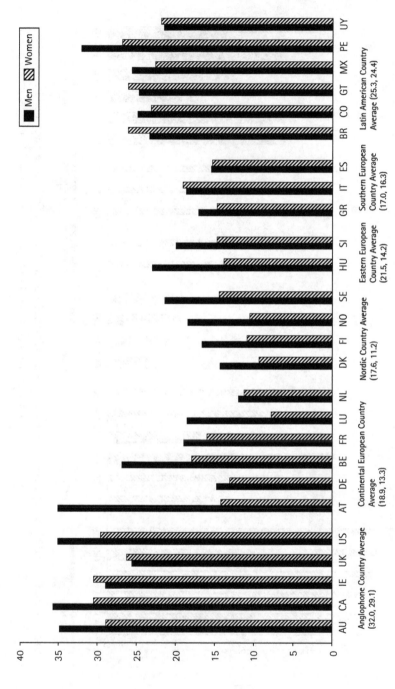

FIGURE 10.3 Poverty Rates by Gender: Low Labor Market Status, Post-tax–Post-transfer Income (early-middle 2000s)

Note: Country group averages are unweighted.

Some datasets in the LIS archive report only after-tax income. To maximize cross-national comparability, the study is limited to after-tax income throughout. Unfortunately, this approach clearly lessens the degree of redistribution reported relative to a comparison of pre-tax/pre-transfer income versus post-tax/post-transfer income. In this case, the results are likely to be similar either way, because most poor families in these countries have fairly limited tax liabilities.

In all of our analyses, we use a relative poverty line set at 50 percent of national median disposable income among all persons, adjusted for family size.

Demographic and Labor Market Variables

The study sample is limited to persons aged 25–54. Although elderly women are at elevated risk for poverty (as we noted earlier), we restrict these empirical analyses to prime-age adults, simply to contain the scope of our presentation. To highlight the high risk of poverty among single parents, we present poverty rates of single heads of households with children below the age of 18 in the household.

Results

Gender Differences in Household Poverty Rates

Figure 10.1 reports poverty rates by gender.[8] For each country, the left bar indicates men's poverty rates; the right bar indicates women's poverty rates. The total height of the bars represents poverty rates pre-transfers. The patterned parts of the bars illustrate poverty reduction through transfers. Finally, the solid parts of the bars report the post-transfer poverty rates for men and women. This figure reveals a telling story of the role of public income transfers in addressing poverty and its interaction with gender.

Among prime-age adults, the prevalence of "pre-transfer" poverty varies markedly across these countries, ranging from a low of 10–15 percent in the Netherlands to a high of 28–32 percent in Hungary, Brazil, and Uruguay.[9] Substantial variation in "pre-transfer" poverty across the country groupings is also evident, with country clusters showing fairly homogeneous poverty rates.

Income transfers reduce poverty substantially, as indicated by the poverty-reduction results. Post-transfer poverty rates are much lower than pre-transfer rates everywhere. The country clusters again show consistent patterns with respect to "post-transfer" poverty rates. It is evident, of course, that accounting for transfers causes these country cluster's poverty rates to reorder substantially. Indeed, the percentage of poverty reduced by transfers varies sharply across them. Clearly, these 26 countries, and these country groups, vary both by the level of poverty prior to transfers and by the extent to which income transfers pull otherwise poor households out of poverty.

Before income transfers are taken into account, the pattern with respect to gender is remarkably uniform: with the exception of the two Eastern European countries, women are everywhere more likely to be poor than are men—although in general the differences are relatively small. Women's "pre-transfer" poverty rates are higher than men's by one percentage point or less in Denmark and Finland and, on the high end, by about four to five percentage points across the Anglophone and Continental countries, and in Colombia and Guatemala. In Slovenia, women and men are equally likely to be poor and, in Hungary, men are slightly more likely to be poor than are women.

After accounting for income transfers, the gender picture becomes more favorable for women. In all countries, when we shift from "pre" to "post" poverty, the gender gap narrows, reversing direction entirely in the four Nordic countries and Guatemala. Clearly, the overall finding is that, across these countries, income transfers are disproportionately reducing women's prevalence of poverty.

Gender Differences in Poverty Rates—Among Single Parent Households

Much prior literature on poverty establishes that family type (and/or household structure), interacted with gender, dramatically affects the likelihood of poverty within countries. Our findings confirm that single-parent households—which are overwhelmingly female headed in all of these countries—face the greatest risk of poverty (see Figure 10.2).

Figure 10.2 reports poverty rates among single-parent households disaggregated by gender. The first crucial result is that women are far more prevalent in this family-type group than are men. In this age group (25–54), single parents constitute about 2 to 5 percent of women in Greece, Hungary, Italy, Luxembourg, the Netherlands, Slovenia, and Spain; and 6–10 percent or higher in the other countries (results calculated but not shown). In contrast, in most of these countries, less than 1–2 percent of men are single fathers. In fact, as evident in Figure 10.2, in fully 10 of the 26 countries, we have less than 30 cases of single fathers in these LIS datasets, hence we report "not available" (n.a.) rather than a poverty rate. Clearly, single parenthood, and its associated economic hazards, is demonstrably more prevalent among women throughout these countries.

Among single mothers across all of our study countries, the prevalence of post-transfer poverty is marked. In the 16 countries in which we can compare poverty rates among single mothers with those of single fathers, these mothers are more likely to be poor nearly everywhere, and sometimes dramatically so. Two Anglophone countries especially stand out—Canada and the United States—where single mothers are more than 20 percentage points more likely to be poor than are single fathers.

Gender Differences in Poverty Rates—Among Those with Low Labor Market Attachment

Finally, in the third figure, we report the difference between women's and men's poverty rates among adults with lower labor market attachment, as defined by their earnings (see Figure 10.3). Low labor market attachment (a person-level measure) is defined as having earnings in the bottom fifth of each country's earnings distribution, including those with zero earnings.

A counterintuitive gendered story emerges when looking at differences between women's and men's poverty rate among adults with weak labor market attachment. In most of these countries—Ireland, the United Kingdom, Italy, and three Latin American countries are exceptions—women with weak links to employment are *less* likely to be poor than are their male counterparts. This result is not, however, unexpected—because many more women than men in this age group (especially among parents) are out of the labor market; a large share of these women are part-nered with men with substantial labor market attachment and sufficient income to keep their households out of poverty. In contrast, among men in this age range who are weakly attached to the labor market—a less common occurrence—a higher proportion have no partners (and no second income), while substantial numbers share their homes with partners who also have no or weak connections to the labor market.

This finding has disconcerting implications for women and their risk of poverty. Women might gain from receiving economic support from their partners (in the short term), but their economic dependency on their male partners' income also carries an array of risks. This dependency, coupled with the disadvantages women face in the labor market, leaves many of these women at elevated risk of poverty in the event that they lose access to their partner's income. Women's reliance on income that "comes through" their partners can be especially problematic later in life, when women rely on pension entitlements (their or their partners) that penalize them for their weaker earnings histories during their earlier years.

Conclusion

Our review of the literature and our empirical analyses shed light on gendered poverty outcomes. Our findings reveal how gender intersects with various social institutions to shape women's risk of poverty, both absolutely and relative to men's. While the relationship between gender and poverty is complex, several elements of this relationship are evident.

First, overall, women face a higher risk of poverty than do men, due to several economic and social factors. In our empirical analysis, we found that, before income transfers are taken into account, poverty outcomes with respect to gender are remarkably uniform: in nearly all countries included in our study, women are more likely to be (relatively) poor than are men—although in general the differences are fairly small. However, public income transfers matter for reducing poverty disparities by gender. After accounting for income transfers, the picture becomes more favorable for women. In all 26 countries, when we shift from pre-transfer to post-transfer poverty, the poverty gender gap narrows. In a few countries, it reverses direction entirely. Clearly, across these countries, income transfers—even with their shortcomings vis-à-vis women's disadvantage—play a key role in reducing women's market-generated poverty.

Second, family structure matters—most especially, single parenting. Among single mothers, the heightened poverty risk is driven by the lack of a partner's income coupled with the disadvantages women face in the labor market. Our comparison of poverty rates among single mothers, with those of single fathers, show that single mothers are more likely to be poor (than are single fathers) nearly everywhere and sometimes dramatically so. Two Anglophone countries especially stand out—Canada and the United States—where single mothers are more than 20 percentage points more likely to be poor than are single fathers.

Third, many women are economically dependent on their male partners. A key facet of the poverty risk faced by women is illustrated by our analysis of men and women with weak labor attachment. Nearly everywhere, these women are less likely than their male counterparts to be poor—and often by a substantial magnitude. As noted earlier, this finding has a double-edged-sword aspect to it. On the one hand, it highlights the extent to which men "provide" for their female partners, reducing women's likelihood of being poor. On the other hand, the "income transfers" that women receive within their families, and that keep them out of poverty, are inherently unstable; women's economic well-being depends on their partners' continued economic success and on their families remaining intact. Notably, much of this economic disadvantage stems from women's disproportionate performance of unpaid care work. Importantly—as much research has established—women's dependency on their male partners' income during their prime-age years places them at heightened poverty risk during their elderly years.

Fourth, national contexts matter—and they matter a lot. While the focus of this analysis concerns gender differentials, it is crucial to emphasize that women—as well as men—report widely varying levels of poverty across countries. Gender clearly matters for women's well-being but so does one's home country. Women's and men's poverty outcomes, across these countries, are undoubtedly shaped by an array of country-specific institutions, including social policy designs.

Although the concept of the "feminization of poverty" may not adequately characterize the interplay between poverty and gender, poverty—in countries at diverse levels of economic development—undoubtedly has a gendered cast to it. Nevertheless, extensive work lies ahead for scholars of gender and poverty. Further empirical analyses of gender and poverty are much needed, especially analyses that use high-quality data, incorporate noneconomic metrics—such as constrained capabilities and social exclusion—and capture both dynamics and levels. Finally, scholars would do well to carry out more fine-grained policy analyses aimed at identifying and evaluating the ways in which, and the extent to which, poverty-alleviation policies and strategies account for and respond to gender differences in the causes, natures, and consequences of poverty.

NOTES

1. The World Bank ranks countries into four income categories—high, upper-middle, lower-middle, and low—based on per capita GDP. As of the early-mid 2000s, 19 of these 26 countries were classified as high-income countries. Hungary, Mexico, and Uruguay were classified as upper-middle income countries. Brazil, Colombia, Guatemala, and Peru were classified as lower-middle income countries. The LIS Database contains no low-income countries.

2. See section "Data, Methods, and Analytical Strategy," for a description of the LIS data.

3. Section IV of this chapter is based on empirical work carried out collaboratively with Markus Jäntti and reported in Gornick and Jäntti 2010a, 2010b. We are grateful to Markus Jäntti for his invaluable input, especially his contributions to the design and construction of the results presented in Figures 10.1–10.3.

4. Following the convention in cross-national research, we refer to Canada as Anglophone, although it is officially bilingual, part Anglophone and part Francophone.

5. In 2009, LIS added five new Latin American datasets to its archive—from Brazil, Colombia, Guatemala, Peru, and Uruguay—and the analyses reported here were among the first to use these datasets.

6. Detailed information on the original surveys, including sample sizes, is available at http://www.lisdatacenter.org/our-data/lis-database/by-country/.

7. For a review of LIS-based research on gender gaps in labor market outcomes, see Gornick (2004).

8. In the three figures, the countries are abbreviated as follows: Australia (AU), Canada (CA), Ireland (IE), United Kingdom (UK), United States(US); Austria (AT), Belgium (BE), Germany (DE), France (FR), Luxembourg (LU), Netherlands (NL); Denmark (DK), Finland (FI), Norway (NO), Sweden (SE); Hungary (HU), Slovenia (SI); Greece (GR), Italy (IT), Spain (ES); Brazil (BR), Colombia (CO), Guatemala (GT), Mexico (MX), Peru (PE), Uruguay (UY).

9. The ranges reported refer to the poverty rates of men and women, respectively.

REFERENCES

Barnes, Matt, Christopher Heady, Sue Middleton, Jane Millar, Fotis Papadopoulos, Graham Room, and Panos Tsakloglou. 2002. *Poverty and Social Exclusion in Europe*. Northampton, MA: Edward Elgar.

Benería, Lourdes. 2003. *Gender, Development, and Globalisation: Economics as if All People Mattered*. London: Routledge.

Bradbury, Bruce and Markus Jäntti. 1999. *Child Poverty across Industrialized Nations*. Economic and Social Policy Series No. 71. Paris: UNICEF.

Brady, David and Denise Kall. 2008. "Nearly Universal, but Somewhat Distinct: The Feminization of Poverty in Affluent Western Democracies, 1969–2000." *Social Science Research* 37:976–1007.

Brickell, Katherine. 2010. "Gender, Poverty and Work in Cambodia." Pp. 458–62 in *The International Handbook of Gender and Poverty: Concepts, Research, Policy*, edited by S. Chant. Northampton, MA: Edward Elgar.

Budowsky, Monica. 2010. "Poverty, Gender and Old Age: Pension Models in Costa Rica and Chile." Pp. 226–31 in *The International Handbook of Gender and Poverty: Concepts, Research, Policy,* edited by S. Chant. Northampton, MA: Edward Elgar.

Casper, Lynne, Sara McLanahan, and Irwin Garfinkel. 1994. "The Gender Poverty Gap: What Can We Learn From Other Countries?" *American Sociological Review* 59:594–605.

Castel, Robert. 1991. "De l'Indigence a l'Éxclusion, la Désaffiliation. Précarité du Travail et Vulnérabilité Relationnelle." In *Face a l'Éxclusion: Le Modele Français,* edited by J. Donzelot. Paris: Editions Esprit.

Carr, Marilyn and Martha Atler Chen. 2002. "Globalization and the Informal Economy: How Global Trade and Investment Impact on the Working Poor." Working Paper on the Informal Economy (Employment Sector 2002/1). Geneva: International Labor Organization.

Chant, Sylvia. 2003. "New Contributions to the Analysis of Poverty: Methodological and Conceptual Challenges to Understanding Poverty from a Gender Perspective." Serie Mujer y Desarrollo #47. Santiago: CEPAL-ECLAC.

Chant, Sylvia. 2007. *Gender and Generation and Poverty: Exploring the "Feminization of Poverty" in Africa, Asia and Latin America.* Northampton, MA: Edward Elgar.

Chant, Sylvia, ed. 2010. *The International Handbook of Gender and Poverty: Concepts, Research, Policy.* Northampton, MA: Edward Elgar.

Chen, Martha, Joann Vanek, Francie Lund, James Heintz, with Renana Jhabvala and Christine Bonner. 2005. *Progress of the Worlds Women—2005.* New York: UNIFEM.

Christopher, Karen. 2002a. "Single Motherhood, Employment, or Social Assistance: Why Are U.S. Women Poorer than Women in Other Affluent Nations?" *Journal of Poverty* 6:61–80.

Christopher, Karen. 2002b. "Welfare State Regimes and Mothers' Poverty." *Social Politics* 9:60–86.

Christopher, Karen. 2002c. "Caregiving, Welfare States and Mothers' Poverty." Pp. 113–32 in *Child Care and Inequality: Re-thinking Carework for Children and Youth,* edited by F. Cancian, D. Kurz, A. London, R. Reviere, M. Tuominen. New York: Routledge Press.

Collins, Jane L. and Victoria Mayer. 2011. *Both Hands Tied: Welfare Reform and the Race to the Bottom of the Low-Wage Market.* Chicago: University of Chicago Press.

Falkingham, Jane, Maria Evandrou, and Athina Vlachantoni. 2010. "Gender, Poverty and Pensions in the United Kingdom." Pp. 232–40 in *The International Handbook of Gender and Poverty: Concepts, Research, Policy,* edited by S. Chant. Northampton, MA: Edward Elgar.

Folbre, Nancy. 1994. *Who Pays for the Kids? Gender and the Social Structures of Constraint.* London: Routledge.

Gallie, Duncan and Serge Paugam. 2004. "Unemployment, Poverty, and Social Isolation: An Assessment of the Current State of Social Exclusion Theory." Pp. 34–53 in *Resisting Marginalization: Unemployment Experience and Social Policy in the European Union.* London: Oxford University Press.

Goldberg, Gertrude Schaffner, ed. 2010. *Poor Women in Rich Countries: The Feminisation of Poverty over the Life Course.* New York: Oxford University Press.

Gornick, Janet C. and LaDonna Pavetti. 1990. "A Demographic Model of Poverty Among Families with Children: A Comparative Analysis of Five Industrialized Countries Based on Microdata from the Luxembourg Income Study." LIS Working Paper No. 65. Luxembourg.

Gornick, Janet C. 2002. "Against the Grain: 'Social Exclusion' and American Political Culture." Pp. 77–88 in *Beyond Child Poverty: The Social Exclusion of Children,* edited by A. Kahn and S. Kamerman. New York: Columbia Institute for Child and Family Policy.

Gornick, Janet C. 2004. "Women's Economic Outcomes, Gender Inequality, and Public Policy: Lessons from the Luxembourg Income Study." *Socio-Economic Review* 2:213–38.

Gornick, Janet C. and Markus Jäntti. 2009. "Child Poverty in Upper-Income Countries: Lessons from the Luxembourg Income Study." Pp. 339–38 in *From Child Welfare to Child Well-being: An International Perspective on Knowledge in the Service of Making Policy*, edited by S. Kamerman, S. Phipps, and A. Ben-Arieh. New York: Springer.

Gornick, Janet C. and Markus Jäntti. 2010a. "Women, Poverty, and Social Policy Regimes: A Cross-National Analysis." LIS Working Paper No. 534. Luxembourg.

Gornick, Janet C. and Markus Jäntti. 2010b. "Women, Poverty, and Social Policy Regimes: A Cross-National Analysis." Pp. 63–95 in *Social Security, Poverty and Social Exclusion in Rich and Poorer Countries. International Studies on Social Security*, edited by P. Saunders and R. Sainsbury. Vol. 16. Antwerp: Intersentia.

Heintz, James. 2010. "Women's Employment, Economic Risk and Poverty." Pp. 434–39 in *The International Handbook of Gender and Poverty: Concepts, Research, Policy*, edited by S. Chant. Northampton, MA: Edward Elgar.

Huber, Evelyne, John Stephens, David Bradley, Stephanie Moller, and Francois Nielsen, 2001. "The Welfare State and Gender Equality." LIS Working Paper No. 279. Luxembourg.

Jackson, Cecile. 1999. "Social Exclusion and Gender: Does One Size Fit All?" *European Journal of Development Research* 11:125–46.

Jackson, Cecile and Richard Palmer-Jones. 2000. "Rethinking Gendered Poverty and Work". Pp. 145–70 in *Gendered Poverty and Well-Being*, edited by S. Razavi. Malden, MA: Blackwell.

Kabeer, Naila. 2003. *Gender Mainstreaming in Poverty Eradication and the Millennium Development Goals: A Handbook for Policy-makers and Other Stakeholders*. London: Commonwealth Secretariat.

Klett-Davies, Martina. 2007. *Going It Alone: Lone Motherhood in Late Modernity*. Burlington, VT: Ashgate.

McLanahan, Sara, Lynne Casper, and Annemette Sorensen. 1995. "Women's Roles and Women's Poverty in Eight Industrialized Countries." Pp. 258–78 in *Gender and Family Change in Industrialized Countries*, edited by K. Mason and A. Jensen. Oxford: IUSSP/Oxford University Press.

Morissens, Ann. 1999. "Solo Mothers and Poverty: Do Policies Matter? A Comparative Case Study of Sweden and Belgium." LIS Working Paper No. 210. Luxembourg.

Ng, Roxanna. 2008. "Homeworking: Dream Realized or Freedom Constrained? The Globalized Reality of Immigrant Garment Workers." Pp. 95–101 in *Daily Struggles: The Deepening Racialization and Feminization of Poverty in Canada*, edited by M. A. Wallis and S. Kwok. Toronto: Canadian's Scholars' Press.

Nichols-Casebolt, Ann and Judy Krysik. 1997. "The Economic Well-Being of Never- and Ever-Married Single Mother Families: A Cross National Comparison." *Journal of Social Service Research* 23:19–40.

Orsini, Kristian, Felix Büchel, and Antje Mertens. 2003. "Is Mothers' Employment an Effective Means to Fight Family Poverty? Empirical Evidence from Seven European Countries." LIS Working Paper No. 363. Luxembourg.

Pearson, Ruth. 2010. "Women's Work, Nimble Fingers and Women's Mobility in the Global Economy." Pp. 421–26 in *The International Handbook of Gender and Poverty: Concepts, Research, Policy*, edited by S. Chant. Northampton, MA: Edward Elgar.

Perrons, Diane. 2010. "Gender, Work and Poverty in High-Income Countries." Pp. 409–14 in *The International Handbook of Gender and Poverty: Concepts, Research, Policy*, edited by S. Chant. Northampton, MA: Edward Elgar.

Pressman, Steven. 1998. "The Gender Poverty Gap in Developed Countries: Causes and Cures." *Social Science Journal* 35:275–87.

Pressman, Steven. 2002. "Explaining the Gender Poverty Gap in Developed and Transitional Economies." *Journal of Economic Issues* 36:17–40.

Pressman, Steven. 2003. "The Feminist Explanations for the Feminization of Poverty." *Journal of Economic Issues* 37:353–61.

Razavi, Shahra. 2000. "Gendered Poverty and Well-Being: Introduction." Pp. 1–25 in *Gendered Poverty and Well-Being*, edited by S. Razavi. Malden, MA: Blackwell.

Razavi, Shahra and Silke Staab. 2010. "Gender, Poverty and Inequality: The Role of Markets, States and Households." Pp. 427–33 in *The International Handbook of Gender and Poverty: Concepts, Research, Policy*, edited by S. Chant. Northampton, MA: Edward Elgar.

Sandström, Susanna and Timothy Smeeding. 2005. "Poverty and Income Maintenance in Old Age: A Cross-National View of Low Income Older Women." *Feminist Economics* 11:163–98.

Sen, Amartya. 1999. *Developed as Freedom*. New York: Anchor Books.

Sen, Gita. 2000. "Engendering Poverty Alleviation: Challenges and Opportunities." Pp. 269–76 in *Gendered Poverty and Well-being*, edited by S. Razavi. Malden, MA: Blackwell.

Sen, Gita. 2010. "Poor Households or Poor Women: Is There a Difference?" Pp. 101–4 in *The International Handbook of Gender and Poverty: Concepts, Research, Policy*, edited by S. Chant. Northampton, MA: Edward Elgar.

Solera, Cristina. 1998. "Income Transfers and Support for Mothers' Employment: The Link to Family Poverty Risks: A Comparison between Italy, Sweden and the UK." LIS Working Paper No. 192. Luxembourg.

Sorensen, Annemette. 1994. "Single Mothers, Low Income and Women's Economic Risks. The Cases of Sweden, West Germany and the United States." *European Sociological Review* 10:173–88.

Sugden, Robert. 1993. "Welfare, Resources, and Capabilities: A Review of Inequality Reexamined by Amartya Sen." *Journal of Economic Literature* 31:1947.

Vera-Sanso, Penny. 2010. "Gender, Urban Poverty and Ageing in India: Conceptual and Policy Issues." Pp. 220–25 in *The International Handbook of Gender and Poverty: Concepts, Research, Policy*, edited by S. Chant. Northampton, MA: Edward Elgar.

Vosko, Leah F., Martha MacDonald, and Iain Campbell. 2011. "Introduction: Gender and the Concept of Precarious Employment." Pp. 1–25 in *Gender and the Contours of Precarious Employment*, edited by L. Vosko, M. MacDonald, and I. Campbell. New York: Routledge.

Wong, Irene, Irwin Garfinkel, and Sara McLanahan. 1993. "Single-Mother Families in Eight Countries: Economic Status and Social Policy." *Social Service Review* 67:177–97.

Wright, Robert. 1995. "Women and Poverty in Industrialized Countries." *Journal of Income Distribution* 5:31–46.

CHAPTER 11

··

LIFE, DEATH, AND RESURRECTIONS

The Culture of Poverty Perspective

··

JESSI STREIB, SAUNJUHI VERMA,
WHITNEY WELSH, AND LINDA M. BURTON

THIS chapter is a critical treatise on the culture of poverty thesis. The thesis has lived many lives in scholarship about the poor, mostly in the United States, as it is repeatedly put to rest only to be resurrected again when a new wave of poverty research emerges. For example, a decade into the millennium and over a half century since the thesis emerged in the scholarly literature, sociologists Mario Small, David Harding, and Michele Lamont (2010) edited a volume of the *ANNALS of the American Academy of Political and Social Science* on new ways of studying culture and poverty. After a fierce backlash against the culture of poverty argument in the 1960s and 1970s, the edited volume revived academic and policy interests in the culture of poverty, albeit from a "new perspective." Selective reactions to the *ANNALS* volume and its claim of offering a new perspective on culture and poverty were aptly reflected in a statement by an urban anthropologist with whom we consulted: "How many lives has this cat [referring to the culture of poverty] lived anyway? Surely it is more than nine!" This scholar's sentiments matched our own. The thesis has been resurrected in many forms, some of which merely reflect a play on words, or a reconceptualization of culture, but not the overall thesis (Vaisey 2010). Others attempt to sporadically revive the culture of poverty as a way of thinking about the poor by arguing that the thesis has been deeply misunderstood (Harvey and Reed 1996).

The culture of poverty argument also lives, dies, and is reborn time and again in the public imagination and discourse. For example, shortly after the publication of Small, Harding, and Lamont's (2010) special issue of the *ANNALS*, policy-makers, pundits, and average U.S. citizens debated the culture of poverty in the media. Each attached their own meaning to the thesis. A *New York Times* (Cohen 2010) article seemed to celebrate, or at least eye with curiosity, the idea that cultural explanations of poverty, once "That Which Must Not Be Named" were now being discussed again. An NPR (2010) report raised the issue of whether the culture of poverty argument is an "insult that blames the victims of institutional racism." An earlier book took a very different stance when it claimed that inner city poverty stems from a culture that devalues work and whose occupants may be genetically inferior (Herrnstein and Murray 1994).

In this chapter we consider the many lives, deaths, and reincarnations of the culture of poverty thesis. We begin with a short intellectual history of the thesis and then show how the argument has been interspersed throughout U.S. history and applied to various groups. We illustrate that while the culture of poverty perspective is used often in the United States, it also ebbs and flows in countries as diverse as England and Bahrain. After discussing the public reproduction of the culture of poverty thesis, we turn our attention toward the main focus of this chapter: its scholarly reproduction. We begin with the observation that at the center of the culture of poverty argument is a binary whereby segments of the poor, racial minorities, and immigrants are positioned as having a deviant, morally suspect culture that undermines their potential upward mobility whereas white middle- and upper-class Americans are positioned as having a normal, morally upstanding culture that secures their class position. We argue that this binary receives little explicit support from academics, but that four routine scholarly practices implicitly and inadvertently reproduce it: (1) missing and false comparison groups, (2) the selection of one-sided research agendas, (3) biased interpretations of research findings, and (4) limited theoretical alternatives. Together, these practices engender a specter of support for the culture of poverty thesis, subtly breathing life into an argument that is regularly declared dead. We then draw upon exemplary work to suggest frameworks for avoiding these issues. We conclude by maintaining that the culture of poverty should either be put to rest or allowed to live based on its own merits, and suggest ways to end the unintentional resurrection of what may be social scientists' most infamous paradigm.

THE CULTURE OF POVERTY ARGUMENT

The culture of poverty is a loosely formulated theory associated with Oscar Lewis's (1959, 1966) studies of impoverished Latinos in the 1950s and 1960s. Lewis defined the culture of poverty as a set of adaptations that offer a solution to the problems of poverty in the short term but perpetuate poverty in the long term. Lewis named nearly six dozen adaptations, including feelings of dependency and helplessness, a present-time orientation, unemployment, a lack of class consciousness, out-of-wedlock child-rearing, female-headed households, and a general mistrust of institutions. According to Lewis, these adaptations become habitual for those who live in long-term poverty, are passed down to subsequent generations, and create a cycle of intergenerational poverty that is difficult to escape even when structural conditions change. In the wake of World War II, when theories invoking biological inferiority had largely been discredited, this turn to culture was initially well received. As the perspective gained recognition—first through Lewis's work, then through Michael Harrington's best-selling *The Other America,* and finally through the Moynihan Report—the authors' claims that the culture of poverty stemmed from structural inequities dropped out of the public discourse, and the poor were viewed as mired in a culture of poverty of their own making (see O'Connor this volume). In addition, in some Americans' minds, the culture of poverty thesis became tied to race, specifically to African Americans.

That Americans linked the culture of poverty to race was not surprising given that the theory gained popularity during a time of aggravated racial turmoil. The decades following World War II saw a huge migration of African Americans from the American South to the American North (see Wilson this volume). These new arrivals mainly settled in large predominately white cities, making their influx all the more noticeable. Legal and informal residential segregation practices then channeled them into old and rundown neighborhoods near the city center (again increasing their visibility), which were soon bursting at the seams from overcrowding (Massey and Denton 1993). As the demographics shifted, African Americans became more politically active, raising their profiles locally as well as nationally through the Civil Rights and various nationalist movements. African Americans also garnered attention in the 1960s for their participation in urban revolts, which surprised and unsettled the white establishment. In the wake of the revolts, poverty became entrenched in northern African American neighborhoods as the larger community retreated from those precincts, and everyone who could afford to leave left (Wilson this volume).

Into this charged atmosphere Daniel Moynihan, the Assistant Secretary of Labor under President Johnson, delivered his controversial conclusion on class and racial inequality—that is, the African American community was characterized by a "tangle of pathology." Moynihan designated growing rates of out-of-wedlock childbearing as the center of the pathology, and, like Lewis, believed that the culture of the black poor would preclude their upward mobility even if all structural barriers were removed. The report, meant to bolster support for President Johnson's War on Poverty initiatives, instead provoked a firestorm of controversy, as academics, community activists, and civil servants alike lined up to dispute and denounce its findings (see, e.g., Billingsley 1968; Ryan 1971; Stack 1974). The backlash was so fierce that no serious scholars of poverty ventured anywhere near culture for decades. The past few years, however, have begun to see a backlash to the backlash, with Princeton sociologist Douglas Massey (2014:611) lamenting that "sociology did itself a grave disservice when it demonized and ostracized Lewis (1966) following the 1966 publication of his book, *La Vida: A Puerto Rican Family in the Culture of Poverty.*" Others, however, still avoid talking about poverty and culture together.

The Public Reproduction of Culture of Poverty Arguments

While the culture of poverty argument is most often associated with Lewis's and Moynihan's writings in the tumultuous 1960s, the argument itself was neither new to the mid-twentieth century nor confined to scholarly journals. Rather, we show that these arguments have been deployed and reproduced by the public throughout American history and in countries across the world. Here we name several time periods and locations where the culture of poverty thesis has surfaced, demonstrating that it is repeatedly reproduced even when it is not named as such.

Decades before Lewis's (1959) first major writing on the culture of poverty was published, Americans used a similar framework to describe Asian immigrants, including those from the Philippines, Korea, Vietnam, China, and Japan. Many Asian immigrants entered the United States through Angel Island, an island in the San Francisco Bay known as the "Ellis Island of the West." Here, American immigration officials detained and processed immigrants. The officials, like many of their contemporaries, considered Asian immigrants to be filthy, immoral, unassimilable, and therefore suitable only for low-wage jobs. More broadly, government officials drew upon beliefs about Asian immigrants' cultural traits to limit their access to property ownership and citizenship. Some American thinkers of the time, including sociologist Robert E. Park, argued that Asian immigrants' culture would also keep them in poverty even if legal and informal restrictions were removed (Lee and Yung 2010).

Asian immigrants were not the only group accused of having norms, values, and behaviors that prevented their mobility. For much of the twentieth century, Italian Americans were accused of the same. Italian Americans did not achieve socioeconomic parity with whites until the 1970s—much slower than other ethnic groups (Alba and Abdel-Hady 2005). Before achieving socioeconomic parity, the rhetoric deployed to explain the disparity was strikingly similar to that used decades later by proponents of the culture of poverty perspective: Italian Americans were said to have congenitally low intelligence, no interest in education, and were thus destined to remain in the lower strata of the working class. They were also considered predisposed to criminality, in large part because they lacked self-control and were often at the mercy of their emotions. For the same reasons, they were thought to have many children, and certainly more than they could afford (Gans 1962; Whyte 1943). However, once Italian Americans acquired economic parity with their white peers, these cultural condemnations waned and were instead applied to other groups.

In recent decades, the culture of poverty argument has been applied to America's poor in general and minority poor in particular. In 1996, President Bill Clinton worked with congressional Republicans to sign the Personal Responsibility and Work Opportunity Reconciliation Act. This welfare reform bill was based upon key assumptions embedded in the culture of poverty framework—that poverty resulted from the poor's inferior work ethic, women's inability to remain chaste, and the poor's disinclination to marry (Daguerre 2008). More recently, congressman and 2012 vice presidential candidate Paul Ryan was quoted as explaining that poverty derives from a "tailspin of culture, in our inner cities in particular, of men not working and just generations of men not even thinking about working or learning the value and the culture of work" (Isquith 2014). Contemporary calls for drug testing welfare recipients and cutting food stamps echo elements of culture of poverty arguments—that the poor are prone to criminality, irresponsibility, and indolence—and that changing their situation through governmental assistance will not improve their outlook but make them worse. Policymakers' focus on welfare and inner cities also highlights who they think is engaged in a culture of poverty—the black poor.

The culture of poverty argument, however, is not only deployed in the United States. In post-Thatcher England, unions deteriorated, and many working-class jobs disappeared. As the working class's economic conditions worsened, some British people changed their views of the white working class. Rather than seeing them as the morally righteous "salt of the earth," they instead came to see them as morally inferior "Chavs." Chavs—an acronym standing for "council housing and violent"—are framed as having a unique and cohesive culture that is distant from that of the middle class. Men in this group are labeled as aggressive, violent, lazy, and dumb; women are viewed as unruly, loud, tasteless, and promiscuous. The image of the Chav is used to imply that segments of the white working class are primitive, barbaric, morally flawed, and irresponsible. Their class position is viewed as the justified result of their inferior culture, and their culture is viewed as locking them in the lower class even if structural conditions change (Jones 2011). In Scotland, the same phenomena occurs, but the stigmatized group is instead referred to as "Neds" (non-educated delinquents) (Young 2012).

Likewise, the culture of poverty argument is perpetuated in Bahrain, a small country in the Middle East. In Bahrain, nearly 85 percent of the labor force consists of foreign workers, predominately from South Asia. Most lack access to citizenship and to avenues of upward mobility. Nevertheless, locals attribute foreigners' class position to their culture—foreign workers are framed as violent, uneducated, lacking a work ethic, and from unstable families (Gardner 2010). In a similar fashion, Filipino migrants are framed as deviant by the Philippine state; low-wage workers are characterized as embodying a morally scrupulous culture that is in need of state intervention (Guevarra 2010). National training programs emphasize the need for transforming the domestic workforce into ideal global workers by reshaping their values and behaviors rather than emphasizing their structural exclusion from education and the domestic labor market (Guevarra 2010). In England, Scotland, Bahrain, the Philippines, and countries across the globe, elements of the culture of poverty argument are retold and reproduced. In each case, the poor are blamed for their poverty.

It is not surprising that the culture of poverty argument receives such long and widespread support given the functions it serves. Culture of poverty arguments justify exclusion, relieve agencies and citizens of an obligation to help the poor, and enhance the image of the middle class as morally upstanding citizens who deserve their class position. Policymakers can use the argument as a rationale to leave exclusionary policies in tact; middle-class laypeople can use the argument to feel virtuous and innocent. In scholarly communities, however, there is less incentive to reproduce culture of poverty arguments. Nevertheless, scholars keep the culture of poverty argument alive.

THE SCHOLARLY REPRODUCTION
OF CULTURE OF POVERTY ARGUMENTS

In the public, the culture of poverty argument is *explicitly* reproduced through political declarations and repeated stereotypes. Until the last few years, however, the scholarly community took pains to avoid explicitly endorsing culture of poverty arguments. At least since Oscar Lewis (1959, 1966) published his thesis on the culture of poverty, scholars have criticized both his specific scholarship and the larger idea that the poor, minorities, and immigrants have inferior values, norms, and behaviors that lock them into lower class positions (Bourgois 2001; Duneier 1999; Watkins-Hayes and Kovalsky this volume). Nevertheless, we argue that while academics typically lend little *explicit* support to culture of poverty arguments, key elements of the argument are *implicitly* reproduced by routine scholarly practices. Thus, while scholars proclaim the death of the culture of poverty, they simultaneously give it life.

At the center of the culture of poverty thesis is a binary: segments of the poor, racial minorities, and immigrants are positioned as having a deviant, morally suspect culture that undermines their potential upward mobility whereas white middle- and upper-class Americans are positioned as having a normal, morally upstanding culture that secures their class position. We argue that although this binary receives little explicit support from academics, four scholarly practices inadvertently reproduce it: (1) missing and false comparison groups, (2) the selection of one-sided research agendas, (3) biased interpretations of research findings, and (4) limited theoretical alternatives. Together, these practices engender a specter of support for the culture of poverty thesis, implicitly reproducing ideas associated with the culture of poverty argument.

Below we provide examples of ways that missing and false comparison groups, one-sided research agendas, biased interpretations of research findings, and limited theoretical alternatives bolster the binary of culturally suspect disadvantaged groups and culturally superior advantaged groups. We then provide examples of research that disrupts these common practices. Our intention is not to single out any particular study but to illuminate general patterns. We also emphasize that many of these patterns are not the fault of an individual scholar but occur due to the theoretical and methodological traditions of academic fields and the collective lack of reflexivity on specific issues. Finally, arguments about the culture of poverty use "culture" to mean anything from a subgroup with shared norms, values, and behaviors to a group with an overlapping set of beliefs and strategies that are used in fragmented, contradictory, and heterogeneous ways (Small et al. 2010). In this chapter, we take an agnostic view of how to conceptualize culture. We often refer to culture as more homogeneous and cohesive than it is, simply because this is the way it has historically been referred to in culture of poverty debates.

Missing and False Comparison Groups

One way that the culture of poverty thesis is implicitly supported is by the failure to use a comparison group. Writing of Oscar Lewis's version of the culture of poverty, sociologist Eduardo Bonilla-Silva (1993:35) revealed how this occurs: "Lewis recognized that 'people with a culture of poverty are aware of middle-class values, talk about them, and even claim some of them as their own, but on the whole they do not live by them' (ibid: xlvi). *The untested assumption is that the 'middle-class' live by them*" (italics added). Yet, despite Bonilla-Silva's criticism and that of others (Lamont and Small 2008; Young 2004), the practice of assuming that segments of poor, nonwhite, and immigrant groups are uniquely deviant continues. This occurs not only because individual studies lack a white middle-class American comparison group, but also because existing studies of the white American middle class are not regularly considered in the culture of poverty debate.

One example of this trend is in studies about culture, poverty, and education. One strand of the culture of poverty argument suggests that segments of poor, black, American youth disengage in school and create an oppositional culture whereby status is created through distancing oneself from formal learning (Fordham and Ogbu 1986; Ogbu 2003). Many scholars question the accuracy of this claim (Carter 2005; Harris 2011). More relevant to this chapter, however, is that white middle- and upper-class youth could also be viewed as having an oppositional culture in regards to education. Many middle- and upper-class students regularly distance themselves from academic learning and publicly sanction their peers who do not conceal their academic investments (Khan 2011; Tyson, Darrity, and Castellino 2005). Elite, historically white colleges have long been reputed to be epicenters of academic learning, but students at these universities regularly create status systems that reward distance from academic commitments (Karabel 2005). Today, wealthy students at elite colleges report socializing more than studying (Arum and Roksa 2011), and some upper-middle-class and elite white women report learning more about beauty-work than academic work (Armstrong and Hamilton 2013; Holland and Eisenhart 1992). Given that many privileged white students engage in a status system that rewards behaviors that are in competition with school and learning, they could be considered to be engaging in an oppositional culture. They, however, are rarely labeled as having one, nor are many of these studies included in the culture of poverty debate. Leaving them out casts segments of the black poor as particularly culturally deviant as they are seen as uniquely disinterested in education.

A culture of poverty is also thought to be characterized by negative relations between men and women. Prominent works, such as Elijah Anderson's (1990) *Streetwise*, document that young black poor men and women have little trust in each other and use each other to gain status through sexual relations. Again, however, if we look at relationships between the sexes among the white American middle- and upper-classes, we find that the black American poor look less unique. White middle- and upper-class teenagers and young adults also talk about participating in a hook-up culture: one where respect between the sexes can be lacking, hooking up is partly about status, and sexual assault is a regular occurrence (Armstrong, Hamilton, and Sweeney 2006; Wade and Heldman 2012). Among these youth, cheating in committed relationships is viewed simply as a normal part of being young and not overly deviant (Wilkins and Dalessandro 2013). Likewise, ethnographies of poor black and Latino men sometimes frame them as culturally deviant due to their drug use (Anderson 1990; Bourgois 2003; Vehnkatesh 2008), but white youths from higher classes use drugs at similar rates (Johnston et al. 2008; Wightman, Schoeni, and Schulenberg 2012). While it is challenging for single ethnographies to study multiple groups, the lack of comparison to extant scholarship on other classes creates a skewed view in which only one group is viewed as culturally deviant.

Variants of the immigration literature also uphold the American white middle-class as culturally upstanding while casting nonwhite and poorer immigrants as culturally deviant. This, however, is accomplished through a false reference group rather than a missing one. In aspects of the American immigration literature, poor immigrants of color are compared to the white settlers who founded the United States. The representation of the white settlers, however, is too often false. Comparisons emphasize that poor immigrants of color unfairly and immorally extract native whites' resources while overlooking that white settlers did the same to native groups (Ignatiev 2009; Jung 2009). Other studies of immigration more explicitly reproduce the binaries present in the culture of poverty argument. Segmented assimilation theory suggests that immigrants will become upwardly mobile if they take on the culture of the American "mainstream"—the white middle class—while they will become downwardly mobile if they adopt the culture of the "underclass"— poor black communities (Alba and Nee 2003). In this case, the cultural distinctions between the white middle class and black underclass are more assumed than tested but are reproduced nonetheless.

One-Sided Research Agendas

The binary of a culturally upstanding white American middle class whose efforts secure their class position and a culturally deviant minority and immigrant poor whose behaviors and values undermine their mobility is reinforced by the types of research agendas repeatedly engaged in and avoided. For example, the central studies in the culture of poverty debate focus on poor blacks and Hispanics (Anderson 1990; Bourgois 2003; Hannerz 1969; Lewis 1966; Liebow 1967; Massey and Denton 1993; Rainwater 1970; Stack 1974; Wilson 1996; Young 1999). Even though many of these studies conclude that blacks and Hispanics are not mired in a culture of poverty, they engage in the culture of poverty debate when studying these groups. There are more poor whites than poor blacks in the United States (National Center for Children in Poverty 2007), but few studies ask whether poor whites are engaged in a culture of poverty. When studies of poor whites are conducted, they are often regionalized, suggesting that the cultural problems pertaining to poor whites are limited to Appalachia rather than to poor whites as a whole. More often, studies of poor whites avoid the culture of poverty debate altogether as authors stress the structural issues or discrimination that they face (McDermott 2006; Nelson and Smith 1999) or praise them for the same behaviors that poor blacks are criticized for, such as understanding structural constraints and creating oppositional cultures (MacLeod 1995; Willis 1977). Classic studies of whites at the lower end of the class structure also tend to focus on the working class—who are popularly coded white— rather than the poor. These books use empathetic frameworks to paint working-class whites as making reasonable and heart-wrenching adaptations to their economic conditions (Rubin 1976, 1994; Sennett and Cobb 1972; Skeggs 1997). The racialized focus and framing of research agendas may reproduce the idea that minorities have a culture of poverty and that whites do not.

Similarly, many studies analyze how the culture of the poor prevents their mobility (Bourgois 2003; Harding 2010; Massey and Denton 1993; Smith 2007; Wilson 1996; Young 1999). Few, however, ask how the culture of the middle class encourages down- ward mobility or prevents upward mobility. Surely, however, this is a possibility given the relatively high rates of mobility of individuals born into the middle of the class structure (Urahn et al. 2012). As noted, middle-class individuals engage in some of the same behaviors as the poor, but studies do not attribute them to their lack of further upward mobility.

Another way that the one-sided nature of research agendas offer implicit support for the binary embedded in cultural of poverty arguments is by repeatedly asking how the practices of the white American middle class would benefit minorities and the poor but not asking how the practices of minorities and the poor would benefit the white middle class. For example, middle-class children are more likely to be involved in organized—usually fee-paying—activities whereas poor children are more likely to create their own informal activities (Lareau 2003). Many studies have examined the potential academic—thus potentially mobility enhancing—benefits of organized activ- ities for children of all classes (Bodovski and Farkas 2008; Cheadle 2008; Henderson 2013; Roksa and Potter 2011). Few have done the same for unorganized activities despite that these activities may teach skills that are useful for upward mobility such as cre- ativity, initiative, and the ability to get along well with an age-diverse group (Lareau 2003). Similarly, working-class parents' more hands-off and hardened parenting style is thought to teach children resiliency and perseverance (Kusserow 2004). Though these traits may be widely beneficial to people across classes, scholars tend not to study whether middle-class children suffer from a lack of resilience. In these cases, aspects of the culture of the middle class are cast as potentially universally useful whereas aspects of the culture of the poor are not.

Similarly, there is a long history of considering poor families dysfunctional (Moynihan 1965). On average, the poor now marry less and divorce more than their middle- and upper-classes counterparts (Cherlin 2010; Ellwood and Jencks 2004). Researchers often ask why the poor marry less (e.g., Edin and Kefalas 2005; Wilson 1996). While a legitimate question, researchers tend not to also ask how middle-class families could benefit from the strengths of poor families. For example, poor families tend to spend more of their leisure time with each other (Lareau 2003; Petev 2013), and women at the bottom of the income distribution report warmer relationships with their mothers than those at the top (Wharton and Thorne 1997). Indeed, among married couples in which each spouse was raised in a different social class, those from privileged class backgrounds tend to cast their spouse's poor family as warmer, more fun, and less emotionally distant (Streib 2015b). These advantages may be linked to mobility as families that are emotionally close may share more economic, social, and cultural resources. Yet, despite these potential advantages, researchers tend to ask why poor families do not look like middle-class ones without also asking the reverse.

In another example, people of color, compared to whites, tend to have more accurate perceptions of structural constraints to mobility (Kluegel and Smith 1986; Hunt and Bullock this volume). Research questions often center on whether and how blacks' insights prevent their mobility (Ogbu 1983). Even when scholars answer that blacks' realism about the opportunity structure does not minimize their academic striving (Harris 2008), the question is rarely reframed to ask how whites might benefit from more accurate perceptions of the class structure. Similarly, college students from minority, poor, and working-class families tend to view college as primarily about academic learning and credentials, whereas upper-middle- and upper-class white students tend to place greater emphasis on using college for socializing and self-discovery (Armstrong and Hamilton 2013; Grisby 2009; Stuber 2011). Academics, however, seldom ask whether disadvantaged groups' orientation toward college offers benefits to all class groups.

Similarly, the selection of research questions concerning immigrant and native populations tend to assume that the former's behaviors are potentially problematic while the latter's are not. Classic assimilation theory positions immigrants as having a potentially problematic culture unless they adopt the cultural practices of the white American middle class (Park 1925). For instance, the skill set of immigrants in navigating multiple countries, cultural norms, languages, and political structures is overlooked (Ong 1999; Lan 2006). Instead, their cultural asymmetry to the white middle class is critiqued as a hindrance to upward mobility (Alba and Nee 2003, Bean and Stevens 2003). More recently, segmented assimilation theory suggests that poor blacks are mired in a culture of poverty and that immigrants' own culture can help them avoid it (Alba and Nee 2003; Brubaker 2004). In addition to problematically assuming that poor blacks live in a culture of poverty, these theories also suffer from assuming that whites have cultural elements that could help immigrants' mobility projects but not vice versa. Such assumptions may not be accurate. For example, immigrant groups tend to engage in grassroots organizing, collective claims making, legislation reform, and public demonstrations for basic rights to a greater extent than American middle-class whites, and these strategies may facilitate opportunities for social mobility (Das Gupta 2007). Research agendas, however, tend to focus on why immigrants engage less in white middle-class forms of political participation such as voter registration and holding political office (Calavita 1992; Das Gupta 2007; Hing 1993). Without focusing on the reverse, only one group's culture is problematized.

Biased Interpretations of Research Findings

Interpretations of research findings also lend implicit support to the culture of poverty binary when they assume that the cultural practices of poor people of color are problematic whereas those of middle- and upper-class whites are beneficial. For example, when poor women engage in hook-up culture they are viewed as jeopardizing their chances of mobility (Anderson 1990); when upper-middle and upper-class women engage in hook-up culture they are viewed as using hook-ups as a strategy to secure their mobility (Hamilton and Armstrong 2009). When poor black teenagers party, they are viewed as not thinking about their future (Anderson 1990); when upper-class white teenagers party, they are portrayed as networking and entering into marriage markets (Armstrong and Hamilton 2013). Working-class parents are more likely to value conformity and obedience in their children; these values are thought to train their children for jobs in which they are managed (Kohn 1969). Middle-class parents are more likely to value self-direction in their children; these values are thought to teach children to be managers (Kohn 1969). Although values and practices can contradict—in aspects of their lives, working-class parents allow their children more self-direction whereas middle-class parents emphasize greater obedience (Weininger and Lareau 2009)—it is rarely suggested that working-class parents teach their children to be managers and middle-class parents teach their children to be managed. In addition, one could surmise that the experience of being raised by a managerial parent teaches children to follow their managerial parents' orders, making them easily managed rather than managers. Without detailed longitudinal data, it is impossible to know which assumptions are correct. In the absence of the data needed to make these claims, it is remarkable that the common interpretations problematize only the culture of the poor and working class.

Similar interpretations privilege American whites over immigrant groups. When white middle- and upper-class Americans consume a large variety of culture they are viewed as engaging in a practice that maintains their privileged position (Khan 2011; Peterson and Kern 1996). Immigrants hold a large variety of culture—some from their original country, and some from their new one—but their cultural omnivoreness is generally viewed as a liability to their upward mobility rather than an asset (Agarwal 1991; Das Gupta 2007; Grewal and Kaplan 1994). In a more specific example, traveling abroad is viewed as an asset for the class reproduction of middle- and upper-middle-class Americans, but traveling across national borders and knowing home and second languages is viewed as a potential barrier to upward mobility for poor immigrants (Alba and Nee 2003; Brubaker 2004; Rivera 2011). It is possible that these similar activities have different implications for different groups, but, again, in the absence of evidence, it is remarkable that privileged groups' culture is so often viewed as maintaining their privilege whereas disadvantage groups' culture is viewed as a cause for their disadvantage.

Limited Theoretical Alternatives

Though the culture of poverty theory has been proclaimed dead, theories that exist in its stead also posit that the poor's use of culture locks them in poverty whereas the middle class' use of culture keeps them in the middle class. For decades, social isolation theory (Massey and Denton 1993; Wilson 1987, 1996) suggested that segments of the poor were geographically segregated from the middle class, and as a result the segregated poor developed distinct cultural norms, values, and behaviors. The types of alternative culture the poor developed offered them avenues for status and the ability to navigate their social milieu, but deterred their upward mobility as their new culture was at odds with that of the middle class. Social isolation theory has been challenged as scholars have demonstrated that the poor are never fully isolated from middle-class culture (Duneier 1992; Edin and Kefalas 2005; Newman 1999). Instead, scholars now argue that the cultural landscape of the poor is marked by cultural heterogeneity (Harding 2007, 2010). That is, the poor are viewed as having access to both alternative and mainstream cultural elements. However, such variety is considered problematic. The frames and scripts in alternative and mainstream culture are conflicting and contradictory, and the poor sometimes go back and forth between using both. Without sticking to mainstream culture, the poor are unlikely to be upwardly mobile.

In a different vein, Bourdieu's (1977, 1984) mismatch theory also maintains that the culture used by the poor prevents their mobility. He argues that individuals internalize aspects of culture—worldviews, perceptions of reality, and practical strategies—that help them succeed in their own classed environment. The poor and middle class then develop some distinct aspects of culture due to their different class locations. He emphasizes that institutions which serve as gatekeepers to the middle class reward the culture the middle class uses while penalizing the culture that the poor uses. Due to this institutional bias, cultural differences between the poor and middle class are likely to lead to class reproduction for each social class.

Social isolation, cultural heterogeneity, and cultural mismatch theories are all theories of how culture is used by the poor (and the middle class) to maintain the poor's poverty. Theories of how the poor may use culture for upward mobility are more limited. Cultural mobility scholars (DiMaggio 1982) argue that those born into social class disadvantage can learn to use the culture rewarded by middle-class institutions. Code-switching theory (Pattillo 1999) suggests the same. However, these theories do not disrupt the binary inherent in the culture of poverty argument. Instead, they reinforce it by suggesting that some poor people can use the culture associated with the middle class to gain mobility, but that the culture associated with the poor is only associated with remaining impoverished. Only by assimilating can the poor become middle class.

Though each of these theories of culture and social class inequality has much to offer and effectively describes many instances in the social world, the existing theoretical landscape is unbalanced. None of the theoretical alternatives to the culture of poverty argument explain how in instances when the culture of the poor and middle class differ, the poor can use culture in any way other than to trap themselves in poverty. None explain how the middle class can use culture to deter their further upward mobility or to facilitate their downward mobility. The default assumption is that when the poor and middle class use culture in different ways, the poor's culture will keep them poor and the middle-class' culture will prevent them from being poor. Without theories that explain how cultural differences between the classes can facilitate the poor's upward mobility and the middle class' downward mobility, scholars are likely to unreflexively interpret their data in ways that reproduces the binary at the heart of the culture of poverty argument regardless of if it is true.

Disrupting the Binary

Aspects of the culture of poverty argument are then implicitly reproduced by scholarly practices that uphold the notion that white middle-class Americans have a culture that maintains their privilege while nonwhite, poor, and immigrants possess cultural traits that detract from theirs. However, not all scholarly practices have missing or false reference groups, one-sided research agendas, biased assumptions, or theoretical limitations. Many of these practices are challenged. For instance, researchers no longer see the culture associated with the middle class as entirely beneficial to the poor. This is partly because researchers have found that the same culture held by different groups does not necessarily yield the same outcomes. For example, poor black women are often criticized for entering parenthood at "young" ages, where young is defined in relation to the age when middle-class white women tend to give birth. Researchers have found, however, that poor black women who give birth at "young" ages tend to have equal or better health and academic outcomes for themselves and their children compared to if they gave birth at the same age as their white middle-class counterparts (Geronimus 2003). Similarly, poor parents and parents of color who adopt the parenting style associated with the white middle class are not rewarded and may even be penalized by their children's teachers (Dumais et al. 2012). Poor children who go to a museum may see little change in their grades; middle-class children who go to a museum may benefit more (Meier Jaeger 2011). Bangladeshi immigrants in the United Kingdom (Blackledge 2001), Turkish immigrants in Germany (Becker 2010) and former Soviet Republic immigrants in Israel (Leopold and Shavit 2013) are not rewarded by teachers for their cultural capital, even if it is high cultural capital in their home countries.

Other approaches also challenge the idea that the culture of the middle class is necessarily advantageous for mobility. Older studies conceptualized the teaching of middle-class culture to the poor via role models as helpful for the latter's mobility (Anderson 1990; Wilson 1996). Now that approach is questioned. Middle-class "role models" who attempt to teach the poor to be more "cultured" are viewed as potentially harming the poor's mobility options (Pattillo 2007). Similarly, studies of upward mobility—though rarely incorporated into the culture of poverty literature—also undermine the idea that middle-class culture is a necessary precursor to mobility. People born into poverty who enter the middle class as adults regularly maintain many of the values, frames, and scripts they learned in their class of origin but are upwardly mobile anyway (Karp 1986; Streib 2015b; Stuber 2005).

Taking a different approach, economists and psychologists have also disrupted the binary. Economists find, for example, that both the rich and the poor use culture to their detriment. When either group faces scarcity—often time-scarcity for the rich and money-scarcity for the poor—they act in ways that worsen their situation (Shah, Mullainathan, and Shafir 2012). Psychologists highlight that people in the middle class tend to be independent, whereas people in poverty tend to be interdependent. They argue that both approaches are associated with some mobility-enhancing and some mobility-detracting strategies (Piff et al. 2010; Snibbe and Markus 2005; Stephens, Markus, and Townsend 2007; Stephens, Markus, and Phillips 2014). The binary that the culture of the poor is problematic whereas the culture of the middle class is not is then destabilized as the culture of the latter is not viewed as universally good or necessary for upward mobility.

Scholars are also able to dismiss the binary inherent in the culture of poverty argument by taking a more macro and historical perspective that includes an analysis of power. By focusing on how poverty is made likely for some groups and not others via national policies, laws, histories, and hegemonic forces, it is possible to see any deviant behaviors among disadvantaged groups as having a minimal impact on their class position compared to broader social forces (Brady 2009). For example, when Lewis (1966) and Moynihan (1965) were writing, black women had children out of wedlock more than white poor and middle-class women. Yet, whereas each author locates single motherhood as part of a culture of poverty and as responsible for keeping black families locked in poverty, neither fully takes into account the many forces that were likely to keep black women in poverty regardless of their motherhood practices. Educational apartheid, employment discrimination, white violence against blacks, and the remnants of legal segregation combined to make upward mobility unlikely regardless of family structure. The laws, polices, and economic conditions that have changed—ones that Lewis predicted a segment of poor individuals would not be able to take advantage of—include those such as deindustrialization and mass incarceration that continue to lock groups in poverty with little regard to their behavior.

In addition, scholars have moved beyond the culture of poverty debates by examining how groups are constructed as culturally superior and inferior through their relationship to one another. This literature looks at how groups are labeled, evaluated, and reconstructed through micro- and macroprocesses. British social theorists, for example, show how the middle class constructs the poor as excessive and disgusting in order to maintain their own position as normal and deserving (Lawler 2005; Skeggs 2004). Studies on migration patterns show that female employers construct domestic migrant workers as docile, obedient, and less agentic, while positioning themselves as skilled professionals entering the workforce (Lan 2006). States also engage in labeling processes that uphold the binary. The Philippines, for example, constructs its emigrants as national heroes for working abroad and sharing remittance that alleviate poverty at home (Rodriguez 2010). At the same time, the Filipino state constructs emigrants as commodities for export, facilitating other states' ability to label Filipinos as a stigmatized group that is undeserving of high pay (Rodriguez 2010). These studies draw our attention away from the values and behavior of the poor and to the ability of groups in power to label the poor in ways that reaffirm existing hierarchies. Thus, whereas some sets of studies inadvertently provide implicit support for the binary embedded in the culture of poverty thesis, others undermine it.

Conclusion

The culture of poverty argument casts a specter on poverty scholarship—a specter that lurks in the background even when not named, and one that continues to live on despite widespread declarations that the idea has been put to rest. That the idea continues to be a part of public discourse is not surprising as it justifies the position of those in power while leaving them unaccountable for assisting the economically marginalized. That the culture of poverty argument continues to infiltrate scholarly discourse, however, may be more surprising, as the same segment of scholars who proclaimed its death keep it alive. In this chapter, we argued that scholars have not killed the idea as thoroughly as they believed. Instead they unintentionally breathe life into it.

In the following, we lay out several ways that the routine reproduction of the culture of poverty argument may be avoided by scholars. Our point is not that the binary inherent in the culture of poverty argument is never correct, but merely that it should not be *unintentionally* reproduced through missing comparison groups, one-sided research agendas, biased interpretations of research findings, and limited theoretical alternatives. Others have suggested countering culture of poverty arguments by emphasizing frames rather than values or considering culture as a loose collection of elements rather than a cohesive whole (Small et al. 2010). These approaches, while having other commendable attributes, will not disrupt the unreflexive and unintentional reproduction of the binary central to the culture of poverty argument. In addition to following the lead of the scholarship that is disrupting the binary, we suggest the following alternatives.

1. *Develop theories of how culture facilitates upward mobility for the poor.* A key reason why research agendas are one-sided and interpretations of research findings are biased is that the theories available to researchers are also one-sided. Theories of how culture is used in class reproduction dwarf theories of how culture is used for mobility. This theoretical bias primes researchers to ask some questions and not others, and

to consider their findings as having some implications and not others. Developing a toolkit of how culture is used both for class reproduction and mobility would challenge scholars to weigh their evidence rather than unreflexively applying theories that suggest cultural differences between the classes keeps the poor in poverty.

2. *Expand the cannon.* While the above strategy is difficult, this strategy is not. Just as women's studies became gender studies and race studies expanded to include research on whites, the study of culture and poverty should be reframed as the study of culture and class. Reimagining the canonical culture and poverty literature in this light would force comparisons to existing studies of how culture is used by poor people who become upwardly mobile and to how middle- and upper-class people deploy culture. Such comparisons would raise questions about the conclusions drawn in some of the culture and poverty literature and force a partial reinterpretation of the role of culture in the class reproduction of the poor. Furthermore, given that poverty is often coded black while other classes are coded as whites, broadening the cannon may also remind researchers that the study of culture and poverty should include the study of all racial groups.

3. *Consider counterfactuals.* Another easy strategy to avoid unreflexively reproducing the binary that the poor's culture prevents their mobility and the middle-class' culture secures their privilege is to ask counterfactual questions. If we lack the evidence to substantiate how cultural differences between the classes matter, would we interpret our results differently if the cultural strategies were used by members of different classes? Given the constraints the poor face, if they refrained from using specific cultural strategies or did more to mimic the middle class, would their mobility prospects change? If the poor did resemble the middle class more, would the middle class reinvent itself to create greater cultural distance from the poor?

4. *Generate more sophisticated understandings of when cultural similarities and differences between the classes facilitate the poor's mobility.* One of the assumptions in the culture of poverty thesis is that if poor people resembled middle-class people their chances of upward mobility would increase. However, gatekeepers may not reward culture equally for all classes, and the same culture used in different-classed environments may lead to different results (Geronimus 2003; Meier Jaeger 2011). More work should be done to understand when cultural similarities between classes are associated with similar outcomes for all class groups. Similarly, some work shows that cultural *differences* between class groups may be associated with mobility-enhancing outcomes (Streib 2015a). Asking when cultural similarities and differences are rewarded by gatekeepers and for whom may lead to research agendas that challenge the binary at the center of the culture of poverty argument.

5. *Consider cross-national variation in culture and class.* Much of the culture of poverty literature is based on American subjects. Americans, however, are the most individualistic people in the world, place an unusually strong emphasis on self-sufficiency, and exhibit comparatively little class consciousness (Henrich, Heine, and Norenzayan 2010). The implications of culture may vary in settings in which gatekeepers have less individualistic views. Cross-national studies could also reveal which cultural adaptations to poverty, if any, are universal, which are context specific, and which are most

associated with the intergenerational transmission of poverty. Given different structural, economic, institutional, and demographic contexts of countries around the world, cross-national research (or even cross-context research within countries) could be used to generate theories of the scope conditions under which culture plays a causal role in keeping the poor in poverty.

6. *Include comparison groups and check one-sided research agendas.* The need for these strategies is clear. However, implementing them requires substantial changes to current research practices. Ethnography, for example, is typically single-sited. Multisite ethnographies, however, would better allow researchers to compare how culture is used across class and to what effect. Similarly, researchers tend to avoid asking questions about how the middle class could more effectively use culture, as scholars' concern lies more with the poor. While we sympathize with this reasoning, we believe it has the unintended consequence of further problematizing the poor and valorizing the middle class.

7. *Test the culture of poverty argument.* Despite many heated debates about the culture of poverty perspective, some of its key claims have gone untested. Lewis argued that (1) a small segment of individuals in deep poverty develop and internalize cultural adaptations that (2) are passed down through generations and (3) prevent upward mobility even when structural conditions change. Much evidence has indicated that the poor do adapt to their class conditions (just as the middle class adapts to theirs) while also maintaining many mainstream values (Bourgois 2003; Dunier 1992; Edin and Kefals 2005; Geronimus 2003; Liebow 1967; Stack 1974). Some research has demonstrated that parents attempt to, and sometimes successfully do, pass down cultural adaptations to their class conditions (Calarco 2014; Lareau 2003; Kusserow 2004). However, research has generally ignored the last claim—that the poor cannot adapt to structural change. To fully understand the theory, this must be tested.

The culture of poverty argument should be maintained or defeated based upon its empirical accuracy. In this chapter, we have instead argued that scholars unintentionally maintain the theory through routine research practices. If researchers wish to dampen the argument's unintentional resurrection, scholarly routines must be changed and greater reflexivity must be enforced. If these and other changes do not happen, the culture of poverty argument will go through more cycles of life, death, and resurrection.

References

Agarwal, Priya. 1991. *Passage from India: Post-1965 Indian Immigrants and Their Children: Conflicts, Concerns, and Solutions.* Palos Verdes, CA: Yuvati.

Alba, Richard and Dalia Abdel-Hady. 2005. "Galileo's Children: Italian Americans' Difficult Entry into the Intellectual Elite." *Sociological Quarterly* 46:3–18.

Alba, Richard and Victor Nee. 2003. *Remaking the American Mainstream: Assimilation and Contemporary Immigration.* Cambridge, MA: Harvard University Press.

Anderson, Elijah. 1990. *Streetwise: Race, Class, and Change in an Urban Community.* Chicago: University of Chicago Press.

Armstrong, Elizabeth, Laura Hamilton, and Brian Sweeney. 2006. "Sexual Assault on Campus: A Multilevel, Integrative Approach to Party Rape." *Social Problems* 53(4):483–99.

Armstrong, Elizabeth and Laura Hamilton. 2013. *Paying for the Party: How College Maintains Inequality.* Cambridge, MA: Harvard University Press.

Arum, Richard and Josipa Roksa. 2011. *Academically Adrift: Limited Learning on College Campuses.* Chicago: University of Chicago Press.

Bean, Frank and Gillian Stevens. 2003. *America's Newcomers and the Dynamics of Diversity.* New York: Russell Sage Foundation.

Becker, Birgit. 2010. "The Transfer of Cultural Knowledge in the Early Childhood: Social and Ethnic Disparities and the Mediating Role of Familial Activities." *European Sociological Review* 26(1):17–29.

Billingsley, Andrew. 1968. *Black Families in White America.* New York: Prentice Hall/Spectrum.

Blackledge, Adrian. 2001. "The Wrong Sort of Capital? Bangladeshi Women and their Children's Schooling in Birmingham, U.K." *International Journal of Bilingualism* 5(3):345–66.

Bodovski, Katerina and George Farkas. 2008. "'Concerted Cultivation' and Unequal Achievement in Elementary School." *Social Science Research* 37(3):903–19.

Bonilla-Silva, Eduardo. 1993. "Squatters, Politics, and State Responses: The Political Economy of Squatters in Puerto Rico, 1900–1992." PhD dissertation, University of Wisconsin.

Bourdieu, Pierre and Jean-Claude Passeron. 1977. *Reproduction in Education, Society, and Culture.* New York: Sage.

Bourdieu, Pierre. 1984. *Distinction.* Cambridge, MA: Harvard University Press.

Bourgois, Phillipe. 2001. "Culture of Poverty." Pp. 11904–7 in *International Encyclopedia of the Social & Behavioral Sciences,* edited by Neil Smelser and Paul Bates. Oxford: Pergamon.

Bourgois, Phillipe. 2003. *In Search of Respect: Selling Crack in El Barrio.* New York: Cambridge University Press.

Brady, David. 2009. *Rich Democracies, Poor People: How Politics Explain Poverty.* New York: Oxford University Press.

Brubaker, Rogers. 2004. "The Return of Assimilation?" Pp. 116–31 in *Ethnicity Without Groups,* edited by Rogers Brubaker. Cambridge, MA: Harvard University Press.

Calarco, Jessica. 2014. "Coached for the Classroom: Parents' Cultural Transmission and Children's Reproduction of Educational Inequalities." *American Sociological Review* 79(5):1015–37.

Calavita, Kitty. 1992. *Inside the State: The Bracero Program, Immigration, and the INS.* New York: Routledge.

Carter, Prudence. 2005. *Keepin' It Real: School Success Beyond Black and White.* New York: Oxford University Press.

Cheadle, Jacob. 2008. "Educational Investment, Family Context, and Children's Math and Reading Growth from Kindergarten through Third Grade." *Sociology of Education* 81(1):1–31.

Cherlin, Andrew. 2010. *The Marriage Go-Round: The State of Marriage and the Family in America Today.* New York: Alford Knopf.

Cohen, Patricia. 2010. "'Culture of Poverty' Makes a Comeback." *New York Times,* October 17. Retrieved December 15, 2014 (http://www.nytimes.com/2010/10/18/us/18poverty.html?pagewanted=all).

Daguerre, Anne. 2008. "The Second Phase of US Welfare Reform, 2000–2006: Blaming the Poor Again?" *Social Policy and Administration* 42(4):362–78.

Das Gupta, Monisha. 2007. *Unruly Immigrants: Rights, Activism, and Transnational South Asian Politics in the United States.* Durham, NC: Duke University Press.

DiMaggio, Paul. 1982. "Cultural Capital and School Success: The Impact of Status-Culture Participation on the Grades of U.S. High-School Students." *American Sociological Review* 47(2):189–201.

Dumais, Susan, Richard Kessinger, and Bonny Ghosh. 2012. "Concerted Cultivation and Teachers' Evaluation of Students: Exploring the Intersection of Race and Parents' Educational Attainment." *Sociological Perspectives* 55(1):17–42.

Duneier, Mitchell. 1992. *Slim's Table.* Chicago: University of Chicago Press.

Duneier, Mitchell. 1999. *Sidewalk.* New York: Farrar, Strauss, and Giroux.

Edin, Kathryn and Maria Kefalas. 2005. *Promises I Can Keep: Why Poor Women Put Motherhood Before Marriage.* Berkeley: University of California Press.

Ellwood, David and Christopher Jencks. 2004. "The Uneven Spread of Single-Parent Families: What Do We Know? Where Do We Look for Answers?" Pp. 3–77 in *Social Inequality*, edited by Katherine Neckerman. New York: Russell Sage Foundation.

Fordham, Signithia and John Ogbu. 1986. "Black Students' School Success: Coping with the 'Burden of Acting White.'" *Urban Review* 18(3):176–206.

Gans, Herbert. 1962. *The Urban Villagers.* New York: Free Press of Glencoe.

Gardner, Andrew. 2010. *City of Strangers: Gulf Migration and the Indian Community in Bahrain.* Ithaca, NY: Cornell University Press.

Geronimus, Arline. 2003. "Damned if You Do: Culture, Identity, Privilege and Teenage Childbearing in the United States." *Social Science and Medicine* 57(5):881–93.

Grewal, Inderpal and Caren Kaplan, eds. 1994. *Scattered Hegemonies: Postmodernity and Transnational Feminist Practice.* Minneapolis: University of Minnesota Press.

Grisby, Mary. 2009. *College Life Through the Eyes of Students.* New York: SUNY.

Guevarra, Anna Romina. 2010. *Marketing Dreams, Manufacturing Heroes: The Transnational Labor Brokering of Filipino Workers.* New Brunswick, NJ: Rutgers University Press.

Hamilton, Laura and Elizabeth Armstrong. 2009. "Gendered Sexuality in Young Adulthood: Double Binds and Flawed Options." *Gender & Society* 23:589–616.

Hannerz, Ulf. 1969. *Soulside: Inquiries into Ghetto Culture and Community.* Chicago: University of Chicago Press.

Harding, David. 2007. "Cultural Context, Sexual Behavior, and Romantic Relationships in Disadvantaged Neighborhoods." *American Sociological Review* 72(3):341–64.

Harding, David. 2010. *Living the Drama: Community, Culture, and Conflict among Inner-City Boys.* Chicago: University of Chicago Press.

Harrington, Michael. 1962. *The Other America: Poverty in the United States.* New York: Scribner.

Harris, Angel. 2008. "Optimism in the Face of Despair: Black-White Differences in Beliefs about School as a Means for Upward Social Mobility." *Social Science Quarterly* 89(3):608–30.

Harris, Angel. 2011. *Kids Don't Want to Fail: Oppositional Culture and the Black-White Achievement Gap.* Cambridge, MA: Harvard University Press.

Harvey, David and Michael Reed. 1996. "The Culture of Poverty: An Ideological Analysis." *Sociological Perspectives* 39(4):465–95.

Henderson, Morag. 2013. "A Test of Parenting Strategies." *Sociology* 47(3):542–59.

Henrich, Joseph, Steven Heine, and Ara. Norenzayan. 2010. "The Weirdest People in the World?" *Behavioral and Brain Sciences* 33:61–135.

Herrnstein, Richard and Charles Murray. 1994. *Bell Curve: Intelligence and Class Structure in American Life*. New York: Simon and Schuster.

Hing, Bill Ong. 1993. *Making and Remaking Asian America through Immigration Policy: 1850-1990*. Palo Alto, CA: Stanford University Press.

Holland, Dorothy and Margaret Eisenhart. 1992. *Educated in Romance: Women, Achievement, and College Culture*. Chicago: University of Chicago Press.

Ignatiev, Noel. 2009. *How the Irish Became White*. New York: Routledge.

Isquith, Elias. 2014. "Paul Ryan: Poverty Due to 'Real Culture Problem' in American's 'Inner Cities.'" *Salon*, March 12.

Johnston, Lloyd, Patrick O'Malley, Jerald Bachman, John Schulenberg. 2008. *Monitoring the Future: National Results on Adolescent Drug Use*. Bethesda, MD: US Department of Health and Human Services.

Jones, Owen. 2011. *Chavs: The Demonization of the Working Class*. New York: Verso.

Jung, Moon Kie. 2009. "The Racial Unconscious of Assimilation Theory." *Du Bois Review* 6(2):375–95.

Karabel, Jerome. 2005. *The Chosen: The Hidden History of Admission and Exclusion at Harvard, Yale, and Princeton*. Boston: Houghton Mifflin.

Karp, David. 1986. "You Can Take the Boy Out of Dorchester, but You Can't Take Dorchester Out of the Boy: Toward a Social Psychology of Mobility." *Symbolic Interactionism* 9(1):19–36.

Khan, Shamus. 2011. *Privilege: The Making of an Adolescent Elite at St. Paul's School*. Princeton, NJ: Princeton University Press.

Kluegel, James and Eliot Smith. 1986. *Beliefs about Inequality: Americans' Views of What Is and What Ought to Be*. New York: A. de Gruyter.

Kohn, Melvin. 1969. *Class and Conformity: A Study in Values*. Homewood, IL: Dorsey Press.

Kusserow, Adrie. 2004. *American Individualisms: Child Rearing and Social Class*. New York: Palgrave MacMillan.

Lamont, Michèle and Mario Luis Small. 2008. "How Culture Matters: Enriching Our Understandings of Poverty." Pp. 76–102 in *The Colors of Poverty: Why Racial and Ethnic Disparities Persist*, edited by David Harris and Ann Lin. New York: Russell Sage Foundation.

Lan, Pei-Chia. 2006. *Global Cinderellas: Migrant Domestics and Newly Rich Employers in Taiwan*. Durham, NC: Duke University Press.

Lareau, Annette. 2003. *Unequal Childhoods*. Berkeley: University of California Press.

Lawler, Steph. 2005. "Disgusting Subjects: The Making of Middle-Class Identities." *Sociological Review* 53(3):429–46.

Lee, Erika and Judy Yung. 2010. *Angel Island: Immigrant Gateway to America*. New York: Oxford University Press.

Leopold, Liliya and Yossi Shavit. 2013. "Cultural Capital Does Not Travel Well: Immigrants, Natives, and Achievement in Israeli Schools." *European Sociological Review* 29(3):450–63.

Lewis, Oscar. 1959. *Five Families: Mexican Case Studies in the Culture of Poverty*. New York: Basic Books.

Lewis, Oscar. 1966. *La Vida: A Puerto Rican Family in the Culture of Poverty San Juan and New York*. New York: Vintage Books.

Liebow, Elliot. [1967] 2003. *Tally's Corner: A Study of Negro Streetcorner Men*. New York: Rowman & Littlefield.

Massey, Douglas and Nancy Denton. 1993. *American Apartheid: Segregation and the Making of the American Underclass*. Cambridge, MA: Harvard University Press.

Massey, Douglas. 2014. "Filling the Meso-Level Gap in Stratification Theory." *Socio-Economic Review* 12(3):610–14.

McDermott, Monica. 2006. *Working-Class White: The Making and Unmaking of Race Relations*. Berkeley: University of California Press.

Meier Jaeger, Mads. 2011. "Does Cultural Capital Really Affect Academic Achievement? New Evidence from Combined Sibling and Panel Data." *Sociology of Education* 8(4):281–98.

Moynihan, Daniel. 1965. *The Negro Family: The Case for National Action*. Washington, DC: Office of Policy Planning and Research, U.S. Department of Labor.

National Center for Children in Poverty. 2007. "By Race, White Children Make Up the Biggest Percentage of American's Poor." New York: Columbia University.

Nelson, Margaret and Joan Smith. 1999. *Working Hard and Making Do: Surviving in Small Town America*. Berkeley: University of California Press.

Newman, Katherine. 1999. *No Shame in My Game: The Working Poor in the Inner City*. New York: Knopf/Russell Sage Foundation.

Ogbu, John 1983. "Minority Status and Schooling in Plural Societies." *Comparative Education Review* 27:168–90.

Ogbu John. 2003. *Black American Students in an Affluent Suburb: A Study of Academic Disengagement*. New York: Lawrence Erlbaum.

Ong, Aihwa. 1999. *Flexible Citizenship: The Cultural Logics of Transnationality*. Durham, NC: Duke University Press.

NPR. 2010. "Reconsidering the 'Culture of Poverty.'" October 20. Retrieved December 15, 2014 (http://www.npr.org/templates/story/story.php?storyId=130701401).

Park, Robert. 1925. *The City*. Chicago: University of Chicago Press.

Pattillo, Mary. 1999. *Black Picket Fences: Privilege and Peril among the Black Middle Class*. Chicago: University of Chicago Press.

Pattillo, Mary. 2007. *Black on the Block: The Politics of Race and Class in the City*. Chicago: University of Chicago Press.

Piff, Paul, Michael Kraus, Stéphane Côté, and Dachner Keltner. 2010. "Having Less, Giving More: The Influence of Social Class on Prosocial Behavior." *Journal of Personality and Social Psychology* 99(5):771–84.

Peterson, Richard and Roger Kern. 1996. "Changing Highbrow Taste: From Snob to Omnivore." *American Sociological Review* 61(5):900–907.

Petev, Ivaylo. 2013. "The Association of Social Class and Lifestyle Persistence in American Sociability, 1974 to 2000." *American Sociological Review* 78(4):633–61.

Rainwater, Lee. 1970. *Behind Ghetto Walls: Black Families in a Federal Slum*. Somerset: Aldine.

Rivera, Lauren. 2011. "Ivies, Extracurriculars, and Exclusion: Elite Employers' Use of Educational Credentials." *Research in Social Stratification and Mobility* 29:71–90.

Rodriguez, Robyn. 2010. *Migrants for Export: How the Philippine State Brokers Labor to the World*. Minneapolis: University of Minnesota Press.

Roksa, Josipa and Daniel Potter. 2011. "Parenting and Academic Achievement: Intergenerational Transmission of Educational Advantage." *Sociology of Education* 84(4):299–321.

Rubin, Lillian. 1976. *Worlds of Pain: Life in the Working-Class Family*. New York: Basic Books.

Rubin, Lillian. 1994. *Life on the Fault Line: America's Working-Class Speaks about the Family, the Economy, Race and Ethnicity.* New York: Harper Collins.

Ryan, William. 1971. *Blaming the Victim.* New York: Pantheon.

Sennett, Richard and Jonathon Cobb. [1972] 1993. *The Hidden Injuries of Class.* New York: W.W. Norton.

Shah, Anuj, Sendhil Mullainathan, Eldar Shafir 2012. "Some Consequences of Having Too Little." *Science* 338:682–85.

Skeggs, Beverly. 1997. *Formations of Class & Gender: Becoming Respectable.* London: Sage.

Skeggs, Bev. 2004. *Class, Self, Culture.* New York: Routledge.

Small, Mario, David Harding, and Michele Lamont. 2010. "Reconsidering Culture and Poverty." *The ANNALS of the American Academy of Political and Social Science* 629:6–27.

Smith, Sandra. 2007. "Lone Pursuit: Distrust and Defensive Individualism among the Black Poor." New York: Russell Sage Foundation.

Snibbe, Alana and Helen Rose Markus. 2005. "You Can't Always Get What You Want: Educational Attainment, Agency, and Choice." *Journal of Personality and Social Psychology* 88:703–20.

Stack, Carol. 1974. *All Our Kin.* New York: Harper.

Stephens, Nicole, Helen Rose Markus, L. Taylor Phillips. 2014. "Social Class Culture Cycles: How Three Gateway Contexts Shape Selves and Fuel Inequality." *Annual Review of Psychology* 65:611–34.

Stephens, Nicole, Helen Rose Markus, and Sarah Townsend. 2007. "Choice as an Act of Meaning: The Case of Social Class." *Journal of Personality and Social Psychology* 93(5):814–30.

Streib, Jessi. 2015a. "Explanations of How Love Crosses Class Lines: Cultural Complements and the Case of Cross-Class Marriages." *Sociological Forum* 30(1):18–39.

Streib, Jessi. 2015b. *The Power of the Past: Understanding Cross-Class Marriages.* New York: Oxford University Press.

Stuber, Jenny. 2005. "Asset and Liability? The Importance of Context in the Occupational Experiences of Upwardly Mobile White Adults." *Sociological Forum* 20(1):139–66.

Stuber, Jenny. 2011. *Inside the College Gates: How Class and Culture Matter in Higher Education.* New York: Lexington Books.

Tyson, Karolyn, William Darrity, and Domini Castellino. 2005. "It's Not 'A Black Thing:' Understanding the Burden of Acting White and Other Dilemmas of High Achievement." *American Sociological Review* 70(4):582–605.

Urahn, Susan, Erin Currier, Diana Elliott, Lauren Wechsler, Denise Wilson, and Daniel Colbert. 2012. "Pursuing the American Dream: Economic Mobility Across the Generations." Washington, DC: Pew Charitable Trusts.

Vaisey, Stephen. 2010. "What People Want: Rethinking Poverty, Culture, and Educational Attainment." *Annals of the American Academy of Political and Social Science* 629:75–101.

Vehnkatesh, Sudhir. 2008. *Gang Leader for a Day: A Rogue Sociologist Takes to the Streets.* New York: Penguin Books.

Wade, Lisa and Caroline Heldman. 2012. "Hooking Up and Opting Out: What Students Learn about Sex in their First Year of College." Pp. 128–45 in *Sex for Life: From Virginity to Viagra, How Sexuality Changes Throughout Our Lives*, edited by John DeLamater and Laura Carpenter. New York: New York University Press.

Weininger, Elliott and Annette Lareau. 2009. "Paradoxical Pathways: An Ethnographic Extension of Kohn's Findings on Class and Childrearing." *Journal of Marriage and Family* 71(3):680–95.

Wharton, Amy and Deborah Thorne. 1997. "Why Mothers Matter: The Effects of Social Class and Family Arrangements on African American and White Women's Perceived Relations with their Mothers." *Gender & Society* 11(5):656–81.

Whyte, William Foote. 1943. *Street Corner Society: The Social Structure of an Italian Slum.* Chicago: University of Chicago Press.

Wightman, Patrick, Robert Schoeni, and John Schulenberg. 2012. "Socioeconomic Status and Substance Use Among Young Adults: A Comparison across Constructs and Drugs." *Journal of Studies on Alcohol and Drugs* 73(5):772–82.

Wilkins, Amy and Cristen Dalessandro. 2013. "Monogamy Lite: Cheating, College, and Women." *Gender & Society* 27(5):728–51.

Wilson, William Julius. 1987. *The Truly Disadvantaged: The Inner City, the Underclass, and Public Policy.* Chicago: University of Chicago Press.

Wilson, William Julius. 1996. *When Work Disappears: The World of the New Urban Poor.* New York: Knopf.

Wilson, William Julius. 2009. *More Than Just Race: Being Black and Poor in the Inner City.* New York: W.W. Norton.

Young, Alford, Jr. 1999. "The (Non)Accumulation of Capital: Explicating the Relationship of Structure and Agency in the Lives of Poor Black Men." *Sociological Theory* 17(2):201–27.

Young, Alford, Jr. 2004. *The Minds of Marginalized Black Men.* Princeton, NJ: Princeton University Press.

Young, Robert. 2012. "Can Neds (or Chavs) be Non-delinquent, Educated, or Even Middle Class? Contrasting Empirical Findings with Cultural Stereotypes." *Sociology* 46(6):1140–60.

CHAPTER 12

THE HISTORICAL ORIGINS OF POVERTY IN DEVELOPING COUNTRIES

SAMBIT BHATTACHARYYA

INTRODUCTION

THE recent economic growth record of the developing world has been the subject of many discussions. Indeed, some nations in the developing world have been growing at an enviably rapid pace. In spite of such dynamism in some developing economies, the gap between the rich and the poor nations of the world is wider than ever. According to a recent estimate, 1.4 billion people are trapped in extreme poverty and reside in developing countries (IFAD 2011). At the macro level, the latest World Bank estimates suggest that the divide between rich and poor nations is even more striking. Norway, the world's richest nation with an annual per capita income of $84,290 is 496 times richer than Burundi, the world's poorest country with a per capita income of $170.

In this chapter I explore the genesis of this divergence. During the second half of the previous century, the vast majority of the intellectual efforts by economists and social scientists in the quest for growth were focused on exploring the post–World War II period. However, simple plots of GDP per capita across nations show that there is very little change in the relative positions of countries since the war (see Figure 12.1). The difference in living standards in India and the United Kingdom hardly changed since the war. The gap between Ghana or Tanzania and the industrial West widened during this period. The only exception, however, is China as the Chinese economy showed immense dynamism since the 1970s and is rapidly catching up with the industrial West.[1] In spite of such dynamism, the gap between China and the industrial West still remains significant. Therefore, the genesis of this gap cannot be the postwar period. To trace the origin of divergence, we need to look further back in time.

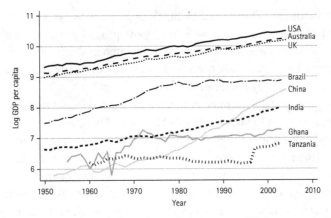

FIGURE 12.1 Evolution of Per Capita Income across Nations, 1950–2005

In order to systematically analyze the root causes of poverty in developing countries, I start with a review of the theories of root causes (geography, disease, colonial history, slave trade, culture, and technology) of poverty. Following which, I present a novel, unified framework that unites these theories. The central thesis is that Western Europe benefited from favorable geography that led to highly productive agriculture, food surpluses, and institutions conducive to development. In contrast, Africa continues to suffer from unfavorable geography and disease. Institutional weaknesses in Latin America and Russia explain their relatively weak long-term economic performance. I also argue that these historical factors matter for contemporary patterns of development across the globe.

The main contribution of the chapter is to present a novel, unified framework. The framework links root causes such as geography, disease, colonial institutions, and technology in order to describe the history of long-term development in Western Europe and North America. It is also used to assess what went wrong in Africa, Latin America, and Russia.

The chapter is organized as follows. In the next section, I start with a critical analysis of the existing theories of root causes of poverty. The third section presents a unified framework for Western Europe relating factors such as geography, disease, colonial history, and knowledge in explaining economic progress. The fourth section applies this framework to explain the history of poverty in Africa, Latin America, and Russia and is followed by concluding statements.

Theories of Root Causes of Poverty

Institutions and Development

Economists, philosophers, and other social scientists have been grappling with the role of institutions in delivering prosperity at least since the days of the European and

Scottish Enlightenment. The role of institutions in reducing poverty and promoting development has been articulated well in elegant prose by Adam Smith. In Smith's words, "Little else is required to carry a state to the highest degree of opulence from the lowest barbarism, but peace, easy taxes and tolerable administration of justice; all the rest being brought about by the natural course of things."

Even though many scholars since Adam Smith have referred to the role of institutions, it is perhaps due to the works of Nobel Laureate Douglass North in the 1980s that institutions and development theory returned to the center stage of mainstream economics. North (1994) defines institutions as humanly devised constraints that structure human interaction. He also classifies these constraints into formal and informal and shows that they depend on the enforcement characteristic. The constraints and the enforcement characteristics taken together form the incentive structure of a society and are crucial to innovation, investments, poverty reduction, and prosperity.

The institutions and development theme has also been advanced by Evans (1995) and Amsden (2001). Evans (1995) distinguishes between developmental and predatory states in developing nations and analyzes their impact on economic development. Amsden (2001), on the other hand, highlights the importance of flexible institutions that allow ingenious and more independent industrial policy in developing countries.

Following Douglass North's and others' work on economic institutions, many of the recent empirical studies test the statistical significance of institutional variables in explaining the variation in living standard across countries. Knack and Keefer (1995) and Hall and Jones (1999) are some of the early studies to use institutions and governance as explanations of the variation in poverty and prosperity across nations. They use measures of institutions as explanatory variables in a regression model with GDP per capita as a dependent variable and show that they are statistically significant.

Even though many of the early empirical studies report statistical significance, questions were raised about the direction of causality in the relationship between institutions and economic performance. One could argue that causality runs from institutional quality to economic performance. However, one could also argue that richer nations are better able to afford good institutions, and therefore causality runs from GDP per capita to institutional quality. Acemoglu, Johnson, and Robinson (2001) were perhaps the first to put forward an empirically validated causal explanation in this literature. They assert that the Europeans resorted to different styles of colonization depending on the feasibility of settlement. In a tropical environment, the settlers had to deal with malaria and yellow fever, and they faced a high mortality rate. This prevented them from settling in tropical environments, and resource extraction became the most important, if not the only, activity in these colonies. In order to support these activities, the colonizers erected institutions that were extractive in nature. On the other hand, in temperate conditions European settlers felt more at home and decided to settle. In these places they erected institutions characterized by strong protection of property rights and efficient enforcement of contracts. These institutions persisted over time and influenced the incentive structure in these societies. Therefore, the shaping of the incentive structure during the colonial period has a long-term impact on economic development, which is reflected by the current standard of living of these places.

Using data on European settler and clergy mortality rates from the colonies Acemoglu et al. (2001) show that indeed there is a negative correlation between settler mortality and current institutional quality. Furthermore, they also show that institutional quality has a positive impact on the current level of development. This leads them to conclude colonial institutions systematically influence the living standards of citizens in the former European colonies.

In a paper published the following year, Acemoglu, Johnson, and Robinson (2002) show that the economic fortunes of the former European colonies reversed after colonization. Colonies that were prosperous prior to European colonization became poorer, whereas economically backward colonies became prosperous after colonization. They attribute this "reversal of fortune" to institutional reversal. They argue that economically effective institutions of previously prosperous tropical colonies were replaced by extractive institutions after colonization. These institutions persisted over time and are not conducive to capitalism. In contrast, in settler colonies strong property rights and contracting institutions were set up that were conducive to capitalism. They also argue that this reversal of fortune provides strong evidence in favor of the dominance of the institutions view, and it nullifies the role of factors such as geography. Note that the influence of geography remained unchanged both before and after colonial intervention. The institutions however experienced a reversal after colonization.

The "reversal of fortune" argument was not limited to the economics literature. Lange, Mahoney, and vom Hau (2006) argue that the reversal of fortune had more to do with the style of colonialism than colonialism per se. They argue that mercantilist Spain extensively colonized regions that were more prosperous and populous. Mercantilist and extractive policies of Spanish colonialism were extremely harmful to these colonies. In contrast, liberal British colonialism targeted areas that were sparsely populated and less developed. They set up institutions that were liberal and conducive to capitalism. Therefore, these colonies experienced rapid development under British colonialism.

Note that Lange et al. (2006) are not unique in comparing British and Spanish colonial institutions. North (1989) and La Porta et al. (1999) also present a similar argument. North (1989) contrasts the evolution of British common law and its influence on colonies, such as the United States, with the centralized institutional enforcement mechanism of Spain and its influence on South American colonies. La Porta et al. (1999) in contrast focus on the influence of British and Spanish legal origins.

A series of empirical papers followed these two influential papers. Rodrik, Subramanian, and Trebbi (2004) test the institutions hypothesis against statistical proxies of the geography and trade hypotheses respectively. They find that institutions are the only dominant factor explaining the difference in living standards across countries. Bhattacharyya (2009b) estimates the impact of different types of institutions on growth. He shows that "market creating institutions" such as property rights and contracts are the key for prosperity. Regulatory institutions matter only up to a certain point, whereas political institutions, such as democracy, do not seem to matter. In a similar vein, Acemoglu and Johnson (2005) test the relative importance of property rights and contracting institutions and find that the former is relatively more important than the latter.

Independently, Engerman and Sokoloff (2001) focus on the roles of initial endowment and distribution of political power in shaping institutions. Comparing North and South America they write, "While all [New World colonies] began with an abundance of land and other resources relative to labour, at least after the initial depopulation, other aspects of their factor endowments varied—contributing to extreme differences in the distributions of land holdings, wealth, and of political power" (p. 3).

They argue that the climatic conditions of North American colonies were favorable to growing grains and keeping livestock. The production technology involved with these agricultural activities exhibited limited economies of scale in production. Therefore, small family-sized farms were preferred over large landholdings. This led to a more equitable distribution of land and wealth. This had a profound impact on the initial distribution of political power and political institutions. These political institutions honored the right of citizens to own private property and hence protected them. They also enforced contracts. The property rights and contracting institutions taken together were key ingredients for the creation of a thriving local market economy. The local market economies were also well connected to the European economies on the other side of the Atlantic and delivered shared prosperity. This in turn created a culture of more equitable distribution of political power that helped these institutions to persist and thrive. The idea of a property-owning democracy with universal male suffrage was unprecedented in the political history of the world. The success of these institutions in North America later led to the adoption of these institutions in Western Europe.

In contrast, climatic conditions in South America and the Caribbean Islands were conducive to cash crops such as sugar, tobacco, rubber, and cotton. This continent was also home to a vast amount of mineral resources. Production technology involved in the planting and harvesting of cash crops and the extraction of mineral resources can benefit from large economies of scale. Therefore, large plantations and mines were set up in these regions. These plantations and mines were owned by a minority group of European colonizers and run by large armies of cheap slave labor. The working population in these colonies was extremely poor and had no political rights or power. Any revolt by the enslaved workers was often brutally quashed by the colonial masters. This led to an unequal initial distribution of wealth and political power in these colonies. The highly concentrated landholdings and extreme inequality in Mexico, Colombia, and Peru during the colonial period are supportive of Engerman and Sokoloff's (2001) theory on the Americas. This skewed distribution of wealth and political power contributed to the development of political and economic institutions that were exploitative and extractive in nature. These institutions persisted over time and continue to inhibit the development of markets, an advanced capitalist economy, and conditions for sustained economic growth in South America.

The debate on institutions and development in political science is somewhat dominated by sociologist Seymor Martin Lipset's (1959) "modernization hypothesis," which says that as countries develop, their quality of institutions, education, and health service improves simultaneously. In other words, the causality runs from living standards to institutions and not the other way around. However, this view has been challenged by recent research. A potent counterargument is that institutions diverge not in a systematic manner as outlined by Lipset (1959) but rather due to exogenous shocks at critical historical junctures. Barrington Moore (1966), in his famous work on institutions, outlines that events such as the Russian Revolution, the American Civil War, and many others were critical junctures in history which shaped future institutions and economic trajectories. This is commonly known as the "critical juncture hypothesis." Thelen (1999, 2000) also makes a case for the critical juncture thesis in explaining German labor history and institutions. Thelen (1999) also presents a survey of the critical juncture literature in politics.

Another strand of the institutions literature is inspired by the works of Giovanni Arrighi, Terence Hopkins, and Immanuel Wallerstein. Arrighi et al. (1989), in their book entitled *Anti-systemic Movements*, argue that antisystemic movements or revolutions arising out of class struggle in a capitalist society could be transient as the institutions of class characterized by old Marxists are in a constant state of flux. They argue that in a capitalist world economy, due to the rapid change in technology and the mode of production, groups and institutions are constantly recreated, remolded, and eliminated.

Institutions of Slave Trade and Development in Africa

A large literature also links the institutions of the slave trade and the poverty trap in Africa. The major contributors are Inikori (1977, 1992), Manning (1981, 1982), and Miller (1988).

Inikori (1992) argues that a vast majority of slaves that were exported were free individuals captured by force. The capture took a number of forms, notably kidnapping, raids organized by the state, warfare, pawning, via the judicial procedures, tributes and so forth. Firearms were imported from the Europeans in exchange for slaves particularly during the period 1750 to 1807, which were used for capturing more slaves (Inikori 1977). Inikori (1992) also shows that the rise of Atlantic slave trade led to more capturing and the expansion of the African slave trade. The increase in the trade for captives institutionalized banditry and corruption for more than 300 years on the continent thus weakening institutions, which in turn retarded socioeconomic development (Inikori 2000).

Manning's argument is similar to Inikori's; however, his work focuses on Dahomey, which is roughly the area around the Bight of Benin during the period 1640 to 1860 (Manning 1981, 1982). He observes that the immense increase in slave prices with a price elasticity of supply of 1.5 created the incentive for capturing more slaves. Institutions (which included warfare, raiding, kidnapping, judicial procedures, and tributes) were set up from 1640 to 1670 in this area, which was conducive to capturing slaves. The state became an active participant in the collection and delivery of slaves, which is further evidence favoring Inikori's argument. Miller (1988) also provides a similar account in the case of Angola.

More recently, Nunn (2008), using regression models, shows that the slave trade prevented state development, encouraged ethnic fractionalization, and weakened legal institutions. Through these channels, the slave trade continues to affect current economic development in Africa. However, Bhattacharyya (2009c) shows that Nunn's empirical evidence is not robust because it did not include certain variables such as disease and geography.

Geography and Development

Jared Diamond's influential book entitled *Guns, Germs and Steel* is perhaps the most comprehensive account of the role of geography in economic development in recent times.

In his book, Diamond (1997) asks: Why did history unfold so differently on different continents? He argues that geography and biogeography influenced humanity in contrasting ways on different continents. Geographic conditions and climate in different continents created different endowments for food and livestock. In the Eurasian plain, especially in Southwest Asia by the Mediterranean, the climate was best suited for the development of a large number of edible wild grains and large mammals. Diamond (1997) follows University of Chicago archeologist James Henry Breasted by calling this region the "Fertile Crescent."[2] Early hunter-gatherers domesticated a large number of edible wild grains and resorted to a sedentary agriculturally based lifestyle.[3] They also domesticated a large number of large mammals and used them for their milk, meat, and muscle power. Milk and meat from domesticated animals became a reliable source of protein, which increased productivity of agricultural labor. Large domesticated animals' muscle power in agriculture also boosted agricultural productivity and contributed to food surpluses. This farming technology, knowledge, domesticated crops and animals, and surplus food traveled along the same latitude to other parts of the Eurasian plain. These animals and crops thrived in the geographic conditions of Western Europe. Western Europe has glaciated, extremely fertile soil, reliable rainfall, and very few debilitating tropical diseases. These conditions were ideally suited for further development of these crops and domesticated animals. Agricultural productivity improved even further, which consistently contributed to food surpluses. A reasonably long history of sedentary agriculture along with animal domestication led to frequent outbreaks of epidemic diseases. This helped the Eurasian population develop vital immunity against many epidemic diseases. Powered with immunity and food surpluses, these societies experienced population growth. Societal structure became more complex, and sedentary lifestyles led to the development of guns, steel swords, sea-worthy vessels, and so forth. When the non-Europeans in the Americas and Africa came into contact with the Europeans during colonial conquest, the former were unable to offer much resistance to the latter, as the latter were powered with guns, steel swords, horses, ocean-navigable ships, and germs. Many of the Native American population perished from alien Eurasian diseases such as small pox. As a result, over time, the Europeans became more and more prosperous relative to the rest of the world.

Diamond's thesis of the origin of productive agriculture in the Fertile Crescent is also supported by archeobotanists Daniel Zohary and Maria Hopf. Zohary and Hopf (2000) in their book *Domestication of Plants in the Old World* presents evidence that the extensive spread of wild barley was confined to the Fertile Crescent. They also show that the wild ancestors of modern wheat (the emmer wheat and the einkorn wheat) and wild ancestors of other crops originated in the Fertile Crescent.

Similar to Diamond's theory on the role of geography, Olsson and Hibbs (2000) and Gallup and Sachs (2000) emphasize the role of agriculture in explaining current levels of development. Olsson and Hibbs (2000) show that on average nations with a long history of agriculture tend to be richer than nations with a relatively short history of agriculture. Highly productive and organized agriculture began in Europe approximately 9,000 years ago. In contrast, agriculture in equatorial and subequatorial Africa started approximately 2,000 to 1,800 years ago. The length of agricultural history is also correlated with the development of the state. Europe acquired some form of government much earlier than Africa. Therefore, it is not surprising that contemporary Europe is far more economically advanced than contemporary Africa. Gallup and Sachs (2000), however, focus on the influence of soil quality on agricultural productivity and economic development. They argue that high relative humidity and high nighttime temperatures in the tropics cause high plant respiration and slows down plant growth. This deficiency in plant growth in the tropics is also related to the lack of nutrients in tropical soil. Humid tropical soils (alfisols, oxisols, and ultisols) are typically low in nutrients and organic matters. This limits plant growth and also causes soil erosion and acidification. In addition the lack of frost allows a greater number of pests to survive and breed. These factors have a debilitating impact on agricultural productivity and inhibit economic progress. In contrast European and temperate regions are blessed with extremely fertile, glaciated soil and more frost days to eliminate pests. Therefore, agricultural productivity is much higher.

Geography can also impose severe constraints on trade and commerce (Sachs and Warner 1995; Sachs and Warner 1997; Gallup et al. 1998). Many countries are landlocked and as a result have limited or no access to ports and ocean-navigable waterways, which limits their ability to trade. Access to a port or major markets in such situations often involves crossing international borders, which makes the cost of transportation relatively high. Limited international trade in these economies confines all commercial activities to small internal markets. This causes an inefficient division of labor and underdevelopment. Inland Africa and some Central Asian countries are perhaps good examples of the perils of unfavorable geography (Collier and Gunning 1999).

Even though Jared Diamond's influential book brought the role of geography and climate back to center stage, by no means is Diamond's work the first. The climate and geography argument may be traced as far back as Montesquieu ([1748] 1989). He argues that the population in the tropics is not industrious enough largely due to the energy-sapping heat. Natural availability of food in abundance also makes tropical people idle. This has a direct and negative effect on human productivity and hence economic growth. In a recent study, Parker (2000) supports Montesquieu's argument. According to his thesis, an individual's desire to maximize utility is dependent on motivation; homeostasis; and neural, autonomic, and hormonal adjustments. These physiological factors are governed by the hypothalamus. The activity of the hypothalamus is heavily dependent on thermodynamics. In hot conditions, the hypothalamus secretes hormones that negatively affect motivation and enterprise; whereas in cold climates, individuals are naturally hard working. These tendencies affect the steady state level of income in these two regions. The average steady state income in a cold climate is naturally higher than the average steady state in a hot climate. Hence, climate explains two-thirds of the per capita income differences between the tropics and temperate regions.

Disease and Development

Demographers have long talked about the role of mortality and fertility in transforming a society. The idea of how mortality and fertility shape a society at least goes back to Malthus. When societies are faced with high birth rates without a significant increase in food production, then it is likely that the mortality rate will rise. In contrast, an increase in food production would be followed by a significant increase in the birth rate as the society is better able to support a larger population. In recent times a more sophisticated version of this theory has evolved which is commonly known as the theory of "demographic transition." The demographic transition theory suggests that as societies become more economically advanced, they then focus more and more on the quality of life for newborns rather than their quantity. The survival rate of newborns in an economically advanced society improves alongside life expectancy. As a result, households concentrate more on quality of life rather than how many children are born and both fertility and mortality decline. The transition from an economically backward high-fertility and high-mortality equilibrium to an economically advanced low-fertility and low-mortality equilibrium is commonly known as the demographic transition.

Disease influences both mortality and fertility and therefore delays demographic transition. Therefore, in an environment of high-disease incidence, a society could be trapped in a low-level equilibrium, which is often referred to as the "poverty trap." Bhattacharyya (2011) presents a model that outlines the mechanism through which disease could impact development. High-disease incidence increases mortality and therefore affects individuals' savings and investment decisions. If the probability of survival into the future is low, then individuals are more likely to focus on current consumption and save less for the future. As a result of low savings, investments in the future would suffer. Furthermore, morbidity could also be high in an environment where debilitating diseases, such as malaria, are prevalent. Therefore, low labor productivity would also be an issue. These factors taken together would lead to a poverty trap (Gallup et al. 1998).

The link between disease and economic development is empirically established by Gallup and Sachs (2001), Bloom and Sachs (1998), and Gallup et al. (1998). Gallup and Sachs (2001) point out that the countries with intensive malaria grow 1.3 percentage points slower per person per year than countries without malaria, and a 10 percentage point reduction in malaria might result in a 0.3 percentage point increase in annual per capita income growth. Bloom and Sachs (1998) also claim that the high incidence of malaria in sub-Saharan Africa reduces the annual growth rate by 1.3 percentage points a year. In other words, eradication of malaria in 1950 would have resulted in a doubling of current per capita income. Sachs (2003) reports a strong and negative effect of malaria on economic progress even after controlling for institutions and openness.

More recently, Bhattacharyya (2009c) showed that the fundamental cause of lack of development in Africa is malaria. Using an empirical model and the instrumental variable method of estimation to estimate the long-term impact of malaria, the slave trade, and institutions on living standards in Africa, he finds that malaria is the only statistically significant explanatory variable. Factors such as the slave trade and institutions are statistically insignificant. The purported link between the slave trade and current living standards through institutional quality also breaks down in the presence of malaria. Bhattacharyya's finding is also a confirmation of a long list of earlier research findings in the field of tropical medicine which asserts that malaria in Africa is different than malaria in the rest of the world (Kiszewski et al. 2004). Malaria in Africa is vector based, and tropical countries are saddled with diseases that present a much bigger challenge for the local population relative to temperate countries.[4] These diseases are a product of tropical biology, and it is somewhat misplaced to brush off the disease argument by claiming it to be endogenous to institutional and state capacity. In other words, financially well-resourced states could easily overpower malaria. Hence it is not the severity of the disease but institutional weakness which is the root cause of African underdevelopment. It is important to note here that in spite of the billions pumped into research in tropical medicine to eradicate these diseases over the last and the current century, it is still proving illusive. Strategies such as vector control also turned out to be unsuccessful. Therefore, the endogeneity argument often bandied about in the economics literature seems somewhat ill-informed. Kiszewski et al. (2004) present an excellent summary of the research in tropical medicine.

Technology and Development

The technology and human capital theory of development was formalized in economics by Joseph A. Schumpeter (1934). In his book entitled *The Theory of Economic Development*, he describes the notion of "creative destruction" and how it is central to the process of economic development. He argues that every enterprise in a capitalist economy is constantly searching for new ideas to outsmart their competitors. A commercially viable new idea comes with the privilege of enjoying monopoly profit in a particular product range. Therefore, product differentiation is the key to success, and constant innovation is the main driver of product differentiation. The process of creative destruction and product differentiation may render previous products obsolete and thus leave their market open to capture. This round the clock dynamism of the capitalist economy creates incentives for entrepreneurs to invest in R&D in their quest for a larger market share. Schumpeter argues that this is what creates value and keeps capitalism marching forward.

Historian Joel Mokyr in his influential book *The Lever of Riches* also credits new technology for the success of capitalism. He identifies technological progress as the lifeblood of economic progress in all human societies. He writes, "Technological progress predated capitalism and credit by many centuries, and may well outlive capitalism by at least as long" (1990:6). He, however, puts more emphasis on the complementary role played by invention and innovation in the success of a society. Using anecdotal evidence from European and Chinese history, he shows that both invention and innovation must go hand in hand for a society to be successful. Even though in the short run, one could make up for the other, in the long run, one could not survive without the other.

Supporting the technology and human capital view of development, Glaeser et al. (2004) focus on the causes of success of some former European colonies. They argue that when the European settlers migrated to the New World, they took their knowledge and human capital with them and not the institutions. The Anglo-Saxon colonies of the North received migrants predominantly from industrial Britain and Western Europe. Consequently their migrant stock had relatively high levels of knowledge and human capital. In contrast, the Spanish and Portuguese colonies of the South received migrants predominantly from the not so industrial European South. Consequently, their migrant stock had relatively low levels of knowledge and human capital. These differences in knowledge and human capital persisted and continue to explain the difference in living standards in these former colonies. Therefore, human capital could be more fundamental than institutions behind the success of the northern New World colonies. Even though their argument seems feasible, Bhattacharyya (2009b) shows that it is statistically difficult to identify these effects.

Another strong case for the human capital and development view is put forward by Galor and Moav (2006). They argue that after the Industrial Revolution in Britain, the factory system became the dominant model of production. The three major factors used in the factory system of production were land, labor, and capital. However, land became secondary relative to the other two factors over time. The owners of labor were the workers, and the owners of capital and land were the capitalists. The society also became segmented along these lines of ownership, and this gave rise to a class society. The owners of labor were part of the working class, and the owners of capital and land were part of the capitalist class. However, over time the class society broke down. Galor and Moav associate this demise of the class society to technological progress. At the start of the Industrial Revolution production technology was fairly basic, and therefore the demand for skilled labor was low. However, the demand for labor shifted more toward skilled labor as production and machineries became more complex near the latter part of the Industrial Revolution. In order to maintain their profit levels, capitalists started investing in schooling to create a steady supply of skilled workers. This is in sharp contrast to the early part of the Industrial Revolution when the use of child labor in factories was rife.[5] During the latter part of Industrial Revolution Britain experienced the rise of the Victorian do-gooders—a group of entrepreneurs actively engaging in philanthropy to improve public welfare through building schools, hospitals, and proper sanitation. Therefore, technology not only helped the economic progress of the society, but it also brought about changes in political and social institutions.

Galor and Moav (2006) also provide empirical evidence in favor of their theory using the voting patterns of the legislators on England's education reform, the Balfour Act of 1902. This bill was meant to create a publicly supported secondary school system. They show that legislators' support for this bill is positively correlated with the industrial skill-intensity level of the counties. Legislators representing counties with high industrial skill-intensity levels overwhelmingly supported this bill, whereas the others did not. By assuming that the legislators received financial backing from the industrialists in their respective counties, Galor and Moav argue that the voting result reflects the capitalists', who owned skill-intensive industries, eagerness to invest in human capital.

Culture and Development

Max Weber's seminal work entitled *The Protestant Ethic and the Spirit of Capitalism* is perhaps one of the earliest scholarly works highlighting the importance of religion and culture. Weber (1930) argues that Protestantism's, and especially Calvinism's, emphasis on industry, thrift, and frugality, along with its moral approval of risk taking and financial self-development, created a social environment conducive to investment and the accumulation of private capital. These values sowed the seeds of modern capitalism. Weber's views are rejected by Tawney (1926) who argues that it was secularism and not Protestantism which bolstered the forward march of industrial England in the sixteenth century.

Other noteworthy theories of culture are due to Landes (1998) and Clark (2007). Landes (1998) argues that religious tolerance of Protestantism is one of the key virtues which facilitated capitalism. Clark (2007), on the other hand, emphasizes the role of religion and middle-class virtues of thrift and hard work. In spite of their intellectual appeal, the supporting evidence provided by these authors is often found unreliable (Allen 2008).

UNIFIED FRAMEWORK

In the previous section we observed that multiple factors may have influenced the process of economic development or the lack of it. Therefore, it is unlikely that a process as complex as economic development may have been driven by one single factor. In this section I present a novel, unified framework similar to Bhattacharyya (2009a, 2011) to show that it was not one factor but a series of factors that created the difference between success and failure throughout human history.[6] The idea here is to construct a framework to explain the Western European and later North American success story. The unified framework emphasizes the important roles of geography, disease, trade, and institutions in the development of Western Europe and North America. In the next section I will compare this framework with African, Latin American, and Russian historical narratives to identify why they fell behind. I discuss the roles of the abovementioned factors in turn. Table 12.1 also provides a summary of factors that may have influenced development across the globe.

Western Europe

Western Europe benefited from the transfer of seeds and agricultural technology from the East. Organized and productive agriculture started in the Fertile Crescent approximately 11,000 years ago (Diamond 1997). Local populations domesticated wild varieties of modern wheat and barley, which were plentiful in the Fertile Crescent. They also domesticated large mammals that were a reliable source of protein. These crops migrated westward to Europe along with humans. As a result, organized agriculture started in Europe around 9,000 years ago. Agriculture, food surpluses, and sedentary lifestyles increased human population in Europe. Increased population created more pressure on cultivable land, which led to frequent armed conflicts between villages and tribes. Armed conflicts and warfare necessitated the creation of a more complex and hierarchical institutions within the society. Armed conflicts also led to technological progress, especially in metallurgy, which had a direct positive externality on agriculture. Agricultural productivity improved further, and human society became more complex relative to hunter-gatherers.

In spite of such progress, humans in Western Europe were not as advanced as modern industrial societies. Due to intensive agriculture and increased population density, humans were living side by side to domesticated animals and other humans. This led to more frequent outbreaks of deadly and infectious diseases such as cholera, the bubonic plague, and small pox. Even though these frequent outbreaks took a heavy toll on the human population in Western Europe, it also boosted immunity. Furthermore, it also necessitated the development of the art of alchemy and early medicine to treat diseases.

In the Middle Ages, investments in science and technology coupled with increased immunity boosted human population even further. Growing demand for food

Table 12.1 History and Poverty around the Globe

Western Europe	North America	South America	Africa	Russia
Glaciated fertile soil →	Glaciated fertile soil but land abundant and labor-scarce society →	Fertile soil but land abundant and labor-scarce society →	Infertile soil, low agricultural productivity, and high disease incidence →	Glaciated fertile soil →
Food surplus →	European migration and settlement →	Spanish and Portuguese conquest, European migration and settlement →	Land abundant and labor-scarce society →	Land abundant but labor-scarce society →
Population growth →	Migration of European technology and institutions →	Geographic endowment conducive to plantations and mining precious metals →	Disease and low agricultural productivity continues to be a major constraint to development →	Landed elite holds enormous power over the royal court because they supply labor, recruits for the army, and tax revenue →
Conflict, technological progress, and stronger institutions →	Land abundance and smaller family farms to cultivate crops such as wheat and corn leads to more egalitarian initial income distribution →	Small group of colonial owners of plantations and mines run by large number of native American labor or African slave labor →	European contact, plunder, and colonial institutions →	Skewed distribution of economic and political power →
Conflict-induced need for more government revenue →	More egalitarian distribution of political power →	Skewed distribution of economic and political power →	Exploitative and autocratic political institutions →	Exploitative and authoritarian political institutions →
Exploration of the Atlantic route and hunt for precious metals →	More inclusive and democratic political institutions →	Exploitative and autocratic political institutions →	Weak property rights and contracting institutions →	Weak property rights and contracting institutions →
Plunder and import of precious metals lead to inflation →		Expropriation of private property with weak property rights and contracting institutions →	Atlantic slave trade weakens institutions →	Any democratic tendencies vehemently resisted by the landed elite →
Mercantilist policy to stop outflow of precious metals and rising inflation →				Disastrous war with Japan in 1905 and then with Germany in 1914 →
Atlantic trade in manufacturing →				

(Continued)

Table 12.1 Continued

Western Europe	North America	South America	Africa	Russia
Induces institutional change and rise of capitalist institutions →	Atlantic trade with Europe and the rest of the world →	Atlantic trade in primary products and metals with Europe and the rest of the world →	Poverty trap due to geography, disease, and institutional failure	Russian Revolution in 1917 and the formation of Soviet Union in 1922 →
More inclusive political institutions that sustain the progress of capitalist development →	Successful capitalism and shared prosperity	Unsuccessful capitalism and decline due to institutional failure		Planned economy experiencing early success but suffers from inefficiency →
Successful capitalism along with inclusive political institutions lead to shared prosperity				Weak property rights, lack of innovation, and decline →
				Collapse of Soviet Union in 1989 and recovery →
				Questions over current political institutions →
				Institutions and the economy modernizing rapidly

necessitated intensive agriculture and the exploitation of increasing returns to scale in agricultural production. Farm sizes became larger and larger. New farming tools coupled with new farming techniques increased agricultural productivity even more. Protection of food surpluses and agricultural land from frequent armed invasions by other villages and tribes necessitated the creation of full-time military forces. A complex reorganization of society took place at this point. Leaders of military forces started gaining more prominence in society. In return for their military service, the leaders established the right to expropriate a part of the agricultural produce. This is what modern societies would call taxation. With taxation came the need for accounting and documenting who is paying what and when. As a result, institutions became more formalized.

Toward the later part of the Middle Ages as population density increased, so increased the greed of the European feudal elites to bolster their coffers by waging wars and acquiring new territory. During this period Western Europe experienced virtually unabated armed conflicts. The increasing predominance of the military within society gave rise to a new kind of social organization. Feudal elites forged coalitions often along ethnic lines and increasingly appeared to be united as an imperial nation-state under the monarch.

Frequent conflicts and the culture of waging wars weakened the coffers of the Western European monarchs. They started looking elsewhere for more riches to plunder. The Spanish and the Portuguese monarchs commissioned exploratory voyages intended to discover direct trading routes to the East and eliminate the Arab middleman. They were also inspired by the tales of great riches (especially precious metals such as gold) in the East. Their quest for precious metals was satisfied, albeit accidentally, not from the East but by reaching the shores of South America. Francesco Pizzaro's ransom in terms of gold to free Atahualpa after the battle of Cajamarca is perhaps a testament to the Western European imperial glut for precious metals.

The opening of the trade routes across the Atlantic led to large-scale exploitation of gold and silver mines in South America. This steady flow of metals into Europe (especially Portugal and Spain) led to inflation, and the monarchs by default adopted mercantilist policies (Bhattacharyya 2011). Monarchs wanted to prevent precious metals from leaving the country, so they restricted import of manufactured goods. The focus shifted from importing manufactured goods from India and China to exporting manufactured goods.

Increasingly, from the seventeenth century onward, Western European monarchs engaged in naval conflicts with one another for control over trade routes. Trade companies were established to wrest control of the trades routes: first it was the Portuguese, then the Spanish, followed by the Dutch, French, and English. Finally, the English prevailed over the rest and established themselves as the supreme naval and military power of Europe. The English imperial fortunes were bolstered by acquiring new land to expand the empire, increased tax revenue, and sometimes outright plunder.

The English merchants and monarchs developed a symbiotic relationship over this period. Merchants trading on the high seas required the support of the military and the monarch. The monarch in return also required the support of the merchants for credit, tax revenue, and a share of the plunder from the colonies. This symbiotic relationship galvanized through the development of new economic and political institutions. The merchants demanded more political rights and protection from expropriation by the monarchs and the elites. Their newfound economic power enabled them to impose more "checks and balances" on the monarch, protect property rights, establish Parliament, and seek more political power. These institutions were pivotal to the success of capitalism and the Industrial Revolution. Unfettered and sometimes favorable access to overseas markets in other parts of the empire without doubt helped the cause of the Industrial Revolution.

Britain's involvement in the triangular trade of the Atlantic economy may have helped the Industrial Revolution (Findlay 1990) even though conclusive evidence on this remains elusive. Cotton textile, sugar, rum, and guns produced in Manchester, Liverpool, and other parts of industrial England were traded for slaves in Africa until abolition.[7] Merchants and slave traders would exchange these goods with African warlords and slave raiders in return for slaves. These slaves would be exported to the Caribbean and the American South to work in sugar and cotton plantations respectively. Raw sugar and cotton from the New World would then be exported back to England for processing in the industrial mills.

The capitalist economic institutions survived and were bolstered by more representative political institutions. These economic and political institutions were key to the success of capitalism in England. These institutions and the ideas related to the Industrial Revolution also spread to the continental European West and contributed to the success of capitalism there.

In summary, the success of Western Europe is due to multiple factors. To start with, the long history of successful agriculture and overcoming diseases was one. This was followed by military conquests and unstoppable imperial glut for precious metals. This gave rise to maritime trade, new institutions, the Industrial Revolution, and capitalism. These institutions continue to be the cornerstones of capitalism's success in the European West.

North America

North America prior to European colonization was land abundant and labor scarce. The disease environment in North America was conducive to European settlement. Mercantilist policies, fertile land, and the pursuit of religious freedom were the main drivers of European settlement in this part of the world. The first English settlers arrived in 1607 and established Jamestown colony in Virginia. Subsequently, they also claimed Canada.

These colonies attracted settlers who came armed with Western knowledge and Western institutions. They were also blessed with extremely fertile temperate soil. Since the first settlement in Jamestown, productive agriculture, Western technology and institutions, and the Atlantic trade helped North America leapfrog during the next two centuries to an advanced capitalist economy.

Why Africa, Latin America, and Russia Fell Behind

Africa

Agriculture in Africa began almost 7,000 years after agriculture in Europe. Therefore, the history of agriculture in Africa is fairly recent. African soil is also not as fertile as the glaciated soil of Europe. As a result, the continent became trapped in the cobwebs of unfavorable geography. Furthermore, tropical diseases, such as malaria and yellow fever, also created almost insurmountable challenges for development on the African continent. Bhattacharyya (2009c, 2011) presents evidence and describes the challenges Africa faced over the long run.

To summarize, the African development story is a poverty trap due to almost insurmountable constraints imposed by geography and diseases. These constraints did not allow accumulation of food surpluses and population growth, which are essential for the development of a complex society, institutions, and economy. After European contact, Africa's engagement with the slave trade further distorted institutional incentives and reinforced the poverty trap (Inikori 1977, 1992, 2000). Many of these institutions and diseases still persist and continue to exert negative impacts on economic development in Africa.

South America

South America was also a settler colony after European conquest. However, the non-European population density in the South was relatively higher than the North. Furthermore, it was also well endowed with mineral resources and commercial crops that are suitable for plantations. Therefore, the initial endowments of resources were quite different between North America and Central and South America.

The colonizers in South America also came from Europe in pursuit of fertile land, mercantilism, and religious freedom. However, the initial endowment dictated the type of institutions that were set up in these colonies. After overpowering the Mayas and the Incas, colonizers took control of the mines. They also set up plantations in the tropical climates. These mines and plantations were run with slave labor from Africa as there was a labor scarcity. Many of the native population perished from alien European diseases such as small pox. This type of colonization led to high inequality and perverse institutions—institutions that were extractive and exploitative. These institutions persisted over time and continue to exert negative influences on the economies in Latin America.

Russia

Russia fell behind Western Europe but not due to geography. Russia, especially modern-day Ukraine, is endowed with extremely fertile, glaciated soil. Agricultural output in this part was at least as good as Western Europe. However, there were institutional weaknesses that imposed constraints and did not allow the economy to prosper to its full potential.

Landed elites in Russia had enormous power and influence over the royal court in tsarist Russia. They were vigorously opposed to democratic pressure from the merchants and the masses. Their opposition was based on the fear that any form of democratization might lead to a loss of their exclusive control over land. Land was the main asset from which the Russian elite made their wealth.

This opposition to democratic pressure created a highly unequal society that had implications for both political and economic institutions. A skewed distribution of economic and political power created institutions that were not conducive to capitalist development. Bitter power struggles within the society led to sharp polarization and armed revolutions. The creation of the Soviet Union and a socialist economy also altered incentives. The Soviets attempted to replace economic incentives with social incentives. It worked for a while, however, it harmed economic incentives to innovate over the long run. As a result, the Soviet economy struggled from the 1970s onward. The legacy of these institutions continues to exert negative influences on Russia's economies.

CONCLUDING REMARKS

In this chapter I explored the long-term origins of poverty in developing countries. I started with an analysis of causality and the existing theories of causality used in previous studies. That section also presented the perspective on causality used in the chapter. This is followed by a unified framework relating factors such as geography, disease, colonial history, and technology in explaining the process of development in Western Europe and the New World colonies. The final section applied this framework to explain why Africa, Latin America, and Russia fell behind.

The overwhelming evidence from research on the root causes of development and poverty suggest that the explanation comprises not a single factor but a combination of factors. This is not surprising given that the process of economic development is complex and very closely related to the evolution of our species. The latest research indicates that perhaps we should spend more time and scientific energy on integrating these different factors. These factors have played out in different ways in different parts of the world. Therefore, economic history is not independent of geography, society, politics, and the order in which these factors played out.

NOTES

1. Another recent success story is South Korea. See Milanovic (2005).
2. James Henry Breasted was the first to use the term "Fertile Crescent" in his book *Ancient Records of Egypt* published in 1906. The Fertile Crescent spans part of modern-day Israel, Palestine, and the Jordan valley. For further reference see the map in Diamond (1997:135).
3. Note that even though most human societies experienced a transition from being hunter-gatherers to sedentary agriculture-based societies, there are quite a few exceptions to this rule. See Diamond (2012) for a list.
4. In epidemiology literature, a vector is defined as an agent (person, animal, or microorganism) that carries and transmits an infectious pathogen to another living organism.
5. Dickensian stories of the Oliver Twists of early industrial England are a chilling testament of industrial practice during that time.
6. Note that these sections draw on a variety of historical accounts, notably Diamond (1997); Engerman and Sokoloff (2001); and Acemoglu, Johnson, and Robinson (2005).
7. Note that these goods were also sold to the other parts of the empire.

REFERENCES

Acemoglu, Daron and Simon Johnson. 2005. "Unbundling Institutions." *Journal of Political Economy* 113(5):949–95.

Acemoglu, Daron, Simon Johnson, and James Robinson. 2001. "The Colonial Origins of Comparative Development: An Empirical Investigation." *American Economic Review* 91(5):1369–1401.

Acemoglu, Daron, Simon Johnson, and James Robinson. 2002. "Reversal of Fortune: Geography and Institutions in the Making of the Modern World Income Distribution." *Quarterly Journal of Economics* 117:1231–94.

Acemoglu, Daron, Simon Johnson, and James Robinson. 2005. "The Rise of Europe: Atlantic Trade, Institutional Change and Economic Growth." *American Economic Review* 95(3):546–79.

Allen, Robert, C. 2008. "A Review of Gregory Clark's A Farewell to Alms: A Brief Economic History of the World." *Journal of Economic Literature* 46(4):946–73.

Amsden, Alice, H. 2001. *The Rise of "The Rest": Challenges to the West from Late-Industrializing Economies.* New York: Oxford University Press.

Arrighi, Giovanni, T. Hopkins, and Immanuel Wallerstein. 1989. *Anti-systemic Movements.* London: Verso.

Bhattacharyya, Sambit. 2009a. "Institutions, Diseases and Economic Progress: A Unified Framework." *Journal of Institutional Economics* 5(1):65–87.

Bhattacharyya, Sambit. 2009b. "Unbundled Institutions, Human Capital, and Growth." *Journal of Comparative Economics* 37:106–20.

Bhattacharyya, Sambit. 2009c. "Root Causes of African Underdevelopment." *Journal of African Economies* 18(5):745–80.

Bhattacharyya, Sambit. 2011. *Growth Miracles and Growth Debacles: Exploring Root Causes.* Cheltenham: Edward Elgar.

Bloom, David and Jeffrey Sachs. 1998. "Geography, Demography, and Economic Growth in Africa." *Brookings Papers on Economic Activity* 2:207–95.

Clark, Gregorey. 2007. *A Farewell to Alms: A Brief Economic History of the World.* Princeton, NJ: Princeton University Press.

Collier, Paul and Jan W. Gunning. 1999. "Explaining African Economic Performance." *Journal of Economic Literature* 37(1):64–111.

Diamond, Jared. 1997. *Guns, Germs and Steel: The Fate of Human Societies.* New York: W.W. Norton.

Diamond, Jared. 2012. "What Makes Countries Rich or Poor?" *New York Review of Books*, June 12, pp. 70–75.

Engerman, Stanley and Kenneth Sokoloff. 2001. "Inequality, Institutions, and Differential Paths of Growth Among New World Economies." Working Paper, University of California, Los Angeles.

Evans, Peter, B. 1995. *Embedded Autonomy: States and Industrial Transformation.* Princeton, NJ: Princeton University Press.

Findlay, Ronald. 1990. *"The Triangular Trade" and the Atlantic Economy of the Eighteenth Century: A Simple General-Equilibrium Model.* Princeton, NJ: Department of Economics Princeton University.

Gallup, John and Jared Sachs. 2000. "Agriculture, Climate, and Technology: Why Are the Tropics Falling Behind?" *American Journal of Agriculture Economics* 82:731–37.

Gallup, John and Jared Sachs. 2001. "The Economic Burden of Malaria." *American Journal of Tropical Medicine and Hygiene* 64(1–2):85–96.

Gallup, John, Jared Sachs, and Andrew Mellinger. 1998. "Geography and Economic Development." NBER Working Paper No. 6849, December.

Galor, Oded and Omer Moav. 2006. "Das Human-Kapital: A Theory of the Demise of the Class Structure." *Review of Economic Studies* 73:85–117.

Glaeser, Edward, Rafael LaPorta, Florencio Lopez-de-Silanes, and Andrei Shleifer. 2004. "Do Institutions Cause Growth?" *Journal of Economic Growth* 9:271–303.

Hall, Robert and Charles Jones. 1999. "Why Do Some Countries Produce So Much More Output Per Worker Than Others?" *Quarterly Journal of Economics* 114(1):83–116.

IFAD. 2011. *Rural Poverty Report: New Realities, New Challenges, New Opportunities for Tomorrow's Generation.* Rome: United Nations.

Inikori, J. 1977. "The Import of Firearms into West Africa, 1750–1807: A Quantitative Analysis." *Journal of African History* 18:339–68.

Inikori, Joseph. 1992. *The Chaining of a Continent: Export Demand for Captives and the History of Africa South of the Sahara, 1450–1870.* Mona, Jamaica: Institute of Social and Economic Research, University of the West Indies.

Inikori, Joseph. 2000. "Africa and the Trans-Atlantic Slave Trade." Pp. 389–412 in *Africa Volume 1: African History before 1885*, edited by T. Falola. Durham, NC: Carolina Academic Press.

Kiszewski, Anthony, Andrew Mellinger, Andrew Spielman, Pia Malaney, Sonia Sachs, and Jared Sachs. 2004. "A Global Index Representing the Stability of Malaria Transmission." *American Journal of Tropical Medicine and Hygiene* 70(5):486–98.

Knack, Stephen and Philip Keefer. 1995. "Institutions and Economic Performance: Cross-country Tests using Alternative Institutional Measures." *Economics and Politics* 7(3):207–27.

Landes, David. 1998. *The Wealth and Poverty of Nations: Why Some Are So Rich and Some So Poor.* London: Abacus.

Lange, Matthew, James Mahoney, and Matthias vom Hau. 2006. "Colonialism and Development: A Comparative Analysis of Spanish and British Colonies." *American Journal of Sociology* 111(5):1412–62.

La Porta, Rafael, Florencio Lopez-de-Silanes, Andrei Shleifer, and Robert Vishny. 1999. "The Quality of Government." *Journal of Law, Economics and Organization* 15(1):222–79.

Lipset, Seymour. 1959. "Some Social Requisites of Democracy: Economic Development and Political Legitimacy." *American Political Science Review* 53:69–105.

Manning, Patrick. 1981. "The Enslavement of Africans: A Demographic Model." *Canadian Journal of African Studies* 15(3):499–526.

Manning, Patrick. 1982. *Slavery, Colonialism and Economic Growth in Dahomey, 1640–1960.* Cambridge: Cambridge University Press.

Milanovic, Branko. 2005. *World Apart: Measuring International and Global Inequality.* Princeton, NJ: Princeton University Press.

Miller, David, J. 1988. *Way of Death: Merchant Capitalism and the Angolan Slave Trade, 1730–1830.* Madison: University of Wisconsin Press.

Mokyr, Joel. 1990. *The Lever of Riches: Technological Creativity and Economic Change.* New York: Oxford University Press.

Montesquieu, Charles-Louis. [1748] 1989. *The Spirit of Laws.* New York: Cambridge University Press.

Moore, Barrington. 1966. *Injustice: The Social Bases of Obedience and Revolt.*: White Plains, NY: M. E. Sharpe.

North, Douglass, C. 1989. "Institutions and Economic Growth: An Historical Introduction." *World Development* 17(9):1319–32.

North, Douglass, C. 1994. "Economic Performance through Time." *American Economic Review* 84(3):359–68.

Nunn, Nathan. 2008. "The Long-Term Effects of Africa's Slave Trades." *Quarterly Journal of Economics* 123(1):139–76.

Olsson, Ola and Douglas Hibbs. 2000. "Biogeography and Long-Run Economic Development." Working Paper in Economics No. 26, Göteborg University.

Parker, Philip. 2000. *Physioeconomics: The Basis for Long-Run Economic Growth.* Cambridge, MA: MIT Press.

Rodrik, Dani, Arvind Subramanian, and Franscesco Trebbi. 2004. "Institutions Rule: the Primacy of Institutions over Geography and Integration in Economic Development:" *Journal of Economic Growth* 9:131–65.

Sachs, Jared. 2003. "Institutions Don't Rule: Direct Effects of Geography on Per Capita Income." NBER Working Paper No. 9490, February.

Sachs, Jared and Andrew Warner. 1995. "Natural Resource Abundance and Economic Growth." NBER Working Paper No. 5398, December.

Sachs, Jared and Andrew Warner. 1997. "Sources of Slow Growth in African Economies:" *Journal of African Economies* 6(3):335–76.

Schumpeter, Joseph. 1934. *The Theory of Economic Development.* Cambridge, MA: Harvard University Press.

Smith, Adam. [1776] 1976. *The Wealth of Nations*. Edwin Cannan ed. Chicago: University of Chicago Press.

Tawney, Richard. 1926. *Religion and the Rise of Capitalism*. London: John Murray.

Thelen, Kathleen. 1999. "Historical Institutionalism in Comparative Politics." *American Review of Political Science* 2:369–404.

Thelen, Kathleen. 2000. "Timing and Temporality in the Analysis of Institutional Evolution and Change." *Studies in American Political Development* 14:101–8.

Weber, Max. 1930. *The Protestant Ethic and the Spirit of Capitalism*. London: Allen and Unwin.

Zohary, Daniel, Maria Hopf, and Ehud Veiss. 2000. *Domestication of Plants in the Old World*. New York: Oxford University Press.

CHAPTER 13

··

THE DYNAMICS
OF POVERTY

··

ANIRUDH KRISHNA

KADIJJA Nantoga was 45 years old when I met her, in 2004, in a village of central Uganda. Ten years previously, Kadijja and her husband had held full-time jobs in a coffee-processing plant. They owned the house in which they lived and cultivated a plot of land. Their daughter and son attended private schools. Kadijja's saga of misfortunes began in 1996. First, her husband died as a result of a road accident. Ten other people riding in the same *matatu* (minibus) were also killed or fatally wounded. Overnight, the family lost one of its primary earners. No monetary compensation was paid. Kadijja had to spend a great deal of money for her husband's funeral ceremony. "But we could still manage," she told me, "because I had my job, and we owned some land, some cows, and a few goats." Five years after her husband's death, Kadijja was laid off from work. Disease had devastated the local coffee crop, and the processing factory was shut down. With her job gone, Kadijja lost her steady income. Worse, her expenses shot up at the same time. Her 10-year-old son was stricken by an illness that was never clearly diagnosed, even though she spent large amounts of money and consulted different healers and doctors. Kadijja was forced to sell her cows and goats and ultimately her land in order to pay for these medical treatments, but they did not help save her son's life. Two years after he had fallen ill, he died. She lives with her daughter now in the house that she still owns. They have no other assets and no steady income. They get by precariously from one day to the next, working for wages whenever some opportunity arises but are often forced to look for handouts.

Kadijja has fallen into abject and chronic poverty. She is hardly alone in this respect. Many others in her village community have also become impoverished. Moreover, versions of her story were repeated in every one of more than 400 rural and urban communities that I studied in countries as diverse as India, Kenya, Uganda, Peru, and the United States (Krishna 2010).

Scholars examining these trends in other countries, including both developing and advanced industrialized countries, have also found that poverty creation and poverty reduction occur in tandem. Many people fall *into* poverty, even as many others around them move out of poverty.

Poverty is essentially dynamic in nature: it simultaneously ebbs and grows. The pool of poverty is constantly refreshed by these parallel and opposite flows. Poverty knowledge and poverty policy are both assisted by understanding better the nature of poverty dynamics. Rather than considering it only as a stock measured at a particular point in time, poverty is more appropriately studied by looking at the underlying flows.

An example will help make this point clearer. Consider a hypothetical country in which the national stock of poverty fell from 35 percent in the year 2000 to 29 percent in 2010. How should one interpret this six percentage point reduction? Is it an encouraging or discouraging result? More to the point, should the same poverty policies be continued over the next 10 years? Questions such as these cannot be answered adequately without identifying the constituent poverty flows. The observed 6 percent reduction in the stock of poverty could have come about in a number of different ways, for instance:

> *Alternative A*: 6 percent of the population escaped poverty, and no one fell into poverty over this 10-year period; *or*
>
> *Alternative B*: 16 percent of the population escaped poverty while 10 percent concurrently fell into poverty; *or*
>
> *Alternative C*: 24 percent escaped poverty and 18 percent fell into poverty.

All three of these flow configurations (as well as many others) can produce the same 6 percent reduction in the stock of poverty. However, these different alternatives are hardly similar in nature. Considerably different policies are required to deal with each of them. If Alternative A represents the true state of affairs, then, indeed, the observed reduction is an encouraging outcome; the policies that helped bring it about should be continued and strengthened. But if Alternative C is a truer depiction of the underlying poverty flows, then the prognosis is very different: the high and unchecked rate of poverty descents gives cause for grave concern, urgently requiring the introduction of a different set of interventions. Static studies, focused on stocks, do not help distinguish between these alternative scenarios.

Poverty dynamics studies that examine flows in both directions are essential for calculating both the risk of falling into poverty in any community (or region or country) and the probability that some currently poor individual will escape poverty in years to come.

A second and equally important reason for studying poverty dynamics is to identify the reasons associated, respectively, with poverty escapes and poverty descents. Critically, these two poverty flows are *not symmetric* in terms of reasons. People move out of poverty on account of one set of reasons. They fall into poverty on account of a different set of reasons. Thus, two sets of poverty policies need to be implemented in parallel: one set of policy responses is required to promote more escapes; a second set is required to block descents into poverty. The faster the pace of descents in some regions, the more urgently will policies of the second type be required. But where descents are fewer in number, resources should be concentrated, instead, on promoting more escapes from poverty.

Different combinations of poverty policies are required, therefore, depending upon the relative rates of escape and descent. Information about poverty flows is essential for determining what needs to be done.

Poverty dynamics studies also assists in other ways to gain a deeper understanding of the diverse facets of poverty. For instance, chronic and intergenerationally poor people cannot be readily identified, except through examining poverty dynamics.[1] Policymakers have been predisposed to assume, often mistakenly, that people's experiences of poverty are temporary affairs, small dips from which they will generally recover relatively quickly. Studies of poverty stocks do not provide the additional evidence that can help sustain or dispel these unfounded assumptions. Distinguishing between transitory and chronic poverty—how many experience poverty only for relatively short periods and how many others remain persistently poor—is only possible when people's situations are studied, not just at one point in time but through repeated observations made over extended periods; in other words, by examining the dynamics of poverty.

Similarly, understanding social mobility, in particular, examining how far people escaping poverty actually rise—do they typically rise only a little above the poverty line, remaining mostly near-poor, or do many rise higher, becoming prosperous—is only feasible by examining poverty dynamics, keeping track of the same individuals over longer periods of time. Analyses of stocks alone do not help here as well.

To summarize, investigating poverty dynamics is necessary for serving at least the following four objectives: (1) estimating the risk of impoverishment and the probability of escaping poverty; (2) identifying the reasons associated, respectively, with poverty descents and escapes; (3) distinguishing between transient and chronic poverty; and (4) examining the social mobility prospects of individuals in different economic situations.

DIVERSE APPROACHES

Compelling reasons exist, therefore, for carefully investigating poverty flows. Unfortunately, the same rationale which makes these studies worthwhile quite often hinders the undertaking of poverty dynamics studies.

Long-period studies are particularly difficult to mount. Few researchers and few grant-making agencies have been willing to make long-period commitments toward constructing the required data sets, pledging resources for 10 or 20 years or longer. Therefore, relatively few poverty dynamics data sets are available, particularly for developing country contexts. Even among richer countries of the world, poverty dynamics remains a relatively understudied area, and "until recently, only a few countries (for example, the U.S., Canada, Germany, and Great Britain) had either a short- or a long-term panel" enabling an examination of poverty flows (Burkhauser 2009:718).

Encouragingly, however, investigations of poverty flows, including some longer term studies, have been taken up in increasing numbers more recently. Diverse approaches and different measurement strategies have been adopted by these studies.

Three types of approaches are distinguished in this chapter. Each approach has its merits and drawbacks; none is uniquely best in all situations and for all purposes. Depending upon the specific questions guiding any particular study and depending as well upon the prior availability of baseline data, one or another method of studying poverty dynamics will be preferred.

Panel Data Studies: The approach most often taken for studying poverty dynamics is to construct a panel data set, measuring the incomes (or consumption expenditures) of the same individuals (or households) at two or more points in time separated by an interval of some years. Individuals who escape poverty and who become poor, respectively, can be identified, and the probabilities of escape and descent can be calculated.

Relatively long-period panel data are available for some richer countries, enabling these examinations to span multiple time periods and to identify succeeding episodes— or "spells" of poverty, consecutive years in which a household or individual is poor. In the United States, the Panel Study of Income Dynamics (PSID) was begun in 1968 with 4,800 households and their 18,000 members, selected initially to be statistically representative of the entire nation. These family members have been tracked regularly with new household members and spin-off households being added on. Currently, the PSID has data for over 60,000 individuals, among whom information for some is available continuously for periods exceeding 30 years.[2] Two other nationally representative data sets—the Survey of Income and Program Participation (SIPP) and the National Longitudinal Survey of Youth (NLSY)—have been consulted by other researchers. A host of useful findings have been generated by studies drawing upon these longitudinal data sets.[3] The European Community Household Panel (ECHP) has similarly involved the annual interviewing of a panel of roughly 60,500 nationally representative households in 12 European Union countries, covering a wide range of topics, with data collected from 1994 to 2001, and other data sets, covering different topics and smaller numbers of OECD countries, are also available.[4]

Comparable panel data sets are not yet available for developing countries. Because this enterprise has been commenced more recently within such countries and has not been as well resourced, the few panel data sets available for such countries are usually not nationally representative, instead focusing on particular communities or regions. Typically they span much shorter intervals, often no more than three to five years (Deaton 1997; Dercon 2005). Such short intervals make it difficult to examine the effects of national policies and particularly household strategies to cope with poverty. Household strategies are usually made over generational time horizons. For instance, people invest in the education of their children so that when these children come of age they are better able to escape poverty. Farmers make improvements incrementally upon their agricultural fields, leveling the land and digging irrigation canals, so that they can reap a bigger harvest in years to come. In order to understand better what households do by themselves, relatively long periods of time need to be considered. Summarizing the available evidence for low-income countries, Addison, Hulme, and Kanbur (2009:11–12) note that "if we wish to take a longer, inter-generational, or dynastic, perspective, then panels of 20 years or more are needed by definition. ... Quantitative panel-based analysis on poverty dynamics [in developing countries is to date], therefore, largely an analysis of fairly short-run fluctuations in well-being and poverty."

Another shortcoming, common to both long- and short-period panel data sets, relates to their inability, usually, to identify events and reasons associated with escapes and descents. What we get from panel studies are consumption or income (or less often, asset ownership) data at two points in time, with additional information being provided in some cases about household characteristics and about local, regional, and national conditions prevailing at the starting and ending points. Analysts can use such data to compare some characteristics of households who fell into poverty with those who successfully avoided descents, for instance, initial education levels and landholdings can be compared. However, without being informed about microlevel processes and events, they are unable to deduce why some landholding or educated households fell into poverty while others did not, or why the effects of the same regional characteristics, of national policies or macroevents, were distributed so unevenly across different households.

Household (or idiosyncratic) events, while micro in nature, can have large cumulative impacts, often overwhelming the effects of larger (or covariate) events,[5] but since virtually "no attention is focused on the events which lead people into and out of poverty, it has proved very difficult [using panel data approaches] to trace the processes whereby people may suddenly or gradually escape poverty" (Bane and Ellwood 1986:4). Or as Sawhill (1988:1085) puts it, also in a U.S. context, "We are swamped with facts about people's incomes and about the number and composition of people who inhabit the lower tail [of the income distribution], but we don't know very much about the processes that generate these results."

A third issue, not exclusively related to panel studies but especially germane in developing country contexts, has to do with the inappropriateness of incomes or consumption expenditures as measures of poverty and well-being. For poor people in such contexts, incomes and consumption expenditures are often highly unstable quantities that fluctuate substantially from month to month and year to year (Chambers, Longhurst, and Pacey 1991). "In all panel data sets on developing countries currently available, large consumption fluctuations mean that a large number of households [are recorded to] move in and out of poverty. ... One needs to be cautious about interpreting [such] evidence on widespread poverty transitions" (Dercon 2005:23). For instance, a panel study undertaken in rural China found that as much as "half of the average severity of poverty ... was directly due to inter-temporal variability in consumption" (Jalan and Ravallion 2000:88).

Analysts, including Carter and Barrett (2006) and Sherraden (1991), have suggested that one can do better by moving away from a consumption-based index, instead adopting an assets- or capabilities-based measure. In fact, participatory exercises in which people have been asked to describe what it means to them to be poor have repeatedly produced lists of assets as indicators of relative poverty, only rarely mentioning consumption or income. More accurately, these exercises have produced lists of functionings and capabilities in the sense implied by Amartya Sen (1981, 1999), who regards capabilities as the substantive freedoms people enjoy to lead the lives they have reason to value. Capabilities defined in this manner are more closely related than income or consumption to people's own understandings of what it means to be poor (Kanbur and Squire 1999).

Assets- and capabilities-based measures are also useful for making the important distinction, proposed by Carter and May (2001), between *structural* and *stochastic poverty*. The structural poor are those who lack adequate asset endowments. While their income and consumption levels fluctuate from year to year, on average these levels are well below the poverty line. The stochastic poor, on the other hand, have sufficient asset endowments, so their incomes on average are above the poverty line. In some particular month or year, consumption and incomes could be below the poverty line, as a result of short-term effects that produce such fluctuations. Distinguishing people's usual (or structural) conditions from short-term fluctuations is better assisted when poverty measures are grounded in capabilities and assets rather than being based entirely on calculations of incomes or consumption expenditures.

Participatory Poverty Assessments and Ethnographic Studies: A second method of investigation, involving participatory poverty assessments, works more closely with people's own understandings, and it performs comparatively better by way of coming to grips with the complex and contextualized nature of poverty. Some good exemplars of this approach in developing country contexts are provided by Chambers (1995); Narayan et al. (2000); and Salmen (1987).

While possessing the potential to examine household-level processes and events, participatory poverty assessments have, however, not usually undertaken such analytical exercises. They have helped illuminate to a considerable extent the correlates and conditions associated with poverty as this notion is understood by the people concerned, taking a broad rather than a narrowly materialistic interpretation of this term, but they have not gone further to isolate processes, events, and household strategies associated with escapes from or descents into poverty.[6]

A third group of studies, ethnographic in nature, are more promising in this regard. They have more to say, both about the extents of movement in both directions and about the natures of processes, events, and household strategies involved. Attwood (1979); Eder (1999); Jodha (1988); Moser (2009); Perlman (2011); Van Schendel (1981); and Wadley (1994) present results for different developing country contexts, while Newman (1988) is an example from the United States.

However, while participatory poverty assessments are often conducted on a fairly large scale, ethnographic examinations have been undertaken usually on a much smaller scale, quite often considering just a single village or urban community, with the researcher visiting this community repeatedly over extended periods of time. The resulting knowledge is very important, because it helps identify the nature of processes affecting different households. The restricted scale of such studies, however, presents a new set of problems: it does not become clear which identified trend operates only in the village or community examined, and which other trends have influence over a wider area, thereby acquiring larger policy relevance.

In sum, each of these has particular strengths and notable weaknesses. Panel data studies use clear and transparent definitions and measures of poverty, but being based on consumption or income criteria, they are susceptible to damaging short-term fluctuations, and they can be unrelated to people's own conceptions of poverty. Because of this reason and because they do not usually record and examine event histories, panel data studies have been unable to uncover how and why people go down different pathways, with some rising out of poverty and others simultaneously becoming poor. Participatory poverty assessments, on the other hand, are more closely allied to people's own ideas and their understandings of poverty. Typically, however, such studies do not adopt a diachronic perspective. They do not construct prospectively (nor reconstruct retrospectively) the trajectories traversed by different households. Ethnographic studies have undertaken more process tracing than either panel studies or participatory assessments, but many lack a clear definition and poverty cutoff, and their tiny scale makes it hard to pick out special effects from more general poverty dynamics.

Mixed-method studies: A combination of research methods—statistical and ethnographic in nature—can be more useful, helping uncover not only the numbers who escaped but also the processes whereby these numbers were generated. Studies that employ qualitative as well as quantitative methods are suggested for these reasons (Kanbur 2003). Mixed-method studies—undertaking, for instance, panel studies of income or consumption (or assets and capabilities) while also collecting detailed household event histories—are increasingly conducted with a view to providing a more comprehensive picture of poverty dynamics.

Less common so far within richer countries, mixed-method studies have taken off rapidly, particularly within the last decade, in a variety of developing country contexts. Diverse methodologies have been developed.[7]

The results of one such study, presented by Davis and Baulch (2011), are illustrative of the nature of pathways taken by households moving into or out of poverty. Rather than being sudden or smooth, these transitions are usually worked out incrementally over longer periods of time. Jagged or "saw-toothed" movements—in which households or individuals move up (or down) in one time period only to fall back (or move upward) in the succeeding period—are more common in practice than single-step or regularly upward (or downward) sloping trajectories.

The lives of poor people are more complicated than two-point panel data sets would appear to suggest. Events of different types affect households' economic fortunes in different ways. Positive events—some household member gets a job, someone else lands a beneficial supply contract—tend to have buoyant effects, moving households upward. But households also experience negative or adverse events, such as illnesses, job losses, droughts, and so on, which counteract and reverse positive events. Rather than any single event being determinative of a households' poverty status, it is the *balance of events*—positive and negative—occurring over a period of time that more critically affects its fate. Studying poverty dynamics using a mix of methods helps identify those processes and events that matter most in any particular context.

In a series of inquiries using one particular mixed-methods approach—the stages-of-progress methodology—that I helped develop together with colleagues in different countries, poverty dynamics were examined for a total of more than 35,000 households in various parts of India, Kenya, Uganda, Peru, and the United States. Developed initially in 2002, this retrospective methodology has been used as well by other researchers and organizations, both academic and policy oriented, for supporting a range of research and programming efforts.[8] Applied within diverse community settings, rural and urban, with the participation of the people concerned, it helps identify—relatively quickly, reliably and cost-effectively—the extent of movements in and out of poverty and the reasons associated with both types of poverty flows.

The space available does not permit full development and support of this methodology. A necessarily brief account is presented here.[9] *Stages-of-progress* involves a seven-step retrospective research process. Households' economic conditions are assessed using a community-generated scale of relative wealth developed in a participatory setting. Assets and capabilities acquired sequentially as a household moves out of dire poverty constitute these stages of progress, which are remarkably similar across communities in the same region. Households' poverty status in previous time periods are recalled by community groups in terms of the same sequence of stages— and it is independently verified by the households concerned. A random sample of 25–30 percent is drawn from each of the following categories of households: those who have fallen into poverty, others who have moved out of poverty, and still others who have remained poor or remained not poor over the period examined. Detailed event-history interviews are undertaken separately with two members of each such household. Further triangulation is made possible by consulting with the assembled community groups. Events and processes and household characteristics commonly associated with descent (and with escape) are identified in this manner. Chronically poor households are also identified and the characteristics and events that have held them back are identified.

Taken together, poverty dynamics studies following different approaches and measurement methods have helped extend the frontiers of poverty knowledge in different directions. As Blank (2008:243), summarizing a discussion of alternative methods, concludes: "there is no 'right' way to develop poverty thresholds or resource measures." The use of multiple modes of inquiry helps unearth a richer variety of facts.

KEY FINDINGS

Four sets of results are briefly highlighted here, corresponding respectively to the reasons, discussed earlier, which make poverty dynamics necessary to investigate. Probably because these results are so new, theory building has not kept pace with results generation, a concern that I will address toward the end of this chapter.

> 1. *Poverty creation and poverty reduction occur everywhere in tandem. Focusing on moving people out of poverty will not be effective unless descents into poverty are simultaneously controlled.*

In every context examined—no matter how high or low the country's economic growth rate or its per capita income—escapes from poverty and descents into poverty have occurred in parallel, underlining our earlier observation that poverty is essentially dynamic in nature. A sample of these results is presented in Table 13.1. The first row shows that in Kwa-Zulu Natal, South Africa, 10 percent of a representative sample of over 1,000 households escaped poverty between 1993 and 1998, but more than twice as many households, 25 percent, fell into poverty during the same period of time. In Egypt similarly, 6 percent of the studied sample of households came out of poverty between 1997 and 1999, but many more households, 14 percent, fell into poverty, enlarging the stock of the poor.

Descents into poverty are common as well within richer countries. An examination conducted within 14 OECD countries refers to the "two faces of poverty" that "are evident in all of the countries analyzed, but their relative importance varies. On average across all countries, about five percent of the population, not previously poor, entered poverty each year" (OECD 2001:39, 48). For the United States, McKernan and Ratcliffe (2002) found that the likelihood of falling into poverty in a year averaged 2.8 percent

Table 13.1 Poverty Dynamics: Some Examples

Area	Study	Period	Sample Size (households)	Escaped Poverty	Fell into Poverty
South Africa	Carter and May (2001)	1993–1998	1,171	10%	25%
Egypt	Haddad and Ahmed (2003)	1997–1999	347	6%	14%
India	Bhide and Mehta (2004)	1970–1982	3,139	23%	13%
Kenya	Krishna et al. (2004)	1978–2003	1,706	18%	19%
Uganda	Krishna et al. (2006b)	1994–2004	2,631	14%	12%
Bangladesh	B. Sen (2003)	1987–2000	379	26%	18%

in the 1970s, rising slightly to 3.0 percent in the 1980s and further to 4.2 percent during the first half of the 1990s.

An accumulating body of evidence shows that large numbers of households fall into poverty every year—and it is not only borderline households that are affected by these flows. Even formerly well-to-do households have fallen deeply into poverty. Households in Rajasthan, India, that fell into poverty have lost all or large parts of the productive assets that they previously owned. Many have become entirely landless, and they see little hope of climbing back to their previous economic positions (Krishna 2004). Of the 344 Ugandan households that fell into poverty in the study mentioned earlier, as many as 24 percent can no longer afford food and clothes, and another 29 percent have pulled their children out of school. They have fallen so deeply into poverty that moving out is at best a remote possibility.

It is not only in remote or "left-behind" communities that descents into poverty have occurred in large numbers. In capital cities and other current-day foci of economic growth, large numbers of people have fallen into poverty. In Nairobi, the capital city of Kenya, and in Mombasa, its second-largest city, 10 percent of a random sample of households fell into poverty between 1990 and 1998 (Kristjanson et al. 2009). Less than one-third of these households were able to bounce back over the next eight-year period.

These findings have a clear policy implication: Even large successes in raising people out of poverty can have little net impact. Unless descents into poverty are concurrently controlled, worldwide poverty will not fall appreciably.

Controlling descents into poverty assumes even greater policy relevance because of results which show how the probability of descent has risen over time. Krishna (2010:63–66) reports these results for a group of developing countries, finding that compared to a previous period the risk of falling into poverty has everywhere increased.

Similarly disturbing trends are reported for the United States by (Hacker 2006:12–13), who comments that "while the gaps between the rungs on the ladder of the American economy have increased, what has increased even more quickly is how far people slip down the ladder when they lose their financial footing. The chance that families will see their incomes plummet has risen." Particularly among the lower half of the income distribution, insecurity and volatility have increased together with increasing inequality in the United States (Western et al. 2012).

> 2. *Escapes from poverty and descents into poverty are asymmetric in terms of reasons. Two sets of poverty policies are required in parallel: one set to address the microlevel reasons associated with descents into poverty, and another set to promote the different set of reasons associated with escapes from poverty. Bad health and high health care costs constitute the single most important reason for falling into poverty (and for remaining poor). Poverty cannot be reduced sustainably without having effective, accessible, and affordable health care in place.*

Consistently, studies of poverty dynamics have revealed that discrete events, rather than any particular household characteristics, are closely associated with both poverty flows. While one set of events is related to descents into poverty, a different set of events is associated with escapes.

This asymmetry of reasons between escapes and descents is a basic and recurrent feature. In one of the earliest studies of poverty dynamics, Bane and Ellwood (1986) found that events associated with the commencement of a spell in poverty in the United States were different in nature from other events that helped end households' spells in poverty. Subsequent investigations carried out in other contexts have continued to uphold this important finding.[10]

People usually fall into poverty over a period of time, bit-by-bit, and not all of a sudden. A number of factors contribute to poverty descents and they differ in importance within and across countries. A chain of everyday events, rather than any single catastrophe, is most often involved (Davis and Baulch 2011; Krishna and Lecy 2008).

The leading culprit almost everywhere is poor health care. Several other factors are also associated with falling into poverty, but in terms of frequency and magnitude the effects of ill health and health care expenses predominate in every region examined. Ill-health imposes a double burden on households—when high-treatment costs combine with loss of earning power—and it has the biggest influence on becoming poor (and remaining in poverty). Table 13.2 presents the relative importance of different reasons for poverty descents in the regions I examined.

Table 13.2 **Principal Reasons for Descent into Poverty**

Reasons	Rajasthan, India	Gujarat, India	Western Kenya	Andhra Pradesh, India	Central and Western Uganda	Puno and Cajamarca, Peru
Share of Descending Households (percent)						
Poor health and health-related expenses	60	88	74	74	71	67
Marriage/dowry expenses	31	68		69	18	29
Funeral-related expenses	34	49	64	28	15	11
High-interest private debt	72	52		60		
Drought/ irrigation failure/ crop disease	18			44	19	11

Note: The total percentages reported in each column add up to more than 100 because more than one reason was involved in most cases. Cells that are blank represent factors that were not significant in the regions concerned.

Source: Adapted from Krishna (2010).

In every region studied, ill health and high health care expenses were implicated in the largest number of descents into poverty. For instance, 88 percent of people who fell into poverty in 36 villages in India's Gujarat province, a region that has experienced very high growth rates, placed the blame principally upon health care costs. In Peru, 67 percent of the recently impoverished in two provinces cited ill health, hard-to-reach medical facilities, and high health care costs. (In comparison, it must be mentioned that drunkenness, drug abuse, and laziness together accounted for no more than 3 percent of all poverty descents in any of these regions.)

People are not poor because they wish to be poor or because of some character defect. Most have become poor due to influences beyond their personal control, including, particularly, health care. Households who have remained persistently poor have also disproportionately experienced health-related events involving major expenditures.

Once families are hit by a health crisis, it is often hard to recover. One major illness typically reduces family income by up to one-fifth. Successive illnesses ensure an even faster spiral into persistent poverty (Xu et al. 2003). Millions of people in poorer countries as well as several richer ones are living one illness away from poverty. Public health researchers have concluded that a "medical poverty trap" operates in many countries, including several rich ones.[11]

Poverty is lowest in those countries and communities where residents can get a loved one's illness treated without having to lose their shirts. Sweden, Denmark, Japan, and all other countries with single-digit poverty rates have invested in high-quality, universally accessible health care—and they started making these investments well before their average incomes rose to become among the highest in the world (Kangas and Palme 2005; Macinko, Shi, and Starfield 2004; Milly 1999; Scruggs and Allan 2006).

Improving health care will reduce future poverty by stemming the inflow. It will also improve the prospects of the existing poor. People who know that they are protected against downslides will more readily take risks and invest in their futures.

Simultaneously, another set of policies will help improve poor people's prospects of escaping poverty in the future. Table 13.3 presents the household-level reasons for escape identified in the event histories of thousands of households who escaped poverty in the different contexts that I studied. Note how these reasons for escape are qualitatively different from the reasons for descent that we examined earlier.

In general, more than one reason was associated with each household's escape from poverty. The cumulative effect of multiple positive stimuli pushed households above the poverty cutoff, helping offset the downward pulls of negative events.

Diversification of income sources—through the urban informal sector and separately through crops and livestock—has served as the most important avenue of escape in every developing country region studied. In fact, diversification of livelihood sources is a more widespread household strategy, associated both "with success at achieving livelihood security under improving economic conditions as well as with [preventing or alleviating] livelihood distress in deteriorating conditions" (Ellis 1998:2).

Table 13.3 Principal Reasons for Escaping Poverty

Reasons	Rajasthan, India	Gujarat, India	Kenya (country sample)	Andhra Pradesh, India	Central and Western Uganda	Puno and Cjamarca, Peru
Share of Households Escaping Poverty (percent)						
Diversification of income (informal sector)	58	35	77	51	52	44
Diversification of income (crops and livestock)	39	29	64	48	41	69
Private-sector employment	7	32	9	7	9	8
Public-sector employment	11	39	11	10	6	5
Government/NGO assistance	8	6	3	7	3	4

Note: The total percentages reported in each column add up to more than 100 because more than one reason was involved in most cases.

Source: Adapted from Krishna (2010).

Households have diversified their income sources employing multiple means. Many have intensified and diversified their agricultural activities. Others have started small business enterprises on the side. The largest number of households escaped poverty, however, by sending one or more of their members to work in the informal sector in a city.

Mostly, quite modest natures of gains have been made by such people. Prospects for more substantial advancement are limited because

> work in the informal economy cannot be termed "decent" compared to recognized, protected, secure and formal employment. Most cases of child labor are to be found in the informal economy, often in the most hidden and hazardous forms of work, including forced labor and slavery. On the whole, average incomes in the informal economy are much lower than in the formal economy. The working poor are concentrated in the informal economy. (ILO 2002:25–30)

There is, however, no better alternative for many. For people who live in rural areas, still the majority of the poor in most developing countries, the city quite often contains the most viable pathways out of poverty. Within cities, a vast and growing informal sector has served as the principal creator of new positions and opportunities, helping funnel people's escapes from dire poverty, but at the same time imposing a low glass ceiling upon their future prospects.

3. The longer people remain in poverty, the more difficult it becomes for them to escape poverty at a later date. Large numbers of people across the world are trapped in chronic poverty. Far from being a transient phenomenon, falling into poverty has become a long-term condition for many.

Short spells in poverty are more easily overcome; longer spells tend to translate into chronic poverty. Bane and Ellwood (1986), a pioneering study in many respects, first presented this result, finding that the probability of escaping poverty falls progressively as the spell in poverty increases: from 0.45 for a one-year spell to 0.29 for a two-year spell to 0.21 for a four-year spell. Considering a longer time period, Stevens (1999) found similarly that the rates of escaping poverty fall consistently as the spell in poverty gets prolonged. Further and germane to the policy discussion on transient versus chronic poverty, she also found that "the bulk of those currently poor are in the midst of a lengthy stay in poverty" (Stevens 1999:559), thereby establishing the presence within the United States of chronic poverty. Studies undertaken in developing countries also show how whole families can remain poor for their entire lifetimes (ODI 2005; Hulme and Shepherd 2003). Poverty is often passed on from parents to children and grandchildren. Such chronically poor people are estimated to number between 320 and 400 million across the world (ODI 2014).

People become and remain chronically poor not for of lack of trying or because nothing happens to change their lifestyles. More often, for them, one step forward is followed by two steps back.

Some who fall into poverty are able to bounce back, that is, in some cases the flow into poverty gets reversed, but many households who fall into poverty become persistently poor. Of all households who fell into poverty during the period 1979 to 1994 in the 36 rural Ugandan communities that I examined, only one-third had emerged out of poverty by 2004. The remaining two-thirds of newly impoverished households became persistently poor. A similar result was observed in communities of Peru: of households that fell into poverty between 1979 and 1994 more than half were still poor 10 years later (Krishna et al. 2006a).

A poverty trap, corresponding to a low-level equilibrium, tends to ensnare many freshly impoverished people (Carter and Barrett 2006). Chronic poverty is thus not only inherited; it is also brought into being when people falling into poverty are unable to move out.

Studies show that there is a spatial dimension to chronic poverty, which is found more often in rural than in urban areas. It is especially acute in remote rural regions. A hard core of chronic poverty is frequently found among forest dwellers and mountain folks. Lack of transportation, schools, and clinics combine to keep people trapped in chronic poverty, which is multidimensional in nature—the chronically poor are more often sick, they are less often educated, and they find it hard to connect with market opportunities.

These handicaps are made worse by social exclusion and political discrimination directed toward members of particular ethnic groups. In India, for instance, scheduled castes (former untouchables) and scheduled tribes (indigenous people) have been historically discriminated against and still carry a higher burden of poverty. Similarly, African Americans and Hispanics in the United States are more likely to endure extended spells of poverty (Corcoran 1995; Stevens 1999). Gender discrimination is another concern in many countries. Female-headed households are among the poorest of the poor, being (or becoming) chronically poor in a vast number of cases.

A third chronic poverty trap has to do with civil wars and limited citizenship (Collier 2007). Prolonged civil strife with refugees moving across borders has given rise to persistent poverty, especially in sub-Saharan Africa, where the chronic poor can constitute between 15 and 20 percent of the entire population (CPRC 2009).

Having little or no education, lacking roads and communication, isolated, and often socially discriminated or refugees to boot, the chronic poor have few means to avail themselves of the benefits of economic growth. Targeted policies are required to assist these people. Improving health care and especially education is critical; illiterate people are many and their wages are low. Building better connections to outlying areas is another policy priority.

> 4. The small amount of evidence collected in developing countries to date shows that social mobility is limited: relatively few people escaping poverty have become rich. Most remain marginally above the poverty cutoff, liable to reversals of fortune on account of adverse events.

Research in respect of this last reason motivating poverty dynamics studies is the least well advanced; relatively little is known so far about social mobility in developing countries. Even in the West, where social mobility has been studied for a longer time and different schools of thought have emerged, "the transmission of economic success across generations remains something of a black box" (Bowles, Gintis, and Groves 2005:3).

The few studies of poverty dynamics in developing countries that have examined a relatively long time-horizon have consistently shown, however, that while many people have moved out of poverty, only a tiny number were able to rise high (Krishna 2010; Moser 2009; Perlman 2011; Quisumbing 2007). As we saw earlier, most have been absorbed within low-paying positions. Those who escaped poverty have mostly found positions working as maids, gardeners, chauffeurs, pushcart vendors, security guards, rickshaw pullers, mason's assistants, and the like. Hardly anyone became a software engineer, university professor, business magnate, or airline pilot. Further investigations showed that even the sons and daughters of these maids and pushcart vendors were rarely able to achieve higher paying positions (Krishna 2013).

Global statistics tend to uphold the same dismal conclusions. Between 1981 and 2005, the number of people living in acute poverty (below $1.25 per day) fell by 500 million across the world (Chen and Ravallion 2007). Simultaneously, the numbers of those in near-poverty (between $1.25 and $2) went up by an even larger number: 600 million. The entire reduction in the numbers of the acutely poor seems to have been absorbed thus within the ranks of the near-poor, with those escaping poverty climbing above but still remaining close to the poverty line.

The nature of pathways available for escaping poverty in developing country settings—principally, the urban informal sector and small-scale agriculture intensification—are such that only quite limited gains can usually be achieved. Doing better in the future will require investing in more effective promotional policies, including higher quality education and more easily available career information. Research in this particular area is still quite limited, because longer period studies are few in number. It needs to be advanced so that more robust conclusions can be generated in the future.

FUTURE DIRECTIONS

Longer period data need to be assembled in order to undertake more fine-grained analyses than have been possible in the past. Studies that extend over the life course of individuals are especially important in this regard.

In addition to further research using diverse approaches, especially different mixed-methods ones, future work on poverty dynamics also needs to deal better with theory development. Studying poverty dynamics has helped make clear that no collection of individuals—whether aggregated at the national level, the regional level, or even at the community level—moves up or moves down all together. This simultaneous ebb and flow is the essence of poverty. It is at the core of what needs to be influenced in order for poverty to be reduced.

Why such disparate pathways are traveled by so many households has been little explored so far by poverty theories. The theories that exist are mostly focused on explaining differences in aggregate poverty across countries. Factors such as colonialism, bad macroeconomic policies, failed states, geographic location, resource endowments, catastrophic events, and the like, have been put forward to account for why aggregate poverty is larger in some countries and smaller in others. Such country-level knowledge is certainly useful and important. But it does not help explain why some households in one country or region or community move upward and out of poverty, while other households in the *same* country, region, and community—operating under the same national economic and political conditions—fall into poverty concurrently. Microevents, rather than national economic trends, help explain these ubiquitous divergent experiences: people, and not countries, escape poverty and become poor.

Microlevel theories need to be developed that can help us understand better and, to the extent possible, help predict poverty dynamics in the future. Even in the United States, with a longer tradition of investigating household poverty dynamics, much of the research has been descriptive rather than theoretical (Western et al. 2012). Some earlier theories had made a beginning in this direction, but since they squared poorly with data subsequently assembled by poverty dynamics studies, they have largely become discredited. For example, a "culture of poverty" theory sought to explain individual poverty in terms of a distinct culture that poor individuals inherit from their parents (Lewis 1968). Lacking empirical support, such studies and those relying on differences in inherent intelligence, have been mostly put aside and forgotten (Duncan 1984; Esping-Anderson 2005). Newer theories have yet to take their place.

In addition to theories that help us understand better why diverse positive and negative microlevel events take place and why these affect some individuals and households more than others, another group of theories is required that can help trace the nature of macro-micro links—helping make the connection between national and international events, on the one hand, and outcomes at the household level, on the other hand, while also identifying intermediate links. Absent such chains of connection and causation, we are reduced to making bland and ultimately meaningless statements, such as "growth is good for the poor," which may well be true in some abstract and general sense, although there will be many unaccounted exceptions.[12] How the effects of national economic growth are transmitted to different individuals, through what channels and via which filters, needs to be better understood in order to give the agenda of pro-poor growth more theoretical and better empirical content. At present, the available theories are largely inadequate, making it hard to identify the conditions in which national economic growth will or will not translate into robust and widespread poverty reduction.

Notes

1. Chronic poverty is experienced by people who remain poor for much or all of their lives, many of whom will pass on their poverty to their children (ODI 2005).
2. See psidonline.isr.umich.edu. McKernan and Ratcliffe (2002) provide a useful review of studies that draw upon these data.
3. See Cellini, McKernan, and Ratcliffe (2008) for a review of studies drawing upon each of these data sets.
4. See circa.europa.eu/irc/dsis/echpanel/info/data/information.html. Also see OECD (2001).
5. Morduch (2005) calculated that microlevel factors, observed at the household and individual levels, accounted for between 75 and 96 percent of the total variance in household income. Similarly, Binayak Sen (2003:522) found that household- and individual-level factors were much more important, compared to village- and district-level factors, for explaining differences in people's incomes in rural Bangladesh. See also Krishna and Lecy (2008).
6. "There appear to be no studies," of this genre, conclude Moore, Chaudhary, and Singh (1998:6) after reviewing a group of such studies "that clearly separate (a) the indicators of poverty identified by poor people from (b) their understandings of the causes of poverty."
7. Shaffer (2013) provides an extensive review.
8. Investigators associated with the following institutions have adapted and utilized this methodology: BRAC, CARE, CIP, the World Agro-forestry Center, the government of Kenya,

the International Food Poverty Research Center, the Food and Agriculture Organization of the United Nations, the International Livestock Research Institute, SEWA, Uppsala University (Sweden), University of Edinburgh (UK), Humboldt University (Germany), and most notably, the World Bank, whose ladder-of-life method is a rough-and-ready adaptation of stages-of-progress.

9. For further development of these arguments and a detailed exposition of the methodology see the author's larger study (Krishna 2010).

10. See, for example, Barrett and McPeak (2005); Baulch and McCulloch (2002); McKernan and Ratcliffe (2002); and Sen (2003).

11. The general case is presented by Whitehead, Dahlgren, and Evans (2001); Labonte and Schrecker (2007); Xu et al. (2003); and Farmer (1999). Himmelstein et al. (2005) present the evidence for the United States; Zhao (2006) for China; and EQUITAP (2005) for another group of countries in Asia.

12. See, for instance, Dollar and Kraay (2000).

REFERENCES

Addison, Tony, David Hulme, and Ravi Kanbur. 2009. "Poverty Dynamics: Measurement and Understanding from an Interdisciplinary Perspective." Pp. 3–26 in *Poverty Dynamics: Interdisciplinary Perspectives*, edited by Addison, Hulme, and Kanbur. Oxford: Oxford University Press.

Attwood, Donald. W. 1979. "Why Some of the Poor Get Richer: Economic Change and Mobility in Rural West India." *Current Anthropology* 20 (3):495–516.

Bane, Mary J. and David T. Ellwood. 1986. "Slipping into and out of Poverty: The Dynamics of Spells." *Journal of Human Resources* 21(1):1–23.

Barrett, Christopher and John G. McPeak. 2005. "Poverty Traps and Safety Nets." Chapter 7 in *Poverty, Inequality and Development: Essays in Honor of Erik Thorbecke*, edited by Alain de Janvry and Ravi Kanbur. Amsterdam: Springer.

Baulch, Bob and Neil McCulloch. 2002. "Being Poor and Becoming Poor: Poverty Status and Poverty Transitions in Rural Pakistan." *Journal of Asian and African Studies* 37 (2):168–85.

Bhide, Shashank and Asha Kapur Mehta. 2004. "Chronic Poverty in Rural India, issues and Findings from Panel Data." *Journal of Human Development* 5(2):195–209.

Blank, Rebecca M. 2008. "How to Improve Poverty Measurement in the United States." *Journal of Policy Analysis and Management* 27(2):233–54.

Bowles, Samuel, Herbert Gintis, and Melissa Osborne Groves. 2005. "Introduction." Pp. 1–22 in *Unequal Chances: Family Background and Economic Success*, edited by Samuel Bowles, Herbert Gintis, and Melissa Osborne Groves. Princeton, NJ: Princeton University Press.

Burkhauser, Richard V. 2009. "Deconstructing European Poverty Measures: What Relative and Absolute Scales Measure." *Journal of Policy Analysis and Management* 28(4):715–24.

Carter, Michael R. and Julian May. 2001. "One Kind of Freedom: Poverty Dynamics in Post-apartheid South Africa." *World Development* 29(12):1987–2006.

Carter, Michael R. and Christopher B. Barrett. 2006. "The Economics of Poverty Traps and Persistent Poverty: An Asset-Based Approach." *Journal of Development Studies* 42(2):178–99.

Cellini, Stephanie R., Signe-Mary McKernan, and Caroline Ratcliffe. 2008. "The Dynamics of Poverty in the United States: A Review of Data, Methods, and Findings." *Journal of Policy Analysis and Management* 27(3):577–605.

Chambers, Robert. 1995. *Poverty and Livelihoods: Whose Reality Counts.* Discussion Paper 347. Institute of Development Studies, Brighton.

Chambers, Robert, R. Longhurst, and A. Pacey. 1981. *Seasonal Dimensions to Rural Poverty.* London: Frances Pinter.

Chen, Shaohua and Martin Ravallion. 2007. *The Changing Profile of Poverty in the World. 2020 Focus Brief on the World's Poor and Hungry People.* Washington, DC: International Food Policy Research Institute.

Collier, Paul. 2007. *The Bottom Billion: Why the Poorest Countries are Failing and What Can Be Done About It.* Oxford: Oxford University Press.

Corcoran, Mary. 1995. "Rags to Riches: Poverty and Mobility in the United States." *Annual Review of Sociology* 21:237–67.

Davis, Peter and Bob Baulch. 2011. "Parallel Realities: Exploring Poverty Dynamics Using Mixed Methods in Rural Bangladesh." *Journal of Development Studies* 47(1):118–42.

Deaton, Angus. 1997. *Analysis of Household Surveys: A Microeconometric Approach to Development Policy.* Baltimore, MD: Johns Hopkins University Press.

Dercon, Stefan. 2005. "Risk, Insurance, and Poverty: A Review." Pp. 9–37 in S. Dercon, ed., *Insurance against Poverty.* Oxford: Oxford University Press.

Dollar, David and Aart Kraay. 2000. "Growth Is Good for the Poor." *Journal of Economic Growth* 7:195–225.

Duncan, Greg J. 1984. *Years of Poverty, Years of Plenty.* Ann Arbor: University of Michigan, Institute for Social Research.

Eder, J. 1999. *A Generation Later: Household Strategies and Economic Change in the Rural Philippines.* Honolulu: University of Hawaii Press.

Ellis, Frank. 1998. "Household Strategies and Rural Livelihood Diversification." *Journal of Development Studies* (35):1–38.

EQUITAP. 2005. *Paying Out-of-Pocket for Health Care in Asia: Catastrophic and Poverty Impact.* Equitap Project Working Paper No. 2. Retrieved September 7, 2015 (http://www.researchgate.net/publication/23778503_Paying_Out-of-Pocket_for_Health_Care_in_Asia_Catastrophic_and_Poverty_Impact).

Esping-Andersen, Gosta. 2005. "Education and Equal Life-Chances: Investing in Children." Pp. 147–63 in *Social Policy and Economic Development in the Nordic Countries,* edited by Olli Kangas and Joakim Palme. New York: Palgrave Macmillan.

Farmer, Paul. 1999. *Infections and Inequalities: The Modern Plagues.* Berkeley: University of California Press.

Hacker, Jacob. 2006. *The Great Risk Shift.* New York: Oxford University Press.

Haddad, Lawrence and Akhter Ahmed. 2003. "Chronic and Transitory Poverty: Evidence from Egypt, 1997–99." *World Development* 31(1):71–85.

Himmelstein, David, Elizabeth Warren, Deborah Thorne, and Steffie Woolhandler. 2005. "Illness and Injury as Contributors to Bankruptcy." *Health Affairs,* February 2.

Hulme, David and Andrew Shepherd. 2003. "Conceptualizing Chronic Poverty." *World Development* 31(3):403–24.

ILO. 2002. *Decent Work and the Informal Economy.* Geneva: International Labor Office. Retrieved September 7, 2015(www.ilo.org/public/english/standards/relm/ilc/ilc90/pdf/rep-vi.pdf).

Jalan, Jyotsna and Martin Ravallion. 2000. "Is Transient Poverty Different? Evidence for Rural China." *Journal of Development Studies* 36(6):82–99.

Jodha, Narpat S. 1988. "Poverty Debate in India: A Minority View." *Economic and Political Weekly,* November, pp. 2421–28.

Kanbur, Ravi, ed. 2003. *Q-Squared: Combining Qualitative and Quantitative Methods in Poverty Appraisal.* Delhi: Permanent Black.

Kanbur, Ravi and Lyn Squire. 1999. "The Evolution of Thinking about Poverty: Exploring the Interactions." Retrieved September 7, 2015 (http://siteresources.worldbank.org/INTPOVERTY/Resources/WDR/evolut.pdf)

Kangas, Olli and Joakim Palme. 2005. "Coming Late—Catching Up: The Formation of a 'Nordic Model.'" Pp. 17–59 in *Social Policy and Economic Development in the Nordic Countries,* edited by Olli Kangas and Joakim Palme. New York: Palgrave Macmillan.

Krishna, Anirudh. 2004. "Escaping Poverty and Becoming Poor: Who Gains, Who Loses, and Why? People's Assessments of Stability and Change in 35 North Indian Villages." *World Development* 32(1):121–36.

Krishna, Anirudh. 2010. *One Illness Away: Why People Become Poor and How They Escape Poverty.* Oxford: Oxford University Press.

Krishna, Anirudh. 2013. "Stuck in Place: Investigating Social Mobility in 14 Bangalore Slums." *Journal of Development Studies* 49(7):1010–28.

Krishna, Anirudh and Jesse Lecy. 2008. "The Balance of All Things: Explaining Household Poverty Dynamics in 50 Villages of Gujarat, India." *International Journal of Multiple Research Methods* 2(2):160–75.

Krishna, Anirudh, Patricia Kristjanson, Judith Kuan, Gustavo Quilca, Maren Radeny, and Alicia Sanchez-Urrelo. 2006a. "Fixing the Hole in the Bucket: Household Poverty Dynamics in Forty Communities of the Peruvian Andes." *Development and Change* 37(5):997–1021.

Krishna, Anirudh, Daniel Lumonya, Milissa Markiewicz, Firminus Mugumya, Agatha Kafuko, and Jonah Wegoye. 2006b. "Escaping Poverty and Becoming Poor in 36 Villages of Central and Western Uganda." *Journal of Development Studies* 42(2):346–70.

Kristjanson, Patricia, Nelson Mango, Anirudh Krishna, Maren Radeny, and Nancy Johnson. (2009). "Understanding Poverty Dynamics in Kenya." *Journal of International Development* 22(7):978–96.

Labonte, Ronald and Ted Schrecker. 2007. "Globalization and Social Determinants of Health:" Part 1: *Globalization and Health* 3(5):1–10; Part 2, *Globalization and Health* 3(6):1–17; Part 3, *Globalization and Health* 3(7):1–15.

Lewis, Oscar. 1968. *La Vida.* London: Panther Books.

Macinko, James, Leiyu Shi, and Barbara Starfield. 2004. "Wage Inequality, the Health System, and Infant Mortality in Wealthy Industrialized Countries, 1970–1996." *Social Science and Medicine* (58):279–92.

McKernan, Signe-Mary and Caroline Ratcliffe. 2002. "Transition Events in the Dynamics of Poverty." Washington, DC: Urban Institute.

Milly, Deborah, J. 1999. *Poverty, Equality, and Growth: The Politics of Economic Need in Postwar Japan.* Cambridge, MA: Harvard University Press.

Moore, Mick, Madhulika Choudhary, and Neelam Singh. 1998. "How Can We Know What They Want? Understanding Local Perceptions of Poverty and Ill-Being in Asia." *IDS Working Paper 80.* Brighton: Institute of Development Studies.

Morduch, Jonathan. 2005. "Consumption Smoothing Across Space: Testing Theories of Risk-Sharing in the ICRISAT Study Region of South India." Pp. 38–58 in, *Insurance against Poverty*, edited by Stefan Dercon. Oxford: Oxford University Press.

Moser, Caroline. 2009. *Ordinary Families, Extraordinary Lives: Assets and Poverty Reduction in Guayaquil, 1978-2004*. Washington, DC: Brookings Institution Press.

Narayan, D., R. Patel, K. Schafft, A. Rademacher, and S. Koch-Schulte. 2000. *Voices of the Poor: Can Anyone Hear Us?* New York: Oxford University Press.

Newman, Katherine S. 1988. *Falling from Grace: Downward Mobility in the Age of Affluence*. Berkeley: University of California Press.

ODI. 2005. *The Chronic Poverty Report 2004–05*. Overseas Development Institute, UK. Retrieved September 7, 2015 (http://static1.squarespace.com/static/539712a6e4b06a6c9b892bc1/t/55a8f6d9e4b02a02236696a7/1437136601716/CPR1_ReportFull.pdf).

ODI. 2014. *The Chronic Poverty Report, 2014-15: The Road to Zero Extreme Poverty*. Overseas Development Institute, UK. Retrieved September 7, 2015 (http://static1.squarespace.com/static/539712a6e4b06a6c9b892bc1/t/539b1fe3e4b0d7588ce6ead8/1402675171712/Chronic+Poverty+report+-+full+report.pdf).

OECD. 2001. "When Money is Tight: Poverty Dynamics in OECD Countries." Retrieved September 7, 2015 (http://www.oecd.org/els/emp/2079296.pdf).

Perlman, Janice. 2011. *Favela: Four Decades of Living on the Edge in Rio de Janeiro*. Oxford: Oxford University Press.

Quisumbing, Agnes R. 2007. "Poverty Transitions, Shocks, and Consumption in Rural Bangladesh: Preliminary Results from a Longitudinal Household Survey." CPRC Working Paper 105. Manchester: Chronic Poverty Research Centre.

Salmen, Lawrence. 1987. *Listen to the People: Participant-Observer Evaluation of Development Projects*. New York: Oxford University Press.

Sawhill, Isabel V. 1988. "Poverty in the U.S.: Why Is It So Persistent?" *Journal of Economic Literature* 26:1073–1119.

Scruggs, Lyle and James P. Allan. 2006. "The Material Consequences of Welfare States: Benefit Generosity and Absolute Poverty in 16 OECD Countries." *Comparative Political Studies* 39(7):880–904.

Sen, Amartya. 1981. *Poverty and Famines: An Essay on Entitlement and Deprivation*. Oxford: Clarendon Press.

Sen, Amartya. 1999. *Development as Freedom*. New York: Random House.

Sen, Binayak. 2003. "Drivers of Escape and Descent: Changing Household Fortunes in Rural Bangladesh." *World Development* 31(3):513–34.

Shaffer, Paul. 2013. "Ten Years of "Q-Squared": Implications for Understanding and Explaining Poverty." *World Development* 45:269–85.

Sherraden, Michael. 1991. *Assets and the Poor: A New American Welfare Policy*. Armonk, NY: M.E. Sharpe.

Stevens, Ann Huff. 1999. "Climbing Out of Poverty, Falling Back In: Measuring the Persistence of Poverty Over Multiple Spells." *Journal of Human Resources* 34(3):557–88.

Van Schendel, W. 1981. *Peasant Mobility: The Odds of Life in Rural Bangladesh*. Assen, Netherlands: Van Gorcum.

Wadley, Susan. 1994. *Struggling with Destiny in Karimpur, 1925-1984*. Berkeley: University of California Press.

Western, Bruce, Dierdre Bloom, Benjamin Sosnaud, and Laura Tach. 2012. "Economic Insecurity and Social Stratification." *Annual Review of Sociology* 38:341–59.

Whitehead, Margaret, Goran Dahlgren, and Timothy Evans. 2001. "Equity and Health Sector Reforms: Can Low-Income Countries Escape the Medical Poverty Trap?" *The Lancet*, September 8, pp. 833–36.

Xu, Ke, David B. Evans, Kei Kawabata, Riadh Zeramdini, Jan Klavus, and Christopher J. L. Murray. 2003. "Household Catastrophic Health Expenditure: A Multi-country Analysis." *The Lancet*, July 12, pp. 111–17.

Zhao, Zhongwei. 2006. "Income Inequality, Unequal Health Care Access, and Mortality in China." *Population and Development Review* 32(3):461–83.

SECTION III

PLACE AND CONTEXT

CHAPTER 14

PEOPLE AND PLACES LEFT BEHIND

Rural Poverty in the New Century

DANIEL T. LICHTER AND KAI A. SCHAFFT

INTRODUCTION

RURAL poverty is a global problem, and a persistent and distinctive American problem—one with a long history. In 1964, for example, President Lyndon B. Johnson declared the War on Poverty, not from the littered streets or in front of boarded storefronts in a big-city slum, but from the porch of a rundown shack in rural Appalachia. At the time, this was a clear signal that rural America was where people and places were most deeply affected by poverty and disadvantage (Ziliak 2012). Despite its association in the public imagination with *urban* America, poverty has always been higher in nonmetropolitan (nonmetro) than metropolitan (metro) areas (Brown and Schafft 2011; Lichter and Jensen 2002). Yet, the nation's attention is usually deflected from rural problems by the residential blight, economic decline, and racial transformation of America's oldest inner cities (e.g., Detroit and St. Louis). Most Americans have had little, if any, exposure to day-to-day life in declining rural areas, much less to those "out of the way" places that have suffered most historically from population and economic decline and cultural isolation (e.g., Appalachia or the Mississippi Delta).[1]

Poverty in America has proved an especially intractable problem. In the later years of his presidency, Ronald Reagan declared: "In the sixties we waged a war on poverty, and poverty won" (Lemann 1988:37). This applause line had its intended effect on uncritical audiences, containing a clear political message regarding the wisdom of public expenditures on poverty alleviation. It was also a thinly veiled statement about the etiology of poverty (cf., Shucksmith and Schafft 2012; Tickamyer 2007). Poverty is sometimes viewed as a *cultural* phenomenon, the product of shared behaviors in which individuals are largely held responsible for their economic circumstances. Indeed, policy debates usually privilege individual-level explanations of poverty with accompanying market-based solutions (Somers and Block 2005). Yet, the 1960s brought significant expansions in social programs aimed at expanding services for the poor, including the creation of Medicare and Medicaid, Head Start, the National Education Corps, the Fair Housing Act, the Model Cities Program, and Job Corps (Massey and Sampson 2009).

The longer-term picture, however, has not been quite so sanguine, either in terms of public commitment to anti-poverty programs or in terms of continuing reductions in poverty (O'Connor 2001; Somers and Block 2005). To be sure, poverty rates in non-metro America have been cut in half, dropping from 33 percent in 1959 to 17 percent in 2011 (Farrigan 2013). But most of the decline occurred in the 1960s (see Figure 14.1). In fact, the rural poverty rate in 1971 was 17.2 percent, virtually the same as in 2011. Metropolitan poverty rates also have shown scant progress, moving from slightly above 15 percent in 1959 to slightly below by 2011. The past 40 years have therefore brought little if any reduction in poverty, at least as officially measured by the federal government.

This chapter has several specific objectives. First, we discuss the strengths and weaknesses of the U.S. official poverty measure—based on absolute money (rather than in-kind) income—for assessing material disadvantage in rural areas. Second, we highlight six key features of contemporary rural poverty that distinguish it from big-city or inner-city poverty (or suburban poverty, for that matter). Third, and finally, we give some international context to current poverty patterns in rural America, providing a comparative assessment of theory, measurement, and policy on rural disadvantage in the United States and countries of the European Union (EU), with a particular focus on the United Kingdom. Although an extended discussion of rural poverty in developing country contexts is beyond the scope of this chapter, we nevertheless sketch out key comparative issues regarding rural poverty globally. We highlight alternative approaches to the social welfare state, to conceptualizing poverty, and to better understanding the implications for rural people and places. An overarching goal is to

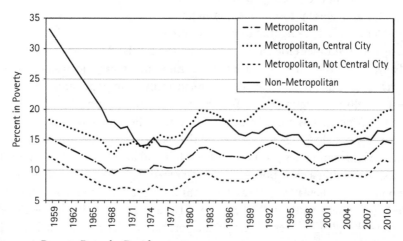

FIGURE 14.1 Poverty Rates by Residence, 1959–2011

Source: Current Population Survey.

highlight the unique issues faced by rural people and places in the new century—in the United States and elsewhere—and to raise the profile of disadvantaged rural populations for scholarly and policy audiences alike.

MEASURING RURAL POVERTY

The official U.S. poverty line was established in 1964 during the Johnson Administration using recommendations provided by the president's Council on Economic Advisors. Based on absolute money income, poverty income levels were based, first, on a minimum cost per day for food (e.g., an "economy food plan") and, second, on the assumption that low-income households typically spent about one-third of their income on food. Poverty income cutoffs reflect household differences in family size, age of family head, and number of children under 18 years of age; and they are adjusted each year for changes in the cost of living. This definition is quite unlike measurement schemes used in Europe, where low income or poverty is typically benchmarked against a national median or average income (i.e., a relative measure of poverty), or in low-income developing countries, where poverty is extreme by any absolute and relative measure (e.g., shares of people living on $1 or $2 a day).

If the statistical evidence in the United States showing higher rural poverty is straightforward, the interpretation is often unclear. In 2013, a family income of over $19,530 was required for a family of two adults and one child to escape poverty, whether they lived in Manhattan, New York or Manhattan, Kansas; Philadelphia, Pennsylvania or Philadelphia, Mississippi. The official poverty line does not adjust for spatial differences in the cost of living (e.g., transportation, housing). It ignores in-kind income, such as housing vouchers and food stamps, and other programs that benefit low-income populations. It fails to consider place-to-place differences in consumption, the basket of goods that define the Current Price Index, which is used to adjust the poverty income thresholds from one year to the next. It does not take into account the cost of employment (e.g., clothing, transportation, or union dues), nor does it consider the income lost to alimony or child support. And neither does it adjust for state and local differences in taxes, such as property taxes, state income taxes, or sales taxes, all of which can place an enormous burden on the poor.

If the assumption is correct that money goes farther in rural America, then should the result be less material deprivation? The empirical evidence suggests otherwise. Higher percentages of rural people face food insecurity (Coleman-Jensen et al. 2012), and a larger share of rural people have inadequate housing, if defined by percentages without plumbing, running water, or electricity. Unlike their urban counterparts, rural people typically lack access to reliable or affordable public transportation. About 40 percent of rural residents lack access to any public transportation in their communities (Stommes and Brown 2008). The rural poor also are more likely to fall through the welfare safety net, as smaller eligible shares of the rural poor receive cash assistance, food stamps, or public housing.

The problem of low family income is compounded by physical isolation, inadequate infrastructure (e.g., lack of safe drinking water), and limited institutional resources and social support services (Burton, Garrett-Peters, and Eason 2011; Jensen, McLaughlin, and Slack 2003; Tickamyer 2007). The rural poor often lack basic services that their urban counterparts take for granted. A large share, for example, live in so-called food deserts (Schafft, Jensen, and Hinrichs 2009; Ver Ploeg et al. 2009); that is, areas with limited access to full-scale grocery stores and fresh fruits and vegetables. Others lack access to health care—doctors and hospitals—even if they have health insurance or the income to purchase it on the market (Burton et al. 2013). The underground economy (e.g., bootlegging, drugs, bartering, and odd jobs), often a response to hardship, is thriving in many rural areas (Jensen, Cornwell, and Findeis 2010; Reding 2009; Sherman 2009). Rural people also are more likely to be exposed to environmental toxins (e.g., herbicides and insecticides) or face long-standing traditions of race discrimination and economic oppression (Lichter and Brown 2011; Saenz 2012). Finally, rural places, in contrast to urban areas, are often assumed to be backward and antimodern (Corbett 2007), and their residents frequently socially stigmatized as hillbillies, rednecks, trailer trash, and so forth (Lichter and Brown 2011; Theobald and Wood 2010; Wray 2006). Evidence of higher rates of rural poverty—despite its many flaws—is consistent with multiple indicators showing that rural people, especially the poor, face extraordinary material and cultural deprivation.

Key Dimensions of U.S. Rural Poverty Today

The demography of America's rural areas is rapidly changing, the stock of human capital has eroded, and rural America has been on the frontline of economic globalism. In the following sections we identify six distinct characteristics of rural poverty that are critical to better understanding the rural disadvantage: (1) spatially concentrated rural poverty, (2) persistent poverty, (3) work and poverty (e.g., the growth of the working poor), (4) poverty among historically disadvantaged rural minorities and immigrant newcomers, (5) rural family instability and poverty, and (6) access to public welfare and the safety net.

Spatially Concentrated Poverty

Most previous research on concentrated poverty has focused on neighborhood poverty in the nation's largest cities (Massey 1996; Reardon and Bischoff 2011). But poverty is also highly concentrated in rural regions and small towns across the United States, especially those that have large concentrations of racial and ethnic minority populations, such as the Mississippi Delta, Appalachia, or Indian country. As in the nation's cities, rural poverty became more spatially concentrated during the 2000s (Lichter, Parisi, and Taquino 2012; Farrigan and Parker 2012) after declining during the 1990s (Lichter and Johnson 2009). The rise in so-called rural ghettos (Burton et al. 2011; Eason 2012) implies that the rural poor are increasingly cordoned off, marginalized, or excluded from middle-class and affluent segments of society. The number of poor rural places—those with poverty rates over 20 percent—increased by over 30 percent during the 2000s. In the late 2000s, over 35 percent of the nonmetro poor lived in these poor places. In contrast, about 30 percent of the metro poor lived in poor communities (Lichter, Parisi, and Taquino 2011).

Rural poverty concentration is reinforced by the selectivity of migration, that is, by differences in the socioeconomic characteristics of people who move in and out of rural areas. This is usually conceptualized in terms of "brain drain": rural areas typically lose their most highly educated and skilled workers to metro labor markets (Carr and Kefalas 2009; Lichter, McLaughlin, and Cornwell 1995). Significantly, not only are the nonpoor most likely to move from poor communities, but economically disadvantaged movers are most likely to move *into* poor communities. The implications are obvious: The poor are not simply becoming poor "in place," but the effects of the economic downturn and chronic unemployment and low wages are reinforced by socioeconomic differentials associated with in- and outmigration (Fitchen 1995; Foulkes and Schafft 2010).

The spatial concentration of the rural poor people—and their growing separation from the rural nonpoor—can thus be self-reinforcing (Fitchen 1995; Foulkes and Schafft 2010; Schafft 2006). Of course, the retention and attraction of the "best and brightest" have much to do with negative perceptions of job opportunities—jobs with a future—and the quality of life in rural communities (e.g., the lack of cultural amenities). Migration processes are arguably driven by the conditions of local opportunity and economic development, which underlie the recent acceleration of concentrated rural poverty. Unfortunately, the 2000s ushered in a new spatial balkanization of America's population along economic and class lines.

PERSISTENCE

Rural poverty is characterized in part by its persistence over time (Partridge and Rickman 2007). Intragenerational and intergenerational poverty has gone hand in hand with the persistence of poverty in many economically depressed rural areas (Duncan 1997). The Economic Research Service in the U.S. Department of Agriculture has classified 386 counties as persistently poor, which are defined as counties having poverty rates exceeding 20 percent in each decade since 1970. Of these, 340 are nonmetro counties. Overall, only 4 percent of metro counties are persistently poor, compared with 13 percent of micropolitan counties (i.e., nonmetro counties with places of 10,000 or more) and 18 of noncore counties (i.e., other mostly rural counties). The overwhelming share (280 counties) of persistently poor nonmetro counties is located in the U.S. South

(Farrigan 2013). These counties tend to be disproportionately comprised of African Americans and Hispanics. Many chronically poor counties face high rates of unemployment and slow job growth, especially in occupational and industrial sectors of the economy that pay less than a living wage.

Chronic rural poverty, measured at the community level, is reinforced by ongoing demographic processes, including immobility among the most disadvantaged, who languish behind in rural areas. Yet, the problem in Appalachia, and in other regions of chronic poverty, is much less a matter of selective out-migration of the "best and brightest," but of attracting skilled workers in search of good jobs that make use of their education and training, good schools for their children, and cultural amenities that make life more enriching and satisfying. Rural residence, in fact, may be endogenous if those groups most at risk of poverty are most likely to move to or stay in rural areas.

Persistence is also reflected in intergenerational patterns of poverty. In general, the past decade was marked by a slowdown in upward intergenerational mobility, that is, the children at the bottom of the income distribution are less likely than in the past to move up in the income distribution during adulthood (Beller and Hout 2006). This is perhaps unsurprising during a period of growing income inequality in America, when America's class boundaries have become more rigid and less permeable. We are not aware of any studies that have shown rural-urban differences or temporal differences of changing intergenerational poverty in rural areas. Yet, it seems clear that patterns in rural areas are reinforced by shared risk factors for poverty between parents and children (e.g., race and ethnicity, low education, and family dynamics, including nonmarital fertility).

WORKING POOR

To "play by the rules" typically means to work for a living rather than rely on the government for subsistence. To do otherwise suggests moral lassitude in America's "blame the victim" culture (Brady, Fullerton, and Moren 2010; Prins and Schafft 2009; Rank 2005). Rural America is usually associated with self-reliance, independence, and hard work. Despite rural poverty concentration, most recent studies show that a larger share of the rural rather than the urban poor are in the labor force (Lichter and Jensen 2002). That is, larger shares of workers in rural America are poor: they work hard but are rewarded less.

Unemployment rates are similar in metro and nonmetro areas, and rates followed similar upward trajectories during the 2007–2009 Great Recession and its aftermath (Kusmin 2011). By the second quarter of 2011, the unemployment rate was 8.2 percent in nonmetro areas and 9.2 percent in metro areas. Metro areas, however, had a higher employment rate (58.5 percent) than in nonmetro areas (55.4 percent), in part because of the larger retiree population in rural areas. The postrecession employment recovery has also been slower in nonmetro areas, at least through the two quarters of 2012 (Kusmin 2012).

These figures indicate that higher rates of nonmetro poverty than metro poverty are not due to differentials in employment or unemployment, but rather to higher rates of part-time unemployment and lower wage rates in rural areas (Lichter and Jensen 2002; Slack 2010). In perhaps the most comprehensive study on this topic, Slack (2010) documented the share of all poor families over the 1979 to 2003 period with at least one family member who worked at least 27 weeks or more in the past year. In 2003, 43.5 percent of poor rural families included a worker compared with 37.5 percent in metro areas. The rural poor are disproportionately comprised of the working poor. Declines in metro-nonmetro gap in working poverty declined from 15.3 percent to 6.0 percent over the study period, but this was due largely to increases in working poverty in metro areas rather than to large declines in nonmetro areas.

At the same time, work is essential for avoiding poverty. For example, Slack (2010) showed that only 6.6 percent of nonmetro workers were poor in 2003. Still, this percentage was higher than the percentage of poor workers in metro areas (4.7), and there was little evidence of convergence over the 1979 to 2003 period. Moreover, in the multivariate analysis of working poverty, the nonmetro "effect" was .484, indicating that nonmetro workers were 1.62 times more likely than metro workers to be poor. The relative risk of working poverty was substantial even when controlling for family labor supply, employment characteristics, gender, family status, and other demographic covariates (Slack 2010).

Comparative patterns of employment and unemployment arguably misrepresent economic hardship in rural America. Previous studies suggest that rural areas suffer disproportionately from *under*employment (Lichter 1989; Slack and Jensen 2002). Slack and Jensen (2002) defined underemployment using the labor utilization framework (Clogg and Sullivan 1986), which is made up of discouraged workers, unemployed workers, involuntarily part-time workers, the working poor, and the "overeducated" (i.e., those whose education level is much higher than others with a similar job). They found that the underemployment rate was 16.2 percent in 2000 compared with 15.5 in metro central cities and 11.3 in metro suburban areas (Jensen and Slack 2003). Rates of rural underemployment skyrocketed during the late 2000s recession (Slack 2014).

Work and poverty are inextricably linked in rural America. High poverty in rural America, however, cannot be reduced to an issue of low attachment to the labor force. Instead, the empirical literature tells us that work is less highly rewarded in rural areas, even for people with similar demographic backgrounds, education levels, and job characteristics.

RURAL MINORITIES AND IMMIGRANTS

The nation's minority and immigrant populations are highly concentrated (and highly visible) in the nation's largest cities (Lichter 2012; Saenz 2012). Yet, a metro-centric approach risks ignoring the empirical fact that some of America's most impoverished

Table 14.1 Economic and Educational Attainment Status of U.S. Racial and Ethnic Groups by Metropolitan Status, 2006–2008

	Metro					Nonmetro				
	All	White	Black	Indian	Latino	All	White	Black	Indian	Latino
Economic Status										
Poverty rate										
Total	13.1	10.5	24.7	25.3	21.2	16.1	13.7	34.0	31.1	26.6
Under 18	18.2	13.6	34.5	32.8	28.0	22.2	18.2	45.7	38.3	33.2
Median income	54,756	59,027	36,700	41,400	42,319	41,053	42,986	23,799	30,812	33,500
Educational Attainment										
<HS	14.9	12.3	18.6	23.1	39.0	18.3	16.4	30.5	25.6	45.3
HS grad	13.3	28.0	32.5	30.2	27.3	18.6	37.6	38.8	36.4	28.6
Some college	27.6	28.2	30.5	31.8	20.7	27.3	27.9	22.3	28.9	18.4
Bachelor's +	29.5	31.5	18.4	14.8	13.0	17.1	18.1	8.4	9.1	7.6

Source: Brown and Schafft (2011); U.S. Census 2006–2008 American Community Survey Three-Year Estimates, Tables B15002; B15002A-D; C150021; C17001; C17001A-D; and C1700.

minority populations live in rural areas. Table 14.1, using American Community Survey three-year estimates, shows the economic and educational attainment status of selected racial and ethnic groups in metro and nonmetro areas. For each racial and ethnic group, nonmetro poverty rates exceeded their metro counterparts. For example, among African Americans living in rural areas, the poverty rate was 34 percent compared with 25 percent in metro areas. Some of the difference reflects differences in education. Among nonmetro blacks, over 30 percent lack a high school education compared with less than 20 percent in metro areas. The exceptionally low education levels of rural Hispanics, in particular, undoubtedly contribute to their high rates of poverty (27 percent). About 45 percent of rural Hispanics lack a high school education.

A sobering portent of the future of rural minority populations is contained in today's child poverty rates (Table 14.1). For example, nearly 46 percent of nonmetro African American children live in poverty, as do over 38 percent of American Indians and 33 percent of Latinos. Among the nation's rural minority children, poverty rates exceed their counterparts in metro areas; rural minority children also are overrepresented among the rural minority poor (i.e., race-specific poverty rates are larger among children than among the total population). Rural minority children clearly are among the most economically vulnerable populations in America.

Average poverty rates—even for rural minorities—sometimes hide substantial geographic variation. For example, among Native American Indians, poverty is geographically concentrated and persistent, which separates them from the economic mainstream and good jobs (Snipp 1989). On Indian reservations, poverty is often extreme. For example, in South Dakota, Ziebach County had a poverty rate of 49.9 percent, based on 2011 estimates provided by the Census Bureau's Small Area Income and Poverty

Estimates program. Ziebach County is a remote rural county (i.e., it is coded as a 9 in the ERS's 1–9 Rural-Urban Code) in North Central South Dakota. It also is home of the Pine Ridge Indian Reservation, with a population that is 77.6 percent American Indian (U.S. Census Bureau 2013c).

Geographic disparities are also evident among rural African American populations. In 2011, African Americans in the rural South experienced exceptionally high rates of poverty—higher on average than their inner city metro counterparts (36.0 vs. 30.8 percent) (U.S. Census Bureau 2013a). More significantly, averages in the South hide the extreme cases (Poston et al. 2010). In Louisiana, for example, the highest poverty rates in 2011 were observed in East Carol and Madison Counties (Economic Research Service 2013a). These two counties are located on the Mississippi River, in the Delta in the northeast corner of the state. East Carol was 64.8 percent black in 2010, while Madison County was 60.6 percent black (U.S. Census 2013b). Extreme black poverty in the rural South is a historical legacy of the slave and plantation economy (Poston et al. 2010).

More recently, interest in rural minority populations has grown with the diaspora of America's native- and foreign-born Hispanic populations (Massey 2008). In 1990, over 90 percent of U.S. Hispanics lived in just 10 states, gateways in the Southwest and some states with large immigrant populations, like Miami, Chicago, and New York City. Today, many rural and small towns have become new immigrant destinations (Lichter 2012). Hispanics have moved in large numbers to work in agriculture and food processing in America's heartland, in the Southeast, and in the Northwest (Johnson and Lichter 2010). America's rural aging-in-place native white population is being replaced rapidly by young immigrant populations in the family-building stage of the life course.

In 2011, the poverty rate among nonmetro Hispanics was 30.2 percent, well above the national figure for Hispanics (24.9 percent) (U.S. Census Bureau 2013d). Ordinarily, spatial and social mobility go hand in hand; to get somewhere in life you have go elsewhere. Yet, Hispanic in-migrants to new immigrant destinations often have exceptionally high rates of poverty, especially in rural areas (Raffaelli et al. 2012). A large number of small towns have been transformed into majority-minority communities, and many of these have also experienced big upticks in poverty. New Hispanic immigrant populations are "at risk" of poverty by virtue of low levels of education, few job skills, and limited English-language ability, which sometimes leads to a white backlash and job discrimination and exploitation (e.g., wage theft).

At the same time, rural Hispanic poverty has been highly concentrated in areas of traditional settlement (Colonias along the borderland) (Slack et al. 2006). Averages hide wide place-to-place disparities. Starr County is located at the southern-most tip of Texas, just to the north of Tamaulipas county Mexico. It is 95 percent Hispanic, with an overall poverty rate in 2011 of 36.3 percent, based on the 2007–2011 American Community Survey (Economic Research Service 2013). Like East Carol County, Louisiana, and Ziebach County, South Dakota, Starr County is unfamiliar territory to most Americans. The shifting geography of poverty will arguably be an increasingly salient dimension of racial and ethnic inequality as America is transformed racially over the next 40 years (Lichter 2013; Massey 2008).

FAMILY CHANGE

The conventional wisdom is that strong families and kinship networks are a source of strength in rural America. Indeed, stable families are sometimes viewed as safe havens from the economic and social dislocations associated with a rapidly urbanizing society (Lichter and Brown 2011). But rural areas have not been immune to changing urban values, normative expectations about marriage and family life, and sexual behavior and fertility. Rapid rural family change has placed unprecedented upward demographic pressure on poverty and inequality (Snyder and McLaughlin 2004). The reality is that rural and urban families—their structure and processes—look remarkably similar to each other. More significantly, evidence of substantial rural-urban convergence over the past 20 years largely reflects unprecedented changes in rural rather than urban families (Lichter and Graefe 2011).

There are some notable differences, however. For example, a recent study by the National Campaign to Prevent Teen and Unwanted Pregnancy (2012) found that the teen birth rate in rural counties was nearly one-third higher than that in America's suburban and urban areas. The majority of rural teen births are to whites (63 percent), unlike the nation's large cities of over one million, where the overwhelming share of teen births is to minority women (84 percent). This is not a matter of race and ethnicity. Even if the discussion is restricted to white teenagers, the birth rate was more than twice as high in rural areas than in major urban centers. Moreover, although both rural and urban areas experienced declines in teen pregnancy and childbearing between 1990 and 2010, declines were substantially slower in rural counties. The large majority of teen births are to unmarried mothers. Higher rates of rural teen nonmarital fertility, according to the authors of the National Campaign study, are not due to differences in education or economic background, or to more permissive values and sexual behavior. Rather, they largely reflect the lack of reproductive health services (including access to abortion providers) and comprehensive sex education in the classroom. Rural teen birth rates are especially high in southern Bible Belt states, where pregnancy-prevention programs could benefit an underserved rural population.

Family change and poverty rates are clearly inextricably linked (Edin and Kissane 2010). Nationally, the poverty rate among persons living in female-headed families was 34.2 percent in 2011 (U.S. Census Bureau 2013d). It is even higher in rural areas (41.6 percent). For rural persons living in married couple families, the poverty rate was 7.9 percent, a figure comparable to their metro counterparts (7.3 percent). Not only has family change been especially rapid in rural areas, but the putative economic consequences, at least as measured in poverty rates, also prey most heavily on "at risk" families. This point is sometimes overlooked in studies of rural poverty (see Lichter and Jensen 2002), where the emphasis is usually placed on economic development and job growth, not healthy or strong families. For rural single mothers, they typically have fewer quality opportunities for employment, and they also have less access to work supports, including dependable and affordable childcare and transportation. Also, their knowledge of eligibility requirements for cash assistance and other government programs is often limited.

Changing rural family patterns have also affected children's vulnerability to poverty. The nonmetro poverty rate for female-headed families with children was 50.7 percent in 2011 compared with 41.2 percent in metro areas (U.S. Census Bureau 2013e). The overall poverty rate for nonmetro children in 2011 was 25.9 percent, and nearly 40 percent of all rural children were below 200 percent of the poverty line. The corresponding poverty rate for metro children was 21.2 percent. The rate was 29.2 percent inside principal cities in 2011.

The disproportionately high rates of poverty for rural children has potentially significant implications for their developmental trajectories, for their cognitive development and academic achievement, and for their ability to escape poverty as the transition to productive (or not) adult roles (Duncan, Ziol-Guest, and Kalil 2010). The long-term deleterious consequences of childhood poverty in rural areas are reinforced by underresourced schools, a growing drug epidemic in rural areas, and low educational or academic expectations. High rates of poverty among today's rural children provide a portent of the future.

THE SAFETY NET

Rural people, as we have documented here, experience disproportionately high rates of poverty—poverty that is often chronic, intergenerational, spatially concentrated, and reinforced by family demographic processes and the lack of local job opportunities. The implications of these distinct disadvantages are compounded by issues of race and ethnicity, which typically go unrecognized in an urban-centric literature on inequality. Yet, the rural poor are often underserved by America's social safety net. The War on Poverty has seemingly been replaced by a War on Welfare, which is reflected in cutbacks in America's safety net, and more tangibly, the dollar amount of cash assistance to welfare beneficiaries (Rank 2005; Tickamyer 2006).

Interestingly enough, government transfer payments to individuals accounted for 24.8 percent of total nonmetro personal income and 16.3 percent of metro personal income in 2011 (Economic Research Service 2013). But this primarily reflects rural America's large retirement-age population, which has raised the cost of Social Security and Medicare and Medicaid expenditures, and the lower average income from earnings in rural areas. Retirement and medical benefits alone accounted for roughly 75 percent of all government payments to rural persons.

Government transfers to nonmetro areas mask the fact that the rural residents eligible for government assistant are less likely to receive help from the government, and the cash receipt is often substantially lower (Lichter and Jensen 2002). Some of the rural-urban difference was made up by SNAP (Supplemental Nutrition Assistance Program, i.e., food stamps), which is based on money income, which means that states with low TANF (Temporary Assistance for Needy Families) levels are (partially) compensated with above-average dollar amounts of food stamps. Still, the monthly average dollar value of food stamps per recipient was only $124 in 2009, which greatly benefited the poor, especially those with incomes less than one-half the poverty income threshold (Tiehen, Jolliffe, and Gundersen 2012).

Rural people, and especially the rural poor, are disproportionately represented in the South and in states located in the agricultural heartland (e.g., South Dakota), which typically have less generous cash assistance programs or other government subsidies (e.g., housing vouchers). This is important because states have great latitude in determining how TANF is implemented (i.e., eligibility requirements, payment levels, assets allowed, including automobiles, work requirements, earnings disregards, and time limits). For example, our calculations from the three-year file of the American Community Survey (2009–2011) revealed that only 2.5 percent of households in heavily rural Mississippi received public cash assistance, compared with 3.3 percent in New York state. Moreover, despite much higher rates of rates of family poverty in Mississippi than New York (17.5 vs. 11.5), the average cash assistance received per recipient in Mississippi was $2,605 compared with $4,039 in New York. The federal government helped make up the difference with food stamps. In Mississippi, 16.3 percent of its population received food stamps compared with 13.8 percent in New York.[2]

These data illustrate a familiar story of unmet need in rural America but also of all disadvantaged families. The limited availability of cash assistance and food stamps is hardly the only problem. About 15 percent of American families have no health insurance; 22 percent are not in the labor force. In Mississippi and New York, 17.9 and 11.6 percent, respectively, are without health insurance. And the percentages are higher yet among nonworkers (25.8 and 15.4 percent, respectively). To be sure, the expansion of America's largest public assistance program, the Earned Income Tax Credit (EITC), has played an important role in ameliorating poverty. But EITC is limited to families with workers and the benefits are graduated by earnings. Therefore, the comparative benefits of EITC tend to favor urban over rural areas, where wages are lower. Rural areas and states (like Mississippi) have rates of labor force nonparticipation, unemployment (especially among disadvantaged minorities), and low wages that limit EITC participation and average dollars received.

Finally, we have emphasized the benefit (or lack of benefits) from government transfers. Another understudied topic that affects the ability of the poor to provide for basic needs is burdensome state and local taxes. In many states, but especially in the South and largely rural states (South Dakota, Wyoming, New Hampshire, Alaska), highly regressive sales taxes (even on food and clothing) take a disproportionate bite out of the buying power of low-income families. As documented by Newman and O'Brien (2011), sales taxes often have to "make up" for the lack of state income and corporate taxes, which are etched into state tax laws and often require a super-majority vote in state legislatures to change. This clearly indicates another pernicious aspect of current definitions of poverty; it is based upon pretax rather than posttax income.

WHAT CAN BE LEARNED FROM EUROPE
AND VICE VERSA?

Comparative local area studies of poverty in the United States and Europe are surprisingly sparse despite many shared demographic dimensions of the problem, which suggests new opportunities for mutual understanding and collaboration. This scholarly disconnect is due, at least in part, to country-to-country differences in the conceptualization and measurement of poverty. In the United States, the poverty line is an absolute measure denoting a specified level of income below which one is considered to be poor; the emphasis is placed on whether basic needs for food, shelter, and clothing are met. European poverty scholars, however, typically emphasize relative measures of poverty (Brady 2005). Poverty thresholds are typically set at 60 percent of average family income (adjusted for purchasing power of different currencies). While unambiguous interpretations of comparative rural poverty in Europe and the United States are made difficult by conceptual and measurement differences, if measured in absolute terms, rural poverty on the whole is considerably lower in Europe than in the United States (Shucksmith 2012; Tickamyer 2007).

European scholars and policymakers often focus on the concept of *social exclusion* which emphasizes how individuals and groups are prevented from full participation in economic, political, and civic life (Milbourne 2004; Shucksmith 2012; Walker and Walker 1997). The conceptual utility of social exclusion has attracted far less attention in the United States among rural scholars and government agencies (Commins 2004; Shucksmith and Schafft 2012). The concept of social exclusion "emphasizes dynamic social processes, the multi-dimensional nature of disadvantage and inequality, and the importance of local context in shaping and reproducing the social logic that regulates the distribution of resources and power" (Molnár and Schafft 2003:55–56). Its conceptual focus illuminates the systemic factors that limit individuals or groups from full participation in the civic, economic, and cultural realms of social life. Not surprisingly, the emphasis on social exclusion in Europe is expressed by the use of myriad indicators of material deprivation, including the quality of housing, levels of homelessness, access to public services, or on welfare provisions rather than on income or relative income (Cloke, Marsden, and Mooney 2007).

Avoiding poverty in rural European communities (or elsewhere) does not ensure social inclusion (Commins 2004; Palacios 2007), and critics of the concept of social exclusion argue that the concept risks overemphasizing social-boundary formation, and it suggests that a "cohesive society undifferentiated by class or social division" (Shucksmith and Schafft 2012:107) from which some are "excluded." More recently in political debates in the United Kingdom, the concept has lost some currency, with both Conservative and Liberal sides of the governing coalition emphasizing, as in the United States, more individual and "cultural" explanations of poverty, and disincentives for welfare dependency (Shucksmith and Schafft 2012).

To be sure, relative poverty measures are more conceptually consistent with concepts like social exclusion. In 2011, there were nearly 120 million people or 24 percent of the population who lived in relative poverty in the 27 countries comprising the EU (Eurostat 2011). Published breakdowns of European poverty by urbanity are difficult to locate, however, and peer-reviewed papers are virtually nonexistent. Fortunately, Eurostat now provides a rural-urban typology that defines three types of regions: predominantly urban, intermediate, and predominantly rural. Data show that rural poverty in Europe (as a relative measure) is on average higher than urban poverty; indeed, 24 of 30 EU countries had higher rural poverty than average, while the lowest rates tended to be in intermediate areas (i.e., akin perhaps to suburban or exurban areas in the U.S. case) (Eurostat 2013). The highest rates of rural poverty are found in Lithuania, Latvia, Romania, and Bulgaria (see Figure 14.2), where relative poverty rates exceed 25 percent in rural areas. With the establishment and expansion of the European Union, it is more important than ever to build a comparative understanding of rural poverty (Shucksmith 2012).

Poverty in the EU, as in the United States, reflects local, national, and international labor market processes or other structural causes, it is experienced disproportionately by minority populations (both native and foreign born), and it is often highly concentrated and persistent (Tickamyer 2007). This has been most pronounced in the new transition economies of the Central and Eastern European countries from the old Soviet bloc (Brown and Schafft 2003). The expansion of the European Union has

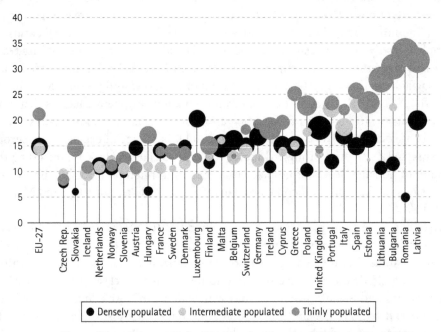

FIGURE 14.2 Share of Population at Risk of Poverty, by Degree of Urbanization, 2009

Source: Eurostat (http://ec.europa.eu/eurostat/).

contributed, as in the United States, to new international labor flows (mostly from east to west) into rural areas to work in agriculture, fishing, and "green jobs." The growth of unskilled or uneducated laborers from Bulgaria, Romania, Poland, and other parts of Eastern and Southern Europe to work in agriculture in the North and West is a new but understudied feature of rural poverty in Europe (e.g., McAreavey 2012). The policy implications for immigrant incorporation and cultural integration are similar to those in new immigrant destinations in the rural United States.

Yet, compared with the North American case, the research literature on rural poverty in Europe is surprisingly underdeveloped. In the United States, published empirical studies of rural poverty—in sociology, demography, economics, and policy sciences—are comparatively abundant and well developed, perhaps owing to the U.S. land grant tradition of many publicly funded state universities such as Iowa State, Penn State University, and others. These institutions, which came about through the Morrill Act in 1862, were established with experiment-station research programs emphasizing the needs of rural people and communities. There is no clear organizational or funding counterpart to the Morrill Act in Europe, which means that the overwhelming share of poverty research studies on rural European countries have adopted a decidedly urban-centric approach to the problem. The rural European poverty literature is often idiosyncratic, emphasizing local or regional case studies that lack the geographic reach necessary to build a cumulative knowledge base that informs our understanding of rural poverty in Europe or its differences from the United States.

The rural poverty literature from the United Kingdom is probably the most well developed in Europe. But, interestingly enough, rural areas in the United Kingdom are sometimes viewed as places for the affluent—for the gentry who desire a safe haven and the quietude of the countryside. Indeed, in many rural studies in England, the emphasis is less on the rural poor and more about the political tactics used by the rural gentry or economic elite to effectively exclude economically disadvantaged populations. Rural places are to be preserved rather than transformed. Similar processes are sometimes the topic of study in America's rural resort communities, for instance in tests of the so-called gangplank hypothesis where affluent urban-origin migrants seek to pull up the gangplank to prevent others from changing their communities (Smith and Krannich 2000). Rural retirement communities, in particular, often have strong incentives to attract the "right kind" of people who preserve the status quo (and property values and low taxes).

RURAL POVERTY IN THE GLOBAL SOUTH: EMERGENT TRENDS AND ISSUES

Approximately 1.4 billion people around the world live in extreme poverty, with incomes of $1.25 or less per day (IFAD 2010). Of this population, some two-thirds live in rural areas in developing countries. Extreme poverty in rural areas has declined over time; in 1988, 54 percent of the rural population in developing nations lived in extreme poverty, while by 2010 that figure had dropped to 35 percent (IFAD 2010). While some progress has been made in reducing the incidence of rural poverty globally, wealth and income inequality has increased during the same time period. Currently nearly half the world's wealth is controlled by 1 percent of the population, a figure that is equivalent to 65 times the wealth held by the lower economic half of the world's population (Fuentes-Nieva and Galasso 2014).

With regard to developing countries, the term "development" is a contested concept because it is connected to historical legacies of colonial domination and the normative first world assumptions regarding the trajectories of social and economic modernization (Ballard 2012; McMichael and Morarji 2010; Peet and Hartwick 2009). These assumptions have had mixed and contradictory outcomes for the well-being of people and nations located on the peripheries of the global economy. This is particularly the case with regard to economic liberalization policies imposed upon postcolonial nations (often by global lending institutions such as the World Bank and the International Monetary Fund) on governance, education, land use, and social safety nets (Bello 2008; Dao 2004; McMichael 2011; Patel and McMichael 2004; Prashad 2013). For these reasons, the "Global South" has increasingly been used to refer to the countries of Latin America, Africa, and Asia on the global economic peripheries, a term employed in part to problematize the development discourse, while emphasizing "asymmetry and inequality amidst intensifying global interdependency" (Sparke 2007:117).

For much of the post–World War II development era, rural areas in the Global South were seen as lags on development or as export platforms for industrial agriculture, whereas economic modernization was understood to be largely driven by urbanization and industrialization (McMichael 2011). In the Global South, about 80 percent of rural households are involved in some form of agriculture as a form of household provisioning, paid labor, and/or market production (IFAD 2010). In many countries, however, long-term urban biases in governance and in expenditures on education, health care, housing, and sanitation have directly contributed to the economic and political marginalization of the extreme poor, in rural areas and elsewhere (Ballard 2012; Dao 2004). Under these conditions, as a recent IFAD report states,

> . . . agriculture in developing countries has operated in the context of low global prices for food products coupled, in many countries, with unfavourable domestic environments. Low levels of investment in agriculture, inappropriate policies, thin and uncompetitive markets, weak rural infrastructure, inadequate production and financial services and a deteriorating national resource base have all contributed to creating an environment in which it has been risky and unprofitable for small holders to participate in agricultural markets. (IFAD 2010:14)

This occurred in the context of highly subsidized agricultural production in OECD countries, indebtedness, and the subsequent need for agriculture geared toward export rather than domestic production. Unilateral trade liberalization pushed by the North created conditions in many developing nations in which smallholders struggled with depressed market prices for the goods produced, increased input costs, and reduced credit access (Bello 2008; Byerlee et al. 2007; Peine 2010).

Thinking on the relative prioritization of different agricultural production models has shifted somewhat in recent years, however, and rural areas are now increasingly recognized as sites of economic resiliency, with smallholder agriculture in both rural and urban fringe areas acknowledged as an important means of combating poverty, increasing food security, enhancing household livelihood strategies, and creating community assets consistent with local economic and cultural rationalities (Byerlee et al. 2007; IFAD 2010; Lerner and Eakin 2011; Thorpe and Sahan 2013).

This perspective was only reinforced by the food crisis in the late 2000s, when in 2006 to 2008 global food prices doubled, thrusting the most vulnerable around the world into new depths of insecurity (Bello 2008; Byerlee et al. 2007). The crisis in food price increases is also creating new global concerns about rising demands for food in the context of not only increasing land, water, and energy scarcities but also changing and unpredictable environmental conditions associated with climate change, which is predicted to have the harshest impacts on areas experiencing the most intense concentrations of extreme poverty, notably sub-Saharan Africa (Hertel, Burke, and Lobell 2010).

By many counts, climate change arguably represents one of the most significant long-term risks of deepening the vulnerability of poor people in developing nations because of the increased probability of droughts, extreme weather events, and reduced food security. Uneven in its effects, agricultural yields in places dependent upon rainfall, in some areas, may be halved by 2020. Globally, however, climate change may place as many as 49 million additional people at risk of hunger (IFAD 2008). Climate change as an anthropogenic event (IPCC 2007) casts new attention not only on increased vulnerability for poor populations but also on the consequences of different agricultural practices for mitigating and/or exacerbating social, environmental, and climatic impacts.

Under these circumstances, heated debates continue regarding the most appropriate policy directions, with some advocating continued trade liberalization and global market integration while improving price incentives and supports for smallholder farmers (Byerlee et al. 2007). Others raise serious concerns about the exclusionary practices of market-based development and its contradictory outcomes (Ballard 2012; Bello 2008; Sparke 2007; White et al. 2012).

Conclusion

High rates of rural poverty have been a persistent problem around the globe. In the United States, rural people and places are often overlooked among scholars and policymakers, who view poverty as largely an urban and minority problem. This is reinforced by a neoliberal economic perspective that dominates thinking today about the root causes of poverty and inequality (Somers and Block 2005; Tickamyer 2007). Economists dominate the poverty research and policy community—in the United States and elsewhere; their theoretical approach and ideological policy lens emphasizes choice rather than the ascriptive constraints of place (i.e., opportunity). Most of the scholarly interest in rural communities and poverty resides with rural sociologists and geographers, who emphasize the constraints of place over choices. Rural poverty reflects the lack of opportunities—good schools and stable jobs—that serve to concentrate poverty and reproduce it generation to generation. Not surprisingly, they also tend to emphasis place-based policy (e.g., economic development) rather than policies directed at individuals, regardless of where they happen to live (e.g., punitive welfare policies).

The global reality is that the boundaries of rurality and urbanity are rapidly blurring (Lerner and Eakin 2011; Lichter and Brown 2011; Shucksmith, Brown, and Vergunst 2011). Improvements in communication and transportation, the emergence of global markets for labor and goods, and government devolution has accelerated the breakdown of urban and rural distinctions. Poverty arguably must be seen as part of an interconnected system of economic and social relations that perpetuate the disadvantaged circumstances found in historically disadvantaged rural communities (e.g., Brown and Schafft 2011). We see this when poor and powerless rural communities become dumping grounds for urban toxic waste, sites for America's prison populations, and the target of exploitation of natural resources (e.g., fracking for natural gas). And we see it in the nations of the Global South where rural populations have born the brunt of structural adjustment and trade liberalization policies that have impoverished small-scale agricultural producers, and gutted social safety nets, while reinforcing conditions for uneven wealth accumulation. The problem of rural poverty cannot be neatly separated from the larger political economy, yet it is typically cordoned off from other scholarship on poverty and inequality.

In the final analysis, this chapter is a call for new research on rural people and places left behind in a globalizing economy supported by neoliberal economic policy (where the poor are blamed for their current economic circumstances). Reducing poverty in America—rural or urban—requires political will, especially during a period of growing political polarization, fiscal austerity, rising antitax and antigovernment sentiment, and new racial and ethnic antagonisms. Paradoxically, as we learned from Thomas Frank's *What's the Matter with Kansas*, rural voters often support cultural and political agendas that seemingly work against their collective economic interests (Frank 2005; cf., Sherman 2009). As a starting point, improving the circumstances of the rural poor will therefore require greater commitment to public engagement and information outreach than we have seen to this point.

NOTES

1. This chapter was completed, in part, while the first author was a visiting fellow at the Netherlands Interdisciplinary Demographic Institute (NIDI) in Den Haag. The support of NIDI is gratefully acknowledged. The authors also acknowledge the support of the Cornell Population Center, and Penn State's Children, Youth and Family Consortium. We are grateful for the helpful comments of the editors, external reviewers, and Sharon Sassler.

2. To put these figures in national perspective, only 2.8 percent of all American households received cash assistance and 11.7 percent received food stamps. The annual average dollar amount of cash assistance was $3,860.

REFERENCES

Ballard, Richard. 2012. "Geographies of Development: Without the Poor." *Progress in Human Geography* 36(5):563–72.

Beller, Emily and Michael Hout. 2006. "Intergenerational Social Mobility: The United States in Comparative Perspective." *The Future of Children* 16:19–36.

Bello, Walden. 2008. "Manufacturing a Food Crisis: How Free Trade is Destroying Third World Agriculture—and Who is Fighting Back." *The Nation* 286(21):16–21.

Brady, David. 2005. "The Welfare State and Relative Poverty in Rich Western Democracies, 1967–1997." *Social Forces* 83:1329–64.

Brady, David, Andrew S. Fullerton, and Jennifer Moren. 2009. "Putting Poverty in Political Context: A Multi-Level Analysis of Adult Poverty across 18 Affluent Democracies." *Social Forces* 88:271–99.

Brady, David, Andrew S. Fullerton, and Jennifer Moren. 2010. "More Than Just Nickles and Dimes: A Cross-national Analysis of Working Poverty in Affluent Democracies." *Social Problems* 57:559–85.

Brown, David L. and Kai A. Schafft. 2003. "Social Exclusion in Rural Areas of East Central Europe during Post Socialism." *Eastern European Countryside* 9:27–45.

Brown, David L. and Kai A. Schafft. 2011. *Rural People and Communities in the 21st Century: Resilience and Transformation.* New York: Polity.

Burton, Linda M., Daniel T. Lichter, Regina S. Baker, and John M. Eason. 2013. "Inequality, Family Processes, and Health in the 'New' Rural America." *American Behavioral Scientist* 57(8):1128–51.

Burton, Linda M., Raymond Garrett-Peters, and John Major Eason. 2011. "Morality, Identity, and Mental Health in Rural Ghettos." *Social Disparities in Health and Health Care* 1:91–110.

Byerlee, Derek, Alain de Janvry, Elisabeth Sadoulet, Robert Townsend, and Irina Klytchnikova. 2007. *World Development Report 2008: Agriculture for Development.* Washington, DC: International Bank for Reconstruction and Development/ World Bank.

Carr, Patrick J., and Maria J. Kefalas. 2009. *Hollowing Out the Middle: The Rural Brain Drain and What It Means for America.* Boston: Beacon Press.

Clogg, Clifford C. and Teresa A. Sullivan. 1983. "Labor Force Composition and Underemployment Trends, 1969–1980." *Social Indicators Research* 12:117–52.

Cloke, Paul, Terry Marsden, and Patrick Mooney. 2007. *Handbook of Rural Studies*. New York: Sage.

Coleman-Jensen, Alisha, Mark Nord, Margaret Andrews, and Steven Carlson. 2012. *Household Food Security in the United States in 2011*. Economic Research Report No. ERR-141. Washington, DC: Economic Research Service, USDA.

Commins, Patrick. 2004. "Poverty and Social Exclusion in Rural Areas: Characteristics, Processes and Research Issues." *Sociologia Ruralis* 44:60–75.

Corbett, Michael. 2007. *Learning to Leave: The Irony of Schooling in a Coastal Community*. Halifax, Nova Scotia: Fernwood.

Dao, Minh Quang. 2004. "Rural Poverty in Developing Countries: An Empirical Analysis. *Journal of Economic Studies* 31(5/6):500–508.

Duncan, Cynthia M. 1997. *Worlds Apart: Why Poverty Persists in Rural America*. New Haven, CT: Yale University Press.

Duncan, Greg J., Kathleen M. Ziol-Guest, and Ariel Kalil. 2010. "Early-Childhood Poverty and Adult Attainment, Behavior, and Health." *Child Development* 81:306–25.

Eason, John M. 2012. "Extending the Hyperghetto: Toward a Theory of Punishment, Race, and Rural Disadvantage." *Journal of Poverty* 16:274–95.

Economic Research Service. 2013a. "Percent of Total Poplulation in Poverty, 2013." Retrieved June 20, 2013 (http://www.ers.usda.gov/data-products/county-level-data-sets/poverty.aspx).

Economic Research Service. 2013b. "Rural Income, Welfare, and Poverty Briefing Room." Retrieved March 31, 2013 (http://webarchives.cdlib.org/sw1rf5mhok/http://ers.usda.gov/Briefing/IncomePovertyWelfare/PovertyDemographics.htm).

Edin, Kathryn and Rebecca Joyce Kissane. 2010. "Poverty and the American Family: A Decade in Review." *Journal of Marriage and Family* 72:460–79.

Eurostat. 2011. *Eurostat Regional Yearbook 2011*. Luxembourg: Publications Office of the European Union.

Farrigan, Tracey and Timothy Parker. 2012. "The Concentration of Poverty Is a Growing Rural Problem." *Amber Waves* 10(4):1–4.

Farrigan, Tracy. 2013. *Rural Poverty and Well-being*. Washington DC: Economic Research Service, USDA.

Fitchen, Janet M. 1995. "Spatial Redistribution of Poverty through Migration of Poor People to Depressed Rural Communities." *Rural Sociology* 60:181–201.

Foulkes, Matt and Kai A. Schafft. 2010. "The Impact of Migration on Poverty Concentration in the United States, 1995–2000." *Rural Sociology* 75:90–110.

Frank, Thomas. 2005. *What's the Matter with Kansas: How Conservatives Won the Heart of America*. New York: Holt.

Fuentes-Nieva, Ricardo and Nicholas Galasso. 2014. *Working for the Few: Political Capture and Economic Inequality*. Oxford: Oxfam.

Hertel, Thomas W., Marshall B. Burke, and David B. Lobell. 2010. "The Poverty Implications of Climate-Induced Crop Yield Change by 2030." *Global Environmental Change.* 20:577–85.

Intergovernmental Panel on Climate Change (IPCC). 2007. *Climate Change 2007: Synthesis Report. Contribution of Working Groups I, II and III to the Fourth Assessment Report of the Intergovernmental Panel on Climate Change*. Geneva: IPCC.

International Fund for Agricultural Development (IFAD). 2008. *Climate Change: Building the Resilience of Poor Rural Communities*. Rome: IFAD.

International Fund for Agricultural Development (IFAD). 2010. *Rural Poverty Report 2011*. Rome: IFAD.

Jensen, Leif and Tim Slack. 2003. "Underemployment in America: Measurement and Evidence." *American Journal of Community Psychology* 32:21–31.

Jensen, Leif, Gretchen T. Cornwell, and Jill L. Findeis. 2010. "Informal Work in Nonmetropolitan Pennsylvania." *Rural Sociology* 60:91–107.

Jensen, Leif. Diane K. McLaughlin, and Tim Slack. 2003. "Rural Poverty: The Persisting Challenge." Pp. 118–31 in *Challenges for Rural America in the Twenty-First Century*, edited by D. L. Brown and L. E. Swanson. University Park: Pennsylvania State University Press.

Johnson, Kenneth M. and Daniel T. Lichter. 2010. "Growing Diversity among America's Children and Youth: Spatial and Temporal Dimensions." *Population and Development Review* 36:151–76.

Kusmin, Lorin. 2011. *Rural America at a Glance, 2011 Edition*. Economic Information Bulletin Number 85. Washington, DC: Economic Research Service, USDA.

Kusmin, Lorin. 2012. *Rural America at a Glance, 2012 Edition*. Economic Information Bulletin Number 21. Washington, DC: Economic Research Service, USDA.

Lemann, Nicholas. 1988. "The Unfinished War." *Atlantic Monthly* , December, pp. 37–56.

Lerner, Amy M. and Hallie Eakin. 2011. "An Obsolete Dichotomy? Rethinking the Rural-Urban Interface in Terms of Food Security and Production in the Global South." *Geographical Journal* 177(4):311–20.

Lichter, Daniel T. 1989. "Race, Employment Hardship, and Inequality in the American Nonmetropolitan South." *American Sociological Review* 54:436–46.

Lichter, Daniel T. 2012. "Immigration and the New Racial Diversity in Rural America." *Rural Sociology* 77:3–35.

Lichter, Daniel T. 2013. "Integration or Fragmentation? Race and the American Future." *Demography* 50:359–91.

Lichter, Daniel T. and David L. Brown. 2011. "Rural America in an Urban Society: Changing Spatial and Social Boundaries." *Annual Review of Sociology* 37:565–92.

Lichter, Daniel T. and Deborah R. Graefe. (2011). "Rural Economic Restructuring: Implications for Children, Youth, and Families." Pp. 25–39 in *Economic Restructuring and Family Wellbeing in Rural America*, edited by K. Smith and A. Tickamyer. University Park: Pennsylvania State University Press.

Lichter, Daniel T. and Leif Jensen. 2002. "Rural America in Transition: Poverty and Welfare at the Turn of the Twenty-First Century." Pp. 77–110 in *Rural Dimensions of Welfare Reform: Welfare, Food Assistance, and Poverty in Rural America*, edited by B. Weber, G. Duncan, L. Whitener. Kalamazoo, MI: W. E. Upjohn Institute.

Lichter, Daniel T. and Kenneth M. Johnson. 2009. "Immigrant Gateways and Hispanic Migration to New Destinations." *International Migration Review* 43:496–518.

Lichter, Daniel T. and Kenneth M. Johnson. 2007. "The Changing Spatial Concentration of America's Rural Poor Population." *Rural Sociology* 72:331–58.

Lichter, Daniel T., Diane K. McLaughlin, and Gretchen Cornwell. 1995. "Migration and the Loss of Human Resources in Rural America." Pp. 235–56 in *Investing in People: The Human Capital Needs of Rural America*, edited by L. J. Beaulieu and D. Mulkey. Boulder, CO: Westview.

Lichter, Daniel T., Domenico Parisi, and Michael C. Taquino. "The Geography of Exclusion: Race, Segregation, and Concentrated Poverty." *Social Problems* 59:364–88.

Massey, Douglas S. 1996. "The Age of Extremes: Concentrated Affluence and Poverty in the Twenty-First Century." *Demography* 33:395–412.

Massey, Douglas S. 2008. *New Faces in New Places*. New York: Russell Sage Foundation.

Massey, Douglas S. and Robert J. Sampson. 2009. "Moynihan Redux: Legacies and Lessons." *The Annals of the American Academy of Political and Social Science*. 621:6–27.

McAreavey, Ruth. 2012. "Resistance or Resilience? Tracking the Pathway of Recent Arrivals to a New Rural Destination." *Sociologia Ruralis* 52:488–507.

McMichael, Philip. 2011. *Development and Social Change: A Global Perspective*. Thousand Oaks, CA: Pine Forge Press.

McMichael, Philip and Karuna Morarji. 2010. "Development and its Discontents." Pp. 233–41 in *Contesting Development: Critical Struggles for Social Change*, edited by Philip McMichael. New York: Routledge.

Milbourne, Paul. 2004. *Rural Poverty: Marginalisation and Exclusion in Britain and the United States*. London: Routledge.

Molnár, Emilia and Kai A. Schafft. 2003. "Social Exclusion, Ethnic Political Mobilization, and Roma Minority Self-Governance in Hungary." *East Central Europe/L'Europe Du Centre Est* 30:53–74.

National Campaign to Prevent Teen and Unintended Pregnancy. 2013. "Teen Childbearing in Rural America." Retrieved May 1, 2013 (http://www.thenationalcampaign.org/resources/pdf/ss/ss47_teenchildbearinginruralamerica.pdf).

Newman, Katherine S. and Rourke L. O'Brien. 2011. *Taxing the Poor: Doing Damage to the Truly Disadvantaged*. Berkeley and Los Angeles: University of California Press.

O'Connor, Alice. 2001. *Poverty Knowledge: Social Science, Social Policy, and the Poor in Twentieth-Century U.S. History*. Princeton, NJ: Princeton University Press.

Palacios, Simon Pedro Izara. 2007. "Welfare Benefits and Social Exclusion in Southern Spain." *South European Society & Politics* 12:165–82.

Partridge, Mark D. and Dan S. Rickman. 2007. "Persistent Rural Poverty: Is It Simply Remoteness and Scale?" *Review of Agricultural Economics* 29:430–36.

Patel, Rajeev and Philip McMichael. 2004. "Third Worldism and the Lineages of Global Fascism: The Regrouping of the Global South in the Neoliberal Era." *Third World Quarterly* 25(1):231–54.

Peet, Richard and Elaine Hartwick. 2009. *Theories of Development: Contentions, Arguments, Alternatives*. New York: Guilford Press.

Peine, Emelie. 2010. "Corporate Mobilization on the Soybean Frontier of Mato Grosso, Brazil." Pp. 132–45 in *Contesting Development: Critical Struggles for Social Change*, edited by Philip McMichael. New York: Routledge.

Poston Jr., Dudley L., Joachim Singelmann, Carlos Siordia, Tim Slack, Bruce A. Robertson, Rogelio Saenz, and Kayla Fontenot. 2010. "Spatial Context and Poverty: Area-Level Effects and Micro-Level Effects on Household Poverty in the Texas Borderland and Lower Mississippi Delta." *Applied Spatial Analysis and Policy* 3:139–62.

Prashad, Vijay. 2013. *The Poorer Nations: A Possible History of the Global South*. New York: Verso.

Prins, Esther S. and Kai A. Schafft. 2009. "Individual and Structural Attributions for Poverty and Persistence in Family Literacy Programs: The Resurgence of the Culture of Poverty." *Teachers College Record* 111:2280–310.

Raffaelli, Marcela, Steve P. Tran, Angela R. Wiley, Maria Galarza-Heras, Vanja Lazarevic. 2012. "Risk and Resilience in Rural Communities: The Experiences of Immigrant Latina Mothers." *Family Relations* 61:559–70.

Rank, Mark R. 2005. *One Nation Underprivileged: Why American Poverty Affects Us All*. New York: Oxford University Press.

Reardon, Sean F. and Kendra Bischoff. 2011. "Income Inequality and Income Segregation." *American Journal of Sociology* 116:1092–1153.

Reding, Nick. 2009. *Methland: The Death and Life of an American Small Town.* New York: Bloomsbury.

Saenz, Rogelio. 2012. "Rural Race and Ethnicity." Pp. 207–23 in *International Handbook of Rural Demography*, edited by L. J. Kŭlcsár and K. J. Curtis. Dordrecht, the Netherlands: Springer.

Schafft, Kai A. 2006. "Poverty, Residential Mobility and Student Transiency within a Rural New York School District." *Rural Sociology* 71:212–31.

Schafft, Kai A., Eric B. Jensen, and C. Clare Hinrichs. 2009. "Food Deserts and Overweight Schoolchildren: Evidence from Pennsylvania." *Rural Sociology* 74:153–77.

Sherman, Jennifer. 2009. *Those Who Work, Those Who Don't: Poverty, Morality and Family in Rural America.* Minneapolis: University of Minnesota Press.

Shucksmith, Mark. 2012. "Class, Power and Inequality in Rural Areas: Beyond Social Exclusion?" *Sociologia Ruralis* 52:377–97.

Shucksmith, Mark, David L. Brown, and Jo Vergunst. 2012. "Constructing the Rural-Urban Interface: Place Still Matters in a Highly Mobile Society." Pp. 287–303 in *Rural Transformations and Rural Policies in the US and the UK*, edited by M. Shucksmith, D. L. Brown, S. Shortall, J. Vergunst, and M. E. Warner. New York: Routledge.

Shucksmith, Mark and Kai A. Schafft. 2012. "Rural Poverty and Social Exclusion in the US and the UK." Pp. 100–116 in *Rural Transformations and Rural Policies in the US and the UK*, edited by M. Shucksmith, D. L. Brown, S. Shortall, J. Vergunst, and M. E. Warner. New York: Routledge.

Slack, Tim. 2010. "Working Poverty across the Metro-Nonmetro Divide: A Quarter Century in Perspective, 1979–2003." *Rural Sociology* 75:363–87.

Slack, Tim. 2014. "Work in Rural America in the Era of Globalization." Pp. 573–90 in *Rural America in a Globalizing World: Problems and Prospects for the 2010s*, edited by C. Bailey, L. Jensen, and E. Ransom. Morgantown: West Virginia University Press.

Slack, Tim and Leif Jensen. 2002. "Race, Ethnicity, and Underemployment in Nonmetropolitan America: A 30-Year Profile." *Rural Sociology* 67:208–33.

Slack, Tim, Joachim Singelman, Kayla Fontenot, Dudley Poston, Rogelio Saenz, and Carlos Siordia. 2006. "Poverty in the Texas Borderland and Lower Mississippi Delta: A Comparative Analysis of Differences by Family Type." *Demographic Research* 20:353–76.

Smith, Michael D. and Richard S. Krannich. 2000. "'Culture Clash' Revisited: Newcomer and Longer-Term Residents' Attitudes toward Land Use, Development, and Environmental Issues in Rural Communities in the Rocky Mountain West." *Rural Sociology* 65:396–421.

Snipp, C. Matthew. 1989. *American Indians: First of the Land.* New York: Russell Sage Foundation.

Snyder, Anastasia R. and Diane K. McLaughlin. 2004. "Female-Headed Families and Poverty in Rural America." *Rural Sociology* 69:127–49.

Somers, Margaret R. and Fred Block. 2005. "From Poverty to Perversity: Ideas, Markets, and Institutions over 200 Years of Welfare Debate." *American Sociological Review* 70:260–87.

Sparke, Matthew. 2007. "Everywhere But Always Somewhere: Critical Geographies of the Global South." *The Global South* 1(1–2):117–26.

Stommes, Eileen S. and Dennis M. Brown. 2002. "Transportation in Rural America: Issues for the 21st Century." *Rural America* 16(4):2–10.

Theobald, Paul and Kathy Wood. 2010. "Learning to Be Rural: Identity Lessons from History, Schooling, and the U.S. Corporate Media." Pp. 17–33 in *Rural Education for the Twenty-First Century: Identity, Place and Community in a Globalizing World*, edited by Kai A. Schafft and Alicia Youngblood Jackson. University Park: Pennsylvania State University Press.

Thorpe, Jodie and Erinch Sahan. 2013. "Power, Rights, and Inclusive Markets: Public Policies that Support Small Scale Agriculture." Oxfam Briefing Note. Oxford: Oxfam.

Tiehen, Laura, Dean Jolliffe, and Craig Gundersen. 2012. *Alleviating Poverty in the United States: The Critical Role of SNAP Benefits,* ERR-132, USDA, Economic Research Service, April.

Tickamyer, Ann R. 2007. "Rural Poverty." Pp. 411–26 in *Handbook of Rural Studies*, edited by P. Cloke, T. Marsden, and P. Mooney. New York: Sage.

U.S. Census Bureau. 2013a. "POV41: Region, Division and Type of Residence—Poverty Status for All People, Family Members and Unrelated Individuals by Family Structure: 2011." Retrieved June 20, 2013. (http://www.census.gov/hhes/www/cpstables/032012/pov/toc.htm).

U.S. Census Bureau 2013b. *American Factfinder*. Retrieved June 21, 2013 (http://factfinder2.census.gov/faces/nav/jsf/pages/index.xhtml).

U.S. Census Bureau. 2013c. *American Factfinder*. Retrieved June 20, 2013 (http://factfinder2.census.gov/faces/tableservices/jsf/pages/productview.xhtml?pid=DEC_10_DP_DPDP1).

U.S. Census Bureau. 2013d. "POV42: Region, Division and Type of Residence—Poverty Status for People in Families by Family Structure: 2011." (http://www.census.gov/hhes/www/cpstables/032012/pov/POV42_000.htm).

U.S. Census Bureau. 2013e. "POV43: Region, Division and Type of Residence—Poverty Status for People in Families with Related Children Under 18 by Family Structure: 2011." Retrieved June 21, 2013 (http://www.census.gov/hhes/www/cpstables/032012/pov/POV43_100.htm).

Ver Ploeg, Michele, Vince Breneman, Tracey Farrigan, Karen Hamrick, David Hopkins, Phillip Kaufman, Biing-Hwan Lin, Mark Nord, Travis A. Smith, Ryan William, Kelly Kinnison, Carol Olander, Anita Singh, and Elizabeth Tuckermanty. 2009. *Access to Affordable and Nutritious Food—Measuring and Understanding Food Deserts and Their Consequences: Report to Congress.* Administrative Publication No. (AP-036). Washington DC: Economic Research Service, USDA.

Walker, Alan and Carol Walker. 1997. *Britain Divided: The Growth of Social Exclusion in the 1980s and 1990s.* London: Child Poverty Action Group.

Wray, Matt. 2006. *Not Quite White: White Trash and the Boundaries of Whiteness.* Durham, NC: Duke University Press.

Ziliak, James (Ed.). 2012. *Appalachian Legacy: Economic Opportunity After the War on Poverty.* New York: Brookings Institution Press.

CHAPTER 15

POOR NEIGHBORHOODS
IN THE METROPOLIS

MARY PATTILLO AND JOHN N. ROBINSON III

INTRODUCTION

THE image of a poor neighborhood in the United States is inevitably one of a place located within city boundaries. While this portrayal has long distinguished U.S. cities from those in Europe, Latin America, Africa, and some Asian countries, where poverty is more often concentrated at the urban periphery, spatial patterns have recently begun to converge. Hence, our primary goal in this chapter is to argue for a metropolitan scope for the study of neighborhood poverty—or what Hanlon, Vicino, and Short (2006) call the "new metropolitan reality"—as opposed to one that is fixated on the central city. Thinking about poverty in the metropolis has four advantages: it recognizes the new reality in the United States where the proportion of people who are poor (i.e., the poverty rate) is higher in cities than in suburbs, but the number of poor people (i.e., the poor population) is greater in suburbs than in cities (Kneebone and Berube 2013); it brings into view sprawling metropolitan areas in the U.S. South and West, and especially their growing Latino populations; and it highlights the fact that poor neighborhoods are the products of a metropolitan and global political economy and not the simple aggregation or "selection" of poor residents. The fourth advantage of a metropolitan focus is that it allows for more accurate international comparisons.[1]

This chapter proceeds as follows. First we argue that it is only possible to understand neighborhood poverty in the metropolis through the integration of three bodies of research—the political economy of place, the economic causes of concentrated poverty, and household mobility patterns—which are often seen as separate theoretical paradigms. Second, we explore recent population trends in the United States that support this new metropolitan perspective on poverty. Next, we look at neighborhood poverty on the ground by highlighting the ethnographic research on poor neighborhoods in particular places; in that section we also highlight empirical gaps in the literature and reiterate the need for theoretical integration. Finally, we briefly introduce the research on the effects of poor neighborhoods on residents in order to question if current policy approaches are equipped to address the new metropolitan reality of poverty.

CAUSES OF NEIGHBORHOOD POVERTY

There are numerous causes of the uneven geography of poverty within metropolitan areas. Here, we focus on three explanations that have received extensive scholarly treatment: the political economy of place, the labor market changes shaping the inner city, and household mobility patterns. While these literatures have generally developed along separate trajectories, we argue for the importance of their synthesis.

Political Economy of Place

A political economy approach to the metropolis begins with recognizing urban space as configured by the demands of capitalist production and accumulation; the commodification of space; and the resulting social conflicts between people and groups with unequal political, economic, and symbolic resources. Pioneered in the work of French social theorist Henri Lefebvre and elaborated by French and British sociologists Manuel Castells and David Harvey, among others, political economy theory illustrates how local formations such as homelessness, gated communities, malls, downtown office buildings, condo conversions, informal settlements, and foreclosures are all manifestations of "uneven development" (Smith 1984) linked to capitalist processes such as labor reproduction; financialization; and the globalization of law, consumption, and information (Sassen 2001). As a result of these processes, some groups have privileged and unbridled access to urban resources—effective sanitation, clean water, reliable electricity, good schools—and others are completely excluded, through price, law, violence, and other forms of repression in which state and capitalist actors collude. This political economy approach has been applied widely to cities in Latin America (Portes and Roberts 2005; Portes and Walton 1976), Europe (Brenner 2004), and in explicitly cross-national comparisons (Castells 1985; see Walton 1993 and Zukin 1980 for reviews).

Logan and Molotch (1987) largely set the agenda for the political economy of urban places in the United States. They argue that the poor have a different economic relationship to urban landscapes than elites, deriving "use value" where elites are interested primarily in "exchange value." In other words, housing and land not only provide a sense of home and community but are also commodities in local property markets. Additionally, the need to improve the profitability of land-use stands central to the ways in which coalitions of economic and political elites (or "growth machines") govern cities, which in turn shapes the neighborhood contexts within which poor households pursue their livelihoods. Thus, seeking to achieve the highest possible return on land investments, elites aim for increasing rents, making it difficult for poor people to occupy urban space. Relegating poor people to the least attractive land concentrates poverty, which later can be the justification for the wholesale displacement of poor people through urban renewal if and when such land once again shows potential for profit (Hyra 2008; Hirsch 1983).

The state plays a key role in growth machines primarily through two levels of policymaking: local and federal (the regional, or metropolitan, scale will be discussed in a later section). The local sphere is uniquely relevant to land use in the United States because the authority to control land use is among the powers commonly delegated from states to local governments (Miller 2008; Orfield 2005). Indeed, the jurisdiction of local government over matters pertaining to land use is widely regarded as "the essence of home rule" (Barron 2002/2003:2318), a term that refers to the culturally entrenched idea in the United States that "local government, the government closest to the people, is the best government," and why "local citizens oppose nearly anything that would threaten the existence, powers, services or autonomy of their local governments" (Norris 2001:562). Moreover, a large body of research indicates that the U.S. metropolitan landscape has experienced ongoing governmental fragmentation and diffusion of authority, thereby frustrating attempts to coordinate metropolitan-wide antipoverty efforts (Adams 2008; Miller 2008; Dreier, Mollenkopf, and Swanstrom 2004; Agnew and Smith 2002; Doherty and Stone 1999; Burns 1994).

Land-use practices are shaped by more than growth or antigrowth alone; discrimination also determines how urban space is allocated, as exemplified by popular protests against subsidized housing in particular neighborhoods and communities (Scally and Koenig 2012; Nguyen, Basolo, and Tiwari 2013; Goetz 2008). Likewise, through inclusionary or exclusionary zoning, regulation of land use can either open up or close off neighborhoods and municipalities to housing that is affordable to economically diverse populations (Orfield 2005; Briggs 2005). Such policies directly create or dismantle barriers of access to nonpoor neighborhoods.

Cities and suburbs also vary in how capable they are of addressing the socioeconomic needs of their residents (Weir 2011; Orfield 2002), and this bears directly on revenues and expenses. The primary responsibility of local government is to collect property taxes. More expensive property, accessible only to higher income buyers, translates into more fiscal resources with which to address resident demands (Orfield 2002). The presence of high-income populations often means fewer demands for social services. On the other hand, low-cost property, with low-income residents generates less revenue but greater need for public services. Hence, the fragmentation of municipalities and lack of collective resource sharing or coordinated services means that some places will have low tax burdens and high-quality services and amenities, while others will have to tax their already struggling residents just to maintain basic services, and will over time lose their more affluent residents, leading to further segregation by income.

The federal government is also a key player in such patterns. Before the Depression and the New Deal, the federal government was not a major actor in addressing local poverty, but through the 1930s and by the late 1960s the amount of federal aid going to cities had reached historic levels (Wilson and Aponte 1985). Federal antipoverty initiatives have been characterized by differential investment, regulation, and enforcement across space, which has together promoted and exacerbated class segregation and poverty concentration. There is a robust literature on how the imbalanced placement of federally funded public housing along with the federal subsidization of highways and suburban home construction and financing have worked to concentrate poverty in some places and limit it in others (Turner, Popkin, and Rawlings 2009; Bennett, Smith, and Wright 2006; Gotham 2002; Roisman 1995; Schill and Wachter 1995; Jackson 1985; Hirsch 1983). Even more specifically, discriminatory practices against African Americans in home appraisals for the purpose of federal mortgage insurance, in the implementation of the GI Bill, and in unscrupulous bank practices have created inequalities across places by race (Satter 2009; Freund 2007; Katznelson 2005; Squires 1994; Jackson 1985). The 2008 housing crisis is perhaps the most explicit illustration of how global capitalism shapes urban inequality (Aalbers 2012; Rugh and Massey 2010), leaving low- to moderate-income neighborhoods with boarded-up homes while the neighborhoods of financiers have grown richer. Moreover, new capitalist technologies have expanded residential mortgage debt into developing and emerging market countries for the extraction of profit from middle-income people and places across the globe (Sassen 2012).

Therefore, the political economy perspective is foundational for understanding the causes of the uneven geography of poverty because it foregrounds the commodification of space, the use of places for the generation of profit, the management of labor through the control of space, and the coordination of governance regimes and capitalist interests to create landscapes of advantage and disadvantage. This conceptual framework is crucial for putting in context the economic and mobility factors that also create high-poverty neighborhoods.

Economic Changes

Scholarship on the economic transformation of the U.S. inner city builds on the political economy of place, even though it is "not explicitly anchored in the urban political economy tradition" (Walton 1993:316). In *The Truly Disadvantaged*, Wilson (1987) showed that between 1960 and 1980 the number of high-poverty neighborhoods grew substantially, and the proportion of poor people living in poor neighborhoods also grew. These trends led to what Wilson called "concentration effects," the finding that poor residents living in high-poverty neighborhoods were worse off on many social measures than poor residents living in lower poverty neighborhoods. Wilson identified the relocation of industry out of the urban core, leaving inner city communities without either the economic benefits or social stability of regular employment, as the structural change most responsible for the rise of concentrated urban poverty (see also Sugrue 1996). This transformation had many layers, including deindustrialization (Harrison and Bluestone 1988), plus the movement of remaining low-skill manufacturing jobs to suburban areas and beyond, leaving urban poor (black) households—who were less likely to own cars (Kasarda 1990)—in a situation of "spatial mismatch" with respect to jobs for which they were qualified (Kain 1968, 1965). Simultaneously, the urban core increasingly became the site of high-skilled, white-collar employment, creating a growing skills mismatch between poorly educated urban households and the nearest jobs (Kasarda 1990; see also Neckerman and Kirschenman 1991).

In her study of 12 poor areas in England and Wales, Lupton (2003) similarly stresses the importance of changes in the economy. She lists the "disappearance of work" as one of the key causes of concentrated poverty and reports that "the 1970s and 1980s were periods of catastrophic employment decline. Two distinct processes were underway: the ongoing decline of traditional industries and the collapse of the manufacturing sector" (2003:46). Hence, Wilson's (1996) "new urban poverty" thesis, and the abundant scholarship that draws on it, highlights structural changes in the labor market that led to high rates of unemployment, labor market nonparticipation, and income poverty in neighborhoods with low-skilled residents, with broad reverberations beyond neighborhoods to political and social institutions (Anyon 1997; Judd and Swanstrom 1994).

Household Mobility

While political economy provides a macro-account for how places are made and sustained, and economic arguments show how places change around people, a third and even more proximate element in shaping neighborhood poverty is how families change in and move through places as a result of their own economic and residential mobility. Household-level factors influence neighborhood poverty in two main ways: through changes in household poverty status (i.e., economic mobility), and through household movement and settlement (i.e., residential mobility). For example, the increase in the number of high-poverty neighborhoods through the 1970s and 80s was due partly to the loss of stable employment in the urban core, which plunged many households into poverty (Jargowsky 1997). Likewise, Quillian (1999) finds that during the early 1980s recession, changes in household-poverty status caused a substantial increase in the number of extremely poor neighborhoods. Hence, even when families do not move, a neighborhood's poverty rate can increase if their and their neighbors' socioeconomic fortunes decline.

Patterns of movement and settlement also transform neighborhoods. Wilson posited that macrolevel forces, like the 1980s recession, did not alone cause a spike in neighborhood poverty rates but rather occurred simultaneous to the out-migration of black middle-income households, presumably to white neighborhoods (see also Jargowsky

1997; Gramlich et al. 1992; Jargowsky and Bane 1991; Greene 1991). There has been vigorous debate about the importance of black middle-class out-migration for explaining the increase in high-poverty neighborhoods in the 1970s and 1980s and, perhaps, into the 1990s. High and stable rates of black/white segregation even for middle-class blacks highlights the importance of residential segregation for concentrating poverty, especially in African American neighborhoods (South et al. 2005; Massey et al. 1994; Denton and Massey 1988; Massey and Denton 1987; Massey 1979). On the other hand, evidence of increasing class segregation among African Americans in the 1970s and 1980s supports the out-migration thesis (Massey and Fischer 2003; Massey and Eggers 1990).

Reconciling these poles, Quillian (1999) finds that middle-class blacks were significantly more likely than poor blacks to move to white nonpoor neighborhoods from 1970 to 1990, but the white neighborhoods to which they moved were experiencing rapid white population loss and increases in poverty at the same time. Hence, while the out-migration of nonpoor blacks has contributed to the increase in high-poverty (black) neighborhoods, black middle-class households largely settled in either white neighborhoods that were experiencing a racial and class transition or in black nonpoor neighborhoods that were often adjacent to areas of high poverty (Sharkey 2011; Sampson 2011; Pattillo-McCoy 2000). Quillian (2012) also calls attention to a "third segregation" in which blacks and Hispanics experience heightened neighborhood poverty due to their proximity to poor other-race households. That is, for example, even when blacks and Hispanics live around whites, they tend to live around *poor* as opposed to affluent whites. Finally, the probability of moving into a high-poverty neighborhood is much greater and the probability of leaving a high-poverty neighborhood is much lower for blacks and Latinos of all classes than for whites (Sampson and Sharkey 2008; South et al. 2005).

To summarize our framework for understanding the stratification of places in the metropolis, it rests on the assertion that neighborhoods, cities, and regions are the spatial instantiations of efforts to generate profits through (dis)investments in land, labor, and the infrastructure necessary to sustain capitalism. Withholding resources from some places allows for their accumulation in others and also serves to spatially marginalize and barely maintain an unnecessary, surplus, or exploited labor force. At the same time, post–World War II deindustrialization and the resulting decline in jobs for central city residents has been a primary driver of concentrated poverty in the United States and Europe. The particular mechanisms in Latin American, Asian, and African cities (and even postcommunist Eastern European cities) are similar but are more tied to international economic policies that have caused both intra- and international urban migrations (Auyero 2011; Logan 2008; Portes and Roberts 2005; Simone 2010, 2004). Finally, changing neighborhood demographics—household-level downward mobility plus in the case of the U.S. nonpoor blacks leaving poor neighborhoods but not fully escaping the holds of racial segregation and neighborhood disadvantage—further contributed to increases in concentrated poverty. In the next section, we discuss demographic trends that illustrate the new metropolitan reality of urban poverty.

TRENDS IN METROPOLITAN POVERTY

The "new urban poverty" framework that was applicable to the period from about 1970 through the 1990s must be significantly revised in order to account for the new metropolitan reality of the twenty-first century. As the geographic scope of poverty has changed over time, so too has the prevalence of high-poverty neighborhoods. Jargowsky (1997) first documented that concentrated poverty had doubled in U.S. cities from 1970 to 1990, but later showed that the population living in high poverty neighborhoods had declined by 24 percent in the 1990s (Jargowsky 2003). Why did concentrated poverty decline so dramatically during the 1990s? Many scholars point to the importance of economic over residential mobility as the answer. Cooke (2010) and Wagmiller (2011), for example, both find that household-level economic mobility was a strong predictor of decline in neighborhood poverty rates, while residential mobility proved mostly insignificant. In other words, the strong economy in the 1990s was the primary driver in reducing neighborhood poverty. Hence, it is not surprising that major economic crises in the 2000s pushed trends in the opposite direction. Kneebone et al. (2011) show that, although the situation has not returned to 1990 levels, the number of high-poverty neighborhoods increased from 2000 to 2009. Notably, concentrated poverty rose twice as much in suburban areas as in cities, and these trends were particularly pronounced in the Midwest and South.

Taking a metropolitan perspective requires us to recognize how relationships among central cities and suburbs shape neighborhood poverty. Three interrelated factors are important for understanding the suburban context of poverty: inner-ring suburban decline, geographic sprawl, and Hispanic immigration (Weir 2011).[2] First, a growing body of work confirms that inner-ring suburbs are now host to problems of social and economic decline typically associated with the inner city (Hanlon 2009; Leigh and Lee 2005; Lucy and Phillips 2000, 2006). According to Orfield (2002), "at-risk" suburbs, many of them inner ring, account for 56 percent of the suburban population and 40 percent of the entire metropolitan population. These can be long-established poor suburbs or declining industrial hubs, but what unites them is high social need and limited fiscal resources (Mikelbank 2004). Closer to the urban core, inner suburbs have been associated with more migrants from the central city, more residential overcrowding, more welfare recipients, and more female-headed households, resulting in a deeper form of economic distress than found elsewhere in suburbia (Holliday and Dwyer 2009).

However, some have challenged the idea that inner suburbs house the lion's share of suburban poverty. Hanlon et al. (2006) and Hanlon (2009) show that many inner suburbs—particularly those in the Northeast—are affluent, and some struggling suburbs are not in the inner ring. Therefore, "postwar" more accurately describes suburbs that are beset by the kinds of problems usually attributed to those in the inner ring. Likewise, Holliday and Dwyer (2009) find that although inner suburbs hold the largest share of the suburban poor *population*, the modal suburban poor *neighborhood* is located in a suburb composed of housing built after 1970, which is often not in the inner ring. Forty percent of poor suburban neighborhoods are located in areas built after 1970, and their racial and geographic profile contrasts sharply with that of poor inner suburbs, containing fewer minorities and twice as many whites, and including semirural areas at the edge of the metropolis (Holliday and Dwyer 2009; Orfield 2002). Thus, suburban poverty is not limited to a declining inner ring but exists in various forms across the suburban landscape (Dwyer 2010).

Inner-ring suburbs and sprawl are two sides of the same coin. Sprawl fuels the growth of suburban poverty through a "demand-supply nexus" that promotes green-field development and, consequently, disinvestment in and "devalorisation" of some older and closer-in suburbs (Short et al. 2007). According to Briggs (2005), this trend has been marked by rates of land consumption two times the rate of population growth, particularly in the Northeast and Midwest where population growth has been slow. To combat sprawl, some states have implemented "urban growth boundaries," which limit the amount of developable land at the edge and promote infill in central cities and older inner-ring suburbs (Pendall et al. 2005; Orfield 2005). These policies have been most successful in places where they are mandatory, are part of comprehensive statewide or metropolitan-wide planning, and are subject to oversight and enforcement—features that tend to undermine local home rule (Orfield 2005) and may result in gentrification or NIMBYism (Pendall et al. 2005).

Finally, increased Hispanic immigration to the suburbs has also been a key trend in new metropolitan poverty. Most Hispanic immigrants now migrate directly to suburban areas, bypassing the city (Singer et al. 2008). This is noteworthy because Hispanic households are the least likely to escape high-poverty neighborhoods once they live in them and are far more likely than whites to move into them (South et al. 2005). The new Hispanic immigrant boomtowns feature low-wage employment, higher levels of poverty, greater Hispanic-white segregation, and considerable linguistic isolation, distinguishing them from the established destinations in which second-generation Hispanics are more likely to live (Lichter et al. 2010; Crowley et al. 2006; Kandel and Parrado 2005). Hanlon (2009) finds that Hispanics mostly settle in western inner-ring suburbs in which up to 45 percent of residents are Hispanic (such as outside Los Angeles), and southern ones with a more mixed demographic and a slightly poorer economic profile (such as the suburbs of Washington, DC and Atlanta), where their population nearly tripled between 1980 and 2000 (Holliday and Dwyer 2009). The size, growth, and socioeconomic situation of the Hispanic population will be a primary driver of metropolitan patterns of poverty and inequality in the future.

NEIGHBORHOOD EXPERIENCES

While poor neighborhoods are commonly assumed to be bad places to live, poor people's attachments to their neighborhoods is a common theme in the literature (Arena

2012; Pattillo 2007; Bennett et al. 2006; Venkatesh 2000; Gans 1962). In this section we turn to the (primarily qualitative) literature that describes the lived reality in poor neighborhoods. We lay out three major paradigms in the study of poor neighborhoods, one that emphasizes their *disadvantage*, a second that emphasizes the *assets and resilience* of neighborhood residents and institutions, and a third that attempts a balance by focusing on the structural and cultural *heterogeneity* within and between poor neighborhoods. Although there is empirical support for all three characterizations, most nonetheless emphasize one or another position.[3] We also offer suggestions for new research and theoretical directions.

The "disadvantaged" paradigm—rooted in a long tradition (Clark 1965; Du Bois 1899; Addams 1895; Booth 1891)—stresses the pathologies of poor neighborhoods. Authors in this camp do not intend to blame poor people for their plight, minimize their humanity, or downplay the heroic survival strategies that residents develop. Instead, they seek to expose the harsh realities in poor neighborhoods to generate outrage that might compel the public to action.

Wacquant (2008) provides a fitting example of this approach, writing: "The hyperghetto of century's end is a despised and loathed space from which nearly everyone is desperately trying to escape" (2008:62). He details how poor black Chicago residents generally lack checking accounts, often report not having a best friend, and live in places where "commercial establishments are as scarce as abandoned buildings are plentiful" (2008:122). Such depictions apply equally to nonblack U.S. neighborhoods. In Los Angeles, Salvadorans and Guatemalans, for example, face the "shattering experience" of migrating to the deteriorated, crime-ridden public housing projects in the city (Hamilton and Chinchilla 2001:53). This scholarship features descriptions of absence, isolation, and abandonment (Desmond 2012a; Barnes 2005; Cummings 1998;Wilson 1996; Kotlowitz 1991), that worsen the individual experience of financial and material hardship (Desmond 2012b; MacLeod 2009; Rosen and Venkatesh 2008; Edin and Lein 1997), and that are exacerbated by the omnipresence of violence by neighbors and/or the police (Rios 2011; Jones 2010; Goffman 2009; Miller 2008; Popkin 2000; Anderson 1999; Bourgois 1995).

Outside of the United States, Roy (2003) chronicles life in squatter settlements on the outskirts of Calcutta. Employing a political economy theoretical framework, Roy shows how communism that is "as comfortable with global capital as with the sons of the soil" (2003:10) leads to welfare state retrenchment, rural-to-urban "distress migration," and the emergence of the shantytowns where Roy did her fieldwork. There Roy met Mala and her family and wrote: "There is no infrastructure in this settlement—no running water, no toilets, and no electricity. The railway tracks are ominously close, and when she is away, Mala often has to tie some of her children to the post of the bed to ensure that they do not get run over by the trains" (2003:79–80). Elsewhere, Auyero (2000a) finds that the survival strategies of Argentinian shantytown residents are undermined by interpersonal violence, state repression, and mass unemployment, thereby plunging such neighborhoods even deeper into social isolation. Indeed, the international literature sometimes argues explicitly that the disadvantaged perspective is the only valid treatment of neighborhood poverty. For example, De la Rocha (2006) finds that macroeconomic changes have diminished the capacity of the Mexican urban working poor to maintain networks of social exchange. The theoretical implication here is that researchers should focus less on survival among the urban poor and more on the structural transformations that "erode their capacity for survival" (De la Rocha 2001:72).

Studies that stress the disadvantaged character of poor neighborhoods argue that allowing such places to persist is nothing short of criminal. Writing about poor neighborhoods in the developing world, Mike Davis's (2006:47) words are so strong that one can nearly smell them: "[T]he principal function of the Third World urban edge remains as a human dump. In some cases, urban waste and unwanted immigrants end up together, as in such infamous 'garbage slums' as the aptly named Quarantina outside Beirut, Hillat Kusha outside Khartoum, Santa Cruz Meyehualco in Mexico City, the former Smoky Mountain in Manila, or the huge Dhapa dump and slum on the fringe of Kolkata" (also see Biehl 2005; Caldeira 2000; Roberts 2005; Brockerhoff and Brennan 1998; Scheper-Hughes 1992). Such depictions are meant to be difficult to read so that apathy is not an option.

The assets and resilience paradigm is partly a response to this singular focus on disadvantage, which some scholars argue contributes (unintentionally) to the stigma that attaches to poor people and poor places (Baeten 2001; di Leonardo 1998; Gans 1995). However, a focus on assets comes from the same empirical observations that yield stories of despair. Hence, Wacquant's alarming appraisal of the South Side of Chicago is countered by Pashup et al.'s (2005) findings that some poor black families in Chicago chose not to relocate to more affluent neighborhoods when offered the money to do so because they were too busy to look for an apartment or because they rejected outright the requirement of moving to a predominately white neighborhood to receive the subsidy. Fully another third of nonmovers feared leaving the familiarity of their neighborhoods, which suggests that a sense of familiarity is an important psychological asset. Such findings call into question the notion that escape, fueled by uniform suffering and oppression, is the predominant ethos in these neighborhoods. Disadvantage exists alongside leisure, hope, familiarity, comfort, and resilience.

Sánchez-Jankowski (2008), Venkatesh (2000), and Small (2004) write about multiethnic public housing projects in Los Angeles, New York, Chicago, and Boston as places with high levels of social capital from which residents obtain emotional and instrumental benefits. Feldman and Stall (2004) and Williams (2004) show how such networks are mobilized for political activism. On the international front, Simone (2004) describes economic sophistication and ingenuity in four cities in Africa and the Middle East where structured informal economies provide stability where the state cannot. Auyero (2000b) highlights the "problem-solving networks" established between poor families and local political brokers in Buenos Aires that help shantytown residents acquire valuable goods. Finally, the everyday resistance to an antipoverty initiative by laid-off urban workers in Harbin, China, helped change the rhetoric of national policymakers (Cho 2010). Many ethnographies document how residents of poor neighborhoods survive and, sometimes, thrive (Elliott et al. 2007; Furstenberg 1999; Newman 1999). Without romanticizing poverty or the racial exclusion that often creates it, such accounts focus on how people take what good they can find in their neighborhoods and use it to get ahead.

Other studies focus on the human capacity for creativity, despite oppression. Focusing on how "segregation" has begotten "congregation," Lipsitz (2011:126) writes: "It is not that members of aggrieved groups are likely to like each other more than members of other groups like each other, but rather that their linked fate requires them to recognize 'something left to love' in each other as a means of preserving it in themselves." That "something left to love" is the motivation for public art, urban gardening, and community beautification efforts in U.S. cities (Wherry 2011; White 2011, 2010; Medoff and Sklar 1994); as well as for the iconization of criminal bosses in Kingston, Jamaica, through dance-hall lyrics, street dances, and murals (Jaffe 2012); and even for the absurdist humor and storytelling practices Brazilian women employ to cope with the hardships of everyday life in *favelas* (Goldstein 2003).

The empirical findings of intense disadvantage alongside rejuvenating assets and resilience have produced a literature that emphasizes the heterogeneity in poor neighborhoods. For example, Jargowsky (1996:598) presents an array of demographic portraits of high-poverty neighborhoods across the country and concludes that "the popular and politically exploitable image of ghettos as places where everyone drops out of school, where no one works, and where everyone receives welfare is a gross distortion of reality." Newman and Chen (2007) make a similar ethnographic observation about the invisible population of workers in poor New York neighborhoods. Small and McDermott (2006) look at the relationship between the number of commercial establishments and neighborhood poverty, and find that the number of businesses per capita actually increases as neighborhood poverty rates increase, and that "whether high-poverty neighborhoods are deprived of organizations or not depends greatly from city to city" (p. 1713). Finally, characterizing findings from a comprehensive study of urban marginality across Europe (Musterd et al. 2006), Musterd (2008:109–10) concludes:

> [T]here is more difference than commonality between the various local contexts. We found neighbourhoods in contexts where integration was supported by strong welfare states, well-functioning labour markets and strong local social support networks (Hoogvliet, Rotterdam); neighbourhoods where the welfare state was still trying to redistribute affluence, but where the labour market failed; however, where local social networks did offer opportunities (St Pauli, Hamburg) or cases where local social networks hardly offered support (La Courneuve, Paris). We also found examples of deprived neighbourhoods, where the role of the state was almost absent, but where the labour market still offered chances (Pool Farm, Birmingham). Incidentally, we even found examples of neighbourhoods that come close to the experiences in the black ghetto in the USA, since there appeared to be no welfare state intervention, no labour market opportunities and no local support networks (Scampia, Naples).

This body of work illustrates that there is no archetypal, representative poor neighborhood (Small and Feldman 2011; Sessoms and Wolch 2008; Small 2007, 2008; Abu-Lughod 1997), thereby challenging any blanket characterization across the United States and surely across countries.

Even when places seem demographically and structurally very similar, heterogeneity and contingency are important. Studying two Mexican American neighborhoods in California, Dohan (2003) finds distinct strategies for making ends meet in otherwise similar places. In Los Angeles, residents combined work in the low-wage formal economy with informal and illegal work (hustling), whereas residents of the San José barrio used "overwork" as their way to survive and get ahead. While these two neighborhoods had much in common, each generated mutually distinct local "common-senses" about the most appropriate and reasonable ways to respond to a low-wage labor market. Even within the same neighborhood, Harding (2010) finds that young men in Boston's poor neighborhoods are exposed to a wide range of possible life trajectories, indeed a greater variety than boys who live in nonpoor neighborhoods.

Hence, the findings about life in poor neighborhoods range from the most harrowing to the most inspiring, and include all the local and individual contingencies in between. Still, this review uncovers some important gaps in our knowledge. For example, while there is a large and growing literature on urban marginality in the Global South (Simone 2010; Smart and Smart 2003), ethnographic detail on the lived experiences in poor neighborhoods in Europe is lacking. Important gaps remain in the U.S. literature also. Facing the new metropolitan reality of poor neighborhoods requires a shift in both data collection and theoretical approach. Empirically, it shifts attention to research on the suburbs, on the southern and western regions of the United States, and on poor white neighborhoods. Theoretically, it demands a tighter integration of the political economy approach into studies of poverty and place. We discuss each of these later.

While demographers have empirically revealed the nature of growing poverty in the suburbs, qualitative research on suburban poverty is very limited. This void is at least partially explained by the difficulty of describing "the suburbs" as a distinct entity. According to Murphy (2010), suburbs that look very similar to central city poor areas have different needs from suburbs that have recently become poor due to the sudden departure of a major employer; and both of those types of suburbs are different from ones that are generally affluent but have hidden pockets of intense poverty. In this way, the diversity of suburban poverty thwarts attempts to fit it into the symbolic landscape of inner city poverty discourse that is shared among researchers, funders, and policymakers.

Nonetheless, the existing research on suburban poverty offers some important new themes to be explored. In her ethnographic account of life in the St. Louis suburb of East St. Louis, Hamer (2011) details what it means not to have a car in areas with no public transportation: "Those nuisances [of not having a car] magnify into Shakespearean agonies, torturing East St. Louisans twenty-four/seven in their daily personal interactions, in their professional options, and in their sense of self-worth and full participation in the opportunities and benefits of national life" (2011:58). In other research,

Murphy and Wallace (2010), Zuberi (2010), Allard (2009), and Allard and Roth (2010) find that the social and youth services infrastructure in the suburbs is thin, stretched financially, and often exhibits prohibitive barriers to utilization or participation. On the positive side, Briggs et al. (2010) and Rubinowitz and Rosenbaum (2000) highlight the significantly increased feelings of safety for poor families who moved to nonpoor suburbs through housing-opportunity programs. Given the lower densities, greater travel distances, greater proportion of single-family homes, and a host of other differences in the built environment and social composition, there is considerable room for new research on suburban poor neighborhoods and their effects.

Other gaps in the literature are even wider. Qualitative research on the western region of United States (with the exception of Los Angeles) and the (nonrural) South is limited (for an exception see Federal Reserve Bank and Brookings 2008; Robinson 2014; Rushing 2009; for a review of research on the urban South, see Lloyd 2012). Mainly because of Hurricane Katrina, there are a growing number of studies of poverty in New Orleans (Arena 2012; Gotham 2007; Gotham and Greenberg 2013), and the West and the South both appear in research on the national transformation of public housing (Fraser et al. 2012; Kleit and Carnegie 2011; Tester et al. 2011; Popkin, Levy, and Buron 2009; Fraser and Kick 2007; Kleit 2005; Bayor 2003), yet few of these studies offer textured ethnographic portraits of people's lived experience. Likewise, the qualitative study of white (not to mention Asian or Native American) poverty in cities and suburbs is nearly nonexistent (for an exception see Hartigan 1999), and the quantitative research is also thin (for exceptions see Jargowsky 1997; Krivo and Peterson 1996). Research on whites more frequently emphasizes their "working-class" identities (McDermott 2006; Carr 2005; Kefalas 2003; Ehrenreich 2001; Fine and Weis 1998). Hence, the new directions awaiting young researchers are clear.

The need for more conversation across theoretical frameworks is as important as new empirical studies. *Urban Fortunes*, the foundational text in U.S. urban political economy studies, and *The Truly Disadvantaged*—which holds the same position in the study of changing labor markets, economic and residential mobility, and neighborhood effects—were both published in 1987, and they seemed to have inspired a generation (or two) of scholarship that is largely independent of one another (for some exceptions see Marwell 2007; Pattillo 2007; Barnes 2005). One challenge lies in the unit, or scale, of analysis. Studying the political economy of urban regions directs researchers to the resources, social networks, interests, and decisions of local and nonlocal elites (e.g., multinational corporation executives, city boosters, federal policymakers, foundations, elected officials) and as made manifest in contracts, plans, investments, laws, and financial practices. In contrast, documenting the local impact of a changing labor market or how movement across neighborhoods affects racial or class segregation takes individuals and small geographic areas as the units of analysis. Yet, we argue that these two perspectives must be joined in order to fully understand why and how poor and rich neighborhoods are formed and maintained.

As one example, in his study of the gentrification of poor African American neighborhoods in New York and Chicago, Hyra (2008) documents the increase in foreign direct investment and the centralization of corporate headquarters and their highly paid professional workers as the crucial global context for the dramatic rise in neighborhood property values and on-the-ground battles over cultural and residential displacement in these two cities. Amplifying our point about the need for theoretical integration, Hyra writes:

> While some scholars view external neighborhood factors, such as economic globalization, federal policy, and citywide politics, as the driving forces related to inner city revitalization, others contend that internal variables, including neighborhood-based organizational efforts, are more important. . . . To focus on either external or internal factors is shortsighted. (p. 20)

The new metropolitan reality makes it untenable to focus on neighborhoods as discrete geographic, economic, or political formations since the movement of poor people across the metropolis (and, indeed, across metropolises across the world) illustrates the mutual constitution of places; poverty is concentrated in (or confined to) one place because wealth is concentrated (or protected) in another.

Scholars of European urbanization generally have a stronger critical political economy tradition as illustrated in the Marxist urbanist theories discussed earlier and in the language of urban "social exclusion" (Mingione 1996). Moreover, recent debates about "ghettos" in Europe (Peach 2009; Wacquant 2008) illustrate the benefits of comparative research for foregrounding considerations of citizenship, (post-) colonial histories, and employment policies. This is also the case in the research on cities in Latin America, Asia, and Africa, where the international political economy is always present in the analysis of even the most local experiences. This model of linking the interests and actions of government and capitalist actors to the description of neighborhood labor markets and household mobility needs to become the new orthodoxy in the study of poor neighborhoods in the metropolitan context.

NEIGHBORHOOD EFFECTS AND POLICY RESPONSES

Central to the study of neighborhood poverty is the question of if it actually matters. That is, do neighborhoods have effects above and beyond the impact of individual characteristics or national political and economic contexts? There is an abundance of research on neighborhood effects in the United States that generally finds that living in a high-poverty neighborhood does lead to worse life outcomes for residents (Galster 2012; Sharkey and Elwert 2011; Sanbonmatsu et al. 2011; Wodtke, Harding, and Elwert 2011; Sampson, Sharkey, and Raudenbush 2008; Ellen, Mijanovich, and Dillman 2001; Sampson, Morenoff, and Gannon-Rowley 2002). The field has grown to include European and other advanced capitalist cities, where neighborhood effects appear to be weaker (or some argue nonexistent) owing to a more robust welfare state (Maloutas and Fujita 2012; van Ham 2012; Kauppinen 2007; Musterd and Murie 2002), and to cities in developing countries (Villarreal and Braulio 2006; Montgomery and Hewett 2005). Still, debates remain over issues of data, method (especially how to approach selection bias, see Sampson 2011), and the magnitude and diversity of findings. Instead of repeating the findings about how neighborhoods do or do not matter, we weigh in on this subject with an eye toward how existing policies in the United States can address the new realities of neighborhood poverty.

Policy responses to neighborhood effects fall under four general domains: (1) deconcentration through mobility, (2) place-based investments in poor people and neighborhoods, (3) revitalization or gentrification, and (4) metropolitan strategies of regional governance. All of these approaches attempt to decrease neighborhood concentrations of poverty thereby eliminating their negative effects. How well can these approaches handle the changing geography of poverty?

Mobility strategies involve using public subsidies (called "Housing Choice Vouchers" in the United States) to move poor people from high poverty neighborhoods to low-poverty neighborhoods, with an emphasis on suburban destinations. This has been the strategy used by courts (Popkin et al. 2003; Rubinowitz and Rosenbaum 2000), and legislators (Sanbonmatsu et al. 2011; Briggs, Popkin, and Goering 2010) to combat racial and economic segregation, with generally positive outcomes. However, low take-up rates in mobility programs and frequent moves by poor families back to poor neighborhoods in the city signal that the preference for and the ability to sustain suburban living are not uniform across all poor people (as they are not among nonpoor people). Additionally, Latinos' and other immigrants' low usage of Housing Choice Vouchers will make it difficult to serve them using this tool (Troche-Rodriguez 2008). New research aimed at improving this policy approach should focus on *for whom* such mobility programs are the most desirable and effective. At the same time, even if there is a population of poor families that wants to move out of the city, critics highlight the coercive nature of mobility policies, the disruption they cause to families' social networks and sense of place and belonging, and the counterproductive nature of deconcentration itself, which can accelerate urban decline, provide the impetus for gentrification, support unsustainable sprawl, and undermine possibilities for class- or race-based political coalitions (Imbroscio 2004, 2008; Goetz 2003).

Place-based investment strategies—such as the Harlem Children's Zone and the New Hope Experiment (Tough 2008; Duncan, Huston, and Weisner 2007)—make investments in the people who live in high poverty neighborhoods and the institutions that serve them. These include federal programs (e.g., Promise Neighborhoods, the newest model from the Obama administration), local foundation-led and community-based initiatives (see Kubisch et al. 2011), and systemic approaches such as those that support tight labor markets or living wages (Wilson 1996). Critics of mobility programs prefer systemic approaches because they eliminate the trauma of moving, meet people where they are, and recognize the social and economic assets that exist for families in poor neighborhoods (Pattillo 2009). While suburbs, and perhaps even cities in the South and West, may not be conducive to place-based investment efforts because of their geographic sprawl and lower densities, systemic improvements in wages, schools, and health care (along the lines of a strong welfare state model) would be effective no matter the geography or target population (with the possible exception of undocumented immigrants).

Another kind of place-based initiative focuses less on existing residents in poor neighborhoods and more on making such places attractive to middle-class and affluent people. The neutral word for such efforts is "revitalization," but "gentrification" is the more charged description. HOPE VI (as well as its Obama-era Choice Neighborhoods program), which either renovates or demolishes and redevelops public housing in U.S. cities, is a national example of a revitalization strategy, since nearly all HOPE VI projects include new housing for nonpoor (and sometimes quite affluent) new residents. While HOPE VI is funded under the rubric of public housing, estimates are that fewer than half of the original residents return to the completed developments (Chaskin et al. 2012; Joseph and Chaskin 2012; Popkin et al. 2004;). It is generally a bricks-and-mortar program to make these areas of the city attractive to new middle-income buyers, rather than one that invests in the skills or well-being of poor people (Levy and Woolley 2007; Manjarrez, Popkin, and Guernsey 2007). These approaches are not likely to be successful in emerging poor areas because they are irrelevant to places like the suburbs that lack public housing.

Finally, metropolitan strategies recognize the relationship of poor neighborhoods to nonpoor and, especially, affluent neighborhoods in the metropolis. Those relationships can be exclusionary or inclusionary, mutually beneficial, or antagonistically competitive. In the United States, regional approaches have been studied in Oregon, New Jersey, Maryland, California, and Minnesota, and the greater Boston and Washington, DC areas (Orfield 2002, 2005; Goetz et al. 2005; Pendall et al. 2005). An even longer history of regionalism exists in Europe (Booth and Jouve 2005; Brenner 2004), and the Organisation for Economic Cooperation and Development (OECD) has published dozens of "territorial reviews" that evaluate urban regional coordination in developed and developing cities (OECD 2014). In the U.S. cases, state-level legislation or regional housing agreements aim to reduce sprawl and metropolitan fragmentation in order to promote an equitable distribution of affordable housing, with specific attention to opportunities for blacks and Latinos. Like the systemic interventions discussed previously, regional strategies are comprehensive policies aimed at reducing neighborhood concentrations of poverty. Because such policies aim toward redistribution of people and resources, however, they pose significant political challenges (Briggs 2005; Dreier et al. 2004).

Conclusion

This chapter presents a synthesis of existing research and puts new considerations on the table, especially the topics of suburban poverty and the centrality of the regional political economy. Trends show that concentrated poverty in central cities, although still disproportionately high, has declined slightly since the 1980s and 90s. Conversely, suburban areas have seen rapid increases in neighborhood poverty but have not become universally distressed. Instead, the patterns are quite heterogeneous. Heterogeneity also characterizes the recent work on the lived experiences of urban poor residents, which increasingly moves beyond defining poor neighborhoods primarily in terms of their disadvantage. Tossing out the notion that there is one archetypal description of a poor neighborhood in the metropolis complicates the effectiveness of public policies, which currently have a heavy focus on cities and on public housing.

This chapter also raises a more fundamental question: How should our understanding of suburbs change in response to trends documented in research on the new metropolitan reality? In the United States, suburbs are typically perceived as sites of social and economic privilege in relation to distressed central cities. This contrast often serves to distinguish the U.S. metropolitan landscape from its European and Global South counterparts, which generally feature the opposite pattern. However, the suburbanization of U.S. neighborhood poverty together with the gentrification of U.S. cities calls into question these traditional distinctions. Will our lay language catch up with the changing geography of neighborhood poverty? Or will the myth of suburban privilege remain symbolically resonant, even if empirically incorrect? These questions loom as researchers continue to try to understand and rectify the unequal geography of the metropolis.

Notes

1. Defining neighborhood poverty in a cross-national perspective is challenging, as is establishing a clean distinction between "poor" and "nonpoor" neighborhoods and, indeed, defining "poverty" or "neighborhoods" at all. Therefore, we do not propose an absolute definition of "poor neighborhoods." However, as a loose guide, when discussing the demographic research in the United States, a neighborhood poverty rate of at least 20 percent or 40 percent indicates a poor or high-poverty neighborhood, respectively. "Concentrated poverty" refers to the proportion of poor households in a city or metropolitan area that lives in poor neighborhoods (see Wolch and Sessoms 2005; and Sessoms and Wolch 2008 for discussion of measurement and definition). Because we do not conduct any original data analysis in this review, we use the general terms "poor neighborhoods" and "high-poverty neighborhoods" for all areas above the 20 percent threshold, and we use "concentrated poverty" as a way to reference the relegation of poor families to poor neighborhoods in a metropolis.
2. Weir also adds "demographic inversion," or the process by which affluent households move back to central cities and poorer households move to the suburbs (also see Ehrenhalt 2008).
3. Vale (1997) offers a useful framework that encompasses all three depictions simultaneously. He argues that poor neighborhoods are best analyzed as "empathological places;" that is, places "where profound ambivalence is the ruling emotional response

... where the fear of remaining is counterbalanced by the fear of departure, where the ties of friendship are inextricably juxtaposed with the incursions of unwanted outsiders" (pp. 159–60).

REFERENCES

Abu-Lughod, Janet. 1997. "The Specificity of the Chicago Ghetto: Comment on Wacquant's 'Three Pernicious Premises.'" *International Journal of Urban and Regional Research* 21:357–62.

Aalbers, Manuel B. 2012. *Subprime Cities: The Political Economy of Mortgage Markets*, Vol. 55. Malden, MA: Wiley-Blackwell.

Adams, Carolyn Teich. 2008. *Restructuring the Philadelphia Region: Metropolitan Divisions and Inequality*. Philadelphia: Temple University Press.

Addams, Jane. 1895. *Hull-House Maps and Papers, a Presentation of Nationalities and Wages in a Congested District of Chicago, Together with Comments and Essays on Problems Growing out of the Social Conditions*. New York: T.Y. Crowell, Hull-House Association.

Agnew, John A. and Jonathan M. Smith. 2002. *American Space/American Place: Geographies of the Contemporary United States*. New York: Routledge.

Allard, Scott W. 2009. *Out of Reach: Place, Poverty, and the New American Welfare State*. New Haven, CT: Yale University Press.

Allard, Scott W. and Benjamin Roth. 2010. *The Social Service Challenges of Rising Suburban Poverty*, edited by B. Institute. Washington, DC: Brookings Institute Press.

Anderson, Elijah. 1999. *Code of the Street: Decency, Violence, and the Moral Life of the Inner City*. New York: W.W Norton.

Anyon, Jean. 1997. *Ghetto Schooling: A Political Economy of Urban Educational Reform*. New York: Teachers College Press, Teachers College, Columbia University.

Arena, John. 2012. *Driven from New Orleans: How Nonprofits Betray Public Housing and Promote Privatization*. Minneapolis: University of Minnesota Press.

Auyero, Javier. 2000a. *Poor People's Politics: Peronist Survival Networks and the Legacy of Evita*. Durham, NC: Duke University Press Books.

Auyero, Javier. 2000b. "The Logic of Clientelism in Argentina: An Ethnographic Account." *Latin American Research Review* 35(3):55–81.

Auyero, Javier. 2011. "Researching the Urban Margins: What Can the United States Learn from Latin America and Vice Versa?" *City & Community* 10(4):431–36.

Baeten, Guy. 2001. "Clichés of Urban Doom: The Dystopian Politics of Metaphors for the Unequal City—A View from Brussels." *International Journal of Urban and Regional Research* 25(1):15.

Barnes, Sandra L. 2005. *The Cost of Being Poor: A Comparative Study of Life in Poor Urban Neighborhoods in Gary, Indiana*. Albany: State University of New York Press.

Barron, David J. 2003. "Reclaiming Home Rule." *Harvard Law Review* 116(8):132.

Bayor, Ronald H. 2003. "The Second Ghetto: Then and Now." *Journal of Urban History* 29(3):238–42.

Bennett, Larry, Janet L. Smith, and Patricia A. Wright. 2006. *Where Are Poor People to Live?: Transforming Public Housing Communities*. Armonk, NY: M.E. Sharpe.

Biehl, João Guilherme. 2005. *Vita: Life in a Zone of Social Abandonment*. Berkeley: University of California Press.

Booth, Charles. 1891. *Labour and Life of the People*. London and Edinburgh: Williams and Norgate.

Booth, Philip and Bernard Jouve. 2005. *Metropolitan Democracies: Transformations of the State and Urban Policy in Canada, France and the* [Sic] *Great Britain*. Aldershot, Hampshire, England; Burlington, VT: Ashgate.

Bourgois, Philippe I. 1995. *In Search of Respect: Selling Crack in El Barrio*. Cambridge; New York: Cambridge University Press.

Brenner, Neil. 2004. *New State Spaces: Urban Governance and the Rescaling of Statehood*. Oxford; New York: Oxford University Press.

Briggs, Xavier de Souza, ed. 2005. *The Geography of Opportunity: Race and Housing Choice in Metropolitan America*. Washington, DC: Brookings Institution Press.

Briggs, Xavier de Souza, Susan J. Popkin, and John M. Goering. 2010. *Moving to Opportunity: The Story of an American Experiment to Fight Ghetto Poverty*. New York: Oxford University Press.

Brockerhoff, Martin and Ellen Brennan. 1998. "The Poverty of Cities in Developing Regions." *Population and Development Review* 24(1):40.

Burns, Nancy. 1994. *The Formation of American Local Governments: Private Values in Public Institutions*. New York: Oxford University Press.

Caldeira, Teresa. 2000. *City of Walls: Crime, Segregation, and Citizenship in São Paulo*. Berkeley, CA: University of California Press.

Carr, Patrick J. 2005. *Clean Streets: Controlling Crime, Maintaining Order, and Building Community Activism*. New York: New York University Press.

Castells, Manuel. 1985. *The City and the Grassroots: A Cross-Cultural Theory of Urban Social Movements*: Berkeley: University of California Press.

Chaskin, Robert, Mark L. Joseph, Sara Voelker, and Amy Dworsky. 2012. "Public Housing Transformation and Resident Relocation: Comparing Destinations and Household Characteristics in Chicago." *Cityscape* 14(1):183–214.

Cho, Mun Young. 2010. "On the Edge between "the People" and "the Population": Ethnographic Research on the Minimum Livelihood Guarantee." *China Quarterly* 201(1):20–37.

Clark, Kenneth Bancroft. 1965. *Dark Ghetto; Dilemmas of Social Power*. New York: Harper & Row.

Cooke, Thomas. 2010. "Residential Mobility of the Poor and the Growth of Poverty in Inner-Ring Suburbs." *Urban Geography* 31(2):179–193.

Crowley, Martha, Daniel T. Lichter, and Zhenchao Qian. 2006. "Beyond Gateway Cities: Economic Restructuring and Poverty among Mexican Immigrant Families and Children." *Family Relations* 55(3):345–60.

Cummings, Scott. 1998. *Left Behind in Rosedale: Race Relations and the Collapse of Community Institutions*. Boulder, CO: Westview Press.

Davis, Mike. 2006. *Planet of Slums*. London; New York: Verso.

De la Rocha, Mercedes González. 2001. "From the Resources of Poverty to the Poverty of Resources? The Erosion of a Survival Model." *Latin American Perspectives* 28(4):72–100.

De la Rocha, Mercedes González. 2006. "Vanishing Assets: Cumulative Disadvantage among the Urban Poor." *Annals of the American Academy of Political and Social Science* 606(1):68–94.

Denton, Nancy A. and Douglas S. Massey. 1988. "Residential Segregation of Blacks, Hispanics, and Asians by Socioeconomic Status and Generation." *Social Science Quarterly* 69(4):797–817.

Desmond, Matthew. 2012a. "Disposable Ties and the Urban Poor." *American Journal of Sociology* 117(5):1295–1335.

Desmond, Matthew. 2012b. "Eviction and the Reproduction of Urban Poverty." *American Journal of Sociology* 118(1):88–133

Di Leonardo, Micaela. 1998. *Exotics at Home: Anthropologies, Others, American Modernity.* Chicago: University of Chicago Press.

Dohan, Daniel. 2003. *The Price of Poverty: Money, Work, and Culture in the Mexican-American Barrio.* Berkeley: University of California Press.

Doherty, Kathryn M. and Clarence N. Stone. 1999. "Local Practice in Transition: From Government to Governance." Pp. 154–88 in *Dilemmas of Scale in America's Federal Democracy,* edited by M. Derthick. New York: Cambridge University Press.

Dreier, Peter, John H. Mollenkopf, and Todd Swanstrom. 2004. *Place Matters: Metropolitics for the Twenty-First Century.* Lawrence: University Press of Kansas.

Du Bois, W. E. B. 1899. *The Philadelphia Negro: A Social Study Together with a Special Report on Domestic Service by Isabel Eaton.* Philadelphia. Published for the University.

Duncan, Greg J., Aletha C. Huston and Thomas S. Weisner. 2007. *Higher Ground: New Hope for the Working Poor and Their Children.* New York: Russell Sage Foundation.

Dwyer, Rachel E. 2010. "Poverty, Prosperity, and Place: The Shape of Class Segregation in the US." *Social Problems* 57:114–137.

Edin, Kathryn and Laura Lein. 1997. *Making Ends Meet: How Single Mothers Survive Welfare and Low-Wage Work.* New York: Russell Sage Foundation.

Ehrenhalt, Alan. 2008. "Trading Places: The Demographic Inversion of the American City." *New Republic,* August 13.

Ehrenreich, Barbara. 2001. *Nickel and Dimed: On (Not) Getting by in America.* New York: Metropolitan Books.

Ellen, Ingrid Gould, Tod Mijanovich, and Keri-Nicole Dillman. 2001. "Neighborhood Effects on Health: Exploring the Links and Assessing the Evidence." *Journal of Urban Affairs* 23(3&4):18.

Elliott, Delbert S. 2007. *Good Kids from Bad Neighborhoods: Successful Development in Social Context.* Cambridge; New York: Cambridge University Press.

Federal Reserve Bank and Brookings. 2008. *The Enduring Challenge of Concentrated Poverty in America: Case Studies from Communities across the US.* Richmond: Federal Reserve Bank.

Feldman, Roberta M. and Susan Stall. 2004. *The Dignity of Resistance: Women Residents' Activism in Chicago Public Housing.* Cambridge, UK; New York: Cambridge University Press.

Fine, Michelle and Lois Weis. 1998. *The Unknown City: Lives of Poor and Working Class Young Adults.* Boston: Beacon Press.

Fraser, James, Ashley Brown-Burns, Josh Bazuin, and Deirdre Oakley. 2012. "In the Neighborhood: Hope VI and the Production of Difference." Unpublished Manuscript.

Fraser, James C. and Edward L. Kick. 2007. "The Role of Public, Private, Non-Profit and Community Sectors in Shaping Mixed-Income Housing Outcomes in the US." *Urban Studies* 44:2357–77.

Freund, David M. P. 2007. *Colored Property: State Policy and White Racial Politics in Suburban America.* Chicago: University of Chicago Press.

Furstenberg, Frank F. 1999. *Managing to Make It: Urban Families and Adolescent Success.* Chicago: University of Chicago Press.

Galster, George C. 2012. "The Mechanism(s) of Neighbourhood Effects: Theory, Evidence, and Policy Implications." Pp. 23–56 in *Neighbourhood Effects Research: New Perspectives,* edited by M. van Ham, D. Manley, N. Bailey, L. Simpson and D. Maclennan. Dordrecht: Springer Science and Business Media B.V.

Gans, Herbert J. 1962. *The Urban Villagers; Group and Class in the Life of Italian-Americans.* New York: Free Press of Glencoe.

Gans, Herbert J. 1995. *The War against the Poor: The Underclass and Antipoverty Policy.* New York: BasicBooks.

Goetz, E. G., K. Chapple, and Barbara Lukemann. 2005. "The Rise and Fall of Fair Share Housing: Lessons from the Twin Cities." Pp. 247–65 in *The Geography of Opportunity,* edited by X. d. S. Briggs. Washington, DC: Brookings Institution Press.

Goetz, Edward. 2008. "Words Matter: The Importance of Issue Framing and the Case of Affordable Housing." *Journal of the American Planning Association* 74(2):222–29.

Goetz, Edward G. 2003. *Clearing the Way: Deconcentrating the Poor in Urban America.* Washington, DC: Urban Institute Press.

Goffman, Alice. 2009. "On the Run: Wanted Men in a Philadelphia Ghetto." *American Sociological Review* 74(3):19.

Goldstein, Donna M. 2003. *Laughter out of Place: Race, Class, Violence, and Sexuality in a Rio Shantytown,* Vol. 9. Oakland: University of California Press.

Gotham, Kevin Fox. 2002. *Race, Real Estate, and Uneven Development: The Kansas City Experience, 1900–2000.* Albany: State University of New York Press.

Gotham, Kevin Fox. 2007. *Authentic New Orleans: Tourism, Culture, and Race in the Big Easy.* New York: New York University Press.

Gotham, Kevin Fox and Miriam Greenberg. 2013. *Crisis Cities: Disaster and Redevelopment in New York and New Orleans.* New York: Oxford University Press.

Gramlich, Edward, Deborah Laren, and Naomi Sealand. 1992. "Moving into and out of Poor Urban Areas." *Journal of Policy Analysis and Management: [Journal of the Association for Public Policy Analysis and Management]* 11(2):273–87.

Greene, Richard. 1991. "Poverty Area Diffusion: The Depopulation Hypothesis Examined." *Urban Geography* 12(6):526–41.

Hamer, Jennifer. 2011. *Abandoned in the Heartland: Work, Family, and Living in East St. Louis.* Berkeley: University of California Press.

Hamilton, Nora and Norma Stoltz Chinchilla. 2001. *Seeking Community in a Global City: Guatemalans and Salvadorans in Los Angeles.* Philadelphia: Temple University Press.

Hanlon, Bernadette. 2009. "A Typology of Inner-Ring Suburbs: Class, Race, and Ethnicity in US Suburbia." *City & Community* 8(3):221–46.

Hanlon, Bernadette, Thomas Vicino, and John Rennie Short. 2006. "The New Metropolitan Reality in the Us: Rethinking the Traditional Model." *Urban Studies* 43(12):15.

Harding, David J. 2010. *Living the Drama: Community, Conflict, and Culture among Inner-City Boys.* Chicago; London: University of Chicago Press.

Harrison, Bennett and Barry Bluestone. 1988. *The Great U-Turn: Corporate Restructuring and the Polarizing of America.* New York: Basic Books.

Hartigan, John. 1999. *Racial Situations: Class Predicaments of Whiteness in Detroit.* Princeton, NJ: Princeton University Press.

Hirsch, Arnold R. 1983. *Making the Second Ghetto: Race and Housing in Chicago, 1940–1960.* Cambridge, Cambridgeshire; New York: Cambridge University Press.

Holliday, Amy L. and Rachel E. Dwyer. 2009. "Suburban Neighborhood Poverty in US Metropolitan Areas in 2000." *City & Community* 8(2):155–176.

Hyra, Derek S. 2008. *The New Urban Renewal: The Economic Transformation of Harlem and Bronzeville*. Chicago: University of Chicago Press.

Imbroscio, David. 2008. "'[U]Nited and Actuated by Some Common Impulse of Passion': Challenging the Dispersal Consensus in American Housing Policy Research." *Journal of Urban Affairs* 30(2):111–30.

Imbroscio, David. 2004. "Fighting Poverty with Mobility: A Normative Policy Analysis." *Review of Policy Research* 21(3):447–61.

Jackson, Kenneth T. 1985. *Crabgrass Frontier: The Suburbanization of the United States*. New York: Oxford University Press.

Jaffe, Rivke. 2012. "The Popular Culture of Illegality: Crime and the Politics of Aesthetics in Urban Jamaica." *Anthropological Quarterly* 85(1):79–102.

Jargowsky, Paul A. 1996. "Beyond the Street Corner: The Hidden Diversity of High-Poverty Neighborhoods." *Urban Geography* 17(7):25.

Jargowsky, Paul A. 1997. *Poverty and Place: Ghettos, Barrios, and the American City*. New York: Russell Sage Foundation.

Jargowsky, Paul A. 2003. "Stunning Progress, Hidden Problems: The Dramatic Decline of Concentrated Poverty in the 1990s." The Brookings Institution. http://www.brookings.edu/~/media/research/files/reports/2003/5/demographics-jargowsky/jargowskypoverty.pdf. Accessed June 23, 2014.

Jargowsky, Paul A. and Mary Jo Bane. 1991. "Ghetto Poverty in the United States 1970–1980." Pp. 235–74 in *The Urban Underclass*, edited by C. Jencks and P. E. Peterson. Washington, DC: Brookings Institution Press.

Jones, Nikki. 2010. *Between Good and Ghetto: African American Girls and Inner-City Violence*. New Brunswick, NJ Rutgers University Press.

Joseph, Mark L. and Robert Chaskin. 2012. "Mixed-Income Developments and Low Rates of Return: Insights from Relocated Public Housing Residents in Chicago." *Housing Policy Debate* 22(3):377–405

Judd, Dennis R. and Todd Swanstrom. 1994. *City Politics: Private Power and Public Policy*. New York: HarperCollins.

Kain, John F. 1965. "The Effect of the Ghetto on the Distribution and Level of Nonwhite Employment in Urban Areas." Pp. 260–71 in *Proceedings of the Social Statistics Section*, edited by ASA. Washington, DC.

Kain, John F. 1968. "Housing Segregation, Negro Employment, and Metropolitan Decentralization." *Quarterly Journal of Economics* 82(2):175–97.

Kandel, William and Emilio A. Parrado. 2005. "Restructuring of the US Meat Processing Industry and New Hispanic Migrant Destinations." *Population and Development Review* 31:447–71.

Kasarda, John D. 1990. "Structural Factors Affecting the Location and Timing of Urban Underclass Growth." *Urban Geography* 11(3):234–64.

Katznelson, Ira. 2005. *When Affirmative Action Was White: An Untold History of Racial Inequality in Twentieth-Century America*. New York: W.W. Norton.

Kauppinen, Timo M. 2007. "Neighborhood Effects in a European City: Secondary Education of Young People in Helsinki." *Social Science Research* 36(1):421.

Kefalas, Maria. 2003. *Working-Class Heroes: Protecting Home, Community, and Nation in a Chicago Neighborhood*. Berkeley: University of California Press.

Kleit, Rachel Garshick. 2005. "Hope Vi New Communities: Neighborhood Relations in Mixed-Income Housing." *Environment and Planning A* 37:1413–41.

Kleit, Rachel Garshick and Nicole Boehme Carnegie. 2011. "Integrated or Isolated?: The Impact of Public Housing Redevelopment on Social Network Homophily." *Social Networks* 33(2):101–76.

Kneebone, Elizabeth and Alan Berube. 2013. *Confronting Suburban Poverty in America.* Washington, DC: Brookings Institution Press.

Kneebone, Elizabeth, Carey Nadeau, and Alan Berube. 2011. "The Re-Emergence of Concentrated Poverty: Metropolitan Trends in the 2000s." The Brookings Institution. http://www.brookings.edu/~/media/research/files/papers/2011/11/03%20poverty%20knee-bone%20nadeau%20oberube/1103_poverty_kneebone_nadeau_berube.pdf. Accessed June 24, 2014.

Kotlowitz, Alex. 1991. *There Are No Children Here: The Story of Two Boys Growing up in the Other America.* New York: Doubleday.

Krivo, Lauren J. and Ruth D. Peterson. 1996. "Extremely Disadvantaged Neighborhoods and Urban Crime." *Social Forces* 75(2):30.

Kubisch, Anne C., Patricia Auspos, Prudence Brown, and Tome Dewar. 2011. *Listening to Voices from the Field III: Lessons and Challenges from the Two Decades of Community Change Efforts.* Washington, DC: The Aspen Institute.

Leigh, N. G. and S. Lee. 2005. "Philadelphia's Space in Between: Inner-Ring Suburb Evolution." *Opolis* 1(1):13–32.

Levy, Diane K. and Mary Woolley. 2007. "Relocation Is Not Enough: Employment Barriers among HOPE VI Families." Vol. 6, edited by Metropolitan Housing and Communities Center at the Urban Institute. Washington, DC: Urban Institute Press.

Lichter, Daniel T., Domenico Parisi, Michael Clark Taquino, and Steven Michael Grice. 2010. "Residential Segregation in New Hispanic Destinations: Cities, Suburbs, and Rural Communities Compared." *Social Science Research* 39:215–30.

Lipsitz, George. 2011. *How Racism Takes Place.* Philadelphia: Temple University Press.

Lloyd, Richard. 2012. "Urbanization and the Southern United States." *Annual Review of Sociology* 38:483–506.

Logan, John R. and Harvey Luskin Molotch. 1987. *Urban Fortunes: The Political Economy of Place.* Berkeley: University of California Press.

Logan, John R. 2008. *Urban China in Transition.* Malden, MA; Oxford: Blackwell.

Lucy, William H. and David L. Phillips. 2000. *Confronting Suburban Decline: Strategic Planning for Metropolitan Renewal.* Washington, DC: Island Press.

Lucy, William H. and David L. Phillips. 2006. *Tomorrow's Cities, Tomorrow's Suburbs.* Chicago, IL: American Planning Association Chicago.

Lupton, Ruth. 2003. *Poverty Street: The Dynamics of Neighbourhood Decline and Renewal*: Policy Press.

MacLeod, Jay. 2009. *Ain't No Makin' It: Aspirations & Attainment in a Low-Income Neighborhood.* Boulder, CO: Westview Press.

Maloutas, Thomas and Kuniko Fujita. 2012. *Residential Segregation in Comparative Perspective*: Ashgate.

Manjarrez, Carlos A., Susan J. Popkin, and Elizabeth Guernsey. 2007. "Poor Health: Adding Insult to Injury for Hope VI Families." Vol. 5, edited by Metropolitan Housing and Communities Center at the Urban Institute. Washington, DC: the Urban Institute Press.

Marwell, Nicole P. 2007. *Bargaining for Brooklyn: Community Organizations in the Entrepreneurial City.* Chicago: University of Chicago Press.

Massey, Douglas. 1979. "Effects of Socioeconomic Factors on the Residential Segregation of Blacks and Spanish Americans in Us Urbanized Areas." *American Sociological Review* 44:1015–22.

Massey, Douglas and Nancy A. Denton. 1987. "Trends in the Residential Segregation of Blacks, Hispanics and Asians." *American Sociological Review* 52:802–25.

Massey, Douglas and Mitchell L. Eggers. 1990. "The Ecology of Inequality: Minorities and the Concentration of Poverty, 1970–1980." *American Journal of Sociology* 95(5):1153–88.

Massey, Douglas and Mary Fischer. 2003. "The Geography of Inequality in the United States, 1950–2000." *Brookings-Wharton Papers on Urban Affairs* 2003(1):40.

Massey, Douglas S., Andrew Gross, and Kumiko Shibuya. 1994. "Migration, Segregation, and the Geographic Concentration of Poverty." *American Sociological Review* 59:425–45.

McDermott, Monica. 2006. *Working-Class White: The Making and Unmaking of Race Relations*. Berkeley: University of California Press.

Medoff, Peter and Holly Sklar. 1994. *Streets of Hope: The Fall and Rise of an Urban Neighborhood*. Boston: South End Press.

Mikelbank, Brian A. 2004. "A Typology of US Suburban Places." *Housing Policy Debate* 15(4): 935–64.

Miller, Jody. 2008. *Getting Played: African American Girls, Urban Inequality, and Gendered Violence*. New York: New York University Press.

Mingione, Enzo. 1996. *Urban Poverty and the Underclass*. Cambridge, MA: Wiley-Blackwell.

Montgomery, Mark and Paul C. Hewett. 2005. "Urban Poverty and Health in Developing Countries: Household and Neighborhood Effects." *Demography* 42(3):397–425.

Murphy, Alexandra K. 2010. "The Symbolic Dilemmas of Suburban Poverty: Challenges and Opportunities Posed by Variations in the Contours of Suburban Poverty." *Sociological Forum* 25(3):541–69.

Murphy, Alexandra K. and Danielle Wallace. 2010. "Opportunities for Making Ends Meet and Upward Mobility: Differences in Organizational Deprivation across Urban and Suburban Poor Neighborhoods." *Social Science Quarterly* 91(5):1164–86.

Musterd, Sako. 2008. "Banlieues, the Hyperghetto and Advanced Marginality: A Symposium on Loic Wacquant's Urban Outcasts." *City* 12(1):107–14.

Musterd, Sako and Alan Murie. 2002. "The Spatial Dimensions of Urban Social Exclusion and Integration: Final Report." 4th Framework Programme on Targeted Socio-Economic Research of the European Union.

Musterd, Sako, Alan Murie, and Christian Kesteloot. 2006. *Neighborhoods of Poverty: Urban Social Exclusion and Integration in Europe*. New York: Palgrave MacMillan.

Neckerman, Kathryn M. and Joleen Kirschenman. 1991. "Hiring Strategies, Racial Bias, and Inner-City Workers." *Social Problems* 38(4):433–47.

Newman, Katherine S. 1999. *No Shame in My Game: The Working Poor in the Inner City*. New York: Knopf and the Russell Sage Foundation.

Newman, Katherine S. and Victor Tan Chen. 2007. *The Missing Class: Portraits of the near Poor in America*. Boston, MA: Beacon Press.

Nguyen, M. T., V. Basolo, and Abhishek Tiwari. 2013. "Opposition to Affordable Housing in the USA: Debate Framing and the Responses of Local Actors." *Housing, Theory and Society* 30:107–30.

Norris, Donald F. 2001. "Prospects for Regional Governance under the New Regionalism: Economic Imperatives versus Political Impediments." *Journal of Urban Affairs* 23(5):15.

Orfield, Myron. 2002. *American Metropolitics: The New Suburban Reality*. Washington, DC: Brookings Institution Press.

Orfield, Myron. 2005. "Land Use and Housing Policies to Reduce Concentrated Poverty and Racial Segregation." *Fordham Urban Law Journal* 33(3):101–59.

OECD. 2014. "OECD Territorial Reviews." http://www.oecd-ilibrary.org/urban-rural-and-regional-development/oecd-territorial-reviews_19900759. Accessed June 23, 2014.

Pashup, J., K. Edin, G. J. Duncan, and K. Burke. 2005. "Participation in a Residential Mobility Program from the Client's Perspective: Findings from Gautreaux Two." *Housing Policy Debate* 16(3–4):361–92.

Pattillo, Mary. 2007. *Black on the Block: The Politics of Race and Class in the City*. Chicago: University of Chicago Press.

Pattillo, Mary. 2009. "Investing in Poor Black Neighborhoods 'as Is.'" Pp. 31–46 in *Public Housing and the Legacy of Segregation*, edited by M. A. Turner, S. J. Popkin, and L. Rawling. Washington, DC: Urban Institute Press.

Pattillo-McCoy, Mary. 2000. "The Limits of Out-Migration for the Black Middle Class." *Journal of Urban Affairs* 22:225–41.

Peach, Ceri. 2009. "Slippery Segregation: Discovering or Manufacturing Ghettos?" *Journal of Ethnic and Migration Studies* 35(9):1381–95.

Pendall, Rolf, Arthur C. Neslon, Casey J. Dawkins, and Gerrit J. Knaap. 2005. "Connecting Smart Growth, Housing Affordability, and Racial Equity." Pp. 219–46 in *The Geography of Opportunity*, edited by X. d. S. Briggs. Washington, DC: Brookings Institution Press.

Popkin, Susan J. 2000. *The Hidden War: Crime and the Tragedy of Public Housing in Chicago*. New Brunswick, NJ: Rutgers University Press.

Popkin, Susan J., Diane Levy, and Larry Buron. 2009. "Has Hope Vi Transformed Residents' Lives? New Evidence from the Hope Vi Panel Study." *Housing Studies* 24(4):477–502.

Popkin, Susan J., George C. Galster, Kenneth Temkin, Carla Herbig, Diane K. Levy and Elise K. Richer. 2003. "Obstacles to Desegregating Public Housing: Lessons Learned from Implementing Eight Consent Decrees." *Journal of policy analysis and management: [the journal of the Association for Public Policy Analysis and Management]* 22(2):22.

Popkin, Susan J., Bruce Katz, Mary K. Cunningham, Karen D. Brown, Jeremy Gustafson and Margery Austin Turner. 2004. "A Decade of Hope VI: Research Findings and Policy Challenges." edited by The Urban Institute and the Brookings Institution. Washington, DC: Urban Institute Press.

Portes, Alejandro and John Walton. 1976. *Urban Latin America: The Political Condition from above and Below*, Vol. 10: Austin: University of Texas Press Austin.

Portes, Alejandro and Bryan R Roberts. 2005. "The Free-Market City: Latin American Urbanization in the Years of the Neoliberal Experiment." *Studies in Comparative International Development (SCID)* 40(1):43–82.

Quillian, Lincoln. 1999. "Migration Patterns and the Growth of High-Poverty Neighborhoods, 1970–1990." *American Journal of Sociology* 105(1):37.

Quillian, Lincoln. 2012. "Segregation and Poverty Concentration: The Role of Three Segregations." *American Sociological Review* 77(3):354–79.

Rios, Victor M. 2011. *Punished: Policing the Lives of Black and Latino Boys*. New York: New York University Press.

Roberts, Bryan R. 2005. "Globalization and Latin American Cities." *International Journal of Urban and Regional Research* 29(1):110–23.

Robinson, Zandria. 2014. *This Ain't Chicago: Race, Class, and Regional Identity in the Post-Soul South.* Chapel Hill: The University of North Carolina Press.

Roisman, Florence. 1995. "Intentional Racial Discrimination and Segregation by the Federal Government as a Principal Cause of Concentrated Poverty: A Response to Schill and Wachter." *University of Pennsylvania Law Review* 143:1351–78.

Rosen, Eva and Sudhir Venkatesh. 2008. "A 'Perversion' of Choice: Sex Work Offers Just Enough in Chicago's Urban Ghetto." *Journal of Contemporary Ethnography* 37(4):417–41.

Roy, Ananya. 2002. *City Requiem, Calcutta: Gender and the Politics of Poverty*, Vol. 10. Minneapolis: University of Minnesota Press.

Rubinowitz, Leonard S. and James E. Rosenbaum. 2000. *Crossing the Class and Color Lines: From Public Housing to White Suburbia.* Chicago: University of Chicago Press.

Rugh, Jacob S. and Douglas S Massey. 2010. "Racial Segregation and the American Foreclosure Crisis." *American Sociological Review* 75(5):629–51.

Rushing, Wanda. 2009. *Memphis and the Paradox of Place: Globalization in the American South.* Chapel Hill: University of North Carolina Press.

Sampson, Robert J. 2011. *Great American City: Chicago and the Enduring Neighborhood Effect.* Chicago; London: University of Chicago Press.

Sampson, Robert J., Jeffrey D. Morenoff, and Thomas Gannon-Rowley. 2002. "Assessing "Neighborhood Effects": Social Processes and New Directions in Research." *Annual Review of Sociology* 28:443–78.

Sampson, Robert J. and Patrick Sharkey. 2008. "Neighborhood Selection and the Social Reproduction of Concentrated Racial Inequality." *Demography* 45(1):1–29.

Sampson, Robert J., Patrick Sharkey, and Stephen Raudenbush. 2008. "Durable Effects of Concentrated Disadvantage on Verbal Ability among African-American Children." Pp. 845–53 in *National Academy of Sciences*, Vol. 105.

Sanbonmatsu, Lisa, Jens Ludwig, Lawrence F. Katz, Lisa Gennetian, Greg Duncan, Ronald C. Kessler, Emma Adam, Thomas W. McDade and Stacy Tessler Lindau. 2011. "Moving to Opportunity for Fair Housing Demonstration Program—Final Impacts Evaluation." Washington, DC: U.S. Department of Housing and Urban Development, PD&R.

Sánchez-Jankowski, Martín. 2008. *Cracks in the Pavement: Social Change and Resilience in Poor Neighborhoods.* Berkeley: University of California Press.

Sassen, Saskia. 2001. *Global Networks, Linked Cities.* New York: Routledge.

Sassen, Saskia. 2012. "Expanding the Terrain for Global Capital." Pp. 74–96 in *Subprime Cities: The Political Economy of Mortgage Markets*, edited by M. B. Aalbers.

Satter, Beryl. 2009. *Family Properties: Race, Real Estate, and the Exploitation of Black Urban America.* New York: Metropolitan Books.

Scally, Corianne Payton and Richard Koenig. 2012. "Beyond Nimby and Poverty Deconcentration Reframing the Outcomes of Affordable Rental Housing Development." *Housing Policy Debate* 22(3):435.

Scheper-Hughes, Nancy. 1992. *Death without Weeping: The Violence of Everyday Life in Brazil.* Berkeley: University of California Press.

Schill, Michael H. and Susan M. Wachter. 1995. "The Spatial Bias of Federal Housing Law and Policy: Concentrated Poverty in Urban America." *University of Pennsylvania Law Review* 143(5):58.

Sessoms, Nathan and Jennifer Wolch. 2008. "Measuring Concentrated Poverty in a Global Metropolis: Lessons from Los Angeles." *Professional Geographer* 60(1):70–86.

Sharkey, Patrick. 2011. "Spatial Disadvantage and Downward Mobility among the (New?) Black Middle Class." Paper presented at the Annual Meeting of the American Sociological Association Las Vegas, Nevada.

Sharkey, Patrick and Felix Elwert. 2011. "The Legacy of Disadvantage: Multigenerational Neighborhood Effects on Cognitive Ability." *American Journal of Sociology* 116(6):1934–81.

Short, John Rennie, Bernadette Hanlon, and Thomas Vincino. 2007. "The Decline of Inner Suburbs: The New Suburban Gothic in the United States." *Geography Compass* 1(3):641–56.

Simone, AbdouMaliq. 2004. *For the City yet to Come: Changing African Life in Four Cities.* Durham, NC: Duke University Press Books.

Simone, AbdouMaliq. 2010. *City Life from Jakarta to Dakar: Movements at the Crossroads.* New York: Routledge.

Singer, Audrey, Susan W. Hardwick, and Caroline B. Brettell. 2008. "Twenty-First Century Gateways: Immigrant Incorporation in Suburban America." edited by Brookings. Washington, DC: Brookings Institute Press.

Small, Mario Luis. 2004. *Villa Victoria: The Transformation of Social Capital in a Boston Barrio.* Chicago: University of Chicago Press.

Small, Mario Luis. 2007. "Is There Such a Thing as 'the Ghetto'?" *City* 11(3):413–21.

Small, Mario Luis. 2008. "Four Reasons to Abandon the Idea of "the Ghetto." *City & Community* 7(4):389–98.

Small, Mario Luis and Jessica Feldman. 2011. "Ethnographic Evidence, Heterogeneity, and Neighborhood Effects after Moving to Opportunity." Pp. 57–77 in *Neighborhood Effects Research: New Perspectives,* edited by M. Van Hamm, D. Manley, N. Bailey, L. Simpson and D. Maclennan. Dordrecht: Springer.

Small, Mario Luis and Monica McDermott. 2006. "The Presence of Organizational Resources in Poor Urban Neighborhoods: An Analysis of Contextual Effects." *Social Forces* 84(3):1697–1724.

Smart, Alan and Josephine Smart. 2003. "Urbanization and the Global Perspective." *Annual Review of Anthropology* 32:263–85.

Smith, Neil. 1984. *Uneven Development: Nature, Capital, and the Production of Space.* New York: Blackwell.

South, Scott J., Kyle Crowder, and Erick Chavez. 2005. "Exiting and Entering High-Poverty Neighborhoods: Latinos, Blacks and Anglos Compared." *Social Forces* 84(2):873–900.

Squires, Gregory D. 1994. *Capital and Communities in Black and White: The Intersections of Race, Class, and Uneven Development.* Albany: SUNY Press.

Sugrue, Thomas J. 1996. *The Origins of the Urban Crisis: Race and Inequality in Postwar Detroit.* Princeton, NJ: Princeton University Press.

Tester, Griff, Erin Ruel, Donald C. Reitzes and Deirdre Oakley. 2011. "Sense of Place among Atlanta Public Housing Residents." *Journal of Urban Health* 88(3):436–53.

Tough, Paul. 2008. *Whatever It Takes: Geoffrey Canada's Quest to Change Harlem and America.* Boston: Houghton Mifflin.

Troche-Rodriguez, Madeline. 2008. "Latinos and Their Housing Experiences in Metropolitan Chicago: Challenges and Recommendations." *Harvard Journal of Hispanic Policy* 21:17–33.

Turner, Margery Austin, Susan J. Popkin, and Lynette Rawlings. 2009. *Public Housing and the Legacy of Segregation.* Washington, DC: Urban Institute Press.

Vale, Lawrence J. 1997. "Empathological Places: Residents' Ambivalence toward Remaining in Public Housing." *Journal of Planning Education and Research* 16(3):159–75.

van Ham, Maarten. 2012. *Neighborhood Effects Research: New Perspectives*, edited by M. van Ham, D. Manley, N. Bailey, L. Simpson and D. Maclennan. Dordrecht: Springer Science and Business Media.

Venkatesh, Sudhir Alladi. 2000. *American Project: The Rise and Fall of a Modern Ghetto*. Cambridge, MA: Harvard University Press.

Villarreal, Andrés and Braulio FA Silva. 2006. "Social Cohesion, Criminal Victimization and Perceived Risk of Crime in Brazilian Neighborhoods." *Social Forces* 84(3):1725–53.

Wacquant, Loic. 2008. *Urban Outcasts: A Comparative Sociology of Advanced Marginality*. Malden, MA: Polity Press.

Wagmiller, Jr. Robert L. 2011. "Why Did Poverty Become Less Geographically Concentrated in the 1990s?" *Social Science Quarterly* 92(3):710–34.

Walton, John. 1993. "Urban Sociology: The Contribution and Limits of Political Economy." *Annual Review of Sociology* 19:301–20.

Weir, Margaret. 2011. "Creating Justice for the Poor in the New Metropolis." Pp. 237–56 in *Justice and the American Metropolis*, edited by C. R. Hayward and T. Swanstrom. Minneapolis: Regents of the University of Minnesota.

Wherry, Frederick F. 2011. *The Philadelphia Barrio: The Arts, Branding, and Neighborhood Transformation*. Chicago; London: University of Chicago Press.

White, Monica M. 2010. "Shouldering Responsibility for the Delivery of Human Rights: A Case Study of the D-Town Farmers of Detroit." *Race Ethnicity: Multidisciplinary Global Perspectives* 3(2):189–211.

White, Monica M. 2011. "D-Town Farm: African American Resistance to Food Insecurity and the Transformation of Detroit." *Environmental Practice* 13(4):406–17.

Williams, Rhonda Y. 2004. *The Politics of Public Housing: Black Women's Struggles against Urban Inequality*. New York: Oxford University Press.

Wilson, William Julius. 1987. *The Truly Disadvantaged*. Chicago: University of Chicago Press.

Wilson, William Julius. 1996. *When Work Disappears: The World of the New Urban Poor*. New York: Knopf: Distributed by Random House.

Wilson, William Julius and Robert Aponte. 1985. "Urban Poverty." *Annual Review of sociology* 11:231–58.

Wodtke, Geoffrey, David Harding, and Felix Elwert. 2011. "Neighborhood Effects in Temporal Perspective: The Impact of Long-Term Exposure to Concentrated Disadvantage on High School Graduation." *American Sociological Review* 76(5):713–36.

Zuberi, Anita. 2010. "Limited Exposure: Children's Activities and Neighborhood Effects in the Gautreaux Two Housing Mobility Program." *Journal of Urban Affairs* 32(4):405–23.

Zukin, Sharon. 1980. "A Decade of the New Urban Sociology." *Theory and Society* 9(4):575–601.

CHAPTER 16

SEGREGATION AND THE PERPETUATION OF DISADVANTAGE

DOUGLAS S. MASSEY

THE discipline of sociology emerged along with urban industrialism in the late nineteenth and early twentieth centuries. From the very beginning, residential segregation in cities was a topic of central interest, especially to sociologists at the University of Chicago. It was the Chicago School's theories of urbanism that first developed segregation as a discrete field of sociological inquiry. Indeed, the foundational text in American sociology, Robert E. Park and Ernest W. Burgess's *Introduction to the Science of Sociology* (1921), treated patterns and processes of spatial segregation extensively. The first journal article on the subject of residential segregation was published in 1928 by Ernest Burgess in the *Annals of the American Academy of Political and Social Science*.

In their conceptual models, Chicago School theorists viewed spatial relations as fundamental to social relations and geographic location as a key factor in social stratification (Bulmer 1985; Park 1926). Even though research on residential segregation regularly followed the release of each decennial census, however, and while trends and patterns of both black and immigrant segregation were carefully monitored, during the 1960s and 1970s the study of segregation gradually became detached from analyses of social stratification; and the connection disappeared entirely during the heyday of the status attainment model, which conceived of stratification as an intergenerational process played out within families but not necessarily neighborhoods (Massey 2001).

Although research on residential segregation emerged first in the United States in the 1920s, after 1960 it was extended to other traditional countries of immigration such as Canada (Darroch and Marson 1971; Newman, Mezoff, and Richmond 1973; Balakrishnan 1976, 1982), Australia (Jones 1967; Timms 1969; Burnley 1972, 1976; Lee 1973; Peach 1974), and Israel (Klaff 1973, 1977). As these traditional immigrant-receiving countries were joined by new receiving nations in Europe, research on residential segregation spread to other nations in the 1970s, including Britain (Jones 1976;

Woods 1976, 1979; Prandy 1980; Peach 1982), Belgium (DeLannoy 1975), Germany (O'Loughlin 1980; O'Loughlin and Glebe 1980), the Netherlands (Drewe, van der Knaap, and H. M. Rodgers 1975). As in the United States, however, these studies of segregation were largely divorced from research on processes of social stratification and focused instead on the prospects for immigrant integration and assimilation (Massey 1981).

A turning point came with the 1987 publication of William Julius Wilson's *The Truly Disadvantaged*, which noted the growing concentration poverty in black neighborhoods and argued that concentrated disadvantage was critical to understanding the perpetuation of black poverty. In 1993 Douglas Massey and Nancy Denton followed up with *American Apartheid*, which argued that spatially concentrated poverty stemmed from a pernicious interaction between high segregation and rising inequality. They demonstrated that the geographic concentration of poverty inevitably followed from rising rates of poverty in highly segregated groups. Since then, segregation has featured prominently in sociological explanations of how advantage and disadvantage are perpetuated over time and across the generations (see Massey 2007; Peterson and Krivo 2012; Sampson 2012; Sharkey 2013).

In the remainder of this chapter I outline the historical origins of segregation, summarize early substantive and theoretical work done on the subject at the University of Chicago, and describe the most commonly used measure of segregation. I then describe the social mechanisms by which residential segregation is produced, focusing on the paradigmatic case of African Americans in the twentieth century. I then outline newer mechanisms that have arisen to promote racial-ethnic segregation in the twenty-first century and describe how it operates to promote socioeconomic inequality through the spatial concentration of poverty. After reviewing current levels and trends with respect to both racial and class segregation in cities around the world, I close with a discussion of implications for the future.

SEGREGATION AS A SOCIAL FACT

Segregation refers to the separation of socially defined groups in space. A social group may be distinguished by any trait, but studies of segregation have most commonly focused on those defined on the basis of race, class, and ethnicity, although patterns of segregation by age, religion, family status, and occupation have also been studied (White 1987). The geographic separation of social groups in residential space began with the emergence of the first cities around 10,000 years ago. The agricultural revolution liberated a small share of human beings from the daily need to find food themselves and enabled them to take up new occupations, thereby creating new forms of social differentiation and stratification that were expressed geographically (Massey 2005a).

Within preindustrial cities, religious and political elites typically occupied the center, surrounded closely by merchants, artisans, scribes, and craftsmen, whereas common laborers inhabited the urban periphery and outcasts were relegated to positions outside the city walls (Sjoberg 1960). Since mortality exceeded fertility, preindustrial cities could only be maintained through constant in-migration, typically from a large agrarian hinterland composed of diverse peoples, cultures, and languages, giving rise to origin groups that tended to cluster together residentially to yield ethnic segregation. At the same time, economies of agglomeration led to segregation by occupation, as specific crafts and guilds clustered within defined districts or along specific streets (Massey 2005a).

Segregation is thus a natural outgrowth of forces unleashed by urbanism; but it can also be imposed politically whenever a government decides to restrict certain groups to particular residential areas by fiat, as when Jews were consigned to the ghetto in medieval Venice or when special quarters were set aside for Europeans in colonial cities (Nightingale 2012). Prior to the nineteenth century, the potential for ecological segregation was limited, however, as all residents, rich or poor, had to live within walking distance of the things they needed on a daily basis (Hershberg et al. 1979). Residential densities were also limited by the inability to build very far upward with bricks and mortar (Massey 2005a).

It was the Industrial Revolution that dramatically increased the size and scale of cities and generated new economic stratification and social differentiation to increase the potential for residential segregation. With industrialization densities skyrocketed as structural steel enabled skyscrapers to reach new heights; economic inequality surged as huge fortunes were created through mass production; places of work and residence diverged as workers began to commute to jobs on railroads, subways, and trolleys; and all this occurred in a context of burgeoning ethnic diversity as steamships and railroads brought in waves of immigrants from around the globe.

Although many measures of residential segregation have been proposed over the years, the most commonly used remains the index of dissimilarity (Massey and Denton 1988). For any two groups, this index gives the relative proportion of majority and minority members that would have to exchange neighborhoods to achieve an even residential distribution. In an even distribution, each neighborhood has the same social composition as the urban area as a whole, and when the proportion to be moved is expressed as a percentage, the index varies from 0 (complete integration) to 100 (total segregation). If a city is composed 80 percent of Group A members and 20 percent of Group B members, for example, the dissimilarity index would equal 0 if every neighborhood were 80 percent comprised of A members and 20 percent comprised of B members. It would equal 100 if A and B members shared no neighborhood in common, so that all areas were either 100 percent A members or 100 percent B members.

Index values above 60 are generally considered to be "high," those between 30 and 60 "moderate," and those under 30 "low" (Massey and Denton 1993). In preindustrial cities, levels of segregation between ethnic groups generally fell within the low to moderate range, whereas in industrial cities they rose into the moderate and high range (Hershberg et al. 1979; Massey 1985). Much of the segregation in early industrial cities was generated through market processes identified by the Chicago School. Competition for spatial advantage produced geographic variation in land prices, home values, and rents (Burgess 1925); and spatial variation in the cost of real estate, in turn, separated people and functions geographically according to their ability to pay, yielding segregation by social class and land use. To the extent that wealth and income vary socially between groups, of course, segregation by race and ethnicity was produced as well.

The Chicago School viewed residential segregation as resulting from impersonal market forces, with neighborhoods being created and changed through a staged process of "ecological succession" (Park 1925, 1926). The first stage was "invasion," in which a new group entered a neighborhood dominated by pre-existing social group. Invasion was followed by "conflict" as the two groups struggled for spatial advantage, and this phase gave way to "consolidation" as members of the new group steadily replaced the original inhabitants to change the composition and character of the neighborhood. The final "climax" stage occurred when the new social group fully displaced the original inhabitants to create a new "natural area."

MANUFACTURING SEGREGATION
IN AMERICA

Although segregation by income, race, and ethnicity may indeed be created through impersonal market forces, segregation also stems from structures and actions that work outside markets. Over time it became clear that certain social groups, such as African Americans, experienced levels of segregation that were far too extreme to be attributed solely to market forces operating on intergroup differences in wealth and income. Levels of occupational segregation generally fell into the low or moderate range despite large income differentials between occupational categories, and black segregation did not decline with rising economic status (Massey and Denton 1993). Although ethnic segregation at times ventured into the high range, with dissimilarities in the range of 60 to 65, by 1920 black segregation had reached levels of 80 or above throughout the industrial North. As dissimilarity indices rose upward toward 100, it became less and less likely that segregation was being produced by impersonal market forces alone (Lieberson 1981).

As noted earlier, segregation can be imposed politically, such as when local authorities set aside different zones for different social groups. Politically mandated racial segregation did occur in U.S. cities for a brief time in the early twentieth century. In 1910 the Baltimore City Council became the first to pass an ordinance establishing separate neighborhoods for black and white residents, and similar laws mandating the spatial separation of the races soon spread to other cities throughout the nation

(Massey and Denton 1993). In 1917, however, the U.S. Supreme Court declared these laws to be unconstitutional, and government-mandated residential segregation ended in the United States (Rice 1968). From that point on, the residential segregation of African Americans was achieved by other mechanisms.

The earliest tool used to limit the expansion of black neighborhoods was violence. In the early years of the twentieth century, the entry of African Americans into white neighborhoods was often met by mob violence and vigilante attacks; and with black populations growing rapidly through in-migration from the rural South, white-on-black race riots swept the nation with increasing fury (Massey and Denton 1993). The destruction of property prompted the real estate industry to develop new institutional methods to enforce racial segregation without disrupting commerce. One such method involved embedding deed restrictions in property titles to prohibit rental or resale to African Americans. This method only dealt with properties on a case-by-case basis, however, and the industry responded by inventing restrictive covenants—private contracts that covered entire geographic areas in which owners mutually agreed not to rent or sell to African Americans. Once a majority of homeowners in an area approved a covenant, it became binding and was enforceable in court should anyone violate its provisions. In 1924 the National Association of Real Estate Brokers stated in its code of ethics that "a realtor should never be instrumental in introducing into a neighborhood ... members of any race or nationality ... whose presence will clearly be detrimental to property values in that neighborhood" (Helper 1969:201), and in 1927 the Chicago Real Estate Board developed a model covenant for use by realtors across the nation (Philpott 1978).

As the New Deal gained momentum in the wake of the Great Depression of the 1930s, the federal government increasingly intervened in the political economy of the United States and thus became progressively implicated in the perpetuation of racial segregation (Katznelson 2005). The Federal Housing Administration (FHA) and later the Veterans Administration (VA), for example, until 1950 recommended that covenants be applied to all properties purchased with FHA or VA mortgages (Jackson 1985). In addition, both agencies mandated the use of "residential security maps" that color-coded neighborhoods according to their credit worthiness. Red was used to indicate risky property that was ineligible for government-insured loans and, of course, black and mixed neighborhoods were invariably coded red, thus institutionalizing the practice of "redlining" in the lending industry (Jackson 1985). The FHA underwriting manual justified these practices by stating that "if a neighborhood is to retain stability, it is necessary that properties shall continue to be occupied by the same social and racial classes" (Jackson 1985:208).

Black residential segregation was also perpetuated privately by rampant discrimination against African Americans in the sale and rental of homes. One study of real estate practices in the 1950s revealed pervasive bias against black home seekers in virtually all American cities (Helper 1969), and a survey of real estate agents in Chicago revealed that 80 percent refused to sell property to African Americans in white neighborhoods while 68 percent refused even to rent to them. Most agents (56 percent) relied on a flat refusal to stop black entry into an area, though a minority (24 percent) employed subterfuges, such as telling black home seekers that a unit was sold when it was not. In addition to these hard and soft refusals, real estate agents also engaged in a subtler form of discrimination known as "steering" in which African Americans were systematically channeled into neighborhoods that were poorer, blacker, more dilapidated, and closer to existing black neighborhoods than the neighborhoods shown to comparable whites (Saltman 1979; Pearce 1979).

Discrimination in the sale and rental of homes was not outlawed until the Fair Housing Act of 1968; discrimination in mortgage lending was not prohibited until the 1974 Equal Credit Opportunity Act; and redlining was only banned in 1977 by the Community Reinvestment Act (see Metcalf 1988). Although these laws outlawed discrimination, however, they contained few enforcement provisions, generally placing the onus on individual victims to prove that they had suffered discrimination in court. As a result, discrimination did not cease so much as become clandestine after the Civil Rights Era (Massey and Denton 1993).

Such discrimination cannot be observed directly, of course, and must be assessed indirectly using "audit studies" in which black and white testers trained by investigators pose as home seekers and inquire about the availability of housing or loans from a sample of realtors or lenders (Blank and Massey 2006). After the encounter they report their experiences, and their reports are analyzed to detect differences on the basis of race. Audits were initially undertaken mainly by local fair-housing groups; one review concluded that "racial discrimination continues to be a dominant feature of metropolitan housing markets in the 1980s" (Galster 1990a:172) and that racial steering occurred in as many as half of all transactions (Galster 1990b).

Although audit studies continue to be carried out by private fair housing groups, eventually the U.S. Department of Housing and Urban Development launched its own nationwide audit program (see Wienk et al. 1979; Yinger 1995; Turner et al. 2002), with audits conducted in 1977, 1988, and 2000, and each documenting significant discrimination against African Americans (Turner et al. 2002). A comparison of results from 1977 and 1988 revealed little change in rates or patterns of discrimination; and although the incidence of white-favored marketing generally fell between 1988 and 2000, the likelihood of racial steering rose; and the decline in white favoritism was greater in sales than in rental markets (Ross and Turner 2004).

From 1945 to 1970, rapid black population growth propelled by in-migration brought about the spillover of black home seekers into adjacent white neighborhoods despite ongoing discrimination, resulting in a moving color line that gradually shifted in space. By the 1960s expanding black neighborhoods had begun to encroach on districts in which prominent white citizens had place-bound investments such as hospitals, universities, or businesses, leading local authorities to turn to federal urban renewal and public housing programs to shore up the walls of the ghetto (Hirsch 1983; Bauman 1987). Local development authorities were granted the power of eminent domain to gain control of land on the leading edge of black residential expansion. After evicting black residents and shunting them off to public housing projects, the authorities then converted the land to institutional, commercial, or upscale residential uses, thereby blocking expansion of the ghetto toward the threatened district (White 1980; Hays 1985; Massey and Denton 1993).

These government interventions came to an end after 1968 when fair-housing advocates drew upon new civil rights laws to sue local development authorities to prevent further destruction of black neighborhoods. Thereafter local authorities increasingly turned to zoning as a means of forestalling the entry of poor minorities into white residential areas. Although the competition for spatial advantage generates geographic variation in real estate values, it does not automatically follow that high- and low-cost housing must be located in different residential areas. In areas where land prices are high, developers can erect multiunit structures to amortize the costs over a large number of buyers or renters (Glaeser and Gyourko 2008).

What prevents this strategy from being implemented is zoning that limits the density of residential construction (Pendall 2000). In general, the more restrictive the density zoning regime in a given area, the fewer the housing units allowed per acre of land; and the higher the cost of homes, the fewer the number of households that can afford to live in them (Glaeser, Gyourko, and Saks 2005). Recent studies have uncovered a strong causal relationship between restrictive density zoning and both class and racial segregation (Rothwell and Massey 2009, 2010). As times have changed and legal environments have shifted, the mechanisms promoting segregation in U.S. metropolitan areas have adjusted (Massey 2005b).

SEGREGATION AND STRATIFICATION

Sociologists have identified two fundamental mechanisms of stratification—exploitation and exclusion (Tilly 1998; Massey 2007). Exploitation occurs when people in one social group expropriate a resource produced by members of another group to prevent them from realizing the full value of their labor in helping produce it. The most extreme form of exploitation is slavery, and, short of this, exploitation is achieved by discrimination achieved by the imposition of social mechanisms that systematically reduce the rewards to investments of time and resources by members of a disfavored out-group. Exclusion occurs when a dominant social group restricts access to a scarce resource, either through outright denial or by exercising monopoly control that requires subordinate group members to pay rent in return for access. Racially targeted violence, deed restrictions, covenants, redlining, biased marketing, and restrictive zoning clearly constitute mechanisms of exclusion barring African Americans from entry to certain neighborhoods, while channeling them to disadvantaged neighborhoods, and compelling them pay more than whites to attain certain homes and reside in certain neighborhoods clearly constitute discrimination.

Through segregation, mechanisms of exploitation and discrimination become more efficient, given that dominant groups can easily disinvest in a subordinate group by disinvesting in a place and can easily target a segregated group for invidious treatment (Massey and Denton 1993). During the wave of subprime lending that accompanied the recent housing bubble, for example, black neighborhoods were singled out for predatory lending in a process of "reverse redlining" that systematically stripped home equity from black communities, to the point where black-white dissimilarity emerged the strongest single predictor of the number and rate of postbubble foreclosures in U.S. metropolitan areas (Rugh and Massey 2010; Rugh, Albright, and Massey 2015), causing black wealth to plummet after 2007 (Taylor et al. 2010).

Residential segregation also leaves minority group members vulnerable to economic shocks that increase poverty and inequality within the group, since the extra poverty created among segregated groups during any downturn will be concentrated in a restricted geographic space (Massey 1990). For example, if the black poverty rate rises from 10 percent to 20 percent in the course of a recession, in cities where blacks and whites live in separate neighborhoods, the spatial concentration of poverty necessarily doubles for all African Americans; but if blacks and whites are evenly distributed across neighborhoods, then the rise in black poverty will be spread out and buffered by the presence of whites. As a consequence, if blacks are a relatively small minority and the white poverty does not rise very much, the neighborhoods inhabited by black residents will experience little change in the concentration of poverty. Later work showed that this mechanism of poverty concentration is further exacerbated by class segregation (Massey and Fischer 2000) and that spatially concentrated disadvantage ultimately stems from a three-way interaction between racial segregation, class segregation within race, and class segregation between racial groups (Quillian 2012).

When poverty is concentrated geographically, of course, anything associated with poverty is also concentrated in space, yielding high concentrations of crime, welfare dependency, substance abuse, and disrupted families to create a uniquely disadvantaged social environment (Massey, Gross, and Eggers 1991). Exposure to high rates of crime and social disorder, in turn, have serious negative consequences for individuals and families on a wide range of dimensions: reducing access to employment, lowering incomes, increasing dependency, raising crime exposure to crime and violence, undermining educational achievement, compromising health, and generally impairing the formation of cognitive and behavioral skills (Massey 2004; Sampson 2012; Massey et al. 2013).

Opportunities and resources are always distributed unevenly in space, and in market societies people move residentially to access them. Those who are segregated, however, cannot move freely to access resources and often find themselves isolated from opportunities for social and economic advancement (Massey and Denton 1985). Historically, most ethnic groups have achieved social mobility by translating socioeconomic gains into residential gains (Massey and Mullan 1984). As income rises, families move into safer neighborhoods with higher home values, better schools, lower insurance costs, and social networks that connect people to jobs and education, thus putting themselves and especially their children in a better position to move even further up the socioeconomic ladder. By interspersing economic and residential mobility, people ratchet themselves up the socioeconomic ladder step by step, a mobility strategy that is curtailed under conditions of high residential segregation (Massey and Denton 1993).

For these reasons, segregation has been called the structural linchpin of racial stratification in the United States (Pettigrew 1979; Bobo 1989), just as it was in the Union of South Africa under apartheid (Clark and Worger 2011). Whereas segregation in South Africa was achieved by fiat under the Group Areas Act of 1950, however, such a strategy was unavailable in the United States after 1917 and, as we have seen, the spatial separation of blacks and whites was achieved through a combination of discriminatory and exclusionary actions enacted formally and informally in the public and private spheres. Despite the contrast in causal mechanisms, however, the outcome in terms of segregation was much the same, as shown in Figure 16.1, which plots trends in average levels of black residential dissimilarity within urban areas of South Africa (from Christopher 1990) and the United States (from Massey et al. 2009). In cases where South African census dates did not correspond to U.S. census dates, the American indices were adjusted by interpolation between the bracketing U.S. census dates.

As can be seen, in 1911 black-white dissimilarities averaged between 60 and 65 in both countries (65 in South Africa and 62 in the United States). In the United States, however, segregation levels rose steadily over the ensuing decades to achieve a dissimilarity of 77 by 1951, where it remained until 1970. In contrast, South African segregation fell between 1911 and 1921 and lagged well behind U.S. segregation until 1950 when, spurred by the Group Areas Act, black segregation levels rose rapidly to surpass those observed in the United States, reaching an average dissimilarity of 82 in 1970. Thereafter the paths diverged, as segregation levels began to decline in the United States in response to civil rights legislation while segregation continued to rise under apartheid in South Africa, reaching a value of 88 in 1985 compared with 68 in the United States.

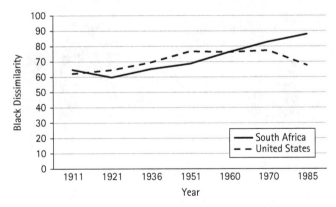

FIGURE 16.1 Average Black Dissimilarity Indices in United States and South African Urban Areas 1911–1985

Sources: For South Africa, Christopher (1990); and for the United States, Massey et al. (2009).

SEGREGATION IN THE WORLD TODAY

While studies of ethnic and racial segregation have long been undertaken in the United States and other traditional countries of immigration, the subject has more recently engaged social scientists in other nations (Massey 1985). Studies of Israeli segregation, for example, have traditionally focused on spatial separation between Jews of European and Middle Eastern origins; but later work has concentrated on Arab-Jewish segregation. In Europe, the subject of segregation rose to prominence when the continent was transformed by mass immigration in the late twentieth century, turning many nations into multiracial/multiethnic societies in the course of a few years and creating deep concerns about assimilation. More recently, scholars have begun to consider levels and patterns of segregation in other multiracial societies, such as Brazil and Mexico, and have also turned their attention to segregation on the basis of class.

Racial-Ethnic Segregation in North America

Although Canada, like the United States, has a long tradition of immigration, it was only in the final decades of the twentieth century that it became a multiracial society through mass immigration from new origin countries in Africa, the Caribbean, and Asia. At the same time, the United States experienced a dramatic rise in immigration from Asia and Latin America that transformed its traditional black-white dichotomy into a complex multihued mosaic. Since the close of the Civil Rights Era, levels of black-white dissimilarity have generally fallen in U.S. urban areas. Figure 16.2 shows average levels of residential segregation in metropolitan areas of the United States in

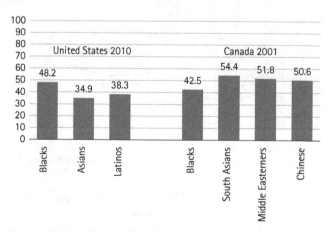

FIGURE 16.2 Average Dissimilarity Indices for Major Race-Ethnicity Groups in the United States and Canada

Sources: For the United States: Author's computation from census data; and for Canada, Walks and Bourne (2006).

2010 (computed by the author from census data) and for Canada in 2001 (from Walks and Bourne 2006). As indicated by the left-hand bars, by 2010 the average level of black-white dissimilarity had fallen to around 48 (from a peak of 77 forty years earlier), compared with levels of 35 for Asians and 38 for Latinos. Despite the massive entry of immigrants from abroad, levels of Latino and Asian segregation have generally remained stable or increased slightly since 1970 (Massey et al. 2009).

The indices in Figure 16.2 are simple arithmetic averages computed across a large number of metropolitan areas, however, many of which contain few minority group members. When weighted averages are computed that weight each area by the size of its minority population, the black dissimilarity index rises to 60, the lower threshold for high segregation. In contrast, segregation levels for black Canadians are and have always been moderate (cf. Fong 1996), with an average dissimilarity index of 42.5 in 2001. Unlike the their counterparts in the United States, moreover, Asians in Canada are more segregated than blacks, with South Asians being highest at 54.4 followed by Middle Easterners at 51.8 and Chinese at 50.6. Although Asians are the least segregated of all major racial-ethnic groups in the United States, they are the most segregated in Canada, yet never approaching the high range.

On average, segregation levels in North American metropolitan areas thus appear to be converging on levels in the moderate range of segregation, with averages in the range of 35 to 55. Nonetheless, in a subset of U.S. metropolitan areas historically characterized by a high degree of segregation across multiple geographic dimensions simultaneously, segregation levels have declined little over the decades, and in the case of Latinos have actually increased (Massey 2004; Wilkes and Iceland 2004; Massey and Rugh 2014). As of 2010, these "hypersegregated" metropolitan areas contained almost half of all urban African Americans and a fifth of urban Latinos, and were converging on dissimilarity values around 60—more than enough segregation to perpetuate poverty by creating separate and highly unequal social worlds for blacks and Hispanics relative to whites (see Peterson and Krivo 2012; Sampson 2012; Sharkey 2013). Recent work by Massey and Rugh (2014) indicates that such high levels of segregation are produced and sustained by restrictive density-zoning regimes in suburbs combined with high levels of antiblack and anti-Latino sentiment in certain metropolitan areas.

Racial-Ethnic Segregation in Europe

Whereas levels of segregation in North America have been falling or holding steady, in Europe they have been rising and Figure 16.3 summarizes the situation in selected European nations using the latest available data. The left-hand bars show average levels of dissimilarity in Stockholm between people originating in Ethiopia, Somalia, Turkey, and the Middle East relative to native Swedes in the year 2000 (from Andersson 2007). Despite its egalitarian economic structure and strong social supports, levels of residential segregation in Sweden are remarkably high. The least segregated group shown, Ethiopians, display a dissimilarity index of 62, compared with values of 65 for Iraqis

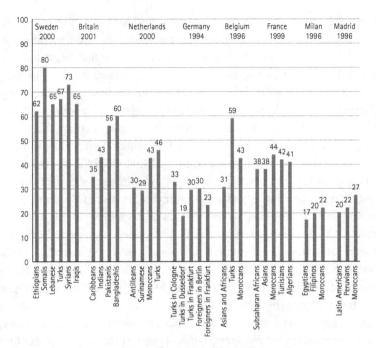

FIGURE 16.3 Residential Dissimilarities for Immigrant Groups in Europe

Sources: For Sweden, Andersson (2007); for Britain, Peach (2007); for the Netherlands, Musterd and Ostendorf (2007); for Germany, Kemper (1998) and van Kempen (2005); for Belgium, Arbaci (2008); for France, Ke Shon (2011); and for Milan and Madrid, Arbaci (2008).

and Lebanese, 67 for Turks, and 80 for Somalis. By way of contrast, dissimilarities for Germans and Poles in Stockholm stood at just 17 and 28, respectively, whereas the index for Chileans was 51 (all not shown).

Thus groups that are Christian and white (e.g., Poles) display low levels of segregation; those that are darker skinned but still Christian (Chileans) evince moderate levels of segregation; those that are black and Christian (Ethiopians) display an index just into the high range; those that are dark-skinned and Muslim display levels of segregation clearly in the high range (Turks); and those that are black and Muslim (Somalis) display an extreme level of segregation that is comparable to that experienced by Africans under apartheid or African Americans before the Civil Rights Era. Although levels of segregation in Sweden may be rather high, to the extent that the Swedish welfare state mitigates inequality, the potential for the spatially concentrated poverty is muted.

As the next set of bars to the right shows, we observe a similar though less extreme pattern of residential segregation in Britain (from Peach 2007). Persons of Caribbean origin (typically Christians of mixed European and African origins) display a very moderate level of segregation with a dissimilarity index of just 35 relative to white Britons. Indians, who are Hindus or Sikhs that exhibit a variety of skin tones but are generally darker than Britons, display a dissimilarity index of 43, still well within the moderate range. Among migrants from the Indian subcontinent who are Muslim, however, segregation levels approach or reach the high range, with dissimilarities of 56 for Pakistanis and 60 for Bangladeshis (whose skin tone is often quite dark). Given the starker economic inequalities observed in Britain than Scandinavia and other European countries (Smeeding 2005), this residential pattern creates real potential for the concentration of poverty among Muslims.

The next set of bars to the right depicts average levels of residential dissimilarity between immigrant origin groups and nongroup members in Amsterdam, The Hague, and Rotterdam (from Musterd and Ostendorf 2007). As in Britain, residential dissimilarities for the two Caribbean-origin groups—persons from the Antilles and Suriname—are on the border between the low and moderate ranges with values of 30 and 29, respectively. In contrast, the index for Moroccans is 43 and that for Turks is 46. These higher but still moderate levels of dissimilarity are likely lower than those reported for Britain because the dissimilarity indices measure segregation between minority group members and all others rather than between minority members and whites.

The bars in the middle of the figure present dissimilarities for Turks and all foreigners relative to Germans in selected cities circa 1994 (from Kemper 1998 and van Kempen 2005). Compared with Turks in Sweden and the Netherlands, those in Germany do not appear to be particularly segregated. Turks in Dusseldorf exhibited a dissimilarity index of just 19, compared to respective values of 30 and 33 for Turks in Frankfurt and Cologne. In Berlin foreigners taken together evinced an index value of 30, compared with 23 for all foreigners in Frankfurt. Although Turks in Germany may not be very segregated, however, those in Belgium approach the high range with a dissimilarity index of 59 relative to Belgians. In contrast, the dissimilarity for Moroccans is just 43 and only 31 for Asians and Africans combined (see next set of bars to the right, from Arbaci [2008]).

The segregation of Moroccans, Asians, and Africans is also moderate in metropolitan areas of France, as indicated by the third set of bars from the right, which show average levels of dissimilarity between selected immigrant origin groups and persons of French nationality born in France (from Ke Shon 2011). Whereas sub-Saharan Africans and Asians (which here include Turks) both display index values of 38, the dissimilarities for Algerians, Tunisians, and Moroccans are 41, 42, and 44, respectively—all squarely in the moderate range. Finally we consider levels of segregation in Italy and Spain, by graphing levels of residential dissimilarity between native citizens and persons of immigrant origin in Milan and Madrid in 1996 (from Arbaci 2008). In both cases, segregation levels are universally in the low range no matter which immigrant group is considered. In Milan dissimilarity levels range from 17 among Egyptians to 20 among Filipinos to 22 among Moroccans, whereas in Madrid they extend from 20 for Latin Americans generally to 22 for Peruvians and to 27 for Moroccans.

Given differences in the size and definition of the spatial units used in computing dissimilarity indices across countries and the variability in the reference groups (all others versus whites or natives), one must be cautious in drawing hard conclusions from the foregoing statistics. In general, levels of racial-ethnic segregation in European cities appear to be quite variable, ranging from very low to very high levels depending on the group and the setting. On the whole, levels of residential segregation appear to be greater in northern than southern Europe, and within most nations segregation is greater for Muslims than for other religious groups. Holding religion constant, segregation also appears to be greater for darker skinned nationalities in most places.

In general, then, European cities do not exhibit very high segregation levels comparable to those observed for African Americans in the United States before the Civil Rights Era or in hypersegregated metropolitan areas today. Nonetheless, relatively high levels of segregation beyond what can easily be attributed to neutral market forces prevail for Africans and Muslim-origin groups in Sweden, for Bangladeshis and Pakistanis in Britain, and for Turks in Belgium. Black Caribbeans are moderately segregated in Britain and the Netherlands; and Muslims from North Africa and the Middle East are moderately segregated in the Netherlands, Germany, France, Spain, and Italy. Given that minority groups in most European countries generally have higher rates of poverty, unemployment, and dependency, segregation must be playing some role in concentrating disadvantage throughout the region and perpetuating poverty, but research documenting these connections is not nearly as well developed as in the United States.

Religious Segregation in Israel

Although Israel remains quite divided on the basis of both class and Jewish ethnicity (Ashkenazim versus Sephardim), by far the most salient cleavage is between Arabs and Jews. Figure 16.4 draws on work by Falah (1996) to show trends in Jewish-Arab residential dissimilarity in five Israeli urban areas that contain significant numbers of both groups. Arab-Jewish segregation within cities has always been high in Israel and appears to be increasing over time, rising from a dissimilarity index of

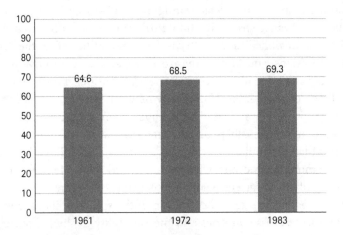

FIGURE 16.4 Average Jewish-Arab Dissimilarity in Five Israeli Cities

Source: Falah (1996).

around 65 in 1961 to 69 in 1983. Owing to a lack of data, more recent calculations are not available, but given Israel's steady polarization on the issue of Palestine, a decline would be surprising.

Most of the segregation between Arabs and Jews, however, occurs not within Israeli cities but between them. Within the state of Israel, Arabs and Jews concentrate in very different towns and cities. Moreover, within the entire zone of Israeli control, spatial segregation is mostly between Jews living in Israel proper and its annexed areas and Arabs living in occupied territories, communities that are now separated by a physical wall (Yiftachel and Yacobi 2005), a spatial configuration that some observers consider a kind of "apartheid" (Carter 2007; Yiftahel 2001, 2009; Engler 2010). According to Yiftachel (2006), this state of affairs is created by an "ethnocratic" state whose policies privilege Jews over Arabs in the control of land, access to resources, investment for development, and the distribution of political power. Whatever label is used, it is clear that residential segregation plays a central role in perpetuating poverty, exclusion, and the concentration of disadvantage for Arabs.

Racial-Ethnic Segregation in Developing Nations

In addition to South Africa, scholars have examined levels and patterns of racial and ethnic segregation in other developing nations. Figure 16.5 updates the earlier data reported for South Africa with computations based on the post-apartheid census of 2001 (from Christopher 2005) and adds dissimilarity indices computed for minority groups in Brazil (from Telles 1992), Argentina (from Groisman and Suarez 2009), and Mexico (from Monkkonen 2010). The figures for South Africa represent average

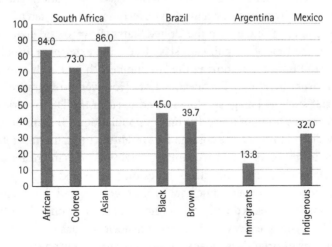

FIGURE 16.5 Average Racial-Ethnic Dissimilarity Indices in Selected Developing Nations

Sources: For South Africa, Christopher (2005); for Brazil, Telles (1992); for Argentina, Groisman and Suarez (2009); and for Mexico, Monkkonen (2010).

dissimilarities computed between Africans and non-Africans, colored persons and noncolored persons (in South African parlance, "colored" are persons of racially mixed origins), and Asians and non-Asians in urban areas of South Africa. Recall that, in 1985, a few years before the demise of apartheid, average black dissimilarity in South African cities stood at 88 (see Figure 16.1). As shown in Figure 16.5, the residential situation of Africans changed little by 2001, when the index stood at 84, compared with values of 86 for Asians and 73 for those labeled colored. With the steady decline of black segregation in the United States since the Civil Rights Era, South Africa is now the undisputed world leader in racial-ethnic segregation, apartheid or not, and that the spatial separation of whites from the black and colored populations constitutes a primary mechanism by which socioeconomic resources continue to be reserved disproportionately for white citizens.

The largest African-origin populations outside Africa are in Brazil, which historically has adhered to an ideology of racial mixture and intergroup tolerance that viewed race as a complex, multicategory continuum ranging from white European and black Africans rather than a stark black-white dichotomy (Telles 2004). As shown in Figure 16.5, this more fluid ideology appears to yield levels of segregation that are very moderate compared with those observed historically in the United States. The average black dissimilarity in metropolitan areas of Brazil stood at just 45, compared to a value of 40 for those identified by the census as "brown" (again people of mixed origins).

Although levels of racial segregation may be lower in Brazil than in the United States, the degree of socioeconomic inequality between the races is much higher, and rich and poor tend to live in very different neighborhoods. As a result, concentrations of urban poverty in Brazil generally exceed those observed in the United States (Szwarcwald et al. 2000). Whereas concentrated poverty in Brazil is produced by moderate racial segregation, high class segregation, and great racial inequality, in the United States it is produced by high racial segregation, moderate class segregation, and lower racial inequality. However produced, concentrated poverty can be expected to have the same deleterious outcomes in Brazil as in the United States (Szwarcwald et al. 2000).

In Argentina, the lack of a significant slave trade, the extermination of indigenous people, and mass immigration during the late nineteenth and early twentieth centuries created an overwhelmingly European nation. However, immigration from neighboring countries such as Paraguay, Bolivia, and Peru in the late twentieth and early twenty-first centuries brought a sizeable brown population of Indians and mestizos to Argentinian society. However, the column for Argentina in Figure 16.5 refers to segregation between immigrants and natives among neighborhoods in greater Buenos Aires and reveals very little segregation, with an index only of around 14.

Although Mexico was shaped somewhat by immigration and slavery, its slave trade was relatively small and ended early, while the volume of immigration from Europe was modest. The principal cleavage in Mexico historically has been between Creoles (persons of European origin), mestizos (persons of mixed European and Indian origins), and indigenous people. Since the revolution of 1910–1920, however, the principal distinction has been between Indians and all others. The bar on the right side of

Figure 16.5 shows the average level of dissimilarity between Indians and non-Indians in Mexican urban areas during the year 2000 to reveal a moderate level of indigenous segregation, with an average dissimilarity index of 32. Thus levels of racial-ethnic segregation in Latin America generally appear to be modest compared with those in South Africa or the pre–civil rights United States, though high levels of intergroup economic inequality can be expected to produce significant concentrations of poverty.

Class Segregation in the Americas

Since the publication of Wilson's *Truly Disadvantaged* in 1987, social scientists have become increasingly interested in segregation by class and socioeconomic status, as concentrated poverty is now seen to stem from an interaction between class segregation within groups, class segregation within groups, and racial segregation (Quillian 2012). Although class segregation has become a central topic of study in the United States (see Massey and Fischer 2003; Fischer et al. 2004; Reardon and Bischoff 2011), little work on the subject exists for Europe; but a recent compilation of studies by Roberts and Wilson (2009) offers a window on class segregation in cities of the Americas. Figure 16.6 summarizes their results by showing selected dissimilarity indices for the poor versus nonpoor persons, variously defined, in selected large urban areas of the Americas.

The definition of poverty, of course, is subjective and varies from country to country and in response to data availability. In their analysis of metropolitan Buenos Aires, Groisman and Suarez (2009) identified poor families using a factor scale of poverty,

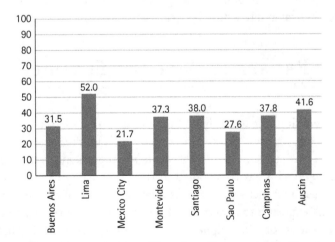

FIGURE 16.6 Residential Dissimilarities of Poor from Nonpoor in the Americas circa 2000

Sources: For Buenos Aires, Groisman and Suarez (2009); for Lima, Peters (2009); for Mexico City, Villareal and Hamilton (2009); for Montevideo, Katzman and Retamoso (2009); for Santiago, Sabatini et al. (2009); for Sao Paulo, da Gama Torres and Mirandola Bichir (2009); for Campinas, Pinto da Cunha and Jimenez (2009); and for Austin, Flores and Wilson (2009).

and Peters (2009) used a similar scale of socioeconomic status to identify poor households in Lima. In Mexico City, however, Villareal and Hamilton (2009) defined the poor as those who earned less than twice the minimum wage. In other cases scholars relied on educational data. In Montevideo, Katzman and Retamoso (2009) defined the poor as those with less than a primary education; in Santiago they were those not finishing high school (Sabatini et al. 2009); in Sao Paulo they were those not completing eighth grade (da Gama Torres and Mirandola Bichir 2009); and in Campinas, Brazil, dissimilarities were computed between those below and above the average educational level (Pinto da Cunha and Jimenez 2009). By way of comparison, Flores and Wilson (2009) computed residential dissimilarity in Austin, Texas between those who had and had not completed high school, and we present this information on the far right of Figure 16.6.

As seen in Figure 16.6 the lowest level of segregation between poor and nonpoor are in Mexico City and Sao Paulo, Brazil, with respective dissimilarities of 21.7 and 27.6, both in the low range. The two highest levels of class segregation are in Lima, Peru, and Austin, Texas, where the poor versus nonpoor dissimilarities were 52.0 and 41.6, respectively. In the remaining urban areas, the segregation of the poor was in the lower reaches of the moderate range, with values of 31.5 in Buenos Aires, 37.3 in Montevideo, 37.8 in Campinas, and 27.6 in Sao Paulo. The fact that class segregation is so elevated in an American metropolitan area such as Austin may surprise some, but levels of socioeconomic segregation have generally increased in recent decades. With the exception of a respite in 2000 after the economic boom of the 1990s, the degree of income segregation and class isolation has risen steadily in the United States (see Massey et al. 2009; Lichter et al. 2011; Reardon and Bischoff 2011; Fry and Taylor 2012). In other words, as black segregation has fallen in the United States, and as Asian and Hispanic segregation have held steady, the degree of class segregation has risen to create an urban mosaic defined by a complicated interaction between race and class.

Prospects for the Future

At present all developed nations have become countries of immigration, whether they choose to recognize this reality officially or not; and international migration has turned globally connected cities everywhere into multiracial, multiethnic metropolises (Massey et al. 1998) as it has contributed to rising inequality (Massey 1996). Recent work has demonstrated that segregation is a key determinant of concentrated urban poverty and that exposure to concentrated poverty and its correlates undermine life chances along a variety of salient dimensions to constitute a critical link in the production and reproduction of disadvantage. Given the importance of segregation in the process of stratification, its accurate and timely measurement represents and important goal for social scientists around the world. Unfortunately, outside North America, a few countries in Europe, and even fewer countries in the developing world, little information on racial-ethnic segregation exists; and statistics on trends and levels of class segregation are even rarer. As a result, a critical feature of contemporary stratification systems necessary to understanding the production and reproduction of inequality is understudied and poorly understood.

The data considered here indicate that levels of segregation are rising in many, though not all, nations of Europe, and in some places certain groups have already reached high levels of segregation as measured by the dissimilarity index. In general, segregation levels tend to be greater in northern than southern Europe and for dark-skinned non-Christian groups, especially Muslims. In the United States, levels of racial segregation are falling for blacks and holding steady for Hispanics and Asians despite rapid increases in those populations. Levels of racial-ethnic segregation in Europe and the United States thus appear to be converging in the moderate range, joining other multiracial societies in the Western Hemisphere such as Canada, Brazil, Mexico, and Argentina.

Paradoxically, however, as racial segregation has moderated in the United States, class segregation has risen and now equals or exceeds the relatively high levels of class segregation that have historically prevailed in many Latin American cities. Unfortunately the combination of rising income inequality, growing income segregation, and declining but still significant racial segregation is a formula for the geographic concentration of poverty, which recent work suggests is a critical nexus in the reproduction of disadvantage, not only in the United States but in any society that exhibits this combination of attributes. Whether concentrated poverty becomes endemic to societies in the twenty-first century depends very much on future trends in racial and class segregation as well as inequality, and at this juncture the signs are troubling.

REFERENCES

Andersson, Roger. 2007. "Ethnic Residential Segregation and Integration Processes in Sweden." Pp. 61–90 in *Residential Segregation and the Integration of Immigrants: Britain, the Netherlands and Sweden*, edited by Karen Schönwälder. Discussion Paper SP IV 2007-602. Berlin: Wissenschaftszentrum Berlin für Sozialforschung.

Arbaci, Sonia. 2008. "(Re)Viewing Ethnic Residential Segregation in Southern European Cities: Housing and Urban Regimes as Mechanisms of Marginalisation." *Housing Studies* 23(4):589–613.

Balakrishnan, T. R. 1976. "Ethnic Residential Segregation in the Metropolitan Areas of Canada." *Canadian Journal of Sociology* 1:481–98.

Balakrishnan, T. R. 1982. "Changing Patterns of Ethnic Residential Segregation in the Metropolitan Areas of Canada." *Canadian Review of Sociology and Anthropology* 19:92–110.

Bauman, John F. 1987. *Public Housing, Race, and Renewal: Urban Planning in Philadelphia, 1920–1974.* Philadelphia: Temple University Press.

Blank, Rebecca M. and Douglas S. Massey. 2006. "Assessing Racial Discrimination: Methods and Measures." Pp. 61–80 in *Fairness in the Housing Market*, edited by John Goering. Lanham, MD: Rowman and Littlefield.

Bobo, Lawrence. 1989. "Keeping the Linchpin in Place: Testing the Multiple Sources of Opposition to Residential Integration." *International Review of Social Psychology* 2:305–23.

Bulmer, Martin. 1985. *The Chicago School of Sociology: Institutionalization, Diversity and the Rise of Sociological Research*. Chicago: University of Chicago Press.

Burgess, Ernest W. 1925. "The Growth of the City: An Introduction to a Research Project." Pp. 47–62 in *The City*, edited by Robert E. Park and Ernest W. Burgess. Chicago: University of Chicago Press.

Burgess, Ernest W. 1928. "Residential Segregation in American Cities. *Annals of the American Academy of Political and Social Science* 140:105–15.

Burnley, Ian H. 1972. "European Immigrant Settlement Patterns in Metropolitan Sydney 1947–1966." *Australian Geographical Studies* 10:61–78.

Burnley, Ian H. 1976. "Southern European Populations in the Residential Structure of Melbourne 1947–1971." *Australian Geographical Studies* 14:116–32.

Christopher, A. J. 1990. "Apartheid and Urban Segregation Levels in South Africa." *Urban Studies* 27:328–35.

Christopher, A. J. 2005. "The Slow Pace of Desegregation in South African Cities, 1996–2001." *Urban Studies* 42:2305–20.

Clark, Nancy L. and William H. Worger. 2011. *South Africa: The Rise and Fall of Apartheid*. 2nd ed. London: Longman.

da Gama Torres, Haroldo, and Renata Mirandola Bichir. 2009. "Residential Segregation in Sao Paulo: Consequences for Urban Policies." Pp. 145–68 in *Urban Segregation and Governance in the Americas*, edited by Bryan R. Roberts and Robert H. Wilson. New York: Palgrave Macmillan.

Darroch, A. Gordon and Wilfred G. Marson. 1972. "The Social Class Basis of Ethnic Residential Segregation: The Canadian Case." *American Journal of Sociology* 77:491–510.

DeLannoy, W. 1975. "Residential Segregation of Foreigners in Brussels." *Bulletin Societé Belge d'Etudes Geographiques* 44:215–38.

Drewe, Paul, G. A. van der Knaap, G. Mik, and H. M. Rodgers. 1975. "Segregation in Rotterdam: An Explorative Study on Theory, Data, and Policy." *Tijdschrift voor Economische en Social Geografie* 66:204–16.

Engler, Yves. 2010. *Canada and Israel: Building Apartheid*. Winnepeg, MB: Fernwood.

Falah, Ghazi. 1996. "Living Together Apart: Residential Segregation in Mixed Arab-Jewish Cities in Israel." *Urban Studies* 33:823–57.

Fischer, Claude S., Gretchen Stockmayer, Jon Stiles, and Michael Hout. 2004. "Distinguishing the Geographic Levels and Social Dimensions of U.S. Metropolitan Segregation, 1960–2000." *Demography* 41:37–59.

Flores, Carolina and Robert H. Wilson. 2009. "Changing Patterns of Residential Segregation in Austin." Pp. 187–204 in *Urban Segregation and Governance in the Americas*, edited by Bryan R. Roberts and Robert H. Wilson. New York: Palgrave Macmillan.

Fong, Eric. 1996. "A Comparative Perspective on Racial Residential Segregation: American and Canadian Experiences." *Sociological Quarterly* 37:199–226.

Fry, Richard and Paul Taylor. 2012. "The Rise of Residential Segregation by Income." Washington, DC: Pew Center on Social and Demographic Trends.

Galster, George C. 1990a. "Racial Discrimination in Housing Markets during the 1980s: A Review of the Audit Evidence." *Journal of Planning Education and Research* 9:165–75.

Galster, George C. 1990b. "Racial Steering by Real Estate Agents: Mechanisms and Motives." *Review of Black Political Economy* 19:39–63.

Glaeser, Edward L. and Joseph Gyourko. 2008. *Rethinking Federal Housing Policy: How to Make Housing Plentiful and Affordable.* Washington, DC: AEI Press.

Glaeser, Edward L., Joseph Gyourko, and Raven E. Saks. 2005. "Why Have Housing Prices Gone Up?" *American Economic Review* 95:21–39.

Groisman, Fernando and Ana Lourdes Suarez. 2009. "Residential Segregation in Greater Buenos Aires." Pp. 39–54 in *Urban Segregation and Governance in the Americas,* edited by Bryan R. Roberts and Robert H. Wilson. New York: Palgrave Macmillan.

Hays, R. Allen. 1985. *The Federal Government and Urban Housing: Ideology and Change in Public Policy.* Albany: State University of New York Press.

Helper, Rose. 1969. *Racial Policies and Practices of Real Estate Brokers.* Minneapolis: University of Minnesota Press.

Hershberg, Theodore, Alan N. Burstein, Eugene P. Ericksen, Stephanie Greenberg, and William L. Yancey. 1979. "A Tale of Three Cities: Blacks and Immigrants in Philadelphia: 1850–1880, 1930 and 1970." *Annals of the Academy of Political and Social Science* 441:55–81.

Hirsch, Arnold R. 1983. *Making the Second Ghetto: Race and Housing in Chicago, 1940–1960.* Cambridge: Cambridge University Press.

Jackson, Kenneth T. 1985. *Crabgrass Frontier: The Suburbanization of the United States.* New York: Oxford University Press.

Jones, F. Lancaster. 1967. "Ethnic Concentration and Assimilation: An Australian Case Study." *Social Forces* 45:412–23.

Jones, Philip N. 1976. "Colored Minorities in Birmingham, England." *Association of American Geographers* 66:89–103.

Katzman, Ruben and Alejandro Retamoso. 2009. "Residential Segregation in Montevideo: Challenges to Education Equality." Pp. 97–120 in *Urban Segregation and Governance in the Americas,* edited by Bryan R. Roberts and Robert H. Wilson. New York: Palgrave Macmillan.

Katznelson, Ira. 2005. *When Affirmative Action Was White: An Untold History of Racial Inequality in Twentieth-Century America.* New York: W.W. Norton.

Kemper, Frans Josef. 1998. "Residential Segregation and Housing in Berlin: Changes Since Unification." *GeoJournal* 46:17–28.

Ke Shon, Jean-Louis Pan. 2011. "Residential Segregation of Immigrants in France: An Overview." *Population and Societies* 477 Institut National d'Études Démographiques, April.

Klaff, Vivian Z. 1977. "Residence and Integration in Israel: A Mosaic of Segregated Peoples." *Ethnicity* 4:103–21.

Klaff, Vivian Z. 1978. "Ethnic Segregation in Urban Israel" *Demography* 10:161–84.

Lee, Trevor R. 1973. "Ethnic and Social Class Factors in Residential Segregation: Some Implications for Dispersal." *Environment and Planning* 5:477–90.

Lichter, Daniel T. Lichter, Domenico Parisi, and Michael C. Taquino. 2011. "The Geography of Exclusion: Race, Segregation, and Concentrated Poverty." Working Paper Series No. 11-16. Ann Arbor, MI: National Poverty Center.

Lieberson, Stanley. 1981. *A Piece of the Pie: Blacks and White Immigrants Since 1880.* Berkeley: University of California Press.

Massey, Douglas S. 1981. "Dimensions of the New Immigration to the United States and the Prospects for Assimilation." *Annual Review of Sociology* 7:57–85.

Massey, Douglas S. 1985. "Ethnic Residential Segregation: A Theoretical Synthesis and Empirical Review." *Sociology and Social Research* 69:315–50.

Massey, Douglas S. 1990. "American Apartheid: Segregation and the Making of the Underclass." *American Journal of Sociology* 95:1153–88.

Massey, Douglas S. 2004. "Segregation and Stratification: A Biosocial Perspective." *The DuBois Review: Social Science Research on Race* 1:1–19.

Massey, Douglas S. 2005a. *Strangers in a Strange Land: Humans in an Urbanizing World.* New York: W.W. Norton.

Massey, Douglas S. 2005b. "Racial Discrimination in Housing: A Moving Target." *Social Problems* 52:148–51.

Massey, Douglas S. 2007. *Categorically Unequal: The American Stratification System.* New York: Russell Sage Foundation.

Massey, Douglas S., Len Albright, Rebecca Casciano, Elizabeth Derickson, and David N. Kinsey. 2013. *Climbing Mount Laurel: The Struggle for Affordable Housing and Social Mobility in an American Suburb.* Princeton, NJ: Princeton University Press.

Massey, Douglas S., Joaquín Arango, Graeme Hugo, Ali Kouaouci, Adela Pellegrino, and J. Edward Taylor. 1998. *Worlds in Motion: International Migration at the End of the Millennium.* Oxford: Oxford University Press.

Massey, Douglas S. and Nancy A. Denton. 1985. "Spatial Assimilation as a Socioeconomic Outcome." *American Sociological Review* 50:94–105.

Massey, Douglas S. and Nancy A. Denton. 1988. "The Dimensions of Residential Segregation." *Social Forces* 67:281–315.

Massey, Douglas S. and Nancy A. Denton. 1993. *American Apartheid: Segregation and the Making of the Underclass.* Cambridge, MA: Harvard University Press.

Massey, Douglas S. and Nancy A. Denton. 1996. "The Age of Extremes: Concentrated Affluence and Poverty in the 21st Century." *Demography* 33:395–412.

Massey, Douglas S. and Mary J. Fischer. 2000. "How Segregation Concentrates Poverty." *Ethnic and Racial Studies* 23:670–91.

Massey, Douglas S. and Mary J. Fischer. 2003. "The Geography of Inequality in the United States 1950–2000." Pp. 1–40 in *Brookings-Wharton Papers on Urban Affairs 2003*, edited by William G. Gale and Janet Rothenberg Pack. Washington, DC: Brookings Institution.

Massey, Douglas S. and Brendan P. Mullan. 1984. "Processes of Hispanic and Black Spatial Assimilation." *American Journal of Sociology* 89:836–73.

Massey, Douglas S., Jonathan Rothwell, and Thurston Domina. 2009. "Changing Bases of Segregation in the United States." *Annals of the American Academy of Political and Social Science* 626:74–90.

Massey, Douglas S. and Jacob S. Rugh. 2014. "Segregation in Post–Civil Rights America: Stalled Integration or End of the Segregated Century?" *The DuBois Review* 11(2):205–32.

Metcalf, George R. 1988. *Fair Housing Comes of Age.* New York: Greenwood Press.

Monkkonen, Paavo. 2010. "Measuring Residential Segregation in Urban Mexico: Levels and Patterns." Working Paper 2010-05. Berkeley: Institute of Urban and Regional Development.

Musterd, Sako and Wim Ostendorf. 2007. "Spatial Segregation and Integration in the Netherlands." Pp. 41–60 in *Residential Segregation and the Integration of Immigrants: Britain, the Netherlands and Sweden*, edited by Karen Schönwälder. Discussion Paper SP IV 2007-602. Berlin: Wissenschaftszentrum Berlin für Sozialforschung.

Newmann, Brigitte, Richard Mezoff, and Anthony H. Richmond. 1973. *Immigrant Integration and Urban Renewal in Toronto.* The Hague: Martinus Nijhoff.

Nightingale, Carl H. 2012. *Segregation: A Global History of Divided Cities.* Chicago: University of Chicago Press.

O'Loughlin, John. 1980. "Distribution and Migration of Foreigners in German Cities." *Geographical Review* 70:253–75.

O'Loughlin, John and Guenther Glebe. 1981. "The Location of Foreigners in Dusseldorf: A Causal Analysis in a Path Analytic Framework." *Geographische Zeitschrift* 69:81–97.

Park, Robert E. 1925. "The City: Suggestions for the Investigation of Human Behavior in the Urban Environment." Pp. 1–46 in *The City*, edited by Robert E. Park and Ernest W. Burgess. Chicago: University of Chicago Press.

Park, Robert E. 1926. "The Urban Community as a Spatial Pattern and a Moral Order." Pp. 3–18 in *The Urban Community*, edited by Ernest W. Burgess. Chicago: University of Chicago Press.

Park, Robert E. and Ernest W. Burgess. 1921. *Introduction to the Science of Sociology.* Chicago: University of Chicago Press.

Peach, Ceri. 1974. "Ethnic Segregation in Sydney and Intermarriage Patterns." *Australian Geographical Studies* 12:219–29.

Peach, Ceri. 1982. "The Growth and Distribution of the Black Population in Britain 1945–1980." Pp. 23–442 in *The Demography of Immigrants and Minority Groups in the United Kingdom*, edited by D. A. Coleman. New York: Academic Press.

Peach, Ceri. 2007. "Sleepwalking into Ghettoisation? The British Debate over Segregation." Pp. 7–40 in *Residential Segregation and the Integration of Immigrants: Britain, the Netherlands and Sweden*, edited by Karen Schönwälder. Discussion Paper SP IV 2007-602. Berlin: Wissenschaftszentrum Berlin für Sozialforschung.

Pearce, Diana M. 1979. "Gatekeepers and Homeseekers: Institutional Patterns in Racial Steering." *Social Problems* 26:325–42.

Pendall, Rolf. 2000. "Local Land-use Regulation and the Chain of Exclusion." *Journal of the American Planning Association* 66:125–42.

Peterson, Ruth D. and Lauren J. Krivo. 2012. *Divergent Social Worlds: Neighborhood Crime and the Racial-Spatial Divide.* New York: Russell Sage Foundation.

Pettigrew, Thomas F. 1979. "Racial Change and Social Policy." *Annals of the American Academy of Political and Social Science* 441:114–31.

Philpott, Thomas. 1978. *The Slum and the Ghetto: Neighborhood Deterioration and Middle Class Reform, Chicago 1880–1930.* New York: Oxford University Press.

Pinto da Cunha, Jose Marcos, and Maren Andrea Jimenez. 2009. "The Process of Cumulative Disadvantage: Concentration of Poverty and the Quality of Public Education in the Metropolitan Region of Campinas." Pp. 169–86 in *Urban Segregation and Governance in the Americas*, edited by Bryan R. Roberts and Robert H. Wilson. New York: Palgrave Macmillan.

Prandy, Kenneth. 1980. "Residential Segregation and Ethnic Distance in English Cities." *Ethnicity* 7:367–89.

Quillian, Lincoln. 2012. "Segregation and Poverty Concentration: The Role of Three Segregations." *American Sociological Review* 77(3):354–79.

Reardon, Sean F. and Kendra Bischoff. 2011. "Income Inequality and Income Segregation." *American Journal of Sociology* 116:1092–1153.

Rice, Roger L. 1968. "Residential Segregation by Law, 1910–1917." *Journal of Southern History* 64:179–99.

Rothwell, Jonathan and Douglas S. Massey. 2009. "The Effect of Density Zoning on Racial Segregation in U.S. Urban Areas." *Urban Affairs Review* 44:799–806.

Rothwell, Jonathan and Douglas S. Massey. 2010. "Density Zoning and Class Segregation in U.S. Metropolitan Areas." *Social Science Quarterly* 91:1123–43.

Ross, Stephen L. and John Yinger. 2002. *The Color of Credit: Mortgage Discrimination, Research Methodology, and Fair-Lending Enforcement*. Cambridge, MA: MIT Press.

Rugh, Jacob S. and Douglas S. Massey. 2010. "Racial Segregation and the American Foreclosure Crisis." *American Sociological Review* 75:629–51.

Rugh, Jacob S., Len Albright, and Douglas S. Massey. 2015. "Race, Space, and Cumulative Disadvantage: A Case Study of the Subprime Lending Collapse." *Social Problems* 62:186–218.

Sabatini, Francisco, Guillermo Wormald, Carlos Sierralta, and Paul A. Peters. 2009. "Residential Segregation in Santiago: Scale-Related Effects and Trends 1992–2001." Pp. 121–44 in *Urban Segregation and Governance in the Americas*, edited by Bryan R. Roberts and Robert H. Wilson. New York: Palgrave Macmillan.

Saltman, Juliet. 1979. "Housing Discrimination: Policy Research, Methods, and Results." *Annals of the American Academy of Political and Social Science* 441:186–96.

Sampson, Robert J. 2012. *Great American City: Chicago and the Enduring Neighborhood Effect*. Chicago: University of Chicago Press.

Smeeding, Timothy M. 2005. "Public Policy, Economic Inequality, and Poverty: The United States in Comparative Perspective." *Social Science Quarterly* 86:955–83.

Szwarcwald, C., F. I. Bastos, C. Barcellos, M. D. Pina, and M. A. Esteves. 2000. "Health Conditions and Residential Concentration of Poverty: A Study in Rio de Janeiro, Brazil." *Journal of Epidemiological Community Health* 54:530–36.

Sharkey, Patrick. 2013. *Stuck in Place: Urban Neighborhoods and the End of Progress Toward Racial Equality*. Chicago: University of Chicago Press.

Sjoberg, Gideon. 1960. *The Pre-Industrial City: Past and Present*. Glencoe, IL: Free Press.

Taylor, Paul, Rakesh Kochhar, Richard Fry, Gabriel Velasco, and Seth Motel. 2011. *Wealth Gaps Rise to Record Highs between Whites, Blacks and Hispanics*. Washington, DC: Pew Social and Demographic Trends.

Telles, Edward E. 1992. "Residential Segregation by Skin Color in Brazil." *American Sociological Review* 57(2):186–97.

Telles, Edward. 2004. *Race in Another America: The Significance of Skin Color in Brazil*. Princeton, NJ: Princeton University Press.

Timms, Dundan W. C. 1969. "The Dissimilarity between Overseas-Born and Australian-Born in Queensland: Dimensions of Assimilation." *Sociology and Social Research* 53:363–75.

Turner, Margery A., Stephen L. Ross, George C. Galster, and John Yinger. 2002. *Discrimination in Metropolitan Housing Markets: National Results from Phase I*. Washington, DC: U.S. Department of Housing and Urban Development.

van Kempen, Ronald. 2005. "Segregation and Housing Conditions of Immigrants in Western European Cities." Pp. 190–209 in *Cities of Europe: Changing Contexts, Local Arrangement and the Challenge to Urban Cohesion*, edited by Yuri Kazepov. Oxford: Blackwell.

Villareal, Andres and Erin R. Hamilton. 2009. "Residential Segregation in the Mexico City Metropolitan Area." Pp. 73–96 in *Urban Segregation and Governance in the Americas*, edited by Bryan R. Roberts and Robert H. Wilson. New York: Palgrave Macmillan.

Walks, R. Alan and Larry S. Bourne. 2006. "Ghettos in Canada's Cities? Racial Segregation, Ethnic Enclaves, and Poverty Concentration in Canadian Urban Areas." *Canadian Geographer* 50(3):273–97.

White, Michael J. 1980. *Urban Renewal and the Residential Structure of the City*. Chicago: Community and Family Studies Center.

White, Michael J. 1987. *American Neighborhoods and Residential Differentiation*. New York: Russell Sage Foundation.

Wienk, Ronald, Cliff Reid, John Simonson, and Fred Eggers. 1979. *Measuring Racial Discrimination in American Housing Markets: The Housing Market Practices Survey*. Washington, DC: U.S. Department of Housing and Urban Development.

Wilkes, Rima and John Iceland. 2004. "Hypersegregation in the Twenty-First Century." *Demography* 41:23–36.

Wilson, William Julius. 1997. *The Truly Disadvantaged: The Inner City, the Underclass, and Public Policy*. Chicago: University of Chicago Press.

Woods, Robert I. 1976. "Aspects of the Scale Problem in the Calculation of Segregation Indices: London and Birmingham." *Tijdschrift voor Economische en Social Geografie* 67:169–74.

Woods, Robert I. 1979. "Ethnic Segregation in Birmingham in the 1960s and 1970s." *Ethnic and Racial Studies* 2:455–76.

Yiftachel, Oren. 2001. "From 'Peace' to Creeping Apartheid: The Emerging Political Geography of Israel/Palestine." *Arena* 16:13–24.

Yiftachel, Oren. 2006. *Ethnocracy: Land, and the Politics of Identity Israel/Palestine*. Philadelphia: University of Pennsylvania Press.

Yiftachel, Oren. 2009. "Theorizing 'Gray Space': The Coming of Urban Apartheid?" *Planning Theory* (8)1:88–100.

Yiftachel, Oren and Yacobi, H. 2005. "Walls, Fences and 'Creeping Apartheid' in Israel/Palestine." Pp. 138–58 in *Against the Wall: Israel's Barrier to Peace*, edited by Michael Sorkin. New York: Greenwood Press.

Yinger, John. 1995. *Closed Doors, Opportunities Lost: The Continuing Costs of Housing Discrimination*. New York: Russell Sage Foundation.

CHAPTER 17

....

URBAN POVERTY, RACE, AND SPACE

....

WILLIAM JULIUS WILSON

THROUGH the second half of the 1990s and into the early years of the twenty-first century, public attention to the plight of poor, inner-city residents seemed to wane. There was scant media attention paid to the problem of concentrated urban poverty (neighborhoods in which a high percentage of the residents fall beneath the federally designated poverty line), little or no discussion of inner-city challenges by mainstream political leaders, and even an apparent quiescence on the part of ghetto residents themselves. This was dramatically different from the 1960s, when the transition from legal segregation to a more racially open society was punctuated by social unrest that sometimes expressed itself in violent terms, as seen in the riots that followed the assassination of Dr. Martin Luther King Jr.

But in 2005, Hurricane Katrina exposed concentrated poverty in New Orleans. When television cameras focused on the flooding, the people trapped in houses and apartments, and the vast devastation, many Americans were shocked to see the squalid living conditions of the poor. Of course, the devastation of Katrina was broadly visited upon the residents of New Orleans, black and white, rich and poor, property owner and public housing tenant alike. But while many residents were able to flee, the very poor, lacking automobiles or money for transportation and lodging, stayed to wait out the storm with tragic results. And through Katrina, the nation's attention became riveted on these poor urban neighborhoods.

If television cameras had focused on the urban poor in New Orleans, or in any inner-city ghetto, before Katrina, I believe the initial reaction to descriptions of poverty and poverty concentration would have been unsympathetic. Public opinion polls in the United States routinely reflect the notion that people are poor and jobless because of their own shortcomings or inadequacies. In other words, few people would have reflected on how the larger forces in society—including segregation, discrimination, a lack of economic opportunity, and failing public schools—adversely affect the inner-city poor. However, because Katrina was clearly a natural disaster that was beyond the control of the inner-city poor, Americans were much more sympathetic. In a sense, Katrina turned out to be something of a cruel natural experiment, wherein better-off Americans could readily see the effects of racial isolation and chronic economic subordination.

Despite the lack of national public awareness of the problems of the urban poor prior to Katrina, social scientists have rightly devoted considerable attention to concentrated poverty because it magnifies the problems associated with poverty in general: joblessness, crime, delinquency, drug trafficking, broken families, and dysfunctional schools. Neighborhoods of highly concentrated poverty are seen as dangerous, and therefore they become isolated, socially and economically, as people go out of their way to avoid them (Jargowsky 1994).

In this chapter, I discuss the political, economic, and cultural forces that contributed to the emergence and persistence of concentrated poverty in black inner cities, areas that have the highest levels of concentrated poverty. I highlight, first of all, the political forces that adversely affected black inner-city neighborhoods, including those that were explicitly racial in nature and those that were ostensibly nonracial. Secondly, I focus on the impersonal economic forces that accelerated neighborhood decline in the black inner city and increased disparities in race and income between cities and suburbs. Thirdly, I consider two types of cultural forces that contribute to racial inequality: (1) belief systems of the broader society that either explicitly or implicitly give rise to racial inequality, and (2) cultural traits that emerge from patterns of intragroup interaction in settings created by racial segregation and discrimination. I then turn to an examination of the impact of the recent rise of immigration on areas of concentrated urban poverty, including some surprising positive impacts. I conclude this chapter by suggesting a new agenda for America's inner city poor, based on the analysis I put forth in the following sections.

THE IMPACT OF POLITICAL FORCES
ON INNER-CITY BLACK NEIGHBORHOODS

Since 1934, with the establishment of the Federal Housing Administration (FHA), a program necessitated by the massive mortgage foreclosures during the Great Depression, the U.S. government has sought to enable citizens to become homeowners by underwriting mortgages. In the years following World War II, however, the federal government contributed to the early decay of inner-city neighborhoods by withholding mortgage capital and making it difficult for these areas to retain or attract families who were able to purchase their own homes. But the FHA selectively administered the mortgage program by formalizing a process that excluded certain urban neighborhoods using empirical data that suggested a probable loss of investment in these areas. "Redlining," as it came to be known, was assessed largely on racial composition. Although many neighborhoods with a considerable number of European immigrants were redlined, virtually all black neighborhoods were excluded. Homebuyers hoping to purchase a home in a redlined neighborhood were universally denied mortgages, regardless of their financial qualifications. This severely restricted opportunities for building or even maintaining quality housing in the inner city, which in many ways set the stage for the urban blight that many Americans associate with black neighborhoods. This action was clearly motivated by racial bias, and it was not until the 1960s that the FHA discontinued mortgage restrictions based on the racial composition of the neighborhood (Bartelt 1993; Katz 1993; Kelley 1993; Sugrue 1993).

Subsequent policy decisions worked to trap blacks in these increasingly unattractive inner cities. Beginning in the 1950s, the suburbanization of the middle class, already underway with government-subsidized loans to veterans, was aided further by federal transportation and highway policies that included the building of freeway networks through the heart of many cities, which had a devastating impact on the neighborhoods of black Americans. These developments not only spurred relocation from the cities to the suburbs among better-off residents, the freeways themselves also "created barriers between the sections of the cities, walling off poor and minority neighborhoods from central business districts" (Katz 1993:462).[1] For instance, a number of studies have revealed how Richard J. Daley, the former mayor of Chicago, used the Interstate Highway Act of 1956 to route expressways through impoverished African American neighborhoods, resulting in even greater segregation and isolation (Hirsch 1983; Cohen and Taylor 2000; Mohl 2000). A lasting legacy of that policy is the 14-lane Dan Ryan Expressway, which created a barrier between black and white neighborhoods (Cohen and Taylor 2000).

Another particularly egregious example of the deleterious effects of highway construction is Birmingham, Alabama's interstate highway system, which curved and twisted to bisect several black neighborhoods rather than taking a more direct route through some predominantly white neighborhoods. The highway system essentially followed the boundaries that had been established in 1926 as part of the city's racial zoning law, although these boundaries were technically removed a few years before the highway construction began in 1956 (Connerly 2002).

At the same time, government policies such as mortgages for veterans and mortgage interest tax exemptions for developers enabled the quick, cheap production of massive amounts of tract housing and drew middle-class whites to the suburbs (Sampson and Wilson 1995). A classic example of this effect of housing-market incentives is the mass-produced suburban Levittown neighborhoods that were first erected in New York and later in Pennsylvania, New Jersey, and Puerto Rico. The homes in these neighborhoods were manufactured on a large scale, using an assembly line model of production, and were arranged in carefully engineered suburban neighborhoods that included many public amenities, such as shopping centers and space for public schools. These neighborhoods represented an ideal alternative for people who were seeking to escape cramped city apartments and were often touted as "utopian communities" that enabled people to live out the "suburban dream." Veterans were able to purchase a Levittown home for a few thousand dollars with no money down, financed with low-interest mortgages guaranteed by the Veterans Administration. However, the Levitts would not initially sell to African Americans. The first black family moved into Levittown, New York, in 1957, having purchased a home from a white family (Baxandall and Ewen 1999), and they endured harassment, hate mail, and threats for several months after moving in. Levittown, New York, remains a predominantly white community today. Here, once again, we have a practice that denied African Americans the opportunity to move from segregated inner-city neighborhoods.

Explicit racial policies in the suburbs reinforced this segregation by allowing suburbs to separate their financial resources and municipal budgets from those of the cities. In the nineteenth and early twentieth centuries, strong municipal services in cities were very attractive to residents of small towns and suburbs; as a result, cities tended to annex suburbs and surrounding areas. But the relations between cities and suburbs in the United States began to change following the Great Depression; the century-long influx of poor migrants who required expensive services and paid relatively little in taxes could no longer be profitably absorbed into the city economy. Annexation largely ended in the mid-twentieth century as suburbs began to successfully resist incorporation. Suburban communities also drew tighter boundaries through the use of zoning laws, discriminatory land-use controls, and site selection practices, which made it difficult for inner-city racial minorities to access these areas because these practices were effectively used to screen out residents on the basis of race.

As separate political jurisdictions, suburbs also exercised a great deal of autonomy through covenants and deed restrictions. In the face of mounting pressure for integration in the 1960s, "suburbs chose to diversify by race rather than class. They retained zoning and other restrictions that allowed only affluent blacks (and in some instances Jews) to enter, thereby intensifying the concentration and isolation of the urban poor" (Katz 1993:461–62).[2] Although these policies clearly had racial connotations, they also reflected class bias and helped reinforce the exodus of white working-class and middle-class families from urban neighborhoods and the growing segregation of low-income blacks in inner-city neighborhoods.

Federal public housing policy contributed to the gradual growth of segregated black ghettos as well. The federal public housing program's policies evolved in two stages that represented two distinct styles. The Wagner Housing Act of 1937 initiated the first stage. Concerned that the construction of public housing might depress private rent levels, groups such as the U.S. Building and Loan League and the National Association of Real Estate Boards successfully lobbied Congress to require, by law, that for each new unit of public housing erected, one "unsafe or unsanitary" unit of public housing must be destroyed.

The early years of the public housing program produced positive results. Initially, the program mainly served intact families temporarily displaced by the Depression or in need of housing after the end of World War II. For many of these families, public housing was the first step on the road toward economic recovery. Their stays in the projects were relatively brief because they were able to accumulate sufficient economic resources to move on to private housing.

The passage of the Housing Act of 1949 marked the beginning of the second policy stage. It instituted and funded the urban renewal program, designed to eradicate urban slums, and therefore was seemingly nonracial. However, the public housing that it created "was now meant to collect the ghetto residents left homeless by the urban renewal bulldozers" (Condon 1991). A new, lower income ceiling for public housing residency was established by the federal Public Housing Authority, and families with incomes above that ceiling were evicted, thereby restricting access to public housing to only the most economically disadvantaged segments of the population.

This change in federal housing policy coincided with the Second Great Migration of African Americans from the rural South to the cities of the Northeast and Midwest, which lasted 30 years—from 1940 to 1970. This mass movement of African Americans was even larger and more sustained than the First Great Migration, which began at the turn of the twentieth century and ended during the Great Depression, and had a more profound impact on the transformation of the inner city. As the black urban population in the North grew, pressure mounted in white communities to keep blacks out. Suburban communities, with their restrictive covenants and special zoning laws, refused to permit the construction of public housing. And the federal government acquiesced to opposition to the construction of public housing in the neighborhoods of organized white groups in the city. Thus, units were overwhelmingly concentrated in the overcrowded and deteriorating inner-city ghettos—the poorest and least powerful sections of cities and metropolitan areas. In short, public housing became a federally funded institution that isolated families by race and class, resulting in high concentrations of poor black families in inner-city ghettos (Sampson and Wilson 1995).[3]

In the last quarter of the twentieth century, one of the most significant changes in these neighborhoods was the out-migration of middle-income blacks (Wilson 1987). Before the 1970s, African American families faced extremely strong barriers when they considered moving into white neighborhoods. Not only did many experience overt discrimination in the housing market, some were violently attacked. Although even today fair-housing audits continue to reveal the existence of discrimination in the housing market, fair-housing legislation has reduced the strength of these barriers. At the same time, middle-income African Americans have increased their efforts to move from concentrated black poverty areas to more desirable neighborhoods throughout the metropolitan area, including white neighborhoods (Quillian 1999).

This pattern represents an important change in the formation of neighborhoods. In the earlier years, communities undergoing racial change from white to black tended to experience an increase in population density, as a result of the black migration from the South. Because of the housing demand, particularly in the late stages of the succession from white to black, homes and apartments in these neighborhoods were often subdivided into smaller units (Quillian 1999).

However, 1970 marked the end of the Great Migration wave of blacks from the South to northern urban areas, and two developments affected the course of population movement to the inner cities after that time. Improvements in transportation made it easier for workers to live outside the central city, and industries gradually shifted to the suburbs because of the increased residential suburbanization of the labor force and the lower cost of production. Because of the suburbanization of employment and improvements in transportation, inner-city manufacturing jobs were no longer a strong factor pulling migrants to central cities (Quillian 1999). So with the decline of industrial employment in the inner city, the influx of southern black migration to northern cities ceased, and many poor black neighborhoods, especially those in the Midwest and Northeast, changed from densely packed areas of recently arrived migrants to communities gradually abandoned by the working and middle classes (Wilson 1987; Wilson 1996; Quillian 1999).

Other factors contributed to the decay of black inner cities. Beginning in 1980, when Ronald Reagan became president, sharp spending cuts in direct aid to cities dramatically reduced budgets for general revenue sharing—unrestricted funds that can be used for any purpose—urban mass transit, economic development assistance, urban development action grants, social service block grants, local public works, compensatory education, public service jobs, and job training. Many of these programs were designed to help disadvantaged individuals gain some traction in attaining financial security (Caraley 1992). It is telling that the federal contribution was 17.5 percent of the total city budgets in 1977 but only 5.4 percent by 2000 (Wallin 2005). These cuts were particularly acute for older cities in the East and Midwest that largely depended on federal and state aid to fund social services for their poor populations and to maintain aging infrastructure.

The decline in federal support for cities since 1980 coincided with an increase in the immigration of people from poorer countries—mainly low-skilled workers from Mexico—and whites steadily moving to the suburbs. With minorities displacing whites as a growing share of the population, the implications for the urban tax base were profound. According to the U.S. Census Bureau, in 2000 the median annual household income for Latinos was about $14,000 less than that of white households. With a declining tax base and the simultaneous loss of federal funds, municipalities had trouble raising enough revenue to cover basic services such as garbage collection, street cleaning, and police protection. Some even cut such services in order to avoid bankruptcy (U.S. Department of Housing and Urban Development 1999).

This financial crisis left many cities ill-equipped to handle three devastating public health problems that emerged in the 1980s and disproportionately affected areas of concentrated poverty: first, the prevalence of drug trafficking and associated violent crime; second, the acquired immunodeficiency syndrome (AIDS) epidemic and its escalating public health costs; and third, the rise in the homeless population, not only individuals, but entire families as well (Caraley 1992). Although drug addiction, drug-related violence, AIDS, and homelessness are found in many American communities, their impact on the black ghetto is profound. A number of fiscally strapped cities have watched helplessly as these problems—aggravated by the reduction of citywide social services as well as high levels of neighborhood joblessness—have reinforced the perception that cities are dangerous places to live and have perpetuated the exodus of working- and middle-class residents. Thus, while poverty and joblessness, and the social problems they generate, remain prominent in ghetto neighborhoods, many cities have fewer and fewer resources with which to combat them.

Finally, policymakers have indirectly contributed to concentrated poverty in black inner-city neighborhoods with decisions that have decreased the attractiveness of low-paid jobs and accelerated the relative decline in the wages of low-income workers. In particular, in the absence of an effective labor market policy, policymakers have tolerated industry practices that undermine worker security—including the erosion of benefits and the rise of involuntary part-time employment.

In sum, federal government policies, even those that are not explicitly racial, have had a profound impact on black inner-city neighborhoods. These impacts have been felt in many cities across the country, but they perhaps have been felt more in the older central cities of the Midwest and Northeast—the traditional Rust Belt—where depopulated, high-poverty areas have experienced even greater problems.

THE IMPACT OF ECONOMIC FORCES ON INNER-CITY BLACK NEIGHBORHOODS

Older urban areas were once the hubs of economic growth and activity, and were therefore major destinations for people in search of economic opportunity. However, the economies of many of these cities have since been eroded by complex economic transformations and shifting patterns in metropolitan development. These economic forces are typically considered nonracial—in the sense that their origins are not the direct result of actions, processes, or ideologies that explicitly reflect racial bias. But nevertheless, they have accelerated neighborhood decline in the inner city and widened gaps in race and income between cities and suburbs (Fox and Treuhaft 2006).

Since the mid-twentieth century, the mode of production in the United States has shifted dramatically from manufacturing to one increasingly fueled by finance, services, and technology. This shift has accompanied the technological revolution, which has transformed traditional industries and brought about changes that range from streamlined information technology to biomedical engineering (Fox and Treuhaft 2006; Joy 2000).

In the last several decades, almost all improvements in productivity have been associated with technology and human capital, thereby drastically reducing the importance of physical capital (Wilson 1996). With the increased globalization of economic activity, firms have spread their operations around the world, often relocating their production facilities to developing nations that have dramatically lower labor costs (Fox and Treuhaft 2006).

These global economic transformations have adversely affected the competitive position of many U.S. Rust Belt cities. For example, Cleveland, Detroit, Philadelphia, Baltimore, and Pittsburgh perform poorly on employment growth, an important traditional measure of economic performance. Nationally, employment increased by 25 percent between 1991 and 2001, yet job growth in these older central cities did not exceed 3 percent (Fox and Treuhaft 2006).

With the decline in manufacturing employment in many of the nation's central cities, most of the jobs for lower skilled workers are now in retail and service industries (for example, store cashiers, customer service representatives, fast food servers, and custodial work). Whereas jobs in manufacturing industries typically were unionized, relatively stable, and carried higher wages, positions for workers with low to modest levels of education in the retail and service industries tend to provide lower wages, be unstable, and lack the benefits and worker protections—such as workers' health insurance, medical leave, retirement benefits, and paid vacations—typically offered through unionization. This means that workers relegated to low-wage service and retail firms are more likely to experience hardships as they struggle to make ends meet. In addition, the local economy suffers when residents have fewer dollars to spend in their neighborhoods (Wilson 1996; Fox and Treuhaft 2006).

Beginning in the mid-1970s, the employment balance between central cities and suburbs shifted markedly to the suburbs. Since 1980, over two-thirds of employment growth has occurred outside the central city: manufacturing is now over 70 percent suburban, and wholesale and retail trade is just under 70 percent (U.S. Department of Housing and Urban Development 1999). The suburbs of many central cities, developed originally as bedroom localities for commuters to the central business and manufacturing districts, have become employment centers in themselves. For example, in Detroit, Philadelphia, and Baltimore, less than 20 percent of the jobs are now located within three miles of the city center (Fox and Treuhaft 2006).

Accompanying the rise of suburban and exurban economies has been a change in commuting patterns. Increasingly, workers completely bypass the central city by commuting from one suburb to another. "In the Cleveland region, for example, less than one-third of workers commute to a job in the central city and over half (55 percent) begin and end in the suburbs" (Fox and Treuhaft 2006:32).

Sprawl and economic stagnation reduce inner city residents' access to meaningful economic opportunities and thereby fuel the economic decline of their neighborhoods. For example, in Cleveland, although entry-level workers are concentrated in inner city neighborhoods, 80 percent of the entry-level jobs are located in the suburbs. And there is little public transportation between these neighborhoods and jobs (Fox and Treuhaft 2006).

In addition to the challenges in learning about and reaching jobs, there is persistent racial discrimination in hiring practices, especially for younger and less experienced minority workers.[4] This racial factor affects black males especially seriously. Today, most of the new jobs for workers with limited education and experience are in the service sector, which includes jobs that tend to be held by women, such as wait staff, sales clerks, and nurse's aides. Indeed, "employment rates of young black women now exceed those of young black men, even though many of these women must also care for children" (Holzer, Offner, and Sorensen 2003). The shift to service jobs has resulted in a greater demand for workers who can effectively serve and relate to the consumer. Many employers in an extensive study in Chicago, conducted by my colleagues and I, felt that, unlike women and immigrants (who have recently expanded the labor pool for service sector jobs), inner-city black males lack these qualities. Instead, low-skilled black males are perceived as dangerous or threatening (Wilson 1996).

In the past, all black men had to demonstrate was a strong back and muscles for heavy lifting and physical labor in a factory, at a construction site, or on an assembly line. They did not have to interact with customers. Today, they have to search for work in the service sector, and employers are less likely to hire them because they have to come into contact with the public. Consequently, black male job seekers face rising rates of rejection. This may well account for the higher dropout rate and lower academic achievement of black males in comparison with black females. Black males are far less likely than black females to see a strong relationship between their schooling and postschool employment.

With the departure of higher income families, the least upwardly mobile in society— mainly low-income people of color—are left behind in neighborhoods with high concentrations of poverty and deteriorating physical conditions. These neighborhoods offer few jobs and typically lack basic services and amenities, such as banks, grocery stores and other retail establishments, parks, and quality transit (Wilson 1987; Wilson 1996; Fox and Treuhaft 2006). Typically, these communities also suffer from substandard schools, many with run-down physical plants. Two of the most visible indicators of neighborhood decline are abandoned buildings and vacant lots. According to one recent report, there are 60,000 abandoned and vacant properties in Philadelphia, 40,000 in Detroit, and 26,000 in Baltimore (Fox and Treuhaft 2006).

The Impact of Cultural Forces on Inner-City Black Neighborhoods

In addition to racial and nonracial political and economic forces, cultural forces have also contributed to or reinforced racial inequality. Two types of cultural forces are in play: (1) national views and beliefs on race; and (2) cultural traits—shared outlooks, modes of behavior, traditions, belief systems, worldviews, values, skills, preferences, styles of self-presentation, etiquette, and linguistic patterns—that emerge from patterns of intragroup interaction in settings created by discrimination and segregation and that reflect collective experiences within those settings.

Racism has historically been one of the most prominent American cultural frames and has played a major role in determining how whites perceive and act toward blacks.

At its core, racism is an ideology of racial domination with two key features: (1) beliefs that one race is either biologically or culturally inferior to another; and (2) the use of such beliefs to rationalize or prescribe the way that the "inferior" race should be treated, as well as to explain their social position as a group and their collective accomplishments. In the United States today there is no question that the more categorical forms of racist ideology—in particular, those that assert the biogenetic inferiority of blacks—have declined significantly, even though they still may be embedded in institutional norms and practices. For example, school tracking, the practice of grouping students of similar capability for instruction, tends to not only segregate African American students but often also results in placing some black students in lower level classes, even though they have the cultural capital—requisite skills for learning—to compete with students in higher level classes.

However, there has emerged a form of what some scholars refer to as "laissez faire racism," a perception that blacks are responsible for their own economic predicament and therefore undeserving of special government support (Bobo, Kluegel, and Smith 1997). The idea that the federal government "has a special obligation to help improve the living standards of blacks" because they "have been discriminated against for so long" was supported by only one in five whites in 2001 and has not exceeded support by more than one in four since 1975 (Bobo et al. 2012:54). Significantly, the lack of white support for this idea is not related to background factors such as level of education or age.

The vast majority of social scientists agree that as a national cultural frame, racism, in its various forms, has had harmful effects on African Americans as a group. Indeed, considerable research has been devoted to the effects of racism in American society. However, there is little research and far less awareness of the impact of emerging cultural frames in the inner city on the social and economic outcomes of poor blacks. Note that distinct cultural frames in the inner city have not only been shaped by race and poverty but in turn often also shape responses to poverty, including responses that may contribute to the perpetuation of poverty. Moreover, an important research question for social scientists is the following: How much of the framing of racial beliefs at the national level is based on the actual observed cultural traits among the inner-city black poor, and how much of it is the result of biased media reports and racial stereotypes?

In my own earlier work, I have discussed at length how several factors determine the extent to which communities, as areas bounded by place, differ in outlook and behavior (Wilson 1978, 1996). These factors include the degree to which the community is socially isolated from the broader society;[5] the material assets or resources controlled by members of the community; the benefits and privileges the community members derive from these resources; their accumulated cultural experiences from current as well as historical, political, and economic arrangements; and the influence members of the community wield because of these arrangements.

Culture is closely intertwined with social relations in the sense of providing tools (skills, habits, and styles) and creating constraints (restrictions or limits on behavior or outlooks) in patterns of social interaction (Tilly 1998). These constraints include cultural frames (shared visions of human behavior) developed over time through the processes of in-group meaning making (shared views on how the world works) and decision-making (choices that reflect shared definitions of how the world works)[6]—for example, in the inner-city ghetto, cultural frames define issues of trust/street smarts and "acting black" or "acting white"—that lead to observable group characteristics.[7]

One of the effects of living in racially segregated neighborhoods is exposure to group-specific cultural traits (cultural frames, orientations, habits, and worldviews as well as styles of behavior and particular skills) that emerged from patterns of racial exclusion and that may not be conducive to factors that facilitate social mobility. For example, research has found that some groups in inner-city black neighborhoods put a high value on "street smarts," the behaviors and actions that keep them safe in areas of high crime (Anderson 1990). Street smarts may be an adaptation to living in unsafe neighborhoods. In this environment, it is wise to avoid eye contact with strangers and keep to yourself. This mind-set may also lead someone to approach new situations with a certain level of skepticism or mistrust. Although such an approach is logical and smart in an unsafe neighborhood, the same behavior can be interpreted as antisocial in another setting. Moreover, this street-smart behavior may, in some cases, prevent individuals from performing well during a job interview, creating a perception that they are not desirable job candidates.

Other concrete examples from the writings of sociologists Elijah Anderson (1999) and Sudhir Venkatesh (2006) on the ghetto experience might prove even more illuminating. Each author reveals the existence of informal rules in the inner-city ghetto that govern interactions and shape how people engage one another and make decisions. This decision-making is influenced partly by how people come to view their world over time—what we call "meaning making." It is important to remember that the processes of meaning making and decision making evolve in situations imposed by poverty and racial segregation—situations that place severe constraints on social mobility. Over time, these processes lead to the development of informal codes that regulate behavior.

First of all, Anderson (1999) talks about the "code of the street," an informal but explicit set of rules developed to govern interpersonal public behavior and regulate violence in Philadelphia's inner-city ghetto neighborhoods, where crime is high and police protection is low. Anderson argues that the issue of respect is at the root of the code. In a context of limited opportunities for success, some individuals in the community, most notably young black males, devise alternative ways to gain respect that emphasize manly pride, ranging from simply wearing brand-name clothing, to having the "right look" and talking the right way, to developing a predatory attitude toward neighbors. Anderson points out, however, that no one residing in these troubled neighborhoods is unaffected by the code of the street—especially young people, who are drawn into this negative culture both on the streets and in the schools as they must frequently adopt "street" behavior as a form of self-defense. As Anderson puts it, "the code of the street is actually a cultural adaptation to a profound lack of faith in the police and the judicial system—and in others who would champion one's personal security" (1999:34).

A related informal but regulated pattern of behavior was described by Sudhir Venkatesh (2006) in his study of the underground economy in ghetto neighborhoods. Venkatesh points out that "the underground arena is not simply a place to buy goods and services. It is also a field of social relationships that enable off-the-books trading to occur in an ordered and predictable manner" (2006:381). This trading often results in disagreements or breaches because there are no laws on the books, but "in situations ostensibly criminal and often threatening to personal security, there is still a structure in place that shapes how people make decisions and engage one another" (2006:377). In other words, informal rules actually govern what would appear on the surface to be random underground activity. These rules stipulate what is expected of those involved in these informal exchanges and where they should meet. Just as Anderson describes a "code of the street," Venkatesh (2006) talks about a "code of shady dealings."

Like Anderson (1999) in his effort to explain the emergence of the code of the street, Venkatesh (2006) argues that the code of shady dealings is a response to circumstances in inner-city ghetto neighborhoods, where joblessness is high and opportunities for advancement are severely limited. Furthermore, both Anderson and Venkatesh clearly argue that these cultural codes ultimately hinder integration into the broader society and are therefore dysfunctional. In other words, they contribute to the perpetuation of poverty.

Anderson finds that for some young men the draw of the street is so powerful that they cannot take advantage of legitimate employment opportunities when they become available. Likewise, Venkatesh maintains that adherence to the code of shady dealings impedes social mobility. The "underground economy enables people to survive but can lead to alienation from the wider world" he states (2006:385).[8] For example, none of the work experience accrued in the informal economy can be listed on a resume for job searches in the formal labor market, and time invested in underground work reduces time devoted to accumulating skills or contacts for legitimate employment.

However, an adequate explanation of cultural attributes in the black community must explore the origins and changing nature of attitudes and practices going back decades, even centuries. From a historical perspective, it is hard to overstate the importance of racialist structural factors. Aside from the enduring effects of slavery, Jim Crow segregation, public school segregation, legalized discrimination, residential segregation, the FHA's redlining of black neighborhoods in the 1940s and 1950s, the construction of public housing projects in poor black neighborhoods, employer discrimination, and other racial acts and processes, there is the impact of political, economic, and policy decisions that were at least partly influenced by race, as discussed previously.

For all of these reasons more weight should be given to structural causes of racial inequality, despite the dynamic interrelationships of structure and culture, because they continue to play a far greater role in the subjugation of black Americans and other people of color. In addition, culture is less casually autonomous than social structure in the sense that it more often plays a mediating role in determining African Americans' chances in life. In other words, residents of the inner-city ghetto develop ways, often quite creative, to adjust and respond to chronic racial and economic subordination, as reflected in meaning-making and decision-making processes, including those result-ing in the development of informal codes that regulate behavior. However, when one considers the combined historical impact of the structural factors, one has to include how they influence cultural responses over time.

Unfortunately, historical analyses of origins and the changing nature of attitudes and practices in black inner-city neighborhoods are complex and difficult. For example, sociologist Kathryn Neckerman (2007) had to conduct years of research to provide the historical evidence to explain why so many black youngsters and their parents lose faith in the public schools. She shows in her book, *Schools Betrayed* (2007), that a century ago, when African American children in most northern cities attended schools along-side white children, the problems commonly associated with inner-city schools—low achievement and dropping out—were not nearly as pervasive as they are today.

Neckerman carefully documents how city officials responded to increases in the African American student population: by introducing and enforcing segregation between black and white children in the city schools. And she discusses at length how poor white immigrant children—whose family circumstances were at least as impov-erished as their black counterparts—received more and better resources for their edu-cation. "The roots of classroom alienation, antagonism, and disorder can be found in school policy decisions made long before the problems of inner-city schools attracted public attention," states Neckerman:

> These policies struck at the foundations of authority and engagement, making it much more difficult for inner-city teachers to gain student cooperation in learn-ing. The district's history of segregation and inequality undermined the schools' legitimacy in the eyes of its black students; as a result, inner-city teachers struggled to gain cooperation from children and parents, who had little reason to trust the school. (2007:174)

Clearly, we can more fully understand the frustration and current cultural dynamics in inner-city neighborhoods, in this case with reference to public schools, if we under-stand the history that work like Neckerman's uncovers.

THE LATINO PARADOX: CONCENTRATED POVERTY AND THE RISE OF LATINO IMMIGRATION

As I mentioned previously, the declining white population in urban areas has had sig-nificant implications for the urban tax base as the median household income of blacks and of the growing number of Latinos is significantly below the median income of white households. Accordingly, because of the declining tax base and the simultaneous

loss of federal funds, many municipalities have experienced difficulty in raising sufficient revenue to cover basic services such as street cleaning, garbage collection, and
police protection. Nonetheless, as we shall soon see, several notable positive developments for urban areas have accompanied the rise of the immigrant population.

Foreign immigration, especially from Mexico, increased by more than 50 percent
between 1990 and 2000, resulting in a rapid growth in immigrant enclaves in large
cities (Sampson 2012). According to a report by the Pew Hispanic Center, the most significant growth in immigration occurred in the mid-1990s, reaching its peak at the end
of the decade (Passel, Cohn, and Gonzales-Berrera 2012). Although annual immigrant
flows from Mexico declined sharply after 2005, in the wake of a weakening U.S. job
market and heightened border enforcement, the number of immigrants from Mexico
remains high at approximate 12 million (Passel et al. 2012).

It is noteworthy, as Robert Sampson's (2012) impressive research so clearly reveals,
that areas of concentrated immigration are among the safest in the city, and the process
of immigrant diffusion revitalized and increased the population of a number of deteriorating inner-city neighborhoods. Sampson states:

> Among the public, policy makers, and many academics, a common expectation is
> that the concentration of immigrants and the influx of foreigners drive up disorder
> and crime because of the assumed propensities of these groups to commit crimes
> and settle in poor, presumably disorganized communities. . . . Yet increases in immi-
> gration are correlated with less crime, and immigrants appear to be less violent than
> those born in America, particularly when they live in neighborhoods with high
> numbers of other immigrants. (2012:252)

Immigration has rejuvenated such inner-city neighborhoods as Queens in
New York, the Lower West Side of Chicago, pockets of the North and South Sides
of Chicago, Bushwick in Brooklyn, and large strips of south central Los Angeles and
has lowered their crime rates. "It follows," states Sampson, "that the spatial 'externalities' associated with immigration are multiple in character and constitute a plausible
mechanism to explain some of the ecological variation in crime rates of all groups in
the host city" (2012:253).

What should be underlined is that although the links between economic hardship
and homicide are similar for blacks, Latinos, and Haitians, and although concentrated
disadvantaged and neighborhood social processes predict similar patterns of violence
across racial and ethnic groups, immigrants tend to be less violent, especially if they
reside in concentrated immigrant enclaves. The research of Moreoff, Sampson, and
Raudenbush (2001) revealed that residing in a neighborhood of concentrated immigration, even after adjusting for a series of correlated factors such as an individual's
immigrant status and poverty, was directly related to lower rates of violence. In short, it
appears that immigration is "protective" against violence.

Moreover, as Sampson points out, increases in immigration are also linked to crime
decreases in neighborhoods that are proximate to the center of Mexican immigration

such as the middle and near southern section of Chicago and the far northwestern areas of the city "that have been predominantly white" (Sampson 2012:255). Sampson hypothesizes that the spillover "immigration effects" may eventually spread to other Chicago neighborhoods near immigration centers, including the black neighborhood of Englewood. In Chicago, "crime dropped in the 1990s as immigration surged" (Sampson 2012:253).

Because immigration results in the spread of diverse and formerly external cultures, this logically implies that the spatial process of diffusion has a cultural overtone. Referring to the subculture of violence in the black inner-city depicted in Anderson's "code of the street" discussed earlier, where shared expectations for "saving face" and demanding respect in the "street culture" often lead to violent reactions to otherwise petty encounters such as perceived insults and slights, Sampson theorizes that "if one does not share the cultural attribution or perceived meaning of the event, violence is less likely. Outsiders to the culture, that is, are unlikely to be caught in the vicious cycle of interaction (and reaction) that promote violence" (2012:257). In other words, it may be hypothesized that current immigration is resulting in greater perceptibility of competing nonviolent mores that are diffused through social interaction and affect not only immigrant communities but also depress violent behavior in general.

However, more research is needed on the lasting effects of immigration on crime. Moreoff et al. (2001) found (after accounting for differences in individual, neighborhood, and family background) that first-generation immigrants (those born outside the United States) in Chicago were 45 percent less likely to commit violent crimes than third-generation Americans. Accordingly, the *Latino paradox*—"whereby Latinos do much better on various social indicators, including violence, than blacks and apparently even whites, given relatively high levels of disadvantaged" (Sampson 2012:251)—is driven mainly by first-generation immigrants. If the sharp drop in Latino immigration to the United States that began in 2005 represents a long-term rather than a short-term pattern, rates of violence in Latino communities could increase significantly; and the structural and related cultural problems that drive high-crime rates in the inner-city African American community could conceivably, over time, have similar and notable effects in Latino communities, effects that offset the positive impacts of the first generation on inner-city neighborhoods, including their nonviolent mores.

POLICY IMPLICATIONS

For those committed to fighting inequality, especially those involved in multiracial coalition politics, the lesson from this discussion of key political, economic, and cultural forces is to fashion a new agenda that gives more scrutiny to both racial and nonracial policies. Given the devastating recent economic downturn in the United States, it is especially important to scrutinize fiscal, monetary, and trade policies that may have long-term consequences for our national and regional economies. We must ameliorate the primary problem feeding concentrated poverty: inner-city joblessness. The ideal solutions would be economic policies that produce a tight labor market—that is, one in which there are ample jobs for all applicants. More than any other group, low-skilled workers depend upon a strong economy, particularly a sustained tight labor market. Moreover, fiscal and monetary policies to stimulate noninflationary growth and increase the competitiveness of American goods on both the domestic and international markets would be welcome, as well as a national labor market strategy to make the labor force, including the black and Latino labor force, more adaptable to changing economic opportunities. These are universal policies that are designed to address the problems of all groups who are struggling economically.

However, this new agenda should also include an even sharper focus on traditional efforts to fight poverty, including programs that are targeted at the most disadvantaged racial groups, to ensure that their unique problems are adequately addressed. I refer especially to the following:

- Combating racial discrimination in employment, which is especially devastating during slack labor markets.
- Revitalizing poor, urban neighborhoods, including eliminating abandoned buildings and vacant lots, to make them more attractive for economic investment that would help improve quality of life and create jobs in the area.
- Promoting job-training programs to enhance employment opportunities for inner-city residents.
- Improving public education to prepare inner-city youngsters for higher paying and stable jobs in the new economy.
- Strengthening unions to provide the higher wages, worker protections, and benefits typically absent from low-skilled jobs in retail and service industries.

In short, this new agenda would reflect a multipronged approach that attacks inner-city poverty on various levels, an approach that recognizes the complex array of factors that have contributed to the crystallization of concentrated urban poverty and limited the life chances of so many inner-city residents. The emphasis here is on structural, not cultural solutions, because cultural factors, although they may have some autonomous force once they emerge, are largely a reaction to structural impediments.

CONCLUSION

In this chapter, I have presented a framework that focuses on political, economic, and cultural factors that contribute to the emergence and persistence of concentrated urban black poverty. I highlighted, first of all, explicitly racial and ostensibly nonracial political forces that adversely affected black neighborhoods, which was followed by a discussion of impersonal economic forces that accelerated neighborhood decline in black inner cities and increased racial disparities between cities and suburbs. Secondly, I considered two types of cultural forces that contribute to racial inequality: (1) belief systems of the broader society that either explicitly or implicitly contributed to racial inequality, and (2) cultural traits that arise from patterns of intragroup interaction in settings shaped by racial segregation and discrimination. I then examined the impact of the recent sharp rise in immigration on concentrated urban poverty areas and the challenges they pose for future research. I concluded this chapter with a set of policy recommendations that would constitute a new agenda for addressing the problems of America's inner-city poor, based on the analyses I put forth in this chapter.

NOTES

1. Also see Bartelt (1993); Sugure (1993); Anderson (1994); and Crowder, Scott, and Chavez (2006).
2. For a good discussion of the effects of housing discrimination on the living conditions, education, and employment of urban minorities, see Yinger (1995).
3. Also see Hirsch (1983); Hummon and Muller (1991); Bartelt (1993); Sugrue (1983).
4. See, for example, Kirschenman, Neckerman (1991); Holzer 1995; Wilson (1996); Bertrand and Mullainathan (2002); Pager (2003); Pager and Karafin (2009); Pager, Western, and Sugie (2009); Pager, Western, and Bonikowski (2009).
5. In other societies social isolation may exist in certain inner-city neighborhoods even though the levels of concentrated poverty do not match those inherent in American ghettos. For example, there is evidence that the long term jobless in the Dutch inner cities of Rotterdam and Amsterdam—particularly the immigrants with weak labor-force attachment from Surinam and Indonesia—have experienced sharply decreasing contact with conventional groups and institutions in Dutch society despite levels of ethnic and class segregation far below those of large inner cities in the United States. In response to this development, several Dutch social scientists have discussed the problems of weak labor attachment and social isolation in the Netherlands in precisely the theoretical terms outlined in my book *The Truly Disadvantaged* (1987). See Engbersen (1990); Engbersen, Schuyt and Timmer (1990); Kloosterman (1990); and Schuyt (1990).
6. My discussion of the concept of culture owes a great deal to the work of Lamont and Small (2008). Also see Small, Harding, and Lamont (2010).
7. There is mixed evidence for the outcomes of "acting white" as it applies to education. One of the most well-known studies of this concept was published by Fordham and Ogbu (1986). They studied African American students at a high school in Washington, D.C. and concluded that the fear of acting white was one of the major factors undermining student achievement. On the other hand, Carter (2003) and Cook and Ludwig (1998) do not support the idea that students who avoided "acting white" held lower educational aspirations. Moreover, Tyson, Darity Jr., and Castellino (2005), drawing from interviews and data collected in eight North Carolina public schools, found that "black adolescents are generally achievement oriented and racialized peer pressure against high academic achievement is not prevalent in all schools" (2005:582). Also Downey and Ainsworth-Darnell (2002) have discounted the oppositional culture hypothesis. Roland Fryer (2006) presents yet another perspective. He found that a high Grade Point Average presents a social disadvantage for Hispanics and blacks in integrated schools and public schools, but he saw no such effect in schools that were segregated (80% or more black) or private. He also noticed a marked difference in this effect among black boys and black girls; black

boys in public, integrated schools were particularly susceptible to social ostracism as their GPAs increased, and were penalized seven times more than black students (including both genders) overall.

8. For another excellent study of how activities in the underground economy can adversely affect inner-city residents see Wacquant (1998).

REFERENCES

Anderson, Elijah. 1990. *Street Wise: Race, Class, and Change in an Urban Community*. Chicago: University of Chicago Press.

Anderson, Elijah. 1999. *Code of the Street: Decency, Violence, and the Moral Life of the Inner City*. New York: W.W. Norton.

Anderson, Martin. 1964. *The Federal Bulldozer: A Critical Analysis of Urban Renewal, 1949–1962*. Cambridge, MA: MIT Press.

Bartelt, David W. 1993. "Housing the 'Underclass.'" Pp. 118–57 in *The "Underclass" Debate: Views from History*, edited by Michael B. Katz. Princeton, NJ: Princeton University Press.

Baxandall, Rosalyn and Elizabeth Ewen. 1999. *Picture Windows: How the Suburbs Happened*. New York: Basic Books.

Bertrand, Marianne and Sendhil Mullainathan. 2002. "Are Emily and Jane More Employable than Lakisha and Jamal? A Field Experiment on Labor Market Discrimination." *American Economic Review* 94(4):991–1013.

Bobo, Lawrence D., James R. Kluegel, and Ryan A. Smith. 1997. "Laissez-Faire Racism: The Crystallization of a Kinder, Gentler, Antiblack Ideology." Pp. 15–44 in *Racial Attitudes in the 1990s*, edited by Steven A. Tuch and Jack K. Martin. Westport, CT: Praeger.

Bobo, Lawrence D., Camille Z. Charles, Maria Kryson, and Alicia D. Simmons. 2012. "The Real Record on Racial Attitudes." Pp. 38–83 in *Social Trends in American Life: Findings from the General Social Survey Since 1972*, edited by Peter V. Marsden. Princeton NJ: Princeton University Press.

Caraley, Demetrios. 1992. "Washington Abandons the Cities." *Political Science Quarterly* 107(Spring):1–30.

Carter, Prudence L. 2003. "'Black' Cultural Capital, Status Positioning, and Schooling Conflicts for Low-Income African American Youth." *Social Problems* 50:136–55.

Cohen, Adam and Elizabeth Taylor. 2000. *American Pharaoh: Mayor Richard J. Daley—His Battle for Chicago and the Nation*. Boston: Little, Brown.

Condon, Mark. 1991. "Public Housing, Crime and the Urban Labor Market: A Study of Black Youth in Chicago." Working Paper Series No. H-91-3. Malcolm Wiener Center, John F. Kennedy School of Government. Cambridge, MA: Harvard University.

Connerly, Charles E. 2002. "From Racial Zoning to Community Empowerment: The Interstate Highway System and the African American Community in Birmingham, Alabama." *Journal of Planning Education and Research* 22:99–114.

Cook, Philip J. and Jens Ludwig. 1998. "The Burden of Acting White: Do Black Adolescents Disparage Academic Achievement?" Pp. 375–400 in *The Black-White Test Score Gap*, edited by Christopher Jencks and Meredith Phillips. Washington, DC: Brookings Institution Press.

Crowder, Kyle, Scott J. South, and Erick Chavez. 2006. *American Sociological Review* 71:72–94.

Downey, Douglas B. and James W. Ainsworth-Darnell. 2002. "The Search for Oppositional Culture among Black Students." *American Sociological Review* 67:156–64.

Engbersen, Godfried. 1990. "The Making of the Dutch Underclass? A Labour Market View." Paper presented at the Workshop on Social Policy and the Underclass, University of Amsterdam, the Netherlands, August.

Engbersen, Godfriend, Kees Schuyt, and Jaap Timmer. 1990. "Cultures of Unemployment: Long-Term Unemployment in Dutch Inner Cities." Working paper 4. Leiden: Vakgroep Sociologie Rijksuniversiteit.

Fordham, Signithia and John Ogbu. 1986. "Black Students' School Success: Coping with the Burden of 'Acting White.'" *Urban Journal* 18(3):176–206.

Fox, Radhika K. and Sarah Treuhaft. 2006. *Shared Prosperity, Stronger Regions: An Agenda for Rebuilding America's Older Core Cities*. Report prepared for Policy Link. Oakland, CA.

Fryer, Roland G. 2006. "'Acting White:' The Social Price Paid by the Best and Brightest Minority Students." *Education Next* 6:53–59.

Hirsch, Arnold R. 1983. *Making the Second Ghetto: Race and Housing in Chicago, 1940–1960*. Cambridge: Cambridge University Press.

Holzer, Harry. 1995. *What Employers Want: Job Prospects for Less Educated Workers*. New York: Russell Sage.

Holzer, Harry J., Paul Offner, and Elaine Sorensen. 2003. "What Explains the Continuing Decline in Labor Force Activity Among Young Black Men?" Paper presented for the Color Lines Conference, Harvard University, August 30.

Jargowsky, Paul. 1994. "Ghetto Poverty among Blacks in the 1980s." *Journal of Policy Analysis and Management* 13:288–310.

Joy, Bill. 2000. "Why the Future Doesn't Need Us." *Wired* 8:238–62.

Katz, Michael B. 1993. "Reframing the 'Underclass' Debate." Pp. 440–78 in *The "Underclass" Debate: Views from History*, edited by Michael B. Katz. Princeton, NJ: Princeton University Press.

Kelley, Robin D. G. 1993. "The Black Poor and the Politics of Opposition in a New South City." Pp. 293–333 in *The "Underclass" Debate: Views from History*, edited by Michael B. Katz. Princeton, NJ: Princeton University Press.

Kirschenman, Joleen and Kathryn Neckerman. 1991. "'We'd Love to Hire Them, But . . . The Meaning of Race for Employers." Pp. 203–34 in *The Urban Underclass*, edited by Christopher Jencks and Paul E. Peterson. Washington, DC: Brookings Institution.

Kloosterman, Robert C. 1990. "The Making of the Dutch Underclass? A Labour Market View." Paper presented at the Workshop on Social Policy and the Underclass, University of Amsterdam, the Netherlands, August.

Lamont, Michèle and Mario Luis Small. 2008. "How Culture Matters: Enriching Our Understanding of Poverty." Pp. 76–102 in *The Colors of Poverty*, edited by Ann C. Lin and David R. Harris. New York: Russell Sage Foundation.

Mohl, Raymond. 2000. "Planned Destruction: The Interstates and Central City Housing." Pp. 226–45 in *From Tenements to Taylor Homes: In Search of an Urban Housing Policy in Twentieth-Century America*, edited by John F. Bauman, Roger Biles, and Kristin Szylvian. University Park: Pennsylvania State University Press.

Moreoff, Jeffrey D., Robert J. Sampson, and Stephen Raudenbush. 2001. "Neighborhood Inequality, Collective Efficacy and the Spatial Dynamics of Urban Violence." *Criminology* 39:517–60.

Muller, Edward K. 1991. "Public Housing Isolation and the Urban Underclass." *Journal of Urban History* 17:264–29.

Neckerman, Kathryn. 2007. *Schools Betrayed*. Chicago: University of Chicago Press.

Neckerman, Kathryn M. and Joleen Kirschenman. 1991. "Hiring Strategies, Racial Bias, and Inner-City Workers." *Social Problems* 38:433–47.

Quillian, Lincoln. 1999. "Migration Patterns and the Growth of High-Poverty Neighborhoods, 1970–1990." *American Journal of Sociology* 105:1–37.

Pager, Devah. 2003. "The Mark of a Criminal Record." *American Journal of Sociology* 108:937–75.

Pager, Devah and Diana Karafin. 2009. "Bayesian Bigot? Statistical Discrimination, Stereotypes, and Employer Decision-Making." *Annals of the American Academy of Political and Social Sciences* 621:70–93.

Pager, Devah, Bruce Western, and Bart Bonikowski. 2009. "Discrimination in a Low-Wage Labor Market: A Field Experiment." *American Sociological Review* 74:777–99.

Pager, Devah, Bruce Western, and Naomi Sugie. 2009. "Sequencing Disadvantage Barriers to Employment Facing Young Black and White Men with Criminal Records. *Annals of the American Academy of Political and Social Sciences* 623:195–213.

Passel, Jeffrey, D'Vera Cohn, and Ana Gonzalez Barrera. 2012. "Net Migration from Mexico Falls to Zero—and Perhaps Less." Pew Hispanic Center Report, April 23.

Sampson, Robert J. and William Julius Wilson. 1995. "Toward a Theory of Race, Crime, and Urban Inequality." Pp. 37–54 in *Crime and Inequality*, edited by John Hagan and Ruth Peterson. Stanford, CA: Stanford University Press.

Schuyt, Kees. 1990. "The New Emerging Underclass in Europe: The Experience of Long-Term Unemployment in Dutch Inner Cities." Paper presented at the Workshop on Social Policy and the Underclass, University of Amsterdam, the Netherlands, August.

Small, Mario Luis, David J. Harding, and Michèle Lamont. 2010. "Reconsidering Culture and Poverty." *Annals of the American Academy of Political and Social Sciences* 629:6–27.

Sugrue, Thomas J. 1993. "The Structure of Urban Poverty: The Reorganization of Space and Work in Three Periods of American History." Pp. 85–117 in *The "Underclass" Debate: Views from History*, edited by Michael B. Katz. Princeton, NJ: Princeton University Press.

Tilly, Charles. 1998. *Durable Inequality*. Berkeley: University of California Press.

Tyson, Karolyn, William Darity Jr., and Domini R. Castellino. 2005. "It's Not a 'Black Thing': Understanding the Burden of Acting White and Other Dilemmas of High Achievement." *American Sociological Review* 70:582–605.

U.S. Department of Housing and Urban Development. 1999. *The State of Cities*. Washington, DC: GPO.

Venkatesh, Sudhir Alladi. 2006. *Off the Books: The Underground Economy of the Urban Poor*. Cambridge, MA: Harvard University Press.

Wacquant, Loic. 1998. "Inside the Zone: The Social Art of the Hustler in the Black American Ghetto." *Theory, Culture & Society* 15(2):1–36.

Wallin, Bruce A. 2005. "Budgeting for Basics: The Changing Landscape of City Finances." Discussion paper, the Brookings Institution Metropolitan Policy Program. Washington, DC, August.

Wilson, William Julius. 1987. *The Truly Disadvantaged: The Inner City, the Underclass, and Public Policy*. Chicago: University of Chicago Press.

Wilson, William Julius. 1996. *When Work Disappears: The World of the New Urban Poor*. New York: Alfred A. Knopf.

Yinger, John. 1995. *Closed Doors, Opportunities Lost: The Continuing Costs of Housing Discrimination*. New York: Russell Sage Foundation.

SECTION IV

CAUSES AND THE REPRODUCTION OF POVERTY

CHAPTER 18

SINGLE AND COHABITING
PARENTS AND POVERTY

CHRISTINA M. GIBSON-DAVIS

THE last century has witnessed profound changes in how households are formed and maintained. Around the globe, family sizes have decreased as fertility rates have dropped; fewer people are marrying, and when, they do so, they marry at later ages; and divorced households, in many countries, are now common. Little doubt exists that, at the beginning of the twenty-first century, the global familial landscape looks quite different than it did 100 years ago.

Perhaps no change has been as far-reaching as the decoupling of marriage from fertility. This separation can take many forms: married, childless unions; same-sex couples who adopt children; or the use of surrogates and other techniques to raise children with no biological relationship to the parents. But arguably the most common manifestation of this decoupling is the children who are born and raised outside of a state-recognized marital union. A key indicator of this decoupling is the percentage of children born out of wedlock (known as the nonmarital fertility ratio, or the NMFR). The NMFR has risen dramatically in the past few decades, and a recent report on marriage and fertility patterns in 31 diverse countries found that children born out of wedlock now constitute a sizeable fraction of births. Across the 31 countries, the NMFR averaged more than 30 percent, with particularly high percentages found in Western Europe (Sweden's NMFR, 54 percent) and Latin America (Columbia's NMFR, 85 percent) (Child Trends 2013).

The rise of the NMFR, and the emergence of two other family structures that highlight the separation of marriage from fertility—never married mothers residing apart from the biological father, and romantically involved cohabiting couples raising children together—has become a matter of public and policy concern because of the high correlation between these types of nonmarital family units and poverty. For many countries, childhood poverty is disproportionately concentrated among one parent and cohabiting households (Heuveline and Weinshenker 2008; Gornick and Jäntti 2012). A simple comparison of poverty rates makes this point clear. In Brazil, the household poverty rate for two-parent homes with children was 25 percent; for single-parent households, it was 35 percent. In Taiwan, the disparity was even greater: 5 percent versus 21 percent.[1] Even by U.S. standards, which tend to have relatively high-poverty rates compared with the rest of the industrialized world, the difference in poverty rates was striking: 11.8 percent for all households, and 31 percent for single-parent households (DeNavas-Walt, Proctor, and Smith 2012).

The strong correlation between poverty rates and nonmarital family structures—which, in this chapter, refer to children who live with a never-married parent, usually the mother, or with cohabiting parents—is not surprising, given that married parents tend to have many sociodemographic advantages (e.g., higher earnings, more education) than single or cohabiting parents (Heuveline and Weinshenker 2008; Perelli-Harris et al. 2010). But, as the hoary social science cliché indicates, correlation is not causation. Nonmarital family structure, by itself, is not the primary driver of either a country or an individual's poverty rate, nor does it explain between-country variation in poverty levels. Many other factors, including employment practices and tax and transfer programs, explain far more variance in both country- and individual-level poverty rates (Rainwater and Smeeding 2003; Gornick and Jäntti 2010; Gornick and Jäntti 2012).

This is not to say, however, that nonmarital family structures are economically benign. They can have indirect economic consequences through their association with poverty: children who grow up in poor households are more likely to be poor as adults, have weaker labor force attachments, and are less likely to marry as adults (Duncan et al. 1998; Ribar 2004; Bradshaw, Hoelscher, and Richardson 2007). These cross-generational effects suggest that, at least in the American context, the rise of nonmarital family structures has contributed to economic inequality (McLanahan and Percheski 2008).

In what follows, I address the association between nonmarital family structures, poverty, and inequality. I begin by briefly describing marriage and fertility patterns around the world, and how these patterns exhibit characteristics of the so-called second demographic transition in which marriage and fertility have become increasingly disconnected. I then explain why nonmarital families tend to be poorer than marital families, but why the correlation between poverty and nonmarital family structures does not causally explain between- or within-country variation in poverty rates. I discuss some methods for addressing high poverty rates among nonmarital household structures, and argue that policies other than marriage promotion would be far more effective at reducing poverty for nonmarital households. I conclude by briefly discussing some implications of nonmarital fertility for economic inequality.[2]

THE SECOND DEMOGRAPHIC TRANSITION

Most countries of the world now exhibit at least some elements of the so-called second demographic transition (Lesthaeghe 2010). The first demographic transition was the decline of mortality and fertility that began in the early nineteenth century. The second demographic transition, emerging in the early nineteenth century and accelerating into the twentieth, is characterized by the separation of fertility from marriage and the emergence of other household types besides the conventional two parent married household (van de Kaa 1987; Lesthaeghe and Johan 1988). The second demographic transition has five key components: decreases in fertility, increases in cohabitation, a rise in the age at first marriage, increases in divorce, and increases in nonmarital fertility. Societies that have fully entered into the second demographic transition have large proportions of children being raised in nonmarital households and have loosened the once-tight connection between marriage and fertility (Lesthaeghe 1995).

Though the second demographic transition was first identified in Western Europe, it now characterizes most industrialized and emerging economies, including the United States; Canada; Mexico; Australia; New Zealand; East and Southeast Asia; Central, Eastern, and Southern Europe; Russia; and Latin America (Sobotka 2008; Lesthaeghe 2010; Perelli-Harris and Gerber 2011; Cherlin 2012). All of these regions and countries have seen sharp drops in fertility, with many below replacement levels (the level of fertility needed to maintain a constant population), an increasing age at first marriage, and an increase in divorce. Most areas have also seen a dramatic rise in nonmarital fertility and births within cohabiting relationships.

Even countries where not all the elements of the second demographic transition are present have nevertheless seen some changes in family structure that are consistent with the second demographic transition. For example, North Africa and the Middle East are still characterized by the absence of cohabitation, near universal marriage, and very few out-of-wedlock births. Nevertheless, both regions have seen a decline in fertility and a postponement of age at first marriage (Cherlin 2012; Engelen and Puschmann 2011). Similarly, in China and Japan, nonmarital fertility is relatively rare, but both countries have seen a dramatic drop in fertility rates, a postponement of age at first marriage, and an increased rate of divorce (Morgan, Zhigang, and Hayford 2009; Wang and Zhou 2010).

Only a handful of countries have family formation patterns that are inconsistent with the second demographic transition. India has had a drop in fertility, but marriage rates are quite high, most people marry at quite young ages, and nonmarital fertility is rare (Dommaraju 2011). Sub-Saharan Africa is one of the few regions of the world that has not had a drop in fertility; it also has very high rates of marriage and very little divorce (Conley, McCord, and Sachs 2007).

These few exceptions notwithstanding, the world is generally moving toward family formation patterns consistent with the second demographic transition. The next sections of this chapter discuss the implications of two of these factors—the decrease in fertility, and the increase in single-parent homes as manifested through a rise in nonmarital births and cohabiting parents—for poverty and economic well-being.

Separation of Fertility from Marriage

The Rise of Nonmarital Births

Perhaps no indicator best represents the separation of marriage from fertility then the percentage of births born out of wedlock (as mentioned, known as the nonmarital fertility ratio, or the NMFR). In many countries, it is commonplace for a child to be born to unmarried parents; in a handful of countries, particularly those in South America and Northern Europe, it is the norm. Figure 18.1 presents the NMFR for 31 countries.

The NMFR ranged from a low of 1 percent (Japan) to a high of 85 percent (Columbia). Most countries had double-digit NMFRs, and in 18 of the 31 countries examined, at least one-third of all children were born out of wedlock. The NMFR comprised the majority of births in the four South American countries (Bolivia, Columbia, Peru, and Chili), and in Mexico, Sweden, and France.

What is most notable about the NMFR is how fast it has risen. Figure 18.2 compares the proportion of births born out of wedlock for select European countries, the United States, and Canada between 1980 and 2011.[3]

As Figure 18.2 makes clear, the past 30 years have seen a dramatic increase in the NMFR. With the exception of countries that already had a high NMFR in 1980 (e.g., Iceland, Sweden, Denmark), countries have seen their NMFR at least double, if not triple or quadruple, in the past 30 years. The biggest jump occurred in the Netherlands,

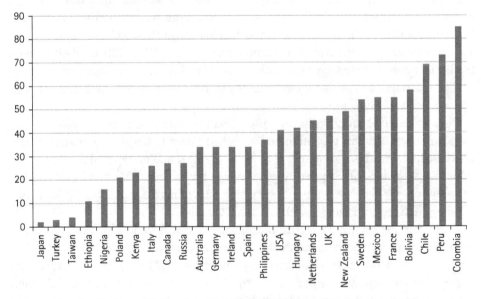

FIGURE 18.1 Proportion of Births Born Nonmaritally, Various Countries

Note: Years measured varies between 2008 and 2011.

Source: Child Trends (2013; Figure 5).

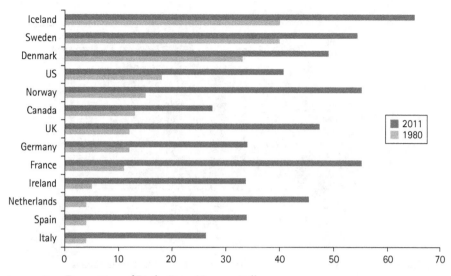

FIGURE 18.2 Proportion of Births Born Nonmaritally

Note: Data for Canada is from 2010.

Source: 1980 figures: Ventura (2009). 2011 figures: Statistics Europe; Statistics Canada, Centers for Disease Control National Vital Statistics.

where the NMFR increased more than 11 times between 1980 and 2011 (from 4 to 45 percent). Large increases were also seen in Spain (from 4 to 34 percent) and France (5 to 55 percent).

This dramatic rise in nonmarital births has stimulated numerous debates about the consequences of single-parent households for poverty (though not all nonmarital births are born to single parents, a point discussed in more detail later). Many policy-makers and politicians, particularly in the American context, have pointed to the rise of single-parent households as a primary reason for high poverty rates among children (Amato and Maynard 2007; Rector 2010).

It is true that, on an individual level, single-parent status is one of the most important correlates with poverty. In most places around the globe, children living with one parent have higher poverty rates than children living with two parents, particularly if the family is headed by a woman (Bradbury and Jäntti 1999; Beaujot and Liu 2002; Rainwater and Smeeding 2003; Chen and Corak 2008; Heuveline and Weinshenker 2008). A cross-national study indicated that, on average, single mothers are estimated to be 2.7 times more likely to be poor than other women (Brady and Burroway 2012).

The correlational evidence of the association between poverty and single-parent households is compelling. Gornick and Jäntti (2012) using data from the Luxembourg Income Study, which collects economic and demographic data across industrialized and emerging economics, found that mother-only households have considerably higher poverty rates than two-parent households (see Figure 18.3). They defined poverty as households having market income (e.g., income from earnings, pensions, and cash property) that is below 50 percent of the median household income for that country.

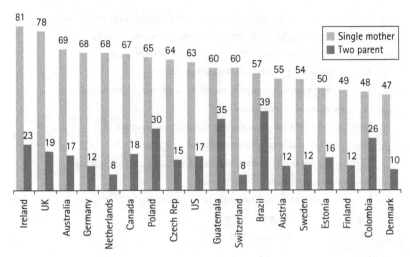

FIGURE 18.3 Market Poverty Rates, Single Mother vs. Two-parent Households

Notes: Poverty rates are households that have market income that is below 50 percent of the median household income for that country.

Source: Gornick and Jäntti (2012; Table 3).

As the Figure 18.3 illustrates, poverty rates for mother-headed households are extremely high, ranging from 81 percent (Germany) to 47 percent (Denmark). Father-only households (results not shown) have slightly lower poverty rates than mother-only households but are still more likely to be poor than two-parent households. Disparities between mother-headed households and two-parent households were quite pronounced and existed across all regions represented in this graph: Northern Europe, Australia, North America, South America, and the former Soviet Republics.

However, despite the correlational associations, most researchers believe that single-parent homes do not cause an increase in poverty levels, either on an individual or country level. This point is illustrated in Figure 18.4, which plots the American NMFR against overall poverty rate and child poverty rates from 1980 to 2011 (here, poverty rate refers to the official poverty threshold as defined by the American government). If the NMFR had a causal effect on poverty rates, then one would expect the poverty rates to rise with the NMFR. However, as the figure indicates, very little covariance exists between the NMFR and poverty rates. Between 1980 and 2011, the American NMFR rose steadily, while poverty rates oscillated (around 14 percent for the overall rate and 20 percent for the child poverty rate). A far more important determinant of U.S. poverty rates was the strength of the U.S. economy, with increases in the poverty rate corresponding to the recessions of early 1980s, early 1990s, early 2000s, and late 2000s.

Though this figure is meant to be illustrative only, it does demonstrate what has been found across industrialized countries: a rise in out-of-wedlock fertility, with its accompanying rise in single-parent families, does not directly translate into increased poverty or a weakened economy (Rainwater and Smeeding 2003). Moreover, the relative prevalence of single-parent families does not explain variation in poverty rates across countries; the relatively high poverty rate of the United

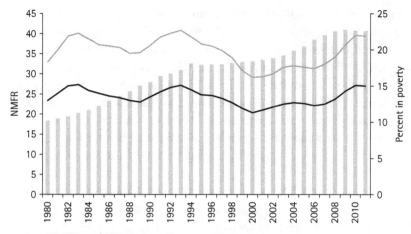

FIGURE 18.4 NMFR and U.S. Poverty Rates, 1980–2011

Source: U.S. Census Bureau, NMFR, U.S. National Vital Statistic Poverty Rates.

States, for example, cannot be explained because the United States has more out-of-wedlock births than its European peers (Gornick and Jäntti 2010, 2012). Instead, most of the variance in poverty rates between the United States and its European peers can be accounted for by employment and social safety net policies (a point discussed in more detail later). Put succinctly, out-of-wedlock births and the proportion of single-parent homes play very little role in explaining within or between country variation in poverty rates (Rainwater and Smeeding 2003).

Another piece of evidence arguing against the causal effect of single-parent homes on poverty rates is demonstrated by the lack of correlation between nonmarital birth and poverty rates in developing countries. India, for example, has very low rates of nonmarital fertility (less than 1 percent in 2005, the last year for which numbers are available) but has extremely high poverty rates (33 percent of its population living on less than $1.25 a day). Similar points can be made about countries in sub-Saharan Africa, such as Rwanda, Angola, or Botswana. These countries have very high poverty rates, yet almost no out-of-wedlock births, and few would argue that their high poverty rates are caused by nonmarital fertility.

Of course, it would be surprising if any one factor was universally responsible for poverty rates around the globe or within any given country. And little doubt exists that the association between single-parent households and lack of economic resources for the majority of countries is quite robust. But the evidence suggests that though single parent households are a reliable marker for poverty, particularly for children, they do not, by themselves, cause its levels to rise.

Births within Cohabiting Unions

The rise in the NMFR can also be seen as a marker for another indication of the decoupling of marriage from fertility: the increase in the proportion of births born to cohabiting parents.[4] Though cohabitation can be defined in various ways, here I refer to two opposite sex romantically involved adults who share living quarters. Cohabiting parents account for more than 50 percent of all first births in Norway and France and at least a third of all first births in Austria, the UK, and the Netherlands (Perelli-Harris et al. 2010). In the United States, the proportion of births to cohabiting parents is about 20 percent (Wildsmith, Steward-Streng, and Manlove 2011), similar to Russia's 17 percent (Perelli-Harris and Gerber 2011). This rise in cohabiting parents has largely occurred over the past 30 years, which has seen a three- to four-fold increase in the proportion of births born to cohabiting parents (Kennedy and Bumpass 2008; Perelli-Harris et al. 2012).

The associations of cohabitating families with poverty and economic well-being are similar to those discussed earlier: strongly correlational, but not necessarily causal. Trends in cohabiting births do not correlate well with trends in poverty (as an example, cohabitating births could be substituted for the NMFR in Figure 18.3, and the figure would look remarkably unchanged). Heuveline and Weinshenker (2008), in one of the few studies to examine aggregate impacts of cohabitation on economic well-being internationally, found that the proportion of children living with cohabiting parents did not have a strong association on a country's level of poverty, nor did it explain variation in poverty rates across countries.

Like single-parent households, though, cohabiting parent households are more likely to be poor than married-parent households, as they have higher poverty rates and lower household incomes (Lichter, Qian, and Crowley 2005; Manning and Brown 2006; Heuveline and Weinshenker 2008). Across 11 North American and European countries, cohabiting parents had an average poverty rate of 13 percent, whereas married parents had a poverty rate of 8 percent.[5] The difference varied greatly by country, though: Sweden's poverty rate was the same for married and cohabiting households (2.3 percent), whereas the United States had much higher rates for cohabiting versus married families (30 percent vs. 14 percent) (Heuveline and Weinshenker 2008). Cohabiting parents also fared better economically than single-parent households. Nevertheless, evidence consistently indicates that married and cohabiting households are not economically equivalent, and that a two-parent household by itself does not necessarily shield children from economic risk.

WHY NONMARITAL FAMILIES ARE POOR

If nonmarital family structures do not causally impact poverty rates, why, then, are they so strongly associated with high levels of poverty? Most of the reason can be explained by who forms nonmarital family structures, and how they compare, demographically, to those in married-parent families. Married parents, relative to single or cohabiting parents, have completed more education, come from more economically advantaged backgrounds, have higher levels of physical and mental health, wait longer to have children, and make different behavioral choices (Carlson, McLanahan, and England 2004; Heuveline and Weinshenker 2008; Kalil and Ryan 2010; Perelli-Harris et al. 2012). All of these advantages likely contribute to differences in levels of economic resources. Note, however, that these demographic advantages stem from who selects into marriage, rather than a benefit of marriage per se.

Nevertheless, the economic impact of these differences can be large. As one example consider that single and cohabiting parents have completed less education than married parents, a difference which has been found in the United States (Kalil and Ryan 2010), Canada (Kerr, Moyser and Beaujot 2006), Europe (Perelli-Harris et al. 2010), and Russia (Perelli-Harris and Gerber 2011). A large-scale American birth-cohort study found that among married mothers, 18 percent did not have a high school diploma, compared to 41 percent of cohabiting mothers and 49 percent of single mothers. The same study indicated that 36 percent of married mothers had at least a bachelor's degree, as compared to 2 percent of cohabiting and single mothers (Kalil and Ryan 2010). Education in turn directly affects wages. In 2011, the median earnings for an American woman without a high school diploma was $15,000; for a woman with at least a bachelor's degree, it was $45,000 (U.S. Census Bureau 2012). Over the course of her lifetime, a woman with a BA will earn $1.2 million more than a woman who is a high school dropout. With these types of economic advantages, it is easy to see why married families are less likely to be poor than mother-only households.

Higher levels of economic resources found among married parents may also, to a lesser extent, stem from advantages that accrue to marriage itself. There are several reasons why marriage might be economically beneficial. First, married men earn more money than unmarried men, as found in the United States, Germany, and Britain (Ginther and Zavodny 2001; Bardasi and Taylor 2008; Pollmann-Schult 2011). American married fathers earn more money than American single or cohabiting fathers (Glauber 2008). Estimates of the U.S. marriage premium range between 3 and 10 percent (Hersch and Stratton 2000; Lundberg and Rose 2000; Killewald 2013). Marriage premiums have been found for white, Hispanic, and black men (Glauber 2008; Hodges and Budig 2010). Part of this marriage premium likely occurs because of selection: married men bring higher human capital to the marketplace and are able to command higher wages. But part of this marital advantage also stems from married fathers ability to rely on a married partner to support them in their work effort. They benefit from either a stay-at-home spouse who addresses domestic chores or a spouse who works but can share in the household and child-rearing tasks (Lundberg and Rose 2000). Theoretically, cohabiting fathers should also enjoy the same wage premium, but cohabiting relationships may not be as effective at promoting workforce attachment (Killewald 2013).

A second economic advantage for married-parent households is that they can take advantage of economies of scale (Thomas and Sawhill 2005). When an adult joins a family, many costs remained unchanged (e.g., mortgage, rent, utilities, etc.), with the added advantage that the new adult can contribute economically. In a one-parent household, all the fixed costs of maintaining a household must be borne by one person. These costs can be offset if the single parent has other adults living in the household, but research suggests that coresident adults are more likely to make in-kind, rather than monetary, contributions (Sarkisian and Gerstel 2004). Though economies of scale should theoretically be possible for cohabiting couples, studies in the United States, Sweden, and Norway (Heimdal and Houseknecht 2003; Lyngstad, Noack, and Tufte 2011), indicate that cohabiting couples do not pool resources to the same extent as do married couples, which diminishes their ability to take advantage of economies of scale.

Marriage likely increases incomes in another way: it facilitates the buildup of wealth (Zagorsky 2005; Vespa and Painter 2011). Married parents are able to take advantage of higher earnings and economies of scale and channel that money into assets and savings (Wilmoth and Koso 2004). Moreover, marriages are more stable than other types of unions (Osborne and McLanahan 2007; Wu and Musick 2008), and their durability encourages long-term financial planning and investment (Waite and Gallagher 2000).

Two other factors explain the marriage advantage, specifically for single-parent households relative to two-parent unions. Single-parent families may be less able to manage the twin tasks of breadwinning and child-rearing (McLanahan and Sandefur 1994). Single parents must provide both economic and emotional resources for their children—having to provide both can compromise their ability to provide either (Thomson, Hanson, and McLanahan 1994). Without the presence of another adult to aid in domestic work, single parents can find it difficult to maintain a strong attachment to the labor force.

A final factor explaining higher poverty rates is specific to single mothers: in addition to facing a human capital gap, they also face a gender wage gap. Though this gap has decreased over time, it is endemic to most industrialized countries (Weichselbaumer and Winter-Ebmer 2005). A recent OECD report indicates that the gap (measured as the percent of male wages earned by women) ranges from 20 percent (Australia, Hungary, Italy) to 50 percent (Canada and Japan) (Polachek and Xiang 2009). The gender wage gap is determined by many factors: women tend to select lower paying occupations, for example, and may accumulate less experience in a particular field. Nevertheless, part of the gender gap appears to result from wage discrimination (Burda, Hamermesh, and Weil 2012).

To summarize, most of the economic advantages of marriage stem from the characteristics of those who marry rather than marriage per se, and positive selection into marriage accounts for most of its economic benefits (Chapple 2009; Thomson and McLanahan 2012). Nevertheless, it is also appears that marriage has a small, yet positive, effect on a family's economic well-being (Ribar 2004). In general, unmarried parents have lower levels of human capital and cannot take advantage of economies of scale. They also do not benefit from a married-male wage premium or the accumulation of assets that comes from a long-lasting partnership. Single parents must divide their time between the marketplace and the home, and single mothers face the gender wage gap. Cumulatively, these factors contribute to the economic disparity between marital and nonmarital household structures.

MARRIAGE AS POVERTY REDUCER

If marriage has so many economic benefits, should marriage be employed as a poverty-reduction tool? This question has been raised most prominently in the United States, as researchers have struggled to identify the causal effects of marriage on economic well-being (Lichter and Crowley 2004; Sigle-Rushton and McLanahan 2004; Foster and Kalil 2007). Some American researchers have conducted simulations in which an unwed mother was "married" to a demographically similar man (Sigle-Rushton and McLanahan 2002; Thomas and Sawhill 2002). Because the only factor that changed was the mother's marital status, any resulting differences in her poverty levels must have occurred because of her marriage. Results from these simulations studies found that poverty rates decreased considerably.

However, these simulation studies cannot be interpreted to mean that unwed mothers marrying in the real world would see any reduction in poverty. First, it is unclear that policies can be used to persuade parents to marry, as marriage rates are relatively insensitive to policy levers. There are a few exceptions: Austria, for example, saw a 350 percent increase in 1987 in marriage rates, right before a marriage-subsidy program was abolished (Frimmel, Halla, and Winter-Ebmer 2012). But the Austrian government eliminated the subsidy (nearly $3,000 per couple) because it was too expensive. More modest policy efforts to promote marriage have largely been ineffective. The United States tried to induce marriage among low-income adults, through changes to its welfare system and the Earned Income Tax Credit (EITC), a refundable tax credit for the working poor. These promarriage changes have, by most accounts, had little effect on marriage rates (Ellwood 2000; Blank 2007; Graefe and Lichter 2008). Another approach tried by the United States to encourage marriage—providing relationship-skills and premarriage counseling to adults with a shared birth—likewise had minimal effects (Wood et al. 2012).

A more fundamental problem exists, however, in assuming that marriage by itself would cause poverty rates to decrease. The economic advantages of marriage adhere only under certain circumstances—namely, when a marriage is high quality and long-lasting. Indeed, evidence from the United States suggests that mothers who marry and then divorce are economically worse off than if they had never married at all (Lichter, Graefe. and Brown 2003). Marital disruption is one of the primary means by which women, both in the United States and in Western Europe, enter into poverty (D'Ambrosio, Deutsch and Silber 2011). Moreover, the most economically beneficial marriages are those that involve a man with relatively strong attachment to the labor force (Lichter et al. 2003). However, many unmarried mothers may have difficulties in finding a partner with sufficient levels of human capital to successfully engage in the workforce (Wilson 1987, 1996). Research has found that unmarried mothers, relative to women without children, marry men with lower earned income and weaker labor force participation rates (Graefe and Lichter 2007; Lichter and Graefe 2007).

Additionally, studies that have projected economic benefits to marriage have tacitly assumed that marriages among unwed mothers would function in ways that facilitate income growth and reduce poverty. Yet the expectations of how marriage operates are largely based on studies where the sample population married first and then had children. Given the differences between those who select single parenthood and those who do not, it is not clear that marriage would function in the same way for a mother who had her child first and then married.

In sum, marriage is an uncertain means to reduce poverty. First, it is not clear that large numbers of unmarried parents could be convinced to marry and if unmarried mothers would have the kinds of marriages (e.g., stable, with sufficient levels of earnings) that promote economic well-being. Perhaps most fundamentally, however, it is not known how marriages among unwed parents would operate and if marriages among parents would, indeed, be economically beneficial.

Addressing Poverty among Nonmarital Households

As this chapter has indicated, nonmarital households generally have higher poverty rates and lower incomes than marital households. The previous section argued that encouraging marriage among single and cohabiting parents is an uncertain strategy for reducing poverty. In this section, I examine some policy solutions that offer more promise for addressing the economic realities of nonmarital household structures.

The provision of public and private transfers has been found to be extremely effective at reducing poverty among nonmarital family structures. To demonstrate this point, Figure 18.5 returns to the analysis presented by Gornick and Jäntti (2012) to illustrate how transfers affect the poverty rate of single-mother households. Transfers included two types: government and private. Government transfers include policies such as childcare subsidies, paid parental leave, or child allowances through cash or tax benefits. Private transfers refer primarily to the provision of child support, usually provided by a nonresident father. The figure presents two poverty rates: the first is the same used in Figure 18.4 and defines poverty rates based on market income alone. The second poverty rate measures poverty rates after transfer income (net of taxes) has been included.

As illustrated by Figure 18.5, transfers reduce poverty rates quite dramatically. Government and private transfers in Denmark, Sweden, Finland, Switzerland, the Netherlands, Poland, and Austria reduced the poverty rate by more than 60 percent. Transfers in the United Kingdom, Australia, Guatemala, and Ireland reduce it by more than 50 percent. The United States, Canada, and Columbia stand out as outliers because of their small reductions in poverty, and because single mothers in those countries have high rates of poverty even after transfers.

A similar analysis examined how after-tax transfer policies affected the poverty rates of cohabiting couples with children (Heuveline and Weinshenker 2008). Across the 15 countries, transfer policies reduced poverty rates among cohabiting families by 6.5 percentage points. The largest reductions in poverty rates were found for Finland, Australia, and Sweden (Heuveline and Weinshenker 2008).

Scholars believe that it is these country-level differences in transfers policies, rather than family structure per se, that explains the high poverty rates among nonmarital families. The United States is perhaps the best example of this. The United States has, by international standards, a relatively average number of children born of wedlock (see Figure 18.1)—its NMFR falls in the moderate range. Likewise, the before-transfer poverty rate of American single-parent households, when compared to other countries, is again about average (see Figure 18.5). What makes the United States stand out from other countries, however, is that its transfers policies do relatively little to reduce poverty among single-parent households. In the United States, transfers reduce poverty by only 12 percentage points, or by 20 percent. In Denmark, by contrast, government and private transfers reduce the poverty rate by 38.5 percentage points, or 469 percent (see Figure 18.5).

For the United States, the ineffectiveness of transfers in reducing poverty rates among single-parent households is not surprising given that the United States targets

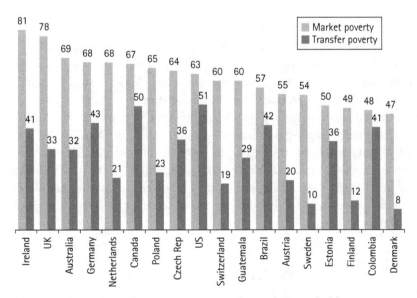

FIGURE 18.5 Market vs. Transfer Poverty Rates, Mother-only Households

Notes: Market poverty includes only market income. Transfer poverty includes market and transfer income (net of taxes). Households are poor if income falls below 50 percent of median income for that country.

Source: Gornick and Jäntti (2012; Table 3).

its social safety net primarily to the elderly (through Medicare and Social Security) and to those who are temporarily separated from the workforce (unemployment insurance). And these transfer programs have been quite effective; the poverty rate among Americans under the age of 65 fell precipitously after Congress expanded Medicare and Social Security in the mid-1960s (the poverty rate for those 65 and older remains well below the poverty rate for those under 18). The United States, when compared to other European countries, provides relatively little support to single-parent families, and this lack of support translates into high poverty rates.

Scholars have worked to identify the types of transfer programs that might be most effective in reducing poverty among nonmarital households. For example, countries that offer paid parental leave and provide publicly funded childcare for young children had lower poverty rates for single mothers relative to partnered mothers (Misra et al. 2012). Other work (Brady and Burroway 2012) suggests that policies universal in nature, that is, offered to all citizens, had larger effects on the poverty rates of single mothers than did targeted policies, that is, those offered to single mothers in particular. Examples of universal policies are pensions, unemployment insurance, and the provision of health care, whereas targeted policies include family assistance and childcare grants.

Another possible avenue to reduce poverty is to strengthen maternal employment, as employment significantly lowers poverty risk among female-headed households. A study done across 11 industrialized nations compared poverty rates of single mothers with low earnings (earnings that were in the bottom quintile for female earnings in that country) as compared to single mothers with medium to high earnings (earnings that were not in the bottom quintile) (Gornick and Jäntti 2010). The average difference in poverty rates was stark: 95 percent for the low earners versus 41 percent for the high earners. Once transfers were taken into account, the average poverty rate for high-earning single mothers fell to 14 percent. Policies that have been shown to encourage female employment include paid maternity leave, childcare subsidies, and school schedules consistent with ordinary work hours (Misra et al. 2012).

It is important to note that even in the presence of transfers and strong labor market attachment, single-parent households are still more likely to be poor than married-parent households (Gornick and Jäntti 2010). And countries that have generous transfer policies face other trade-offs, including higher taxes and increasing levels of public debt. Nevertheless, providing transfers and strengthening employment ties has proven to be an effective means of reducing poverty among nonmarital households.

WHAT'S AT STAKE

This chapter has made the argument that the growth of nonmarital family structures has not impacted a country's well-being, and, while strongly correlated with individual levels of poverty, does not by itself account for much poverty variance. It might be concluded that nonmarital family structures are largely irrelevant to discussions of poverty and that policymakers interested in reducing poverty should focus their attention elsewhere.

However, two factors are important to keep in mind when evaluating the relevance of nonmarital family structures for poverty. First, family structure, because it is so closely correlated with poverty, is an important determinant of the life chances of children (McLanahan and Sandefur 1994). Children who grow up in poverty in the industrialized world are less likely to finish school and have lower earnings and higher poverty rates as adults (Corak 2006; Bradshaw et al. 2007). Notably, they are also more likely to have an out-of-wedlock birth (Duncan et al. 1998). These cross-generational effects are important because it means that as increasing fractions of children grow up in nonmarital households, with its corresponding association with poverty, then an increasing percentage of children are at risk for compromised well-being as adults. Note that the important transmitter of disadvantage is poverty and not necessarily nonmarital family structure. Nevertheless, nonmarital family structure warrants special consideration because it is such a strong indicator of poverty—it demarcates the children most at risk of compromised life outcomes as adults and is a strong indicator that the cycle of disadvantage will be perpetuated.

Another reason to consider family structure in discussions of poverty is that family structure has important, and likely increasing, effects on economic and social inequality. Family structure matters for inequality because family structure has become increasingly stratified by social class (as proxied by education). In the United States, for example, the rise in single and cohabiting parenthood has been disproportionately concentrated among less-well-educated adults (Isen and Stevenson 2011). Women with a bachelor's degree have seen almost no change in their family formation patterns and, by and large, only have children in the context of marriage. Class disparities in fertility patterns are less pronounced elsewhere, but research confirms that class differences in family structure in Europe and Russia are growing (Perelli-Harris et al. 2010; Perelli-Harris and Gerber 2011). Insofar as only the better educated are choosing marriage, then any benefits of marriage, even if small, will be disproportionately concentrated among individuals who are already socioeconomically advantaged.

Scholars who have investigated how family structure might affect inequality have found that increases in nonmarital households account for an 11 to 56 percent rise in income inequality (see McLanahan and Percheski 2008 for a list of these studies in the United States). The connection between family structure and income inequality is important for two reasons. First, like poverty, income inequality directly impacts the life chances of future generations. Children in lower positions in society may have limited access to the schools, health care, and other public goods that they need to thrive. Second, income inequality may impact overall economic growth (Rajan 2011). The impact of economic inequality on economic growth remains a matter of debate (De Dominicis, Florax and De Groot 2008), but it is possible that nonmarital family structures may someday directly influence a country's financial health.

CONCLUSION

Most countries around the globe, with a few notable exceptions, are moving in the direction of decreased fertility and more nonmarital family structures. This chapter has argued that these two factors have had mixed effects on poverty and economic well-being. Decreasing fertility has led to reductions in poverty and increases in financial well-being. The rise of nonmarital family structures has had more ambiguous effects: almost no aggregate impact, but likely a small (but unknown) increase in individual poverty rates.

Given that reductions in fertility have had large positive economic impacts on poverty rates, and that the rise of nonmarital family structures has had (at most) a small negative impact, it could be concluded that changes in modern family structure have, on the whole, been beneficial. Yet, in many industrial and emerging economies, policymakers and scholars alike have raised concerns about the state of the modern family and suggest that modern family arrangements have negative consequences for families and for society.

This concern about the modern family, particularly the rise of fertility outside of marriage, is not misplaced but rather misinformed. Children living in single- and cohabiting-parent homes should be a matter of national interest because they have disproportionately higher poverty rates and lower median incomes than children in other family arrangements. The poverty they experience as children will likely affect their well-being as adults, as childhood poverty has been associated with decreased adult wages and increased likelihood of single parenthood. Single- and cohabiting-parent households therefore serve as an important mechanism through which the intergenerational transmission of poverty occurs.

At the same time, it is likely that family structure qua family structure accounts for only a small fraction of the causal variation in poverty rates. More important factors include labor force attachment and transfer payments; it is these factors that can explain much more of the variance in both country- and individual-level poverty rates. As evidence of their importance, strong labor force attachment and generous transfer payments can greatly reduce the poverty rates of one-parent households (in some countries, by more than two-thirds). In contrast, policies that have addressed marital status have also been associated with decreases in poverty but only on paper. There has yet to be an effective marriage-intervention program that has induced people to marry and lowered their poverty rates as a result.

The impact of labor market participation and transfer programs, in fact, undermines the argument that family structure by itself causes poverty: if one-parent households were poor simply because they had only one parent, then addressing factors other than their marital status would be ineffective. Instead, a more appropriate way to conceptualize the role of nonmarital family structures in poverty rates is to acknowledge that they identify the group of children most at risk of poverty. These children merit special attention because the consequences of growing up poor in a rich country are great. But, as this chapter has argued, the way they merit special attention is not through marriage, but through policies and programs that facilitate their family's economic health.

Notes

1. Author's calculations using data from the Luxembourg Income Study.
2. In this review, I have tried to include data from as many countries as possible. However, most of the work on nonmarital family structures has been concentrated on a select group of countries, particularly those in Western Europe and North America. Where possible, I have included research from emerging economies and other regions. Much work remains to be done, however, on how nonmarital family structures affect poverty and inequality outside the Western or European context.
3. Data on the 1980 NMFR not available for all countries examined in Figure 18.1.
4. Cohabiting unions between adults without children have also risen dramatically (Cherlin 2010; Kasearu and Kutsar 2011). This chapter only discusses cohabiting unions that involve children.
5. To the best of my knowledge, very little research has been done on the associations between cohabitation and poverty levels for countries outside the United States and Western Europe.

References

Amato, P. R. and R. A. Maynard. 2007. "Decreasing Nonmarital Births and Strengthening Marriage to Reduce Poverty." *The Future of Children* 17:117–41.

Bardasi, E. and M. Taylor. 2008. "Marriage and Wages: A Test of the Specialization Hypothesis." *Economica* 75:569–91.

Beaujot, R. and J. Liu. 2002. "Children, Social Assistance and Outcomes: Cross National Comparisons." Luxembourg Income Study Working Paper No. 304. Luxembourg.

Bradbury, B. and M. Jäntti. 1999. "Child Poverty across Industrialized Nations." Innocenti Occassional Papers, Economic and Social Policy Series, no. 71. Florence, Italy, UNICEF.

Bradshaw, J., P. Hoelscher, and D. Richardson. 2007. "An Index of Child Well-Being in the European Union." *Social Indicators Research* 80:133–77.

Brady, D. and R. Burroway. 2012. "Targeting, Universalism, and Single-Mother Poverty: A Multilevel Analysis across 18 Affluent Democracies." *Demography* 49:719–46.

Burda, M., D. S. Hamermesh and P. Weil. 2012. "Total Work and Gender: Facts and Possible Explanations." *Journal of Population Economics*: 1–23.

Carlson, M. J., S. McLanahan and P. England. 2004. "Union Formation in Fragile Families." *Demography* 41:237–61.

Chapple, S.. 2009. "Child Well-Being and Sole-Parent Family Structure in the OECD: An Analysis." OECD Social, Employment and Migration Working Papers, No. 82. OECD Publishing.

Chen, W.-H. and M. Corak. 2008. "Child Poverty and Changes in Child Poverty." *Demography* 45:537–53.

Cherlin, A. J. 2010. "Demographic Trends in the United States: A Review of Research in the 2000s." *Journal of Marriage and Family* 72:403–19.

Cherlin, A. J. 2012. "Goode's World Revolution and Family Patterns: A Reconsideration at Fifty Years." *Population and Development Review* 38:577–607.

Child Trends. 2013. *World Family Map*. Bethesda, MD.

Conley, D., G. C. McCord, and J. D. Sachs. 2007. "Africa's Lagging Demographic Transition: Evidence from Exogenous Impacts of Malaria Ecology and Agricultural Technology." National Bureau of Economic Research.

Corak, M. 2006. "Do Poor Children Become Poor Adults? Lessons from a Cross-Country Comparison of Generational Earnings Mobility." *Research on Economic Inequality* 13:143–88.

D'Ambrosio, C., J. Deutsch, and J. Silber. 2011. "Multidimensional Approaches to Poverty Measurement: An Empirical Analysis of Poverty in Belgium, France, Germany, Italy and Spain, Based on the European Panel." *Applied Economics* 43:951–61.

De Dominicis, L., R. J. G. M. Florax, and H. L. F. De Groot. 2008. "A Meta-Analysis on the Relationship between Income Inequality and Economic Growth." *Scottish Journal of Political Economy* 55:654–82.

DeNavas-Walt, C., B. D. Proctor, and J. C. Smith. 2012. "Income, Poverty, and Health Insurance Coverage in the United States: 2011." Current Population Reports, P60-243. Washington, DC: U.S. Census Bureau.

Dommaraju, P. 2011. "Marriage and Fertility Dynamics in India." *Asia-Pacific Population* 26:21.

Duncan, G. J., J. Brooks-Gunn, W. J. Yeung, and J. Smith. 1998. "How Much Does Childhood Poverty Affect the Life Chances of Children?" *American Sociological Review* 63:406–23.

Ginther, D. K. and M. Zavodny. 2001. "Is the Male Marriage Premium Due to Selection? The Effect of Shotgun Weddings on the Return to Marriage." *Journal of Population Economics* 14:313–28.

Glauber, R. 2008. "Race and Gender in Families and at Work: The Fatherhood Wage Premium." *Gender & Society* 22:8–30.

Gornick, J. C. and M. Jäntti. 2010. "Child Poverty in Upper-Income Countries: Lessons from the Luxembourg Income Study." Pp. 339–68 in *From Child Welfare to Child Well-being: An International Perspective on Knowledge in the Service of Making Policy*, edited by S. B. Kamerman, S. Phipps, and A. Ben-Arieh. New York: Springer.

Gornick, J. C. and M. Jäntti. 2012. "Child Poverty in Cross-National Perspective: Lessons from the Luxembourg Income Study." *Children and Youth Services Review* 34:558–68.

Graefe, D. R. and D. T. Lichter. 2007. "When Unwed Mothers Marry: The Marital and Cohabiting Partners of Midlife Women." *Journal of Family Issues* 28:595–622.

Heimdal, K. R. and S. K. Houseknecht. 2003. "Cohabiting and Married Couples' Income Organization: Approaches in Sweden and the United States." *Journal of Marriage and Family* 65:525–38.

Hersch, J. and L. S. Stratton. 2000. "Household Specialization and the Male Marriage Wage Premium." *Indus. & Lab. Rel. Rev.* 54:78.

Heuveline, P. and M. Weinshenker. 2008. "The International Child Poverty Gap: Does Demography Matter?" *Demography* 45:173–91.

Hodges, M. J. and M. J. Budig. 2010. "Who Gets the Daddy Bonus? Organizational Hegemonic Masculinity and the Impact of Fatherhood on Earnings." *Gender & Society* 24:717–45.

Isen, A. and B. Stevenson. 2011. "Women's Education and Family Behavior: Trends in Marriage, Divorce and Fertility." Pp. 107–42 in *Demography and the Economy* edited by J. B. Shoven. Chicago: University of Chicago Press.

Kalil, A. and R. M. Ryan. 2010. "Mothers' Economic Conditions and Sources of Support in Fragile Families." *The Future of Children* 20:39–61.

Kasearu, K. and D. Kutsar. 2011. "Patterns Behind Unmarried Cohabitation Trends in Europe." *European Societies* 13:307–25.

Kennedy, S. and L. Bumpass. 2008. "Cohabitation and Children's Living Arrangements: New Estimates from the United States." *Demographic Research* 19:1663–92.

Kerr, D., M. Moyser, and R. Beaujot. 2006. "Marriage and Cohabitation: Demographic and Socioeconomic Differences in Quebec and Canada." *Canadian Studies in Population* 33:83–117.

Killewald, A. 2013. "A Reconsideration of the Fatherhood Premium: Marriage, Coresidence, Biology, and Fathers' Wages." *American Sociological Review* 78:96–116.

Lesthaeghe, R. 1995. "The Second Demographic Transition in Western Countries: An Interpretation." Pp. 17–62 in *Gender and Family Change in Industrialized Countries*, edited by K. O. Mason and A.-M. Jensen. Oxford: Clarendon Press.

Lesthaeghe, R. 2010. "The Unfolding Story of the Second Demographic Transition." *Population and Development Review* 36:211–51.

Lesthaeghe, R. and S. Johan. 1988. "Cultural Dynamics and Economic Theories of Fertility Change." *Population and Development Review* 14:1–45.

Lichter, D. T. and D. R. Graefe. 2007. "Men and Marriage Promotion: Who Marries Unwed Mothers?" *Social Service Review* 81:397–421.

Lichter, D. T., D. R. Graefe, and R. B. Brown. 2003. "Is Marriage a Panacea? Union Formation among Economically Disadvantaged Mothers." *Social Problems* 50:60–86.

Lichter, D. T., Z. Qian, and M. L. Crowley. 2005. "Child Poverty among Racial Minorities and Immigrants: Explaining Trends and Differentials." *Social Science Quarterly* 86:1037–59.

Lundberg, S. and E. Rose. 2000. "Parenthood and the Earnings of Married Men and Women." *Labour Economics* 7689–710.

Lyngstad, T. H., T. Noack, and P. A. Tufte. 2011. "Pooling of Economic Resources: A Comparison of Norwegian Married and Cohabiting Couples." *European Sociological Review* 27:624–35.

Manning, W. D. and S. L. Brown. 2006. "Children's Economic Well-Being in Married and Cohabiting Parent Families." *Journal of Marriage and Family* 68:345–62.

McLanahan, S. and C. Percheski. 2008. "Family Structure and the Reproduction of Inequalities." *Annual Review of Sociology* 34:257–76.

McLanahan, S. and G. D. Sandefur. 1994. *Growing up with a Single Parent: What Hurts, What Helps*. Cambridge, MA: Harvard University Press.

Morgan, S. P., G. Zhigang, and S. R. Hayford. 2009. "China's Below-Replacement Fertility: Recent Trends and Future Prospects." *Population and Development Review* 35:605–29.

Misra, J., S. Moller, E. Strader, and E. Wemlinger. 2012. "Family Policies, Employment and Poverty among Partnered and Single Mothers." *Research in Social Stratification and Mobility* 30:113–28.

Osborne, C. and S. McLanahan. 2007. "Partnership Instability and Child Well-being." *Journal of Marriage and Family* 69:1065–83.

Perelli-Harris, B. and T. P. Gerber. 2011. "Nonmarital Childbearing in Russia: Second Demographic Transition or Pattern of Disadvantage?" *Demography* 48:317–42.

Perelli-Harris, B., et al. 2010. "The Educational Gradient of Childbearing within Cohabitation in Europe." *Population and Development Review* 36:775–801.

Perelli-Harris, B., et al. 2012. "Changes in Union Status during the Transition to Parenthood in Eleven European Countries, 1970s to Early 2000s." *Population Studies* 66:167–82.

Polachek, S. W. and J. Xiang. 2009. "The Gender Pay Gap across Countries: A Human Capital Approach." SOEP papers on Multidisciplinary Panel Data Research. Berlin, Germany.

Pollmann-Schult, M. 2011. "Marriage and Earnings: Why Do Married Men Earn More Than Single Men?" *European Sociological Review* 27:147–63.

Rainwater, L. and T. M. Smeeding. 2003. *Poor Kids in a Rich Country: America's Children in Comparative Perspective.* New York: Russell Sage.

Rajan, R. G. 2011. *Fault Lines: How Hidden Fractures Still Threaten the World Economy.* Princeton, NJ: Princeton University Press.

Rector, R. 2010. "Marriage: America's Greatest Weapon against Child Poverty." *Backgrounder No. 2465.* Washington, DC, Heritage Foundation.

Ribar, D. C. 2004. "What Do Social Scientists Know about the Benefits of Marriage? A Review of Quantitative Methodologies." Discussion Paper No. 998, IZA. Bonn, Germany.

Sarkisian, N. and N. Gerstel. 2004. "Kin Support among Blacks and Whites: Race and Family Organization." *American Sociological Review* 69:812–37.

Sigle-Rushton, W. and S. McLanahan. 2002. "For Richer or Poorer? Marriage as an Anti-Poverty Strategy in the United States." *Population. English Edition* 57:509–26.

Sobotka, T. 2008. "The Diverse Faces of the Second Demographic Transition in Europe." *Demographic Research* 19:171–224.

Thomas, A. and I. Sawhill. 2002. "For Richer or for Poorer: Marriage as an Antipoverty Strategy." *Journal of Policy Analysis and Management* 21:587–99.

Thomas, A. and I. V. Sawhill. 2005. "For Love and Money? The Impact of Family Structure on Family Income." *The Future of Children* 15:57–74.

Thomson, E., T. L. Hanson and S. McLanahan. 1994. "Family Structure and Child Well-Being: Economic Resources Vs. Parental Behaviors." *Social Forces* 73:221–42.

Thomson, E. and S. McLanahan. 2012. "Reflections on 'Family Structure and Child Well-Being: Economic Resources Vs. Parental Socialization.'" *Social Forces* 91:45–53.

U.S. Census Bureau. 2012. "Pinc-03. Educational Attainment—People 25 Years Old and Over, by Total Money Earnings in 2011, Work Experience in 2011, Age, Race, Hispanic Origin, and Sex." Retrieved February 28, 2012. (http://www.census.gov/hhes/www/cpstables/032011/perinc/toc.htm).

van de Kaa, D. J. 1987. "Europe's Second Demographic Transition." *Population Bulletin* 42:1–59.

Vespa, J. and M. A. Painter. 2011. "Cohabitation History, Marriage, and Wealth Accumulation." *Demography* 48:993–1004.

Wang, Q. and Q. Zhou. 2010. "China's Divorce and Remarriage Rates: Trends and Regional Disparities." *Journal of Divorce & Remarriage* 5:257–67.

Waite, L. and M. Gallagher. 2000. *The Case for Marriage.* New York: Doubleday.

Weichselbaumer, D. and R. Winter-Ebmer. 2005. "A Meta-Analysis of the International Gender Wage Gap." *Journal of Economic Surveys* 19:479–511.

Wildsmith, E., N. R. Steward-Streng and J. Manlove. 2011. "Childbearing Outside of Marriage: Estimates and Trends in the United States." Childs Trend Research Brief. Washington, DC.

Wilmoth, J. and G. Koso. 2004. "Does Marital History Matter? Marital Status and Wealth Outcomes among Preretirement Adults." *Journal of Marriage and Family* 64:254–68.

Wilson, W. J. 1987. *The Truly Disadvantaged: The Inner City, the Underclass, and Public Policy.* Chicago: University of Chicago Press.

Wilson, W. J. 1996. *When Work Disappears: The World of the New Urban Poor.* New York: Vintage Books.

Wu, L. L. and K. Musick. 2008. "Stability of Marital and Cohabiting Unions Following a First Birth." *Population Research and Policy Review* 27:713–27.

Zagorsky, J. L. 2005. "Marriage and Divorce's Impact on Wealth." *Journal of Sociology* 41:406–24.

....

CHAPTER 19

JOB-FINDING AMONG THE POOR

Do Social Ties Matter?

....

SANDRA SUSAN SMITH

INTRODUCTION

....

IN *Getting Paid*, Mercer Sullivan (1989) charts the work trajectories of three adolescent, male cliques—one black, one Hispanic, and one white—each growing up in different, but contiguous, Brooklyn neighborhoods. According to Sullivan, white youths transitioned to skilled and unskilled blue-collar jobs from light construction and cleaning of local businesses; government-sponsored summer jobs; work as part-time building superintendents; and temporary, off-the-books jobs in local factories and warehouses. Hispanic youths transitioned to manual labor and clerical work; and black youths transitioned to clerical and service sector jobs primarily from government-sponsored youth summer employment, if they were able to find work at all.[1]

Jay MacLeod also describes the divergent paths to adulthood that black and white adolescents from one, low-income neighborhood took. In the third edition of *Ain't No Makin' It* (2011), we learn that despite the "Brothers'" commitment in adolescence to hard work and an ideology of meritocracy, as adults they were surprisingly less successful than their white counterparts, the Hallway Hangers, in finding stable, well-paying jobs, even though the Hallway Hangers' low aspirations and expectations led them to drop out of school, shun hard work, abuse drugs and alcohol, and collectively thumb their noses at the wider society they blamed for their inability to get ahead.

Deirdre Royster's *Race and the Invisible Hand* presents another stark contrast in the career trajectories of working-class black and white youth. These youths had attended the same vocational program in the same high school and had similar aspirations and levels of academic achievement. Yet as they transitioned from high school to employment, it was the young, white men who found well-paid, union jobs doing the work for which they had been trained. Their black counterparts, in contrast, had great difficulty making the transition to similar positions, and so they often settled for low-level service sector work that offered lower wages and less security.

While many factors account for the divergent trajectories of these otherwise similar groups of young men, each author—Sullivan, MacLeod, and Royster—highlights one factor in particular—social networks. In each case, how smoothly the transition occurred was conditioned by the extent and nature of youths' connections to adults who could either hire them or act as intermediaries on their behalf. White youths, who experienced smoother transitions, had such networks; Hispanic and black youths, who entered the labor market in fits and starts, most often did not.

Although debate has recently been rekindled about whether network effects are causal (see Mouw 2003), the weight of the evidence suggests that social ties can make a difference above and beyond other factors of importance.[2] A number of studies indicate that in relative and absolute terms, the poor rely heavily on social networks for job-finding. They both search for work through personal connections at high rates, but many primarily find work this way as well. For instance, drawing from a sample of the poor from two neighborhoods in Santiago, Chile, Espinoza (1999) finds that 72 percent of workers found their jobs through personal contacts. Drawing from the Atlanta Social Survey on Urban Inequality, Green, Tigges, and Brown (1995) report that whereas 74 and 37 percent of the nonpoor searched for work through friends and relatives, respectively, 81 and 49 percent of the poor did. Furthermore, while 43 percent of the nonpoor found work through friends or relatives, 66 percent of the poor did.[3] Drawing from the Multi-City Survey of Urban Inequality, Elliot and Sims (2001) also report high rates of personal contact use. Between 70 and 80 percent of blacks searched for work through kith and kin, and between 39 and 52 percent found work this way. Among Hispanics, 85 percent of job seekers searched for work through personal contacts, and between 68 and 75 percent found work this way (see also Falcon 1995).

Evidence also suggests that without networks, poor job seekers are significantly less likely to find work. In an ethnographic study of the working poor, Katherine Newman (1999) shows that among applicants to Burger Barn, whether black or Latino, those who applied without the assistance of a personal contact were significantly less likely to be hired. In another study, Newman and Lennon (1995) show that whereas just 11 percent of recent nonreferral applicants were hired at Burger Barn, 33 percent of recent referrals were. According to these authors:

> Networks of friends and family members who already have jobs play an important role in making it possible to find low wage jobs. Put slightly differently, people who have been isolated from job networks are more likely to be rejected when they search for work, even when their human capital is equivalent. It has long been

recognized that "contacts" of this kind are crucial in getting jobs in higher skilled and better paying jobs. This new research suggests that contacts are important even in the minimum wage, low skilled sector of the economy. Indeed, these findings suggest that whenever labor markets are slack, possession of a functioning social network will advantage job seekers, while the absence of this resource will handicap applicants. (1995:8)

Their findings are consistent with those reported by others who study nonpoor workers—referrals are more likely than nonreferrals to be hired (Petersen, Saporta, and Seidel 2000; Coverdill 1998; Fernandez and Weinberg 1997; but see Fernandez and Fernandez-Mateo 2006).

There is mixed evidence, however, that using personal contacts improves poor job seekers' income (Korenman and Turner 1996). For instance, drawing from the Boston Survey, Falcon (1995) finds that those who found work through personal contacts earned significantly less than nonreferrals, net of important controls. Drawing from the Atlanta Social Survey, Green, Tigges, and Browne (1995) show that while whites' incomes benefit from help from an inside referrer, and while both whites and blacks benefit by having a greater number of employed contacts, blacks' incomes are negatively associated with help finding work from neighborhood ties or relatives. Elliot and Sims (2001) also find that neighborhood ties are associated with lower weekly earnings. These findings suggest that among the poor, social networks enable survival in part by connecting others to jobs. They do little to facilitate mobility, however, because they lack access to information and influence around "good" jobs. If this is the case, what kinds of ties help the poor get ahead?

WHAT KINDS OF TIES HELP THE POOR GET AHEAD?

The literature contrasts contacts that provide social support and thus enable survival and those that provide social leverage and thus enable mobility. Briggs, for instance, defines social support as a form of social capital "that helps one 'get by' or cope" (1998:178). These forms of support facilitate survival, reducing the likelihood of going without food, shelter, clothing and emotional support (Dominguez 2011; Dominguez and Watkins 2003; Espinoza 1999; Lee and Aytac 1998; Hogan, Eggebeen, and Clogg 1993; Eggebeen 1992; Parish, Hao, and Hogan 1991; Hofferth 1984; Stack 1974). They do not, however, provide individuals with the opportunity to achieve mobility. Mobility, Briggs contends, is the realm of social leverage (Boissevain 1974), a form of social capital that enables individuals "'to get ahead' or change one's opportunity set through access to job information, say, or a recommendation for a scholarship or loan" (1998:178). Research indicates that although social support among the poor is both insufficient

(Benin and Keith 1995; Hogan et al. 1993; Jayakody et al. 1993) and on the decline in some contexts (see Brewster and Padavic 2002 for an analysis of the decline in social support with work requirements associated with welfare in the United States), not surprisingly, the poor are far more likely to gain social support than social leverage from friends, relatives, and acquaintances (Dominguez 2003; Espinoza 1999; Stack 1974). But poor isolates lack both (Wacquant and Wilson 1989).

Interestingly, the literature discusses social support and social leverage in such a way that suggests that the poor either have contacts that provide social support or they have contacts that provide social leverage (Briggs 1998). Whereas social support networks are networks of affection and survival, social leverage networks allow for upward mobility. Two important interventions correct this misrepresentation. First, Dominguez and Watkins (2003) note that among the poor, contacts that provide social support might also provide the type of assistance that enables mobility. They state, "We find that social capital that improves opportunities for upward mobility can be obtained from relationships that provide advice, contacts, and encouragement to get ahead" (2003:111). Contacts who provide social support can also provide social leverage. Those who provide social support might also seek to limit kith and kin's mobility, for fear that they might lose critical social resources as a result, an issue first raised in Stack's *All Our Kin*.

Dominguez and Watkins (2003) also note that although some contacts are not well positioned to provide social leverage, the type of support they can provide allows friends and relatives to take advantage of emerging opportunities for mobility. Through the provision of free or cheap childcare, for example, relatives or friends make it possible for single mothers to take advantage of job opportunities that might otherwise be out of reach (Harris 1993; Stoloff et al. 1999), although there is evidence that these types of supports are on the decline (Brewster and Padavic 2002). Contacts might not be able to provide job information or shape the hiring process in favor of their job-seeking tie, but they might be able to provide transportation on a regular basis, facilitating job seekers' efforts to get to work on time. Thus, although it is typical to study networks of social support separately from networks providing social leverage, these divisions are not always appropriate, as research by Dominguez and Watkins (2003) indicates. Networks providing social support and social leverage can be one and the same, and networks providing social support often provide the foundation upon which individuals can take advantage of social leverage.

Another important distinction made in the literature is that between networks that provide opportunities for lateral and vertical mobility; this distinction maps on to notions of social support (survival) and social leverage (mobility). In *No Shame in My Game*, a study of Harlem's young, working poor, Katherine Newman contends that most network members *could* offer opportunities for lateral mobility—the movement from one job to another of similar status, typically low-wage, dead-end jobs. Few networks of Harlem's working poor, however, could offer opportunities for vertical mobility—jobs that pay more and that offer security, benefits, and a chance for a comfortable retirement. Whereas opportunities for lateral mobility can originate from networks providing social support, opportunities for vertical mobility emerge from networks offering social leverage. Thus, even when the poor have networks of relations capable of providing job opportunities, formal and informal, as many do (Dohan 2003; Menjivar 2000; Espinoza 1999; MacLeod 2011), they often lack access to networks that might provide information or possibly recommend hires for good jobs (Gowan 2010; Espinoza 1999; Newman 1999; for a discussion of what a "good" job is, see also Kalleberg, Reskin, and Hudson 2000; and Jencks, Perman, and Rainwater 1988).

The Role of Weak Ties

The type of job contact that has received the most research attention as a beneficial source of job information and influence has been the "weak" tie. Very simply, weak ties are those that are socially, emotionally, and often physically distant (Marsden and Campbell 1984). They are acquaintances, friends of friends, people with whom our social lives infrequently overlap. Most importantly, they are bridges to new opportunities and resources, because they provide information that individuals could not obtain through strong ties, such as relatives and close friends. Following homophily/ heterophily principles, whereas strong ties tend to link individuals with similar attributes (homophily), weak ties are more likely to function as bridges between dissimilar actors (heterophily), people and groups offering new and different information, thereby increasing opportunities for mobility (Granovetter 1995, 1981).

Granovetter (1981) contends that individuals of low socioeconomic status are less likely to benefit from weak ties because their weak ties are more likely to be acquaintances of friends and family members occupying similar positions in the social structure and not bridges to new opportunities and resources for labor market mobility and advancement. Other researchers predict the opposite, however. Lin, Ensel, and Vaughn (1981) and Lin and Dumin (1986) contend that an interaction exists between an individuals' social structural position and returns to the use of weak ties. Relative to high-status job seekers, low-status jobs seekers will garner greater benefits from the use of weak ties over strong. They reason that high-status individuals are likely to experience a "ceiling effect" that limits the structural advantage that weak ties theoretically provide. As individuals approach this ceiling, their weak ties provide no additional benefits over strong ties because their weak ties are unlikely to provide bridges to those more highly placed in the social structure to facilitate further advancement. Indeed, in this context, they contend that strong ties may actually be more beneficial. They argue, however, that the ceiling effect does not exist for low-status job seekers. For these individuals, the use of weak ties over strong may provide substantial benefits because weak ties are more likely than strong ties to provide links to positions that are structurally different and in all likelihood higher, because for those of low status, most other positions are higher.

Some researchers have also argued that members of minority groups are disadvantaged in the labor market because they lack weak, wide-ranging ties (Kasinitz and Rosenberg 1996; Campbell 1988; Mier and Giloth 1985). For example, to explain the almost total exclusion of black residents from 3,600 private sector, blue-collar jobs in their community, the Red Hook section of Brooklyn, Philip Kasinitz and Jan Rosenberg (1996) contend that black job seekers lack connections to and references from weak ties—non-blacks and/or noncommunity residents—who might serve as credible gatekeepers on their behalf. Similarly, Robert Mier and Robert Giloth (1985) explain underrepresentation of Latinos in manufacturing jobs in the Pilsen neighborhood of Chicago, a predominantly Latino community. They find that because employers' primary method of recruitment was through employee referrals, and employees predominantly of Eastern European ancestry tended to refer like-others, Latino residents were consequently shut out of the hiring process. The authors suggest that only through the mobilization of weak ties will Pilsen Latinos be able to access the opportunities in their community as their strong ties are not linked to jobs in Pilsen. Studies such as these indicate that members of minority groups may indeed benefit from the use of weak over strong ties to advance their labor market prospects. Thus, it appears that the networks of Latinos and blacks generally lack the types of ties essential for providing access to opportunities for labor market advancement.

To date, few studies have systematically examined this weak tie contingency. To the extent that studies have, they mostly provide evidence negating any contingency (Marsden and Hurlbert 1988). Interestingly, even Lin and colleagues (1986, 1981b, 1981a) find no evidence that low-status job seekers benefit in ways that high-status job seekers do not; and Elliot (1999) has found that, although rarely mobilized, weak ties provide no benefit over strong ties or over more formal matching methods among less-educated urban workers. My own examination of this question revealed that the benefits of social resources, like weak versus strong ties, appear largely contingent on the social structural location of job seekers mobilizing them, less on any benefits inherent in different types of job contacts (Smith 2000).

Others provide evidence highlighting the importance of *strong* ties among the poor. A wonderful empirical example is Edwina Uehara's (1990) examination of the effect of network structures on the ability and willingness of poor black women who have recently lost their jobs to mobilize their ties for instrumental aid, with network structures characterized by social closure that facilitate this type of assistance. She discovered that women embedded in high-density, high-intensity networks were more likely to engage in generalized exchanges than women embedded in networks low in both because the former were better able to control each other's behavior through tracking, monitoring, and sanctioning, which created an environment of trustworthiness that promoted extensive exchanges. In *Keeping It in the Family*, Margaret Grieco (1987) presents a solid case for the central role that strong ties play in the job-finding process. In *Fragmented Ties*, Cecilia Menjivar's Salvadoran respondents reported that they would not help someone with job-finding assistance if they did not know them well. Paul's (2012) study of Filipino migrants to Hong Kong and Singapore revealed the same preference for helping those with whom they had strong versus weak ties. And in prior work, I found that social capital activation among the black poor was associated with strong ties between job seekers and jobholders. The use of weak ties was infrequently in evidence (Smith 2008). Thus, while a number of researchers provide anecdotal evidence of the effect that weak ties have on job-finding and mobility among the poor (Dominguez 2011; Newman 1999; Briggs 1998), empirical evidence based on quantitative and qualitative data analysis fails to show this. So, if weak ties don't make much of a difference, what types of ties do?

Network Structure and Composition

In her discussion of ties that enable vertical mobility, Newman (1999) points to the role that extended family members used to play in the lives of the working poor. According to Newman (1999), among the black, working poor, many older relatives—aunts, uncles, and grandparents, for instance—currently hold, or once held, jobs in the public sector. More than one generation ago, these jobs provided opportunities for upward mobility for many blacks, leading to the expansion of the black middle class. However, as the public sector has shrunk, many fewer opportunities exist about which to inform those of the younger generation, and so older kin are unable to provide the type of information and influence that once brought a generation of blacks into the lower middle class (see also Anderson 1999).

Newman's argument is consistent with Nan Lin's theory of social resources—resources accessible through one's direct and indirect ties (1999:468). Lin (1999) posits that social resources exert an effect on the outcome of an instrumental action (social resources proposition); that social resources, in turn, are affected by the original position of ego (strength of positions proposition); and that social resources are also affected by the use of weaker rather than stronger ties (strength of ties proposition) (1999:470). Again, while evidence is mixed about the utility of weak ties, studies examining the effect of contact status are revelatory (more recently, see Lin, Lee, and Ao, 2013). They indicate that greater social resources lead to better jobs. Specifically, having contacts of higher SES status leads to jobs with higher occupational prestige and better income. These findings have been reported as well in studies conducted in the United States (Marsden and Hurlbert 1988; Lin, Ensel, and Vaughn 1981; Ensel 1979); the Netherlands (Moerbeek, Utle, and Flap 1996; Volker and Flap 1996; DeGraaf and Flap 1988); East and West Germany (Wegener 1991); Taiwan (Hsung, Sun, and She 1986; Hsung and Hwang 1992); and China (Bian 1997).

For members of disadvantaged groups, we can also attribute poorer employment outcomes to network structure and composition. To date, an extensive literature does not exist on racial and ethnic differences in the structure and composition of personal networks. But we do know that relative to Latinos and blacks, whites tend to have a larger number of personal contacts, more kin and nonkin, and greater sex diversity, meaning a greater proportion of their ties are of the opposite sex (Marsden 1987). Relative to whites, blacks report stronger ties with neighbors. Blacks have more neighbors, contact them more frequently, and rely on them more heavily for social support (Lee, Campbell, and Miller 1991). Finally, comparing blacks, whites, Mexicans, and Puerto Ricans residing in poor neighborhoods, a higher proportion of blacks' and whites' networks are composed of educated ties, and a higher proportion of whites' and Mexicans' networks are composed of employed ties (Smith 1997).

A more extensive literature exists that compares the personal networks of different classes of urban blacks (Hurlbert, Beggs, and Haines 1998; Tigges, Browne, and Green 1998; Smith 1995; Fernandez and Harris 1992; Wacquant and Wilson 1989; Oliver 1988). These studies have generally found that, relative to the network structure and composition of nonpoor and working poor blacks, those of the nonworking poor place them at greater risk of social isolation and militate against finding employment, especially good jobs. The most disadvantaged urban blacks are less likely than those in the "mainstream" to have a best friend, partner, spouse, or discussion partner (Tigges et al. 1998; Wacquant and Wilson 1980), and their networks tend to be composed of strong, redundant, dense, and multistranded ties that are kin based and spatially concentrated in their neighborhoods (Smith 1995; Fernandez and Harris 1992; Oliver 1988). Moreover, nonworking poor blacks or those residing in high- or extreme-poverty neighborhoods are less likely to have educated or employed social ties (Tigges et al. 1998; Smith 1995; Wacquant and Wilson 1989).

Racial and ethnic differences in the structure and composition of personal networks have important implications for persisting labor market inequalities. A substantial minority of blacks and Latinos live in racially and economically segregated neighborhoods in which a significant proportion of residents have unstable connections to the labor market. Not only would it be difficult for job seekers from such communities to access "new" information about jobs generally, it would also be highly improbable that their contacts would share information about "good" jobs in particular. Indeed, while previous research has found that disadvantaged white youths garner significantly higher wages when connected to jobs by personal contacts (Korenman and Turner 1996), personal contact use among disadvantaged black and Latino youths offers no significant wage advantage (Korenman and Turner 1996; Falcon 1995; Green, Tigges, and Browne 1995). Moreover, blacks who are embedded in segregated networks are more likely to find poorer paying, racially segregated jobs compared to the jobs of blacks embedded in racially mixed networks (Braddock and McPartland 1987).

In terms of gender, previous research has shown that while women and men do not differ in terms of the size of their personal contacts (Moore 1990; Marsden 1987; Fischer 1982), other aspects of the structure and composition of their networks do vary. Relative to men's networks, women's are denser and lack occupational range. Women's networks are composed of a higher proportion of kin (Moore 1990; Marsden 1987; Wellman 1985; Fischer and Oliker 1983; Fischer 1982; Bott 1971), more types of kin, and a larger number of neighbors (Moore 1990). Men's networks are composed of significantly more friends, advisors, and coworkers, even among employed women and men. In addition, their friendship networks tend to be more diverse than those of women (Moore 1990). Analogously, although men and women have virtually the same number of organizational affiliations, the size and types of organizations to which they belong differ substantively. Women tend to belong to smaller organizations devoted to domestic or community affairs while men tend to belong to larger, economically oriented organizations (McPherson and Smith-Lovin 1982).

What consequences arise from gender differences in network structure and composition? Research suggests that women garner lower wage returns than men because they obtain information about jobs from other women (Hanson and Pratt 1991), have networks that are less likely to contain high-status or influential individuals (Brass 1985), and tend to find jobs through nonsearch methods (Campbell and Rosenfeld 1985). Thus, they are routed to female-dominated and sex-segregated occupations (Stoloff, Glanville, and Bienenstock 1999; Drentea 1998; Hanson and Pratt 1991), usually resulting in lower wages and fewer advancement opportunities (Baron and Bielby 1984; Bielby and Baron 1984, 1986). Moreover, women's networks have less occupational range than men's although not significantly less status diversity (Stoloff, Glanville, and Bienenstock 1999; Campbell 1988). Li, Savage, and Warde (2008), who study social mobility and social capital in the British context, also report that women and ethnic minorities are less likely to have diverse networks and networks of high-status contacts. In sum, women appear less likely than men to be embedded in networks that can provide opportunities for status, income, and occupational advancement. Like members of minority groups, they lack network range and diversity and so have difficulty accessing and mobilizing well-placed and influential contacts hypothesized to affect employment outcomes positively.

Among immigrants, help by co-ethnics is assumed to be helpful in terms of job information and influence (Amuedo-Dorantes and Mundra 2008; Aguilera 2002, 2003; 2005; Aguilera and Massey 2003; Sanders et al. 2002; Sanders and Nee 1996). More recent research, however, has tested the idea that bridging ties matter more for upward mobility and integration by examining the effect of having native contacts on immigrants' employment outcomes (Kanas and van Tubergen 2009; Putnam 2000; Hagan 1998). For instance, drawing from qualitative interviews with Albanian immigrants in Greece, Iosifides and colleagues (2007) examine the effect that social capital in its various forms has on the social, economic, and institutional incorporation of Albanians in Greece. They find that although Albanians' links to the native population were few and relatively weak, in the rare instances where these links were stronger, Albanian immigrants reported that greater social integration into Greek society was facilitated.

Others also find that ties to natives matter. Drawing from a large-scale survey data set, Kanas and van Tubergen (2009) has shown that among immigrants in Netherlands—specifically Turkish, Moroccan, Surinamese, and Antillean immigrants—associating with Dutch natives during free time and through organizational affiliations increased immigrants' odds of employment and was associated with higher occupational status. Similarly, drawing from the 2002 wave of the SPVA, Lancee (2010) examined the effect of bridging and bonding social capital on the economic outcomes of immigrants to the Netherlands from Turkey, Morocco, the Antilles, and Suriname. He found that bridging social networks—those that linked immigrants to the native population—were positively associated with both employment and income—bonding social capital was not. Using the Fourth National Survey of Ethnic Minorities, Kahanec and Mendola (2008) investigated how tie strength and ethnic networks affected six immigrant groups' economic outcomes—Caribbeans, Indians, African Asians, Pakistanis, Bangladeshis, and Chinese. They found that while contact with family members back home increased the likelihood of self-employment, formal membership in a club or organization increased the likelihood of paid employment. Furthermore, while speaking to non-English friends was associated with a higher likelihood of self-employment, having a mixed network member or a nonethnic network member was associated with paid employment. And Kanas, van Tubergen, and Van der Lippe (2011) examined how having social contacts with natives affected immigrants' chances of employment in the German context. Using the German Socio-economic Panel, they have shown that while strong ties with family, friends, and neighbors and active volunteering did not affect employment status, contact with native Germans did. Thus, results from a meta-analysis indicate that having access to diverse, wide-ranging, bridging ties, especially those of higher social and economic status, significantly improves chances that the poor and marginalized might achieve mobility.

WHERE ARE LEVERAGEABLE TIES FORGED?

How do people make leveraging ties, and how might this process of tie formation inform our understanding of network inequality? These are the simple yet centrally important questions that motivate Mario Small's *Unanticipated Gains: Origins of Network Inequality in Everyday Life*, and the answers to these questions are the basis for the organizational embeddedness perspective that Small puts forward as a necessary corrective to conventional theories of network inequality that focus solely on individual actors' network structure and composition and their purposeful action. Specifically, Small contends that the quality and quantity of connections that individuals make, and the resulting social capital that they have access to, are in large part a function of the organizations in which they are embedded and routinely participate. It is in the organizational context and as a result of organizational processes that inequalities in personal networks emerge and are reproduced, despite individuals' purposive action. Organizations, then, are key to understanding social inequalities.

Small makes three major points. First, organizations matter. This contention would surprise few, since for decades urban poverty scholars have theorized the importance of neighborhood organizations and institutions (Saegaret et al. 2001; Wilson 1987). But Small *shows* this. Drawing from the Fragile Families Study, Small shows that, all things considered, poor and nonpoor mothers who enrolled their children in childcare centers had more friends than mothers whose children were not enrolled. Moreover, because of center membership and the ties formed in this context, to varying degrees, poor and nonpoor mothers experienced greater material and psychological well-being than mothers without center connections.

Second, organizations matter because of how their formal and informal practices and procedures bring people together. Drawing from the Childcare Centers and Families Survey and in-depth interviews with center parents, Small finds that to the extent that childcare centers institutionalize rules and procedures that encourage and/or mandate attendance, interaction, and collaboration among parents, they create opportunities and inducements for individuals similar in many ways to get to know one another and rely on each other for instrumental action and emotional support. Small discovered that many centers bring parents together to help chaperone children during field trips to museums, zoos, parks, and the like; help organize fundraising events; undertake spring cleaning; and, in some cases, assist with hiring decisions. When they do, ties between parents often form. While some do not develop beyond acquaintanceships, many often evolve into close friendships. In centers that focus little of their efforts on activities that bring parents together, parents have many fewer opportunities to meet, chat, and collaborate, and so they are also less likely to make friends.

Importantly, Small also informs us, parents do not only benefit from the friendships they make in the context of centers. They are also advantaged by the resources they have access to as a result of the interorganizational relationships their childcare centers develop on their behalf. Through their relationships with resource-rich entities, centers broker resources—information (nutrition, safety, domestic violence, childcare, housing, and education), services (such as legal aid, health care, housing support, employment training), and material goods (such as health insurance, meals, tickets to cultural and entertainment events, employment, scholarships). Mothers gained access to these resources through center-organized collaborative meetings, information sessions, workshops, and referrals to other organizations. Thus, organizational embeddedness not only shapes individuals' personal networks, but it also shapes their access to valuable resources that affect individuals' quality of life and life chances.

Third, Small contends that organizations are made to matter often by mandates from the state and/or supraorganizational bodies of authority. Drawing from center case study data, Small explains that not all childcare centers provide opportunities and inducements for parents to participate in center activities, nor do they all broker valuable resources. Some centers, notably for-profits, do not have to. Parents at for-profit establishments could afford to have outsourced what parents in other centers were asked to volunteer to do in an effort to save money (e.g., chaperoning children on field trips). Moreover, parents at for-profit centers had the requisite social, cultural, and financial capital that made moot questions or concerns about access to information about childcare providers, quality education, health care, culture, and the like. For government and private nonprofits, however, getting parents to participate and brokering ties with other organizations were essential—and often mandated. Pressures to involve parents and form interorganizational ties derived from the authority of the state and of the powerful nonprofit sector. With government retrenchment, federal support for social services has declined. To compensate, these entities mandate that the childcare centers under their charge facilitate more parental involvement in day-to-day operations. They also mandate that centers make connections with resource-rich organizations that might provide parents access to the information, services, and material goods they need to survive and in some cases thrive. Thus, it was among those centers with a clear social service mandate that mothers were recruited to assist through parenting associations and that parents gained access to resources through other organizations. Here, Small puts forward a clear and convincing argument that the roots of network inequality are to be found in the state and other powerful institutions, which shape the extent and nature of interactions the exist within institutional contexts. Again, while Small is not the first to contend that organizations matter for the development of ties of social support and leverage, he is one of the first to show how and why this is so. Needed now are cross-national comparative studies to advance our understanding of the ways that different cultural and political economic contexts shape social capital creation and development through their influence on organizations.

WHAT DO LEVERAGING TIES DO? WHY ARE THEY EFFECTIVE?

Reports of the incidence of network search for finding jobs vary considerably, a function of differences in the populations surveyed and the types of questions posed to respondents (Granovetter 1995). Despite the range of rates researchers report, it is clear that network search is pervasive (see, for instance, Falcon and Melendez 2001; Green, Tigges, and Diaz 1999; Granovetter 1995; Marsden and Campbell 1990; Holzer 1987a, 1987b; Corcoran, Datcher, and Duncan 1980a, 1980b). Among some populations, like the poor, it exceeds 80 percent (Green et al. 1999; Holzer 1987a, 1987b). There are three reasons why this is so. First, compared to other methods of job searching, networking through one's friends, family members, and acquaintances is relatively costless; it generally takes little effort or time to learn about job opportunities from those with whom we already have relations because we are close to them and/or we see them with some regularity.

That network search increases the odds of getting a job, and does so relatively quickly, also helps explain its ubiquity as a search strategy (Petersen et al. 2000; Blau and Robins 1990; Holzer 1987a, 1987b; Wielgosz and Carpenter 1987). Personal intermediaries are not only in a position to inform jobseekers about whether employers are hiring (Fernandez et al. 2000; Fernandez and Weinberg 1997; Granovetter 1995), they also identify job seekers who are well-suited for positions, while screening out unsuitable jobseekers; they inform job seekers about the least competitive times to apply; they instruct job seekers on how to complete applications or write appropriate résumés; they provide tips on successful interviewing techniques; and they personally vouch for the applicants they refer (Smith 2007; Neckerman and Fernandez 2003; Fernandez et al. 2000; Fernandez and Weinberg 1997; Wanous 1980). Not surprisingly, then, job seekers who find out about job opportunities through personal intermediaries are more likely to get an interview and to get hired, and they spend less time searching than those who employ other search strategies (Petersen et al. 2000; Coverdill 1998; Newman and Lennon 1995; Fernandez and Weinberg 1997; Blau and Robins 1990; Holzer 1987a, 1987b; Wielgosz and Carpenter 1987; but see Fernandez and Fernandez-Mateo 2006).

Finally, finding work through personal intermediaries also increases the likelihood of *keeping* the job. This, too, might explain its ubiquity. Once hired, referrals receive more on-the-job training from personal contacts (Bishop and Abraham 1993; Bailey and Waldinger 1991; Grieco 1987), which helps them learn tasks faster. They are also more likely to make innovative suggestions and to stay late to complete work (Bishop and Abraham 1993). For these reasons, employers are more likely to perceive referrals as having better interaction and motivation skills (Bishop and Abraham 1993). The end result is that referrals have longer job tenures than nonreferrals; they are less likely to quit or be fired (Neckerman and Fernandez 2003; Fernandez and Weinberg 1997; but see Fernandez, Castillo, and Moore 2000). In summary, searching through friends and relatives—or activating one's personal social capital—is one of the most effective ways of finding work *and keeping it*, for the nonpoor and poor alike.

What Conditions Facilitate Social Capital Activation?

Most research on the leveraging ties of the poor focus on the poor's access to such ties. What has been taken for granted is that if the poor have access to ties that can make a difference, those ties can and will be mobilized for instrumental purposes (Lin 1999; Granovetter 1995). Increasingly, however, scholars are calling into question this assumption (Paul 2012; Smith 2010, 2007, 2005; Menjivar 2000; Newman 1999). Cecilia Menjivar (2000), for instance, finds distrust and noncooperation among the Salvadoran immigrants she studied. Although the majority of her respondents found out about their jobs through friends, relatives, or acquaintances, the jobholders among them were often hesitant to provide job recommendations. Stack's (1974) classic ethnographic study of the coping strategies that families in one poor black community employed to survive persistent poverty and racism showed that residents developed extensive networks of relationships with kin and nonkin alike and that these relationships were built on and characterized by ongoing obligations of typically generalized exchange. Within these networks, residents regularly gave and received goods, services, and resources from family members and friends. They also proactively networked to increase the number of their exchange partners in hopes of building networks large and stable enough to receive a constant flow of resources that would sustain them through good times and bad. But the middle class among them often refused to take part in these obligations of exchange, fearing that doing so might reverse the gains they had made in economic and social status.

My research on the process of finding work represents one of the only systematic studies of jobholders' decision-making processes, and from this we might glean important insights (Smith 2007, 2005). Through in-depth interviews with low-income, young black men and women, I found that jobholders overwhelmingly treated requests for job-seeking help with great skepticism and distrust. Because most perceived the U.S. stratification system to be open (see Young 2004; Hochschild 1995), much like cultural deficiency theorists and conservative commentators (McWhorter 2005, 2000; Patterson 1998; Thernstrom and Thernstrom 1998; Mead 1986), they largely understood black joblessness as a function of defeatism and resistance, individual and cultural. It is through this lens that they most often made sense of job-seeking relations' unemployment and job-seeking behaviors—job seekers they knew were too unmotivated to accept assistance, required great expenditures of time and emotional energy, or would act too irresponsibly on the job—and these interpretations shaped decision-making about whether to help and what form help should take. As a result, even when they could help, many were loath to do so. Feelings of distrust and a corresponding reluctance to assist were most intense among jobholding residents of neighborhoods of concentrated disadvantage—neighborhoods marked by high to extreme rates of poverty and other "negative" social indicators, including welfare dependence, persistent joblessness, high rates of incarceration, and female-headship.

To explain this finding, I drew from social disorganization theory, which advises that social capital mobilization is less likely to occur among residents of communities characterized by concentrated disadvantage. This is because concentrated disadvantage also breeds pervasive distrust (Sampson 2012; Aguilar 1984; Suttles 1968; Carstairs 1967; Foster 1967; Liebow 1967; Banfield 1958). Chronic economic hardship and a history of exploitation diminish both individual (Pearlin et al. 1981) and collective efficacy (Morenoff, Sampson, and Raudenbush 2001; Sampson, Morenoff, and Earls 1999), leading to high rates of crime, substance abuse, violence, and neglect. The vulnerability and pervasive distrust that residents experience in this context fuel individualistic approaches to getting things done, as illustrated in more recent accounts, such as Elijah Anderson's *Code of the Street* (1999) and Furstenberg et al.'s *Managing to Make It* (1999). Thus, relative to poor residents of comparatively affluent communities, I theorized, the likelihood of mobilizing one's network of social relations for job-finding in neighborhoods characterized by concentrated disadvantage is low. And indeed, new evidence supports this argument. Using the General Social Survey, Hamm and McDonald (2015) investigated the likelihood that respondents recently provided job-finding help to others. Net of a number of important controls, black residents of neighborhoods of concentrated poverty were significantly less likely to help than members of other ethnoracial groups and community contexts.

Others have also found a reluctance to assist among the poor. In *No Shame in My Game*, for instance, Katherine Newman (1999) notes that among the low-wage workers she studied, personal contacts were vital to the job-matching process, but assistance was not always forthcoming. Fearing that their referrals would prove unreliable and would compromise their reputations with employers, a few of her subjects denied help to their job-seeking ties. And, using a unique data set of contacts, Trimble (2013) finds that contacts who think job seekers are "good" workers help more than contacts who think job seekers are "poor" workers. Access, therefore, did not guarantee mobilization (also see Royster 2003 for a brief discussion of reluctance among working-class black, job contacts).

Some scholars have also begun to examine the conditions that facilitate social capital activation outside the United States, and this research, too, highlights contacts' reluctance to help (Marin 2012; Paul 2012; Trimble 2013). For instance, drawing from 95 interviews with Filipino, migrant, domestic workers in Hong Kong and Singapore, Paul (2012) finds that when these migrant workers were pressed to help family members and close friends back home with migration assistance, they often declined to do so. Migrants were less likely to help if they had had negative helping experiences in the past; if they were uncertain about prospective migrants' commitment to working overseas; if the prospective migrant was not a close family member; if they had poor relations with potential employers; and if they were not well-connected with locals in the host country who could provide information and influence. Thus, although we often take for granted that immigrants rely heavily on social networks during the migratory process, what recent evidence suggests is that, even among immigrants, help cannot be assumed (see also Menjivar 2000).

Conclusion

Do social ties matter to the poor? It is clear from the literature that they do. Social networks enable the poor to survive, and, under particular circumstances, they also facilitate mobility. The vast majority of the poor search for work through personal contacts, and most of these job-seekers find work this way as well. Although the poor's job contacts tend to provide opportunities for lateral mobility, with wages no better and often worse than they might have gotten otherwise, such opportunities do stave off spells of unemployment and joblessness, and for this reason alone have great value to the poor.

To the extent that the poor have access to ties that provide opportunities for mobility, they are likely embedded in networks of diverse, wide-ranging ties of higher social and economic status. Although weak ties have often been the focus of study and posited to be the panacea to the poor's social capital deficits, the empirical evidence does not support this view. Weak ties are rarely used, and when they are deployed, they tend *not* to yield better outcomes. That the poor are not advantaged by weak ties would not surprise Granovetter, who has theorized that among the poor, weak ties are not likely to be bridges to new information and influential contacts. But for those, like Lin, who have argued otherwise, such findings call for a reconsideration of the role of weak ties for mobility.

The poor, however, do appear to benefit from embeddedness in networks characterized by strong, overlapping ties, both for survival and for mobility. When networks are unable to act in this capacity, it is often because they lack the essential resources for instrumental action. But as more recent research suggests, their networks might also be unwilling to act as a source of social capital. In other words, even where there is access, social capital mobilization is not guaranteed. Instead, it seems contingent on a number of factors, most notably the perceived risks and costs, especially to reputation, that those in a position to help consider when making decisions about whether to help and what types of help to provide. This particular area of research is relatively new, but it has infused debates with new life by challenging unquestioned assumptions and providing new insights, especially about the logics of assistance that the poor (and nonpoor) deploy.

Despite some exciting new developments, much more research is needed that takes into consideration the role that social networks play in shaping the life chances of the poor across national contexts. Increasingly, researchers report findings from studies undertaken outside the United States, most notably in China, Russia, and Northern Europe. This is an encouraging sign, especially because these studies have yielded important insights. But few of these studies focus on the poor, and outside of China, almost none of this research is being conducted in the developing world. Such efforts should be encouraged as most of the world's population live in such contexts, and opportunities for extensions abound.

NOTES

1. Direct all correspondence to Sandra Susan Smith at the e-mail address listed above. sandra_smith@berkeley.edu

2. In two widely cited papers, Ted Mouw (2006; 2003) proposes that the effects of social capital are not causal but instead spurious. Mouw argues that because individuals become friends with others in nonrandom ways—like attracts like—the social capital effects found in previous research are likely instead selection effects resulting from social homophily. Mouw's argument, however, focuses solely on supply-side evidence. Although he acknowledges that demand-side studies have provided strong evidence that referrals are significantly more likely than nonreferrals to make it through every stage of the hiring process (Yakubovich and Lup 2006; Fernandez and Sosa 2005; Fernandez et al. 2000; Petersen et al. 2000; Fernandez and Weinberg 1997), he intimates that because these findings are based on case studies of individual firms, they do not carry as much weight as those reported from large-scale surveys of randomly selected respondents, where the evidence is less clear (2003). In response to Mouw's powerful critique, researchers have primarily responded by altering their methodological approaches, typically examining within-individual variation in hiring outcomes (Obukhova 2012; Obukhova and Lan 2012; Fernandez and Galperin 2014; Yakubovich 2005; but see Lin et al. (2012) and McDonald (2012), who adopted different approaches

to address Mouw's concern). These supply-side studies have also produced strong evidence that network effects are causal. For instance, Yakubovich (2005) examined within-actor differences in the effect of weak versus strong ties on the odds of getting hired. His was the first study to provide a direct test of the strength-of-weak-ties proposition, showing that job seekers were more likely to find work through their weak ties than their strong ties. Obukhova and Lan's (2012) study of the school-to-work transitions of 291 university graduates revealed that "for those who use their social networks to search, applications submitted to job opportunities identified through their networks are more likely to result in an interview, an offer, and an acceptance than applications submitted to opportunities identified through formal methods and even through university intermediaries" (2012:13). And Fernandez and Galperin's (2012) examination of repeat applicants at one large, retail bank reveals that when applicants applied as referrals, they were substantially more likely to get interviews and job offers than when they had applied as nonreferrals. Having a personal contact made a huge difference. Although the jury is still out, Mouw's critiques have inspired a host of studies designed to address the methodological flaws associated with prior work, and these more recent studies are providing compelling evidence that networks do, indeed, have a causal effect on employment outcomes, especially getting jobs, above and beyond other important factors.

3. A significantly higher percentage of the poor also searched for work through state employment agencies and private employment services.

REFERENCES

Aguilar, John L. 1984. "Trust and Exchange: Expressive and Instrumental Dimensions of Reciprocity in a Peasant Community." *Ethos* 12(1):3–29.

Aguilera, Michael B. 2002. "The Impact of Social Capital on Labor Force Participation: Evidence from the 2000 Social Capital Benchmark Survey." *Social Science Quarterly* 83(3):853–74.

Aguilera, Michael B. 2003. "The Impact of the Worker: How Social Capital and Human Capital Influence the Job Tenure of Formerly Undocumented Mexican Immigrants." *Sociological Inquiry* 73(1):52–83.

Aguilera, Michael B. 2005. "The Impact of Social Capital on the Earnings of Puerto Rican Migrants." *Sociological Quarterly* 46(4):569–92.

Aguilera, Michael B. and Douglas S. Massey. 2003. "Social Capital and the Wages of Mexican Migrants: New Hypotheses and Tests." *Social Forces* 82(2):671–701.

Amuedo-Dorantes, Catalina and Kusum Mundra. 2008. "Social Networks and their Impact on the Earnings of Mexican Migrants." *Demography* 44(4):849–63.

Anderson, Elijah. 1999. *Code of the Street: Decency, Violence, and the Moral Life of the Inner City*. New York: W.W. Norton.

Bailey, Thomas and Roger Waldinger. 1991. "Primary, Secondary, and Enclave Labor Markets: A Training Systems Approach." *American Sociological Review* 56:432–45.

Banfield, Edward C. 1958. *The Moral Basis of a Backward Society*. New York: Free Press.

Baron, James N. and William T. Bielby. 1984. "Organizational Barriers to Gender Equality: Sex Segregation of Jobs and Opportunities." Pp. 233–51 in *Gender and the Life Course*, edited by Alice Rossi. New York: Aldine de Gruyter.

Benin, Mary and Verna M. Keith 1995. "The Social Support of Employed African American and Anglo Mothers." *Journal of Family Issues* 16(3):275–97.

Bian, Yanjie. 1997. "Bringing Strong Ties Back In: Indirect Ties, Network Bridges, and Job Searches in China." *American Sociological Review* 62(3):366–85.

Bielby, William T. and James N. Baron. 1984. "A Woman's Place Is with Other Women: Sex Segregation within Organizations." Pp. 27–55 in *Sex Segregation in the Workplace*, edited by Barbara F. Reskin. Washington, DC: National Academy.

Bielby, William T. and James N. Baron. 1986. "Men and Women at Work: Sex Segregation and Statistical Discrimination." *American Journal of Sociology* 91:759–99.

Bishop, John and Katharine G. Abraham. 1993. "Improving Job Matches in the U.S. Labor Market." *Brookings Papers on Economic Activity: Microeconomics* 1:335–400.

Blau, David M. and Philip K. Robins. 1990. "Job Search Outcomes for the Employed and Unemployed." *Journal of Political Economy* 98(3):637–55.

Boissevain, Jeremy. 1974. *Friends of Friends: Networks, Manipulators and Coalitions*. New York: St. Martin's Press.

Bott, Elizabeth. 1971. *Family and Social Networks: Roles, Norms, and External Relationships*. 2nd ed. New York: Free Press.

Braddock, Jomills Henry II, and James M. McPartland. 1987. "How Minorities Continue to Be Excluded from Equal Employment Opportunities: Research on Labor Markets and Institutional Barriers." *Journal of Social Issues* 43(1):5–39.

Brass, Daniel. 1985. "Men's and Women's Networks: A Study of Interaction Patterns and Influence in an Organization." *Academy of Management Journal* 28:327–43.

Brewster, Karin L. and Irene Padavic. 2002. "No More Kin Care? Change in Black Mothers' Reliance on Relatives for Child Care, 1977–1994." *Gender and Society* 16(4):546–63.

Briggs, Xavier de Souza. 1998. "Brown Kids in White Suburbs: Housing Mobility and the Many Faces of Social Capital." *Housing Policy Debate* 9(1):177–221.

Campbell, Karen E. 1988. "Gender Differences in Job-Related Networks." *Work and Occupations* 15:179–200.

Campbell, Karen E. and Rachel A. Rosenfeld. 1985. "Job Search and Job Mobility: Sex and Race Differences." *Research in the Sociology of Work* 3:147–74.

Carstairs, G. Morris. 1967. *The Twice-Born: A Study of a Community of High Caste Hindus*. Bloomington: Indiana University Press.

Corcoran, Mary, Linda Datcher, and Greg J. Duncan. 1980a. "Information and Influence Networks in Labor Markets." In *Five Thousand American Families: Patterns of Economic Progress*, vol. 8, edited by Greg J. Duncan and James N. Morgan. Ann Arbor, MI: Institute for Social Research.

Corcoran, Mary, Linda Datcher, and Greg J. Duncan. 1980b. "Most Workers Find Jobs through Word of Mouth." *Monthly Labor Review*, August, pp. 33–35.

Coverdill, James E. 1998. "Personal Contacts and Post-Hire Job Outcomes: Theoretical and Empirical Notes on the Significance of Matching Methods." *Research in Social Stratification and Mobility* 16:247–69.

DeGraaf, Nan Dirk and Hendrik Derk Flap. 1988. "With a Little Help from My Friends." *Social Forces* 67(2):452–72.

Dohan, Daniel. 2003. *The Price of Poverty: Money, Work, and Culture in the Mexican American Barrio*. Berkeley: University of California Press.

Dominguez, Silvia. 2011. *Getting Ahead: Social Mobility, Public Housing, and Immigrant Networks*. New York: New York University Press.

Dominguez, Silvia and Celeste Watkins. 2003. "Creating Networks for Survival and Mobility: Social Capital among African-American and Latin-American Low-Income Mothers." *Social Problems* 50(1):111–35.

Drentea, Patricia. 1998. "Consequences of Women's Formal and Informal Job Search Methods for Employment in Female-Dominated Jobs." *Gender and Society* 12:321–38.

Eggebeen, David J. 1992. "From Generation unto Generation: Parent-Child Support in Aging American Families." *Generations* 16(3):45–49.

Elliot, James R. 1999. "Social Isolation and Labor Market Insulation: Network and Neighborhood Effects on Less-educated Urban Workers." *Sociological Quarterly* 41(2):199–216.

Elliot, James R. and Mario Sims. 2001. "Ghettos and Barrios: The Impact of Neighborhood Poverty and Race on Job Matching among Blacks and Latinos." *Social Problems* 48(3):341–61.

Ensel, Walter M. 1979. *Sex, Social Ties, and Status Attainment* Albany: State University of New York at Albany Press.

Espinoza, Vicente. 1999. "Social Networks among the Urban Poor: Inequality and Integration in a Latin American City." Pp. 147–84 in *Networks in the Global Village: Life in Contemporary Communities*, edited by Barry Wellman. Boulder, CO: Westview Press.

Falcon, Luis M. 1995. "Social Networks and Employment for Latinos, Blacks, and Whites." *New England Journal of Public Policy* 11(1):17–28.

Fernandez, Roberto, Emilio Castilla, and Paul Moore. 2000. "Social Capital at Work: Networks and Employment at a Phone Center." *American Journal of Sociology* 105(5):1288–1356.

Fernandez, Roberto and Isabel Fernandez-Mateo. 2006. "Networks, Race, and Hiring." *American Sociological Review* 71(1):42–71.

Fernandez, Roberto and Roman V. Galperin. 2014. "The Causal Status of Social Capital in Labor Markets." Pp. 445–62 in *Research in the Sociology of Organizations: Contemporary Perspectives on Organizational Social Network Analysis*, edited by Daniel J. Brass, Giuseppe (Joe) Labianca, Ajay Mehra, Daniel S. Halgin, and Stephen P. Borgatti. Bingley: Emerald.

Fernandez, Roberto and David Harris. 1992. "Social Isolation and the Underclass." Pp. 257–94 in *Drugs, Crime, and Social Isolation: Barriers to Urban Opportunity*, edited by Adele V. Harrell and George E. Peterson. Washington, DC: Urban Institute Press.

Fernandez, Roberto and M. Lourdes Sosa. 2005. "Gendering the Job: Networks and Recruitment at a Call Center." *American Journal of Sociology* 111(3):859–904.

Fernandez, Roberto and Nancy Weinberg. 1997. "Sifting and Sorting: Personal Contacts and Hiring in a Retail Bank." *American Sociological Review* 62:883–902.

Fischer, Claude. 1982. *To Dwell among Friends: Personal Networks in Town and City*. Chicago: University of Chicago Press.

Fischer, Claude and Stacey Oliker. 1983. "A Research Note on Friendship, Gender, and the Life Cycle." *Social Forces* 62:124–32.

Foster, George M. 1967. *Tzintzuntzan*. Boston: Little, Brown.

Furstenberg, Frank F., Jr., Thomas D. Cook, Jacquelynne Eccles, Glen H. Elder, Jr., and Arnold Sameroff. 1999. *Managing to Make It: Urban Families and Adolescent Success*. Chicago: University of Chicago Press.

Gowan, Teresa. 2010. "What's Social Capital Got to Do with It? The Ambiguous (and Overstated) Relationship between Social Capital and Ghetto Underemployment." *Critical Sociology* 37(1):47–66.

Granovetter, Mark S. 1981. "Toward a Sociological Theory of Income Differences." Pp. 11–49 in *Sociological Perspectives on Labor Markets*, edited by Ivar Berg. New York: Academic Press.

Granovetter, Mark S. 1995. *Getting a Job: A Study of Contacts and Careers*, 2nd ed. Chicago: University of Chicago Press.

Green, Gary P., Leann M. Tigges, and Irene Browne. 1995. "Social Resources, Job Search, and Poverty in Atlanta." *Research in Community Sociology* 5:161–82.

Green, Gary P., Leann M. Tigges, and Daniel Diaz. 1999. "Racial and Ethnic Differences in Job-Search Strategies in Atlanta, Boston, and Los Angeles." *Social Science Quarterly* 80(2):263–78.

Grieco, Margaret. 1987. *Keeping It in the Family: Social Networks and Employment Chance.* London and NY: Tavistock.

Hagan, Jacqueline M. 1998. "Social Networks, Gender and Immigrant Settlement: Resource and Constraint." *American Sociological Review* 63(1):55–67.

Hamm, Lindsay and Steve McDonald. 2015. "Helping Hands: Race, Neighborhood Context, and Reluctance in Providing Job-Finding Assistance." *The Sociological Quarterly* 56: 539–57.

Hanson, Susan and Geraldine Pratt. 1991. "Job Search and the Occupational Segregation of Women." *Annals of the Association of American Geographers* 81(2):229–53.

Harris, Kathleen Mullan. 1993. "Work and Welfare among Single Mothers in Poverty." *American Journal of Sociology* 99:317–52.

Hochschild, Jennifer L. 1995. *Facing Up to the American Dream: Race, Class, and the Soul of the Nation.* Princeton, NJ: Princeton University Press.

Hofferth, Sandra L. 1984. "Kin Networks, Race, and Family Structure." *Journal of Marriage and the Family* 46:791–806.

Hogan, Dennis P., David J. Eggebeen, and Clifford C. Clogg. 1993. "The Structure of Intergenerational Exchanges in American Families." *American Journal of Sociology* 98(6):1428–58.

Holzer, Harry J. 1987a. "Informal Job Search and Black Youth Unemployment." *American Economic Review* 77(3):446–52.

Holzer, Harry J. 1987b. "Job Search by Employed and Unemployed Youth." *Industrial and Labor Relations Review* 40(4):601–11.

Hsung, R.-M. and Y.-J. Hwang. 1992. "Job Mobility in Taiwan: Job Search Methods and Contacts Status." XII International Sunbelt Social Network Conference, San Diego, February.

Hurlbert, Jeanne S., John J. Beggs, and Valerie A. Haines. 1998. "Exploring the Relationship between the Network Structure and Network Resources Dimensions of Social Isolation: What Kinds of Networks Allocate Resources in the Underclass?" Paper presented at the Social Capital and Social Network Conference, Duke University, Durham, NC.

Iosifides, Theodoros and Mari Lavrentiadou, Electra Petracou, and Antonios Kontis. 2007. "Forms of Social Capital and the Incorporation of Albanian Immigrants in Greece." *Journal of Ethnic and Migration Studies* 33(8):1348–61.

Jayakody, Rukmalie, Linda M. Chatters, and Robert Joseph Taylor. 1993. "Family Support to Single and Married African American Mothers: The Provision of Financial, Emotional, and Child Care Assistance." *Journal of Marriage and the Family* 55(May):261–76.

Jencks, Christopher, Lauri Perman, and Lee Rainwater. 1988. "What Is a Good Job? A New Measure of Labor Market-Success." *American Journal of Sociology* 93:1322–57.

Kahanec, Martin and Mariapia Mendola. 2008. "Social Determinants of Labor Market Status of Ethnic Minorities in Britain." Centro Studi Luca D'Agliano Development Studies Working Papers. No. 253.

Kalleberg Arne L., Barbara Reskin, and Ken Hudson. 2000. "Bad Jobs in America: Standard and Nonstandard Employment Relations and Job Quality in the United States." *American Sociological Review* 65:256–78.

Kanas, Agnieszka and Frank van Tubergen. 2009. "The Impact of Origin and Host Country Schooling on the Economic Performance of Immigrants." *Social Forces* 88(2):893–915.

Kanas, Agnieszka, Frank van Tubergen, and Tanja Van der Lippe. 2011. "The Role of Social Contacts in the Employment Status of Immigrants: A Panel Study of Immigrants in Germany." *International Sociology* 26(1):95–122.

Kasinitz, Philip and Jan Rosenberg. 1996. "Missing the Connection: Social Isolation and Employment on the Brooklyn Waterfront." *Social Problems* 43(2):180–96.

Korenman, Sanders and Susan C. Turner. 1996. "Employment Contacts and Minority-White Wage Differences." *Industrial Relations* 35(1):106–22.

Lancee, Bram. 2010. "The Economic Returns of Immigrants' Bonding and Bridging Social Capital: The Case of the Netherlands." *International Migration Review* 44(1):202–26.

Lee, Yean-Ju and Isik A. Aytac. 1998. "Intergenerational Financial Support among Whites, African Americans, and Latinos." *Journal of Marriage and the Family* 60(May):426–41.

Li, Yaojun, Mike Savage, and Alan Warde. 2008. "Social Mobility and Social Capital in Contemporary Britain." *British Journal of Sociology* 59(3):391–411.

Liebow, Elliot. 1967. *Tally's Corner: A Study of Streetcorner Men.* Boston: Little, Brown.

Lin, Nan. 1999. "Social Networks and Status Attainment." *Annual Review of Sociology* 25:467–87.

Lin, Nan and Mary Dumin. 1986. "Access to Occupational through Social Ties." *Social Networks* 8:365–85.

Lin, Nan, Walter M. Ensel, and John C. Vaughn. 1981. "Social Resources and Strength of Ties: Structural Factors in Occupational Status Attainment." *American Sociological Review* 46(4):393–405.

Lin, Nan, Hang Young Lee, and Dan Ao. 2013. "Contact Status and Finding a Job: Validation and Extension," Pp. 21–41 in *Social Capital in Three Societies: The Context of Socioeconomic and Cultural Institutions*, edited by Nan Lin, Yang-chih Fu, and Chih-jou Jay Chen. New York: Routledge.

Lin, Nan, John C. Vaughn, and Walter M. Ensel. 1981. "Social Resources and Occupational Status Attainment." *Social Forces* 59:1163–81.

MacLeod, Jay. 2011. *Ain't No Makin' It*, 3rd ed. Boulder, CO: Westview Press.

Marin, Alexandra. 2012. "'Don't mention it': Why People Don't Share Job Information, When They Do, and Why It Matters." *Social Networks* 34:181–92.

Marsden, Peter V. 1987. "Core Discussion Networks of Americans." *American Sociological Review* 52:122–31.

Marsden, Peter V. and Karen E. Campbell. 1984. "Measuring Tie Strength." *Social Forces* 63:482–501.

Marsden, Peter V. and Jeanne S. Hurlbert. 1988. "Social Resources and Mobility Outcomes: A Replication and Extension." *Social Forces* 66(4):1038–59.

McPherson, Miller J. and Lynn Smith-Lovin. 1982. "Women and Weak Ties: Differences by Sex in the Size of Voluntary Organizations." *American Journal of Sociology* 87:883–904.

McWhorter, John. 2000. *Losing the Race: Self-Sabotage in Black America.* New York: Harper Perennial.

McWhorter, John 2005. *Winning the Race: Beyond the Crisis in Black America.* New York: Gotham Books.

Mead, Lawrence M. 1985. *Beyond Entitlement: The Social Obligations of Citizenship.* New York: Free Press.

Menjivar, Cecilia. 2000. *Fragmented Ties: Salvadoran Immigrant Networks in America.* Berkeley: University of California Press.

Mier, Robert and Robert Giloth. 1985. "Hispanic Employment Opportunities: A Case of Internal Labor Markets and Weak-Tied Social Networks." *Social Science Quarterly* 66:296–309.

Moerbeek, H., W. Utle and Henk Flap. 1996. "That's What Friends Are For: Ascribed and Achieved Social Capital in the Occupational Career." European Social Networks Conference, London.

Moore, Gwen. 1990. "Structural Determinants of Men's and Women's Personal Networks." *American Sociological Review* 55:726–35.

Morenoff, Jeffrey, Robert J. Sampson, and Stephen W. Raudenbush. 2001. "Neighborhood Inequality, Collective Efficacy, and the Spatial Dynamics of Urban Violence." *Criminology* 39(3):517–58.

Mouw, Ted. 2003. "Social Capital and Finding a Job: Do Contacts Matter?" *American Sociological Review* 68:868–98.

Mouw, Ted. 2006. "Estimating the Causal Effect of Social Capital: A Review of Recent Research." *Annual Review of Sociology* 32:79–102.

Neckerman, Kathryn M. and Roberto M. Fernandez. 2003. "Keeping a Job: Network Hiring and Turnover in a Retail Bank." *Research in the Sociology of Organizations* 20:299–318.

Newman, Katherine S. 1999. *No Shame in My Game: The Working Poor in the Inner City*. New York: Knopf and Russell Sage Foundation.

Newman, Katherine S. and Chauncy Lennon. 1995. "Finding Work in the Inner City: How Hard Is It Now: How Hard Will It Be for AFDC Recipients?" Working Paper no. 76. New York, Russell Sage Foundation.

Obukhova, Elena. 2012. "Motivation vs. Relevance: Using Strong Ties to Find a Job in Urban China." *Social Science Research* 41:570–80.

Obukhova, Elena and George Lan. 2012. "Do Job-Seekers Benefit from Contacts? A Within-Individual Test with Contemporaneous Searches." *Management Science* 59(10):2204–16.

Oliver, Melvin L. 1988. "The Urban Black Community as Network: Toward a Social Network Perspective." *Sociological Quarterly* 29:623–45.

Parish, William, Lingxin Hao, and Dennis P. Hogan. 1991. "Family Support Networks, Welfare, and Work among Young Mothers." *Journal of Marriage and the Family* 53:203–15.

Patterson, Orlando. 1998. *The Ordeal of Integration: Progress and Resentment in America's "Racial" Crisis*. New York: Basic Civitas.

Paul, Anju Mary. 2012. "Differentiated Social Capital Mobilization in the Migration Decision." Working paper, University of Michigan.

Pearlin, Leonard I., Elizabeth G. Menaghan, Morton A. Lieberman, and Joseph T. Mullan. 1981. "The Stress Process." *Journal of Health and Social Behavior* 22(4):337–56.

Petersen, Trond, Ishak Saporta, and Marc-David L. Seidel. 2000. "Offering a Job: Meritocracy and Social Networks." *American Journal of Sociology* 106(3):763–816.

Putnam, Robert. 2000. *Bowling Alone: The Collapse and Revival of American Community*. New York: Simon and Schuster.

Royster, Deirdre. 2003. *Race and the Invisible Hand: How White Networks Exclude Black Men from Blue-Collar Jobs*. Berkeley: University of California Press.

Saegert, Susan, J. Phillip Thompson, Mark R. Warren, eds. 2001. *Social Capital in Poor Communities*. New York: Russell Sage Foundation.

Sampson, Robert J. 2012. *The Great American City: Chicago and the Enduring Neighborhood Effect*. Chicago: University of Chicago Press.

Sampson, Robert, Jeffrey Morenoff, and Felton Earls. 1999. "Beyond Social Capital: Spatial Dynamics of Collective Efficacy for Children." *American Sociological Review* 64(5):633–60.

Sanders, Jimy M. and Victor Nee. 1996. "Immigrant Self-Employment: The Family as Social Capital and the Value of Human Capital." *American Sociological Review* 61(2):231–49.

Sanders, Jimy M., Victor Nee, and Scott Sernau. 2002. "Asian Immigrants' Reliance on Social Ties in a Multiethnic Labor Market." *Social Forces* 81(1):281–314.

Small, Mario Luis. 2010. *Unanticipated Gains: Origins of Network Inequality in Everyday Life*. New York: Oxford University Press.

Smith, Sandra Susan. 1995. "Poverty Concentration and Social Networks: Implications for Joblessness." Paper presented at the annual meetings of the American Sociological Association, Washington, D.C.

Smith, Sandra Susan. 1997. "Social Capital and Employment Probabilities: The Case of Chicago's Urban Poor." Paper presented at the annual meetings of the American Sociological Association, Toronto, Canada.

Smith, Sandra Susan. 2000. "Mobilizing Social Resources: Race, Ethnic, and Gender Differences in Social Capital and Persisting Wage Inequalities." *Sociological Quarterly* 41(4):509–37.

Smith, Sandra Susan. 2005. "'Don't Put My Name on It': Social Capital Activation and Job-Finding Assistance among the Black Urban Poor." *American Journal of Sociology* 111(1):1–57.

Smith, Sandra Susan. 2007. *Lone Pursuit: Distrust and Defensive Individualism among the Black Poor*. New York: Russell Sage Foundation.

Smith, Sandra Susan. 2008. "A Question of Access or Mobilization? Understanding Inefficacious Job Referral Networks among the Black Poor." Pp. 157–81 in *Social Capital: Advances in Research*, edited by Nan Lin and Bonnie Erickson. New York: Oxford University Press.

Smith, Sandra Susan. 2010. "A Test of Sincerity: How Black and Latino Service Workers Make Decisions about Making Referrals." *Annals of the American Academy of Political and Social Science* 629:30–52.

Stack, Carol. 1974. *All Our Kin: Strategies for Survival in a Black Community*. New York: Harper Colophon Books.

Stoloff, Jennifer A., Jennifer L. Glanville, and Elisa Jayne Bienenstock. 1999. "Women's Participation in the Labor Force: The Role of Social Networks." *Social Networks* 21:91–108.

Sullivan, Mercer. 1989. *Getting Paid: Youth Crime and Work in the Inner City*. Ithaca, NY: Cornell University Press.

Suttles, Gerald. 1968. *The Origins of the Urban Crisis: Race and Inequality in Postwar Detroit*. Princeton, NJ: Princeton University Press.

Thernstrom, Stephan and Abigail Thernstrom. 1998. *America in Black and White: One Nation, Indivisible*. New York: Simon & Schuster.

Tigges, Leann M., Irene Browne, and Gary P. Green. 1998. "Social Isolation of the Urban Poor: Race, Class, and Neighborhood Effects on Social Resources." *Sociological Quarterly* 39:53–77.

Trimble, Lindsey. 2013. "Ask and You Shall Receive: Social Network Contacts' Provision of Help during the Job Search." *Social Networks* 35:593–603.

Uehara, Edwina. 1990. "Dual Exchange Theory, Social Networks, and Informal Social Support." *American Journal of Sociology* 96(3):521–57.

Volker, Beat and Henk Flap. 1996. "Getting Ahead in the GDR: Human Capital and Social Capital in the Status Attainment Process under Communism." *Acta Sociologica* 42 (1):17–34.

Wacquant, Loic and William Julius Wilson. 1989. "The Cost of Racial and Class Exclusion in the Inner City." *Annals of the American Academy of Political and Social Science* (January):8–25.

Wanous, John P. 1980. *Organizational Entry: Recruitment, Selection, and Socialization of Newcomers*. Reading, MA: Addison-Wesley.

Wegener, Bernd. 1991. "Job Mobility and Social Ties: Social Resources, Prior Job and Status Attainment." *American Sociological Review* 56:1–12.

Wellman, Barry. 1985. "Domestic Work, Paid Work and Net Work." Pp. 159–91 in *Understanding Personal Relationships*, edited by Steve Duck and Daniel Perlman. London: Sage.

Wielgosz, John B. and Susan Carpenter. 1987. "The Effectiveness of Alternative Methods of Searching for Jobs and Finding Them: An Exploratory Analysis of the Data Bearing upon the Ways of Coping with Joblessness." *American Journal of Economics and Sociology* 46(2):151–64.

Wilson, William Julius. 1987. *The Truly Disadvantaged: The Inner City, the Underclass, and Public Policy*. Chicago: University of Chicago Press.

Young, Alford Jr. 2004. *The Minds of Marginalized Black Men: Making Sense of Mobility, Opportunity, and Future Life Chances*. Princeton, NJ: Princeton University Press.

Yakubovich, Valery. 2005. "Weak Ties, Information, and Influence: How Workers Find Jobs in a Local Russian Labor Market." *American Sociological Review* 70(3):408–21.

Yakubovich, Valery and Daniela Lup. 2006. "Stages of the Recruitment Process and the Referrer's Performance Effect." *Organization Science* 17(6):710–23.

CHAPTER 20

....

EDUCATION

....

EMILY HANNUM AND YU XIE

KEY CONCEPTS

....

Poverty

In the poverty literature, poverty is typically measured by comparing resources to needs, and families or individuals are considered poor if they fall below some threshold (Foster 1998:335).[1] Economists, and, to some degree, sociologists, interested in the economic and social welfare of populations and individuals have brought multiple conceptual approaches to the study of poverty and proposed a variety of strategies to operationalize the concept (for a review, see Grusky and Kanbur 2006; Smeeding, this volume).

One line of distinction in existing approaches has been in the selection of the relevant welfare measure (World Bank 2011). Income is a common choice, the use of which may be justified on the grounds that income is essential in societies with market economies (Borgeraas and Dahl 2010); consumption is another common choice. A different approach, popularized by Sen and others, focuses on capabilities or endowments (Bourguignon 2006; Nussbaum 2006; Sen 1999, 2006). This approach is associated with efforts to define poverty as a failure to reach minimally acceptable levels in multiple dimensions—different monetary and nonmonetary attributes necessary for functioning (for example, see Bourguignon and Chakravarty 2003; Bourguignon 2006; for a critical discussion of child-focused multidimensional indicators of poverty, see Dercon 2012; Marlier and Atkinson 2010; Nussbaum 2006; Thorbecke 2005). A second area of distinction in approaches has to do with selecting the poverty line—the threshold below which a given household or individual will be classified as poor—and the poverty indicators (World Bank 2011). The poverty line can be defined in absolute, relative, or subjective terms (Borgeraas and Dahl 2010:73; Brady 2003; World Bank 2011; Yoshikawa, Aber, and Beardslee 2012:273). Poverty indicators often include one or more of a trio of measures that quantify the incidence, depth, and severity of poverty developed by Foster, Greer, and Thorbecke (1984) that have become "the workhorse" of applied work on poverty across the world (Grusky and Kanbur 2006:5), but other measures have been proposed.[2]

Poverty has been a core concept of interest in research on educational inequality. However, the conceptualization of poverty in empirical educational research does not always, or even usually, conform to definitions and measures that are prevalent in the poverty literature. To further muddy the waters, the educational literature subscribes to no uniform set of alternative conceptualizations. At the national level, measures of national economic development such as per capita gross domestic product (GDP) or gross national product (GNP) are much more commonly used than direct measures of poverty in analyses of educational expansion or achievement. Economic inequality, typically in some form of national Gini coefficient, is another related concept that is also much more commonly found in comparative educational expansion or achievement studies than direct measures of poverty.

At the community and family levels, researchers have employed a broad set of variables related to poverty, some detailed and some crude. Some have consisted of interval-level measures of the underlying welfare concepts used in the construction of poverty measures, and some have consisted of other proxies.[3] For example, as indicators of community or household poverty, studies have employed measures such as community per capita income, percentage of poor in schools or percentage on free or reduced-price lunches, household income, wealth or consumption, and income-to-needs ratios.

At the family level, sociologists have employed the concepts of class and socioeconomic status (SES). The latest work on microclasses has closely linked the approaches of class and SES (Weeden and Grusky 2005), the key difference being that the former is categorical, implying distinct boundaries, while the latter is gradational, or continuous. Notions of class have obvious parallels to the concept of impoverishment, but class identification can also carry other, sometimes controversial, connotations related to degree of structural marginalization, social milieu, and culture (Bourdieu 1973; Grusky and Kanbur 2006; Wilson 1987, 2006). SES indices, based on estimated interval scores at a detailed occupation level, have long been used in sociology (Duncan 1961; Hauser and Warren 1997). Such SES indices are intended to indicate a person's position in a vertical social hierarchy, often measured by occupational prestige, which has been shown to be invariant over time and across societies (Treiman 1977). While scholars have generally not treated low values of the SES indices as proxies for poverty, the concept of household socioeconomic status—whether measured formally as a score or simply encompassing some combination of adult occupational, economic, and educational characteristics—is directly related to the concept of poverty and is widely used in quantitative studies of educational attainment.

Finally, in the burgeoning comparative literature on educational opportunity and achievement, still different measures for studying economic welfare have been developed to overcome data limitations. For example, much of the available comparative data on educational access and attainment has come from demographic surveys or population censuses that lacked detailed income or expenditure data. Filmer and

Pritchett (1999, 2001) developed a proxy for long-run wealth of the household from asset information, using principal components analysis.

In the comparative achievement literature, the fact that surveys are administered to students or children rather than parents or household heads poses further barriers to collecting data related to poverty. Researchers have developed proxies for household socioeconomic status and economic welfare that could be reliably reported by children themselves. One solution is a composite index of socioeconomic status that builds on questions children can answer. For example, the OECD has developed a comparable measure of "Economic, Social and Cultural Status" (ESCS), a composite of parental occupational status, parental education, and household possessions, for the Program for International Student Assessment (PISA) data (Ladd 2012). "Poverty" is defined as below the "low ESCS" line set at one standard deviation below the mean (Ladd 2012).

Another approach, in dealing with the same problem, has been to use books in the home as a proxy for household income. Economists have argued that the number of books in the home is reliably related to household income (Schütz, Ursprung, and Woessmann 2008:287–88). Analyzing Progress in International Reading Literacy Study (PIRLS) data from six countries, Schütz et al. (2008:287–88) found that the relationship between household income and books at home did not vary significantly across countries. Schütz et al. (2008) and Hanushek and Woessmann (2011) argue that this finding constitutes evidence of the validity of using the books-at-home variable as a proxy for family background in cross-country comparisons.

As is evident from these examples, there persists a lack of agreement about how to operationalize household poverty for the study of children's developmental, behavioral, and educational outcomes. There is also a lack of agreement about the set of controls that should be included in empirical studies of this relationship in order to determine the "true" or net effect of household poverty (Aber et al. 1997). These issues are unlikely to be resolved anytime soon, given an emerging conceptualization of poverty as encompassing an interrelated set of circumstances (Huston and Bentley 2010).

Education

In essence, education is the process of learning. Although education can and does take place outside educational institutions, for our purposes in this chapter, we limit our discussion to formal education. Before we discuss further the relationship between poverty and education, let us first understand three important functions of education in almost every modern society: (1) imparting knowledge, (2) socializing children, and (3) transmitting family advantage or disadvantage.

There is near-consensus in the economics literature, under the rubric of "human capital theory," that education imparts useful knowledge and makes a person receiving education more productive in the labor market (Becker 1964; Mincer 1974). According to this view, the secular increase in educational attainment over time is a major driving force behind technological advances and economic growth at the societal level

(Goldin and Katz 2008). At the individual level, it is also rational for families to invest in children's education, as this is likely to yield good economic returns (Becker and Tomes 1986). Indeed, a large literature has shown that education, particularly college education, yields high economic returns—evidence consistent with but not necessarily supporting the interpretation that formal education makes workers more productive in their work (for a review, see Hout 2012).

One of the prominent features of the industrialization that began in the eighteenth century is the gradual relocation of daily activities, economic as well as noneconomic, from families to formal institutions (Thornton, Axinn, and Xie 2007). Because students spend most of their waking hours in school, away from home and away from parents, they are strongly influenced by their educational experiences, as well as by the attitudes and behaviors of their peers. For example, the Stouffer hypothesis predicts that educated persons tend to hold more liberal views, and a secular increase in educational attainment would make a society more liberal over time (Davis 1980).

Finally, education serves to transmit social advantages or disadvantages from one generation to the next. While economists emphasize economic benefits as the main motivating factor behind education, sociologists have long recognized the social significance of education. In the United States, Lareau's fieldwork among European American and African American families in the mid-Atlantic region indicates that middle-class parents, for example, practice "concerted cultivation" parenting styles, as compared to "natural growth" parenting styles of the working-class parents, the former being more conducive to education (Lareau 2011). Numerous sociological studies have found that a higher level of education is a cultural norm, rather than an economic investment, for high-SES parents (reviewed in Brand and Xie 2010). Sociologist Collins (1979) articulated this view most forcefully, arguing that education's function is mainly to serve as a credential and thus allow the elite class to differentiate their children from those from working-class family backgrounds. We will return to this topic in discussing the dual roles of education in intergenerational mobility later.

Synthesis

Overall, there are many competing ideas in the poverty and education literatures about how best to conceptualize and measure poverty, and emerging research on poverty and child welfare suggests that poverty must necessarily be viewed as multidimensional in form. Lack of uniformity in conceptualization and measurement obviously poses challenges to building a knowledge base about how poverty affects educational outcomes. Moving forward, there is a clear need for further work to test and establish the dimensions of poverty most relevant to children's education. It may be that different dimensions of poverty matter in different contexts, but this point, too, can be theorized and tested. In contrast, while scholars hold different interpretations of the meaning and significance of educational credentials, there is less disagreement on measurement. Despite recognition that quality of education probably varies tremendously across countries, school systems, and schools, scholars tend to default to measures of attainment, enrollment, and achievement.

IMPACT OF POVERTY ON EDUCATION

Conceptually, poverty or its proxies at the national, community, or household level could shape educational chances for children. In this section, we consider the literature on how poverty operates at each level. However, few studies on global patterns of educational expansion and national differences in achievement have focused on national poverty or related indicators. Presumably, researchers have assumed that national-level poverty affects educational outcomes primarily through poverty at more localized levels—communities and families. For this reason, we discuss briefly the literature on national characteristics and educational outcomes before devoting most of our discussion to community and family poverty.

Poverty at the National Level

Surprisingly, we did not find research that addressed explicitly the impact of national poverty on educational expansion or achievement. However, several strands of related work exist and deserve mention here. One strand of related work has emerged as part of the world society perspective, which focuses on the rise of global forces in shaping educational expansion. This literature has incorporated national measures of economic development, modernization, and position in the world system into analyses of the course of educational expansion across countries, but results have been mixed depending on indicators utilized and specifications (Meyer et al. 1977; Meyer, Ramirez, and Soysal 1992; Schofer and Meyer 2005).[4] For example, Meyer et al. (1977:250) found that the national economic development indicator per capita kilowatt-hours of energy use was related to subsequent tertiary educational expansion, net of controls for the "self-generating" process of educational expansion linked to prior population characteristics of schools and the population without education. However, per capita GNP was not related to tertiary expansion in this specification; both variables were marginally significant for secondary expansion; and neither variable significantly predicted primary expansion. Schofer and Meyer (2005:915) investigated the role of per capita GDP and a Gini coefficient for inequality, among many other factors, in shaping national patterns of higher educational expansion, but showed no effect net of other variables in their models in recent decades.

Another strand of work has linked national characteristics to individual enrollment and attainment by drawing on household surveys. Analyzing a combined sample of 222,853 children living in 340 districts in 30 countries from the Demographic and Health Surveys and the Pan Arab Project for Family Health of the League of Arab States,

Huisman and Smits (2009) investigated whether children aged 8 to 11 were enrolled in school at the time of the interview. A bivariate analysis showed a significant relationship with per capita GDP, indicating higher enrollment probabilities in wealthier countries. This association was present only for boys in specifications including district- and family-level socioeconomic, demographic, and educational characteristics.

A different body of research compares educational achievement across nations using comparative data such as the Program for International Assessment (PISA), Trends in International Mathematics and Science Study (TIMSS), and the Progress in International Reading Literacy Study (PIRLS). National characteristics considered in much of this work have been institutional features of schools and education systems (for a review, see Hanushek and Woessmann 2011). As in the case of the educational expansion literature, we did not find studies of achievement that had focused on national poverty as an analytic concept or had sought to make a strong causal argument about the effect of poverty on achievement. However, in this literature, many studies have employed concepts related to national poverty such as economic inequality, usually measured in the form of a Gini coefficient, and development level, usually measured as GDP per capita. These variables have been employed as control variables and sometimes as focal variables.

For example, in a country-level analysis using PISA math data from 27 affluent countries, Condron (2011: Figures 1, 2, and 3) showed that national economic inequality (measured in the form of the Gini index) was negatively associated with average achievement and with percentage of students scoring above the highest math-proficiency level, and positively related to the percentage of students scoring in the lowest math-proficiency level. Consistent with these findings, a multilevel analysis of science achievement among 107,834 fifteen-year-olds in 41 countries using PISA data showed that students had higher science scores if they lived in wealthier countries and if they lived in countries with more equal distributions of household income (smaller Gini coefficients) (Chiu 2007:515). Chiu's (2007) GDP per capita results were robust to specification; the wealth distribution results became insignificant in the most extensive specification that included proxies for prior achievement, country-level variables, family demographic structure, family socioeconomic status, family cultural possessions and communications, and various interactions between country-level and student-level variables. Chiu (2010) produced similar findings for GDP per capita and inequality in multilevel analyses of PISA math achievement among 107,975 fifteen-year-olds in 41 countries, though the Gini coefficient becomes insignificant once measures of SES and other family background characteristics are included. In contrast, also using PISA math achievement data, Hanushek and Woessmann (2011) show a negative coefficient for GDP per capita, but these authors' specifications included a large number of institutional variables that might be correlated with GDP per capita, as well as family background variables.

In summary, some of the studies that contain measures of national development and inequality suggest, unsurprisingly, that opportunity and achievement tend to be better in wealthier, more equal countries, but these findings are sensitive to model specification.

Few studies have treated development and inequality as core analytic variables, and we found no studies that directly addressed national rates or depth of poverty per se as factors affecting educational expansion or achievement. Disadvantage at the national level might simply signal aggregated economic disadvantages of households, communities, and school systems within countries, but poverty and underdevelopment at the national level may bring disadvantages that do not simply represent aggregations of impoverished households and communities. Problems disproportionately faced by the poorest countries—such as indebtedness, dependence on foreign aid and technical assistance, brain drain, violent conflict, and weak governance structures—may shape their capacity to invest in education and reap returns on educational investments. Additional work is needed to understand the attributes of poverty at the national level that might be associated with educational expansion and opportunity.

Community and Neighborhood Poverty

Unlike the case of poverty at the national level, there are well-established lines of research about community poverty effects on education. In the United States, there are long-standing traditions in sociology, economics, and psychology that investigate links between neighborhood conditions and various social welfare outcomes (for reviews, see Bradley and Corwyn 2002; Leventhal and Brooks-Gunn 2003; Sampson, Morenoff, and Gannon-Rowley 2002; Sampson 2009). These studies often focus on urban settings and have sought to investigate direct effects of concentrated poverty on outcomes, as well as mechanisms in the form of institutional resources; environmental contamination; disorder, crime, and violence; norms and collective efficacy; routine activity, and social ties and interactions (Bradley and Corwyn 2002; Leventhal and Brooks-Gunn 2000, 2003; Sampson et al. 2002; Sampson 2009).

The literature pertaining to children and youth outcomes goes beyond education to include behavioral, physical health, and psychological welfare outcomes. Studies suggest that a wide range of child and adolescent outcomes is associated with concentrated disadvantage. These outcomes include infant mortality, low birth weight, teenage childbearing, dropping out of high school, child maltreatment, and adolescent delinquency (Leventhal and Brooks-Gunn 2003; for reviews, see Sampson et al. 2002). Based on extensive review of empirical studies, Levanthal and Brooks-Gunn (2000:330) indicate that, for children and adolescents, residing in a low-SES neighborhood adversely affects behavioral and emotional well-being, especially externalizing behavior problems among young children and delinquency and problem behavior among adolescents. With regard to educational outcomes, a number of studies using longitudinal data and propensity-score methods have found that exposure, especially extended exposure, to poor neighborhoods in the United States leads to poor educational outcomes (Harding 2003; Wodtke, Harding, and Elwert 2011). Analysis of experimental data from the Moving to Opportunity for Fair Housing Demonstration New York site showed that moving from high- to low-poverty neighborhoods had positive effects on 11 to 18-year-old boys' achievement scores compared with those of their peers in high-poverty neighborhoods (Leventhal and Brooks-Gunn 2004).

Beyond the neighborhood effects literature focused on the United States and other developed countries, there has also been research on community effects on educational opportunity in developing countries. This literature has tended to focus on a different set of themes and often on issues salient to rural communities. Conceptualization has not been very comprehensive or consistent. In the cross-national literature, most studies have few options in measuring community attributes related to education, and they tend to make use of survey data collected for other purposes to measure community attributes. Huisman and Smits's (2009) 30-country analysis of enrollment among 8- to 11-year-olds highlights the average distance to school in rural areas and the district teacher-child ratio as consistently significant in their associations with enrollment. Community infrastructure has also been shown to be associated with enrollment. For example, in one study of rural Bangladesh, roads and rural electrification were associated with increased school participation for rural girls (Khandker 1996). In one province in northwest China, odds of completing junior high school and transitioning to high school were lower in the poorest communities, isolated communities, and communities providing lower levels of community support for schooling (Cherng and Hannum 2013). Community economic and social resources were also systematically related to student math scores (Adams 2006).

Scholars focusing on the United States have highlighted the importance of further research on why low SES neighborhoods matter for youth—research that goes beyond measures of low SES to directly assess theoretically driven, well-specified underlying processes (Leventhal and Brooks-Gunn 2003:30). Scholars have also indicated the importance of considering that neighborhood effects vary based on other contexts in which youth function. For example, Harding et al. (2010) suggest that youth educational outcomes be viewed as a function of neighborhood context, neighborhood exposure, individual vulnerability to neighborhood effects, and non-neighborhood educational inputs. More work is needed to extend well-theorized neighborhood effects literature to rural communities, and more work is needed to theorize the community effects literature focused on rural communities in developing countries.

Household Poverty

Cross-nationally, household poverty has been linked to poorer educational access and attainment in many studies. Using asset indices developed from Demographic and Health Surveys from 35 countries, Filmer and Pritchett (1999) constructed a ranking of households within each country and defined "poor" as the bottom 40 percent. They then assessed the links between poverty and educational outcomes. They found a prominent pattern in many countries in which much of the deficit in universal basic education is among the poor. Huisman and Smits (2009) used Filmer and Pritchett's general approach for measuring wealth, but they employed different cutoffs for designating poverty and analyzed enrollment at ages 8 to 11 in a combined sample of 222,853 in 30 countries from the Demographic and Health Surveys and the Pan Arab Project for Family Health of the League of Arab States. Huisman and Smits (2009) found that two indicators of socioeconomic status—parents' education and household wealth—remain strongly predictive even in specifications controlling for other family background and structural effects, along with district educational, demographic, and economic characteristics. From a different perspective, the effectiveness of conditional cash-transfer programs in a variety of settings in Latin America for enrollment and attainment demonstrates the critical role played by economic deprivation in shaping educational opportunity for the poor (Valencia Lomelí 2008).[5]

However, the manner in which household poverty relates to educational opportunity and attainment manifests very differently across contexts. For example, Filmer and Pritchett (1999:93) report four different regional educational attainment profiles of the poor: low ever-enrollment and high dropout in Western and Central Africa; low ever-enrollment and low dropout in South Asia; high ever-enrollment and high early-dropout in Latin America and the Caribbean; high ever-enrollment and late dropout in Eastern and Southern Africa or very late dropout in East Asia and the Pacific and Middle East, North Africa, and Central Asia. Echoing the importance of context at the community level, Huisman and Smits (2009) report significant interaction effects in their models indicating that the effects of many household-level variables varied across districts with different educational facilities and between urban and rural areas.

Constructs related to poverty have also been linked to academic achievement. Using PISA reading score data from 15-year-olds in the United States and the 13 OECD countries that scored higher than the United States, Ladd (2012:209) showed that reading achievement was strongly correlated with the Economic, Social and Cultural Status (ESCS) socioeconomic index in all 14 countries. Using books in the home as a proxy for household economic status, Hanushek and Woessmann (2011) concluded that the association of achievement with this indicator of economic status was robust across the board in countries analyzed in the TIMSS-95 and TIMSS-Repeat, net of controls for age, gender, family status, immigration and parent immigration status, and test cycle (Hanushek and Woessmann 2011:118, Figure 2.2). Chiu's (2007:515) analysis of science achievement in the PISA data also showed a significant coefficient for books. In the United States, the education gap between rich and poor is increasingly pronounced: Reardon (2011) compiled achievement data over 50 years and showed a dramatic rise in the achievement gap between children at the 10th and 90th percentiles of the income distribution.

Why are children in poor households disadvantaged? In the United States and in low- and middle-income countries, household poverty, variously measured, is a well-established risk factor for many outcomes for children that could help or hinder capacity to function in school, including physical health, and language and cognitive development, though specific causal processes are not yet well established (Engle and Black 2008; Grantham-McGregor et al. 2007; Walker et al. 2011; Yoshikawa et al. 2012:273). For example, in a survey conducted among rural children in an impoverished region of northwest China, the poorest children were at elevated risk of being chronically under-nourished, living in food insecure households, and lacking access to vision correction (Hannum, Liu, and Frongillo 2012; Hannum and Zhang 2012; Yu and Hannum 2007). In interviews in the same region, children reported deep concerns about lacking essential school materials; lacking adults at home who had the educational experience to assist them with homework or school problems; and distress about money and the burden of their school costs on their parents (Hannum and Adams 2008).

Naudeau et al. (2011) found, via a literature review and in an empirical analysis of data from Cambodia and Mozambique, that children's cognitive development delays are common in poor countries; that these delays are associated with socioeconomic status; and that socioeconomic gradients remain even after accounting for mediating factors such as nutrition and parenting. The poorest children may also be at risk for exposure to environmental toxins that impede development (for a review, see Walker et al. 2011). Moreover, multiple developmental risks associated with poverty are likely to co-occur (Grantham-McGregor et al. 2007; Walker et al. 2011).

The "toxic stress"—or experiences of severe, uncontrollable, and chronic adversity—associated with child poverty in many contexts can strain children's capacity for behavioral functioning (de Walque 2011). For example, in the United States, Gershoff and her colleagues (2007) analyzed a national sample of 21,255 kindergarteners from the Early Childhood Longitudinal Study, and, as income increased, parental invest-ments and resources for the child increased, which enhanced academic skills. At the same time, higher income was associated with reduced material hardship and stress, and fewer child behavior problems. Using data from a sample of rural adolescents in 100 villages in northwest China, Davidson and Adams (2013) linked a cumulative adversity index measuring stressful life events to elevated scores on an internalizing problems scale.

The timing of impoverishment may also be important for children (Boyden and Cooper 2007), with evidence suggesting that earlier poverty experiences can be more damaging than later ones for children's developmental outcomes (Alderman 2011; Bird 2007; Engle 2012). Assessing literature for the United States available through the middle of the 1990s, Brooks-Gunn and Duncan (1997) concluded that children who experience poverty during their preschool and early school years have lower rates of school completion than children and adolescents who experience poverty only in later years. Guo's (1998) analysis using National Longitudinal Survey of Youth data from the United States distinguished development tests from achievements, and showed that long-term poverty had substantial influences on both but with differ-ent time patterns. The younger ages were a more crucial period for the development of cognitive ability than early adolescence, but poverty experienced in adolescence appeared more influential to adolescent achievement than poverty experienced ear-lier in life.

Moreover, poor children are likely to attend schools and classrooms with fewer resources. For example, in the United States, children living in poverty tend to be concentrated in schools with inadequate resources and poorly skilled teachers (Murnane 2007:162). State educational spending has long been correlated positively with state per capita income, though the association has weakened over the last 50 years (Cascio and Reber 2013). Per pupil expenditures vary tremendously. Considering per pupil current expenditures for public elementary and secondary education in fiscal year 2008, instruction expenditures ranged from $3,886 in Utah to $11,572 in New York (Zhou and Johnson 2010). Even within districts, variation may be high. For example, a study of 89 public elementary schools in a large, north central, urban district in the United States indicates considerable disparities in per pupil spending (Condron and Roscigno 2003). However, many studies have debated the seemingly straightforward, logical link between school resources and achievement, ever since the publication of the Coleman Report (Coleman et al. 1966), whose result that between-school resource variation mattered little for explaining variation among individual students remains "the seminal finding in U.S. sociology of education" (Gamoran and Long 2007:23). This result has stimulated much debate about whether and how school resources matter in the United States (Greenwald, Hedges, and Laine 1996; Hanushek 1994, 1996; Hedges, Laine, and Greenwald 1994a, 1994b; e.g., see Murnane 1991; Wenglinsky 1997) and in other countries, both developing and industrialized (Baker, Goesling, and Letendre 2002; Gamoran and Long 2007; Heyneman and Loxley 1982; Heyneman 1975), with some evidence suggesting that school resources may explain more variation in student achievement in poor countries than in rich countries.

Yet, even in developing country settings where school resources are thought to matter more for student outcomes, it has been difficult for researchers to pin down specific resources that matter. Drawing on a systematic review of studies published between 1990 and 2010 in the education and economics literatures, Glewwe et al. (2011) sought to investigate which specific school and teacher characteristics appeared to have strong positive impacts on learning and time in school. The authors concluded, "The estimated impacts on time in school and learning of most school and teacher characteristics are statistically insignificant, especially when the evidence is limited to the 'high quality' studies. The few variables that do have significant effects—e.g. availability of desks, teacher knowledge of the subjects they teach, and teacher absence—are not particularly surprising and thus provide little guidance for future policies and programs."

Gamoran and Long (2007) have argued that it is critical to understand pathways of within-school inequality, and others have suggested that the organization or culture of schools or classrooms may be critical in shaping the experiences of poor children. Part of the story may be the different capacities and strategies available to poor and non-poor families to support their children's schooling. For example, qualitative research in the United States has indicated that the evaluative standards of school systems favor the nonpoor, meaning that school systems tend to engage with and evaluate favorably the intervention and child-rearing strategies of the middle class and the learning styles of their children (Lareau and Weininger 2003; Lareau 1987, 2000, 2011).

However, given the high degree of variability in achievement that occurs within schools and the difficulty of identifying specific resource variables in schools that can explain poverty effects on student achievement, it is not surprising that many studies have emerged that highlight the importance of deprivations in children's lives outside schools as a key contributor to socioeconomic achievement disparities. Ladd (2012:206–8) showed results from bivariate regressions suggesting that fully 40 percent of the state variation in reading scores and 46 percent of the state variation in math scores in the United States are associated with variation in child poverty rates. Ladd also presented results of state fixed-effect panel regressions, which account for long-standing state differences, and which show associations between changes in state child poverty rates and changes in test scores, especially for math. Reardon's (2011) work in the United States has also highlighted the importance of nonschool factors in the income gap in achievement: the national achievement gap was large when children entered kindergarten and did not appear to increase or decrease materially as children progressed through school. Another line of influential research in this vein is the "summer setback" literature, which showed that socioeconomic differences in learning tended to emerge in the summer, rather than during the school year (Downey, von Hippel, and Broh 2004; Entwisle and Alexander 1992; Heyns 1978).

In summary, unsurprisingly, household economic disadvantage, variously conceptualized and measured, is associated with poorer access to schools, poorer performance in schools, and poorer attainment. The patterns by which this relationship manifests vary by context, and the mechanisms—both within and outside schools—remain an active topic of research. Important directions for research include future work investigating the family-school relations and within-school practices and environments that lead to disparate outcomes in schools. There is also a need for research to further investigate the contextual factors experienced by poor children—constraints to physical health and psychological well-being—that make it difficult for them to receive full access to education.

IMPACT OF EDUCATION ON POVERTY

Education is widely viewed as an effective weapon against poverty. For example, Sen (e.g., 2013) has credited investments in education, along with other dimensions of human capital, as a key to China's economic success relative to India. More broadly, research has suggested that at the national level, under the right institutional conditions, an increase in overall levels of educational attainment can serve as an engine promoting economic growth (Goldin and Katz 2008). At the individual level, education functions as a channel of mobility that breaks the intergenerational influences of parental advantages or disadvantages (Yamaguchi 1983). Most of the research on the topic focuses on the impact of education on outcomes at the individual level, such labor outcomes as employment, occupational attainment, and income, and the odds of avoiding poverty in adulthood. We thus limit our review to the impact at the individual level.

Education and Individual Economic Outcomes

As we discussed earlier, poverty is commonly defined as a categorical status derived from measures of interval-measured economic well-being, using either an absolute or a relative threshold. Thus, determinants of economic well-being are also determinants of poverty. A large literature in economics and sociology has well documented the strong role of education in determining earnings and other measures of economic well-being (i.e., Brand and Xie 2010; Goldin and Katz 2008; Hout 2012; Krueger and Lindahl 2001; Mincer 1974; Psacharopoulos 1981). However, the actual rate of return to education may differ substantially by context. In a study of international comparisons, Psacharopoulos (1981:330) found the rate of return to one year of education to vary between 5.9 percent (for Canada) and 22.8 percent (for Malaysia). China had a very low return in the early years of its economic reform (at 2 percent in 1988), and it was almost doubled to 4 percent in 1995 (Hauser and Xie 2005). Overall, the rate of return tends to be higher in less developed countries than in more economically advanced countries (Psacharopoulos 1981) and is a positive function of the rate of economic growth (Chiswick 1971:28).

As recognized by Fischer and Hout (2006), education has become the single most important determinant for a whole host of social outcomes in a modern society. It affects not only earnings but also other important social outcomes such as marriage (Thornton et al. 2007), health (Link et al. 1998), subjective well-being (Dolan, Peasgood, and White 2008), and numerous other outcomes (Fischer and Hout 2006; for a review, see Hannum and Buchmann 2005). It is thus likely that education exerts, in addition to its direct effects, indirect effects that reduce poverty through many other pathways. For example, analyzing U.S. Current Population Survey data, Diprete and Buchmann (2006) find that the returns to higher education for women and men go beyond returns in the labor market, to include a higher standard of living and insurance against poverty.

Educational Interventions

Beyond studies drawing on observational data from surveys or censuses that investigate the links between years of education and various economic outcomes are a number of studies that have undertaken experiments to determine the impact of particular educational interventions. Prominent in recent years are studies of early childhood education interventions, driven by the concept of an early critical period in life for development, from which patterns of advantage and disadvantage accumulate. For example, Alderman and Vegas (2011:178) suggest that early childhood education programs can be viewed as a component of poverty-reduction and social-protection strategies (see also Engle et al. 2011 for a similar argument).

This argument can be made on the basis of many studies showing the short-term impact of interventions on development or educational performance, coupled with the cumulative nature of education, and its role in shaping employment and income opportunities. For example, Engle and her colleagues (Engle et al. 2007, 2011) have conducted systematic reviews of early childhood intervention programs. The 2007 review considered 35 studies of programs implemented in developing countries since 1990, of which 20 met inclusion criteria for rigor and showed evidence that early interventions promote child development outcomes (Engle et al. 2007). The 2011 review considered effectiveness trials and program assessments of parenting support and education, preprimary or preschool centers, conditional cash-transfer programs, educational media for children, and interventions for children at high risk. Results showed that parenting education and support can improve children's cognitive and psychosocial development, and that center-based early learning programs usually improve children's cognitive functioning, readiness for school, and school performance (Engle et al. 2011). In both kinds of interventions, Engle et al. report that effects are larger for children in more disadvantaged circumstances.

Given the challenge associated with obtaining long-term follow-up, there are fewer studies that have investigated directly the longer term educational or poverty impact of such programs. In a review of the literature that evaluated the effects of the Perry Preschool Program, a program combining half-day preschool intervention for four-year-olds with weekly home visits by preschool teachers, Yoshikawa and his colleagues (2012:280) found that the program resulted in higher earnings among program children as adults and reduced their likelihood of receiving welfare. Heckman and his colleagues (2013) recently reanalyzed the data from the Perry Preschool Program and concluded that the treatment benefits of the program came mainly from enhancing children's noncognitive skills instead of their cognitive skills.

Walker (2011: Table 4.1) summarizes U.S. early childhood intervention programs, including the Perry Preschool Program; the Abecedarian Project, in which 111 high-risk infants were randomly assigned to experimental or control groups and 104 were measured at age 21; the Chicago Child Parent Centre Project, a matched comparison of children attending intervention preschools and kindergarten with alternative kindergarten (no preschool), and with 1,389 of 1,539 followed up at age 24; the Nurse Home Visitation Program, in which 400 pregnant women enrolled and were randomly assigned to comparison, visits in pregnancy, or visits in pregnancy and up to age two, and in which 310 were followed up at age 19; and the Infant Health and Development Program, in which 985 low birth weight preterm infants in eight sites were randomized to intervention or follow-up only, and in which 636 were measured at age 18. Among these, all measured some form of educational attainment outcome, and the first three showed significant educational benefits. All but the last measured some form of income and employment, but only the Perry Preschool Program showed consistent, direct economic welfare effects.

In short, scholars have argued that the short-term impacts of early interventions coupled with the cumulative nature of education suggest that early interventions could be viewed as a tool for addressing intergenerational poverty transmission. More studies are needed to revisit sites of early childhood intervention to collect direct evidence of the long-term impact of early education on economic outcomes.

Synthesis: Dual Roles of Education in Modern Society

In summary, education is extremely important in modern society, both to the individual and to the society. For intergenerational transmission of economic advantages or disadvantages, including family poverty, education has dual roles. On the one hand, education is an agent of social stratification in that family economic background, such as poverty status, has a strong effect on a child's educational attainment. That is, the distribution of educational outcomes is unevenly distributed by family SES, severely disadvantaging children who grow up in poor families. On the other hand, education also serves as a social equalizer, as it provides a universalistic credential that is recognized and rewarded by a modern society. There is a substantial income payoff to investments in education; evidence suggests that the payoff is especially strong for those who traditionally complete low levels of schooling (Krueger and Lindahl 2001:1130). That is, even though persons from poor families face more difficulties in obtaining higher levels of education, they reap economic rewards when they do (Brand and Xie 2010). In other words, education is an effective way to avoid or to transition out of poverty. This dual role of education was succinctly summarized by Hauser (1971:144) in reference to the United States:

> [E]ducational attainment serves both to transmit the advantages or disadvantages of status of origin and to weaken the relationship between it and subsequent achievement. On the one hand, the most important way in which families influence the adult achievement of their offspring is by their effect on their children's educational attainment. On the other hand, privileged birth is no guarantee of high educational attainment: the rewards of education go to those who are educated, and for many persons of lowly origin educational attainment is the high road to success.

Although Hauser's statement was in reference to social stratification in the contemporary United States, we believe that it is applicable to most modern societies with a market economy.

DISCUSSION AND CONCLUSIONS

This chapter reviewed literature linking poverty to education and education to poverty, with the intention of synthesizing key findings and highlighting promising directions for future research. Focusing first at the macrolevel, we found surprisingly little theoretical or empirical literature linking national poverty rates or trends to educational expansion, opportunity, or achievement. The lack of attention to whether and how national poverty inhibits educational expansion, and whether and what kinds of educational expansion protect against national poverty are surprising omissions in the literature. This is especially so given the robust interest in the impact of other dimensions of national context and world system position on educational expansion, and given the degree of attention that has been paid to education for economic growth and other aspects of social development (Hannum and Buchmann 2005). The reasons for this lack of attention probably have to do with the complexity of teasing out cause and effect at the national level, versus community or family levels. However, from both the perspective of theory building about education for development and from the perspective of informing educational development policy, it is important to understand whether and how depth of national impoverishment matters. National poverty may simply signal aggregated economic disadvantages of households, communities, and school systems within countries. However, poverty and underdevelopment at the national level might imply disadvantages that do not simply represent aggregations of impoverished households and communities. Problems such as indebtedness, dependence on foreign aid and technical assistance, brain drain, violent conflict, and weak governance structures may shape both the capacity to invest in education and to reap returns on educational investments. The links in both directions between national poverty rates and educational provision are theoretically significant and policy relevant, and deserve further research.

At the mezzo level, literature on neighborhood poverty suggests the importance of investigating both direct effects of concentrated poverty on outcomes and mechanisms in the form of institutional resources; disorder, crime and violence; norms and collective efficacy; routine activity, and social ties and interactions; and environmental contamination (Bradley and Corwyn 2002; Leventhal and Brooks-Gunn 2000, 2003; Sampson et al. 2002; Sampson 2009). Frameworks linking community, household, and school contexts in the U.S. neighborhood effects literature exist, but these frameworks do not mesh well with the circumstances of rural community poverty that remain significant from a global perspective. The existing literature on community effects in developing countries does tend to focus on rural poverty, and this work has suggested the potential importance of community infrastructure, isolation, and distance to schools, school district teacher-pupil ratios, and community support for schooling (Cherng and Hannum 2013; Huisman and Smits 2009; Khandker 1996). However, this line of work remains fairly descriptive compared to the highly theorized urban neighborhood effects literature. Our understanding of community poverty would benefit from attention to theorizing community effects in ways that can accommodate both urbanized and rural settings in which poor children are educated around the world.

Moving to a household perspective, while there is agreement across many studies that household poverty or low socioeconomic status is linked to poorer educational outcomes, there is a continuing lack of agreement over the best approaches for defining and operationalizing childhood poverty in a manner that is parsimonious, feasible, and takes into account the multidimensional nature of poverty-related risk. However, lack of agreement about conceptualization and measurement of childhood poverty makes a synthesis of findings difficult and serves as a significant barrier to knowledge accumulation. Moreover, existing cross-national work on educational outcomes that does use common definitions of household poverty suggests that specific risks associated with household poverty vary across contexts; research also suggests that the impact of poverty on children may differ for children at different ages. Importantly, multiple developmental risks associated with poverty are likely to co-occur, and their impact could be additive or interactive (Grantham-McGregor et al. 2007; Walker et al. 2011). For example, impact of household poverty may also differ depending on community context, and vice versa. In addition, the poorest children may also be at risk for exposure to environmental toxins that impede development, with likely implications for educational readiness, performance, and behaviors (Walker et al. 2011); these exposures remain largely unexplored in the social science literature on childhood poverty. In short, a complicated task lies ahead in teasing out the impact of household poverty on children's education. In the words of Boyden and Cooper (2007:6), the "long-cherished premise that poverty can be ascertained according to uni-dimensional measures is increasingly contested and countered. Multidimensional definitions of poverty are now being advocated and accepted, thereby gradually moving away from definitions resting solely on income or consumption shortfall."

Finally, moving to the level of the child, a substantial subset of the exciting literature on the impact of early childhood interventions for poverty alleviation has focused on short-term effects on children's education, development, or behaviors, with the expectation that these effects should cumulate as children age. While such expectations are logical and plausible, there would be great value to additional studies that revisit participants in earlier interventions to directly observe their long-term economic impact.

Overall, to address the limitations described in this chapter and move forward theoretically, a multilevel framework for understanding the impact of poverty on children's education is needed. The framework needs to specify the underlying dimensions of poverty that might matter, in both households and communities, and their potential interactions. The framework needs to accommodate the possibility that impacts differ for children at different ages. Finally, it needs to accommodate the elements of national context that might buffer or exacerbate community and household poverty effects.

NOTES

1. Additional approaches not discussed here include subjective poverty, or falling below a subjective perception of "the amount of income it takes to barely get by," and asset poverty, defined as wealth minus debt (Yoshikawa, Aber, and Beardslee 2012:273).

2. For example, see Brady (2003) for a series of new measures of relative poverty targeting developed countries; for a discussion of conceptualizing poverty indicators in a social exclusion framework, see Marlier and Atkinson (2010).

3. For a summary, see Ladd's 2011 presidential address to the Association for Public Policy Studies and Management (Ladd 2012 [2011]).

4. For example, models presented are not set up to show gross effects of inequality or per capita GDP, and then effects net of potential mechanisms of impact. Because these measures have been included as control variables with many other control variables, their substantive significance is difficult to ascertain.

5. However, Valencia Lomelí (2008) also notes that the effectiveness of conditional cash-transfer programs for promoting learning is largely unknown: there is little evidence about whether conditional cash-transfer programs succeed in improving the academic achievement of the poor students who receive them.

References

Aber, J. Lawrence, Neil G. Bennett, Dalton C. Conley, and Jiali Li. 1997. "The Effects of Poverty on Child Health and Development." *Annual Review of Public Health* 18(1):463–83.

Adams, Jennifer H. 2006. "Community Matters in China," edited by Emily Hannum and Bruce Fuller. *Research in the Sociology of Education* 15:15–41.

Alderman, Harold, ed. 2011. *No Small Matter: The Impact of Poverty, Shocks, and Human Capital Investments in Early Childhood Development.* Washington, D.C.: World Bank Publications. Retrieved September 19, 2015 (http://dx.doi.org/10.1596/978-0-8213-8677-4).

Alderman, Harold and Emiliana Vegas. 2011. "The Convergence of Equity and Efficiency in ECD Programs." Pp. 155–76 in *No Small Matter: The Impact of Poverty, Shocks, and Human Capital Investments in Early Childhood Development*, edited by Harold Alderman. Washington, D.C.: World Bank Publications. Retrieved September 19, 2015 (http://dx.doi.org/10.1596/9780821386774_CH05).

Baker, D. P., B. Goesling, and G. K. Letendre. 2002. "Socioeconomic Status, School Quality, and National Economic Development: A Cross-National Analysis of the 'Heyneman-Loxley Effect' on Mathematics and Science Achievement." *Comparative Education Review* 46(3):291–312.

Becker, Gary S. 1964. *Human Capital: A Theoretical and Empirical Analysis, with Special Reference to Education.* New York: Columbia University Press.

Becker, Gary S. and Nigel Tomes. 1986. "Human Capital and the Rise and Fall of Families." *Journal of Labor Economics* 4(3):S1–39.

Bird, Kate. 2007. *The Intergenerational Transmission of Poverty: An Overview.* London: Overseas Development Institute. Retrieved June 8, 2012 (http://papers.ssrn.com/sol3/papers.cfm?abstract_id=1629262).

Borgeraas, Elling and Espen Dahl. 2010. "Low Income and 'Poverty Lines' in Norway: A Comparison of Three Concepts." *International Journal of Social Welfare* 19(1):73–83.

Bourdieu, Pierre. 1973. "Cultural Reproduction and Social Reproduction." Pp. 71–112 in *Knowledge, Education, and Cultural Change: Papers in the Sociology of Education*, edited by British Sociological Association and Richard K. Brown. London: Tavistock. Distributed in the U.S. by Harper & Row, Barnes & Noble Import Division.

Bourguignon, Francois. 2006. "From Income to Endowments: The Difficult Task of Expanding the Income Poverty Paradigm." Pp. 76–102 in *Poverty and Inequality*. Palo Alto, CA: Stanford University Press.

Bourguignon, Francois and Satya R. Chakravarty. 2003. "The Measurement of Multidimensional Poverty." *Journal of Economic Inequality* 1(1):25–49.

Boyden, Jo and Elizabeth Cooper. 2007. *Questioning the Power of Resilience: Are Children up to the Task of Disrupting the Transmission of Poverty?* London: Overseas Development Institute. Retrieved September 19, 2015 (http://dx.doi.org/10.2139/ssrn.1753009).

Bradley, Robert H. and Robert F. Corwyn. 2002. "Socioeconomic Status and Child Development." *Annual Review of Psychology* 53(1):371–99.

Brady, David. 2003. "Rethinking the Sociological Measurement of Poverty." *Social Forces* 81(3):715–51.

Brand, Jennie E. and Yu Xie. 2010. "Who Benefits Most from College? Evidence for Negative Selection in Heterogeneous Economic Returns to Higher Education." *American Sociological Review* 75(2):273–302.

Brooks-Gunn, Jeanne and Greg J. Duncan. 1997. "The Effects of Poverty on Children." *The Future of Children* 7(2):55–71.

Cascio, Elizabeth U. and Sarah Reber. 2013. "The Poverty Gap in School Spending Following the Introduction of Title I." *American Economic Review* 103(3):423–27.

Cherng, Hua-Yu Sebastian and Emily C. Hannum. 2013. "Community Poverty, Industrialization, and Educational Gender Gaps in Rural China." Gansu Survey of Children and Families Working Papers. Retrieved June 6, 2013 (http://repository.upenn.edu/gansu_papers/41/).

Chiswick, Barry R. 1971. "Earnings Inequality and Economic Development." *Quarterly Journal of Economics* 85(1):21–39.

Chiu, Ming Ming. 2007. "Families, Economies, Cultures, and Science Achievement in 41 Countries: Country-, School-, and Student-Level Analyses." *Journal of Family Psychology* 21(3):510–19.

Chiu, Ming Ming. 2010. "Effects of Inequality, Family and School on Mathematics Achievement: Country and Student Differences." *Social Forces* 88(4):1645–76.

Coleman, James S. et al. 1966. *Equality of Educational Opportunity: Summary Report*. U.S. Department of Health, Education, and Welfare, Office of Education.

Collins, Randall. 1979. *The Credential Society: An Historical Sociology of Education and Stratification*. New York: Academic Press.

Condron, Dennis J. 2011. "Egalitarianism and Educational Excellence: Compatible Goals for Affluent Societies?" *Educational Researcher* 40(2):47–55.

Condron, Dennis J. and Vincent J. Roscigno. 2003. "Disparities within: Unequal Spending and Achievement in an Urban School District." *Sociology of Education* 76:18–36.

David J. Harding. 2003. "Counterfactual Models of Neighborhood Effects: The Effect of Neighborhood Poverty on Dropping Out and Teenage Pregnancy." *American Journal of Sociology* 109(3):676–719.

Davidson, Shannon and Jennifer Adams. 2013. "Adversity and Internalizing Problems among Rural Chinese Adolescents: The Roles of Parents and Teachers." *International Journal of Behavioral Development* 37(6):530–41.

Davis, James A. 1980. "Conservative Weather in a Liberalizing Climate: Change in Selected NORC General Social Survey Items, 1972–78." *Social Forces* 58(4):1129–56.

De Walque, Damien. 2011. "Conflicts, Epidemics, and Orphanhood: The Impact of Extreme Events on the Health and Educational Achievements of Children." Pp. 85–113 in *No Small*

Matter: The Impact of Poverty, Shocks, and Human Capital Investments in Early Childhood Development, edited by Harold Alderman. Washington, D.C.: World Bank Publications. Retrieved September 19, 2015 (http://dx.doi.org/10.1596/9780821386774_CH03).

Dercon, S. 2012. "Understanding Child Poverty in Developing Countries: Measurement and Analysis." Pp. 52–72 in *Childhood Poverty: Multidisciplinary Approaches*, edited by J. Boyden and M. Bourdillon. New York: Palgrave Macmillan.

DiPrete, Thomas A. and Claudia Buchmann. 2006. "Gender-Specific Trends in the Value of Education and the Emerging Gender Gap in College Completion." *Demography* 43(1):1–24.

Dolan, Paul, Tessa Peasgood, and Mathew White. 2008. "Do We Really Know What Makes Us Happy? A Review of the Economic Literature on the Factors Associated with Subjective Well-Being." *Journal of Economic Psychology* 29(1):94–122.

Downey, Douglas B., Paul T. von Hippel, and Beckett A. Broh. 2004. "Are Schools the Great Equalizer? Cognitive Inequality during the Summer Months and the School Year." *American Sociological Review* 69(5):613–35.

Duncan, Otis Dudley. 1961. "A Socio-Economic Index for All Occupations." Pp. 109–38 in *Occupations and Social Status*, edited by Albert J. Reiss. New York: Free Press.

Engle, Patrice L. 2012. "Poverty and Developmental Potential." Pp. 129–47 in *Childhood Poverty: Multidisciplinary Approaches*, edited by J. Boyden and M. Bourdillon. New York: Palgrave Macmillan.

Engle, Patrice L. and Maureen M. Black. 2008. "The Effect of Poverty on Child Development and Educational Outcomes." *Annals of the New York Academy of Sciences* 1136(1):243–56.

Engle, Patrice L. et al. 2007. "Strategies to Avoid the Loss of Developmental Potential in More than 200 Million Children in the Developing World." *The Lancet* 369(9557):229–42.

Engle, Patrice L. et al. 2011. "Strategies for Reducing Inequalities and Improving Developmental Outcomes for Young Children in Low-Income and Middle-Income Countries." *The Lancet* 378(9799):1339–53.

Entwisle, Doris R. and Karl L. Alexander. 1992. "Summer Setback: Race, Poverty, School Composition, and Mathematics Achievement in the First Two Years of School." *American Sociological Review* 57(1):72–84.

Filmer, Deon and Lant Pritchett. 1999. "The Effect of Household Wealth on Educational Attainment: Evidence from 35 Countries." *Population and Development Review* 25(1):85–120.

Filmer, Deon and Lant H. Pritchett. 2001. "Estimating Wealth Effects without Expenditure Data—or Tears: An Application to Educational Enrollments in States of India." *Demography* 38(1):115–32.

Fischer, Claude S. and Michael Hout. 2006. *Century of Difference: How America Changed in the Last One Hundred Years*. New York: Russell Sage Foundation.

Foster, James E. 1998. "Absolute versus Relative Poverty." *American Economic Review* 88(2):335–41.

Foster, James, Joel Greer, and Erik Thorbecke. 1984. "A Class of Decomposable Poverty Measures." *Econometrica* 52(3):761–66.

Gamoran, Adam and Daniel A. Long. 2007. "Equality of Educational Opportunity: A 40-Year Retrospective." Pp. 23–47 in *International Studies in Educational Inequality, Theory and Policy*, edited by Richard Teese, Stephen Lamb, Marie Duru-Bellat, and Sue Helme. Amsterdam: Springer Netherlands. Retrieved September 19, 2015 (http://dx.doi.org/10.1007/978-1-4020-5916-2_2).

Gershoff, Elizabeth T., J. Lawrence Aber, C. Cybele Raver, and Mary Clare Lennon. 2007. "Income Is Not Enough: Incorporating Material Hardship into Models of Income Associations with Parenting and Child Development." *Child Development* 78(1):70–95.

Glewwe, Paul W., Eric A. Hanushek, Sarah D. Humpage, and Renato Ravina. 2011. *School Resources and Educational Outcomes in Developing Countries: A Review of the Literature from 1990 to 2010*. National Bureau of Economic Research. Retrieved September 19, 2015 (http://www.nber.org/papers/w17554).

Goldin, Claudia Dale and Lawrence F. Katz. 2008. *The Race between Education and Technology*. Cambridge, MA: Harvard University Press.

Grantham-McGregor, Sally et al. 2007. "Developmental Potential in the First 5 Years for Children in Developing Countries." *The Lancet* 369(9555):60–70.

Greenwald, Rob, Larry V. Hedges, and Richard D. Laine. 1996. "The Effect of School Resources on Student Achievement." *Review of Educational Research* 66(3):361–96.

Grusky, David B. and Ravi Kanbur. 2006. "The Conceptual Foundations of Poverty and Inequality Measurement." Pp. 1–29 in *Poverty and Inequality*, edited by David B. Grusky and Ravi Kanbur. Stanford, CA: Stanford University Press.

Guo, Guang. 1998. "The Timing of the Influences of Cumulative Poverty on Children's Cognitive Ability and Achievement." *Social Forces* 77(1):257–87.

Hannum, Emily and Jennifer Adams. 2008. "Beyond Cost: Rural Perspectives on Barriers to Education." Pp. 156–71 in *Creating Wealth and Poverty in China*, edited by Deborah Davis and Feng Wang. Stanford, CA: Stanford University Press. Retrieved September 19, 2015 (http://repository.upenn.edu/cgi/viewcontent.cgi?article=1006&context=gansu_papers).

Hannum, Emily and Claudia Buchmann. 2005. "Global Educational Expansion and Socio-Economic Development: An Assessment of Findings from the Social Sciences." *World Development* 33(3):333–54.

Hannum, Emily, Jihong Liu, and Edward A. Frongillo. 2014. "Poverty, Food Insecurity and Nutritional Deprivation in Rural China: Implications for Children's Literacy Achievement." *International Journal of Educational Development* 34:90–97.

Hannum, Emily and Yuping Zhang. 2012. "Poverty and Proximate Barriers to Learning: Vision Deficiencies, Vision Correction and Educational Outcomes in Rural Northwest China." *World Development* 40(9):1921–31.

Hanushek, Eric A. 1996. "School Resources and Student Performance." Pp. 43–73 in *Does Money Matter*, edited by Gary T. Burtless. Washington, DC: Brookings Institution Press.

Hanushek, Eric A. 1994. "Money Might Matter Somewhere: A Response to Hedges, Laine, and Greenwald." *Educational Researcher* 23(4):5–8.

Hanushek, Eric A. and Ludger Woessmann. 2011. "The Economics of International Differences in Educational Achievement." Pp. 89–200 in *Handbook of the Economics of Education*, vol. 3, edited by Eric A. Hanushek, Stephen Machin, and Ludger Woessmann. Amsterdam; London: Elsevier. Retrieved September 19, 2015 (http://www.sciencedirect.com/science/article/pii/B9780444534293000028).

Harding, David J., Lisa Gennetian, Christopher Winship, Lisa Sanbonmatsu, and Jeffrey R. Kling. 2010. *Unpacking Neighborhood Influences on Education Outcomes: Setting the Stage for Future Research*. National Bureau of Economic Research. Retrieved September 19, 2015 (http://www.nber.org/papers/w16055).

Hauser, Robert M. and John Robert Warren. 1997. "Socioeconomic Indexes for Occupations: A Review, Update, and Critique." *Sociological Methodology* 27(1):177–298.

Hauser, Robert Mason. 1971. *Socioeconomic Background and Educational Performance*. Washington, DC: American Sociological Association.

Hauser, Seth M. and Yu Xie. 2005. "Temporal and Regional Variation in Earnings Inequality: Urban China in Transition between 1988 and 1995." *Social Science Research* 34(1):44–79.

Heckman, James, Rodrigo Pinto, and Peter Savelyev. 2013. "Understanding the Mechanisms Through Which an Influential Early Childhood Program Boosted Adult Outcomes." *American Economic Review* 103(6):2052–86.

Hedges, Larry V. Richard D. Laine, and Rob Greenwald. 1994a. "An Exchange: Part I: Does Money Matter? A Meta-Analysis of Studies of the Effects of Differential School Inputs on Student Outcomes." *Educational Researcher* 23(3):5–14.

Hedges, Larry V., Richard D. Laine, and Rob Greenwald. 1994b. "Money Does Matter Somewhere: A Reply to Hanushek." *Educational Researcher* 23(4):9–10.

Heyneman, Stephen P. 1975. *Influences on Academic Achievement in Uganda: A "Coleman Report" from a Non-Industrial Society*. Chicago: University of Chicago.

Heyneman, Stephen P. and William A. Loxley. 1982. "Influences on Academic Achievement across High and Low Income Countries: A Re-Analysis of IEA Data." *Sociology of Education* 55(1):13–21.

Heyns, Barbara. 1978. *Summer Learning and the Effects of Schooling*. New York: Academic Press.

Hout, Michael. 2012. "Social and Economic Returns to College Education in the United States." *Annual Review of Sociology* 38(1):379–400.

Huisman, Janine and Jeroen Smits. 2009. "Effects of Household- and District-Level Factors on Primary School Enrollment in 30 Developing Countries." *World Development* 37(1):179–93.

Huston, Aletha C. and Alison C. Bentley. 2010. "Human Development in Societal Context." *Annual Review of Psychology* 61:411–37.

Khandker, Shahidur R. 1996. *Education Achievements and School Efficiency in Rural Bangladesh*. Washington, D.C: World Bank. Retrieved September 19, 2015 (http://elibrary. worldbank.org/doi/book/10.1596/0-8213-3593-6).

Krueger, Alan B. and Mikael Lindahl. 2001. "Education for Growth: Why and for Whom?" *Journal of Economic Literature* 39(4):1101–36.

Ladd, Helen F. 2012. "Education and Poverty: Confronting the Evidence." *Journal of Policy Analysis and Management* 31(2):203–27.

Lareau, Annette. 1987. "Social Class Differences in Family-School Relationships: The Importance of Cultural Capital." *Sociology of Education* 60(2):73–85.

Lareau, Annette. 2000. *Home Advantage: Social Class and Parental Intervention in Elementary Education*. 2nd ed. Lanham, Md: Rowman & Littlefield.

Lareau, Annette. 2011. *Unequal Childhoods: Class, Race, and Family Life*. Berkeley: University of California Press.

Lareau, Annette and Elliot B. Weininger. 2003. "Cultural Capital in Educational Research: A Critical Assessment." *Theory and Society* 32(5):567–606.

Leventhal, Tama and Jeanne Brooks-Gunn. 2000. "The Neighborhoods They Live in: The Effects of Neighborhood Residence on Child and Adolescent Outcomes." *Psychological Bulletin* 126(2):309–37.

Leventhal, Tama and Jeanne Brooks-Gunn. 2003. "Children and Youth in Neighborhood Contexts." *Current Directions in Psychological Science* 12(1):27–31.

Leventhal, Tama and Jeanne Brooks-Gunn. 2004. "A Randomized Study of Neighborhood Effects on Low-Income Children's Educational Outcomes." *Developmental Psychology* 40(4):488.

Link, Bruce G., Mary E. Northridge, Jo C. Phelan, and Michael L. Ganz. 1998. "Social Epidemiology and the Fundamental Cause Concept: On the Structuring of Effective Cancer Screens by Socioeconomic Status." *Milbank Quarterly* 76(3):375–402.

Marlier, Eric and A. B. Atkinson. 2010. "Indicators of Poverty and Social Exclusion in a Global Context." *Journal of Policy Analysis and Management* 29(2):285–304.

Meyer, John W., Francisco O. Ramirez, Richard Rubinson, and John Boli-Bennett. 1977. "The World Educational Revolution, 1950–1970." *Sociology of Education* 50(4):242–58.

Meyer, John W., Francisco O. Ramirez, and Yasemin Nuhoglu Soysal. 1992. "World Expansion of Mass Education, 1870–1980." *Sociology of Education* 65(2):128–49.

Mincer, Jacob A. 1974. "Schooling and Earnings." Pp. 41–63 in *Schooling, Experience, and Earnings*. New York: Columbia University Press.

Murnane, Richard J. 1991. "Interpreting the Evidence on Does Money Matter." *Harvard Journal on Legislation* 28:457.

Murnane, Richard J. 2007. "Improving the Education of Children Living in Poverty." *The Future of Children* 17(2):161–82.

Naudeau, Sophie, Sebastian Martinez, Patrick Premand, and Deon Filmer. 2011. "Cognitive Development among Young Children in Low-Income Countries." Pp. 9–50 in *No Small Matter: The Impact of Poverty, Shocks, and Human Capital Investments in Early Childhood Development, Human Development Perspectives*. Washington, D.C.: World Bank Publications. Retrieved September 19, 2015 (http://dx.doi.org/10.1596/9780821386774_CH01).

Nussbaum, Martha M. 2006. "Poverty and Human Functioning: Capabilities as Fundamental Entitlements." Pp. 47–75 in *Poverty and Inequality*, edited by David B. Grusky and Ravi Kanbur. Stanford, CA: Stanford University Press.

Pritchett, Lant. 2001. "Where Has All the Education Gone?" *World Bank Economic Review* 15(3):367–91.

Psacharopoulos, George. 1981. "Returns to Education: An Updated International Comparison." *Comparative Education* 17(3):321–41.

Reardon, Sean F. 2011. "The Widening Academic Achievement Gap between the Rich and the Poor: New Evidence and Possible Explanations." Pp. 91–116 in *Whither Opportunity? Rising Inequality, Schools, and Children's Life Chances*, edited by Greg J. Duncan and Richard J. Murnane. New York: Russell Sage Foundation Publications.

Sampson, Robert J. 2009. "Racial Stratification and the Durable Tangle of Neighborhood Inequality." *Annals of the American Academy of Political and Social Science* 621(1):260–80.

Sampson, Robert J., Jeffrey D. Morenoff, and Thomas Gannon-Rowley. 2002. "Assessing 'Neighborhood Effects': Social Processes and New Directions in Research." *Annual Review of Sociology* 28(1):443–78.

Schofer, Evan and John W. Meyer. 2005. "The Worldwide Expansion of Higher Education in the Twentieth Century." *American Sociological Review* 70(6):898–920.

Schütz, Gabriela, Heinrich W. Ursprung, and Ludger Woessmann. 2008. "Education Policy and Equality of Opportunity." *Kyklos* 61(2):279–308.

Sen, Amartya. 1999. *Commodities and Capabilities*. Delhi, NY: Oxford University Press.

Sen, Amartya. 2006. "Conceptualizing and Measuring Poverty." Pp. 30–46 in *Poverty and Inequality*, edited by David B. Grusky and Ravi Kanbur. Stanford, CA: Stanford University Press.

Sen, Amartya. 2013. "Why India Trails China." *New York Times*. Retrieved June 19, 2014 (http://www.nytimes.com/2013/06/20/opinion/why-india-trails-china.html).

Thorbecke, Erik. 2005. *Multidimensional Poverty: Conceptual and Measurement Issues*. Brasilia: UNDP International Poverty Centre International Conference on "The Many Dimensions of Poverty," August 29–31. Retrieved September 19, 2015 (http://econweb.arts.cornell.edu/et17/Erik%20Thorbecke%20files/Multi1.pdf).

Thornton, Arland, William G. Axinn, and Yu Xie. 2007. *Marriage and Cohabitation*. Chicago: University of Chicago Press.

Treiman, Donald J. 1977. *Occupational Prestige in Comparative Perspective*. New York: Academic Press.

Valencia Lomelí, Enrique. 2008. "Conditional Cash Transfers as Social Policy in Latin America: An Assessment of Their Contributions and Limitations." *Annual Review of Sociology* 34(1):475–99.

Walker, Susan. 2011. "Promoting Equity through Early Child Development Interventions for Children from Birth through Three Years of Age." Pp. 115–54 in *The Impact of Poverty, Shocks, and Human Capital Investment in Early Childhood Development*, edited by Harold Alderman. Washington DC: The World Bank. Retrieved September 19, 2015 (http://dx.doi.org/10.1596/9780821386774_CH04).

Walker, Susan P. et al. 2011. "Inequality in Early Childhood: Risk and Protective Factors for Early Child Development." *The Lancet* 378(9799):1325–38.

Weeden, Kim A. and David B. Grusky. 2005. "The Case for a New Class Map." *American Journal of Sociology* 111(1):141–212.

Wenglinsky, Harold. 1997. "How Money Matters: The Effect of School District Spending on Academic Achievement." *Sociology of Education* 70(3):221–37.

Wilson, William J. 1987. *The Truly Disadvantaged: The Inner City, the Underclass, and Public Policy*. Chicago: University of Chicago Press.

Wilson, William J. 2006. "Social Theory and the Concept 'Underclass.'" Pp. 103–16 in *Poverty and Inequality*. Palo Alto, CA: Stanford University Press.

Wodtke, Geoffrey T., David J. Harding, and Felix Elwert. 2011. "Neighborhood Effects in Temporal Perspective: The Impact of Long-Term Exposure to Concentrated Disadvantage on High School Graduation." *American Sociological Review* 76(5):713–36.

World Bank. 2011. "Poverty Analysis—Measuring Poverty." *Poverty Reduction and Equity*. Retrieved February 28, 2013 (http://go.worldbank.org/0C60K5UK40).

Yamaguchi, Kazuo. 1983. "The Structure of Intergenerational Occupational Mobility: Generality and Specificity in Resources, Channels, and Barriers." *American Journal of Sociology* 88(4):718–45.

Yoshikawa, Hirokazu, J. Lawrence Aber, and William R. Beardslee. 2012. "The Effects of Poverty on the Mental, Emotional, and Behavioral Health of Children and Youth: Implications for Prevention." *American Psychologist* 67(4):272–84.

Yu, Shengchao and Emily Hannum. 2007. "Food for Thought: Poverty, Family Nutritional Environment, and Children's Educational Performance in Rural China." *Sociological Perspectives* 50(1):53–77.

Zhou, Lei and Frank Johnson. 2010. *Revenues and Expenditures for Public Elementary and Secondary Education: School Year 2007–08 (Fiscal Year 2008)*. Washington, DC: Department of Education. Retrieved September 9, 2014 (http://nces.ed.gov/pubs2010/2010326.pdf).

CHAPTER 21

···

EMPLOYMENT AND THE WORKING POOR

···

JÉRÔME GAUTIÉ AND SOPHIE PONTHIEUX

In a worldwide perspective, working poverty may appear as a widespread phenomenon. In 2010, about 942 million workers aged 15 years and older were living with their families on less than $2 per person per day—the poverty line defined by the World Bank—that is, nearly one in three workers worldwide (ILO 2011). Among them, more than a half (an estimated 476 millions) lived on less than $1.25, the extreme poverty threshold. It is worth noting, symmetrically, that among all persons aged 15 and older leaving in poverty, about 60 percent were considered employed according to the International Labour Office (ILO) definition. Extreme working poverty remains largely a rural phenomenon, as about 80 percent of poor workers under the $1.25 poverty line lived in rural areas, employed for most of them in the low-productivity subsistence agricultural sector. Another important feature of working poverty is that poor workers lived in families with significantly higher number of dependant nonworkers (3.6 against 2.1 for nonpoor workers). Countries with the highest share of agriculture, and which have not yet made their demographic transition, have the highest share of working poor. Overall, the issue of working poverty is, in a way, just a dimension of the more global economic development issue (see Chapter 22 in this *Handbook*).

In industrialized countries (notably OECD countries) there are almost no working poor if one refers to the World Bank absolute poverty thresholds. Still, it is in those countries that working poverty has been construed as a specific social issue, introducing both a paradox and a challenge.

The paradox derives from the fact that in wealthy countries, according to a widely shared view, work—or more precisely, employment, which refers to the social and legal status attached to the work activity—should allow one to avoid poverty. Poverty should become a residual phenomenon restricted to persons out-of-work, supported, under some conditions, by social assistance. One has to remember that in the early stages of industrialization, in particular during the nineteenth century, the association between work and poverty was, on the contrary, a "normal" situation. According to the "iron law of wages"—an expression usually attributed to the German philosopher and socialist political activist Ferdinand Lassalle—real wages were stuck at the subsistence level, any increase above this level induces an increase in the labor supply, following Malthus's demographic theory, and a subsequent wage decline. Even if Karl Marx was critical of this alleged law, he also contributed to the strong association in social representations between (manufacturing) work and poverty, referring, not without ambiguity, to the "pauperization" of the working class—the so-called proletarians. It is only at the end of the nineteenth century that the virtuous circle between productivity and real wage increases became more evident, even if the significant increase in workers' standard of living was to come later. Henry Ford's introduction of a "five dollars a day" on the eve of World War II was a first step. Far beyond its anecdotal appearance, it is the best illustration of the emergence of "welfare capitalism" in the American context, which relied on the will of big manufacturers to create the loyal and productive workforce they needed for their development. This workforce was conceived—in particular by Ford himself—as mainly male. The "male breadwinner" model is a correlative of the affluent worker. The second decisive step was the introduction of welfare states along with full-employment policies—what could be coined as the Beveridgian paradigm—the two reports of British social scientist and politician William Beveridge issued during World War II (Beveridge 1942, 1944) giving maybe the best formulation of the new underpinnings of advanced industrialized democracies—with, of course, important national diversity. In modern welfare state democracies, "unemployment" became the key issue, and therefore full employment was defined as the highest priority for public economic policy. Poverty was then considered explicitly mainly as a risk deriving from non-employment, whether temporary (because of sickness, workplace accident, etc.) or permanent (old age, incapacity). Social insurance and social assistance where therefore conceived as complements to "employment"—employment being the best route out of poverty.

The view that "most of the poor do not work" (Mead 1993:ix) prevailed in OECD countries until the early 1990s. But growing empirical evidence put in light that working poverty had not disappeared and seemed even to increase in many nowadays "postindustrialized" economies. This constitutes a real challenge for both social scientists and policymakers.

The chapter is structured in two sections. The first is dedicated to definition and measurement issues, which are not only technical: the diversity of statistical definitions of working poverty reflects national specificities in the labor market functioning and social protection systems, and beyond, reveals also how the issue is shaped by political and social representations. The second section assesses the factors impacting working poverty—both at individual and household levels—and its potential remedies in terms of public policies, insisting also on the importance of national contexts.

The Working Poor: Definition and Measurement Issues

Overview of the Problems of Definition

While the "working poor" may be quite easily described as a person who is a worker and who is poor, there is a long way from the "obviousness" of the notion to an operational definition—that is, one that can be used to measure the extent of the problem. Working poverty being at the intersection of "work" and "poverty," an operational definition necessarily depends on the criteria used to define each of these terms.

What Does "Poor" Mean?

Poverty may be approached in various ways (for an overview: Atkinson 1998; see also Chapters 2 and 4), but statistical approaches are basically interested in defining a threshold or a line that can be used to divide a population into the poor and nonpoor. This division can rely on "objective" approaches (monetary poverty, material deprivations) or subjective approaches (perceptions). Working poverty statistics are almost always implemented as monetary poverty (an exception can be found in Airio 2008, who compares different poverty measures over European countries).

There are in turn two main ways to measure monetary poverty.

- The first one consists in evaluating the income families need to cover the costs of living, *that is,* shelter, food, clothing, and basic needs; this is the so-called absolute approach, used in the United States to define the poverty line in the 1960s in the context of the War on Poverty. The income needed was adjusted for different types of families, and the amount defined in this way at the time has been updated annually using the Consumer Price Index. It has been widely discussed and criticized in the past decades for drawing a very low the poverty line (see Short 2011), and various alternative measures have been implemented (see e.g., Dalaker 2005; Citro and Michael 1995; Iceland 2000 for an application to working poverty).
- The second one, the "relative approach," considers poverty as not being able to live a "normal life" considering regional and contemporary prevailing standards. In this approach, poverty is identified by comparing a household income level with the general income level, then depends on the income distribution. More precisely, the poverty threshold is defined as a percentage of the median income, equivalized using a weighting (an equivalence scale) that allows taking into account the size and composition of the households. This is the method implemented for European statistics (see Atkinson et al. 2002). Since the beginning of the 2000s, the threshold is set at 60 percent of the median equivalized income (it was 50 percent previously), and the equivalence scale (OECD-modified scale) counts the first adult in a household with a weight of 1, the next

adults with a weight of 0.5 each, and children (less than 14 years old) with a weight of 0.3. This approach, as well as the way it is implemented, is not without critics: for the relative approach itself, the main objection is that it is more of an indicator of inequalities at the bottom of the income distribution than an indicator of absolute deprivation. Moreover, even if incomes and standards of living increase significantly, poverty will not disappear or even decrease as long as the income distribution remains unchanged. Concerning the implementation, most critics are concerned with the measurement of income, which can be imprecise, and the equivalence scale. Another line of criticism is the difficulty of using such a definition for cross-country comparisons because the poverty rates do not reflect the differences between national income levels—as illustrated by the low poverty rates of some of the most recent EU member states from Central and Eastern Europe.

To finish with differences between the American and European approaches to monetary poverty, a last one is worth underlining: official figures include social transfers net of social contributions and taxes on income in Europe while they are computed pretax pretransfer in the United States.

What Does "Worker" Mean?

In addition to the different approaches to poverty, a particular problem is that there is no official or generally agreed definition of "a worker:" Is it someone actually working, or someone whose "normal" situation is (or should be) to be employed, therefore all the "suppliers" in the labor market—that is, the whole labor force? But there is one constraint: to be operational, a statistical approach to working poverty requires a consistent period of observation for "work" and for poverty. Since monetary poverty is assessed on the basis of annual incomes, the operational definition must use an approach to work based on individuals yearly activity or employment status. This discards the widely used ILO categories (employment, unemployment, inactivity), which are based on a person's status during the week before data collection.

But moreover, to get an operational definition, one needs to define the amount of time spent in the labor market and/or in employment required to qualify as "a worker." This is where the main statistical approaches diverge.

The Diversity of Definitions and Its Consequences

Different Current Definitions of the Statistical Category "Working Poor"

It would be an exaggeration to say that there are as many definitions of the working poor as studies on the working poor, but there are many of them (see e.g., Peña-Casas and Latta 2004; updated in Crettaz and Bonoli 2011). We will focus on the two "official" statistical approaches: the one implemented by the Bureau of Labor Statistics (BLS) for the United States, and the one implemented by Eurostat for the European Union.

The first statistical implementation of the notion of working poor was proposed in the United States by the BLS at the end of the 1980s. In the statistics and analysis published by the BLS on the working poor, workers are defined as individuals who have participated in the labor market for at least half of a reference period of one year (i.e., 27 weeks or more), either employed or unemployed (cf. Klein and Rones 1989). It is not a "positive" definition: as the authors make clear, this threshold of half a year is arbitrary, used only to discard those who are only marginally active.

In the European Union, the approach takes a different turn, obvious even in the labeling of the phenomenon, which is not "working poverty" but "in-work poverty," an indicator introduced in 2005 in the European portfolio of social indicators (European Commission 2009). Here, workers are defined as individuals who have spent at least seven months in employment during the reference period. So there is a profound difference between the two main approaches, one relying on a norm of participation in the labor market, the other relying on a norm of employment.

How to account for this diversity? It shows how a question that appears to be the same may actually refer to different construed social problems in different national contexts and political conceptions. In the United States, the absence of any explicit employment record criterion to define a "worker" results from the more or less explicit assumption that an individual who was in the labor market for at least six months must have been employed at least during a certain period. At the same time, the poor constitute the population of interest, and the need to distinguish between the poor rather than between workers might result from a long-term view of poverty due to lack of work. The issue of working poverty actually appeared in a context about whether the poor were willing to work—a recurring issue in the United States, along with the risk of discouraging them from working or helping the wrong people—that is, those who do not deserve assistance because they do not try hard enough (Danziger and Gottschalk 1995:12). The focus of these studies was therefore not, it is worth underlining, workers' poverty. This is a significant difference in perspective than the European approach. In Europe, long-term unemployment and (involuntary) unemployment, and working poverty are considered separate problems. Underlying the Eurostat definition, the basic question is more explicit: Does work protect one from poverty (or: does it pay enough to work)? "Workers in-work" are the population of interest. This is also coherent with the focus on "job quality," which is one of the agendas of the "European employment strategy" defined at the European level.

The Impact of Definitions on Assessing the In-work Poverty Phenomenon

The definitions of poverty (poverty line) and work (quantity of work required to qualify as a worker) have necessarily a big impact on the measured level of working poverty. The magnitude of the problem is then very difficult to compare across countries: if

we stick with the two main approaches described, the European and American poverty rates of workers may differ because of the American lower (absolute) poverty line
and because of the European stricter definition of "workers." Moreover, depending on
the definition, not only the magnitude but also the scope of working poverty and its
explaining factors—labor market factors (unemployment, low pay, part-time jobs, self-
employment, etc.) and family factors (dependent children, single-parent families, etc.)
may diverge (see the section "The Determinants of Working Poverty") For instance,
Eurostat's strict employment criterion (i.e., only those who have worked at least seven
months in a year are considered workers) results in a lower impact of unemployment
and "employment precariousness" on working poverty, since many workers with low
employment records during the year of reference are excluded. It therefore induces at the
same time a greater contribution of family factors (versus labor market factors). Another
consequence is that the population of working poor may decline when unemployment
increases, whereas it tends to be the opposite when the U.S. definition is adopted.

The impact of changing the definition of workers can be illustrated by comparing
the poverty rates of workers and labor market characteristics of the working poor using
different definitions, as in Ponthieux (2010:311–16), for a sample of countries in the
European Union. The comparison shows that using the strict Eurostat definition rather
than the more encompassing BLS definition can divide the number of working poor
almost by two in some countries and the poverty rate of workers by as much as 1.5
(this is the case for Germany and France, for instance). As for the composition of the
working-poor population, moving from the BLS definition to the Eurostat definition
causes an increase in the number of workers who are steadily employed, and significant
changes in the shares of low-paid employment, part-time work, and self-employment.
Using one or the other definition also results in changing the working poor's household
structure, especially the number of one-person households and families with children.
Of course, the impact of changing the definition is not of the same magnitude for all
countries, depending on labor market conditions, institutions, employment policies,
social transfers, and gender (in)equality.

The sensitivity to the definition can also be illustrated by comparing the poverty
rate of U.S. workers in the mid-2000s in the BLS "Profile of the Working Poor" and in
the dedicated chapter of the OECD "Employment Outlook": about 5 percent according to the BLS (2005), versus about 12 percent according to the OECD (2009:180). In
this example, *all* the components of the definition are different: the BLS applies the
official poverty line and defines workers as people who were in the labor force for at
least 27 weeks; the OECD uses a relative poverty threshold (50 percent of the median
equivalized income) and defines workers as people who have a job.

Another issue, independent from the definition of workers adopted, is the "hybrid"
nature of the statistical category, as it mixes elements from both individual and household levels. While workers are identified on the basis of their individual characteristics
of activity, the same is not true of the identification of poor individuals, based on income
variables measured at the household level, under the assumption of income pooling
and equal sharing within households. In consequence, all the members of the same

household are poor or not poor. The "working poor" are then statistically a combination of "working individuals" and "poor households." This would not be a problem if the population of interest were the poor, and the question was to assess whether they are employed or participating in the labor market. But the population of interest is that of workers, and the aim is to analyze the relationship between their economic activity and their poverty. The double-level construction of the category makes it quite difficult to analyze, since the same individual economic activity may or may not result in poverty, depending on family configurations—themselves determining many social transfers.

This complexity has been acknowledged for a long time as placing a specific constraint on the analysis of the phenomenon (cf. Danziger and Gottschalk 1986). As a consequence, a working-poor individual's poverty cannot be directly linked to their individual economic activity, and a significant proportion of individuals in unfavorable situations of activity do not appear as working poor. It results in a particular paradox when it comes to gendered analysis: while women are highly overrepresented among low-wage workers and, on average, more generally benefit from less favorable labor market characteristics than men, which results in lower earnings, they are not, when considered as a whole, especially overrepresented among the working poor (discussed later in the chapter). More generally, the link between work and poverty, blurred by the household effect, becomes difficult to interpret at the individual level. This is especially a problem for the European approach focused on the "does work pay enough" issue. It also limits the scope of cross-country comparisons because working poverty can be driven more or less by market factors or by the households' structure. Ideally, one would want to assess poverty on the basis of individual well-being, but a methodology remains to be found.

The Working Poor: A Brief Statistical Portrait and Evolutions

Who are the working poor? In order to avoid misleading comparisons, the "statistical" portrait proposed here, limited to (post)industrialized countries, will actually not display figures but rather characterize the populations in terms of over- or underrepresentation. The portrait drawn here is based on the most recent available descriptive statistics from the BLS's "Profile of the Working Poor" (2012), the European Commission's "Employment and Social Developments in Europe" (2011: Chapter 4), and the OECD's "Employment Outlook" (2009: Chapter 3). However, working poverty characteristics are mostly time invariant (see for instance Cummings 1965), hence, using any descriptive statistics from the 1980s would change the numbers but not dramatically change the picture.

Starting with demographic characteristics, all descriptive statistics show that single persons and persons living with dependent children, especially single parents (most often mothers) are significantly overrepresented among the working poor. More generally, individuals who are the only earner in their household, especially women, face higher risks of working poverty. However, in most countries, men tend to be overrepresented in the population of working poor. No clear pattern emerges in terms of age: this may be a consequence of the fact that younger workers often cohabit with their parents, hence their lower status in the labor market or employment may not show due to the fact that poverty is assessed at the household—not individual—level. As for ethnic origin, this dimension is rarely taken into account in European statistics, but it matters significantly in the United States, where Blacks and Hispanics face a much higher risk of being working and poor than whites and Asians. Individuals with low educational attainment are generally overrepresented, hence, not surprisingly, low-skilled jobs also tend to be overrepresented.

In terms of labor market and employment status, low-work intensity, either in the form of alternating spells of employment and unemployment or in the form of part-time work, is overrepresented. However, a profound difference between the European Union and the United States, due to the difference in the definition of workers, is that a large majority of European working poor actually work all year-round. The majority of the working poor are wage workers, but the self-employed are generally overrepresented, especially in southern countries, where self-employment is associated with higher shares of the agricultural sector. Among wage workers, those who work year-round but in low-paid jobs also tend to be overrepresented.

But, as already pointed out, this does not mean that less educated individuals, part-time workers, low-wage workers, or persons experiencing unemployment spells will necessarily end up among the working poor. It depends essentially on their household's composition, especially on the number of dependants and whether they are the only earner.

How has the risk of working poverty evolved in the 2000s? One could expect that the financial and economic crises resulted in a significant increase in the size of the problem. It is actually so in the United States, where the working-poor rate rose from a rather steady 5 percent until 2007 to 7.2 percent in 2010 (BLS 2012). But in Europe, due to the definition of workers as persons employed at least seven months a year, hence excluding those in the most precarious status, the in-work poverty rate has remained mostly stable and even has decreased in some countries (European Commission 2011; Eurostat 2012): it went from 9.3 percent in 2005, down to 8.4 percent in 2010—if all the 27 member states are considered—and from 7.3 percent to 7.9 percent in the EU15 (i.e., the EU before the inclusion of Eastern and Central Europe members).

ASSESSING THE CAUSES OF WORKING POVERTY AND POTENTIAL REMEDIES

The Determinants of Working Poverty: A Complex Bundle of Factors

The combination of labor market and household factors and the difficulties it raises in the analysis are generally acknowledged in the literature (e.g., Danziger and Gottshalk 1986, for the United States; Bardone and Guio 2005, for the EU).

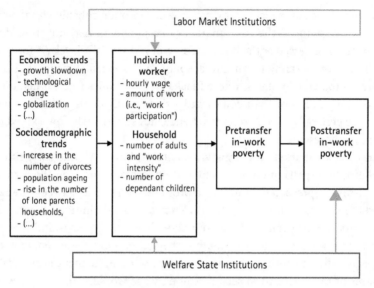

FIGURE 21.1 Determinants of Working Poverty

The issue was already behind Rowntree's analysis of poverty ([1901] 2000) when he distinguished poverty due to low earnings from poverty due to large families. Figure 21.1 tries to map the different factors that may have an impact on working poverty. The issue is quite complex as many factors interplay, making it difficult to disentangle exogenous from endogenous variables. Both labor market and welfare state institutions—comprehensively defined here as covering both cash transfers and the provision of services—play crucial roles in shaping working poverty. We will begin by analyzing the determinants of low individual earnings at the worker's (individual) level before turning to the combination of factors at household level, at which working poverty is measured.

Low Earnings at the Individual Level

Individuals' earnings over a given period (e.g., the year) are simply the combination of two elements: the average hourly wage and the number of hours worked over the period (*work participation*, according to OECD terminology), resulting from the number of days worked over the period (*work participation on the extensive margin*) and the average, daily working time (*work participation on the intensive margin*) (OECD 2009). The shift from advanced industrialized economies to "postindustrialized" economies has put pressure on both wages (with the increase in inequalities) and work participation (with the rise of flexible insecure jobs and intermittent employment). Many factors have been at play here, and their respective roles are often still debated. Things are a bit different in the case of the self-employed, who do not earn wages; their earnings result directly from their business profits. Because most of the self-employed are "self-employed" all year-round, whether they make a profit or not, work participation and intermittent employment do not have the same meaning as in the case of employees.

From the early 1980s, several OECD countries have witnessed a sharp increase in wage inequality, with a decline of the low-skilled worker's wages in relative and even in some cases (as in the United States) absolute terms. Globalization and competition with low labor-costs countries have played a role here, especially in the manufacturing sector. Nevertheless, many economists pointed at another main driver of increasing inequalities: skill-biased technological change—new technologies, in particular computers, requiring higher skill levels (Acemoglu 2002). But, this thesis has also been criticized by both economists and sociologists (Card and DiNardo 2002; Handel 2007). New production processes, both in manufacturing and service sectors also require more "soft" (or "social" or "noncognitive") skills, which are usually correlated with "hard" skills acquired in the education system. If, up to the beginning of the 2000s, the economic literature focused on the shift of labor demand away from less educated workers, more recent research insists rather on the polarization induced by technological change, evidenced by the growth in employment among both the highest skilled (professional and managerial) and lowest skilled (in particular personal services), with declining employment in the middle of the distribution of skills and wages—manufacturing and routine office jobs being the most affected by new technologies (Autor et al. 2006; Goos et al. 2009). Off-shoring has also played a role in the polarization process (facilitated by new technologies, such as use of the Internet for some routine service activities), as well as the rise in inequalities, which has induced an increase in the demand of low-paid personal services by high-paid workers.

Polarization and deindustrialization have induced a shift away from better paid and more secure jobs (epitomized by the "male breadwinner," blue-collar job in the automotive industry) to lower paid and more insecure jobs. Increased competition—resulting not only from globalization but also from the deregulation of many sectors (such as transportation, finance, public utilities, etc.)—and new work organization (such as the "just-in-time" process) induced an increase in flexibility and therefore job insecurity. In particular, the number of temporary workers has increased in most of the countries, pushing many workers, in particular youth, into a low-pay/no-pay cycle.

As all OECD countries were more or less affected by these global trends, the outcomes in terms of low pay and working poverty have been quite dissimilar across them. While wage inequalities, measured by the 9th to 1st deciles wage ratio among full-time workers, have increased dramatically in liberal countries such as the United States, Canada, and the United Kingdom since the 1970s (reaching respectively 5.0, 3.7, and 3.6 in 2010), they have increased much less, or even declined, in Nordic European countries (where the 9th/1st wage ratio was 2.2 in Sweden and 2.8 in Denmark in the same year), in continental Europe (2.2 in Italy, 2.9 in France, 3.2 in Germany), and Japan (3.0) (OECD 2012: statistical appendix). The share of low-wage workers—defined as those earning less than two-thirds of the median wage—was also contrasted across countries, ranging, in the mid-2000s, from 9 to 11 percent in Denmark, France, or Italy, to about 15 percent in Japan, over 20 percent in the UK and Germany, and even 25 percent in the United States.

Both labor market and welfare state institutions play a role in explaining these differences across countries. Empirical evidence suggests that the most important influence on the observed differences in low-wage work is the country's wage-setting institutions—covering unions, collective-bargaining systems, and minimum wages—(Gautié and Schmitt 2010). In particular, centralized wage bargaining (such as in Scandinavian countries) has a significant negative impact on low-wage work and pretransfers in-work poverty (see Keese et al. 1998; Lohmann 2009). In countries like France, where unionization is very low (about 5 percent in the private sector), the expansion of low-wage work was limited by the legal extension of industry collective agreements and an active minimum wage policy. The positive role of unions has been put in light in more liberal countries like the United States, where Brady et al. (2011) found that state-level unionization has a strong negative impact on working poverty (see also Appelbaum et al. [2003] on the role of unions in the low-wage labor market in the United States). As a consequence, deunionization, as well as the decline of the federal minimum wage both in real terms (as opposed to nominal) and relative terms (as compared to the median wage), may have played an important role in the increase of inequalities and the subsequent high level of low-pay work—even more crucial than technological changes according to Card and DiNardo (2002).

Welfare state institutions (including here labor market policies) may have an important impact on the supply side of the low-pay/low-skills labor market. The availability and generosity of government allowances (such as unemployment benefits and social assistance) may impact directly the reservation wage and, therefore, the effective floor for wages in the low-wage labor market. For instance, a decent level of pensions may prevent the elderly from being forced to take low-paid "bridge-jobs" to (full) retirement (Ruhm 1990). Since the mid-1990s, OECD countries have tended to reduce the generosity of out-of-work benefits and to promote "activation policies" to put beneficiaries back to work, sometimes based on a "work first" strategy (like the United States did with the Personal Responsibility and Work Opportunity Act in 1996), where any job is considered better than no job. These policies have been also implemented in Europe, and may partly explain the positive correlation across European countries between the number of jobs created and the number of working poor in the 1990s. Whether these policies have actually increased the number of low-wage workers and working poor, trapped in dead-end jobs, is still debated (Andress and Lohmann 2008).

The Combination of Factors at the Household Level

When poverty is measured at the household level, the household's structure and composition play a crucial role in the explanation of in-work poverty. Two key factors are the number of household members of working age and their work participation on the one hand, and the number of dependant children on the other hand.

One of the most important demographic trends that may have impacted dramatically on working poverty is the rise in the number of households with dependent children headed by a single parent—a mother in most cases. This is particularly the case in the United States, where the number of families headed by single mothers increased from 12.8 percent in 1970 to 26.2 percent in 2010 (and from 37.1 percent in 1971 to 52.8 percent in 2010 among African Americans) (Edelman 2012). The phenomenon is less widespread in Europe and Japan.

In Europe, due to the definition of the poverty line as a percentage of the median income, another compositional effect has played a greater role: the rise in the number of dual-earner households. It contributed to the increase in the median income and therefore the poverty line, all the more that the increase in workforce participation (as defined above—i.e., in terms of total hours worked over a given period) has been higher among skilled women, who tend to be partners of skilled men. This, in countries where women's education level and participation in the labor market underwent large changes, automatically led many male breadwinner, traditional households to fall under the poverty line (Marx and Nolan 2012). Symmetrically, low-skilled men's participation in the workforce tended to decline during the same decades because of increasing unemployment and the rise of intermittent and temporary employment (discussed earlier). This contributed to an increase in employment polarization among households in European countries as well as in other OECD countries (Gregg et al. 2010); that is, an increasing share of households with two full-time workers versus jobless or low work-intensity households therefore bringing a high risk of working poverty. These trends led European policymakers to build a new indicator, household "work intensity," which takes into account both the intensive and extensive margin of work participation of all working-age members—for instance, the indicator reaches 100 percent for a household with two adults working full time, 75 percent if the second earner works part time, 25 percent for a couple with only one worker employed full time but during only six months over the year. As one could expect, the risk of poverty is negatively correlated to households' work intensity (European Commission 2011).

The number of dependent children is also a potential key factor of working poverty because the total income has to be distributed among more persons, but also—more indirectly—because children and/or the cost of childcare may lower women's work participation and therefore the household's earnings.

When combining labor market factors and household circumstances, it is worth mentioning that the overlap between low-paid employment and working poverty is weak in most industrialized countries (Marx and Nolan 2012). In the same line of analysis, Gardiner and Millar (2006) show that between working longer hours, living with other people, and relying on social transfers, it is the second (i.e., living arrangements) that better protects the low paid against poverty. Why is this so? Mostly because low earnings are often those of "secondary" earners in a household, hence, assuming incomes are pooled in households, low earners are poor when they live alone or when they are the primary (or only) earner in their household. This also explains why single parents, mostly women, face a disproportionate risk of working poverty (and also of poverty without work), combining the average lower position of women in the labor market and no counterbalance to their low earnings in their household. This also shows the limits of Gardiner and Millar's conclusions: they suggest that the household is the best protection against poverty, but this remains true only as long as the household's members stay together. In case of separation or divorce, or any splitting up of the household, the most fragile members in terms of individual earnings will no longer benefit from the "protection" other earners offer. To that extent, avoiding financial dependency on other household members may be a better solution for decreasing the risk of falling into poverty.

More generally, given labor market inequality between men and women, the household factor that tends to protect women against poverty—to a smaller extent—works the other way around for men. For a sample of EU countries, Ponthieux (2010) shows that while women are significantly more affected than men by "employment problems" (defined as holding any labor market status other than full-time, year-round, not low-paid employment), their poverty rate is lower in almost all the countries covered. She shows that if individuals were to live only on their own earnings, women would be much more at risk of poverty than men. Using a slightly different methodology Peña-Casas and Ghailani (2011) reach a similar conclusion.

The Decisive Role of Welfare States

At the household level, social transfers have to be taken into account on top of earnings. If labor market institutions may have an important role regarding pretransfer in-work poverty, welfare institutions are indeed a key factor regarding posttransfer poverty (Lohmann 2009; Brady et al. 2010; OECD 2009; European Commission 2011). According to the OECD (2009), net social transfers cut the poverty rate before transfers by almost half on average among the working-age population but with large differences across countries: more than two-thirds in countries like Denmark, France, and Sweden; but less than one-third in Canada, Japan, Korea, Spain, and the United States. Focusing on the working population, and with a sample restricted to European countries, Lohmann (2009) finds lower differences between pre- and posttransfer poverty rates (as one could expect) but with an even larger dispersion across countries: while the net reduction of the poverty rate amounts between 47 and 56 percent in countries like Denmark, Sweden, France and Germany, it falls to between 7 and 14 percent in Southern European countries like Italy, Spain, and Portugal.

Beyond the issue in terms of poverty reduction, differences in welfare states may account for the large differences both in the level and composition of the (posttransfer) working-poor population across OECD countries—see for instance Crettaz and Bonoli (2011) and Crettaz (2011). In liberal countries like the United States, where the welfare state is residual—in the sense that social transfers consist mainly in safety nets, in particular with no family benefits—the percentage of low-wage workers living in poverty is relatively high, and having children impacts also significantly on working poverty. The incidence of poverty is very high among single-parents families (26 percent of the families maintained by a woman in the workforce were under the poverty line in 2010; BLS 2012), which, moreover, represent a higher share of households than other countries, as mentioned earlier (see Chapter 18 in this volume).

At the opposite end, in Nordic European countries, such as Sweden and Denmark, the welfare state is much more developed. This means not only generous monetary transfers (often on an universalistic basis) but also a high provision of services—in particular, family services, such as childcare, which accounts for up to 2 percent of the GDP in Denmark, for instance, the highest by far among OECD countries (Lohmann 2009). In-work poverty remains residual in this context, with a clear life-course dimension—young workers make up a large share of the working poor—while household work intensity (which is on average high) and the number of children play a much lesser role. Continental European countries such as Germany, France, and the Netherlands, for instance, are also characterized by a relatively low share of working poverty, even if some of them (like Germany) may have a high share of low-wage workers (see earlier discussion). This is because most low-wage workers are "second earners" and therefore live in nonpoor households. As the tax and benefit system is favorable to households with children, the number of children is not an important factor regarding poverty. Low work participation, but also being young, plays a greater role. In Southern European countries (such as Spain, Portugal, and Italy), the welfare state is much less generous and also much less redistributive as we have seen. In particular, the tax and benefit system does not much take into account family type and composition. Even if the participation rate of women has increased rapidly in the 1990s and the 2000s, in 2009, many adults (in particular in Spain) still live in households with medium work intensity (40–50 percent) (European Commission 2011)—meaning that the traditional, male breadwinner household remains more present than in the United States and other continental and Northern European countries. As a result, in this context, low work intensity and the number of children remain important factors regarding working poverty.

Public Policies to Tackle In-work Poverty

Some Issues at Stake

When turning to policies fighting working poverty, one must first keep in mind that the working poor are not an easy population to target. This results from the fact that, on the one hand, the size and composition of the corresponding population may be very sensitive to the definition adopted (see the first section of this chapter), and, on the other hand, for a given definition and in a given country, the population of working poor may be quite heterogeneous.

Another crucial element is that, as working poverty is a multifaceted problem (a term coined over 25 years ago by Danziger and Gottschalk 1986), resulting from multiple factors, as emphasized in the previous sections, not one but a combination of tools may be needed. One has to also consider that some factors that may have an important impact on working poverty—like sociodemographic trends, such as the rise in the divorce rate and in the number of single-parent households—may be partly or largely beyond the scope of public policy. Furthermore, the nature of working poverty differs across countries. Thus, overall, as Crettaz put it, "there is no one-size-fits all policy mix: each country must find its own combination of policies" (2011:200).

But the combination of factors at play also implies that identifying the working poor's problems to be tackled is not just a technical issue. As Marx and Nolan point out (2012): "*Whether their risk of financial poverty status is construed as a problem of insufficient breadwinner earnings or as a problem of partner non-participation makes a fundamental difference as to what type of policy action is to be examined and possibly favoured.*" As already suggested, there is in fact a complex interaction between the diagnoses of working poverty—and even, in the first place, the definition of working poverty itself—and the way it is construed as a social issue in political debates. Statistical definitions and indicators are never neutral; they are already shaped by social representations. For instance, introducing an indicator of "work intensity at household level"—as mentioned earlier—means that policymakers (or at least experts) have already identified low participation of household members as *an*—if not *the*—issue. All in all, it is not easy to assess that certain definitions and/or indicators lead to better social policies to address in-work poverty, as normative views play an important role in assessing the phenomenon in the first place.

Accounting for the ideological underpinnings of policies to alleviate working poverty is beyond the scope of this chapter. Because Chapters 31, 32 and 35, for example, in this *Handbook* are dedicated to policies aimed at alleviating poverty, and which may therefore impact in-work poverty, we will focus here on more specific policy tools that address only a limited number of potential factors. We will insist on the fact that the relevance and effectiveness of these tools depend on national contexts.

Minimum Wage, In-work Benefits, and Activation Policies

A first set of tools targets low earnings. These are mainly legal minimum wages (MWs) as well as "living wages"—usually set at the local level to cover businesses receiving public assistance or having contracts with local public authorities (subcontractors, service providers with public procurement, etc.). Concerning MWs, there has been a revival of interest since the mid-1990s among both economists and policymakers (see, for instance, Vaugham-Whitehead 2009, for Europe) regarding the context of growing inequalities and increasing shares of low-wage work in many OECD countries. As a result, some countries have decided to introduce a national minimum wage, such as the United Kingdom in 1999, Ireland in 2000, and Germany in 2015. New theoretical and empirical research in particular had highlighted that MWs could have a sizable impact on inequalities and low wages without hurting necessarily employment (Card and Krueger 1995; Manning 2003). In the postindustrialized countries characterized by employment polarization and the rise of personal services (as depicted previously), the MW could indeed be a good tool to redistribute resources from highly paid consumers to low-paid service providers (Freeman 1996). The potential negative impact on employment is still hotly debated, and recent literature has focused on other arguments to cast doubt on the effectiveness of MWs to alleviate working poverty. The main drawback is that this instrument is not well targeted for the objective. As pointed out, even in the United States, the overlap between low wage and working poverty is overall relatively weak. According to Formby et al. (2010) more than 85 percent of low-income families (defined as those below twice the official poverty line) were not directly affected by the 41 percent increase in the federal minimum wage between 2007 and 2009. In Europe in the mid-2000s, if the share of the working poor living in a household with at least one low-wage worker was about 50 percent on average, symmetrically, the share of low-wage workers living in a poor household was on average less than 10 percent (OECD 2009). Moreover Marx, Marchal, and Nolan (2012) show that either in Europe or the United States—adopting the 60 percent median income poverty line definition—the net income packages at MW levels are below this threshold, and often by a wide margin, for lone parents and sole breadwinners with dependent children. Filling the gap would require a big increase in the MW in most countries, with potential strong negative side effects. Overall, if the MW remains a key instrument to ensure decent wages, other tools must be used to decrease significantly in-work poverty in OECD countries.

The role of in-work benefits (IWB), such as the pioneer American Earned Income Tax Credit (EITC), has increased notably since the mid-1990s. Both the characteristics of the beneficiaries and the benefit design can vary significantly across countries (OECD 2009; Immervoll and Pearson 2009). Countries such as Canada, Ireland, New Zealand, the United Kingdom, and the United States implement IWB schemes that are means-tested on family (rather than individual) income. In many countries only families with children can benefit from IWB. The use of these kinds of schemes faces important dilemmas. When targeted at families, they may have a sizable positive impact on the household income, but they may also have some potential negative influence on second earners in the family incentive to work. As for individual-based IWB, they may reduce workers' incentive to work more hours, as well as move up the wage ladder and invest in human capital. Another issue is that employers may take advantage of the IWB scheme by lowering wages. As a consequence, this kind of plan has to be supplemented by a legal minimum wage set at an appropriate level. But beyond these potential risks, it is worth noting that if IWB schemes have proved efficient as redistributive tools in countries where wage inequalities are important, such as the United Kingdom and the United States, simulations tend to show that the cost-effectiveness of similar plans is much lower in countries with more compressed earning distribution (Immervoll et al. 2007; Marx et al. 2012).

Finally, since low work intensity at the household level may be an important factor in in-work poverty, one should consider all the policies aimed at increasing work participation of adult members of poor households. In many countries, this has been one of the objectives of activation policies (including the introduction of IWBs and/or their increase), sometimes in association with a degree of labor market deregulation, specifically to facilitate the use of temporary workers. As mentioned, this may have simply contributed to transform out-of-work poverty into in-work poverty. As a consequence, other routes have been proposed, in particular in Europe, with the European "social inclusion" agenda based more on a "capability approach." As summarized by Nicaise (2011:21), this approach, clearly inspired by the Nordic countries experience, consists "*not just on transferring as many people into work through financial incentives, but on investing in people so as to strengthen their participation in society in all areas of life.*" In particular, the provision of support services, beginning with available and affordable childcare and other family supports, as well as adequate information and guidance for employment mobility and training, is a key element to "empower" the working poor and give them a chance to move out of poverty (see, among many, Edelman 2012; Ray et al. 2010).

REFERENCES

Acemoglu, Daron. 2002. "Technical Change, Inequality and the Labor Market." *Journal of Economic Literature* 40(1):7–72.

Airio, Ilpo. 2008. "Change of Norm? In-Work Poverty in a Comparative Perspective." *Studies in social security and health* 92. Helsinki: Social Insurance Institution.

Andress Hans-Jürgen and Henning Lohmann, eds. 2008. *The Working Poor in Europe—Employment, Poverty and Globalization.* Northampton, MA: Edward Elgar.

Appelbaum, Eileen, Annette Bernhardt, and Richard J. Murnane, eds. 2003. *Low-Wage America: How Employers Are Reshaping Opportunity in the Workplace.* New York: Russell Sage Foundation.

Atkinson, Anthony B. 1998. *Poverty in Europe.* Oxford: Blackwell.

Atkinson, Tony, Bea Cantillon, Eric Marlier, and Brian Nolan. 2002. *Social Indicators—The EU and Social Inclusion.* Oxford: Oxford University Press.

Autor David H., Lawrence F. Katz, and Melissa S. Kearney. 2006. "The Polarization of the US Labor Market." *American Economic Review* 96(2):189–94.

Bardone Laura and Anne-Catherine Guio. 2005. "In-work Poverty." Eurostat, *Statistics in Focus* 5.

Beveridge, William. 1942. "Social Insurance and Allied Services." London: His Majesty Stationary Office.

Beveridge, William. 1944. "Full Employment in a Free Society." London: His Majesty Stationary Office.

Brady, David, Regina S. Baker, and Ryan Finnigan. 2011. "When Unionization Disappears: State-level Unionization and Working Poverty in the US." *American Sociological Review* 78:872–96.

Brady, David, Andrew S. Fullerton, and Jennifer Moren Cross. 2010. "More Than Just Nickels and Dimes: A Cross-National Analysis of Working Poverty in Affluent Democracies." *Social Problems* 57:559–85.

Bureau of Labor Statistics (BLS). 2012. "A Profile of the Working Poor in 2010." Washington, DC: Bureau of Labor Statistics.

Card, David and John E. DiNardo. 2002. "Skilled-Biased Technological Change and Rising Wage Inequality: Some Problems and Puzzles." *Journal of Labor Economics* 20(4):733–83.

Card, David and Alan B. Krueger. 1995. *Myth and Measurement: The New Economics of the Minimum Wage.* Princeton, NJ: Princeton University.

Citro, Constance. F. and Robert T. Michael, eds. 1995. *Measuring Poverty: A New Approach.* Washington, DC: National Academy Press.

Crettaz, Eric. 2011. *Fighting Working Poverty in Post-industrial Economies. Causes, Trade-offs and Policy Solutions*. Cheltenham: Edward Elgar.

Crettaz, Eric and Giuliano Bonoli. 2011. "Worlds of Working Poverty. National Variations in Mechanisms." Pp. 46–69 in *Working Poverty in Europe. A Comparative Approach.*, edited by Neil Fraser, Rodolfo Gutiérrez, and Ramón Peña-Casas. Basingstoke: Palgrave Macmillan.

Cummings, Laurie D. 1965. "The Employed Poor: Their Characteristics and Occupations." *Monthly Labor Review* 88(7):828–35.

Dalaker, Joe. 2005. "Alternative Poverty Estimates in the United States: 2003." Washington, DC: U.S. Census Bureau.

Danziger Sheldon and Peter Gottschalk. 1986. "Work, Poverty and the Working Poor: A Multifaceted Problem." *Monthly Labor Review* 109(9):17–21.

Danziger Sheldon and Peter Gottschalk. 1995. *America Unequal*. New York: Russell Sage Foundation.

Edelman, Peter. 2012. *So Rich, So Poor. Why It's So Hard to End Poverty in America*. New York: New Press.

European Commission. 2009. *Portfolio of Indicators for the Monitoring of the European Strategy for Social Protection and Social Exclusion*. Employment, Social Affairs and Equal Opportunity DG, Brussels. (http://ec.europa.eu/social/main.jsp?catId=756).

European Commission. 2011. "Is Working Enough to Avoid Poverty? In-work poverty Mechanisms and Policies in the European Union." Chapter 4 in *Employment and Social Developments in Europe 2011*. Luxembourg: Publications Office of the European Union.

Eurostat. 2012. *In Work at-risk-of-poverty Rate in the EU*. Retrieved September 20, 2014. (http://epp.eurostat.ec.europa.eu/tgm/table.do?tab=table&init=1&language=en&pcode=ts dsc320).

Freeman, Richard B. 1996. "Minimum Wage as a Redistributive Tool." *Economic Journal* 106(436):639–49.

Formby, John B., John A. Bishop, and Hoseong Kim. 2010. "What's Best at Reducing Poverty? An Examination of the Effectiveness of the 2007 Minimum Wage Increase." Washington, DC: Employment Policy Institute.

Gardiner, Karen and Jane Millar. 2006. "How Low-Paid Employees Avoid Poverty: An Analysis by Family Type and Household Structure." *Journal of Social Policy* 35(3):351–69.

Gautié, Jérôme and John Schmitt, eds. 2010. *Low Wage Work in Wealthy Countries*. New York: Russell Sage Foundation.

Goos Maarten, Alan Manning and Anna Salomons. 2009. "Job Polarization in Europe." *American Economic Review* 99(2):58–63.

Gregg, Paul, Rosanna Scutella, and Jonhatan Wadsworth. 2010. "Reconciling Workless Measures at the Individual and Household Level. Theory and Evidence from the United States, Britain, Germany, Spain and Australia." *Journal of Population Economics*, 23(1):139–67.

Handel, Michael J. 2007. "Computers and the Wage Structure." *Research in Labor Economics* 26:155–96.

Iceland, John. 2000. "Poverty among Working Families: Findings from Experimental Poverty Measures." *Current Population Reports*. Washington, DC: U.S. Census Bureau.

International Labour Office (ILO). 2011. "Working Poverty in the World." Chapter 1A, in *Key Indicators of the Labour Market*, 7th edition. Geneva: ILO.

Immervoll, Hervig, Henrik Jacobsen Kleven, Claus Thustrup Kreiner, and Emmanuel Saez. 2007. "Welfare Reform in Europe: A Microsimulation Analysis." *Economic Journal* 117(516):1–44.

Immervoll, Hervig and Mark Pearson. 2009. "A Good Time for Making Work Pay? Taking Stock of In-Work Benefits and Related Measures across the OECD." OECD Social Employment and Migration Working Papers, No. 81. Paris: OECD.

Keese, Mark, Agnès Puymoyen, and Paul Swaim. 1998. "The Incidence and Dynamics of Low-paid Employment in OECD Countries." In *Low Pay and Earnings Mobility in Europe*, edited by Rita Asplund, Peter J. Sloane, and Ioanis Theodossiou. Northampton, MA: Edward Elgar.

Klein, Bruce W. and Philip L. Rones. 1989. "A Profile of the Working Poor." *Monthly Labor Review* 112(10):3–13.

Lohmann, Henning. 2009. "Welfare States, Labour Market Institutions and the Working Poor: A Comparative Analysis of Twenty European Countries." *European Sociological Review* 25(4):489–504.

Manning, Alan. 2003. *Monopsony in Motion: Imperfect Competition in Labor Markets*. Princeton, NJ: Princeton University.

Marx, Ive, Sarah Marchal, and Brian Nolan. 2012. "Mind the Gap: Net Incomes of Minimum Wage Workers in the EU and the US." IZA Discussion Paper, No. 6510.

Marx, Ive and Brian Nolan. 2012. "In-work Poverty." In *For Better, For Worse, For Richer, For Poorer*, edited by Bea Cantillon, and Frank Vandenbroucke. Oxford: Oxford University Press.

Mead, Lawrence. 1993. *The New Politics of Poverty*. New York: Basic Books.

Nicaise, Ides. 2011. "Building the Tools to Fight In-Work Poverty." Synthesis Report, Peer Review in Social Protection and Social Inclusion, Paris, March31–April 1.

OECD. 2009. "Is Work the Best Antidote to Poverty?" Chapter 3, in *OECD Employment Outlook 2009*. Paris: OECD.

OECD. 2012. *OECD Employment Outlook 2012*. Paris: OECD.

Peña-Casas, Ramon and Mia Latta. 2004. *Working Poor in the European Union*. Dublin: European Foundation for the Improvement of Living and Working Conditions.

Peña-Casas, Ramon and Dalila Ghailani. 2011. "Towards Individualizing Gender In-work Poverty Risks." In *Working Poverty in Europe (Work and Welfare in Europe)*, edited by N. Fraser, R. Guttierez and R. Peña-Casas. London: Palgrave Macmillan.

Ponthieux, Sophie. 2010. "Assessing and Analyzing In-work Poverty Risk." In *Income and Living Conditions in Europe*, edited by A. B. Atkinson and E. Marlier. Luxembourg: EU Publications Office.

Ray, Kathryn, Lesley Hoggart, Sandra Vegeris and Rebecca Taylor. 2010. "Better off Working? Work, Poverty and Benefit Cycling." York: Joseph Rowntree Foundation.

Ruhm Christopher J. 1990. "Bridge Jobs and Partial Retirement." *Journal of Labor Economics* 8(4):482–501.

Rowntree, B. Seebohm. [1901] 2000. *Poverty: A Study of Town Life*. Bristol: Policy Press.

Short Kathy. 2010. *The Research Supplemental Poverty Measure: 2010*. Washington, DC: U.S. Census Bureau.

Vaugham-Whitehead, Daniel, ed. 2009. *The Minimum Wage Revisited in the Enlarged EU*. Northampton, MA: Edward Elgar.

CHAPTER 22

GREAT ESCAPES AND GREAT DIVERGENCES

Growth, Poverty, and Income Inequality on a Global Scale

ROBERT H. WADE

INTRODUCTION

How has the world economy been performing in terms of human well-being? We can measure outcomes in terms of wealth, income, consumption, life expectancy, health, height, education, accommodation, water and sanitation, social inclusion, happiness, and the health of the biosphere. Here we simplify and stick to income or consumption.

This chapter gives a bird's-eye view of global income distribution; patterns of economic growth; the movement of countries in the global income hierarchy; trends in income distribution between countries and between individuals or households; and trends in the incidence of "extreme" and "ordinary" poverty.

It shows that the global income distribution is still highly polarized, reflecting the great divergence between the Western core and "developing countries" that opened up after the Industrial (Energy) Revolution. But thanks to economic growth—the great engine of escape from material deprivation—this divergence has probably been narrowing for several decades by some measures and for the past decade by other measures. The chapter also reports that the proportion of the world's population living in the degree of poverty which kills—"extreme poverty"—has probably fallen over the past several decades; and even the absolute number of people in extreme poverty has probably fallen, despite the world's now much larger total population.

Good news of this kind has been widely taken to validate the general expectations of neoliberalism. The core neoliberal proposition is that "the market"—in which individuals are free to maximize their material advantage, and prices and resource allocation are determined by supply, demand, and profits without government intervention—is the preferred mechanism for achieving human ambitions as compared to the state and politics. Hinder the market and you hurt jobs and the poor. So markets should be free of state controls (including "rights") except in specific circumstances; exchange rates should be determined by the market; the optimum degree of trade openness is maximum openness; state-owned enterprises should be privatized; trade unions (and other labor market frictions, like minimum legal wages) should be minimized; and much more. To the extent that public policy enlarges the scope for private profit-seeking and supply-and-demand-determined prices, economic performance will improve at a national level and above. As Martin Wolf of the *Financial Times* urges in *Why Globalization Works*:

> It cannot make sense to fragment the world economy more than it already is but rather to make the world economy work as if it were the United States, or at least the European Union. . . . The failure of our world is not that there is too much globalization, but that there is too little. The potential for greater economic integration is barely tapped. We need more global markets, not fewer, if we want to raise the living standards of the poor of the world. (Wolf 2004:4)

Since the 1980s the neoliberal paradigm has guided policy prescriptions across many domains in Western economies and in developing economies; and has been strongly advocated by international organizations which claim to think for the world, like the Organisation for Economic Cooperation and Development (OECD) and the World Bank (Fourcade 2009; Wade 2014).

This chapter does not pretend to "test" neoliberal propositions. But its review does suggest that the evidence about economic performance following the shift in the global center of gravity in a neoliberal direction since the 1980s is a lot more ambiguous than commonly claimed. The appropriate degree of confidence in the good news is rather lower than has been the case, and there is a lot of credible bad news. Yet not even the long slump in Western economies, starting in the United States in 2007 and jumping to Europe, has substantially dented the dominant role of neoliberal thinking in Western public policy and Western prescriptions for economic development.

WORLD INCOME AND POPULATION DISTRIBUTION

We begin with a snapshot of world income distribution, shown as the share of the world's population living in countries across the range of average incomes. In Figure 22.1 we see that it has "twin peaks" and a "missing middle." One peak contains 70 percent of the world's population living in countries whose GDP per capita is below PPP$7,500.

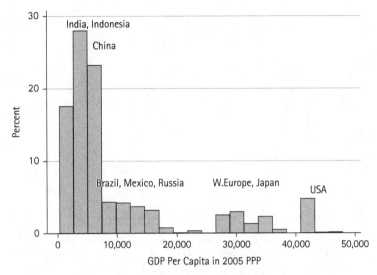

FIGURE 22.1 "International Income Distribution": The Distribution of People According to the GDP Per Capita of the Country in Which They Live (Year 2011)]

Note: GDP shown in 2005 international dollars.

Source: Milanovic (personal communication).

(PPP stands for purchasing power parity, about which more later.) The other peak is the 15 percent who live in countries with GDP per capita above PPP$26,000—the rich world. Only about 1 percent live in countries with average incomes between PPP$17,000 and PPP$26,000. Talk of the "middle-income" countries can be misleading if taken to suggest that they are "midway" between the low- and the high-income countries. In fact, the middle-income countries fall toward the low end.

Figure 22.2 shows how the distribution of population by country average income changed between 1980 and 2008.[1] The income scale is divided into 10 equal (logged) intervals from lowest to highest gross national income per capita. The figure shows that in 1980 just over half the population covered by the sample lived in the three-poorest income deciles (China and India were in the second poorest). Twenty percent lived in countries in the top-four deciles. Notice again, as in Figure 22.1, the underpopulated middle.

Three decades later, China's fast growth lifted it into the fifth income decile and India's into the fourth, bringing a large bloc of people toward the lower middle of the distribution. The "missing middle" remained but over a shorter income range. The percentage in the top-four deciles increased to about 22 percent, and in the middle decile six shrank from about 10 percent to 8 percent.

Table 22.1 shows some of the biggest countries—biggest by population or by share of world GDP (at market exchange rates). The disproportion between population shares and GDP shares is striking and raises the question of how the relatively small population of the developed countries got to have such a high share of world GDP. The United

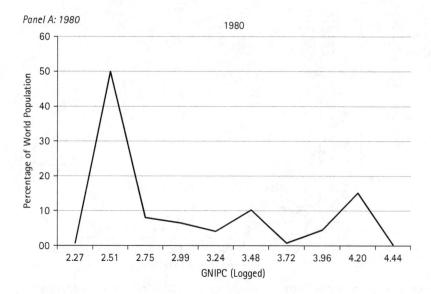

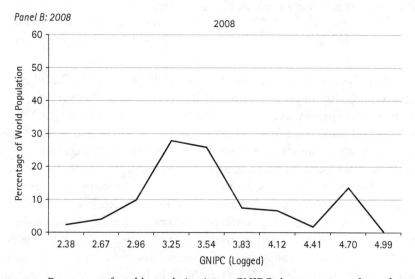

FIGURE 22.2 Percentage of world population in ten GNIPC clusters, 1980 and 2008]

Note: Market exchange rates are adjusted by the World Bank's Atlas method

Source: Korzeniewicz (2012).

States remains the biggest economy by far; between 1980 and 2010 its GDP relative to that of the second-biggest economy declined hardly at all, from 2.5 to 2.4. Other striking points include China's large gain in GDP share to make it by 2010 the second-biggest economy; India's very small share relative to its population; and the small and fairly constant shares in world GDP of Brazil and South Africa, which are often grouped with China and India as members of the BASIC (Brazil, South Africa, India, China) vanguard of emerging market economies challenging Western dominance.

Table 22.1 Major Economies, Share of World Population and GDP at Market Exchange Rates (percentages)

	Population 2010	GDP 1980	GDP 2010
USA	4.5%	25.1%	22.9%
China	19.4%	1.7%	9.4%
Japan	1.8%	9.9%	8.7%
Germany	1.2%	8.2%	5.2%
Brazil	2.8%	2.1%	3.4%
India	17.8%	1.7%	2.7%
South Africa	0.7%	0.7%	0.6%

Source: OECD (2013).

GROWTH AND GEOGRAPHICAL DISTRIBUTION

We take growth in per capita incomes to be normal, but on a scale of millennia it is unprecedented (Deaton 2013). Britain after the Industrial Revolution made the first great escape into more or less continuous growth, thereby increasing the competence and income differential with rival economies. By the late nineteenth century, the northwestern Europeans and North Americans had more or less eliminated the gap, and the resulting core of the world economy continued to open wider gaps with the rest of the world—the "periphery," much of it colonies of Europeans, Americans, and Japanese. Only after the Second World War did growth in average incomes become normal on a world scale and an explicit objective of government policy. Since 1960 the average country has experienced an average income growth of around 1.5 percent a year, a rate that doubles a country's economy in 47 years.

The half century after the Second World War saw a pronounced growth slowdown. The growth rate of world gross domestic product (GDP) per capita fell by a third between 1955 to 1980 and 1980 to 2007, from an average of about 2.2 percent to 1.7 percent. For the OECD as a whole, and for the United States, Europe, and Japan separately, the rate of growth per head fell in every decade from 1960–1973, 1973–1979, 1979–1990, and 1990–2004. The fall in 1990–2004 is especially telling because, by this time, the 1980s policies of squeezing inflation, deregulating, privatizing, liberalizing trade and capital movements had worked themselves into macroeconomic stabilization and free markets; yet the promised upturn in economic growth, in line with neoliberal expectations, did not appear.

In 2003 to 2008 world output grew much faster than during the previous quarter century, at about 2.3 percent (compared to a 1992–2008 average of 1.7 percent). For the first time ever, middle- and low-income countries grew several percentage points faster than the high-income countries (OECD 2013). Commentators celebrated the "great convergence" ("rise of the South") and the West's "great moderation," the latter meaning solid growth rates with low inflation and high employment. They interpreted both trends as evidence for the core neoliberal proposition about free or freer markets (and the linked proposition about democracy being good for economic growth). The crash of 2008 revealed what was in plain sight of those with eyes to see, that much of the growth and high corporate profits in the earlier part of the decade came from unsustainable debt on the balance sheets of households and/or governments, especially in the United States, Britain, and Southern Europe. Plautus, the third-century BC playwright, expressed the mechanism when he had one of his characters declare, "I am a rich man, as long as I do not repay my creditors." The high global growth rates of 2003 to 2008 are unlikely to be regained any time soon, unless based again on unrestrained debt.

The world growth trend hides large variations between regions and classes. Growth in the South is more erratic than in a typical developed country, with periods of relatively fast growth followed by deeper and longer recessions (Reddy and Minoiu 2009; Pritchett and Summers 2014). Indeed, a majority of the world's countries (56 percent) experienced negative growth of GDP per person from 1980 to 2000; though not, of course, a majority of the world's population. Sub-Saharan Africa, with almost 1 billion people, had an average income in the mid-2000s barely above the level of 1980, despite most states receiving foreign aid and loans to implement neoliberally informed Washington Consensus structural-adjustment programs for many years. Latin America, with 550 million people, experienced much the same long-term stagnation at a higher income level. Many countries of the former Soviet Union, after more than 20 years of transition to capitalism, remain at about the same average income as when the transition started.

On the other hand, the North (Western Europe and North America) grew faster than these other regions in the 1980s and 1990s. Also, China from the 1980s and India from the 1990s have grown very fast from a very low base. But they and most other emerging market economies slowed markedly after 2010, suggesting that their growth is still fairly closely dependent on, and coupled to, growth in the North, as in colonial times.

The fact is that, after six decades of explicit efforts around the world to promote economic development and three decades of global public policy to liberalize markets, the average income for the South is still only around 20–25 percent of that of the North in PPP terms, and more like 10–15 percent in foreign exchange rate (FX) terms, especially if one takes out one country, China.

Nevertheless, we can celebrate that the combination of China's and India's 37 percent share of world population and their fast growth over the past two to three decades means that, while the average country grew at 1.5 percent a year in the half century after 1960, the average person lived in a country growing at 3 percent a year, a doubling time of around 23 years, or one generation (Deaton 2013:235).

INCOME INEQUALITY WITHIN COUNTRIES

A large majority of the world's population lives in countries where income dispari-ties are higher than they were a generation ago. One study compared income distribu-tions in the 1960s and 1990s in 73 countries and found that about two-thirds of them containing about two-thirds of their population experienced an increase in inequality, while only about 10 percent of them containing 5 percent of their population experi-enced a fall (Corea and Kiiski 2001). All the countries which were OECD members in the mid-1980s had experienced an increase in the Gini coefficient by 2010, with the possible exception of Greece.

Trends in industrial wage inequality within countries confirm the broad trend. Wage data has an advantage over income data because pay is a much less ambiguous variable; it has been collected systematically by the United Nations since the early 1960s and gives many more observation points for each country than any data set on incomes. It is a useful way to get at the impacts of changes in trade policy and trade flows, or of manufacturing innovation, and the like. The disadvantage of pay data is that it treats only a small part of the economy of many developing countries and provides only a proxy for incomes and expenditure. This is not as limiting as it may seem because what is happening to pay rates in formal-sector activity reflects larger trends, including income differences between countries and income differences within countries (since the pay of unskilled, entry-port jobs in the formal sector is closely related to the oppor-tunity cost of time in the informal or agricultural sectors).

Pay inequality in a large sample of rich and poor countries was stable from the early 1960s to the early 1970s, declined until around 1980–1982, and increased sharply from 1980–1982 to the early 2000s. The countries within continents showed closely correlated movements in pay dispersions, suggesting macroregional forces at work. Since the early 2000s, regional trends have been more varied; Latin America's pay inequality fell after 2000, and China's peaked in the mid-2000s. James K. Galbraith and associates present analyses of pay disper-sions at the University of Texas, Inequality Project website http://utip.gov.utexas.edu.

Countries tend to form high-income and low-income inequality clusters. Most developed countries are in the low-inequality cluster, and most developing countries are in the high-inequality cluster (roughly one-and-a-half to twice as high). Among the developed countries, the Anglos are at the high end (the United Kingdom's and United States' Gini before taxes and transfers were around 0.45 and 0.49 in the mid-2000s and 0.33 and 0.38 for disposable income). At the low end of developed countries are east and central European countries, coming from a history of communism; and also Scandinavia, where the Gini for disposable income was around 0.23–0.26 in the mid-2000s (down from around 0.42 before taxes and transfers, indicating the redistributive power of the state). Japan's Gini (pre and post) were around 0.44 and 0.32.

China's Gini was around 0.48 in the mid-2000s (the figures for pre- and posttaxes and transfers are not much different). But the China Household Finance Survey, from Southwestern University of Finance and Economics, Chengdu, finds China's Gini to be about 0.6, the higher figure reflecting determined effort by the surveyors to get information about the richest households. One cannot compare this much higher figure for China with official Gini in other countries, however, because a similarly determined effort in other countries—India and the United States, for example—would probably yield significant increases in their Gini. India's Gini is given officially as around 0.35; but this is based on the distribution of consumption, and other calculations based on income suggest a figure of around 0.54. Brazil is around 0.55, South Africa around 0.65.

Changes in within-country distribution tend to be small relative to the two big Gini clusters, and membership of the clusters shows considerable stability through the second half of the twentieth century. Contrary to what one might expect from the Kuznets inverted U hypothesis (inequality rises in the early stages of development, flattens out, and then falls as rural-urban differentials fall and now better educated citizens demand redistribution), there has been little movement from the high-inequality to the low-inequality cluster as countries become richer. On the other hand, the United States—with its history as a hybrid industrial-plantation economy—has been rising out of the low-inequality cluster and by 2000 was well into the zone between the low-inequality and the high-inequality clusters (Korzeniewicz and Moran 2009).

In short, within-country inequality has generally increased over the past several decades, to the point where vertical inequality has accounted for a rising (still minority) share of total between-country and within-country inequality. The mechanism is a combination of technological change (expressing Moore's law, the steady doubling in the power of microchips) and neoliberal globalization (market integration across the world). This combination has raised the mobility of goods, capital, and to a degree labor, and boosted the capacity of corporate (especially financial) sectors to raise the share of profits and squeeze the share of wages via deregulation in high-profit activities, informalization of work in low-profit activities, and credit booms based on house mortgages and lending from developed to developing countries. Imports of manufactures assembled in China have knocked out jobs and depressed wages in many high- and middle-income countries (Brazil, for one), even as executive and professional remuneration in those countries soars. Around the world the winners use the rhetoric of "efficiency," "flexibility," "innovation," "a rising tide lifts all boats," and "government must live within its means just like a household," sprinkling neoliberal ideas like holy water to justify their riches and kick away the ladder for others.

Income Inequality between Countries and All People

In the past decade world income distribution has become a hot topic of debate in international economics and in sociology. Disagreement about trends should be no surprise, given the collage of economic performance by region. Different measures emphasize different parts of the collage.

Much of the debate is mathematical, far removed from people's experience of inequality, and focuses less on the "facts" than on the measures. It turns out that the only valid short answer to the question, "What is the trend of world income distribution?" is, "It depends on which of several plausible measures and samples we choose." Whereas we could get better data on the poor to the extent that the poverty headcount would command general agreement, there is no best measure of world income inequality. Different measures are useful for answering different questions.

The results vary according to which of three core measures of inequality are used: Concept 1: inter- or between-country, using average incomes (this could be called the UN General Assembly measure, one country one vote); Concept 2: inter-country, like Concept 1, but countries weighted by population; and Concept 3: global interpersonal, covering all the world's people as though the world was one country (Milanovic 2005, 2009).

Several other choices also affect the results. Incomes in different currencies may be converted into a common numeraire using market exchange rates or PPP conversion factors. The results also depend on the choice of statistic for calculating dispersion—an integral measure over the whole distribution (such as the Gini coefficient), or a ratio of top decile to bottom decile, or average income of a region relative to that of the North. And, of course, the country sample and the time period matter.

Concept 1: Inequality: Distribution between Unweighted Countries

Concept 1 gives China the same weight as Uganda. It has the great advantage that it requires little information about each country, just per capita GDP or GNP. Of course, we should not weight countries equally if interested simply in relative well-being of people. But we should weight them equally—treat each country as analogous to a laboratory test observation—if interested in convergence or divergence of countries rather than people. We might want to test the effects of different government policies on growth—to see whether (unweighted) countries with more open trade regimes grow faster than those with less open ones, for example (Wade 2013a).

The spread of average incomes between countries is not falling over time. The Gini for unweighted intercountry income distribution held fairly steady from 1960 to 1980, increased steeply from 1980 to 2000, and fell from 2000 to 2007, leaving a large net increase in inequality since 1980 (Figure 22.3). Is the increase in inequality due only to the collapse of Africa? No. With Africa excluded, the Gini fell from the mid-1960s to the early 1980s and then increased steeply. Angus Deaton summarizes the trend: "there has been little or no narrowing of income inequalities between countries; for every country with a catch-up story there has been a left-behind story" (2013:219).

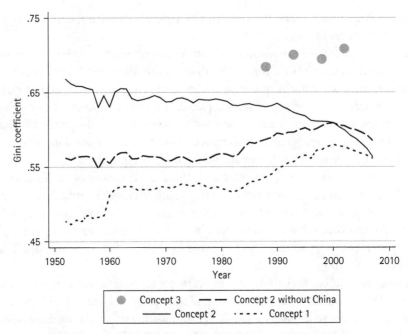

FIGURE 22.3 Trends in the Three Concepts of International Inequality, 1950–2007

Note: Results incorporate PPP data from the 2005 round of the International Comparison Project

Source: Milanovic (2009).

Concept 2: Inequality: Distribution between Weighted Countries

Intercountry income inequality, using PPP dollars, population weights, and the Gini coefficient, was fairly stable from 1960 to the early 1990s and then fell right up to 2007. This is good news: it suggests that the centuries-old trend to income divergence between countries—when weighted by population—has finally gone into reverse.

But here the global Gini conceals as much as it reveals. If we take out just one case, China, the population-weighted intercountry Gini *rises* after 1980 up to 2000, when it, too, begins to turn down; so it goes mostly in the *opposite* direction to the trend with China included. Falling income inequality between population-weighted countries is a function of China's fast growth since the early 1980s, not a *generalized* tendency of the world economy, which could be attributed to a generalized process of neoliberal globalization. If we took out India (which accounts for 18 percent of the world's population and has grown fast toward median world income since the 1990s), the increase in between-country inequality among the remainder would be stronger.

However, this Concept 2 measure is interesting mainly as an approximation to income distribution among all the world's people or households regardless of which country they live in. We would not be interested in measuring income inequality in the

United States by calculating the average income for each state weighted by its population if we had data for all U.S. households.

Concept 3: Inequality: Global Interpersonal Income Distribution

To calculate interpersonal or global income distribution, one way would be to take each population-weighted country's average GDP and its internal income distribution, and then calculate the combined between-country and within-country inequalities across the whole sample. As noted, between-country population-weighted distribution measured by the Gini became more equal after 1980 with China included and more unequal with China excluded. And as noted, within-country distributions generally became more unequal.

But combining between-country and within-country measures is a blunt way to get at global income distribution between all the world's people. A better way, in principle, is to aggregate up from thousands of surveys of household income and expenditure. Branko Milanovic used the resources of the World Bank to do this for five-yearly intervals from 1988 to 2008. He found that the global Gini index remained more or less unchanged over this 20-year period, in the range of 0.71 to 0.76. This rough stability results from the combination of relatively fast growth in the incomes of the median world income deciles in 1988 (especially in China) and relatively very slow growth in the incomes of country deciles which were around the 85th percentile of the global income distribution in 1988 (mainly the Western working and lower-middle classes) (Lakner and Milanovic 2013).

Of course, this method of calculating global income distribution, too, has its problems. It undercounts free public services such as education, health, and infrastructure that add to welfare but are not counted in household consumption. And there are big problems of comparability between household surveys.

However, we can be reasonably confident in saying that global interpersonal PPP income or consumption distribution (using the Gini coefficient) has probably *not* become significantly more equal during the period of intense globalization since 1980.[2]

Polarization or Relative Gap Measure

The Gini coefficient is a measure of dispersion across the whole of the distribution. It can mislead by obscuring what is happening to major components and by giving more weight to what is happening in the middle than at the extremes. Simple "polarization" measures can compensate.

Most such measures show the income caravan of countries to be lengthening. For example, with countries grouped into deciles by their PPP GDP per capita, the ratio between top and bottom deciles almost doubled during the 1960–2000 period, from 19 to 1 to 37 to 1 (Milanovic 2005:53). The average income (market exchange rates) of the 10 richest countries to that of the 10 poorest soared from 34 times in 1962 to 92 times in 1980 to 271 times in 2008 (Korzeniewicz 2012). Polarization would look even more dramatic if we took the remuneration of the top 1 percent of the world's population over the median, or over the average of the bottom 10 percent's.

The Absolute Income Gap

The standard measures of inequality refer to relative incomes, not absolute incomes. To see why relative measures impart a conservative bias, take two countries: A, with a per capita income of $30,000 (e.g., United States and Denmark); and, B, with a per capita income of $1,000 (e.g., Philippines and Syria). Their relative income is 30:1 and the absolute gap is $29,000. If A's per capita income increases by 1 percent to $30,300 and B's also increases by 1 percent to $1,010, the relative gap remains constant and so "inequality" as normally defined remains constant; but the absolute gap widens from $29,000 to $29,290. If B jumped to 6 percent growth while A continued at 1 percent, the absolute gap would widen until year 35 and B would not catch up until year 70. If B grew at 4 percent and A grew at 2 percent, the absolute gap would widen for 140 years and catch-up would take the best part of two centuries.

No one questions that world absolute income gaps have been increasing fast—as between, for example, the average income of the top 10 percent of world income recipients (countries and individuals) and that of the bottom 10 percent, between the top 10 percent and the intermediate 60 percent, and between average incomes in North America and Europe and those in developing country regions. If, as some evidence suggests, people commonly think about inequality in absolute rather than relative terms—for example, those at the lower end feel more resentful and more inclined to migrate as absolute gaps increase even as relative incomes become more equal—our answer to the question, "What is happening to income inequality?" should not be blind to absolute gaps.

POVERTY

Poverty has attracted more attention from the "international community" than inequality, as in the World Bank's motto, "Our dream is a world free of poverty." One reason is that acting to reduce poverty boosts our sense of "doing good in the world," while acting to reduce inequality inevitably raises questions about the appropriateness of the income of those who voice their concern. Inequality sounds ominously "political" to international organizations like the World Bank, which claim to be "apolitical," whereas "poverty" sounds safe.

To get a tangible idea of the distribution of economic hardship around the world we could use the number of hours of work needed for an adult male entry-level employee at McDonald's to earn the equivalent of one Big Mac. In the "core" zone of Western Europe, North America, and Japan, the figure in 2007 was in the range of 15–30 minutes; in Seoul–Taipei–Singapore, 47–51 minutes; San Jose (Costa Rica) and Santiago (Chile), 1 hour 25 minutes; Shanghai 1 hour 48 minutes; Delhi 3 hours; Hyderabad (India) 3 hours 54 minutes. Remember that a job at McDonald's is well up the prestige ranking in low-income countries; most people work in less desirable jobs.

Counting the number of people living below an income poverty line gives us a measure of the incidence (but not the degree of severity) of poverty, and we can measure trends in global poverty by summing the number of people living below a standard international poverty line and tracing the headcount across time. The World Bank is the main source of the poverty numbers.

To get the world extreme poverty headcount, the World Bank first defines an international extreme poverty line (IEPL) for a given base year by using PPP exchange rates to convert the purchasing power of an *average* of the official national poverty lines of a set of low-income countries into the U.S. dollar amount needed to have the same notional purchasing power over a standard bundle of goods and services in the United States in the benchmark year. In its first global poverty estimation, this procedure yielded a conveniently understandable PPP$1 a day for the base year of 1985. Then the Bank uses PPP conversion factors to estimate the amount of local currency, country by country, needed to have the same purchasing power in the same year as in the U.S. base case. So by this method, Rs. 10 may have the same purchasing power over a standard basket of goods and services in India in 1985 as US$1 in the United States in the same year. This gives an IEPL expressed in domestic currency (Rs. 10 per day in the Indian example, which may well differ from India's national poverty line).

From household surveys, the Bank then estimates the number of people in the country living on less than this IEPL in the base year. It sums up the country totals to get the world total of people living in extreme poverty. Then it uses national consumer price indices to keep real purchasing power constant across time and adjusts the IEPL for each country upward with inflation. As well as the extreme poverty headcount (people living on less than PPP$1 a-day, updated) the Bank also estimates the ordinary poverty headcount by simply doubling the extreme poverty line, a rather arbitrary procedure. Currently the extreme poverty line is $1.25; the ordinary poverty line is $2.50.

In 2008, the World Bank presented revised estimates of countries' GDPs and world poverty headcounts, based on the international price survey of 2005. Table 22.2 summarizes the numbers before and after the revised estimates with and without China. The size of the revisions suggests the fragility of the poverty numbers.

The numbers living in extreme poverty show a pronounced fall between 1981 and 2005, with both the pre-2005 PPP exchange rates and the ones based on the 2005 price survey and extrapolated from 2005. This is good news, indicating substantial progress in cutting the number of people living in extreme poverty. The bad news is that, according to the new estimates, hundreds of millions more people have been living in extreme

Table 22.2 Key World Poverty Numbers

	Including China					
	1981		2002		2005	
	Number (bn)	Percentage	Number (bn)	Percentage	Number (bn)	Percentage
Old estimate @ $1.08	1.5	41	1.1	20	0.9	17
New estimate @ $1.25	1.9	52	1.6	31	1.4	25
New estimate @ $2.50	2.7	75	3.3	62	3.1	57

	Excluding China					
	1981		2002		2005	
	Number (bn)	Percentage	Number (bn)	Percentage	Number (bn)	Percentage
Old estimate @ $1.08	0.9	32	0.9	23	0.9	22
New estimate @ $1.25	1.1	40	1.2	31	1.2	28
New estimate @ $2.50	1.8	66	2.6	66	2.6	63

Note: Percentage refers to population of the developing world. "Old" refers to PPP conversion using pre-2005 price data.

Source: Chen and Ravallion 2008. See also World Bank PovcalNet (www.worldbank.org/research/PovcalNet/jsp/index).

poverty than earlier estimated, so the extreme poverty problem was and remains much worse than had been thought. As the World Bank's "poverty czars" summarize, "While the new data suggest that the developing world is poorer than we thought, it has been no less successful in reducing the incidence of absolute poverty since the early 1980s" (Chen and Ravallion 2008:33).

More bad news is that the fall in the number under $1.25 a day is due entirely to China. Take out China and the number in extreme poverty increased (though the proportion of the developing world population still fell substantially from 40 percent to 28 percent). Still more bad news is the sheer number of people living on less than the scarcely generous PPP$2.50 a day, almost 3 billion by 2010— more than 40 percent of the world's population. Moreover, the number of people living below this threshold increased substantially between 1981 and 2005, which implies a big bunching between $1.25 and $2.50 a day. People in this income band remain very vulnerable to shocks such as the steep rise in food and fuel prices after 2005, and the global economic crisis of 2008.

The geographical distribution of extreme poverty has changed. In 1981, East Asia (including China) had the highest proportion of its population in extreme poverty (78 percent, using the new estimates for the PPP$1.25 line), then South Asia (59 percent), then sub-Saharan Africa (54 percent). By 2005, the rank order was sub-Saharan Africa (51 percent), South Asia (40 percent), East Asia (17 percent).

So if we take the World Bank poverty numbers at face value, the record of reducing world poverty is mixed. However, we should not take the numbers at face value. While the Bank generally presents its numbers as "without a doubt," it should provide health warnings to consumers.

Margin of Error

Several reasons suggest that the margin of error is significant. First, the poverty head-count is sensitive to the precise level of the international poverty lines. The curve of the number of people living at each level of income or consumption is steep at the point of intersection of the $1-a-day line, meaning that small shifts in the line make large changes in the number of people below it.

Second, the poverty headcount is sensitive to the reliability of household surveys. Some countries survey income, others, expenditure, others, consumption, and merging the results is not straightforward. The available surveys are of widely varying quality, different countries use different formats; and the same country may change the format from one survey to another. For example, surveys may use different reporting periods ("your income in the past week, or past month").

Third, by far the two most important countries for the overall trend, China and India, have PPP-adjusted income figures that contain even more guesswork than for most other big countries. The government of China declined to participate in all the rounds of the International Comparison Program (ICP) until 2005, so the PPP estimations for China have been based on econometric interpolation rather than real data; and India's have been based on extrapolations from the 1985 price survey. The lack of reliable price surveys for countries accounting for over a third of the world's population—hence the lack of reliable evidence on the purchasing power of even average incomes, let alone incomes of the poor—compromises any statement about levels and trends in world poverty.

Note that other world variables are also subject to large but unquantified margins of error. The absolute income per capita of the poorest countries is implausibly close to the survival minimum, which probably reflects substantial undercounting of agricultural, informal, and black activities. The per capita income of the richest countries may be underestimated because of deficiencies in measuring inflation and quality improvements, and undercounting at the top. Income and wealth recorded in tax havens are readily hidden.

Downward Bias

Other sources of error may bias the poverty numbers downward, making the number of poor people seem lower than it is; and the bias may increase over time, making the trend look rosier than it is.

First, the Bank's IEPL probably underestimates the income or expenditure needed for an individual (or household) to avoid periods of food-water-clothing-shelter consumption too low to maintain health. And it avoids altogether the problem that basic needs include unpriced public goods like clean water and health care. The Bank's line refers to purchasing power over an "average consumption" bundle, not to a basket of goods and services that makes sense for measuring poverty (though "$1 a day" does have intuitive appeal to a Western audience being asked to support aid). Suppose it costs Rs. 30 to buy an equivalent bundle of food in India (defined in terms of calories and micronutrients) as can be bought in the United States with $1; and that it costs only Rs. 3 to buy an equivalent bundle of services (haircuts, massages) as $1 in the United States (Reddy and Pogge 2005). Current methods of calculating purchasing power parity, based on an *average* consumption bundle of food, services, and other things, may yield a PPP exchange rate of, say, PPP$1 = Rs. 10, meaning that Rs. 10 in India buys the equivalent average consumption bundle (food, services, etc.) as $1 in the United States. But the poor person, spending most income on food, can buy with Rs. 10 only a third of the food purchasable with $1 in the United States. To take the IEPL for India as Rs. 10 therefore biases the number of poor downward.

We have no way of knowing what proportion of food-water-clothing-shelter needs the Bank's international poverty line captures. But we can be fairly sure that had the Bank used a basic needs poverty line rather than its present one (an average of the national poverty lines of a set of low-income countries) the number of absolute poor would rise, because the national poverty lines equivalent to a global basic needs poverty line would probably rise, perhaps by 25 to 40 percent. A 25 to 40 percent increase in a basic-needs-based international poverty line would, for the reason mentioned earlier, increase the world total of people in extreme poverty by a large fraction, probably by at least 25 to 40 percent.

In short, we can be reasonably sure that switching from the Bank's IEPL to one reflecting the purchasing power necessary to achieve elementary human capabilities would substantially raise the number of people in poverty.

The second reason for suspecting that the Bank's poverty numbers make the trend look too rosy relates to the effects of changes in average consumption patterns as average incomes rise. Worldwide average consumption patterns are shifting toward services whose prices relative to food and shelter are lower in poor than in rich countries, giving the false impression that the cost of the basic consumption goods required by the poor is falling. As Indians become wealthier and consume more services relative to food, a rupee appears to buy more than it used to; and so the PPP value of Indian incomes goes up. But poor Indians continue to spend most of their income on food, and for them the purchasing power of rupees has not increased. Part of the apparent fall in the number of people below a poverty line defined in PPP-adjusted rupees is therefore a statistical illusion.

All these problems have to be resolved in one way or another in any estimate of world poverty, whoever makes it. But the fact that the World Bank is the near-monopoly provider introduces a third source of possible downward bias. The number of poor people is politically sensitive. The Bank's many critics on the Right and Left like to use the poverty numbers as a stick to beat the Bank. The chairman of a taskforce established by the U.S. Congress to report on the multilateral economic organizations described the fall in the proportion of the world's population in extreme poverty from 28 percent in 1987 to 24 percent in 1998 as a "modest" decline (Meltzer 2001). Former U.S. Treasury Secretary Paul H. O'Neill asserted that the Bank had accomplished "precious little" (Institutional Investor 2002). This critique then provides justification for U.S. control of the Bank. Understandably, the Bank highlights the fall in the poverty numbers when responding to criticism from powerful member states in order to show that it is doing a good job. On the other hand, when trying to enlist support for a bold initiative, it may highlight the magnitude of persisting poverty to show that it needs more support.

The enormous increase in the poverty numbers made in the wake of the 2005 ICP price survey adds to the sense of being in quicksand. Angus Deaton, one of the world experts in this subject, argues that the increase is due mostly to the statistical technique for recalibrating the IEPL. The line is calculated as the average national poverty lines of a sample of low-income countries, one of which was India, whose national line was one of the lowest in the sample. When India's average income reached the middle-income threshold, its national poverty line was removed from the sample—causing the sample average, hence the IEPL, to rise, causing the global extreme poverty headcount to rise. Having said this, Deaton also states, "It is all very confused, at least to me" (personal communication, December 27, 2009). However, the Bank has recently put its poverty computations online in a way that enables others to recalculate poverty numbers with different assumptions (available at PovcalNet).

In sum, the international poverty lines have a weak link with the income needed to sustain basic human capabilities. But we know enough about trends in other variables—life expectancy, heights, and other nonincome measures—to be confident that "objective" poverty headcounts have, indeed, fallen dramatically over the past 20 to 30 years. Moreover, the magnitude of world population increase is so large that the Bank's poverty numbers would have to be huge underestimates for the world poverty *rate* not to have fallen.

CONCLUSIONS

This chapter has accented ambiguities and indeterminacies in our knowledge about growth, inequality, and poverty, stemming in particular from measurement difficulties and from differences in measures of what is ostensibly the same thing ("poverty," "inequality"). In addition to those ambiguities noted earlier, we can add here that two of the world's experts on PPP calculations, Angus Deaton and Alan Heston, estimate the error on either side of the PPP exchange rate at about 25 percent; meaning that, for example, the aggregate Chinese economy in PPP terms is somewhere between 56 percent and 94 percent of the aggregate American economy (Deaton 2013:228). With reference to the revised PPP exchange rates calculated on the basis of the 2005 price survey (which led to a change in China's PPP GDP per capita in 2005 from $6,7605 using the pre-2005 PPP exchange rate, to $4,090 for the same year, 40 percent down, and a change in India's corresponding figure from $3,450 to $2,220), Deaton and Heston remark, "it is hard not to speculate about which previously established econometric results survive the incorporation of these revisions" (Deaton and Heston 2009).

It is also worth bringing out the implication of an earlier point made about the Gini coefficient—the workhorse measure of inequality. By calculating only changes in relative incomes and ignoring changes in absolute gaps it undermeasures increases in inequality. If individual or country A has an income of $100 and B has $200 in time 1, and A has $200 and B has $400 in time 2, the Gini says that inequality remains constant (allowing the government to claim that "growth is inclusive", as the government of India regularly does). But the absolute gap increased from $100 to $200. A more "progressive" Gini formula would include both relative and absolute gaps, and world inequality would be at a higher level and rising more than according to the standard, "conservative" measure (Subramanian and Jayaraj 2013).

In short, confidence in trends in PPP incomes, inequality, and poverty should be limited by the certainty of wide uncertainty (DeMartino 2011). Still, we can be reasonably confident about several substantive conclusions. First, for all the uncertainties around the extreme poverty numbers, the headcount trend has been downward, as supported by nonincome data (such as life expectancy and child mortality). It is even possible that the number of people living in extreme poverty could be reduced to a tiny fraction of the world's population by 2030. Elimination of humanity's ancient scourge would be a triumph of the first half of the twenty-first century.

Second, "the rise of the South" is mainly the "rise of the East," and the latter is mainly "rise of China," with India coming along some way behind. The commonly heard image of "the new, fast-evolving [economically] multipolar world" is an exaggeration fueled by extrapolating what has changed and overlooking what has not changed—always the temptation of pundits and academics heralding the turning points of history. The United States remains by far the weightiest economy in terms of GDP, capital markets, technology, and innovation, and the idea of China as the emerging superpower has some way to go before it can even be called simplistic.

Third, average income inequality among countries not weighted by population increased after the 1980s and probably declined somewhat in the 2000s. Inequality among countries weighted by population probably remained more or less constant from 1960 to 1990 and fell thereafter as the Chinese and Indian giants grew fast toward the median in the 1990s and 2000s, more than offsetting the falling behind of other national economies.

Fourth, the much faster growth of low- and middle-income countries in 2003–2010, compared to the high-income countries, was fueled by unsustainable credit growth in the United States and parts of Western Europe. Their sharp growth slowdown since 2010 suggests that their growth remains substantially dependent on the North's. Some big developing countries may experience financial crises in the coming years as monetary policy in the United States tightens, starting a third phase of the global crisis that began in the United States in 2007.

Fifth, within-country market income inequality has increased in most countries over the past several decades; hence the period since the 1980s has been called the "second age of inequality," following the first one in the several decades before 1929.

To end, let us consider the likely negative consequences of some of the aforementioned trends continuing—a lengthening income caravan of countries, an increasing share of world production from a small number of big developing countries, higher or constant inequality within countries, and images of the good life in the West available on every internet connection. One result, intensified by civil and inter-state wars, is intense pressure to escape from zones of disorder and economic stagnation into Western zones of order and economic opportunity.

Another result is gridlock in global governance. Many more developing countries have entered the ranks of the world's biggest 20 countries by GDP, demanding more voice in global governance. Earlier the biggest countries by GDP were also the richest by GDP per head (and also almost all of Western culture). Now the correlation between GDP and GDP per head has broken down, producing much greater divergence of interests among countries sitting at the top table of global governance. The lagging states are frustrated because of their failure to catch up and are less inclined to accept the fairness of the Western-dominated order. For example, the four big BRICs (Brazil, Russia, India, and China) have a combined share of world GDP of 24.5 percent, compared to the 13.4 percent share of the four big EU economies (Germany, France, Britain, and Italy); but they have a combined share of IMF votes of only 10.3 percent, compared to the EU4's 17.6 percent (Wade 2013b; Vestergaard and Wade 2012, 2013; Wade and Vestergaard 2015). Western states' continued blocking of reform in the IMF and World Bank has spurred the BRICS (including South Africa) to create the New Development Bank and the Contingent Reserve Arrangement (a form of pooling some foreign-exchange reserves to be available as a source of emergency loans, described by some as a "mini-IMF").

The within-country trends raise financial fragility and the likelihood of multi-country financial crises. Both the 1929 crash and the 2008 crash were preceded, in the United States and Britain, by sharp increases in income concentration and stagnant incomes for the bulk of the population. They were inequality crises, or wages crises, as much as debt crises; increasing inequality and stagnant wages raised the supply and demand for credit, resulting in a credit boom, a house price boom, and rising debt-to-income ratios (Wade 2009a; Sington 2010).[3] When the elite accrues a rising share of national income and also—thanks to globalization—moves capital and enterprises readily across borders, the impetus to crisis is strengthened, as in the buildup to 2008. The elite can translate affluence into influence to prevent tighter constraints (think of the erosion of the Dodd-Frank Act's attempt to apply discipline to U.S. financial markets after 2008) and can count on taxpayer or shareholder bailouts to protect themselves from losses should high leverage go horribly wrong.

Similarly, as the rungs on the ladder move further apart, the elite has more incentive to fortify its position by supporting state policies and institutions that in one way or another place a glass floor beneath their children, thus raising the cost to children born to nonelite parents. Intergenerational social mobility in the United States and Britain is probably the lowest of the major North American and European economies.[4] The implications for democracy are captured in a statement by Louis Brandeis, U.S. Supreme Court justice from 1916 to 1939: "We must make our choice. We may have democracy or we may have wealth concentrated in the hands of a few, but we can't have both" (Wade 2012).

Neoliberalism's framing of "the market versus the state" helps conceal the way that "the market" operates according to the pricing, marketing, production, and remuneration strategies of oligopolistic corporations rather than according to the textbook picture of competing enterprises—none of whom can shape the outcomes. Wolf's prescription for "more market" is an invitation to more corporate power, less collective bargaining, and more super-elites shrugging off the responsibilities of social compacts. When the market does not generate employment for the labor force growing in sub-Saharan African by 8 million people a year, and in South Asia by 1 million a month, the economically excluded are likely to direct their anger at government (not the market) and are more likely to turn to extremism and violence; and in response, governments become more capricious. Decay of democracy and erosion of trust in national governments are all too likely. We see this in the dramatic decline in public confidence in governing classes in Europe. A Eurobarometer poll in 2013 recorded trust in national governments at 25 percent, down from 41 percent in 2007 (Barber 2014). No doubt recession, unemployment, and stagnant or falling living conditions partly account for this slump. But underlying these factors is voters' frustration that they exert less influence than ever over the decisions of elites and live on stagnant incomes as income is sluiced up to the top.

Still, it seems likely that the life expectancy of neoliberalism is beginning to shrink. The concatenation of climate change, wealth concentration, "precariate" jobs, and multicountry financial crashes will eventually produce politics and policies that rein in the plutocrats, as did the Bretton Woods regime in the wake of the calamities of the first half of the twentieth century. Perhaps President Obama's declaration, in a speech on December 4, 2013, that inequality is "the defining challenge of our time" is a harbinger of wider acceptance of the idea of a "fate-sharing community"—provided middle- and low-income groups organize to countervail the efforts of the wealthy to dress self- and class-interest in the neoliberal language of national and global interest.

NOTES

1. Figure 22.1 uses PPP exchange rates to commensurate average incomes in different currencies. Figure 22.2 uses lagged-market exchange rates. To compare incomes in different currencies a common numeraire has to be used. Indian rupees, Brazilian real, British pounds could be converted into U.S. dollars at (lagged) market-exchange rates. But typically, a given amount of currency in a developing country buys a bigger bundle of goods and services in that country than it buys in the United States when the currency is converted to dollars at market-exchange rates. Hence, poor Americans feel rich when they go to India, and rich Indians feel poor when they go to the United States. The PPP methodology attempts to correct market-exchange rates for this difference in the purchasing power of currencies. In principle, PPP exchange rates should be used for comparing levels of material well-being among countries. Market-exchange rates should be used for comparing the ability of people in one country to purchase goods and services produced in another (for example, comparing the ability of Ugandans and French to import, repay foreign debt, or represent themselves in the WTO in Geneva and at the UN in New York). For explanations of PPP methodology see Deaton (2013); Deaton and Heston (2009).

2. Hung and Kucinskas 2011 use inequality between Indian states, and Chinese provinces, divided into rural and urban areas, as a proxy for within-country inequality in these two countries, and find that adding these measures to more standard measures of within- and between-country inequality, global interpersonal income inequality declined between 1980 and 2005; but it increased strongly when China and India are taken out. Their paper is a salutary reminder of wide margins of uncertainty in our knowledge of trends, when different measures of much the same thing produce substantially different results.

3. Of course a credit boom and resulting financial fragility can occur separately from high inequality. The UK, Australia, Iceland, Ireland, and Spain all had housing-price booms over the 2000s at levels of inequality less than the United States, though most of them experienced sharp increases in inequality.

4. Contrary to the image of the United States as the land of opportunity, intergenerational mobility is lower than in much of Western Europe and Canada, and has either fallen or remained about the same for children born between 1971 and 1986. Britain is almost as low as the United States. See Blanden et al. 2005 and Chetty et al. 2014.

REFERENCES

Barber, Tony. 2014. "To Revive Trust in Europe, Rebuild Faith in Democracy." *Financial Times*, January 2.

Blanden, Jo, Paul Gregg, and Stephen Machin. 2005. *Intergenerational Mobility in Europe and North America*. London: LSE, Centre for Economic Performance.

Chen, Shaohua and Martin Ravallion. 2008. "The Developing World Is Poorer Than We Thought, but No Less Successful in the Fight against Poverty." Policy Research Working Paper No. 4703, August. Washington, DC, World Bank.

Chetty, R., et al. 2014. "Is the United States Still the Land of Opportunity? Recent Trends in Intergenerational Mobility." Working Paper No. 19844. Cambridge, MA, National Bureau of Economic Research.

Corea, Giovanni A. and Sampsa Kiiski. 2001 "Trends in Income Distribution in the Post–World War II Period." Discussion Paper No. 89. Helsinki, WIDER.

Deaton, Angus. 2013. *The Great Escape: Health, Wealth, and the Origins of Inequality.* Princeton, NJ: Princeton University Press.

Deaton, Angus and Alan Heston, 2009. "Understanding PPPs and PPP-based National Accounts." Working Paper No. 14499. Cambridge, MA, National Bureau of Economic Research.

DeMartino, George. 2011. *The Economist's Oath: On the Need for and Content of Professional Economic Ethics.* New York: Oxford University Press.

Fourcade, Marion. 2009. *Economists and Societies: Discipline and Profession in the United States, Britain and France, 1890s to 1990s.* Princeton, NJ: Princeton University Press.

Hung, Ho-Fung and Jaime Kucinskas. 2011. "Globalization and Global Inequality: Assessing the Impact of the Rise of China and India, 1980–2005." *American Journal of Sociology* 116(11):1478–1513.

Institutional Investor. 2002. "Poor Choices." September 1.

Korzeniewicz, Roberto. 2012. "Trends in World Income Inequality and the 'Emerging Middle.'" *European Journal of Development Research* 24(2):205–22.

Korzeniewicz, Roberto and Timothy P. Moran. 2009. *Unveiling Inequality: A World-Historical Perspective.* New York: Russell Sage Foundation.

Lakner, Christoph and Branko Milanovic. 2013. "Global Income Distribution: From the Fall of the Berlin Wall to the Great Recession." Policy Research Working Paper No. 6719. Washington, DC, World Bank.

Meltzer, Allan H. 2001. "The World Bank One Year after the Commission's Report to Congress." Hearings before the Joint Economic Committee, U.S. Congress, March 8.

Milanovic, Branko. 2005. *Worlds Apart: Measuring International and Global Inequality.* Princeton, NJ: Princeton University Press.

Milanovic, Branko. 2009. "Global Inequality Recalculated: The Effect of New 2005 PPP Estimates on Global Inequality." Working Paper No. 5061. Washington, DC: World Bank.

OECD. 2013. *Shifting Wealth: The Recalibration of Global Development.* Paris: OECD.

Pritchett, L. and L. Summers. 2014. "Asiaphoria Meets Regression to the Mean." NBER Working Paper 20573, October.

Reddy, Sanjay and Camelia Minoiu. 2009."Real Income Stagnation of Countries, 1960–2001." *Journal of Development Studies* 45(1):1–23.

Reddy, Sanjay and Thomas Pogge. 2005. "How *Not* to Count the Poor." Retrieved December 10, 2014 (http://www.columbia.edu/~sr793/count.pdf).

Sington, David. 2010. *The Flaw.* Documentary film.

Subramanian, S. and D. Jayaraj. 2013. "Economic Inequality in India: Value-neutral Measurement." *Challenge* 56(4):26–37.

Vestergaard, Jakob and Robert H. Wade. 2012. "Establishing a New Global Economic Council: Governance Reform at the G20, the IMF and the World Bank." *Global Policy* 3(1):257–69.

Vestergaard, Jakob and Robert H. Wade. 2013. "Protecting Power: How Western States Retain Their Dominant Voice in the World Bank's Governance Reforms." *World Development*, 46:153–64.

Wade, Robert H. 2009a. "The Global Slump: Deeper Causes and Harder Lessons." *Challenge* 52(5):5–24.

Wade, Robert H. 2009b. "From Global Imbalances to Global Reorganisations." *Cambridge Journal of Economics* 33:539–62.

Wade, Robert H. 2012. "Why has income inequality remained on the sidelines of public policy for so long?" *Challenge* 55(3):21–50.

Wade, Robert H. 2013a. "Trade Liberalization and Economic Growth: Does Trade Liberalization Contribute to Economic Prosperity?" In *Controversies in Globalization*, edited by P. Haas et al. 2nd ed. Washington, DC: Sage.

Wade, Robert H. 2013b. "The Art of Power Maintenance: How Western States Keep the Lead in Global Organizations." *Challenge* 56(1):5–39.

Wade, Robert H. 2014. "Growth, Inequality, and Poverty: Evidence, Arguments, and Economists." Chapter 12 in *Global Political Economy*, 4th ed., edited by John Ravenhill. Oxford: Oxford University Press.

Wade, Robert H. 2015. "Why is the IMF at an Impasse, and What Can Be Done About It?" *Global Policy*, September.

Wolf, Martin. 2004. *Why Globalization Works: The Case for the Global Market Economy*. New Haven, CT: Yale University Press.

CHAPTER 23

....

INTERGENERATIONAL
MOBILITY

....

LIANA FOX, FLORENCIA TORCHE,
AND JANE WALDFOGEL

INTRODUCTION

INTERGENERATIONAL mobility is an important goal in both developed and developing countries as it indicates opportunity for children to move beyond their social origins and obtain a status not dictated by that of their parents. Intergenerational mobility has been considered through various disciplinary lenses, but a common feature is that mobility tends to be measured by the extent of association between parents' and adult children's socioeconomic status (measured by social class, occupation, earnings, or family income). Stronger associations mean more intergenerational transmission of advantage (often referred to as persistence) and less mobility, whereas weaker associations indicate less persistence and more mobility.

This chapter provides an overview of current research on intergenerational mobility. The chapter begins with theoretical and methodological approaches to measuring intergenerational mobility. Drawing on research in economics and sociology, the chapter reviews the evidence on the degree of mobility and persistence as well as possible underlying mechanisms. The chapter concludes with an international comparison of mobility in wealthy and developing countries and directions for future research.

THEORY

Researchers interested in understanding intergenerational persistence typically ground their analyses in Becker and Tomes's (1979) human capital model, which explains parents' decisions about investments in children and how those investments influence children's future outcomes. This model states that parents maximize a Cobb-Douglas utility function in allocating their lifetime earnings between their own consumption and investment in their children. The Becker and Tomes model expands previous human capital models that only explained inequality within a single generation as a stochastic process of luck and ability. Their model assumes that families maximize a utility function spanning several generations, which determines the amount of resources they will invest in their children, which then influences a child's future lifetime earnings.

Without going too far into mathematical notation, the basic model of intergenerational human capital accumulation can best be presented in a couple of equations.[1] Equation (1) shows the budget constraint parents face in the first generation:

$$Y_{t-1} = C_{t-1} + I_{e-1},$$

(1)

where parent's lifetime earnings (Y_{t-1}) are split between parent's own consumption (C_{t-1}) and investment in their children's human capital (I_{t-1}). Parents will then maximize this equation subject to their own propensity to invest in their children and their knowledge of the child's anticipated endowments and market luck.

Children's lifetime earnings are subsequently a function of parent's lifetime earnings (Y_{t-1}), child's endowment (e_t) and market luck (u_t):

$$Y_t = a\left[(1+r)I_{t-1} + \lambda e_t + u_t\right],$$

(2)

where the influence of parent's income is determined by the propensity of parents to invest in their children (a) and the return on human capital investment (r) and endowments are influenced by the degree of inheritability of parent's endowments (λ). Endowments include genetically inherited traits such as race, height, weight, perceived beauty, IQ, and ability; and environmentally inherited, "family culture" items such as reputation, connections, skills, and goals provided by family environment. Market luck (u_t) is assumed to be a phenomenon that parents are likely to have some prior knowledge of before investing in their child's human capital.

The Becker and Tomes model clearly points out that the intergenerational transmission of economic status occurs through multiple processes, not just direct investment in children's human capital. Utilizing this framework, intergenerational persistence can change for three reasons: (1) changes in the relative investments in children in rich and poor families; (2) changes in the payoff to investments in human capital; and (3) changes in the returns to endowments or heritability of endowments (Mayer and Lopoo 2004). Increased progressivity of investments in children from public provision of education or universal health care would have an equalizing impact on a child's future outcomes. Alternatively, thinking of height as an endowment that is typically perceived to be genetically determined, environmental factors such as nutrition also play a role. As nutrition in a country improves, disparities in height will likely decline and therefore the heritability of this endowment will decrease, which means that income inequalities based on height will be reduced and intergenerational persistence will decrease.

In 1986, Becker and Tomes expanded their model to include the notion of credit constraints. In this expansion they found that parents with low earnings are most likely to lack access to credit markets and as a result would be unable to optimally borrow against their lifetime earnings to invest in their children. As a result, Becker and Tomes hypothesized that mobility would be limited among low-earning families. In turn, high rates of intergenerational persistence at the bottom end of the earnings distribution, which gradually declined as credit constraints lessened at higher levels of earnings, would lead to a concave relationship between parent and child earnings. This implies that initial investments in children's human capital will have the largest impact on out-comes (Mayer and Lopoo 2008). While this hypothesis has been extensively studied, most researchers acknowledge that they cannot fully test this assumption. In fact, some empirical work has found a convex intergenerational association (e.g., Behrman and Taubman 1990). In 2004, Grawe argued against the usage of nonlinearities in inter-generational elasticity as a test of credit constraints, stating that there is no compelling theoretical reason to assume why the relationship between parent and child log earn-ings would be linear in the first place, and that nonlinearities may emerge from other factors. Therefore, the presence of nonlinearities in intergenerational elasticity is not evidence of credit constraints. Other researchers such as Mazumder (2005a, 2005b) and Mulligan (1997) have used some measure of actual wealth as a proxy for credit constraints but have found conflicting results.

Additional criticisms of the Becker and Tomes model by Solon (1999) are that it fails to taken into account intergenerational bequests and *inter vivos* transfers, which could factor heavily into children's human capital accumulation patterns. Intergenerational transfers could be a source of credit for human capital investment or could provide funds for entrepreneurship, both of which would boost children's future incomes and increase disparities among children. Additionally, the model ignores the division of resources between multiple children and interactions among kids. Finally, the role of assortative mating is ignored in this model.

Economic Approaches to Estimating Intergenerational Mobility (IGM)

Early economic analysis of mobility focused on father-son pairs and on individual earnings. Over the last two decades, the study of economic mobility has expanded in three related directions: considering total family income, including daughters, and considering the role of assortative mating in the mobility process. Earnings provide a cleanly identified measure of well-being strictly based on the labor market. As a result, it does not include those who are not working or nonearnings resources, such as financial assets and public and private transfers. These additional resources are most important at either extreme of the economic distribution—among the "underclass" poorly attached to the labor market (Grusky and Weeden 2008) and among the "overclass," whose income largely depends on returns to capital. By focusing on the family rather than the individual or the occupational group as the unit of analysis, measures of total family income assess the economic position of those not in the labor force and include a more comprehensive measure of economic well-being. Furthermore, this measure accounts for family-level dynamics, such as spousal selection (assortative mating) and intrahousehold division of labor, and for institutional arrangements that may mediate the consequences of economic factors on the household's well-being. Given that women's labor market engagement is still weaker than men's, income mobility may provide a more comprehensive account for women. Many of the estimation issues discussed in this chapter are particularly acute when it comes to studying mobility for women, given their lower and more intermittent labor force participation rates (Torche 2015).

Research on intergenerational correlations of poverty (surveyed in Jenkins and Siedler 2007) welfare recipiency (Page 2004) and worklessness (Macmillan 2011) highlight the various ways through which researchers would find a strong correlation in income but not necessarily earnings. However, even when considering family income as opposed to individual earnings, many family-level studies restrict the sample to two-parent families (Mayer and Lopoo 2005) and treat cohabiting partners as two separate families, which would tend to overstate mobility (Aaberge et al. 2002). To the extent that female-headed households are disproportionately low income, exclusion of these families could introduce a bias to estimates of intergenerational persistence (Peters 1992). These selection issues are especially problematic as the share of the population in these family structures increases over time.

While income and earnings are two different measures of economic status, the same methods can be applied to both measures so they are discussed jointly in the following section. Additional methods for focusing on poverty transmission are also examined.

Measurement of Earnings and Income Mobility

Classically, intergenerational economic mobility is measured by estimating the elasticity of children's earnings (or income) with respect to the same measure for their parents, by regressing the log of children's earnings on the log of parent's earnings:[2]

$$\log(Y_{child})_i = \alpha + \beta_1 \log(Y_{parent})_i + \varepsilon_i \qquad (3)$$

where β is the intergenerational elasticity (IGE). The elasticity captures the average percent change in children's earnings associated with a percent change in parents' earnings. For example, an elasticity of 0.4 indicates that if fathers' earnings differ by 10 percent, their children's earnings will, on average, differ by 4 percent. Higher elasticities (i.e., β's closer to 1) indicate greater reliance on parents' income and therefore lower mobility. Estimates of "consensus" rates of intergenerational income and earnings persistence in the United States have changed considerably as data and methodology have improved, ranging from 0.2 in the 1980s to 0.4 in the late 1990s to as high as 0.6 in the 2000s (and back down to 0.34 in 2014). These findings suggest that regression to the mean is not occurring as rapidly as previously thought and family background plays a large role in determining economic outcomes. Reconciling this wide range of estimates requires an in-depth examination of evolving methodologies over time.

Recent work has moved beyond the focus on elasticities in several distinct ways. One critique of elasticities is that they are by definition affected by the underlying distribution of earnings or income over which they are estimated. If the underlying distribution has changed over time or differs between two groups, estimates that account for such change or differences would be preferable. For this reason, some analyses have instead used the intergenerational correlation coefficient:

$$\varphi = \beta * \left(\frac{\sigma_{parent}}{\sigma_{child}} \right) \tag{4}$$

which adjusts elasticities by the ratio of the standard deviation (σ) in income between the two generations. While elasticities are unbounded, the correlation is bounded by 0 and 1, where 0 indicates no intergenerational association and 1 indicates perfect association. This accounts for differing variance in income over time and produces a measure not affected by changes in cross-sectional inequality (Björklund and Jäntti 2009).[3]

A further concern about elasticities is that they do not take into account possible nonlinearities in mobility. Recent research by Chetty et al. (2014a) highlights the importance of using rank specifications (i.e., rank in income distribution relative to others in the same birth cohort) rather than the typical logged specification as previous research has consistently found a nonlinear relationship between logged parent and child income while Chetty et al. (2014a) find a strong linear relationship between parent and child rank relations. One straightforward solution is the use of quantile regression to estimate elasticities at various points in the initial income distribution. Quantile regression provides a conditional probability of mobility, given a particular level of parental income. Utilizing this method, researchers have found that both the lowest and highest income families experience a greater deal of "stickiness" than do middle-income families (Hertz 2005; Grawe 2004a; Eide and Showalter 1999). Couch and Lillard (1998) found stronger intergenerational persistence at the top and bottom of income distribution than at the middle, while Eide and Showalter (1999) found that fathers' income is more persistent among sons with low earnings than among sons with high earnings. These results suggest that the standard elasticity methodology that measures the average association may be obscuring patterns at different points in the distribution.

However, quantile regression still does not get at the direction of mobility, only the magnitude. For this reason, transition matrices have been used to complement both mean and quantile regression results to provide context as to the amount of upward versus downward mobility. To address limitations in current measures and allow direct comparisons of subgroups, Bhattacharya and Mazumder (2011) developed a new methodology to calculate rates of upward and downward intergenerational mobility that overcomes the sensitivity of transition matrices to choice of cut-points (i.e., whether to use quartiles or quintiles) and instead allows the emphasis to be on the magnitude of the upward or downward mobility, given a certain starting point in the income distribution.

Another methodological solution to the nonlinear relationship between income in two generations is to examine the persistence of extreme negative outcomes, such as poverty or welfare dependence, rather than simply measuring the overall degree of correlation in incomes. Researchers typically adjust income using a ratio of family income to a family-specific poverty threshold (Jenkins and Siedler 2007). This ratio is then analyzed using binary definitions of whether a family's income falls below a poverty threshold or not or grouped into three categorical outcomes: whether a given family was never poor, ever poor, or persistently poor (for at least half the observed outcome years). Similar definitions are used to examine the persistence of intergenerational welfare benefit receipt as well. Poverty transition tables estimate the likelihood of an individual experiencing poverty as an adult given that they were poor in childhood (Gibbons and Blanden 2006; Corcoran 2001; Corcoran and Adams 1997).

Patterns and Trends of Earnings and Income Mobility

Economists and sociologists have been attempting to measure intergenerational mobility for decades, but new methods continue to challenge previous findings (Solon 1999; Black and Devereux 2011). Early research (Blau and Duncan 1967, Becker and Tomes 1979, 1986) indicated that the United States had considerable mobility from one generation to the next with intergenerational elasticities of around 0.2. Early estimates did not have access to nationally representative longitudinal surveys, so instead researchers had to rely on unique samples that were very homogenous (e.g., Behrman and Taubman 1985) and often only had a single year of income for each generation. Subsequent research found that homogenous samples biased estimates of IGE downward (Solon 1992) and that single-year estimates of income or earnings were quite poor predictors of permanent income status (Solon 1992; Zimmerman 1992). Alternatively, instrumental variable (IV) estimates that used father's education or occupation as an instrument for father's earnings can lead to omitted variable bias resulting in an overestimation of IGE (Solon 1992). Using any estimate of annual earnings as a proxy for permanent earnings results in measurement error, due to both reporting error (i.e., rounding, recollection bias) and transitory variance (i.e., fluctuations in current earnings from permanent, long-run value). Both reporting error and transitory variance lead to attenuation bias toward 0 (Solon 1992, 1999; Zimmerman 1992). Single-year estimates of income were especially prone to substantial attenuation bias due to substantial fluctuations in income from year to year.

In the 1990s and 2000s, research methodologies for measuring intergenerational mobility progressed substantially, leading to a new consensus estimate of about 0.4 in the 1999 *Handbook of Labor Economics* (Solon 1999). Following Solon's and Zimmerman's findings, most subsequent research was done on nationally representative samples and used averages of multiple years of log fathers' earnings in the estimation of IGE to better proxy permanent earnings. New forms of bias including life-cycle variation in income, nonlinearities and group differences were all explored at length in the literature.

Throughout the life course, earnings follow an inverted U-shaped pattern, starting low when individuals are young and have little experience, and growing rapidly until middle age, where growth flattens out and starts to decline around retirement age. Due to this life-cycle variation in earnings, the age at which earnings are measured matters quite a bit for the estimation of intergenerational mobility. To help reduce life-cycle bias, an average of several consecutive years of earnings information is typically used as a proxy for permanent lifetime earnings.

Haider and Solon (2006) found that systematic heterogeneity exists across individuals in their rates of earnings growth over the life cycle. Highly educated individuals will have more years of low earnings during years while they are in school but will experience much steeper wage growth trajectories than other members of their cohort. Therefore, if earnings are measured at a young age, the perceived difference in permanent earnings status (with current earnings as a proxy for permanent earnings) will understate the true difference in status. Conversely, if earnings are measured late in life, the difference in current earnings will overstate permanent lifetime earnings due to amplification bias. As a result, earnings should ideally be measured from both generations while they are in their 30s to 40s (Grawe 2006; Haider and Solon 2006). In addition to observing both generations at similar ages in midcareer, estimates should be age-adjusted to account for age differences within a sample (Solon 1992; Bratberg et al. 2007).

Recent work using administrative data has re-estimated IGE to be around 0.6 instead of the previously agreed-upon elasticity of 0.4 (Mazumder 2005a, 2005b). This is due to bias resulting from persistent transitory fluctuations and measurement error of parental earnings. Utilizing Social Security earnings data matched with the 1984 Survey of Income and Program Participation (SIPP) data, Mazumder (2005a) finds that short-term averages (4–5 years) of earnings data are inadequate proxies of permanent earnings as there is serial correlation in transitory shocks. An isolated single-year (or even partial-year) shock such as unemployment continues to impact earnings for years after the event occurs. As a result, if income is measured in any of the years surrounding a negative shock, earnings will be biased downward. However, subsequent research has found differing results. Chetty et al. (2014a) find much less attenuation bias than Mazumder and conclude that there is little difference in IGEs based on five-year versus 15-year averages. Even in the absence of administrative data, Mazumder's (2005a) findings have important ramifications for future work. He found that if one has a short panel (i.e., less than 20 years of earnings data per generation), family income is a better measure than father's earnings because families can use spousal earnings or nonearnings forms of income such as asset income or government transfers to smooth consumption in periods when earnings are low.

CURRENT ESTIMATES AND TRENDS OVER TIME

Current estimates indicate that the persistence of economic inequality in the United States is particularly strong, especially at the top and bottom of the income distribution (Hertz 2005). The best current estimates of intergenerational elasticity (IGE) of children's earnings with respect to their parents' earnings are between 0.34 and 0.6 (Solon 1999; Mazumder 2005a; Black and Devereux 2011; Chetty et al. 2014a). This degree of association means that the disadvantage of living in a family with earnings that are half the national average would take five generations to phase out (Mazumder 2005b). This lack of mobility is especially troubling when one considers the rigidities that exist at both the bottom and top of the income distribution (Hertz 2005; Grawe 2004a; Eide and Showalter 1999).

While the current portrait of intergenerational mobility appears rather bleak, the question remains whether this has always been the case, or whether mobility has decreased in recent years as inequality has increased. Availability of longer panels of longitudinal data has made empirical investigation of trends in mobility possible both through the National Longitudinal Surveys (NLS) and the Panel Study of Income Dynamics (PSID). However, there remains quite a bit of debate on this topic and direct comparison of various studies can be difficult as studies examine different cohorts and time periods. Generally, trend analyses based on the PSID find no statistically significant trends in the intergenerational elasticity of earnings for U.S. cohorts born between 1952 and 1975, a finding probably due to small sample sizes (Lee and Solon 2009; Hertz 2007; and Beller and Hout 2006), while analyses using the NLS show a decline in mobility between cohorts born in the late 1940s/early 1950s and those born in the early 1960s (Levine and Mazumder 2002; Bloome and Western 2011). Recent research using administrative data finds stable rates of rank-based intergenerational mobility for cohorts born between 1971 and 1993 (Chetty et al. 2014b).

With a handful of exceptions (e.g., Chadwick and Solon 2002; Jäntti et al. 2006), most intergenerational economic analyses have been restricted to examining the outcomes of men. Given women's lower and more intermittent labor force participation rates, women's earnings may be a poor proxy for economic well-being, while excluding nonemployed women results in a biased sample. To address these methodological challenges, Chadwick and Solon (2002) focus on family income as opposed to individual earnings and find women to have lower intergenerational elasticities (between 0.35 and 0.49) than men (between 0.43 and 0.58). The authors conclude that assortative mating plays an important role in the transmission process. Extending this work, Mayer and Lopoo (2004) present evidence that intergenerational elasticity trends over time vary by gender. They find that sons' intergenerational elasticity of earnings increases for those born 1949–1953 and then declines for those born 1954–1965, while daughters' intergenerational elasticity increases for those born before 1958–1961 and then declines. However, they do not find statistically significant linear trends, and their choice of endpoints is crucial for finding their trends. In more recent work, Mazumder (2005a) finds that in short run, daughter's IGE may appear to be greater than son's IGE, but in the long run they are the same.

Recent research confirms that significant disparities exist by race, with a very low rate of upward mobility for blacks from the bottom of the income distribution. Using quantile regression, Hertz (2005) finds that 30 percent of whites born into the top decile remain there in adulthood, compared with only 4 percent of blacks. The situation is reversed when examining persistence in the bottom decile, with 17 percent of whites remaining compared with 42 percent of blacks. Similarly, Bhattacharya and Mazumder (2011) find that blacks experience much less upward mobility than whites.

Consistent with findings of strong persistence of economic status in the bottom of the income distribution, research using binary or ordered outcomes finds strong persistence of poverty across generations in both the United States and the United Kingdom. In the United States, Corcoran and Adams (1997) found that both white and black children who grew up in poverty are at a higher risk for adult poverty than non-poor children and that risk increased as the duration of childhood poverty increased. Long-term childhood poverty was found to be especially detrimental for black children (Corcoran 1995). Examining UK data, Gibbons and Blanden (2006) estimate that men who experienced poverty at age 16 were nearly twice as likely (19 vs. 10 percent) to be poor as adults than those who did not experience poverty. They find that the persistence of poverty sharply increases for boys growing up in the 1980s versus the 1970s.

Research on the intergenerational transmission of welfare dependency has been very limited and is based on small samples and potentially problematic (with often only one to three years of data) measures of welfare participation (e.g., Gottschalk 1990; McLanahan 1988; and Levine and Zimmerman 1996). Page (2004) finds that earlier analyses underestimated the true persistence in welfare recipiency and that the intergenerational correlation is 0.30, meaning that women who experience a period of welfare receipt in childhood are three times as likely as other women to receive welfare in adulthood.

SOCIOLOGICAL ANALYSES OF MOBILITY

While the economic approach focuses on earnings and income mobility, sociological approaches rely on occupations, collapsed into highly aggregated *social classes* or ranked into a one-dimensional *occupational status* hierarchy. Occupations have many advantages for the analysis of mobility. At the practical level, collecting information about occupations is relatively easy and faces fewer issues in terms of recall, reliability, refusal, and stability than measures of earnings of income. Furthermore, information about parents can be reported retrospectively by adult children. At the substantive level, jobholding is the most important social and economic role held by most adults outside their immediate family (Hauser and Warren 1997; Hauser 2010). However, the correlation between occupations and socioeconomic standing depends on the degree of inequality that exists within and between occupations in a particular society (Bloome and Western 2011). Additionally, like earnings, occupational measures are restricted to those in the labor force.

Classes are categorical groupings based on specific occupational assets—different skills, authority in the workplace, ownership of business, among others—that determine life chances. Because they involve different types of assets, classes are differentially affected by economic and institutional factors such as technological change, the labor market, and welfare policy (Breen and Whelan 1996). By differencing the type and not only the amount of occupational resources, the class perspective claims to focus on causes of economic disparities, not only their surface manifestation (Portes and Hoffman 2003).

The most widely used class classification was devised by Erikson, Goldthorpe, and Portocarero (1979) and is known as the EGP or CASMIN (Comparative Analysis of Social Mobility in Industrialized Countries) class schema. The EGP classification is based on different types of "employment relations." First, a distinction is made among employees, the self-employed, and employers. Among employees, a further distinction is made between a "service relationship"—a long-time exchange entailing a comprehensive compensation package and career prospects, which characterizes highly skilled professional and managerial occupations—and a "labor contract relationship" involving a short-term specific exchange of time or product for pay that characterizes manual, low-skill occupations. Classes are claimed to be defined by the varying amounts of these relationships. In its most detailed formulation, the EGP classification distinguishes 12 classes, but it is usually collapsed into 7 or 5 groups for comparative analysis (Erikson and Goldthorpe 1992; Breen 2005). In the seven-class formulation, this schema distinguishes: professionals and managers, clerical workers, the self-employed, farmers, skilled manual workers, unskilled manual workers, and farm workers.

MEASUREMENT OF CLASS MOBILITY

Given that classes entail occupational assets that vary in kind and not only in amount, the analysis of class mobility is not restricted to movements up and down in a socioeconomic hierarchy. Rather, it considers barriers to mobility emerging from the ownership of different kinds of assets such as property ownership, sector barriers (for example between agricultural and non-agricultural sectors), or authority in the workplace. Analysis of the intergenerational class association treats classes as nominal (although orderable) categories. The basic information is the "mobility table," a cross classification of parents' (class or origin) and adult children's class (class of destination), in which the cells are the frequencies in each bivariate combination.

At the most basic level, the mobility table provides information on total observed flows between classes of origins and classes of destination, called "absolute mobility." Measures of absolute mobility include, for instance, the proportion of individuals that remain in the same class of their parents ("immobile"), and—if a ranked order of classes is assumed—the proportion that moves upward or downward, gaining or losing status. Absolute mobility flows can be meaningfully divided into two dimensions. The first dimension is the transformation of the class structure over time, called *structural mobility*, and expressed in disparity in the marginals of the mobility table. Structural mobility is interpreted as a consequence of exogenous economic and demographic factors such as technological change, economic policy, foreign trade, fertility, and immigration (Hout 1989). The most important of these factors during the twentieth century is the transformation from an agricultural to a service-based economy. This transformation has led to a significant upgrade in national class structures, creating "room at the top"—in the professional and managerial classes—and reducing positions in agriculture and unskilled manual occupations, thereby inducing a large amount of upward class mobility.

The second dimension of mobility, called *relative mobility* refers to the association between origins and destinations, net of structural changes. Relative mobility indicates the level of *social fluidity*, or "equality of opportunity," in a society. Relative mobility is measured through odds-ratios in the mobility table, which are insensitive to marginal changes, and is modeled by means of log-linear models (e.g., Hauser 1978; Hout 1983). Relative mobility or social fluidity is a measure analogous to the intergenerational correlation coefficient in that it captures intergenerational association net of changes in the distribution of the variables in either generation.

PATTERNS AND TRENDS OF CLASS MOBILITY

Researchers have found that the *pattern* of relative class mobility is remarkably similar across advanced countries. The common pattern of mobility has been summarized in a "core model" of fluidity, which includes the following effects: "Hierarchy" (status differences between classes), "inheritance" (class-specific propensity to remain in the class of origin), "sector" (barrier between agricultural and non-agricultural classes), and affinities/disaffinities between specific pairs of classes (Erikson and Goldthorpe 1992). The similarity in the pattern of class mobility appears to further extend to countries with different historical traditions and levels of development such as Japan, Korea, Chile, and Brazil (Ishida 1993; Park 2004; Torche 2005; Ribeiro 2007).

In contrast to the pattern of social fluidity, the strength of the intergenerational association—that is, the level of "social fluidity"—varies substantially across advanced industrial countries. Findings from the 1970s indicated that the most fluid countries were the former Czechoslovakia, Australia, Japan and the United States, while during the 1980s and 1990s the most fluid were Poland, Sweden, and Hungary (Erikson and Goldthorpe 1992; Breen and Luijkx 2004b) (the United States was not included in this latter comparison).

The strength of class mobility has also changed over time. In the United States, class mobility has remained constant over time or may have declined somewhat (Beller 2009). In contrast, class mobility has increased in most—but not all—European countries (Breen and Luijkx 2004a). Growing class fluidity in European countries is largely driven by a weaker influence of parental class on children's educational attainment (Breen at al. 2009).

OCCUPATIONAL STATUS MOBILITY

Occupational status ranks occupations based on the mean level of earnings and the mean level of education of occupational incumbents and produces a one-dimensional scale. Occupational status provides a good proxy for long-term economic standing because it remains relatively stable over the individual occupational career, such that a single measure is claimed to yield adequate information of long-run standing. For this reason, some economists have claimed that status may be a better indicator of permanent income than single-year income measures (Goldberger 1989; Zimmerman 1992). However, measures of status are still affected by reporting error and short-term fluctuation. It is therefore still recommended to account for measurement error by averaging across measures, as it is routinely done with measures of income or earnings mobility. Research suggests that measurement error results in a 15–20 percent downward bias in the intergenerational association (Bielby et al. 1977). Surprisingly (and reassuringly) no substantially higher measurement error was found in retrospective reports of parental status than in contemporary reports about own status.

PATTERNS AND TRENDS OF OCCUPATIONAL STATUS MOBILITY

A long tradition of "status attainment" research starting in the 1960s has examined the intergenerational stratification process using occupational status of parents and children (Blau and Duncan 1967). Occupational status mobility is captured by a regression model in which adult child's status is regressed on parental status. Over the last few decades, the intergenerational status association in the United States has ranged between .30 and .45 for white men, with an average value close to .40. The occupational status association is much weaker (and more imprecisely estimated) for black men (Blau and Duncan 1967; Hauser et al. 2000). There is some indication that the occupational status association has declined from the 1960s to the 1980s, but evidence is weak and formal tests of trends are usually missing (Grusky and DiPrete 1990; Beller and Hout 2006).

The "status attainment" tradition has also investigated mechanisms in the intergenerational mobility process (Blau and Duncan 1967; Sewell and Hauser 1975). Using path analysis, researchers have modeled the individual life course, including parents' resources, children's education, children's occupational status in first and current jobs. Other factors, such as family structure, number of siblings, rural origins, cognitive ability, and significant others' influences, have also been included as potential mediators in the transmission of advantage across generations. This line of research has found that education is the main factor in both the reproduction of status across generations and upward mobility (Hout and DiPrete 2006). Education is the main vehicle for reproduction because advantaged parents are able to afford more education for their children which in turn pays off in the labor market. But education is also the main vehicle for mobility because factors other than parental resources account for most of the variance in educational attainment, extricating individuals from their social origins. In the United States, the "direct" effect of parental status, once education is accounted for, is not zero but very minor (Blau and Duncan 1967; Sewell et al. 1969; Sewell and Hauser 1975). The concern with mechanisms in the mobility process emphasized by the "status attainment" approach in the 1960s and 1970s has been revived by recent analyses of economic mobility (e.g., Eide and Sholwater 1999; Bowles and Gintis 2002; Blanden et al. 2007), with a novel emphasis on early health and childhood circumstances as a mediating factor in the intergenerational reproduction of advantage (Currie 2009; Carvalho 2012).

DISCREPANCIES IN MOBILITY FINDINGS BASED ON DIFFERENT MEASURES OF SOCIOECONOMIC STANDING

The distinction between social class, occupational status, earnings, and income mobility is not just disciplinary, nor is it trivial. Specifically, empirical analyses show divergent results depending on which measure is used. The United States consistently ranks as the least fluid country of the advanced industrial world when earnings/income mobility is evaluated, but it emerges as relatively fluid in terms of class mobility. Furthermore, while a strong negative correlation exists between cross-sectional inequality and earnings mobility at the national level, there does not seem to be an association between economic inequality and class mobility (Erikson and Goldthorpe 1992; Björklund and Jäntti 2000; Breen and Luijkx 2004b; Blanden 2013). Other important discrepancies in the analysis of occupational versus earnings mobility exist. For example, while educational attainment accounts for most—about 85 percent—of the intergenerational association of occupational status, it accounts for only about half of the intergenerational association of total family income (Torche 2016). This suggests that family income may be a more comprehensive measure of socioeconomic standing, insofar as it includes extra-occupational assets and family processes such as assortative mating.

What may explain such divergent results between occupational and economic mobility? Different measures of economic standing will provide a disparate evaluation of intergenerational mobility to the extent that the distributions of these measures are not perfectly correlated and, crucially, to the extent that deviations across distributions are strongly correlated across generations (Björklund and Jäntti 2000). Blanden (2013) shows that dimensions of income not explained by social class are transmitted across generations, which explains divergences in measures of economic and occupational mobility in the United Kingdom. The problem may be due to the fact that classes are highly aggregated groupings, which miss important variation in socioeconomic advantage. One solution would be to use more detailed occupations, or "microclasses" (Weeden and Grusky 2005; Jonsson et al. 2009), but the problem may still persist if deviations across distributions are strongly correlated across generations. This discrepancy is relevant not because it proves one or another measure of standing is "better" but because it highlights the importance of a multidimensional approach to the analysis of mobility.

Mechanisms

While mobility trends in the United States remain somewhat unclear, understanding the mechanisms that promote or hinder mobility is much clearer. Björklund and Jäntti (2009) and others have documented the sizable role played by inherited parental characteristics, such as intelligence and other cognitive and noncognitive skills, but also stress that the role of such factors is augmented by environmental factors that act both independently and in interaction with inherited factors. Thus, the fact that a portion of intergenerational persistence is due to genetic factors does not mean that environmental factors do not play a role.

Among environmental factors, education is clearly one of the most important. As indicated in the Becker and Tomes theoretical model, one of the most important channels through which parents promote their children's position in society is through their support and investment in their child's education. This investment begins in early childhood and continues throughout childhood into adolescence and young adulthood. In terms of policy responses to promote mobility, then, there is a strong case to be made for interventions beginning in the early years of a child's life. Instituting a comprehensive system of high-quality, affordable early care and education as well as support for paid parental leave in the first 12 months following birth and strong work-family policies thereafter would greatly improve child outcomes, with particular benefits for children from low-income families (Waldfogel 2004; Esping-Anderson 2004). There is also an important role for reforms after school entry. Educational reforms such as eliminating (or at least significantly delaying) tracking, standardizing curricula, improving school facilities, institutionalizing a system of high expectations for all students, and recruiting experienced teachers in schools serving low-income students could further help promote upward mobility and reduce educational disparities (Björklund and Jäntti 2009; Esping-Anderson 2004; Corak 2006; Telles and Ortiz 2008).

Additionally, more is being learned about pathways through which parental income affects child health, which in turn affects future economic and other outcomes (Currie 2009, 2011). Again, this process begins early in childhood (indeed, prenatally) and continues throughout childhood and adolescence into young adulthood. Universal health care would promote the well-being of children and eliminate the credit constraints that parents face in providing basic health care (Jencks and Tach 2006). There is also an important role for policies to improve prenatal health and early child health (Currie 2009, 2011).

Equality of opportunity is also hampered by the unequal distribution of wealth. Wealth is not only more unevenly distributed than income, but also historic discrimination in wealth accumulation policies has resulted in very large disparities across racial and ethnic groups that cannot be accounted for by age or educational attainment (Scholz and Levine 2004; Oliver and Shapiro 2006; Conley 1999). Direct taxation of wealth would compensate for the reduced progressivity of the income tax system and would help reduce some of the historical legacy of racism in the United States (Wolff 2002).

INTERNATIONAL COMPARISONS
AMONG RICH NATIONS

International comparisons are informative for evaluating the extent to which societies offer fair outcomes for individuals (Bratberg et al. 2007). In particular, international comparisons may yield clues as to how income status is transmitted and why persistence varies across countries. As discussed in Garfinkel et al. (2010), it is highly unlikely that the degree of endowment transmission should vary by country, so international comparisons may also reveal differences in equality of opportunity between countries.

International comparisons of intergenerational mobility can be extremely difficult to make due to differences in data availability. While Nordic countries have excellent sources of rich administrative data spanning generations with very little measurement error, most countries do not even have nationally representative longitudinal surveys spanning more than 40 years. For many countries, single years of cross-sectional data are the only available option, so researchers must create synthetic panels or use two-stage IV regressions with parent's education or occupation as an instrument for parents' earnings.

Assuming researchers are able to find or create data sets covering similar time periods, definitions for key terms such as "income" or "earnings" can be nearly impossible to equivalize due to differences in tax and transfer systems and the very perception of what constitutes income or earnings. Another important data quality point is life-cycle bias which makes the age of observation very important, especially for international comparisons. In a review of international estimates, Grawe (2006) found that Germany and Finland seem to have very low rates of intergenerational elasticities, but researchers were actually looking at fairly old fathers, which would be expected to produce downward-biased estimates of intergenerational elasticities. Often researchers are unable to identically match ages of both generations and therefore have to estimate the potential direction and magnitude of the bias (Haider and Solon 2006).

While the challenges to comparative analysis are great, considerable research has been undertaken in the past decade comparing the United States to other wealthy countries. Corak (2006) finds that the United States and the United Kingdom have the strongest rates of intergenerational earnings persistence with an elasticity of 0.50, while France and Germany are the next with elasticities of 0.41 and 0.32, respectively. Sweden follows at 0.27, while Canada, Finland, Norway, and Denmark all have intergenerational elasticities less than 0.20. Similarly, in an analysis of intergenerational wage and education persistence in 14 European OECD countries, Causa et al. (2009) find that intergenerational wage and education persistence is lower in Nordic countries while wage persistence is higher in Southern European countries and the United Kingdom, and educational persistence is higher in Southern European countries, Luxembourg, and Iceland.

In a review of existing research on cross-country research on occupational and income mobility, Beller and Hout (2006) find that the United States occupies a middle ground in occupational mobility, with Canada, Norway, and Sweden experiencing greater mobility; and Ireland, Portugal, Great Britain, Germany, Italy, and France experiencing less mobility. In comparison, the United States ranks near the bottom of income mobility, with comparable rates with Great Britain, but lower mobility than Canada, Finland, Sweden, Norway, and possibly Germany. Beller and Hout find that the middle of the income distribution in the United States looks very similar to other countries, but that there is considerably more persistence at both the top and bottom of the income distribution in the United States, which accounts for its low overall ranking.

To investigate cross-country comparisons of mobility at different points in the income distribution, Grawe (2004b) used quantile regression to obtain estimates of persistence in the United States, Canada, Germany, and the United Kingdom (as well as Malaysia, Ecuador, Nepal, Pakistan, and Peru). Grawe finds that the United States and Canada have less persistence at the top of the distribution and more at the bottom of the distribution than Germany and the United Kingdom. Furthermore, North American children from above-average income families experience more mobility than Europeans, while North American children from below-average income families experience less mobility than Europeans.

These cross-country comparisons support several conclusions about mobility in the United States and the nature of the relationship between cross-sectional inequality and intergenerational mobility. First of all, the United States clearly ranks fairly low in terms of intergenerational mobility, although it is also clear that how the United States compares to other countries depends on what point in the distribution one considers. Individuals in the middle of the income distribution have similar rates of mobility in the United States as in European countries, and children at the top of the distribution may actually experience more mobility in the United States than they do in countries such as the United Kingdom or Germany. However, the weight of the evidence also suggests that that there is less mobility for children from low-income backgrounds in the United Kingdom than in peer countries.

Second, while there is not an exact mapping between intergenerational mobility and cross-sectional inequality at the national level, there appears to be a negative relationship between the two: as inequality increases, intergenerational mobility decreases. This relationship has been coined the "Great Gatsby Curve," although in a review of the literature, Jäntti and Jenkins (2015) suggest that more research is required before the veracity of this relationship can be accurately estimated. Björklund and Jäntti (2009) undertake a comprehensive review of cross-national estimates and find that Nordic countries have the lowest levels of cross-sectional inequality and the highest levels of intergenerational mobility while France, Italy, the United Kingdom and the United States all have high inequality and low mobility. Germany falls in between the two groups. However, several individual countries do not fit the pattern, such as Canada and Australia, which have relatively high inequality and high mobility (Beller and Hout 2006; Smeeding, Erikson, and Jäntti 2011).

INTERGENERATIONAL MOBILITY IN THE DEVELOPING WORLD

Although most mobility analysis is focused on the advanced industrial world, an incipient literature on mobility in the developing world exists, particularly in Latin America, and, most recently, in South and East Asia. Lacking long-term panels that allow direct examination of parent-children pairs, researchers have used a variety of strategies to obtain a limited but still informative understanding of mobility.

The study of intergenerational mobility has grown in Latin America in the last decade, prompted by better data and a renewed concern with equality of opportunity in context of very high levels of economic inequality (De Ferranti et al. 2004; Torche 2014). Although analysis is still limited to a handful of countries and data and analytical techniques vary in quality, one conclusion appears clear: economic

mobility is much more limited in Latin American countries than in advanced industrialized countries. The intergenerational earnings elasticity reaches around 0.6 and
0.7 in Brazil and between .57 and .73 in Chile (Dunn 2007; Ferreira and Veloso 2006;
Nunez and Miranda 2010). Given the lack of long-term panels, these figures are
obtained from a two-sample instrumental variable approach (TSIV) (Arellano and
Meghir 1992; Angrist and Krueger 1992). This approach combines information from
two samples to obtain a predicted value of parents' earnings and is known to produce somewhat inflated measures of association. However, research using an identical strategy in the United States produces estimates of intergenerational elasticity
between 0.42 and 0.52 (Björklund and Jäntti 1997). This indicates a much stronger
level of intergenerational persistence in Latin America. Further evidence is provided by Grawe (2004) who compares mobility in the United States, Canada, United
Kingdom, Germany, Malaysia, Vietnam, Pakistan, Mexico, and Peru and found the
strongest associations in the Latin American countries.

In terms of country-level factors associated with mobility, comparative analysis
across Latin American countries finds a negative association between mobility and
cross-sectional inequality. However, a surprisingly weak association between mobility
and public spending in education is found in Latin America (Dahan and Gaviria 2001).
This finding contrasts with the United States and other advanced industrial countries,
where public spending in education has a positive association with mobility (Mayer
and Lopoo 2008; Blanden 2013). The discrepancy is likely due to the fact that educational spending is more targeted to higher levels of schooling in Latin America, which
tends to favor affluent families whose children are more likely to reach postsecondary
education.

CLASS MOBILITY IN LATIN AMERICA

Comparative analysis of class mobility exists in Brazil, Chile, and Mexico (Torche
2014). In Brazil, the analysis of class mobility started in the 1970s, enabled by high-
quality retrospective data on parental occupation. Studies described the enormous
process of upward mobility pushed by the fast transformation from an agricultural to
industrial economy (Pastore 1981; Scalon 1999; Pastore and Silva 2000). More recent
work concentrates on relative mobility and reports an increase in Brazilian class fluidity (Ribeiro 2007; Torche and Ribeiro 2010), similar to the one recently found in
Europe. Researchers have found the opposite trend in Mexico: a decline in mobility in
recent decades attributed to economic crisis and structural adjustment reforms since
the 1980s (Zenteno and Solis 2006). In Chile, Torche (2005) found surprisingly high
levels of class fluidity in spite of high economic inequality. However, Torche also finds
a close isomorphism in the patterns of mobility and inequality: income concentration
among the professional elite is matched by restricted mobility to and from the elite.

Analysis of mobility is more limited in other developing regions and findings are usually inconsistent given data constraints and varying methodologies. Recent analyses of economic mobility in urban China indicate that earnings persistence is very high, with elasticities close to 0.6 (Gong et al. 2012; Quheng et al. 2012). Recent literature about India also indicates high levels of educational and occupational persistence across generations, although with some improvement as education expands and benefits a larger proportion of the population (Emran and Shilfi 2012; Motiram and Singh 2012; Azam and Bhatt 2012). Given the historical role of caste in determining opportunities in the Indian context, researchers have examined the role of caste in the mobility process. In spite of policies aimed at improving the status of low-caste members, several recent studies find very limited educational and, particularly, occupational mobility among disadvantaged castes and tribes (Majumder 2010; Motiram and Singh 2012), although a breaking down of caste-based barriers to socioeconomic mobility has been documented (Hnatkovska et al. 2013). Though the literature on social mobility elsewhere in South Asia is thin, a few recent studies document substantial intergenerational persistence in terms of wealth and occupation and a sizable urban/rural mobility barrier in Bangladesh, Nepal, Vietnam, and Pakistan (Asadullah 2012; Emran and Shilpi 2011; Javed and Irfam 2012).

Most of the work on intergenerational social mobility in Africa is focused on South Africa and considers educational rather than socioeconomic mobility. The literature indicates that educational mobility for nonwhite South Africans increased in the 1950s and 1960s as the education system opened to all races; however, inherited status of education has become increasingly important over time and educational mobility has stalled for the most recent cohorts of nonwhite South Africans (Thomas 1996; Burns and Keswell 2012). Literature from elsewhere in the African continent also show a pattern of increased educational mobility in the reform-oriented postindependence period followed by static or declining rates of educational mobility for the most recent cohorts (see Peil 1990 on Nigeria, Sierra Leone, and Zimbabwe; Binzel 2011 on Egypt). More recently, Burns and Keswell (2012) find lower levels of intergenerational educational mobility for recent cohorts of South African nonwhite girls compared to boys.

In addition, there is some evidence that colonial power matters for predicting contemporary patterns of social mobility. In a comparative study of five former French and British colonies during the period preceding and following independence, Bossuroy and Cogneau (2008) find occupational and educational mobility are significantly more restricted in the French colonies (Guinea, Cote D'Ivoire, and Madagascar) than the British ones (Uganda and Ghana). The authors argue that differing colonial policies on centralization, infrastructure development, and educational reform may have continued to play a role in mobility in the postcolonial era, particularly with respect to access to education, rural to urban migration, and the transition from agricultural to nonagricultural work.

In sum, mobility analysis in the developing world suggests that in spite of substantial educational expansion and economic transformation, relative mobility tends to be low compared with advanced industrial countries, and strong ascriptive barriers such as gender, caste, race, and rural residence shape mobility opportunity.

CONCLUSION: POLICY IMPLICATIONS
AND FUTURE AREAS OF RESEARCH

Cross-country comparisons may help inform discussion of public policies or institutions that may be beneficial for promoting mobility. In this interdisciplinary review, we found suggestive evidence of a negative relationship between intergenerational mobility and cross-sectional inequality. Although none of the studies discussed in this chapter explicitly tested causal relationships, several policies have been shown to be causally related to decreased cross-sectional inequality. The top policy associated with increased intergenerational mobility has been mentioned throughout this chapter: educational reform. Progressive education financing at all levels from early care to higher education promotes upward mobility and decreased persistence of family background (Solon 2002). Esping-Anderson (2004) concludes that the reason Nordic countries have the greatest intergenerational mobility is due to universal, high-quality childcare. Björklund and Jäntti (2009) also point to evidence about specific education reforms that led to more mobility in Nordic countries such as Sweden and Finland. Ermisch, Jäntti, and Smeeding (2012) use a life-course approach to examine the underlying mechanisms through which intergenerational advantage is passed and find that while cross-country differences in the SES gradient appear in early childhood, these disparities do not increase as children age and that there are many later stages (such as during labor market entry) where policy intervention has the potential to diminish disadvantage. Causa et al. (2009) find a positive cross-country correlation between mobility and redistributive policies such as progressive tax-and-transfer systems and universal benefits such as health care. Causa et al. (2009) also find a positive cross-country correlation between mobility and wage-setting institutions that compress earnings distributions, such as union density and the rate of wage replacement through the transfer system.

In terms of future research, our review highlights four areas that would particularly benefit from future study. First, it is clear that more attention to gender and family structure is warranted, as studies based solely on males and married couple families have been shown to provide an incomplete and biased picture of mobility. Second, it is striking that the intergenerational mobility literature has barely engaged the geographic mobility—migration—literature, even though increased rates of global migration mean that immigrants will be a larger share of the population in many developed and developing countries. Third, continued cross-disciplinary dialogue is needed. While to date most mobility studies use one single measure of socioeconomic standing—such as earnings, family income, class, and occupational status—we know that findings vary across measures used. To the extent that different measures of socioeconomic standing capture different dimensions of life chances, it is essential to consider analyses from different disciplines and investigate potential discrepancies in findings. Fourth, as more countries of the world gather acceptable-quality data, international comparative analysis of mobility is needed to further understand the association between institutional arrangements and equality of opportunity.

NOTES

1. Notation in these simplified equations comes from Solon (1999) and Mulligan (1997).
2. While income and earnings are two different concepts, the same methods can be applied to both measures so they are discussed jointly.
3. The issue of the underlying distribution of earnings or income is also relevant when estimating IGE by race. Hertz (2005) found that the pooled estimate of IGE will be greater than either of the separate black versus white within-group estimates (0.53 pooled, 0.35–0.44 white, 0.32–0.42 black). This is attributable to greater within group variance in earnings than in the population as a whole. This is consistent with Borjas (1992) who suggested that within group differences could bias the overall estimate of IGE.

REFERENCES

Aaberge, Rolf, Anders Björklund, Markus Jäntti, Marten Palme, Peder J. Pedersen, Nina Smith, and Tom Wennemo. 2002. "Income Inequality and Income Mobility in the Scandinavian Countries Compared to the United States." *Review of Income and Wealth* 48(4):443–69.

Angrist, Joshua D., and Alan B. Krueger. 1992. "The Effect of Age at School Entry on Educational Attainment: An Application of Instrumental Variables with Moments from Two Samples." *Journal of the American Statistical Association* 87(418):328–36.

Arellano, Manuel, and Costas Meghir. 1992. "Female Labour Supply and On-the-Job Search: An Empirical Model Estimated Using Complementary Data Sets." *The Review of Economic Studies* 59(3):537–59.

Asadullah, Niaz M. 2012. "Intergenerational Wealth Mobility in Rural Bangladesh." *The Journal of Development Studies*, 48(9):1193–208.

Azam, Mehtabul, and Vipul Bhatt. 2012. "Like Father, Like Son? Intergenerational Education Mobility in India." *Working Paper 6549*. Bonn: Institute for the Study of Labor.

Becker, Gary S., and Nigel Tomes. 1979. "An Equilibrium Theory of the Distribution of Income and Intergenerational Mobility." *Journal of Political Economy* 87(6):1153–89.

_____. 1986. "Human Capital and the Rise and Fall of Families." *Journal of Labor Economics* 4(2): S1–39.

Behrman, Jere R., and Paul Taubman. 1985. "Intergenerational Earnings Mobility in the United States: Some Estimates and a Test of Becker's Intergenerational Endowments Model." *Review of Economics and Statistics* 67:144–51.

_____. 1990. "The Intergenerational Correlation Between Children's Adult Earnings and Their Parents' Income: Results from the Michigan Panel Survey of Income Dynamics." *Review of Income and Wealth* 36(2):115–27.

Beller, Emily. 2009. "Bringing Intergenerational Social Mobility Research into the Twenty-first Century: Why Mothers Matter." *American Sociological Review* 74:507–28.

Beller, Emily, and Michael Hout. 2006. "Intergenerational Social Mobility: The United States in Comparative Perspective." *The Future of Children* 16(2):19–36.

Bhattacharya, Debopam, and Bhashkar Mazumder. 2011. "A Nonparametric Analysis of Black-White Differences in Intergenerational Income Mobility in the United States." *Quantitative Economics* 2:335–79.

Bielby, William, Robert Hauser, and David Featherman. 1977. "Response Errors of Black and Nonblack Males in Models of the Intergenerational Transmission of Socioeconomic Status." *American Journal of Sociology* 82:1242–88.

Binzel, C. 2011. "Decline in Social Mobility: Unfulfilled Aspirations among Egypt's Educated Youth." IZA Discussion Paper 6139.

Björklund, Anders, and Markus Jäntti. 1997. "Intergenerational Mobility in Sweden Compared to the United States." *American Economic Review* 87(5):1009–18.

_____. 2000. "Intergenerational Mobility of Socio-Economic Status in Comparative Perspective." *Nordic Journal of Political Economy* 26(1):3–32.

_____. 2009. "Intergenerational Mobility and the Role of Family Background." Pp. 491–521 in *Oxford Handbook of Economic Inequality*, edited by W. Salverda, B. Nolan and T. Smeeding. Oxford, UK: Oxford University Press.

Black, Sandra E., and Paul J. Devereux. 2011. "Recent Developments in Intergenerational Mobility." Pp. 1487–1541 in *Handbook of Labor Economics*, Volume 4B, edited by Orley Ashenfelter and David Card. Amsterdam: Elsevier Science BV.

Blau, Peter M., and O. D. Duncan. 1967. *The American Occupational Structure*. New York, NY: Wiley.

Blanden, Jo. 2013. "Cross-Country Rankings in Intergenerational Mobility: A Comparison of Approaches from Economics and Sociology." *Journal of Economic Surveys* 27(1):38–73.

Blanden, Jo, Paul Gregg and Lindsey Macmillan. 2007. "Accounting for Intergenerational Income Persistence: Noncognitive Skills, Ability and Education." *The Economic Journal* 117:C43–C60.

Bloome, Deirdre, and Bruce Western. 2011. "Cohort Change and Racial Differences in Educational and Income Mobility." *Social Forces* 90(2):375–95.

Borjas, George J. 1992. "Ethnic Capital and Intergenerational Mobility." *Quarterly Journal of Economics* 107(1):123–50.

Bossuroy, Thomas, and Denis Cogneau. 2008. "Social Mobility and Colonial Legacy in Five African Countries." *Working Paper 2008-10*. Paris: Developpement, Institutions et Mondialisation.

Bowles, Samuel, and Herbert Gintis. 2002. "The Inheritance of Inequality." *Journal of Economic Perspectives* 16(3):3–30.

Bratberg, Espen, Oivind A. Nilsen, and Kjell Vaage. 2007. "Trends in Intergenerational Mobility Across Offspring's Earnings Distribution in Norway." *Industrial Relations* 46(1):112–28.

Breen, Richard, and Christopher Whelan. 1996. *Social Class and Social Mobility in Ireland*. Dublin: Gill and McMillan.

Breen, Richard, Ruud Luijkx, Walter Muller and Reinhard Pollak. 2009. "Nonpersistent Inequality in Educational Attainment: Evidence from Eight European Countries." *American Journal of Sociology* 114(5):1475–1521.

Breen, Richard, and Ruud Luijkx. 2004a. "Social Mobility in Europe between 1970 and 2000." Pp. 37–75 in *Social Mobility in Europe*, edited by R. Breen. Oxford: Oxford University Press.

_____. 2004b. "Conclusions." Pp. 383–410 in in *Social Mobility in Europe*, edited by R. Breen. Oxford: Oxford University Press.

Breen, Richard. 2005. "A Weberian Approach to Class Analysis." Chapter 2 in *Approaches to Class Analysis*, edited by E. O. Wright. Cambridge: Cambridge University Press.

Burns, Justine, and Malcolm Keswell. 2012. "Inheriting the Future: Intergenerational Persistence of Educational Status in KwaZulu-Natal, South Africa." *Economic History of Developing Regions* 27(1):150–75.

Carvalho, Leandro. 2012. "Childhood Circumstances and the Intergenerational Transmission of Socioeconomic Status." *Demography* 49:913–38.

Causa, Orsetta, Sophie Dantan, and Asa Johansson. 2009. Intergenerational Social Mobility in European OECD Countries." *Working Paper 709, Economics Department*. Paris: OECD.

Chadwick, Laura, and Gary Solon. 2002. "Intergenerational Income Mobility among Daughters." *American Economic Review* 92(1):335–44.

Chetty, Raj, Nathaniel Hendren, Patrick Kline, and Emmanuel Saez. 2014a. "Where is the Land of Opportunity? The Geography of Intergenerational Mobility in the United States." National Bureau of Economic Research (NBER) Working Paper 19843. Cambridge, MA.

Chetty, Raj, Nathaniel Hendren, Patrick Kline, Emmanuel Saez and Nicholas Turner. 2014b. "Is the United States Still a Land of Opportunity? Recent Trends in Intergenerational Mobility." National Bureau of Economic Research (NBER) Working Paper 19844. Cambridge, MA.

Conley, Dalton. 1999. *Being Black, Living in the Red: Race, Wealth and Social Policy in America.* Berkeley, CA: University of California Press.

Corak, Miles. 2006. "Do Poor Children Become Poor Adults? Lessons from a Cross Country Comparison of Generational Earnings Mobility." *Research on Economic Inequality* 13(1):143–88.

Corcoran, Mary. 1995. "Rags to Rags: Poverty and Mobility in the United States." *Annual Review of Sociology* 21:237–67.

_____. 2001. "Mobility, Persistence and the Consequences of Poverty for Children: Child and Adult Outcomes." Pp. 127–61 in *Understanding Poverty*, edited by S. Danziger, and R. Haveman. New York: Russell Sage Foundation.

Corcoran, Mary, and Terry Adams. 1997. "Race, Sex and the Intergenerational Transmission of Poverty." Pp. 461–517 in *Consequences of Growing Up Poor*, edited by G. J. Duncan and J. Brooks-Gunn. Russell Sage Foundation, New York.

Couch, Kenneth, and Dean Lillard. 1998. "Sample Selection Rules and the Intergenerational Correlation of Earnings." *Labour Economics* 5:313–29.

Currie, Janet. 2009. "Healthy, Wealthy and Wise: Is There a Causal Relationship between Child Health and Human Capital Development?" *Journal of Economic Literature* 47(1):87–122.

_____. 2011. "Inequality at Birth: Some Causes and Consequences." *American Economic Review* 101(3):1–22.

Dahan, Momi, and Alejandro Gaviria. 2011. "Sibling Correlations and Intergenerational Mobility in Latin America." *Economic Development and Cultural Change* 49(3):537–54.

De Ferranti, David, Francisco Ferreira, Guillermo Perry, and Michael Walton. 2004. *Inequality in Latin America and the Caribbean. Breaking with History?* Washington DC: World Bank.

Dunn, Christopher. 2007. "The Intergenerational Transmission of Lifetime Earnings: Evidence from Brazil." *The B.E. Journal of Economic Analysis and Policy* 7(2): Article 2.

Eide, Eric, and Mark Showalter. 1999. "Factors Affecting the Transmission of Earnings Across Generations: A Quantile Regression Approach." *Journal of Human Resources* 34(2):253–67.

Emran, Shahe, and Forhand Shilpi. 2011. "Intergenerational Occupational Mobility in Rural Economy: Evidence from Nepal and Vietnam." *Journal of Human Resources* 46(2):427–58.

_____. 2012. "Gender, Geography and Generations: Intergenerational Educational Mobility in Post-reform India." World Bank Working Paper 6055.

Erikson, Robert, John Goldthorpe, and Lucienne Portocarero. 1979. "Intergenerational Class Mobility in Three Western European Societies." *British Journal of Sociology* 30(4):415–41.

Erikson, Robert and John Goldthorpe. 1992. *The Constant Flux.* Oxford: Oxford University Press.

Ermisch, John, Markus Jäntti, and Timothy M. Smeeding. 2012. *From Parents to Children: The Intergenerational Transmission of Advantage.* New York: Russell Sage Foundation.

Esping-Anderson, Gosta. 2004. "Unequal Opportunities and the Mechanisms of Social Inheritance." Pp. 289–314 in *Generational Income Mobility in North America and Europe,* edited by M. Corak. Cambridge University Press.

Ferreira, Sergio, and Fernando Veloso. 2006. "Intergenerational Mobility of Wages in Brazil." *Brazilian Review of Econometrics* 26:181–211.

Garfinkel, Irwin, Timothy Smeeding, and Lee Rainwater. 2010. *Wealth and Welfare States: Is America a Laggard or Leader?* Oxford, U.K.: Oxford University Press.

Gibbons, Stephen, and Jo Blanden. 2006. *The Persistence of Poverty Across Generations: A View from Two British Cohorts.* The Policy Press on behalf of the Joseph Rowntree Foundation, Bristol, UK.

Goldberger, Arthur. 1989. "Economic and Mechanical Models of Intergenerational Transmission." *American Economic Review* 79(3):504–13.

Gong, Honge, Andrew Leigh, and Xin Meng. 2012. "Intergenerational Income Mobility in Urban China." *Review of Income and Wealth* 58(3):481–503.

Gottschalk, Peter. 1990. "AFDC Participation Across Generations." *American Economic Review* 80(2):367–71.

Grawe, Nathan D. 2004a. "Reconsidering the Use of Nonlinearities in Intergenerational Earnings Mobility as a Test of Credit Constraints." *Journal of Human Resources* 39(3):813–27.

_____. 2004b. "Intergenerational Mobility for Whom? The Experience of High- and Low-Earning Sons in International Perspective." Pp. 58–89 in *Generational Income Mobility in North America and Europe,* edited by M. Corak. Cambridge University Press.

_____. 2006. "Lifecycle Bias in Estimates of Intergenerational Earnings Persistence." *Labour Economics* 13(5):551–70.

Grusky, David, and Thomas DiPrete. 1990. "Recent Trends in the Process of Stratification." *Demography* 27:617–37.

Grusky, David, and Kim Weeden. 2008. "Are There Social Classes? A Framework for Testing Sociology's Favorite Concept." Chap. 2 in *Social Class: How Does It Work?* edited by A. Lareau and D. Conley. New York: Russell Sage.

Haider, Steven, and Gary Solon. 2006. "Life-Cycle Variation in the Association between Current and Lifetime Earnings." *American Economic Review* 96(4):1308–20.

Hauser, Robert. 1978. "A Structural Model of the Mobility Table." *Social Forces* 56(3):919–53.

_____. 2010. "Intergenerational Economic Mobility in the United States: Measures, Differentials, and Trends," Working Paper 98–12 University of Wisconsin-Madison Center for Demography and Ecology.

Hauser, Robert, and John Warren. 1997. "Socioeconomic Indexes for Occupations: A Review, Update and Critique." In *Sociological Methodology,* Vol. 27, edited by A. Raftery. San Francisco: Jossey-Bass.

Hauser, Robert, John R. Warren, Min-Hsiung Huang, and Wendy Carter. 2000. "Occupational Status, Education, and Social Mobility in the Meritocracy." Pp. 179–229 in *Meritocracy and*

Economic Inequality, edited by K. Arrow, S. Bowles, and S. Durlauf. Princeton: Princeton University Press.

Hertz, Thomas. 2005. "Rags, Riches and Race: The Intergenerational Economic Mobility of Black and White Families in the United States." Pp. 165–91 in *Unequal Chances: Family Background and Economic Success,* edited by S. Bowles, H. Gintis and M. Osborne Groves. Princeton: Princeton University Press.

_____. 2007. "Trends in the Intergenerational Elasticity of Family Income in the United States." *Industrial Relations* 46(1):22–50.

Hnatkovska, Viktoria, Amartya Lahiri, and Paul Sourabh. 2013. "Breaking the Caste Barrier: Intergenerational Mobility in India." *Journal of Human Resources* 48(2):435–73.

Hout, Michael. 1983. *Mobility Tables.* Beverly Hills, CA: Sage.

_____. 1989. *Following in Father's Footsteps.* Cambridge, Mass: Harvard U. Press.

Hout, Michael, and Thomas DiPrete. 2006. "What Have We Learned: RC28's Contribution to Knowledge About Social Stratification." *Research in Social Stratification and Mobility* 24:1–20.

Ishida, Hiroshi, and John Goldthorpe. 1993. *Social Mobility in Contemporary Japan.* Stanford CA: Stanford University Press.

Jäntti, Markus, Bernt Bratsberg, Knut Røed, Oddbjorn Raaum, Robin Naylor, Eva Österbacka, and Anders Björklund. 2006. "American Exceptionalism in a New Light: A Comparison of Intergenerational Earnings Mobility in the Nordic Countries, the United Kingdom and the United States." Discussion Paper 1938. Bonn: IZA.

Jäntti, Markus, and Stephen P. Jenkins. 2015. "Chapter 10—Income Mobility." Pp. 807–935 in *Handbook of Income Distribution Volume 2A,* edited by A. B. Atkinson and F. Bourguignon. Elsevier.

Jencks, Christopher, and Laura Tach. 2006. "Would Equal Opportunity Mean More Mobility?" Pp. 3–20 in *Mobility and Inequality. Frontiers of Research in Sociology and Economics,* edited by S. Morgan, D. Grusky, and G. Fields. Stanford: Stanford University Press.

Jonsson, Jan, David Grusky, Matthew Di Carlo, Reinhard Pollak, and Mary Brinton. 2009. "Microclass Mobility: Social Reproduction in Four Countries." *American Journal of Sociology* 114(4):977–1036.

Javed, Sajid A., and Mohammed Irfan. 2012. "Intergenerational Mobility: Evidence from Pakistan Panel Household Survey." Pakistan Institute of Development Economics Working Paper PSDPS 5.

Jenkins, Stephen P., and Thomas Siedler. 2007. "The Intergenerational Transmission of Poverty in Industrialized Countries." Working Paper 75 Chronic Poverty Research Centre.

Lee, Chul-In, and Gary Solon. 2009. "Trends in Intergenerational Income Mobility." *Review of Economics and Statistics* 91(4):766–72.

Levine, David I., and Bhash Mazumder. 2002. "Choosing the Right Parents: Changes in the Intergenerational Transmission of Inequality Between 1980 and the Early 1990s." Working Paper Series WP-02-08, Federal Reserve Bank of Chicago.

Levine, Phillip B., and David J. Zimmerman. 1996. "The Intergenerational Correlation in AFDC Participation: Welfare Trap or Poverty Trap?" *Institute for Research on Poverty Discussion Paper* 1100-96. University of Wisconsin-Madison.

McLanahan, Sara. 1988. "Family Structure and Dependency: Early Transitions to Female Household Headship." *Demography* 25:1–16.

Macmillan, Lindsey. 2011. "Measuring the Intergenerational Correlation of Worklessness." *Centre for Market and Public Organisation Working Paper* 11/278. University of Bristol.

Majumder, Rajarhi. 2010. "Intergenerational Mobility in Educational and Occupational Attainment: A Comparative Study of Social Classes in India." *Margin: The Journal of Applied Economic Research* 4(4):463–494.

Mayer, Susan E., and Leonard M. Lopoo. 2004. "What Do Trends in the Intergenerational Economic Mobility of Sons and Daughters in the United States Mean?" Pp. 90–118 in *Generational Income Mobility in North America and Europe,* edited by M. Corak. Cambridge University Press.

_____. 2005. "Has the Intergenerational Transmission of Economic Status Changed?" *Journal of Human Resources* 40(1):169–85.

_____. 2008. "Government Spending and Intergenerational Mobility," *Journal of Public Economics* 92:139–58.

Mazumder, Bhashkar. 2005a. "Fortunate Sons: New Estimates of Intergenerational Mobility in the United States Using Social Security Earnings Data." *Review of Economics and Statistics* 87(2):235–55.

_____. 2005b. "The Apple Falls Even Closer to the Tree than We Thought: New and Revised Estimates of Intergenerational Inheritance of Earnings." Pp. 80–99 in *Unequal Chances: Family Background and Economic Success,* edited by S. Bowles, H. Gintis and M. Osborne Groves. Princeton: Princeton University Press.

Motiram, Sripad, and Ashish Singh. 2012. "How Close Does the Apple Fall to the Tree? Some Evidence on Intergenerational Occupational Mobility from India." Working Paper 2012/101 UNU-WIDER.

Mulligan, Casey B. 1997. *Parental Priorities and Economic Inequality.* Chicago: University of Chicago Press.

Nunez, Javier, and Leslie Miranda. 2010. "Intergenerational Income Mobility in a Less-Developed, High-Inequality Context: The Case of Chile." *The B.E. Journal of Economic Analysis and Policy* 10(1):Article 33.

Oliver, Melvin L., and Thomas M. Shapiro. 2006. *Black Wealth/White Wealth: A New Perspective on Racial Inequality.* New York: Routledge.

Page, Marianne E. 2004. "New Evidence on the Intergenerational Correlation in Welfare Participation." Pp. 226–44 in *Generational Income Mobility in North America and Europe,* edited by M. Corak. Cambridge University Press, Cambridge.

Park, Hyunjoon. 2004. "Intergenerational Social Mobility among Korean Men in Comparative Perspective." *Research in Social Stratification and Mobility* 20:227–53.

Pastore, Jose. 1981. *Inequality and Social Mobility in Brazil.* Madison: University of Wisconsin Press.

Pastore, Jose, and N. Silva. 2000. *Social Mobility in Brazil* (in Portuguese). Sao Paulo: Makron.

Peil, Margaret. 1990. "Intergenerational Mobility through Education: Nigeria, Sierra Leone and Zimbabwe." *International Journal of Educational Development* 10(4):311–25.

Peters, Elizabeth. 1992. "Patterns of Intergenerational Mobility in Income and Earnings." *Review of Economics and Statistics* 74(3):456–66.

Portes, Alejandro, and Kelly Hoffman. 2003. "Latin American Class Structures: Their Composition and Change During the Neoliberal Era." *Latin-American Research Review* 38(1):41–82.

Quheng, Deng, Bjorn Gustafsoon, and Li Shi. 2012. "Intergenerational Income Persistency in Urban China." IZA Discussion Paper 6907.

Ribeiro, Celso C. 2007. *Social Structure and Social Mobility in Brazil* (in Portuguese). Sao Paulo: Edusc.

Scalon, Maria. 1999. *Social Mobility in Brazil: Patterns and Trends.* Rio de Janeiro: Revan-Iuperj-UCM.

Scholz, John Karl, and Kara Levine. 2004. "U.S. Black-White Wealth Inequality." Pp. 895–929 in *Social Inequality,* edited by K. Neckerman. New York: Russell Sage.

Sewell, William, and Robert Hauser. 1975. *Education, Occupation, and Earnings: Achievement in the Early Career.* New York: Academic Press.

Sewell, William H., Archibald O. Haller, and Alejandro Portes. 1969. "The Educational and Early Occupational Attainment Process." *American Sociological Review* 34(1):82–92.

Smeeding, Timothy M., Robert Erikson, and Markus Jäntti. 2011. *Persistence, Privilege and Parenting: The Comparative Study of Intergenerational Mobility.* New York: Russell Sage Foundation.

Solon, Gary. 1992. "Intergenerational Income Mobility in the United States." *American Economic Review* 82(3):393–408.

_____. 1999. "Intergenerational Mobility in the Labor Market." Pp. 1761–1800 in *Handbook of Labor Economics,* Vol. 3, edited by O. Ashenfelter and D. Card. Amsterdam: Elsevier Science BV.

_____. 2002. "Cross-Country Differences in Intergenerational Earnings Mobility." *Journal of Economic Perspectives* I16(3):59–66.

Telles, Edward, and Vilma Ortiz. 2008. *Generations of Exclusion: Mexican Americans, Assimilation and Race.* New York: Russell Sage Foundation.

Thomas, Duncan. 1996. "Education Across Generations in South Africa." *American Economic Review Papers and Proceedings* 86(2):330–34.

Torche, Florencia. 2005. "Unequal but Fluid: Social Mobility in Chile in Comparative Perspective." *American Sociological Review* 70:422–50.

_____. 2014. "Social Mobility in Latin America." *Annual Review of Sociology* 40:619–42.

_____. 2015. "Analyses of Intergenerational Mobility: An Interdisciplinary Review." *Annals of the American Academy of Political and Social Science* 657(1):37–62.

_____. 2016. "Education and the Intergenerational Transmission of Advantage in the US." in *Education, Occupation and Social Origins: A Comparative Analysis of the Transmission of Socio-Economic Inequalities,* edited by F. Bernardi and G. Ballarino. Cheltenham: Edward Elgar.

Torche, Florencia, and Carlos Costa-Ribeiro. 2010. "Pathways of Change in Social Mobility: Industrialization, Education and Growing Fluidity in Brazil." *Research in Social Stratification and Mobility* 28(3):291–307.

Waldfogel, Jane. 2004. "Social Mobility, Life Chances and the Early Years." Center for the Analysis of Social Exclusion Working Paper No. 88. (http://sticerd.lse.ac.uk/dps/case/CP/CASEPaper88.pdf).

Weeden, Kim, and David Grusky. 2005. "The Case for a New Class Map." *American Journal of Sociology* 111(1):141–212.

Wolff, Edward. 2002. *Top Heavy: The Increasing Inequality of Wealth in America and What Can be Done About It.* New York: New Press.

Zenteno, Rene, and Patricio Solis. 2006. "Continuities and Discontinuities in Occupational Mobility in Mexico" (in Spanish). *Estudios Demograficos y Urbanos* 21(3):515–46.

Zimmerman, David. 1992. "Regression Toward Mediocrity in Economic Stature." *American Economic Review* 82(3):409–29.

CHAPTER 24

ECONOMIC PERFORMANCE, POVERTY, AND INEQUALITY IN RICH COUNTRIES

DAVID BRADY AND MARKUS JÄNTTI

INTRODUCTION

POVERTY scholars have long emphasized the role of economic performance in poverty reduction (Brady 2009; Gordon 1972). In her masterful history of twentieth-century American poverty scholarship, O'Connor (2001) highlights the prevailing, recurring concern with economic growth and the business cycle. Indeed, there has seemingly always been a group of scholars stressing economic and job growth as the key strategies to combat poverty. For instance, in the series of volumes reviewing American poverty research that emanate from the Institute for Research on Poverty, there has routinely been a chapter on economic performance or business cycles (e.g., Blank 1994, 2009; Ellwood and Summers 1986; Freeman 2001; Tobin 1994). Also, many contemporary scholars emphasize the primacy of economic performance for alleviating poverty (Blank 2000, 2009; Bluestone and Harrison 2000; Balke and Slottje 1993; Sawhill 1988; Williams 1991). For instance, the first sentence of Blank, Danziger, and Schoeni's (2006:1) book on working poverty reads: "Fluctuations in the economy have a strong effect on the extent of poverty and well-being among low-income families."

The central thesis of this research is that poverty rises and falls with the business cycle and economic performance. By the business cycle, we are referring to macroeconomic fluctuations in economic growth, unemployment, and employment. Scholars typically conceive of economic performance as slightly broader than the business cycle, and incorporate longer term economic development (typically captured by rising gross domestic product [GDP] per capita) and perhaps the industrial composition of the labor force. The reasons why economic performance matters are straightforward. Higher economic growth and a lower unemployment rates result in more individuals employed. Because a job is one of the most effective ways to remove a household from poverty (Rainwater and Smeeding 2004), macroeconomic performance should directly influence individual poverty. Moreover, as unemployment declines and economic growth increases, this means firms are hiring, there is greater demand for workers, and wages are likely to rise. As a result, improving economic performance should reduce poverty among the employed as well. In short, there have always been strong arguments for why macroeconomic context matters to poverty.

Despite the long-standing interest in and intuitive logic of these relationships, there has been some fluctuation in exactly how important economic performance is to poverty (Freeman 2008; Haveman and Schwabish 2000). For example, writing in 1986 about the United States, Ellwood and Summers (1986:79) argued that "[e]conomic performance is the *dominant* determinant of the poverty rate" (emphasis added). In the late 1980s and early 1990s however, American poverty researchers began to question whether economic performance was as good a predictor of poverty as it had been in the past (Blank 2000; Blank and Blinder 1986). Nevertheless, by the late 1990s, economists returned to emphasizing the salience of economic performance. While economic performance was not as effective at reducing poverty in the 1970s and 1980s, Haveman and Schwabish (2000) conclude that economic performance became more effective again in the 1990s. As they write (p. 425), "Strong economic growth and high employment again appear to be effective antipoverty policy instruments." Similarly, Blank (2000) writes: "A strong macroeconomy matters more than anything else," and "the first and most important lesson for anti-poverty warriors from the 1990s is that sustained economic growth is a wonderful thing" (pp. 6, 10).

While impressions of the effectiveness of economic performance have fluctuated in the United States over time, there is even greater variation in the effectiveness of economic performance across rich countries (Brady 2009). This variation partly reflects the varying definitions and meanings of poverty across countries. Because most international researchers use relative measures of poverty while U.S. researchers often use the official measure of poverty, this could account for differing conclusions about the effectiveness of economic performance (DeFina 2004). In addition, countries differ massively in their social policies and institutions, and these social policies and institutions are likely to interact with and mediate the effects of economic performance (Lohmann 2009). As a result, and like many questions regarding poverty, there are reasonable bases for expecting that conclusions drawn from the United States do not necessarily generalize to other rich countries.

As illustrated by the temporally and cross-nationally varying effectiveness of economic performance, a rich literature on economic performance and poverty exists. Although poverty researchers have consistently been interested in questions regarding economic performance, there is a fair amount of debate within the field.

This chapter reviews the literature on how economic performance influences poverty in rich countries. In terms of economic performance, we examine the effects of the business cycle, economic growth, unemployment rates, and GDP per capita. While the principal focus of our essay is on poverty, because of the close links between income poverty and income inequality, we also incorporate literature on income inequality. Because Wade's chapter in this volume explores the role of economic growth and economic development in poverty and inequality in developing countries, we concentrate on rich countries. The first section explains the statistical models used to estimate the effects of economic performance on poverty. We concentrate on panel regression models across countries and within countries over time. We devote attention to the particular challenges of panel estimation, stationarity, measurement error, and causality. The next sections discuss studies assessing the effects of economic performance on poverty and income inequality. We consider both studies of within-country and between-country variation. Therefore, a central focus of our review is to highlight the methodological challenges and uncertainties regarding the effects of economic performance on poverty.

STATISTICAL AND ECONOMETRIC ISSUES

The "canonical" model has poverty (or an income distribution statistic) y be a linear function of a vector of L control variables z (including an intercept) and a vector of K variables that measure economic progress x for a country i in year t:

$$y_{it} = x_{it}' b + z_{it}' g + a_i + e_{it} \tag{1}$$

The dependent variable might be vector valued, in which case the parameter vectors b and g would be matrices. For now, we focus on a single income distribution statistic (i.e., scalar-valued y). The term a is an intercept that varies across countries. The error term e captures deviations of y from its expected or projected value, given x, z, and, possibly, a, and is most often assumed to have a constant variance s^2. It is in general unnecessary to assume e to be normally distributed. If it were, conditional on x, z, and a, the dependent variable would also be normally distributed, which, considering the dependent variables we discuss are income distribution statistics, might be an odd assumption to make. The parameters of main interest are the coefficients on the economic variables, b.

Note that the aforementioned postulates two-dimensional data—the country and time dimensions—but it can easily be extended to include groups within countries as well. For instance, some scholars analyze variation across states or cities and over time (within countries). The country-year dimensions are sufficient for the discussion here, however. Note also that the parameters b and g are assumed to be constant across countries (and time). However, the earlier setup is sufficiently general to allow for the possibility of varying coefficients—for example, by adding country interactions in x and/ or z so we do not need to discuss that option separately here.

There are many problems in estimating the parameters in equation (1) that are well understood, such as whether the country intercept a is correlated with either z or x (or parts thereof, the "fixed" vs. "random" effects cases). We discuss later a number of issues that affect the possibility to obtain accurate estimates and perform accurate statistical inference on the parameters. We discuss, in order, "traditional" panel-data issues (random vs. fixed effects; multilevel models); panel problems related to time series (unit roots, cointegration, dynamic models); problems related to the measurement of both dependent and explanatory variables (measurement errors, proxy variables, sampling and correlated samples); and, finally, whether coefficients can be given causal interpretations.

Fixed or Random Effects

For consistent estimation of b and g, the data must be reasonably well behaved. In general, we would treat x and z to be fixed, that is, nonstochastic, although it is often sufficient to make the other random variables in the model conditional on those. A key question is whether a can be treated as a "random" or "fixed" effect. This terminology is a little misleading, although well established and refers to whether a has a zero correlation with x and z (note that it need not be independent).

If a is "fixed," the parameters cannot be consistently estimated by applying least-squares to equation (1) directly as this leads to omitted-variable bias. The solution is to take the mean- or first-differences of the data. Which of these is preferable depends on the properties of the error term e—if they are serially uncorrelated, the two are equivalent for purposes of estimating b and g, but the two procedures induce somewhat different dependence between consecutive observations that need to be taken into account in calculating the variance matrix of the estimator.[1]

It is well-known that the presence of fixed, as opposed to random, effects can and should be tested for using a so-called Hausman test. The Hausman test relies on asymptotic results (Hausman 1978). Cross-country time series typically have both a small number of countries and relatively short time series. It is not clear how well the Hausman test performs in small samples so some caution needs to be applied. However, mean and first differencing of the data typically disposes of a lot of variance in both the dependent and explanatory variables, so it is prudent to carefully statistically test for the presence of fixed effects.

A possibly underappreciated problem is that the contrasting of only a fixed versus random effects model against each other in the context of equation 1 may mask other problems of misspecification. For instance, suppose there are both a country-level intercept and a country-level trend (random or fixed), or that the coefficients on the other variables vary by country. It is hard to tell a priori how the Hausman test will perform and doing more diagnostic checking is probably a good idea.

Stationarity and Cointegration

The typical application in examining the importance of economic performance for poverty involves a relatively small number of time periods. The chief reason for this is that internationally comparable time series on poverty tends to stretch back no further than 1970 or so.[2] Moreover, many data sources do not provide annual information.[3] Perhaps for these reasons, the time series properties of y, x, and z are often not discussed at length.[4]

In the time-series statistics and econometrics literatures, it is well-known that if each of two time series y_t and x_t are *integrated*, regressing y on x will result in regression results that appear to indicate a very strong relationship between the two even if, in fact, they are unrelated. It is possible for two or more integrated time series to be associated despite their being integrated, a phenomenon known as *cointegration*, when they share at least one common so-called stochastic trend. Detecting both integration and cointegration requires analysts to use regression techniques and statistical tests that have nonstandard properties—in the sense of what applies to stationary data (Hendry 1995).

Problems associated with applying methods to study potentially nonstationary data on income distribution and its covariates are discussed critically by Parker (2000). Jäntti and Jenkins (2010) suggest the use of parametric models that may be more amenable to time-series methods than the "raw" income distribution, such as poverty rates or Gini coefficients, which are often logically bounded (and cannot therefore be cointegrated with unbounded variables).

There is by now a substantial body of statistical methods that allow for the analysis of the time-series properties of cross sections of time series (Arellano 2003; Hsiao 2014; Cameron and Trivedi 2005). These include tests for whether a collection of country-level times series x_{it} should be considered integrated, and how to test for and estimate cointegrated models in panel data. The important point here is that, even if working with short time series (i.e., T is small) that may suffer from low statistical power, the problems caused by nonstationarity (of the particular type of integratedness) are present even in very short time series. They may just be hard to detect and deal with, but they lead to distorted statistical conclusions all the same. Moreover, in most of the applications we are considering in this chapter, both n and T are small.

Measurement Errors

The conventional wisdom about how measurement errors in the variables in a regression equation affect estimates is that only measurement errors in the right-hand-side variables (x and z) are cause for concern. Measurement errors in the dependent variable y are considered to lead to decreased explanatory power for the regression—that is, lower R^2—but not lead to inconsistent parameter estimates. It is useful to recall that the conventional wisdom applies to "classical" measurement errors, meaning here errors that are independent of (not only orthogonal to) the true values and that have a constant variance. It is well-known that such errors in explanatory variables cause downward bias in the parameter estimates.[5]

Measurement errors in one variable also lead to inconsistencies in the parameter estimates for other variables (sometimes referred to as "contamination bias") and lead to inflated estimates of the residual variance.

However, classical measurement errors—independent of the true value and constant variance—should be considered a best-case scenario. Suppose, for instance, that one of the explanatory variables is the unemployment rate. The estimate of the unemployment rate is

$$\check{u}_{it} = \#\,\text{unemployed} / \#\,\text{labor force} = U_{it} / L_{it} \tag{2}$$

However, U is a sum of binomial variables, the variance of which are $u(1-u)$ so the standard deviation of $\hat{u}$ is $(u(1-u)/L)^{1/2}$. This renders the measurement errors affecting the observed variable both heteroscedastic—its variance varies from year to year and across countries with both sample size and the true level of unemployment—and makes it, of course, a function of the true value of the unemployment rate, so the two cannot be independent.

To make matters potentially worse, suppose that the unemployment rate (a right-hand-side variable) is estimated from the same data as both another right-hand-side variable—say, the share of single-mother families—and the dependent variable—say, the poverty rate. Then measurement errors are nonclassical and correlated across variables. However, it is possible that measurement errors of the type discussed here—those due to sampling—are small enough to be safely ignored. Even if they are not, they can easily be estimated so that both the estimator and its variance's inconsistency can be corrected by using the known error variances.[6]

In the case of variables that measure business cycles and economic performance, which are under discussion here, sampling errors are not necessarily the main concern.[7] For both national accounts data and inflation, the key issue is if the empirical measurements capture the true underlying data. National accounts data in particular are subject to frequent revisions, even decades after initial publication. The standard deviations of such revisions are typically of an order of magnitude comparable to (but somewhat smaller than) the standard deviations of prediction errors (Öller and Tallbom 1996).

Causality

The possibly most difficult question discussed here relates to whether the relationship between the economic variables and the income distribution statistics can be considered causal. To the best of our knowledge, there is no study that utilizes quasi-experimental evidence of the sort now popular in empirical economics (Angrist and Pischke 2008). An example of this would be a study that compares the effect of an employment shock induced by, for instance, the closure of a large establishment on local poverty or inequality rates, using nearby localities that have not experienced a plant closure as a control group. The problem is partly that one cannot randomly assign economic performance to places. Moreover, the problem is also that most "random" economic shocks that could be exploited as instruments or discontinuities are probably correlated both with the independent variable (economic performance) and the outcome (poverty) in a variety of observable and unobservable ways.

However, even the much less demanding concept of Granger causality, which addresses the predictive capacity of different time series for each other, has received little attention in these types of models. One fairly common strategy employs models with fixed effects for both states/countries and time. For example, Brady and colleagues (2013) utilize two-way fixed-effects models to assess the effects of state-level economic growth, unemployment, and GDP per capita for individual-level working poverty in the United States from 1991 to 2010. In their analyses, fixed effects are included for U.S. states and for years, which allows them to net out the stable unobserved differences between states and the generic changes over time.

Empirical Literature

Although this *Handbook* examines a variety of conceptualizations and measures of poverty, here we concentrate primarily on income poverty. Although a few scholars have examined the effects of economic performance on other measures of poverty (e.g., consumption, Meyer and Sullivan 2011), most studies of economic performance have focused on income poverty. That said, this does not mean we need to exclusively examine poverty indices. Models that account for the parameters of parametric distribution functions, such as Metcalf (1969), Thurow (1970) or, recently, Jäntti and Jenkins (2010), can be used to examine the importance of economic progress on poverty. Models that account for the evolution of inequality indices, such as Beach (1977) or Blinder and Esaki (1978), can also be used in conjunction with other information to draw inferences of how poverty varies with economic performance.

We also focus on studies that use regression models and leave aside studies that use decomposition methods, such as shift-share analysis. This is not always a straightforward distinction to make, as decomposition analyses can often easily be rephrased in terms of regressions. The studies we examine can be categorized along many different dimensions: which countries are covered; which time periods are covered, and whether time periods are compared; analyses on between- and/or within-country variation; which measures of poverty are utilized; whether the analyses account for inequality; whether the study focuses on business-cycle indicators alone or in combination with structural aspects of the economy (e.g., the sectoral distribution); whether economic performance is evaluated for poverty overall or decomposed for specific demographic groups; and what control variables are considered. Perhaps above all, previous studies vary considerably in how they address the aforementioned methodological issues and challenges.

We start by discussing studies that explicitly model income poverty and then discuss (more briefly) studies that focus on income inequality. The focus of the inequality studies is what we can learn from the determinants of inequality about income poverty. While not necessarily a lot, some of the findings can be used to deduce how economic progress or cyclical variation affects income poverty. The review of the literature that follows is also organized by whether the studies are comparative or examine only one country.

Within-Country Studies—Poverty

Perhaps the most prolific and visible literature on economic performance and poverty within countries concentrates on the United States. As noted, many have written about how the business cycle and economic performance shape trends in U.S. poverty (e.g., Balke and Slottje 1993; Blank 1994, 2000, 2009; Blank and Blinder 1986; Ellwood and Summers 1986; Freeman 2001; Hall 2006; Tobin 1994; Williams 1991). Several studies examine historical trends in the United States as a whole, others examine regional variation over time, and still others pool regional or state and temporal variation. As mentioned, much of the literature debates how the effects of economic performance on poverty have changed over time.

In one example, Gundersen and Ziliak (2004) conclude that economic performance has substantial effects on poverty in the United States. They (2004:78, 83) write, "Aggregate business cycle and economic growth do, in fact, 'lift all boats.' A strong macroeconomy at both the state and national levels reduces the number of families with incomes below the poverty line and the severity of poverty." Similar to other studies that find the unemployment rate is the most important aspect of economic performance (e.g., Williams 1991), Gundersen and Ziliak (2004:73) find: "A one-percentage-point decrease in the unemployment rate leads to a 4.5% decline in the short-run poverty rate." Analyzing the United States between 1963 and 2008, Meyer and Sullivan (2011) find that both income and consumption poverty are negatively associated with the unemployment rate and GDP per capita. Using data on regions in the United States over time, Freeman (2008) finds that poverty is sensitive to unemployment rates and growth. Hence, these studies conclude that poverty does follow the business cycle and is sensitive to macroeconomic conditions.

In one of the more recent contributions, Blank (2009) analyzes the relationship between economic performance and poverty in the United States over a 44-year period. Blank (2009:63) argues forcefully and unequivocally: "Maintaining a high-employment economy, with stable or growing wages and jobs that are readily available to less-educated workers, continues to be the most important anti-poverty policy for this country." Reflecting the methodological discussions above, she estimates a regression model with the dependent variable of poverty (for the entire United States, and for specific groups like single mothers, families, children, race/ethnic minorities, etc.). Blank concentrates much of her focus on the coefficient for the macrolevel unemployment rate, and how this coefficient changes over time. She also adjusts for the lagged dependent variable, earnings inequality, and the declining value of the poverty threshold, among other factors. From her analysis, she concludes that there is a strong positive relationship between the unemployment and poverty rates. Specifically, a two-point rise in the unemployment rate leads to a .9 point increase in the poverty rate. The unemployment rate had a much weaker relationship with poverty in the 1980s but became more influential in the 1990s and 2000s. She also finds that unemployment has a particularly strong effect on the poverty of children, blacks, and single mothers. Blank (2009:84) ultimately concludes: "these regressions demonstrate that poverty remains very responsive to the economic cycle." From this evidence, she argues: "Maintaining a strong economy and low unemployment is most important for the long-term economic well-being of low-wage workers ... the best policy we can pursue for the poor is to keep unemployment low and the economy strong" (p. 86).

In contrast, a few scholars are more skeptical. DeFina (2004) concludes that the effects of economic performance depend heavily on the particular poverty measure used. For several reasonable alternative poverty measures within the United States, DeFina finds no effect of the unemployment rate but a strong effect of earnings growth. Analyzing individuals nested in U.S. states from 1991 to 2010, Brady and colleagues (2013) find that a state's unemployment rate is positively associated with relative working poverty. However, contrary to expectations, they find that economic growth is surprisingly (and robustly) positively associated with working poverty. They also find no effect of a rising state-level GDP per capita.

There are far fewer time-series-based studies of the determinants of poverty within countries outside the United States. This reflects, at least in part, the fact that because of the War on Poverty in the United States, there are both long time series of poverty and a policy-oriented interest in understanding it evolution over time. A recent exception is Ayala, Cantó, and Rodríguez (2013) who examine the effects of the business cycle (in terms of both unemployment and inflation) on poverty in Spain using regional and quarterly data. They find that the unemployment rate increases and inflation decreases poverty. They also find that the effects depend on the concentration of unemployment within the household. Their evidence further suggests that the poverty-increasing effect of unemployment is magnified in cyclical downturns, that is, the impact is asymmetric.

Comparative Studies—Poverty

There is a rich tradition in comparative welfare state research to use regression-based methods to examine the determinants of poverty across countries (in general, using time series of cross sections or multilevel models of individuals nested in countries). As the term suggests, the focus is often on how welfare states and political arrangements are related to poverty. Typical welfare state covariates include the generosity of different kinds of welfare state benefits; the relative sizes of traditionally vulnerable population groups, such as single-mother households or the elderly; the political composition (in terms of Left, Center, and Right parties) of governments; and measures of the strength of labor unions, such as union density. Many of these studies also inform us about economic performance—typically measured by both business cycles and long-term economic performance, such as recent economic growth and unemployment—and measures of economic structure, such as the sectoral distribution of either production or the labor force. However, in this literature, economic performance is often treated as a set of control variables rather than the true object of interest. Moreover, this literature has generally found that the welfare state is more important than economic performance for poverty.

Within his broader study of poverty across rich democracies, Brady (2009) uses data from the Luxembourg Income Study (LIS 2015) to compare different explanations for variations in poverty rates across countries. His analyses show that the sectoral distribution of employment, especially the share in manufacturing, significantly influences poverty. Also, female labor-force participation significantly reduces poverty. Brady also shows that economic growth reduces poverty, while productivity and unemployment are insignificant in all models. Even though he provides evidence of some effects for economic performance and economic structure, the primary objective is to estimate the importance of the welfare state.

Scruggs and Allan (2006) estimate both relative and absolute (defined using price deflators, PPPs and 40 percent of U.S. median income in 1986 as the poverty line) poverty across countries from the mid-1980s to 2000. They use data on disposable income from the LIS. Part of the contribution of their work is to examine not only national accounts based aggregates, such as income per capita, economic growth, and central government spending, but also to include specific measures of the generosity of the welfare state. All their regressions include market income poverty, income per capita, union density, legislative veto points, liberal or socialist regime, and income growth rate across the past five years. These measures are often insignificant, with signs that vary, but seem to have greater impacts on absolute than relative poverty. For instance, neither market income poverty nor economic growth have a particularly consistent or large effect on relative poverty, but the coefficients are largely statistically significant and are the expected sign for absolute poverty (positive for market income poverty, and negative for income per capita). The main object of interest in their paper, however, is the scores for unemployment, sickness, and pension benefit generosity.

Also using data from LIS, Misra and colleagues (2012) compare how household- and country-level, family-policy variables affect the poverty of partnered and single mothers. It is something of a stretch to think of things like average employment, family allowances, parental leave generosity and childcare availability as measures of economic performance—indeed, hitherto we have considered them measures of the welfare state. Moreover, the data are at the individual level when we have mostly considered country-level outcomes. Nonetheless, what emerges from their results is that family allowances and employment levels are important, and largely similar, determinants of poverty for both partnered and unpartnered mothers. To the extent that employment is influenced by economic performance, it could indirectly influence the poverty outcomes they study.

Brady, Fullerton, and Cross (2009) use individual-level data on working-age adults to estimate multilevel models that incorporate country-level and individual-level variables to predict the incidence of individual relative poverty based on disposable income. The individual-level covariates include household structure, household employment, and presence of the elderly and children. The country-level variables include economic growth, unemployment, and manufacturing employment, as well as a welfare state index. The latter is composed of (relative to GDP) social welfare expenditures, social security transfers, and government expenditures, as well as public health spending as share of total. The welfare state index turns out to be substantially and statistically significantly related to lower poverty, whereas the economic variables do not appear to be consequential.

On balance, some comparative research finds that economic performance is just as, if not more, important as the welfare state to poverty. For example, Hauser and colleagues (2000) argue that unemployment is more important than social policy in explaining trends in poverty in Western Europe. Brady and colleagues (2009) find that the country-level variables welfare state generosity and union density significantly reduce individual-level poverty. However, they also find that individual-level employment is the most powerful predictor of individual-level poverty. Similarly, Brady and colleagues (2010) do not find powerful direct effects of economic performance on working poverty. However, they do find that having multiple earners in the household is an important individual-level predictor of working poverty. They also find that economic performance clearly influences whether an individual is in an employed household. Because individual-level employment (or having multiple earners) is likely driven partly by economic performance, economic performance likely still indirectly, but powerfully, shapes poverty.

Despite these contributions, there are good reasons to suspect that welfare states and other institutions mediate and moderate the effects of economic performance on poverty. For example, a few studies examine the recent economic crisis of 2008 and assess whether this sharp change in economic performance had adverse effects on poverty. Using the EU-SILC, De Beer (2012) finds substantial variation across the EU in how at-risk poverty responded to the crisis.

Related Research on Income Inequality

As mentioned, the literature on income inequality is also relevant here because income poverty and income inequality are closely connected. As a result, we now review some of the research on how economic performance is related to income inequality.

The typical study examines a time series of annual data on either the income shares of quintile or quartile groups, or some inequality index such as the Gini coefficient, where the income shares and inequality indices are usually estimated from household survey data. The dependent variables are regressed against a number of macroeconomic variables, possibly including both contemporaneous and lagged values (e.g., Burniaux et al. 2006). The findings from these studies are reviewed by Parker (1998) and their methods are discussed critically by Parker (2000).

Most of the earlier studies, including Metcalf (1969), Thurow (1970), Beach (1977), and Blinder and Esaki (1978), used data for the United States.[8] Other studies include Nolan (1988–1989) using UK data, Björklund (1991) using Swedish data, and Buse (1982) and Beach and McWatters (1990) using Canadian data. These studies have typically found that unemployment had a regressive impact on the income distribution and that inflation had no statistically significant association with it.

Studies such as Ashworth (1994), Parker (1996), and Mocan (1999), were motivated by the premise that, if the explanatory variables are nonstationary, then the estimators of the regression parameters have nonstandard distributions. The argument was that statistical inference that mistakenly uses standard asymptotic results could and did lead to erroneous conclusions. The authors applied the framework of dynamic econometrics (Hendry 1995) to the analysis of macroeconomic variables and income quantile group shares or inequality indices. Specifically, they examined whether each time series had a unit root and if this was the case, they proceeded to model their cointegration relations.

It can be inappropriate to examine whether inequality indices and income shares have unit roots, because most commonly used indicators of inequality have logical bounds. It may also be inappropriate to assume that the relationship between income inequality and macroeconomic variables is linear. One of the lessons of Metcalf (1969), Thurow (1970), and McDonald (1992) is that by regressing the distributional parameters on macroeconomic variables one may incorporate nonlinear relationships between distributional characteristics, such as the Gini coefficient, and macroeconomic factors even though the estimating equations are linear.

There is a large literature on the determinants of inequality within countries. Studies have been done on the United States (e.g., Nielsen and Alderson 1997), and the United Kingdom (Jäntti and Jenkins 2010; Taylor and Driffield 2005). Interesting within-country studies have also been done on many individual countries, such as South Korea (Lee, Kim, and Cin 2013), and Australia (Leigh 2003; Gaston and Rajaguru 2009). Like the poverty literature, there is also a large literature comparing inequality across countries. Although this literature is less focused on short-term variation in the business cycle, it has often emphasized the role of long-term economic development and sectoral change. Because economic performance contributes to such long-term economic developments, it stands to reason that economic performance could be relevant to cross-national variation in income inequality. Moreover, even though this literature also finds that welfare state and labor market institutions are essential, this does not mean economic performance is irrelevant.

For example, Gustafsson and Johansson (1999) examine factors that caused the rise in household income inequality in rich democracies to vary over time. Broadly, they find that five key variables drove the rise in income inequality: employment in industry, imports from developing countries, public consumption, unionization, and the size of the youth population. Because the sectoral composition of the economy is important, economic performance likely plays a role in variation in income inequality.

Focused on detecting the role of economic globalization, Alderson and Nielsen (2002) find that foreign direct investment (FDI), North-South trade, and immigration have played key roles in driving up income inequality. Direct investment affects income inequality by (1) accelerating deindustrialization, (2) weakening the bargaining position of labor, and (3) altering the distribution of income between labor and capital and the demand for unskilled labor. North-South trade and net migration also positively affect income inequality. Alderson and Nielsen also conclude that the recent inequality experience of rich countries is associated with (1) the long-term labor force shift from the agriculture to the nonagricultural sectors; (2) demographic transition; (3) the continuing spread of education with development; (4) deunionization; (5) the decline of wage-setting coordination; (6) variation in the degree to which welfare states decommodify labor; (7) the growth of female labor-force participation; and (8) deindustrialization. Interestingly, they find that strongest effect on inequality corresponds to the share of the labor force in agriculture. Though slightly less important than labor market and welfare state institutions, they conclude that FDI, North-South trade, and immigration did contribute to the rise in income inequality.

Even among studies emphasizing the role of politics, economic performance remains important. For example, Pillai (2011) shows that income inequality is closely related to the level of democracy. Low-income countries benefit from increased trade. As the countries move toward free trade, income inequality tends to fall. Still, per capita GDP also tends to have an inverse relationship with inequality in all the data sets analyzed. FDI does not seem to be playing the role the literature specifies for it. It creates more inequality and furthers the divide rather than working toward reducing it in low-income countries.

CONCLUSION

This essay examines how economic performance and the business cycle influence poverty in rich countries. For a long time, there has been an extensive literature on how poverty is shaped by economic growth, unemployment rates, economic development, and labor market structure. This literature also has strong links to literatures on welfare states and income inequality. Much of the interest in the effects of economic performance on poverty has been fueled by links between American public policy, the War on Poverty, and academic poverty research. The literature features within-country studies of over-time variation, cross-sectional between-country studies, studies pooling historical and cross-national variation, and increasingly, multilevel studies of individuals nested in countries and time.

There has been considerable debate about how much, when, and under what conditions economic performance drives poverty. American poverty researchers often highlight the relationship between economic performance and the official U.S. poverty rate or absolute measures of poverty, material deprivation, and consumption. The U.S. literature stands out for being most optimistic about the poverty-reducing effects of improved economic performance. For instance, a number of studies provide evidence that official U.S. poverty is strongly associated with the unemployment rate and economic growth. International scholars often fail to find as robust relationships when studying other countries besides the United States, comparing between rich countries, or studying relative poverty and other outcomes. Instead, such researchers tend to find the welfare state is more important than economic performance and that economic performance has only a relatively modest effect on poverty. Even within the United States, it is widely understood that there has been substantial over-time fluctuation in the strength of the relationship between economic performance and poverty. On balance, however, comparativists have increasingly acknowledged that economic performance surely affects individual employment, and individual employment is one of the most important predictors of individual poverty. Therefore, economic performance likely has some contextual, albeit often indirect, influence on the probability of individual or household poverty. Just how large this effect is, and how this effect compares with other contextual influences on poverty, continues to warrant further research and scrutiny.

This essay devotes considerable attention to the statistical models used to estimate the effects of economic performance on poverty. We concentrate on panel regression models across countries and within countries over time and discuss the particular challenges of panel estimation, stationarity, measurement error, and causality. Like many literatures, our view is that scholars should be more aware of the assumptions behind their models and the limitations of their statistical evidence. Progress is occurring in statistically untangling how economic performance and poverty are related, however, the literature still lacks the sorts of stronger causal evidence that is increasingly prominent in empirical economics. Even in the event that scholars can come closer to identifying the causal effects of economic performance, it will remain important to scrutinize even more fundamental methodological issues. We especially highlight the absolutely essential role of careful measurement and sound comparison. Racing ahead to identify causal effects will not be nearly as productive if it comes with sacrificing measurement and comparison.

We conclude by highlighting one central weakness in the literature: the tendency for advocates of economic performance to inflate their conclusions. Especially among American poverty researchers, one routinely finds bold rhetoric about how economic performance and/or the business cycle "have a strong effect on the extent of poverty" (Blank et al. 2006:1); "is the dominant determinant of the poverty rate" (Ellwood and Summers 1986:79); "matters more than anything else" (Blank 2000:6); "is a wonderful thing" (Blank 2000:10); "do, in fact, 'lift all boats'" (Gundersen and Ziliak 2004:78, 83); "continues to be the most important anti-poverty policy for this country" (Blank

2009:63); and, finally, "is most important for the long-term economic well-being of low-wage workers ... [and] the best policy we can pursue for the poor." (Blank 2009:84). It is noteworthy that one does not find such strong rhetoric in the international litera-ture or in literatures using alternative measures of poverty. Indeed, there is a rather striking imbalance between the strong American rhetoric for economic performance on one side, and the methodological, measurement, and cross-national caution on the other side.

Indeed, our literature review shows that many studies fail to find unequivocal sup-port for the power of economic performance to shape poverty. A broader perspective incorporating literature on the welfare state and income inequality provides even less certainty about the effects of economic performance. Therefore, one limitation of the literature is that proponents of economic performance have not sufficiently engaged with critical studies about the effects of economic performance. More generally, the literature would benefit from greater methodological rigor and caution. At a minimum, future scholars can improve the literature with (a) more depth about the assumptions and limitations of the statistical models used in these literatures; (b) more study of cases besides the United States; (c) more attention to alternative measures of poverty and the limitations of the official U.S. measure; (d) more cross-national comparison; (e) more consideration of the interactive influence of welfare states and political institutions; and (f) more incorporation of the indirect influence through individual employment. For research on economic performance to advance, we need to move beyond trium-phant rhetoric about economic growth. One promising direction is to more fully utilize the extensive cross-national data sets like the Luxembourg Income Study to scrutinize the effects of economic performance on various measures of poverty in many countries in many time periods.

The next generation of research on economic performance has the potential to be more international, more interdisciplinary, and more responsive to skepticism. To the extent that research follows such a path, there are strong reasons to believe we can gain an even better understanding of how economic performance shapes poverty.

NOTES

1. First differencing makes two consecutive observations correlated but induces no further correlation. Mean differencing makes all observations within a country correlated across each other.
2. An exception to this is the World Top Income Database (Atkinson et al. 2011). See, for example, Roine, Vlachos, and Waldenström (2009) for a study that uses those data.
3. The periodicity of different data sources is discussed in the third section.
4. Note that the time series properties of e, while related to those of y, are not the main worry for stationarity.
5. More precisely, parameter estimates can easily be shown to be downward inconsistent, that is, converge improbability not to the true values of the parameters but to a constant that is closer in absolute value to zero than then true value.

6. See Cameron and Trivedi (2005); see also Jäntti and Jenkins (2010) for an application.
7. Curiously, even though important cyclical variables, such as the rate of inflation, build on sampled data (in the case of inflation, on prices of sampled goods), sampling errors are rarely discussed, which contrasts sharply with data on employment.
8. The U.S. studies include Blank and Blinder (1986) who also examine the poverty rate, and Cutler and Katz (1991) who also examine the effects on consumption inequality. The studies by, for example, Mocan (1999), Ashworth (1994), and Parker (1996) used methods of dynamic econometrics discussed in this chapter.

REFERENCES

Alderson, Arthur S. and Francois Nielsen. 2002. "Globalization and the Great U-Turn: Income Inequality Trends in 16 OECD Countries." *American Journal of Sociology* 107:1244–99.

Ashworth, John. 1994. "An Empirical Examination of Macroeconomic Activity and Income Distribution in the United States." Economics Working Paper No. 130. Durham, U.K. University of Durham.

Atkinson, Anthony B., Thomas Piketty, and Emmanuel Saez. 2011. "Top Incomes in the Long Run of History." *Journal of Economic Literature* 49:3–71.

Ayala, Luis, Olga Cantó, and Juan G Rodríguez. 2013. "Poverty and the Business Cycle: The Role of the Intra-Household Distribution of Unemployment." Unpublished manuscript, Universidad Rey Juan Carlos.

Balke, Nathan S. and Daniel J. Slottje. 1993. "Poverty and Change in the Macroeconomy: A Dynamic Macroeconometric Model." *Review of Economics and Statistics* 75:117–22.

Beach, Charles M. 1977. "Cyclical Sensitivity of Aggregate Income Inequality." *Review of Economics and Statistics* 59:56–66.

Beach, Charles M. and Catherine J. McWatters. 1990. "Factors Behind the Changes in Canada's Family Income Distribution and the Share of the Middle Class." *Relation Industrielles* 45:118–33.

Björklund, Anders. 1991. "Unemployment and Income Distribution: Time-Series Evidence from Sweden." *Scandinavian Journal of Economics* 93:457–65.

Blank, Rebecca M. 1994. "The Employment Strategy: Public Policies to Increase Work and Earnings." Pp. 168–204 in *Confronting Poverty*, edited by S. H. Danziger, G. D. Sandefur, and D. H. Weinberg. Cambridge, MA: Harvard University Press.

Blank, Rebecca M. 2000. "Fighting Poverty: Lessons from Recent U.S. History." *Journal of Economic Perspectives* 14:3–19.

Blank, Rebecca M. 2009. "Economic Change and the Structure of Opportunity for Less-Skilled Workers." Pp. 63–91 in *Changing Poverty, Changing Places*, edited by M. Cancian and S. H. Danziger. New York: Russell Sage Foundation.

Blank, Rebecca and Alan Blinder. 1986. "Macroeconomics, Income Distribution and Poverty." Pp. 180–208 in *Fighting Poverty*, edited by S. H. Danziger and D. H. Weinberg. Cambridge, MA: Harvard University Press.

Blank, Rebecca M., Sheldon H. Danziger, and Robert F. Schoeni. 2006. *Working and Poor.* New York: Russell Sage Foundation.

Blinder, Alan and Howard Esaki. 1978. "Macroeconomic Activity and Income Distribution in the Post-War United States." *Review of Economics and Statistics* 60:604–9.

Bluestone, Barry and Bennett Harrison. 2000. *Growing Prosperity: The Battle for Growth With Equity in the 21st Century.* New York: Houghton Mifflin.

Brady, David. 2009. *Rich Democracies, Poor People: How Politics Explain Poverty.* New York: Oxford University Press.

Brady, David, Regina S. Baker, and Ryan Finnigan. 2013. "When Unionization Disappears: State-Level Unionization and Working Poverty in the U.S." *American Sociological Review* 78:872–96.

Burniaux, Jean-Marc, Flavio Padrini, and Nicola Brandt. 2006. "Labour Market Performance, Income Inequality and Poverty in OECD Countries." OECD Economics Department Working Paper No. 500. Paris, France.

Buse, Adolf. 1982. "The Cyclical Behavior of the Size Distribution of Income in Canada 1947–1978." *Canadian Journal of Economics* 15:189–204.

Cameron, A. Colin and Pravin K. Trivedi. 2005. *Microeconometrics: Methods and Applications.* Cambridge: Cambridge University Press.

Cutler, David M. and Lawrence F Katz. 1991. "Macroeconomic Performance and the Disadvantaged." *Brookings Papers on Economic Activity* 10:1–74.

De Beer, Paul. 2012. "Earnings and Income Inequality in the EU during the Crisis." *International Labour Review* 151:313–31.

DeFina, Robert H. 2004. "The Impacts of Unemployment on Alternative Poverty Indices." *Review of Income and Wealth* 50:69–85.

Ellwood, David T. and Lawrence Summers. 1986. "Poverty in America: Is Welfare the Answer or the Problem." Pp. 78–105 in *Fighting Poverty: What Works and What Doesn't,* edited by S. H. Danziger and D. H. Weinberg. Cambridge, MA: Harvard University Press.

Freeman, Donald G. 2008. "Poverty and the Macroeconomy: Estimates from U.S. Regional Data." *Contemporary Economic Policy* 21:358–71.

Freeman, Richard B. 2001. "The Rising Tide Lifts. . ." Pp. 97–126 in *Understanding Poverty,* edited by In S. H. Danziger and R. H. Haveman. New York and Cambridge, MA: Russell Sage Foundation and Harvard University Press.

Gaston, Noel and Gulasekaran Rajaguru. 2009. "The Long-Run Determinants of Australian Income Inequality." *Economic Record* 85:260–75.

Gordon, David M. 1972. *Theories of Poverty and Underemployment: Orthodox, Radical, and Dual Labor Market Perspectives.* Lexington, MA: Lexington Books.

Gundersen, Craig and James P. Ziliak. 2004. "Poverty and Macroeconomic Performance across Space, Race, and Family Structure." *Demography* 41:61–86.

Gustafsson, Björn and Mats Johansson. 1999. "In Search of Smoking Guns: What Makes Income Inequality Vary over Time in Different Countries?" *American Sociological Review* 64:585–605.

Hall, Robert E. 2006. "The Macroeconomy and Determinants of the Earnings of Less-Skilled Workers." Pp. 89–112 in *Working and Poor,* edited by R. M. Blank, S. H. Danziger, and R. F. Schoeni. New York: Russell Sage Foundation.

Hauser, Richard and Brian Nolan with Konstanze Morsdorf and Wolfgang Strengmann-Kuhn. 2000. "Unemployment and Poverty: Change Over Time." Pp. 25–46 in *Welfare Regimes and the Experience of Unemployment in Europe,* edited by D. Gallie and S. Paugam. New York: Oxford University Press.

Haveman, Robert and Jonathan Schwabish. 2000. "Has Macroeconomic Performance Regained Its Antipoverty Bite?" *Contemporary Economic Policy* 18:415–27.

Hendry, David. 1995. *Dynamic Econometrics.* Oxford: Oxford University Press.

Jäntti, Markus and Stephen P Jenkins. 2010. "The Impact of Macroeconomic Conditions on Income inequality." *Journal of Economic Inequality* 8:221–40.

Lee, Hae-Young, Jongsung Kim, and Beom Cheol Cin. 2013. "Empirical Analysis on the Determinants of Income Inequality in Korea." *International Journal of Advanced Science and Technology* 53:95–109.

Leigh, Andrew. 2003. "What Affects Inequality? Evidence from Time Series Data." Presentation to the Australian Social Policy Conference, University of New South Wales, Sydney.

Lohmann, Henning. 2009. "Welfare States, Labour Market Institutions and the Working Poor: A Comparative Analysis of 20 European Countries." *European Sociological Review* 25:489–504.

Luxembourg Income Study Database (LIS). 2015. Luxembourg. (http://www.lisdatacenter.org).

McDonald, James B. 1992. "The Distribution of Income and Efficient Estimation." Pp. 123–37 in *Research on Economic Inequality*, Vol. 2, edited by D. J. Slottje. Greenwich, CT: JAI Press.

Metcalf, Charles E. 1969. "The Size Distribution of Personal Income during the Business Cycle." *American Economic Review* 59:657–68.

Meyer, Bruce D. and James X. Sullivan. 2011. "Consumption and Income Poverty over the Business Cycle." National Bureau of Economic Research Working Paper No. 16751. Cambridge, MA.

Mocan, H. Naci. 1999. "Structural Unemployment, Cyclical Unemployment and Income Inequality." *Review of Economics and Statistics* 81:122–35.

Nolan, Brian. 1988–1989. "Macroeconomic Conditions and the Size Distribution of Income: Evidence from the United Kingdom." *Journal of Post Keynesian Economics* 11:196–221.

O'Connor, Alice. 2001. *Poverty Knowledge*. Princeton, NJ: Princeton University Press.

Öller, Lars-Erik and Christer Tallbom. 1996. "Smooth and Timely Business Cycle Indicators for Noisy Swedish Data." *International Journal of Forecasting* 12:389–402.

Parker, Simon. 1996. "Explaining the Determinants of US Income Inequality, 1948–90." Economics Working Paper No. 163. Durham, U.K.: University of Durham.

Parker, Simon. 1998–1999. "Income Inequality and the Business Cycle: A Survey of the Evidence and Some New Results." *Journal of Post Keynesian Economics* 21:201–25.

Parker, Simon. 2000. "Opening a Can of Worms: The Pitfalls of Time-Series Regression Analyses of Income Inequality." *Applied Economics* 32:221–30.

Pillai, Archana. 2011. "Impact of Political Regime and Economic Openness on Income Inequality: A Tale of Low-Income and OECD Countries." Tech. rep. Institute of Management Technology, Hyderabad, India.

Rainwater, Lee and Timothy Smeeding. 2004. *Poor Kids in a Rich Country*. New York: Russell Sage Foundation.

Roine, Jesper, Jonas Vlachos, and Daniel Waldenström. 2009. "The Long-Run Determinants of Inequality: What Can We Learn from Top Income Data?" *Journal of Public Economics* 93:974–88.

Sawhill, Isabel V. 1988. "Poverty in the U.S.: Why Is It So Persistent?" *Journal of Economic Literature* 26:1073–1119.

Scruggs, Lyle and James P. Allan. 2006. "The Material Consequences of Welfare States: Benefit Generosity and Absolute Poverty in 16 OECD Countries." *Comparative Political Studies* 39:880–904.

Taylor, Karl and Nigel Driffield. 2005. "Wage Inequality and the Role of Multinationals: Evidence from UK Panel Data." *Journal of Labour Economics* 12:223–49.

Thurow, Lester C. 1970. "Analyzing the American Income Distribution." *American Economic Review* 60:261–69.

Tobin, James. 1994. "Poverty in Relation to Macroeconomic Trends, Cycles, and Policies." Pp. 147–67 in *Confronting Poverty*, edited by S. H. Danziger, G. D. Sandefur, and D. H. Weinberg. Cambridge, MA: Harvard University Press.

Williams, Donald R. 1991. "Structural Change and the Aggregate Poverty Rate." *Demography* 28:323–32.

SECTION V

CONSEQUENCES

CHAPTER 25

....

MATERIAL DEPRIVATION
AND CONSUMPTION

....

BASAK KUS, BRIAN NOLAN,
AND CHRISTOPHER T. WHELAN

INTRODUCTION

....

RESEARCH on poverty in rich counties has relied primarily on household income to capture living standards and to distinguish those in poverty. This is also true of official poverty measurement and monitoring for policy purposes. However, as awareness of the limitations of income as the sole means of capturing both levels of poverty and the underlying processes has been increasing, there has been a fundamental shift toward a multidimensional approach. However, a variety of obstacles, relating to the conceptual and empirical underpinnings of existing research, lie in the path of such implementation (Grusky and Weeden 2007; Kakwani and Silber 2007; Thorbecke 2007). In this chapter we provide an overview of the advantages of supplementing information relating to income with additional data relating to lifestyle deprivation and consumption.

In a developing country context, manifest material deprivation and inadequate levels of consumption have always been central to the conceptualization of poverty and living standards, and direct measures of failure to meet "basic needs" are commonly used alongside income-based measures such as the World Bank's "dollar a day" standard. In contrast, both research and official poverty monitoring in rich countries typically relies primarily on household income. Recently, though, an increasing awareness of the limitations of using income has been reflected in a focus on the role which non-monetary measures of deprivation can play in capturing and understanding poverty and exclusion. This is illustrated most strikingly by the fact that the poverty reduction target for 2020 adopted by the European Commission in 2010 includes as one component a direct measure of material deprivation (Nolan and Whelan 2011; European Commission 2011) This is part of a broader interest, at both research and policy levels, in developing multidimensional approaches to measuring and monitoring poverty and exclusion, on the understanding that no single indicator can be expected to adequately capture such complex concepts.

In this chapter we first provide an overview of recent research on material deprivation, seen primarily as a means to go "beyond income" in capturing poverty and exclusion. We then focus on measuring deprivation, with some illustrations using comparative data for the countries of the EU, the broadest set of rich(er) countries for which comparative data are available. The mismatch between low income and measured deprivation is discussed, incorporating both longitudinal and cross-sectional perspectives.

In responding to the issues raised by the somewhat different pictures provided by income and deprivation, we first subject the notion of multidimensionality to critical scrutiny. Our starting point is that the case for a multidimensional approach has to be argued and demonstrated rather than assumed. We then proceed to focus on the measurement issues raised in the implementation of multidimensional approaches. In particular, we seek to establish what can be learned from recent attempts to develop measures that can be decomposed by dimension. The issues involved will once again be addressed with illustrative applications using comparative material-deprivation data for European countries. We will proceed to deal with a range of literature that focuses on conceptual and empirical issues relating to the contrast between income and consumption. Finally some key conclusions in relation to poverty, material deprivation, and consumption will be highlighted.

Going Beyond Income
in Capturing Poverty

Most research on poverty takes as a point of departure the definition that people are in poverty when "their resources are so seriously below those commanded by the average individual or family that they are, in effect, excluded from ordinary living patterns, customs and activities" (Townsend 1979). Poverty from this starting point has two core elements: it is about inability to participate, which is attributable to inadequate resources. While most quantitative research employs income to distinguish the poor, this reliance on income has been increasingly questioned, and, in that context, the potential uses of direct measures of deprivation have come to the fore. While the use of nonmonetary indicators in monitoring living conditions or quality of life has a long history, their use in capturing deprivation and poverty received a major impetus with Townsend's pioneering British study (1979). As these indicators became more widely available, they underpinned a more radical critique: reliance on income actually fails to identify those who are unable to participate in their societies due to lack of resources (Ringen 1988). Since then an extensive research literature on measures of material deprivation in OECD countries has grown; the review by Boarini and Mira d'Ercole (2006) lists over a hundred studies covering a wide range of countries. In Europe, the widespread adoption of the terminology of social exclusion/inclusion reflected inter alia a concern that focusing simply on income misses an important part of the picture, while reinforcing an interest in material deprivation and, more broadly, in multidimensional approaches to measuring poverty and exclusion (Nolan and Whelan 2007; Burchardt, Le Grand, and Piachaud 2002; Boarini and Mira D'Ercole 2006; Bradshaw and Finch 2003). There has also been significant interest in measuring and investigating material deprivation in OECD countries outside Europe, as in Headey (2008), Saunders, Naidoo, and Griffits (2007), and Scutella, Wilkins, and Kostenko (2009) for Australia; and Jensen et al. (2002) and Perry (2011) for New Zealand. The use of deprivation indicators in a U.S. context has been more limited until recently (though see Mayer and Jencks 1989; Mayer 1993; Baumann 1998, 1999, 2003), leading Blank to conclude: "We should catch up with our European cousins and, like them; work to develop multiple measures of economic deprivation" (2008:252).

A much more limited set of cross-country studies employs nonmonetary indicators to capture and analyze poverty and exclusion in a comparative perspective. Studies covering a few countries using national data sources include Halleröd et al.'s (2006) analysis of Britain, Finland and Sweden; Saunders and Adelman (2006) on Australia and Britain; and Mayer's (1993) comparison of the United States with Canada, Sweden, and Germany. Drawing on a variety of sources and studies with somewhat different definitions and measurement procedures, Boarini and Mira d'Ercole (2006) present a range of comparative data for OECD countries on the percentage of households unable to satisfy "basic needs" and basic leisure activities, lacking various consumer durables, in poor housing conditions, and so forth. There are also now a significant number of comparative studies for the EU, starting with the pre-enlargement countries covered by the European Community Household Panel Survey, and, more recently, studies making use of data emerging from the EU Statistics on Income and Living Conditions (EU-SILC) data-generation process from the mid-2000s.[1] The study by Fusco, Guio, and Marlier (2010) were carried out in association with Eurostat with a particular eye to the use of deprivation indicators in the EU's social inclusion process, with such a material-deprivation indicator being adopted at the EU level in 2010, based on a set of nine deprivation items.

Measuring Deprivation

The material-deprivation indicator adopted by the EU is based on data from the ambitious EU-SILC data-gathering process; these exceptionally rich comparative data on deprivation from this source will be used here to illustrate some core issues and approaches in measuring deprivation, in particular the special module on deprivation included with the 2009 wave of EU-SILC. We focus as far as possible on *enforced deprivation.* Where the question format allows, we count an individual/household only when they indicate they lack an item because they cannot afford it. In other cases, where this information is not available, but where it is implausible that absence occurs on a voluntary basis, absence is taken as sufficient to constitute deprivation. Response rates tend to be extremely high for such items, and the key measurement issues tend to relate to reliability, particularly cross-national reliability.

The recent EU-SILC data allow four distinct dimensions of deprivation to be identified via factor analysis, the most commonly adopted approach, which provides a solid basis (in terms of measured reliability) for comparative European analysis (see Nolan and Whelan 2011; Whelan and Maître 2012a):

- *Basic deprivation* comprises items relating to enforced absence of clothes, a leisure activity, a holiday, a meal with meat or a vegetarian alternative, adequate home heating, or shoes.
- *Consumption deprivation* comprises three items: enforced absence of a personal computer, an Internet connection, or a car. (It is obviously a rather limited measure, and it would be preferable to have a number of additional items.)
- *Health* is captured by three items relating to the health of the Household Reference Person (HRP). These include current self-defined health status, restrictions on current activity, the presence of a chronic illness.
- *Neighborhood environment* is captured by the quality of the neighborhood/area environment with a set of five items that including, for example, litter, damaged public amenities, and pollution.[2]

Table 25.1 shows the levels of deprivation on these dimensions across 20 European countries, together with conventional relative income poverty rates using the 60 percent of the median threshold (termed "at-risk-of-poverty rates" in the EU's social indicators, or ARP for short here). For ease of interpretation, we have ordered countries by gross national disposable income per head (GNDH).[3] The measures were constructed using prevalence weighting across the countries included, weighting each item by the proportion of households as a whole possessing an item or not experiencing the type of deprivation in question. Scores were normalized on each of these dimensions so that they have a potential range running from 0—indicating that the household is deprived of none of the items included in the index—to 1, indicating that they are deprived of all the items.

In Table 25.1, we observe rather modest variation across countries in relative income poverty rates. There is no clear relationship between the ARP measure and GNDH as captured by income per capita. In contrast, the basic deprivation dimension shows much greater variation and also varies systematically by income level. The intraclass correlation coefficient (ICC) captures the proportion of the total variance accounted for by between-country differences and can also be interpreted as the expected correlation between two randomly drawn households within a particular country (Hox 2010:14–15). In the case of basic deprivation, the ICC value of .244 indicates that

Table 25.1 Deprivation Dimensions and Relative Income Poverty
(ARP) by Country, EU–SILC 2009

	Basic	Consumption	Health	Neighborhood	ARP
	Mean	Mean	Mean	Mean	%
Luxembourg	.052	.011	.164	.124	14.9
Norway	.031	.023	.170	.065	11.7
Netherlands	.052	.022	.176	.176	11.1
Austria	.093	.049	.242	.137	12.0
Denmark	.044	.039	.141	.141	13.2
Germany	.128	.054	.195	.105	15.5
Belgium	.098	.058	.184	.147	14.6
Finland	.044	.049	.085	.085	13.8
United Kingdom	.099	.042	.196	.214	17.3
France	.118	.048	.217	.217	12.9
Spain	.111	.075	.213	.135	19.5
Ireland	.095	.077	.152	.144	15.0
Italy	.114	.041	.192	.177	18.4
Iceland	.040	.001	.134	.081	15.0
Cyprus	.129	.040	.192	.153	16.2
Greece	.161	.113	.170	.201	19.7
Slovenia	.132	.042	.203	.154	11.3
Portugal	.249	.114	.278	.164	17.9
Czech Republic	.126	.083	.211	.174	8.6
Malta	.198	.026	.166	.216	15.1
Slovakia	.171	.138	.280	.251	11.0
Estonia	.137	.103	.237	.128	19.7
Hungary	.314	.164	.290	.200	12.4
Poland	.205	.137	.248	.134	17.1
Lithuania	.253	.127	.203	.137	2.6
Latvia	.297	.172	.252	.221	25.7
Romania	.413	.351	.198	.198	22.4
Bulgaria	.465	.256	.153	.229	21.8
Intraclass correlation (ICC)	.244	0.117	.015	.043	

Source: European Union Survey of Income and Living Conditions, 2009.

between-countries variation accounts for 24.4 percent of the variance in economic
stress while within-country variation captures 75.6 percent. The consumption deprivation measure is also associated with income level, but variation across country is
more modest with an ICC value of .112. The remaining dimensions exhibit very weak
correlations with income per capita in the country, with ICC values of .046 and .018
respectively for neighborhood deprivation and health. Correlations between the deprivation dimensions are modest: there are interrelated risks rather than strongly overlapping patterns of deprivation. Not only does the importance of cross-national variation

differ across these dimensions, it is clear that socioeconomic patterning in relation to these relatively distinct outcomes must also differ significantly. The basic deprivation measure is by far the most reliable measure available for comparative European analysis of deprivation and displays the highest average correlation with the other dimensions of deprivation. It comes closest to capturing a form of generalized deprivation in which those deprived on that dimension are also significantly more likely to be deprived on a range of other dimensions. If one's interest is in capturing exclusion from customary patterns of living due to lack of resources, what is required is a measure of deprivation that is significantly related to but by no means identical to income. Further analysis shows that basic deprivation is the dimension most closely correlated with disposable household income and national disposable income per capita. It is also the deprivation outcome most closely associated with subjective economic stress, for which measures are also available in EU-SILC. However, reflecting the mediating role of national reference groups, the impact of an absolute increase in basic deprivation is actually stronger in high-income and low-inequality countries (Delhey and Kohler 2006; Fahey 2007; Whelan and Maître 2009, 2013).

Earlier studies such as Kenworthy, Epstein, and Duerr (2011) have suggested a weak relationship between deprivation and GDP at country level. However, multilevel analysis by Whelan and Maître (2012a) shows basic deprivation to be systematically related to both gross national disposable income per capita and to a lesser degree income inequality (as reflected in the Gini coefficient), as well as a range of socioeconomic factors. Patterns of social stratification by class, education, unemployment, marital disruption, and number of children are significantly sharper in less prosperous countries with lower levels of national disposable income per head. Correspondingly, cross-national differences in basic deprivation are significantly greater among disadvantaged groups than among their more favored counterparts.

POVERTY AND THE MISMATCH
BETWEEN INCOME AND DEPRIVATION

Going back to Ringen (1988), the mismatch between low income and measured deprivation at a point in time has been highlighted as a concern with respect to reliance on income-based poverty measures. The highest correlation with income relates to basic deprivation. In Table 25.2 we breakdown the correlation between equivalent disposable income for individuals and basic deprivation by country. The average population weighted correlation is -.358 while the median correlation is -.307. The range of correlations goes from a low of -.141 in Iceland to a high of -.521 in Bulgaria. There is a clear tendency for correlations to be higher in the less affluent counties. The lowest correlations are observed for the affluent countries normally allocated to the social democratic welfare regime. For Denmark, Finland, Iceland, the Netherlands, and Norway

Table 25.2 Correlation between Equivalent
Disposable Income and Basic Deprivation

Country	Correlation
Luxembourg	-.249
Norway	-.180
Netherlands	-.209
Austria	-.330
Denmark	-.149
Germany	-.149
Belgium	-.274
Finland	-.204
United Kingdom	-.260
France	-.262
Spain	-.345
Ireland	-.309
Italy	-.305
Iceland	-.141
Cyprus	-.287
Greece	-.440
Slovenia	-.349
Portugal	-.374
Czech Republic	-.297
Malta	-.294
Slovakia	-0364
Estonia	-.377
Hungary	-.417
Poland	-.328
Lithuania	-.328
Latvia	-.349
Romania	-.400
Bulgaria	-.521
Population weighted average	-.358
Median correlation	.307

Source: European Union Survey of Income and Living
Conditions, 2009.

the average correlation is -.177. In contrast for the six least affluent counties, the correlation is -.396. The correlation is clearly significant but very far from perfect. The level of the association appears to be influenced by national income levels and, to some extent, to by welfare regime. The findings suggest that the relationship is influenced by the extent to which current disposable income serves as an adequate proxy for longer term command over resources and the extent to which needs are satisfied predominantly through market mechanisms relative to welfare state intervention.

For many, the solution to the income-deprivation mismatch has been seen to lie in using longitudinal measures of income, on the basis that low income at a point in time may not be an accurate reflection of "permanent" income or living standards. On this basis, it may be argued that by paying appropriate attention to the longitudinal aspects of income poverty, or income and wealth, one can avoid the need for nonmonetary indicators and multidimensional approaches. Panel research has shown that movements in and out of poverty are a great deal more frequent than had been supposed, and that a far greater proportion of the population experience poverty at some point than suggested by cross-sectional studies.[4] By extending the measure of income poverty over time, the expectation would be that such a measure would be more strongly related to deprivation, reducing the income poverty–deprivation mismatch.

Implicit in this approach is the assumption that deprivation measures are more stable than income over time, with the consequence that current levels of deprivation is a significantly better indicator of persistent deprivation than current income is of its longitudinal counterpart. Given this, the mismatch problem, evident at the cross-sectional level, would be largely resolved by taking poverty experience over time into account. However, contrary to expectations, the level of mismatch at the longitudinal level is no less than for point-in-time measures (Whelan, Layte, and Maître 2004). Further investigation by Whelan and Maître (2006) estimated models of dynamics incorporating structural and error components, which were found to perform equally well in accounting for poverty and deprivation dynamics. Short-term changes over time in deprivation (at the individual/household level) are very weakly related to corresponding variations in income, with measurement error in each contributing, while, in contrast, mean deprivation over a period is highly correlated with income averaged over a period (Berthoud et al. 2004; Berthoud and Bryan 2011). However, there is no evidence that differences in the determinants of poverty and deprivation persistence found in cross-sectional analysis are a consequence of there being more error in the measurement of income than deprivation. Although income poverty and deprivation are substantially correlated, even when measured over reasonable periods of time and allowing for measurement error, they continue to tap relatively distinct phenomenon (Breen and Mosio 2004, Whelan and Maître 2006.

We should stress that we are not proposing a sole reliance on deprivation measures. Income continues to be a crucial indicator, and deprivation measures are of limited value unless we can develop an understanding of the manner in which they are related to longer term accumulation and erosion of resources over time. It is perhaps worth keeping in mind that, viewed from a broader sociological perspective on social stratification, the fact that the complexities of such processes are far from being adequately captured by a single indicator relating to current disposable income is unsurprising. Nolan and Whelan (2011:108–19) review a range of evidence demonstrating that social class differentiation is significantly sharper where we focus on joint exposure to income poverty and deprivation and where we employ longitudinal rather than cross-sectional measures.[5] Ultimately, as Goldthorpe (2010) argues, issues such as this must be addressed within a broader framework relating to the socially structured nature of disadvantage and social inequality.

While continuing efforts to develop a more adequate understanding of the dynamics relating income and deprivation are a priority—if poverty continues to be defined in terms of "exclusion from a minimally acceptable standard of living through a lack of resources"—the longitudinal measures of income poverty currently available cannot be taken on their own as providing valid measures of the underlying construct: direct measures of material deprivation continue to be a valuable complement. If one wants to use both indicators of deprivation or consumption and low income to capture levels of and trends in poverty and identify those most at risk, what is the best way of doing so? More broadly, if one wants to incorporate various dimensions of poverty or exclusion rather than be confined to one (notably income), how is this best approached?

MULTIDIMENSIONAL POVERTY

A particularly ambitious statement of what a multidimensional approach to poverty measurement should encapsulate is provided by Tomlinson and Walker:

> Poverty is not just the absence of income or even the material deprivation that accompanies it. It is both of these and everything that follows from them: the hassle; the hard work; the stress; the budgeting; the conflict; the shame; the degraded environment; the isolation; the helplessness; the ill-health; the misfortune—and much else that, taken together, is both a reasoned and involuntary responses to hardship and which may, quite often, serve to exacerbate it. (2009:20)

By these standards pretty well all measures of poverty constructed at the national level will fail the "multidimensionality" test. Providing such a multidimensional account of poverty could be realistically achieved only by a mixed approach combining both quantitative and qualitative techniques. A particularly good example of the value of such a multipronged approach is provided by childhood poverty and deprivation. A recent strand of research explores the impact of poverty from the perspective of children. In an in-depth study of 40 children (aged 10 to 17) from low-income families, Ridge (2002) found that effects of poverty and disadvantage can permeate every aspect of a child's life—material, social, and emotional. Impacts that were specific to children included limited access to their own economic resources, access to transportation, and the importance of friendship. However, a clear distinction needs to be maintained between *understanding* the multifaceted nature of poverty, which clearly requires a mixed-method approach, and *identifying* those exposed to multidimensional deprivation (Nolan and Whelan 2007). It is clear that national quantitative-based measures cannot deliver on the former objective. However, it does not follow that adult indicators cannot be successful in identifying children exposed to multidimensional deprivation. For example, Whelan and Maître (2012b) employing both adult and childhood national deprivation measures have shown that the former are largely successful in capturing those exposed to childhood deprivation.

A variety of analytic strategies have been employed in efforts to develop quantitative, multidimensional approaches. These include latent class analysis (De Wilde 2004; Moisio 2004; Grusky and Weeden 2007; Whelan and Maître 2005); structural equation modeling (Carle, Bauman, and Short 2009; Tomlinson, Walker, and Williams 2008); item response theory (Capellari and Jenkins 2007); and self-organizing maps (Pisati et al. 2010). In practical application, one rather straightforward approach has been to focus attention on those who are measured both on low income and experiencing high levels of deprivation—what has been termed the "consistently poor" (see Nolan and Whelan 1996). By contrast, the poverty target adopted in 2010 by the European Union includes in the target population those who meet any one of three criteria—being below an income threshold, above a deprivation threshold, or in a "workless" household. (For an in-depth examination of this target see Nolan and Whelan 2011).

This illustrates the contrast between what Atkinson (2003) terms the *union* approach, which includes all those deprived in relation to any of a set of dimensions, and the *intersection* approach, which requires that an individual is deprived on each of the dimensions under consideration. While the former typically produces very high estimates of multidimensional poverty, the latter generally results in extremely low estimates. This distinction has received little explicit discussion in the social policy literature on poverty and social exclusion. However, the dilemma it presents is captured in Room's (1999:171) discussion of notions of *continuity* and *catastrophe* in the social exclusion literature, and it is also recognized in Levitas et al.'s (2007) distinction between "social exclusion" and "deep exclusion." The former refers to restriction of access to any of a wide range of commodities and services necessary for full participation in the society. "Deep exclusion," on the other hand, focuses on deprivation across more than one dimension of disadvantage, resulting in severe negative consequences for quality of life, well-being, and future life chances.

Recently, Alkire and Foster (2007, 2010, 2011a, 2011b) have sought to develop alternatives to the union, intersection, and unidimensional approaches, extending the Foster, Greer, and Thorbecke (1984) class of indices widely employed with income poverty measures. Their approach has mostly been applied in the context of less developed counties (Alkire and Santos 2010; Alkie and Seth 2011), but Whelan, Nolan, and Maître (2014) have applied it to the EU, once again employing the data on deprivation from the 2009 special module in EU-SILC. The focus is on five dimensions comprising ARP, basic deprivation, consumption deprivation, health, and neighborhood environment. Thresholds have been chosen for the remaining dimensions to produce numbers "poor" on each dimension as close as possible to the number below the national ARP threshold. The Alkire and Foster approach involves a dual cutoff approach. This involves choices by analysts employing the approach in relation to the appropriate threshold for each deprivation dimension included in the analysis and a decision on the number of dimensions on which an individual must be deprived to be classified as "poor."

Once an individual is identified as poor, the aggregation step builds upon the standard Foster, Greer and Thorbecke methodology. Nonpoor individuals are excluded from further analysis so information on the nonpoor does not affect the measure. Our focus here is on the *adjusted head count ratio* that is defined as $M_o = \mu(g^O(k))$, or the mean of the censored deprivation matrix. M_o has a potential range of values from 0 to 1. Where no one in the population experiences any of the deprivations the value is 0, and where all individuals experience deprivation on all items the value is 1. In column (i) of Table 25.3, we can see that the observed range of values goes from .019 in Iceland to .291 in Romania. The ICC is .129, indicating the proportion of variance accounted for by between-country differences. Values generally increase as country income levels decline. For the three-lowest income countries, the adjusted head count

Table 25.3 Multidimensional Poverty by Country, EU–SILC 2009

	(i) MD Adjusted Head Count Ratio	(ii) Union	(iii) Intersection
Luxembourg	.054	.381	.001
Norway	.060	.434	.001
Netherlands	.060	.434	.001
Austria	.083	.465	.004
Denmark	.054	.387	.002
Germany	.107	.489	.006
Belgium	.091	.423	.007
Finland	.066	.409	.002
United Kingdom	.105	.544	.002
France	.081	.438	.001
Spain	.102	.531	.002
Ireland	.096	.455	.002
Italy	.092	.512	.002
Iceland	.030	.310	.000
Cyprus	.078	.438	.001
Greece	.136	.606	.004
Slovenia	.082	.446	.004
Portugal	.171	.617	.005
Czech Republic	.102	.569	.003
Malta	.088	.522	.001
Slovakia	.158	.668	.005
Estonia	.123	.551	.002
Hungary	.240	.770	.006
Poland	.157	.637	.005
Lithuania	.170	.611	.008
Latvia	.253	.731	.016
Romania	.313	.821	.006
Bulgaria	.289	.808	.012

Source: European Union Survey of Income and Living Conditions, 2009.

ratio (AHR) ranges between .25 and .31. In other words, the multidimensionally poor experience an aggregate level of deprivation that reaches over 25 to 31 percent of that which would be observed if multidimensional poverty was universal and all poor individuals were deprived on all items. Clearly the M_0 is a great deal more successful in capturing cross-country variation than the ARP indicator.

The figures for M_0 can be contrasted with those for those for the union and intersection counts for the five dimensions involved in our analysis as set out in columns (ii) and (iii). For the former, where all individuals experiencing deprivation on any of the dimensions is counted, the levels range from a lows of .381 in Luxembourg and .387 in Denmark to highs of .808 and .821 in Bulgaria and Romania respectively. The figures in relation to the intersection of the dimensions, involving deprivation on all five dimensions, provide a sharp contrast. Here the counts range from scores of effectively zero in most affluent countries to .012 in Bulgaria and .016 in Latvia. The fact that the income variable is defined in relative terms contributes to the extreme nature of our results. However, they are generally consistent with earlier research focusing on multiple deprivation in the European Union (Tsakloglou and Papadopouous 2002; Whelan, Layte, and Maître 2002; Whelan and Maître 2005). The Adjusted Head Count Ratio (AHCR) clearly provides a middle ground between the union approach, where in excess of 40 percent of individuals in most EU countries are counted as deprived, and the intersection approach, where hardly any one is counted as multiply deprived even in the least affluent countries.

DECOMPOSITION OF MULTIDIMENSIONAL POVERTY BY DIMENSION

One of the advantages of the M_0 measures is that it is decomposable in terms of deprivation dimensions. In Table 25.4 we show this decomposition broken down by country. It is clear that there is substantial variation across countries in the relative importance of dimensions. In the more affluent countries, basic and consumption deprivation play a modest role; the dimensions making the greatest contribution are the ARP indicator and health deprivation. The neighborhood dimension has its highest values in relatively affluent countries, such as the Netherlands and the United Kingdom. Multidimensional poverty is influenced by both deprivation levels and the association between dimensions. Individuals are counted as poor only where they are deprived on two or more dimensions. High levels of deprivation on individual dimensions together with low levels of association produce low levels of poverty. For the more affluent countries, the distribution of levels of deprivation and the degree of association between income poverty and health are sufficient to lead to these factors dominating while others play a much less significant role.

Table 25.4 Decomposition of the Adjusted Head Count Social Exclusion Ratio by Dimension by Country EU–SILC 2009

	ARP	Basic	Consumption	Health	Neighborhood	Total
	%	%	%	%	%	%
Luxembourg	.276	.173	.146	.227	.178	1.0
Norway	.281	.128	.220	.258	.112	1.0
Netherlands	.199	.107	.133	.242	.246	1.0
Austria	.190	.205	.180	.265	.160	1.0
Denmark	.236	.111	.226	.254	.172	1.0
Germany	.215	.228	.193	.228	.136	1.0
Belgium	.224	.186	.181	.228	.177	1,0
Finland	.265	.092	.243	.269	.132	1.0
United Kingdom	.212	.174	.136	.234	.240	1.0
France	.206	.233	.179	.228	.154	1.0
Spain	.238	.154	.216	.237	.156	1.0
Ireland	.203	.154	.243	.217	.182	1.0
Italy	.238	.208	.116	.230	.208	1.0
Iceland	.243	.143	.125	.325	.166	1.0
Cyprus	.257	.197	.153	.278	.116	1.0
Greece	.223	.208	.214	.176	.179	1.0
Slovenia	.173	.247	.156	.262	.162	1.0
Portugal	.161	.286	.211	.226	.116	1.0
Czech Republic	.130	.164	.201	.282	.215	1.0
Malta	.210	.286	.119	.183	.202	1.0
Slovakia	.108	.184	.238	.243	.226	1.0
Estonia	.230	.153	.250	.246	.126	1.0
Hungary	.094	.289	.220	.205	.192	1.0
Poland	.170	.242	.241	.226	.120	1.0
Lithuania	.201	.321	.234	.220	.119	1.0
Latvia	.179	.256	.225	.187	.154	1.0
Romania	.134	.329	.309	.123	.106	1.0
Bulgaria	.144	.347	.240	.120	.150	1.0

Source: European Union Survey of Income and Living Conditions, 2009.

For countries in the middle range of affluence, individual dimensions contribute more evenly. However, the role of the consumption dimension remains modest in a number of cases, and the role of neighborhood environment remains variable. In France and Spain the ARP measure, basic deprivation, and health contribute relatively evenly, while the impact of consumption and neighborhood environment are weaker. In Italy all dimensions, other than consumption, make a proportionate contribution. For Greece and Ireland we observe a relatively uniform distribution across dimensions. For the Czech Republic and Slovakia the contribution of ARP is weaker than in most counties, while the impact of health is stronger than the other dimensions. For most of the remaining less affluent counties, basic deprivation in particular, but also consumption deprivation, come to play an important role. For Romania and Bulgaria the basic deprivation rates are .329 and .347, and the combined basic and consumption deprivation rates are .638 and .587. In the latter case, the comparable figures for the Netherlands and Denmark are .240 and .337.

Multidimensional poverty, defined in the foregoing manner, varies systematically across sociodemographic groups. The impact of key factors such as social class and age group varies significantly across counties; the former plays a more significant role in less affluent countries, and the latter has its most substantial influence in their more affluent counterparts. National income levels are important in accounting for cross-national variation both in themselves and in the manner in which they interact with key socioeconomic variables. In contrast, income inequality and welfare-regime effects have no additional impact once we control for the foregoing factors (Whelan et al. 2014).

In relation to outcomes such as subjective economic stress, there is a significant loss of explanatory power in subsuming different deprivation profiles under the multidimensional poverty label rather than focusing on a variable such as basic deprivation chosen on the grounds of particular theoretical considerations (Whelan and Maître 2012b). Similarly, the variable impact of socioeconomic factors across countries with different aggregate income levels derives, in part, from corresponding differences in the dominant multidimensional profiles. One is not exactly comparing like with like. However, focusing on current outcomes rather than also including drivers to some extent to guard against the dangers to which Ravallion (2011) directs attention, that is, recognizing that poverty is multidimensional does not necessarily imply the use of a multidimensional poverty index rather than a focus on a range of multiple indicators, as in the case of the Millennium Development Goals. The possibility exists that the former approach may lead to confusion rather than clarity.

Obviously, the extent to which aggregation may create difficulties is related to the choice of dimensions included in the analysis and the extent to which it is reasonable to assign weights, whether equal or unequal. This is something that must be determined on the basis of substantive rather than technical considerations. The breadth of the dimensions employed in applying this method to developing countries (Alkire and Santos 2010; Alkire and Seth 2011) present substantially greater difficulties in this respect than the deprivation analysis relating to European countries that we have discussed in this chapter. We have also made clear that the choice of dimensions to include in the analysis and the thresholds for the dimensions included and the weights to apply lie with the analyst rather than deriving from the method. Any such findings can be subjected to sensitivity analysis in order to assess the robustness of the findings. If a multidimensional index of this kind is utilized, it is clearly preferable that it is constructed so that it characterized by a range of desirable axiomatic properties rather than on an ad hoc basis. However, the construction of such an index is not an alternative to the development of improved indices for individual dimensions. Nor is this the only approach to tapping such dimensionality: for example, latent class approaches focusing on distinctive risk profiles rather than patterning of current outcomes offer a different but complementary perspective (Grusky and Weeden 2007; Whelan and Maître 2010b).

CONSUMPTION AND POVERTY

Consumption has become a subject of heightened interest recently in the literatures on poverty and inequality (Ringen 1988; Cutler and Katz 1991; Slesnick 1991, 1994, 2001; Mayer and Jencks 1993; Johnson 2004; Johnson, Smeeding, and Torrey 2005; Krueger and Perri 2006; Brewer, Goodman, and Leicester 2006; Meyer and Sullivan 2003, 2004, 2007, 2010, 2011, 2012). Building on the existing criticism of the accuracy of income as an indicator of people's real conditions and material well-being, various scholars have argued that consumption must be taken into consideration when determining the poverty status.

The focus on consumption as a measure of well-being has been particularly prominent in economics, in part due to several influential analyses by Nobel laureate economists Milton Friedman and Franco Modigliani, in the 1950s and 1960s, which argued that consumption expenditures constitute a more accurate indicator of economic well-being since they are more stable than current incomes across time. According to Friedman's (1957) "permanent income hypothesis," temporary changes in income do not really affect consumption decisions since individuals base their consumption choices on a long-term view of their income. Similarly, Modigliani's "life-cycle thesis" argues that "consumption and saving decisions of households at each point of time reflect a more or less conscious attempt at achieving the preferred distribution of consumption over the life cycle, subject to the constraint imposed by the resources accruing to the household over its lifetime" (1966:162). In other words, both theories hold that individuals and households tailor their consumption patterns to their needs independently of their incomes.[6]

More recently, American economist Slesnick (1991, 1994, 2001) argued quite forcefully in favor of shifting the focus of poverty and inequality studies to consumption. Meyer and Sullivan (2003, 2007) argued, likewise, that consumption provides a more appropriate measure of well-being than income for those with few resources.

In sociology, on the other hand, a consumption-based view of poverty and well-being has never really taken hold. Sociological interest in consumption has largely remained limited to qualitative studies examining its relationship to status (e.g., Veblen 1899; Bourdieu 1984). Although Ringen (1988:263) argued that income provides an "indirect" measure of poverty and consumption a "direct" one, and that "one only needs to introduce some very simple and tentative information in the standard of consumption to demonstrate the inadequacy of relying on income information alone in the measurement of poverty," the poverty and consumption link has remained rather neglected, and there have been very few quantitative and comparative studies on the subject to

Table 25.5 Consumption Expenditure Per Household in the First Income Quintile (mean value in PPS) versus Top Cutoff Income Level, First Quintile (in PPS)

	Income			Consumption		
	1995	1999	2005	1994	1999	2005
Belgium	8,211	9,842	10,164	18,933	18,699	18,929
Germany	8,169	10,141	11,039	11,132	12,490	14,388
Ireland	5,452	6,964	9,102	13,083	27,102	18,272
Greece	3,843	4,677	6,515	10,285	12,570	18,617
Spain	4,522	5,478	7,037	12,690	13,955	16,874
France	7,537	8,685	9,852	13,843	15,457	18,069
Italy	5,335	6,655	8,394	11,321	19,290	N/A
Luxembourg	12,943	14,319	19,103	26,190	26,921	21,139
Netherlands	7,527	9,740	11,368	12,449	17,522	22,694
Austria	8,766	9,506	12,210	21,697	17,124	24,766
Portugal	3,411	4,335	5,001	6,049	8,195	8,375
Finland	:	8,166	9,794	9,247	10,021	13,085
United Kingdom	6,885	7,793	10,338	11,906	14,347	18,941

Source: European Union Survey of Income and Living Conditions, 2009.

date. This is rather surprising for even a cursory look at income and consumption statistics in selected European nations shows quite clearly that our poverty estimates are likely to change significantly when consumption is brought into the picture. Data from Eurostat on income and consumption included in Table 25.5 gives a good preliminary sense about the discrepancy between income and consumption measures in selected European nations. The mean consumption expenditure of households in the first income quintile (in purchasing power standard) seems to be significantly lower than the top cutoff income level (in PPS) for households in the first quintile.

THE PROS AND CONS
OF CONSUMPTION-BASED MEASURES

Several theoretical and empirical reasons have been advanced for taking into account what families actually consume when determining their poverty status. First, at a broad theoretical level, it is argued that families and individuals "derive material well-being from the actual consumption of goods and services rather than from the receipt of income *per se*" (Johnson 2004:2). As noted, even when their income drops, families and individuals may still be able to sustain their levels of consumption by relying on their savings or by taking advantage of various public and private mechanisms. Official poverty measures relying on income statistics, however, ignore various public and private mechanisms such as access to credit, increasing availability of affordable consumption products, or social transfers that affect what people are able to consume. Second, consumption can be divided into meaningful categories, such as food and housing, which makes it easier to get a sense of the actual nature of deprivation (Meyer and Sullivan 2010). And third, research has shown that consumption-based measures of well-being differ substantially from those based on income.

At the same time, using consumption as an indicator of poverty and other aspects of well-being raises a set of challenges and problems. Conceptually, consumption may not fully reflect a family's true well-being but simply mask the long-term challenges of increasing indebtedness given that it has remained largely credit-reliant over the past few decades in both advanced and developing nations. There are also major difficulties concerned with defining "consumption" in operational terms, collecting the data necessary to construct an appropriate measure, and setting appropriate parameters for measurement (equivalence scale, measurement unit, and cost-of-living adjustments).

First, consumption measures are often based on family-expenditure data. The difficulty of obtaining complete, accurate, and comparable data on family expenditures renders adoption of a consumption-based index problematic (Smeeding 2009). Expenditure surveys are seen as among the most "difficult and expensive surveys" (Deaton and Grosh 2000).[7] Moreover, as Smeeding (2009) notes, many countries collect consumption data solely for the purpose of providing weights for measuring the consumer price index, rather than capturing an accurate picture of consumption trends and habits. Largely due to these reasons, consumer expenditure surveys often rely on small sample sizes. Various sampling and nonsampling errors (e.g., differences in respondents' interpretation of questions, inability or unwillingness of the respondents to provide the required information, handling of missing data, etc.) may occur. As a result of these combined factors, the collected data might not provide an accurate representation of the consumption levels and habits of the population.

Second, consumption measures always involve some degree of imputation (Cutler and Katz 1991; Deaton and Grosh 2000; Slesnick 2001). Deaton and Grosh (2000) warn that such imputations need to be done with great care to avoid erroneous interpretations of the results in cases where such imputations have an important effect on the total consumption measure. The question of choice versus need remains unresolved in consumption-based measures of poverty (Smeeding 2009). The treatment of medical expenses deserves careful attention, for instance. As pointed out by Meyer (2007) and Meyer and Sullivan (2011), high medical expenses may be taken to reflect a higher standard of living, which would be erroneous. Similarly, how to reflect the consumption flow derived from home ownership is also debated among researchers.

Third, choice of the equivalence scale might also affect the results on the relative standard of living of different families. A lower equivalence scale implies that the family's resources will be adjusted upward, and vice-versa. Similarly, the choice of the unit of measurement affects the poverty rate and its composition (see Jencks, Mayer, and

Swingle 2004). Finally, as Jencks et al. (2004) demonstrated, different price indexes (or cost-of-living adjustments) lead to a variety of changes in well-being and poverty.

All the choices researchers have to make in addressing these various challenges concerned with collecting and constructing a consumption measure will inevitably affect poverty measures, and there is no consensus on how to resolve these issues (see Cutler and Katz 1992; Deaton and Grosh 2000; Jonhson 2012; Slesnick 1991, 1994, 2001). Differences in specific measures and parameters used lead researchers to different conclusions regarding poverty trends. For instance, speaking about poverty trends in the United States, Slesnick (1991, 1994, 2001) argues that consumption data show that from 1980 through 1995 poverty fell considerably more than the corresponding income poverty rates. Similarly, examining shifts in the rate of poverty for those 65 and over between 1972 and 2004 while employing varying measures based on income and consumption, Meyer and Sullivan (2007) argue that consumption-based measures of poverty suggested greater improvements in well-being than are evident in alternative income-based measures. Other scholars dispute these findings. Similarly, focusing on inequality trends in the United States, Krueger and Perri (2005) note that while both measures of inequality indicate an increase in inequality over the 1980s, consumption inequality increased at a slower rate and remained flat, while income inequality continued to rise throughout the 1990s. Cutler and Katz (1992), on the other hand, argue that consumption poverty in the United States rose more than income poverty during the 1970s, while the distributions of income and consumption have remained relatively flat since the early 1980s.

As noted, neither the methodological challenges that concern the use of consumption-based measures nor the conflicting findings that result from them undermine the usefulness of consumption measures for the measurement of poverty. However, given that these findings might have substantial implications for social policies designed to deal with poverty and related issues, it is important to proceed with caution when interpreting data. The use of both consumption and income measures together may be the best course of action in order to fully examine the levels of and trends in poverty (Johnson 2004).

Conclusions

The central message of this chapter is that research on poverty in rich counties is undergoing a fundamental shift away from reliance on household income to capture living standards and distinguish those in poverty toward incorporation of a variety of nonmonetary indicators within a multidimensional framework, feeding through to practice in official poverty measurement and monitoring for policy purposes. This reflects increasing recognition of the limitations of relying solely on income in capturing poverty and studying the underlying processes that create it, and of the potential richness of multidimensional perspectives and approaches incorporating nonmonetary indicators.

This shift, though under way for quite some time, has been gathering momentum and is perhaps best exemplified by the fact that the European Union has chosen to frame its 2020 poverty-reduction target in terms of what is in effect a (rather crude) multi-dimensional measure of which low income is only one of three constituent elements.

Material deprivation as measured by a set of nonmonetary deprivation indicators provides one of the additional elements in this measure, illustrating the new promi-nence which such deprivation measures have attained in poverty research and practice in OECD countries. This chapter has shown, using comparative data for the countries of the EU for illustration, how material deprivation indicators can be used to capture specific dimensions or aspects of deprivation, such as in basic everyday necessities, durables, housing, and the local neighborhood. Those affected by these particular forms of deprivation can then to be identified, opening new possibilities for teasing out the potentially distinctive causal processes at work. It also provides a basis for capturing the extent of multiple deprivations across these dimensions—how often these different forms or aspects of deprivation go together—which may be less than is often assumed. This type of analysis of specific aspects of deprivation and of multiple deprivation pro-vides the base for new insights in making comparisons across countries, in tracking changes over time, and in framing policies to respond to the situation and needs of different groups.

We have indicated our agreement with the view that accepting that poverty is mul-tidimensional does not automatically imply that one must opt for a multidimensional poverty index rather than focusing on multiple indicators. Combining indicators across a variety of dimensions into a "headline" summary index then provides a basis for highlighting overall trends and differences across countries, though there is inevi-tably a loss of information in doing so. Aggregation choices, whether in relation to such indices or the utilization of information relating to both income and deprivation by the analyst in relation to substantive as well as technical choices. Ultimately such decisions must be justified on the basis of the extent to which they increase our understanding of the underlying processes generating poverty and inform policy choices. Both the dimensions under consideration and the context in which they are employed, in terms of the level of development of the counties in which they are applied, are likely to have a crucial bearing on what can be considered appropriate. However, as we have argued, where it is deemed appropriate to construct a multidimensional index, it is clearly desirable that it should be done on a transparent basis with clearly identified properties.

While it has been highly productive to date and is moving forward rapidly, this developing field faces a variety of obstacles. Both its conceptual and empirical under-pinnings urgently require further development. Conceptually, there needs to be much greater clarity in precisely why a multidimensional approach is appropriate or help-ful in answering the particular question or questions being posed. Empirically, vari-ous sophisticated methodological approaches are being developed and applied, but there is as yet little clear understanding or consensus about their advantages and disadvantages, and the settings in which one versus another would be more satisfac-tory or appropriate. The use of nonmonetary deprivation indicators and application of multidimensional-measurement approaches to poverty measurement will not converge on a single "best" approach, but a greater degree of methodological consensus is attainable and desirable. Similarly, at this point in time, the use of both consumption and income measures together may be the best course of action in order to fully examine the levels of and trends in poverty (Johnson 2004). Much has been learned to date from these approaches to improve the study of poverty and exclusion, and their use is set to increase in the future. Here we have argued that exploiting the full potential of such approaches will depend not only on technical progress but also on successfully locating their use within broader theoretical perspectives relating to the structured nature of disadvantage and inequality.

NOTES

1. See Nolan and Whelan (2011) for a detailed set of references.
2. For an alternative analysis of the dimensionality of deprivation employing the EU-SILC 2009 special deprivation module and a comprehensive discussion of the data base see Guio, Gordon, and Marlier (2012).
3. Sweden has been excluded from the analysis due to serious missing data problems in relation to the deprivation items.
4. See Breen and Moisio (2004) and Jarvis and Jenkins (1999).
5. For empirical support for these claims see Whelan, Watson, and Maître (2010).
6. See Deaton (2005) for an extensive discussion on Modigliani's "life-cycle thesis."
7. Deaton and Grosh (2000) note that in the United States, the Consumer Expenditure Survey (CEX) costs about five times as much per household as the current population survey (CPS), which is the main source for data on income, earnings, and employment.

REFERENCES

Alkire, Sabina and James Foster. 2007. *Counting and Multidimensional Poverty Measurement.* Working Paper No. 7. Oxford: Oxford Poverty and Human Development Initiative, University of Oxford.

Alkire, Sabina and James Foster. 2011a. "Understandings and Misunderstandings of Multidimensional Poverty Measurement." *Journal of Economic Inequality* 9:289–314.

Alkire, Sabina and James Foster. 2011b, "Counting and Multidimensional Poverty." *Journal of Public Economics* 95:476–87.

Alkire, Sabina and Maria Emma Santos. 2010. "Acute Multidimensional Poverty: A New Index for Developing Countries." Oxford Poverty and Human Development Initiative Working Paper 38. Oxford: University of Oxford.

Alkire, Sabina and S. Seth Suman. 2011. "Decomposing India's MPI by State and Caste: Examples and Comparisons." Oxford Poverty and Human Development Initiative. Oxford: University of Oxford.

Atkinson, Anthony. 2003. "Multidimensional Deprivation: Contrasting Social Welfare and Counting Approaches." *Journal of Economic Inequality* 1:51–65.

Atkinson, Anthony, B. B. Cantillon, Eric Marlier, and, Brian Nolan. 2002. *Social Indicators: The EU and Social Inclusion.* Oxford: Oxford University Press.

Bauman, Kurt. 1998. "Direct Measures of Poverty as Indicators of Economic Need: Evidence from the Survey of Income and Program Participation." Population Division Technical Working Paper No. 30. Washington, DC: U.S. Census Bureau.

Bauman, Kurt. 1999. "Extended Measures of Well-being: Meeting Basic Needs." Current Population Reports P70–67. Washington, DC: U.S. Census Bureau.

Bauman, Kurt. 2003. "Extended Measures of Well-being: Living Conditions in the United States." Current Population Reports P70–87. Washington, DC: U.S. Census Bureau.

Berthoud, Richard, Bryan, Mark, and Elena Bardasi. 2004. "The Dynamics of Deprivation: The Relationship between Income and Material Deprivation over Time." Research Report No. 219. London: Department for Work and Pensions.

Berthoud, Richard and Mark Bryan. 2011. "Income. Deprivation and Poverty: A Longitudinal Analysis." *Journal of Social Policy* 40(11):135–56.

Blank, Rebecca. 2008. "How to Improve Poverty Measurement in the United States." *Journal of Policy Analysis and Management* 27:233–54.

Bradshaw, Jonathan and Naomi Finch. 2003. "Overlaps in Dimensions of Poverty." *Journal of Social Policy* 32:513–25.

Boarini, Romina and Marco Mira d'Ercole. 2006. "Measures of Material Deprivation in OECD Countries." OECD Social Employment and Migration Working Papers No. 37. Paris: OECD.

Brewer, Mike, Alissa Goodman, and Andrew Leicester. 2006. *Household Spending in Britain: What Can It Teach Us about Poverty?* London: Institute for Fiscal Studies.

Breen, Richard and Pasi Moiso. 2004. "Overestimated Poverty Mobility: Poverty Dynamics Corrected for Measurement Error." *Journal of Economic Inequality* 2:171–91.

Burchardt, Tania, Julian Le Grand, and David Piachaud. 2002. "Degrees of Exclusion: Developing a Dynamic, Multidimensional Measure." Pp. 30–43 in *Understanding Social Exclusion*, edited by J. Hills, J. Le Grand, and D. Piachaud. Oxford: Oxford University Press.

Cappellari, Lorenzo and Stephen P. Jenkins. 2007. "Summarising Multiple Deprivation Indicators," in *Poverty and Inequality: New Directions*, edited by J. Micklewright and S. P. Jenkins. Oxford: Oxford University Press.

Carle, Adam C., Kurt J. Bauman, and Kathleen S. Short. 2009. "Assessing the Measurement and Structure of Material Hardship in the United States." *Social Indicators Research* 92:35–35.

Cutler, David M. and Lawrence F. Katz. 1991. "Macroeconomic Performance and the Disadvantaged." *Brooklyn Papers on Economic Activity* 2:1–14.

Deaton, Angus. 2005. "Franco Modigliani and the Life Cycle Theory of Consumption." *Banca Nazionale del Lavoro Quarterly Review* 58(233–34):91–107.

Deaton, Angus and Margaret M. Grosh. 2000. "Consumption." In *Designing Household Survey Questionnaires for Developing Countries: Lessons from 15 Years of the Living Standards Measurement Study*, edited by Margaret Grosh, and Paul Glewwe. New York: Oxford University Press.

Delhey, Jan and Ulrich Kohler. 2006. "From Nationally Bounded to Pan-European Inequalities? On the Importance of Foreign Countries as Reference Groups." *European Sociological Review* 22:125–4.

Dewilde, Caroline. 2004. "The Multidimensional Measurement of Poverty in Belgium and Britain: A Categorical Approach." *Social Indicators Research* 68:331–69.

European Commission. 2011. *Employment and Social Developments in Europe 2001.* Brussels: DG Employment, Social Affairs and Equal Opportunities.

Fahey, Tony. 2007. "The Case for an EU-wide Measure of Poverty." *European Sociological Review* 23:35–47.

Foster, James, Joel Greer, and Erik Thorbeck. 1984. "A Class of Decomposable Poverty Measures." *Econometrica* 52:761–66.

Friedman, Milton. 1957. *A Theory of the Consumption Function.* Princeton, NJ: Princeton University Press.

Fusco, Alfredo, Anne-Catherine Guio, and Eric Marlier. 2010. *Characterising the Income Poor and the Materially Deprived in European Countries.* In *Income and Living Conditions in Europe,* edited by A. B. Atkinson and E. Marlier. Luxembourg: Publications Office of the European Union.

Goldthorpe, John H. 2010. "Analysing Inequality: A Critique of Two Recent Contributions from Economics & Epidemiology." *European Sociological Review* 26(6):731–44.

Grusky, David B. and Kim A. Weeden. 2007. "Measuring Poverty: The Case for a Sociological Approach." In *The Many Dimensions of Poverty,* edited by N. Kakawani and J. Silber. Basingstoke, UK: Palgrave Macmillan.

Guio, Anne-Catherine, David Gordon, and Eric Marlier. 2012. "Measuring Material Deprivation in the EU: Indicators for the Whole Population and Child Specific Indicators." Eurostat Methodological and Working Papers. Luxembourg: Publications Office of the European Union.

Halleröd, Björn, Daniel Larsson, David Gordon, and Veli Matti Ritakallio. 2006. "Relative Deprivation: A Comparative Analysis of Britain, Finland and Sweden." *Journal of European Social Policy* 16:328–45.

Headey, Bruce. 2008. "Poverty is Low Consumption and Low Wealth Not Just Income." *Social Indicators Research* 89:23–29.

Hox, Joop. 2010. *Multilevel Analysis: Techniques and Applications.* 2nd ed. New York: Routledge.

Jarvis, Sarah and Stephen P. Jenkins. 1999. "Low Income Dynamics in the 1990s in Britain." *Fiscal Studies* 18:123–42.

Jencks, Cristopher, Susan E. Mayer, and Joseph Swingle. 2004. "Can We Fix the Federal Poverty Measure So It Provides Reliable Information about Changes in Children's Living Conditions?" Harvard University Faculty Research Working Paper Series, September 2004.

Jensen, John, Matt Spittal, S. Crichton, Sathi G. Sathiyandra, and Vasantha Krishnan. 2002. "Direct Measures of Living Standards: the New Zealand ELSI Scale." Wellington, Ministry of Social Development.

Johnson, David S. 2004. "Measuring Consumption and Consumption Poverty: Possibilities and Issues." Prepared for Reconsidering the Federal Poverty Measure, American Enterprise Institute.

Johnson, David S., Timothy M. Smeeding, and Barabara Boyle Torrey. 2005. "Economic Inequality through the Prisms of Income and Consumption." *Monthly Labor Review.* April. Washington, DC: U.S. Bureau of Labor Statistics.

Kakwani, Nanak C. and Jacques Silber, eds. 2007. *The Many Dimensions of Poverty* Basingstoke, UK: Palgrave Macmillan.

Kenworthy, Lane, Jessica Epstein, and Daniel Duerr. 2011. "Generous Social Policy Reduces Material Deprivation." In *Progress for the Poor,* edited by L. Kenworthy. Oxford: Oxford University Press.

Krueger, Dirk and Fabrizio Perri. 2006. "Does Income Inequality Lead to Consumption Inequality? Evidence and Theory." *Review of Economic Studies* 73:163–93.

Levitas, Ruth, Christina Panatzis, Eldin Fahmy, David Gordon, Eva Lyod, and Demy Patsios. 2007. *The Multidimensional Analysis of Social Exclusion.* London: Social Exclusion Unit.

Mayer, Susan E. 1993. "Living Conditions among the Poor in Four Rich Countries." *Journal of Population Economics* 6:261–86.

Mayer, Susan E. and Christopher Jencks. 1989. "Poverty and the Distribution of Material Hardship." *Journal of Human Resources* 24:88–114.

Mayer, Susan E. and Christopher Jencks. 1993. "Recent Trends in Economic Inequality in the United States: Income vs. Expenditures vs. Material Well-Being." In *Poverty and Prosperity in America at the Close of the Twentieth Century*, edited by D. Papadimitriou and E. Wolfe. London: Macmillan.

Meyer, Bruce D. and James X. Sullivan. 2003. "Measuring the Well-being of the Poor Using Income and Consumption." Working Paper No. 976. Cambridge, MA: National Bureau of Economic Research.

Meyer, Bruce D. and James X. Sullivan. 2004. "Consumption for the Poor: What We Know and what We Can Learn." Paper prepared for the ASPE-initiated workshop on Consumption among Low Income Families. Washington, DC, November 5.

Meyer, Bruce D. and James X. Sullivan. 2007. "Consumption and Income Poverty for Those 65 and Over." Paper prepared for the 9th Annual Joint Conference of the Retirement Research Consortium "Challenges and Solutions for Retirement Security." Washington, DC, August 9–10.

Meyer, Bruce D. and James X. Sullivan. 2010. "Five decades of consumption and income poverty." Working Paper 09.07. Chicago: Harris School of Public Policy Studies.

Meyer, Bruce D. and James X. Sullivan. 2011. "Consumption and Income Poverty over the Business Cycle." Working Paper No. 16751. Washington, DC: National Bureau of Economic Research.

Meyer, Bruce D. and James X. Sullivan. 2012. "Measuring Poverty: Income, Consumption and the New U.S. Poverty Measure." Unpublished paper.

Moisio, Pasi. 2004. "A Latent Class Application to the Multidimensional Measurement of Poverty." *Quantity and Quality* 38:703–17.

Nolan, Brian and Christopher T. Whelan. 2007. "On the Multidimensionality of Poverty and Social Exclusion." In *Inequality and Poverty Re-Examined*, edited by J. Micklewright and S. Jenkins. Oxford: Oxford University Press.

Nolan, Brian and Christopher T. Whelan. 2011. *Poverty and Deprivation in Europe*. Oxford: Oxford University Press.

Perry, Bryan. 2011. *Material, Poverty, Hardship and Living Standards in New Zealand: A Brief Overview*, 2nd ed. Bristol: Peter Townsend Conference.

Pisati, Maurizio, Christopher T. Whelan, Mario Lucchini, and Bertrand Maître. 2010. "Mapping Patterns of Multiple Deprivation Using Self Organising Maps: An Application to EU-SILC Data for Ireland." *Social Science Research* 39:405–18.

Ravallion, Martin. 2011. "On Multidimensional Indices of Poverty." *Journal of Economic Inequality* 9:235–48.

Ridge, Tess. 2002. *Childhood Poverty and Social Exclusion*. Bristol: Policy Press.

Ringen, Stein. 1988. "Direct and Indirect Measures of Poverty." *Journal of Social Policy* 17:351–66.

Room, Graham. 1999. "Social Exclusion, Solidarity and the Challenge of Globalisation." *International Journal of Social Welfare* 8:166–74.

Saunders, Peter and Laura Adelman. 2006. "Income, Poverty, Deprivation and Exclusion: A Comparative Study of Australia and Britain." *Journal of Social Policy* 35:559–84.

Saunders, Peter, Yuvisthi Naidoo, and Megan Griffits. 2007. *Towards New Indicators of Disadvantaged Deprivation and Exclusion in Australia.* Sydney: Social Policy Research Centre, University of New South Wales.

Scutella, Rosanna, Roger Wilkins, and Weiping Kostenko. 2009. "Poverty and Social Exclusion in Melbourne." Working Paper No. 26/09. Melbourne Institute of Applied Economics and Social Research.

Slesnick, Denial T. 1991. "The Standard of Living in the United States." *Review of Income and Wealth* 37(4):363–86.

Slesnick, Denial T. 1994. "Consumption, Needs and Inequality." *International Economic Review* 35(3):677–703.

Slesnick, Denial T. 2001. *Consumption and Social Welfare: Living Standards and Their Distribution in the United States.* Cambridge: Cambridge University Press.

Smeeding, Timothy M. 2009. "New Comparative Measures of Income, Material Deprivation, and Well-being." *Journal of Policy Analysis and Management* 28(4):745–52.

Thorbecke, Erik. 2007. "Multidimensional Poverty: Conceptual and Measurement Issues." In *The Many Dimensions of Poverty,* edited by N. Kakawani and J. Silber. Basingstoke, UK: Palgrave Macmillan.

Tomlinson, Mark and Robert Walker. 2009. *Coping with Complexity: Child and Adult Poverty.* London: Child Poverty Action Group.

Tomlinson, Mark, Robert Walker, and Glenn Williams. 2008. "Measuring Poverty in Britain as a Multi-dimensional Concept, 1991 to 2003." *Journal of Social Policy* 37:597–620.

Townsend, Peter. 1979. *Poverty in the United Kingdom: A Survey of Household Resources and Standards of Living.* Harmondsworth: Penguin.

Tsakloglou, Panos and Fotis Papadopoulos. 2002. "Poverty, Material Deprivation and Multidimensional Disadvantage during Four Life Stages: Evidence from the ECHP." In *Poverty and Social Exclusion in Europe,* edited by C. Heady, M. Barnes, J. Millar, S. Middleton, P. Tsakloglou, and F. Papadopoulos. Cheltenham: Edward Elgar.

Veblen, T. 1899. *The Theory of the Leisure Class: An Economic Study of Institutions.* New York: Macmillan.

Whelan, Christopher T., Richard Layte, and Bertrand Maître. 2004. "Understanding the Mismatch between Income Poverty and Deprivation: A Dynamic Comparative Analysis." *European Sociological Review* 20:287–301.

Whelan, Christopher T. and Bertrand Maître. 2005. "Economic Vulnerability, Social Exclusion and Social Cohesion in an Enlarged European Community." *International Journal of Comparative Sociology,* 46:215–39.

Whelan, Christopher T. and Bertrand Maître. 2006. "Comparing Poverty and Deprivation Dynamics: Issues of Reliability and Validity." *Journal of Economic Inequality* 4:303–23.

Whelan, Christopher T. and Bertrand Maître. 2009. "Europeanization of Inequality and European Reference Groups." *Journal of European Social Policy* 19:117–3.

Whelan, Christopher T. and Bertrand Maître. 2010. "Comparing Poverty Indicators in an Enlarged EU." *European Sociological Review* 26:713–73.

Whelan, Christopher T., Dorothy Watson, and Bertrand Maître. 2010. "Validating the ESeC Class Schema: Cross-sectional and Dynamic Analysis of Income Poverty and Deprivation." In *The European Socio-economic Classification,* edited by David Rose and Eric Harrison. London: Routledge.

Whelan, Christopher T. and Bertrand Maître. 2012a. "Understanding Material Deprivation: A Comparative European Analysis." *Research in Social Stratification and Mobility* 30(4):489–503.

Whelan, Christopher T. and Bertrand Maître. 2012b. "Identifying Childhood Deprivation: How Well Do National Indicators of Poverty and Social Exclusion in Ireland Perform?" *Economic and Social Review* 43:251–72.

Whelan, Christopher T. and Bertrand Maître. 2013. "Material Deprivation, Economic Stress and Reference Groups in Ireland an Analysis of EU-SILC." *European Sociological Review* 29(6):1162–74.

Whelan, Christopher T., Brian Nolan, and Bertrand Maître. 2014. "Multidimensional Poverty in Europe: An Application of the Adjusted Headcount Approach." *Journal of European Social Policy* 24(2):183–97.

CHAPTER 26

HUNGER AND FOOD INSECURITY

CHRISTOPHER B. BARRETT AND ERIN C. LENTZ

INTRODUCTION

ONE consistent message across all the available global-scale measures is that food insecurity is overwhelmingly concentrated in the developing countries. By the United Nations Food and Agriculture Organization's (FAO) estimates, only 16 million of the world's 868 million food insecure individuals—just 2 percent of the global total—live in developed countries (FAO 2012). Food insecurity nonetheless exists in wealthy countries. For example, in any given year, the U.S. Department of Agriculture (USDA) estimates that 10–15 percent of U.S. households are food insecure, with approximately one-third of these households experiencing moderate to severe hunger. Indeed, rates of household food insecurity and "very low" food security have both increased considerably during the recent recession and "jobless recovery." The most recent USDA estimates are that the share of (very) food insecure households in the United States increased from 10.1 (3.0) percent in 1999 to 14.5 (5.4) percent in 2010 (Coleman-Jensen et al. 2011). Since the 2008 economic downturn, the number of food insecure individuals in the United States has held steady at roughly 50 million; at that scale, food insecure Americans would comprise the 25th most-populous nation on earth if they were a country unto themselves. So while the prevalence of food insecurity is overwhelmingly larger in the developing countries, even the wealthiest and most powerful nations still face considerable challenges in eradicating domestic poverty and food insecurity.[1]

Food insecurity remains widespread today in large measure because extreme poverty remains widespread, and vice versa. But the relationship between poverty and food insecurity is complex and bidirectional. Food insecurity, especially that manifests in malnutrition, which results in ill-health and lethargy, contributes to individuals remaining trapped in poverty (Thomas and Strauss 1997). In turn, poverty contributes to poor nutrition and health.

In the past 10 to 15 years, numerous researchers have found that early experiences of food insecurity can have a lasting impact on people's lives and even on their children's lives. In a review of maternal and child undernutrition, Bhutta et al. (2008:340) write "height-for-age at 2 years was the best predictor of human capital and . . . undernutrition is associated with lower human capital. We conclude that damage suffered in early life leads to permanent impairment and might also affect future generations." Krishna (2007) documents how poor health, commonly associated with undernutrition, can lead to chronic impoverishment. Victora et al. (2008:340), reviewing findings on maternal and child undernutrition and human capital and risk of adult diseases, find "undernutrition [at two years of age] was strongly associated . . . with shorter adult height, less schooling, reduced economic productivity, and—for women—lower offspring birth weight."

Prenatal insults experienced in utero, such as maternal undernutrition, illness, or smoking or drinking habits, can result in lasting health effects, disability, and lower educational attainment and adult wages for unborn children. The fetal origins hypothesis—also known as the Barker hypothesis for Barker's (1992) work linking undernutrition of pregnant women with the later health of their adult children—posits that the effects of the in utero environment are lasting and can be latent for many years. In a recent review of findings, Almond and Currie (2011) write that much of the findings are associational rather than causal, although this is changing rapidly as evidence mounts. Furthermore, undernutrition in the early years may impact future generations as, for example, children born to mothers who were themselves undernourished as children are more likely to suffer low birth weight (Victora et al. 2008; Berhman et al. 2009).

This intergenerational transmission of undernutrition is closely related to the concept of nutritional poverty traps. A nutritional poverty trap occurs when individuals' physical work capacity declines more rapidly than wages once the wages (and the nutrition it can buy) falls below a critical level. Thus, in equilibrium there will be some critical asset holding such that those with at least that level obtain employment and reach a nonpoor standard of living, while those below that critical level will remain mired in poverty and malnutrition (Dasgupta and Ray 1986, 1987; Dasgupta 1993, 1997).

Yet, the causes of food insecurity are many. Not all food insecurity is related to household-level poverty. Over 25 percent of Indian children living in households from the highest income quintile had weight—for—age lower than two standard deviations below the reference group mean, a measure of wasting (Horton et al. 2010). Indeed, food insecurity remains stubbornly high in the face of increasing income and falling poverty rates in some places (e.g., India) but has fallen dramatically with increases in income and reductions in poverty in other countries (e.g., China). Micronutrient (vitamin and mineral) deficiencies, for example, can be related to cultural beliefs about the appropriateness of certain foods, a lack of information on what is required for a healthy diet, or due to weak bargaining power within the household.

In the remainder of this chapter, we first discuss concepts and definitions related to food security. We then review the major approaches to measuring food insecurity and discuss both why measurement matters and why it remains so challenging.

We provide a historical overview of hunger and food insecurity before turning to a discussion on the causes of hunger and food insecurity. Lastly, we discuss interventions intended to reduce hunger and food insecurity and indicate directions for future research.

CONCEPTS AND DEFINITIONS

One of the most tangible manifestations of poverty is a diet insufficient to keep someone healthy. The term "hunger" is popularly used as shorthand for this condition. But more precisely used, however, "hunger" refers specifically to the physical discomfort caused by a lack of food. Because this is both a relatively narrow measure of nutritional deprivation and a difficult one to measure, policymakers and scientists more commonly focus on the broader concept of "food insecurity" and its complement "food security."

Food security is inherently unobservable and difficult to define but both intrinsically and instrumentally important. Humans have a physiological need for the nutrients supplied by food. Many development programs, projects, and policies therefore include food security objectives. But food is also a source of pleasure apart from its physiological necessity. Since both biological needs for food and psychic satisfaction from food vary markedly among and within populations, it is difficult to pin down precise, operationalizable measures of food security. Moreover, the concept of food security encompasses more than current nutritional status, capturing as well vulnerability to future disruptions in one's access to adequate and appropriate food (Barrett 2002). This forward-looking, uncertainty-based dimension of food security adds further complexity to the concept.

This complexity has given rise to scores, if not hundreds, of different definitions of the term "food security." Definitions have evolved with thinking about the proximate manifestations and direct and indirect causes and consequences of food insecurity. But there remains much variation and imprecision in these terms as used in practice (Headey and Ecker 2013).

The most commonly used definition was agreed upon at the 1996 World Food Summit and holds that food security represents "a situation that exists when all people, at all times, have physical, social and economic access to sufficient, safe and nutritious food that meets their dietary needs and food preferences for an active and healthy life." Food insecurity exists when this condition is not met. Of course, by that standard, the world has only known food insecurity.

Food security is commonly conceptualized as resting on three pillars: availability, access, and utilization. Some analysts add a fourth pillar, stability, to this listing. As Webb et al. (2006) note, these concepts are inherently hierarchical, with availability necessary but not sufficient to ensure access, which is in turn necessary but not sufficient for effective utilization, none of which ensure stability of food security over time.

Availability reflects the supply side of the food security concept. In order for all people to have "sufficient" food, there must be adequate availability. While adequate availability is necessary, however, it does not ensure universal access to "sufficient, safe and nutritious food," so it is not a sufficient condition for food security.

Hence the second pillar of the food security concept: access. Access is most closely related to social science concepts of individual or household well-being: What is the range of food choices open to the person(s), given their income, prevailing prices, and formal or informal safety net arrangements through which they can access food? As the Nobel laureate Amartya Sen (1981:1, emphasis in original) famously wrote: "[S]tarvation is the characteristic of some people not *having* enough food to eat. It is not the characteristic of there *being* not enough food to eat. While the latter can be a cause of the former, it is but one of many *possible* causes." Access reflects the demand side of food security, as manifest in uneven inter- and intrahousehold food distribution and in the role that food preferences play, reflecting sociocultural limits on what foods are consistent with prevailing tastes and values within a community. Access also underscores problems of uninsured risk exposure and recourse to safe coping mechanisms to mitigate the effects of adverse shocks such as unemployment spells, price spikes, or the loss of livelihood-producing assets. Through the access lens, food security's close relationship to poverty and to social, economic, and political disenfranchisement comes into clearer focus for those who look for such mechanisms as structural explanations of human deprivation. But because access is an inherently multidimensional concept, its measurement is especially troublesome and commonly proxied by simple indicators such as per capita income.

Utilization reflects concerns about whether individuals and households make good use of the food to which they have access. Do they consume nutritionally essential foods they can afford or do they choose a nutritionally inferior diet? Are the foods safe and properly prepared, under sanitary conditions, to deliver their full nutritional value? Is their health such that they absorb and metabolize essential nutrients? While undernutrition reflects insufficient dietary energy (caloric) intake, utilization concerns foster greater attention to dietary quality, especially micronutrient deficiencies associated with inadequate intake of essential minerals and vitamins (NRC 2005).

Stability captures the susceptibility of individuals to food insecurity due to interruptions in availability, access, or utilization. The temporal aspect of stability links to the distinction between chronic and transitory or acute food insecurity. Chronic food insecurity reflects a long-term lack of access to adequate food and is typically associated with structural problems of availability, access, or utilization. Transitory or acute food insecurity, by contrast, is associated with sudden and temporary disruptions in availability, access or, less commonly, utilization. The most common transitory food insecurity is seasonal, recurring quite predictably, especially among rural populations during the period preceding harvest, when grain stocks run low and food prices typically hit annual peaks (Devereux, Vaitla, and Hauenstein-Swan 2008). Some transitory food insecurity is regular but not periodic, as in the case of regular droughts that routinely strike semiarid regions. The most serious episodes of transitory food insecurity are commonly labeled "famine," which is itself an elusive concept typically, but not always, associated with a critical food shortage, mass undernutrition or starvation, and excess mortality (Devereux 1993; Ravallion 1997).

MEASUREMENT

Thus defined and conceptualized, food security—and its complement, food insecurity—is inherently unobservable. In practice, therefore, analysts use proxy measures across different levels of aggregation, such as food availability at the national or regional level; food expenditures, coping strategies index, and dietary diversity measures at the household level; and hunger, undernutrition, underweight, and malnutrition at the individual level. Researchers from different disciplines naturally gravitate toward different measures, which implicitly emphasize distinct dimensions of the food security challenge.

All measures have their flaws. Food availability neglects waste and the inevitably unequal distribution of food within a population. Access measures such as the coping strategies index (Maxwell 1996; Maxwell et al. 1999; Maxwell et al. 2003) and food expenditure and dietary diversity measures (Arimond and Ruel 2004) rely on household or individual responses to questions about approaches to respond to shocks and past consumption, respectively, to understand the distribution of food insecurity. Other access measures use income, consumption or expenditures as proxies of food insecurity. Yet, access and availability measures generally ignore micronutrient (i.e., mineral and vitamin) shortfalls that affect a far greater number of people and are strongly linked to a range of disabilities, diseases, and premature mortality. Various anthropometric measures—such as weight-for-height, weight-for-age or mid-upper-arm circumference—are commonly used, especially for children, with measures at least two standard deviations below global reference values widely interpreted as signaling serious problems of wasting (low weight-for-height), underweight (low weight-for-age) or stunting (low height-for-age). These measures are the joint product, however, of nutrition and health status, thus identified problems are often due to factors unrelated to nutrient intake. Malnutrition refers to the ensemble of undernutrition, overweight and obesity and micronutrient (mineral and vitamin) deficiencies, thereby reflecting the full "triple burden" of nutritional problems faced by many poor communities (Pinstrup-Andersen 2007). Overweight and obesity are commonly measured using the body mass index, a measure widely acknowledged as flawed because it fails to control for body-frame type or the distribution of weight between fat and muscle.

Measurement matters for at least three major reasons. First, each measure captures and neglects different phenomena intrinsic to the elusive concept of food security, thereby subtly influencing prioritization among food security interventions. Historically, reliance on national food availability estimates has predictably focused attention on food aid shipments and agricultural-production strategies to increase food supplies in the short and long term, respectively. Over roughly the past quarter century, Sen's (1981) core thesis—that food access accounts for most food insecurity—has focused increased attention on individual-specific income, hunger, and anthropometric data, which naturally reinforces food security strategies based on poverty reduction, food price, and social protection policies.

Second, observational data necessarily report on the past. But policymakers are most interested in the likely future effects of prospective interventions. Given its "at all times" element, an ideal food security indicator would reflect the forward-looking time series of probabilities of satisfying the access criteria (Barrett 2002). The degree of stability of observed measures over time and their predictability affects analysts' ability to translate estimates into defensible prescriptions on behalf of those whose food security is most tenuous.

Third, insofar as food insecurity measures diagnostically inform actions, they must be readily associated with targetable characteristics of vulnerable households and individuals and remediable causal factors that lead to food insecurity. National-level measures inherently lend themselves only to addressing national-scale food availability shortfalls, not intranational access and utilization concerns. The research frontier today therefore revolves around the development of cross-nationally comparable, longitudinal monitoring and analysis at household and individual levels. Over the past decade or so, research has moved increasingly toward survey-based measures to improve the disaggregated identification of food insecure subpopulations and their targetable characteristics and behaviors.

The most widely cited food insecurity figures are the "undernourishment" estimates generated by the FAO, derived from national-level food balance sheets and strong assumptions about the intranational distribution of food across individuals. Alternative measures, such as those reported to Congress each year by the USDA, often differ radically from FAO estimates. For example, in October 2012, the FAO estimated that the number of undernourished people in developing countries was 852 million (FAO 2012). A few months earlier, the USDA estimated a figure of 802 million food insecure people living in developing countries (Rosen et al. 2012). And the FAO estimate for Asia was nearly 30 percent higher than USDA's (563 vs. 398 million) while that for Sub-Saharan Africa was more than one-third lower (239 vs. 357 million). Such discrepancies make even macroscale geographic targeting difficult for policymakers.

The global figures mask considerable heterogeneity among and within regions, especially in trends. In China and Southeast Asia, scores of millions fewer people suffer undernutrition than a generation ago due to broad-based, rapid economic growth. In other regions, including South Asia, and parts of east and southern Africa, undernutrition rates have fallen even while the number of undernourished has increased due to population growth. And in some regions, such as Central Africa, both numbers and rates have increased.

These measures also ignore how membership in the ranks of the food insecure changes over time. The FAO's newly revised 2012 measure defines undernourishment as energy deficiency lasting over a year (FAO 2012). As a result, they ignore the suffering of those who experience transitory periods of food security but know they face a significant likelihood of being food insecure again in the near future. The "churning" of those who experience transitory food insecurity means both that the FAO measures, which capture only chronic but not seasonal or periodic food insecurity, and other cross-sectional estimates underestimate the population that is at significant risk of experiencing food insecurity over any multiyear period.

Continued reliance on contested national food availability measures reflects the limited availability and timeliness of household and individual data collected in nationally representative surveys, especially in the low-income countries in which food insecurity is most widespread and severe. A growing literature proves the value of survey data that capture objective dietary, economic, and health indicators as well as subjective measures of adequacy, risk exposure, and sociocultural acceptability (Bickel et al. 2000; Frongillo and Nanama 2006; Smith, Alderman, and Aduayom 2006; Wunderlich and Norwood 2006). Food security measures based on household and individual data routinely generate higher estimates of food insecurity than those derived from more aggregate data. The differences seem attributable not only to differences in intra- and interhousehold nutrient distribution but also in the resulting estimates of nutrient availability. Not surprisingly, survey-based estimates of food insecurity are more strongly correlated with poverty estimates, the most convincing of which are likewise generated from household survey data.

Beyond the increased precision that more disaggregated evidence allows, individual and household-level survey-based measures permit reasonably accurate predictions of who is most likely to be affected adversely by potentially harmful shocks, such as food price increases, drought, or slumping demand for wage labor. Survey data-based predictions of community-level variables, such as child undernutrition, can even underpin catastrophic insurance contracts that trigger payouts when most needed (Chantarat et al. 2007). By contrast, aggregate food availability is a poor predictor of other food insecurity indicators. As but one striking example, the FAO's estimate of the world's undernourished population has increased by 9 percent globally in spite of its 12 percent rise in global food production per capita since 2007 (Barrett 2010).

Nonetheless, even when agencies utilize the same data, they may come to different conclusions about the need for assistance. For example, in 2012 in the Sahel, the United Nations World Food Programme and the Famine Early Warning System Network reached contrasting conclusions about the severity of food insecurity due to differences in measures (food security vs. malnutrition) and in whether measures should capture acute or acute and chronic conditions, among other factors (Amaral et al. 2012). While variations in assessments are not uncommon, large and persistent differences, such as those observed in the Sahel, can create confused messages and ultimately slow assistance where needed.

Although the most severe food insecurity is typically associated with disasters such as drought, floods, war, or earthquakes, most food insecurity is not associated with catastrophes but rather with chronic poverty (Barrett 2010). The rapidly growing global population affected by disasters is merely a modest fraction of the undernourished, who in turn represent a minority of those living in poverty at any given time. While good data remain elusive, it is widely believed that only a small fraction of hunger-related deaths worldwide are caused by humanitarian emergencies while the vast majority are associated with chronic or recurring hunger and malnutrition. Similarly, in every country, rates of child stunting—reflecting chronic undernutrition—far exceed those of child wasting—indicating short-term, acute undernutrition—with the difference greatest in the poorest countries (see Figure 26.1).

What also comes through clearly in the best-statistical-fit curves depicted in Figure 26.1 is the negative-but-weak relationship between per capita gross national income and both stunting and wasting measures. While the chronic indicator, stunting, has a steeper negative slope than does the more transitory measure, wasting, at very low levels of national income, the dispersion around both curves is considerable; and the slope is close to zero once countries hit the "upper middle income" range, defined by the World Bank as over roughly $4,000 per capita. This suggests that income growth is only weakly correlated with improvements in child nutritional status and almost exclusively over the low-income and lower middle-income ranges. This underscores the importance of distributional concerns to patterns of food security.

Because most food insecurity is seasonal or regular but aperiodic—that is, associated with temporary unemployment, episodes of ill health, or other recurring adverse events—people anticipate such possibilities. They engage in precautionary behaviors to try to mitigate their risk. Hence the empirical regularity that perceptions-based survey

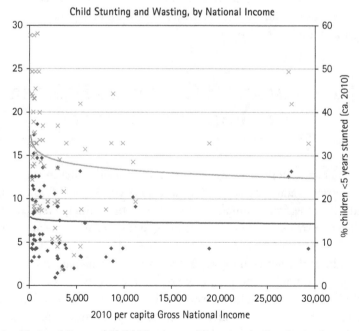

FIGURE 26.1 National Rates of Child Wasting and Stunting, by Per Capita Income

Source: UNICEF (2012): http://data.un.org. Authors' own calculations.

measures consistently find food insecurity rates several times higher than related hunger or insufficient intake measures (NRC 2005). Food insecurity remains widespread today in large measure because poverty and economic vulnerability remain widespread, and vice versa (Dasgupta 1997; Carter and Barrett 2006).

Perceptions data may not suffice to capture utilization problems, such as those associated with micronutrient malnutrition. The prevalence of micronutrient deficiencies is imprecisely known; very rough estimates suggest that iodine, iron, vitamin A, and zinc shortfalls alone affect at least 2 billion people, disproportionately women and children. This leads to increased risk of both chronic and infectious disease, aggravates diseases' effects, and leads to irreversible loss of cognitive and physical function, especially during the crucial 1,000-day period from conception until the child reaches age two, during which children are biologically vulnerable and thus heavily dependent on caregiver knowledge to utilize foods appropriately (Darnton-Hill et al. 2005; World Bank 2006; Horton, Alderman, and Rivera 2008). These irreversible effects contribute to persistent poverty, reinforcing the consequences of food insecurity.

To summarize, a range of measures of food insecurity exist, many of them inconsistent with one another. Over time, experts have come to favor survey-based measures, especially those that incorporate perceptions measures that more comprehensively reflect the psychology and expectations of food security, not just past dietary patterns, thereby reflecting increasingly nuanced understandings of food insecurity. But the considerable difficulties and expense involved in fielding large-scale, regular individual and household nutrition and food security surveys precludes their use in generating large-scale measures of food insecurity. Coarse approximations based on intrinsically contestable methods therefore continue to dominate the global policymaking discourse about hunger and food insecurity.

HISTORICAL OVERVIEW OF HUNGER AND FOOD INSECURITY

For most of human history, lives were short and unhealthy due in large measure to insufficient nutrient intake. Thomas Malthus's (1998 (1798)) well-known explanation for this predicament was that human population growth routinely overtaxed the capacity of the earth to provide sufficient food, leading to routine food insecurity and regular famines.

Since the eighteenth century, however, a few dozen countries have enjoyed an unprecedented escape from hunger and premature death due largely to dramatic advances in food availability and associated income growth broadened access to a satisfactory diet. Synergistic interactions arise as increased consumption requires increased food production, which becomes more feasible as people grow bigger, stronger, healthier, and more energetic because they eat more—of course, only up to a point now commonly exceeded in an era of exploding obesity rates. The reinforcing feedback between nutritional status and productivity points to a nutritional poverty trap. Several scholars argue that the escape from the nutritional poverty trap helped catalyze the unprecedentedly rapid and widespread advance of living standards over the past 300 years (Dasgupta 1993, 1997; Fogel 2004).

Much of this progress traces back to increased food availability made possible by agricultural technological change associated with plant breeding, improved agronomic practices such as intercropping and crop rotations, irrigation, and the emergence of mechanical implements and chemical fertilizers. As a direct result, food security has often been equated with food availability indicators, typically measured in terms of satisfaction of dietary energy requirements, that is, calories per person per day. Indeed, at the time of the World Food Conference of 1974, food security was widely viewed as a problem of insufficient and unstable production. And because domestic food production represents the overwhelming majority of food availability in virtually every country, increased variability in domestic food production significantly increases national-level food consumption instability (Diakosavvas 1989).

Such measures create an inherent conceptual link to food self-sufficiency, that is, whether a country produced enough food to feed its population adequately. However, self-sufficiency implies letting the domestic market equilibrate local demand and supply, which can lead to high prices and widespread hunger for countries with poor endowments of fertile land and plentiful water. Strictly availability-based measures pay scant attention to the economic (in)efficiency or environmental consequences of producing one's own diet rather than trading internationally for food according to economic laws of comparative advantage based on natural resource endowments.

Moreover, distributional problems commonly lead to food insecurity despite sufficient aggregate food availability. This is true at the national level and the household and individual levels. Although food is plentiful at the global level, food availability is insufficient in some poor countries, especially without significant external assistance. International trade is helpful but of limited use in relieving aggregate food insecurity in some low-income countries because, in part, limited export-earning and international-borrowing capacity constrain current account deficits.

Over the past quarter century, the major shift in thinking about food insecurity has therefore been toward the close linkage between poverty (rather than low agricultural productivity) and food insecurity. Put differently, emphasis is on consumption rather than production. This second generation of thinking on food security, focused more on the demand side and on issues of access by vulnerable people to food, stems directly from the pathbreaking work of Sen (1981). Ironically, Sen explicitly eschewed the concept of food security, focusing instead on the "entitlements" of individuals and households. Sen's seminal work helped shift the focus from supply-side issues associated with aggregate food availability toward the levels of individual and household access to food, and thus to the role of (perhaps idiosyncratic) demand failure brought about by lost employment, adverse movement in the terms of trade, production failure, termination of transfers, or other forms of "entitlement failure." Sen's concept of "entitlements" represents the commodity bundles that a person can rightfully make her own, through production, trade, or transfers. Sen (1981) explains hunger as the failure of an individual's entitlements to provide a commodity bundle offering sufficient nutrients and famine as the result of widespread entitlement failures. Sen thus placed increased emphasis on not only traditional economic variables of incomes and prices but equally on human rights and on the legal institutions of the state, as well as the moral and social norms of cultures.

The entitlements approach has been critiqued by some as apolitical, ahistorical, excessively legalistic, and economistic (de Waal 1989; Baro and Deubel 2006). Most recent analysts have encouraged efforts to incorporate power and vulnerability into conceptualizations of food insecurity, although these have gained little traction, not least of which because of the added layers of measurement challenge these concepts introduce. One consequence has been increased focus on understanding the proximate threats to food security in an integrated fashion. The emergent third-generation view of food security builds on food availability and entitlements as a summary of food access. Chambers (1989:34) identifies two dimensions of vulnerability, a driver of food insecurity: "an external side of risks, shocks and stress to which an individual or household is subject; and an internal side which is defenselessness, meaning a lack of means to cope without damaging loss." Individuals with excessive risk exposure and without access to noninjurious coping mechanisms are the most food insecure. Both risk exposure and the availability of noninjurious coping mechanisms depend heavily on structural patterns of control of (financial, human, and natural) resources and on access to markets, technologies, and finance. Food security is thus closely related to poverty and to social, economic, and political disenfranchisement (Drèze and Sen 1990).

CAUSES OF HUNGER AND FOOD INSECURITY

Many factors can result in availability, access, or utilization failures. Indeed researchers have identified sources of food insecurity ranging from macrostructural factors, such as globalization or episodes of widespread unemployment or high food prices, to microlevel factors, such as household bargaining power (Hoddinott and Haddad 1995; McMichael 1995; Scanlan 2009). In many instances food insecurity is likely the result of a complex combination of availability, access, and utilization failures. Devereux (2009), for example, argues that famines—the most severe form of food insecurity—cannot be attributed to a single cause and that famines result from a varying mix of production failures (e.g., due to natural disasters or environmental changes), exchange failures (i.e., market failures or poverty) and response failures (i.e., accountability failures by governments and international agencies).

Production failures, trade barriers, poor governance, and so forth may result in availability failure, meaning that adequate and appropriate food cannot reach the target population. Likewise, conflict, poverty, inaccessible markets, information failures, liquidity constraints, or sociocultural norms, and so on may limit food access for an entire community, for a household, or for an individual within a household. Utilization failures may be due to poor health, poor sanitation, or lack of knowledge about food preparation or nutrition. Stability is commonly interlinked with access, as the intent of the stability pillar is to ensure continuous access. For example, food price spikes can undermine stable access to food. Chronic food security is generally linked to structural problems, while acute food insecurity is typically associated with rapid onset shocks. In complex emergencies, individuals suffering from chronic or seasonal food insecurity may suddenly face acute food insecurity. Already weak coping mechanisms may collapse and individuals' nutritionals status can face a rapid and precipitous decline.

Yet, most food insecurity is due to chronic or seasonal poverty, not due to catastrophic events, such as earthquakes, floods, or war that disrupt food production and distribution at scale, although these events can result in episodes of severe food insecurity (Barrett 2010). Devereux et al. (2008) point to regular seasonal shortages and associated price increases as a source of food insecurity for landless laborers and smallholder farmers. Krishna (2004) highlights the sizeable entry and exit of households into and out of poverty in India. Wilde and Nord (2005:430–31) find that U.S. food stamp eligible households "do not come in constant 'secure' and 'insecure' varieties. Instead, it appears that unobserved hardships strike from time to time, with large effects both on [food stamp] program participation and food security."

When faced with dire choices, individuals or households may choose food insecurity rather than losing assets, such as seed stock, livestock, or land (de Waal 1989; Conway 1998; Hoddinott 2006). While this strategy protects productive assets, it puts at risk the nutrition of the most vulnerable family members. Malnutrition during the first thousand days from the start of a woman's pregnancy until her child's second birthday can have lasting consequences (Victora et al. 2008). Further, different household members may make different choices about how to allocate resources. Hoddinott and Haddad (1995) find that in Côte d'Ivoire mothers' control of income is associated with increased spending on food. In one of very few studies from a developed country, Kenney (2008) finds that U.S. children are less likely to be food insecure if their mother controls the household's pooled income than if their father does or both parents jointly control income. Yet, this is not universally the case. Cultural rules regarding parental responsibility shape these outcomes (Kenney 2008). For example, in Bangladesh, increases in fathers' income led to increased spending on food, but increased income for mothers did not. And among pastoralists in northern Kenya and southern Ethiopia, Villa et al. (2011) find that male household heads adjust their own diets to buffer family members' dietary diversity against adverse income shocks.

INTERVENTIONS TO REDUCE HUNGER
AND FOOD INSECURITY

Given the strong, bidirectionally causal relationship between poverty and food insecurity, food assistance programs expressly aimed at reducing hunger and undernutrition are commonly viewed as an important element of holistic poverty-reduction strategies in addition to their more direct role addressing food insecurity. Food assistance encompasses any publicly financed direct food, cash, or voucher transfers, or food subsidies that serve as de facto transfers, for the purpose of increasing the quality or quantity of food consumed to improve recipients' health and nutritional status.

Carefully designed food assistance programs, and related nutritional interventions, have been identified by the Copenhagen Consensus (2008) as among the highest return investments available worldwide. But, as Barrett (2002:2105) writes, "[t]he impulse to action is strong but does not guarantee success. Most nations have implemented food assistance programs of some sort, but many of these have proved expensive, ineffective, or both." One of the key reasons is that food assistance programs are quite small relative to the broader, commercial and semisubsistence food systems on which people rely for daily nourishment. Therefore, any public food assistance policy or program must be designed to integrate effectively with the private food production and distribution system.

International food aid receives disproportionate attention. International food aid deliveries are actually quite modest relative to private and domestic sources of supply. Globally, 85–90 percent of global cereals production is consumed in the country in which it is grown in any given year; only 11–12 percent of global food production is internationally traded in any given year even though trade has been growing faster than output over the past 40 years (Lentz and Barrett 2012). International food aid is far smaller still, amounting to less than one-quarter of 1 percent of total food production and only 1.9 percent of commercial international food trade. Moreover, most international food aid is now purchased primarily in developing countries, not in donor countries, with much of it bought in surplus regions of the recipient country under "local purchase" programs (Lentz et al. 2013). Even the poorest countries rely heavily on their own agricultural production systems and on regional trade networks to satisfy food demand.

Global food aid amounts to less than $5 billion annually now, as compared to, for example, nearly $90 billion spent by the U.S. government each year on public feeding programs (school breakfast and lunch programs, Supplemental Nutrition Assistance Program, etc.). And even in the countries with the largest food assistance programs, these are small compared to the broader food economy. For example, India's targeted public distribution system comprised only about 16 percent of total food grains produced in 2009–2010 (Government of India 2011), while the United States' domestic food assistance programs account for less than 10 percent of a food economy of more than $1 trillion annually. For this reason, the performance of the domestic, private food-production and distribution systems matter more to food security than do national, public food-assistance policies and programs, which in turn matter more than international food aid. In designing and evaluating food assistance policy, it is crucial to keep this ordering of the key sources of populations' diet firmly in mind.

Food assistance policies and programs can nonetheless provide essential social protection, filling in the gaps left by the private (for-profit) food system and informal (not-for-profit) social safety nets to ensure the food security of vulnerable individuals, households, and communities. A growing literature underscores the importance of social protection for economic growth and poverty reduction (Carter and Barrett 2006, 2007; Alderman, Hoddinott, and Kinsey 2006; Barrett, Carter, and Ikegami 2011). The safety net provided by food assistance and other social protection programs reduces individuals' and households' catastrophic risk exposure and encourages savings, investment, and adoption of improved technologies, all of which contribute to increased incomes and enhanced food availability and access.

In order for government agencies and civil society institutions to offer effective food assistance programs, they must have the clear legal obligation and political commitment to protect the fundamental human right to food, as enshrined in the "International Covenant on Economic, Social and Cultural Rights," as well as adequate resources to implement such protection. Effective, direct food security interventions depend on targeting the vulnerable subpopulation(s) and the causes of insecurity, as well as prompt response. Where data collection is timely, causal factors can be robustly associated with food insecurity measures, and where predictive models have demonstrable accuracy, preventive measures can substantially reduce unnecessary human suffering. The long-term consequences of crises can be limited where appropriate policies and institutions are already in place, such as social protection schemes to cushion people in times of adversity and early childhood health programs to protect the most vulnerable from even short-lived interruptions in essential nutrient intake.

Automatic stabilizing and safety net programs are important means of circumventing inconsistent or inadequate government and donor response. Political and economic elites are rarely severely affected by crises, nor do they suffer chronic food insecurity. Because they rarely face intense, immediate political pressure, slow, halting or incompetent government and donor response is a recurring problem. For example, the median delivery time for emergency food aid from the United States, the main global food donor, is nearly five months due to legislative restrictions on procurement and shipping (Barrett and Maxwell 2005). And even prescient early warning systems often go unheeded (Lautze et al. 2012).

For example, in the Niger crisis of 2004–2005, below-normal rains and anticipated locust attacks led to a low cereals harvest that elicited prompt government and United Nations appeals for emergency assistance in November 2004. But global response was anemic. By July 2005, the Niger situation was finally attracting graphic global media coverage that led to a significant global response, much of which arrived with the next harvest. These delays are both deadly and expensive. In Niger, quite apart from the still-unclear human health toll and lives lost to delays, the cost per beneficiary for World Food Programme deliveries more than tripled from February to August 2005, from $7 to $23, due to far greater need for supplemental and therapeutic foods instead of cheaper, bulk commodities; and the need for airlifts and other quicker, but more expensive, logistical support (Chantarat et al. 2007). Poorly conceptualized or implemented relief programs can adversely affect communities, leaving them more vulnerable to food insecurity by displacing commercial food trade, affecting local prices, or distorting incentives and behaviors. Hence the need for prearranged financing facilities, social protection programs such as employment guarantee schemes, and other ready-made responses to emergent food security crises.

Perhaps the most important factor determining the efficacy of food security interventions is the quality of targeting (Lentz and Barrett 2008). Does assistance reach intended beneficiaries? Good targeting is exceedingly difficult. Even so-called self-targeting designs, such as public employment schemes that pay below-market wages or subsidization of inferior foods not desired by the food secure, experience leakage (Barrett and Clay 2003; Coady, Grosh, and Hoddinott 2004). The neediest individuals are not always easily identified, even in participatory or community-based targeting efforts, for example, due to social isolation or discrimination. Further, the need for political buy-in often leads to targeting a broader population for food assistance programs (Pinstrup-Andersen 1993).

Effective targeting is usually based on a mixture of geographic indicators, observable individual or household characteristics, program restrictions (such as work requirements), or community consultations (Coady et al. 2004). Identifying the most needy prospective recipients and the optimal form of assistance involves tradeoffs across time, efficacy, and cost and commonly requires triangulation using multiple indicators across time and levels of aggregation. In responding to transitory food insecurity associated with sudden natural disasters (e.g., earthquakes, hurricanes), careful and expensive data collection may be inappropriate, especially for short-lived interventions. By contrast, careful targeting is essential for long-term programs that address more common chronic food insecurity.

The greatest food security gains typically come indirectly, however, through policies that promote poverty reduction through asset building, employment creation, and productivity growth among the poor, as well as safety nets to safeguard the vulnerable nonpoor. Where food availability remains limiting, as is true of dozens of low-income countries, efforts to boost crop productivity, especially of micronutrient-rich foods, and improve food-marketing systems merit prioritization. Hence the resurgence of interest in pursuing a new Green Revolution to end hunger, especially in sub-Saharan Africa and South Asia (Conway 1998; Cullather 2010; AGRA 2013). The original Green Revolution led to improved food security for urban populations, primarily due to lower cereals prices; however, its impact on the rural poor was mixed, with some farmers and landless laborers experiencing increased hunger (Conway 1998). Conway (1998) argues that future efforts to improve productivity should incorporate conservation techniques and pay more attention to distributional effects. The Alliance for a Green Revolution in

Africa (AGRA), a novel partnership between the Gates and Rockefeller Foundations, aims to sustainably strengthen agricultural value chains, focusing on breadbasket areas within Africa. Yet, there remain disputes as to whether a new Green Revolution can improve food security. Cullather (2010) warns that although the Green Revolution is commonly portrayed as a technocratic approach it was, in fact, a highly political undertaking. He argues, "tantalizing one-time solutions distract from the inequities of power that perpetuate poverty and hunger" (Cullather 2010:270).

Food insecurity and broader concerns about the role of food in people's lives can also catalyze social movements. Examining recent social movements such as Food Sovereignty, Slow Food, and Fair Trade, McMichael (2009) writes that peasants have mobilized to advocate for biodiverse and sustainable agriculture and against industrial agriculture. These peasant movements arose in response to "the human and ecological wake created by the 'globalisation' of the corporate food regime" (McMichael 2009:148). The Right to Food movement advocates for reform of both short-term and long-term food security interventions and repositions beneficiaries as rights-holders, and donors and participant governments as duty-bearers (De Schutter 2009). The Right to Food movement in India, through legal action and campaigning, has played a major role in shaping Indian social protection programs, including the establishment of the 2005 National Rural Employment Guarantee Act and the 2005 Right to Information Act (Devereux et al. 2008). Other social movements seeking to change to underlying structural factors, such as the Brazilian Landless Workers Movement (MST), may indirectly impact food security by increasing assets, income, or access to services.

FUTURE DIRECTIONS FOR RESEARCH

There is a great deal that we do not yet understand about food security. At the most basic level, simply measuring food insecurity in an accurate and timely fashion remains challenging. Developing and assessing innovative measurements, such as dietary recall or subjective perceptions, and innovative measurement techniques, such as the use of sentinel sites, will continue to be important areas for future research (Barrett 2010; Headey and Ecker 2013).

A second, related research frontier concerns comparative impact evaluation. Despite the enormous sums spent on food assistance programs and policies over the years, there exists relatively little rigorous evidence comparing among interventions to establish what works best for which objective and, therefore, what should be the highest priority interventions given scarce resources. Moreover, there are relatively few studies that offer long-term results to establish long-run payoffs as well as those during a short period of program evaluation (Hoddinott et al. 2008; Behrman et al. 2009). Finally, it is difficult to do benefit-cost analysis effectively in the absence of clear counterfactuals and solid methods for controlling for nonrandom placement and selection effects. Because most food insecurity interventions are expressly targeted at those most vulnerable to food insecurity, failure to control adequately for such effects automatically biases the estimated impacts of any intervention in the direction of finding no or adverse effects. There is a pressing need for more careful attention to both confounding variables and explicit comparison among alternative interventions in empirical work on food insecurity.

Yet, social protection and food assistance programs remain critical means to address food insecurity. Clear analyses of what food security interventions work in what institutional and cultural context—and whether such approaches are replicable—can contribute to a relatively small literature of carefully documented findings. For example, the small but growing body of evidence of the causal link between nutritional status during the first thousand days and long-term outcomes has the potential for major implications in the design and implementation of effective social protection policies (Almond and Currie 2011). Policymakers and researchers are just beginning to grapple with how to translate research findings on the first thousand days into practice.

Furthermore, the link between poverty and food security indicates that poverty-alleviation efforts can mitigate food insecurity, especially for lower income individuals and households. This emerging understanding is reflected in the recent interest in harnessing smallholder agricultural growth for nutrition. Whether a new Green Revolution could be the means to achieve improved smallholder nutrition in an environmentally sustainable and equitable manner is similarly emerging as an important area for research. The links between poverty alleviation and food security also create an opportunity to examine potential knock-on effects of poverty-alleviation programs and policies, or of related social movements, on food insecurity as well as the limits of these factors to address food insecurity, perhaps resulting from distributional inequities, political power, or behavioral and cultural practices.

NOTE

1. This chapter draws significantly on Barrett (2010), Barrett and Lentz (2010), and Lentz and Barrett (2012).

REFERENCES

AGRA. 2013. "AGRA's Strategy for an African Green Revolution." Retrieved September 6, 2014 (http://www.agra.org/agra/en/who-we-are/agras-strategy-for-an-african-green-revolution//).

Alderman, Harold, John Hoddinott, and B. Kinsey. 2006. "Long Term Consequences of Early Childhood Malnutrition." *Oxford Economic Papers* 58:450–74.

Almond, Douglas and Janet Currie. 2011. "Killing Me Softly: The Fetal Origins Hypothesis." *Journal of Economic Perspectives* 23:153–72.

Amaral, Cristina, Gary Eilerts, Laouali. Ibrahim, Joyce Luma, and Jean Senahoun. 2012. "Reflections from a Joint Multiple-Agency Examination of the Sahel Food Security Crisis." FAO August 21, Situation Update.

Arimond Mary and Marie T. Ruel. 2004. "Dietary Diversity is Associated with Child Nutritional Status: Evidence from 11 Demographic and Health Surveys." *The Journal of Nutrition* 134(10):2579–85.

Barker, David J. 1992. *The Fetal and Infant Origins of Adult Disease*. London: British Medical Journal Books.

Baro, Mamadou and Tara F. Deubel. 2006. "Persistent Hunger: Perspectives on Vulnerability, Famine and Food Security in Sub-Saharan Africa." *Annual Review of Anthropology* 35:521–38.

Barrett, Christopher B. 2002. "Food Security and Food Assistance Programs." *Handbook of Agricultural Economics* 2:2103–90.

Barrett, Christopher B. 2010. "Measuring Food Insecurity." *Science* 327:825–28.

Barrett, Christopher B., Michael. R. Carter, and M. Ikegami. 2011. "Poverty Traps and social protection." Cornell University working paper.

Barrett, Christopher B. and Daniel C. Clay. 2003. "Self-targeting Accuracy in the Presence of Imperfect Factor Markets: Evidence from Food-for-Work in Ethiopia." *Journal of Development Studies* 39:152–80.

Barrett, Christopher B. and Erin C. Lentz. 2010. "Food Insecurity." In: *The International Studies Encyclopedia*, edited by Denemark, R. A., vol. IV. Chichester: Wiley-Blackwell.

Behrman, Jere R., Maria C. Calderon, Samuel H. Preston, John Hoddinott, Reynaldo Martorell, and Aryeh D. Stein. 2009. "Nutritional Supplementation in Girls Influence the Growth of Their Children: Prospective Study in Guatemala." *American Journal of Clinical Nutrition* 90:1372–79.

Bhutta, Zulfiqar A., Tahmeed Ahmed, Robert E. Black, Simon Cousens, Kathryn G. Dewey, Elsa Giugliani, Batool A. Haider, Betty Kirkwood, Saul S. Morris, H. P. S. Sachdev, and Meera Shekar. 2008. "What Work? Interventions for Maternal and Child Undernutrition and Survival." *The Lancet* 371:417–40.

Bickel, Gary, Mark Nord, Cristofer Price, William Hamilton, and John Cook. 2000. *Guide to Measuring Household Food Security, Revised 2000*. Alexandria, VA: USDA Food and Nutrition Service.

Carter, Michael R. and Christopher B. Barrett. 2006. "The Economics of Poverty Traps and Persistent Poverty: An Asset-Based Approach." *Journal of Development Studies* 42:178–99.

Carter, Michael R. and Christopher B. Barrett. 2007. "Asset Thresholds and Social Protection." *IDS Bulletin* 38:34–38.

Chambers, Robert. 1989. "Vulnerability, Coping and Policy (Editorial Introduction)." *IDS Bulletin* 20(2):34–40.

Chantarat Sommarat, Christopher Barrett, Andrew Mude, and Callum Turvey. 2007. "Using Weather Index Insurance to Improve Drought Response for Famine Prevention." *American Journal of Agricultural Economics* 89(5):1262–68.

Coady, David P., Margaret Grosh, and John Hoddinott. 2004. "Targeting Outcomes Redux." *World Bank Research Observer* 19:61–85.

Conway, Gordon. 1998. *The Doubly Green Revolution: Food for All in the 21st Century*. Ithaca, NY: Cornell University Press.

Cullather, Nick. 2010. *The Hungry World: America's Cold War Battle against Poverty in Asia*. Cambridge, MA: Harvard University Press.

Darnton-Hill, Ian, Patrick Webb, Philip W. J. Harvey, Joseph M. Hunt, Nita Dalmiya, Mickey Chopra, Madeline J. Ball, Martin W. Bloem, and Bruno de Benoist. 2005. "Micronutrient Deficiencies and Gender: Social and Economic Costs." *American Journal of Clinical Nutrition* 81:1198–1205.

Coleman-Jensen, Alisha, Mark Nord, Margaret Andrews, and Steven Carlson. 2011. "Household Food Security in the United States in 2010." USDA Economic Research Service Report No. 125.

Copenhagen Consensus. 2008. "Copenhagen Consensus 2008—Results." Copenhagen Consensus Center, pp. 1-6.

Dasgupta, Partha. 1993. *An Inquiry Into Well-being and Destitution*. Oxford: Clarendon Press.

Dasgupta, Partha. 1997. "Nutritional Status, the Capacity for Work, and Poverty Traps." *Journal of Econometrics* 77:5-37.

Dasgupta, Partha and Debraj Ray. 1986. "Inequality as a Determinant of Malnutrition and Unemployment: Theory." *Economic Journal* 96:1011-34.

Dasgupta, Partha and Debraj Ray. 1987. "Inequality as a Determinant of Malnutrition and Unemployment: Policy." *Economic Journal* 97:177-88.

De Schutter, Olivier. 2009. "Promotion and Protection of All Human Rights, Civil, Political, Economic, Social and Cultural Rights, Including the Right to Development: The Role of Development Cooperation and Food Aid in Realizing the Right to Adequate Food: Moving from Charity to Obligation." Human Rights Council: 10th session: Agenda item 3. February 11. Retrieved March 26, 2013 (http://www.wunrn.com/news/2009/02_09/02_23_09/022309_special_files/SR%20Food%20Report%20to%20UN%202009.pdf).

De Waal, Alex. 1989. "Famine Mortality: A Case Study of Darfur, Sudan 1984-5." *Population Studies* 43:5-24.

Devereux, Stephen. 1993. *Theories of Famine*. New York: Harvester Wheatsheaf.

Devereux, Stephen. 2009. "Why Does Famine Persist in Africa?" *Food Security* 1:25-35.

Devereux, Stephen, Bapu Vaitla, and Samuel Hauenstein Swan. 2008. *Seasons of Hunger: Fighting Cycles of Quiet Starvation among the World's Rural Poor*. London: Pluto Press.

Diakosavvas, Dimitris. 1989. "On the Causes of Food Insecurity in Less Developed Countries: An Empirical Evaluation." *World Development* 17(2):223-35.

Drèze, Jean and Amartya Sen. 1990. "Introduction." In *The Political Economy of Hunger: Volume 1: Entitlement and Wellbeing*," edited by J. Dreze and A. Sen. Oxford: Oxford University Press.

FAO. 2011. *State of Food Insecurity 2011*. Rome: FAO.

FAO. 2012. *The State of Food Insecurity in the World 2012*. Rome: FAO.

Fogel, Robert W. 2004. *The Escape from Hunger and Premature Death, 1700-2100: Europe, America, and the Third World*. Cambridge: Cambridge University Press.

Frongillo, Edward A. and Simeon Nanama. 2006. "Development and Validation of an Experience-based Measure of Household Food Insecurity within and across Seasons in Northern Burkina Faso." *Journal of Nutrition* 136:1409-19.

Government of India. 2011. *Annual Report 2010-2011: Department of Food and Public Distribution*. Ministry of Consumer Affairs, Food and Public Distribution. New Delhi.

Headey, Derek and Olivier Ecker. 2013. "Rethinking the Measurement of Food Security: from First Principles to Best Practice." *Food Security* 5(3):327-43.

Hoddinott, John. 2006. "Shocks and Their Consequences across and within Households in Rural Zimbabwe." *Journal of Development Studies* 42:301-21.

Hoddinott, John and Lawrence Haddad. 1995. "Does Female Income Share Influence Household Expenditures? Evidence from Côte d'Ivoire." *Oxford Bulletin of Economics and Statistics* 57:77-96.

Hoddinott, John, John A. Maluccio, Jere R. Behrman, Rafael Flores, and Reynaldo Martorell. 2008. "Effect of a Nutrition Intervention during Early Childhood on Economic Productivity in Guatemalan Adults." *The Lancet* 371:411-16.

Horton, Susan, Harold Alderman, and Juan Rivera. 2008. *Copenhagen Consensus 2008 Challenge Paper: Hunger and Malnutrition.* Copenhagen Consensus Center.

Horton, Susan, Meera Shekar, Christine Donald, Ajay Mahal, and Jana Krystene Brooks. 2010. "Scaling Up Nutrition: What Will it Cost?" *The World Bank's Directions in Development: Human Development Series.*

Kenney, Catherine T. 2008. "Father Doesn't Know Best? Parents' Control of Money and Children's Food Insecurity." *Journal of Marriage and Family* 70:654–69.

Krishna, Anirudh. 2004. "Escaping Poverty and Becoming Poor: Who Gains, Who Loses, and Why?" *World Development* 32:121–36.

Krishna, Anirudh. 2007. "Poverty and Health: Defeating Poverty by Going to the Roots." *Development* 50:63–69.

Lautze, Sue, Winnie Bell, Luca Alinovi, and Luca Russo. 2012. "Early Warning, Late Response (Again): The 2011 Famine in Somalia." *Global Food Security* 1:43–49.

Lentz, Erin C. and Christopher B. Barrett. 2008. "Improving Food Aid: What Reforms Would Yield the Highest Payoff?" *World Development* 36:1152–72.

Lentz, Erin C. and Christopher B. Barrett. 2012. "The Economics and Nutritional Impacts of Food Assistance Policies and Programs." Background paper prepared for FAO's 2013 State of Food Security and Agriculture.

Lentz, Erin Christopher B. Barrett, Miguel Gomez, and Daniel Maxwell. 2013. "On the Choice and Impacts of Innovative International Food Assistance Instruments." *World Development* 49:1–8.

Malthus Thomas R. 1998 (1798). *An Essay on the Principle of Population.* The Electronic Scholarly Project: http://www.esp.org.

Maxwell, Daniel, Clement Ahiadeke, Carol Levin, Margaret Armar-Klemesu, Sawudatu Zakariah, and Grace M. Lamptey. 1999. "Alternative Food-security Indicators: Revisiting the Frequency and Severity of Coping Strategies." *Food Policy* 24:411–29.

Maxwell, Daniel G., Ben Watkins, Robin Wheeler, and Greg Collins. 2003. "The Coping Strategies Index: A Tool for Rapidly Measuring Food Security and the Impact of Food Aid Programs in Emergencies." Nairobi, Kenya: CARE and World Food Programme.

Maxwell, Daniel G. 1996. "Measuring Food Insecurity: The Frequency and Severity of 'Coping Strategies.'" *Food Policy* 21:291–303.

McMichael, Philip. 1995. *Food and Agrarian Orders in the World-economy.* Westport, CT: Greenwood.

McMichael, Philip. 2009. "A Food Regime Genealogy." *Journal of Peasant Studies* 36:139–69.

National Research Council. 2005. *Measuring Food Insecurity and Hunger, Phase 1 Report.* Washington, DC: National Academies Press.

Pinstrup-Andersen, Per. 1993. *The Political Economy of Food and Nutrition Policies.* Wallingford: CABI.

Pinstrup-Andersen, Per. 2007. "Agricultural Research and Policy for Better Health and Nutrition in Developing Countries: A Food Systems Approach," *Agricultural Economics* 37, S1:187–98.

Ravallion, Martin. 1997. "Famines and Economics." *Journal of Economic Literature* 35:1205–42.

Sen, A. 1981. *Poverty and Famines.* Oxford: Clarendon Press.

Rosen, Stacey; Birgit Meade, Shahla Shapouri, Anna D'Souza, and Nicholas Rada. 2012. "International Food Security Assessment." Outlook No. (GFA-23) 71, July.

Scanlan, Stephen J. 2009. "New Direction and Discovery on the Hunger Front: Toward a Sociology of Food Security/Insecurity." *Humanity and Society* 33:292–316.

Smith, Lisa C., Harold Alderman, and Dede Aduayom. 2006. *Food Insecurity in Sub-Saharan Africa: New Estimates from Household Expenditure Surveys.* Research Report 14. IFPRI: Washington, DC.

Thomas, Duncan and John Strauss. 1997. "Health and wages: Evidence on men and women in urban Brazil." *Journal of Econometrics* 77(1):159–85.

UNICEF. 2012. *The State of the World's Children 2012.*

Victora, Cesar G., Linda Adair, Caroline Fall, Pedro C. Hallal, Reynaldo Martorell, Linda Richter, and Harshpal S. Sachdev. 2008. "Maternal and Child Undernutrition: Consequences for Adult Health and Human Capital." *The Lancet* 371:340–57.

Villa, Kira M., Christopher B. Barrett, and David R. Just. 2011. "Whose Fast and Whose Feast? Intrahousehold Asymmetries in Dietary Diversity Response among East African Pastoralists." *American Journal of Agricultural Economics* 93(4):1062–81.

Webb, Patrick, Jennifer Coates, Edward A. Frongillo, Beatrice L. Rogers, Anne Swindale, and Paula Bilinsky. 2006. "Measuring Household Food Insecurity: Why It's So Important and Yet So Difficult to Do." *Journal of Nutrition* 136:1404–8.

Wilde, Parke and Mark Nord. 2005. "The effect of food stamps on food security: a panel data approach." *Applied Economic Perspectives and Policy* 27:425–32.

World Bank. 2006. *Repositioning Nutrition as Central to Development.* Washington, DC: World Bank.

Wunderlich, Gooloo S. and Janet L. Norwood. 2006. *Food Insecurity and Hunger in the United States: An Assessment of the Measure.* Washington, DC: National Academy Press.

CHAPTER 27

POVERTY AND CRIME

PATRICK SHARKEY, MAX BESBRIS, AND MICHAEL FRIEDSON

THE relationship between poverty and crime is complex. There is substantial evidence indicating that poverty is associated with criminal activity, but it is less clear that this relationship is causal or that higher levels of poverty in a neighborhood, a city, or a nation necessarily translate into higher levels of crime. Perhaps the most powerful illustration of this empirical reality comes from the simple observation made by Lawrence Cohen and Marcus Felson several decades ago in introducing their "routine activities theory" of crime. During the 1960s, when poverty and racial inequality were declining in American cities, the crime rate was rising (Cohen and Felson 1979). The experience during the economic downturn from 2008–2012 provides a more recent example. Despite the rise in poverty and sustained unemployment over these years, crime has not risen in any remarkable way. The implication is that in order to understand the relationship between poverty and crime it is necessary to move beyond the assumption that more poor people translates directly into more crime.

One of the major shifts in criminological thinking, spurred in large part by Cohen and Felson's ideas, is an expansion of focus beyond the characteristics or the motivations of potential offenders and toward a broader view of what makes an incident of crime more or less likely. This entails a shift from a focus on who is likely to commit a crime toward a focus on when, where, and why a crime is likely to occur (Birkbeck and LaFree 1993; Katz 1988; Wikström and Loeber 2000). The basic insight of routine activities theory is that the likelihood of a crime occurring depends on the presence of a motivated offender, a vulnerable victim, and the absence of a capable guardian (Sampson and Wikström 2008). Whereas traditional approaches to understanding crime focus primarily on the first element of this equation, the offender, these approaches ignore the two other moving parts: the vulnerable victim, and the presence or absence of capable guardians (Wikström et al. 2012).

The "situational" perspective on crime has important implications for understanding the complexities of the relationship between poverty and crime. It forces one to consider how poverty affects the motivations of offenders, how poverty affects the vulnerability and attractiveness of potential targets, and how poverty affects the presence of capable guardians. We will consider each of these issues throughout the chapter. The research that we review reinforces the point that crime cannot be understood primarily in terms of individual characteristics, incentives, or resources. It has to be understood in terms of situations, attachments, networks, and contexts. This insight is central to a wide range of research in the field, and it frames our approach to considering the relationship between poverty and crime.

In this chapter we review theory and evidence on the relationship between poverty and crime at the level of the individual and at the level of the community. We make no attempt to be comprehensive, but instead we focus on major patterns of findings in the literature and important theoretical and empirical advances and developments. The research that we review considers criminal activity and violent behavior, using self-reports or official records of violent offenses (homicide, assault, rape), property crime (burglary, theft, vandalism), and in some cases delinquency or victimization. This approach, which reflects the dominant focus of research in criminology and sociology, places less emphasis on (or ignores completely) other types of less visible, underreported or understudied criminal activity or deviant behavior, including crime or abuse committed by police or elected officials, domestic violence, crimes committed in prison, and many types of financial or "white-collar" crime. It is important to acknowledge that the disproportionate focus on what might be thought of as "street crime" is likely to lead to biased conclusions about the overall strength of the relationship between poverty and crime. This bias arises due to the dearth of research on crime occurring outside of low-income communities (most notably white-collar crime) and because of the use of official records to measure criminal activity. Official reports of arrests reflect some combination of criminal activity, enforcement, and reporting. These are potential sources of bias that are present in much of the criminological literature and thus are present in this review as well.

The chapter proceeds with a review of the literature on individual- or family-level poverty and crime. Although the literature demonstrates a consistent association between poverty and crime, there are multiple interpretations of this association that have been put forth in the literature. Poverty may lead directly to some types of criminal activity. However, the link between poverty and crime also may be spurious, or it may be mediated by other processes related to labor force attachment, family structure, or connections to institutions like the military or the labor market. We then move to the level of the neighborhood or community. Again, the literature shows a consistent positive association between community-level poverty and crime, although the functional form of this relationship is less settled. A prominent strand of research has argued that community-level social processes play a central role in mediating the association between poverty and crime, generating resurgent interest in the importance of social cohesion, informal social control, and other dimensions of community organization that help explain the link between poverty and crime.

Our review of the literature concludes by highlighting three shifts of thinking about the relationship between poverty and crime: (1) a shift away from the idea that criminal activity is located within the individual, and toward a perspective that locates the potential for criminal activity within networks of potential offenders, victims, and guardians; (2) a shift away from a focus on individual motivations and toward a focus on situations that make crime more or less likely; and (3) a shift away from a focus on aggregated deprivation as an explanation for concentrations of crime and toward a consideration of community social processes that make crime more or less likely.

INDIVIDUAL POVERTY AND CRIME

Evidence for a positive association between individual or family poverty and criminal offending is generally strong. A review of 273 studies assessing the association between different dimensions of social and economic status (SES) and offending concludes that there is consistent evidence from multiple national settings that individuals with low income, occupational status, and education have higher rates of criminal offending (Ellis and McDonald 2001). However, evidence based on self-reported data on delinquent behavior is less consistent (Tittle and Meier 1990; Wright et al. 1999). A recent study based on comparable surveys conducted in Greece, Russia, and Ukraine showed no consistent association between social and economic status and various self-reported measures of delinquent or criminal behavior (Antonaccio et al. 2010).

Given this conflicting evidence, it is important to clarify that the claims made in this section are based primarily on research that examines poverty or economic resources and that considers criminal offending as an outcome. Evidence for an association between economic resources and crime is more consistent across settings and is generally quite strong, particularly in the United States (Bjerk 2007). As a whole, however, the studies reviewed do not appear to provide strong evidence that these relationships are causal, nor is the overall association between poverty and crime particularly surprising—this association is consistent with virtually all individual- and family-level theories of criminal behavior. Poverty is associated with self-control and cognitive skills (Hirschi and Gottfredson 2001), with family structure and joblessness (Matsueda and Heimer 1987; Sampson 1987), with children's peer networks (Haynie 2001; Haynie, Silver, and Teasdale 2006), and with the type of neighborhoods in which families reside and the types of schools that children attend (Deming 2011; Wilson 1987). The association between individual poverty and criminal offending may reflect some combination of all of these pathways of influence.

Alternatively, poverty may have direct effects on crime if the inability to secure steady or sufficient financial resources leads individuals to turn to illicit activity to generate income or if relative poverty in the midst of a wealthy society generates psychological strain (Merton 1938). The "economic model of crime," put forth formally by economist Gary Becker (1974) and elaborated and refined by an array of criminologists (Clarke and Felson 1993; Cornish and Clarke 1986; Piliavin et al. 1986), suggests that crime can be explained as the product of a rational decision-making process in which potential offenders weigh the benefits and probable costs/risks of committing a crime or otherwise becoming involved in criminal activities (Becker 1974). Much of the research assessing the economic model of crime has focused on deterrence, or the question of whether raising the costs of criminal behavior reduces crime. However, the theory also has direct implications for the study of poverty and crime, as it suggests that individuals lacking economic resources should have greater incentives to commit crime. Despite the abundance of evidence for an association between economic resources and criminal offending, there is little convincing research demonstrating a direct causal effect. For instance, the experimental programs that are most frequently cited for evidence on the effect of income on various social outcomes—such as the income maintenance experiments of the 1970s or the state-level welfare reform experiments of the 1990s— did not assess impacts on crime (Blank 2002; Munnell 1987).

There are, however, a small number of studies that provide persuasive, if not definitive, evidence supporting a direct causal relationship between individual economic resources and crime. One example is a recent study that exploits differences in cities' public assistance payment schedules in order to assess whether crime rises at periods of the month when public assistance benefits are likely to be depleted. As predicted by the economic model, crimes that lead to economic gain tend to rise as the time since public assistance payments grows, while other types of crime not involving economic gain do not increase (Foley 2011). Another example comes from a set of experimental studies in which returning offenders from Georgia and Texas were randomly assigned to receive different levels of unemployment benefits immediately upon leaving prison, while members of the control group received job-placement counseling but no cash benefits (Berk, Lenihan, and Rossi 1980; see also Rossi, Berk, and Lenihan 1980). Although the results are generalizable only to returning offenders, they show that modest supplements of income reduce subsequent recidivism.

A larger base of evidence suggests that unemployment (and underemployment or low wages) is causally related to criminal offending, with a stronger relationship between unemployment and property crime as compared with violent crime (Chiricos 1987; Fagan and Freeman 1999; Grogger 1998; Levitt 2001; Raphael and Winter-Ebmer 2001). This finding from the quantitative literature finds support in ethnographic studies arguing that the absence of stable employment and income are important factors leading to participation in informal and illicit profit-seeking activity, ranging from drug distribution and burglary to participating in informal or underground economic markets (Bourgois 1995; Venkatesh 2006; Wright and Decker 1994).

The evidence linking unemployment with criminal behavior can be interpreted in multiple ways. Economists studying this relationship tend to view criminal activity as a substitute for employment in the formal labor market. From this perspective, individuals who cannot find work or whose wages are low, relative to opportunities in the informal or illicit labor market, are likely to choose criminal activity as an alternative (or supplemental) source of income (Fagan and Freeman 1999; Grogger 1998). Criminological and sociological perspectives acknowledge the importance of income as a mechanism underlying the relationship between joblessness and crime but view employment as one of many social bonds that connect individuals to other individuals and to institutions in ways that reduce the likelihood that they will become involved in criminal activity. In their life-course model of deviance and desistance, Robert Sampson and John Laub describe the set of attachments that individuals form at different stages in the life course, including college attendance, military service, and entrance into marriage (Sampson and Laub 1993, 1996; Laub and Sampson 2003). The formation and maintenance of individuals' bonds to romantic partners and family, to employers and institutions, and the informal social controls that arise from these social bonds do not only reduce the probability of criminal activity but also help explain patterns of desistance over time. Marriage and employment, for example, can alter the offending trajectory of individuals by serving as turning points from the past to the present, by increasing supervision and responsibilities, and by transforming roles and identities (Laub and Sampson 2003).

The implication is that the relationship between poverty and crime may not be direct and causal; it is plausible that this relationship may be indirect or even spurious. Unemployment is only one characteristic that may confound the relationship between poverty and crime, but there are many others. Growing up in a single-parent household or in a community dominated by single-parent households is strongly related to criminal activity and also is associated with poverty (Sampson 1987; Sampson and Wilson 1995). Association with delinquent peers is another potential confounder, as are cognitive skills, work ethic, and exposure to environmental toxins like lead or environmental stressors like violence (Anderson 1999; Matsueda 1982, 1988; Nevin 2007; Reyes 2007; Stretesky and Lynch 2001).

This discussion leaves us with three possible models of the relationship between individual or family poverty and crime. The first model posits that this relationship is direct and causal. In this model, which is reflected in the economic model of crime, poverty and the inability to secure stable and well-paid employment in the formal labor market provide greater incentives for individuals to commit crimes in order to generate income and associated benefits. The second model posits that the relationship between poverty and crime is mediated by other processes, such as the formation of social attachments to romantic partners, jobs, or institutions like the military. The third model posits that the association between poverty and crime is spurious and is the result of bias due to confounding factors. This model would suggest that poverty is linked with crime because it is associated with other criminogenic characteristics of the family or the individual.

The evidence available provides the strongest support for the first two models. Poverty is likely to be linked to crime both because the poor have greater incentives to commit crime and because poverty affects individuals' environments, their relationships, their developmental trajectories, and their opportunities as they move through different stages of the life course. The strongest evidence in support of this conclusion comes from the literature on unemployment, wages, and crime. However, there is very little convincing evidence that focuses purely on the direct effect of poverty on crime. We consider this to be an important gap in the literature.

COMMUNITY POVERTY AND CRIME

Despite the myriad ways that individual poverty may be linked with individual criminal activity, the aggregation of individuals who have greater incentives or propensity to commit crime does not necessarily lead to more crime in the aggregate. One simplistic illustration of why this is the case emerges when we return to the situational framework of offenders, victims, and guardians with which we began the chapter. Focusing in particular on the presence of attractive and vulnerable victims, one might conclude that in areas where poverty is concentrated there are likely to be fewer attractive victims vulnerable to potential offenders (Hannon 2002). If one were to consider only the second dimension of the crime equation, one might arrive at the hypothesis that in periods where poverty is rising or in places where poverty is concentrated there should be fewer crimes committed. Just as with theories that focus only on the prevalence of motivated offenders, this hypothesis is simplistic and incomplete.

Theories that focus exclusively on the number of potential offenders or the number of potential victims within a community are equally deficient because they do not consider the ecological context in which criminal activity takes place. Moving beyond the individual-level analysis of crime requires a consideration of social organization within the community; the enforcement of common norms of behavior by community residents, leaders, and police; the structure and strength of social networks within a community; and the relationships between residents, local organizations, and institutions within and outside the community (Sampson 2012; Sampson and Wikström 2008).

An illustrative example comes from the Moving to Opportunity (MTO) program, a social experiment that randomly offered vouchers to public housing residents in five cities that allowed them to move to low-poverty neighborhoods. The most common reason that families gave for volunteering for the program was that they wanted their children to be able to avoid the risks from crime, violence, and drugs in their origin neighborhoods (Kling, Liebman, and Katz 2007). However, when data on criminal activity were analyzed years later, the results showed that youth in families who had moved to neighborhoods with lower poverty were no less likely to report having been victimized or "jumped," seeing someone shot or stabbed, or taking part in violent activities themselves (Kling, Liebman, and Katz 2007; Kling, Ludwig, and Katz 2005). A complicated set of findings emerged, with very different patterns for girls and boys. Whereas girls reported feeling more safe in their new communities, boys in families that moved to low-poverty neighborhoods were less likely to have been arrested for violent crimes but more likely to be arrested for property crimes, to have a friend who used drugs, and to engage in risky behaviors themselves (Clampet-Lundquist et al. 2006; see also Sharkey and Sampson 2010).

The results from Moving to Opportunity reveal the complex ways in which individuals and aspects of their social environments interact to make crime more or less likely. Boys in families that moved to new environments may have changed their behavior with new opportunities for property crime available to them, but they may also have been subject to greater scrutiny from their new neighbors and from law enforcement. Girls in the same families were likely to be seen in a different light by neighbors and police, leading to different behavioral and social responses (Clampet-Lundquist et al. 2006). The interaction between the characteristics of youths themselves; the types of potential targets that existed in their new communities; and the level of supervision, suspicion, and policing in the new communities created an unexpected pattern of behavior within the new environment.

This example highlights the complexity of community-level models of poverty and crime. In an attempt to synthesize some of the core ideas that have been put forth in the criminological literature on community-level crime, we focus on three stylized facts that guide our discussion of the community-level relationship between poverty and crime. First, crime is clustered in space to a remarkable degree (Sampson 2012). This empirical observation has been made repeatedly by scholars in different settings and in different times, but the study of space and crime has been refined considerably in recent years. Crime is not only spatially clustered at the level of the neighborhood or community, but it is concentrated in a smaller number of "hot spots" within communities (Block and Block 1995; Sherman 1995; Sherman, Gartin, and Buerger 1989). The spatial dimension of crime leads to questions about the underlying mechanisms that might explain why certain spaces or areas appear to be criminogenic. Over the past few decades, the concentration of poverty has emerged as a primary explanatory mechanism.

This leads to our second stylized fact: the level of poverty in a community is strongly associated with the level of crime in the community (Patterson 1991; Krivo and Peterson 1996). This relationship is found not only in the United States but also in nations such as the Netherlands and Sweden, where the levels of concentrated poverty and violent crime are substantially lower (e.g., Sampson and Wikström 2008; Weijters, Scheepers, and Gerris 2009). Despite the robustness of this relationship across contexts, there is conflicting evidence on the functional form of this relationship. One of the central arguments in William Julius Wilson's classic book *The Truly Disadvantaged* (1987) was that urban poverty in the United States transformed in the post–civil rights period, and the new type of concentrated neighborhood poverty that emerged during this period led to the intensification of an array of social problems including a sharp rise in violent crime. Sampson and Wilson (1995) argue that areas of concentrated poverty provide a niche where role models for youth are absent and residents are less fervent in enforcing common norms of behavior, leading to elevated levels of crime. This argument has served as a primary explanation for the rise and concentration of urban crime from the 1960s through the 1990s, but it has been challenged recently by research investigating the form of the relationship between neighborhood poverty and crime. Analyzing data on neighborhood crime from 25 cities in 2000, Hipp and Yates (2011) find no evidence that crime rises sharply in extreme-poverty neighborhoods. All types of crime rise with the level of poverty in the neighborhood, but for most types this relationship levels off as the neighborhood poverty rate reaches 30 percent or higher. As the most rigorous study conducted to date on the form of the relationship between neighborhood poverty and crime, we believe the findings from this article should provoke further theoretical and empirical investigations into this important issue.

Discussions about the functional form of the relationship between community poverty and crime lead directly into a broader discussion about the mechanisms underlying this relationship. An extensive ethnographic literature demonstrates how the threat of violence can come to structure interpersonal interactions and outlooks in areas of extreme poverty, creating the need for individuals to take strategic steps to avoid violence (Anderson 1999; Harding 2010). The emergence of patterned responses to community-level poverty and violence involving the adoption of unique frames and repertoires of action becomes visible in this research, with consequences that can affect individual behavior and reinforce the atmosphere of threat, further weakening informal social controls and trust within the community (Anderson 1999; Small, Harding, and Lamont 2010).

The importance of community trust, social cohesion, and informal social controls has been theorized and analyzed in a resurgent literature on community social processes and crime and violence. The third stylized fact about communities and crime is that social processes at the level of the community appear to play a central role in mediating the association between poverty and crime. In their classic work on the organization of communities and rates of juvenile delinquency, Shaw and McKay (1942) argued that community organization is lower and crime and delinquency are higher in neighborhoods with low social and economic status, high levels of ethnic heterogeneity, and high levels of residential mobility. In the last few decades these ideas have served as the basis for a resurgent interest in the role that structural characteristics of communities play in facilitating informal social controls, in strengthening or weakening community organization, and in increasing or reducing crime (Sampson and Groves 1989; Sampson, Raudenbush, and Earls 1997).

The research of Robert Sampson and several colleagues lies at the heart of this resurgence. With the concept of collective efficacy, Sampson builds on the ideas of Shaw and McKay but puts forth a more refined theory of the role of community-level social processes in influencing patterns of crime and violence. In addition to the three dimensions of communities on which Shaw and McKay focused, this research analyzes the importance of family structure and rates of family disruption as central factors influencing the capacity of a community to supervise and monitor teenage peer groups and to establish intergenerational lines of communication, social cohesion, and informal social controls. The "social process turn" (Sampson, Morenoff, and Gannon-Rowley 2002) in research on neighborhoods and crime leads to a new understanding of the link between neighborhood poverty and crime. According to this perspective, neighborhood poverty is associated with criminal activity not because of the aggregation of motivated offenders, but rather because of community-level dynamics that create an environment in which informal social controls over activity in public space are weakened. Community-level poverty is linked with family structure, residential mobility, the density of housing, labor force detachment, physical disorder, legal cynicism, civic and political participation, and community organization, all of which are associated with crime (Hagan and Peterson 1995; Krivo and Peterson 1996; Sampson 2012; Sampson and Lauritsen 1994).

Comparative research is beginning to assess whether the focus on community social processes is applicable in different national settings. Some research using the same methods developed to study collective efficacy in Chicago suggests that the basic relationships are similar in very different places. For instance, in comparable studies conducted in Chicago and Stockholm, neighborhood collective efficacy was found to have a remarkably similar, inverse association with violent crime (Sampson and Wikström 2008). However, such similarities do not suggest that models of poverty, collective efficacy, and community violence can be blindly transferred across national contexts. In a study of Belo Horizonte, Brazil, Villarreal and Silva (2006) find that neighborhood social cohesion is not predictive of crime rates. In a context in which national policies have led to a retrenchment of public sector employment and the welfare state (Portes and Hoffman 2003), the authors argue that informal networks of reciprocity and exchange are central to community sustainability but also have led to a proliferation of informal labor market activity and have emerged at a time of rising crime and violence. This study provides an example of how the relationships among neighborhood social cohesion, neighborhood poverty, and crime may vary across different local or national contexts.

Summary of the Evidence and Three Shifts of Thinking

The evidence we have reviewed suggests a set of core findings that characterize the relationship between poverty and crime at the level of the individual and the community. First, poverty is strongly associated with crime at both levels of analysis. In the rational choice, or economic model, of crime, the individual-level relationship between poverty and criminal behavior is assumed to be direct and causal, but most theoretical models do not make this assumption. We have uncovered very little empirical research that provides convincing evidence for a direct causal relationship between individual poverty and criminal activity. Some suggestive research is consistent with a causal relationship, but most research does not assess it directly. Instead, most theoretical and empirical evidence suggest that poverty is linked with criminal behavior through individual characteristics and conditions associated with poverty, such as joblessness, family structure, peer networks, psychological strain, or exposure to intensely violent environments.

At the level of the community, there is again a strong relationship between poverty and aggregated rates of crime. However, the most prominent theoretical and empirical work on the topic suggests that this relationship is mediated by community-level social processes that facilitate social cohesion and trust and that act to limit criminal activity in the community. Poverty is thus viewed as one of several characteristics of communities that lead to the breakdown of community organization, in turn leading to higher rates of crime.

These findings lead us to identify three interrelated shifts of thinking that are central to understanding the relationship between poverty and crime. These shifts of thinking reflect the insights of criminologists that have been developed over the past several decades, but they may be less familiar to poverty researchers. The first is a shift away from thinking of the potential for crime as lying within the individual offender and instead thinking of the potential for crime as lying within networks of potential offenders, victims, and guardians situated within a diverse group of contexts and settings (Papachristos 2011; Wikström et al. 2012). The field of criminology has a long history of locating the source of criminal activity within the individual. Without denying the importance of individual characteristics in affecting the propensity for criminal activity, and without denying the agency of individual offenders, we argue that the traditionally dominant focus on the offender has stifled progress in understanding variation in crime across places and over time.

This point reflects a second shift of thinking, which involves moving from a focus on individual motivations to a focus on situations (Wikström et al. 2012). Applied to the study of poverty and crime, this shift moves away from the idea that crime is driven primarily by economic calculations. While economic benefit is one important motivation for potential offenders, even the rational choice paradigm has been extended to consider other types of noneconomic rewards arising from criminal offending (e.g., Cornish and Clarke 1986). The situational approach to crime, by contrast, expands beyond the motivations of individuals to consider the interactions of offenders, victims, and guardians. The role of poverty as a predictor of criminal offending is much more complex in the situational approach to crime. Poverty may produce more motivated offenders, fewer potential victims (for at least some types of crime), and less effective community guardians. Considered together, one would still expect an association between poverty and crime, but the mechanisms underlying this association are more complex than the economic model suggests.

The third shift of thinking moves beyond a focus on aggregated deprivation as an explanation for concentrations of crime and toward a consideration of community social processes (Sampson, Morenoff, and Gannon-Rowley 2002). Concentrated poverty is one of several characteristics of communities, along with others such as high levels of residential mobility, that tend to disrupt processes of informal social control and social cohesion within communities, or collective efficacy (Sampson, Raudenbush, and Earls 1997). The breakdown of collective efficacy provides the context for the emergence of crime and violence within the community, as informal controls over public space are less effective and violations of collective norms of behavior become common.

These three shifts of thinking reflect the findings from a complex theoretical and empirical literature on the relationship between poverty and crime. In the most simplistic model of this relationship, individual poverty causes individuals to commit more crime and the aggregation of poor individuals in a community, a city, or a nation translates directly into more crime. The experience of the United States over the last 50 years demonstrates that this model is not adequate. When poverty is high, crime does not necessarily rise with it. In critiquing the direct, linear, causal model of poverty and crime, we acknowledge that we do not have an equally simple model to replace it. Instead, we argue that the relationship is complex, that it is driven by a number of different mediating mechanisms, and that these mechanisms vary depending on the level of analysis (e.g., individuals, neighborhoods, nations, etc.). While this may not be a particularly satisfying conclusion, the evidence available suggests that it is the most realistic.

REFERENCES

Anderson, Elijah. 1999. *Code of the Street: Decency, Violence, and the Moral Life of the Inner City.* New York: W. W. Norton.

Antonaccio, Olena, Charles R. Tittle, Ekaterina Botchkovar, and Maria Kranidiotis. 2010. "The Correlates of Crime and Deviance: Additional Evidence." *Journal of Research in Crime and Delinquency* 47(3):297–28.

Becker, Gary S. 1974. "Crime and Punishment: An Economic Approach." Pp. 1–54 in *Essays in the Economics of Crime and Punishment* edited by Gary S. Becker and William M. Landes. Cambridge: National Bureau of Economic Research.

Berk, Richard A., Kenneth J. Lenihan and Peter H. Rossi. 1980. "Crime and Poverty: Some Experimental Evidence from Ex-Offenders." *American Sociological Review* 45(5):766–86.

Birkbeck, Christopher and Gary LaFree. 1993. "The Situational Analysis of Crime and Deviance." *Annual Review of Sociology* 19:113–37.

Bjerk, David. 2007. "Measuring the Relationship between Youth Criminal Participation and Household Economic Resources." *Journal of Quantitative Criminology* 23(1):23–39.

Blank, Rebecca M. 2002. "Evaluating Welfare Reform in the United States." *Journal of Economic Literature* 40(4):1105–66.

Block, Richard and Carolyn R. Block. 1995. "Space, Place and Crime: Hot Spot Areas and Hot Places of Liquor-Related Crime." Pp. 145–83 in *Crime and Place*, edited by J. E. Eck and D. Weisburd (Crime Prevention Studies, Vol. 4). Washington, DC: Criminal Justice Press.

Bourgois, Philippe. 1995. *In Search of Respect: Selling Crack in El Barrio.* Cambridge: Cambridge University Press.

Chiricos, Theodore G. 1987. "Rates of Crime and Unemployment: An Analysis of Aggregate Research Evidence." *Social Problems* 34(2):187–212.

Clampet-Lundquist, Susan, Kathryn Edin, Jeffrey R. Kling, and Greg J. Duncan. 2006. "Moving At-Risk Teenagers Out of High-Risk Neighborhoods: Why Girls Fare Better Than Boys." Working paper No. 509. Princeton, NJ: Industrial Relations Section, Princeton University.

Clarke, Ronald V. and Marcus Felson. 1993. *Routine Activity and Rational Choice: Advances in Criminological Theory.* New Brunswick, NJ: Transaction.

Cohen, Lawrence E. and Marcus Felson. 1979. "Social Change and Crime Rate Trends: A Routine Activity Approach." *American Sociological Review* 44(4):588–608.

Cornish, Derek B. and Ronald V. Clarke. 1986. *The Reasoning Criminal: Rational Choice Perspectives on Offending.* Secaucus, NJ: Springer-Verlag.

Deming, David J. 2011. "Better Schools, Less Crime?" *The Quarterly Journal of Economics* 126:2063–2115.

Ellis, Lee and James N. McDonald. 2001. "Crime, Delinquency, and Social Status: A Reconsideration." *Journal of Offender Rehabilitation* 32(3):23–52.

Fagan, Jeffrey and Richard B. Freeman. 1999. "Crime and Work." *Crime and Justice* 25:225–90.

Foley, Fritz. 2011. "Welfare Payments and Crime." *Review of Economics and Statistics* 93(1):97–112.

Grogger, Jeff. 1998. "Market Wages and Youth Crime." *Journal of Labor Economics* 16(4):756–91.

Hagan, John and Ruth D. Peterson. 1995. "Criminal Inequality in America: Patterns and Consequences." Pp. 14–36 in *Crime and Inequality*, edited by John Hagan and Ruth D. Peterson. Stanford, CA: Stanford University Press.

Hannon, Lance. 2002. "Criminal Opportunity Theory and the Relationship between Poverty and Property Crime." *Sociological Spectrum* 22:363–81.

Harding, David J. 2010. *Living the Drama: Community, Conflict, and Culture among Inner-City Boys.* Chicago: University of Chicago Press.

Haynie, Dana L. 2001. "Delinquent Peers Revisited: Does Network Structure Matter?" *American Journal of Sociology* 106(4):1013–57.

Haynie, Dana L., Eric Silver, and Brent Teasdale. 2006. "Neighborhood Characteristics, Peer Networks, and Adolescent Violence." *Journal of Quantitative Criminology* 22(2):147–69.

Hipp, John and Daniel Yates. 2011. "Ghettos, Thresholds, and Crime: Does concentrated poverty really have an accelerating increasing effect on crime?" *Criminology* 49(4):955–90.

Hirschi, Travis and Michael Gottfredson. 2001. "Self-Control Theory." Pp. 81–96 in *Explaining Criminals and Crime: Essays in Contemporary Criminological Theory*, edited by Raymond Pasternoster and Ronet Bachman. Cary: Roxbury.

Katz, Jack. 1988. *The Seductions of Crime: Moral and Sensual Attractions in Doing Evil.* New York: Basic Books.

Kling, Jefrey, Jeffrey Liebman, and Lawrence Katz. 2007. "Experimental Analysis of Neighborhood Effects." *Econometrica* 75(1):83–119.

Kling, J. R., J. Ludwig, and L. Katz. 2005. "Neighborhood Effects on Crime for Female and Male Youth: Evidence from a Randomized Housing Voucher Experiment." *Quarterly Journal of Economics* 120(1):87–130.

Krivo, Lauren J. and Ruth D. Peterson. 1996. "Extremely Disadvantaged Neighborhoods and Urban Crime." *Social Forces* 75(2):619–48.

Laub, John H. and Robert J. Sampson. 2003. *Shared Beginnings, Divergent Lives: Delinquent Boys to Age 70.* Cambridge, MA: Harvard University Press.

Levitt, Steven D. 2001. "Alternative Strategies for Identifying the Link between Unemployment and Crime." *Journal of Quantitative Criminology* 17(4):377–90.

Matsueda, Ross L. 1982. "Testing Control Theory and Differential Association: A Causal Modeling Approach." *American Sociological Review* 47(4):489–507.

Matsueda, Ross L. 1988. "The Current State of Differential Association Theory." *Crime & Delinquency* 34(3):277–306.

Matsueda, Ross L. and Karen Heimer. 1987. "Race, Family Structure, and Delinquency: A Test of Differential Association and Social Control Theories." *American Sociological Review* 52(6):826–40.

Merton, Robert K. 1938. "Social Structure and Anomie." *American Sociological Review* 3(5):672–82.

Munnell, Alicia H. 1987. *Lessons from the Income Maintenance Experiments.* Boston: Federal Reserve Bank of Boston.

Nevin, Rick. 2007. "Understanding International Crime Trends: The Legacy of Preschool Lead Exposure." *Environmental Research* 101(3):315–36.

Papachristos, Andrew V. 2011. "The Coming of a Networked Criminology?" *Advances in Criminological Theory* 17:101–40.

Piliavin, Irving, Rosemary Gartner, Craig Thornton, Ross L. Matsueda. 1986. "Crime, Deterrence, and Rational Choice." *American Sociological Review* 51(1):101–19.

Patterson, E. Britt. 1991. "Poverty, Inequality, and Community Crime Rates." *Criminology* 29(4):755–76.

Portes, Alejandro and Kelly Hoffman. 2003. "Latin America Class Structures: Their Composition and Changes during the Neoliberal Era." *Latin America Research Review* 38:41–82.

Raphael, Steven and Rudolf Winter-Ebmer. 2001. "Identifying the Effect of Unemployment on Crime." *Journal of Law and Economics* 44(1):259–83.

Reyes, Jessica Wolpaw. 2007. "Environmental Policy as Social Policy? The Impact of Childhood Lead Exposure on Crime." Working Paper 13097. Cambridge, National Bureau of Economic Research.

Rossi, Peter H., Richard A. Berk, and Kenneth J. Lenihan. 1980. *Money, Work, and Crime: Some Experimental Results.* New York: Academic Press.

Sampson, Robert J. 1987. "Urban Black Violence: The Effect of Male Joblessness and Family Disruption." *American Journal of Sociology* 93(2):348–82.

Sampson, Robert J. 2012. *Great American City: Chicago and the Enduring Neighborhood Effect.* Chicago: University of Chicago Press.

Sampson, Robert J. and Byron Groves. 1989. "Community Structure and Crime: Testing Social Disorganization Theory." *American Journal of Sociology* 94(4):774–802.

Sampson, Robert J. and John H. Laub. 1993. *Crime in the Making: Pathways and Turning Points through Life.* Cambridge, MA: Harvard University Press.

Sampson, Robert J. and John H. Laub. 1996. "Socioeconomic Achievement in the Life Course of Disadvantaged Men: Military Service as a Turning Point, circa 1940–1965." *American Sociological Review* 61:347–67.

Sampson, Robert J. and Janet L. Lauritsen. 1994. "Violent Victimization and Offending: Individual-, Situational-, and Community-level Risk Factors." Pp. 1–114 in *Understanding and Preventing Violence: Social Influences* (Vol. 3), edited by Albert J. Reiss Jr. and Jeffrey Roth. (National Research Council.) Washington, DC: National Academy Press.

Sampson, Robert J., Jeffrey D. Morenoff, and Thomas Gannon-Rowley. 2002. "Assessing 'Neighborhood Effects': Social Processes and New Direction in Research." *Annual Review of Sociology* 28:443–78.

Sampson, Robert J. and Per-Olof Wikström. 2008. "The Social Order of Violence in Chicago and Stockholm Neighborhoods: A Comparative Inquiry." Pp. 97–119 in *Order, Conflict, and Violence*, edited by I. Shapiro, S. Kalyvas, and T. Masoud. New York and Cambridge: Cambridge University Press.

Sampson, Robert J., Stephen W. Raudenbush, and Felton Earls. 1997. "Neighborhoods and Violent Crime: A Multilevel Study of Collective Efficacy." *Science* 277:918–24.

Sampson, Robert J. and William Julius Wilson. 1995. "Toward a Theory of Race, Crime, and Urban Inequality." Pp. 37–54 in *Crime and Inequality*, edited by John Hagan and Ruth D. Peterson. Stanford, CA: Stanford University Press.

Sharkey, Patrick and Robert J. Sampson. 2010. "Destination Effects: Residential Mobility and Trajectories of Adolescent Violence in a Stratified Metropolis." *Criminology* 48:639–81.

Shaw, Clifford and Henry McKay. 1942. *Juvenile Delinquency and Urban Areas: A Study of Rates of Delinquency in Relation to Differential Characteristics of Local Communities in American Cities*. Chicago: University of Chicago Press.

Sherman, Lawrence W. 1995. "Hot Spots of Crime and Criminal Careers of Places." Pp. 35–52 in *Crime and Place*, edited by J. E. Eck and D. Weisburd. (Crime Prevention Studies, Vol. 4). Washington, DC: Criminal Justice Press.

Sherman, Lawrence W., Patrick R. Gartin, and Michael E. Buerger. 1989. "Hot Spots of Predatory Crime: Routine Activities and the Criminology of Place." *Criminology* 27(1):27–55.

Small, Mario, David J. Harding, and Michele Lamont. 2010. "Reconsidering Culture and Poverty" *Annals of the American Academy of Political and Social Science* 629(1):6–27.

Stretesky, Paul B. and Michael J. Lynch. 2001. "The Relationship between Lead Exposure and Homicide." *Archives of Pediatric and Adolescent Medicine* 155:579–82.

Tittle, Charles R. and Robert F. Meier. 1990. "Specifying the SES/Delinquency Relationship." *Criminology* 28:271–99.

Venkatesh, Sudhir. 2006. *Off the Books: The Underground Economy of the Urban Poor*. Cambridge, MA: Harvard University Press.

Villarreal, A. and B. F. Silva. 2006. "Social Cohesion, Criminal Victimization and Perceived Risk of Crime in Brazilian Neighborhoods." *Social Forces* 84(3):1725–53.

Weijters, Gijs, Peer Scheepers, and Jan Gerris. 2009. "City and/or Neighbourhood Determinants?: Studying Contextual Effects on Youth Delinquency." *European Journal of Criminology* 6(5):439–55.

Wikström, Per-Olof H., Dietrich Oberwittler, Kyle Treiber, and Beth Hardie. 2012. *Breaking Rules: The Social and Situational Dynamics of Young People's Urban Crime*. Oxford: Oxford University Press.

Wikström, Per-Olof H. and Rolf Loeber. 2000. "Do Disadvantaged Neighborhoods Cause Well-Adjusted Children to Become Adolescent Delinquents? A Study of Male Juvenile Serious Offending, Individual Risk and Protective Factors, and Neighborhood Context." *Criminology* 38(4):1109–42.

Wilson, William J. 1987. *The Truly Disadvantaged*. Chicago: University of Chicago Press.

Wright, Richard T. and Scott H. Decker. 1994. *Burglars on the Job: Streetlife and Residential Break-Ins*. Boston: Northeastern University Press.

Wright, Bradley R. Entner, Avshalom Caspi, Terrie E. Moffitt, Richard A. Miech, and Phil A. Silva. 1999. "Reconsidering the Relationship between SES and Delinquency: Causation but Not Correlation." *Criminology* 37(1):175–94.

CHAPTER 28

....

POVERTY AND INFORMAL ECONOMIES

....

FRANCOIS BONNET AND SUDHIR VENKATESH

INTRODUCTION

....

INFORMAL economic activity is a significant part of world production and distribution. The most comprehensive recent study is by Elgin and Oztunali (2012), in which the shadow economy is estimated to be approximately 23 percent of world GDP. Informal economies occupy a central role in the lives of the poor. Low-income households depend on various forms of unregulated work to make ends meet. Criminal activities such as drug trafficking, theft, or credit card fraud typically make headlines because of the risks involved and the deleterious impact on communities. For the urban poor, these activities can bring significant resources into the home—and they carry significant social costs, but they do not constitute the bulk of underground revenue generation.

Criminal activities are only a small subset of the ways in which informal economies penetrate the lives of low-income households. Much more common are socially legitimate activities, such as hairstyling or gypsy cab driving, whose principal legal infraction arises because individuals fail to report their income to the state and other regulatory agencies. Among these socially legitimate activities, some lack certification and licenses, while others depend on the infringement of regulation to be competitive (e.g., labor laws, sanitation codes). For all, their formalization could require not only a complete overhaul of the activity, but it also may end up creating additional costs that might eclipse the benefits for individual participants.

There are several phrases commonly used to describe informal economic activities, including the black market, underground economy, and shadow economy. Their particular meaning varies by country of usage and by social context.[1] There are some important distinctions in usage that we address in this chapter. In most definitions, constituent economic activity typically refers to unregulated income generation that are de jure illegal or that are legal but whose mode of operation does not fall under a formal regulatory body.

The purpose of this essay is to understand how the informal economy matters in the context of poverty and social inequality. We divide the presentation in three sections. The first section presents a brief history of the concept and related theoretical perspectives and controversies. The second deals with the informal economic activities among the urban poor. Finally, we conclude by reviewing methodological challenges and research priorities for the coming period of social science research on the urban poor.

Defining Informal Economies

The Informal Economy between Informal Activities and the Informal Sector

The concept of informal economic revenue generation appears under a variety of conceptual guises (Losby et al. 2002:1; Venkatesh 2008). Attention to such activities became popular in the social science literature after the Second World War as global national productivity seemed to be running alongside a second, parallel stream of commerce that was suggestive of the kind of traditional highly localized economies one found in premodern civilizations (Valentine 1978; Marable 1983; Fusfield and Bates 1984).

The first author to (explicitly) mention informal economic activities is Keith Hart (1973), a social anthropologist. During the 1960s, Hart conducted fieldwork among the Frafras, a group of poor Ghanaian migrants who moved about from rural districts to Accra (Ghana's capital) in search of material opportunities. Hart wrote, "Does the 'reserve army of urban unemployed and underemployed' really constitute a passive, exploited majority in cities like Accra, or do their informal economic activities possess some autonomous capacity for generating growth in the incomes of the urban (and rural) poor?" (Hart 1973:61).

Hart had identified practices rather than a coherent system of material interrelationships. Hart was studying income generation using the household as a unit of analysis. He described how poor people facing a context of low wages, inflation, and lack of safety nets would engage in creative ways to make ends meet. At the same time, the International Labor Organization (ILO) launched the World Employment Program, which spurred a set of studies in the third world. The Kenya Report (ILO 1972) featured an entire chapter (pp. 223–32) on the "informal sector" (defined as tax evasion and lack of government regulation) that emphasized its innovativeness and dynamism.

Hart's research did not speak of the informal economy but of "informal economic activities" or "income opportunities." By contrast, ILO's Kenya Report, focusing on firms (not households), aimed at describing an entire economic *sector*. Specifically, in the ILO's view, developing economies featured a "modern sector," which looked like a capitalist, rational, formal, modern, Western economy, and a "traditional sector," with small units of production, low productivity, and little state regulation (Lautier 1994).

This initial distinction between practices and economic sector would open up a fertile analytic debate for decades. Viewed as *activities*, the informal sector becomes a hodgepodge of activities that are only linked to one another by their common auspice as helping individuals make sporadic revenue necessary for survival. Various social scientists pursued these adaptive mechanisms because they helped to counter a dominant discourse that portrayed the poor as lazy or unable to work (see Stack 1974; Valentine 1978). By contrast, those who viewed the unregulated practices as a distinct *sector* tended to focus on the formal properties of constituent markets: how big they were, what kinds of pricing and contracts defined them, and what models were needed to estimate their impact on any particular nation. While these two lines of thought are not necessarily mutually exclusive, in practice, there have been two distinct streams of social science activity in which the research has not engaged one another in any significant manner. One school of thought, rooted in the discipline of economics, has focused on measurement and national-level impact. By contrast, another—at the intersection of sociology and anthropology—has sought to determine the practical consequence of such economies on the daily lives of those in low-income households and communities.

Among those who see the informal economy as a distinct sector, there has been a tendency to simply rule out all activities that are by definition illegal. Thus, the influential work of Castell and Portes (1989) does not include a wide range of behavior, from drug trafficking to sex work, as falling within the "informal economy." Scholars distinguish licit from illicit exchange in order to separate "informal" from "criminal" pursuits (Centano and Portes 2006). That is, Portes and Castells (1989) differentiate criminal economies from clandestine exchange that would otherwise be legitimate if licenses were obtained and revenue was reported to government bodies. For those who adopt this perspective, "crime" constitutes a more serious moral as well as a legal violation, and so must be kept distinct. Most literature reviews (Losby et al. 2002; Chen et al. 2002; Gërxhani 2004) exclude criminal activities from a meaningful definition of the informal economy.

Such differentiation of economic pursuits by the legitimacy of the good or service being exchanged ultimately has limited analytic purchase. We would hold that a priori definitional distinctions between licit and illicit is only marginally helpful when trying to understand social inequality and poverty—we will return to this issue in our concluding discussion of methodology. In fact, such a framework falls under sharp criticism by the in situ concrete overlap among legitimate and various illegitimate practices that characterize the daily lives of low-income households (Valentine 1978; Edin and Lein 1997; Venkatesh 2006). In practice, studies show that for poor people, a variety of resources come into the home—monetary, barter, shared property and assets, and so forth. These goods and services cannot be neatly differentiated by their licit or illicit provenance.

Thus, as a foundation for sociological analysis, making such distinctions will be only minimally helpful. Rather than differentiating one practice from another on the basis of moral criteria, it may be more fruitful to consider the ways that informal economies (including criminal enterprises) participate in the full economic profile of a society and the overall social reproduction of the poor. Other scholars have adopted the view that the entire range of unregulated work should be considered without a priori analytic bias; this view has tended to support an examination of the impact of informal work on households and individuals (Gaughan and Ferman 1987).

Three Types of Informal Economies and Their Corresponding Problems

Within the diversity of informal activities, we distinguish three types, each of which corresponds to a distinct scientific problem. The first is the informal economy in the third world, to which corresponds a problem of development. The second is the "second economy" in the Soviet Union, which complicates the question of the relationship between formal and informal. The third is the informal economy in contemporary Western societies.

The informal economy has first been studied in the third world (ILO 1972; Hart 1973) in the context of development studies. Early economic theories of development, based on Rostow's stages of growth model, conceptualize development as a sequence of stages, from traditional rural economy to advanced postindustrial societies of mass consumption. An entire field of study has been devoted to the fate of rural migrants to rapidly developing cities who are less pulled by the development of industry than pushed by misery, desertification, mechanization of agriculture, unfair competition from mechanized and subsidized Western agriculture, and the consequences of structural adjustment programs. Many of these urban dwellers live in informal settlements (slums) and live off informal activities. Debates mostly concern the question of whether the informal economy is an obstacle or an opportunity for development.

A second context of scholarly study of the informal economy is the "second economy" in Soviet Union before the fall of communism in Eastern Europe. Grossman (1977:25) defined the second economy as the set of activities that were for private gain and/or that were against the law. This definition included theft of state property, corruption, and crime, but also—and more interesting to Grossman—economic exchange where "demand-and-supply relations reign almost supreme." Some of these transactions were tolerated if they remained discreet, some were actively prosecuted, and some "economic crime" was met with the firing squad (Grossman 1977). Doctors, teachers, and tailors moonlighted for private gain; construction, home repair, and renting apartments were most likely done in "semilegal" ways (Katsenelinboigen 1977; 1990); creative ways of stealing from the company were found to supplement the income of indispensable employees, such as good chauffeurs; and illegal flea markets made available goods that were impossible to find otherwise (Grossman 1977; Katsenelinboigen 1990). For instance, a kiosk woman in Romania was renting her one copy of *Newsweek* by the hour (Sampson 1987:136). As Grossman (1977:29) argues: "The enormous variety and occasional complexity of illegal and semi-legal activities . . . appear to be limited only by human ingenuity, though, naturally, the most ingenious schemes, being pre-sumably also the more successful ones, tend to escape identification by Soviet authori-ties and detached observer alike." Instead of being a residue of presocialist mentality, the "second economy" was thriving. What made the second economy so fascinating to Russian émigrés and American economists was that it worked under the supply-and-demand market assumptions of modern capitalism, disproving the viability of a centrally planned economy not only because it addressed its shortcomings, but also because it was an "island of capitalism" in nature (Sampson 1987). Grossman (1977:40) and Stark (1989:657) analyzed the second economy as (respectively) a "spontaneous surrogate economic reform" and a "force of marketization."

A third line of research on informal economies focuses on advanced postindustrial societies. Here, the efforts can be subdivided in several categories. On the one hand, Sassen and others have focused on informalization in global cities (see discussion of structuralist perspectives below). They do not necessarily equate informalization with the urban poor, but they are careful to note that such economic spheres have very unstable work arrangements and can be exploitative. A second line of inquiry has focused specifically on the urban poor (Stack 1974; Valentine 1978; Fusfield and Bates 1984; Venkatesh 2006; Duneier1999). This research has continued apace since the 1960s when scholars realized that pockets of poverty persisted midst postwar affluence. In this tradition, the growth of an informal sector is linked to the demise of Fordist models of employment (job security, strong unions) and the persistence of concen-trated poverty that requires individuals to look for alternate means of social reproduc-tion. Informality is a means of survival among disenfranchised populations but also a factor reproducing their alienation from the social mainstream. As such, scholars view informal economies as both cause and consequence of inequality. A final area of inquiry focuses primarily on macroeconomic effects of informal economic activity. Here, the principal concern has been to understand how much revenue and manpower is not accounted for in standard economic models—and, in turn, what tax loss is being incurred by governments. There is only tangential concern in such studies for the fate of low-income populations.

Theoretical Perspectives and Controversies

The typology of Chen, Jhabvala, and Lund (2002:6) offers a useful starting point for a discussion of the relationship of informality and inequality. The authors outline a three-part categorization of informal economic activity based on the premise that the informal economy and mainstream economy must be thought of in relationship to one another. This relationship is *dualist, legalist, or structuralist* depending on the relation-ship of illegitimate and legitimate modes of exchange.

1. The *dualist* (or *development*) perspective on informal economies builds on the central theoretical contributions of dual labor market theory (Doeringer and

Piore 1971). This perspective adheres to a conventional labor market classification. Namely, the primary sector includes well-paying legitimate jobs; a secondary sector is based on unskilled, temporary employment; and finally the informal sector and the illegal criminal sector make up the remainder (see also Losby et al. 2002). In the dualist perspective, the informal economy is thought to function more or less independently of the legitimate sector. There is relatively little interest among proponents of this view for overlaps and permeable boundaries.

This perspective tends to conflate informal economic activity with the survival practices of low-income populations—as opposed to, say, white-collar underground revenue generation, organized crime, or gambling across income strata. The poor are presumed to work irregularly, if at all, in legitimate jobs, and so the informal economy becomes their principal space for earning revenue for basic survival (Marcelli, Pastor, and Joassart 1999). The notion is that the informal economy is a safety net for the poor (see also Ferman, Henry, and Hoyman 1987; Stack 1974).

Not surprisingly, perhaps, dualist perspectives draw a sharp contrast between the informal economy of developing countries, where basic survival is a concern for a much larger sub-population (compared to developed countries), and advanced industrialized countries, where the externalities of market vicissitudes occasionally drive people into the underground sector. For instance (and according to estimations), the informal economy represents 12 percent of the GDP of OECD countries, 25 percent of the former Soviet Union's, and 44 percent of Africa's (Gerxhani 2004:268).

A drawback of this perspective is that it ignores the many ways in which low-income populations are central to both formal and informal economies. Low-income populations are critical both in terms of provision of labor in the mainstream economy and as consumers. Despite the recognition of the use of unregulated work for survival, the dualist perspective can lead to arbitrary and rigid classifications that isolate the poor into a distinct economic realm.

In addition, informality is a legal construct, not an indicator of vulnerability. There are many ways in which nonmainstream activities can be undertaken by individuals who are not in materially disadvantageous positions. And some such activities may be quite rewarding despite the risks involved. Examples include successful street vendors and food-carts, off-the-book plumbing and home maintenance service, and high-end sex work.[2]

2. The *legalist* (or *neoliberal*) perspective originates in the work of Hernando De Soto (1989). Unlike the dualist perspective, the legalist view places heavy emphasis on the role of the state, particularly in terms of state regulations that support the creation and maintenance of economic activity. Indeed, in this view, some scholars have gone so far as to write, "the relationship of the informal economy and the state is, by definition, one of inevitable conflict" (Centano and Portes 2006:30).

De Soto argued that informal economies were neither a function of poverty nor a structural necessity of late capitalism. Instead, he suggested that informality is a choice made by rational actors facing a legal environment that hinders creative entrepreneurship. Thus, if the state is not seen as welcoming particular forms of material gain, those so interested will move underground to pursue their interests.

De Soto focused specifically on the Peruvian context. He argued that the country's poor would forgo developing their ventures in an unregulated realm if they believed that the state could operate in a uncorrupt fashion. Instead, low-income persons found government bureaucracies with little interest in supporting their needs. To model their argument, De Soto and his team of researchers conducted an experiment. They established a small clothing factory as a means of gauging the challenges of working with the Peruvian state bureaucracy. Using bribes only when absolutely necessary, it took 289 man-days to complete the task, which De Soto found to be an unnecessarily long time. In this manner, De Soto argued that the informal economic activities of the poor were the behavior of market actors rationally responding to economic incentives.

The legalist perspective holds that low-income populations can be understood as more than simply survivalists—which is the dominant characterization of the dualist view. Instead, the poor are innovators and rational actors who are realizing aspirations that would be recognizable to anyone in that society. What the poor lack however—and what distinguishes them from other classes—is support from the state for their property rights and enforcement of the contracts they develop in their petty accumulation strategies. Without this backing, the poor are assigned to work in economic sectors that are inherently stable and on the societal margins.

Adherents to this legalist perspective also argue that the informal economy should not necessarily be viewed as a social problem. Instead of being policed and eradicated, it should be supported and formalized (see Gerxhani 2004:286–92 for a discussion). And, conversely, limiting the deleterious consequences of excessive state regulation would help reduce the number of low-income households who end up turning away from the mainstream for their material pursuits. In other words, in the legalist perspective, advancing the interests of low-income populations is best pursued by formalizing their inclusion into the economy via state-based supports.

Formalization includes giving economic actors on the fringes access to modern legal institutions of capitalism such as credit, legitimate property rights, bankruptcy laws, commercial laws, and the power of enforceable contracts—all of which can support regulated accumulation.[3]

A criticism of the legalist perspective is the failure to discuss how the basic organization of capitalism creates the conditions for some families to rely on informal work, where violence and extortion are ever present, and where women and children are particularly likely to suffer exploitation (Davis 2006:179). Competition among the poor makes income minimal, which explains why many people turn to "gambling, pyramid schemes, lotteries, and other quasi-magical forms of wealth appropriation" (Davis 2006:183).

In addition, simply legitimating the commerce of low-income populations by granting property rights and official titles may not be feasible as a policy approach to inequality (Gilbert 2002). While the formalization of informal activities is a key medium to enable poor people to trade their assets—as proponents of the legalist perspective contend—it is not the case that all economic actors who work informally want to accumulate capital and enter mainstream markets. Many may prefer the capacity for flexible work, on a temporary basis, that enables them to bring resources into the home as needed. The rigidity of wage labor that is recorded on the books, and the expense of contracts, may end up increasing their vulnerability.

3. The *structuralist* (or *neo-Marxist*) perspective, championed by Castells and Portes (1989; Portes and Sassen-Koob 1987) deviates from both dualist and legalist perspectives. The informal economy in advanced countries enables capitalists to reproduce "uncontrolled, exploitative relationships of production" by doing away with labor unions, and labor, health, and environmental regulations. Capitalists are thus able to cut costs and increase their competitiveness (Portes and Walton 1981) "under the auspices of government tolerance" (Castells and Portes 1989:27). Workers— especially, but not only, undocumented migrants—experience "downgraded labor" (Sassen-Koob 1984). In this perspective, informalization is a logical development of the shifting needs of capitalism. The need to reduce the production costs of commodities motivates industrialists to use informality as a cost-saving principle (Sassen 1994, 1997).

The structuralist perspective has been particularly attractive for scholars observing so-called global cities in which the fast pace of economic change results in off-the-books activity that is virtually impossible to regulate through conventional means. Informality enables newcomers, such as immigrants and undocumented workers, to quickly establish a foothold via their inclusion in mainstream economic circuits— albeit in a way that can be exploitative.

Structuralists criticize dualist perspectives by equating the informal economy with poverty. As Castells and Portes write, "We depart from the notions of economic dualism and social marginality which have been so pervasive in the development literature" (1989:12). Portes and Sassen-Koob (1987) make a distinction between informal entrepreneurs and informal workers; the former are more likely to benefit from informality (no taxes, no regulations, no unions), and the latter are more likely to be exploited. The distinction between entrepreneur and workers is a notable attempt at defining the informal economy because it underlines how the label "informal economy" mixes up vastly different situations.[4]

The idea of the informal economy as fundamentally exploitative and being functional to the needs of late capitalism contrasts with the notion that informality may be understood as a "popular economy," or a "counter-economy." In this latter view, the formal sector is the locus of capitalism, rational calculation, and contractual relations, while the informal economy gives rise to solidarity, deepened and enhanced social bonds, in particular at the local and familial level (Lautier 1994). In England for instance, research of 511 respondents from poor and rich neighborhoods found that the rich and the poor equally use off-the-books labor. However, the rich favor market-like economic relations, and they quit using informal arrangements once their needs have been met. Such instrumentalism is not present among the lower income populations, for whom informal arrangements are means to strengthen social relations among friends and relatives (Williams and Windebank 2001).

The American version of this can be traced back to the post-1960s societal concern with the social exclusion of the native black population. The state of black America led to concerns that an alternative form of capitalism—criminal, immoral, primitive—was holding back social progress in low-income ghettos. A dominant view was that an "underground economy" saturated black, urban communities such that mainstream economic progress was being hampered. Against this perspective, various scholars argued that black Americans were more than capable of sustaining legitimate, mainstream forms of accumulation (Cross 1969; Fusfeld and Bates 1984; Gaughan and Ferman 1987). Some anthropologists suggested that the material foundations of black ghettos as a whole should be thought of via the dualist perspective: as different, not necessarily as deficient (Hannerz 1969; Stack 1974). In subsequent periods, studies of the underground economy in the United States became primarily opportunities to publicize the hardships among the low-income populations. The proliferation of studies of the urban underclass (see essays in Jencks and Peterson 1991) pointed to debilitating effects of organized criminal activities for low-income neighborhoods in general and for urban youth in particular. One strand of research focused on the consequences of informalization on youth who, in their adolescent years, began drifting away from mainstream work toward illegal enterprises. As youth dropped out of school and entered illicit economies, it became more difficult for them to re-establish their pathways in socially legitimate economies at a later date (Bourgois 1996). Other work has examined the effects on adult populations (Anderson 1990; Duneier 1994) by looking at the ways in which informal economies prevent black and Latino men and women from accumulating the social and economic capital necessary to create long-term stability for themselves and their families. The writings on global cities (Abu Lughod 1999; Sassen 2001) extended this argument by noting the ways that immigrants in urban centers became drawn into informal labor markets (and simultaneously excluded from the high-growth sectors of the urban economy).

Thus, in these early considerations, the focus was on the articulation of economic and political systems. Scholars were interested in the role that the underground economy played in generating inequities, but they were not necessarily concerned (as they are today) with strategies to reintegrate earners and workers who toiled on the margin. Instead, the underground economy was interpreted in political-economic terms via a contentious relationship to the broader capitalist economy. It was seen by some as a potential space through which people could create more humanistic forms of economic exchange. For others, it might be the hotbed of socially revolutionary activity (see Lautier 1994).

What Types of Regulation Emerge from Informality?

At its core, an informal economic action is an exchange of a good or service between (at least) two parties that occurs via some form of nonstate based regulation. The simplicity of this transaction belies a complex social structure that enables multiple exchanges to occur on a daily basis and, for the most part, in smooth fashion. In the formal economy, the institutional apparatus of conflict resolution is ultimately backed by the state's capacity for coercive violence. However, unlike the mainstream economy, in which a battery of institutions—from courts and licensing agencies to exchanges and tax authorities—regulate and provide stability to the parties by disseminating information on prices and by specifying resources for disputes, the underground economy typically has no such identifiable structure that can house buyers and sellers. In the informal economy, no such institutional apparatus exists. Instead, a variety of other venues, from community courts to third-party brokers (Lewicki et al. 1992) might exist to help individuals address conflicts and ensure that justice is meted out (Merry 1990, 1993; Venkatesh 2007, 2013a; Bourgois 1996). Attentiveness to the ways that such mediation and dispute resolution occurs can also shed light on the ways that informal economies reproduce conditions of inequality in a given society.

To begin, the absence of the state leads to three types of problems that arise in the context of informal economies. The most common disagreements occur over pricing and contracts. Buyer and seller each recall a different promise of payment or pricing structure; two traders might argue over a revenue split and so on. A second source of dispute occurs over property rights: two individuals might argue over the right to occupy a public space, such as a park or a street corner, or they might haggle over intrusions that result from competitive bidding and marketing of services to potential clients. A third conflict may arise over the appropriate form of mediation or punishment for a given infraction.

Such problems are not inherently destabilizing. However, for the poor, their occurrence can be detrimental for two reasons. First, the ubiquity of underground markets means that such problems are prevalent and demand a significant amount of the energy of low-income households. As the poor spend more time and resources managing highly localized economies that provide resources and opportunities, there is little left for more productive purposes. As a consequence, informal economies by nature are almost always localized, idiosyncratic, and difficult to integrate into the wider society at any scale (Rauch and Evans 2000). Second, the repeated use of nonstate-based means of resolving conflicts can pose serious threats to the ability of poor households to function in the wider society. That is, paradoxically, the more that poor populations are able to show innovativeness and ingenuity with respect to their investments and engagement in the informal economy, the easier it is for the dominant society to view them as unfit to participate in the legitimate sphere (Castells and Laserna 1989). A common problem arises in the United States because the poor end up failing to support the law enforcement institutions of the state—preferring instead to rely on their own dispute mediators. This becomes one factor among others that exacerbates the crisis of legitimacy of police in poor communities (Meares 2002, 2008).

In low-income environments, the forms of regulatory response that one finds to such conditions are twofold. On the one hand, a vibrant redistributive justice movement over the past two decades has created para-state mechanisms of redress in which the state participates alongside other institutions but agrees to share authority over mediation and punishment (Muncie 2007). These include local community-policing initiatives that are common in the United States and community courts that offer reduced sentences for individuals who are willing to work with community-based organizations to reduce the likelihood of future involvement in criminal activities (Merry 1990). There are also many highly localized cases in which nonstate-based methods of redress help local citizens to cope with the disputes that arise over informal economic activities (Venkatesh and Kasimir 2007; McRoberts 2005).

It should be noted that the forms of community-based redress, involving the state or not, do not necessarily signal an entirely different culture or way of life. For example, some regulatory movements are modeled after (neoclassical) market economic structures. De Soto argues that informal entrepreneurs operating outside the purview of legal regulations "spontaneously" create rules derived from the logic of the market economy (De Soto 1989:xviii). Similarly, Katsenelinboigen (1990) inferred from his study of the second economy in the USSR that a market economy derived from human nature ("human psychology has not changed," and "people have natural vices"). In fact, the little we know about informal regulations of informal activities suggests that conflict resolution is grounded in interpersonal ties (Venkatesh 2006). Trading parties must rely on implicit norms or a priori codes that specify fair conduct, expected valuation, acceptable currency, and methods of redress for grievances. For instance, in the case of the second economy in the former Soviet Union, personal ties were central to the functioning of the second economy. Corruption was widespread, but one had to know who to bribe; corruption often involved bringing gifts, which personalized relations (Grossman 1977). Sampson (1987) stresses the importance of primary ties and of friendships to reduce the risk of being reported to the authorities; he notes that underground factories were often run by Jews who relied on ethnic solidarity to avoid legal troubles. How these social functions of exchange are carried out can tell us quite a bit about the overall lives of the poor.

THE INFORMAL ECONOMY
IN THE EVERYDAY LIFE OF THE POOR

Underground exchange in poor neighborhoods shapes not just the lives of buyers and sellers of goods and services but also the wider population who come into contact with those engaged in unreported trading. The inclusion of underground economies in scholarly work becomes a means for scholars to raise a host of concerns about life in poverty.

Informal economies appear consistently in studies of law enforcement and policing. Urban policing strategy is overwhelmingly shaped by the behavior of those involved in illegal economic pursuits (Skogan 2003, 2006; Fung 2006; Moskos 2008; Venkatesh 2008; Jackall 2009). However, these studies typically do not offer a substantive analysis of the economic activities per se, other than to note their existence and significance for the dynamics of local policing. Similarly, illicit exchange can be a means to talk about the wider social organization of urban poor communities. Several studies have suggested that the presence of informal economies can create social divisions that pit various households against one another. Elijah Anderson's work (1999) differentiates families in urban, poor social contexts via two different value orientations. In their efforts to live according to mainstream values, "decent" families are waged in a battle with those adopting a "street" orientation; the latter are those whose lives are centrally embedded in informal economies. Decent families worry about children who are playing with their "street" counterparts; they must navigate public spaces where underground entrepreneurs congregate; they suffer the continuous presence of law enforcement and an atmosphere of criminality. Venkatesh (2007) and Meares and Kahan (1998) also adopt a neighborhood-level focus; however, their respective studies focus on those who, via outreach, community organizing, mediation, or protest engage the sellers of informal economic goods in an effort to restore public safety. They do not make value judgments that differentiate "decent" from "street" households, and, instead, they examine the ways that informal economic activity creates social problems that require a collective response.

A number of scholars have examined the impact of underground exchange and criminal opportunity on individuals (Khoury 1995; Fitzpatrick 1997; Vega and Gil 1999; Wilson 2009). Alford Young's ethnographic study of marginalized black men (2004) suggests that individual perceptions of mobility and decisions to pursue economic paths are framed with an understanding of the potential sources of illegal revenue generation in existence. Philippe Bourgois's research on young men in Spanish Harlem similarly examines the role that underground economies play in motivating young men to choose socially legitimate work pathways (Bourgois 1996). Although Bourgois's study is based on a group of crack-cocaine dealers, the two authors are similar in pointing to the ways that informal exchange serves as an ever-present specter that haunts every young man and woman in urban, poor neighborhoods. Even if they never participate directly, they make their decisions with an awareness that such opportunities exist and are being chosen by peers and acquaintances. The work of Kathryn Edin and Laura Lein has examined the interplay of individual and household contexts in assessing the role that informal economies play in the lives of the urban poor (Edin and Lein 1997). In such studies, it becomes clear that individual decisions to pursue opportunities for illegitimate gain are framed by the pressures that stem from the needs of the overall household.

Informal Activities Reward Specific Skills

Drawing on Wilson and Portes (1980) and Portes and Bach (1980), Thery (2014) conceptualizes informal activities as an economic space where specific skills get rewarded—skills that are not rewarded by the formal economy. For instance, the moral and physical ability to exert extreme violence is not rewarded in the formal labor market, but it is valuable to criminal endeavors (Bourgois 1996; Contreras 2012). "Street smarts" is another example of skills that are useful to informal endeavors but inadequate to most high-productivity service jobs that are available in contemporary global cities.

For instance, not all women are willing to sell sex, but those who do may earn more than what their marginal productivity in the legitimate economy would have them earn. Weitzer's (2005, 2009) reviews suggest that most of the literature on sex workers is about work conditions as opposed to economic activities. Little is known about pricing, about how much sex workers really earn, what do they do with the earnings, and what kind of professional career develops after sex work (for an exception, see Rosen and Venkatesh 2008). The literature about customers, which is less developed, focuses on their motivations to patronize sex workers and to what extent they abuse them (Monto 2000; Kern 2000; Macleod et al. 2008); and little is known about third parties, such as pimps (see nonetheless Decker 1979:238–58; Hoigard and Finstad 1992; O'Connell Davidson 1998; Chapkis 2000; all references found in Weitzer 2005:227). Another aspect of third-party involvement that might be studied under the heading of the informal economy is sex trafficking. But sex trafficking studies are less interested in the economics of trafficking and more interested in the critique of human/women's right abuse (Farley et al. 2003) or in the deconstruction of the critique (Bernstein 2012). Sex work exemplifies how what is defined as criminal by a given state varies in time and space. Consider the example of sex work. Both the act of buying sex and selling sex are illegal in most parts of the United States, Africa, the Arab world, and Asia, with extreme variations in enforcement. In Canada, Argentina, Brazil, and most of Western Europe, only pimping is illegal. In Germany, the Netherlands, Turkey, and many Latin American countries, sex work is legal and regulated; in Sweden and Norway, selling sex is not illegal per se, but buying sex is. The economy of sex work is shaped by the legal context: the sector may be entirely informalized by way of its criminalization or may give rise to a two-tier market in countries that authorize sex work, with a formal sector regulated by the state and an informal sector. Prostitution, drug trafficking, and gambling are quintessentially economic activities that happen to be often illegal and therefore operate outside the state's regulation.

The study of gambling—another activity that is transactional in nature and arbitrarily informalized by way of state regulation—also illustrates how the literature tends to overlook its "informal economy." Instead of looking at gamblers as economic actors, many authors have focused on the more pathological aspects of gambling, such as related alcohol abuse (Welte et al. 2001), psychological disorders (Petry 2005), the impact of new technologies and their enhancing effect of the gambling experience

(Schull 2005), or the relationship between casino gambling and street crime (Miller and Schwartz 1998). A variation on the focus on the pathological aspects of gambling is to organize the literature as a debate between functional analyses of gambling and anomie/alienation perspectives (Frey 1984). The sociology of gambling departs from the pathologizing perspective to focus on the different subjective experiences and the different subcultures of gambling (Neal 1998; Aasved 2003) and the "seductions of gambling" and the thrill associated with it (Cosgrave 2006). What comes closer to an "informal economy" perspective is the body of work that examines legalization and the state regulation of gambling (Eadington 1976; Cosgrave and Klassen 2001; Cosgrave 2006). An example of a study of the informal economy of gambling can be found in Light (1977). Light studies numbers gambling among the African American urban poor—a community notoriously deprived of financial services. Light describes how numbers gambling work alongside usury to provide access to credit to community residents.

A prominent empirical vehicle to study the underground economy is via the practices of street gangs and the drug economies they control. Illicit drugs are an undoubtedly significant component of the informal economy (on the economics of drug trade see Caulkins and Reuter 1998; Reuter 2003; Reuter and Caulkins 2004; Leeson 2007), and gangs are sometimes part of this economy. Fagan (1996) argues that American gangs became more involved with the drug trade with the crack cocaine epidemic. Dominant theoretical perspectives in the study of gangs in sociology emphasize social disorganization perspectives (which emphasize explanations in terms of poverty, victimization, nonnuclear family structures, and so on) and control theories (which argue that criminals, at heart, act impulsively) (Wood and Alleyne 2010:103). Psychological explanations of the gang phenomenon stress that gang members are more likely to exhibit psychopathic tendencies and have low IQs (Wood and Alleyne 2010:106). Research in these perspectives tends to not see gangs as (informal) economic actors. Bourgois's (1996) ethnography, for instance, depicts gang members who have to exert violence to prove their masculinity. Costanza and Helms's (2012) statistical study of gang activity and aggregate homicides demonstrated a correlation between the two. Gang violence is at the forefront of Huff's (1996) edited volume. Even when violence is not central to the argument, we often know little about gang members' involvement in the informal economy (for instance Smith 2006:212–13). An important literature grew in reaction to these perspectives and took a keen interest in the informal economic activities of gangs—especially the drug trade.

During the crack epidemics, ethnographers found that gangs were displaying a new entrepreneurial spirit (Sanchez-Jankowski 1991; Padilla 1992; Venkatesh 1997; Venkatesh and Levitt 2000), leading gang members to make more rational, business-minded decisions. Venkatesh (1997) described the "corporatization" of the gang, and Padilla (1992) and Venkatesh and Levitt (2000) wrote about the emergence of the franchise model of drug selling among gangs. Ethnographers showed that this economic organization provided fewer opportunities for women and deteriorated sex-work conditions (Maher and Daly 1996) and resulted in the gross exploitation of street-level operatives (Padilla 1992; Fagan 1996)—especially ex-convicts unable to find legitimate employment

(Scott 2004)—including the routine use of violence to enforce contracts in the absence of a third-party to regulate business disputes (Venkatesh and Levitt 2000).

Some have argued that the rise of the drug trade and the entrepreneurial shift among gangs occurred in light of the deindustrialization of the United States and the lack of opportunities for young black males in the formal economy (Fagan 1997; Coughlin and Venkatesh 2003). Young, urban black males saw drugs as a main source of income and status (Anderson 1990); gangs with more adult members were more likely to be criminal. The "institutionalization of drug markets" and the "second economies" that derived from it have had a "redistributive function" (Fagan 1996:62–65). In this conception, informal economies reward specific types of skills, creativity, and agency.

CONCLUSION

This chapter outlined some of the key theoretical and analytic trends in the study of inequality and underground economies. To conclude the chapter, we turn to some of the implications for future research by addressing methodological issues and research-design challenges. We do so because systematic social science research on inequality presupposes an institutionalized recording of activity. In the United States, some common forms of documentation that inform our understanding of inequality include assessments of labor force participation by the Bureau of Labor Statistics, shifts in public welfare expenditures by the Department of Health and Human Services, and local trends in health care utilization by each state's public health division.

None of these established data streams exist for underground economic activities. Indeed, much of the informal economy by definition elides the very institutions that are responsible for producing such assessments. For this reason, we should not be surprised that substantive discussions of informal economic activity can be dominated by concerns over definition, generalizability, and validity and reliability of data (Kanbur 2009). Alice Sindzingre (2006:60) describes the contemporary situation well by addressing the challenges that researchers face:

> Definitional problems also stem from the plurality of methodologies aimed at quantifying informal activities. There is no unique statistical aggregate that corresponds to the concept of informal economy. Statistical certainty is limited to the sub-sectors, such as the types of enterprises or employment that fulfill certain criteria of size, organization, payment of particular taxes, and so on.

As Sindzingre notes, with respect to informal economies, there is no accepted data set, either within a single national context or globally, that might enable multiple researchers to offer competing explanations and shape theoretical propositions with a robust analytic exchange. For this reason, treatments of informal economic activity appear in several guises, though they are limited in terms of producing

representative findings. Perhaps the most common approach is to draw on qualitative research based on successful access to a set of individuals who are actively
involved in hidden economic exchange. The advantages of this kind of methodological posture are several: extended interviews and/or observation can enable
researchers to understand the shifting ways poor households draw on underground
economies to make ends meet (Edin and Lein 1997); qualitative research can also
highlight the complex interplay between illegitimate and legitimate economic circuits (Venkatesh 2013a, 2013b); and single case studies typically demonstrate the significance of informal economic activity for the poor beyond their de jure criminal
dimension (Duneier 1999). Qualitative research presents some notable challenges,
however. To begin, it is not always easy to link qualitative studies; an ethnographic
study of textile workers in India and in the United States may employ different
definitions of informality—one finding that criminal operations must be included,
the other finding them irrelevant—and so comparisons become problematic (Patel
1990; see also NCEUS 2008); even if the group (say, a "gang") and the definition are
similar, the research may have occurred in such widely different geographic circumstances (say, postcommunist Ukraine and modern-day Britain) that it becomes
difficult to draw generalizations.

A second common research design appears in the work of contemporary economists. To adjust to the difficulties of comparing case studies that were conducted in
different times and places, economists will use complex estimation procedures to
draw inferences from existing data sets that document other aspects of the economy
(Torgler and Schneider 2007; Elgin and Oztunali 2012). A common method is to
make creative use of data from national GDP or tax reports. Torgler and Schneider's
study (2007) demonstrates both the strengths and limitations of this perspective.
Torgler and Schneider draw on financial reporting from different countries to construct a multinational, informal economic data set that enables basic comparison
across countries of many different political and economic histories. This type of
study can alert officials about tax-revenue loss or the large-scale social exclusion of a
particular segment of society. They can be valuable for shaping social policies, such
as labor protections or progressive tax distribution, which might ameliorate inequality (cf. Portes 1994). They can also enable local officials to spur economic growth by
helping isolate those individuals who may need documentation, licensing, insurance,
credit, and other kinds of immediate economic catalysts (Amin 1994). However, like
most others who use estimation methods, Schneider's construct does not incorporate
any criminalized economies or even an estimate of household production. In other
words it is limited to the behavior of organized firms. This is a common attribute
of estimation models, and there may be significant consequences for any attempt
to draw conclusions about social inequality. Most importantly, the activities of low-
income populations may never make it into the official financial reporting of firms
but are quite actively represented in informal domestic production and distribution,
as well as in crime.

Finally, a third means of assessing informal economies is to launch large-scale surveys of a particular population of interest, such as small businesses of individual entrepreneurs (Chen et al. 2004; Crowell 2003). Macrosurveys are extraordinary useful for understanding how informality shapes an entire economic industry. This sectoral-based view can offer insight into the difficulties that low-income workers have in securing meaningful wages and stable employment. However, most attempts to give a broad overview face difficulty securing cooperation from their informants—whether individuals or firms—and so generalizability within and across a geographic region or commercial industry is compromised (Borotav, Yelden, and Kose 2000; Narayana 2006).

NOTES

1. In the aftermath of the most recent European financial crisis, the self-employed Greek citizen who earns money, but who fails to pay his taxes, drew attention throughout the Continent as an example of spreading informal economic entrepreneurship. The symbol of the Greek black marketer played a pivotal role in speeches by European officials who cited Greece's inability to support rational, modern, bureaucratic commerce.

2. The small size of economic units—often an item in defining informality—is also not relevant: many professionals (doctors, lawyers) and most shopkeepers are self-employed or have a small staff. Even the criteria of avoiding state regulation is weak. Most formal firms routinely disregard regulations and laws: banks launder money, industries pollute, arms dealer smuggle weapons; nonprofits, political parties, and bureaucracies organize clientelism and corruption. In particular, systematic tax evasion by the richest and most established individuals and firms is widespread: about 8 percent of the global financial wealth of households is held in tax havens (Zucman 2013).

3. Another characteristic of De Soto's work is the way the state is perceived. In the development literature, the state is unable to control its territory, hence the informal economy: it is because the state cannot field enough civil servants, or cannot pay them adequately, that corruption, clientelism, and lack of manpower give way to the rise of informal activities. De Soto argues instead that the informal economy exists because the state is too controlling, hence the need for deregulation, or, more precisely, to formalize informality by undoing regulations.

4. It is worth mentioning the work of David Stark (1989), who makes an important contribution in this regard by challenging modernization theories—both capitalist and Marxist—that perceive informal and second economies as relics of a preindustrial or presocialist past. By contrast, Stark (1989:639) argues is that "[i]nformalization is a product of the modern and the bureaucratic." The informal economy is a consequence of "regulatory bureaucratization," and the second economy is an "alternative institution in which skills and effort find a higher rate of returns." In other words, the informal economy can also be constituted by the active agency of individuals who exercise preferences in relationship to a wide field of economic opportunities—legitimate and informal. The informal economy in any society would hence help the analyst understand not only the scope conditions of the wider economy—who it serves, what kind of commerce it can support, and so on—but also the ways in which individual entrepreneurs might move to unregulated domains to pursue their economic interests.

REFERENCES

Aasved, Mikal. 2003. *The Sociology of Gambling*. Springfield, IL: Charles C. Thomas.

Abu-Lughod, Janet L. 1999. *New York, Chicago, Los Angeles: America's Global Cities*. Minneapolis: University of Minnesota Press.

Amin, Ash. 1994 "The Difficult Transition from Informal Economy to Marshallian Industrial District." *Area* 13–24.

Anderson Elijah. 1999. *Code of the Street: Decency, Violence, and the Moral Life of the Inner City*. New York: W.W. Norton.

Anderson, Elijah. 1990. *Streetwise. Race, Class and Change in an Urban Community*, Chicago: University of Chicago Press.

Bernstein, Elizabeth. 2012. "Carceral Politics as Gender Justice? The 'Traffic in Women' and Neoliberal Circuits of Crime, Sex, and Rights." *Theory and Society* 41(3):233–59.

Boratav, Korkut, Erinç Yeldan, and Ahmet Köse. 2000. "Globalization, Distribution and Social Policy: Turkey, 1980–1998." *CEPA and The New School for Social Research, Working Paper Series* 20:113–14.

Bourgois, Philippe. 1996. *In Search of Respect: Selling Crack in El Barrio*. Cambridge: Cambridge University Press.

Castells, Manuel and Roberto Laserna. 1989. "The New Dependency: Technological Change and Socioeconomic Restructuring in Latin America." *Sociological Forum* 4(4):535–60.

Castells, Manuel and Alejandro Portes. 1989. "World Underneath: The Origins, Dynamics, and Effects of the Informal Economy." Pp. 11–37 in *The Informal Economy: Studies in Advanced and Less Developed Countries*, edited by A. Portes, M. Castells, and L. A. Benton. Baltimore, MD: Johns Hopkins University Press.

Caulkins, Jonathan and Peter Reuter. 1998. "What Can We Learn from Drug Prices?" *Journal of Drug Issues* 28(3):593–612.

Centeno, Miguel A. and Alejandro Portes. 2006. "The Informal Economy in the Shadow of the State". Pp. 23–48 in *Out of the Shadows: Political Action and the Informal Economy in Latin America*, edited by Patricia Fernandez-Kelly and Jon Shefner. University Park: Pennsylvania State University.

Chapkis, Wendy. 2000. "Power and Control in the Commercial Sex Trade." In *Sex for Sale: Prostitution, Pornography, and the Sex Industry*, edited by R. Weitzer. New York: Routledge.

Chen, Martha A., Renana Jhabvala, and Frances Lund. 2002. *Supporting Workers in the Informal Economy: A Policy Framework*. Geneva: International Labor Organization.

Chen, Martha A., Joann Vanek and Marilyn Carr. 2004. *Mainstreaming Informal Employment and Gender in Poverty Reduction: A Handbook for Policy-Makers and Other Stakeholders*. London: Commonwealth Secretariat.

Contreras, Randol. 2012. *The Stickup Kids: Race, Drugs, Violence, and the American Dream*. Berkeley: University of California Press.

Cosgrave, James F., ed. 2006. *The Sociology of Risk and Gambling Reader*. New York: Routledge.

Cosgrave, Jim and Thomas R. Klassen. 2001. "Gambling against the State: The State and the Legitimation of Gambling." *Current Sociology* 49(5):1–15.

Costanza, S. E. and Ronald Helms. 2012. "Street Gangs and Aggregate Homicides: An Analysis of Effects during the 1990s Violent Crime Peak." *Homicide Studies* 16(3):280–307.

Coughlin, Brenda C. and Sudhir Alladi Venkatesh. 2003. "The Urban Street Gang after 1970." *Annual Review of Sociology* 29:41–64.

Cross, Theodore L. 1969. *Black Capitalism: Strategy for Business in the Ghetto*. New York: Atheneum.

Crowell, Daniel W. 2003. *The SEWA Movement and Rural Development: The Banaskantha and Kutch Experience*. New Delhi: Sage.

Davis, Mike. 2006. *Planet of Slums*. London: Verso.

De Soto, Hernando. 1989. *The Other Path*. New York: Basic Books.

De Soto, Hernando. 2000. *The Mystery of Capital*. New York: Basic Books.

Decker, John. 1979. *Prostitution: Regulation and Control*. Littleton, CO: Rothman.

Doeringer, Peter B. and Michael Piore. J. 1971. *Internal Labor Markets and Manpower Analysis*. London: ME Sharpe Inc.

Duneier, Mitchell. 1994. *Slim's Table: Race, Respectability, and Masculinity*. Chicago: University of Chicago Press.

Duneier, Mitchell. 1999. *Sidewalk*. London: Macmillan.

Eadington, William R. 1976. *Gambling and Society: Interdisciplinary Studies on the Subject of Gambling*. Springfield, IL: Charles C. Thomas.

Edin, Kathryn and Laura Lein. 1997. *Making Ends Meet: How Single Mothers Survive Welfare and Low-Wage Work*. London: Russell Sage Foundation.

Elgin, Ceyhun and Oguz Oztunali. 2012."Shadow Economies around the World: Model Based Estimates." Bogazici University Department of Economics Working Papers 5.

Fagan, Jeffrey. 1996. "Gangs, Drugs and Neighborhood Change." Pp. 39–74 in *Gangs in America*, edited by C. Ronald Huff. 2nd ed. Thousand Oaks, CA: Sage.

Farley Melissa, Ann Cotton, Jacqueline Lynne, Sybille Zumbeck, Frida Spiwak, Maria E. Reyes, Dinorah Alvarez, and Ufuk Sezgin. 2003. "Prostitution and Trafficking in Nine Countries: Update on Violence and Posttraumatic Stress Disorder." *Journal of Trauma Practice* 2(3/4):33–74.

Ferman, Louis A., Stuart Henry, and Michele Hoyman. 1987. "Issues and Prospects for the Study of Informal Economies: Concepts, Research Strategies, and Policy." *Annals of the American Academy of Political and Social Science* 493(1):154–72.

Fitzpatrick, Kevin M. 1997. "Aggression and Environmental Risk among Low-Income African American Youth." *Journal of Adolescent Health* 21:172–78.

Frey, James H. 1984. "Gambling: A Sociological Review." *Annals of the American Academy of Political and Social Science* 474:107–21.

Fung, Archon. 2006. "Varieties of Participation in Complex Governance." *Public Administration Review* 66(1):66–75.

Fusfeld, Daniel R. and Timothy M. Bates. 1984. *The Political Economy of the Urban Ghetto*. Chicago: SIU Press.

Gaughan, Joseph P. and Louis A. Ferman. 1987. "Toward an Understanding of the Informal Economy." *Annals of the American Academy of Political and Social Science* 493:15–25.

Gërxhani, Klarita. 2004. "The Informal Sector in Developed and Less Developed Countries: A Literature Survey." *Public Choice* 120(3–4):267–300.

Gilbert, Alan. 2002. "On the Mystery of Capital and the Myths of Hernando De Soto: What Difference Does Legal Title Make?" *International Development Planning Review* 24(1):1–19.

Grossman, Gregory. 1977. "The 'Second Economy' of the USSR." *Problems of Communism* 26(5):25–40.

Hannerz, Ulf. 1969. *Soulside: Inquiries into Ghetto Culture and Community*. New York: Columbia University Press.

Hart, Keith. 1973. "Informal Income Opportunities and Urban Employment in Ghana." *Journal of Modern African Studies* 11(1):61–89.

Hoigard, Cecilie and Liv Finstad. 1992. *Backstreets: Prostitution, Money, and Love*. University Park: Pennsylvania State University Press.

Huff, Ronald C., ed. 1996. *Gangs in America*. 2nd ed. Thousand Oaks, CA: Sage.

International Labor Office. 1972. *Employment, Income and Equality: A Strategy for Increasing Productivity in Kenya*. Geneva: ILO.

Jackall, Robert. 2009. *Street Stories: The World of Police Detectives*. Cambridge, MA: Harvard University Press.

Jencks, Christopher and Paul E. Peterson, eds. 1991. *The Urban Underclass*. Washington, DC: Brookings Institution Press.

Kanbur, Ravi. 2009. "Conceptualising Informality: Regulation and Enforcement." No. 4186. IZA discussion papers.

Katsenelinboigen, Aron. 1990. *The Soviet Union: Empire, Nation, and System*. New Brunswick: Transaction.

Katsenelinboigen, Aron. 1977. "Coloured Markets in the Soviet Union." *Europe-Asia Studies* 29(1):62–85.

Khoury, Wavel. 1995. "Cultural Conflicts and Problem Behaviors of Latino Adolescents in Home and School Environments." *Journal of Community Psychology* 23(2):167–79.

Lautier, Bruno. 1994. *L'économie informelle dans le tiers monde* [The informal economy in the Third World]. Paris: La Découverte.

Leeson, Peter T. 2007. "An-arrgh-chy: The Law and Economics of Pirate Organization." *Journal of Political Economy* 115(6):1049–94.

Lewicki, Roy J., Stephen E. Weiss, and David Lewin. 1992. "Models of Conflict, Negotiation and Third Party Intervention: A Review and Synthesis." *Journal of Organizational Behavior* 13(3):209–52.

Light, Ivan. 1977. "Numbers Gambling among Blacks: A Financial Institution." *American Sociological Review* 42(6):892–904.

Losby, Jan L., John F. Else, Marcia E. Kingslow, Elaine L. Edgcomb, Erika T. Malm, and Vivian Kao. 2002. *Informal Economy Literature Review*. Newark: Institute for Social and Economic Development (ISED) and Washington: Aspen Institute.

Macleod Jan, Melissa Farley, Lynn Anderson, and Jacqueline Golding. 2008. *Challenging Men's Demand for Prostitution in Scotland*. Glasgow: Women's Support Project.

Maher, Lisa and Kathleen Daly. 1996. "Women in the Street-Level Drug Economy: Continuity or Change?" *Criminology* 34(4):465–91.

Marable, Manning. 1983. *How Capitalism Underdeveloped Black America*. New York: Pluto.

Marcelli, Enrico A., Manuel Pastor Jr., and Pascale Joassart. 1999. "Estimating the Effects of Informal Economic Activity: Evidence from Los Angeles County." *Journal of Economic Issues* 33(3):579–607.

McRoberts, Omar M. 2005 *Streets of Glory: Church and Community in a Black Urban Neighborhood*. Chicago: University of Chicago Press.

Meares, Tracey. 2002. "Praying for Community Policing." *California Law Review* 90(5):1593–634.

Meares, Tracey. 2008. "Legitimacy of Police among Young African-American Men." *Marquette Law Review* 92(4):651.

Meares, Tracey and Dan Kahan. 1998. "Law and (Norms of) Order in the Inner City." *Law and Society Review* 32(4):805–38.

Merry, Sally Engle. 1990. *Getting Justice and Getting Even: Legal Consciousness among Working-Class Americans*. Chicago: University of Chicago Press.

Miller, William J. and Martin D. Schwartz. 1998. "Casino Gambling and Street Crime." *Annals of the American Academy of Political and Social Science* 556:124–37.

Monto, Martin. 2000. "Why Men Seek out Prostitutes." In *Sex for Sale: Prostitution, Pornography, and the Sex Industry*, edited by R. Weitzer. New York: Routledge.

Moskos, Peter. 2008. *Cop in the Hood*. Princeton, NJ: Princeton University Press.

Muncie, John. 2007. "Youth Justice and the Governance of Young People: Global, International, National, and Local Contexts." Pp. 17–56 in *Youth, Globalization, and the Law*, edited by Sudhir Alladi Venkatesh and Ronald Kassimir. Stanford, CA: Stanford University Press.

Narayana, M. R. 2006. "Formal and Informal Enterprises: Concept, Definition, and Measurement Issues in India." Pp. 93–120 in *Linking the Formal and Informal Economy: Concepts and Policies*, edited by Basudeb Guha-Khasnobis, Ravi Kanbur and Elinor Ostrom. New York: Oxford University Press.

National Commission for Enterprises in the Unorganised Sector (NCEUS). 2008. *Report on Definitional and Statistical Issues Relating to Informal Economy*. New Delhi.

Neal, Mark. 1998. "You Lucky Punters! A Study of Gambling in Betting Shops." *Sociology* 32(3):581–600.

O'Connell Davidson, Julia. 1998. *Power, Prostitution, and Freedom*. Ann Arbor: University of Michigan Press.

Padilla, Felix. 1992. *The Gang as an American Enterprise*. New Brunswick, NJ: Rutgers University Press.

Patel, B. B. 1990. *Workers of Closed Textile Mills: A Study in Ahmedabad*. Ahmedabad: Gandhi Labour Institute.

Petry, Nancy M. 2005. *Pathological Gambling: Etiology, Comorbidity, and Treatment*. Washington, DC: American Psychological Association.

Portes, Alejandro. 1994. "When More Can Be Less: Labor Standards, Development, and the Informal Economy." *Contrapunto: The Informal Sector Debate in Latin America* 113–29.

Portes, A. and R. L. Bach. 1980. "Immigrant Earnings: Cuban and Mexican Immigrants in the United States." *International Migration Review* 14(3):315–41.

Portes, Alejandro and Saskia Sassen-Koob. 1987. "Making It Underground: Comparative Material on the Informal Sector in Western Market Economies." *American Journal of Sociology* 93(1):30–61.

Portes, Alejandro and John Walton. 1981. *Labor, Class, and the International System*. New York: Academic Press.

Rauch, James E. and Peter B. Evans. 2000. "Bureaucratic Structure and Bureaucratic Performance in Less Developed Countries." *Journal of Public Economics* 75(1):49–71.

Reuter, Peter. 2003. "The Political Economy of Drug Smuggling." Pp. 128–47 in *The Political Economy of the Drug Industry*, edited by Menno Vellinga. Gainesville: Florida University Press.

Reuter, Peter and Jonathan Caulkins. 2004. "Illegal Lemons: Price Dispersion in the Cocaine and Heroin Markets." *UN Bulletin on Narcotics* LVI(1–2):141–65.

Rosen, Eva and Sudhir Alladi Venkatesh. 2008. "A 'Perversion' of Choice. Sex Work Offers Just Enough in Chicago's Urban Ghetto." *Journal of Contemporary Ethnography* 37(4):417–41.

Sampson, Steven L. 1987. "The Second Economy of the Soviet Union and Eastern Europe." *Annals of the American Academy of Political and Social Science* 493(1):120–36.

Sanchez-Jankowski, Martin. 1991. *Islands in the Street: Gangs and American Urban Society*. Berkeley: University of California Press.

Sassen, Saskia. 1994. "Informal Economy: Between New Developments and Old Regulations." *Yale Law Journal* 103(8):2289–304.

Sassen, Saskia. 2001. *The Global City: New York, London, Tokyo*. Princeton, NJ: Princeton University Press.

Sassen-Koob, Saskia. 1984. "Notes on the Incorporation of Third World Women into Wage-Labor through Immigration and Off-Shore Production." *International Migration Review* 18(4):1144–67.

Schull, Natasha Dow. 2005. "Digital Gambling: The Coincidence of Desire and Design." *Annals of the American Academy of Political and Social Science* 597(1):65–81.

Scott, Greg. 2004. "'It's a Sucker's Outfit': How Urban Gangs Enable and Impede the Reintegration of Ex-Convicts." *Ethnography* 5(1):107–40.

Sindzingre, Alice. 2006. "The Relevance of the Concepts of Formality and Informality: A Theoretical Appraisal." Pp. 58–74 in *Linking the Formal and Informal Economy: Concepts and Policies*, edited by B. Guha-Khasnobis, R. Kanbur, and E. Ostrom. New York: Oxford University Press,

Skogan, Wesley G. 2004. *Community Policing: Can It Work?* Stamford, CT: Thomson Wadsworth.

Skogan, Wesley G. 2006. *Police and Community in Chicago: A Tale of Three Cities*. Oxford: Oxford University Press.

Smith, Robert Courtney. 2006. *Mexican New York: Transnational Lives of New York Immigrants*. Berkeley: University of California Press.

Stack, Carol B. 1974. *All Our Kin: Strategies for Survival in a Black Community*. New York: Basic Books.

Stark, David. 1989. "Bending the Bars of the Iron Cage: Bureaucratization and Informalization in Capitalism and Socialism." *Sociological Forum* 4(4):637–64.

Thery, Clement. 2014. *Larry's Clique: The Informal Side of the Housing Market in Low-Income Minority Neighborhoods*. Unpublished dissertation, Department of Sociology, Columbia University.

Torgler, Benno and Schneider, Friedrich G. 2007. "Shadow Economy, Tax Morale, Governance and Institutional Quality: A Panel Analysis." CES working paper, No. 1923.

Valentine, Betty Lou. 1978. *Hustling and Other Hard Work*. New York: Free Press.

Vega, William and Andres Gil. 1999. "A Model for Explaining Drug Use Behavior among Hispanic Adolescents." *Conducting Drug Abuse Research with Minority Populations: Advances and Issues* 14(1–2):57–74.

Venkatesh, Sudhir A. 1997. "The Social Organization of Street Gang Activity in an Urban Ghetto." *American Journal of Sociology* 103(1):82–111.

Venkatesh, Sudhir A. 2006. *Off the Books: The Underground Economy of the Urban Poor*. Cambridge, MA: Harvard University Press.

Venkatesh, Sudhir A. 2008. *Gang Leader for a Day: A Rogue Sociologist Takes to the Streets*. New York: Penguin.

Venkatesh, Sudhir A. 2013a. *Floating City: A Rogue Sociologist Lost and Found in New York's Underground Economy*. New York: Penguin.

Venkatesh, Sudhir A. 2013b. "Underground Markets as Fields in Transition: Sex Work in New York City." *Sociological Forum* 28(4):682–99.

Venkatesh, Sudhir Alladi and Ronald Kassimir, eds. 2007. *Youth, Globalization, and the Law*. Redwood, CA: Stanford University Press.

Venkatesh, Sudhir A. and S. D. Levitt. 2000. "Are We a Family or a Business? History and Disjuncture in the Urban Street Gang." *Theory and Society* 29:427–62.

Weitzer, Ronald. 2005. "New Directions in Research on Prostitution." *Crime, Law and Social Change* 43:211–35.

Weitzer, Ronald. 2009. "Sociology of Sex Work." *Annual Review of Sociology* 35:213–34.

Welte, John, Grace Barnes, William Wieczorek, Marie-Cecile Tidwell and John Parker. 2001. "Alcohol and Gambling Pathology Among U. S. Adults: Prevalence, Demographic Patterns and Comorbidity." *Journal of Studies on Alcohol* 62(5):706–12.

Williams, Colin and Jan Windebank. 2001. "Reconceptualising Paid Informal Exchange: Some Lessons from English Cities." *Environment and Planning* 33(1):121–40.

Wilson, Kenneth L. and Alejandro Portes. 1980. "Immigrant Enclaves: An Analysis of the Labor Market Experiences of Cubans in Miami." *American Journal of Sociology* 86(2):295–319.

Wilson, William J. 2009. *More than Just Race: Being Black and Poor in the Inner City*. New York, NY: W.W. Norton.

Wood, Jane and Emma Alleyne. 2010. "Street Gang Theory and Research: Where Are We Now and Where Do We Go From Here?" *Aggression and Violent Behavior* 15(2):100–111.

Zucman, Gabriel. 2013. "The Missing Wealth of Nations: Are Europe and the US Net Debtors or Net Creditors?" *Quarterly Journal of Economics* 128(3):1321–64.

CHAPTER 29

··

SOCIAL CLASS, POVERTY, AND THE UNEQUAL BURDEN OF ILLNESS AND DEATH

··

RONALD J. ANGEL

Two Centuries of Increasing Life Expectancy

SINCE the beginning of the Industrial Revolution, technological progress and productivity gains have vastly increased the world's aggregate wealth. Alongside these gains, improvements in public health and medical science have greatly improved the overall health of the human population (Bharmal et al. 2012; Easterlin 2000; Elo 2009; Morbidity and Mortality Weekly Report 1999; Preston 1996; Wilmoth 1998). In the developed world, the modern welfare state ensures a basic level of material security to all citizens, and life expectancy has increased to historically unprecedented levels (CIA 2011; Esping-Andersen 1990, 1999; Tuljapurkar, Li, and Boe 2000; UNESCO 2010). Developed nations have not been the only beneficiaries of improving living standards; the populations of developing nations have benefited as well, if not to the same degree (Easterlin 2000; United Nations 2011a). In 1955 life expectancy at birth for the world's population was approximately 47; by 2005 it had increased to 66 (United Nations 2011a). During that same period the proportion of the world's population living in countries with life expectancies below 50 decreased from 60 to only 7 percent, and the proportion living in countries with life expectancies of 70 or older increased from 1 to over 50 percent (United Nations 2011a).

These dramatic increases in life expectancy are the result of a complex set of economic, political, and social changes, the health effects of which are as yet incompletely understood (Elo 2009; Link and Phelan 1995; Phelan et al. 2010). What is certain, though, is that while increases in productivity and advances in public health and medicine have increased the health of the world's population generally, not all nations or groups have benefited equally. Today a baby born in Japan can expect to live for more than 82 years, and in the United States a newborn can expect to live for at least 77 years (CIA 2011; United Nations 2011b). On the other hand, a child born in Afghanistan can expect to live 45 years, and a child born in Angola only 39 years, numbers that reflect high infant mortality as well as high disease burdens among both children and adults.

Moreover, urbanization and economic development are complex processes with varying health consequences for different groups. Although urban residents have greater access to health care providers than rural residents, lower income urban residents in the developing world have health profiles that are no better than those of impoverished rural residents (Montgomery 2009). Despite the greater access of urban residents to care providers of all sorts, the care available to those with little income is often of low quality (Das and Hammer 2007). As Amartya Sen, the winner of the 1998 Nobel Prize in Economics points out, the health of a population is as much the result of social inequalities and injustice and the lack of true democracy as the result of pathogens and infectious agents (Sen 1999).

This chapter provides a survey of major themes related to the association among social factors that generate and maintain poverty and that determine health outcomes among different income groups. It does not focus on psychological traits or individual biological vulnerabilities. Rather it deals with institutional and structural factors that result in different illness risk profiles for different income groups. The literature on poverty and health is immense, and it is impossible to touch upon all the debates and methodological challenges or to deal with even a small number of the specific health outcomes in one chapter. Rather, this chapter presents an overview of theoretical considerations related to the attempt to understand how poverty and the factors that generate it also undermine health. Following Sen (1999) and others mentioned later, this chapter is informed by the perspective of social medicine in which social, political, and economic factors are as important in assessing health risks as are clinical factors.

Chapter Structure

The chapter is divided into various sections. I begin with a general discussion of the social class factors that affect health. Clearly income is an important component of social class, but although income is correlated with such components of wealth as housing quality and the ownership of stocks, bonds, and other property, wealth differentials among racial and ethnic groups are far larger than differentials in income (Loucks et al. 2009; McFadden et al. 2008). A focus on income alone, then, ignores important aspects of social class defined in terms of wealth, social capital, and political power that affect individuals' and communities' ability to act as agents on their own behalf.

I then briefly discuss the meaning and measurement of poverty and the potential ways in which poverty undermines health. Mounting evidence suggests that early life deprivation has lifelong negative health consequences. Yet definitively identifying the mechanisms through which social factors affect health remains complicated. That complexity is revealed in what has been termed the "Hispanic paradox," which I discuss briefly. This paradox refers to the fact that although Hispanics have high levels of poverty and low educational levels, their life expectancy is similar to that of non-Hispanic whites.

I then move on to a brief examination of the association among poverty, mental illness, and mental health care. Poverty is clearly associated with increased mental health risks, especially in the developing world in which poor individuals are often exposed to stressors associated with extreme poverty, a lack of basic necessities, and political upheaval. Unfortunately, although the need for services is high in both the developed and developing nations, the availability of mental health services is often inadequate or nonexistent, again especially in the developing world. As is the case for mental health care, dental health care reflects a social class and income gradient. Low-income children and adults suffer from a wide range of health problems related to dental disease, again especially in the developing world.

After a discussion of these health differentials within and between the developed and developing world, I move on to a discussion of the concept of "social capital" and what has been termed the "new morbidity." Social capital refers to the power that group membership provides individuals and communities. The "new morbidity" refers to the range of social, behavioral, and psychological problems that are influenced by social factors. The chapter ends with two sections that reflect on the health implications of health care reform for poor and minority Americans and the potential role of non-governmental and faith-based organizations in enhancing the health of disadvantaged individuals and communities.

PERSISTENT SOCIALLY BASED INEQUITIES IN HEALTH

The levels and extent of poverty in the least developed nations clearly dwarf those within developed nations. Diseases such as malaria, leishmaniasis (the sand fly's bug), schistosomiasis (snail fever), trypanosomiasis (sleeping sickness), river blindness, and the other tropical diseases that affect impoverished populations are largely absent from developed nations. Yet social class disparities in morbidity and mortality burdens remain significant even in the richest nations (Babones 2008; Elo 2009; Marmot et al. 1991). In the United States and Britain, for example, individuals with lower levels of education and in the lower occupational strata have higher coronary heart disease risk than those with more education or in higher occupational strata (Loucks et al. 2009; McFadden et al. 2008; Ramsay et al. 2008). One might expect that at a certain level of economic development, large differences in morbidity and mortality among social groups would disappear. After all, rich nations can afford to provide basic nutrition, education, housing, and medical care to all citizens. Affluence alone, though, does not eliminate social class disparities in illness and the risk of death. In all developed nations, individuals with lower levels of education, less income and wealth, and fewer social characteristics of the upper classes face an elevated risk of most negative health outcomes (Montgomery 2009). These differences can be observed even in nations with near universal access to health care (Elo 2009). A core question for public health professionals and researchers who deal with the consequences of social inequality, then, relates to the sources of the disparities in disease and death associated with differences in wealth and other social class characteristics.

THE MEANING AND MEASUREMENT OF POVERTY

Before we proceed, it is necessary to at least briefly discuss the core construct dealt with in the chapter, poverty. The first definition on the Merriam-Webster free, online dictionary is "the state of one who lacks a usual or socially acceptable amount of money or material possessions." Such a definition seems straightforward, yet when one employs the concept of "poverty" in the context of outcomes like health, the complexity of both the concept and its operationalization becomes clear. Given space limitations it is not possible to summarize the major theoretical and practical considerations in the operationalization of the concept of poverty; yet some general sense of how the concept is approached is necessary.

In general terms one can conceive of poverty in either an absolute or relative sense. Most of us are familiar with the poverty thresholds employed by the U.S. government to determine the number of individuals in poverty and to establish program eligibility. These thresholds are an example of an attempt to define an absolute level of poverty below which one is considered poor. This approach has serious shortcomings since it fails to consider changes over time in what is minimally necessary for a dignified existence in particular social contexts, and it also fails to include the impact of taxes, transfers, and other adjustments that affect individuals' and families' well-being (Brady 2003; Sen 1976). The World Bank's definition of extreme poverty as subsistence on less than the equivalent of one dollar a day is another well-known measure of absolute poverty that reflects a level of material deprivation that is so extreme as to be life threatening. It is a level of material want that robs individuals of their basic dignity.

Relative definitions of poverty, such as income deciles, and more complicated measures that include such aspects of income distribution as the number or proportion of individuals below the median income and the extent of extreme poverty among them, rank individuals and groups relative to one another (Brady 2003, 2005; Sen 1976; Smeeding, Rainwater, and Burtless 2001). Of course, the level of consumption of someone in the lowest decile in a developed nation can be far higher than that of someone in a higher decile in a developing country. That fact, in addition to the reality that cash income or its equivalent alone does not provide complete information about an individual or group's quality of life, has led some, primarily in the field of development, to propose social definitions of "poverty" that include many other dimensions of well-being, including the quality of one's housing, one's educational level, one's economic opportunities, one's access to credit, and logically, even one's health. Researchers in this tradition have proposed various multidimensional definitions and measures of poverty, including subjective measures of one's satisfaction with one's level of material well-being (Kakwani and Silber 2008; Rojas 2008; see this entire volume). The notion of poverty as multidimensional has given rise to the concept of "social exclusion" (Sen 1999, 2000). This concept draws attention to the fact that poverty can result from social factors including racism, sexism, or associated factors that systematically prevent individuals or groups from obtaining what they need to live a decent and dignified life.

Separating the independent impact of poverty on health is theoretically and methodologically difficult because of the fact that the two are so highly correlated. Measures such as infant and adult mortality rates and morbidity from acute illness can be used as measures of a nation's level of "poverty" or level of development. Although health outcomes are routinely modeled as if the effect of those predictors can be identified and isolated, the truth is that health is a highly endogenous social phenomenon. Researchers and mathematical modelers are constantly forced to deal with the fact that although poverty and variables such as education and labor force participation are correlated, it is almost impossible to unambiguously determine which causes which.

For theoretical, as well as practical operational reasons then, one might usefully ask whether a focus on "poverty" in relation to health is not in fact a focus more generally on social class or at least the impact of lower class membership, defined as class analysts have traditionally dealt with the concept. Such a focus refers to those structured economic and historically determined social, economic, and political processes that determine an individual's or a group's capacity to act as agents on their own behalf and to control the circumstances of their lives, including those that determine health levels. Later I will discuss this possibility in relation to the concept of "social capital."

A growing body of research suggests that the discrimination that marginalized and excluded groups experience can undermine both physical and mental health (Williams and Mohammed 2009). One example are the Roma, one of the ethnic groups that are known collectively as gypsies, who face exclusion and discrimination in many European nations where they often lack access to adequate health care (Hajioff and McKee 2000). The relevance of race and factors associated with the history of racial exclusion in the United States is demonstrated by a large body of research. In the United States, minorities, who are disproportionately poor, face seriously elevated risks of illness, disability, and premature death (CDC 2011a). These disparities are reflected in racial differences in life expectancy. In 2008 life expectancy at birth for white males was 79.8 years and for white females, 80.8 years. For black males life expectancy at birth was only 70.9 years and for black females 77.4 years (U.S. Census Bureau 2012a). These racial disparities in life expectancy reflect racial differences in morbidity. In 2009 African American adults were almost twice as likely as non-Hispanic white adults to report diabetes (13.2 percent vs. 7.7 percent) (Ostchega et al. 2000). Homicide represents the fourth-leading cause of death for black males but is not among the 10-leading causes for white males (Kaiser Family Foundation 2011). Significant state variation in overall mortality rates for African Americans further illustrate the complexity inherent in assessing the causes of racial and social class differences in mortality (Bharmal et al. 2012).

CHILDHOOD POVERTY
AND ADULT OUTCOMES

New research is beginning to reveal the extent and permanence of the damage that childhood poverty inflicts on individuals throughout life (Conroy, Sandel, and Zuckerman 2010; Evans and Kim 2007; Shonkoff, Boyce, and McEwen 2009; Victora et al. 2008). As is readily observable in developing nations, a lack of adequate nutrition during the prenatal period and the early years of life result in stunted growth and shorter adult height, and lower vitality in adulthood. Early childhood deprivation and the stress that accompanies poverty have negative consequences for a wide range of adult outcomes including educational attainment, labor force participation, and health (Duncan, Ziol-Guest, and Kalil 2010; Evans and Kim 2007; Hayward et al. 2000; Victora et al. 2008).

Although an understanding of the specific mechanisms by which malnutrition and other early stressors affect adult health provides useful insights, the ultimate insight that one draws from this new research is a reaffirmation of what Rudolf Carl Virchow, one of the founders of social medicine observed in the nineteenth century, noted. In reporting on a typhus epidemic in Upper Silesia, then a part of Prussia, Virchow offered the observation that a history of oppression and a lack of democracy and freedom, in addition to malnutrition, low education, and the lack of other necessities that guarantee a dignified and decent life left the population demoralized and highly susceptible to disease and its consequences. A core tenet of social medicine is that while disease is clearly the result of pathological processes and infectious agents, the exposure to those agents, as well as the host's immunity and ability to respond depend on a wide range of social institutions, not solely those associated with medicine (Brown and Fee 2006; Waitzkin 2011). The clear association between poverty and the exposure to infectious disease can be easily seen in the vulnerability of impoverished populations, such as those of Haiti and Rwanda, to cholera, tuberculosis, and many other diseases, including those referred to as "neglected tropical diseases" (Alsan et al. 2011; Montgomery 2009).

The specific mechanisms by which prenatal and childhood deprivations and other traumas produce permanent vulnerabilities remain matters of ongoing investigation, but two major possibilities may be at work independently or in combination. First, it is possible that deprivation or trauma that occurs at developmentally sensitive ages interferes with normal development giving rise to lifelong vulnerabilities. Or second, it may be that poverty is associated with a greater number of illnesses and trauma throughout life resulting in an accumulation of their negative effects (Conroy et al. 2010; Shonkoff et al. 2009). It is also likely that certain individuals with specific genetic vulnerabilities suffer more serious long-term negative effects than those without such vulnerabilities (Caspi et al. 2002; Caspi et al. 2005; Caspi, et al. 2003).

A detailed review of the specific physiological mechanisms by which childhood deprivation affects specific disease outcomes in adolescence, adulthood, and later life is clearly beyond the scope of this chapter. Several summaries of and empirical exemplars of current knowledge are available (e.g., Conroy et al. 2010; Shonkoff et al. 2009). The core lesson for social and health policy that emerges from this research, though, again reaffirms the core insight of social medicine, which is that social, political, and economic factors are as central to the determination of health and illness as are aging, pathogenic processes, and disease agents (Brown and Fee 2006; Sen 1999; Waitzkin 2011). While a focus on physiological mechanisms promises to provide useful information on the specific pathways through which deprivation at any age causes illness, it is important to retain social medicine's focus on social institutions, inequality, and powerlessness and not lose sight of potentially controversial topics with an excessive focus on individual genetic vulnerabilities. The identification of genetic factors that increase the vulnerability of certain individuals to the stressors that accompany poverty may be of theoretical interest, but it is of questionable practical value. Policy cannot be focused solely on the most vulnerable among the poor, even if they can be accurately identified. All humans victimized by poverty face serious risks to their health and well-being. It is the poverty that must be addressed, in addition to disease and specific individual health risk factors.

THE HISPANIC PARADOX

One of the difficulties in assessing the sources of poverty and social class factors in mortality is illustrated by a phenomenon that has been termed the "Hispanic paradox" (Markides and Coreil 1986; Markides and Eschbach 2005; U.S. Census Bureau 2012b). This term refers to the surprisingly long life-expectancy at birth and at older ages among Hispanics in the United States, despite their relatively unfavorable socioeconomic profile. In 2007, while life expectancy at birth for the non-Hispanic white population was 78.2, it was 80.9 for Hispanics, but only 73.2 for blacks (Blue 2011). This longer life-expectancy reflects favorable mortality from heart disease and cancer and occurs despite the fact that nearly a quarter of the Hispanic population has no regular source of care and over 40 percent lack health insurance (U.S. Census Bureau 2012b; Wilper et al. 2009). In addition, one quarter of Hispanics, the same fraction as blacks, fall below the official government poverty line (Angel and Angel 2009). Hispanics also suffer from extremely low levels of education, another major health risk. In 2010 while nearly 88 percent of whites and 84 percent of blacks had graduated from high school, only 63 percent of Hispanics were high school graduates (CDC 2011b). Given the educational, health insurance, and poverty profiles of the Hispanic population, one would expect to observe mortality rates and life expectancies much more similar to those of the black population.

Several possible explanations for this longevity advantage among Hispanics have been offered. The Hispanic population includes a large number of immigrants who might be selected for better health. A possible mechanism for an immigrant health advantage arises from the fact that Hispanic immigrants report lower rates of smoking which may contribute to their lower mortality (Livingston, Minushkin, and Cohn 2012). In addition to factors that might actually result in lower mortality, there are potential problems in the correct identification of the population at risk since not all Hispanics are readily identifiable as such. Life expectancy could be overestimated if a significant number of ill Mexican-origin individuals return to Mexico to die reducing the number of recorded deaths (U.S. Census Bureau 2012b). In all likelihood, all of these factors are at play in determining Hispanics' favorable mortality experience.

Despite life expectancies that are comparable to those of non-Hispanic whites, this population suffers from substantial morbidity of the sort associated with poverty (Angel and Angel 2006). The prevalence of diagnosed diabetes is far higher among Hispanic adults than among non-Hispanic white adults. Again, there are significant differences among specific Hispanic groups. Mexican and Puerto Rican adults are far more likely to report diabetes compared to Central or South American adults (13.8 percent, 16.7 percent, and 7.3 percent respectively). Studies of older Hispanics find elevated rates of disability and greater need for assistance living in the community than is the case for non-Hispanic whites (CDC 2012a, 2012b; Markides and Eschbach 2005). These apparently conflicting morbidity and mortality patterns in a subpopulation with high levels of poverty, low education, and a large fraction of immigrants illustrates the difficulties inherent in understanding the association among social factors and health.

POVERTY, MENTAL ILLNESS, AND HEALTH CARE

Individuals who are exposed to the stresses associated with chronic poverty, neighborhood instability, violence, political upheaval, and natural disasters often face the stark reality that treatment for the emotional and mental consequences of those traumatic conditions and events is unavailable or inadequate. In Africa, as in the rest of the developing world, mental health services are for the most part unavailable even though the need for such services is great (Bird et al. 2011; Lund 2010; see issue 6, volume 22 of International Review of Psychiatry). Data on the prevalence of mental illness in developing nations has been scarce. One recent initiative, the World Health Organization (WHO) World Mental Health Survey (WMH), attempts to assess the prevalence of various mental disorders in an ever-growing number of developing and eight developed countries using a common methodology to not only assess compara- tive patterns of illness but to also assess treatment access (Kessler and Ustun 2008; WHO 2004). These studies show that although there is wide variation in the prevalence of specific mental disorders rates of mental illness are high in all nations. They also show that although the likelihood of receiving treatment increases with the severity of the disorder, the likelihood of receiving treatment is lower in developing than devel- oped countries (WHO 2004).

An important finding from these studies is that individuals with serious mental ill- nesses function less well and earn substantially less than healthy individuals (Levinson et al. 2010). This finding again illustrates the fact that it is difficult to determine causal- ity when it comes to illness and social risk factors. These studies also reveal another important pattern. As the world's population grows, it is increasingly concentrated in megacities in which migrants and poor residents are exposed to the stresses associated with poverty, high crime rates, and other stressors that increase rates of anxiety and mental and emotional disorders (Andrade et al. 2012).

In many parts of the world, mental illness is stigmatized. In Uganda, for example, despite the fact that the country has a formal policy that guarantees the rights of the mentally ill, in practice the mentally ill often suffer physical and emotional abuse (Cooper et al. 2010). In addition, mental health services tend to be of low quality, reflecting a lack of trained mental health professionals. Those services that are avail- able are concentrated in the largest city, Kampala, leaving poorer rural residents who make up 88 percent of the country's population with no services. Mental illness and the response to it are affected by other social factors including gender, that are related to poverty and powerlessness. Given women's subordinate position, they suffer from multiple vulnerabilities associated with poverty and their relative lack of power relative to men. Likewise, in the United States low-income women in poor neighborhoods face serious role strains that undermine their mental health and interfere with their effec- tiveness as parents (Belle 1990; Klebanov, Brooks-Gunn, and Duncan 1994).

Although we as yet do not understand the specific mechanisms through which adverse life circumstances affect health, a large body of evidence suggests that chronic adversity has serious mental health impacts. For example, Latina women who experi- ence abuse at the hands of their intimate partners are at elevated risk of depression and posttraumatic stress disorder (PTSD). A history of such trauma increases the risk of negative outcomes, while a greater sense of mastery and higher income reduce it (Rodriguez et al. 2008).

Unfortunately in this overview it is impossible to summarize the massive literature on mental illness and its association with poverty and the risk factors that are associ- ated with it. There is a great need for research to guide policy, but the difficulties inher- ent in isolating the predictors of mental illness present major problems. What is clear is that relatively mild mental disorders are common and that serious illnesses represent a major challenge for national health systems (Kessler and Ustun 2008). Unfortunately, as in other areas of life, those with the fewest material resources are the ones who are exposed to the most serious mental health risks, and they are also those with the least power to demand their rights.

POVERTY AND DENTAL HEALTH

Oral health is a major component of overall general health and access to dental care is highly dependent on income. Socioeconomic differentials in oral health and access to dental care exist both within developed nations and between developed and developing nations (Do 2012; Marmot and Bell 2011). These differentials have serious implications for the health of populations. A growing body of research, for example, shows that untreated periodontitis increases the risk of coronary heart disease (Bahekar et al. 2007; Humphrey et al. 2008). Dental care is expensive, and low-income families find it difficult to pay for even when it is available. Although in the United States dental health has improved in recent years as a result of greater access to dental care at all ages, low-income individuals continue to suffer lifelong consequences of poor oral health (Dye and Thornton-Evans 2010).

Of special note is what cavities and tooth decay mean for the health of children. They are among the major health problems of childhood, and children in low-income families and minority families remain at elevated risk of inadequate dental care (Paradise 2009). In the developing world where access to medical care in general is limited among the more impoverished segments of society, the poor are at seriously elevated risk of suffering the negative consequences of poor oral health. In Africa, cavities, periodontal diseases, noma, an opportunistic infection that results from compromised immune functions that can result in massive facial disfigurement, oro-facial trauma resulting from violence and accidents, the oral manifestations of HIV infection, cleft lips and palates, and oral cancer cause major suffering (WHO 2009b).

THE NEW MORBIDITY

The phrase "the new morbidity" was introduced 35 years ago by Robert Haggerty and colleagues in their treatment of childhood behavioral and emotional problems (CDC 2012b). Similar to the positions espoused by Amartya Sen and Rudolph Virchow, the concept of new morbidity emphasizes the fact that illness results from the interaction of biological, environmental, and psychological factors, many of which are related to social class and poverty. Regardless of the overall level of mortality, the lower strata of society bears a disproportionate burden of disease and illness (Link and Phelan 1995; Phelan, Link, and Tehranifar 2010). In the past when the rich could afford the high-fat and high-carbohydrate diets that today we attempt to avoid, the rich were fat and the poor were thin. In developed nations today, and increasingly in developing nations, the poor increasingly suffer from what used to be the diseases of affluence (CDC 2012a; Markides and Eschbach 2005). Those in the lower social strata, which include a disproportionate number of minority group members, suffer from obesity, hypertension, and diabetes at higher rates than the rich (Braveman et al. 2010; Marquezine et al. 2008; Stamatakis et al. 2010; Zaninotto et al. 2009).

The persistence of disparities inevitably leads us to ask whether such differentials are inevitable, or whether more basic social changes might eliminate them. Jo Phelan and Bruce Link have developed a conceptual perspective which they refer to as "fundamental cause" theory to explain the persistence of disparities in health and illness, despite innovations such as vaccinations that have greatly reduced morbidity and mortality from traditional causes such as infectious disease (Link and Phelan 1995; Phelan et al. 2010). They begin with the observation that in any historical period certain causes of illness and death predominate. For example, before antibiotics and modern public health initiatives acute infectious illnesses, as well as malnutrition and related factors, caused greater misery and death among the poor than among the rich.

In a morbidity and mortality regime in which chronic diseases are the major cause of illness and death, the rich can afford the preventive care, better diets, and lifestyles that can prevent them or mitigate their consequences. Regardless of the major causes of disease and death in any nation or historical period, then, social inequalities inevitably result in higher morbidity and mortality rates among the lower classes. Given the fact that few societies are completely egalitarian in terms of material resources, the risk of illness and its negative consequences will continue to be greater for those with fewer resources. The logical conclusion again reiterates the message of Amartya Sen and Rudolph Virchow, that the elimination of health disparities demands nothing short of redistribution and directly dealing with the large social class inequalities in material and nonmaterial resources. In a period of serious anti-welfare-state sentiment and the ongoing dominance of neoliberal market-based social policies, such possibilities face serious challenges.

Although Phelan and Link do not employ the term "social capital," their theory is very similar in drawing attention to the potentially complex nexus of social factors that place certain groups at risk of poorer health in any particular morbidity and mortality regime. The concept of social capital has been employed in many disciplines to refer to the advantages and power associated with group membership. The utility of the concept is that it emphasizes the fact that, although material wealth conveys power, it is associated with a more complex set of sources of power and influence that are not strictly material and that are associated with an individual's and a group's ability to control important aspects of their lives. In the realm of health it is affects one's ability to avoid or deal with risk.

Social capital arises from one's connections to others, and it affects individuals' and groups' ability to act as effective agents to further their own interests, largely by enhancing a groups' or individuals' access to material capital (Bourdieu 1986). A lack of social capital, therefore, can increase the risk of poverty and thereby the risk of poor health. Social capital is a characteristic of groups rather than individuals, but it has direct individual benefits. High levels of social capital are associated with safer neighborhoods, greater political influence, and greater material wealth (Fukuyama 2001; Guiso, Sapienza, and Zingales 2004; Sampson and Groves 1989; Samson 1999; Vieno et al. 2010; Zak and Knack 2001). James Coleman was one of the first to demonstrate the significance of social capital by showing that it keeps high school students from dropping out (Coleman 1988). Others have shown that it fosters individual occupational and social mobility (Burt 1992; Lin 1999). The social support that accompanies social capital protects health (Berkman et al. 2000; Fujiwara and Kawachi 2008; James, Schulz, and Olphen 2001). At the community level it results in greater neighborhood stability and more effective community action (Agnitsch, Flora, and Ryan 2006; Portney and Berry 1997; Saegert, Thompson, and Warren 2001; Silverman 2004; Temkin and Rohe 1998). At the national level it is associated with higher levels of economic development (Knack and Keefer 1997; Portes and Landolt 2000; Woolcock 2002).

Social capital theorists have been careful to emphasize that social capital has value in that it can be translated into material and social power. One might, in fact, conclude that the concept does not add much to explanations based solely on income and wealth. Pierre Bourdieu, for example, notes that social capital can only be understood in terms of its association with cultural capital and material capital (Bourdieu 1986; Light 2004). By cultural capital, Bourdieu primarily refers to education but also to other aspects of one's ability to navigate and influence one's social and political environment. Ultimately, the concept of social capital, like the concept of the new morbidity, emphasizes the complex multifactorial origins of health vulnerabilities. It also raises both theoretical and practical questions as to its source and whether it can be fostered in situations and among groups who lack it. The theoretical ties among social capital, and cultural and material capital underscore the need for effective political action and the beneficent protection and support of an enlightened welfare state in order to deal with persistent inequalities in disease and death.

Poverty and Health Care Reform in the United States

Although the focus of this chapter is global, it is informative to discuss the implications of health care reform in the United States for the health of low-income individuals and families. The United States is unique among developed nations in not providing a basic package of health care to all of its citizens (Reid 2009). Although individuals without health insurance, and even noncitizens, have access to charity and emergency care, such care is often unavailable and lacks the continuity that insured individuals enjoy (Institute of Medicine 2001, 2002). The evidence clearly shows that a lack of health insurance results in an elevated risk of illness and death (Institute of Medicine 2001; U.S. Census Bureau 2012c). Treating illness or conditions that have been neglected is expensive and represents a major social cost (Institute of Medicine 2003).

The overrepresentation of minority group families and individuals among the uninsured has other potential long-term consequences. Given the changing racial and ethnic demography of the country and higher fertility among minority Americans, the labor force of the future will be increasingly African American and Latino (Angel and Angel 2009; Institute of Medicine 2002). These individuals will be called upon to pay for Social Security, Medicare, defense, public education, the repair of infrastructure, and much more. If the productivity of that future labor force is undermined by low levels of education and less than optimal health, not only will their own earnings capacities be harmed, but the prosperity of the nation as a whole will also be placed in jeopardy.

Many nations have developed universal health care systems based on employer and employee contributions, yet even as they look to a greater reliance on the market, they rely on public financing to assure universal coverage (Hassenteufel and Palier 2007; Reid 2009). The United States has developed a system in which employer-based group health insurance is the major source of coverage for most middle-class Americans. Yet the number of employers offering health plans is dropping, down from 69 percent in 2010 to 60 percent in 2011 (Kaiser Family Foundation 2011). Since not all workers enroll even when a plan is offered, only 65 percent of workers in firms that offer health plans participate. The outcome of this arrangement is that a large fraction of the U.S. population does not have any form of coverage. This is particularly true among young childless adults who do not qualify for Medicare or Medicaid. In 2009, 16.7 percent of the population had no coverage of any sort. Among individuals 18 to 34, approximately 30 percent lacked coverage (Shetterly et al. 1998). The Patient Protection and Affordable Care Act signed into law by President Obama in March 2011 increases coverage by extending Medicaid to poor childless adults and providing subsidized coverage to low-income individuals and families through state insurance exchanges. Even then, though, we will not have universal health care. One clear benefit that came into effect in 2010 is the option to allow young adults to remain on their parents' plans until age 26.

HEALTH: A RIGHT OR A MARKET COMMODITY?

The response to the health care reform legislation clearly illustrates the extent of opposition to any federal mandate intended to assure universal coverage. The opposition reflects basic philosophical differences, as well as a fairly pervasive lack of understanding of the nature of health care financing and the consequences of lacking coverage. From a policy perspective that optimizes market solutions to social problems, health can be conceived of as a personal responsibility and the social goods that optimize it, such as good nutrition and medical care, commodities that like any other one can consume to the extent that one can afford them. On the other hand, one might conceive of the material factors that foster good health as basic human rights that represent collective responsibilities to be provided by the state. From this perspective, access to material resources such as adequate nutrition, decent housing, and education, that guarantee good health represent basic "social rights," without which one cannot exercise his or her civil and political rights (Marshall 1950). Since at least the Second World War, health and the material factors necessary to maintain it have increasingly come to be seen as social rights in developed and even developing nations. Except for the United States, all developed nations provide citizens some basic level of health care as a core welfare state right (Reid 2009). The growing extent and cost of programs that protect social rights at a time of protracted fiscal crises have led to inevitable attempts to control those costs and reduce the size of welfare states (Palier 2010).

The philosophy that health is so basic to human life and welfare that it should be fostered at public expense has become common in the post–World War II era. That philosophy is embodied in major multilateral international treaties and agreements. The preamble to the constitution of the World Health Organization, which was drafted in 1946, defines health very broadly and states clearly that it is a basic human right that governments should guarantee:

> Health is a state of complete physical, mental and social well-being and not merely the absence of disease or infirmity. . . . The enjoyment of the highest attainable standard of health is one of the fundamental rights of every human being without distinction of race, religion, political belief, economic or social condition. . . . Governments have a responsibility for the health of their peoples which can be fulfilled only by the provision of adequate health and social measures. (WHO 1946:2)

Article 25 of the Universal Declaration of Human Rights adopted by the UN General Assembly in 1948 includes the statement:

> Everyone has the right to a standard of living adequate for the health and well-being of himself and of his family, including food, clothing, housing and medical care and necessary social services, and the right to security in the event of unemployment, sickness, disability, widowhood, old age or other lack of livelihood in circumstances beyond his control. (United Nations 1948)

Most nations of the world, and certainly the vast majority of developed nations, provide at least basic health care to their populations (Reid 2009). Clearly, many developing nations lack the resources to provide adequate care to all of their citizens and, as mentioned later, developed nations contribute to health care in developing nations through governmental assistance and the actions of private nongovernmental and faith-based organizations. In this scenario the United States stands out in not providing universal coverage as a matter of principle.

GLOBAL HEALTH: INTERNATIONAL CHALLENGES FOR THE TWENTY-FIRST CENTURY

Although the health levels of human populations have improved in many ways and for many individuals in recent decades, the world faces major threats that could halt or even reverse those improvements (WHO 2009a). It is only possible to mention a few. Malnutrition remains a major problem. It can result from a lack of food that results in starvation, or the ill effects of too much food, and a diet that contains too many calories, fats, carbohydrates, salt, and so forth that can result in obesity and its complications, including diabetes. Famines and droughts continue to plague humanity, often as the result of war and political conflict. Global warming and the rise in sea levels may result in more serious storms, flooding, and crop failures that can only exacerbate serous food shortages in many parts of the world. Refugees and internally displaced peoples suffer serious stresses and threats to health, while lacking access to adequate medical care.

Old and new potentially deadly tropical diseases, including Ebola and other hemorrhagic fevers continue to pose major threats to human health and even survival. Although antiretroviral drugs are effective against HIV/AIDS, they are still too expensive or unavailable to the poorest inhabitant of many parts of the world. Although penicillin and newer antibiotics at one time promised to end the scourge of infectious disease, today the world faces the danger of growing antibiotic resistance and the prospect of superbugs that defy all attempts at treatment. Finally, a major problem that continues to plague the world and affect low-income individuals is the lack of access to high-quality care and the lack of the newest and most effective pharmaceuticals.

CIVIL SOCIETY AND THE NONGOVERNMENTAL RESPONSE

Today many organizations, including the Red Cross, Doctors without Borders, and numerous other international NGOs like the Clinton Foundation and the Bill and Melinda Gates Foundation provide health care or help finance research into global health issues and provide health care for people who would otherwise do without (American Public Health Association 2008). The core question has to do with whether such organizations can make a major difference or whether their efforts are only palliative. As in the case of education, if the state does not build and maintain the infrastructure needed to provide care to its population, can nongovernmental and even international actors substitute. There is reason not to place too much hope in the capacities of such nongovernmental efforts. Civil society organizations can function effectively only in situations in which a beneficent and efficient state provides security, resources, and the rule of law that makes it possible for providers of services to effectively carry out their objectives (Angel et al. 2012). In addition, given the magnitude of the task of building a health care system that educates doctors, nurses, and other medical professionals and provides clinics, primary, secondary, and tertiary hospitals, as well as the technology to make them function, only the state has the resources and authority.

Nonetheless, despite their limitations nongovernmental and faith-based organizations operate in almost all areas of service delivery in all parts of the world, and their activities probably do more good than harm. The growth in the number of such civil society organizations has been impressive, and the movement clearly indicates a desire among people in both the developed and developing world to change things for the better (Boli and Thomas 1999). Such a desire and such a movement should be optimized. In addition to providing services directly to individuals in need, civil society organizations can advocate for the poor and go beyond dealing with immediate and short-term medical needs to further the ends of social medicine and work toward improving the general condition of the poorest segments of the world's population. The possibilities should continue to be explored.

Conclusion: The Challenge

The evidence is overwhelming then that poverty, measured in either absolute or relative terms, undermines physical and mental health and undermines individuals' and groups' quality of life. Poverty in the developing world is far deeper and affects many more individuals than in the developed world. The residents of the poorest nations suffer more illnesses and live shorter lives than the citizens of richer countries. Yet even within developed nations, including those with universal health care systems, those at the bottom of the income distribution have poorer health and higher mortality rates than those higher up. What is more impressive, though, is that there is convincing evidence that inequality, independent of a nation's level of wealth, has similar effects. In highly unequal societies certain individuals exist at the margins and are excluded from the benefits of full social citizenship. Such exclusion undermines physical and mental health. In addition, as the literature reviewed in this chapter has shown, poverty and inequality and their negative health consequences are part of a package that includes race, ethnicity, gender, cultural differences, and other social factors that place certain groups at elevated risk of exclusion, illness, and death in all parts of the world.

Although there is ongoing debate as to the potential causes of the negative health effects of poverty, and the many complicated conceptual and methodological issues involved in determining the mechanisms that give rise to the association, the basic correlation among indicators of poverty and negative health outcomes remains indisputable. This basic and consistent finding reaffirms the lessons of Amartya Sen, Rudolph Virchow, and T. H. Marshall. Even as research into the genetic basis of disease and the complex interactions of genes and environment reveal new and important findings, the basic truth of social medicine remains and brings us back to the inherently political nature of health and illness. As noted earlier, from an epidemiological perspective, a host and the disease agents that make him or her ill are brought together in an environment that is socially, biologically, and physically constructed. Separating the host from the agents of illness requires changing the social as well as the physical environment. Individuals who lack basic nutrition, education, shelter, and health care suffer and die unnecessarily. Even as the health of the world's population has improved, certain groups have been left behind, and the majority of those are members of the segment of the human population with few political or economic resources.

The challenge, then, if we are to eliminate or reduce health disparities and improve the health of the least advantaged members of humanity goes beyond clinical medicine, with all the difficulties that implies. Modern genetics and clinical science have made great strides in furthering our understanding of the causes of disease and in improving human health, but their benefits will continue to disproportionately benefit the rich if the social institutions and political structures that deny certain segments of humanity their basic social rights and access to the necessities of a dignified and healthy life remain intact. In a period of global fiscal austerity, when sovereign debt levels seem unsupportable and calls for deep reductions in spending for social programs dominate political discourse, ensuring the health and welfare of the poorest members of humanity represents a major challenge.

References

Agnitsch, Kerry, Jan Flora, and Vern Ryan. 2006. "Bonding and Bridging Social Capital: The Interactive Effects on Community Action." *Community Development: Journal of the Community Development Society* 37:36–51.

Alsan, Marcella M., Michael Westerhaus, Michael Herce, Koji Nakashima, and Paul E. Farmer. 2011. "Poverty, Global Health, and Infectious Disease: Lessons from Haiti and Rwanda." *Infectious Disease Clinics of North America* 25:611–22.

American Public Health Association. 2008. "Strengthening Health Systems in Developing Countries." Washington, DC. Retrieved September 6, 2014 (http://www.apha.org/policies-and-advocacy/public-health-policy-statements/policy-database/2014/07/23/09/09/strengthening-health-systems-in-developing-countries).

Andrade, Laura Helena, Yuan-Pang Wang, Solange Andreoni, Camila Magalhães Silveira, Clovis Alexandrino-Silva, Erica Rosanna Siu, Raphael Nishimura, James C. Anthony, Wagner Farid Gattaz, Ronald C. Kessler, and Maria Carmen Viana. 2012. "Mental Disorders in Megacities: Findings from the São Paulo Megacity Mental Health Survey, Brazil." *PLoS ONE* 7:e31879.

Angel, Ronald J. and Jacqueline L. Angel. 2006. "Diversity and Aging in the United States." Pp. 94–110 in *Handbook of Aging and the Social Sciences*, edited by R. Binstock and L. George. 6th ed. New York: Academic Press.

Angel, Ronald J and Jacqueline L. Angel. 2009. *Hispanic Families at Risk: The New Economy, Work, and the Welfare State*. New York: Springer.

Angel, Ronald J., Holly Bell, Julie Beausoleil, and Laura Lein. 2012. *Community Lost: The State, Civil Society and Displaced Survivors of Hurricane Katrina*. New York: Cambridge University Press.

Babones, Salvatore J. 2008. "Income Inequality and Population Health: Correlation and Causality." *Social Science & Medicine* 66:1614–26.

Bahekar, Amol Ashok, Sarabjeet Singh, Sandeep Saha, Janos Molnar, and Rohit Arora. 2007. "The Prevalence and Incidence of Coronary Heart Disease Is Significantly Increased in Periodontitis: A Meta-Analysis." *American Heart Journal* 154:830–37.

Belle, Deborah. 1990. "Poverty and Women's Mental Health." *American Psychologist* 45:385–89.

Berkman, Lisa F., Thomas Glass, Ian Brissette, and Teresa E. Seeman. 2000. "From Social Integration to Health: Durkheim in the New Millennium." *Social Science & Medicine* 51:843–57.

Bharmal, Nazleen, Chi-Hong Tseng, Robert Kaplan, and Mitchell D. Wong. 2012. "State-Level Variations in Racial Disparities in Life Expectancy." *Health Services Research* 47:544–55.

Bird, Philippa, Maye Omar, Victor Doku, Crick Lund, James Rogers Nsereko, Jason Mwanza, and the MHaPP Research Programme Consortium. 2011. "Increasing the Priority of Mental Health in Africa: Findings from Qualitative Research in Ghana, South Africa, Uganda and Zambia." *Health Policy and Planning* 26:357–65.

Blue, Laura. 2011. "The Ethnic Health Advantage." *Scientific American* 301:30–32.

Boli, John and George M. Thomas. 1999. *Constructing World Culture: International Nongovernmental Organizations since 1875*. Stanford, CA: Stanford University Press.

Bourdieu, Pierre. 1986. "The Forms of Capital." Pp. 241–58 in *Handbook of Theory and Research for the Sociology of Education*, edited by J. G. Richardson. New York: Greenwood.

Brady, David. 2003. "Rethinking the Sociological Measurement of Poverty." *Social Forces* 81:715–52.

Brady, David. 2005. "The Welfare State and Relative Poverty in Rich Western Democracies, 1967–1997." *Social Forces* 83:1329–64.

Braveman, Paula A., Catherine Cubbin, Susan Egerter, David R. Williams, and Elsie Pamuk. 2010. "Socioeconomic Disparities in Health in the United States: What the Patterns Tell Us." *American Journal of Public Health* 100:S186–S196.

Brown, Theodore M. and Elizabeth Fee. 2006. "Rudolf Carl Virchow: Medical Scientist, Social Reformer, Role Model." *American Journal of Public Health* 96:2104–5.

Burt, Ronald S. 1992. *Structural Holes: The Social Structure of Competition*. Cambridge, MA: Harvard University Press.

Caspi, Avshalom, Joseph McClay, Terrie E. Moffitt, Jonathan Mill, Judy Martin, Ian W. Craig, Alan Taylor, and Richie Poulton. 2002. "Role of Genotype in the Cycle of Violence in Maltreated Children." *Science* 297:851.

Caspi, Avshalom, Terrie E. Moffitt, Mary Cannon, Joseph McClay, Robin Murray, HonaLee Harrington, Alan Taylor, Louise Arseneault, Ben Williams, Antony Braithwaite, Richie Poulton, and Ian W. Craig. 2005. "Moderation of the Effect of Adolescent-Onset Cannabis Use on Adult Psychosis by a Functional Polymorphism in the Catechol-O-Methyltransferase Gene: Longitudinal Evidence of a Gene X Environment Interaction." *Biological Psychiatry* 57:1117–27.

Caspi, Avshalom, Karen Sugden, Terrie E. Moffitt, Alan Taylor, Ian W. Craig, HonaLee Harrington, Joseph McClay, Jonathan Mill, Judy Martin, Antony Braithwaite, and Richie Poulton. 2003. "Influence of Life Stress on Depression: Moderation by a Polymorphism in the 5-HTT Gene." *Science* 301:386–89.

Centers for Disease Control and Prevention (CDC). 2011a. "CDC Health Disparities and Inequalities Report—United States, 2011." Morbidity and Mortality Weekly Report 60 (Suppl). Atlanta, GA. Retrieved February 15, 2012 (http://www.cdc.gov/mmwr/pdf/other/su6001.pdf.).

Centers for Disease Control and Prevention (CDC). 2011b. "Morbidity and Mortality Weekly Report: QuickStats: Percentage of Adults Aged ≥18 Years Who Ever Received a Diagnosis of Diabetes, by Race/Ethnicity and Hispanic Subpopulation." National Health Interview Survey, United States, 2009, Retrieved February 2, 2012 (http://www.cdc.gov/mmwr/preview/mmwrhtml/mm6028a7.htm?s_cid=mm6028a7_w).

Centers for Disease Control and Prevention (CDC). 2012a. "Leading Causes of Death in Males United States, 2007." Retrieved February 16, 2012 (http://www.cdc.gov/men/lcod/).

Centers for Disease Control and Prevention (CDC). 2012b. "National Vital Statistics Reports, Vol. 59, No. 9." September 28, 2011. Retrieved February 16, 2012 (http://www.cdc.gov/nchs/data/statab/lewk3_2007.pdf).

Central Intelligence Agency (CIA). 2011. *The World Factbook, Country Comparison: Life Expectancy at Birth*. Washington, DC. Retrieved February 5, 2012 (https://www.cia.gov/library/publications/the-world-factbook/rankorder/2102rank.html).

Coleman, James S. 1988. "Social Capital in the Creation of Human Capital." *American Journal of Sociology* 94:S95–S120.

Conroy, Kathleen, Megan Sandel, and Barry Zuckerman. 2010. "Poverty Grown Up: How Childhood Socioeconomic Status Impacts Adult Health." *Journal of Developmental & Behavioral Pediatrics* 31:154–60. doi: 10.1097/DBP.0b013e3181c21a1b.

Cooper, Sara, Joshua Sebunnya, Fred KigoziI, Crick Lund, Alan Flisher, and The Mhapp Research Programme Consortium. 2010. "Viewing Uganda's Mental Health System through a Human Rights Lens." *International Review of Psychiatry* 22:578–88.

Das, Jishnu and Jeffrey Hammer. 2007. "Location, Location, Location: Residence, Wealth, and the Quality of Medical Care in Delhi, India." *Health Affairs* 26:w338–w351.

Do, L. G. 2012. "Distribution of Caries in Children." *Journal of Dental Research* 91:536–43.

Duncan, Greg J., Kathleen M. Ziol-Guest, and Ariel Kalil. 2010. "Early-Childhood Poverty and Adult Attainment, Behavior, and Health." *Child Development* 81:306–25.

Dye, B. A. and G. Thornton-Evans. 2010. "Trends in Oral Health by Poverty Status as Measured by Healthy People 2010 Objectives." *Public Health Reports* 6:817–30.

Easterlin, Richard A. 2000. "The Worldwide Standard of Living since 1800." *Journal of Economic Perspectives* 14:7–26.

Elo, I. T. 2009. "Social Class Differentials in Health and Mortality: Patterns and Explanations in Comparative Perspective." Pp. 553–72 in *Annual Review of Sociology*, vol. 35, *Annual Review of Sociology*. Palo Alto: Annual Reviews.

Esping-Andersen, Gøsta. 1990. *The Three Worlds of Welfare Capitalism*. Princeton, NJ: Princeton University Press.

Esping-Andersen, Gøsta. 1999. *Social Foundations of Postindustrial Economies*. Oxford; New York: Oxford University Press.

Evans, Gary W. and Pilyoung Kim. 2007. "Childhood Poverty and Health." *Psychological Science* 18:953–57.

Fujiwara, Takeo and Ichiro Kawachi. 2008. "Social Capital and Health: A Study of Adult Twins in the U.S." *American Journal of Preventive Medicine* 35:139–44.

Fukuyama, Francis. 2001. "Social Capital, Civil Society And Development." *Third World Quarterly* 22:7–20.

Guiso, Luigi, Paola Sapienza, and Luigi Zingales. 2004. "The Role of Social Capital in Financial Development." *American Economic Review* 94:526–56.

Hajioff, S. and M. McKee. 2000. "The Health of the Roma People: A Review of the Published Literature." *Journal of Epidemiology and Community Health* 54:864–69.

Hassenteufel, Patrick and Bruno Palier. 2007. "Towards Neo-Bismarckian Health Care States? Comparing Health Insurance Reforms in Bismarckian Welfare Systems." *Social Policy and Administration* 41:574–96.

Hayward, Mark D., Eileen M. Crimmins, Toni Miles, and Yu Yang. 2000. "The Significance of Socioeconomic Status in Explaining the Racial Gap in Chronic Health Conditions." *American Sociological Review* 65:910–30.

Humphrey, Linda, Rongwei Fu, David Buckley, Michele Freeman, and Mark Helfand. 2008. "Periodontal Disease and Coronary Heart Disease Incidence: A Systematic Review and Meta-analysis." *Journal of General Internal Medicine* 23:2079–86.

Institute of Medicine. 2001. *Coverage Matters: Insurance and Health Care*. Washington, DC: National Academy Press.

Institute of Medicine. 2002. *Care without Coverage: Too Little, Too Late*. Washington, DC: National Academy Press.

Institute of Medicine. 2003. *Hidden Costs, Value Lost: Uninsurance in America*. Washington, DC: National Academy Press.

James, Sherman A., Amy J. Schulz, and Juliana van Olphen. 2001. "Social Capital, Poverty, and Community Health: An Exploration of Linkages." Pp. 165–88 in *Social Capital and Poor Communities*, edited by S. Saegert, J. P. Thompson, and M. R. Warren. New York: Russell Sage Foundation.

Kaiser Family Foundation and Health Research and Educational Trust. 2011. "Employer Health Benefits: 2011 Summary of Findings." Washington, DC. Retrieved February 18, 2012 (http://ehbs.kff.org/pdf/8226.pdf).

Kakwani, Nanak and Jacques Silber. 2008. "Introduction: Multidimensional Poverty Analysis: Conceptual Issues, Empirical Illustrations and Policy Implications." *World Development* 36:987–91.

Kessler, Ronald C. and T. Bedirhan Ustun. 2008. "The WHO World Mental Health Surveys: Global Perspectives on the Epidemiology of Mental Disorders." New York: Cambridge University Press.

Klebanov, Pamela Kato, Jeanne Brooks-Gunn, and Greg J. Duncan. 1994. "Does Neighborhood and Family Poverty Affect Mothers' Parenting, Mental Health, and Social Support?" *Journal of Marriage and Family* 56:441–55.

Knack, Stephen and Philip Keefer. 1997. "Does Social Capital Have an Economic Payoff? A Cross-Country Investigation." *Quarterly Journal of Economics* 112:1251–88.

Levinson, Daphna, Matthew D. Lakoma, Maria Petukhova, Michael Schoenbaum, Alan M. Zaslavsky, Matthias Angermeyer, Guilherme Borges, Ronny Bruffaerts, Giovanni de Girolamo, Ron de Graaf, Oye Gureje, Josep Maria Haro, Chiyi Hu, Aimee N. Karam, Norito Kawakami, Sing Lee, Jean-Pierre Lepine, Mark Oakley Browne, Michail Okoliyski, José Posada-Villa, Rajesh Sagar, Maria Carmen Viana, David R. Williams, and Ronald C. Kessler. 2010. "Associations of Serious Mental Illness with Earnings: Results from the WHO World Mental Health Surveys." *British Journal of Psychiatry* 197:114–21.

Light, Ivan. 2004. "Social Capital for What?" Pp. 19–33 in *Community-Based Organizations: The Intersection of Social Capital and Local Context in Contemporary Urban Society*, edited by R. M. Silverman. Detroit, MI: Wayne State University Press.

Lin, Nan. 1999. "Social Networks and Status Attainment." *Annual Review of Sociology* 25:467–87.

Link, Bruce G. and Jo Phelan. 1995. "Social Conditions as Fundamental Causes of Disease." *Journal of Health and Social Behavior* Special Issue 35:80–94.

Livingston, Gretchen, Susan Minushkin, and D'Vera Cohn. 2012. "Hispanics and Health Care in the United States." Pew Hispanic Center and the Robert Wood Johnson Foundation. Retrieved February 16, 2012 (http://www.pewhispanic.org/files/reports/91.pdf).

Loucks, Eric B., John W. Lynch, Louise Pilote, Rebecca Fuhrer, Nisha D. Almeida, Hugues Richard, Golareh Agha, Joanne M. Murabito, and Emelia J. Benjamin. 2009. "Life-Course Socioeconomic Position and Incidence of Coronary Heart Disease: The Framingham Offspring Study." *American Journal of Epidemiology* 169:829–36.

Lund, Crick. 2010. "Mental Health in Africa: Finding from the Mental Health and Poverty Project." *International Review of Psychiatry* 22:547–49.

Markides, K. S. and J. Coreil. 1986. "The Health of Hispanics in the Southwestern United States: An Epidemiologic Paradox." *Public Health Rep* 101:253–65.

Markides, Kyriakos S. and Karl Eschbach. 2005. "Aging, Migration, and Mortality: Current Status of Research on the Hispanic Paradox." *Journals of Gerontology Series B: Psychological Sciences and Social Sciences* 60:S68–S75.

Marmot, M. and R. Bell. 2011. "Social Determinants and Dental Health." *Advances in Dental Research* 23:201–6.

Marmot, M. G., S. Stansfeld, C. Patel, F. North, J. Head, I. White, E. Brunner, A. Feeney, and G. Davey Smith. 1991. "Health Inequalities among British Civil Servants: The Whitehall II Study." *The Lancet* 337:1387–93.

Marquezine, Guilherme Figueiredo, Camila Maciel Oliveira, Alexandre C. Pereira, José E. Krieger, and José G. Mill. 2008. "Metabolic Syndrome Determinants in an Urban Population from Brazil: Social Class and Gender-Specific Interaction." *International Journal of Cardiology* 129:259–65.

Marshall, T. H. 1950. *Citizenship and Social Class: And Other Essays.* Cambridge: Cambridge University Press.

McFadden, Emily, Robert Luben, Nicholas Wareham, Sheila Bingham, and Kay-Tee Khaw. 2008. "Occupational Social Class, Risk Factors and Cardiovascular Disease Incidence in Men And Women: A Prospective Study in the European Prospective Investigation of Cancer and Nutrition in Norfolk (EPIC-Norfolk) Cohort." *European Journal of Epidemiology* 23:449–58.

Montgomery, Mark R. 2009. "Urban Poverty and Health in Developing Countries." *Population Bulletin* 64. Retrieved May 7, 2012 (http://www.prb.org/pdf09/64.2urbanization.pdf).

Morbidity and Mortality Weekly Report. 1999. "Ten Great Public Health Achievements— United States, 1900–1999." *JAMA: Journal of the American Medical Association* 281:1481.

Ostchega, Y., T. B. Harris, R. Hirsch, V. L. Parsons, and R. Kington. 2000. "The Prevalence of Functional Limitations and Disability in Older Persons in the US: Data from the National Health and Nutrition Examination Survey III." *Journal of the American Geriatrics Society* 48:1132–35.

Palier, Bruno. 2010. *A Long Goodbye to Bismarck? The Politics of Welfare Reform in Continental Europe.* Amsterdam: Amsterdam University Press.

Paradise, Julia. 2009. "Oral Health Coverage and Care for Low-Income Children: The Role of Medicaid and Chip." Kaiser Commission on Medicaid and the Uninsured. Washington, DC: Kaiser Foundation. Policy Brief 7681-03. Retrieved May 15, 2012 (http://www.kff.org/medicaid/upload/7681-03.pdf).

Phelan, Jo C., Bruce G. Link, and Parisa Tehranifar. 2010. "Social Conditions as Fundamental Causes of Health Inequalities." *Journal of Health and Social Behavior* 51:S28–S40.

Portes, Alejandro and Patricia Landolt. 2000. "Social Capital: Promise and Pitfalls of its Role in Development." *Journal of Latin American Studies* 32:529.

Portney, Dent E. and Jeffrey M. Berry. 1997. "Mobilizing Minority Communities: Social Capital and Participation in Urban Neighborhoods." *American Behavioral Scientist* 40:632–44.

Preston, Samuel H. 1996. "American Longevity: Past, Present, and Future." Policy Research Paper 36. Maxwell School of Citizenship and Public Affairs, Syracuse University, New York.

Ramsay, Sheena E., Peter H. Whincup, Richard Morris, Lucy Lennon, and S.G. Wannamethee. 2008. "Is Socioeconomic Position Related to the Prevalence of Metabolic Syndrome?: Influence of Social Class across the Life Course in a Population-Based Study of Older Men." *Diabetes Care* 31:2380–82.

Reid, T. R. 2009. *The Healing of America: A Global Quest for Better, Cheaper, and Fairer Health Care*. New York: Penguin Books.

Rodriguez, Michael A., MarySue V. Heilemann, Eve Fielder, Alfonso Ang, Faustina Nevarez, and Carol M. Mangione. 2008. "Intimate Partner Violence, Depression, and PTSD among Pregnant Latina Women." *Annals of Family Medicine* 6:44–52.

Rojas, Mariano. 2008. "Experienced Poverty and Income Poverty in Mexico: A Subjective Well-Being Approach." *World Development* 36:1078–93.

Saegert, Susan, J. Phillip Thompson, and Mark R. Warren. 2001. "Social Capital and Poor Communities." New York: Russell Sage Foundation.

Sampson, Robert J. and W. Byron Groves. 1989. "Community Structure and Crime: Testing Social-Disorganization Theory." *American Journal of Sociology* 94:774.

Samson, Robert J. 1999. "What "Community" Supplies." Pp. 241–79 in *Urban Problems and Community Development*, edited by R. F. Ferguson and W. T. Dickens. Washington, DC: Brookings Institution.

Sen, Amartya. 1976. "Poverty: An Ordinal Approach to Measurement." *Econometrica* 44:219–31.

Sen, Amartya. 1999. *Development as Freedom*. New York: Random House.

Sen, Amartya. 2000. *Social Exclusion: Concept, Application, and Scrutiny*, vol. 1. Manila, Philippines: Asian Development Bank.

Shetterly, S. M., J. Baxter, N. E. Morgenstem, J. Grigsby, and R. F. Hamman. 1998. "Higher Instrumental Activities of Daily Living Disability in Hispanics Compared with Non-Hispanic Whites in Rural Colorado: The San Luis Valley Health and Aging Study." *American Journal of Epidemiology* 147:1019–27.

Shonkoff, Jack P., W. Thomas Boyce, and Bruce S. McEwen. 2009. "Neuroscience, Molecular Biology, and the Childhood Roots of Health Disparities." *JAMA: Journal of the American Medical Association* 301:2252–59.

Silverman, Robert Mark. 2004. *Community-based Organizations: The Intersection of Social Capital and Local Context in Contemporary Urban Society*. Detroit, MI: Wayne State University Press.

Smeeding, Timothy M., Lee Rainwater, and Gary Burtless. 2001. "U.S. Poverty in a Cross-national Context." Pp. 162–89 in *Understanding Poverty*, edited by S. H. Danziger and R. H. Haveman. New York and Cambridge, MA: Russell Sage Foundation and Harvard University Press.

Stamatakis, E., P. Zaninotto, E. Falaschetti, J. Mindell, and J. Head. 2010. "Time Trends in Childhood and Adolescent Obesity in England from 1995 to 2007 and Projections of Prevalence to 2015." *Journal of Epidemiology and Community Health* 64:167–74.

Temkin, Kenneth and William M. Rohe. 1998. "Social Capital and Neighborhood Stability: An Empirical Investigation." *Housing Policy Debate* 9:61–88.

Tuljapurkar, Shripad, Nan Li, and Carl Boe. 2000. "A Universal Pattern of Mortality Decline in the G7 Countries." *Nature* 405:789–92.

U.S. Census Bureau. 2012a. "Table 105. Life Expectancy by Sex, Age, and Race: 2008." In *Statistical Abstract of the United States*. Washington, DC: U.S. Census Bureau. Retrieved February 5, 2012 (http://www.census.gov/compendia/statab/2012/tables/12s0105.pdf).

U.S. Census Bureau. 2012b. "Table 155. Health Insurance Coverage Status by Selected Characteristics: 2008 and 2009." Retrieved September 6, 2015 (http://www.google.com/url?sa=t&rct=j&q=&esrc=s&source=web&cd=1&ved=0CB4QFjAAahUKEwi1h7Wo8OLHAhWBEZIKHYrlAqk&url=http%3A%2F%2Fwww.census.gov%2Fcompendia%2Fstatab%2F2012%2Ftables%2F12s0155.xls&usg=AFQjCNG4kW7B9Wro1tWbPOmaFSnfIxEUhQ&bvm=bv.102022582,d.aWw).

U.S. Census Bureau. 2012c. "Table 229. Educational Attainment by Race and Hispanic Origin: 1970 to 2010." Retrieved September 6, 2015 (http://www.census.gov/compendia/statab/2012/tables/12s0229.pdf).

UNESCO. 2010. "Adult and Youth Literacy: Global Trends in Gender Parity." In *UIS Fact Sheet*. Montreal, Quebec: UN Educational, Scientific and Cultural Organization. UIS Fact Sheet, September 2010, No. 3. Retrieved February 5, 2012 (http://www.uis.unesco.org/FactSheets/Documents/Fact_Sheet_2010_Lit_EN.pdf).

United Nations. 1948. "Universal Declaration of Human Rights." New York: United Nations. Retrieved September 6, 2015 (http://www.un.org/en/documents/udhr/).

United Nations. 2011a. "World Mortality Report 2007." New York: United Nations, Department of Economic and Social Affairs, Population Division. Retrieved February 5, 2010 (http://www.un.org/esa/population/publications/worldmortalityreport2007/WORLD%20MORTALITY%20REPORT.PDF).

United Nations. 2011b. "World Population Prospects: The 2010 Revision, Volume I: Comprehensive Tables. St/Esa/Ser.A/313, Table S.16. Life Expectancy at Birth, Both Sexes Combined, By Country For Selected Periods." New York: United Nations, Department of Economic and Social Affairs. Retrieved December 15, 2012 (http://esa.un.org/wpp/Documentation/pdf/WPP2010_Volume-I_Comprehensive-Tables.pdf).

Victora, Cesar G., Linda Adair, Caroline Fall, Pedro C. Hallal, Reynaldo Martorell, Linda Richter, and Harshpal Singh Sachdev. 2008. "Maternal and Child Undernutrition: Consequences for Adult Health and Human Capital." *The Lancet* 371:340–57.

Vieno, Alessio, Maury Nation, Douglas D. Perkins, Massimiliano Pastore, and Massimo Santinello. 2010. "Social Capital, Safety Concerns, Parenting, and Early Adolescents' Antisocial Behavior." *Journal of Community Psychology* 38:314–28.

Waitzkin, Howard. 2011. *Medicine and Public Health at the End of Empire*. Boulder, CO: Paradigm.

Williams, David R. and Selina A. Mohammed. 2009. "Discrimination and Racial Disparities in Health: Evidence and Needed Research." *Journal of Behavioral Medicine* 32:20–47.

Wilmoth, John R. 1998. "The Future of Human Longevity: A Demographer's Perspective." *Science* 280:395.

Wilper, Andrew P., Steffie Woolhandler, Karen E. Lasser, Danny McCormick, David H. Bor, and David U. Himmelstein. 2009. "Health Insurance and Mortality in US Adults." *American Journal of Public Health* 99:2289–95.

Woolcock, Michael. 2002. "Social Capital in Theory and Practice: Where Do We Stand?" Pp. 18–39 in *Social Capital and Economic Development: Well-Being in Developing Countries*, edited by J. Isham, T. Kelly, and S. Ramaswamy. Northampton, MA: Edward Elgar.

World Health Organization (WHO). 1946, "Constitution of the World Health Organization." P. 2. New York: World Health Conference. Retrieved February 5, 2012 (http://whqlibdoc. who.int/hist/official_records/constitution.pdf).

World Health Organization (WHO). 2004. "Prevalence, Severity, and Unmet Need for Treatment of Mental Disorders in the World Health Organization World Mental Health Surveys." *Journal of the American Medical Association* 291:2581–90.

World Health Organization (WHO). 2009a. "An Assessment of Interactions between Global Health Initiatives and Country Health Systems." *The Lancet* 373:2137–69.

World Health Organization, Regional Office for Africa (WHO). 2009b. "Oral and Dental Health." Retrieved May 15, 2012 (http://www.afro.who.int/en/clusters-a-programmes/dpc/non-communicable-diseases-managementndm/programme-components/oral-health. html).

Zak, Paul J. and Stephen Knack. 2001. "Trust and Growth." *Economic Journal* 111:295–321.

Zaninotto, P., J. Head, E. Stamatakis, H. Wardle, and J. Mindell. 2009. "Trends in Obesity among Adults in England from 1993 to 2004 by Age and Social Class and Projections of Prevalence to 2012." *Journal of Epidemiology and Community Health* 63:140–46.

SECTION VI

POLICIES, SOLUTIONS, AND RESPONSES

CHAPTER 30

AID AND GLOBAL POVERTY

SIMON FEENY AND MARK McGILLIVRAY

INTRODUCTION

AID, for the purpose of this chapter, is defined as resource transfers from governments of rich countries to relatively poor countries that purportedly are intended to assist the latter achieve higher living standards. Controversies surround aid. The linkage between aid and poverty in developing countries is especially controversial and has been for decades. There were lofty expectations regarding the poverty-reducing impacts of foreign aid in the early 1960s, when activists called on rich countries to transfer 1 percent of their combined incomes to developing countries to help fight poverty. It seemed to many that foreign aid was a golden wand: wave it enough times and it would rid the world of poverty. To others it might not necessarily rid the world of poverty, but it was the single most important thing rich countries could do to pull many millions of people in poor countries out of poverty. Other observers were skeptical or downright hostile toward aid. Many of these people saw aid as no more than an attempt by rich countries to exploit their poorer counterparts in the pursuit of their own political, commercial, and other self-interests. Some even suggested it might do more harm than good by entrenching the positions of inept or corrupt leaders, constraining the operation of private enterprise, and promoting dependency through the displacement of domestic savings. Rich countries did, to some extent, respond to the calls of the pro-aid activists. Few managed to provide aid to the level of 1 percent of their income, but they have certainly allocated substantial amounts of public money to poor countries. The most widely used measure of aid is Official Development Assistance (ODA).[1] ODA levels have climbed considerably since the 1960s. More than $4.3 trillion in ODA has been provided to more than 150 developing countries over the period 1960 to 2011 (OECD 2012). Global ODA increased from $36 million in 1960 to $148 billion in 2010, the highest level ever recorded (OECD 2012).[2] Yet despite these sums of money, some simple empirical facts remain: poverty levels have not fallen appreciably in the last 30 years, and billions of people still live in poverty. The poverty statistics are indeed quite sobering. In 2008, just under 1.3 billion people were living in developing countries in extreme income poverty on less than $1.25 per day. There were just under 2.5 billion living on less than $2.00 per day in 2008, also the highest level ever recorded (World Bank 2012). Present day critics of aid often see these numbers as proof that the skeptics were correct, with some insisting that aid made a bad situation worse and that it is part of the problem and not the solution to global poverty. Yet aid still has its supporters. Some argue that the problem is that donors have simply not provided enough aid, that it has reduced poverty in some countries but not others, and that it can work a lot better if it was more poverty focused.[3] A more nuanced broadly pro-aid case is that poverty would have been much worse in the absence of aid; that we need to be cognizant about what aid can realistically achieve given that, since the 1970s aid has accounted for the equivalent of just 1.5 percent of developing country GDP; and that even if aid can reduce poverty, it is only one of many drivers of poverty.[4] The international community's stance on the Millennium Development Goals, which include the goal of halving the proportion of people living in extreme income poverty by 2015, is consistent with this recognition in that it views aid as one of a number of means by which this goal might be achieved. Whatever basic position might have the most validity, it remains the case that there is widespread disappointment that aid has not done better in terms of its poverty-reducing impact and that links between aid and poverty reduction remain highly controversial.

This chapter re-examines the relationship between aid and poverty in developing countries, attempting to cut through the controversy surrounding the topic. Its concern is not whether donor governments are motivated and actively set out to reduce poverty in developing countries through the provision of aid but with the impact of aid on poverty reduction. It does so mainly by looking at aid and poverty descriptive statistics—the aid and poverty record—and surveying relevant empirical studies. The chapter concludes that an objective and balanced examination of the literature suggests that income poverty would in all probability be higher in the absence of aid, although by how much remains a matter of much speculation. That said, it also argues that aid can play an important but at best marginal role relative to other drivers in promoting poverty reduction in developing countries, irrespective of how high or efficient aid flows might become. The chapter consists of a further four sections.

The second section examines the aid and poverty record, by looking mainly at global data from the 1980s onward. A key question considered in this section is whether the disappointment over the poverty-reducing impact of aid is, in its proper context, disappointment with the efforts of donors to reduce poverty as opposed to disappointment with the impacts of the aid that has actually been provided. It also uses these data to highlight some of the complexities in looking at empirical relationships between aid and poverty, in particular the problem of the "without aid" counterfactual. Unless we can be reasonably confident of what poverty would have been in the absence of aid, that is, knowing the counterfactual, one can say little of its impact on poverty.

The third section looks at the analytics of aid and poverty, highlighting the various ways that one can analyze the impact of the former on the latter. It makes the fundamental point that only a small proportion of aid has been provided directly to poor people, as if it were a form of welfare support. This has profound implications for how the poverty impact of aid is investigated, and how the results of this investigation are interpreted.

The fourth section provides the literature review. It commences by reviewing studies that look directly, in a strictly empirical sense, at the relationship between aid and poverty. The review then looks at studies that do not address poverty directly but instead look at the impact of aid on variables that might drive poverty reduction.

The fifth section concludes, suggesting that in all probability aid has had a marginally positive impact on poverty reduction in developing countries, implying that poverty would be slightly higher in its absence.

THE AID AND GLOBAL POVERTY RECORD

Prior to progressing any further, the ways that aid and poverty are conceptualized and measured in this chapter need to be specified. Aid can be defined and measured in different ways, but as is evident from the discussion in the first section, we focus on ODA. ODA has a specific definition. ODA represents flows that are provided by OECD country governments to countries classified as developing and which are concessional, either being in the form of grants or soft loans. ODA need not go directly from one government to another but can be provided through a multilateral agency (such as the World Bank or the many UN agencies) or a nongovernment agency. This definition, and the reporting consistent with it, is that of the OECD's Development Assistance Committee, the membership of which is made up of 23 OECD countries and the European Union.[5] In order for a flow to be classified as ODA it is supposed to have the promotion of development and welfare in developing countries as its main objective. Many observers of ODA would question with validity whether any particular ODA flow, be it to a country, region, project or program, actually has these outcomes as the main objective. In practice this requirement excludes military assistance as aid or other flows that are clearly nondevelopmental.

Our focus on ODA means that we take no account of so-called South-South development cooperation, including aid from China. Chinese aid has become an important part of the international aid scene, but an absence of reliable information on these flows prevents its inclusion in the analysis of this chapter. Focusing on ODA also means that we take no account of aid during the Marshall Plan. Much of the aid provided during this period would not be classified as ODA, and, even if it was, data availability remains an issue. While the Marshall Plan is judged to have been very successful in rehabilitating countries from the damage caused by World War II, and in doing so undoubtedly lifted large numbers of people out of poverty, we leave it to historical studies to consider its impacts on poverty. These points noted, it remains the case that ODA is by far the largest form of what might be broadly described as development aid, and for this reason our focus covers the vast majority of the aid landscape.

Poverty, like aid, can also be defined in many ways. Contemporary thinking rightly considers poverty to be multidimensional, involving more than just shortfalls in income. We focus on income poverty, measured using the well-known poverty head-count measure. The chapter does not focus on other poverty dimensions, such as those relating to health and education. Aid certainly has the potential to make an impact on poverty in these dimensions.[6] This chapter does not focus on poverty in nonincome dimensions for two reasons. First, there remains ambiguity over poverty lines for these dimensions and, in turn, the extent of poverty within them. Second, there is little if any preexisting literature on the impact of aid on poverty in dimensions other than income. This is not to say that studies have not looked at the impact of aid on nonin-come quality of life achievements. There is, for example, a body of literature examining the impact of aid on health and education achievements.[7] But this literature does not look at impacts by population subgroup within countries, especially those at the bot-tom end of the relevant distributions. There is also a well-established literature looking at the relationships between aid and public sector expenditures on health and educa-tion.[8] It would be difficult to draw inferences from the findings of this literature, for reasons that are explained below.

Let us now consider some simple empirics of the aid and income poverty relation-ship. Figure 30.1 looks at trends in aid and poverty since the earliest year for which comprehensive poverty data are available. The measures of poverty under consider-ation are the widely used $PPP1.25 and $PPP2 poverty headcounts, which show the number of people living on incomes below these respective poverty lines. The former is treated as a measure of extreme income poverty.[9] There are obvious messages about the relationship between aid and poverty from Figure 30.1. Aid volumes trend upward for the period shown, despite stagnating from 1993 to 1996. Extreme income poverty trends downward for the whole period, as does the number of people living on less than $PPP2 per day from 1996. Putting aside the fact that there are many other drivers of poverty reduction (a point considered later), one might be tempted to conclude that aid

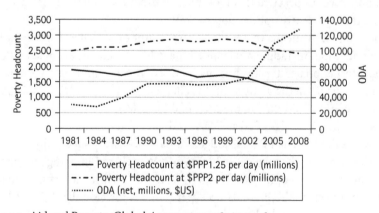

FIGURE 30.1 Aid and Poverty, Global Aggregates, 1981 to 2008

Source: OECD (2012) and World Bank (2012).

is associated with declines in global poverty. It could be equally argued that Figure 30.1 is consistent with the disappointment about the poverty-reducing impact of aid, since the number of people living on less than $PPP2 per day is only slightly lower in 2008 than in 1981, and the declines in extreme income poverty are modest. Perhaps all one can conclude is that the data shown in Figure 30.1 do not support the view that aid is part of the problem with poverty being lower in the absence of this inflow. Measuring aid in constant price per capita terms, per head of recipient country population, does not provide terribly different insights, as Figure 30.2 suggests.[10]

The aid and poverty record in the two regions where poverty has been highest, South Asia and sub-Saharan Africa, is shown in Figures 30.3 to 30.6. The relationship between aid and poverty in South Asia is not especially clear, and identifying a relationship of any type is difficult. Aid to this region might at best be associated with declines in extreme income poverty from 2002. But at the same time, increased aid levels from the

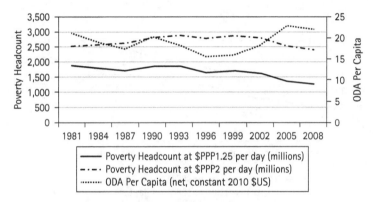

FIGURE 30.2 Aid Per Capita and Poverty, Global Aggregates, 1981 to 2008

Source: OECD (2012) and World Bank (2012).

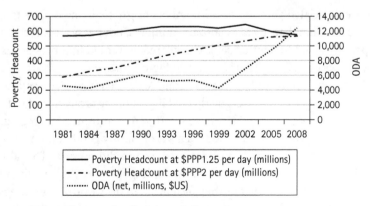

FIGURE 30.3 Aid and Poverty, South Asia, 1981 to 2008

Source: OECD (2012) and World Bank (2012).

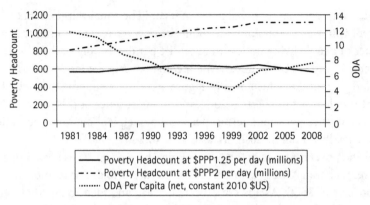

FIGURE 30.4 Aid Per Capita and Poverty, South Asia, 1981 to 2008

Source: OECD (2012) and World Bank (2012).

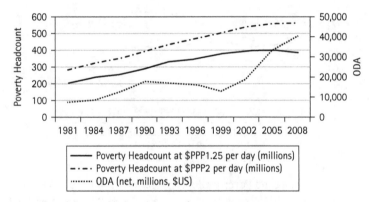

FIGURE 30.5 Aid and Poverty, sub-Saharan Africa, 1981 to 2008

Source: OECD (2012) and World Bank (2012).

late 1990s are associated with increased numbers of people living on less than $PPP2 per day. These trends relate to aid in absolute numbers, not per head of recipient population. If per capita aid to South Asia is considered, lower aid numbers are associated with higher levels of poverty. This is shown in Figure 30.4.

The aid and poverty record in sub-Saharan Africa lends greatest support to the harshest critics of aid, those who argue that aid is part of the problem and not the solution. The picture emerging from Figures 30.5 and 30.6 is far from encouraging. Income poverty declined between 2005 and 2008. This is obviously good news. Yet for most of the years under consideration, as aid increased, so too did poverty. This also applies to the rise in per capita aid from 1999, shown in Figure 30.6. Perhaps the most aid-sympathetic interpretation is that the big push in aid to the world's poorest region from the early 2000s led to a slowing and eventual reversal of the upward trend in income poverty.

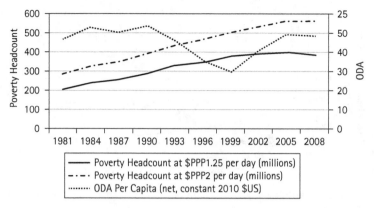

FIGURE 30.6 Aid Per Capita and Poverty, sub-Saharan Africa, 1981 to 2008

Source: OECD (2012) and World Bank (2012).

Arguably the most telling information coming from the simple empirics just pre-sented is that relating to per capita aid, shown in Figures 30.2, 30.4, and 30.6, . Whether aid may rise, fall, or remain the same in absolute terms does not matter so much from a general development-effectiveness perspective. What matters from this perspective are levels relative to the number of people at the receiving end in the recipient country. The number of people at the receiving end can be defined in many ways. It could simply be treated as the total population of the receiving country or the number of people living below and close to the chosen poverty line. Irrespective of what is the most appropriate measure of aid, it is clear that per capita aid, both globally and to South Asia and sub-Saharan Africa, has fallen for much of the period under question. It is lower in 2008 than in 1981 for both South Asia and sub-Saharan Africa. This might suggest that the criticisms of aid are best leveled not at the incremental impact of the aid actually pro-vided but at the efforts of donor governments in seeking to fight poverty in developing countries.

A more incisive way of looking at the aid-poverty relationship, one that gets us closer to drawing conclusions about the impact of aid on poverty, is to examine scatter plots of these two variables. Scatter plots are shown in Figures 30.7 and 30.8, which focus on the poverty headcount based on the $PPP1.25 poverty line.[11] Figure 30.7 combines regional aid and poverty data, while Figure 30.8 combines data for all individual coun-tries for which requisite data are available.[12] In each case aid is measured in per capita terms. A line of best fit is included in these charts, which most closely resembles the relationship evident in the data. What is clear from the data is that higher aid levels are associated with lower poverty levels.

Supporters of aid might like this association, but it does not mean that aid has been effective in reducing poverty or that poverty would have been higher in aid's absence. There are many determinants of poverty reduction, of which aid might (but might not) be one. The relationships shown in these figures might be driven by other variables and have nothing to do with aid. As such, the associations shown in these

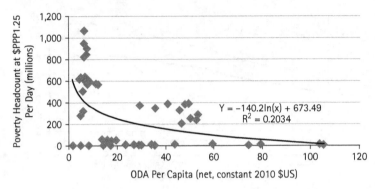

FIGURE 30.7 Scatter Plot of ODA Per Capita and Poverty Headcount at $PPP1.25 Per Day, Developing Country Regions

Source: OECD (2012) and World Bank (2012).

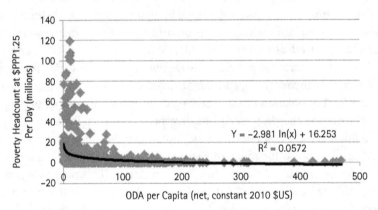

FIGURE 30.8 Scatter Plot of ODA Per Capita and Poverty Headcount at $PPP1.25 per day, All Developing Countries

Source: OECD (2012) and World Bank (2012).

figures could well be spurious. A further complicating factor is that donors might respond to higher levels of poverty with more aid, with poverty leading to more aid rather than more aid leading to less poverty. If this were the case, we might observe a positive relationship between aid and poverty, irrespective of the impact of the former on the latter. The higher-aid-higher-poverty associations shown in a number of Figures 30.1 to 30.8 could actually be due to donors responding to higher poverty levels with more aid. In order to confidently answer the questions of whether poverty is higher, unchanged, or lower owing to aid we need to know what levels of poverty would have prevailed in the absence of aid. Put differently, we need to be able to speculate with accuracy the "no aid" poverty counterfactual. We address this in the remainder of this chapter.

THE ANALYTICS OF AID AND POVERTY: HOW CAN AID IMPACT POVERTY?

Analyzing the impact of aid on poverty would be relatively straightforward if it was given directly to poor people, as if it were a form of welfare support, either by donor governments or agents acting on their behalf. What would matter is the amount provided and how the poor used it. The amount of aid would have to be sufficient to lift the recipients to, or above, an appropriate poverty line, and it would need to be used in a way that kept them on or above this line when the aid money ceased. Yet aid is not by and large given directly to poor people, nor do donor government agencies necessarily target poor people directly.[13] Among the reasons for this is that they are often difficult to reach and attempting to do so comes with high risk, especially when donor country governments and taxpayers demand observable results and value for money (McGillivray et al. 2013).

Aid is instead provided mostly to recipient country governments, civil society, or even to the private sector in recipient countries by donor governments either bilaterally or through multilateral organizations in various forms with a range of specific purposes, some of which will have little direct relationship with poverty reduction. Donors can also provide aid directly, typically using private sector contracting organizations. The specific purposes for which aid is provided do not relate to high-level foreign policy or other objectives donors might pursue in the provision of aid per se but rather to areas or sectors to which it is directed in recipient countries. Among those identified by the OECD's Development Assistance Committee (DAC), and under which OECD donor nations report, include health, education, water, sanitation, public sector administration, human rights, conflict prevention, transport, communications, banking and financial services, trade policy, mining, tourism, agriculture, and forestry (OECD 2012). While it is not uncommon for donors to identify poverty reduction in developing countries as an overall objective motivating the provision of aid, it is not among the specific purposes of aid under which donor nations report as an examination of OECD (2012) makes evident.

This has clear implications for how the poverty impact of aid is investigated, and how the results of this investigation are interpreted. One approach would be to speculate on the drivers of income poverty reduction and ask which forms of aid are likely to address these drivers. It is often claimed that in the context of income poverty, among the reasons why many poor people are poor is a lack of education, low levels of health, and a lack of access to basic services. If this is so, then it would seem reasonable to look for empirical associations between the levels of aid to these sectors and income poverty headcounts through the application of regression analysis, say by using cross country data and after controlling for other drivers of poverty. For example, analysis could be undertaken of the association between education aid and income poverty. Regression analysis could provide an overall association between education aid and income poverty, or an estimate of the total impact of the former on the latter, in that there is no attempt to establish the various causal channels through which such an association might arise. It could be, for instance, be that education aid augments domestic expenditure on primary schooling and thereby allows poor people to obtain more highly paid employment, or that it enables those involved in the delivery of pro-poor services to do so more efficiently, or a combination of these and other impacts.

While such an approach might seem intuitively appealing, it is not without its difficulties. Other forms of aid might have some impact on income poverty. This might not only lead to an incomplete picture of the overall impact of aid on poverty but also deem the results of the empirical analysis biased and misleading owing to omitted variable bias, a well-known problem with regression analysis. There are also good reasons for expecting that education aid, or for that matter aid for health, water, and sanitation, might not have any impact on income poverty or that this impact varies so much across countries that looking for an empirical association from cross-country data is a fruitless exercise. It is reasonably well established that health and education expenditures, along with spending on the provision of water and sanitation services, can have pro-rich biases, and, as a consequence, do not reach those living in income poverty (World Bank 2004). Alternatively, aid can be fungible, which is said to be the case if the recipient has the ability to use aid for purposes other than those intended by the donor (McGillivray and Morrissey 2001). If this is the case, a donor might allocate a given amount of aid to augment the recipient government's own expenditure in a particular area, but the recipient allocates part or all the funds elsewhere, or all the funds to the area intended by the donor but decreases its own expenditure in that area. The net result is that total expenditure in the intended area, donor and recipient, increases but by less than the amount of aid provided. This, like a pro-rich bias in recipient-government expenditure, does not necessarily mean that aid has not had an impact on poverty, positive or otherwise, simply that it cannot necessarily be inferred from an empirical association between a particular form of aid and poverty, however poverty relevant the former might be.

An important driver of poverty is economic growth, the year-on-year growth in real per capita national income. Ravallion and Chen (1997), Dollar and Kraay (2002), and Kraay (2006) are among the better known studies that examine this link. There is some debate over the process through which growth can reduce poverty. Some argue that high rates of growth per se are negatively associated with poverty: countries that achieve such growth will in general have fewer people living in poverty than would otherwise be the case. Others argue that growth is a necessary, but not sufficient, condition for poverty reduction, and that it is sufficient if the incomes of the poor grow as national incomes grow for growth to be termed pro-poor.[14] A measure of the extent to which economic growth results in poverty reduction is the growth elasticity of poverty (GEP) (Bourguignon 2004). The GEP is defined as the percentage change in the incidence of poverty in response to a one percentage increase in per capita income. The GEP will understandably vary across countries, with estimates ranging anywhere from -2.0 to -5.0 (Ravallion and Chen 1997; Bruno Ravallion, and Squire 1998; Bhalla 2002; Adams 2003, 2004). This in turn suggests that a 10 percent increase in economic growth, for example, will lead to a decrease in the proportion of people living in extreme income poverty in the country in question of anywhere between 20 and 50 percent. A widely used global GEP is -2.0 (Collier and Dollar 2001, 2002).

Bourguignon (2004) demonstrates in a theoretical context that the GEP depends on changes in per capita income levels and the distribution of relative incomes or income inequality. Son and Kakwani (2004) find using empirical analysis that the GEP is smaller in countries with low levels of per capita income and in countries with higher levels of inequality. De Janvry and Sadoulet (2000) also report a positive empirical association between the GEP and levels of secondary schooling.

The preceding discussion points to two ways that the impact of aid on poverty can be assessed empirically. The first is to look at the association between aid and economic growth in recipient countries, after controlling for the impact of other variables on the latter, and then draw inferences about the numerical extent of this association for poverty reduction using an appropriate GEP. This essentially amounts to multiplying one coefficient, showing by how much a one-unit change in aid changes the growth rate, by another, the GEP. Looking for an association between aid and growth assumes that most forms of aid will have some impact on economic growth in these countries, positive or otherwise. While not all forms of aid are intended to drive growth, most will have some sort of relationship with it, as a cursory glance of the different types of aid listed previously would suggest. A numerical association between aid and growth might tell us if the former impacts on the latter, and if so, this is useful for advocacy purposes. But by suppressing all the causal channels that lead to this association, it does not tell us why or how this association emerges and as such is not especially useful for devising policies aimed at greater poverty reduction through aid.

The second way that the impact of aid on poverty can be empirically assessed is to look at the former's impact on the GEP or on known drivers of the GEP. If aid impacts on growth of per capita income then it must, by definition influence its level. Aid might have some impact on inequality through an impact on governance, given that good governance can involve the introduction of more inclusive social policies. It might also have some impact on the other known driver of the GEP, secondary schooling, notwithstanding the fungibility issue. Information on an empirical association between aid and the GEP, if there is indeed one, could then be combined with actual growth rates in developing countries to provide an estimate of the extent to which aid has impacted poverty. Put differently, one would obtain an aid-GEP coefficient, which would then be multiplied by an observed economic growth rate to provide an estimate of the extent to which aid has reduced the number of people living in income poverty. Deriving such a coefficient from an analysis of aid and drivers of the GEP would appear to be a more cumbersome task as it would involve information on the coefficient between each driver and the GEP itself.

The discussion thus far has overlooked an obvious point. If it is reasonable to look for a broad association between aid and economic growth, then it would also appear reasonable to look for such an association between aid and income poverty, say using a poverty headcount statistic. This investigation would seek to determine the association between aid and poverty after controlling for the impact on the latter of variables other than aid. Put differently, it would seek to identify what the level of poverty would have been in the absence of aid using historical data. This exercise is subject to the same core criticism of aid and growth studies: it can at best tell us if aid reduces poverty and by how much, but not how. Such an exercise would provide the same basic information as looking at aid and the GEP. It would result in an aid-poverty coefficient, which would be multiplied by the number of people living below the corresponding poverty line to obtain the impact of aid on poverty. Of course it could be the case that aid has no impact on poverty, in which case the aid-poverty coefficient would be zero.

It was mentioned earlier that aid is not by and large given directly to poor people. Some aid is, in addition to a share of humanitarian and emergency relief aid. Conditional cash transfers and microfinance are among a number of forms of aid that can be given directly to people, which include those living in income poverty. Comprehensive aggregate data on these microlevel flows are hard to obtain, but it has been estimated that microfinance has accounted for as much as 10 percent of total aid in any given year. Both have the potential to impact income poverty, to a much greater degree than humanitarian and emergency relief. As such, there are strong grounds for looking for associations between these types of aid and poverty. Poverty impacts of these types of aid cannot be assessed through country-level or cross-country analysis discussed previously. They can, however, be assessed using evidence from field experiments, akin to randomized control trials (RCTs) (Banerjee and He 2003). The challenge in using the results from these field experiments is having a sufficiently large number of them to be able to make judgments about the overall or aggregate impact of aid on poverty.

GOING BEYOND SIMPLE DESCRIPTIVE STATISTICS: A LITERATURE SURVEY

The discussion of the previous section identifies four areas of research that might provide insight into the impact of foreign aid on global poverty. They are research that looks for (1) an empirical association between aid and poverty, seeking to identify what the level of poverty would be in the absence of aid; (2) an empirical association between aid and growth, seeking to identify what the rate of the latter would be in the absence of the former so that inferences can be drawn about the impact of aid on poverty; (3) an empirical association between aid and an appropriate GEP, or on drivers of the GEP, so that this information can be combined with economic growth rates to provide an estimate of the contribution of aid to poverty reduction; and (4) the impacts on poverty of what might be called microinterventions supported by aid, identified through the application of field experiments akin to RCTs. Literature falling into these four areas of research is now considered.

Aid and Poverty

A surprisingly small but growing literature has emerged that examines whether aid impacts income poverty using the econometric analysis of cross-country data. In general, the empirical evidence is encouraging. Asra et al. (2005), Bahmani-Oskooee and Oyolola (2009), and Alvi and Senbeta (2012) all find empirical support for aid reducing headcount poverty.[15] Conversely, Chong et al. (2009) find there is, on average, no association between growth and poverty reduction in developing countries but some weak evidence that foreign aid is effective at reducing poverty in countries with better institutions.[16]

Three other interesting findings from these studies emerge. Firstly, Asra et al. (2005) find that there are diminishing returns to aid. In other words, they find that aid is effective at reducing poverty up to a threshold, beyond which the marginal impact of aid starts to fall. They estimate that this threshold is where aid accounts for 26 percent of a recipient's gross national income (GNI). This finding is in concordance with many studies examining the impact of aid on economic growth discussed later. Secondly, in addition to the poverty (headcount) rate, Alvi and Senbeta (2012) find that foreign aid is associated with a decline in the poverty gap index and squared poverty gap index. These measures reflect the depth and severity of poverty, as well as its incidence, implying that aid is effective at reaching the poorest in developing countries and reducing inequality among the poor.[17] Thirdly, Alvi and Senbeta (2011) find that multilateral aid and aid grants do better in reducing poverty than bilateral aid and aid loans. While multilateral aid is often focused more on poorer countries and freer from political and strategic motives in its allocation, the reasons why it is more effective at reducing poverty are unclear. The finding that grants are more effective than loans would appear to indicate that loans have not been used for activities that benefit the poor in recipient countries.

Aid and Growth

In looking at the literature on aid and growth, it is instructive to distinguish between studies published in the late 1990s and earlier. The earlier studies were largely inconclusive, either finding that aid increased, decreased, or had no impact on growth or a key driver, savings. If an overall conclusion is possible from this literature is it that aid had no impact on growth in recipient countries (McGillivray et al. 2006).

The late 1990s marked a significant change in the aid-growth literature, commencing with the influential study of Burnside and Dollar (2000). Burnside and Dollar's study and most that followed tended to use better data, theory, and empirical techniques than those that preceded them. There have been numerous comprehensive and objective surveys of this more recent aid-growth literature, which consists of scores of studies. These surveys include Morrissey (2001), Clemens et al. (2004), Dalgaard et al. (2004), Addison et al. (2005), McGillivray et al. (2006), and Feeny and McGillivray (2011). All point to the literature concluding that growth would have been lower in the absence of aid. More precisely, they point to almost all studies published since the late 1990s drawing this conclusion and no methodologically valid study concluding that growth would be higher in the absence of aid.[18]

This, of course, does not mean that there are no contrary voices emanating from empirical research circles. Doucouliagos and Paldam (2008) conduct a meta-analysis of the aid-growth literature and find that aid has failed to stimulate income growth. Mekasha and Tarp (2011) look closely at the Doucouliagos and Paldam analysis and suggest that its results are not robust owing to a number of technical issues. Rajan and Subramanian (2008) could not find any association between aid and growth. This widely cited paper has been extremely influential in policy circles and has led some observers to conclude that it is evidence that aid has been ineffective in promoting growth. What is interesting is that Rajan and Subramanian, like Doucouliagos and Paldam (2008), simply could not find a link between aid and growth, which is not to say that such a link does not exist. These studies certainly did not conclude that aid decreases growth in developing countries. That so many other studies have found the link suggests it does in all probability exist and that the observers who want to use the Rajan and Subramanian study as evidence that aid does not work are placing too heavy an emphasis on a single study.

Collier and Dollar (2001, 2002) provide an innovative contribution to the aid impact literature. They quantify the impact of aid on poverty, via its contribution to economic growth in recipient countries and derive what is termed a "poverty efficient" foreign aid allocation. Such an allocation is that which maximizes global poverty reduction subject to a budget constraint, which is simply the total amount of aid available for allocation globally in any particular year. Collier and Dollar find that aid is positively associated with per capita income growth in recipient countries, subject to the quality of the policy regime in them. Based on aid, policy quality, and poverty levels for a sample of 106 developing countries, Collier and Dollar (2002) estimate that aid has lifted 10 million people out of extreme income poverty each year. They also conclude if aid were better directed toward poorer countries with better policies, the number would rise to 19 million per year. The intuition behind this second finding is that by allocating more aid to countries with better policies and, as a result, less to countries with inferior policies, its contribution to global growth is larger, and for this reason its contribution to global poverty reduction is also larger.

Feeny and McGillivray (2011) conduct a broadly similar analysis, albeit focused solely on economic growth. They look at the amounts of aid to recipient countries that are "growth efficient," which maximizes the impact of aid on these countries' per capita income. Feeny and McGillivray find that the growth-efficient aid amount, averaged across recipient countries, is in the vicinity of 20 percent of recipient country GDP. It is possible to extend the findings of Feeny and McGillivray (2011) to calculate an average contribution of aid to recipient country GDP growth. Such a calculation is based on the aid-growth coefficients obtained and the average level of aid relative to GDP developing countries have received since 1970. There calculation suggests that per capita economic growth in these countries would be roughly one percentage point lower in the absence of aid. This number can be combined with the global GEP used by Collier and Dollar (2001, 2002) of -2.0, and data on the number of people living in extreme poverty between 1980 and 2008, the longest period for which data on global poverty are currently available. This combination suggests that aid has lifted 6 million per year or 170 million people in total out of extreme income poverty during this period. This number, which should be treated with healthy skepticism and no more than a rough approximation, is not terribly dissimilar to the estimate of 10 million people per year provided by Collier and Dollar (2002).

Aid on the GEP

There appear to be no studies that look at the relationship between aid and GEPs. A number of studies have, however, looked at the abovementioned GEP determinants, those being inequality, secondary schooling, and per capita income levels. As noted, if aid increases growth in per capita income then it must by definition increase the level of this income. The survey presented earlier of the aid-growth literature leads one to conclude therefore, that aid has a positive impact on the GEP by increasing the level of per capita income. Surveying studies of aid and inequality points to little consensus, unfortunately. Bjørnskov (2009) and Herzer and Nunnenkamp (2012) find that foreign aid is associated with increasing income inequality. Shafiullah (2011) finds that aid actually reduces income inequality in a sample of developing countries while Chong et al. (2009) find aid has no discernible impact. Increases in human capital include improvements in education and health. Few studies have looked at the impact of aid on schooling, and those that have, looked at enrollment per se and not specifically at secondary schooling. They also look only at the impact of education aid and are therefore subject to the criticism noted previously concerning the poverty impact of aid to specific sectors. Of these studies, Dreher et al. (2008) find that aid provided to the education sector of recipient countries is successful at increasing school enrollments. Michaelowa and Weber (2007) find a positive association between aid devoted to education and school enrolment and completion rates. These findings notwithstanding, it is unlikely that these studies offer much insight into the impact of aid on poverty through its impact on the GEP.

Other studies have focused on the impact of aid on the composition of public expenditures. Gomanee, Girma, and Morrissey (2005a) finds that aid improves welfare by increasing the share of public spending devoted to the social sectors. Whether this is good for poverty reduction remains to be seen, given the earlier comment about pro-rich biases of these expenditures in many developing countries. Mosley et al. (2004) provide empirical findings that might, however, provide insights into the impact of aid on the GEP. They find that aid increases the pro-poor orientation of public expenditures in developing countries.

Aid Micro-interventions

Field experiments tend to find that aid has an important and direct impact on well-being in developing countries (Banerjee and He 2003). Studies have found that foreign aid interventions have assisted in achieving some notable global health outcomes. For example, Levine and the What Works Working Group (2004) document 17 successful health interventions that have been funded by aid. For example, the global eradication of smallpox, controlling tuberculosis in China, eliminating polio in the Americas, reducing maternal mortality rates in Sri Lanka, controlling river blindness in Africa, preventing diarrheal disease in Egypt through oral rehydration programs, controlling trachoma in Morocco, reducing guinea worm disease in Africa and Asia, and eliminating measles in Southern Africa. These findings are all well and good and suggest that aid might have reduced poverty in dimensions other than income. Unfortunately, however, field experiments seem not to have looked, or if so not very often, at the impact of aid-supported microinventions on income poverty. As such this literature would appear not to be informative with respect to the specific interest of this chapter.

CONCLUSION

This chapter sought to objectively evaluate the controversial relationship between foreign aid and poverty reduction in developing countries. Three approaches were undertaken to achieve this goal. The first approach was to analyze descriptive statistics and to examine the simple empirical relationship between foreign aid flows and poverty levels through time. The second approach was to examine the analytics of aid and poverty by highlighting the various ways in which foreign aid can potentially impact poverty. Finally, the third approach was to review the increasing number of empirical studies that have examined the aid-poverty relationship. Whether it is possible to conclude that foreign aid reduces poverty in developing countries was a specific focus of the chapter.

The descriptive statistics highlight the trends and simple empirical relationship between aid and poverty. They demonstrate that, over the period 1980 to 2008, aid volumes have trended upward while extreme poverty has tended to fall. This is true if aid is measured in nominal, real, or per capita terms. While this is encouraging from an aid supporter's point of view, relationships between aid and poverty do vary across time periods and geographic regions, and the measures of aid and poverty employed also vary, making it very difficult to draw any robust conclusions. Interpreting the simple bivariate relationship is also difficult. Higher levels of aid being associated with lower levels of poverty could be explained by donors providing more assistance to less poor countries rather than poverty reduction arising as a result of the aid itself. Crucially, the descriptive statistics are unable to provide the counterfactual—or the levels of poverty that would have prevailed in the absence of foreign aid.

In analyzing the analytics of foreign aid and poverty, it is recognized that aid rarely gets provided directly to the poor in developing countries and this has important implications for how the impact of aid on poverty is assessed. Any relationship will be indirect. Regression analysis can help inform us of the impact of aid on income poverty, as well as on known drivers of poverty such as economic growth and improvements in health and education. Importantly, foreign aid could affect the growth elasticity of poverty—or the amount of poverty reduced from a given increase in growth. Unfortunately while regression-based approaches can reveal whether aid is effective at reducing poverty in developing countries, they are unable to reveal how aid achieves this objective, limiting the insights for policymakers.

A thorough and objective reading of the academic literature is encouraging. There is increasing evidence that aid has reduced poverty from empirical studies. Results from these studies suggest that the impact is fairly modest, with aid pulling between 6 and 10 million people out of extreme income poverty per year. Given that the latest data reveal that 1.22 billion people still live in poverty, foreign aid has reduced global poverty by only a very small percentage. Further, these figures suggest that the $4.3 trillion that has been provided in aid between 1960 and 2011 has at best pulled 520 million out of poverty. This equates to a cost in excess of $8,000 in aid to pull a person out of poverty. Whether this is value for the money is subjective and should be evaluated against other ways of reducing poverty. It is certainly of immeasurable importance for those that have been successfully pulled out of poverty, and it is a noteworthy achievement of the international community. It also indicates that increasing the poverty-reducing impacts of aid remains a worthy and important challenge.

We end this chapter with two suggestions for future research on the impact of aid on income poverty. The first concerns the use of poverty data in econometric analysis. It was noted that there has been surprising little use of these data. The data on poverty can always be questioned on the grounds of measurement error and cross-country comparability. But these comments can be made of much of the data used in cross-country empirical analysis and do not alone invalidate the use of poverty data. Much more use of these data would therefore appear to be warranted. It should indeed be a priority for future research. The literature needs more studies of the type discussed in the "Aid and Poverty" section that further develop the methods used by them to provide more informative and empirically rigorous results. The second direction is based on a recognition of one of the principal limitations of these studies: whether they can tell us if aid has impacted poverty and to what extent; yet they cannot identify the mechanisms or channels through which the former impacts the latter. It involves, firstly, seeking to clarify which drivers of poverty-reduction aid can drive and, secondly, seeking to establish the impacts of aid on these drivers. This need not involve purely empirical research. If it is possible to establish these impacts, this will not only tell us the impact of aid on poverty but also guide the design and implication of pro-poverty-reduction aid policies.

NOTES

1. ODA is defined as financial flows to developing countries that are: (1) undertaken by the official sector; (2) have economic development and welfare as their main objective; and (3) provided on concessional financial terms (any loan must have a grant element of at least 25 percent) (OECD 2008). Aid that is overtly military in nature is excluded from ODA.

2. These numbers are in constant 2011 prices. If current price data are used, ODA increased from $4.7 billion in 1960 to $165 billion in 2011. These numbers refer to disbursements of ODA, less repayments of concessional loans.

3. The international development and related literatures abound with works that fall into the pro- and anti-aid positions. Some date back many decades. Not all look specifically at poverty but at aid from a general development-effectiveness positions that consider impacts on economic growth, health, education, governance, and the like. Works that are highly critical of aid include Bauer (1966, 1991), Friedman (1970), Easterly (2006), and Moyo (2009), while those that are supportive albeit often with caveats include Ward (1966), Sachs (2006), and Riddell (2007).

4. This statistic has been obtained by, firstly, taking the average ODA to ratio of each developing country during the period 1970 and 2010 and, secondly, taking the average of these receipts across all developing countries for which GDP data are available. Requisite data were taken from OECD (2012) and World Bank (2012).

5. These countries are Australia, Austria, Belgium, Canada, Denmark, Finland, France, Germany, Greece, Ireland, Italy, Japan, Korea, Luxemburg, the Netherlands, New Zealand, Norway, Portugal, Spain, Sweden, Switzerland, the United Kingdom, and the United States (OECD 2012).

6. The international community's strategy to achieve the Millennium Development Goals relies heavily on the ability of aid to contribute to achievements in health and education and, to this extent, reductions in poverty in these nonincome quality of life dimensions.

7. Studies comprising this relatively small literature include Boone (1996), Kosack (2003), Mosley et al. (2004), Gomanee et al. (2005a, 2005b), Michaelowa and Weber (2007), and Dreher et al. (2008). Results remain a little mixed but tend on balance to support the view that aid is positively associated with higher achievements in health and education.

8. Better known studies of this type include Heller (1975), Pack and Pack (1990, 1993), Gang and Khan (1991), Franco-Rodriguez et al. (1998) and Feyzioglu et al. (1998).

9. The data used to construct Figure 30.1 and those in the remainder of this chapter have been obtained from OECD (2012) and World Bank (2012). The poverty data plotted in Figure 30.1, and those showing global poverty levels, are for the sum of people living below each poverty line in all low- and middle-income countries. The World Bank (2012) only reports these aggregates, and equivalent regional numbers, from 1981. Currently, the latest such data are for the year 2008.

10. This is also the case for measuring total aid (in absolute terms, irrespective of population) in constant price terms, both for all countries combined, those in South Asia and in sub-Saharan Africa.

11. Scatter plots linking aid and $PPP2 poverty headcount reveal the same basic relationships shown in Figures 30.7 and 30.8.

12. Excluded from the data used to plot Figure 30.8 is a handful of small population countries for which per capita aid flows were tremendously high and distorted the overall relationship depicted. That noted, a negative relationship between aid and poverty exists with these countries included.

13. Of all the components of ODA, food and humanitarian aid, which includes emergency relief, tends to be more predominantly allocated directly to poor people. But these forms of aid have constituted roughly 8 percent of total ODA over the period 1960 to 2011 (OECD 2012). Other types of aid, which are not formally considered forms of aid in its reporting, that are given directly to poor people are referred to later in the chapter.

14. Bourguignon (2004) estimates that economic growth explains 26 percent of the variation in changes in poverty headcounts. Kraay (2006), conversely, finds that virtually all of the cross-country variation in changes in poverty is due to cross-country changes in growth.

15. These studies recognize that the aid variable is likely endogenous due to simultaneity bias. While aid might reduce poverty, it is also the case that more aid is allocated to poorer countries. The studies use different techniques to control for the endogeneity of aid.

16. Arvin and Barillas (2002) examine the causality between aid, democracy, and poverty. They find results vary greatly by region, with aid reducing poverty in East Asia and the Pacific but having a detrimental impact in low-income countries. Unfortunately the so-called measure of poverty employed by this study is simply the level of GDP per capita.

17. The poverty gap is the mean shortfall of the total population from the poverty line (counting the nonpoor as having zero shortfall), expressed as a percentage of the poverty line (UN 2003).

18. That the aid-growth literature seems to be in agreement that growth would be lower in the absence of aid does not imply that there is no disagreement among the researchers involved. There is intense disagreement over contingencies to which the aid-growth relationship is subject. Burnside and Dollar (2000) concluded that aid only contributed to growth in countries with "good" economic policies, broadly defined. Subsequent studies struggle to replicate this finding, with others instead pointing to contingencies such as structural vulnerability, political stability, democracy, and climate (McGillivray 2003; Clemens et al. 2004; McGillivray et al. 2006).

References

Adams, Richard, Jr. 2003. "Economic Growth, Inequality and Poverty: Findings from a New Dataset." World Bank Policy Research Working Paper No. 2972. Washington DC: World Bank.

Adams, Jr. Richard. 2004. "Economic Growth, Inequality and Poverty: Estimating the Growth Elasticity of Poverty." *World Development* 32(12):1989–2014.

Addison, Tony, George Mavrotas, and Mark McGillivray. 2005. "Development Assistance and Development Finance: Evidence and Global Policy Agendas." *Journal of International Development* 17(6):819–36.

Alvi, Eskander and Aberra Senbeta. 2012. "Does Aid Reduce Poverty?" *Journal of International Development* 24(8):955–76.

Arvin, B. Mark and Francisco Barillas. 2002. "Foreign Aid, Poverty Reduction and Democracy." *Applied Economics* 34(4):2151–56.

Asra, Abuzar, Gemma Estrada, Yangseon Kim and M. G. Quibria. 2005. "Poverty and Foreign Aid: Evidence from Cross-Country Data." Economics and Research Division, Working Paper Series No. 65. Manila: Asian Development Bank.

Bahmani-Oskooee, Moshen and Maharouf Oyolola. 2009. "Poverty Reduction and Aid: Cross-country Evidence." *International Journal of Sociology and Social Policy* 29(5):264–73.

Banerjee, Abhijit and Ruimin He. 2003. *Making Aid Work*. Cambridge, MA: MIT Press.

Bauer, Peter. 1966. "Foreign Aid: An Instrument for Progress?" Pp. 1–30 in *Two Views on Aid to Developing Countries*, edited by Peter Bauer and Barbara Ward. London: Institute for Public Affairs.

Bauer, Peter. 1991. *The Development Frontier: Essays in Applied Economics*. Hemel Hempstead: Harvester-Wheatsheaf.

Bhalla, Sirjit. 2002. *Imagine There's No Country: Poverty Inequality and Growth in the Era of Globalization*. Washington DC: Institute for International Economics.

Bjørnskov, Christian. 2009. "Do Elites Benefit from Democracy and Foreign Aid in Developing Countries?" *Journal of Development Economics* 92(2):115–24.

Boone, Peter. 1996. "Politics and the Effectiveness of Foreign Aid." *European Economic Review* 40(2):289–329.

Bourguignon, Francois. 2004. "The Growth Elasticity of Poverty Reduction: Explaining Heterogeneity across Countries and Time Periods." World Bank Working Paper. Washington, DC: World Bank.

Bruno, Michael, Martin Ravallion, and Lyn Squire. 1998. "Equity and Growth in Developing Countries: Old and New Perspectives on the Policy Issues." Pp. 98–112 in *Income Distribution and High Growth*, edited by V. Tani and K-Y Chu. Cambridge, MA: MIT Press.

Burnside, Craig and David Dollar. 2000. "Aid, Policies and Growth." *American Economic Review* 90(4):847–68.

Chong, Alberto, Mark Gradstein and Maria-Cecilia Calderón. 2009. "Can Foreign Aid Reduce Income Inequality and Poverty?" *Public Choice* 140:59–84.

Clemens, Michael. Steven Radelet and Rikhil Bhavani. 2004. *Counting Chickens When They Hatch: The Short-Term Effect of Aid on Growth*, Center for Global Development Working Paper Number 44. Washington, DC: Center for Global Development.

Collier, Paul and David Dollar. 2001. "Can the World Cut Poverty in Half? How Policy Reform and Effective Aid Can Meet International Development Goals." *World Development* 29(11):1787–1802.

Collier, Paul and David Dollar. 2002. "Aid Allocation and Poverty Reduction." *European Economic Review* 46(8):1475–1500.

Dalgaard Carl, Henrik Hansen and Finn Tarp. 2004. "On the Empirics of Foreign Aid and Growth." *Economic Journal* 114(496):191–216.

De Janvry, Alain and Elisabeth Sadoulet. 2000. "Growth, Poverty and Inequality in Latin America: A Causal Analysis 1970–94." *Review of Income and Wealth* 46(3):267–87.

Dollar, David and Aart Kraay. 2002. "Growth Is Good for the Poor." *Journal of Economic Growth* 7(3):195–225.

Doucouliagos, Hristos and Martin Paldam. 2008. "Aid Effectiveness on Growth: A Meta Study." *European Journal of Political Economy* 24:1–24.

Dreher, Axel, Peter Nunnenkamp and Rainer Thiele. 2008. "Does Aid for Education Educate Children? Evidence from Panel Data." *World Bank Economic Review* 22(2):291–314.

Easterly, William. 2006. *The White Man's Burden: Why the West's Efforts to Aid have done So Much Ill and So Little Good*. London: Penguin.

Feeny, Simon and Mark McGillivray. 2011. "Scaling-Up Foreign Aid: Will the 'Big Push' Work?" *The World Economy* 4(1):54–73.

Feyzioglu, Tarhan, Vinaya Swaroop and Min Zhu. 1998. "A Panel Data Analysis of the Fungibility of Foreign Aid." *World Bank Economic Review* 12(1):29–58.

Franco-Rodriguez, Susanna, Mark McGillivray and Oliver Morrissey. 1998. "Aid and the Public Sector in Pakistan: Evidence with Endogenous Aid." *World Development* 26:1241–50.

Friedman, Milton. 1970. "Foreign Economic Aid: Means and Objectives." Pp. 63–78 in Jagdish Bhagwati and Richard Eckaus. *Foreign Aid*. Harmondsworth: Penquin Books.

Gang, Ira and Haider Khan. 1991. "Foreign Aid, Taxes and Public Investment." *Journal of Development Economics* 24:355–69.

Gomanee, Karuna, Sourafel Girma, and Oliver Morrissey. 2005a. "Aid, Public Spending and Human Welfare: Evidence from Quantile Regressions." *Journal of International Development* 17(3):299–309.

Gomanee, Karuna, Oliver Morrissey, Paul Mosley, and Arjan Verschoor. 2005b. "Aid, Government Expenditure, and Aggregate Welfare." *World Development* 33(3):355–70.

Heller, Peter. 1975. "A Model of Public Fiscal Behaviour in Developing Countries: Aid, Investment and Taxation." *American Economic Review* 65:429–45.

Herzer, Dierk and Peter Nunnenkamp. 2012. "The Effect of Foreign Aid on Income Inequality: Evidence from Panel Cointegration." Kiel Working Paper No. 1762. Kiel: Kiel Institute for the World Economy.

Kosack, Stephen. 2003. "Effective Aid: How Democracy Allows for Development Aid to Improve the Quality of Life." *World Development* 31:1–22.

Kraay, Aart. 2006. "When is Growth Pro-Poor? Evidence from a Panel of Countries." *Journal of Development Economics* 80(10):198–227.

Levine, Ruth and the What Works Working Group. 2004. *Millions Saved: Proven Successes in Global Health*. Washington, DC: Center for Global Development.

McGillivray, Mark. 2003. "Aid Effectiveness and Selectivity: Integrating Multiple Objectives in Aid Allocations." *DAC Journal* 4(3):23–36.

McGillivray, Mark and Oliver Morrissey. 2001. "Fiscal Effects of Aid." UNU-WIDER Discussion Paper No.2001/61. Helsinki: United Nations University World Institute for Development Economics Research.

McGillivray, Mark, Simon Feeny, Nils Hermes and Robert Lensink. 2006. "Controversies over the Impact of Development Aid: It Works, It Doesn't, It Might, but That Depends . . ." *Journal of International Development* 18(7):1031–50.

McGillivray, Mark, David Fielding, Sebastian Torres, and Stephen Knowles. 2013. *Does Aid Work for the Poor?* Geelong: Deakin University.

Mekasha, T. J. and Fin Tarp. 2011. "Aid and Growth: What Meta-Analysis Reveals." UNU-WIDER Working Paper No. 2011/22. Helsinki: United Nations University World Institute for Development Economics Research.

Michaelowa, Katharina and Anke Weber. 2007. "Aid Effectiveness in the Education Sector: A Dynamic Panel Analysis." Pp. 357–86 in *Theory and Practice of Foreign Aid*, edited by S. Lahiri. Amsterdam: Elsevier.

Morrissey, Oliver. 2001. "Does Aid Increase Growth?" *Progress in Development Studies* 1:37–50.

Mosley, Paul, John Hudson, and Arjan Verschoor. 2004. "Aid, Poverty Reduction and the New Conditionality." *Economic Journal* 114(496):F217–43.

Moyo, Dambisa. 2009. *Dead Aid: Why Aid Is Not Working and How There Is Another Way for Africa*. New York: Farrar, Straus and Giroux.

OECD. 2008. *Is It ODA?* Factsheet. November. Paris: OECD.

OECD. 2012. *International Development Statistics Online*. Paris: OECD.

Pack, Howard and Janet-Rothenberg Pack. 1990. "Is Foreign Aid Fungible? The Case of Indonesia." *Economic Journal* 100:188–94.

Pack, Howard and Janet-Rothenburg Pack. 1993. "Foreign Aid and the Question of Fungibility." *Review of Economics and Statistics* 75:258–65.

Rajan, Raghuram G. and Arvind Subramanian. 2008. "Aid and Growth: What Does the Cross-country Evidence Really Show?" *Review of Economics and Statistics* 90(4):643–65.

Ravallion, Martin and Shaohua Chen. 1997. "What Can New Survey Data Tell Us about Recent Changes in Distribution and Poverty?" *World Bank Economic Review* 11:357–82.

Riddell, Roger. 2007. *Does Foreign Aid Really Work?* Oxford: Oxford University Press.

Sachs, Jeffrey. 2006. *The End of Poverty: Economic Possibilities for Our Time*. London: Penguin.

Shafiullah, Muhammad. 2011. "Foreign Aid and Its Impact on Income Inequality." *International Review of Business Research Papers* 7(2):91–105.

Son, Hyun, H. and Nanak Kakwani. 2004. "Economic Growth and Poverty Reduction: Initial Conditions Matter." International Poverty Centre Working Paper No. 2. New York: United Nations Development Program.

UN. 2003. *Indicators for Monitoring the Millennium Development Goals: Definitions, Rationale, Concepts and Sources*. New York: United Nations.

Ward, Barbara. 1966. "The Decade of Development: A Study in Frustration." Pp. 31–58 in *Two Views on Aid and Development*, edited by Peter Bauer and Barbara Ward. London: Institute of Public Affairs.

World Bank. 2004. *World Development Report 2004: Making Services Work for Poor People*. New York: Oxford University Press.

World Bank. 2012. *World Development Indicators Online Database*. Washington DC: World Bank.

CHAPTER 31

....

THE WELFARE STATES
AND POVERTY

....

CHEOL-SUNG LEE AND INHOE KU

INTRODUCTION

....

MODERN welfare states aim to implement social policies to remedy the suffering caused by ruthless market mechanisms. They provide insurances to allow citizens to prepare for the vicissitudes of life, such as aging, illness, injuries, retirement, and unemployment. In cases in which citizens do not have employment and income to sustain insurance schemes due to those same difficulties, welfare states still provide a certain degree of safety to this less capable population. However, the generosity and spending patterns of welfare states vary widely depending upon their inherent structures, goals, commitments, and capacities. The late twentieth century saw the beginning of ongoing neoliberal trends of market fundamentalism linked with increasing economic globalization in trade, investment, and finance; postindustrial structural transformations of labor market; increasing immigration; rapid aging of the population; and dissolution of traditional family structures. In the face of these structural transformations and pressures, how have different welfare regimes reacted to help stressed populations, especially the poor? Furthermore, how do welfare states in developing countries—which share some structural conditions with developed nations, but feature very different historical backgrounds, such as underdevelopment of economic, social, and political institutions; uneven balance of power between the powerful and the subordinate classes; and vulnerabilities to international pressures—protect their less capable populations under the pressures of globalization and postindustrial economic transformation?

In this article, we critically review existing theoretical and empirical literature on welfare states and poverty, primarily within macrolevel cross-national contexts but also utilizing significant research findings consistent with macrolevel trends on the individual-level basis. In the following sections, we attempt to provide an overview of the relationship between welfare states and poverty outcomes.[1] We initially delineate three welfare state typologies in terms of skill and employment provisions. After briefly discussing the issues of targeting and encompassing welfare institutions, we summarize how demographic transformations affect poverty. In the two sections that follow we report some findings on trends over time regarding poverty in combination with significant findings from existing empirical studies. In the subsequent section we discuss two different types of welfare regimes observed in developing countries—productivist and protectionist welfare regimes—and then discuss their effects on poverty outcomes.

WELFARE REGIME TYPOLOGIES
AND POVERTY

Welfare state scholarship has explored various factors in order to understand the different responses of welfare states to these challenges. One of the useful and popular ideal types to analyze different poverty outcomes across the states is Esping-Andersen's welfare state typologies (1990, 1999). Esping-Andersen, in his celebrated work, *The Three Worlds of Welfare Capitalism*, proposed a novel conceptualization of the welfare state (at that time) focusing on the notion of "decommodification," which refers to "the degree to which individuals, or families, can uphold a socially acceptable standard of living independently of market participation" (p. 37). In this new conceptualization, the welfare state is not merely to secure some basic level of safety net for its citizens, as suggested by previous scholars, but, further, affirmatively to decommodify citizens' life conditions so that they can freely choose not to work, without being concerned about job and income loss. Based on this notion of decommodification, he was able to develop three different types of welfare regimes: liberal, social insurance, and universal welfare states.[2] Based on this classification, in this section, we discuss whether three worlds generate distinctive poverty outcomes especially regarding (1) skill investment and poverty, (2) social policy configuration and poverty, and (3) labor market structure and poverty.

First, in universal (social democratic) welfare states, the long-term incumbent social democratic parties, interwoven with strong labor-linked associations, have consciously sought social and labor market policies based on universal citizenship (Huber and Stephens 2001). The combination of three different aspects of social protection in these countries—generous entitlements, generous transfers, and, importantly, generous opportunities through active labor market policies—has provided the unemployed and employed alike with greater opportunities to maintain stable jobs and incomes. Generous entitlements and replacement rates based on universal citizenship (Korpi and Palme 1998) and sophisticated training programs that allow workers to readjust to rapid technological innovations (Esping-Andersen 1999; Boix 1998; Garret 1998) offer labor market insiders safety nets against the future while also providing outsiders with chances to upgrade their skills. In social democratic countries (and some of the northern tier of continental social insurance countries) that have highly centralized employers' and union organizations, business leaders and employers have also contributed to building employer-sponsored and state-driven "production regimes" (Huber and Stephens 2001) through generous and effective social and labor market policies coupled with a relatively flexible labor market. The "coordinated market economy" in these countries has helped firms maintain international competitiveness by enhancing or reshaping general citizens' skill levels under fierce international competitions and changing industrial structures (Estevez-Abe, Iversen, and Soskice 2001; Hall and Soskice 2001; Mares 2003; Swenson 2002). In these societies, citizens are less likely to experience long-term or permanent poverty across generations (Brady 2009) and wage differences are relatively low, because state- and employer-sponsored public training programs (ALMP) provide ample opportunities for unemployed or low-skilled workers to upgrade obsolete skills. In addition, welfare states in these countries play decisive roles as employers in providing high-quality public service jobs with strong job security, relatively high wages, and fringe benefits based on strong union-based bargaining power (Garrett and Way 1999; Lee, Kim, and Shim 2011). The biggest beneficiaries of this social democratic production regime are low-skilled or unskilled workers and the unemployed at the bottom of the social hierarchy. Therefore, the size of the population under the (either relative or absolute) poverty threshold is minimal in these countries, not only due to low wage differences based on well-configured public education and training system but also due to generous social transfers coupled with training programs.

Employees in continental European welfare states have been well protected in the labor market, as long as they are male, skilled, and the heads of families. The strict labor market regulation; policy competitions between Left parties and Christian Democratic parties (Huber, Ragin, and Stephens 1993); relatively strong labor unions in core industries; and unusually generous (but contribution-based) social insurance systems have jointly provided skilled male breadwinners with strong job and income protection (van Kersbergen 1995; Bussemaker and van Kersbergen 1999). However, in these social-insurance-based continental European countries, unskilled workers, old workers, young workers newly entering the labor market, women, and members of ethnic minorities have suffered from highly exclusive and rigid labor markets configured for the protection of the employment of skilled male breadwinners (Esping-Andersen 1990).[3] In these societies, first, social insurance programs, such as old age and survivor pensions, are responsible for the bulk of public expenditures; they are not based on universal principles but rather distributed following employment history along occupational lines (Esping-Andersen 1999; Korpi and Palme 1998). Second, social-insurance welfare states are less inclined to encourage public sector employment and active labor market policies than their social democratic counterparts, which in turn discourages labor market outsiders from enjoying more job opportunities (Huber and Stephens 2001). In these countries, skill training is more likely to occur within firms and between employers and skilled craft workers (Thelen 2004), as strongly unionized skilled workers have traditionally chosen employers as their skill-training partners in exchange for strong employment protection and earning-related social insurance. Third, under the pressure of rapid technological changes and deindustrialization, social-insurance welfare states encourage or require old and redundant members of the labor force to retire early through compensations—initially in the form of unemployment insurance and subsequently as old-age pensions (Esping-Andersen 1990, 1999).

In sum, the social-insurance model of policy configuration will reinforce existing social hierarchies by segmenting citizens and then predetermining their lifelong risk with strong employment protection, within-firm skill formation, and earning-related insurance with differentiated entitlements. This type of social policy design has two contrasting aspects: on one hand, it makes it difficult for relatively unskilled workers or labor market outsiders to remain competitive or to upgrade their skills, which potentially expose those groups to a higher risk of poverty; but on the other hand, its strong employment protection prevents them from losing jobs and income over relatively long periods of time, which helps them accumulate sufficient employment history to qualify for sufficient pensions. Although insurance schemes are constructed along occupational lines, wage differences across industries and occupations are relatively low in these countries. Therefore, despite some nonuniversal, conservative social-insurance structures, poverty rates are not extremely high in these societies.

Social policies in the liberal residual model are typically based on deregulated labor markets; an extreme imbalance of power between employers and employees; and low solidarity among workers resulting from weak union power. Completely flexible labor markets allow employers to be less committed to their contracts with current employees and less concerned about skill upgrades of workers over time in the face of rapid technological changes, because employers are able to keep recruiting new workers with relevant skills from outside their firms. Based on flexible, deregulated, underunionized labor markets, large service sectors and low-wage industrial sectors develop and persist. In these conditions, unskilled redundant workers periodically lose their jobs depending upon economic cycles, and with poor education, it is difficult for them to get out of "bad jobs" earning low wages with weak worker protection (Baumol 1967; Esping-Andersen 1999). In these countries, welfare policies are regarded as giving away direct, targeted transfers to the "undeserving" poor. Many middle- and upper-class wage earners and employers typically consider welfare policies as free paychecks to "welfare queens" who are irrelevant to their life risks. Training opportunities for the unskilled or labor market outsiders are rare or nonexistent, and, therefore, wage differences across occupations and industries are wide. In these countries, welfare recipients suffer not only strict means-tests but also public disrespect (Soss 1999), and budgets for social policies are much smaller than their counterparts in universal or social-insurance programs (Korpi and Palme 1998). Not surprisingly, the poverty level is highest in these countries (among rich OECD countries).

Table 31.1 summarizes variations in social policy design and labor market structure among three welfare regimes and their average poverty levels, while Figure 31.1 presents a bivariate scatterplot between welfare state generosity (Scruggs 2010), equivalent to

Table 31.1 Social Policy and Labor Market Features and Poverty Level Across Welfare Regimes

Types of Welfare Regimes	Details of Social Policy and Labor Market Configuration	Poverty Level (Mean Level of Overall Head Count Poverty and Poverty Intensity)
Universal Countries	(1) High Co-Investment in Skills and Social Protection for the entire Labor Force (2) Middle class, Skilled and Unskilled Workers Share the Same Conditions of Basic Security Programs (as well as Differentiated Earning Related Programs) (3) Relatively Flexible Labor Market, Late Retirement (4) Skill Upgrade by Retraining, Re-Employment and Public Sector Absorbs Redundant Labor Force (5) High employment	Low
Social Insurance Countries	(1) High Co-Investment in Skills and Social Protection within Firms or Occupations (for Skilled Male-Breadwinners) (2) Occupationally Segmented, Employment-based Insurance + Ungenerous Social Assistance (3) Highly Rigid Labor Market (4) Skill Upgrade by Early Retirement and Families Absorb Redundant Labor Force (5) Low employment, budget austerity	Medium
Residual Countries	(1) Low Co-Investment in Skills and Social Protection (2) Basic Social Insurance + Ungenerous & Means-testing Social Assistance (3) Highly Flexible Labor Market (4) No Social Provision for Skill Upgrade. Low-wage Service Sector Absorbs Redundant Labor Force (5) High employment	High

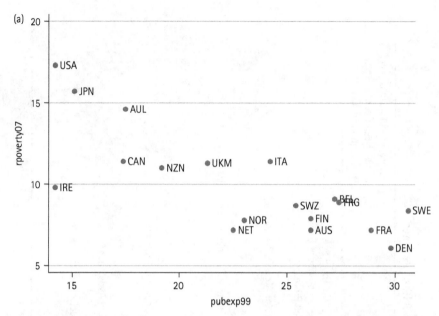

FIGURE 31.1a Public Social Expenditure (% of GDP, 2000) and Relative Poverty (circa 2005)

AUT: Austria, AUL: Australia, BEL: Belgium, CAN: Canada, DNK: Denmark, FIN: Finland, FRA: France, DEU: Germany, IRL: Ireland, ITA: Italy, JPN: Japan, NLD: Netherlands, NZL: New Zealand, NOR: Norway, SWE: Sweden, SWZ: Switzerland, GBR: United Kingdom, USA: United States.
Source: OECD Social Expenditure Database (SOCX) (http://www.oecd.org/social/expenditure.htm).

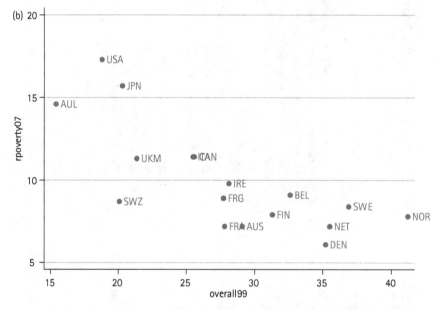

FIGURE 31.1b Decommodification Index (2000) and Relative Poverty (circa 2005)

AUT: Austria, AUL: Australia, BEL: Belgium, CAN: Canada, DNK: Denmark, FIN: Finland, FRA: France, DEU: Germany, IRL: Ireland, ITA: Italy, JPN: Japan, NLD: Netherlands, NZL: New Zealand, NOR: Norway, SWE: Sweden, SWZ: Switzerland, GBR: United Kingdom, USA: United States.
Source: Scruggs 2010 (Decommodification index) and OECD 2008.

Esping-Andersen's decommodification (1990), and relative poverty in 18 rich democracies. In both, total public expenditures on social policies and overall measures of welfare generosity are highly correlated with relative poverty measure in these countries. Social-democratic welfare regimes are mostly clustered at the bottom right corners of two figures, indicating that they are the most effective in shrinking populations under the poverty lines among three types of regimes. However, conservative continental European countries such as France, Austria, Belgium, and Germany are also clustered at the bottom right along with social democratic countries. The Netherlands and Norway (and Ireland) are less ambitious spenders compared to other northern European countries, but their overall generosities are at the top level (with Ireland at the medium level). Overall, their superb records in poverty reduction may reflect their better economic performances in employment and growth than other nations. In both figures, the United States, Japan, and Australia are the stingiest spenders in social policy areas and therefore have the largest population living in poverty. The UK and Canada, thanks to their more generous social assistance programs and more universal nature of insurance programs, have much lower poverty than their liberal peers.

THE EFFECTS OF WELFARE STATES IN REDUCING POVERTY

Critics of welfare states have questioned the effectiveness of government poverty programs. Do welfare states really achieve what they aim to do? Some conservative communitarians (Murray 1984; Mead 1997) and most contemporary economists in the tradition of neoclassical theories believe that big welfare programs retard growth and profits by providing work disincentives. In their argument, poor people in this welfare-poverty trap ultimately end up in permanent poverty. According the "perversity thesis" analyzed by Sommers and Block (2005), welfare states could exacerbate poverty by discouraging work ethics of low-income people and encouraging them to rely on welfare checks. Proponents of "pervisity thesis" contend that such patterns and values of dependency tend to be inherited from parent to child.

Welfare state scholars, however, have effectively countered the perversity thesis with more convincing evidence. For instance, Kenworthy (1999) investigated whether social-welfare programs indeed contribute to reducing poverty. He concludes that, in rich democracies over the period of 1960–1991, the effects on poverty of social-welfare policy extensiveness are robustly negative. Brady, in his several contributions to the field of welfare states and poverty (2005, 2009, 2010), has repeatedly shown that the welfare state's conscious efforts to reduce poverty are significant and substantial.

A more nuanced puzzle in the analysis of welfare states and poverty is the paradox of "targeting": "the greater the degree of targeting, the smaller the redistributive budget." Korpi and Palme (1998:672) explain this paradox by introducing the notion of "configuration of social policy." They expect that the more the nonpoor encompassing the upper and middle classes benefit from social policies, the broader will the base of support for welfare state be. This will eventually lead to bigger redistributive budgets, which result in lower inequality and poverty. However, "because of their low ceilings for earnings replacement, targeted programs and basic security programs stimulate program exit among the middle classes and increase the demand for private insurance" (p. 682). As encompassing institutions "pool the risks" of the entire citizenry by combining flat-rate and earnings-related benefits, they have a larger capacity to reduce poverty. In their study of the types of social policies and their effects on single-mother poverty, Brady and Burroway (2012) support Korpi and Palme's analyses with more detailed analyses on individual-level data. They found that universal social policy contributes significantly to reducing single-mother poverty, while the effects of targeted social policies are either insignificant or less clear.

What, then, drives the development of such encompassing welfare institutions in some countries? Power-resource theorists have long argued that it is labor-linked associational power, such as unions and leftist parties that promote bigger welfare states (Korpi 1983; Esping-Andersen 1985). Huber and Stephens (2001) recently confirmed such an argument that leftist parties, as the representatives of the working- and lower-middle classes, play the key role in expanding the welfare states (along with constitutional structures). While power-resource theorists argue that the emergence of encompassing universal social policies originates from broad working- and middle-class coalitions under the hegemony of the working-class based political parties, institutionalists in the political economy tradition think that such universal welfare systems are an outcome of the electoral system (Persson and Tabellini 2000, 2003). They reason that, on one hand, when voters make choices on candidates based on party lists in a national district under a proportional representation (PR) system, they will favor candidates of the parties who support universal-transfer programs catering to large groups. Politicians will not ignore candidates who represent minority populations, either, because there is no safe district. On the other hand, when voters make choices on individual candidates in regionally segmented districts with a first-past-the-post system, voters are more likely to respond to geographically targeted programs rather than universal welfare systems, which in turn leads party leaders to be more cautious about nominating minority candidates in such districts. Brady contends that it is more comprehensive "institutionalized power relations" that account for an expansion of the welfare state: labor-friendly electoral systems (proportional representative systems) as well as leftist partisan politics (2009).

Welfare States, Aging, and Poverty

Welfare states respond to external shocks and structural transformations of market and civil society, such as economic crises, aging populations, and family dissolution, in different ways and to different degrees. Poverty outcomes vary according to such divergent coping strategies of welfare states.

One of the most serious challenges to welfare states has been an aging population combined with declining fertility. The dependency ratio—the number of elderly people (over 65) relative to the number of people of working age (aged 20–64)—now reaches 20 percent (Canada and the United States) to 30 percent (Japan and Italy). These figures are expected to reach 50 percent in 2025 and 70 percent in 2050 in Japan, and 33 percent in 2025 and 39 percent in 2050 in the United States. The OECD average will be somewhere between these extremes, about 48 percent in 2050. The aging population, therefore, not only slows economic growth due to declining labor supply but also puts a great burden on welfare states by increasing beneficiaries while decreasing contributors (especially regarding pensions and health care).

Welfare states typically readjust entitlement criteria by increasing eligible ages and minimum years of contribution, while decreasing replacement rates, unless they employ higher tax rates for the current labor force. As a result, recipients have to wait longer to receive less. For example in Japan, the replacement rate has been declining dramatically since the 1980s and has now fallen below 60 percent, and the Japanese MHLW predicts that it would decrease to 52 percent in the early 2030 (Shinkawa 2003). To alleviate the burden on the ailing pension system, the Japanese state encouraged the aged population to become re-employed through newly introduced labor market flexibilization laws such as the Labor Dispatching Law and the Stabilization of Elderly Employment Law. However, re-employment of the aged in such low-quality jobs may expose them to higher risk of poverty.

OVER TIME TRENDS IN POVERTY AND THE CHANGING REDISTRIBUTIVE ROLE OF WELFARE STATES

The last few decades have seen rising poverty across many industrialized countries in the Western world and other regions. Welfare states have played a significant role in shaping poverty trends across time and place. Therefore, in principle, the redistributive policies of welfare states should slow down the increasing poverty in market income by benefiting the poor. However, in reality, trends in poverty do not necessarily replicate the same variations observed in the typologies of welfare regimes. In this section, we present some of those unexpected trends and review the existing literature that may account for them.

Figure 31.2 presents changes in the relative poverty rates based on the threshold of 50 percent median income in 21 OECD countries over the past 25 years since the mid-1980s.[4] In the late 2000s, poverty rates calculated with posttax and posttransfer income are the highest (over 15 percent) in Israel, the United States, Turkey, and Japan. Some

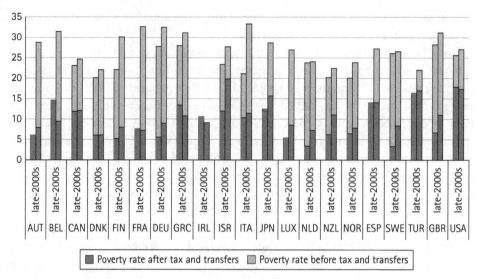

FIGURE 31.2 Poverty Rate Before and After Tax and Transfer in the mid-1980s to mid-2000s among OECD Countries

AUT: Austria, BEL: Belgium, CAN: Canada, DNK: Denmark, FIN: Finland, FRA: France, DEU: Germany, GRC: Greece, IRL: Ireland, ISR: Israel, ITA: Italy, JPN: Japan, LUX: Luxembourg, NLD: Netherlands, NZL: New Zealand, NOR: Norway, ESP: Spain, SWE: Sweden, TUR: Turkey, GBR: United Kingdom, USA: United States.
Source: Constructed by the authors based on OECD Income Distribution Database (Downloaded in 2012 from http://www.oecd.org/social/income-distribution-database.htm).

Anglo-Saxon countries such as Canada, New Zealand, and the UK form the second highest (between 10 and 15 percent), together with Southern European countries including Spain, Italy and Greece. The remaining 11 countries of Scandinavia and Central Europe show lower poverty rates (below 10 percent). Note that the countries with the highest postgovernment poverty rates do not necessarily have high poverty rates based on pretax and pretransfer income. For example, the United States and Sweden have similar pregovernment poverty rates but have very different rates of disposable income poverty. This confirms that tax and transfer systems in welfare states play a significant role in determining poverty rates, as earlier comparative studies have found (Atkinson, Rainwater, and Smeeding 1995; Jäntti and Danziger 2000; Kenworthy 1999; Kim 2000; Mitchell 1991; Smeeding et al. 1990; Smeeding, Rainwater, and Burtless 2001).[5]

Figure 31.2 also shows that poverty rates vary over time. Rates of disposable income poverty increased by 1.6 percentage points on average from 9.3 percent in the mid-1980s to 10.9 percent in the late-2000s. Rising poverty is a recent phenomenon. Earlier studies reported little intertemporal change in poverty levels on average and rather focused on diverse country experience in poverty trends (Burniaux et al. 1998; Forster and Pearson 2002). In fact, the increases in poverty rates were not conspicuous during the earlier decade. From the mid-1980s to the mid-1990s, the simple average of the poverty rate rose very slightly by 0.5 percent. Over the next decade, however, the rising trend intensified, and the average poverty rate increased by 1 percent. This rising trend in poverty was also reported in some recent studies (Förster and D'Ercole 2005;

OECD 2008: Chapter 5; Smeeding 2006).[6] Since the mid-2000s, the average poverty rate remains similar.[7]

Note that the rise in poverty over the period was driven considerably by the steep poverty increases in Israel, Japan, and a couple of English-speaking liberal countries such as New Zealand and the UK. Figure 31.2, however, also presents a slightly unusual picture of the welfare state regimes and changes in poverty over time: Universal countries, not just liberal countries, have suffered dramatic increases in poverty over the past two decades. Finland, Sweden, and the Netherlands all have experienced significant increases in population under the poverty line (after tax and transfer), along with typical liberal countries.

A relatively small number of scholars have paid attention to these new phenomena. Lee et al. (2011) focuses on the collapse of centralized wage-bargaining institutions in the traditional strongholds of social democracy. They found that the strong role of public sector employment in reducing income inequality has been considerably weakened in traditional strongholds of social democracies due to the collapse of wage bargaining and decreasing total employment size in those countries, which may be attributable to an emerging sectoral gap of productivity and consequential sectoral conflicts (between private manufacturing and public service sectors). More studies and scholarly efforts are needed to investigate why and how distributional outcomes have worsened in some welfare regimes.

More generally, the role of changes in market incomes of the lower classes should be examined when accounting for the increase in the relative poverty rates. Among the 21 OECD countries shown in Figure 31.2, the poverty rate of incomes before tax and transfer increased by 4.7 percentage points on average, from 23.0 percent in the mid-1980s to 27.7 percent in the late 2000s. The growing trend in market income poverty mostly happened during the earlier decade. The poverty rate increased by five percentage points on average from the mid-1980s to the mid-1990s and then has remained stable for the subsequent 15 years. The steep rise in the poverty of market incomes was primarily driven by substantial drops of lower income groups. Based on the Luxembourg Income Study data, Immervoll and Richardson (2011) show that market incomes at the 10th percentile in most advanced industrial countries fell substantially until the mid-1990s, with the notable exception of the Netherlands. Income levels at the bottom decile grew strongly during the next decade but still did not reach those of the mid-1980s. Over the same period, median market income grew more or less in some countries and stagnated in other countries.

The steadily growing poverty in the majority of advanced industrial countries cannot be accounted for without considering changes in the redistributive role of welfare states. Taxes and transfers have significant redistributive effects, which vary across countries and over time (OECD 2008). Particularly, public transfers prevent and lessen poverty in various ways. They provide insurance against the risks of falling into poverty, services that the reduce consumption burden, and grant income directly to the poor. Transfers, measured as either a percentage of social spending or other indexes of benefit generosity, are central to cross-country differences in poverty (Brady 2005,

2009; Kenworthy 1999; Moller et al. 2003; Scruggs and Alan 2006).[8] Welfare state transfers also explain much of cross-country variation in poverty of children, women, single mothers, and the elderly (Brady 2004; Brady and Burroway 2012; Brady and Kall 2007; Chzhen and Bradshaw 2012; Heuveline and Weinshenker 2008; Huber et al. 2009; Rainwater and Smeeding 2003). Interestingly, Brady (2005, 2009) finds that social security transfers, together with public health spending, explain away differences in extents of poverty and poverty reduction between the three welfare state regimes. Among transfer programs, sickness benefits, child and family allowances, and pension benefits are found important in accounting for a cross-county variation in poverty while unemployment insurance and means-tested benefits seem to play a weaker role (Backman 2009; Moller et al. 2003; Scruggs and Alan 2006). These studies suggest that a change in poverty trends over time may have reflected the changing role of welfare states.

There have been some indications that welfare states may have become less effective in reducing poverty during the recent decades. Postindustrial transformations of the labor market and the family, expedited by globalization, may have undermined the functioning of welfare states (Esping-Andersen 1999). The recent literature also shows some evidence of welfare state retrenchment. Although earlier studies emphasize the resiliency of the welfare state (Pierson 1994, 1996), by no later than the 1990s, widespread cutbacks are observed in sickness pay, disability pensions, and unemployment benefits (Stephens, Huber, and Ray 1999; Allan and Scruggs 2004). These changes may have reduced the capability of welfare states to tame poverty generated in the market. On the contrary, empirical studies show no significant difference in the effectiveness of welfare states in the 1990s period (Brady 2005) and even find a larger redistributive role of welfare states (Kenworthy and Pontusson 2005). Yet, it may be too early to come to a conclusion.

It is noted that the growth of market-income poverty from the mid-1980s to the mid-1990s was largely mitigated by welfare state redistribution programs. In the mid-1980s, redistribution systems reduced poverty rates by13.7 percent, from 23.0 percent for market income to 9.3 percent for disposable income. The systems show larger poverty-reducing effects in the mid-1990s. They reduced poverty rates by 19.2 percent, from 28.0 percent to 9.8 percent in the mid-1990s. The larger redistribution by welfare states was an automatic response to social needs increased by market turmoil. Lowered market income levels among low-income households generated a larger population eligible for and benefiting from the welfare state systems already in place (Immervoll and Richardson 2011; Kenworthy and Pontusson 2005). Consequently, larger market-income poverty automatically resulted in more poverty reduction by existing systems.

While welfare states nearly offset surging market income poverty until the mid-1990s, they may have become less effective in reducing poverty since then. In the mid-2000s, the OECD countries reduced poverty rates of market income by 17.1 percent, which is less than the 19.2 percentage point reduction in the mid-1990s. Decreased welfare generosity and tightened eligibility in welfare state programs for the working-age population seem to account for the change. This is suggested by the trend in public social expenditure. Among the 29 OECD countries, spending on cash benefits for the nonelderly as a percentage of GDP declined from 5.3 percent in 1995 to 4.5 percent in 2005, while spending on old-age income security shows a continuous upward trend (Immervoll and Richardson 2011). The changes further shifted poverty risk from the elderly to young. The OECD (2008) shows that poverty risks for all age groups older than 50 declined, while the risks for people below 50 increased among OECD countries (see Figure 5.5 of the OECD report). Poverty risks for the elderly significantly decreased. In contrast, poverty rates for children and young adults rose about 25 percent higher than the average in the mid-2000s.

Transfer payments to the elderly population have not been immune to welfare state cutbacks. Old-age pensions, which account for the largest share of income transfers, were changed in many countries after the early 1990s. Pension entitlement was reduced for current and future working populations compared with past generations. The OECD (2007) reports that the average pension promise in the 16 OECD countries fell by 22 percent for men, while it was reduced by 25 percent for women. These pension reforms have large and negative implications for the adequacy of retirement incomes for low-income earners and the elderly. Nevertheless, the reforms did not increase old-age poverty significantly, since most changes did not significantly effect current pensioners and older workers.

In welfare state programs for the nonelderly population, reforms since the 1990s decreased the generosity of social protection for the nonworking population and directly aggravated poverty (Cantillon 2011). Decline in the generosity of unemployment benefits become evident over the 1990s in many countries (Allan and Scruggs 2004). The shares of benefit recipients among unemployed people dropped in a majority of industrialized countries. Changing eligibility rules of unemployment benefit systems, such as the stronger enforcement of job search conditions, contributed to the dwindling shares of benefit recipients. Nor was the incomplete coverage of the growing number of workers in insecure and nonstandard employment adequately addressed. The long-term unemployed have experienced the largest setback in their relative income position. Benefit levels of social assistance and housing support were reduced despite steady earnings growth (Cantillon 2011; Immervoll and Richardson 2011). Among social assistant recipients, however, families with children faced less damaging changes in redistribution systems due to expanded family benefits such as child-related tax credits (Immervoll and Richardson 2011).

By decreasing benefit generosity, welfare states have attempted to strengthen labor force participation rates of recipients. Since the 1990s, many welfare states, including the United States, the United Kingdom, Australia, the Netherlands, and several Nordic countries, have emphasized the need for activation of benefit recipients. The focus on activation and "making work pay," often reinforced by use of negative incentives such as reducing benefits and tightening eligibilities, may have increased poverty among the nonworking population who have difficulties finding employment (Cantillon 2011; Immervoll and Pearson 2009; Vandenbroucke and Vleminckx 2011).

On the other hand, welfare states have been adjusted to accommodate the growing need to support work and reconcile work and family. Based on the "social investment" approach (Esping-Andersen 2002; Morel, Palier, and Palme 2011), policies have become more employment related and service oriented. Spending on childcare and other work-related services has increased compared with spending on cash benefits, which may have distributional implications. An earlier study of distributional effects of in-kind services found relatively small changes in income distribution (Smeeding et al. 1993). Recent studies suggest that social services significantly affect the distribution of economic resources among the population (Castles 2009; Garfinkel, Rainwater, and Smeeding 2006; Paulus, Sutherland, Tsakloglou 2010; Verbist, Forster, and Vaalavuo 2012). Studies show that public services in general are relatively uniformly distributed across income classes and, as a result, lead to a larger increase in the resources of lower income classes than of higher classes (Marical et al. 2006; OECD 2008; Verbist et al. 2012). Verbist et al. (2012) also show that considering public services substantially drops poverty rates in OECD countries. Childcare services and childhood education services, which are recently highlighted in many OECD countries, also reduce child poverty (Forster and Verbist 2012).[9]

The shift from cash transfers to work-related benefits and social services has had some distributional downsides. Thirty years ago, Le Grand (1982) emphasized that social services would fail to achieve equality if inequality of money income is not directly tackled. In general, benefits from social services may improve distribution of disposable economic resources less than cash benefits do (Marical et al. 2006; Esping-Andersen 2009). Work-related services including childcare and parental leave may be less redistributive due to the uneven use of services across income classes. Higher income households tend to use more services than lower income households in most countries while households equally consume services in some Nordic countries. The unequal distribution of service use reflects differences in employment statuses, accessibility to services, and propensities of service use (Ghysels and Van Lancker 2011; Van Lancker and Ghysels 2012) . Particularly, employment support and related social services are more likely to benefit those already employed or ready for employment. Subsidized childcare services tend to be used more by high-income dual-earner families in many countries. In most EU member countries, furthermore, recent employment growth has been largely concentrated in working families with at least one person already employed. It has benefited workless families only marginally and has failed to lower poverty in many European countries, with the exception of a couple of Nordic countries (Cantillon 2011; De Beer 2007). Without addressing employment performance and service use stratified across income classes, work support replacing income support may not reverse worsening poverty trends.[10]

In short, we are forced to conclude that generous welfare states may disproportionally benefit the employed and elderly during turbulent economic periods through generous old-age benefits and strengthened work support, while not effectively assisting the unemployed/nonemployed and the younger population, as the result of its increasingly less efficient job-creation capability or insufficient support for the low-income, out-of-work population. Future research needs to expand its focus on the limitation of the current welfare state structure dealing with these generational gaps as well as so-called Matthew effects of the social investment approach.[11] The fundamental structure of the welfare states, for many reasons, may be more susceptible to sponsoring the old and the employed over the young and labor market outsiders.

WELFARE REGIMES AND POVERTY IN DEVELOPING COUNTRIES

In developing countries, there are several conditions that make it difficult to utilize theories of welfare states (based on rich democracies) in explaining poverty outcomes. First, in most developing countries, governance mechanisms based on democratic accountability and effectiveness have not yet been fully established. In such situations, the state elites are often heavily influenced by, or under the control of, traditional power-holders such as big businesses and landlords. As governance mechanisms are not solid, welfare checks and food stamps are not delivered properly to the poor or targeted recipients, but often directed to the state elites' clientelistic allies. Second, informal sectors based on self-employment and family businesses are overly developed compared with formal sectors based on wage-earner labor consisting of employees hired in the state and state-owned firms, foreign-owned companies, and domestic large businesses. Productivity and wage gaps between these two sectors are strikingly large compared with those of rich democracies. Third, in developing societies, government and financial systems are unstable and ineffective, and therefore highly vulnerable to external economic shocks. Often in these societies, policy autonomy of the state bureaucrats and politicians is far more limited than that of rich democracies due to their vulnerability to external shocks and influences.

Welfare state scholarship has identified two distinct types of welfare regimes in order to explain inequality and poverty trends in developing societies. One is the productivist welfare regime common in East (and some South) Asian countries. These countries have been typically classified as "developmental states" as they direct their state resources to sponsoring entrepreneurship by providing infrastructures, capital, training, and information that cannot be easily obtained by fledgling individual firms. They invest relatively greater state spending on these developmental goals, while allocating minimal resources to social welfare. Basic social insurances were initially provided only to the core state-sector employees, and it was only after they achieved some levels of economic development and political democracy that they began to embrace economically and socially marginalized and vulnerable populations. This type of welfare regime provides universal and highly competitive education for the entire youth population but has been very stingy about other conventional areas, such as pension providing, health care, unemployment benefits, and family allowances.

The other type of regime is the protectionist welfare regime prevalent in Latin American countries and primarily based on import-substitution industries. They have developed relatively large and generous welfare states, but social-insurance schemes were narrowly provided to core, protected formal-sector workers (Malloy 1979). Social-assistance transfers were neither generous nor effective in reaching the poorest populations due to widespread fraud and clientelism. Educational spending is disproportionally allocated to tertiary elite education (Haggard and Kaufman 2009; Rudra 2008). The most deprived populations at the bottom of the social stratum, therefore, did not benefit significantly from social policies, especially social insurances (Huber and Stephens 2012). Poverty rates are extremely high in most Latin American countries compared with those in their East Asian counterparts.

However, globalization and democratization have introduced significant changes in both welfare regimes. In East Asia, the growth of overall social spending has been remarkably upward since the 1980s, but global financial crises in 1997 and 2008 have also caused tremendous ranges of economic and structural transformations in the region. Mass layoffs and early retirements became social norms since 1997. Flexible labor market arrangements, based on nonstandard and substitute workers and on the rapidly aging population, have simultaneously occurred throughout the region. Especially, older generations suffering layoffs and early retirements without pension schemes are most vulnerable to poverty. This phenomenon is most noticeable in South Korea, where the national pension plan was expanded to the entire population just recently (in 1999), while the population is aging faster than anywhere else in the world. Even worse, mass layoffs and flexible employment arrangements became new norms in the labor market, with labor-law reforms resulting from the financial crisis of 1997. The poverty rate for the elderly in this country is 45.1 in 2010 (OECD), which is twice that of the second-tier group countries. This implies that nearly one of two old men at the age of 65 or more is exposed to poverty. In this productivist welfare regime, the impacts of globalization have been deep and pervasive enough to dismantle the fundamental social fabrics of these societies. However, despite the impressive expansion of welfare states since democratization in the 1980s, social policy schemes and implementations are not yet sufficiently generous in their sizes, nor universal enough in scope, to reach the marginalized populations.

In Latin America, where neoliberal privatization and retrenchment of welfare states arrived with democratization in the 1980s and 1990s, leftist parties surged electorally in the 2000s throughout the region. These resurgent leftist partisan politics in Latin America are mainly attributable to market-based reforms in the 1980s and 1990s in this region, which made middle-class employees in the formal sector increasingly vulnerable to poverty (Rudra 2008) and consequently inclined to support leftist parties in the 2000s. Incumbent leftist parties in the region, as democratization provides them with more favorable conditions for implementing redistributive social policies (Huber and Stephens 2012), have attempted to form an electoral majority by building solidarity between the middle and working classes. They not only restored the welfare programs that formerly benefited the middle classes but also introduced ambitious poverty reduction programs, best known as the "conditional cash transfer" (CCT) program. Starting under the Cardoso regime and then expanding even further under the Lula regime in Brazil, CCT became popular in the entire Latin America region and achieved varied successes across countries. Under CCT, poor families are eligible to receive benefits conditioned upon their children's regular school attendance and participation in immunization programs (Hall 2008). Lee (2012) notes that in some developing societies, in which extreme poverty and inequality are entrenched and welfare programs favor workers in the core industries and public sectors (Lee 2005), implementing an effective social-assistance program is no less important than defending an existing social-insurance program (Lee 2012:530). In Brazil, since the mid-1990s, urban (absolute) poverty (population living below $1.25 per day as a percentage of total population) fell from 12 percent to 3 percent in 2008, while rural poverty decreased from 40 percent to 12 percent in 2008. Children's secondary school enrollments skyrocketed from 3 percent in 1992 to 35 percent in 2008 in rural areas, and from 21 percent in 1992 to 55 percent in 2008 in urban areas. Huber and Stephens (2012) show that literacy enhancement through human capital investment is most strongly correlated with reduction in poverty in this region.

CONCLUSION

In this article, we attempted to provide a critical review of the previous literature on the welfare states and poverty. Based on Esping-Andersen's three world typologies, Huber and Stephens's discussion of "production regimes" (2001), and Hall and Soskice's skill investment regimes (2001), we described how three types of welfare states have established different types of institutional configurations for skill and employment provisions and how such institutional configurations lead to variations in poverty. On one hand, since the 1980s, cross-national variations in overall poverty have persisted across countries, confirming conventional knowledge based on Esping-Andersen's welfare regime typology (1990, 1999). On the other hand, the distinction between social insurance countries and universal countries is somewhat less clear than Esping-Andersen's typology suggests, as differences in poverty between universal and social insurance countries are negligible.

We discussed which configurations of social policies reduce poverty more effectively. Recent studies (Korpi and Palme 1998; Brady and Burroway 2012) raise serious questions about the conventional view that targeting the poor should be more effective in reducing the poor. After briefly reviewing the issue on the aging population and the crisis of social insurance, we summarized findings on over-time trends in poverty, which report unexpected stories: while liberal countries maintained their high-poverty rates without significant changes, some universal welfare states have suffered significant increases in poverty rates as well as income inequality. The latest studies report that poverty among work-less families has increased, while this has not been the case for work-rich families. Overall, we conclude that the recent global trends in restructuring welfare states aiming at "social investment" may actually increase poverty.

In the last section, we paid attention to the development of the welfare states in developing countries, in which welfare states have not developed durable social bases, and globalization and economic crises may have even bigger impacts on the retrenchment or expansion of social policies, depending upon their widely varied histories and dynamics of partisan politics (Huber and Stephens 2012). In some countries, the state has conspicuously failed to react properly to rapid demographic changes and flexible labor markets, which has caused the marginalized population (by market mechanisms and demographic changes) to be exposed to high poverty rates. In other countries, especially in Latin America, globalization that has occurred to the consolidation of democracy has contributed to the strengthening of leftist politics and subsequently led to the adoption of innovative family allowance programs in many countries. The contrasting poverty trends in East Asia and Latin America, therefore, offer intriguing policy implications to students of welfare states and social stratification.

Overall, in the welfare state literature, poverty has drawn scholarly attention thanks to increasing availability of more sophisticated, high-quality data, such as the Luxembourg Income Study. Globalization and structural transformational pressures on the traditional welfare states, however, pose new challenges not only to the policy-makers and politicians but also to the welfare state and stratification scholars, as traditional configurations of social policies and labor markets become increasingly unstable and vulnerable. Newly emerging welfare states in the Global South and wide variations in their stratification outcomes also urge welfare state scholars to develop new puzzles and theoretical/analytical tools to investigate them.

NOTES

1. As for the measurement of poverty, we primarily rely on "relative poverty" measure which is typically defined as "households with less than 50% of the median income," because we believe that poverty measure should reflect "each particular society's cultural norms and customary, prevailing standards of necessities" (Brady 2008:35). See Smeeding's piece in this volume for further discussion on poverty measurement.

2. Obviously, a considerable amount of critiques on this regime typology have been made: (1) feminist scholars have criticized Esping-Andersen's typology for its failure to "recognize gender relations and power within the family and outside the family" (Orloff 1993: 314) and for its limitations in accounting for variations in gender outcomes within each regime (Sainsburry 1999); (2) other welfare state scholars also criticized Esping-Andersen's typology for its inability to replicate the same clustering around three regime types when updated measures of decommodification are taken into account (Scruggs 2006).

3. The durable male breadwinner system based on strong family values induced the labor market outsiders or the disadvantaged to rely on the breadwinners. Therefore, family-based reliance-responsibility exchanges in social insurance countries play an important role in keeping their poverty levels low.

4. According to the OECD (2008), the poverty rates based on the OECD income questionnaire are similar to those from the Luxembourg Income Study and the Eurostat in the mid-2000s. However, the OECD estimates show a higher rate (about three to four percentage points) for Germany and a lower rate (about four percentage points) for the United Kingdom.

5. The redistributive role of tax and transfer systems is assessed by the conventional method that compares poverty rates before and after taxes and transfers. As often indicated, the method has some problems. First, pretax and pretransfer income differ from counterfactual income in the absence of tax and transfer systems. The systems affect pretax and pretransfer income by generating behavioral incentive effects on labor supply, family formation, savings, asset accumulation, and other outcomes (Atkinson and Mogensen 1993; Danziger, Haveman and Plotnick 1981; Moffitt 1992). A recent study, which focuses on work disincentive effects of transfer programs in the United States, shows that transfer programs only have a tiny effect on pretransfer poverty (Ben-Shalom, Moffitt, and Scholz 2012). A comparative study also finds no significant effect of transfers on pretransfer poverty (Moller et al. 2003). However, there is a continuing concern that pretransfer old-age poverty unrealistically overstates counterfactual poverty in the absence of public pensions (Bradley et al. 2003; Jesuit and Mahler 2010). Second, the method only includes cash benefits in transfers and does not consider the role of social services. In 2007, public expenditure on social services represents 13 percent of GDP on average among 34 OECD countries, larger than that on cash transfers which amounts to 11 percent, with considerable cross-national variation (OECD 2011; Verbist et al. 2012).

6. Since the mid-1980s, absolute poverty dropped in most welfare states (Scruggs and Alan 2006; Smeeding 2006). Between the mid-1990s and the mid-2000s, when relative poverty noticeably rose, absolute poverty rates substantially declined across many OECD countries (2008:Chapter 5).

7. During this recent period, however, some countries, such as Austria, Finland, and Sweden, showed a significant rise (above 1 percent) in poverty, while a few countries including Greece, Ireland, and Israel experienced a significant decline.

8. Government transfers are effective not only in reducing poverty rates but also in lessening the depth of poverty and the relative deprivation among the poor, although less cross-country variation in poverty reduction is found for the latter two indexes (DeFina and Thanawala 2003). Welfare state transfers also play an important role in reducing absolute poverty and material deprivation (Kenworthy 1999, 2011; Scruggs and Alan 2006).

9. In addition, there is a possibility that social services improve distribution of market income by encouraging work efforts and raising earnings levels among the low-skilled population (Esping-Andersen 2009). However, strong empirical support for this argument remains to be seen (Currie and Gahvari 2008).

10. Working families with employed adults are less likely to be poor. However, the increasing share of working families due to employment growth would not substantially reduce poverty. Transfers play a key role in reducing poverty among the working-age population (Brady, Fullerton, and Moren Cross 2010; Lohmann 2009; Marx, Vandenbroucke, and Verbist 2012; OECD 2009).

11. It refers to the phenomenon that a larger part of welfare state benefits are paid to the middle classes.

REFERENCES

Allan, James P. and Lyle Scruggs. 2004. "Political Partisanship and Welfare State Reform in Advanced Industrial Societies." *American Journal of Political Science* 48(3): 496–512.

Atkinson, Anthony B. and Gunnar Viby Mogensen, eds. 1993. *Welfare and Work Incentives: A North European Perspective.* Oxford: Oxford University Press.

Atkinson, Anthony B., Lee Rainwater, and Timothy M. Smeeding. 1995. "Income Distribution in OECD Countries." Social Policy Studies No. 18, Paris: OECD.

Backman, Olof. 2009. "Institutions, Structures and Poverty—A Comparative Study of 16 Countries, 1980–2000." *European Sociological Review* 25(2): 251–64.

Baumol, William. 1967. "The Macroeconomics of Unbalanced Growth." *American Economic Review* 57: 415–26.

Ben-Shalom, Yonatan, Robert Moffitt, and John Karl Scholz. 2012. "An Assessment of the Effectiveness of Antipoverty Programs in the United States." Pp. 709–49 in *Oxford Handbook of the Economics of Poverty*, edited by P. N. Jefferson. New York: Oxford University Press.

Boix, Carles. 1998. *Political Parties, Growth, and Equality: Conservative and Social Democratic Strategies in the World Economy.* New York: Cambridge University Press.

Brady, David. 2005. "The Welfare State and Relative Poverty in Rich Western Democracies, 1967–1997." *Social Forces* 83(4): 1329–64.

Brady, David. 2009. *Rich Democracies, Poor People: How Politics Explain Poverty.* Oxford: Oxford University Press.

Brady, David and Rebekah Burroway. 2012. "Targeting, Universalism, and Single-Mother Poverty: A Multilevel Analysis across 18 Affluent Democracies." *Demography* 49(2): 719–46.

Brady, David, Andrew S. Fullerton, and Jennifer Moren Cross. "More Than Just Nickels and Dimes: A Cross-National Analysis of Working Poverty in Affluent Democracies." *Social Problems* 57(4): 559–85.

Burniaux, Jean-Marc, Thai-Thanh Dang, Douglas Fore, Michael Forster, Marco Mira d'Ercole, and Howard Oxley. 1998. "Income Distribution and Poverty in Selected OECD Countries." Economic Department Working Papers No. 189. Paris: OECD.

Bussemaker, Jet and Kees van Kersbergen. 1999. "Contemporary Social-Capitalist Welfare States and Gender Inequality." Pp. 15–46 in *Gender and Welfare State Regimes*, edited by D. Sainsbury. New York: Oxford University Press.

Cantillon, Bea 2011. "The Paradox of the Social Investment State: Growth, Employment and Poverty in the Lisbon Era." *Journal of European Social Policy*, 21(5): 432–49.

Castle, Francis G. 2009. "What Welfare States Do: A Disaggregated Expenditure Approach." *Journal of Social Policy* 38(1): 45–62.

Chzhen, Yekaterina and Jonathan Bradshaw. 2012. "Lone Parents, Poverty and Policy in the European Union." *Journal of European Social Policy* 22(5): 487–506.

Currie, Janet and Firouz Gahvari. 2008. "Transfers in Cash and In-Kind: Theory Meets the Data." *Journal of Economic Literature* 46(2): 333–83.

Danziger, Sheldon, Robert Haveman, and Robert Plotnick. 1981. "How Income Transfer Programs Affect Work, Savings, and the Income Distribution: A Critical Review." *Journal of Economic Literature* 19(3): 975–1028.

De Beer, Paul. 2007."Why Work Is Not a Panacea: Decomposition Analysis of EU-15 Countries." *Journal of European Social Policy*, 17(4): 375–88.

Defina, R. H. and K. Thanawala. 2003. "International Evidence on the Impact of Taxes and Transfers on Alternative Poverty Indexes." *Social Science Research* 33: 322–38.

Esping-Andersen, Gøsta. 1985. *Politics Against Markets: The Social Democratic Road to Power*. Princeton: Princeton University Press.

Esping-Andersen, Gøsta. 1990. *The Three Worlds of Welfare Capitalism*. Princeton, NJ: Princeton University Press.

Esping-Andersen, Gøsta. 1999. *Social Foundations of Post-industrial Economies*. New York: Oxford University Press.

Esping-Andersen, Gøsta. 2009. "Economic Inequality and the Welfare State." In *The Oxford Handbook of Economic Inequality*, edited by W. Salverda, B. Nolan, and T. M. Smeeding. Oxford: Oxford University Press.

Esping-Andersen, Gøsta. 2002. *Why We Need a New Welfare State*. New York: Oxford University Press.

Estevez-Abe, Margarita, Torben Iversen, and David Soskice. 2001. "Social Protection and the Formation of Skills: A Reinterpretation of the Welfare State." Pp. 145–83 in *Varieties of Capitalism: The Institutional Foundations of Comparative Advantage*, edited by Peter Hall and David Soskice. New York: Oxford University Press.

Förster, Michael F. and Mira D'Ercole, Marco, Income Distribution and Poverty in OECD Countries in the Second Half of the 1990s (February 18, 2005). OECD Social, Employment and Migration Working Paper No. 22.

Foster, Michael and Mark Pearson. 2002. "Income Distribution and Poverty in the OECD Area: Trends and Driving Forces." OECD Economic Studies No. 34. Paris: OECD.

Forster, M. and G. Verbist. 2012. "Money or Kindergarten? Distributive Effects of Cash versus In-kind Family Transfers for Young Children." OECD Social, Employment and Migration Working Paper No. 135, Paris: OECD.

Garfinkel, Irwin, Lee Rainwater, and Timothy M. Smeeding. 2006. "A Re-examination of Welfare States and Inequality in Rich Nations: How In-kind Transfers and Indirect Taxes Change the Story." *Journal of Policy Analysis and Management* 25(4): 897–919.

Garrett, Geoffrey. 1998. *Partisan Politics in the Global Economy*. New York: Cambridge University Press.

Garrett, Geoffrey and Christopher Way. 1999. "The Rise of Public Sector Unions, Corporatism, and Macroeconomic Performance, 1970–1990." *Comparative Political Studies* 32: 411–34.

Ghysels, Joris and Wim Van Lancker. 2011. "The Unequal Benefits of Family Activation: An Analysis of the Social Distribution of Family Policy among Families with Young Children." *Journal of European Social Policy*, 21(5): 472–85.

Gilbert, Neil. 2004. *Transformation of Welfare State: The Silent Surrender of Public Responsibility*, New York: Oxford University Press.

Haggard, Stephan and Robert R. Kaufman. *Development, Democracy, and Welfare States: Latin America, East Asia, and Eastern Europe*. Princeton, NJ: Princeton University Press.

Hall, Anthony. 2008. "Brazil's Bolsa Familia: A Double-Edged Sword?" *Development and Change* 39: 799–822.

Hall, Peter and David Soskice. 2001. "An Introduction to Varieties of Capitalism." Pp. 1–71 in *Varieties of Capitalism: The Institutional Foundations of Comparative Advantage*, edited by Peter Hall and David Soskice. New York: Oxford University Press.

Heuveline, Patrick and Matthew Weinshenker. 2008. "The International Child Poverty Gap: Does Demography Matter?" *Demography* 45(1): 173–91.

Huber, Evelyne, Charles Ragin, and John D. Stephens. 1993. "Social Democracy, Christian Democracy, Constitutional Structure, and the Welfare State." *American Journal of Sociology* 99: 711–49.

Huber, Evelyne and John D. Stephens. 2001. *Development and Crisis of the Welfare State: Parties and Policies in Global Market.* Chicago: University of Chicago Press.

Huber, Evelyne and John D. Stephens. 2012. *Democracy and the Left: Social Policy and Inequality in Latin America.* Chicago: University of Chicago Press.

Huber, Evelyne, John D. Stephens, David Bradley, and Stephanie Moller. 2009. "The Politics of Women's Economic Independence." *Social Politics: International Studies in Gender, State, and Society* 16(1): 1–39.

Immervoll, Herwig and Mark Pearson. 2009. *A Good Time for Making Work Pay?: Taking Stock of In-work Benefits and Related Measures across the OECD.* OECD Social, Employment and Migration Working Papers, No. 81. Paris: OECD.

Immervoll, Herwig and Linda Richardson. 2011. "Redistribution Policy and Inequality Reduction in OECD Countries: What Has Changed in Two Decades?" Luxembourg Income Study Working Paper Series, No. 571. OECD Social, Employment and Migration Working Papers, No. 122, Paris: OECD.

Jänttiä, Markus and Sheldon Danziger. 2000. "Income Poverty in Advanced Countries." In *Handbook of Income Distribution*, edited by A. B. Atkinson and F. Bourguignon. Amsterdam: Elsevier.

Jesuit, David K. and Vincent A. Mahler. 2010. "Comparing Government Redistribution across Countries: The Problem of Second-Order Effects." *Social Science Quarterly* 91(5): 1390–1404.

Kenworthy, Lane. 1999. "Do Social Welfare Policies Reduce Poverty? A Cross-National Assessment." Social Forces 77: 1119–39.

Kenworthy, Lane 2011. *Progress for the Poor.* Oxford: Oxford University Press.

Kenworthy, Lane and Jonas Pontusson. 2005. "Rising Inequality and the Politics of Redistribution in Affluent Countries." *Perspectives on Politics* 3(3): 449–71.

Kim, Hwanjoon. 2000. "Anti-Poverty Effectiveness of Taxes and Income Transfers in Welfare States." *International Social Security Review* 53(4): 105–29.

Korpi, Walter. 1983. *The Democratic Class Struggle.* London: Routledge and Kegan Paul.

Korpi, Walter and Joakim Palme. 1998. "The Paradox of Redistribution and Strategies of Equality: Welfare State Institutions, Inequality, and Poverty in the Western Countries." *American Sociological Review* 63: 661–87.

Le Grand, Julian. 1982. *The Strategy of Equality: Redistribution and the Social Services.* London: George Allen and Unwin.

Lee, Cheol-Sung. 2005. "Income Inequality, Democracy, and Public Sector Size." *American Sociological Review* 70: 158–81.

Lee, Cheol-Sung. 2012. "Associational Networks and Welfare States in Argentina, Brazil, South Korea, and Taiwan." *World Politics* 64: 507–54.

Lee, Cheol-Sung, Young-Beom Kim, and Jae-Mahn Shim. 2011. "The Limit of Equality Projects: Public Sector Expansion, Sectoral Conflicts, and Income Inequality in Post-Industrial Democracies." *American Sociological Review* 76: 100–24.

Lohman, Henning. 2009. "Welfare States, Labor Market Institutions and the Working Poor: A Comparative Analysis of 20 European Countries." *European Sociological Review* 25(4): 489–504.

Malloy, James M. 1979. *The Politics of Social Security in Brazil.* Pittsburgh: University of Pittsburgh Press.

Mares, Isabela. 2003. *The Politics of Social Risk: Business and Welfare State Development,* New York: Cambridge University Press.

Marx, Ive, Pieter Vandenbroucke, and Gerlinde Verbist. 2012. "Can Higher Employment Levels Bring Down Relative Income Poverty in the EU? Regression-based Simulations of the Europe 2020 Target." *Journal of European Social Policy* 22(5): 472–86.

Mead, Lawrence M. 1997. "Citizenship and Social Policy: T. H. Marshall and Poverty." *Social Philosophy and Policy* 14:197–230.

Mitchell, Deborah. 1991. *Income Transfers in Ten Welfare State*. Aldershot, UK: Avebury.

Moffitt, Robert. 1992. "Incentive Effects of the US Welfare System: A Review." *Journal of Economic Literature* 30(1): 1–61.

Moller, Stephanie, David Bradley, Evelyne Huber, Francois Nielsen, and John D. Stephens. 2003. "Determinants of Relative Poverty in Advanced Capitalist Democracies." *American Sociological Review* 68: 22–51.

Morel, Nathalie, Bruno Palier, and Joakim Palme. 2012. "Beyond the Welfare State as We Know It?" Pp. 1–33 in *Towards a Social Investment Welfare State? Ideas, Policies and Challenges*, edited by N. Morel, B. Palier, and J. Palme. Bristol, UK: Policy Press.

Murray, Charles. 1984. *Losing Ground: American Social Policy, 1950–1980*. New York: Basic Books.

OECD. 2007. *Pension at a Glance: Public Policies across OECD Countries*. Paris: OECD.

OECD. 2008. *Growing Unequal?: Income Distribution and Poverty in OECD Countries*. Paris: OECD.

OECD. 2011. *Divided We Stand: Why Inequality Keeps Rising*, Paris: OECD.

Paulus, Alari, Holly Sutherland, and Panos Tsakloglou. 2010. "The Distributional Impact of In-Kind Public Benefits in European Countries." *Journal of Policy Analysis and Management* 29(2): 243–66.

Orloff, Ann Shola. 1993. "Gender and the Social Rights of Citizenship: The Comparative Analysis of Gender Relations and Welfare States." *American Sociological Review* 58: 303–28.

Persson, Torsten and Guido Tabellini. 2000. *Political Economics: Explaining Economic Policy*. Cambridge, MA: MIT Press.

Persson, Torsten and Guido Tabellini. 2003. *The Economic Effects of Constitutions*. Cambridge, MA: MIT Press.

Pierson, Paul. 1994. *Dismantling the Welfare State?: Reagan, Thatcher, and the Politics of Retrenchment*. Cambridge: Cambridge University Press.

Pierson, Paul. 1996. "The New Politics of the Welfare State." *World Politics* 48(2): 143–79.

Pierson, Paul. 2001. "Post-industrial Pressures on the Mature Welfare States." Pp. 80–104 in *The New Politics of the Welfare State*, edited by P. Pierson. Oxford: Oxford University Press.

Rainwater, Lee and Timothy M. Smeeding. 2003. *Poor Kids in a Rich Country: America's Children in Comparative Perspective*. New York: Russell Sage Foundation.

Rudra, Nita. 2008. *Globalization and the Race to the Bottom in Developing Countries: Who Really Gets Hurt?* Cambridge: Cambridge University Press.

Sainsbury, Diane. 1999. *Gender and Welfare State Regimes*. Oxford: Oxford University Press.

Scruggs, Lyle. 2010. "Welfare State Entitlements Data Set: A Comparative Institutional Analysis of Eighteen Welfare States." Retrieved (http://sp.uconn.edu/~scruggs/wp.htm).

Scruggs, Lyle and James P. Allan. 2006. "The Material Consequences of Welfare States: Benefit Generosity and Absolute Poverty in 16 OECD Countries." *Comparative Political Studies* 39(7): 880–904.

Scruggs, Lyle and James Allan. 2006. "Welfare-State Decommodification in 18 OECD Countries: A Replication and Revision." *Journal of European Social Policy* 16(1): 55–72.

Seccombe, Karen. 2000. "Families in Poverty in the 1990s: Trends, Causes, Consequences, and Lessons Learned." *Journal of Marriage and Family* 62: 1094–1113.

Shinkawa, Toshimitsu. 2003. "The Politics of Pension Retrenchment in Japan." *Japanese Journal of Social Security Policy* 2: 25–33.

Smeeding, Timothy M. 2006. "Poor People in Rich Nations: The United States in Comparative Perspective." *Journal of Economic Perspectives* 20(1): 69–90.

Smeeding, Timothy M., Lee Rainwater, and Gary Burtless. 2001. "U.S. Poverty in a Cross-national Context." In *Understanding Poverty*, edited by S. H. Danziger and Robert Haveman. New York: Russell Sage Foundation.

Smeeding, Timothy M., Lee Rainwater, Martin Rein, Richard Hauser, and Gaston Schaber. 1990. "Income Poverty in Seven Countries: Initial Estimates from the LIS Database." In *Poverty, Inequality and Income Distribution in Comparative Perspective*, edited by T. M. Smeeding, M. O'Higgins, and L. Rainwater. New York: Harvester Wheatsheaf.

Smeeding, Timothy M., Peter Saunders, John Coder, Stephen Jenkins, Johan Fritzell, Aldi J. M. Hagenaars, Richard Hauser, and Michael Wolfson. 1993. "Poverty, Inequality, and Family Living Standards Impacts across Seven Nations: The Effect of Noncash Subsidies for Health, Education and Housing." *Review of Income and Wealth* 39(3): 229–56.

Somers, Margaret R. and Fred Block. 2005. "From Poverty to Perversity: Ideas, Markets, and Institutions over 200 Years of Welfare Debate." *American Sociological Review* 70: 260–87.

Soss, Joe. 1999. "Lessons of Welfare: Policy Design, Political Learning, and Political Action." *American Political Science Review* 93: 363–80.

Stephens, John D., Evelyne Huber, and Leonard Ray. 1999. "The Welfare State in Hard Times." Pp. 164–93 in *Continuity and Change in Contemporary Capitalism*, edited by H. Kitschelt, P. Lange, G. Marks, and J. D. Stephens. Cambridge: Cambridge University Press.

Swenson, Peter. 2002. *Capitalists against Markets: The Makings of Labor Markets and Welfare States in the United States and Sweden*. Oxford: Oxford University Press.

Thelen, Kathleen. 2004. *How Institutions Evolve: The Political Economy of Skills in Germany, Britain, the United States, and Japan*. Cambridge: Cambridge University Press.

Vandenbroucke, Frank and Koen Vleminckx, 2011. "Disappointing Poverty Trends: Is the Investment State to Blame?" *Journal of European Social Policy* 21(5):450–71.

Van Kersbergen, Kees. 1995. *Social Capitalism*. London: Routledge.

Van Lancker, Wim and Joris Ghysels. 2012. "Who Benefits? The Social Distribution of Subsidized Childcare in Sweden and Flanders." *Acta Sociologica* 55(2):125–42.

Verbist, Gerlinde, Michael Forster, and Maria Vaalavuo. 2012. "The Impact of Publicly Provided Services on the Distribution of Resources; Review of New Results and Methods." OECD Social, Employment and Migration Working Papers, No. 130, Paris: OECD.

CHAPTER 32

SOCIAL POLICY, TRANSFERS, PROGRAMS, AND ASSISTANCE

LAURA LEIN, SANDRA K. DANZIGER,
H. LUKE SHAEFER, AND AMANDA TILLOTSON

INTRODUCTION

PUBLIC provision for families in poverty includes programs that provide childcare, income supports, medical assistance, public housing, and employment assistance to family units as well as policies that operate at a more general level to provide workforce and economic development and child welfare and early childhood education and support. Across nations, these policies vary along a number of dimensions (Alber, 2010; Brady, 2009; Prakash and Prokowski, 2011). While the percentage of national GDP devoted to specific assistance programs is one dimension of difference, qualitative variations in the structure and underlying assumptions of benefit programs also have important consequences. Cross-national differences may be further magnified by the fact that poverty measures, which often provide a gateway to programs, also vary across nations (Couch and Pirog, 2010; Besharov and Couch, 2009).

Alternative poverty metrics may also be put forward in intranational debates about poverty policy. These alternatives result in differing estimates of both the incidence and the demographic composition of poverty (Bourguignon and Fields, 1990). In the United States, for example, proposed alternative measures that include the value of transfers or assets and measures based on expenditures rather than income produce different estimates of the proportion of the population in poverty and of the proportion of particular groups, such as families and the elderly, that are poor (Brady, 2003; Smeeding, 2009).

In some nations, supportive programs are universally available and flow from social citizenship (Marshall, 1963); in others, they are targeted, means tested, structured around principles of least eligibility, and instantiate distinctions between the deserving and undeserving poor (Somers and Block, 2005; Brodkin, 1993). Loci of control and implementation also vary: in some nations, programs are developed and implemented entirely at the national level; in others, subnational units of government shape formulation and implementation (Soss, Fording, and Schram, 2008). Policies also vary cross-nationally in the extent to which they protect citizens against market shocks: in some nations, programs aim to incentivize work and connect most benefits to labor market activity; in others, allowance programs that offer minimum benefits to all citizens provide a more distinct alternative to markets (Hacker, 2002; Esping-Andersen, 1990; Handler, 2003). Finally, there is variation in the complexity of available benefit programs. Some nations address poverty through a complex grid of cash and in-kind transfers supplemented by a variety of special-purpose programs, while others provide universal family benefits, public health and childcare, and access to social—or, in American terminology—public housing (Garfinkel, Rainwater, and Smeeding, 2010).

As a standard for comparison, the United States has traditionally been located at one pole on these dimensions, relying primarily on targeted/special purpose and often means- tested programs, many of which allow for substantial state control over benefit levels and program access. Rather than universal provision for childcare, medical care, basic income, employment assistance and social/ public housing, the United States increasingly relies on antipoverty policies that prioritize individual market participation and/or devolve authority to states (Seefeldt and Horowski, 2012; DeParle, 2009; Soss, Fording, and Schram, 2011; Zuberi, 2006). Particularly in the light of the Great Recession, which was characterized by rising poverty and unemployment, contrasts between these policies and those that structure provision in other developed countries became more striking. Some authors, however, have connected these generous welfare states to the economic difficulties of some European nations (Gregg, 2013), while others have raised the possibility that financial crises in developed welfare states have driven retrenchment (Vis, van Kersbergen, and Hyland, 2011).

In this article, we focus intensively on a comparison of poverty policies and programs in four areas. We highlight cash transfer programs, public provision of childcare, publically provided medical care, and public/social housing. We conclude with a brief overview of the ramifications of differing national approaches to poverty in the context of the turn toward neoliberalism and the recent recession.

TRANSFERS

Across nations, cash transfer programs can be grouped into three main categories. First, conditional transfer programs, which are discussed in more detail elsewhere in this volume, provide highly targeted assistance to families and individuals (Slater, 2011). These programs, utilized in developing countries such as Cambodia, Costa Rica, Honduras, and Mexico, target families by income and often, as in Mexico, by geographic location (Garcia and Moore, 2012; Barrientos, 2011; Barrientos and Santibanez, 2009). Transfers are conditioned on a very specific behavioral contract between recipients and the state: recipients may, for example, be required to enroll in medical services or to keep their children in school (Fizbein, Schady, and Feierra, 2009). Failure to meet these requirements results in sanctions (Gonzalez-Flores, Heraclaus, and Winter, 2012).

United States transfer policies constitute a second category that combines targeted and time-limited benefits with behavioral expectations that include mandatory work requirements and sanctions for noncompliance. Since the 1996 passage of the Personal Responsibility and Work Opportunity Reconciliation Act (PRWORA), which transformed AFDC (Aid to Families with Dependent Children) into TANF (Temporary Assistance for Needy Families), means-tested cash assistance transfers in the United States have been restructured as conditional, time-limited benefits that require able-bodies recipients to participate in work activities, ending a 60-year history during which benefits to single mothers were structured as open-ended entitlements (Daguerre, 2008, 2011; Weaver, 2000; Cherry, 2007; Haskins, 2006, 2004; DeParle, 2004). The transition required more mothers to balance low-wage work and family responsibilities (Seefeldt, 2008).

Under AFDC, all applicants whose income fell below the eligibility threshold and had children under the age of 18 were entitled to receive cash assistance. Under TANF, however, the federal contribution changed from a matching grant where the federal government paid a percentage of spending, to a fixed annual block grant (Schott, 2009; Moffitt, 2008). The federal government also imposed a five-year lifetime limit on benefits funded with federal dollars; allowed states to impose "work first" rules that required most recipients to participate in job-seeking activities, such as resume writing, mock interviews, and registering with state employment agencies; and allowed states to impose other additional qualifications for participation, exacerbating existing interstate differences in the structure and amount of benefits (Blank, 2002; Rowe and Giannarelli, 2006; Danziger and Seefeldt, 2003; Danziger, 2010; Seefeldt and Orzol, 2005; Schott and Pavetti, 2011; Seefeldt, Danziger, and Danziger, 2003). TANF also required states to sanction recipients who failed to meet work requirements but gave the states broad discretion on how to structure these sanctions (Bloom and Winstead, 2002; Women's Legal Defense Fund, 2010; Schram et al., 2009).

The initial effect of the transition to TANF, which occurred during a period of economic expansion, was to reduce the size of welfare caseloads and to increase the employment rates of low-income single mothers (Danielson and Klerman, 2008; Danziger et al., 2000). However, when low-wage workers began to improve their pay, they, in some cases, lost means-tested benefits that cost them more than their wage gains (Romich, Simmelink, and Holt, 2007). Despite the severity of the Great Recession, the national TANF caseload grew only slightly (Pavetti and Schott, 2011; Slack, Magnuson, and Berger, 2007). TANF served on average only 26 families for every 100 in poverty in 2013. Just prior to PRWORA, AFDC provided assistance to 68 of every 100 families in poverty (Center on Budget and Policy Priorities, 2015).

As the economy slowed, an increasing number of families became disconnected from cash payments, and the number of families living in extreme poverty doubled. A 2013 study found that in any given month about 1.6 million households with children were living on cash incomes no more than $2 per person day (Shaefer and Edin, 2013). Studies indicate that, depending on the definition of "disconnected," between 13 percent and 20 percent of the population of households in poverty are disconnected both from work and from cash welfare at any one time (Seefeldt and Horowski, 2012; Acs and Loprest, 2004; Slack, Magnuson, and Berger, 2007).

These findings suggest that the initial narrative of TANF's success reflected a specific and time-limited set of labor market conditions rather than the policy's characteristics (Parrott and Sherman, 2007; Scott et al., 2004; Danielson and Klerman, 2008; Cherlin et al., 2009). The low-skill jobs available to many former recipients not only pay low-wages, they often require variable schedules and work hours that complicate planning for childcare and transportation and to produce significant swings in income, are temporary or part time and lack benefits (Henly and Lambert, 2010; Boots, Macomber, and Danziger, 2008; Dworsky and Courtney, 2007; Scott et al., 2004).

While TANF caseloads have fallen in recent years, participation in a unique American program, SNAP (Supplemental Nutrition Assistance Program), is at an all-time high. Formerly known as the Food Stamp Program, it provides means-tested, near-cash benefits restricted to the purchase of food. First piloted 1939–1943 to address the conjuncture of agricultural surpluses and widespread hunger, the program was repiloted in various states from 1961–1964 and was authorized as a federal program in 1964. The program also provides benefits to single, poor individuals without children, although single individuals with no dependents may face work requirements.

After falling in tandem with cash assistance rolls in the late 1990s, SNAP participation began to rise in the early 2000s and exploded during the Great Recession years. An average of 46.6 million individuals—roughly one in seven Americans—accessed SNAP every month in 2012 (Food Research and Action Center, 2013). This growth in SNAP participation during the past few years is largely attributable to a combination of policy changes that have liberalized eligibility (Danielson and Klerman, 2011) coupled with increased unemployment and poverty during the Great Recession years. A family of four could receive a maximum of $688 a month midway through 2012, thanks to a significant, temporary increase in benefits included in the American Recovery and Reinvestment Act (ARRA) of 2009. These increased benefits ended in 2013. There is significant evidence that SNAP has acted as a critical buffer against extreme poverty during the Great Recession period (Shaefer and Edin, 2013; DeParle and Gobeloff, 2010).

Increasingly in the United States, means-tested public benefits are delivered through targeted refundable tax credits. Beneficiaries receive the full amount of the credit, even if it exceeds their income tax liability. The Earned Income Tax Credit (EITC) is the largest such refundable tax credit, targeted at low-income, working families with children, although some very low-income single individuals are eligible. At about $60 billion in total credits in recent years (serving 26 million tax-filing units), the EITC is one of the federal government's two largest means-tested income-maintenance programs (the other is SNAP). The credit amount increases as labor market earnings increase, up to a plateau, where it reaches its maximum level. In 2013, the maximum credit for a family with two children was $5,372, making it a significant benefit. The credit remains at its maximum amount until it begins to decrease in the phase-out range, finally falling to zero at an annual income level around 200 percent of poverty. As of 2015, 26 states plus the District of Columbia have their own EITCs, providing credits to eligible families (Tax Policy Center, 2013).

Most EITC-eligible taxpayers receive the credit (Currie, 2006). Since 1984, EITC benefits have not been included in eligibility calculations for other public welfare programs. Thus, unlike most sources of income, increases in the EITC do not trigger reductions in other public benefits beyond what is related to increased labor force participation and earnings induced by the EITC. It is important to note, however, that EITC receipt is conditional on labor market participation.

One of the interesting aspects of the EITC and other refundable credits is that they are delivered in a yearly lump sum after the recipient files a tax return. This is unlike the United Kingdom's working tax credit, which is included in recipients' paychecks. While some see this as a weakness of the program, research finds that recipients generally seem to like the lump-sum delivery mechanism. Studies that examine how families allocate dollars from their EITC refunds find that families pay back debt, build savings, spend on special consumption (such as family events), and make large purchases, such as cars (Couch, Smeeding and Waldfogel, 2010; Mendenhall et al., 2012; Romich and Weisner, 2000; Shaefer, Song, and Williams Shanks, 2013).

The once-yearly delivery calls into question the degree to which benefits are available when families experience an economic shock such as job loss or marital dissolution. Also, because of the EITC's unique benefit schedule, the tax credit responds to economic shocks in an ambiguous way. For workers in the phase-in or plateau region, lower earnings from a job loss or change in household composition during the year would result in a lower EITC benefit. In contrast, for workers in the higher phase-out range, such economic shocks lead to a higher EITC.

The child tax credit, established in 1997, is a partially refundable tax credit that supports working low-income families with children. Established in 1997, it is worth up to $1,000 per qualifying child, available to families below a certain income threshold (it begins to phase out at $110,000 for married taxpayers filing jointly; $75,000 for single parents), and is refundable based on earnings above a certain minimum threshold.

A third general category of national income-support policies provides families with cash payments on a universal or nearly universal basis. With the exception of the United States, most OECD countries provide two sorts of cash supports for families. First, they provide universal family allowances to dependent children conditioned on income, age, family structure, and family size. Second, the majority of OECD countries, unlike the United States, provide universal or conditional cash grants on the birth or adoption of a child (OECD, 2011). In many cases, these grants are structured as lump-sum payments.

There is variation in the extent of and structure in which these grants support families in poverty, and there have been important changes over time (Starke, 2006). In Britain, for example, one in four children was poor in 1999 when Prime Minister Blair introduced a set of Labour Party antipoverty policy reforms that provided additional cash support for poor families and that aimed to increase the returns for work. The nation saw a 50 percent reduction in child poverty by 2009, although these gains stalled over time and existing transfer programs still pose problems both for single-parent families and for immigrants (Waldfogel, 2013). The Scandinavian countries have traditionally been identified as providing the most nearly universal transfer programs (OECD, 2011; Heclo, 2011). However, changes in the last two decades have arguably created a turn toward selectivism, increasing the returns to labor market participation (Kuivalainen and Niemala, 2010; Kautto et al., 1999).

Childcare Supports

Waldfogel (2006) notes that, across nations, public supports for family childcare take three forms. Parental-leave policies provide early childhood care by allowing one or both parents to remain at home with young children, providing job protection and sometimes cash allowances. Childcare policies provide either allowances or subsidies for childcare or provide for direct public provision of care. A third set of policies, finally, provide cash benefits for the first few years of a child's life, which can be used to purchase childcare or to substitute for foregone earnings.

As in the case of cash transfers, there is a distinction between the United States' system and arrangements that structure benefits in other developed nations (Waldfogel, 2006; Van Hooren, and Becker, 2012; Mahon, 2011; Earle, Mokomane, and Heymann, 2011; White, 2002). In the United States, public provision for childcare is means tested, provided by a complex grid of subsidies and special programs, and varies a great deal across states. In most other developed nations, however, programs are structured as universal entitlements, although there are significant differences in the way public arrangements support childcare in the preschool years (Matthews, 2011).

The childcare system in the United States varies according to state policies that control both access to and funding for programs as well as regulating program quality, while early childhood education programs are funded by a combination of federal, state, and local funds. Subsidized childcare for working parents is funded through block grants to the states; Head Start programs are funded by the federal government; and public prekindergarten programs are supported by state and local public education programs with some support from the federal government. In each case, this assistance is targeted to poor families. None of these are entitlement programs, and, in fact, none come even close to the capacity for serving everyone eligible. Their availability to families in poverty depends not only on funding but also on the presence of facilities— day-care centers, Head Start programs, and local prekindergarten programs that are privately funded or funded at the state and local levels (Blau and Tekin, 2007).

Head Start, one of the best known programs, teaches a developmental curriculum in the context of care for low-income children (Zigler and Valentine, 1979). Many sites have long waiting lists, but according to a 2011 Census working paper, the Head Start program enrolled over 908,000 children in 2007, whereas at its inception in 1965, it served 561,000 children (Laughlin and Davis, 2011).

Variations in state use of federal funding also affect the availability of childcare, and this issue has become more critical as TANF rules have pushed more mothers into the work force (Bainbridge, Myers, and Waldfogel, 2003; Danziger, Ananat, and Browning, 2004; Dunifon, Kalil, and Danziger, 2007; Meyers, Heintze, and Wolf, 2002; Press, Fagan, and Loughlin, 2006). According to one government report, 17 percent of eligible children received childcare subsidies in 2006. According to estimates from 2006, about 15.5 million children were potentially eligible for a child care subsidy, but only one in six received help from the Child Care and Development Block Grant subsidy program (ASPE, 2010). State-level regulations may also make many low-income working families ineligible for childcare support.

TANF work requirements, combined with the nature of low-wage employment, make assistance with childcare provision and costs vital to poor workers. In the United States, almost half of all workers and three-quarters of those at the bottom income quartile do not have paid sick leave on the job that would help them care for children at home. These parents also lack flexible work schedules that would help when childcare issues arise (Boots, Macomber, and Danziger, 2008; Chase-Lansdale et al., 2003; Johnson, Kalil, and Dunifon, 2010).

In terms of overall public provision for childcare as a proportion of GDP, the United States spends comparatively little: its public spending on care for children under the age of three ranks it among nations such as Mexico, the Slovak Republic, and Hungary. While countries such as Israel and New Zealand spend a comparable proportion of GDP on early childhood care, they spend much more for publicly funded preprimary programs that combine education with care. The Scandinavian countries are at the upper end of the expenditure spectrum on both measures (OECD, 2012a). Still, in aggregate terms there is a great deal of variation among developed nations in spending as a proportion of GDP (Gable and Kamerman, 2006.) In 2009, for example, only the Scandinavian nations, France, and the United Kingdom spent more than 1 percent of GDP on childcare; Canada, Greece, and Switzerland spent below 0.3 percent of GDP (OECD, 2012b).

The United States is also an outlier in terms of family leave policy, which allows new parents to take job-protected time off to care for very young children. The Family Medical Leave Act (FMLA) passed in 1993, provides 12 weeks of job-protected, unpaid family leave to individuals with significant work history at firms with more than 50 employees (Garfinkel, Rainwater, and Smeeding, 2010). Less than a fifth of all new mothers are covered under FMLA (Klerman et al., 2013). Low-wage work-ers are less likely to fall into this category and, even when eligible, these workers are less likely able to afford time off without pay (Boushey, 2011; Earle, Mokomane, and Heymann, 2011). Family leave arrangements in other OECD nations differ from those in the United States in three ways. First, leave periods are longer; second, leave in other nations typically provides some degree of wage replacement (Garfinkel, Rainwater, and Smeeding, 2010); finally, access to family and/or medical leave is uni-versal (Waldfogel, 2006).

MEDICAL CARE

Publicly funded health care arrangements also vary among nations. The major distinc-tion is between those nations that offer some form of universal coverage and those that do not. This distinction is not a straightforward function of national income. Writing in 2012, Rodin and de Ferranti (p. 261) note that, apart from the United States, "the 25 wealthiest nations all have some form of universal health coverage ... while sev-eral middle income countries, including Brazil, Mexico and Thailand do so as well." A number of developing countries, including Vietnam, Rwanda, and Ghana are mov-ing toward this goal (Rodin and de Ferranti, 2012; Hu et al., 2008; Chopra et al., 2014; Ewig and Palmucci, 2010). In the United States, the transition to the Affordable Care Act (ACA) passed in 2010 also represents movement in this direction; although, as we note later, structural and political factors make the ultimate extent of progress unclear (Collins, 2010).

Among developed countries that offer universal coverage, there are significant dif-ferences in the structure of provision. In some nations, such as the Nordic countries, the United Kingdom, and Italy, which have national health services, the state serves as the single payer for health care, although individuals can purchase private coverage to provide access to private hospitals and additional services. Other nations, such as Japan, France, and Germany, combine universal insurance requirements with subsidies for low-income individuals.

Prior to the passage of the ACA, the United States had been an outlier among devel-oped nations in terms of provision for medical coverage (Commonwealth Fund, 2012). Private insurance provided by employers had traditionally been the primary source of medical coverage for employed workers, while poor families, unemployed individu-als, and low-wage workers were forced to cope with a fragmented and inadequate sys-tem that left many without coverage and others with only piecemeal access to care (Hacker, 2002). In 2011, Census Bureau figures show that of the estimated 48.6 million uninsured Americans, a disproportionate number were economically disadvantaged (ASPE, 2012).

Publically funded health insurance for poor individuals and families has been pro-vided primarily by three programs: Medicaid, the State Children Health Insurance

Program (SCHIP), and Medicare (Kaiser Family Foundation, 2009). Medicaid, which serves low-income families, children, and—in some states—poor individuals, particularly seniors with no assets but established need for services such as long-term care, is a targeted entitlement program that is funded jointly by the federal government and by states. States have broad authority to set asset and income limits for coverage, resulting in large variations among states (Kaiser Family Foundation, 2013).

One of the biggest expansions of means-tested public assistance in the United States in the past two decades has been through increased access to public health insurance for low-income children. The primary driver of this was passage of the SCHIP in 1997, which provided additional federal funds for states to either expand their Medicaid program or create a new program targeted at low-income working families. As a result, the proportion of children covered by public health insurance has increased significantly. According to official Census Bureau estimates, in 1999, just as SCHIP was beginning to be implemented in most states, about 12 percent of children were uninsured and 23.3 percent were on public insurance, primarily Medicaid/SCHIP. In 2010, during a period of prolonged high unemployment, only 9.4 percent of children were uninsured, with 38.8 percent covered by public insurance. (Kaiser Family Foundation, 2013).

Medicare, finally, is a federally funded program that provides insurance for the vast majority of those who are age 65 or over, for individuals in end-stage renal failure, and for some younger disabled individuals. Different components of Medicare provide hospital coverage; coverage for office visits and outpatient procedures; and prescription drug coverage within certain categories of expenditures. For low-income individuals, some costs related to Medicare may still be problematic, although some very low-income individuals are eligible for Medicaid or other programs to cover some of these expenses.

While the final effects of the Affordable Care Act in providing medical coverage to low- and moderate-income families and individuals remain to be seen, recent years of ACA implementation have brought on a striking expansion of coverage and reduction in the number of families who are uninsured. Prior to ACA, lack of insurance was clearly related to income, and expanding coverage to this group was a key goal of the new law (Todd and Sommers, 2012). The Congressional Budget Office estimates that over 10 years, ACA provisions will lead to coverage for 32 million of the uninsured, or about 94 percent of legal residents (Collins, 2010).

Housing

Affordable housing is a critical need for poor families in virtually all nations, since it impacts many other areas of well-being and because market-rate housing is often unaffordable for low-wage or unemployed workers. Housing provision has been identified as one of the pillars of the modern welfare state (Kemeny, 2003). As the modern industrialized welfare states expanded after World War II, most European countries developed public or social housing programs that provided subsidized housing for middle- and low-income individuals. The significant variations in these programs among nations, however, lead some authors to suggest that Esping-Andersen's welfare regimes model was replicated in housing policy (Esping-Andersen, 2009; Norris and Winston, 2012; Harloe, 1999).

In the United States, the post–World War II housing needs of lower income families were met in four ways that reflected the national preference for complex, targeted arrangements that gave a great deal of priority to market solutions (Turner and Kingsley, 2008). First, institutional and policy interventions, such as the Federal Housing Administration and the GI Bill, expanded home ownership by lowering down payment requirements and providing extended financing, although these advantaged whites over blacks (Katznelson, 2005). Second, public housing units were built with funding by federal, state, and local governments and administered by local housing authorities. Third, the federally funded Section 8 program provided targeted subsidy vouchers (tenant-based vouchers) to allow low-income individuals to rent from private landlords. Finally, the federal government channeled low-interest loans to developers for the construction of income-sensitive private housing (Olsen, 2003). In directly and indirectly subsidized units, rents were capped at 30 percent of family income (project-based vouchers).

Over time in the United States, national investment in all forms of public housing has declined (McCarty, 2014). Lack of routine maintenance and the discovery of problems associated with housing low-income families in these units caused public housing projects to be abandoned in many parts of the country. Between 2010 and 2012, public spending for housing assistance fell by $2.5 billion, or nearly 6 percent. Meanwhile, the number of poor families putting more than 50 percent of their income toward housing has increased significantly (*New York Times*, 2012; National Low Income Housing Coalition, 2012).

A change that began in the 1970s has had broad implications for public housing. Policies in the United States and elsewhere in the developed and the developing world began to converge to place more emphasis on extending home ownership to low-income families as an alternative to public housing (Whitehead and Scanlon, 2012; Forrest and Hirayama, 2009). In the developing world, the World Bank began pressing nations to focus on extending home ownership rather than subsidizing rent in the 1990s (Gilbert, 1997). Nations such as China and Thailand have also moved in this direction (Lee, 2000). In the developed world, the privatization of public housing during the Thatcher administration was an early and well-known policy turn, but over time, the trend toward funding home ownership rather than social/public housing has become more pronounced (Whitehead and Scanlon, 2008). Writing in 2008, however, Malpass noted that "the majority of countries in the European Union have retained some social housing provision, ranging from less than 2 percent of the total stock in Spain, Greece and Estonia to 35 percent in the Netherlands" (p. 15).

THE NEOLIBERAL TURN
AND THE RECESSION

Beginning in the 1980s, political discussion both in the United States and in Europe became focused on the idea of welfare state retrenchment, driven by neoliberal understandings about the primacy of markets (Clarke, 2003; Korpi, 2003; Freeman, Swedenborg, and Topel, 2010). Even in Nordic countries such as Denmark, which had highly developed public-benefits systems and a strong ideological commitment to universal benefits, retrenchment became a political issue. In the United States and Britain, the Reagan and Thatcher administrations became identified with this movement: in both cases, issues of recipient deservingness, the need to force individuals to seek market solutions, and the privatization of public services were central concerns (Pierson, 1994; Daguerre, 2008, 2011).

This set of concerns continued to structure policy discussion in many developed nations through the next two decades, producing what Handler (2003) calls a turn toward contractual rather than universal paradigms of public provision. Under this contractual paradigm, benefits are conditioned on specific behaviors, such as labor market participation, rather than being construed as entitlements derived from citizenship. Over time, this revised paradigm produced retrenchment in some programs in many European welfare states as well as in the United States (Clayton and Pontusson, 1998, 2012; Chzen and Bradshaw, 2012; Starke, 2006; Korpi, 2003). In the case of the United States, the transition from AFDC to TANF and the increased devolution of benefits authority to the states instantiated this paradigm.

On the other hand, this shift led to an increase in other programs such as EITC and increased access to SNAP and public health insurance for children in low-income working families. In fact, federal expenditures on the means-tested safety net have grown considerably since the 1980s but have shifted away from the poorest households and toward those with higher incomes, the disabled, and the elderly (Ben-Shalom, Moffitt, and Scholz, 2012).

The worldwide recession that began in 2007 tested these new arrangements. In the United States, the number of poor families and individuals and the number of those living in extreme poverty rose along with rates of homelessness and near-homelessness. The American Recovery and Reinvestment Act (ARRA, 2009) provided a temporary expansion of benefits by, for example, extending unemployment insurance, increasing SNAP benefits, and increasing TANF emergency funding to states, but these increases were time limited and have expired.

Both in the United States and in European countries that had relied on the expansion of home ownership, such as Ireland, Greece, and Spain, the downturn led to large-scale foreclosures and exacerbated economic difficulties. Prior to the recession, increasing public debt spurred the United States, along with many European countries, to begin to adopt austerity policies that cut public provisions. In the United States, the Deficit

Reduction Act of 2005 (Public Law 109-971) restricted the range of activities that counted toward TANF work participation, so that, for example, most educational activities no longer counted as work. Both the proportion of the caseloads and the types of cases that must meet the more stringent work-participation rates increased. States were thus encouraged to either serve fewer recipients or provide fewer services per case, and these rules further eroded the program's role as a safety net for poor families (Schott, 2009). Retrenchment in the face of sluggish economic growth in the United States results in widespread economic vulnerability but reflects worldwide trends in labor market restructuring and safety net configuration (see also Collins and Mayer, 2010).

REFERENCES

Acs, Gregory and Pamela J. Loprest. 2004. *Leaving Welfare: Employment and Well-being of Families that Left Welfare in the Post-entitlement Era*. Kalamazoo, MI: W.E. Upjohn Institute for Employment Research.

Alber, Jens. 2010. "What European and American Welfare States Have in Common and Where They Differ: Facts and Fictions in Comparisons of the European Social Model and the United States." *Journal of European Social Policy* 20: 102–25.

ASPE. 2010. *Estimates of Child Care Eligibility and Receipt for Fiscal Year 2006*. Washington, DC: Office of the Assistant Secretary for Planning and Evaluation Office of Human Services Policy, U.S. Department of Health and Human Services.

ASPE. 2012. *Overview of the Uninsured in the United States: A Summary of the 2012 Current Population Survey, 09/12*. Washington, DC: Office of the Assistant Secretary for Planning and Evaluation Office of Human Services Policy, U.S. Department of Health and Human Services.

Bainbridge, Jay, Marcia K. Myers, and Jane Waldfogel. 2003. "Child Care Policy Reform and the Employment of Single Mothers." *Social Science Quarterly* 84: 771–91.

Barrientos, Armondo. 2011. "Social Protection and Poverty." *International Journal of Social Welfare* 20: 240–49.

Barrientos, Armondo and Claudio Santibanez. 2009. "Social Policy for Poverty Reduction in Lower-income Countries in Latin America: Lessons and Challenges." *Social Policy and Administration* 43: 409–24.

Ben-Shalom, Yonaton, Robert Moffit, and John Scholz. 2012. "An Assessment of the Effectiveness of Anti-Poverty Programs in the United States." Pp. 709–49 in *The Oxford Handbook of the Economics of Poverty*, edited by Philip Jefferson. New York: Oxford University Press.

Besharov, Douglas J. and Kenneth Couch. 2009. "European Measures of Income, Poverty and Social Exclusion: Recent Developments and Lessons for US Poverty Measurement." *Journal of Policy Analysis and Management* 28: 726–51.

Blank, Rebecca M. 2002. "Evaluating Welfare Reform in the United States." *Journal of Economic Literature* 40: 1105–66.

Blau, David and Erdal Tekin. 2007. "The Determinants and Consequences of Child Care Subsidies for Single Mothers in the USA." *Journal of Population Economics* 20: 719–41.

Bloom, Dan and Don Winstead. 2002. "Sanctions and Welfare Reform." Policy Brief 12, January. Washington, DC: Brookings Institution. Retrieved June 12, 2013 (http://www.brookings.edu/~/media/research/files/papers/2002/1/01welfare%20bloom/pb12.pdf).

Boots, Shelly W., Jennifer Macomber, and Anna Danziger. 2008. "Family Security: Supporting Parents' Employment and Child Development." Washington, DC: Urban Institute.

Bourguignon, Francois and Gary Fields. 1990. "Poverty Measures and Anti-Poverty Policy." *Recherches Economiques de Louvain* 56: 409–27.

Boushey, Heather. 2011. "The Role of Government in Work-Family Conflict." *The Future of Children* 21: 163–90.

Brady, David. 2003. "Rethinking the Sociological Measurement of Poverty." *Social Forces* 81: 715–51.

Brady, David. 2009. *Rich Democracies, Poor People: How Politics Explain Poverty*. New York: Oxford University Press.

Brodkin, Evelyn Z. 1993. "The Making of an Enemy: How Welfare Policies Construct the Poor." *Law and Social Inquiry* 18: 647–70.

Center on Budget and Policy Priorities (CBPP). 2013. "A Quick Guide to SNAP Eligibility and Benefits." Washington, DC: Center on Budget and Policy Priorities. Retrieved June 12, 2013 (http://www.cbpp.org/files/11-18-08fa.pdf).

Chase-Lansdale, P. Lindsay, Robert A. Moffitt, Brenda J. Lohman, Andrew J. Cherlin, Rebekah Levine Coley, Laura D. Pittman, Jennifer Roff, and Elizabeth Vitruba-Drzal. 2003. "Mothers' Transitions from Welfare to Work and the Well-being of Preschoolers and Adolescents." *Science* 299: 1548–52.

Cherlin, Andrew, Bianca Frogner, David Ribar, and Robert Moffitt. 2009. "Welfare Reform in the Mid-2000s: How African-American and Hispanic Families in Three Cities Are Faring." *Annals of the American Academy of Political and Social Science* 621: 178–201.

Cherry, Robert D. 2007. *Welfare Transformed: Universalizing Family Policies That Work*. New York: Oxford University Press.

Chopra, Mickey, Joy E. Lawn, David Sanders, Peter Barron, Salim S. Abdool Karim, Debbie Bradshaw, Rachel Jewkes, Quarraisha Abdool Karim, Alan J. Flisher, Bongani M. Mayosi, Stephen M. Tollman, Gavin J. Churchyard, Hoosen Coovadia for the Lancet South Africa team. 2009. "Achieving the Health Millennium Development Goals for South Africa: Challenges and Priorities." *The Lancet* 374: 1023–31.

Chzhen, Ekaterina and Jonathan Bradshaw. 2012. "Lone Parents, Politics and Poverty in the European Union." *Journal of European Social Policy* 22: 487–506.

Clarke, John. 2003. "Dissolving the Public Realm: The Logic and Limits of Neo-Liberalism." *Journal of Social Policy* 33: 27–48.

Clayton, Richard and Jonas Pontusson. 1998. "Welfare State Retrenchment Revisited: Entitlement Cuts, Public Sector Restructuring, and Inegaliterian Trends in Advanced Capitalist Societies." *World Politics* 51: 67–98.

Collins, Jane and Victoria Mayer. 2010. *Both Hands Tied: Welfare Reform and the Race to the Bottom in the Low-wage Labor Market*. Chicago: University of Chicago.

Collins, Sara. 2010. "How the Affordable Care Act Will Help Low and Moderate Income Families." *Spotlight on Poverty and Opportunity*, June 14. Retrieved June 12, 2014 (http://www.spotlightonpoverty.org/exclusivecommentary.aspx?id=ba21673c-b1ac-44b7-8f76-50e856cdb9b5).

Commonwealth Fund. 2012. "International Profiles of Health Care Systems, 2012." Retrieved May 30, 2013 (http://www.commonwealthfund.org/~/media/Files/Publications/Fund%20 Report/2012/Nov/1645_Squires_intl_profiles_hlt_care_systems_2012.pdf).

Couch, Kenneth and Maureen Pirog. 2010. "Poverty Measurement in the US, Europe and Developing Countries." *Journal of Policy Analysis and Management* 29: 217–26.

Couch, Kenneth, Timothy M. Smeeding, and Jane Waldfogel. 2010. "Fighting Poverty: Attentive Policy Can Make a Huge Difference." *Journal of Policy Analysis and Management* 29: 401–7.

Currie, Janet. 2006. *The Invisible Safety Net: Protecting the Nation's Poor Children and Families*. Princeton, NJ: Princeton University Press.

Daguerre, Anne. 2011. "US Social Policy in the 21st Century: The Difficulties of Comprehensive Social Reform." *Social Policy and Administration* 45: 389–407.

Daguerre, Anne. 2008. "The Second Phase of US Welfare Reform, 2000–2006: Blaming the Poor Again?" *Social Policy and Administration* 42: 362–78.

Danielson, Caroline and Jacob Alex Klerman. 2008. "Did Welfare Reform Cause the Caseload Decline?" *Social Services Review* 82: 703–30.

Danziger, Sandra K. 2010. "The Decline of Cash Welfare and Implications for Social Policy and Poverty." *Annual Review of Sociology* 36: 523–45.

Danziger Sandra K., Mary Corcoran, Sheldon Danziger, Colleen Heflin, Ariel Kalil, Judith Levine, Andrew Rosen, Kristin Seefeldt, Kristine Siefert, and Richard Tolman. 2000. "Barriers to the Employment of Welfare Recipients." Pp. 245–78 in *Prosperity for All? The Economic Boom and African-Americans*, edited by R. Cherry and W. M. Rodgers, III. New York: Russell Sage Foundation.

Danziger, Sandra K., Elizabeth Oltman Ananat, and Kimberly G. Browning. 2004. "Child Care Subsidies and the Transition from Welfare to Work." *Family Relations* 53: 219–28.

Danziger, Sandra K. and Kristin Seefeldt. 2003. "Barriers to Employment and the 'Hard to Serve': Implications for Services, Sanctions, and Time Limits." *Social Policy and Society* 2(2): 151–60.

DeParle Jason. 2004. *American Dream: Three Women, Ten Kids, and a Nation's Drive to end Welfare*. New York: Penguin Books.

DeParle, Jason. 2009. "Slumping Economy Tests Aid System Tied to Jobs." *New York Times*, June 1. Retrieved June 30, 2013 (http://www.nytimes.com/2009/06/01/us/politics/01poverty.html).

DeParle, Jason and Robert Gebeloff. 2010. "Living on Nothing but Food Stamps." *New York Times*, January 2. Retrieved June 1, 2013 (http://www.nytimes.com/2010/01/03/us/03food-stamps.html).

Dunifon, Rachel, Ariel Kalil, and Sandra K. Danziger. 2007. "Maternal Work and Welfare Use and Child Well-being: Evidence from 6 years of Data from the Women's Employment Study." *Children and Youth Services Review* 29: 742–61.

Dworsky, Amy and Courtney, Mark. 2007. "Barriers to Employment among TANF Applicants and Their Consequences for Self-sufficiency." *Families in Society: The Journal of Contemporary Social Services* 88: 379–89.

Earle, Alison, Zita Mokomane, and Jody Heymann. 2011. "International Perspectives on Work-Family Policies: Lessons from the World's Most Competitive Economies." *The Future of Children* 21: 191–210.

Esping-Andersen, Gøsta. 1990. *The Three Worlds of Welfare Capitalism*. Princeton, NJ: Princeton University Press.

Ewig, Christina and Gaston Palmucci. 2010. "Inequality and the Politics of Social Policy Implementation Gender, Age and Chile's 2004 Health Reforms." *World Development* 40: 2490–2504.

Fizbein, Ariel, Norbert Rudiger Schady, and Francisco H. G. Feirra. 2009. *Conditional Cash Transfers: Reducing Present and Future Poverty*. Washington, DC: World Bank.

Food Research and Action Center (2013). "SNAP/Food Stamp Participation." Retrieved July 12, 2013 (http://frac.org/reports-and-resources/snapfood-stamp-monthly-participation-data/).

Forrest, Ray and Yosuke Hirayama. 2009. "The Uneven Impact of Neoliberalism on Housing Opportunities." *International Journal of Urban and Regional Research* 33: 998–1013.

Freeman, Richard B., Birgitta Swedenborg, and Robert Topel. 2010. *Reforming the Welfare State: Recovery and Beyond in Sweden*. Chicago: University of Chicago Press.

Garcia, Marito and Charity Moore. 2012. *The Cash Dividend: The Rise of Cash Transfer Programs in Sub-Saharan Africa*. Washington, DC: World Bank.

Garfinkel, Irving, Lee Rainwater, and Timothy Smeeding. 2010. *Wealth and Welfare States: Is America a Laggard or Leader?* New York: Oxford University Press.

Gable, Steven G. and Sheila B. Kamerman. 2006. "Investing in Children: Public Commitment in Twenty-One Industrialized Countries." *Social Service Review* 80: 239–63.

Gilbert, Alan. 1997. "On Subsidies and Home Ownership: Columbian Housing Policies in the 1990's." *Third World Planning Review* 19: 51–56.

Gonzalez-Flores, Mario, Maria Heracleous, and Paul Winter. 2012. "Leaving the Safety Net: An Analysis of Dropouts in an Urban Conditional Cash Transfer Program." *World Development* 40: 2505–21.

Gregg, Samuel. 2013. *Becoming Europe: Economic Decline, Culture and How America Can Avoid a European Future*. New York: Encounter.

Hacker, Jacob. 2002. *The Divided Welfare State: The Battle over Public and Private Social Benefits in the United States*. New York: Cambridge University Press.

Handler, Joel. 2003. "Social Citizenship and Workfare in the US and Western Europe: From Status to Contract." *Journal of European Social Policy* 13: 229–43.

Harloe, Michael. 1999. *The People's Home: Social Rented Housing in Europe and America*. New York: Wiley.

Haskins Ron. 2006. *Work over Welfare: The Inside Story of the 1996 Welfare Reform Law*. Washington, DC: Brookings Institution.

Heclo, Hugh. 2011. *Modern Social Politics in Britain and Sweden*. 2nd ed. Colchester: European Consortium for Political Research Press.

Henly, Julia and Susan Lambert. 2010. "Schedule Flexibility and Unpredictability in Retail: Implications for Employee Work-Life Outcomes." Working Paper, University of Chicago Work Scheduling Study. Retrieved June 5, 2013 (http://ssascholars.uchicago.edu/work-scheduling-study/files/henly_lambert_unpredictability_and_work-life_outcomes.pdf).

Hu, Shanlian, Shenglan Tang, Yuanli Liu, Yuxin Zhao, Maria-Luisa Escobar, and David de Ferranti. 2008. "Reform of How Health Care Is Paid For in China: Challenges and Opportunities." *The Lancet* 372(9652): 1846–53.

Johnson, Rucker C., Ariel Kalil, and Rachel E. Dunifon. 2010. "Leaving Welfare for Work: How Welfare Reform Has Affected the Well Being of Children." Kalamazoo, MI: W.E. Upjohn Institute for Employment Research.

Kaiser Family Foundation. 2013. "Where Are States today? Medicaid and CHIP Eligibility Levels for Children and Non-disabled Adults." Retrieved July 10, 2013 (http://www.kff.org/medicaid/upload/7993-03.pdf).

Katznelson, Ira. 2005. *When Affirmative Action Was White: An Untold Story of Inequality in Twentieth Century America*. New York: WW Norton.

Kautto, Matti, Borge Hvinden, Mikko Kautto, Staffan Marklund, and Niels Plog. 1999. *Nordic Social Policy: Changing Welfare States*. London: Routledge.

Klerman, Jacob Alex, Kelly Daley, and Alyssa Pozniak. 2013. "Family and Medical Leave in 2012: Technical Report." Abt Associates, prepared for Department of Labor, http://www.dol.gov/asp/evaluation/fmla/FMLA-2012-Technical-Report.pdf.

Kemeny, Jim. 2003. "Korporatism och bostads regimer." *Sociologisk Forskning* 3: 37–56.

Korpi, Walter. 2003. "Welfare State Regress in Western Europe: Politics, Institutions, Globalization and Europeanization." *Annual Review of Sociology* 29: 589–609.

Kuivalainen, Susan and Mikko Niemala. 2010. "From Universalism to Selectivism: The Ideational Turn of Anti-Poverty Policies in Finland." *Journal of European Social Policy* 20: 263–76.

Laughlin, Lynda and Jessica Davis, J. 2011. "Who's in Head Start? Estimating Head Start Enrollment with the ACS, CPS, and SIPP." Working Paper 2011–15. Washington, DC: United States Census Bureau.

Lee, James. 2000. "From Welfare Housing to Home Ownership: The Dilemma of China's Housing Reform." *Housing Studies* 15: 61–76.

Mahon, Rianne. 2011. "Child Care Policy: A Comparative Perspective." *Encyclopedia of Early Childhood Development.* Retrieved May 30, 2013 (http://www.child-encyclopedia.com/documents/MahonANGxp2.pdf).

Malpass, Peter. 2008. "Histories of Social Housing: A Comparative Approach." Pp. 15–29 in *Social Housing in Europe II*, edited by K. Scanlon and C. Whitehead. London: London School of Economics.

Marshall, Thomas Humphrey. 1963. *Class, Citizenship and Social Development.* Chicago: University of Chicago Press.

Matthews, Hannah. 2011. "Child Care Assistance in 2009." Washington, DC: Center for Law and Social Policy.

McCarty, Maggie. 2014. *Introduction to Public Housing.* Washington, DC: Congressional Research Service Report for Congress.

Mendenhall, Ruby, Kathryn Edin, Susan Crowley, Jennifer Sykes, Laura Tach, Katrin Kriz, and Jeffrey R. Kling. 2012. "The Role of the Earned Income Credit in the Budgets of Low-Income Households." *Social Service Review* 86: 367–400.

Meyers, Marcia Kay, Theresa Heintze, and Douglas A. Wolf. 2002. "Child Care Subsidies and the Employment of Welfare Recipients." *Demography* 39: 165–79.

Moffitt, Robert. 2008. "A Primer on Welfare Reform. *Focus* 26: 15–25.

National Low Income Housing Coalition. 2012. "Out of Reach 2012." Washington, DC: National Low Income Housing Coalition. Retrieved August 8, 2012 (http://nlihc.org/sites/default/files/oor/2012-OOR.pdf).

New York Times. 2012. "Editorial: The Affordable Housing Crisis." December 4. Retrieved 30 June 2013 (http://www.nytimes.com/2005/06/16/opinion/16thu4.html).

Norris, Michelle and Winston, Nessa. 2012. "Home Ownership, Housing Regimes and Income Inequalities in Western Europe." Gini Discussion Paper No. 42, May. Retrieved June 10, 2013 (http://aiasbase.nl/uploaded_files/publications/DP42-Norris,Winston.pdf).

OECD. 2011. *Doing Better for Families.* Paris: OECD.

OECD. 2012a. *Economic Policy Reforms 2012: Going for Growth.* Paris: OECD.

OECD. 2012b. *Family Database, PF3.1.* Retrieved June 1, 2013. (http://www.oecd.org/els/soc/PF3.1%20Public%20spending%20on%20childcare%20and%20early%20education%20-%20181012.pdf).

Olsen, Edgar.2003. "Housing Programs for Low-Income Households." Pp. 365–441 in *Means-Tested Transfer Programs in the United States*, edited by Robert Moffit. Chicago: University of Chicago Press.

Parrott, Sharon and Arloc Sherman. 2007. "TANF's Results Are More Mixed than Is Often Understood." *Journal of Policy Analysis and Public Management* 26: 375–81.

Pavetti, Ladonna, Danilo Trisi, and Liz Schott. 2011. "TANF Responded Unevenly to Increase in Need during Downturn." Washington, DC: Center on Budget and Policy Priorities.

Prakesh, Assem and Matthew Prokowski. 2011. "Research Frontiers in Comparative Policy Analysis." *Journal of Policy Analysis and Management* 31: 93–103.

Pierson, Paul. 1994. *Reagan, Thatcher and the Politics of Retrenchment.* New York: Cambridge University Press.

Press, Julie, Jay Fagan, and Lynda Laughlin. 2006. "Taking Pressure off Families: Child-care Subsidies Lessen Mothers' Work-hour Problems." *Journal of Marriage and Family* 68: 155.

Qadeer, Imrana. 2014. "Health Care Systems in Transition III. India Part I. The Indian Experience." *Journal of Public Health Medicine* 22: 25–32.

Rodin, Judith and David DeFerranti. 2012. "Universal Coverage: The Third Global Health Transition." *The Lancet* 380: 861–62.

Romich, Jennifer L., Jennifer Simmelink, and Stephen D. Holt. 2007. "When Working Harder Does Not Pay: Low-Income Working Families, Tax Liabilities, and Benefit Reductions." *Families in Society* 88: 418–26.

Romich, Jennifer L. and Thomas Weisner. 2000. "How Families View and Use the EITC: Advance Payment v. Lump Sum Delivery." *National Tax Journal* 53: 1245–62.

Rowe, Gretchen and Linda Giannarelli. 2006. *Getting on, Staying on, and Getting off Welfare: The Complexity of State-by-State Policy Choices.* Washington, DC: Urban Institute.

Schott, Liz. 2009. "An Introduction to TANF." Washington, DC: Center on Budget and Policy Priorities.

Schott, Liz and LaDonna Pavetti. 2011. "Many States are Cutting TANF Benefits Harshly Despite High Unemployment and Unprecedented Need." Washington, DC: Center on Budget and Policy Priorities. May 19.

Schram, Sanford F., Joe Soss, Richard C. Fording, and Linda Houser. 2009. "Deciding to Discipline: Race, Choice, and Punishment at the Frontlines of Welfare Reform." *American Sociological Review* 74: 398–422.

Scott, Ellen K., Kathryn Edin, Andrew London, and Rebecca Joyce Kissane. 2004. "Unstable Work, Unstable Income: Implications for Family Well-Being in the Era of Time-Limited Welfare." *Journal of Poverty* 8: 61–88.

Seefeldt, Kristin. 2008. *Working after Welfare: How Women Balance Jobs and Family in the Wake of Welfare Reform.* Kalamazoo, MI: W.E. Upjohn Institute for Employment Research.

Seefeldt, Kristin, Sheldon Danziger, and Sandra K. Daniger. 2003. "Michigan's Welfare System." Pp. 351–70 in *Michigan at the Millennium: A Benchmark and Analysis of Its Fiscal and Economic Structure*, edited by C. Ballard, P. Courant, D. Drake, R. Fisher, and E Gerber. Lansing: Michigan State University Press.

Seefeldt, Kristin and Meredith Horowski. 2012. "The Continuum of Connection: Low-income Families and Economic Support during the Great Recession." National Poverty Center Working Paper Series, Nos. 12–11. Ann Arbor: University of Michigan.

Seefeldt Kristin and Sean M. Orzol S. 2005. "Watching the Clock Tick: Factors Associated with TANF Accumulation." *Social Work Research* 29: 215–29.

Shaefer, H. Luke and Kathryn Edin. 2013. "Rising Extreme Poverty in the United States and the Response of Federal Means-Tested Transfers." *Social Service Review* 87: 250–68.

Shaefer, H. Luke, Xioquing Song, and Trina R. Williams Shanks. 2013. "Do Single Mothers in the United States Use the Earned Income Tax Credit to Reduce Unsecured Debt?" *Review of Economics of the Household* 11: 659–80.

Slack, Kristin Shook, Katherine A. Magnuson, and Lawrence M. Berger. 2007. "Editorial: How Are Children and Families Faring a Decade after Welfare Reform? Evidence from Five Non-experimental Panel Studies." *Children and Youth Services Review* 29: 693–97.

Slater, R. 2011. "Cash Transfers, Social Protection and Poverty Reduction." *International Journal of Social Welfare* 20: 250–59.

Smeeding, Timothy. 2009. "New Comparative Measures of Income, Material Deprivation and Well-Being." *Journal of Policy Analysis and Management* 28: 745–52.

Smeeding, Timothy and Jane Waldfogel. 2010. "Fighting Poverty: Attentive Policy Can Make a Huge Difference." *Journal of Policy Analysis and Management* 29: 401–7.

Somers, Margaret and Fred Block. 2005. "From Poverty to Perversity: Ideas, Markets and Institutions over 200 Years of Welfare Debate." *American Sociological Review* 70: 260–87.

Soss, Joe, Richard C. Fording and Sanford Schram. 2008. "The Color of Devolution: Race, Federalism and the Politics of Social Control." *American Journal of Political Science* 52: 536–53.

Soss, Joe, Richard Fording, and Sanford Schram. 2011. *Disciplining the Poor: Neoliberal Paternalism and the Persistent Power of Race.* Chicago: University of Chicago Press.

Starke, Peter. 2006. "The Politics of Welfare State Retrenchment: a Literature Review." *Social Policy and Administration* 40: 104–20.

Tax Policy Center. 2013. *Tax Policy Center Briefing Book.* Retrieved July 9, 2013 (http://www.taxpolicycenter.org/briefing-book/key-elements/family/eitc.cfm).

Todd, Linda and Benjamin Sommers. 2012. "Overview of the Uninsured in the United States: A Summary of the 2012 Current Population Survey Report." ASPE Issue Brief. Retrieved July 9, 2013 (http://aspe.hhs.gov/health/reports/2012/uninsuredintheus/ib.shtml#who).

Turner, Margery Austin and G. Thomas Kingsley. 2008. "Federal Programs for Addressing Low-Income Housing Needs." Washington, DC: Urban Institute.

van Hooren, Franca and Uwe Becker. 2012. "One Welfare State, Two Care Regimes: Understanding Developments in Child and Elderly Care Policies in the Netherlands." *Social Policy and Administration* 46: 83–107.

Vis, Barbara, Kees van Kersbergen, and Tom Hyland. 2011. "To What Extent Did the Financial Crisis Intensify the Pressure to Reform the Welfare State?" *Social Policy & Administration* 45: 338–53.

Waldfogel, Jane. 2006. "International Policies toward Parental Leave and Child Care." *The Future of Children* 11: 98–111.

Waldfogel, Jane. 2013. *Britain's War on Poverty.* New York: Russell Sage Foundation.

Weaver, R. Kent. 2000. *Ending Welfare as We Know It.* Washington, DC: Brookings Institution.

White, Linda A. 2002. "Ideas and the Welfare State: Explaining Child Care Policy Development in Canada and the United States." *Comparative Political Studies* 35: 713–43.

Whitehead, Christine and Kath J. Scanlon, eds. 2008. *Social Housing in Europe II.* London: London School of Economics and Political Science.

Women's Legal Defense Fund. 2010. "The Sanction Epidemic in the Temporary Assistance to Needy Families Program." New York: The Women's Legal Defense and Education Fund. Retrieved June 13, 2013 (http://www.legalmomentum.org/our-work/women-and-poverty/resources—publications/sanction-epidemic-in-tanf.pdf).

Zigler, Edward and Jeanette Valentine. 1979. *Project Head Start: A Legacy of the War on Poverty.* New York: Free Press; Macmillan.

Zuberi, Dan. 2006. *Differences That Matter: Social Policy and the Working Poor in the United States and Canada.* Ithaca, NY: Cornell University Press.

CHAPTER 33

POOR PEOPLE'S POLITICS

FRANCES FOX PIVEN AND LORRAINE C. MINNITE

INTRODUCTION

IT is the right moment to direct attention to the political self-activity of people at the bottom of the world's societies. Inequality is increasing across the globe, even in the European social democracies. And although there has arguably been some progress in reducing the inequality between nations as emerging economies catch up with the West in measures of aggregate national economic growth, inequality within nations is worsening. The rich get richer and as they do, they use their growing political weight to get richer still, usually at the expense of the earnings and living standards and government supports for the poor. "[T]he poor," says Joseph Stiglitz, "are everywhere left behind" (Stiglitz 2013a). Can these left-behind people who are outside the "circle of human concern" (powell and Menendian 2011:5) become a force to help moderate or reverse this pattern?

The core argument of this essay is that political action by the people we call poor, under certain conditions can be a critical influence on public policy. Yet the dynamics governing political action by the poor have received relatively little attention in the social science literature, including scholarship on American politics (for exceptions, see Piven and Cloward 1979; Andrews 2004; Manley et al. 2012; more generally, see Bebbington 2007). This chapter begins with a brief critique of theories about policy development for the poor and then discusses in some detail the development of the dissensus politics arguments of Piven and Cloward that challenge that literature. The purpose of the discussion of the work of Piven and Cloward is to provide a full statement of their argument, as elements of it are sometimes misunderstood or ignored. Their initial insights emerged in the context of the upheavals of the 1960s, and their theories are built upon an historical foundation of cases drawn from the United States. We briefly discuss the extent to which the U.S. focus constrains theoretical usefulness in explaining poverty policy developments in other rich democracies or in the emerging democracies of the developing world, although we do not claim an expertise in the latter literature. We conclude with a few observations on how globalization and the neoliberal assault on the welfare state are producing limited conditions of convergence between rich and poor countries with respect to policy, as the welfare state is under assault in the West with poverty rising, and under construction in a number of emerging economies, especially in Latin America. Thus, the politics of the poor that stem from their interdependent power and their disruptive actions, as well as the policy consequences, can look different depending on the changing institutional and political context.

POVERTY POLICY AND THE POLITICAL AGENCY OF THE POOR

We think neglect of the political agency of the poor in the policy and welfare state literature cripples our ability to understand politics generally, and especially limits our analyses of the politics of policies directed to the poor. Are we correct? Is the politics of the poor in fact neglected? Certainly we have no shortage of theories that attempt to explain how capitalism has been tamed, whether through the systemic imperatives generated by the "logic of industrialism" or by the "power resources" of a growing working class, or by the political processes generated by the institutions of an evolving democratic state. The older family of explanations known as "the logic of industrialism" posits the advance of industry together with urbanization as the motor for the invention of a variety of social security policies.[1] A neo-Marxist variant of the theory emphasizes not industrialization as such, but capitalist industrialization and the imperatives of accumulation and legitimation generated by capitalism (Offe 1972; O'Connor 1973; Gough 1979). Other related theories focus on the political processes through which policies to deal with economic insecurity are initiated and sustained, and, accordingly, emphasize the role of parties and interest groups, unions and reform organizations[2] and the political institutions that shape them.[3]

Our objective here is not to offer a critique of any of the theories in this literature, but rather to make the overall point that they share a common flaw. They tend to give scant analytical attention to the political role of the poor in the evolution (or as it often is, the contraction) of policy. They are able to do this because they choose not to recognize the forms in which political action by the poor typically occurs—mobs and riots, for example, or other forms of protest—as political action. The consequence is to deny the poor any agency. Thus logic of industrialism theorists do write of the new needs that were created by economic growth as traditional community and family arrangements broke down under the impact of economic and social change, but they tell us little about the politics of the people who experienced those needs. And neo-Marxist variants of the logic of industrialism include the imperative of legitimation to explain the dynamics that propel state action in a capitalist society. But just how legitimation translates into political change remains vague and abstract, and certainly there is little examination of how poor people come to think of existing arrangements as illegitimate or what they do about it. As for power resources perspectives, as well as broader political process models, because the poor are rarely a significant voter bloc, and by definition lack the resources on which interest groups rely for influence, theories that focus on the normal contemporary politics generated by parties and interest groups also slight the politics of the poor, although they sometimes emphasize the broader working class (to which the poor may or may not belong, depending on the orientation of the author). We think this is a big oversight. The collective action of poor people themselves is central to understanding the initiation, timing, design, and development of social policies to address poverty.

More recently, David Brady has advanced a more elaborate version of power resources theory that joins power resources to the institutionalist perspective now popular in the social sciences (Brady 2009). He calls the perspective "institutionalized power relations theory," and it has the considerable advantage of taking account of the cumulative effects of the play of power resources on institutional arrangements over time. But while Brady is explicitly interested in the impact of politics on poverty, and specifically the impact of politics on poverty in the rich democracies, the poor themselves remain in the shadows. They are not the actors who announce their own needs and imperatives, and force action in response. As with other power resource and political process theories, the empty spaces that result are filled in by classes and unions, by parties and interest groups or Leftists or reformers, who may on occasion represent the poor, but usually do not. Instead of issuing claims or demands, the poor are depicted as simply presenting problems to be attended to or not by institutional elites.

We propose to begin an effort to remedy the neglect of poor people's politics by focusing specifically on the American case, while also suggesting the relevance of that case to other societies, particularly societies where the poor remain numerous, and perhaps also where electoral-representative arrangements are less developed. We offer two basic justifications for this focus. The first is the persistence of endemic poverty in the United States (DeNavas-Walt, Proctor, and Smith 2013). After falling in the 1960s and early 1970s, poverty levels began to rise again, and rose more or less steadily over the past four decades, in tandem with eroding wages and rollbacks in social programs (Iceland 2013). Stiglitz sums up a wealth of comparative date: "America has more inequality than any other advanced industrialized country, it does less to correct these inequities, and inequality is growing more than in many other countries" (Stiglitz 2013b:31; see also, Brady 2003; Fremstead 2008; Brady, Fullerton, and Cross 2009; Therborn 2102; DeBacker et al. 2013; Edsall 2013a, 2013b; Fremstead 2013; Parrott et al. 2013; and Alvaredo et al. 2013). The United States is presumed to be a leader among rich and democratic nations. Wealth means that the resources exist to reduce poverty, and democracy means, or should mean, that the poor will have at least a measure of influence over the distribution of those resources. If the common sense of the match or mismatch between needs and resources that underlies many of our explanations of social policy elsewhere in the world fails to explain the increase in

American poverty, attention to the politics of the poor casts some light on this expression of "American exceptionalism."[4]

Our second justification is that the politics of the poor in the United States exemplifies the constraints on collective action that result when the poor are not only a minority, but also a culturally stigmatized minority. We see these conditions elsewhere as well. Indeed, even when the poor constitute a significant portion of the population, they are more likely to mobilize behind other identities than "the poor." Thus we see movements of the indigenous, or of racial and ethnic minorities, or of informal workers, or even of the landless. All of these groups are usually preponderantly poor. That they do not rally behind that identity tells us something about the cultural suffocation that has to be overcome by the lowliest if they are to become political actors. True, movements identified as made up of "the poor" did emerge in the United States in the 1960s, inspired by the larger black freedom movement. But it was the federal government's response with the programs called the War on Poverty that named the insurgents as the poor.

THE PIVEN AND CLOWARD THESIS AND THE POLITICS OF THE POOR IN THE UNITED STATES

The line of explanation that we highlight draws on the arguments developed by Frances Fox Piven and Richard Cloward during the past four decades and also considers the arguments of their interlocutors and critics. Unusually, this body of work focused specifically on the politics of the poor, on the American institutional context within which it unfolded, and on the conditions that accounted for the occasional success or the more usual failure of political assertions from below. Piven and Cloward ultimately named the argument a theory of interdependent power (Piven and Cloward 2005). While the poor usually may be ignored, viewed merely as gray masses in the background,[5] they, like virtually everyone else in complex societies are enmeshed in institutions where they play necessary roles as workers or nannies or consumers or beggars or merely as bodies whose quiescence is also necessary. When hardship and broken promises and a measure of hope combine to rouse the poor to anger and defiance, these roles yield them points of potential leverage. They can refuse to work, or to defer to their betters, or to obey the rules of civil society. When they do, their actions cause disruption. If the electoral conditions are favorable, disruption in turn contributes to cleavage and dissensus that can impact policy.

The argument began, however, with the importance of disruption, the emphasis was very much a reflection of unfolding events. Piven and Cloward began to study poor people's politics in the early 1960s when a series of protest movements erupted in the ghetto neighborhoods of American cities. In the preceding decades, millions of African

Americans had crowded into those neighborhoods. Ejected from the still-feudal South where they were no longer needed as agricultural laborers, tenant farmers, or domestics, blacks made their way to the cities. Migration meant they had been effectively liberated from the southern system of oppression that relied in roughly equal parts on legal apartheid and the semi-institutionalized terror of the lynch mob. But life in the increasingly compacted ghettos of the North was also hard. Employment was scarce; the housing was dilapidated and getting worse as more people crowded into the confined ghettos; neighborhood schools were segregated and inferior; and the newcomers were largely excluded from the local political patronage and honorifics that had paved the way for the political integration of earlier waves of urban immigrants from Europe. By the early 1960s, with Freedom Rides, sit-ins and marches spreading in the South, protests erupted in the North as well. The ideas and passions that fueled the civil rights protests in the South had traveled along with millions of largely rural African Americans to the cities of the North.

Northern urban protests were different than those of the southern movement in important ways. In the South, the right to vote and an end to legal segregation had been the principal movement demands. But blacks were allowed to vote in the North, and racial segregation was not enforced by law. As was often said at the time, blacks could sit at integrated drugstore lunch counters, except that they did not have the money for a hamburger. As a consequence, the demands of the northern movement were largely economic and certainly practical. African Americans wanted jobs and better jobs, which meant entry into the trades from which they were barred by white unions and racially biased civil service rules. They wanted housing with heat and hot water. They wanted a voice in the running of the schools their children attended and influence over the police who patrolled their streets. In other words, they wanted economic opportunity and political influence in municipal affairs (Sugrue 2008).

Not only their demands, but the forms of the protest actions they organized were also different. The protestors relied far less on the religious themes so important in the South, or on the ministers who emphasized those themes. The migrants were less tied to the black church and to the Jesus story of humble martyrdom that undergirded the nonviolent strategies of the southern movement. Accordingly, the northern protests were far rowdier, their leaders more flamboyant, and their protest events were more disruptive and sometimes more destructive.

Piven and Cloward's earliest interventions in the 1960s were an effort to explain the rising political tumult in the urban ghettos and also an effort to contribute to the political impact of the movements. Unlike many of the social scientists who later offered explanations of these events,[6] they paid less attention to the causes of civil strife and more attention to its effectiveness as political strategy. Their arguments closely tracked the unfolding events that inspired them, the emergence of unruly protests that took the form of marches and demonstrations, sit-ins and traffic tie-ups, rent strikes, and garbage dumps. The issues were numerous, ranging from civil rights to housing to jobs to schools to welfare. There was a good deal of sympathy for the demands associated with the protests, at least among liberals. But why, these liberal critics asked, ever more impatiently, the obstreperous and flamboyant tactics? Writing in 1963, Piven began the article "Low-Income People and the Political Process" by confronting the critics:

> In recent months, as protests by low-income blacks have escalated, a certain brand of righteous criticism has also escalated that claims to sympathize with the griev-ances of the poor, but not with their disruptive tactics. What poor blacks ought to do, according to this critique, is to seek redress . . . informing themselves . . . negoti-ating with institutional managers for change and backing up these negotiations with informed and disciplined pressure at the polls. (1974:73)

The critics were wrong, Piven argued, because poor blacks were without the resources to influence public policies by conventional methods, whether as individuals or through organizations, and she tried to show how the burgeoning community power literature in sociology, as well as the pluralist literature in political science, provided evidence of that bald fact (however inadvertently, since no one actually focused on the poor). Because the poor lacked the resources and capacities to be effective in "normal" electoral and interest group processes, they were driven to the noisy and disorderly col-lective actions that many observers found reprehensible.

This was not a romantic dismissal of regular politics and formal organizations.[7] Rather it was that disruptive collective action, the mobs, riots, and sit-ins that so dis-mayed the critics, and were in effect the default strategies available if there was to be a politics of the poor. They did not make large claims for what this kind of political action could accomplish. Disruption was simply the withdrawal of a contribution on which others depended, and in this regard the poor were disadvantaged again because their cooperation was less important to major institutions than the cooperation of other groups. As Piven and Cloward later wrote: "Indeed, some of the poor are sometimes so isolated from significant institutional participation that the only 'contribution' they can withhold is that of quiescence in civil life: they can riot" (1979:25). If the potential for poor people's politics was thus closely delimited, it was nevertheless only through the exercise of this disruptive politics that poor people sometimes won something. Amidst the urban uprisings of the 1960s, Piven and Cloward followed up the more general analysis with a series of articles that analyzed the potential for disruptive protests that might win reforms specifically in the American slum housing system and the welfare system (Cloward and Piven 1966, 1968).

One of those articles, based on their empirical analysis of the huge discrepancy between the number of people receiving welfare benefits and the number eligible, called on community organizers, lawyers, advocates, and the poor themselves to pro-mote mass applications by poor people for welfare (Cloward and Piven 1966). Cloward and Piven speculated that the local political and fiscal strains that would result (states and localities paid half the costs and were embroiled in conflict between white eth-nics and minority newcomers) would lead to pressures on the national Democratic administration to modernize and nationalize America's poor relief program. And for a time, black insurgency and the mounting welfare rolls did indeed stir serious interest in a guaranteed income, not only among Democratic leaders worried about the votes of the urban minority poor, but among Republicans and business leaders as well (Steensland 2007; Bach 2013).

The moment of convergence between disruption by the poor and the electoral opportunity created by a national Democratic administration reliant on urban electoral support did not last. As Piven wrote in 1963:

> All of which is to say that it is probably only at certain times in history that the legitimacy if regular political processes is so questioned that people can be mobilized to engage in disruption, for to do so is to violate the implicit "social contract" of major institutions and often to violate the explicit social contract of the law as well. That people are sometimes led to do this, and to run the risks involved, only signifies the paucity of alternatives. If our analysis is correct, disruptive and irregular tactics are the only recourse, short of violence, available to low-income groups seeking to influence public policy. (1974:86)

A DEFIANT POOR AND THE ORIGINS OF POOR RELIEF

A few years later, prodded by their collaboration with the burgeoning "welfare rights" movement, Piven and Cloward attempted to develop an historical perspective on the role of disruptive protests in public policies oriented toward the poor. The resulting history of poor relief gave a major role to the unruly poor in the genesis of these systems and a role also to the quiescence of the poor in the emergence of restrictive and punitive relief practices that forced the poor to accept any work on any terms. In *Regulating the Poor* ([1971] 1993) they traced the origins of poor relief to the disruptive protests of the poor that accompanied the transition from feudalism to capitalism. There were parallels, they argued, between ongoing protests in the United States and their disruptive effects and the politics of the poor that had goaded European authorities into creating the first poor relief systems.

Modern poverty policy originates with the invention of European poor relief arrangements during the transition from feudalism to commercial and then industrial capitalism. The beginnings were uneven and the particular local arrangements often short-lived. But since relief for the poor was a response to recurrent crises, it was typically revived. Those crises originated in crop failures, market downturns, new agricultural practices that displaced the rural poor, or the preemption of local food supplies by the king's armies or urban jobbers. But it was the response of the poor to these devastating hardships that forced local and then national elites to create arrangements to feed the poor, and also to moderate their disorderly behavior (Hammond and Hammond 1917, 1948; de Schweinitz 1964; Piven and Cloward [1971] 1993).

To be sure, only occasionally did the poor rise up in what would today look to us like a social movement. Riots did occur, but infrequently. Instead, starving peasants flocked to the towns in huge numbers in search of alms. Others took to the road as vagabonds. Their numbers were alarming, and so must have been the threat of disease, thievery and disorder they brought with them as they descended on the houses of the better off or surrounded their carriages on the road. Were these elements of a social movement? It was surely collective action, and collective action informed by a sense of at least some rights, rights derived from the Christian obligation to charity perhaps, or from lingering feudal ideas of the lord's obligations to his vassals at times of distress.[8]

A sense of rights also helps explain the defiance implicit in mass begging and vagrancy. Not only was this obviously not the way the poor were supposed to behave, but begging and vagrancy could be brutally punished, and their rise was accompanied by the elaboration of horrific penalties. Punishments, however, were insufficient. In the sixteenth and seventeenth centuries, the growing alarm of elites across Europe gradually gave rise to what the Webb's called "a new statecraft relative to destitution." Poor relief was institutionalized:

> What we see ever-increasingly realized, alike in Germany, the Netherlands, Switzerland, England, and, to some extent, France and Scotland, is that no policy of mere repression availed to stop either mendicancy, on the one hand, or vagrancy on the other; that . . . a systematic and ubiquitous provision had to be made locally by some organ of government for all those who were actually in need of the means of existence, whatever the cause of their destitution. (Webb and Webb 1963:29)

Much of the repertoire of this statecraft created centuries ago remains with us today, particularly evident in American means-tested programs with their miserly benefits, intrusive investigations, and insistence on work tests as a condition for receiving any aid at all. But while there are continuities in poor-serving institutional practices, the dual imperatives of placating a disruptive poor and enforcing low-wage work also demand continuous innovation and adaptation, and that is also evident in the history of relief.[9] Nor is disruptive politics only evident in its impact on poor relief policies. George Steinmetz, for example, sees a strong continuity between the conditions that gave rise to poor relief and the later introduction of unemployment insurance in imperial Germany (Steinmetz 1993).

We should emphasize that the disruption thesis was not put forward so much as a general argument against normal electoral-representative politics or against the party or union or other organizations that were deployed to operate in electoral channels. Rather the justification was explicitly that American political institutions created formidable obstacles to the effective use of electoral channels of influence by the poor, including distorted representational arrangements, plurality voting and the resulting two-party system, the incentives for voter suppression instead of voter mobilization, and the large role of an unelected court (Piven and Cloward 1993:407–80). But this did not mean that the electoral system did not matter. To the contrary, Piven and Cloward argued that the emergence of mass unrest among the poor, and the leverage that disruptive mobilizations could exercise, was very much shaped by electoral politics. The political discourse created by pandering politicians worried about the prospects of defection among voter blocs in their base could encourage or discourage protest, and the effectiveness of the protest movement as it developed was ultimately determined by its impact on electoral politics.

These arguments were developed on the basis of four case studies of uprisings in the American twentieth century, published as *Poor People's Movements: Why They Succeed, How They Fail* ([1977] 1979).[10] Each case showed the interplay between the disruptive protests of hard pressed people who acted out their anger and their hopes in the urban neighborhoods and factories or on the farms, by looting or striking or spilling milk meant for market or sitting-in or rioting. But they gained some of the courage to do so from the words of political leaders who offered encouragement because they depended on their votes. In the 1930s, the escalating protests drove an unbridgeable rift between the Democratic leaders who were pressed to respond and the corporate and financial leaders who, in the uncertain conditions of the early 1930s, party leaders were also trying to woo. In the 1960s, the Civil Rights Movement succeeded in overturning the southern apartheid system, as its sister movement for economic rights in the urban North succeeded in winning a series of gains in welfare state programs and access to employment, because their agitations forced responses from Democratic leaders that ultimately drove the intransigently opposed white South out of the Democratic Party. In the end, it was the movement's success in fracturing the electoral coalitions that underpinned the national regime that made gains possible. This point deserves emphasis.

In the dominant view, two-party competition drives policy toward the center as parties and candidates try to peel off voters from the opposition. This is the so-called median voter theorem of electoral politics (Black 1948; Downs 1957). Less attended to, and more important for an analysis of the relationship between electoral dynamics and movements, is the fact that in a two-party system success is also contingent on holding together unwieldy coalitions of disparate supporters. Protest movements not only raise the price for fealty among particular protest constituencies and their allies or sympathizers, but they also can drive the often powerful groups that oppose them out of the coalition, as the abolitionists drove the South out of the pre–Civil War intersectional political parties, or as an insurgent labor movement drove business out of the New Deal Democratic Party, or as the Civil Rights Movement drove the white racist South out of the Democratic Party.

The key periods of the initiation of contemporary poverty policy in the United States were the 1930s and 1960s. Almost all of the legislation with a significant impact on poverty, whether by providing direct benefits and services or by regulating labor markets, was enacted in two brief periods: between 1933 and 1938, and 1963 and 1968.[11] In the first period, emergency relief and work relief programs were initiated that reached 28 million people, 22.2 percent of the population, and supported them at levels considered astonishingly generous by local elites. Social spending grew from 1.34 percent of GNP in fiscal 1932, to five percent by 1934. In 1935, the Social Security Act legislated old-age pensions, unemployment benefits, and federal grants-in-aid for the uncovered aged, the blind, and orphans. Then, in the same year, the National Labor Relations Act enunciated the right of workers to organize for collective bargaining and created an agency, the National Labor Relations Board, to enforce that right. The Works Progress Administration (WPA) was initiated, providing employment to millions of people in public works projects, and shortly afterward, subsidized housing programs were introduced. And in 1938, the Fair Labor Standards Act established minimum wages and maximum hours for many workers.

These achievements were the result of the coming together of the opportunities created by the still unstable electoral realignment of 1932, when shifts in the urban vote brought a Democratic president and a Democratic Congress to power, and the eruption of the great protest movements of the 1930s. The protests began first, welling up among the desperately poor as economic collapse took its toll in jobs and wages. From time immemorial, hungry people have mobbed and looted food from local markets, and they did this again in the early years of the Depression, although no accurate accounting of these episodes exists, if only because the merchants whose supplies were taken feared that calling the police would lead to the press coverage that would only encourage more episodes (Piven and Cloward 1993; Bernstein 2010). Prodded by desperation, people also flocked to unemployment demonstrations, often organized by Communists, and usually (and often not without reason) labeled riots by the press. Beginning in 1929 and 1930, crowds assembled, raised demands for "bread or wages," and then marched on City Hall, or on such local relief offices as existed.

In the big cities, mobs of people used strong-arm tactics to resist the rising numbers of evictions. In Harlem and the Lower East Side, crowds numbering in the thousands gathered to restore evicted families to their homes. In Chicago, small groups of black activists marched through the streets of the ghetto to mobilize the large crowds that would reinstall evicted families. A rent riot left three people dead and three policemen injured in August 1931, but Mayor Anton Cermak ordered a moratorium on evictions, and some of the rioters got work relief. Later, in August of 1932, Cermak told a House committee that if the federal government didn't send $150 million for relief immediately, it should be prepared to send troops later. In rural areas, farmers armed themselves with clubs and pitchforks to prevent the delivery of farm products to markets where the prices offered frequently did not cover the cost of production (Piven and Cloward 1979:41–180). Even in Mississippi, Governor Theodore Bilbo told an interviewer: "Folks are restless. Communism is gaining a foothold. Right here in Mississippi, some people are about ready to lead a mob. In fact, I'm getting a little pink myself" (Piven and Cloward 1979:109, citing Schlesinger 1957:204–5). By 1934, as employment improved, insurgency was spreading to the factories, mines and other workplaces mainly over the right to form unions.

The period from 1963 to 1968 saw another explosion of poverty legislation. The old-age pension and unemployment benefit programs initiated in the 1930s were expanded to new groups and benefits were raised. The number of women and children receiving Aid to Families with Dependent Children (AFDC) quadrupled. Medicare was created for the elderly, Medicaid for the poor, and new nutritional programs were inaugurated, most importantly the food stamp program. Federal aid was extended to poorer school districts, and new housing subsidies were initiated, while the Equal Opportunity Act of 1964 funded and encouraged the mobilization of the urban poor for a share of local services and patronage. By the mid-1970s, poverty levels by official measures had plummeted to an all-time low. And the civil rights achievements of the era, including the passage of the 24th Amendment to the Constitution striking down poll taxes in federal elections, the Civil Rights Act of 1964, and the Voting Rights Act of 1965, brought an end to the southern caste system.

As in the 1930s, the dynamics of these reforms in poverty were forged by the interplay of electoral politics with protest movements by the poor. The Democratic Party that emerged from the Great Depression was based on an electoral coalition of the Bourbon South and the working class in the big cities of the urban North. The coalition was from its beginning peculiar and fragile, and it was to be strained beyond the breaking point by economic change in the South and the ensuing displacement of rural blacks.

Millions of African Americans, their labor no longer needed on the plantations, had migrated to the cities where they became wage workers and voters. The Civil Rights Movement that emerged in the South in the late 1950s drew much of its early political strength from the resonance of its demands for voting rights and desegregation with the black population that had migrated from the rural South to the northern cities. As the numbers in the cities grew, the movement's agenda expanded to include jobs and income supports, demands that reflected the impoverishment not only of African Americans in the South, but of the newcomers to the cities as well. By the early 1960s, protests spread to the urban ghettos, taking form not only marches and demonstrations and boycotts demanding jobs, housing, and "welfare rights" but also in widespread and destructive rioting in all of America's big cities. Tumult in the cities at a time when the urban black vote was crucial to the prospects of Democratic presidential contenders gave these demands leverage. The Great Society welfare state reforms were the response.

CRITIQUES

Poor People's Movements produced a small furor, mainly among critics on the Left, who were indignant at Piven and Cloward's critical view of what most activists and sympathizers thought of as the hard and grinding work of building enduring membership organizations of the poor, in favor of what appeared to the critics to be the inchoate and unruly protest movements.[12] In effect, the critics faulted the movements Piven and Cloward studied for mobilizing the wrong constituencies with the wrong strategies and espousing the wrong goals, demanding welfare instead of full employment, for example. The movements were blamed for the racial conflict that had been stirred up, and the ensuing racial backlash soon evident in electoral politics.[13] None of this took account, however, of the institutional limits on the politics of the black poor that Piven and Cloward had analyzed. "What was won," they wrote, "must be judged by what was possible. From this perspective the victories were considerable" (1993:xiii).

Finally, the critics complained that the movements had not built formal organizations that would endure. Piven and Cloward were criticized not only because they argued that it was disruptive protests and their electoral repercussions that had won what could be won.[14] They were criticized also because of their conclusions that efforts to build formal organizations at the height of the tumult were mistaken because they turned people away from disruption. In fact, they claimed on the basis of the empirical evidence of their cases that it is only when people are in the streets and making trouble that public and private money and encouragement for organization-building efforts becomes available, proffered by elites precisely because they were anxious to curb disruptive protests in favor of organization and normal politics:

> When the tumult is over, these organizations usually fade, no longer useful to those who provided the resources necessary to their survival. Or the organization persists by becoming increasingly subservient to those on whom it depends. Either way no lesson seems to be learned. Each generation of leaders and organizers acts as if there were no political moral to be derived from the history of failed organizing efforts, nor from the obvious fact that whatever people won was a response to their turbulence and not to their organized numbers. (Piven and Cloward 1993:xii–xiii)

The specific conditions that made protest by the poor possible, including the electoral conditions that gave the protestors a measure of success, were unlikely to persist, according to Piven and Cloward. Indeed, the very successes of the movement drained it of momentum and support, not because of the responses to concrete grievances, but because those responses were never unencumbered by measures intended to co-opt leadership, stripping the movement of whatever legitimacy it enjoyed. Once the disruptive protests subside, the gains made by the movement cease and then are rolled back.

In just this way, the poverty initiatives of the 1930s were whittled back. By 1937, the administration of relief was largely returned to the states and localities, and relief benefits were much less generous. The WPA was not renewed. But some of the most important initiatives—social security, unemployment insurance, and union rights—endured, and seemed to be a permanent part of the American institutional fabric, at least until recently. Many of the poverty initiatives of the 1960s were similarly short-lived. As the protest movements of the 1960s subsided, funds for the poverty programs created by the Economic Opportunity Act were slashed, and welfare benefit levels fell steadily as the states declined to adjust them to inflation. Support for the programs had been fueled by the threat of disruptive protests among the poor, and when the protests faded, the anger of the protestors eased by their victories and their hopes discouraged by growing opposition, many of the programs were also allowed to lapse. From time immemorial there has always been opposition to policies that support the poor. The sharpest opposition arises from employers who see these protections as an interference with low-wage labor markets. But envy and anxiety often make other groups available as opponents, and especially so when the poor are racially or ethnically distinct.

RETRENCHMENT IN THE RICH COUNTRIES, AND WELFARE STATE THEORIES

Maybe times have changed, or rather institutions have changed with the spread of neo-liberal globalization. Maybe the theories that assumed the steady development of the welfare state, including programs to ameliorate poverty, are no longer useful, at least not without major theoretical amendments. Not only in the United States but also in a large number of the rich countries that were earlier the pioneers in creating the welfare state, social spending is under attack, and the buzzword is austerity, meaning cutbacks in welfare state spending and labor "flexibility" or lower labor costs (Blyth 2013; Irwin 2013). The pattern is clearest in beleaguered Greece and Spain where, says Vicente Navarro, "The ECB will not buy Spanish public bonds unless the Spanish government takes tough, unpopular measures such as reforming the labor market, reducing pension benefits, and privatizing the welfare state" (Navarro 2013:5). But the welfare state is also under attack in the United Kingdom, the United States and the other settler countries spawned by the British Empire. Moreover, the emergence of the so-called Eurozone crisis promises the trend will spread to other rich nations that were once heralded as welfare state leaders, with consequences in increased poverty and inequality. Even in Sweden, the exemplar of welfare state generosity, there have been consequential rollbacks in social spending, with resulting increases in poverty and inequality (Olsen 2013).

These developments are not predicted by the main theories of welfare state development, and neither can they be explained by the political action or inaction of the poor. Indeed, France and England have witnessed large-scale riots by the immigrant poor, as well as recurrent protests against austerity policies across Europe. In Greece, where austerity policies have been severe, turmoil reigns, and huge street protests have also unfolded in Spain. But the protestors have so far not halted, much less reversed, the campaign for austerity.

We suspect that what is missing in all our accounts is a theoretical grappling with big changes in the structure of national political institutions that have accompanied globalization and the rise of financial capitalism. The pattern is perhaps most evident in Europe where the authority of national political institutions over financial and currency policies has been usurped by the rise of the European Monetary Union and the Stability Pact by which it is governed, as well as by the European Central Bank (and the Bundesbank with which it is allied), and the International Monetary Fund. Meanwhile the political or electoral representative side of the European Union has lagged far behind. Participation in elections for the European parliament is low, parties are weak, and so is the parliament itself. Bob Jessop has called this kind of state restructuring the "hollowing out" of the state (Jessop 2002).[15]

We ordinarily understand the idea of the nation-state as the institutions with ultimate authority over a territory, its people, and its resources. And we ordinarily associate the existence of a state with a complex of arrangements through which societal demands are mediated upward, and the decisions of political elites are transmitted and enforced. All of our big theories about welfare state development in fact presume the existence of the national state. Our own emphasis on the politics of the poor and poverty policy is no exception. The evidence of Europe suggests hugely important changes in state structures that, as they shift authority upward beyond the reach of the nation-state, also escape the institutional arrangements through which societal demands are transmitted to governmental authorities. This essay is not the place to attempt a more developed analysis of these shifts in governing political structures and their implications for social policy. Rather we simply note them and emphasize their potential importance in explaining recent events.

So, at least for the moment, the future of the welfare state in rich countries seems cloudy and dark, despite mounting opposition to austerity by downwardly mobile middle and working classes. However, an altogether different scenario is offered by policy innovations occurring in the Global South. In many developing countries, including Mexico, Bolivia, Brazil, Turkey, for example, decades-long popular mobilizations among the lower classes have been answered with new and expansive social policy initiatives, a pattern that broadly fits our argument here.[16] These policies, known as conditional cash transfers (or CCTs), tend to take a different form than the welfare state in the West or than the precursor poor relief systems. And already they appear to have had measurable impacts on poverty and inequality (Haggard and Kaufman 2008; Hanlon, Barrientos, and Hulme 2010; Yörük 2012a; Lustig, Lopez-Calva, and Ortiz-Juarez 2012; but see also, Petras and Veltmeyer 2005; Stampini and Tornarolli 2012; and Lo Vuolo 2013). These extraordinary developments in the Global South also demand explanation, and it is here that we think our argument about the politics of the poor may be most useful.

CONCLUSION: PROSPECTS FOR NEW MOVEMENTS OF THE POOR IN THE UNITED STATES

By the 1980s, antipoverty policies and the poor became the foil in a larger campaign led by business and the Republican Right to reverse the policy reforms of the 1960s, but also to roll back those New Deal programs that had endured after the end of the Great Depression and then had greatly expanded, especially during the upheavals of the 1960s.[17] The top priorities of the campaign soon became evident: a massive redistribution of the burden of taxation; the cannibalization of government services through privatization, wage cuts, and enfeebled unions; and the deregulation of business, banks, and financial institutions (Ferguson and Rogers 1986; Blumenthal 2008; Wilentz 2008).

The poor—and especially the minority poor—were an endlessly useful rhetorical foil, a propagandistic distraction used to win elections and make bigger policy gains. A host of new think tanks, political organizations, and lobbyists in Washington, DC carried the message that the country's problems were caused by the poor whose shiftlessness, criminal inclinations, and sexual promiscuity were being indulged by a too-generous welfare system (Reese 2005). The organized Right thus justifies its draconian policies toward the poor with moral arguments. Right-wing think tanks and blogs, for instance, ponder the damaging effect on disabled poor children of becoming "dependent" on government assistance, or they scrutinize government nutritional assistance for poor pregnant women and children in an effort to explain away positive outcomes for infants. Tens of millions of Americans were the audience for this decades-long propaganda drama, a campaign to discredit the broad swath of American social welfare and labor legislation—the American welfare state—by associating it with the deviant minority poor (Gilens 1999). But inevitably, the poor themselves were also part of the audience. And their quiescence as their circumstances worsened and their numbers grew was probably partly owed to the demoralizing impact of sustained public insult (Rainwater 1982; Piven and Cloward 1993:445–49; Korpi and Palme 1998; Soss 2002; Wacquant 2007:163–98).

No matter their hardship, before people can mobilize for defiant collective action, they have to develop a proud and angry identity. They have to go from being hurt and ashamed to being angry and indignant. In the 1930s, many of the jobless tried to hide their travails; hangdog unemployed workers swung empty lunch boxes as they strode down the street so the neighbors would not know. But many of the unemployed also harbored other ideas, half-formed perhaps, about who was to blame for their plight. When those ideas were evoked they could be rallied to rise up with others in anger over their condition.

In the 1960s, welfare recipients also went from being hurt and ashamed to being angry and indignant. When they did, they renamed themselves "mothers" instead of recipients and claimed a right to welfare benefits in the interest of their work as mothers.[18] In other words, ideas about political rights and obligations are not a seamless construct, and people are not simply vessels for elite definitions. Time and again in history even the poor have found the outrage to proclaim not only that their hardships are not of their own making, but that they themselves by their defiance can compel action to alleviate those hardships. Those ideas are of course being promulgated ever more widely in American society and around the world, not necessarily by the very poor but by many groups who find themselves the victims of unregulated neoliberal capitalism. Occupy Wall Street, the Indignados, UKUncut, Mexican and Chilean student protestors are changing the political discourse. This may well augur the reemergence of protest politics among the poor.

NOTES

1. The first generation of such studies included Kerr et al. 1964; Cutright 1965; Wilensky and Lebeaux 1965; Cutright 1967; and Wilensky 1975. Subsequent cross-national research produced evidence to dispute the causal connection between urbanization and industrialization, and the timing of the adoption of national social insurance programs. See, for example, Flora and Alber 1981; and Collier and Messick 1975.

2. Political process approaches owe much to Walter Korpi's "power resource" theory. See Korpi 1983. See also, Stephens 1979; Shalev 1983; Esping-Andersen and Korpi 1984; and Esping-Andersen 1985.

3. This includes state-centric approaches, which emphasize the initiative of bureaucratic actors. See, for example Heclo 1974; and Weir and Skocpol 1985. Building on the state-centered approach, Weir, Orloff, and Skocpol (1988) identify institutional limits, shifting political coalitions and "policy feedbacks" as the key variables in a "institutional-political process" explanation of the welfare state. More recent studies of comparative political economy add a range of "process" and institutional explanations for welfare state spending, further blurring the distinctions between power resources and other political process models, and state-centric and other institutional approaches. See for example, Hicks and Misra 1993; Korpi and Palme 1998; Hicks 1999; Huber and Stephens 2001; and Swank 2002.

4. Disputes about rising levels of poverty in the United States are mainly about alternative poverty measures, particularly the different results when relative and absolute poverty measures are used, and also the impact on estimates of including "in-kind" benefits in calculations of income. On the United States see, for example, Iceland 2013; Fox et al. 2014. Brady (2009) provides a good discussion of comparative poverty levels and the importance of measurement disputes in estimating these levels. See especially Chapters 2 and 3.

5. In the Broadway production of *The Coast of Utopia* by Tom Stoppard, nineteenth-century Russian serfs were portrayed as a simple frieze of gray vaguely human forms, mute and still against a great white expanse. Meanwhile, on the stage the familiar characters of Russian history—Herzen, Bakunin, Tolstoy, Turgenev, and so on—debated the great issues of the day.

6. For example, see the work of scholars such as Ted Robert Gurr ([1970] 2011) who stressed "relative deprivation" explanations of disorder.

7. In subsequent work Piven and Cloward worked to analyze the specific institutional features of the American electoral-representative system that disadvantaged working and poor people generally. See especially Piven and Cloward 1993:407–80; and Piven and Cloward 2000:23–44; see also Piven 2006:19–36; and Piven, Minnite, and Groarke 2009.

8. William Cobbett, a fiery journalist writing at the time of the New Poor Law, which restricted poor relief to the workhouse, defined the restriction as a violation of ancient rights. "Among these rights was . . . the right in case we fell into distress, to have our wants sufficiently relieved out of the produce of the land. . . .. For a thousand years, necessity was relieved out of the produce of the Tithes" (Reitzel 1947, quoted in Thompson 1963:761).

9. On this point see Soss, Fording, and Schram (2011) for an argument that largely accepts the thesis of *Regulating the Poor* but modifies it to incorporate the Foucauldian pattern of self-regulation, which they attribute to the systemic imperatives of neoliberalism. See also Wacquant (2009), who argues that a new paternalist regime of poverty governance in the United States integrating welfare and criminal justice policy has emerged to manage

the effects of deindustrialization by relying on an extremely punitive approach to urban marginality.

10. For a book length review, see Schram 2002; see also the commentaries published as a retrospective symposium on *Poor People's Movements* in the 2003 edition of *Perspectives on Politics* (vol. 1, no. 4, pp. 707–35). We discuss and cite more critical reviews later in the chapter.

11. This discussion draws primarily on the research reported in *Poor People's Movements*.

12. The rise of the "resource mobilization" school in sociology and some of its core assumptions, specifically the view that organizing and organizations are critical to protest movements and their effects, is in opposition to the dissensus politics arguments of Piven and Cloward. While social movement critics tended to focus their arguments on the movement-organization debate (see, for example, McCarthy and Zald 1973; Gamson 1975; Gamson and Schmeidler 1984; Morris 1984; and McAdam 1988; but see Piven and Cloward 1992 for a rejoinder), the study of American electoral politics mostly ignores movements altogether.

13. Jack Beatty, writing in *The Nation*, insisted that "strategies which divide [the working class] are dangerous" (Beatty 1977). Michael Harrington, in the *New York Times Book Review*, said that disruptive protest in the 1960s produced "the mean spirit exploited by people like Richard Nixon" and also that full employment should have been the priority of the welfare rights movement (Harrington 1977). And Eric Hobsbawm in the *New York Review of Books*, concluded of the victories of the 1960s movements, "it is not negligible, but it is not what we wanted" (Hobsbawm 1978). See also, Sleeper (1990) for a strident claim that Piven and Cloward promoted racial polarization and a "radical extension of welfare" in the late 1960s that ultimately inflicted harm on blacks and the poor.

14. See Swank (2006) for a review of a large number of quantitative studies testing Piven and Cloward's theories on the relationship of disruption to poor relief, finding strong support.

15. The literature on the "hollowing out of the state" is ample. See as examples, Brenner 1998; Jessop 2002; Axtmann 2004.

16. See Yörük (2012b:538), who explicitly states that his study of developments in Turkey provides support for Piven and Cloward's thesis that "social assistance is driven by social unrest, rather than social need."

17. See Butler and Germanis (1983), analysts at the conservative Heritage Foundation who argued that proponents of privatization of the Social Security program needed to treat the issue as a political problem if public opposition was ever to be overcome.

18. As it happens, they were unlucky in that this occurred at a time when, influenced by the feminist movement and the fact that women were entering the labor force in large numbers, motherhood was losing prestige.

References

Alvaredo, Facundo, Anthony B. Atkinson, Thomas Piketty, and Emmanuel Saez. 2013. "The Top 1 Percent in International and Historical Perspective." *Journal of Economic Perspectives* 27(3):3–20.

Andrews, Kenneth. 2004. *Freedom Is A Constant Struggle: The Mississippi Civil Rights Movement and Its Legacy.* Chicago: University of Chicago Press.

Axtmann, Roland. 2004. "The State of the State: The Model of the Modern State and its Contemporary Transformation." *International Political Science Review* 25(3):259–79.

Bach, Wendy A. 2013. "Rosado v. Wyman: Litigating the Zeitgeist." Unpublished manuscript.

Beatty, Jack. 1977. "The Language of the Unheard." *The Nation*, October 8.

Bebbington, Anthony. 2007. "Social Movements and the Politicization of Chronic Poverty Policy." *Development and Change* 38:793–818.

Bernstein, Irving. [1960] 2010. *The Lean Years: A History of the American Worker, 1920–1933.* Foreward by Frances Fox Piven. Chicago: Haymarket Books.

Black, Duncan. 1948. "On the Rationale of Group Decision-making." *Journal of Political Economy* 56(1):23–34.

Blumenthal, Sidney. [1986] 2008. *The Rise of the Counter-Establishment: The Conservative Ascent to Political Power.* New York: Union Square Press.

Blyth, Mark. 2013. *Austerity: The History of a Dangerous Idea.* New York: Oxford University Press.

Brady, David. 2003. "Rethinking the Sociological Measurement of Poverty." *Social Forces* 81(3):715–51.

Brady, David. 2009. *Rich Democracies, Poor People: How Politics Explain Poverty.* New York: Oxford University Press.

Brady, David, Andrew S. Fullerton, and Jennifer Moren Cross. 2009. "Putting Poverty in Political Context: A Multi-Level Analysis of Adult Poverty across 18 Affluent Democracies." *Social Forces* 88(1):271–300.

Brenner, Neil. 1998. "Beyond State-Centrism? Space, Territoriality, and Geographic Scale in Globalization Studies." *Theory and Society* 28(1):39–78.

Butler, Stuart and Peter Germanis. 1983. "Achieving a 'Leninist' Strategy." *Cato Journal* 3(2):547–56.

Cloward, Richard A. and Frances Fox Piven. 1966. "The Weight of the Poor: A Strategy to End Poverty." *The Nation*, May 2.

Cloward, Richard A. and Frances Fox Piven. 1968. "Workers and Welfare: The Poor against Themselves." *The Nation*, November 25.

Collier, David and Richard Messick. 1975. "Prerequisites versus Diffusion: Testing Alternative Explanations of Social Security Adoption." *American Political Science Review* 69(4):1299–1315.

Cutright, Phillips. 1965. "Political Structure, Economic Development, and National Social Security Programs." *American Journal of Sociology* 70(5):537–50.

Cutright, Phillips. 1967. "Income Redistribution: A Cross-National Analysis." *Social Forces* 46(2):180–90.

DeBacker, Jason, Bradley Heim, Vasia Panousi, Shanthi Ramnath, and Ivan Vidangos. 2013. "Rising Inequality: Transitory or Permanent? New Evidence from a Panel of U.S. Tax Returns." Washington DC: Brookings Institution. Retrieved July 10, 2013 (http://www. brookings.edu/~/media/Projects/BPEA/Spring%202013/2013a_panousi.pdf).

DeNavas-Walt, Carmen, Bernadette D. Proctor, and Jessica C. Smith. 2013. *Income, Poverty, and Health Insurance Coverage in the United States: 2012.* Current Population Reports. U.S. Department of Commerce, Economics and Statistics Administration, U.S. Census Bureau. Retrieved February 22, 2014 (https://www.census.gov/prod/2013pubs/p60-245.pdf).

de Schweinitz, Karl. 1964. *Industrialization and Democracy: Economic Necessities and Political Possibilities.* New York: Free Press of Glencoe.

Downs, Anthony. 1957. *An Economic Theory of Democracy.* New York: Harper Collins.

Edsall, Thomas. 2013a. "The Hidden Prosperity of the Poor." *New York Times*, January 30. Retrieved July 10, 2013 (http://opinionator.blogs.nytimes.com/2013/01/30/the-hidden-prosperity-of-the-poor/).

Edsall, Thomas. 2013b. "Who Is Poor?" *New York Times*, March 13. Retrieved July 10, 2013 (http://opinionator.blogs.nytimes.com/2013/03/13/who-is-poor/).

Esping-Andersen, Gøsta. 1985. *Politics against Markets: The Social Democratic Road to Power*. Princeton, NJ: Princeton University Press.

Esping-Andersen, Gøsta and Walter Korpi. 1984. "Social Policy as Class Politics in Post-War Capitalism: Scandinavia, Austria, and Germany." Pp. 179–208 in *Order and Conflict in Contemporary Capitalism: Studies in the Political Economy of Western European Nations*, edited by John H. Goldthorpe. Oxford: Clarendon Press.

Ferguson, Thomas and Joel Rogers. 1986. *Right Turn: The Decline of the Democrats and the Future of American Politics*. New York: Hill and Wang.

Flora, Peter and Jens Alber. 1981. "Modernization, Democratization and the Development of Welfare States in Western Europe." Pp. 37–80 in *The Development of Welfare States in Europe and America*, edited by Peter Flora and Arnold J. Heidenheimer. New Brunswick, NJ: Transaction Press.

Fox, Liana, Irwin Garfinkel, Neeraj Kaushal, Jane Waldfogel, and Christopher Wimer. 2014. "Waging War on Poverty: Historical Trends in Poverty Using the Supplemental Poverty Measure." Working Paper 19789. Cambridge, MA: National Bureau of Economic Research. Retrieved February 22, 2014 (http://www.nber.org/papers/w19789.pdf?new_window=1).

Fremstead, Shawn. 2008. "Measuring Poverty and Economic Inclusion: The Current Poverty Measure, the NAS Alternative, and the Case for a Truly New Approach." Washington DC: Center for Economic and Policy Research. Retrieved July 10, 2013 (http://www.cepr.net/documents/publications/2008-12-Measuring-Poverty-and-Economic-Inclusion.pdf).

Fremstead, Shawn. 2013. "Relative Poverty Measures Can Help Paint a More Accurate Picture of Poverty in 21st Century America." CEPR Blog. Washington DC: Center for Economic and Policy Research. Retrieved July 10, 2013 (http://www.cepr.net/index.php/blogs/cepr-blog/relative-poverty-measures-can-help-paint-a-more-accurate-picture-of-poverty-in-21st-century-america).

Gamson, William A. 1975. *The Strategy of Social Protest*. Homewood, IL: Dorsey.

Gamson, William A. and Emilie Schmeidler. 1984. "Organizing the Poor: An Argument with Frances Fox Piven and Richard A. Cloward, *Poor People's Movements: Why They Succeed, How They Fail*." *Theory and Society* 13:567–85.

Gilens, Martin. 1999. *Why Americans Hate Welfare: Race, Media and the Politics of Antipoverty Policy*. Chicago: University of Chicago Press.

Gough, Ian. 1979. *The Political Economy of the Welfare State*. London: Macmillan.

Gurr, Ted Robert. [1970] 2011. *Why Men Rebel*. 40th Anniversary ed. Boulder, CO: Paradigm.

Haggard, Stephan and Robert R. Kaufman. 2008. *Development, Democracy and Welfare States: Latin America, East Asia, and Eastern Europe*. Princeton, NJ: Princeton University Press.

Hammond, John L. and Barbara Hammond. 1917. *The Town Labourer, 1760–1832: The New Civilisation*. London: Longmans, Green.

Hammond, John L. and Barbara Hammond. 1948. *The Village Labourer*, 2 vols. London: Longmans, Green.

Hanlon, Joseph, Armando Barrientos, and David Hulme. 2010. *Just Give Money to the Poor: The Development Revolution from the Global South*. Sterling, VA: Kumarian Press.

Harrington, Michael. 1977. "Disturbance from Below." *New York Times Book Review*, December 11.

Heclo, Hugh. 1974. *Modern Social Politics in Britain and Sweden*. New Haven, CT: Yale University Press.

Hicks, Alexander. 1999. *Social Democracy and Welfare Capitalism: A Century of Income Security Politics*. Ithaca, NY: Cornell University Press.

Hicks, Alexander and Joya Misra. 1993. "Political Resources and the Growth of Welfare in Affluent Capitalist Democracies, 1960–1982." *American Journal of Sociology* 99(3):668–710.

Hobsbawm, Eric J. 1978. "Should the Poor Organize." *New York Review of Books*, March 23. Retrieved February 22, 2014 (http://www.nybooks.com/articles/archives/1978/mar/23/should-the-poor-organize/?pagination=false).

Huber, Evelyne and John D. Stephens. 2001. *Development and Crisis of the Welfare State: Parties and Policies in Global Markets*. Chicago: University of Chicago Press.

Iceland, John. 2013. *Poverty in America: A Handbook*. Berkeley: University of California Press.

Irwin, Neil. 2013. *The Alchemists: Three Central Bankers and a World on Fire*. New York: Penguin Press.

Jessop, Bob. 2002. *The Future of the Capitalist State*. Cambridge, UK: Polity Press.

Kerr, Clark, John T. Dunlop, Frederick H. Harbison, and Charles A. Myers. 1964. *Industrialism and Industrial Man: The Problems of Labor and Management in Economic Growth*. 2nd ed. New York: Oxford University Press.

Korpi, Walter. 1983. *The Democratic Class Struggle*. London: Routledge and Kegan Paul.

Korpi, Walter and Joakim Palme. 1998. "The Paradox of Redistribution and Strategies of Equality: Welfare State Institutions, Inequality, and Poverty in the Western Countries." *American Sociological Review* 63(5):661–87.

Lo Vuolo, Rubén, ed. *Citizen's Income and Welfare Regimes in Latin America: From Cash Transfers to Rights*. New York: Palgrave.

Lustig, Nora, Luis F. Lopez-Calva, and Eduardo Ortiz-Juarez. 2012. "Declining Inequality in Latin America in the 2000s." Policy Research Working Paper 6248. Latin America and the Caribbean Region, Poverty, Equity and Gender Unit, World Bank. Retrieved July 10, 2013 (http://www-wds.worldbank.org/servlet/WDSContentServer/WDSP/IB/2012/10/23/000158349_20121023093211/Rendered/PDF/wps6248.pdf).

Manley, Gregory M., Rachel V. Kutz-Flamenbaum, Deana A. Rohlinger, and Jeff Goodwin, eds. 2012. *Strategies for Social Change*. Minneapolis: University of Minnesota Press.

McAdam, Doug. 1988. *Freedom Summer: The Idealists Revisited*. New York: Oxford University Press.

McCarthy, John D. and Mayer Zald. 1973. *The Trend of Social Movements in America: Professionalization and Resource Mobilization*. Morristown, NJ: General Learning Press.

Morris, Aldon D. 1984. *The Origins of the Civil Rights Movement: Black Communities Organizing for Change*. New York: Free Press.

Navarro, Vincente. 2013. "The Frontal Attack on Social Europe." *International Journal of Health Services* 43(1):1–5.

O'Connor, James. 1973. *The Fiscal Crisis of the State*. New York: St. Martin's Press.

Offe, Claus. 1972. "Advanced Capitalism and the Welfare State." *Politics and Society* 2(4):479–88.

Olsen, Gregg M. 2013. "What's 'Left' in the 'Garden of Sweden'?" *International Journal of Health Services* 43(1):7–30.

Parrott, Sharon, Jimmy Charite, Indivar Dutta-Gupta, and Arloc Sherman. 2013. "Comparison of Benefits for Poor Families to Middle-Class Incomes Is Deeply Flawed." Washington

DC: Center for Budget and Policy Priorities. Retrieved July 10, 2013 (http://www.cbpp.org/files/2-25-13pov.pdf).

Petras, James and Henry Veltmeyer. 2005. *Social Movements and State Power: Argentina, Brazil, Bolivia, Ecuador.* Ann Arbor, MI: Pluto Press.

Piven, Frances Fox. [1963] 1974. "Low-Income People and the Political Process." Pp. 73–88 in *The Politics of Turmoil: Essays on Poverty, Race, and the Urban Crisis*, edited by Richard A. Cloward and Frances Fox Piven. New York: Pantheon Books.

Piven, Frances Fox. 2006. *Challenging Authority: How Ordinary People Change America.* Lanham, MD: Rowman & Littlefield.

Piven, Frances Fox and Richard A. Cloward. [1977] 1979. *Poor People's Movements: Why They Succeed, How They Fail.* With a new introduction by the authors. New York: Vintage Books.

Piven, Frances Fox and Richard A. Cloward. 1992. "Normalizing Collective Protest." Pp. 301–25 in *Frontiers in Social Movement Theory*, edited by Aldon D. Morris and Carol McClurg Mueller. New Haven, CT: Yale University Press.

Piven, Frances Fox and Richard A. Cloward. [1971] 1993. *Regulating the Poor: The Functions of Public Welfare.* Updated ed. New York: Vintage Books.

Piven, Frances Fox and Richard A. Cloward. 2000. *Why Americans Still Don't Vote and Why Politicians Want It That Way.* Boston: Beacon Press.

Piven, Frances Fox and Richard A. Cloward. 2005. "Rule Making, Rule Breaking, and Power." Pp. 33–53 in *Handbook of Political Sociology*, edited by Thomas Janoski, Robert R. Alford, Alexander M. Hicks and Mildred A. Schwartz. New York: Cambridge University Press.

Piven, Frances Fox, Lorraine C. Minnite, and Margaret Groarke. 2009. *Keeping Down the Vote: Race and the Demobilization of American Voters.* New York: New Press.

powell, john a. and Stephen Menendian. 2011. "Beyond Public/Private Understanding of Corporate Power." *Poverty and Race* 20(6):5–8.

Rainwater, Lee. 1982. "Stigma in Income-tested Programs." Pp. 19–46 in *Income-tested Programs: The Case For and Against*, edited by Irwin Garfinkel. New York: Academic Press.

Reese, Ellen. 2005. *Backlash against Welfare Mothers Past and Present.* Berkeley: University of California Press.

Reitzel, William, ed. 1947. *The Autobiography of William Cobbett.* London: Faber and Faber.

Schlesinger, Arthur M., Jr. 1957. *The Age of Roosevelt.* Vol. 1: *The Crisis of the Old Order, 1919–1933.* Boston: Houghton Mifflin.

Schram, Sanford F. 2002. *Praxis for the Poor: Piven and Cloward and the Future of Social Science in Social Welfare.* New York: New York University Press.

Shalev, Michael. 1983. "The Social Democratic Model and Beyond: Two Generations of Comparative Research on the Welfare State." *Comparative Social Research* 6:315–51.

Sleeper, Jim. 1990. *The Closest of Strangers: Liberalism and the Politics of Race in New York.* New York: W.W. Norton.

Soss, Joe. 2002. *Unwanted Claims: The Politics of Participation in the U.S. Welfare System.* Ann Arbor: University of Michigan Press.

Soss, Joe, Richard C. Fording and Sanford F. Schram. 2011. *Disciplining the Poor: Neoliberal Paternalism and the Persistent Power of Race.* Chicago: University of Chicago Press.

Stampini, Marco and Leopoldo Tornarolli. 2012. "The Growth of Conditional Cash Transfers in Latin America and the Caribbean: Did They Go Too Far?" Policy Brief No. IDB-PB-185. Social Sector, Social Protection and Health Division, Inter-American Development Bank. Retrieved July 10, 2013 (http://idbdocs.iadb.org/wsdocs/getdocument.aspx?docnum=37306295).

Steensland, Brian. 2007. *The Failed Welfare Revolution: America's Struggle over Guaranteed Income Policy*. Princeton, NJ: Princeton University Press.

Steinmetz, George. 1993. *Regulating the Social: The Welfare State and Local Politics in Imperial Germany*. Princeton, NJ: Princeton University Press.

Stephens, John D. 1979. *The Transition from Capitalism to Socialism*. London: Macmillan.

Stiglitz, Joseph. 2013a. "Inequality Is a Choice." *New York Times*, October 13. Retrieved February 22, 2014 (http://opinionator.blogs.nytimes.com/2013/10/13/inequality-is-a-choice/?_php=true&_type=blogs&_r=0).

Stiglitz, Joseph E. 2013b. *The Price of Inequality: How Today's Divided Society Endangers Our Future*. New York: W.W. Norton.

Sugrue, Thomas. 2008. *Sweet Land of Liberty: The Forgotten Struggle for Civil Rights in the North*. New York: Random House.

Swank, Duane. 2002. *Global Capital, Political Institutions, and Policy Change in Developed Welfare States*. New York: Cambridge University Press.

Swank, Eric. 2006. "Welfare Reform and the Power of Protest: Quantitative Tests of Piven and Cloward's 'Turmoil-Relief' Hypothesis." Pp. 287–300 in *The Promise of Welfare Reform: Political Rhetoric and the Reality of Poverty in the Twenty-First Century*, edited by Keith M. Kilty and Elizabeth A. Segal. New York: Routledge.

Therborn, Goren. 2012. "The Killing Fields of Inequality." *International Journal of Health Services* 42(4):579–90.

Thompson, E. P. 1963. *The Making of the English Working Class*. New York: Vintage Books, Random House.

Wacquant, Loïc. 2007. *Urban Outcasts: A Comparative Sociology of Advanced Marginality*. Cambridge, UK: Polity Press.

Wacquant, Loïc. [2004] 2009. *Punishing the Poor: The Neoliberal Government of Social Insecurity*. Eng. Lang. Version. Durham, NC: Duke University Press.

Webb, Sidney and Beatrice Webb. 1963. *English Poor Law History, Part 1: The Old Poor Law*. With a new introduction by W. A. Robson, in *English Local Government*, Vols. 7–9. Hamden, CT: Archon Books.

Weir, Margaret, Ann Shola Orloff, and Theda Skocpol. 1988. "Introduction: Understanding American Social Politics." Pp. 3–27 in *The Politics of Social Policy in the United States*, edited by Margaret Weir, Ann Shola Orloff, and Theda Skocpol. Princeton, NJ: Princeton University Press.

Weir, Margaret and Theda Skocpol. 1985. "State Structures and the Possibilities for Keynesian 'Responses' to the Great Depression in Sweden, Britain and the United States." Pp. 107–63 in *Bringing the State Back In*, edited by Peter Evans, Dietrich Rueschemeyer, and Theda Skocpol. New York: Cambridge University Press.

Wilensky, Harold L. 1975. *The Welfare State and Equality: Structural and Ideological Roots of Public Expenditures*. Berkeley: University of California Press.

Wilensky, Harold L. and Charles N. Lebeaux. 1965. *Industrial Society and Social Welfare: The Impact of Industrialization on the Supply and Organization of Social Welfare Services in the United States*. New York: Free Press.

Wilentz, Sean. 2008. *The Age of Reagan: A History, 1974–2008*. New York: Harper Perennial.

Yörük, Erdem. 2012a. "The Politics of the Turkish Welfare System Transformation in the Neoliberal Era: Welfare as Containment and Mobilization of Grassroots Politics." PhD Dissertation, Department of Sociology, Johns Hopkins University.

Yörük, Erdem. 2012b. "Welfare Provision as Political Containment: The Politics of Social Assistance and the Kurdish Conflict in Turkey." *Politics and Society* 40(4):517–47.

CHAPTER 34

WHY AND WHEN DO PEASANTS REBEL?

Origins and Consequences of Rural Collective Action

GUILLERMO TREJO

INTRODUCTION

WHAT do the poor do to overcome poverty in the developing world?[1] In some influential scholarly narratives, the poor are portrayed as passive recipients of foreign aid from the international community or of conditional cash transfer (CCT) programs from domestic governments.[2] In other important narratives, the poor are engaged in clientelistic relationships and sell their votes to political machines in exchange for private goods.[3] In this chapter I explore an alternative account in which the poor take their destiny in their own hands and seek to overcome economic destitution via direct political action. I explore three forms of political action: peaceful protest, armed rebellion, and civil war.

Because the universe of the poor in the developing world is so diverse, in this chapter I narrow down my discussion to rural populations and analyze both classic statements and recent findings in the literature on peasant collective action. The "peasant" category encompasses a wide variety of rural populations, including (1) rural households with no access to land who sell their labor power in exchange for low wages; (2) rural households with access to small land plots who are engaged in subsistence agriculture and consume everything they produce; and (3) rural households with access to land who are able to sell a small surplus of their production but who nonetheless live under a poverty line defined in terms of income and basic capabilities.[4]

A focus on the rural poor in the twenty-first century is not anachronistic. Although the proportion of the world's population living in rural areas has declined rapidly in the last 60 years, the World Bank (2012) reports that by 2012 nearly one-half of the world's population (47 percent) remained in rural settings. And although not all rural populations are poor, most of the world's poor live in rural areas. As the World Bank's (2008) *World Development Report* showed, 75 percent of the world's poor lived in rural settings as of 2008. The study of the rural poor and of rural collective action thus remains a crucially important area of research.

This chapter discusses classic statements and recent findings about peasant collective action from sociology, political science, and economics. While the classic literature has centered on the motivations that drive peasants to take up arms and engage in violent collective action, more recent studies have focused on the organizational infrastructure and the cultural framings that facilitate peasant collective action—both peaceful and violent. This explanatory shift reflects a transition in the study of collective behavior and social movements over the past four decades, by which concerns about the psychological motivations of group action (Gurr 1970) have given way to a focus on the mobilizing and political structures and the ideological frames that enable collective action (McAdam, McCarthy, and Zald 1996; Tarrow 1998). As this chapter shows, some of the most important challenges that we face in expanding our understanding of poor people's collective action are similar to those faced by the broader literature on collective behavior and social movements—namely, the need to integrate micro-individual motivations, meso-level organizational dynamics, and macro-behavior.[5]

The chapter is divided into four sections. In the first part, I discuss some of the most influential responses to a classic question: Why do poor peasants rebel? I cover a wide variety of motivations, including moral indignation (in the face of market reforms); moral outrage (triggered by state repression); pleasure in agency (when the poor perceive that they can make history); greed (in the face of economic opportunities); and rightful resistance (to contest the retraction of vital rights). *Pace* the scholarly effort to find a single driver of peasant collective action, I discuss recent studies that suggest the existence of *multiple* motivations driving individuals toward radical collective action.

Because we cannot draw a straight line from individual motivations to collective action, in the second part I shift the discussion to the meso- and macrolevels and assess theories suggesting that the poor can transform individual motivations into group action only when they have access to the organizational vehicles and the political opportunities to mobilize. Drawing on recent studies of peasant protest, armed insurgency, and civil war, I discuss four lessons that help us rethink dynamics of poor people's movements: (1) The rural poor engage in multiple forms of collective action, not just armed rebellion and revolution. (2) Religion is a surprisingly important source for the creation of the associational networks that enable different forms of peasant collective action. (3) State responses to rural mobilization define whether peasants engage in violent or nonviolent action. (4) The structural characteristics of social networks for peasant mobilization define whether the rural poor are able to collectively resist state repression or co-optation.

In the third section I discuss the long-term economic and political consequences of peasant collective action and whether violent or nonviolent forms of rural mobilization have an impact on land redistribution and democratization. In the concluding section,

I go beyond the peasant world to more broadly assess conditions under which the poor try to overcome their destitution through direct political action.

Why Do the (Rural) Poor Rebel?

For more than half a century, one of the most influential questions in peasant studies has been about the motivations that lead peasants to engage in direct political action. The literature, however, has overwhelmingly focused on armed insurgencies and revolutionary collective action at the expense of more moderate forms of "modular" and peaceful mobilization. Under the influence of modernization theory, scholars of collective action and social movements have assumed for a long time that when peasants overcome the challenges associated with group action, they often engage in radical and violent mobilization, particularly guerrilla warfare. In these classic studies, social protest and nonviolent collective action are typically associated with urban/modern areas but not with traditional rural villages. Hence, the quintessential question about peasant collective action has been about violent revolutionary action—that is, why do peasants rebel? Here is a review of five important individual-level motivations.

Moral Indignation and the Subsistence Ethic

Drawing on E. P. Thompson's (1963 and 1971) moral economy of the English working class, Scott (1977) produced one of the most influential statements in the study of peasant collective action—*The Moral Economy of the Peasant: Rebellion and Subsistence in Southeast Asia*. Scott's classic book has had a major influence in the study of poor peoples' collective action in the developing world. The book suggests that the introduction of commercial agriculture in communities engaged in subsistence agriculture can undermine patron-client relations and the social norms of exchange and reciprocity that allow rural households to survive in the face of economic adversity. In Scott's view, peasants rise up in arms to contest the introduction of market mechanisms and to defend the social norms that characterize their moral economy. He characterizes peasants as risk-averse individuals and groups who defy change and rebel to preserve traditional forms of social exchange and economic sustainability. These are not communities seeking radical transformations but conservative collective actors who engage in violent forms of mobilization to preserve the status quo.

Thompson and Scott's moral economy approach has had a major impact in the interpretation of peasant collective action in the developing world. It has influenced the study of some of the most emblematic past and recent armed insurgencies in Latin America. For example, Womack's (1970) classic study of the Zapatista rebellion during the 1910 Mexican Revolution emphasized the conservative nature of the peasant movement. In the opening pages of his classic study on Zapatismo, Womack unhesitatingly observed: "This is a book about country people who did not want to [change] and therefore got into a revolution." Scott's moral economy had a similar influence in the interpretation of the motivations that led Mayan peasants from the Zapatista National Liberation Army (EZLN) to take up arms in 1994 in opposition to the liberalization of land tenure and the coming into effect of the North American Free Trade Agreement (NAFTA). Historian Adolfo Gilly (1998) and anthropologist June Nash (2001) both interpreted the neo-Zapatista rebellion as a moral uprising of Mexico's most ancient cultural communities against globalization and the marketization of rural life and for the preservation of traditional indigenous norms and ways of life.

The moral economy approach has also had a crucial influence in scholarly interpretations of the most recent wave of antineoliberal mobilization in the developing world. Interpreters of Latin America's unprecedented wave of peasant/indigenous protest in the last quarter of the twentieth century suggest that rural indigenous communities in Bolivia, Ecuador, and Mexico took to the streets to peacefully oppose the commercialization of agriculture and to renegotiate the terms of their incorporation in postauthoritarian contexts on multicultural grounds.[6] These were rural indigenous minorities who learned to defend their community bonds—forged under the auspices of class-based populism—using a new language of multicultural rights (Pallares 2002; Mattiace 2003; Yashar 2005).

The moral economy approach has also influenced the scholarly literature on mass mobilization to contest the privatization of natural resources, including gas, forestry, mining, and water. Simmons (2012) suggests that market-oriented reforms can trigger major episodes of popular mobilization when they affect "subsistence goods"—goods that individuals consider to be materially and culturally essential for their community's survival. She claims that the water and gas wars in Bolivia in the late 1990s resulted from the elite's inability to understand that privatizing these "subsistence resources" could be perceived by some groups—particularly poor peasants—as a major threat to community survival and hence become a trigger for mass mobilization.

Under the influence of the moral economy approach, students of transnational peasant movements suggest that the recent transnational activism against economic globalization has deep roots in global challenges to local moral economies. Edelman (2005) argues that the globalization of agricultural markets, the erosion of the state's capacity to redistribute land and subsidize agricultural production for poor peasants, and the concentration of agricultural production in the hands of major multinational corporations have created new threats to rural moral economies around the globe. In response to these threats, local and national peasant organizations have joined forces to create new transnational movements such as Via Campesina and other cross-national movements working within the framework of the World Social Forum.

Beyond peasant studies, in recent decades the moral economy approach has received important theoretical and empirical support from behavioral economics. The central finding of prospect theory—the influential research program that claims that minimizing losses rather than maximizing gains can be a major driver for human behavior[7]—provides strong analytic and experimental support to Thompson's and Scott's central propositions. In the conceptual language of prospect theory, when peasant communities act collectively in defense of their "moral economy," their actions in favor of the status quo resemble the behavior that individuals seeking to minimize losses display in laboratory experiments.

One important shortcoming in explanations that rely on moral indignation as the only driver for collective action is that authors often fail to explain how movements overcome the organizational and political challenges that frequently inhibit the formation of cycles of protests and armed insurgencies in the developing world. By drawing a straight line from market shocks to moral indignation to collective action, scholars often ignore the collective action problem altogether. Scott (1977:4) himself objected to this move and warned against the temptation of drawing a straight line from moral indignation to mobilization; he was emphatic in calling for closer attention to "intervening factors ... such as alliances with other classes, the repressive capacity of dominant elites, and the social organization of the peasantry itself."

Moral Outrage and Pleasure in Agency

While the moral economy approach suggests that feelings of moral outrage against market reforms may lead peasant communities to take up arms in order to *preserve* the status quo, a new approach based on emotions suggests that feelings of moral indignation against state repression and social injustice can move poor peasants to take up arms to radically *transform* the status quo.

In her influential book *Insurgent Collective Action and Civil War in El Salvador*, Wood (2003) suggests that a dramatic surge in the repressive activities of El Salvador's military state—which acted as guarantor of the interests of a landed oligarchy—gave rise to a widespread sense of moral outrage among peasant communities in the 1970s. As members of Catholic associational networks, which emerged as the preeminent collective vehicles to fight for land redistribution and human rights, Salvadoran peasants joined armed insurgent groups to defend their personal dignity and that of their fellow villagers; they engaged in popular struggles to transform their material and moral conditions of oppression and injustice and to reassert their place in history. Inspired by liberation theology—a seminal Latin American reinterpretation of the Christian gospel, which spoke directly to poor peoples' experiences of exploitation and liberation—Catholic peasants underwent a process of rapid cognitive and emotional liberation, transcended self-regarding views of their own structural condition of exploitation and oppression, and became other-regarding actors who fought for their own and their people's emancipation.

In Wood's important account, partial initial revolutionary victories, including peasants taking over vast hacienda lands where their families had served as peons for generations, gave rise to a sense of ownership and an unprecedented "pleasure in agency" that motivated peasants to be at the forefront of a large-scale civil war. Peasant collective action and the protracted civil war triggered a major wave of de facto land redistribution and became a causal factor for the democratization of El Salvador's oligarchic dictatorship.

Wood's focus on emotions and injustice, together with other studies of emotions and collective action in advanced capitalist democracies (for instance, Goodwin and Jasper 2004), has found strong resonance in the study of social movements among marginalized, stigmatized, and oppressed populations. Scholars have identified moral indignation over government repressive actions and/or negative policy shifts that undermine people's social and economic rights as the crucial drivers for a wide variety of movements, including peasants (Brockett 2005), ethnic minorities (Nash 2001), and urban squatters (Auyero 2004).

As Wood reports, an increasing number of laboratory experiments in behavioral economics have found that other-regarding motivations can lead individuals to engage in high-risk activity and that the pleasure of participation in collective endeavors can be a strong driver for people's engagement in high-risk collective action (Bowles 2008).

While this new emphasis on emotions and solidarity has made an important contribution to restoring agency to the study of social movements of marginalized groups, a significant and yet underdeveloped aspect of these explanations is how poor peasants begin to speak the language of human dignity and historical agency. How do they transform their grievances against government repressive actions and negative policy shifts into a language of moral justice? How do they traverse the process from economic or political shocks to emotional liberation and action? Although in Wood's story liberation theology and Catholic progressive pastoral action are the catalysts in this process of emotional liberation, there is very little discussion of the factors that drove the Catholic Church in El Salvador to become a major agent of social change when it had been a member of the ruling oligarchy for centuries. Because religion plays such an important role in Wood's story and because we know that religious is Janus-faced— every religious tradition has supported conservative *and* progressive movements, pro-elite *and* pro-poor movements—it is crucial to understand the motivations that led Catholic clergy to provide the social infrastructure and the religious narrative for peasant defiance.

Greed

At least since the publication of Mancur Olson's (1966) *The Logic of Collective Action*, economists have suggested that individuals in large groups will not participate in the pursuit of public goods unless leaders provide them with private material incentives. Building on Olson, Popkin (1979) developed his famous critique of Scott's moral economy approach and argued that peasants take part in high-risk revolutionary action only when rebel leaders offer them private access to land or to other selective incentives. In his approach, instrumental rationality—rather than moral values, normative commitments, or communal solidarity—drives *rational* peasants to rebel.

Following Olson and Popkin, economist Paul Collier (2000) and his associates (2005) suggest that greed rather than moral or ideological commitment drives poor young males living in rural and underdeveloped countries to join armed rebel groups and fight civil wars. Based on extensive quantitative cross-national analyses, Collier and his colleagues conclude that a low opportunity cost and the prospect of economic mobility by looting natural resources drive young teenagers to criminal gangs and armed insurgency, particularly in poor countries with failed states, where governments are incapable of policing criminal gangs.[8]

In this influential economic literature, greed and opportunities for looting, rather than grievances, ideology, or moral indignation, drive the rural poor to rebel. For Collier and his associates these are not insurgent groups with clear political ideologies but gangs of organized criminals with clear economic ambitions; they are groups that rebel to plunder. As they seize new territorial controls, these quasi-criminal groups develop ideologies to justify their assault on power. While Collier and his coauthors have added multiple nuances (2005) to the initial suggestion of conceptualizing armed insurgency as a quasi-criminal business (2000), their main point that armed insurgency is a criminal rather than a political phenomenon has remained unchanged.

Although the economic approach to civil war has placed poor, young unemployed men living in rural areas in the developing world as the new revolutionary agent in contemporary civil wars, Collier and his colleagues do not provide any individual-level evidence to support their claim; in fact, their central assertion is simply inferred from the statistical correlation between GDP per capita and the onset of civil war. Moreover, the economic approach has made the strong assumption that nothing other than plundering and economic profit matters in motivating the poor to rebel; ideas, ideologies, emotions, normative convictions, and the organizational bases of rebellion are simply regarded as peripheral factors. Because the statistical associations between economic factors and violence are substantively weak and because models only explain some of the variation in violence, this may be a simplified and untenable assumption.

Grievances

A focus on grievances associated with economic injustice, rather than on economic profit, has led to two important scholarly formulations of why the poor rebel.

In his classic book *Why Men Rebel*, Ted Gurr (1970) suggests that unfulfilled expectations of economic mobility and a sense of relative deprivation can drive people to take up arms. Throughout Gurr's influential scholarly career, he and his associates (1993) have always operationalized relative deprivation in terms of poverty levels. Focusing mainly on ethnic minorities, their analyses in the past two decades have shown that poverty is a strong predictor of ethnic minority rebellions, suggesting that the unfulfilled expectations of poor and marginalized ethnic minorities are an important predictor of insurgent violence.

As an alternative to the relative deprivation argument, students of economic inequality suggest that when the poor perceive that the rich receive more than what they deserve, class differences can lead to class struggle. Muller and Seligson's (1987) pioneering findings from cross-national quantitative studies suggest that income inequality—rather than land inequality—predicts revolutionary collective action. They conjecture that discontent with inequality facilitates the rise of encompassing revolutionary coalitions between urban middle-class sectors and the rural poor that bridge urban centers with the rural countryside. In contrast, Boix's (2008) more extensive cross-national quantitative study suggests that land inequality is a better predictor of armed insurgencies, civil war, and revolution because unequal agrarian societies provide poor peasants with both the motive (discontent) and the opportunity (economic structures with immobile assets—land—that can be de facto expropriated) to take up arms and seize wealth. In Boix's parsimonious explanation, the fixed nature of land explains the revolutionary potential of the rural countryside.

While scholarly approaches based on economic injustice go beyond a narrow economistic view solely based on profits, an important limitation in this literature is that scholars have failed to move beyond testing individual-level predictions using aggregate-level data. As scholars did two decades ago, the current literature continues to deduce the actions of historical actors from correlation coefficients of aggregate national-level data. Although Boix's insightful formal model fleshes out actors and incentives and strategic interaction, we have little microhistorical or survey evidence to know whether and the extent to which perceptions of economic injustice (due to land inequality) combined with opportunities (due to the immobile nature of land) drive peasants to take up arms.

Rightful Resistance

An important insight in conflict studies suggests that when state authorities confront dissident groups with contradictory responses—for example, violently repressing forms of nonviolent dissident action that they had previously tolerated—they stimulate radicalization from below (Lichbach 1987). Building on this insight, different scholars have suggested that elites in authoritarian regimes experiencing partial processes of political liberalization tend to display this type of erratic behavior by which they grant significant economic, political, or ethnic rights to organized groups but then take them away when they fear losing power (Sambanis and Zinn 2006; Trejo 2012). The retraction of fundamental rights can stimulate radicalization from below when these legal changes threaten individual or group self-preservation.[9]

Sambanis and Zinn's (2006) cross-national quantitative study of ethnic civil wars shows that the sudden retraction of autonomy rights granted to ethnic minorities as part of a process of political liberalization can be a strong predictor of the outbreak of violent self-determination movements. Trejo's (2012) study of the neo-Zapatista rebellion in Mexico suggests that the retraction of communal land rights can lead to the outbreak of armed insurgency. Using survey data, he shows that two-thirds of Mexico's peasantry perceived the constitutional reform that ended six decades of land reform and suppressed agricultural subsidies for poor producers as a major threat to their well-being. Yet peasants took up arms only in states where subnational elites used coercive means (e.g., indiscriminate repression) and eliminated basic civil rights and liberties (e.g., the right to protest) to prevent major peasant mobilizations against the reform. Trejo's in-depth interviews with rural Mayan populations from the southern state of Chiapas suggest that peasants took up arms to contest what they perceived to be a dual political and economic reversion that endangered their self-preservation—the restoration of a closed authoritarian regime and a repressive hacienda (plantation) system from which their parents had escaped.

Whereas Scott's approach argues that peasants take up arms to defend their moral economy—the *informal* set of arrangements that guarantee their survival in times of crisis—a rightful resistance approach claims that peasants rebel to defend vital constitutional rights—*formal* institutions that are strategically central to their well-being and self-preservation. Prospect theory provides important analytic and experimental support to the rightful resistance claim. The theory's central experimental finding that when individuals seek to minimize losses they can become risk takers (Kahneman and Tversky 1979) is a plausible explanation of the transformation of poor peasants or marginalized ethnic minorities into radical actors who seek to defend some of their most fundamental rights in the streets or in the mountains.

An important challenge to a rightful resistance approach is to understand why elites decide to eliminate rights they had previously granted. Another challenge is to provide a more systematic explanation of the relevant dimensions of rights that the rural poor consider as fundamental or strategically central to their self-preservation. This is particularly important for the study of poor people's movements. While the poor's material condition of destitution may lead researchers to assume that changes in economic policies are the most relevant dimension for them, it is likely that other dimensions of rights—for example, religious liberties or ethno-linguistic autonomy—can have more relevance than purely economic rights. As Amartya Sen (1999) suggests, poverty is a multidimensional phenomenon and people's perception of destitution may encompass several dimensions of rights and capabilities beyond a narrow sphere of material goods and services.

Multiple Motivations and Unexpected Pathways

In his seminal reinterpretation of violence in civil war, Kalyvas (2006) contends that multiple motivations drive people to engage in war. For Kalyvas the macro- or national-level grievances that scholars often identify as the main drivers of large-scale conflict have little correspondence with the micro-motivations that often drive people to join armed rebel groups on the ground. On the basis of an in-depth exploration of the Greek civil war, Kalyvas concludes that personal vendettas, family conflicts, or local community differences were more commonly cited motivations to go to war than macro-grievances associated with politics or economic changes. While people may frame their local motivations on macro-narratives, personal, nonpolitical issues are often the main driving causes for participating in war.

Because the search for a single mechanism that may explain radical collective action has dominated the study of peasant rebellions for nearly half a century, Kalyvas's distinction between macro- and micro-motivations and his suggestion that multiple local and personal motivations can drive people to war present important theoretical and empirical challenges. Recent important studies of civil war participation echo Kalyvas's challenge. For example, Viterna's (2013) insightful analysis of women's participation in El Salvador's civil war similarly shows that women join armed guerrilla movements for multiple reasons. On the basis of extensive in-depth interviews, she identifies nonconventional motivations for rebel recruitment, including a search for a "sense of adventure" or for an organization where women were less likely to be sexually assaulted—as was the case in the Farabundo Martí National Liberation Front, or FMLN. Based on extensive surveys of ex-combatants in Sierra Leone's civil war, Humphreys and Weinstein (2008) also show that people joined the war for multiple reasons. Perhaps the most surprising finding is that a significant proportion of combatants may have been abducted in the first place. This suggests that in some conflicts there is no room for free agency or free will; young men in rural areas are simply abducted and forced to fight.

WHEN DO THE (RURAL) POOR REBEL?

Influenced by major theoretical developments in the study of collective action and social movements of the past three decades, a significant number of studies of peasant mobilization have slowly moved away from debates about motivations and have focused instead on the organizational factors and political contexts that facilitate or hinder different forms of rural collective action. Under the assumption that grievances are ubiquitous, a number of students of collective behavior and social movements have claimed that the study of contentious politics among marginalized groups should focus on the organizational vehicles and the political opportunities that enable groups to express their grievances in the public arena.[10] Focusing on the meso- and macrolevels of rural collective action, new studies of peasant mobilization have yielded important insights about the conditions under which the rural poor can act collectively to overcome their condition of destitution. Here is a brief discussion of four lessons we have learned from these studies:

Beyond Rebellion: How Peasants Engage in Multiple Forms of Collective Action

One of the most important lessons we have learned in recent decades about the mobilization of the rural poor in the developing world is that peasant collective action is not always violent. Contrary to the commonly held assumption that riots or rebellions are the only forms of collective action available to the rural poor, a significant number of studies have shown that peaceful forms of "modular collective action"[11]—for example, marches, sit-ins, hunger strikes, and major demonstrations—have become part of the collective repertoire in the contemporary rural world. Although students of collective action and social movements in the past have worked under the modernization hypothesis, assuming that urban areas are the arena for peaceful forms of social contestation while rural areas are the site of violent forms of collective action, a wide variety of studies has recently shown that organized and peaceful mobilization can take place in rural areas and violent collective action—including armed insurgency and terrorism—can be part of the contentious repertoire in major metropolitan centers.

These findings have forced us to view the study of rural collective action through a different lens. Rather than simply assume that peasants will engage in violent collective action when they face major external threats to their livelihood, we now look at how rural populations build local, regional, national, and even transnational social movements and combine direct peaceful political action in the streets with legal actions. Studies of the Brazilian Landless Workers' Movement (MST)—the largest social movement in the world—provide extensive evidence of this dual activism in the street and in the courts (Ondetti 2008). An important literature on peasant indigenous mobilization in Latin America in the last quarter of the twentieth century shows that rural populations practice modular forms of collective action that we typically associate with urban areas (Le Bot 1994; Van Cott 2000; Pallares 2002; Mattiace 2003; Yashar 2005; Inclán 2009; Rice 2012; Trejo 2012). To the extent that the rural poor engage in violent revolutionary action, we now trace back the origins of armed insurgencies to prior experiences of peaceful mobilization and try to understand the conditions that explain the escalation from nonviolent protest to violent revolutionary action.

The concept of cycles of protest, initially developed by Sidney Tarrow (1989) to explain dynamics of protest in Italian urban centers, has become a key conceptual tool for the understanding of rural collective action in Latin America. Uncovering the different phases of a cycle of protest has enabled scholars to explain dynamics of radicalization from nonviolence to violence.

For example, Almeida's (2003, 2008) important exploration of the different waves of popular protest El Salvador experienced throughout the twentieth century shows that peasants created important local and regional social networks and "modern" social movements and took part in major cycles of peaceful demonstrations before they took up arms in the late 1970s. Brockett's (2005) influential work presents extensive evidence of multiple cycles of rural and urban peaceful protest in Guatemala and El Salvador prior to the escalation of protest into armed insurgency and civil war. Finally, Trejo's (2012) work on rural indigenous mobilization in Mexico shows that Mayan peasants in the southern state of Chiapas went underground to continue their struggle for land through violent means only two decades into a major cycle of peaceful rural protest.[12] Almeida, Brockett, and Trejo provide original time-series data of protest events that enable them to explain why changes in state repression during protracted cycles of protest stimulated the escalation of peaceful mobilization into violent collective action in Guatemala, El Salvador, and Mexico.[13]

An important challenge in the study of peasant—and poor people's—collective action is to clearly identify and differentiate the distinct forms of mobilization that they adopt. One of the most common observational biases in studies of peasant rebellions and armed insurgencies is that authors fail to recognize the multiple forms of participation that peasants engage in before they take the life-changing decision—for good or for ill—to go underground and take up arms. Recognizing the full extent of this process requires in-depth historical analyses that often involve the systematic collection of protest event data using national and subnational news sources.

Organizations Matter: Why States and Churches Provide the Social Networks for Peasant Mobilization

A second important lesson is that the state and religious institutions play a crucial role in developing the social networks and the organizational infrastructure for the collective action of the rural poor. Unlike in the developed world, where class cleavages are clearly delineated and class identities often serve as a basis for collective action, weak class cleavages in the developing world are seldom sufficient for the aggregation of individuals into groups. In the vast informal sectors of the developing world states and religious institutions, rather than class-based organizations, often play a crucial role in the development of poor people's organizations. States organize the poor because they want votes—particularly in electoral autocracies. As scholars in political science have shown, the poor are the single group most likely to engage in clientelistic relations (Stokes et al. 2013). And churches and religious institutions organize the poor because they want to secure their allegiance. As sociologists of religion have shown, the poor are the primary target for religious reconversion (Norris and Inglehart 2004).

One of the most influential arguments about the major wave of rural indigenous mobilization that took place in Latin America in the last quarter of the twentieth century is that the state corporatist rural unions that authoritarian regimes developed to control the countryside eventually served as the organizational vehicles for the rise of independent indigenous movements. Drawing from in-depth case studies, Yashar (2005) explains that when the states in Bolivia, Ecuador, and Mexico experienced major financial crises and government authorities could no longer continue to use public resources to retain peasant loyalties through clientelistic exchanges, a new generation of leaders seized control over these corporatist unions and turned them into mobilizing vehicles to launch major waves of rural indigenous protest against the marketization of agricultural life and for collective rights.

An alternative argument suggests that churches, rather than states, founded the most enduring social networks for rural indigenous mobilization in Latin America. Trejo (2012) presents extensive quantitative and qualitative evidence showing that rural indigenous protest in Mexico was more intense in areas where the Catholic Church developed Christian base communities (CEBs), economic and social cooperatives, and peasant movements in response to the successful expansion of U.S. mainline Protestant missionaries in the country's most impoverished rural regions. In Trejo's account "the competition for souls" contributed to transform a pro-rich Catholic clergy into progressive institutional actors who became major sponsors of peasant movements for land redistribution.[14]

A wide variety of studies have shown that the grassroots associational networks that the Catholic Church helped develop in some of the most impoverished rural and urban regions in Latin America have persisted through time and have become the social base for some of the most influential progressive movements in the region (Eckstein 1989; Le Bot 1994; Gill 1998; Wood 2003). Because these Catholic-sponsored associational networks have played such a vital role in the mobilization of the poor and have empowered them to resist clientelistic exchanges and engage instead in radical mobilization for material redistribution, it is important to assess in greater detail the structure of these networks. A comparison between socialist (secular) networks and Catholic-sponsored (religious) networks reveals why religious networks can be such a powerful tool for collective mobilization.

Drawing on extensive qualitative interviews, Trejo (2012) provides a reconstruction of the two most common types of network structures that enabled rural indigenous mobilization in Mexico between 1975 and 2000. Figure 34.1 represents the socialist

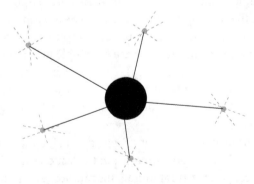

FIGURE 34.1 Socialist Networks in Rural Indigenous Regions in Southern Mexico

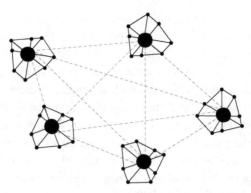

FIGURE 34.2 Catholic Networks in Rural Indigenous Regions in Southern Mexico

networks that served as collective vehicles for peasant mobilization. These were centralized and hierarchical networks where union leaders played a central role (thick dot)
in defining group action but had weak local connections with poorly organized villagers. Defectors from the state-sponsored teachers' and rural unions that had been
created during the era of one-party rule in Mexico led the formation and operation of
these networks.

Figure 34.2 illustrates the structural underpinnings of the Catholic associational
networks that served as the mobilizing vehicles for peasant indigenous mobilization
in Mexico. These were decentralized and horizontal networks with multiple local
leaders who had deep connections to their communities' rich associational lives.
In this figure, catechists played a crucial role (thick dots) as leaders of CEBs—Bible
study groups that gathered 15 to 20 adults in weekly meetings to collectively discuss
their daily lives and their community's economic and political situation in the context
of the Christian gospel. Within their villages, catechists also acted as focal points to
connect different CEBs for the development of social and economic cooperatives for
the provision of public goods and services in their communities. Beyond their villages, catechists became the social entrepreneurs who developed weak and flexible
ties with catechists from other villages and provided the social infrastructure for the
rise of powerful peasant movements for land redistribution and for indigenous rights.

There is extensive evidence from Mexico and Latin America that social movements in which Catholic social networks represent a larger segment of their social
base have been more resilient to state cooptation and coercion than movements that
rely primarily on secular socialist networks. The comparative advantage of the more
resilient movements rests less on religious doctrine and more on the type of social
and political connections that a decentralized network with multiple local leaders
offers. Because local leaders of Catholic decentralized networks are subject to more
effective mechanisms of societal accountability than leaders of centralized networks,
they are less likely to be easily coopted by the state. And because the movement's vitality depends on multiple village leaders, rather than on a single leader, the removal of
one or two of them does not compromise the mobilizing capacity of the group.

Contrary to Marx's ([1844] 1994) famous dictum that "religion is the opium of the people," research about poor people's collective action in the developing world has systematically revealed the Janus-faced nature of religion: it can be a proelite conservative force, but it can also be a major source for the collective mobilization of the poor in favor of economic redistribution (Smith 1996). When U.S. Protestant missionaries have successfully proselytized in Latin America's most impoverished regions, the Catholic Church has experienced a dramatic transformation from a conservative to a progressive actor in favor of the poor. The decentralized and horizontal networks that emerged from these processes have served as one of the most powerful mobilizing vehicles for a wide variety of progressive movements, from peaceful social movements (Santana 1992; Le Bot 1994; and Trejo 2012), to Leftist political parties (Trejo and Bizzarro Neto 2014), and to armed rebel groups (Almeida 2003, 2008; Wood 2003; and Trejo 2012).

While scholars of religion have used ethnographic and qualitative evidence to delineate the structure of religious networks for poor people's movements, an important challenge is to take advantage of the scientific advances in network studies and begin quantifying the ties that bind poor rural parishioners and enable them to be part of major social movements and to participate in major cycles of mobilization. We need to deepen our understanding of the nature of these ties and to explain why these networks are so effective in reshaping ideas, mentalities, and emotions.

Governance and Political Regimes: Why Elite Responses Define the Forms of Peasant Collective Action

A third important lesson is that the political context and the elite responses to social movements and peaceful protest can be a decisive factor in the rise and evolution of cycles of rural protest and in whether peasant movements take a path of violent or nonviolent action. Following scholars of political opportunities and threats in capitalist democracies (Tarrow 1998), students of rural collective action have reconceptualized opportunities and threats in the context of authoritarian regimes. Their central proposition is that when authoritarian elites engage in processes of partial political liberalization by which they introduce government-controlled multiparty elections and grant basic civil rights and liberties, this often gives rise to cycles of peaceful protest. But when authoritarian elites harshly repress movements in the midst of major cycles of peaceful mobilization, this can stimulate the outbreak of major armed insurgencies and civil war.

In his influential study of cycles of mobilization in El Salvador, Almeida (2003, 2008) shows that the partial liberalization of military rule opened a window of opportunity for the organization and mobilization of a wide variety of movements, including poor people's movements in rural and urban areas. After this window closed, these movements had the organizational capacity to remain active in the streets despite renewed authoritarian conditions. However, when military elites tried to contain these movements through indiscriminate lethal repression, peasant movements went underground and launched a civil war. Brockett's (2005) important analysis of collective action in Guatemala also shows that cycles of rural and urban protest and the radicalization of social movements was closely associated with the partial liberalization followed by the punitive autocratization of the country's military regime.[15]

Finally, Trejo's (2012, 2014) work on rural indigenous protest in Mexico shows that the partial liberalization of authoritarian controls and the introduction of government-controlled multiparty elections gave rise to a major cycle of rural indigenous protest in which Leftist opposition parties and Catholic-sponsored rural indigenous movements created powerful socioelectoral coalitions to peacefully advance their causes in the street and through the ballot box. Yet the sudden and punitive reversion of this political liberalization process in southern states—where peasant movements and their Leftist allies opposed the liberalization of land tenure and the end of six decades of land reform—led to the radicalization of rural indigenous movements and to the outbreak of armed insurgency. Radical religious doctrines did not lead members of Catholic-sponsored peasant movements to go underground; rather, it was the punitive governance strategy that subnational elites adopted. Where local elites adopted compensatory measures in favor of poor rural households, members of Catholic rural movements did not take up arms.

A growing cross-national literature has shown that elite reactions to mobilization from below in semiauthoritarian regimes can define the intensity and type of collective action (Hegre et al. 2001; Goldstone et al. 2005). Both the cross-national and subnational analyses suggest that when elites seek to manage protest by means of partial material concessions (carrots) and targeted repression (sticks), the street becomes a major arena for policy negotiation. But when they react to growing protest by eliminating rights they had previously conceded and engage in indiscriminate repression, protestors will more likely go underground and take up arms.

One of the greatest challenges in the study of poor people's collective action is to determine whether political elites are more sensitive to poor people's movements and are more likely to withdraw rights previously granted to them as compared to rights granted to middle- and upper-class opposition groups. Future studies of elite reactions to peaceful cycles of protest should try to understand whether political elites in unequal societies are particularly sensitive to poor people's movements.

Solving the Protest-Repression Puzzle: Why Social Networks Enable Peasant Mobilization in the Face of Repression

While the motivations that lead political elites to co-opt or repress movements from below remain partially unknown, we have made important progress in explaining the structural conditions that enable dissident movements to protest despite state repression. The main intuition comes from social network analysis and suggests that the impact of state repression on the collective action capacity of groups is conditional on the structure of social networks. Whereas social movements organized as centralized and hierarchical networks are more vulnerable to state repression—for instance, the removal of a movement's leader compromises the collective action capacity of the group—movements organized as decentralized and horizontal networks with multiple local leaders are less likely to succumb to state repression—for instance, the removal of one or two leaders does not undermine group action.

Using computational simulation models, Siegel (2011) provides the most general statement of the conditional effect of repression on protest and suggests that individuals who belong to "small world" networks are better equipped to resist state repression. Based on a comparative study of nonviolent movements in Southeast Asia and Africa, Schock (2005) provides important qualitative support for this proposition and shows that decentralized and horizontal movements in the Philippines and South Africa proved more resilient to state repression than those in Burma and China. Trejo's (2012) qualitative evidence previously summarized in Figures 34.1 and 34.2 shows that horizontal and decentralized Catholic social networks with multiple local leaders in Mexico allowed peasant movements to resist state cooptation or repression. These religious networks also served as the basis for recruitment of poor Mayan indigenous communities into the EZLN.

These general theoretical propositions and empirical findings showing the mediating impact of social networks on the ability of social movements to resist state repression have important implications for our understanding of peasant and poor people's movements. If the structural nature of social networks is the key factor that distinguishes resilient from weak movements, then financial or military resources may not be the most important organizational factors for the mobilization of the poor. Rather, *the quality of social connections may be the most important source of power for poor people's movements.*

Explaining how social networks can empower poor people's movements to confront state cooptation and repression is one important example of how meso-level structures (e.g., social networks) can be an important mechanism that connects macroprocesses (e.g., regimes and state repression) with microdecisions (e.g., individual-level risk assessment and decision to protest or rebel). While the moral economy approach would suggest that exogenous challenges to a community's moral economy can transform peasants from risk aversion to risk acceptance, a network approach would suggest that such a transformation would only take place under specific types of network structures that we need to explain rather than assume.

Economic and Political Consequences of Peasant Mobilization

A final question that we must ask is whether peasant movements make a difference for poor peasants and their communities. Do the rural poor affect their well-being when they successfully engage in direct political action and try to overcome their condition of destitution by means of protest, rebellion, or revolution? In their seminal work, Piven and Cloward (1979) suggest that the success of poor people's movements in the United States depends on their capacity for disruption. If we translate this question from the U.S. context to the peasant world, we must ask: Do peasant armed rebellions generate greater individual and social benefits than peaceful collective action?

The literature on peasant studies has focused on the impact of peasant collective action on land redistribution. But we do not have definite answers. While we know that peasant mobilization is associated with greater land redistribution, we do not know whether peaceful protest or armed rebellion is more effective.

A number of recent studies provide evidence of the association between armed rebellions and land redistribution. Based on a new data set on the geography of rebellion during the 1910 Mexican Revolution, Dell (2014) reports the causal impact of armed insurgent activity on land redistribution in the following two decades. Albertus and his colleagues (2013) also find a positive association between armed rebellions and land redistribution in postrevolutionary Mexico. Van der Haar (2005) shows that although the 1992 constitutional reform had put an end to land reform in Mexico, the 1994 Zapatista uprising led to a new postreform wave of land redistribution in the Lacandón rainforest in eastern Chiapas. Wood's (2003) ethnographic work presents evidence of a de facto wave of land redistribution during El Salvador's civil war and of a de jure wave of redistribution after the war. As a cautionary note, however, I should highlight that in his important cross-national analysis of land redistribution in twentieth-century Latin America, Albertus (2014) only finds partial evidence of a positive association between armed insurgencies and land redistribution.

A series of studies of peaceful rural protest find a meaningful association between rural mobilization and land redistribution. Trejo (2012) presents extensive evidence of the endogenous association between protest and land redistribution in the southern state of Chiapas, Mexico, during the two decades prior to the 1994 neo-Zapatista rebellion. Almeida's (2008) work suggests that a major wave of peasant mobilization led to a limited land reform program in El Salvador in the 1970s. Finally, an extensive literature on the Landless Workers' Movement in Brazil shows that the combination of mass mobilization, land occupation, and legal action has made land reform a national issue and has resulted in a piecemeal process of de facto land redistribution to individual households (Ondetti 2008; Wright and Wolford 2003).

Beyond land redistribution, scholars have found that peasant mobilization can have a major impact on the democratization of authoritarian regimes. This is a surprising finding because scholars of comparative political sociology have traditionally associated democratization with the expansion of the industrial bourgeoisie (Moore [1966] 1993), the middle class (Lipset [1960] 1981), and the working class (Rueschmeyer, Stephens, and Stephens 1992; Acemoglu and Robinson 2006) but not with rural collective action. In fact, the political action of rural actors has been associated with the rise of right-wing dictatorship (landowners) or with communist dictatorship (peasants).

Wood's (2000) pioneering comparison of democratization in El Salvador and South Africa suggests that rural mobilization from below can lead to major changes in the political preferences of economic elites. In El Salvador the major peasant uprising and the losses incurred during a decade of civil war led landed and economic elites to consent to the country's democratization. In his influential work on Central America, Lechoucq (2012) suggests that violent rural mobilizations from below also prompted the democratization of Costa Rica, Nicaragua, and Guatemala. In a similar line, Trejo (2012) argues that the 1994 Zapatista uprising and its transformation from a peasant movement demanding land redistribution into a self-determination movement demanding autonomy rights for the country's 65 ethno-linguistic indigenous minorities led Mexico's authoritarian elites to relinquish government controls over elections and to consent to an independent electoral commission to organize free and fair elections. In the Mexican case, Trevizo (2011) offers an alternative narrative in which peasant movements—along with student, urban, workers, and other movements—played a key role in every step of the country's protracted transition to democracy. Rather than assume the antidemocratic nature of rural collective action—as the comparative politics literature has done for decades—these findings suggest that we must inquire about the conditions under which peasant movements can actually become proto-democratic actors.

Peasant Mobilization and Poor People's Movements in the Developing World

Most of the scholarly literature about poverty in the developing world has focused on the policies that governments and the international community adopt to assist the poor in overcoming their condition of destitution. But there is little agency left for the poor in these analyses; in fact, the possibility that the poor may be agents of their own destiny is often simply ignored or grossly underestimated. To the extent that the poor appear as active agents in the scholarly literature, it is as clients involved in vast networks of vote- buying. While these images of the poor as passive recipients or as clients do reflect the realities of the majority of the poor in the developing world, this chapter has tried to underscore a less common but significantly important reality of the poor as collective actors engaged in direct political action to overcome their situation of destitution.

Focusing on poor rural households and on peasant collective action in the developing world, I have analyzed classic and contemporary studies about the motivations that drive the rural poor to act collectively, the social vehicles that enable such actions, and the governance strategies that political elites adopt in response to poor people's movements. The theoretical propositions and empirical findings about peasant collective action can provide important lessons for a more general understanding of the mobilizing capacity of the poor in the developing world. Here are some lessons and ideas for further research in three areas: motivations, social networks, and governance.

Motivations

As I have emphasized in this review, a closer exploration of the motivation of minimizing losses—rather than maximizing gains—is a prominent area of research for the study of poor people's movements. In fact, some of the most important scholarly works about motivations for poor people's action include a wide variety of social mechanisms that could be subsumed under the more general category of actors seeking to minimize losses. The moral economy approach and the powerful idea that a "subsistence ethic" guides peasant collective action are a clear example of actors seeking to minimize loses rather than maximize gains. When peasants act collectively to demand that populist states honor their commitment to continue redistributing land and providing subsidies to poor agricultural producers, their actions are intended to safeguard policies that have functioned as instruments for survival. Peasants also minimize losses when they act collectively to defend what they consider to be "subsistence goods" or "subsistence resources" or when they act to defend rights that they consider to be fundamental for their own individual or group self-preservation.

As proponents of prospect theory have suggested, a closer attention to the framing processes by which goods, resources, and rights become socially accepted as essential for survival or self-preservation is an important area of inquiry.[16] In exploring these processes, however, we should be mindful that the goal of minimizing losses encompasses only one of many types of goals that can drive the poor to act collectively. As several authors studying armed insurgencies have noted, there are multiple motivations driving the poor toward contentious collective action.

Social Networks

In line with recent developments in theories of collective action and social movements, this review has put a strong emphasis on the crucial mediating role that social networks can have in determining the resilience of poor people's movements. I have paid special attention to the role religion can play in the creation of social networks and suggested that the spread of U.S. mainline Protestant churches and the competition for souls in Latin America's most impoverished regions moved Catholic bishops and priests to become major promoters of poor people's associational networks and movements for economic redistribution. A significant number of studies has recently recognized the important role that religious institutions can play in the provision of public goods and social services for the poor, particularly in areas where religious actors are in conflict with the state.[17]

In contrast to a long line of reasoning dating back to the Enlightenment and nineteenth-century Marxism, which suggests that religion reinforces rather than undermines the structural conditions for the perpetuation of poverty, a new scholarly literature shows that clerical actors can become major promoters of poor people's movements when the state or other churches threaten their institutional self-preservation. While states, political parties, and unions can play an important organizing role for the poor, I have tried to underscore the important and often underestimated role that religion can play in the creation of the social infrastructure for poor people's movements. Understanding how different religious traditions have influenced the ability of the poor to engage in direct political action is a major scholarly avenue for future research.

Governance

Following the literature on repression studies, I have strongly suggested in this review that the state's reaction to poor people's movements can play a crucial role in determining the intensity of social mobilization and whether these movements adopt violent or nonviolent courses of action. A number of studies have underscored the importance of political regimes in defining elite governance strategies and have tried to explain why elites in hybrid political regimes—electoral autocracies—more commonly engage in erratic governing behavior, including the expansion and sudden retraction of important rights, thus stimulating movement radicalization. While the study of political regimes and institutions can provide us with important indications of rulers' behavior, future research should pay closer attention to how elites decide whether a movement from below represents a major threat to their hold on power. A closer look at how income and wealth inequalities among social classes and ethnic groups can shape elite responses to social mobilization would increase our ability to understand the dynamics of poor people's movements in the developing world.

NOTES

1. I am grateful to David Brady and Linda Burton for insightful suggestions and to Caroline Domingo for her editorial work. Errors and omissions remain my own.
2. Easterly (2007) provides a critical assessment of this literature relating to why the poor are portrayed as passive recipients of foreign aid from the international community. For influential overviews of conditional cash transfer programs see Díaz-Cayeros, Estévez, and Magaloni (2012) and De La O (2013).
3. Stokes et al. (2013) provide the most comprehensive view of the mechanics of clientelism.
4. Note that I exclude from the discussion those rural households with access to land who are able to sell a large portion of their product and are well above the poverty line.
5. For influential discussions of these challenges in analytic sociology, see Hedstrom and Swedberg (1998), and in political science, see Della Porta (1995).

6. Rural collective action in the developing world often involves peasants traveling from the mountains and the countryside into their country's most proximate urban centers to engage in street protest.

7. For the classic statement, see Kahneman and Tversky (1979). For an early discussion of revolutionary collective action in terms of prospect theory, see Berejikin (1992).

8. While Collier and his colleagues developed the argument that opportunities for looting natural resources lead poor young men to join armed insurgencies, Fearon and Laitin (2003) were the first ones to emphasize that failed states facilitate the expansion of criminal gangs and armed rebel groups.

9. For the initial formulation of the concept of "rightful resistance," see O'Brien's (1996) important work on rural protest in China.

10. This is an assumption shared by rational choice and structuralist theorists. See Lichbach (1996) and McAdam, McCarthy, and Zald (1996). For a critique of this assumption, see Goodwin and Jasper (2004).

11. For the concept of "modular collective action," see Tarrow (1998).

12. Inclán (2009) uses the concept of cycles of protest to explain a new major wave of Zapatista protest while peace negotiations between the federal government and the EZLN were underway.

13. For an influential discussion of the need to establish theoretical and analytical linkages between the study of social movements and civil war, see Tarrow (2007).

14. Note, however, that the spread of neo-Pentecostal and charismatic churches has motivated a different type of Catholic pastoral action: the Catholic charismatic renewal movement. Unlike liberation and indigenous theologies, Catholic charismatic movements do not address questions of material redistribution or engage in the organization of social movements. Instead, they focus on individual spiritual healing and salvation.

15. For a more extensive elaboration of this narrative, see the important work of Lehoucq (2012).

16. The study of "framing" processes in social movement theory can serve as an important guide for inquiry. See Zald (1996).

17. See van Kersbergen and Manow (2009) for a reassessment of the role religion played in the rise of the welfare state in Western Europe. See also Cammett and McLean's (2011) pioneering work on the impact of religion on the provision of social services in the Global South.

REFERENCES

Acemoglu, Daren and J. A. Robinson. 2006. *Economic Origins of Dictatorship and Democracy*. Cambridge: Cambridge University Press.

Albertus, Michael. 2014. *Autocracy and Redistribution: The Politics of Land*. Unpublished Manuscript, University of Chicago.

Albertus, Michael. A. Díaz-Cayeros, B. Magaloni, and B. Weingast. 2013. "Authoritarian Survival and Poverty Traps: Land Reform in Mexico." Typescript, Stanford University.

Almeida, Paul. 2003. "Opportunity, Organizations, and Threat-Induced Contention: Protest Waves in Authoritarian Settings." *American Journal of Sociology* 109(2):345–400.

Almeida, Paul. 2008. *Waves of Protest: Popular Struggle in El Salvador, 1925–2005*. Minneapolis: University of Minnesota Press.

Auyero, Javier. 2004. "The Moral Politics of the Argentine Crowd." *Mobilization* 9(3):311–27.

Berejikin, Jeffrey. 1992. "Revolutionary Collective Action and the Agent-Structure Problem." *American Political Science Review* 86(3):647–57.

Boix, Carles. 2008. "Economic Roots of Civil War and Revolution in the Modern World." *World Politics* 60(3):390–437.

Bowles, Sam. 2008. "Policies Designed for Self-Interested Citizens May Undermine the 'Moral Sentiments': Evidence from Economic Experiments." *Science* 320:1605–09.

Brockett, Charles D. 2005. *Political Movements and Violence in Central America*. Cambridge: Cambridge University Press.

Cammett, Melani and L. McLean. 2011. "The Political Consequences of Non-State Social Welfare in the Global South." *Studies in International Comparative Development* 46(1):1–21.

Collier, Paul. 2000. "Rebellion as a Quasi-Criminal Activity." *Journal of Conflict Resolution* 44(6):839–53.

Collier, Paul, V. L. Elliot, H. Hegre, A. Hoeffler, M. Reynal-Querol, and N. Sambanis. 2005. *Breaking the Conflict Trap: Civil War and Development Policy*. Washington DC: World Bank.

De La O, Ana. 2013. "Do Conditional Cash Transfers Affect Electoral Behavior? Evidence from a Randomized Experiment in Mexico." *American Journal of Political Science* 57(1):1–14.

Dell, Melissa. 2014. "Path Dependence in Development: Evidence from the Mexican Revolution." Typescript, Harvard University.

Della Porta, Donatella. 1995. *Social Movements, Political Violence, and the State: A Comparative Analysis of Italy and Germany*. Cambridge: Cambridge University Press.

Díaz-Cayeros, Alberto, F. Estévez, and B. Magaloni. 2012. "Strategies of Vote-Buying: Poverty, Democracy and Social Transfers in Mexico." Unpublished Manuscript, Stanford University.

Easterly, William. 2007. *The White Man's Burden: Why the West's Efforts to Aid the Rest Have Done So Much Ill and So Little Good*. New York: Penguin Books.

Eckstein, Susan. 1989. *Power and Popular Protest: Latin American Social Movements*. Berkeley: University of California Press.

Edelman, Marc. 2005. "Bringing the Moral Economy back in . . . to the Study of 21st-Century Transnational Peasant Movements." *American Anthropologist* 107(3):331–45.

Fearon, James and D. Laitin. 2003. "Insurgency, Ethnicity and Civil War." *American Political Science Review* 97(1):75–90.

Gill, Anthony. 1998. *Rendering unto Caesar: The Catholic Church and the State in Latin America*. Chicago: University of Chicago Press.

Gilly, Adolfo. 1998. *Chiapas: La razón ardiente. Ensayo sobre la rebelión del mundo encantado*. Mexico City: Era.

Goodwin, Jeff and J. Jasper, eds. 2004. *Rethinking Social Movements: Structure, Meaning, and Emotion*. Lanham: Rowman and Littlefield.

Gurr, Ted. R. 1970. *Why Men Rebel*. Princeton, NJ: Princeton University Press.

Gurr, Ted. R. 1993. *Minorities at Risk: A Global View of Ethnopolitical Conflicts*. Washington DC: United States Institute of Peace Press.

Hedstrom, Peter and R. Swedberg, eds. 1998. *Social Mechanisms: An Analytic Approach to Social Theory*. Cambridge: Cambridge University Press.

Hegre, Havard, T. Ellingsen, S. Gates, and N. P. Gleditsch. 2001. "Toward a Democratic Civil Peace? Democracy, Political Change, and Civil War, 1816–1992." *American Political Science Review* 95(1):33–48.

Humphreys, Macartan and J. Weinstein. 2008. "Who Fights? The Determinants of Participation in Civil War." *American Journal of Political Science* 52(2):436–55.

Inclán, María. 2009. "Sliding Doors of Opportunity: Zapatistas and Their Cycle of Protest." *Mobilization* 14(1):85–106.

Kahneman, Daniel and A. Tversky. 1979. "Prospect Theory: An Analysis of Decision Under Risk." *Econometrica* 47(2):263–91.

Kalyvas, Stathis. 2006. *The Logic of Violence in Civil War.* Cambridge: Cambridge University Press.

Le Bot, Yvon. 1994. *Violence de la modernité en Amérique Latine. Indianité, société et pouvoir.* Paris: Karthala.

Lehoucq, Frabrice. 2012. *The Politics of Modern Central America.* Cambridge: Cambridge University Press.

Lichbach, Mark. 1987. "Deterrence or Escalation? The Puzzle of Aggregate Studies of Repression and Dissent." *Journal of Conflict Resolution* 31(2):266–97.

Lichbach, Mark. 1996. *The Rebel's Dilemma.* Ann Arbor: Michigan University Press.

Lipset, Seymour M. [1960] 1981. *Political Man: The Social Bases of Politics.* Baltimore, MD: Johns Hopkins University Press.

Marx, Karl. [1844] 1994. "Critique of Hegel's Philosophy of Right." In *Marx: Early Political Writings,* edited by J. O'Malley. Cambridge: Cambridge University Press.

Mattiace, Shannan. 2003. *To See with Two Eyes: Peasant Activism and Indian Autonomy in Chiapas, Mexico.* Albuquerque: University of New Mexico Press.

McAdam, Doug, J. McCarthy, and M. N. Zald. 1996. "Introduction: Opportunities, Mobilizing Structures, and Framing Processes—Toward a Synthetic, Comparative Perspective on Social Movements." In *Comparative Perspectives on Social Movements,* edited by D. McAdam, J. McCarthy, and M. Zald. Cambridge: Cambridge University Press.

Moore Jr., Barrington. [1966] 1993. *Social Origins of Dictatorship and Democracy: Lord and Peasant in the Making of the Modern World.* Boston: Beacon Press.

Muller, Edward and M. Seligson. 1987. "Inequality and Insurgency." *American Political Science Review* 81(2):425–52.

Nash, June. 2001. *Mayan Visions: The Quest for Autonomy in an Age of Globalization.* New York: Routledge.

Norris, Pipa and R. Inglehart. 2004. *Sacred and Secular: Religion and Politics Worldwide.* Cambridge: Cambridge University Press.

O'Brien, Kevin. 1996. "Rightful Resistance." *World Politics* 49(1):31–55.

Olson, Mancur. 1966. *The Logic of Collective Action: Public Goods and the Theory of Groups.* Cambridge, MA: Harvard University Press.

Ondetti, Gabriel. 2008. *Land, Protest, and Politics: The Landless Movement and the Struggle for Agrarian Reform in Brazil.* University Park: Pennsylvania University Press.

Pallares, Amalia. 2002. *From Peasant Struggles to Indian Resistance: The Ecuadorean Andes in the Late Twentieth Century.* Norman: University of Oklahoma Press.

Piven, Frances Fox and R. Cloward. 1979. *Poor People's Movements: Why They Succeed, How They Fail.* New York: Vintage Books.

Popkin, Samuel. 1979. *The Rational Peasant: The Political Economy of Rural Society in Vietnam.* Berkeley: California University Press.

Rice, Roberta. 2012. *The New Politics of Protest: Indigenous Mobilization in Latin America's Neoliberal Era.* Arizona: University of Arizona Press.

Rueschmeyer, Dietrich, E. Huber Stephens, and J. Stephens. 1992. *Capitalist Development and Democracy*. Chicago: University of Chicago Press.

Sambanis, Nicholas and A. Zinn. 2006. "From Protest to Violence: Conflict Escalation in Self-Determination Movements." Typescript, Yale University.

Santana, Roberto. 1992. *Les Indiens d'Equateur, citoyens dans l'ethnicité?* Paris: CNRS.

Schock, Kurt. 2005. *Unarmed Insurrections: People Power Movements in Nondemocracies*. Minneapolis: University of Minnesota Press.

Scott, James. 1977. *The Moral Economy of the Peasant: Rebellion and Subsistence in Southeast Asia*. New Haven, CT: Yale University Press.

Sen, Amartya. 1999. *Development as Freedom*. Oxford: Oxford University Press.

Siegel, David. 2011. "When Does Repression Work? Collective Action and Social Networks." *Journal of Politics* 73(4):993–1010.

Simmons, Erica. 2012. "Markets, Movements, and Meaning: Subsistence Resources and Political Protest in Mexico and Bolivia." PhD dissertation, University of Chicago.

Smith, Christian. 1996. "Correcting a Curious Neglect, or Bringing Religion Back In." In *Disruptive Religion: The Force of Faith in Social Movement Activism*, edited by Christian Smith. New York: Routledge.

Smith, Christian. 1998. *Power in Movement*. Cambridge: Cambridge University Press.

Stokes, Susan, Thad Dunning, Marcelo Nazareno, and Valeria Brusco. 2013. *Brokers, Voters, and Clientelism: The Puzzle of Distributive Politics*. Cambridge: Cambridge University Press.

Tarrow, Sidney. 1989. *Democracy and Disorder: Social Conflict, Political Protest and Democracy in Italy, 1965–1975*. New York: Oxford University Press.

Tarrow, Sidney. 2007. "Inside Insurgencies: Politics and Violence in an Age of Civil War." *Perspectives on Politics* 5(3):587–600.

Thompson, Edward P. 1963. *The Making of the English Working Class*. London: Penguin.

Thompson, Edward P. 1971. "The Moral Economy of the English Crowd in the Eighteenth Century." *Past and Present* 50:76–136.

Trejo, Guillermo. 2012. *Popular Movements in Autocracies: Religion, Repression, and Indigenous Collective Action in Mexico*. Cambridge: Cambridge University Press.

Trejo, Guillermo. 2014. "The Ballot and the Street: An Electoral Theory of Social Protest in Autocracies." *Perspectives on Politics* 12(2):332–52.

Trejo, Guillermo and F. Bizzarro Neto. 2014. "Religious Competition and the Rise of the Workers' Party in Brazil." Typescript, University of Notre Dame.

Trevizo, Dolores. 2011. *Rural Protest and the Making of Democracy in Mexico, 1968–2000*. University Park: Pennsylvania University Press.

Van Cott, Donna L. 2000. *The Friendly Liquidation of the Past: The Politics of Diversity in Latin America*. Pittsburgh: Pittsburgh University Press.

Van Der Haar, Gemma. 2005. "Land Reform, the State, and the Zapatista Uprising." *Journal of Peasant Studies* 32(3–4):484–507.

Van Kersbergen, Kees and P. Manow, eds. 2009. *Religion, Class Coalitions, and Welfare States*. Cambridge: Cambridge University Press.

Viterna, Jocelyn. 2013. *Women in War: The Micro-Processes of Mobilization in El Salvador*. Oxford: Oxford University Press.

Womack Jr., John. 1970. *Emiliano Zapata and the Mexican Revolution*. New York: Vintage Books.

World Bank. 2008. *World Development Report*. Washington DC: World Bank.

World Bank. 2012. *World Bank Development Indicators: Rural Environment and Land Use*. Washington DC: World Bank.

Wood, Elisabeth. 2000. *Forging Democracy from Below: Insurgent Transitions in Southern Africa and El Salvador*. Cambridge: Cambridge University Press.

Wood, Elisabeth, J. 2003. *Insurgent Collective Action and Civil War in El Salvador*. Cambridge: Cambridge University Press.

Wright, Angus and W. Wolford. 2003. *To Inherit the Earth: The Landless Movement and the Struggle for a New Brazil*. Oakland: Food First Books.

Zald, Mayer. 1996. "Culture, Ideology, and Strategic Framing." In *Comparative Perspectives on Social Movements*, edited by D. McAdam, J. McCarthy, and M. Zald. Cambridge: Cambridge University Press.

Yashar, Deborah. 2005. *Contesting Citizenship in Latin America: The Rise of Indigenous Movements and the Post-Liberal Challenge*. Cambridge: Cambridge University Press.

CHAPTER 35

··

UNIONS AND POVERTY

··

JAKE ROSENFELD AND JENNIFER LAIRD

ARNOLD Mayer was vice president of the United Food and Commercial Workers International Union (UFCW), a powerful U.S.-based organization that once claimed nearly 1.5 million dues-paying members. He was also a fierce advocate for the federal food stamp program—a targeted government-transfer policy limited to near-poor and very poor individuals. Why? As he described it, "We feel we have a responsibility to end hunger. . . . And the program does create jobs for our members. In the inner cities, they could not maintain food stores without food stamps. There is an ideological interest for us and a self-interest" (Boyarsky, 1981).

In many cases, across disparate institutional environments, we see labor unions acting to curtail poverty—despite the fact that, in the advanced economies at least, very few union members are actually poor. As Mayer so succinctly summarized it, unions' antipoverty efforts derive from a combination of normative and more self-interested motivations. In this chapter we survey the available research about union efforts on behalf of the poor. Are they effective? If so, how? And in those contexts in which unions do reduce poverty levels, what types of institutional arrangements predominate? To answer these questions, we begin our survey in the United States and then move to comparative research on other advanced economies, paying particular attention to Europe. We end by investigating the relatively scant literature on unions and poverty in the developing world.

Ours is the first comprehensive survey of research on unions and poverty. We systematize the available evidence not only by geography but also according to whether the research focuses on indirect or direct linkages between organized labor and poverty. Lobbying the government to maintain funding for an antipoverty program such as food stamps represents an *indirect* effect of unions on poverty. Fighting to expand health insurance coverage for the elderly and raising the minimum wage are other indirect pathways that unions have undertaken on behalf of the poor, and we cover those policy battles below. But as we'll highlight, outside the policy realm unions have combated poverty *directly* as well, for example by increasing the wages of members in certain low-paying occupations above the poverty threshold.

Much of the scholarly evidence on the topic fails to delineate the specific mechanisms connecting unionization rates with levels of economic disadvantage. We illuminate these connections by highlighting examples from the historical record—examples such as Arnold Mayer's efforts to salvage funding for food stamps some three decades ago. Finally, we anchor each of our three sections with a picture based on the most recent data that captures the bivariate relationship between poverty and unionization. These pictures help guide us through the existing research and help reveal where gaps remain in our knowledge about organized labor and poverty throughout the world.

1 UNIONS AND POVERTY IN THE UNITED STATES

The federally financed food stamp program (renamed the Supplemental Nutrition Assistance Program, or SNAP, in 2008) is administered by the Department of Agriculture and provides food coupons to millions of Americans with low or no incomes. Given its means-tested nature, the program lacks a powerful supporting constituency. Lawmakers have repeatedly attacked the program as overly generous and in need of reform. The 1981 budget battle proved no exception, with many politicians eager to rollback financing for food stamps. What some of these politicians—especially those new to Washington, DC—may not have anticipated was the staunch defense of food stamps and other antipoverty programs by key segments of the labor movement. After all, unions rarely represented workers earning poverty-level wages. But defend it they did, repeatedly, during decades of attacks from budget-cutting politicians. During the mid-1970s, for example, organized labor took to the courts to fight for the program's solvency: More than 50 labor unions joined various other organizations and sued the federal government over proposed cuts to food stamps. Half a decade later, unions would threaten court action again. Organized labor's efforts to support food assistance for the disadvantaged, then, represent one avenue through which U.S.-based unions fought against poverty.

In the remainder of this section we analyze the available evidence and systematize the existing scholarly work according to whether it focuses on indirect or direct influences of unions on poverty in the United States. We begin by focusing on indirect effects, largely political in nature, with some efforts proving more successful than others. As we'll demonstrate, organized labor's lobbying on behalf of the food stamp program represents just one of many examples of unions fighting for the poor. We end the section with a snapshot of the relationship between state-level unionization rates and relative poverty in the contemporary United States, as well as an in-depth examination of the most comprehensive quantitative investigation on unions and poverty in the United States to date.

Unions' political efforts on behalf of the poor in America go back well over half a century. According to the labor historian Nelson Lichtenstein, "By the mid-twentieth century, unions also had become important partners in the welfare state and proponents of social policies that promote economic security" (2004:717). In the mid-1960s, longtime labor and civil rights leader A. Philip Randolph along with mentee Bayard Rustin produced "The Freedom Budget," a plan that called on the federal government to expand its investments in "income support, housing, health care, transportation, and urban renewal" (Chappell, 2010:26). George Meany, president of the American Federation of Labor-Congress of Industrial Organizations (AFL-CIO) between 1955 and 1979, called on the federal government to invest in many of the programs outlined in the Freedom Budget. And while the Freedom Budget was a comprehensive proposal meant to pressure lawmakers to take a wide-ranging approach to fighting poverty, many union efforts targeted specific issues.

Take health care: In the United States major labor unions fought to establish a universal, government-run health insurance program. By the 1950s, as labor historian Alan Derickson claims, "labor stood out as virtually the only remaining champion of universal, comprehensive insurance legislation" (1994:1333–34). Derickson argues that to understand the initial rise of universal coverage initiatives in the United States "requires attention to labor, which early on held this to be a cardinal principle" (p. 1334).[1] Ultimately, unions would scale back their ambition after Congress repeatedly failed to pass a universal coverage program, and as unions adjusted to an increasingly disadvantageous organizing context in which offering fringe benefits proved one of union's most powerful—and remaining—incentives to offer potential recruits and retain existing members (Quadagno, 2006: Chapter 2). In the wake of universal coverage, many unions put their political muscle behind passage of Medicare, a program providing health care insurance to seniors. This struggle would succeed in 1965 when President Lyndon Johnson signed Medicare into law. Prior to the program's implementation, nearly half of all elderly Americans lacked health insurance.

A common figure behind many of these political initiatives was the long-standing leader of the United Auto Workers (UAW) Walter Reuther. Reuther believed that union members had a "special responsibility" to assist those "who had been left behind" (Chappell, 2010:26). And by the 1960s, Reuther had leveraged his union's tremendous financial and organizational power into extraordinary political access—especially to President Johnson. According to the historian Kevin Boyle, between November 1963 and November 1964, "Reuther spoke to Johnson by phone or met with him privately well over a dozen times" (1998:192). In Reuther the president found a loyal soldier fighting on behalf of Johnson's War on Poverty programs, with the labor leader promising Johnson that "you can count on us as you lead America into battle against poverty and want" (Boyle, 1998:188).

Reuther's efforts extended beyond supporting the president's initiatives. In 1966, for example, in concert with civil rights organizations and church groups, the labor leader founded the Citizens' Crusade Against Poverty (CCAP), an organization designed to spotlight the problem of food insecurity among the nation's poor. Together with the

Field Foundation, the CCAP comprised "the core of the 'hunger lobby' in the U.S." (DeVault and Pitts, 1984:551). Reuther's CCAP publicized the plight of poor Americans in the South in particular and coordinated with politicians such as then-Senator Robert Kennedy to investigate the extent of malnutrition in states such as Mississippi. The organization, later renamed the Citizens' Board of Inquiry, produced *Hunger, U.S.A.*, a document detailing the "failures of federal policy" in eliminating food insecurity among the nation's poor (Rosenfeld, 2010b:481). The publication helped spur "America's most recent rediscovery of hunger" and pushed politicians to do more to assist Americans suffering from malnutrition (Brown, 1970:116).

Other union-led policy efforts to reduce poverty predate Reuther's leadership. In the summer of 1945 William Green, president of the American Federation of Labor (AFL), lobbied Congress to raise the nation's minimum wage to 72 cents an hour (*New York Times,* 1945). Three decades later George Meany castigated President Jimmy Carter for failing to accede to union demands to increase the minimum wage to $3 per hour. Meany claimed the administration's intransigence on the issue was "a bitter disappointment to everyone who looked to this Administration for economic justice for the poor" (Shabecoff, 1977:48). The overwhelming majority of unionists earned more than the minimum wage, so why did union leaders repeatedly lobby for increasing wage floors? Here too we see the intermingling of normative and self-interested concerns. As Meany voiced it, economic justice for the poor remained a core goal of the labor movement. Left unsaid was a self-interested motivation: establishing a high wage floor helped protect unionized employers from being undercut by nonunion competitors.

In more recent years, many local jurisdictions in the United States have passed "living wage" ordinances, and, similar to minimum wage laws, unions have often been vital supporters of these initiatives. Living-wage ordinances establish a wage floor at a level that covers a worker's daily living expenses. This level is usually significantly higher than the prevailing minimum wage. In the United States, living-wage ordinances usually cover only those businesses that contract with the government or receive government assistance. In the mid-1990s, the American Federation of State, County, and Municipal Employees (AFSCME) teamed up with local civic groups in Baltimore to press the city to require firms that received government subsidies to pay a living wage. The effort succeeded, establishing a blueprint for other unions and community organizations to follow across the country.

The fractured nature of the U.S. labor movement guaranteed that not all unions and certainly not all unionists expended effort to help Americans in need. For example, in the summer of 1969, President Nixon proposed his Family Assistance Plan (FAP) that would have replaced various welfare programs—such as food stamps—with guaranteed cash assistance to the poor.[2] Labor support for Nixon's guaranteed income policy came late, and only after unions had secured key concessions that protected members' interests (Quadagno, 1990:21). In general, however, during decades of debates about poverty policies, major figures in the labor movement fought on behalf of the nation's poor.

What unites these political campaigns on behalf of poverty-reducing policies is that they are *indirect* pathways through which unions have affected poverty: Unions lobby lawmakers to pass particular policies that, over time, help reduce poverty levels, either by raising wage floors or by decommidifying certain basic needs, such as health care for the elderly. The mechanisms here are indirect in that the most proximate cause of the reduction in poverty is the policy unions sought to implement. But over the decades unions in the United States have combated poverty *directly* as well.

For example, while many of the industries unions organized during the American labor movement's heyday were relatively high paying, some were not. As Lichtenstein recounts, unions helped double the wage levels in industries as varied as textiles in New England, California canneries, and department stores in the nation's largest cities (2004:719). Prior to their organization, wages for bottom-rung occupations in these industries were extremely low. Likewise, maritime work was once brutal, disorganized, and temporary—until unions successfully signed up thousands of port employees along much of America's coastline. The result was a wholesale transformation of the industry, and a substantial increase in the standard of living for dock workers.

In these industries and others, unions were able to pull thousands of American workers out of poverty directly by negotiating wage and benefit packages that ensured a decent standard of living. The organization of many of these industries occurred generations ago, during the upsurge in unionization that occurred after passage of the National Labor Relations Act (NLRA) in 1935. What about more recent developments? Is there evidence that unions continue to affect poverty directly?

Case studies along with a comprehensive quantitative examination of poverty levels across the United States provide us with a clear answer: Unions in the United States continue to lift low-wage workers above the poverty line. Take workers in the hotel-casino industry in Nevada. Nevada has two cities heavily reliant on gaming tourism for revenue, Las Vegas and Reno. Reno is largely unorganized; Las Vegas has a strong union presence. In his investigation of poverty-level wages in the hotel-casino industry in both cities, the economist C. Jeffrey Waddoups utilizes census microdata with information on key demographic characteristics and an indicator of whether respondents are employed in the hotel-gaming industry. He finds that median wages for gaming tourism occupations, such as front-desk clerks and baggage porters, are 40 percent higher in Las Vegas than in Reno after controlling for other determinants of wages including education, marital status, and relevant demographic information. As he concludes, "There is little doubt that unionization plays a significant role in decreasing the incidence of poverty-level pay in Las Vegas's hotel-casino industry" (Waddoups, 2001:166).

Or take wage levels in the now largely unorganized agricultural industry along the West Coast. Membership in the once-thriving United Farm Workers union (UFW) has declined by over 60 percent from its peak in the 1970s (Wozniacka, 2011). Falling wages have accompanied falling organization rates. In the early 1980s, a unionized field irrigator earned wages well above the poverty level and received substantial benefits. Just a decade later, a nonunion worker doing the same job earned the minimum wage (at the time, $4.25 per hour) and no benefits. Growing competition between U.S.-based agricultural firms and those in Central and South America pressured employers to shed existing unions—and to shed them quickly. This effort proved effective, and living standards among the thousands of disproportionately immigrant field workers have declined precipitously.[3]

Are the examples provided above representative of a broader pattern? In Figure 35.1 we provide a preliminary snapshot of the relationship between household poverty and unionization across all 50 states and the District of Columbia for two time points, 2003–2004 and 2009–2010.[4] Our definition of poverty differs markedly from the

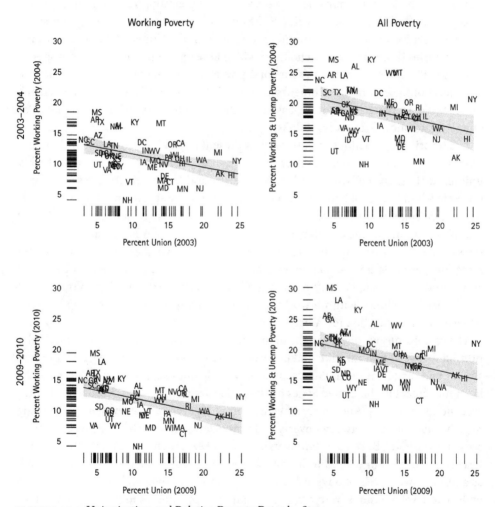

FIGURE 35.1 Unionization and Relative Poverty Rates by State

Notes: Households are considered poor if the household income after government transfers is less than 50 percent of the national median income. Working poor households are those with at least one member who has earned wages or salary during the given survey year. Unemployed poor households are those with no earners during the given survey year. To reduce the influence of outliers, fit lines are estimated using an MM-estimator. Shaded regions represent 95 percent confidence intervals.

Source: State-level union rates come from Hirsh and Macpherson's Unionstates database, based on the CPS. See www. unionstats.com. State-level poverty rates based on household data from the LIS Database, see www.lisdatacenter.org.

U.S. government's absolute poverty thresholds. The official thresholds were first established over a half century ago and have remained largely unadjusted except for inflation.[5] Instead we follow common practice in the comparative poverty literature and employ a relative poverty measure. Our measure defines a household as poor if total household income falls below 50 percent of median national household income. We draw on the Luxembourg Income Study (LIS) for our household poverty data and use the standardized LIS income variable "DPI" (disposable income after taxes and transfers). The DPI measure includes both market income and government transfers, including noncash transfers such as food stamps. Here we are following existing research on the topic, most relevantly David Brady, Regina S. Baker, and Ryan Finnigan's (2013) investigation into relative working poverty and unionization in the United States. Our working poverty series is limited to households in which at least one member earned wages or salary for the given survey year. Our total poverty series makes no such restriction. State-level unionization data come from Barry T. Hirsch and David A. Macpherson's unionstats.com database and are based on the Current Population Survey's (CPS) Outgoing Rotation Group files (ORGs).

The bivariate correlations in both periods present a clear pattern: States with higher unionization rates tend to have lower rates of household poverty. For example, highly unionized states in the Northeast like New Jersey and Connecticut have some of the lowest levels of household poverty. On the other end of the spectrum, Mississippi leads the nation in household poverty in both periods, and the state has one of the lowest unionization rates in the country; only a handful of other southern states have lower rates of labor organization. This broad relationship holds whether we focus on the pre-recession period of 2003–2004, or whether we examine the postrecession period of 2009–2010. And while poverty rates in the "All Poverty" series are higher, given that it includes households with no working members, the negative relationship between poverty and unionization remains.

The correlations we display in the figure are obviously not indicative of a causal relationship between unionization and poverty in the United States. However, all the case studies and historical research presented previously does suggest that for decades the labor movement in the United States has helped lower poverty rates through both indirect and direct routes. And one recent study provides even further evidence of a strong negative relationship between poverty and unionization rates at the state level. In their 2013 article, Brady, Baker, and Finnigan update and expand upon research finding that heavily unionized states tend to have higher levels of government redistribution and, as a result, lower levels of poverty.[6] The authors utilize individual-level LIS data along with state-level measures from a variety of government sources to investigate whether state-level unionization influences working poverty in the United States. Employing a variety of estimation techniques, they find that state-level unionization rates are negatively related to working poverty in 2010, and across the nearly decade-and-a-half between 1991 and 2010. Their models control for a host of individual-level and contextual correlates of poverty, including demographic indicators such as age and race, labor market position variables such as sector, and state-level policy measures such as the state's minimum wage ratio and level of TANF/AFDC (Temporary Assistance for Needy Families and Aid to Families with Dependent Children) funding.[7]

That the negative relationship between unions and poverty remains significant even when controlling for states' minimum wage ratios and TANF/AFDC levels (see Brady et al., 2013: Table 3) suggests that unionization rates reduce working poverty through routes other than labor's political pressure to increase welfare spending on the poor. Whether that route is primarily direct—whether their finding is driven by unions raising wages above the poverty line—awaits further research. Regardless of the precise mechanisms, Brady, Baker, and Finnigan's study stands as the most comprehensive quantitative investigation of unions and poverty in the United States. Further research is needed to strengthen the bridge between their cross-state, quantitative analyses and the robust body of historical and case study research on organized labor's efforts to reduce poverty.

2 UNIONS AND POVERTY IN ADVANCED INDUSTRIALIZED DEMOCRACIES

In the immediate aftermath of the global financial collapse of 2007–2008, many European governments enacted stiff austerity budgets to deal with rising debt levels. These budgetary measures hit the ranks of the poor especially hard, and union leaders responded quickly. Pamela Dooley, an Executive Council member of the Irish Congress of Trade Unions (ICTU) argued that "a massive section of our society is being driven deeper into poverty and the government response is to attack vital public services" (Bradley, 2012:6). ICTU helped organize a demonstration in Belfast to protest the cuts, while the Trades Union Congress (TUC) of Great Britain rallied an estimated 100,000 to turn out for its own anti-austerity march in London. Speaking prior to the rally, Len McCluskey, the general secretary of Unite, the largest British and Irish trade union, remarked that "the government knows full well . . . that millions of low waged workers are just about keeping their heads above water. . . . The poverty that will follow will engulf our communities for generations to come."[8]

Examples of European trade unions lobbying and protesting in support of the poor predates the recent financial crisis. The TUC helped establish the End Child Poverty group in Great Britain over a decade ago. The group's core aim is to eliminate child poverty by 2020, and it has published a series of reports over the years spotlighting Britain's child poverty problem.[9] In the early 1990s, the Confederation of German Trade Unions (DGB) highlighted the problem of poverty in a nation still adjusting to reunification (Gow, 1994). And the European Trade Union Confederation (ETUC) has published research on the poverty-reducing effects of minimum wage increases in certain nations, including England (Hencke, 2007). Thus unions across Europe have consistently publicized the plight of the economically disadvantaged.

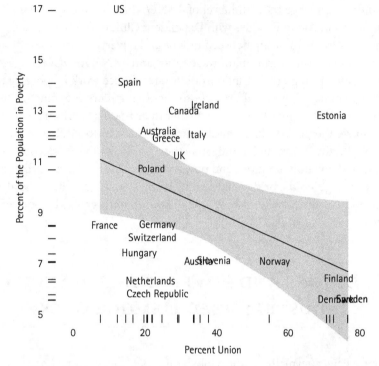

FIGURE 35.2 Unionization and Poverty Rates in OECD Countries, 2003–2005

> *Notes:* The x-axis represents the ration of wage and salary earners that are trade union members divided by the total number of wage and salary earners The y-axis represents the percent of the population living in households with a disposable income that is less than 50 percent of the national median income. To reduce the influence of outliers, fit lines are estimated using an MM-estimator. Shaded regions represent 95 percent confidence intervals.

> *Source:* Poverty estimates are from the LIS Database, see www. lisdatacenter.org. Unionization data from the OECD, see stats.oecd.org.

Figure 35.2 provides preliminary evidence that these and other union efforts against poverty have paid off, at least in recent years. In the figure we present the latest available data on unionization and relative poverty levels for over 20 Organisation for Economic Co-operation and Development (OECD) countries, most of them European. Unionization rates are provided by the OECD, while the relative poverty estimates come from the LIS. We measure poverty as the percent of the population with less than 50 percent of that country's median income, a relative poverty variable commonly used in the cross-national literature. Due to data availability, the measures refer to the 2003–2005 period, a few years prior to the recent global financial crisis. As shown, similar to the pattern displayed in Figure 35.1, the union-poverty correlation is negative. The United States has one of the lowest unionization rates and leads the group in poverty levels. On the other end of the picture lie northern European nations like Finland, Denmark, and Sweden, with unionization rates between 70–80 percent and relative poverty levels below 7 percent.

While the picture is suggestive of a negative relationship between unions and poverty levels across the advanced industrial democracies, there is a counternarrative suggesting that unions actually increase poverty, especially in the highly regulated labor markets of many European countries. From this perspective, the negative relationship between union density and poverty we see in the figure is actually spurious. Why? In recent decades, many European unions have encountered criticism for protecting their members' interests—interests that may disadvantage struggling workers unable to access privileged union jobs.[10] Job protections and high wages enjoyed by union members may make it difficult for young workers in particular to find stable, long-term employment. And some research has found that the relative rigidity of certain European labor markets (an inflexibility driven in part by powerful unions) exacerbates unemployment, especially among the youth and the elderly (Bertola et al., 2002). Young and older workers unable to secure employment may find themselves impoverished, undermining unions' lobbying and advocacy work for the poor by hurting those who—rhetorically at least—unions seek to protect.

Yet other analyses suggest that only the combination of powerful unions and uncoordinated bargaining structures (a relatively rare situation) produces higher unemployment (Nickell, 1997:68). In countries where unions coordinate wage-setting with employers, there is little evidence of a disemployment effect. More recent research provides further evidence against the disemployment thesis. David Brady, Andrew S. Fullerton, and Jennifer Moren Cross's 2010 study of working poverty in the affluent democracies finds that a country's unionization rate has no effect on employment (Brady et al., 2010: Table 3, Model 4). The authors also find that welfare state generosity "does not undermine employment" (p. 559). And while welfare state generosity is obviously not the same as unionization, the two are closely intertwined: a given country's level of unionization is strongly and positively correlated with welfare state generosity (Hicks, 1999; Huber and Stephens, 2001).

Indeed, the very development of the welfare state—and its constitutive redistributive policies—was precipitated by union pressure. Alexander Hicks, in his investigation into the development of a variety of income security policies, argues: "By any standard, the extent of unionization closely aligns with mid-century consolidation of all five major types of income security programs" (1999:116). Unions, along with Leftist political parties, helped institutionalize corporatist arrangements that facilitated the development of robust welfare states. Research has consistently identified this combination of strong labor unions and sustained Leftist political power as key to the initial development of the welfare state. And not only is the establishment of the welfare state dependent on the political environment and strength of labor. Research has found that the extent of government redistribution—in other words, the breadth and depth of the welfare state—is related to unions and Leftist political strength. David Bradley and his colleagues, for example, find that union strength—again, along with the duration of left party governance—significantly reduces posttax, posttransfer inequality through the state's redistributive functions (Bradley et al., 2003:226).

Thus, across the advanced democracies, the extent of welfare state generosity is inextricably linked to labor unions along with Leftist political parties. And welfare state generosity is a powerful predictor of a country's poverty level, as recent comparative research has found. In their analysis of the determinants of poverty across 14 advanced democracies (all but three European nations), Stephanie Moller and her colleagues differentiate the determinants of market-generated poverty from those factors that affect posttax, posttransfer poverty levels (Moller et al., 2003). The authors hypothesize that their measure of the welfare state's reach primarily influences poverty through redistribution—that is, after taxes and transfers. And indeed, welfare state generosity is not a significant factor in explaining pretax/pretransfer poverty (Moller et al., 2003: Table 3), but it is a robust determinant of poverty reduction (Moller et al., 2003: Table 4).

Moller and her colleagues include unionization in their models, and they test whether union strength influences poverty reduction directly, apart from its indirect, negative influence on poverty through welfare state generosity (2003:43). While the degree of wage coordination does seem to reduce market-generated poverty, union density does not (2003: Table 3). However, in their investigation of what determines redistribution (and thus poverty reduction), unionization does play a role, while wage coordination does not: "We conclude that, among labor market institutions, union density is the more significant determinant of redistribution" (2003:43). Is this evidence for a direct effect of unions on poverty in the advanced industrial nations? Not exactly. Their measure of redistribution captures the reduction in poverty achieved through the tax and transfer systems. Heavily unionized nations tend to have tax structures and transfer programs that are particularly effective at redistribution—perhaps due to the political pressure powerful labor movements exert on governments.[11] But that is not evidence for a direct effect of labor unions on market-generated earnings, such as been found in U.S. research on, for example, wages among casino and hotel workers in Nevada (Waddoups, 1999). What Moller and her colleague's study does suggest is that unions affect government redistribution efforts not simply through their influence on welfare state *size* (captured by their measure of generosity) but also through the welfare state's *distributive profile*—that is, the structure of the tax and transfer systems.

Other comparative research buttresses this finding of an indirect role of unions in influencing poverty levels. David Brady, Andrew Fullerton, and Jennifer Moren Cross's investigation into the determinants of working poverty in 18 advanced democracies around the turn of the twenty-first century reveals that "welfare generosity appears to be the principal country-level factor shaping working poverty" (Brady et al., 2010:576). Where do unions fit into their story? Absent a welfare state variable, union density appears to reduce poverty directly. But after including a measure of the welfare state in their analyses, the unionization effect is no longer significant (see their Appendix A). Given the link between union density and welfare state generosity, the authors conclude that unionization "indirectly reduces working poverty" (p. 573).

Further evidence of unions' indirect influence emerges from the same authors' 2009 cross-national examination of working-age poverty (Brady et al., 2009). Similar to their 2010 article, the authors test various individual-level explanations for poverty, including such household composition characteristics as the number of children, the education level of the household head, and whether there are multiple earners in the household. They supplement these predictors with a range of country-level variables including union density, cumulative Left party power, and an index of welfare state generosity. Unlike the study described previously, their focus in this particular investigation is on poverty among all working-age individuals, not simply employed adults.

What do they find? Unionization levels are once again an important contextual factor influencing a country's relative rate of poverty. The United States, for example, has comparatively low unionization rates and comparatively high poverty levels for the years of their study. The authors' analyses suggest that if the United States had either an average unionization rate or a rate of unionization equal to that of Sweden's, "the odds of poverty would decline by a factor of either 1.61 or 4.65" (p. 288). And similar to other comparative research, the duration of a Leftist government is another key factor influencing poverty levels. But both influences—Leftist government and union density— "are channeled indirectly through the welfare state to reduce poverty" (p. 289).

Yet the influence of European unions is not restricted to posttax, posttransfer poverty. Coordinated wage bargaining—at the industry, sector, and national levels—can help raise wages for low-wage nonunion workers. For example, in a recent multilevel investigation of household poverty among employees in 20 European nations, Henning Lohmann finds that the degree of bargaining centralization is negatively related to pretransfer poverty rates among households with at least one employed member (Lohmann, 2009). His analyses include a rich set of individual-level and country-level variables, including basic demographic information such as marital status, immigrant status, and the number of children in the household, supplemented with macrolevel indicators such as the unemployment replacement rate and expenditures on family cash benefits. Whereas "bargaining centralization ... plays no significant role in the explanation of poverty reduction via transfers" it is the one consistent macrolevel variable that reduces pretransfer poverty (p. 499). Research on specific industries, such as retail, supports this general finding that bargaining centralization often improves the conditions of low-skill work, whether through increases in wage rates or increases in the minimum number of hours worked (Carr´e et al., 2009).

Other research has likewise pinpointed "inclusive" wage-setting systems as a key determinant of pay levels among low-skill workers, and therefore of pretransfer poverty rates. Inclusive systems "extend the benefits of ... bargaining power to workers who have relatively little bargaining power in their own right" (Bosch, Mayhew, and Gautie, 2009:91). Inclusive systems, in general, extend "wage gains of the most powerful, generally unionized, workers to those workers with less bargaining power, especially less-skilled and non-union workers" (p. 92). A primary determinant of inclusiveness is centralized bargaining structures in which negotiated wage and benefit settlements are extended to other, oftentimes nonunion workers. Surveying six predominantly European countries, Gerhard Bosch and his colleagues conclude that nations with the most inclusive systems tend to have comparatively low rates of poorly paying jobs. And while inclusiveness may be due to high density rates, as in Denmark, it need not be: other nations with comparatively low density rates have highly centralized bargaining systems that help protect low-wage workers.

In sum, recent comparative research—a literature disproportionately focused on poverty and unionization in European countries—identifies unions as a key influence on a nation's poverty rate. Much of this influence appears indirect: high density rates, in concert with Leftist political parties that are able to secure and sustain power, help shape the redistributive functions of the state in ways that benefit the economically disadvantaged. Meanwhile, centralized wage-setting institutions, which are related to union strength but are not synonymous with union density, help raise wages for low-income nonunion workers, thereby lowering poverty rates.

By contrast, little evidence exists suggesting much of a direct role for unions in lifting people out of poverty. Now, this lack of a finding may highlight an important difference between unions in the relatively unregulated economy of the United States compared with its European peers. Or it may be that the comparative research framework simply cannot detect dynamics occurring in certain nations but not others. Or it may, paradoxically, reflect the greater strength of labor movements in many European nations compared to unions in the United States. After all, multiemployer bargaining arrangements with automatic extensions at the industry-, sector-, or national-level remove the need for unions to intervene directly in the pay rates of low-skill workers. Lacking centralized bargaining, unions in the United States must either organize low-skill workers to raise their wages or lobby policymakers to enact antipoverty legislation. In recent years, both pathways to reducing poverty rates have been largely blocked. Partly as a result, according to most measures, poverty rates in the United States exceed those in the vast majority of European countries.

3 UNIONS AND POVERTY IN THE DEVELOPING WORLD

Great diversity exists between labor movements across the advanced industrialized democracies, and between unions within these nations. But these differences pale in comparison to what we see surveying unions in the developing world. Part of the enormous diversity results from the vast political, economic, and cultural differences between nations grouped within the "developing world" category. And part results from what can only be called a mislabeling of the union term—one that has been placed on organizations that bear almost no relation to common understandings of what a labor union is and does.

Take unionization in contemporary China. The All-China Federation of Trade Unions (ACFTU) claims over 200 million members and has managed to organize notoriously antiunion companies such as Walmart. What explains the federation's apparent success? Independent trade unions in China are banned, and the ACFTU is the only official, state-sanctioned trade union organization in the country. The federation's primary goal is "not so much to protect workers' rights as to strengthen the Chinese Communist

Party's social control" (Liu, 2010:30–31). ACFTU's member unions work in concert with the state to ensure compliance with the governing party and to prevent the emergence of independent trade unions. Thus Walmart and other firms need not worry about labor strife from active, independent unions. And while recent decrees have democratized certain procedures within the ACFTU—such as permitting the direct election of workplace chairs—independent trade unions remain illegal (Liu, 2010:30).

Compare the Chinese case to that of trade unions in South Africa. The Congress of South African Trade Unions (COSATU) was founded in 1985 and remains the largest union federation in the country. Unlike ACFTU in China, COSATU emerged as a key voice challenging state power, playing a leading role in combating the existing Apartheid regime during the late 1980s and early 1990s. All the while member unions operated to improve the economic lives of their members by addressing shop-floor grievances and bargaining for increases in labor's share of available income. These unions proved particularly effective at raising the wages of low-income members (Schultz and Mwabu, 1998).

The organization's fight on behalf of ordinary workers remains to this day. Zwelinzima Vavi is the current secretary general of COSATU and in a recent speech decrying widespread corruption among the ruling elite, he harkened to the revolutionary themes that helped destroy Apartheid: "We are moving towards a society in which the morality of our revolutionary movement—selflessness, service to the people and caring for the poor and vulnerable—is being threatened" (Polgreen, 2012:1). And while controversy has erupted over whether the unions that comprise COSATU have grown too close and comfortable with the ruling African National Congress (ANC) party, similar debates have dominated intralabor discussions in many of the advanced democracies.[12] Meanwhile, recent government crackdowns on striking mine workers in South Africa gained worldwide attention due to their shocking violence. Yet in the aftermath of the bloodshed the government did not attempt to rein in organized labor. Instead, current South African President Jacob Zuma called on unions to work together with businesses and the government to prevent any further violence (Smith and Macalister, 2012).

What, then, can we say about union effects on poverty throughout the developing world? Few decisive findings emerge from the still-scarce literature on organized labor in developing countries. In certain nations, such as Uruguay, collective bargaining rights were granted only recently. In others, such as China, the right to collectively bargain freely remains outlawed. Given that labor movements in many developing countries are comparatively young, if they exist at all, the labor economist Richard Freeman concludes "Most developing country unions are weak" (Freeman, 2009:22).

Figure 35.3 displays poverty and unionization rates for a range of developing nations. Here we draw on information from the World Values Survey (WVS) for our unionization rates. The WVS does not include a national-level poverty measure. Instead, our poverty rates are based on the World Bank's estimates of the fraction of each country's population living on less than $2 per day. The data refer to the 2005–2008 period. Our selection of countries is based partly on data availability and partly on the sample utilized by Nathan Martin and David Brady in their 2007 article on unionization

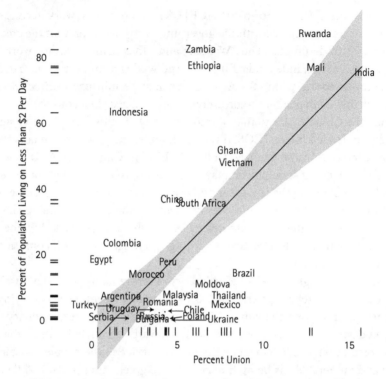

FIGURE 35.3 Unionization and Poverty Rates in LDCs, 2005–2008

Notes: The x-axis represents active union membership rates. The y-axis represents the percent of the population living on less than $2 per day at 2005 international prices. To reduce the influence of outliers, fit lines are calculated using an MM-estimator. Shaded regions represent 95 percent confidence intervals.

Source: Union rates are from the 2005–2008 wave of the World Values Survey, see www.worldvaluessurvey.org. Poverty headcount estimates are from the World Bank. See data.worldbank.org.

predictors in developing countries (Martin and Brady, 2007). Martin and Brady analyze WVS data from the late-1990s. We include those countries with unionization data available in both periods and add those countries not available in the late-1990s but available in the most recent WVS wave. The result is a sample of nearly 30 developing nations.

As shown, the relationship between unionization and poverty for these nations appears positive. Countries such as Rwanda and India have comparatively high unionization rates *and* comparatively high rates of poverty. Countries such as Egypt and Morocco, on the other hand, have almost no union presence at all and very small fractions of their populations living on less than $2 a day.

A few important caveats are in order regarding Figure 35.3. First, it's worth re-emphasizing the vast differences in what "unionization" means in this set of nations. In China, it means membership in a state-controlled organization geared toward greater control over the industrial workforce. In Vietnam, a similar structure exists, with all official unions registered with the state-sanctioned Vietnam General Confederation of Labor (VGCL). Organizing outside the VGCL umbrella remains outlawed. Second, none of the countries examined in the picture have particularly high rates of organization, regardless of what "organization" means in these particular contexts. India's unionization rate of roughly 15 percent is the highest, yet it's a rate of unionization that approaches the lowest seen among the OECD nations. And India's labor force remains predominantly agriculturally based, and a sizable fraction of the nonagricultural workforce is employed in the informal sector. This combination of a disproportionately agricultural-based workforce alongside a sizable informal sector is found in many of the other developing countries in Figure 35.3. Trade unions, independent or not, have a relatively constrained role to play in these types of economies. And finally, due to substantial data limitations, the measure of poverty we use here is absolute rather than relative. This makes comparisons with the prior figures inappropriate.

What the figure does underscore is the enormous diversity in economic development—if not collective bargaining rates—between the developing nations. Countries such as Rwanda and Argentina differ along nearly any dimension one might consider. What they share is the "developing country" categorization, one that, arguably at least, Argentina is close to transcending (the same cannot be said of Rwanda). Figure 35.3 also illuminates the substantial gaps in our knowledge about labor movements and poverty in much of the developing world. There may be patterns in terms of poverty levels and union organization within groups of developing nations obscured by the comprehensive picture we provide. Future research should also consider what role organized labor plays in the development process of these countries, if any, along with basic case studies of trade unions in settings where until recently they were outlawed. As of now, all we can state with much confidence is that there isn't conclusive evidence of a strong relationship between poverty and unionization among our sample of developing countries. Unlike the pattern we observe in the advanced economies, comparatively high unionization rates do not correspond with low rates of poverty. This lack of evidence derives in no small part from the lack of independent unions in some nations and the lack of much union presence of any sort in many others.

4 CONCLUSION

Our survey of the existing literature on organized labor and poverty highlights the political and organizational pathways through which unions reduced poverty in the advanced democracies. These efforts lifted low-wage workers out of poverty directly, through the increased wages that accompanied union membership, or indirectly, by extending contracts to nonunion workers or through a variety of political channels. In the United States, unions' once-formidable organizing efforts uplifted entire occupations. Unions simultaneously lobbied cities, states, and the federal government to enact policies protecting low-wage workers. Some of these efforts proved successful, such as organized labor's steadfast support for passage of the federal Medicare program. Others failed, but even today, despite a hostile political and organizing context, we see many unions fighting for antipoverty measures such as living-wage ordinances and the protection of government health insurance programs.

In many European nations, powerful labor movements helped establish and subsequently enlarge and protect generous welfare states. Research identifies the relative generosity of a nation's welfare state institutions as a key predictor of its poverty rate. Countries with the most generous welfare states generally have lower poverty than those countries with a stingier set of protective institutions. Here we see the critical indirect role unions played in combating poverty. But their influence doesn't end with the size and scope of nation's welfare state. Bargaining centralization, in particular, is associated with reducing poverty rates, especially among unorganized workers whose pay and benefits are patterned on their unionized counterparts' contracts. These mandatory extensions to nonunion workers represent another indirect pathway through which unions influence poverty, since the workers who benefit do so despite not belonging to a union.

The backdrop of these general relationships is the varying fortunes of labor movements in the advanced industrialized countries we survey. In those countries in which unions have been able to instantiate their power in a variety of welfare state and wage-setting institutions, their influence on poverty rates appears durable. Even rather severe declines in density rates, such as those experienced by the Dutch trade movement, have not dislodged the coordinated wage-bargaining and welfare state institutions that simultaneously lift wages and cushion the effects of low-skill employment. In the United States, by contrast, unions' historic role in combating poverty through direct and indirect pathways has diminished. Unlike many of their European peers, unions in the United States were never able to translate their power into the variety of durable policies and bargaining arrangements that protect the poor. This absence of centralized bargaining and comparatively weak welfare state institutions means that unions themselves—through their organizing capacity and political leverage—must remain actively engaged in the fight against poverty. With a private sector density rate now one-seventh of its postwar peak, this capacity and leverage is comparatively fragmented and increasingly diminished.

In the developing world, the picture is much murkier. In many nations, labor movements remain embryonic and thus unable to exert much influence on wages among the poor and nonpoor alike. In others, unions are stillborn, crushed by vicious repression against a free and fair labor movement. And in still others, independent unions have emerged and grown, but their influence remains limited by the fact that most workers remain dependent on subsistence agriculture, the informal economy, or some combination thereof. What remains to be seen is whether the modernization of these nation's economies follows the general path of the United States and Europe in which trade unions helped cushion the effects of a market economy, thereby reducing poverty levels. The absence of an independent labor movement during China's recent and rapid rise suggests that industrialization and the accompanying economic growth need not be accompanied by the emergence of powerful, independent labor movements. If the past experiences of the United States and European nations are any guide, poverty rates in those developing countries where unions have gained a foothold will be comparatively low. Economic modernization unaccompanied by a vibrant labor movement, on the other hand, is likely to produce a growing market society with high levels of economic suffering.

NOTES

1. By contrast, sociologist Jill Quadagno (2004) suggests that union efforts on behalf of national health insurance did not gain momentum until the late 1960s, given the importance many unions placed on their control over fringe benefits, especially during the immediate postwar years.
2. In return, poor Americans—except for mothers of young children—would have to work or enroll in job-training programs.
3. See Chapter 6 of Rosenfeld (2014) for more.
4. All of the figures in this chapter were made using the tile package in R. See Adolph (2012).
5. See Rosenfeld (2010a) for a comparison of "absolute" versus "relative" conceptions of poverty.
6. For an example focused on U.S. states in 1960, see Hicks et al. (1978).
7. AFDC was later replaced by TANF. Both are means-tested transfer programs to the poor; TANF replaces guaranteed cash assistance to certain families with time limits and strict work requirements.
8. See the Unite press release of October 20, 2012, available at http: //www.unitetheunion. org/news__events/latest_news/savage_cuts_will_unleash_a_pov.aspx.
9. See http://www.ecpc.org.uk/ for further information about the group and its efforts.
10. See, for example, Matlack (2005) for a discussion of how unions in France contributed to the country's high rate of joblessness in the early years of the twenty-first century.
11. Leftists governments in particular—recall that the combination of high union density along with sustained rule by Left political parties produces the most generous welfare states.
12. Fierce intraunion arguments in the United States about whether organized labor is too reliant upon the Democratic Party are but one of many examples of this common dynamic.

REFERENCES

Adolph, Christopher. 2012. "tile." R package (faculty.washington.edu/cadolph/software).

Bertola, Giuseppe, Francine D. Blau, and Lawrence M. Kahn. 2002. "Labor Market Institutions and Demographic Employment Patterns." National Bureau of Economic Research Working Paper 9043, National Bureau of Economic Research, Cambridge, MA.

Bosch, Gerhard, Ken Mayhew, and Jerome Gautie. 2009. "Industrial Relations, Legal Regulations, and Wage Setting." Pp. 211–68 in *Low-Wage Work in the Wealthy World*, edited by John Schmitt and Jerome Gautie. Russell Sage Foundation.

Boyarsky, Bill. 1981. "Unlikely Allies Fighting Urban Program Cuts." *Los Angeles Times*, February 15.

Boyle, Kevin. 1998. *The UAW and the Heyday of American Liberalism, 1945–1968*. Ithaca, NY: Cornell University Press.

Bradley, Una. 2012. "Belfast Protest over Austerity Measures." *Irish Times*, October 22.

Brady, David, Regina S. Baker, and Ryan Finnigan. 2013. "When Unionization Disappears: State-Level Unionization and Working Poverty in the U.S." *American Sociological Review* 78:872–96.

Brady, David, Andrew S. Fullerton, and Jennifer Moren Cross. 2009. "Putting Poverty in Political Context: A Multi-Level Analysis of Adult Poverty Across 18 Affluent Western Democracies." *Social Forces* 88:271–300.

Brady, David, Andrew S. Fullerton, and Jennifer Moren Cross. 2010. "More Than Just Nickels and Dimes: A Cross-National Analysis of Working Poverty in Affluent Democracies." *Social Problems* 57:559–85.

Bradley, David, Evelyne Huber, Stephanie Moller, Francois Nielsen, and John D. Stephens. 2003. "Distribution and Redistribution in Postindustrial Democracies." *World Politics* 55:193–228.

Brown, Larry. 1970. "Hunger USA: The Public Pushes Congress." *Journal of Health and Social Behavior* 11:115–26.

Carr′e, Francoise, Chris Tilly, Maarten van Klaveren, and Dorothea Voss-Dahm. 2009. "Retail Jobs in Comparative Perspective." Pp. 211–68 in *Low-Wage Work in the Wealthy World*, edited by John Schmitt and Jerome Gautie. New York: Russell Sage Foundation.

Chappell, Marisa. 2010. *The War on Welfare: Family, Poverty, and Politics in Modern America.* University Park: University of Pennsylvania Press.

Derickson, Alan. 1994. "Health Security for All? Social Unionism and Universal Health Insurance, 1935–1958." *Journal of American History* 80:1333–56.

DeVault, Marjorie L. and James S. Pitts. 1984. "Surplus and Scarcity: Hunger and the Origins of the Food Stamp Program." *Social Problems* 31:545–57.

Freeman, Richard B. 2009. "Labor Regulations, Unions, and Social Protection in Developing Countries: Market Distortions or Efficient Institutions?" National Bureau of Economic Research Working Paper 14789, National Bureau of Economic Research, Cambridge, MA.

Gow, David. 1994. "More Than 7M Germans 'Live in Poverty.'" *The Guardian*, January 21.

Hencke, David. 2007. "Minimum Wage Puts Britain on Top to Combat Worker Poverty." *The Guardian*, May 28.

Hicks, Alexander. 1999. *Social Democracy and Welfare Capitalism: A Century of Income Security Policies.* Ithaca, NY: Cornell University Press.

Hicks, Alexander, Roger Friedland, and Edwin Johnson. 1978. "Class Power and State Policy: The Case of Large Business Corporations, Labor Unions and Governmental Redistribution in the American States." *American Sociological Review* 43:302–15.

Huber, Evelyne and John D. Stephens. 2001. *Development and Crisis of the Welfare State: Parties and Policies in Global Markets.* Chicago: University of Chicago Press.

Lichtenstein, Nelson. 2004. "Trade/Industrial Unions." Pp. 717–21 in *Poverty in the United States: A-K*, edited by Gwendolyn Mink and Alice O'Connor. ABC-CLIO.

Liu, Mingwei. 2010. "Union Organizing in China: Still a Monolithic Labor Movement?" *Industrial and Labor Relations Review* 64:30–52.

Lohmann, Henning. 2009. "Welfare States, Labour Market Institutions and the Working Poor: A Comparative Analysis of 20 European Countries." *European Sociological Review* 25:489–504.

Martin, Nathan D. and David Brady. 2007. "Workers of the Less Developed World Unite? A Multilevel Analysis of Unionization in Less Developed Countries." *American Sociological Review* 72:562–84.

Matlack, Carol. 2005. "Crisis in France." *Bloomberg Businessweek*, November 20.

Moller, Stephanie, David Bradley, Evelyne Huber, Francois Nielsen, and John D. Stephens. 2003. "Determinants of Relative Poverty in Advanced Capitalist Democracies." *American Sociological Review* 68:22–51.

New York Times. 1945. "Revised Pay Policy Is Urged by Green." July 15.

Nickell, Stephen. 1997. "Unemployment and Labor Market Rigidities: Europe versus North America." *Journal of Economic Perspectives* 11:55–74.

Polgreen, Lydia. 2012. "South Africans Suffer as Graft Saps Provinces." *New York Times*, February 18.

Quadagno, Jill. 1990. "Race, Class, and Gender in the U.S. Welfare State: Nixon's Failed Family Assistance Plan." *American Sociological Review* 55:11–28.

Quadagno, Jill. 2004. "Why the United States Has No National Health Insurance: Stakeholder Mobilization against the Welfare State, 1945–1996." *Journal of Health and Social Behavior* 45:25–44.

Quadagno, Jill. 2006. *One Nation, Uninsured: Why the U.S. Has No National Health Insurance.* New York: Oxford University Press.

Rosenfeld, Jake. 2010a. "'The Meaning of Poverty' and Contemporary Quantitative Poverty Research." *British Journal of Sociology* 61:103–10.

Rosenfeld, Sam. 2010b. "Fed by Reform: Congressional Politics, Partisan Change, and the Food Stamp Program, 1961–1981." *Journal of Policy History* 22:474–507.

Rosenfeld, Jake. 2014. *What Unions No Longer Do.* Cambridge, MA: Harvard University Press.

Schultz, T. Paul and Germano Mwabu. 1998. "Labor Unions and the Distribution of Wages and Employment in South Africa." *Industrial and Labor Relations Review* 51:680–703.

Shabecoff, Philip. 1977. "$2.50 Minimum Wage Proposed by Carter in Setback to Labor." *New York Times*, March 25.

Smith, David and Terry Macalister. 2012. "South African Police Shoot Dead Striking Miners." *The Guardian*, August 16.

Waddoups, C. Jeffrey. 1999. "Union Wage Effects in Nevada's Hotel and Casino Industry." *Industrial Relations* 38:577–83.

Waddoups, C. Jeffrey. 2001. "Unionism and Poverty-Level Wages in the Service Sector: the Case of Nevada's Hotel-Casino Industry." *Applied Economics Letters* 8:163–67.

Wozniacka, Gosia. 2011. "United Farm Workers Fight Dwindling Membership." Associated Press, April 20.

CHAPTER 36

···

HOUSING PROGRAMS

···

PETER A. KEMP

INTRODUCTION

STUDIES of income poverty often fail to include analyses of housing expenditure and housing programs, yet housing is one of the basic necessities of life and generally by far the most expensive. This relative neglect has begun to change in the wake of the Great Recession, at the birth of which was the securitization and *en bloc* sale of bundles of subprime mortgage loans that many low-income homebuyers in the United States could scarcely afford to repay.

It goes without saying that housing is a basic necessity for households in most parts of the world. But dwellings have characteristics that, in most advanced economies, have resulted in the introduction of housing programs by governments. The nature and extent of these programs have varied over time and between different countries. But even in the most market-focused advanced economies, these programs are pervasive, even if some interventions are more visible than others. Households living in poverty are the focus of many, but by no means all, of these housing programs.

This chapter considers the nature and role of housing programs for low-income households in the rich democracies. It begins by looking at the characteristics of housing and why these can be problematic for people living in poverty. The second section focuses on the social construction of "the housing question" and considers the ways in which this issue has been conceptualized and debated. The third section focuses on private and public responses to these problematic aspects of housing. Private "solutions" include poor dwelling conditions, undermaintenance, overcrowding, high rent-to-income ratios, and homelessness. Public "solutions" include public health regulations, minimum building standards, rent controls, public housing, housing vouchers, and tax expenditures. However, some of these public solutions have in turn come to be seen as the causes of other "poverty problems"—including high levels of joblessness and ethnic segregation—that have in turn been the subject of policy responses. The fourth section focuses on housing affordability, housing allowances, and mortgage subsidies. The final section presents conclusions on the nature and role of housing programs for the poor.

HOUSING AND POVERTY

Almost by definition, households that are poor find it difficult to afford many of the "essentials" of everyday life, never mind the "nonessentials" that other people may take for granted. Food, water, energy, clothing, travel, and other basic necessities are often expensive. But for most households, and especially the poor, the most expensive necessity is housing. In the advanced economies at least, dwellings are very expensive to build, not only because of the materials and labor that are required to construct them, but also because of the cost of the land on which they are built. Indeed, in central city locations in particular, the purchase price of land is often far higher than the price of building materials and construction. As a result, the cost of housing is typically several times larger than average household incomes. In Britain, for example, the average house price is 5 times the average annual household income and in London it is 11 times average income.

The fact that housing is so expensive, of course, is why the great majority of households are unable to buy their house outright from their income. Instead, they typically either take out a mortgage to buy their home or rent it from a landlord. Purchasing a dwelling with a mortgage or renting from a landlord enables households to obtain a roof over their heads. These solutions to the high cost of housing require households to either make repayments to their lender in the case of homebuyers or rent to their landlord in the case of tenants. However, mortgage payments and rents are typically the largest single item of expenditure in the budgets of most households.

Expenditure on housing generally accounts for a larger share of the budgets of poor households than of better-off ones. Indeed, the proportion of expenditure on housing falls as income rises. The burden of housing expenditure among poor households— measured here as the percentage of disposable income devoted to expenditure on housing (including utilities, maintenance, and building insurance)—is illustrated by data from the European Union's Survey of Income and Living Conditions (EU-SILC). In the 27 countries of the European Union (EU27) in 2010, expenditure on housing averaged 23 percent of disposable income. But among poor households—those whose disposable income was less than 60 percent of the national median—average expenditure on housing was 41 percent (Pittini 2012).

Thus expenditure on housing is generally a bigger burden—and, in fact, often a much bigger burden—for the poor than for the better off. Consequently, households living in poverty are more likely than the nonpoor to have difficulty affording their housing costs. Hence, the poor are more at risk of falling behind on their rent or mortgage payments or having to cut back on other "essentials" in their budget to be able to pay for their housing. The difficulty that some low-income households face in being able to afford their housing has been one of the rationales for the introduction of housing programs such as public housing, rent controls, and housing allowances. A related rationale is that the poorest households are unable to afford to pay an "economic rent," that is, one that would provide landlords with a competitive rate of return; and that without subsidies to cover the gap, developers will not build houses for them.

While mortgage payments or rent may (or may not) be affordable when households take out their mortgage or take on their tenancy, they may subsequently become unaffordable at a later date. Increases in mortgage interest rates, or rent increases during the life of a tenancy, may put pressure on household budgets. And even if their mortgage payment or rent remains unchanged, households that fall on hard times may struggle to afford their housing. Indeed, negative income shocks or unexpected increases in outgoings are among the main reasons why households get into arrears on their rent or mortgage payments.

Households living in poverty often have little or no savings, which limits their ability to pay the rent during periods of unemployment or temporarily reduced incomes. Moreover, the extent to which households can reduce their housing expenditure in the short term is often quite limited. Moving to cheaper accommodation takes time and entails transaction costs that make it less suitable for short-term contingencies (such as unemployment) than for more long-term life changes. Moving to a different home is especially expensive for homeowners. But even for renters, moving typically entails moving costs, paying realtors, and (very often) paying rent in advance and a deposit as security.

Governments have introduced housing programs not only because of housing shortages and the difficulty that low-income households face in paying for their housing; they have also intervened to tackle slum housing, either by demolition or financial assistance to enable owners to upgrade their substandard dwellings. An important reason why such programs are introduced is that substandard housing—and, indeed, the lack of housing—can affect people's health.

In the developed countries, the impact of housing on health was especially apparent in the nineteenth century. Rapid urbanization in Western Europe led to many poor households living in badly designed, poorly ventilated, damp dwellings, many of which had inadequate water and sewage facilities and were severely overcrowded. As housing conditions improved, the link between housing and health became less direct. Nevertheless, it remains "a key social determinant of health and a central component of the relationship between poverty and health" (Shaw 2004:413). Low-income households, perhaps not surprisingly, are more likely than the nonpoor to live in substandard dwellings.

Public health remains a major concern in areas of slum housing in developing countries (UN Habitat 2003). In developed countries, the link between housing and health is now most apparent in relation to homelessness. Homeless people have higher rates of morbidity and premature mortality than do the general population (Fazel et al. 2014). Moreover, Bines (1997) found that rough sleepers (that is, homeless people living on the streets) had worse health than those living in temporary accommodation such as night shelters and hostels. The latter, in turn, had worse health than the general population.

Although there have been many studies of the impact of housing on health, only a minority of them have been based on randomized controlled trials, which control for sample "selection effects." One housing program that was based on randomization is the US Moving to Opportunity (MTO) scheme. An evaluation using MTO data (cited in Gibson et al. 2011) found that there were large and significant reductions in mental health problems and obesity for the treatment group that received a housing voucher limited to low-poverty areas plus counseling. It also found there was a large and significant reduction in obesity among the group receiving an unrestricted voucher but no counseling. These health improvements were relative to the control group, which did not receive either a voucher or counseling but remained in public housing. Meanwhile, a systematic review of the health impact of housing improvements concluded that interventions to improve the warmth and energy efficiency of dwellings had positive impacts on residents' health (Thomson et al. 2009). However, relatively few studies have investigated the causal pathways between housing and health, and it is clear that more (methodologically robust) research is required on the links between housing conditions and health status.

THE HOUSING QUESTION

While the poor are likely to find it difficult to obtain and afford adequate housing, it does not automatically follow that governments will necessarily intervene to tackle these problems. The "housing question"—as an issue of public concern about which many thought something should be done—emerged during the nineteenth century in many of the developed nations. It has been with us ever since. The nature of the issue has changed over time as individual problems were ameliorated and others came into focus. For as Donnison and Ungerson (1982:13–14) have remarked, "The housing problem is never solved: it only changes. That may nevertheless constitute progress. Some problems are nicer to have than others."

However, social problems such as the housing question are social constructs rather than some entirely objective reality that exists independently of our perceptions. In order for social phenomena to become public "problems," they must first be identified and defined as such. What was once considered acceptable, normal, and inevitable may subsequently come to be seen as a social problem to which the energies of the state should be directed. Moreover, policy solutions to particular problems may themselves come to be seen as social problems at a later date.

Housing problems are always with us in part because absolute improvements in housing conditions have been accompanied by rising expectations about what is acceptable. But changes in the definition of housing problems cannot be reduced solely to technological and social progress. Although that progress is clearly important, public perceptions of housing problems—who defines them, how they are defined, and the solutions which those definitions imply—are essentially political and ideological in nature. In consequence, they are also a matter of debate and contestation.

Stakeholders—such as those representing tenants, landlords, homebuilders and mortgage lenders—invariably seek to promote their interests as they interpret them. Along with "think tanks" and other "policy entrepreneurs," stakeholders regularly publish research and policy reports on topics that they claim require government action. The matters at issue include not only whether an issue should be addressed, but also how it should be defined, what is the nature of the problem, what caused it, and how (if at all) it should be tackled. Such debates are invariably rooted in different ideologies and value systems and involve contestation over the distribution of scarce resources. These actors compete for attention in the mass media and, when they are successful in getting "the oxygen of publicity," help bring issues to public attention. This in turn can put pressure on government to "do something" to tackle the alleged problem.

Homelessness provides a good illustration of problem definition. What we mean by "homelessness" is neither straightforward nor universally agreed. Like housing problems more generally, the situations that may be regarded as constituting homelessness are a matter of argument and political debate. Definitions range from being roofless and without any shelter at all to being badly housed. Where the line should be drawn between these two extremes is not value-free. Does homelessness refer only to people sleeping on the streets, or does it also include people using night shelters or living in temporary accommodations such as hostels and boarding houses? Should the definition of homelessness include people who have been threatened with eviction by their family? And should it also include—as some feminists have argued (Watson and Austerberry 1986)—women who are living with abusive partners or in otherwise unsatisfactory relationships?

Perceptions of homeless and what (if anything) should be done about it—and who should do it—vary between different societies and over time. In relation to the former, the contrast between the advanced economies and many developing countries could not be more extreme. The fact that several thousand people sleep rough in central London every night, for example, seems scarcely comparable to the plight of tens of thousands of people losing their homes (not to mention their livelihoods or even their lives) due to a natural disaster or civil conflict in a low-income country. There is very little data on homelessness in developing countries, but estimates suggest that it is widespread and may globally exceed 100 million people (Tipple and Speak n.d.).

In relation to change over time, in medieval Britain official responses to the homeless poor (vagrants) often aimed to deter or punish rather than to help or accommodate them. Numerous statutes were passed making vagrancy or begging illegal, the last of which was enacted in 1824. Rehousing homeless people did not become an explicit goal of housing policy in Britain until the Homeless Persons Act 1977, half a century after government subsidies were first introduced for the provision of social rented housing in order to tackle housing shortages.

This contestation over the nature and definition of a "problem" extends to the issues of who is affected by the problem and who among them should be provided with assistance. For example, when the British homelessness legislation was being enacted, concern was expressed that people might deliberately become homeless to gain access to council housing. In order to prevent such "queue jumping" (as it was termed), the legislation included a clause that ruled out applicants who were deemed to be "intentionally homeless." Some local authorities also expressed concerns that homeless people would move to their area in order to be rehoused under the legislation. To address this concern, the 1977 Act included a clause that confined assistance only to applicants who had a "local connection" to the area. This echoed similar concerns, and a similar official response, to that expressed by local officers under the Poor Laws (Humphreys 1999). Finally, the Act gave a statutory right to be rehoused only to families with children, "vulnerable" people, and the elderly. Again echoing the defunct Poor Laws, "able-bodied" single people and couples had no right to rehousing.

These distinctions in the British homelessness legislation echo a long-running distinction that has often made between "deserving" and "nondeserving" groups of (potential) beneficiaries. Groups typically seen as deserving are the elderly and veterans, while lone parents and the unemployed are often viewed as undeserving. While the "deserving" are seen as fit and proper persons to receive assistance (whether welfare benefits or subsidized housing) the "undeserving" are not seen so charitably. Who should receive help are matters about which different stakeholders will argue in line with their perceived interests and perception of the issue (Schneider and Ingram 1993) and invariably concern the question of who gains and who loses? For example, the Center-Right coalition government elected in 2010 in the UK made a rhetorical distinction between "strivers" (people in work) and "skivers" (welfare claimants). This stereotyping was part of a "mobilisation of bias" (Edelman 1971) strategy to build support for substantial cuts in welfare spending including housing allowances.

These contrasting images of benefit claimants implicitly or even explicitly embody contrasting explanations of the reasons why people are claiming benefits. In general, like poverty more generally, the perceived causes of housing problems can be broadly divided into individual and structural, that is, explanations focused on the characteristics and behavior of individuals and those focused on structural factors (Fitzpatrick et al. 2000). For example, some commentators argue that homelessness is caused by "structural" factors such as poverty, unemployment, and a lack of affordable housing. Others argue that it is caused by the "behavioral" characteristics of the individuals concerned; that they become homeless because of their personal failings, bad luck or inability to cope with adverse events.

Explanations focusing on individual behavior tend to conceptualize homeless and other poor people as active agents who are more or less the architects of their own downfall. In contrast, structural explanations tend to portray the homeless as passive agents who are victims of circumstances over which they have little or no control. Clearly, these different explanations imply different types of policy response to tackle the problem. Thus, if the cause of homelessness is the failings or behavior of the homeless themselves, then the perceived appropriate response might be nothing at all, or punitive actions or perhaps the provision of temporary help from social services or drug and alcohol interventions such as detoxification and rehabilitation. But if the cause is believed to be structural, then the appropriate action is more likely to be seen as interventions that increase the supply of housing or the provision of housing allowances to help the poor afford high rents.

Origins and Development
of Housing Programs

Private Responses

State intervention to tackle the problem of housing was almost nonexistent prior to the nineteenth century. Housing was left to the unregulated market and any difficulties that households encountered in relation to their housing (as in most other areas of their lives) were regarded as their personal problem. Charitable provision, for example almshouses, did exist, but on a very small scale and typically catered to groups of people that were widely regarded as members of the "deserving" poor (such as widows and the frail elderly).

In the case of Britain, the state began to intervene in the housing market to tackle housing conditions in the mid-nineteenth century. However, it did not do so because housing problems had only just appeared, for the evidence suggests that poor housing conditions had existed well before then (Burnett 1986). To some extent, therefore, the emergence of the "housing question," as it became known, was a reflection of a change in attitudes toward conditions that had existed for decades, both in villages and in towns (Holmans 1987). Yet, in part, it was also a response to a material change in the urban housing situation and, in particular, to the sheer scale and concentration of inadequate housing. For the rapid urbanization that occurred during and after the Industrial Revolution in Britain brought with it appalling housing conditions on a wide scale (Gauldie 1974; Wohl 1977).

It is no coincidence that the word "slum" emerged in Britain during the early nineteenth century. In Victorian Britain, areas of slum housing were viewed with suspicion and even fear by many commentators, who saw them as repositories and incubators of incest, promiscuity, criminality, and contagious diseases (Wohl 1977). Overcrowded dwellings and slum housing were the product of the operation of market forces unfettered by government regulation. They enabled the urban poor to reconcile their low incomes with the high cost of housing.

There is a modern parallel here with the informal housing and shanty towns that exist in many developing countries. As in the Industrial Revolution, urban growth in the developing world is often unregulated and left to market forces. In combination with wide-scale poverty, the result in many low-income countries has been the development of slums and shanty towns characterized by the haphazard development of poor-quality dwellings often without adequate water supply or sanitation, with serious consequences for the health and well-being of the residents (UN Habitat 2003). The McKinsey Global Institute (2014) has estimated that 200 million households in the developing world live in slums. While development and international aid agencies may see shanty towns as a "problem" to be tackled, they are also a private "solution" (however inadequate) to the problem of urban poverty.

Public Responses

In Britain, from around 1840 onward, a stream of government reports and nongovernmental publications were published that highlighted the urban housing question. But despite growing public awareness of slum housing conditions, national and local government intervention emerged very slowly and with considerable reluctance. State intervention was contrary to the prevailing Victorian ideology of laissez-faire and self-help. Housing problems were seen as individual failures, even pathological in origin, which could and should only be solved by individual and private or charitable endeavor rather than by government. In so far as intervention did take place, it had a public health orientation and was in part generated by fear of the spread of disease to more wealthy districts and their residents (Fraser 2009).

Official responses to the urban housing question were limited, partial, and often involved discretionary rather than mandatory responsibilities on the part of local governments. In many European countries, the turning point in the origins and development of housing programs was the First World War (Daunton 1990; Pooley 1992). Although economists generally examine the rationale for housing programs in terms of externalities and market failure, the origins of state intervention have more to do with the calculus of politics than of cost-benefit analysis. This can be illustrated with reference to the introduction of rent controls, a development that marked a sharp break with the principles of laissez-faire that had hitherto been so dominant.

Most of the European countries involved in the hostilities introduced rent controls to protect citizens from the sharp increases in rents that occurred in many localities. And after the war, many of these countries also introduced subsidies to encourage housing providers to build homes to tackle the widespread housing shortages (Daunton 1990; Pooley 1992). These housing interventions were generally seen as temporary, after-the-war measures that would be removed once "normalcy" had returned. But far from withdrawing from housing provision, governments in many industrialized countries became ever more deeply involved, even if they did so reluctantly. Although the extent and form of such intervention has varied over time, it has remained of central importance in most of the advanced economies.

The introduction or extension of government intervention in the housing market, especially in the aftermath of the First and the Second World Wars, was often the result of pressure from organized labor and the better paid workers rather than the poorest tenants. Their main demands were for rent controls and social housing construction.

Postwar housing shortages were a prime driver behind such demands. Electoral considerations after the extension of the franchise or even fear of social unrest were among the reasons why governments acceded to such demands (Merrett 1979; Harloe 1995).

Better paid workers rather than the poor were often also the main beneficiaries of social housing programs in Western Europe, particularly in the early years after the world wars. This was partly because better-paid workers in regular employment were often regarded as more "deserving" than the very poor. But it was also because better-off workers could more easily afford the rents of the new social housing. For although the rents were below market levels, the new social housing tended to be built to higher standards of space, amenities, and layout than the private rental housing from which the new tenants were rehoused. Consequently, even with subsidies, the rents were higher than their previous rents (Bowley 1945). By contrast, in the postwar communist countries of Central and Eastern Europe, subsidized public housing—typically built and maintained to low standards and let at very low rents—was the principal method of new housing supply (Hegedus, Lux, and Teller 2012).

The two defining characteristics of social housing are that it is let (1) on the basis of administratively determined housing "need" and (2) at below market rents (Harloe 1995; Stephens et al. 2003). It is not necessarily owned or managed by nonprofit landlords though. In most countries non-profit landlords—for example, local authorities (Britain), municipal housing companies (Sweden), and housing associations (Britain and the Netherlands)—dominate social housing provision. But in others this is less true. For example, although in (West) Germany some social housing is or has been owned by local councils and nonprofit landlords most has been owned by private landlords who have received subsidies in return for an agreement to let the homes for a term of years below market rents and according to certain tenancy allocation rules.

In most of the liberal market economies—in particular, Australia, Canada, New Zealand and the United States—social housing has generally had a minority or "residual" role in the housing market and been targeted at the poor. In contrast, in Austria, Denmark, Sweden, and the Netherlands social housing has generally accommodated a broader range of households (Harloe 1995; Stephens et al. 2003). In countries where the residual model has predominated, social housing has tended to suffer negative public images or be stigmatized, while in countries with a more general needs orientation it has been more popular and constructed to higher standards. Meanwhile, shortage of land and a strong (if not democratic) government in Hong Kong and Singapore resulted in the construction of public housing on a large scale.

Until the 1970s and 1980s, government interventions in the housing market, especially in Europe, tended to take the form of "bricks and mortar" subsidies (such as capital grants and cheap loans) for social housing and rent controls in the private rental market (Doling 1997). While these supply-side interventions were seen by many governments in the aftermath of the two World Wars as the right way to tackle the housing shortage and slum housing, they seemed less appropriate by the 1970s when dwellings had become much less scarce relative to the number of households. Increasingly, the housing question was conceived in terms of affordability more than quantity and quality.

During the last third of the twentieth century, therefore, many of the advanced welfare states began to phase out rent controls and to reduce or even eliminate bricks-and-
mortar subsidies. This, in turn, led to higher rents in both the private rental and the
social housing sectors. In some cases, policymakers sought to help the poorest households cope with these higher rents by introducing or expanding the scope or generosity
of income-related housing-allowance programs. Indeed, the shift from supply-side to
demand-side interventions was related, as the growth in the latter instrument helped
make it possible to achieve the decrease in the former (Kemp 2007a).

It would be wrong to imagine that the shift from supply- to demand-side subsidies in
the housing market was simply a managerial response to the end of large-scale accommodation shortages. It also reflected the rise of neoliberal ideas that occurred after the
postwar "golden age" of economic growth and welfare state development came to an
end in the 1970s. Since then, there has been a renewed belief in the market as an alloca-
tive device and a corresponding decline in the perceived ability of public and other
nonmarket action to tackle public policy concerns. This shift in attitudes has had implications for perceptions of the relative merits of supply- and demand-side subsidies in
housing (Kemp 2007a).

Advocates of market-based approaches argued that housing allowances are more
efficient than bricks-and-mortar subsidies because they can help more households
for a given amount of money. Moreover, it was claimed that bricks-and-mortar subsidies are often "indiscriminate": they assist all tenants living in social housing irrespective of whether they need subsidized rents or not. In contrast, because housing
allowances are income related, they help only households that truly need it. Further,
housing allowances are thought to encourage residential and labor mobility while
rent controls and bricks-and mortar-subsidies inhibit housing moves. Housing allowances are also believed to enable households to exercise choice—an important leitmo-
tif in the neoliberal era—in the housing market. This is because they enable recipients
to move to the accommodation that is best suited to their preferences and circumstances (Kemp 2012). By contrast, social housing is typically allocated on administrative criteria that offer relatively limited scope for the household to choose their
accommodation.

The shift from supply-side to demand-side assistance in housing costs also reflected
the social and economic changes that accompanied the transition from industrial
to postindustrial society. While the class-based social risks associated with postwar
industrial capitalism created a need for mass social housing, the more individualized
"new social risks" (Taylor-Gooby 2005) associated with the shift to postindustrial capitalism have made income-related housing allowances a more relevant type of assistance (Kemp 2007b). Such new social risks include the growth of unemployment since
the 1970s, which led to an increase in the number of households needing help with
their rent or mortgage payments. The increase in part-time work; the growth of more
precarious forms of employment since the 1970s; and the rise of low-paying jobs have
also increased the demand for housing allowances from people on the margins of the
labor market.

Moreover, research has shown that there is considerable movement into and out of poverty over time in many postindustrial economies: although some people are continuously poor for many years, poverty spells are often relatively short (Hills 2004; Leisering and Walker 1998). As a policy instrument targeted at individuals rather than dwellings, housing allowances can provide income support during periods of poverty irrespective of whether it is long-term or transitory.

In Central and Eastern Europe (CEE), the transition from communist to market economies in the 1990s was accompanied by large-scale privatization of public housing. In some countries this involved a right to buy for sitting tenants at very low prices, but in others it occurred through "give-away" privatization. In most CEE countries, public housing now accounts for a very small proportion of the housing stock and of new construction (Hegedus, Lux and Teller 2012).

FROM SOLUTION TO PROBLEM?

Since the 1980s public perceptions of social housing in the liberal market economies (such as Australia, Britain, and the United States) have become less favorable. Social housing, particularly in the United States, became stigmatized and associated with high levels of poverty, social segregation unemployment, crime, and other social problems. Instead of being seen as a solution, social housing had come to be seen as the problem. In this context, housing allowances were viewed as a policy instrument that could help avoid the problems of poverty neighborhoods and the stigma associated with living in them. Indeed, in the United States, the Moving to Opportunity housing-voucher program has explicitly aimed to help low-income households escape from such areas (Briggs, Popkin, and Goering 2010). Meanwhile, a whole raft of programs was introduced to tackle "problem housing estates" in social housing in Britain, France, the Netherlands, the United States, and elsewhere (Power 1997; Schwarz 2010).

However, while income-related housing allowances are now a well-established and increasingly important policy instrument in many advanced welfare states, they have also been subjected to a range of criticisms and pressures for reform. One such pressure has been the rising the cost of housing-allowance programs. Ironically, while the shift away from supply-side subsidies was partly motivated by a desire to use public money more efficiently, the reduction or phasing out of such subsidies has generally led to higher rents and, in turn, higher housing-allowance expenditure. Moreover, housing-allowance caseloads have tended to rise over time, thereby putting further pressures on scheme budgets.

In several countries policymakers and analysts have expressed concern about the possible impact of housing allowances on housing-consumption incentives and, in particular, whether such schemes reduce recipients' incentive to shop around when looking for accommodation in the rental market (Kemp 2007b). Other commentators have suggested that the lack of sufficiently strong incentives to economize on housing costs might encourage housing-allowance recipients to move up-market to higher quality and hence more expensive dwellings (Hills 1991). A related concern is that housing allowances will result in rent inflation in the housing market. The less incentive housing-allowance recipients have to negotiate the rent or shop around for a good deal, the more likely it is that rents will rise. This may be particularly true if the allowance is spent on increasing housing consumption rather than reducing the rent burden (that is, the share of the household budget spent on housing). However, housing allowances are less likely to produce rent inflation in rent-regulated than in unregulated rental markets (Kofner 2007).

These concerns about housing consumption incentives and rent inflation link to the question of the "controllability" of housing-allowance budgets (Priemus and Elsinga 2007). The lack of controllability reflects the fact that housing-allowance programs are typically demand-led and hence expenditure is (to some degree) countercyclical, their costs increasing during economic downturns and falling during upswings. However, it also reflects a more general concern about cost containment in an era of fiscal constraint (Pierson 1994), albeit one that tends to become more urgent during recessions. The rising cost of housing allowances during the Great Recession, for example, was one of the reasons put forward by the UK government when it announced cutbacks in the program in 2010.

Policymakers are also increasingly concerned about the possibility that housing allowances may create work disincentives (Shroder 2002). In part, this concern reflects the fact that they are means tested and may consequently have "poverty trap" effects (Stephens 2005). Concern about possible "unemployment trap" effects may arise where income-related assistance with housing expenditure for people of working age is confined to households in receipt of social assistance (as in Australia or Canada) or the housing supplements in social assistance provide more generous support than the separate housing-allowance scheme (as in Germany).

ASSISTANCE WITH HOUSING COSTS

The social risks tackled by housing allowances are subtly different from those addressed by social housing (Kemp 20007b). The risks covered by social housing include both insufficient or substandard dwellings and high rent-to-income ratios. Depending upon the rules of access to such accommodation, the people benefiting from social housing have included both low- and moderate-income households in conservative- and social-democratic welfare regimes, and—with the exception of Britain prior to the 1980s—the poor in liberal welfare regimes.

The social risks covered by housing allowances are high housing expenditures and, at least indirectly, income risks such as unemployment, sickness and disability, old age, and single parenthood. Housing allowances are focused more on the risk that housing is unaffordable to poor households than that it is substandard or in insufficient supply.

Indeed, while housing allowances help make housing more affordable, they do not necessarily guarantee that recipients live in minimally adequate housing. They are means tested and very largely focused on poor and other low-income households, though the precise extent to which this is the case varies from one country to another (Griggs and Kemp 2012).

Unlike social housing, housing allowances are generally an entitlement to which people with a low income and relatively high housing expenses have a right. However, the United States is an important exception as the Housing Choice Voucher program is not an entitlement-based scheme, and the funds available are cash limited. Consequently, there are queues for housing vouchers among eligible applicants that cannot yet receive one because the money has run out. Only about a quarter of entitled households in the United States receive a voucher (Newman 2007).

But while housing allowances are more typically an entitlement program, they are not necessarily universal schemes open to all low-income households. The risk groups covered by housing allowances vary according to the rules governing such schemes. For example, in some countries (such as Germany and Sweden) housing-allowance schemes include both renters and homeowners, while in others (such as the Netherlands) they are confined to renters. And while in some countries (such as Australia) housing allowances are provided only to recipients of social assistance, in others (such as Britain) they are available to people with incomes above social-assistance levels and to people in low-paid work. Likewise, some types of household may be excluded from eligibility, such as most students in Great Britain or single people and childless couples aged over 28 years in Sweden. Thus, like other means-tested benefits, the groups of people that are eligible for housing allowances may be more or less circumscribed. Such inclusions and exclusions from eligibility are not simply technical matters but also inherently political decisions with potentially important distributional implications (Kemp 2007a).

First, different types of policy instruments have different distributional implications. The actors who gain or lose from rent control, for example, are likely to be somewhat different from those gain or lose from public housing and different again from those who gain or lose from mortgage-interest tax relief. Once a particular policy instrument is introduced, a group of beneficiaries is created who may well see themselves as having an interest in its retention. At the same time, a group of losers is also created who may campaign for the policy instrument to be removed. Thus, as Pierson (1994, 2004), among others, has argued, while interests create policies, policies create interests. Withdrawing that instrument will create new losers, which may make it politically difficult to remove or reform it without transitional arrangements, if at all.

Second, supply- and demand-side subsidies can have different implications for how, and by whom, housing is provided. For example, rent controls have been used to keep private sector rents below market levels. But rent controls reduce landlords' rates of return and in doing so can negatively affect investment in housing. Provision of new social housing at submarket rents has, at times and in some places, affected the ability of private landlords to compete for tenants. Meanwhile, demand-side interventions, such as housing allowances, enable low-income tenants to afford market rents and as such help underwrite the bottom end of the private rental sector.

Third, the way in which help with housing costs is provided can have important social and ideological connotations. Policy instruments that are universal in the sense that they are available to people in certain categories (e.g., homeowners buying a home with a mortgage) irrespective of income tend not to be stigmatized. They are often available in an anonymous way without the need for an application or test of eligibility by the beneficiary. In contrast, housing allowances are typically income related and, therefore, means tested. They have to be applied for by those who wish to receive them, who thereby identify themselves as poor and are defined as "claimants." There is therefore often a stigma associated with receipt of housing allowances, and indeed that stigma is one of the things that account for the low take-up of such schemes. Homeowners in receipt of mortgage interest relief, on the other hand, are not defined or perceived to be "claimants" and there is no stigma attached to this way of subsidizing housing. Indeed, mortgage interest relief and other tax expenditures have been described as part of the "hidden welfare state" (Howard 1997).

Poverty and Housing Affordability

While housing typically takes up the largest share of household budgets, the extent to which it does so tends to vary according to where people live. That is because the cost of housing varies between and often within different regions and localities, and it generally does so more than the cost of other basic necessities and incomes. For example, according to an index based on 100,000 advertisements in the major towns and cities in the UK during the three months to August 2014, the average monthly rent for a furnished double room (including bills such as utilities) ranged from a low of £251 in Batley in the north of England to a non-London high of £569 in Guildford in the south of England and £905 in west central London (spareroom. co.uk 2014). Yet incomes do not vary spatially to anything like the degree to which housing costs vary.

Because of spatial variation in housing costs, households with similar incomes (and similar housing conditions) but different levels of housing expenditure because of where they live will have different levels of disposable incomes after housing expenditure is taken into account. Thus, the purchasing power of disposable income varies due to spatial differences in housing costs. This has implications for income poverty thresholds. If the purpose of poverty thresholds is to identify the income needed to obtain a minimum amount of necessities, then it could be argued that spatial differences in prices should be taken into account in setting such thresholds (Early and Olsen 2012).

Minimum income or poverty thresholds tend to be set at a national level. But since housing costs vary spatially, households with high housing costs and incomes above the national poverty threshold may have lower disposable incomes than those with low housing costs and incomes that are below the poverty threshold. That is why the UK government low-income statistics are calculated on two income poverty measures, one based on poverty before housing costs (BHC), and the other on poverty after housing costs (AHC). The BHC measure is calculated net of income tax and social security taxes and hence corresponds to disposable income. AHC income is simply BHC income minus gross housing expenditure. In both measures, housing allowances are treated as income.

The merits and demerits of these two income measures have been debated. Not surprisingly, as Johnson and Webb (1992:287) have pointed out, "the various protagonists have alighted on the definition of income most favorable to their cause." These two different measures of poverty can produce quite different estimates of the extent to which different types of households are living in poverty. In general, the AHC poverty rate tends to be higher than BHC poverty rate. For example, Fahey et al. (2004) found that the AHC poverty rate was higher than the BHC rate in 12 out of 14 countries in the European Union. Among those 12 countries, the AHC to BHC poverty rate ratio ranged from 1.06 in Spain to 1.62 in Denmark.

A further issue that is both technical and political is how to determine whether housing is so expensive that it is "unaffordable." Two broad approaches to measuring affordability have been prominent in the literature (Hulchanski 1995; Stone 2006; Whitehead 1991). The first is the affordability ratio, which measures housing expenditure as a percentage of income. Implicit in this approach is the assumption that housing is unaffordable when households have a housing expenditure-to-income ratio that is *above* a critical threshold (e.g., 30 percent of income). The second is the residual income approach, which is based on AHC income, that is, the amount of income left after expenditure on housing is deducted. Implicit in this measure is the assumption that housing is unaffordable when AHC income is *below* a critical threshold (e.g., 60 percent of median income—a commonly used measure of income poverty).

The critical thresholds used in both the ratio and the residual income measures of affordability tend to be rules of thumb rather than scientifically or objectively determined. Bramley (2012:134) has argued that there is "a surprising lack of consensus (across time periods, countries, or sectors) on what the right normative ratio standards are, whichever approach is in use." However, this lack of consensus is not really surprising. When policymakers choose to use a particular threshold beyond which housing is deemed not affordable, that is not a neutral or value-free decision; instead, it is a political decision and hence one that is open to contestation and debate. Such measures may be used by pressure groups, for example, to argue for (increased) housing subsidies or (stricter) rent controls in order to make housing more affordable. And when ratios are used in the design of housing allowances, to give another example, the ratio chosen will have income distributional implications. It is likely to determine not only which households are eligible for assistance but also the amount of assistance that they will receive.

IMPACT OF HOUSING ALLOWANCES

Housing allowance programs have developed differently in different developed countries. This variety includes how much of national resources are spent on housing allowances, which types of household are eligible for assistance, and how much assistance they receive. And while some countries have national mandatory programs, others have local or discretionary ones, and some do not have housing-allowance programs at all. Several of the transition economies of Central and Eastern Europe (e.g., the Czech Republic) have introduced housing allowances (Lux and Sunega 2007). Such programs are relatively uncommon in the less developed countries.

Table 36.1 shows expenditure on housing-allowance schemes as a percentage of gross domestic product (GDP) for 10 rich countries in the early 2000s. It is clear from the table that spending on this policy instrument varied widely between them. Leaving aside Canada, which does not have a national scheme, expenditure on housing allowances ranged from 0.1 percent of GDP in both the United States and the Czech Republic to 1.1 percent of GDP in Britain. The latter country and France (0.9 percent) were devoting considerably more of their GDP to housing allowances than any of the other countries. This point is illustrated in the second column of Table 36.1, which shows expenditure on housing allowances in each country expressed as a percentage of the share of GDP spent by Britain. From this it is clear that Sweden was spending about half, the Netherlands a third, Germany a fifth, Australia a quarter, and the United States

Table 36.1 Expenditure as a Percentage of GDP

Country	Housing allowance expenditure as a percentage of GDP [1]	Expenditure on housing allowances as a percentage of the figure for the UK [2]
Australia	0.30	27
New Zealand	0.49	45
Canada	0.02	2
United States	0.10	9
United Kingdom	1.10	100
France	0.92	84
Germany	0.23	21
Netherlands	0.35	32
Sweden	0.57	52
Czech Republic	0.10	9

[1] Excludes housing additions incorporated in social-assistance payments.

[2] Calculated from column 1.

Source: Kemp 2007: Table 12.4.

and Czech Republic only a tenth of the amount that Britain was devoting to housing allowances as a share of GDP.

Table 36.2 shows the percentage of all households and of tenant households that were in receipt of an income-related housing allowance in 15 countries of the European Union in 2007. Across the EU15 as a whole, 9 percent of *all households* were in receipt of housing allowances. However, there was significant variation between different "welfare regime" types (Esping-Andersen 1990), from 3 percent in the Mediterranean countries to 18 percent in the social democratic ones. The proportion of *tenants* in receipt of housing allowances was roughly double that among households as a whole. Housing-allowance receipt was particularly high among tenants in both the liberal (43 percent) and the social democratic (41 percent) welfare regimes, moderately high in the conservative welfare regime (17 percent) and low in the Mediterranean (4 percent) regime (Table 36.2).

Table 36.2 also shows that there is considerable variation not just between welfare regimes but also within them in respect to housing-allowance receipt. This is

Table 36.2 Housing–Allowance Receipt within the EU–15 (2007)

	Percent of all households in receipt	Percent of tenant households in receipt
Mediterranean		
Greece	1.6	6.7
Italy	1.6	5.7
Portugal	6.0	2.3
Spain	1.3	2.3
Conservative		
Austria	4.2	10.5
Belgium	0.8	1.1
France	24.8	53.3
Germany	2.8	4.8
Luxembourg	5.5	0.0
Netherlands	15.2	34.0
Social democratic		
Denmark	21.5	47.0
Finland	20.3	52.7
Sweden	11.7	22.9
Liberal		
Ireland	30.8	38.5
United Kingdom	13.1	47.5
EU-15	9.2	23.0

Source: EU-SILC survey data analyzed by Griggs and Kemp (2012) Table 1.

particularly evident in the conservative countries, where (ignoring Luxembourg) receipt among tenants ranged from only 1 percent in Belgium to 53 percent in France. The figure for Germany is also low, but this is in part explained by the fact that the social-assistance scheme in that country covers "reasonable" housing expenditure (Kofner 2007). Housing-allowance receipt is higher among tenants than among all households because tenants tend to be poorer and more likely to be economically inactive below retirement age than are owner-occupiers. In addition, in some countries—including the Netherlands and Britain—owner-occupiers are not eligible for housing allowances.

Table 36.3 shows the impact of housing allowances for tenant recipients in the 10 EU15 countries for which there was sufficient data. The first two data columns show rent-to-income ratios before and after income from housing allowances is taken into account. Rent-to-income ratios are substantially lower after, compared with before, housing allowances. The reduction in ratios ranges from 9 percentage points in the case of Germany to 25 percentage points in the case of Sweden and 56 percentage points in the case of the UK. Thus, housing allowances can significantly improve housing affordability, though the extent to which they do so varies cross-nationally.

Table 36.3 also shows the impact of housing allowances on recipients' income relative to the national median income for all households. Before housing allowances are taken into account, recipients' incomes as a percentage of the relevant national median income for all households is highest in Ireland (43 percent) and Finland (47 percent). It is lowest in Italy (22 percent) and the UK (3 percent). After housing allowances, income rises the least in Italy and Germany (+8 and +9 percentage points respectively). It increases the most in Sweden and the UK (+22 and +36 percentage points respectively). These findings show that housing allowances can significantly improve disposable incomes and thereby provide an important source of income support (Griggs and Kemp 2012).

These before-and-after comparisons are based on static analyses of benefit impact (Haffner and Boelhouwer 2006). However, the "formal incidence" of housing allowances may not be the same as the "effective incidence" once housing market adjustment is taken into account. As mentioned, one of the concerns expressed by policymakers and analysts is the possibility that housing allowances may be capitalized into higher rents. The extent to which housing allowances result in higher market rents partly depends on the income elasticity of demand for housing. It is also likely to be affected by the proportion of households in receipt of allowances.

If rents rise in response to the introduction or increased generosity of housing allowances, landlords capture part of the benefit from the reform. It follows that rents can also decrease when such programs are terminated or made less generous. In other words, although the formal incidence of a reduction in housing allowances falls entirely on the tenants who are the program recipients, if rents decrease as a result, the effective incidence of cuts may to some extent be shifted to landlords.

Table 36.3 Impact of Housing Allowances on Recipients' Rent-to-Income Ratios and Incomes, 2007

	Rent-to-income ratio—before HA (1)	Rent-to-income ratio—after HA (1)	Recipient income as percent of all household income—before HA (2)	Recipient income as percent of all household income—after HA (2)
Mediterranean				
Italy	0.51	0.39	22	30
Conservative				
Austria	0.43	0.27	33	43
France	0.42	0.20	33	50
Germany	0.39	0.30	38	47
Netherlands	0.48	0.29	36	54
Social democratic				
Finland	0.43	0.27	47	65
Denmark	0.51	0.29	32	48
Sweden	0.62	0.37	26	48
Liberal				
Ireland	0.20	0.07	43	52
United Kingdom	0.59	0.03	3	39

(1) Median rent-to-income ratios.

(2) Median equivalized disposable incomes after housing costs in Euros at purchasing power parities (PPP).

Source: EU-SILC survey data analyzed by Griggs and Kemp 2012: Tables 3 and 4.

The evidence for housing-allowance-induced rent inflation is mixed. The most robust evidence, from the U.S. Experimental Housing Allowance Program (EHAP) in the 1970s, did not find a market-wide increase in rents. That may be because only a small proportion of households were in receipt of an allowance. Also, recipients tended to spend the money on reducing their rental burden (rather increasing their housing consumption) thereby enabling them to increase their expenditure on nonhousing items (Bradbury and Downs 1981). However, several nonrandomized studies have found that housing allowances had an inflationary impact on rents (e.g., Laferrere and Le Blanc 2004; Susin 2002).

MORTGAGE SUBSIDIES

It is not only the poor who benefit from housing programs. A prime example of this is the tax expenditures for which owner-occupiers are entitled in many of the advanced economies. Indeed, there is a wide range of such subsidies (see Table 36.4), and the sums devoted to them in terms of tax income forgone can substantially outweigh the cost of housing-allowance programs. In general, while housing allowances are pro-poor, and hence progressive in their impact on income inequality, tax expenditures are pro-rich and highly regressive.

Depending on the income elasticity of demand and the price elasticity of supply (both of which tend to vary cross-nationally) these tax expenditures may be capitalized into higher house prices. Where that is the case, they do not make it cheaper for first-time buyers to enter the home-ownership market but instead benefit existing owner-occupiers. Nonetheless, this part of the "hidden welfare state" (Howard 1997) is very popular with owner-occupiers and aspiring owner-occupiers, and hence abolishing tax reliefs is politically hazardous.

Cheap loans, loan guarantees, and other forms of financial aid for first-time buyers are relatively common and politically popular in the advanced economies. That governments are keen on such programs reflects a broader and long-standing support for expanding owner-occupation in most of these countries. The pursuit of the "home-ownership dream" has extended to lower income groups in recent years, as witnessed by the "right to buy" for council tenants in Britain. It was also reflected in the promotion of mortgages for "subprime" borrowers in Anglo-America (Langley 2008) prior

Table 36.4 Tax Expenditures for Owner–Occupiers

Program	UK	Denmark	Germany	Netherlands	United States
Imputed rent taxation	No	No	No	Yes for as long as mortgage is being repaid	No
Mortgage interest tax deduction	No	Yes	No	Yes	Yes
Other cost deductions	No	No	No	Yes	Yes
Capital gains tax	No; principal dwelling exempted	Yes; exempted if occupied by owner and land area is limited to 1,400 sq. m.	Yes, if sold within 10 years of acquisition	No	Yes, if dwelling is not owner-occupied for 3 of the last 5 years

Source: Oxley and Haffner (2010) Table 2.

to the Great Recession in 2008. In the latter case, for hundreds of thousands of low-income, subprime borrowers, the dream turned into personal tragedies of mortgage arrears, foreclosure, and negative equity (Schwartz 2010).

CONCLUSIONS

This chapter has considered the nature and role of housing programs that seek to help the poor (and others) gain access to and afford to pay for adequate housing. It also examined they ways in which housing "problems" have been conceived and contested; and the implications of different conceptualizations for how programs are designed, who gains from them, and who does not. It has stressed the fact that, although there are highly technical aspects to housing programs, many of them are also inherently political with distributional implications and ideological connotations. The nature and role of housing programs is not simply the result of cost-benefit analysis considerations but also of political calculi that have significant consequences—including monetary outcomes—for people living in poverty. Housing programs for the poor are often portrayed in negative ways, unlike those that are more universal and from which the better off also benefit. Nevertheless, both types of program have made very substantial contributions to improving the housing circumstances of households living in poverty. It is just that, especially in the liberal market economies, there is still much more that could be done to tackle housing-related income poverty if those societies wished to do so.

REFERENCES

Bines, Wendy. 1997. "The Health of Single Homeless People." Pp. 132–48 in *Homelessness and Social Policy*, edited by R. Burrows, Nicholas Pleace, and Deborah Quilgars. London: Routledge.

Bowley, Marion. 1945. *Housing and the State 1919–1944*. London: George Allen and Unwin.

Bradbury, Katharine L. and Anthony Downs, eds. 1981. *Do Housing Allowances Work?* Washington, DC: Brookings Institution.

Bramley, Glen. 2012. "Affordability, Poverty and Housing Need." *Journal of Housing and the Built Environment* 27:133–51.

Briggs, Xavier de Souza, Susan J. Popkin, and John Goering. 2010. *Moving to Opportunity: The Story of an American Experiment to Fight Ghetto Poverty*. New York: Oxford University Press.

Burnett, John. 1986. *A Social History of Housing*. 2nd ed. London: Routledge.

Daunton, Martin J., ed. 1990. *Housing the Workers*. Leicester, UK: Leicester University Press.

Donnison, David and Clare Ungerson. 1982. *Housing Policy*. London: Penguin Books.

Early, Dirk W. and Edgar O. Olsen. 2012. "Geographical Price Variation, Housing Assistance and Poverty." In *The Oxford Handbook of the Economics of Poverty*, edited by Philip N. Jefferson. Oxford: Oxford University Press. Oxford Handbooks Online version.

Edelman, Murray. 1971. *Politics as Symbolic Action*. Chicago: Markham.

Esping-Andersen, Gøsta. 1990. *The Three Worlds of Welfare Capitalism*. Cambridge: Polity Press.

Fahey, Tony, Nolan, Brian, and Bertrand Maitre. 2004. "Housing Expenditures and Income Poverty in EU Countries. " *Journal of Social Policy* 33:437–54.

Fazel, Seena, John R. Geddes, and Margot Kushel. 2014. "The Health of Homeless People in High-income Countries: Descriptive Epidemiology, Health Consequences, and Clinical and Policy Recommendations." *The Lancet* 384:1529–40.

Fitzpatrick, Suzanne, Peter A. Kemp, and Suzanne Klinker. 2000. *Single Homelessness: An Overview of Research in Britain*. York, UK: Joseph Rowntree Foundation.

Fraser, Derek. 2009. *The Evolution of the British Welfare State*. 4th ed. Basingstoke, UK: Palgrave Macmillan.

Gauldie, Enid. 1974. *Cruel Habitations*. London: George Allen and Unwin.

Griggs, Julia and Peter A. Kemp. 2012. "Housing Allowances as Income Support: Comparing European Welfare Regimes." *International Journal of Housing Policy* 12:391–412.

Gibson, Marcia, Mark Petticrew, Clare Bambra, Amanda J. Sowden, Kath E. Wright, and Margaret Whitehead. 2011. "Housing and Health Inequalities." *Health and Place* 17:175–84.

Haffner, Marietta E. A. and Peter J. Boelhouwer. 2006. "Housing Allowances and Economic Efficiency." *International Journal of Urban and Regional Research* 30:944–59.

Harloe, Michael. 1995. *The People's Home? Social Rented Housing in Europe and America*. Oxford: Blackwell.

Hegedus, Joseph, Martin Lux, and Nora Teller, eds. 2012. *Social Housing in Transition Countries*. London: Routledge.

Hills, John. 1991. *Unravelling Housing Finance*. Oxford: Clarendon.

Hills, John. 2004. *Inequality and the State*. Oxford: Oxford University Press.

Holmans, Alan E. 1987. *Housing Policy in Britain*. London: Croom Helm.

Howard, Christopher. 1997. *The Hidden Welfare State*. Princeton, NJ: Princeton University Press.

Hulchanski, J. David. 1995. "The Concept of Housing Affordability: Six Contemporary Uses of the Housing Expenditure-to-Income Ratio." *Housing Studies* 10:471–91.

Humphreys, Robert. 1999. *No Fixed Abode*. Basingstoke, UK: Macmillan.

Johnson, Paul and Steven Webb. 1992. "The Treatment of Housing in Official Low Income Statistics." *Journal of the Royal Statistical Society*, Series A 155:273–90.

Kemp, Peter A. 2007a. "Housing Allowances in Context." Pp. 1–16 in *Housing Allowances in Comparative Perspective*, edited by Peter A. Kemp. Bristol, UK: Policy Press.

Kemp, Peter A. 2007b. "Housing Allowances in the Advanced Welfare States." Pp. 265–87 in *Housing Allowances in Comparative Perspective*, edited by Peter A. Kemp. Bristol, UK: Policy Press.

Kemp, Peter A. 2012. "Access and Affordability: Housing Allowances." Pp. 23–29 in *International Encyclopedia of Housing and Home*. Vol. 1. Oxford: Elsevier.

Kofner, Stefan. 2007. "Housing Allowances in Germany." Pp. 159–92 in *Housing Allowances in Comparative Perspective*, edited by Peter A. Kemp. Bristol, UK: Policy Press.

Laferrere, Anne and David Le Blanc. 2004. "How Do Housing Allowances Affect Rents? An Empirical Analysis of the French Case." *Journal of Housing Economics* 13:36–67.

Langley, Paul. 2008. *The Everyday Life of Global Finance*. Oxford: Oxford University Press.

Leisering, Lutz and Robert Walker, eds. 1998. *The Dynamics of Modern Society*. Bristol, UK: Policy Press.

Lux, Martin and Petr Sunega. 2007. "Housing Allowances in the Czech Republic in Comparative Perspective." Pp. 239–64 in *Housing Allowances in Comparative Perspective*, edited by Peter A. Kemp. Bristol, UK: Policy Press.

McKinsey Global Institute. 2014. *A Blueprint for Addressing the Global Affordable Housing Challenge*. New York: McKinsey.

Merrett, Stephen. 1979. *State Housing in Britain*. London: Routledge, Kegan Paul.

Newman, Sandra J. 2007. "Housing Allowances American Style: The Housing Choice Voucher Programme." Pp. 87–104 in *Housing Allowances in Comparative Perspective*, edited by Peter A. Kemp. Bristol, UK: Policy Press.

Oxley, Michael and Marrietta Haffner. 2010. *Housing Taxation and Subsidies: International Comparisons and the Options for Reform*. York, UK: Joseph Rowntree Foundation.

Pierson, Paul. 1994. *Dismantling the Welfare State?* Cambridge: Cambridge University Press.

Pierson, Paul. 2004. *Politics in Time*. Princeton, NJ: Princeton University Press.

Pittini, Alice. 2012. *Housing Affordability in the EU*. Brussels: European Social Housing Observatory.

Pooley, Colin G., ed. 1992. *Housing Strategies in Europe, 1880–1930*. Leicester, UK: Leicester University Press.

Power, Anne. 1997. *Estates on the Edge*. Basingstoke, UK: Palgrave Macmillan.

Priemus, Hugo and Marja Elsinga. 2007. "Housing Allowances in the Netherlands." Pp. 193–214 in *Housing Allowances in Comparative Perspective*, edited by Peter A. Kemp. Bristol, UK: Policy Press.

Schneider, Anne and Helen Ingram. 1993. "The Social Construction of Target Populations." *American Political Science Review* 87:234–47.

Schwartz, Alex F. 2010. *Housing Policy in the United States*. 2nd ed. New York: Routledge.

Shaw, Mary. 2004. "Housing and Public Health." *Annual Review of Public Health* 25:397–418.

Shroder, Mark. 2002. "Does Housing Assistance Perversely Affect Self-sufficiency?" *Journal of Housing Economics* 27:381–417.

Stephens, Mark. 2005. "An Assessment of the British Housing Benefit System." *European Journal of Housing Policy* 5:111–29.

Stephens, Mark, Nicola Burns, and Lisa MacKay. 2003. "The Limits of Housing Reform: British Social Rented Housing in a European Context." *Urban Studies* 40:767–89.

Stone, Mark. E. 2006. "What Is Housing Affordability? The Case for the Residual Income Approach." *Housing Policy Debate* 17:151–84.

Susin, Scott. 2002. "Rent Vouchers and the Price of Low-income Housing." *Journal of Public Economics* 83:109–52.

Taylor-Gooby, Peter. 2005. *New Risks, New Welfare*. Oxford: Oxford University Press.

Tipple, A. G. and Suzanne Speak. N.d. *The Nature and Extent of Homelessness in Developing Countries*. Newcastle upon Tyne, UK: University of Newcastle.

Thomson, Hilary, Sian Thomas, Eva Sellstrom, and Mark Petticrew. 2009. "The Health Impacts of Housing Improvement: A Systematic Review of Intervention Studies From 1887 to 2007." *American Journal of Public Health* 99:S681–92.

UN Habitat. 2003. *The Challenge of the Slums*. London: Earthscan.

Watson, Sophie and Helen Austerberry. 1986. *Housing and Homelessness: A Feminist Perspective*. London: Routledge.

Whitehead, Christine M. E. 1991. "From Need to Affordability." *Urban Studies* 28:871–87.

Wohl, Anthony. 1977. *The Eternal Slum*. New Brunswick, NJ: Transaction.

CHAPTER 37

MICROFINANCE AND FINANCIAL INCLUSION

PHILIP MADER

INTRODUCTION

[E]ven though she worked hard to grow her tiny businesses, Rukia was never able to put aside any savings and her dreams remained out of reach. Then, Rukia applied for and received a microloan. . . . Gradually her profits have increased and she has since been able to move her business to a permanent stall on the busy main street outside the market where she attracts even more customers. Thanks to her perseverance and [the microfinance organisation's] loans, Rukia's goal of constructing a house is finally within grasp. "We've already made the foundation and purchased some of the bricks," Rukia states proudly.[1]

Countless success stories like this one are told about microfinance. Summarily, they form a globally recognized narrative about the power of financial services to transform lives in positive ways. Microfinance refers to the provision of financial services to poor and low-income populations, usually in the global South. Microfinance appears as a financial market solution to the social problem of poverty, promising poverty alleviation in a market-friendly and cost-efficient way, and is regarded by many today as a key tool in the portfolio of international development policies. Proponents hope that the financial inclusion of poor and low-income population segments will help them cope better with multifaceted problems of poverty, in particular their uncertain and low incomes.

The activities of the global microfinance sector today directly impact nearly 200 million clients worldwide. Total loans in 2012 amounted to $100.7 billion, equal to roughly two-thirds of global aid, a part of which went to funding microfinance projects.[2] However, for a poverty-alleviation tool of its extraordinary scope and reputation, there is remarkably little consensus about its practical impacts. As a systematic review assessing the entire domain of microfinance-impact studies concluded, until today "it remains unclear under what circumstances, and for whom, microfinance has been and could be of real, rather than imagined, benefit to poor people" (Duvendack et al. 2011:75). This chapter therefore offers a concise examination of the microfinance sector and its practices, explaining its historical origins and rise, discussing and interpreting the results of impact studies, relating the critical debates waged over microfinance, and taking stock of three sets of recent developments: a spate of crises, a new mission, and a growing scope of activity.

OVERVIEW OF MICROFINANCE

Under the heading "What Is Microfinance?" the World Bank's in-house microfinance agency Consultative Group to Assist the Poor (CGAP) explains:

> "Microfinance" is often defined as *financial services for poor and low-income clients* offered by different types of service providers. In practice, the term is often used more narrowly to refer to *loans and other services from providers that identify themselves as "microfinance institutions"* (MFIs). . . . More broadly, microfinance refers to *a movement that envisions a world in which low-income households have permanent access* to a range of high quality and affordable financial services offered by a range of retail providers to finance income-producing activities, build assets, stabilize consumption, and protect against risks. These services include savings, credit, insurance, remittances, and payments, and others. (CGAP 2012; emphasis added)

While merely one possible description, it comes from a key organization linked to the World Bank, which aspires to represent the "consensus" in the microfinance field, and reveals several things. First, microfinance can be understood as *services for* certain populations and *services from* certain providers. Second, it is neither so clear-cut who the clients are—poor or "low income"—nor exactly who the providers are.[3] Third, the focus is on lending, although other services also matter. Fourth, the vision behind microfinance has been adopted by a broader social movement dedicated to promoting it.

The microfinance sector is an amorphous field, constituted by a diverse set of actors at the intersection of the state with the market and civic society. They include the following:

- Microfinance institutions (MFIs), directly working with the clients; some are NGOs or cooperatives, others are strictly for-profit banks, many are in-between.
- International financial institutions (such as the World Bank or Asian Development Bank); they are funders, standardizers, and political promoters of MFIs.
- Governmental development agencies and multilateral development bodies (like USAID or the International Fund for Agricultural Development) that fund and promote MFIs.

- Foundations and philanthropic organizations (such the Gates Foundation or Oxfam) that fund and operate MFIs.
- Specialized for-profit microfinance investment vehicles (MIVs) and investment funds, which are often linked to major banks.
- Transnational private funding and advocacy organizations (such as Accion, Oikocredit, or Kiva).
- Private, wealthy individuals funding and publicly promoting microfinance.
- A broader social movement, including small-scale middle-class investors and active enthusiasts.

The sector rose to global recognition with small loans for entrepreneurship—*micro-credit*—but since at least the mid-2000s the term *microfinance* has dominated. This rephrasing denotes more than a mere semantic change since microfinance also encompasses savings, insurance, and money transfers. At the same time, the justification for offering microfinancial services has shifted: the core mission previously was exclusively to help small enterprises with credit, but today financial services more generally are expected to alleviate poverty through popular participation in the financial sector. The new mission of "financial inclusion" emphasizes savings, sending money, and insurance services but also suggests that poor people's ubiquitous needs (such as housing, water, or consumption) should be served with credit (Mader and Sabrow 2015).

Credit still stands out as the core activity of the microfinance sector. For example, the global scope of microinsurance remains very small (Kiviat 2009; Binswanger-Mkhize 2012) and a major, if not predominant, part of it is credit default or life insurance which is often obligatorily sold with loans, not a loan-independent service like health or crop insurance (Wipf, Kelly, and McChord 2012). Microsavings, meanwhile, are also far less important than often made out to be. Although in 2012 they came to $86.5 billion globally (compared to outstanding loan balances of $100.7 billion), of these savings nearly half were held at two large institutions, Harbin Bank (China) and Bank Rakyat Indonesia—hardly typical microfinance institutions.[4] Practically all MFIs worldwide—even those ostensibly focusing on savings like SafeSave in Bangladesh and MicroSave in India—make loans. Out of 1,263 MFIs reporting to the database MIX, 579 MFIs reported no client savings at all (another 255 had less than $1 million), while 1,255 reported issuing loans (and 978 had lent more than $1 million). Only at 172 MFIs worldwide did clients hold greater savings than the loans they owed.[5]

The focus in microfinance is clearly on credit. Although poor people evidently have fairly little to save (and many of the savings held at MFIs are not from very poor people), MFIs focus on loans for an even simpler reason: lending is more profitable than their other activities. When MFIs do take savings, this service is often tied to credit, such that clients are only allowed to save if they take a loan—worse yet, some parts of what appears as savings are actually *forced savings* (cf. CGAP 2003; Sinclair 2012).[6] Furthermore, the commercialization of microfinance dissuades MFIs from taking savings because it eases MFIs' access to other capital sources; among those MFIs in which commercial MIVs have invested, the share of savings has decreased (Symbiotics 2013).[7] The effort and cost of administering small savings accounts is high, so MFIs often prefer to borrow their capital from larger banks or seek investors; many can even borrow capital without interest from "p2p" funders, like Kiva, or obtain grants from donors.

Economic and Gender Impacts of Microfinance

From the outset, MFIs and other key organizations have argued that poverty alleviation and women's empowerment are the main objectives of microfinance. For instance CGAP (1995:2) explains: "Finance and enterprise systems that serve the majority can be the pivotal links and the levers, enabling the poor to share in economic growth and giving poor people the means to use social services." The idea behind microfinance is that poor people above all lack the financial tools with which to help themselves out of poverty; with hard work and some borrowed capital, they should be able to grow. Muhammad Yunus likened microcredit clients to "bonsai people" in his 2006 Nobel lecture:

> To me poor people are like bonsai trees. . . . There is nothing wrong in their seeds. Simply, society never gave them the base to grow on. All it needs to get the poor people out of poverty [is] for us to create an enabling environment for them. Once the poor can unleash their energy and creativity, poverty will disappear very quickly.[8]

The notion of microfinance as a poverty-alleviating instrument was (and still often is) underpinned by stories of poor individuals investing in their small businesses and gaining material wealth—as with Rukia's story, above. By the 1990s, however, many donors and academics sought more systematic evidence of impact. The most supportive evidence came from studies conducted with World Bank support in Bangladesh, studying "the impact of participation, by gender, in . . . three group-based credit programs on women's and men's labor supply, boys' and girls' schooling, expenditure, and assets" (Pitt and Khandker 1998:960). Pitt and Khandker concluded that "participation in these credit programs, as measured by quantity of cumulative borrowing, is a significant determinant of many of these outcomes. Furthermore, credit provided to women was more likely to influence these behaviors than credit provided to men." They estimated that for every 100 Taka lent to a woman, her household's consumption expenditure—the main poverty indicator used—increased by 18 Taka (11 Taka for men) relative to households who did not borrow. Practitioners broadly welcomed these results as proof of microfinance's success; but the results in fact were far less clear than they first appeared. For instance, when Morduch (1998) and later Roodman and Morduch (2009) adjusted certain parameters, ensuring among other things that the characteristics of borrower households matched those of comparison households, or accounting for women generally receiving much smaller loans, their analysis suggested a slightly negative overall impact from microcredit. Mosley and Hulme's (1998) research found that the poorer the client, the more likely they were to fall deeper into poverty, and only comparatively better-off households stood to benefit from borrowing. Anthropologists in particular meanwhile questioned whether women really gained empowerment through loans, especially because men often appropriated their wives' loans and rising levels of domestic tension and violence were found (Rahman 1999:74).[9]

Pitt and Khandker's contested studies triggered a still-ongoing academic debate over appropriate statistical methods for measuring poverty impact (cf. Duvendack and Palmer Jones 2012), fuelling an enterprise of further studies aiming to resolve the shortcomings of earlier ones. The earlier phase of impact research may be distinguished from a later phase since the mid-2000s which has been dominated by studies using increasingly sophisticated, randomized sampling methodologies (cf. Banerjee and Duflo 2011). The recent spell of randomized controlled trials (RCTs) has drawn upon methods adopted from medical testing in order to eliminate the sources of upward bias which critics and skeptics asserted could account for alleged improvements in poverty indicators, for instance self-selection bias (more success-prone households likelier to apply for loans) and program-placement bias (MFIs lending in settings more conducive to success). By randomizing membership in "treatment" and "control" groups, akin to clinical trials, it was to be ensured that any differences in poverty outcome were actually caused by the intervention itself. RCTs in the social sciences, however, only incompletely reproduce the clinical situation, for instance since "patients" and "doctors" are not double-blinded (both know who received a loan), no "placebo" is administered (to the control group), and therapeutic equivalence is not tested (no comparison of the tested "treatment," microfinance, against another established one) (Mader 2013b).

Instead of clearly demonstrating impact, however, the microfinance RCTs so far have shown very few significant positive differences between the "treatment" and "control" groups; the results of the first two studies were released in 2009. The Indian RCT, conducted in Hyderabad, had partnered with an MFI, agreeing to randomly open branches only in half of certain slum districts where it planned to open new offices (Banerjee et al. 2009). The researchers found no net change in the expenditures of households living in these "treatment" slums relative to "control" slums, indicating that loan availability did *not* make the areas less poor on aggregate. Also, no impacts on women's empowerment and other "social" outcomes were found. The researchers, however, noted that MFI lending made people living here marginally more likely to start a business and increase their overall spending on business purposes, although this did not raise their incomes or assets. They also found that spending on so-called temptation goods (Banerjee et al. 2009:28) decreased, which they interpreted as a successful outcome.[10] In the Philippines RCT, an MFI in Manila randomly gave loans to some marginally creditworthy applicants and denied loans to others (Karlan and Zinman 2009). This research turned up puzzling results: for instance, "treated" businesses shrank and laid off workers. Borrowers' children were more likely to attend school, but only if the borrower was a man. Microcredit did not measurably change households' incomes or consumption levels, yet "self-reported wellbeing, based on responses to standard batteries of questions on optimism, calmness, (lack of) worry, life satisfaction, work satisfaction, job stress, decision making power, and socioeconomic status" worsened significantly (Karlan and Zinman 2009:17).[11] More recent RCTs (such as Augsburg et al. 2012; Crépon et al. 2014) have painted similarly unclear pictures, finding a mixed bag of correlations between certain variables and access to credit but never demonstrating clear-cut poverty-alleviating effects.

In 2011, the British Department for International Development (DFID) published a systematic review summarizing the findings of all available studies on microfinance impact. After considering a total of 2,643 publications, the reviewers short-listed a sample of 58 studies of sufficient quality (in terms of research design and method of analysis) to be reviewed in depth. These studies covered all types of microfinance programs and a variety of different tested outcomes, including gender and economic empowerment. The DFID reviewers concluded that all the studies commonly cited in favor of microfinance were too flimsy to credibly demonstrate positive impact, since,

> . . . almost all impact evaluations of microfinance suffer from weak methodologies and inadequate data, thus adversely affecting the reliability of impact estimates. Nevertheless authors often draw strong policy conclusions generally supportive of microfinance. This may have lead [sic] to misconceptions about the actual effects of programmes, thereby diverting attention from the search for perhaps more pro-poor interventions and more robust evaluations. (Duvendack et al. 2011a:2)

The DFID team argued it had to "come down on the side of 'there is no good evidence for' rather than 'there is no good evidence against the beneficent impact of microfinance'" (Duvendack et al. 2011b:72). Others, like mathematician and microfinance expert David Roodman (2012), have also clarified that "today the best estimate of the impact of microcredit on poverty is zero."

It is worth asking then, given these findings (or lack thereof), exactly why the positive impacts expected by CGAP and Yunus are not materializing, or why microcredit for microenterprise (the key activity of microfinance) may perhaps even generate negative impacts. The problems noted in the literature lie in the micro-, meso- and macrolevels.[12] The issues at the microlevel can be summarized as three interrelated problems: displacement, saturation, and fallacy of composition. *Displacement* (or spillover) refers to how a borrower's microenterprise impinges on other people's microenterprises: a borrower using her loan, for instance, to sell vegetables on a local street usually enters a market with few or no barriers to entry in which others already compete. If this borrower financially succeeds, she likely does so by displacing a (nonborrowing) competitor, and thus the microloan leaves the net local economic situation unchanged. Or, one enterprise does not displace another, but instead both collectively saturate the local market, producing a new distribution, but no growth; that is, market *saturation* occurs.[13] Given displacement and saturation effects, the impact of microfinance may appear exaggeratedly positive when the out-competed nonborrowers are the comparison group. *Fallacy of composition* occurs when an observer (MFI employees, researchers, policymakers) falsely take their individual observations of positive impact among the clients as representative of the entire local economy, which may be stagnant or in decline; a handful of prosperous MFI-financed microenterprises does not equate local economic development.

These issues connect with larger meso-level problems: demand and returns to scale. Microfinance increases the supply of goods and services locally offered by microenterprises, but *demand* generally only rises if overall wealth in the area increases; an issue which microfinance does not address.[14] To make matters worse, microenterprises typically offer products and services whose demand is income inelastic, such that even rising local incomes would create relatively few opportunities for microenterprise expansion. The demand for local farm produce, rickshaw rides, hand-sewn clothes, or haircuts is most likely to remain static while demand for processed foods, motorcycles, urban fashion, or high-tech products (produced by large industry elsewhere) rises. The converse, supply-side, issue is that informal microenterprises show low *returns to scale*; that is, they are inherently hard to grow since there are few feasible means for raising their productivity. For instance, a $100 loan can make the difference between doing nothing and setting up a roadside vegetable stand or buying a sewing machine. The next $100, however, makes comparatively less difference; the vegetable seller could buy at bulk rates or advertise, the tailor could buy a newer machine, but their business remains essentially unchanged, unlike larger industrial enterprises, where additional investments (for instance in machinery) can increase output by a significant factor.

Resting on these issues, finally, are larger problems of economic transformation: *industrial policy* and *entrepreneurship*. Viewed macroeconomically, microfinance spreads credit broadly among many users. However, as scholars like Ha-Joon Chang (2002) argue, successful national economic development hinges on *industrial policy*—deliberately targeting key industries and channeling finance to them (as for instance, historically, happened in South Korea and Taiwan). Milford Bateman (2011) argues that microfinance even actively undermines sustainable development by directing scarce capital to tiny uninnovative, low-productivity undertakings that cannot generate growth. Moreover, microfinance idolizes and misunderstands *entrepreneurship* by supporting practically any autonomous income-generating activity. The ideology behind microfinance suggests everyone is—or should be—an entrepreneur.[15] But, following Schumpeter (1962), it is only select individuals with vision and creativity who create the capitalist dynamic of "creative destruction" that drives economies forward, and while some microfinance clients may be such characters, most probably are not. Most borrowers would likely prefer a decent job, given the choice (Karnani 2007). Worse yet, the tiny loan sizes doled out by MFIs force even the most gifted entrepreneurs into pursuing minimalistic, emulative, noncreative microenterprise activities.

The positive impact which microfinance is supposed to have on women specifically also turns out to be far less clear than commonly assumed. Proponents often cite as evidence for women empowerment the high percentage of female borrowers (over three-quarters are female) and highlight the sheer fact that microloans place significant amounts of cash in many women's hands for the first time. But feminist and anthropological scholars doubt that such borrowing brings empowerment. Microfinance may have a disempowering effect on women since "[w]hen women are constructed as responsible clients," as Katharine Rankin (2001:29) argues, "the onus for development falls squarely on their shoulders." Critics like Nancy Fraser (2013) argue that microfinance politically replaces welfare state paternalism with new, neoliberal forms of oppression. Empowering the female entrepreneur as a new a catalyst for development may appear progressive, but "in traditional patriarchal fashion, women, idealized for their responsibility, are rewarded by being made responsible for more and more labor activities" (Isserles 2003:48).

In practice, instead of MFIs focusing on women as more promising entrepreneurs or better stewards of family money (the "public transcript of microfinance"), Rahman (1999) found it is often the case that MFIs target women because they are weaker. Women's "positional vulnerability" in Bangladesh's rural social hierarchy makes them more pliant borrowers for majority-male MFI staff to manage, and MFIs actively draw on and reinforce these local gendered inequalities through their lending practices. As Karim (2011:84) argues, far from being anathema to microfinance, existing patriarchal structures that suppress women are actually useful ingredients in MFIs' business model:

> Loan recovery technologies deployed by NGOs used public shaming as a form of social control. . . . Women who were unable to pay their loans on time were often publicly humiliated, or the fear of a public humiliation hung over their heads, acting as a form of discipline in their lives." Moreover, women were treated effectively as a tool, in that "NGOs shamed rural men by shaming their wives. (Karim 2011:86)

Moreover, Kabeer (2000:64) found that in Bangladesh a majority of borrowing women practically "exercised little or no control over their loan," and husbands or other male relatives often decided how they should use it. Some women simply had to hand over the loaned money while still bearing the burden of repayment.

HISTORY AND PREHISTORY

The roots of microfinance are often traced back to the lending experiment begun in 1976 in Bangladesh by Muhammad Yunus, who founded the Grameen (Village) Bank in 1983.[16] Yunus and the Grameen Bank won the Nobel Prize for Peace in 2006 and became the public face of microfinance globally. However, Yunus's story is hardly as unique, and microfinance not quite as new, as the commonplace story suggests. Very similar lending experiments were going on in different parts of the world around the same time, particularly in South Asia, where credit as a form of social policy had an institutional lineage dating back to the British colonial administration.[17]

Cooperative credit societies were brought to South Asia by the colonial administration in the late nineteenth and early twentieth centuries as a "transplant of a German idea, with English characteristics, slightly modified to suit conditions in British India" (Turnell 2005:16). Aided with state money, while simultaneously avowing free-market principles and insisting on freedom from state interference,[18] the cooperatives grew to 4 million members by 1930. At the beginning of the twentieth century, prominent cooperatives promoter Henry W. Wolff (1910:520–21) conducted a global survey of cooperatives and specifically lauded the British Indian credit societies for their independence and firmly capitalist ethos, which apparently made them vastly superior to their European counterparts. But ironically, unlike the more solidarity-oriented European cooperatives (many of which survive until today), the British Indian system went into decline around 1925 and wholly collapsed in parts of the subcontinent. The reasons included social imbalances, poor governance, and various departures from the original German model (Turnell 2005). The South Asian co-ops particularly failed in their mission of ousting the moneylender, and instead were often run by landlords, moneylenders, and other elites who used them as sources of patronage and influence (Shah, Rao, and Shankar 2007). After independence, despite these shortcomings, the new South Asian nations drew on the colonial lineage of credit as a social policy and continued to encourage cooperative credit particularly for farmers and artisans. India, especially, operated large, state-driven rural-lending programs. The effect was that the total share of informal credit from moneylenders, traders, and landlords fell by more than half during the 1970s, while households' debt share to formal lenders doubled (Shah et al. 2007).

The Bangladeshi war of independence in 1971, from which a weak and autocratic state emerged, proved a crucial event in the development of modern microfinance. After the war, a catastrophic famine followed in 1973–1974, and throughout the young country newly founded civil society organizations sought to fill the void left by the incapable state, particularly in supporting marginal and recently displaced communities (Zohir 2004). But most of these nascent NGOs lacked funding for large transformative projects, and some discovered short-term loans were one cost-effective way of working with the poor. Thus, a number of nongovernmental relief organizations, such as the Bangladesh Rural Advancement Committee (BRAC), started in 1972, pioneered microfinance before Grameen Bank. It was in this environment that Muhammad Yunus, the son of a jeweler from Chittagong and professor of economics educated at Vanderbilt University, returned from the United States and began experimenting with small rural loans. After initial success, through personal connections, Yunus was able to secure funding from the national Bangladesh Bank and commercial banks. In 1983 the project officially became a government-regulated bank, thanks to a unique ordinance passed by the government of dictator Hussain Muhammad Ershad (Hulme 2009:165).

This new approach to poverty alleviation, with private organizations disbursing small loans for rural entrepreneurship, was also championed by organizations such as Accion and FINCA in Latin America around the same time. It coincided with a series of paradigm shifts in the field of global development. In the 1970s and 1980s, state-driven policies of import-substituting industrial development fell out of favor, while the importance of the informal sector and women's role in development were noted and emphasized; poor women in particular were "discovered" as productive members of society. Also, the "basic needs approach" advocated by the International Labor Organization (targeting the poorest and their most urgent needs first) and the budding NGO sector were recognized as being closer to the lives of poor people than the state and its massive industrial development policies. The new, exciting idea of microcredit matched these new imperatives as a nonstate, women-oriented, grassroots-level intervention that promised to release the productive energies of poor people. It was also a response to the critique of subsidized credit launched by a group of economists who became known as the "Ohio School,"[19] which strongly influenced World Bank policy in the 1980s. Subsidized credit discouraged savings, they argued, actually leading to "redistribution in reverse" (Gonzalez-Vega 1982); therefore, to benefit the poor, credit markets needed to be made competitive and follow market forces (Adams, Douglas, and von Pischke 1984).

Microcredit began to garner serious recognition from the international policy community and economic observers in the 1980s when it began to be used in implementing structural adjustment programs (SAPs). In the context of SAPs orchestrated by multilateral organizations, microcredit played a strategic role in facilitating economic and financial liberalization as a financially steered poverty-alleviation program. The World Bank and the IMF (directly as well as through subsidiaries such as CGAP) employed microcredit to impose an "enabling environment" for financial services, integrated with their development agendas (Weber 2002). In the course of Bolivia's New Economic Program, for instance, from 1986 onward, microloans were deployed in order to assuage resistance to the worst effects of austerity and facilitate the transition of formerly government- or formal-sector employed workers into informal self-employment. Political mainstreaming coincided with the commercial mainstreaming of microfinance. Following the first MFI transformations in the 1980s, in the 1990s a growing number of economically successful microfinance NGOs transformed into for-profit companies. The private for-profit approach to microlending was picked up by the World Bank as a model for the sector, which founded a sub-organization, CGAP, to promote and standardize the template for commercial microfinance (Bateman 2010:16–17).

CGAP, over time, also proposed a broader range of financial activities for MFIs, beyond their traditional focus on entrepreneurship lending. MFIs should aim for a general "provision of credit, savings, and financial services to very poor people" since providing "these services to very poor households creates opportunities for the poor to create, own, and accumulate assets and to smooth consumption" (CGAP 1998:1). The focus of policy actors increasingly shifted in the 1990s from directly supporting MFIs to promoting an *appropriate financial system* for the growth of microfinance providers, primarily through enticing private investors to enter the market. This effort at commercializing microfinance fell onto politically and economically fertile ground in an era of general enthusiasm about financial development paired with an abundance of investment capital. A number of high-profile events finally anchored microfinance in the public imaginary, adding widespread social credence to the increasingly clear business case for microfinance. The Microcredit Summit in 1997 (organized by NGOs, MFIs, and lobby groups), the United Nations' Year of Microcredit in 2005, and particularly the Nobel Prize for Peace awarded to Muhammad Yunus and Grameen Bank in 2006 all raised microfinance's profile among alternative policies in the global development and poverty alleviation toolkit.

Under the new approach that encouraged the entry of private capital (often via subsidies designed specifically to entice commercial investments) the global microfinance sector has grown rapidly since the 1990s (see Table 37.1). While public sector funding for microfinance has continued, and has even grown, major institutional investors have also taken a growing interest particularly since the turn of the millennium (MicroRate 2013). The commercialization of the microfinance sector is ongoing, but today already in many countries the leading MFIs are private companies primarily funded by private capital. The enthusiasm of private, profit-seeking financial investors was further encouraged by a number of stock market share issues by MFIs since the mid-2000s and the emergence of more sophisticated investment tools such as debt collateralization, which improve the liquidity of microfinance investments (Lieberman et al. 2009). Although still fairly small compared to other parts of global finance, with \$100.7 billion in loans (in 2012) the microfinance sector is no longer wholly negligible. The Microcredit Summit Campaign, an advocacy organization, counted 195 million clients served by 3,652 MFIs as of December 2011, and more than three-quarters of the clients were women (Maes and Reed 2012:3). However, the vast majority of MFIs are small or very small, and the industry is highly concentrated: of the 1,262 MFIs reporting their 2012

	1995	2005	2011/12
No. of MFIs	ca. 735[*]	1,228[^]	1,263[^]
No. of loans or borrowers (million)	12.2[*]	48.8[^]	195[†]
Size of loan portfolio (US$ billion)	5.0[*]	18.2[^]	100.7[^]

Sources: [*]World Bank 2001; [†]Maes/Reed 2011; [^]MIX 2013.

FIGURE 37.1 Growth of the microfinance industry

loans to the Microfinance Information Exchange (MIX, a CGAP brainchild), only 50 large MFIs accounted for more than two-thirds of lending worldwide.

RECENT DEVELOPMENTS

Three recent developments in microfinance are worth interpreting in light of the ongoing commercialization and concentration of the microfinance sector. First, a number of crises and collapses have shaken the microfinance field, exposing the tendency of commercial microfinance to push clients into overindebtedness traps; the transformation of some national MFI sectors has come with all the trappings of financial markets. Second, the uncertainty about the impacts of microfinance has fostered the search for a new mission and meaning, such that microfinance is now justified as an integral element of a global push for "financial inclusion," instead of the older, simpler idea of lending for microenterprise. Third, because of its recent expansion beyond its traditional spheres of activity, microfinance is increasingly proposed as useful for addressing a whole range of social problems and is also making headway in the Global North.

Overindebtedness and Collapse

The ongoing transformation and maturation of microfinance into a financial market has brought a series of collapses; the widely reported crisis in India 2010 was only the most recent and severe case.[20] Each collapse appears to have taken the sector by surprise, and industry spokespeople have generally placed the blame on political actors. But the commonalities of the crises suggest they are caused by more fundamental factors inherent to the microfinance business itself. In spite of their geographic dispersion—from Bolivia in 2000 via the crises in Bosnia-Herzegovina, Morocco and Nicaragua in 2007 and 2008, to the huge collapse in the south Indian state of Andhra Pradesh in 2010—the microfinance collapses have shown four common factors: commercialization and growth; competition and overindebtedness; an unsound political economy; and a triggering event.

A first notable feature of the countries that experienced microfinance collapses is that these were fast-growing markets where commercial MFIs dominated. They were leading, exemplary microfinance markets, not backwaters. During the 1980s and 1990s, Bolivia was the global paragon of commercial microfinance, India was the same in the late 2000s, and Morocco was home to several globally renowned MFIs.[21] The underlying problem is that commercialization requires MFIs to seek growth and efficiency (which are supposed to benefit clients via higher outreach and lower cost), but this striving for growth and efficiency often leads MFIs to cut corners and overreach. For instance, among India's leading MFIs before the collapse it was not uncommon for one loan officer to supervise more than 400 clients. Rapid growth also, incidentally, can hide the consequences of bad lending, giving MFIs a false semblance of health, since older, nonperforming loans are numerically eclipsed by new loans that are being repaid on time.

A second feature of these markets was the high level of competition, which amplified the pressure on MFIs to grow and exacerbated the side-effects of growth. The Ohio School economists had suggested competitive credit markets to enhance efficiency and ensure optimal capital allocation, but in practice competition often leads to very poor lending decisions. Since commercial MFIs depend on securing finance from capital markets, they compete in signaling to investors a high likelihood of generating exceptional returns. The most effective means for signaling this is to expand their market share by growing the client base and making larger loans. Competition thereby encourages (or even requires) MFIs to act in ways that in the short term and for each MFI make sense but in the long term and collectively can be disastrous. To illustrate: in a market with several MFIs targeting the same client, each MFI knows that if it does not lend, another will gain the fees and interest payments. Given strong enough competition, even if the client's creditworthiness is doubtful, at least one MFI (and perhaps all) will lend. Perversely, however, if the borrower ever finds herself in repayment trouble—even just temporary trouble—all MFIs will competitively squeeze her for repayments. Competition also extends beyond the other MFIs. In Bolivia and Bosnia-Herzegovina, MFIs and commercial consumer lenders competed for the same clientele. In Nicaragua, MFIs competed against a large state program, and in India they competed against the state-supported "self-help group" model of linking poor borrower groups to commercial banks. Furthermore, ubiquitously there remains the traditional moneylender as a competitor.

Third, the political economies of these locales were conducive to both the growth and subsequent collapse of the microfinance system. In different but comparable ways, desperation rather than opportunity drove many borrowers to take loans. In all locales, a reduction of economic security for low-income populations drove people into debt, generating the high demand for microcredit that attracted MFIs and their investors. In the 1990s, Bolivia's economic reforms thrust multitudes of previously formally employed or transfer-dependent people into the labor market, leaving many with no other option than to self-employ through microenterprise to survive in the country's stagnant economy. For Nicaragua, the 2000s were a period of slow growth and historically relatively low coffee prices. Bosnia-Herzegovina faced not only postwar rebuilding after 1999 but also the construction of a capitalist economy, which European and international donors sought to achieve through microfinance; but their strategy succeeded only in creating a deindustrialized and "infantilized" market economy (Bateman 2007). In India, post-1994 liberalization saw the discontinuation or reduction of various social programs, farmer subsidies, and state lending, which squeezed the livelihoods of the rural poor. Given the lack of economic security and opportunity, it was only a matter of time until many clients became caught in debt traps, which were deepened by the competitive supply of credit.

Fourth, the collapses were all to some extent triggered or accompanied by an external (political or economic) event on which microfinance industry representatives placed the blame. In Bolivia, in 2000, debtor protests arose in the context of successful nationwide campaigning against neoliberal reforms (Marconi and Mosley 2005). In part, they were organized by well-known political activists, and some protestors resorted to desperate means including hunger strikes and building occupations; MFIs mostly blamed the political activists for the crisis (Rhyne 2001). In Nicaragua, in 2008, after six borrowers in a small town were arrested for not repaying, protests ensued and rapidly spread throughout the north of the country, turning violent. This protest movement "No Pago" ("I'm Not Paying") was publicly endorsed by President Daniel Ortega, who accused the MFIs of committing "usury". Again, politics (only the proximate trigger) was blamed for the crisis. The collapses of Bosnia-Herzegovina and Morocco in 2008, meanwhile, were blamed on the global economic downturn (Chen et al. 2010), an explanation that makes the most sense when considering how that credit crunch deprived MFIs of the funds necessary to continue raising the loan balances of their already-overindebted clients.

To understand the interplay of these four factors, it is worth examining the Indian crisis, the deepest and most dramatic one to date. In India, microfinance began expanding in the late 1990s, building on the legacies of colonial cooperative credit and state-lending programs. Indian MFIs were generally founded as NGOs using state and donor money, but within under 10 years many had transformed into private "nonbank financial companies" successfully chasing commercial funding and aiming for share listing on the stock market. Focusing solely on the business of credit, India's hyperefficient MFIs achieved unheard-of growth rates and were well-capitalized by Indian banks and investors from abroad. Showing default rates as low as 0.14 percent in 2008 (nationwide) and posting extraordinary profits, Indian MFIs exemplified the commercial microfinance model's success at generating efficiency, outreach and profitability.[22] Behind the scenes, however, extreme forms of social coercion and multiple borrowing upheld the microfinance miracle; debtors were often driven to take extra loans (including from moneylenders) to survive each successive loan cycle. The boom centered on Andhra Pradesh, a leading neoliberal reform state, where MFIs found many people well-experienced in the management of debt and handily preorganized into borrower groups thanks to the Self-Help Group (SHG) system (the MFIs "poached" these groups) who often also faced extreme and worsening hardships. An ecological crisis (including depleting common resources, unsustainable agricultural change, and climate change) intertwined with the retrenchment of social spending and farmer subsidies to push rural populations to use credit for handling income losses and insecurity or for migrating to cities (Taylor 2011). By the end of the boom, 84 percent of households in Andhra Pradesh held two or more loans (from different sources) and 58 percent had four or more; the median household had three. In late 2010, after two years of droughts and floods afflicting parts of the state, a wave of violence and suicides swept through the ranks of Andhra borrowers, exposing widespread overindebtedness and unleashing a media storm that induced the government of Andhra

Pradesh to temporarily halt all microlending and loan collection.[23] Although the halting effect of the emergency ordinance lasted only five days, widespread repayment defiance took hold, and the MFIs lost an estimated fifth of their nationwide loan portfolio (over $1 billion), for which they blamed the Andhra government.

New Methods and Mission

Rather than retreating from microfinance, or critically reconsidering the suitability of finance-driven approaches to poverty alleviation altogether, since the 2000s the microfinance industry and its funders have reacted to the collapses and deepening questions about impact broadly in three ways. The first is the construction of a new market infrastructure in many countries, particularly those which already experienced collapses. Debt counseling is now supposed to help clients manage and reduce their debts, but its effectiveness is doubtful. For instance, in Bosnia, widespread debt counseling began in 2009, but a 2013 survey still found 69 percent of borrowers "vulnerable" to, "exposed" to, or "concerned" about overindebtedness (Goronja 2014). Credit registries, on the other side, aim to prevent clients from becoming indebted to more than one MFI (cf. McIntosh, Sadoulet, and de Janvry 2006). However, under conditions of intense competition (as described earlier) they may not succeed and might even help one MFI poach another's client. Finally, financial education programs—often supported by large, corporate donors (e.g., cf. MasterCard Foundation 2011)—aim to educate (prospective) clients about the benefits and risks of different financial products, but it is unclear to what extent they actually succeed at improving clients' ability to calculate and plan ahead in practice. Furthermore, there is a risk of "education" merging with marketing and promotion.

A second reaction has been the launching of initiatives for "socially responsible" microfinance—coming together in a "Global Appeal for Responsible Microfinance"[24]—by investor groups and thought leadership organizations. The "Smart Campaign" (initiated by global investor network Accion), "Social Performance Task Force" (spearheaded by CGAP), and "Truelift" (a multistakeholder initiative which, for a fee, assigns a "Pro-Poor Seal of Excellence") are the most prominent in a flurry of new global standards and action plans for responsible, transparent and client-centered microfinance. What unites the initiatives is their emphasis on voluntary participation, an absence of restrictive rules (such as interest rate limits above which lending is considered irresponsible), no measurement of client poverty alleviation, and a lack of mechanisms for sanctioning or exposing transgressors. Citing the example of the Mexican MFI CompartamosBanco, infamous for charging up to 195 percent interest, gaining the Smart Campaign's "Client Protection Certification," critics have argued that the initiatives lack substance and merely serve to deflect criticism from the sector (Sinclair 2014).

Third, and most fundamentally: microfinance has progressively gained a new mission.[25] Earlier, the mission of microfinance was to provide finance for microenterprise (with an explicit focus on *credit*), but lately the goals have broadened and become more diffuse under the mission of "financial inclusion." The new mission asserts access to financial services as a fundamental, ubiquitous need. An early and important marker in this mission shift was CGAP's 2002 annual report, which explained why financial services should be seen as universally applicable and universally necessary tools:

> *Like everyone else,* poor people need and use financial services *all the time.* They need financial services to take advantage of business opportunities, invest in home repairs and improvements, and meet seasonal expenses like school fees and holiday celebrations. They need financial services to prepare for life-cycle events like the wedding of a daughter or the death of a grandmother. They need financial services to cope with emergencies like the sudden death of a wage-earner or a monsoon that wreaks havoc on their village. (CGAP 2001:5, emphasis added)

Unlike microenterprise finance, the financial inclusion mission explicitly endorses credit for survival and consumption, proposing "consumption smoothing" as an important goal in itself: poor people's problem is less that their incomes are low, and more that they are uncertain and volatile, and here microfinance can help. Using finance for income generation is therefore only one financial need the poor have, and MFIs should help them manage their money in whichever way they themselves deem suitable to handle their uncertain lives. Financial inclusion thereby officially inscribes and legitimates practices that were already widespread yet unacknowledged, such as credit for nonproductive purposes. In contrast to the earlier microenterprise mission, it is no longer assumed that poor people need to generate the money for loan repayment via entrepreneurial ventures. Here, they already *have it*, as past or future incomes: "Financial services allow people to reallocate expenditure across time ... if you don't have the ability to pay for things *now*, out of current income, you can pay for them out of *past* income or *future* income, or some combination of both" (CGAP 2000b:2). Taking this logic to the extreme, proponents of the new mission argue, "Not having enough money is bad enough. Not being able to manage whatever money you have is worse" (Collins et al. 2009:184). In this way, with financial inclusion, the goal posts for microfinance have shifted from raising incomes and assets to the more attainable goals of consumption smoothing and financial access for all, such that the troubling issue of (measurable) poverty alleviation disappears from discussion.

Expansion of Scope

In part thanks to the new mission, the hype about microfinance has continued and the sector's scope of activities is still growing. Microlending has gelled with other market-based poverty-alleviation initiatives from the hubristic idea of "social business" serving "humanity's most urgent needs," promoted by Muhammad Yunus (2011), to the idea of a "fortune" for corporations to earn at the "bottom of the pyramid" (Prahalad 2004).

In many places, microlending increasingly is directly linked to the sale of products and services from multinational corporations that are marketed and sold on credit, such as chemically enriched foods, home solar systems, mobile phones, or seeds and farming services.[26] Among the most consequential outgrowths is the expansion of microfinance into goods and services traditionally governed politically as public goods, such as electricity, education, water, and sanitation. Microfinance proponents suggest that poor people should use credit to privately buy access to these goods, rendering public, redistributive solutions obsolete. However, models using microfinance for such goods in practice often go against social values, precipitate local political conflicts, enhance existing inequities, and do not succeed in circumventing the underlying problems related to public sector incapacity (Mader 2011).

Geographically, the scope of microfinance has expanded to the Global North. Grameen America, based in New York and launched with a media buzz in 2008, is only one of numerous microfinance programs now operating in the United States. Muhammad Yunus' new brainchild involves applying to North American poverty the Bangladeshi microfinance model of targeting women (primarily among minority groups) who engage in small, simple, often home-based, income-earning activities. In practice—much as in the Global South—the activities supported in the United States often involve poor people selling goods and services to other poor people.[27] The European Union, meanwhile, funds a growing number of microfinance programs, complementing a plethora of national and subnational schemes, which aim to get the unemployed—particularly youths and ethnic minorities—into self-employment. According to former Italian Minister of Foreign Affairs Giulio Terzi di Sant'Agata (in an uncommonly candid analysis) microfinance is useful as an instrument for keeping volatile populations occupied, and "safeguarding the quality of democracies" by preventing "material distress from encouraging populist deviation and citizen regression" (Foreign Ministry of Italy 2013). Through helping uphold consumption and facilitating self-employment while saddling the poor themselves with social risk, microfinance in Europe serves as a device for austerity facilitation. In Terzi's words: microfinance could "help contain public spending by contributing to the reduction of social buffers, the cost of which rises in times of recession." A 2012 European Investment Fund report, meanwhile, argued that more European public funding should be used to catalyze "the entry of private capital in order to create a self-sustainable market in the long run" (Bruhn-Leon, Eriksson, and Kraemer-Eis 2012:14). Just as previously in the Global South, under conditions of fiscal austerity, taxpayer money may be redirected into microfinance to build and prepare the market for private investors.

CONCLUSION

Microfinance still enjoys popular appeal and growing success as a business and is recently expanding in scope. These factors may obscure the state of crisis which microfinance is in (Guérin et al. 2015)—a crisis that has less to do with symbolic events like Muhammad Yunus's ousting from office as head of Grameen Bank in 2011 (after a spat with the Bangladeshi government), and more with the doubtfulness of it achieving positive social aims. The lack of demonstrable impact (beyond the individual success stories, which are true albeit misleading exceptions), the diverse critiques which highlight its economic and gender-political flaws, and the collapses of major markets all draw into question the idea of microfinance serving as a just and cost-effective poverty-alleviation policy. Certainly, even if public and philanthropic backers were to withdraw, for instance in the wake of even larger and more dramatic collapses than the prior cases, parts of the microfinance sector (which in 2012 earned more than $21 billion in surplus payments from the borrowers[28]) may be able to survive thanks to private, speculative funders seeking high returns. However, in an era increasingly skeptical of financial market solutions to social problems, it is unclear how much longer the sector can retain the public legitimacy on which it has banked so far.

Notes

1. A typical client success story, taken from Accion (2004:8).
2. Public funders accounted for US$21 billion of cross-border funding for microfinance in 2012 (CGAP and MIX 2013. What share of this was declared as aid is unknown. Global aid (Official Development Assistance was US$150.9 billion in 2012 (OECD 2014).
3. In most understandings, "microfinance" providers are formal lenders; as opposed to informal, private moneylenders. Most are at least as formalized as NGOs; at most formal end of the scale, some are registered banks.
4. A standard commercial bank and a part-privatized state development bank.
5. All data here is from 2012; source MIX (2013).
6. Forced savings are parts of loans not fully paid out by the MFI and withheld as collateral but registered as "client savings." These are one of the industry's "dirty little secrets," raising loan interest rates considerably while appearing client-friendly (Sinclair 2012:35–36, 101–102). For instance, when Nigeria's largest MFI, LAPO, was criticized for its 114 percent interest loan rate, management responded by publicly announcing a decrease. At the same time, it silently raised "compulsory" savings from 10 to 20 percent. Clients still had to pay interest on the full loan amount, and the annual effective interest rate for some clients rose to nearly 126 percent (MacFarquhar 2010).
7. From 83 percent voluntary savers as a percentage of active borrowers in 2009 to 57 percent in 2012.
8. Nobel lecture, Oslo, December 10, 2006. Retrieved December 12, 2014, http://www.nobel-prize.org/nobel_prizes/peace/ laureates/2006/yunus-lecture-en.html.
9. Practitioners and development agencies gave little attention to anthropological findings, while economic studies were hotly discussed and new research programs created for economic impact measurement.
10. "Temptation goods" included alcohol, tobacco, betel leaves, gambling, also tea and food consumed outside the home. The economists never wondered whether such declining consumption could adversely affect clients' life satisfaction or the businesses of local microenterprises selling tea or food on the street.

11. The authors, mystifyingly, neglected to interpret this aggregate "reduced happiness" finding in their paper but discussed at length why shrinking businesses may be more efficient.

12. They are only briefly sketched here, drawing on Dichter and Harper (2007), Bateman (2010) and Bateman (2011), where a deeper engagement can be found.

13. Microfinance practitioner and whistle-blower Hugh Sinclair (2012:239–49) suggests that displacement and saturation effects therefore could combine to generate artificial demand for debt, as competitor enterprises are forced to also borrow to remain competitive.

14. MFIs can (and do) lend for consumption, which may raise demand in the short term, but only at the price of interest payments that depress demand even further at a later point in time.

15. Muhammad Yunus (2003:205) for instance says: "I believe that all human beings are potential entrepreneurs. Some of us get the opportunity to express this talent, but many of us never get the chance because we were made to imagine that an entrepreneur is someone enormously gifted and different from ourselves."

16. On the roots of microfinance see, for instance, Counts (2008).

17. For a more detailed version of this historical overview, see Chapter 2 of Mader (2015).

18. Much as the microfinance movement, decades later, has also avowed market principles while using government funds.

19. Many of the economists were based at Ohio State University.

20. This part systematizes the accounts given in Mader (2013a), and Chapters 2 and 5 of Mader (2015).

21. Compare, for instance, the global MFI ranking in MIX (2008).

22. This means that less than 1 in 700 dollars was reported as not repaid; a utopian figure.

23. According to different sources, between 54 and 88 suicides in the space of one month, plus many more attempts.

24. http://www.theglobalappeal.org; retrieved December 12, 2014.

25. As analyzed in depth (in German) in Sabrow and Mader (2014).

26. Cf. Hartmann (2014), in German.

27. The New York Times for instance reports borrowers engaged in home cooking, tailoring, street hawking, or direct selling of cosmetics and products distributed through dubious multilevel marketing schemes (Dewan 2013).

28. For calculations, see Chapter 3 of Mader (2015).

REFERENCES

Accion. 2004. *Accion Ventures: Newsletter of Accion International.* Boston: Accion International.

Adams, Dale W., Douglas H. Graham, and J. D. Von Pischke. 1984. *Undermining Rural Development with Cheap Credit.* London: Westview Press.

Augsburg, Britta, Ralph De Haas, Heike Harmgart, and Costas Meghir. 2012. "Microfinance at the Margin: Experimental Evidence from Bosnia and Herzegovina." EBRD Working Paper No. 146. London: EBRD.

Banerjee, Abhijit, Esther Duflo, Rachel Glennerster, and Cynthia Kinnan. 2009. "The Miracle of Microfinance? Evidence from a Randomized Evaluation." Unpublished paper, May 30 2009. Cambridge: MIT.

Banerjee, Abhijit and Esther Dufo. 2011. *Poor Economics: A Radical Rethinking of the Way to Fight Global Poverty.* New York: Public Affairs.

Bateman, Milford. 2007. "De-industrialization and Social Disintegration in Bosnia." Pp. 207–23 in *What's Wrong with Microfinance?*, edited by Thomas Dichter and Malcolm Harper. Bourton on Dunsmore, UK: Practical Action.

Bateman, Milford. 2010. *Why Doesn't Microfinance Work?* London: Zed Books.

Bateman, Milford, ed. 2011: *Confronting Microfinance: Undermining Sustainable Development.* Sterling, VA: Kumarian Press.

Binswanger-Mkhize, Hans P. 2012. Is There Too Much Hype about Index-Based Agricultural Insurance? *Journal of Development Studies* 48:187–200.

Bruhn-Leon, Birthe, Per-Erik Eriksson, and Helmut Kraemer-Eis. 2012. "Progress for Microfinance in Europe." EIF Research & Market Analysis Working Paper 2012/13. Luxembourg: European Investment Fund.

CGAP. 1995. "The Missing Links: Financial Systems That Work for the Majority." *Focus* No. 3. Washington, DC.

CGAP. 1998. "The Consultative Group to Assist the Poorest: A Microfinance Program." *Focus* No. 1 (1998 rev. ed.). Washington, DC.

CGAP. 2000. "Focus: Raising the Curtain on the 'Microfinancial Services Era.'" Washington DC.

CGAP. 2001. *CGAP Annual Report: July 1, 2001–June 30, 2002.* Washington DC.

CGAP. 2003. *Microfinance Consensus Guidelines: Developing Deposit Services for the Poor* (2nd ed., October 2003). Washington, DC.

CGAP. 2012. "What Is Microfinance?" Washington, DC. Retrieved May 18, 2012 (http://www. microfinancegateway.org/p/site/m/template.rc/1.26.12263/).

CGAP and MIX. 2013. "2013 Survey on Cross-Border Funding for Financial Inclusion" European Microfinance Week 2013, November, 13. Washington, DC. Retrieved December 12, 2014 (http://www.e-mfp.eu/sites/default/files/resources/2014/02/Estelle%20Lahaye_CGAP.pdf).

Chang, Ha-Joon. 2002. *Kicking Away the Ladder: Development Strategy in Historical Perspective.* New York: Anthem Press.

Chen, Greg, Stephen Rasmussen, and Xavier Reille. 2010. "Growth and Vulnerabilities in Microfinance." CGAP Focus Note 61. Washington, DC: CGAP.

Collins, Daryl, Jonathan Morduch, Stuart Rutherford, and Orlanda Ruthven. 2009. *Portfolios of the Poor: How the World's Poor Live on $2 a Day.* Princeton, NJ: Princeton University Press.

Counts, Alex. 2008. *Small Loans, Big Dreams: How Nobel Prize Winner Muhammad Yunus and Microfinance are Changing the World.* Hoboken, NJ: Wiley.

Crépon, Bruno, Florencia Devoto, Esther Duflo, and William Pariente. 2014. "Estimating the Impact of Microcredit on Those Who Take It Up: Evidence from a Randomized Experiment in Morocco." Unpublished paper, May 2014. Cambridge, MA: MIT.

Dewan, Shaila. 2013. "Microcredit for Americans." *New York Times*, October 28.

Dichter, Thomas and Malcolm Harper. 2007. *What's Wrong with Microfinance?* Bourton on Dunsmore: Immediate Technology.

Duvendack, Maren and Richard Palmer-Jones. 2012. "High Noon for Microfinance Impact Evaluations: Re-investigating the Evidence from Bangladesh." *Journal of Development Studies* 48:1864–80.

Duvendack, Maren, Richard Palmer-Jones, James G. Copestake, Lee Hooper, Yoon Loke, and Nitya Rao. 2011a: "Policy Brief: What Is the Evidence of the Impact of Microfinance on the Well-being of Poor People?" London: EPPI-Centre, Social Science Research Unit, Institute of Education, University of London.

Duvendack, Maren, Richard Palmer-Jones, James G. Copestake, Lee Hooper, Yoon Loke, and Nitya Rao. 2011b. "Systematic Review: What Is the Evidence of the Impact of Microfinance on the Well-being of Poor People?" London: EPPI-Centre, Social Science Research Unit, Institute of Education, University of London.

Foreign Ministry of Italy. 2013. "Terzi: Micro Finance to Prevent Social Fragility, Italian Ministry of Foreign Affairs." February. Rome: Italian Ministry of Foreign Affairs. Retrieved December 12, 2014 (http://www.esteri.it/MAE/EN/Sala_Stampa/ArchivioNotizie/Approfondimenti/2013/02/20130201_puntare_microfinanza.htm?LANG=EN).

Fraser, Nancy. 2013. "How Feminism Became Capitalism's Handmaiden—And How to Reclaim It." *The Guardian*, October14.

Gonzalez-Vega, Claudio. 1982. "Cheap Agricultural Credit: Redistribution in Reverse." Colloquium on Rural Finance, Economic Development Institute Discussion Paper No. 10. Washington, DC: World Bank.

Goronja, Nataša. 2014. "IFC Experience with Responsible Microfinance in ECA." Presentation, Tbilisi, Georgia, January 31. Washington, DC, International Finance Corporation. Retrieved December 12, 2014 (https://www.nbg.gov.ge/uploads/prezentacia/lending_standards/natasa_goronja.ppt).

Guérin, Isabelle, Marc Labie, and Jean-Michel Servet (eds.). 2015. *The Crises of Microcredit*. London: Zed Books.

Hartmann, Kathrin. 2014. "Social Business: Können Weltkonzerne Armut Bekämpfen?" Pp. 193–202 in *Rendite machen und Gutes tun? Mikrokredite und die Folgen neoliberaler Entwicklungspolitik*, edited by Gerhard Klas and Philip Mader. Frankfurt am Main: Campus.

Hulme, David. 2009. "The Story of the Grameen Bank: From Subsidized Microcredit to Market Based Microfinance." Pp. 163–70 in *Microfinance: A Reader*, edited by David Hulme and Thankom Arun. New York: Routledge.

Isserles, Robin G. 2003. "Microcredit: The Rhetoric of Empowerment, the Reality of "Development as Usual." *Women's Studies Quarterly* 31:38–57.

Kabeer, Naila. 2000. "Conflicts over Credit: Re-Evaluating the Empowerment Potential of Loans to Women in Rural Bangladesh." *World Development* 29:63–84.

Karim, Lamia. 2011. *Microfinance and Its Discontents: Women in Debt in Bangladesh*. Minneapolis: University of Minnesota Press.

Karlan, Dean and Jonathan Zinman. 2009. "Expanding Microenterprise Credit Access: Using Randomized Supply Decisions to Estimate the Impacts in Manila." Yale Economics Department Working Paper No. 68. Yale University Economic Growth Center Discussion Paper No. 976.

Karnani, Aneel. 2007. "Employment, Not Microcredit, Is the Solution." Ross School of Business Paper No. 1065.

Kiviat, Barbara. 2009. "Why the World's Poor Refuse Insurance." *Time Magazine Business*, September 21.

Lieberman, Ira, Anne Anderson, Zach Grafe, Bruce Campbell, and Daniel Kopf. 2009. "Microfinance and Capital Markets: The Initial Listing/Public Offering of Four Leading Institutions." Pp. 31–80 in *Moving Beyond Storytelling: Emerging Research in Microfinance* (Contemporary Studies in Economic and Financial Analysis, Vol. 92), edited by Todd A. Watkins and Karen Hicks. Bingley: Emerald.

MacFarquhar, Neil. 2010. "Banks Making Big Profits from Tiny Loans." *New York Times*, April 13, 2010.

Mader, Philip. 2011. "Attempting the Production of Public Goods through Microfinance: The Case of Water and Sanitation." *Journal of Infrastructure Development* 3:153–70.

Mader, Philip. 2013a: "Rise and Fall of Microfinance in India: The Andhra Pradesh Crisis in Perspective." *Strategic Change* 22(1–2):47–66.

Mader, Philip. 2013b: "'What Is the Evidence of the Impact of Microfinance . . .?' by Maren Duvendack et al." Pp. 348–52 in *Governance across Borders: Transnational Fields and Transversal Themes*, edited by Leonhard Dobusch, Philip Mader, and Sigrid Quack. Berlin: epubli.

Mader, Philip. 2015. *The Political Economy of Microfinance: Financialising Poverty*. London: Palgrave.

Mader, Philip and Sophia Sabrow. 2015. "All Myth and Ceremony? Examining the Causes and Logic of the Mission Shift in Microfinance from Microenterprise Credit to Financial Inclusion." *Forum for Social Economics* (July 2015).

Maes, Jan P. and Larry R. Reed. 2012. *State of the Microcredit Summit Campaign Report 2012*. Washington, DC: Microcredit Summit Campaign.

Marconi, Reynaldo and Paul Mosley. 2005. "Bolivia during the Global Crisis 1998–2004: Towards a Macroeconomics of Microfinance." Sheffield Economic Research Paper Series 2005007, June.

MasterCard Foundation. 2011. "Taking Stock: Financial Education Initiatives for the Poor." Toronto.

McIntosh, Craig, Elisabeth Sadoulet, and Alain de Janvry. 2006. "Better Lending and Better Clients: Credit Bureau Impact on Microfinance." *BASIS Brief* 45:1–6.

MicroRate. 2013. *The State of Microfinance Investment 2013: Survey and Analysis of MIVs*.8th ed.. Arlington, VA.

MIX. 2008. "2008 MIX Global 100 Composite: Rankings of Microfinance Institutions." Washington, DC: Microfinance Information Exchange. Retrieved December 12, 2014 (http://www.themix.org/sites/default/files/2008%20MIX%20Global%20100%20 updated%20March%202009.pdf).

MIX. 2013. Basic MIX MFI Data Set. Washington, DC. Retrieved December 2, 2013 (http://www.mixmarket.org/crossmarket-analysis-report/download/).

Morduch, Jonathan. 1998. "Does Microfinance Really Help the Poor? New Evidence from Flagship Programs in Bangladesh." Unpublished paper, June 27, 1998. Department of Economics and HIID, Harvard University and Hoover Institution, Stanford University.

Mosley, Paul and David Hulme. 1998. "Microenterprise Finance: Is There a Conflict between Growth and Poverty Alleviation?" *World Development* 26:783–90.

OECD. 2014. "OECD StatExtracts." (Total flows by donor (ODA+OOF+Private) [DAC1]). Paris. Retrieved December 12, 2014 (http://stats.oecd.org).

Pitt, Mark M. and Shahidur R Khandker. 1998. "The Impact of Group-Based Credit Programs on Poor Households in Bangladesh: Does the Gender of Participants Matter?" *Journal of Political Economy* 106:958–96.

Prahalad, C. K. 2004. *The Fortune at the Bottom of the Pyramid: Eradicating Poverty Through Profits*. Philadelphia: Wharton School/Pearson.

Rahman, Aminur. 1999. "Micro-credit Initiatives for Equitable and Sustainable Development: Who Pays?" *World Development* 27:67–82.

Rankin, Katharine N. 2001. "Governing Development: Neoliberalism, Microcredit, and Rational Economic Woman." *Economy and Society* 30:18–37.

Rhyne, Elisabeth. 2001. *Commercialization and Crisis in Bolivian Microfinance*. Bethesda, MD: Development Alternatives.

Roodman, David and Jonathan Morduch. 2009. "The Impact of Microcredit on the Poor in Bangladesh: Revisiting the Evidence." Center for Global Development Working Paper 174.

Roodman, David. 2012. "Think Again: Microfinance." *Foreign Policy*, February 1.

Schumpeter, Joseph. 1962. *Capitalism, Socialism, and Democracy*. New York: Harper Perennial.

Sinclair, Hugh. 2012. *Confessions of a Microfinance Heretic: How Microlending Lost Its Way and Betrayed the Poor*. San Francisco, CA: Berrett-Koehler.

Sinclair, Hugh. 2014. "Smart or Crafty?" Confessions of a Microfinance Heretic Blog, October 7. Retrieved December 12, 2014 (http://blog.microfinancetransparency.com/smart-or-crafty/).

Shah, Mihir, Rangu Rao, and P. S. Vijay Shankar. 2007. "Rural Credit in 20th Century India: An Overview of History and Perspectives." *Economic and Political Weekly* 42:1351–64.

Symbiotics. 2013. "2013 Symbiotics MIV Survey: Market Data & Peer Group Analysis, Market Data & Peer Group Analysis July 2013." Geneva. Retrieved December 12, 2014 (http://www.aboutmicrofinance.com/wp-content/uploads/2013/07/symbiotics-symbiotics-2013-miv-survey-report11.pdf).

Taylor, Marcus. 2011. "'Freedom from Poverty Is Not for Free': Rural Development and the Microfinance Crisis in Andhra Pradesh, India." *Journal of Agricultural Change* 11:484–504.

Turnell, Sean. 2005. "The Rise and Fall of Cooperative Credit in Colonial Burma." Macquarie University Department of Economics Research Papers 0509.

Weber, Heloise. 2002. "The Imposition of a Global Development Architecture: The Example of Microcredit." *Review of International Studies* 28:537–55.

Wipf, John, Eamon Kelly, and Michael McChord. 2012: "Improving Credit Life Insurance." Pp. 197–216 in *Protecting the Poor. A Microinsurance Compendium*. Vol. 2, edited by Craig Churchill and Michal Matul. Geneva: International Labour Organization.

Wolff, Henry W. 1910. *People's Banks: A Record of Social and Economic Success*. London: P. S. King and Son.

World Bank. 2001. *Sustainable Banking with the Poor: A Worldwide Inventory of Microfinance Institutions*. Washington, DC.

Yunus, Muhammad. 2011. *Building Social Business: The New Kind of Capitalism that Serves Humanity's Most Pressing Needs*. New York: Public Affairs.

Zohir, Sajjad. 2004. "NGO Sector in Bangladesh: An Overview." *Economic and Political Weekly* 39:4109–13.

CONCLUSION

Toward a New Paradigm for Understanding Poverty

MARK R. RANK

TOWARD A NEW PARADIGM
FOR UNDERSTANDING POVERTY

IN 1984, John Kenneth Galbraith gave a commencement address to graduating students at American University that was entitled "The Convenient Reverse Logic of Our Time."[1] The central theme of Galbraith's talk was that rather than moving from diagnosis to remedy in social policy, we have witnessed with greater frequency the rise of employing a reverse logic—that of moving from a preferred remedy to an appropriate diagnosis. As Galbraith explained:

> Increasingly in recent times we have come first to identify the remedy that is most agreeable, most convenient, most in accord with major pecuniary or political interest, the one that reflects our available faculty for action; then we move from the remedy so available or desired back to a cause to which that remedy is relevant. (1986:35).

Galbraith went on to illustrate with the example of poverty. Referring to poverty as "our most devastating social failure in this greatly affluent age and land" and "the heaviest burden on our social conscience," he noted that rather than devising social policies that would address the root causes of poverty, we have instead defined the causes of poverty in such a way that are consistent with our preferred policy strategies. These strategies have included cutting back on the role and scope of the federal government, seeking policies that are relatively inexpensive, devolution to the state and local levels, stressing personal responsibility, and so on. Galbraith observed:

> From this need as to remedy we move back to the new cause of poverty. It is that the poor lack motivation—and they lack motivation because they are already unduly rewarded. That cause, once agreed upon, then calls for reduced expenditure on public services and less aid to the disadvantaged. So, in the recent past we have had, as an antipoverty measure, a broad curtailment of income and services to the poor. (p. 36)

This tendency to view the nature of social problems in terms of a desired policy was echoed one hundred years earlier by the French historian Albert Sorel who observed, "There is an eternal dispute between those who imagine the world to suit their policy, and those who correct their policy to suit the realities of the world."

The argument presented in this chapter is that there is a need for a new paradigm in which to understand poverty. The chapters in this handbook represent important pieces of such a paradigm. The old strategies of addressing poverty have rested upon imagining a world that reflects a preferred set of myths, agendas, and policies, whereas a new approach to poverty alleviation must put in place a set of policies that reflect the realities of the world. These policies should be grounded in a new understanding of the nature and meaning of poverty. This chapter is intended to provide the details of such a paradigm. I will focus primarily on the United States, but several dimensions of the new paradigm apply globally across other countries.

The premise for beginning this treatise is a simple one—how we view poverty is critical to guiding how we will address it. Part of America's ineffectiveness in reducing poverty during the past three decades stems from a skewed and incorrect perception of impoverishment. Imagine a doctor treating a patient based upon the wrong diagnosis. The chances are that the prescribed cure will have a negligible effect on the illness and perhaps make the patient worse. Such has been the case with U.S. poverty.

In short, we have followed a paradigm that has reflected a view of the world as many would like to see it rather than being led by a paradigm that reflects the world as it really is. Fundamental change must therefore begin with shifting our understanding of poverty from one based on traditional ways of thinking about it to one based on a new conceptualization.

I begin by briefly describing the major tenets of the "old" paradigm. Much of what I say will be quite familiar, since variations of it can be heard in political sound bites, mainstream policy research, the popular media, or informal discussions with one's neighbors (see Chapter 9, Celeste Watkins-Hayes and Elyse Kovalsky). I then describe the foundations of a new paradigm for comprehending poverty. This paradigm is based upon my prior work and several of the major themes found within this handbook and represents a notable departure from more traditional ways of viewing poverty.

THE OLD PARADIGM

The old paradigm has been the dominant poverty perspective over a prolonged period of time. Indeed, aspects of it have been with us since the beginnings of the country. It is to a large extent a reflection and affirmation of both the free market economic structure and the culture of individualism that have profoundly shaped the ideology of the United States. It has experienced ebbs and flows over time but appears to have been gaining in ascendency since the election of Ronald Reagan in 1980. At its core is the belief that both the causes and solutions to poverty are found within the individual.

This paradigm begins with the key assumption that the American economic system generates abundant economic prosperity and well being for all. The familiar phrases of "rags to riches," "the land of opportunity," or the "American Dream" are emblematic of this. The assumption is not that everyone will be rich, but that with enough hard work and initiative, nearly everyone is capable of achieving and sustaining a modest and comfortable lifestyle (Rank et al. 2014). Given this assumption, poverty becomes largely understood as a result of individual failure.

According to this view, both the causes and solutions to poverty can be found within the context of the individual. With respect to the causes of poverty, they are viewed primarily as a result of individual inadequacies. There is a conservative and a liberal version of this. The conservative version of individual inadequacies tends to focus more heavily on personality characteristics. These would include various character flaws, such as an absence of strong morals, failure to exert responsibility, laziness, an inability to save and plan for the future, a lack of intelligence, addiction to alcohol and/or drugs, and so on (Gilder 2012; Herrnstein and Murray 1994; Sawhill 2003; Schwartz 2000). As a result of these character flaws, individuals are thought to be unable to take advantage of the opportunities that are readily available. In addition, it is believed that government policy exacerbates these problems when it puts in place social programs that do not encourage morality or the incentive to work (Mead 1986, 1992). As Robert Rector and William Lauber wrote in their Heritage Foundation report, *America's Failed $5.4 Trillion War on Poverty*,

> ... the welfare system has paid for non-work and non-marriage and has achieved massive increases in both. By undermining the work ethic and rewarding illegitimacy, the welfare system insidiously generates its own clientele. . . . Welfare bribes individuals into courses of behavior which in the long run are self-defeating to the individual, harmful to children, and increasingly a threat to society. (1995:23)

Consequently, according to the conservative version of the old paradigm, badly designed social welfare programs can encourage people into making destructive decisions during their lives, such as dropping out of school, having children out of wedlock, not getting married, failing to take a low-paying job, engaging in crime, and so on.

The liberal version of the old paradigm tends to focus more on the lack of marketable skills, training, and education, as well as other demographic characteristics that put the poor at a disadvantage in competing in the labor market. The focus is largely on the inadequate human capital that the poor have acquired. This, in addition to particular household characteristics (such as being a single parent or having large numbers of children), hinders the ability of particular Americans to compete in the economy and thereby raises their risk of poverty. Rather than focusing on individual inadequacies as represented by character flaws, the liberal version views individuals as inadequate in terms of their skills, training, and education. As Alice O'Connor notes in Chapter 8 of this volume, the mainstream research community has basically reinforced this approach by focusing on individual and demographic attributes to explain individual behavior such as impoverishment.

What follows from either version is that the poor are by and large at fault for their poverty. This is the result of their not having enough fortitude and morality for getting ahead, making bad judgments in life, and/or because of a failure to acquire the necessary skills to compete in today's economy. The concept of blame permeates the old paradigm.[2] The age old distinction between the deserving and the undeserving poor as discussed by Celeste Watkins-Hayes and Elyse Kovalsky in Chapter 9 is of course central to this—unless the working-age poor have a very good reason to explain their poverty (such as a debilitating illness not brought on by their own doing), they are seen as largely undeserving of help from others. Rather, they have only themselves to blame.

Closely connected to the issue of blame is that the poor are viewed as different from mainstream Americans (see Chapter 5 by Matthew Hunt and Heather Bullock). Perceptions of the poor frequently consist of not being motivated enough, dropping out of high school, having a child out of wedlock, failing to have the qualified skills for a higher paying job, and so forth (rather than working steadily at a low-paying job, trying to be good parents to their children, paying taxes throughout their lives, etc.). The poor are not only to blame for their impoverishment, but they also are portrayed as not playing by the rules and therefore outside the mainstream American experience. These differences can also be physically seen within the popular media, where the poor are often depicted as inner city minority residents, women on welfare, street criminals, the homeless, or taken together, synonymous with what has been labeled the underclass. Such images graphically convey a sense of physical separation from middle America.

In addition to this physical separation, the human dimension of poverty is rarely discussed within the old paradigm, once again creating a distance between the poor and the rest of America. The pain of poverty is largely wiped away. Within the old paradigm, the deeper meaning of poverty is rarely discussed. Rather, poverty is largely viewed through the lens of individual inadequacy. Much of the empirical literature has also reinforced this superficiality. Poverty has routinely been reduced to a set of numbers and correlations.[3] The old paradigm tends to treat poverty in a one dimensional fashion, either as an unflattering stereotype or as a set of regression coefficients.

Turning to solutions, the key according to the old framework is to address personal inadequacies. Again, there is a conservative and a more liberal version of this. The conservative view is that encouraging and rewarding individual initiative and responsibility is critical. These behaviors include working harder, staying married, and not having children out of wedlock. Social policy should reinforce and encourage such behavior. Indeed, the title of the 1996 welfare reform act was the Personal Responsibility and Work Opportunity Reconciliation Act.

On the other hand, cash assistance and generous welfare programs are believed not to be the answer because they often create disincentives for engaging in responsible behavior. Such was the argument made by Alexis de Tocqueville in his 1832 address to the Royal Academic Society of Cherbourg (1983), and such was the argument popularized 150 years later in Charles Murray's book *Losing Ground* (1984). As President George W. Bush noted, "Many are learning it is more rewarding to be a responsible citizen than a welfare client" (Bush, 2002). The distinction between responsibility on the one hand, and the use of welfare on the other, is critical from this perspective. Mainstream economic studies have also devoted considerable attention to the issue of incentives and disincentives within the welfare system, and although the effects have been small, the fact that such a large body of work continues to focus on this question serves to legitimate the issue.

The more liberal solution to poverty according to the old framework is to provide greater opportunities and access to job training and education, while demanding personal responsibility and motivation in return. The concept of the New Democrat epitomizes this view. As Bill Clinton stated in his 1992 Democratic National Convention acceptance speech in New York City, "We offer our people a new choice based on old values. We offer opportunity. We demand responsibility" (1992:226). Or as former Senate Majority Leader Tom Daschle said 10 years later regarding welfare reform, "As we demand responsibility, we need to provide greater opportunity" (Toner, 2002). Thus the focus is on providing opportunities intended to upgrade the poor's limited human capital, with the strong expectation that individuals will make the most of these opportunities.

Finally, from the viewpoint of the old paradigm, our collective responsibility toward poverty is somewhat limited. Since poverty is viewed as the purview of the individual, it is up to the poor themselves to improve their condition. From the conservative view, society and those in authority should use their positions as a moral bully pulpit to encourage the poor to behave in responsible ways. In addition, welfare programs and social policy should be structured in a manner that supports such behavior. Within the liberal version of the old paradigm, society should ensure that the poverty stricken have access to the means of building their education and skills. It is then up to the poor to take advantage of such opportunities. As John Kingdon writes in describing this American approach:

> If unfortunate people were regarded as the victims of forces beyond their control, or simply down on their luck, then we could see our way clear to having government provide for them: "There but for the grace of God go I." But if, in the land of

opportunity, they're responsible for their own condition, then self-help rather than government help is the appropriate prescription. At most, government programs should be designed to enhance opportunity, but nothing more. (1999:37)

Ultimately, the old paradigm reflects and reinforces the myths and ideals of American society—that there are economic opportunities for all, that individualism and self-reliance are paramount, and that hard work is rewarded. It should not be surprising that the dominant paradigm of poverty is a reflection of the overall dominant ideology of America. While there are conservative and liberal versions of this paradigm, both reflect these ideals and myths.

The old paradigm also reflects an overall perceived sense of justice. Opportunities exist for all who are willing to work for them, while the poverty stricken have largely brought their condition upon themselves. Although poverty may be regrettable, it would be a mistake to call it unfair. It is an economic consequence that would appear consistent and in balance with prior actions and behaviors.

It is particularly ironic (and indicative of its strength) that even those in poverty tend to adhere strongly to this paradigm. Surveys have consistently found that the poor tend to reiterate the mainstream values reflected in the old paradigm. Furthermore, those in poverty are often quick to characterize the overall situations of the poor and welfare recipients along the lines of the old paradigm, while carefully distinguishing their own circumstance as different from this pejorative view (Rank 1994). The process of both believing in yet distancing oneself from the common stereotype is often the case for members of stigmatized groups (Goffman 1963).

One of the reasons that American poverty is so high is precisely because of this mind set. The old paradigm offers little in the way of truly understanding and addressing poverty, and in fact, provides a justification for doing so little. The one task that is undertaken is the never ending charge of reforming and analyzing welfare. Yet as we continue to modify the incentives and disincentives that are embedded in the social safety net, poverty remains at the highest levels in the industrialized world. This would appear to be a modern version of Nero fiddling while Rome burns. Fundamental change in confronting poverty must begin with a fundamental change in how poverty is viewed and understood. We now turn to what such a new paradigm might look like.

A New Paradigm

A new paradigm must be built not upon the myths of America but rather upon its realities. It should reflect a fuller appreciation of the meaning of poverty rather than the one dimensional view that we are too often exposed to. It must ultimately stimulate a fundamental shift in how we conceptualize and act toward the problem of poverty. Drawing upon prior work and chapters in this handbook, several themes are highlighted that are intended to lay the foundation for such a paradigm.

POVERTY RESULTS FROM STRUCTURAL FAILINGS

The starting point for a new paradigm is the recognition that American poverty is largely the result of structural failings. There simply are not enough viable opportunities for all Americans. Individual deficiencies, such as the lack of human capital, help explain who is more likely to be left out in the competition to locate and secure such opportunities, but it cannot explain why there is a shortage of opportunities in the first place. In order to answer that question we must turn to the inability of the economic, political, and social structures to provide the supports and opportunities necessary to lift all Americans out of poverty.

The most obvious example of this is the mismatch between the number of decent-paying jobs and the pool of labor in search of such jobs. The failure of the labor market to lift all households out of poverty is substantial. For example, approximately one-third of Americans are working at jobs that pay less than $11.50 an hour. It should be noted that this proportion does not include discouraged workers who have dropped out of the labor force or the over 2 million Americans currently in prison. The inability of the economy to produce enough viable job opportunities can also be seen in the levels of unemployment, which have averaged between 4 and 10 percent during the past 40 years.

Exacerbating this situation is the fact that the American social safety net is extremely weak, resulting in sizeable numbers of families falling through its rather large holes (see Chapter 31 by Cheol-Sung Lee and Inhoe Ku, and Chapter 32 by Laura Lein, Sandra Danziger, Luke Shaefer, and Amanda Tillotson). The United States has also failed to offer the types of universal coverage for childcare, medical insurance, child allowances, or affordable housing that most other developed countries routinely provide. The result is an increasing number of families at risk of economic vulnerability and poverty.

Let us use the analogy of musical chairs to illustrate the relationship between these structural failures and the fact that those who experience poverty tend to have characteristics such as less education or devalued skills. Picture a game of musical chairs in which there are ten players but only eight chairs available at any point in time. Those who are likely to lose at this game tend to have characteristics putting them at a disadvantage in terms of competing for the available chairs (such as less education, fewer skills, single parent families, and so on). However, given that the game is structured in a way such that two players are bound to lose, a deficiency in marketable attributes only explains who loses out, not why there are losers in the first place.

The critical mistake that has been made in the past by those employing the old paradigm is that they have equated the question of who loses at the game with the question of why the game produces losers in the first place. They are, in fact, distinct and separate questions. While deficiencies in human capital and other marketable characteristics help explain who in the population is at a heightened risk of encountering poverty, the fact that poverty exists in the first place results not from these characteristics, but from the lack of decent opportunities and supports in society. By focusing solely on individual characteristics, such as education, we can shuffle people up or down in terms of their being more likely to land a job with good earnings, but we are still going to have somebody lose out if there are not enough decent-paying jobs to go around. In short, we are playing a large-scale version of a musical chairs game in which there are many more players than chairs.

The recognition of this dynamic represents a fundamental shift in thinking from the old paradigm. It helps explain why the social policies of the past three decades have been largely ineffective in reducing the rates of poverty. We have focused our attention and resources on either altering the incentives and disincentives for those playing the game or, in a very limited way, upgrading their skills and ability to compete in the game, while at the same time we have left the structure of the game untouched.

When the overall poverty rates in the United States do in fact go up or down, they do so primarily as a result of impacts on the structural level that increase or decrease the number of available chairs. In particular, the performance of the economy has been historically important. Why? Because when the economy is expanding, more opportunities (or chairs) are available for the competing pool of labor and their families. The reverse occurs when the economy slows down and contracts. Consequently, during the 1930s, early 1980s, or from 2007 onward, when the economy was doing badly, poverty rates went up, while during periods of economic prosperity such as the 1960s or the middle to later 1990s, the overall rates of poverty declined.

Similarly, changes in various social supports and the social safety net available to families will make a difference in terms of how well such households are able to avoid poverty or near poverty. When such supports were increased through the War on Poverty initiatives in the 1960s, poverty rates declined. Likewise, when Social Security benefits were expanded during the 1960s and 1970s, the elderly's poverty rates declined precipitously. Conversely, when social supports have been weakened and eroded, as in the case of children's programs over the past 35 years, their rates of poverty have gone up.[4]

The recognition of poverty as a structural failing also makes it quite clear why the United States has such high rates of poverty compared to other Western countries (see Chapter 24 by David Brady and Markus Jäntti). These rates have nothing to do with Americans being less motivated or less skilled than those in other countries but with the fact that our economy has been producing a plethora of low-wage jobs in the face of global competition and that our social policies have done relatively little to support families compared to our European neighbors. From this perspective, one of the keys to addressing poverty is to increase the labor market opportunities and social supports available to American households.

In sum, a shift in thinking about the causes of poverty from an individually based explanation to a structurally based explanation allows us to distinguish and make sense of two specific questions. First, why does poverty exist? And second, who is more likely to experience poverty? The earlier described musical chairs analogy handles both questions. Poverty exists primarily as a result of a shortage of viable economic opportunities and social supports for the entire population. Given this shortage, a certain percentage of the population is ensured of experiencing poverty. Individuals with a heightened risk of being on the short end of this economic stick will be those who are least able to effectively compete for the limited number of decent economic opportunities. This includes those with fewer marketable skills, less education, ill health, as well as single parents, racial minorities, and/or residents in economically depressed areas (as evidenced in Chapters 13, 14, 15, 16, 17, 18, 19, and 20). A new paradigm recognizes the fundamental distinction between understanding who loses at the game versus understanding how and why the game produces losers in the first place.

Poverty Is a Conditional State that Individuals Move in and Out Of

A second major premise underlying the new paradigm is the recognition of poverty as a conditional state that individuals move in and out of. Within the old way of thinking, we have talked and written about poor people. Yet the term *poor people* is in many respects a misnomer. As we have seen in earlier chapters, the majority of individuals and households move in and out of the state of poverty, rather than remaining *poor people* throughout their lives. In addition, most Americans will experience impoverishment at some point during the life course (Rank 2004; Rank et al. 2014).

Rather than framing the issue as one of poor people, our focus should be on the condition of poverty. This condition affects a very large percentage of the population at some point across the life span. The typical pattern is that individuals may experience poverty for a year or two, get above the poverty line for an extended period of time, and then perhaps experience another spell at some later point (see Chapter 13 by Anirudh Krishna). The recognition of poverty as a conditional state in which a majority of the population will move in and out of is a fundamentally different way of conceptualizing poverty than the static concept of poor people.

One way to illustrate this is with the concept of sickness. Most people are healthy for varying periods of time but periodically experience some kind of illness such as a cold or the flu. In such cases we would not define the lives of these individuals as sick people (even though they have experienced sickness), but rather that they are individuals who occasionally experience the condition of being ill. The appropriate focus is on recognizing the episodic nature of the condition, rather than defining the lives of such individuals in terms of the condition.

Certainly it may be the case that some people are more prone to sickness (just as some people are more prone to poverty). But even in these cases, we would generally not define such individuals as sick people. Only in the case of a chronic disease might we characterize such a person in terms of their illness.

The dynamics of poverty are much the same as that of sickness. Yet the old paradigm of poverty often lumps everyone who experiences poverty into the category of *poor people* or the *underclass*. A quick scanning of the bibliography of books on poverty will reveal a wide variety of titles such as, *Do the Poor Want to Work?*, *Freedom for the Poor*, or *Jobs for the Poor*. The point I am making here is not to deny that people experience periods in their lives when they are poor but that the label of *poor people* reinforces a very static and unchanging image of who encounters poverty. Returning to our analogy, it would not make much sense if we were to define everyone who at some point experienced a sickness as sick people. Yet this would appear to be the case with defining those who have experienced poverty as poor people.

An additional consequence of such labeling is to solidify poverty as a dividing line that separates the population. The old paradigm strengthens the separation between the notions of poor and nonpoor. It fails to recognize the critical point that most Americans are actually both (Rank et al. 2014). Rather than pulling us together, the old paradigm pulls us apart.

Conversely, a new paradigm recognizes that poverty is a conditional state and an economic risk that many Americans will encounter. There is an awareness of the fluid nature of poverty, and the fact that a majority of Americans will experience poverty at some point during their lives. Individuals typically move between the states of being nonpoor and poor during several periods of their life course.

A new paradigm considers the condition of poverty, rather than those who occupy the condition, as harmful and deleterious. As discussed below, poverty has the potential to undermine human well-being and development. It creates a number of problems for those who occupy its ranks. It can result in long-term consequences, depending upon the severity and the length of poverty experienced. This would appear particularly true in the case of children's development. Children who grow up with extended bouts of severe poverty may experience permanent scars in terms of their health, educational attainment, or acquisition of skills and abilities (see Chapter 7 by Vonnie McLoyd, Rosanne M. Jocson, and Abigail Williams).

Once again we can return to our illness analogy. On the one hand, ill health creates temporary pain and suffering for those experiencing it. Yet individuals will generally pass through such a condition, returning to a state of relatively good health. On the other hand, severe health problems such as a heart attack or stroke may produce more lingering damage. Here there may be permanent harm to the heart or brain that will undermine the individual's quality of life in the future. The dynamics of poverty can be understood in a similar fashion. Severe poverty over a prolonged period of time may create permanent damage to individuals and their families.

A second important building block for a new paradigm is therefore the recognition of poverty as a conditional state that individuals move in and out of. It represents an economic risk that most Americans will encounter. The appropriate focus is on the condition of poverty and the temporary and sometimes long-term effects that such a state has upon individuals who pass through it.

Poverty Constitutes Deprivation

A third component of the new paradigm broadens the scope and meaning of poverty from that of low income, to the wider concept of deprivation. As we have seen in prior chapters, poverty acts to deprive individuals and families in a number of ways. A new conception of poverty must recognize that impoverishment represents more than just a shortage of income (Chapter 3 by Barbara Rylko-Bauer and Paul Farmer and Chapter 4 by Rod Hick and Tania Burchardt). This has been emphasized in the attention that European governments and scholars (particularly in England, France, and the Netherlands) have been placing upon the concept of social exclusion or "the inability to participate in the activities of normal living" (Glennerster 2002).

We have seen many illustrations of this in prior chapters. Poverty serves to undermine the quality of life for those inhabiting its ranks. As discussed in Section V, it results in serious compromises and struggles in terms of acquiring basic resources such as food, clothing, shelter, health care, and transportation. These struggles then produce considerable stress in the lives of the poverty stricken and their families.

Poverty also results in reducing the quality of one's health. Poverty is associated with a host of health risks, including undernutrition, elevated rates of heart disease, dental problems, diabetes, lead poisoning, and mental illness as discussed by Ronald Angel in Chapter 29. The result is a decline in one's physical well-being, culminating in a death rate for the poverty stricken that is substantially higher than that for the affluent.

Another area of reduced capabilities lies in the stunted or diminished life chances for children and adults (Chapter 7 by Vonnie McLoyd, Rosanne M. Jocson, and Abigail Williams and Chapter 23 by Liana Fox, Florencia Torche, and Jane Waldfogel). For example, growing up in poverty stricken neighborhoods can result in an inferior education (Chapter 15 by Mary Pattillo and John Robinson and Chapter 20 by Emily Hannum and Yu Xie). Both the quality and quantity of education received are often substandard. There is also a greater exposure to other risks, such as crime, discussed in Chapter 27 by Patrick Sharkey, Max Besbris, and Michael Friedson. These risks, in turn, result in a lowered likelihood of acquiring the necessary skills to compete effectively in the labor market.

In addition, poverty undercuts the ability of adults to build their economic assets, which can affect later life chances. The old saying that it takes money to earn money is certainly true and applies to financial and property assets as well. The ability to build equity in a house or a retirement fund is severely constricted by poverty.

Impoverishment is also closely associated with deprivation in the area of work. Those in poverty may be out of work or employed at part-time or dead-end jobs that simply do not pay enough to support a family (Chapter 21 by Jérôme Gautié and Sophie Ponthieux). In addition, such work is often physically demanding and intellectually deadening. Employment and work have historically been a central part of the American identity. The failure to have a job that supports oneself and/or one's family is a major source of frustration and loss.

Finally, poverty undermines the capability of individuals to fully partake in the freedoms, rights, and opportunities to which all citizens are theoretically entitled. Poverty diminishes one's ability to fully exercise specific rights such as receiving a fair trial or participating in the democratic process.

A new paradigm of poverty must therefore recognize that impoverishment encompasses more than just low income. The lack of income is clearly a critical component of poverty and represents a convenient, logical, and pragmatic starting point and measuring stick. But we must go beyond thinking of poverty solely in terms of low income.[5] This involves incorporating a wider set of experiences and deprivations into our understanding as detailed by Rod Hick and Tania Burchardt in Chapter 4. As Amartya Sen writes, "poverty must be seen as the deprivation of basic capabilities rather than merely as lowness of incomes, which is the standard criterion of identification of poverty" (1999:87). He goes on to note:

> Policy debates have indeed been distorted by overemphasis on income poverty and income inequality, to the neglect of deprivations that relate to other variables, such as unemployment, ill health, lack of education, and social exclusion. Unfortunately, the identification of economic inequality with income inequality is fairly common in economics, and the two are often seen as effectively synonymous. If you tell someone that you are working on economic inequality, it is quite standardly assumed that you are studying income distribution. (p. 108)

An example of bringing several aspects of deprivation to bear upon the measurement of poverty is the United Nations development of a human poverty index for industrialized countries (United Nations Development Programme 2012). This index incorporates four measures: (1) deprivation in survival—the percentage of people not expected to survive to age 60; (2) deprivation in knowledge—the percentage of people aged 16 to 65 who are functionally illiterate; (3) deprivation in income—the percentage of the population below the income poverty line; and (4) social exclusion—the percentage of the total labor force that has been unemployed for 12 or more months. Such an index begins to reflect the wider meaning and scope of poverty.

Finally, conceptualizing poverty in terms of deprivation brings with it a more humane and accessible image. It is sometimes difficult to imagine what $23,834 a year really means (the U.S. poverty line for a family of four in 2013). It may be more intuitive to talk about long-term unemployment, illiteracy, or a shortened life expectancy. Broadening our focus to one of deprivation brings a more human dimension and scale.

Poverty as Injustice

Whereas the old paradigm's moral compass has been largely centered on individual blame, the moral compass of a new paradigm rests upon the notion of injustice. There is a recognition that poverty constitutes an injustice of substantial magnitude. This is based largely upon a juxtaposition of the first and third premises discussed earlier.

We have seen that poverty represents severe deprivation and hardship. This has been documented in countless studies not to mention millions of human lives. The question of justice centers on whether such deprivation is deserved. From the perspective of the old paradigm, the answer is largely yes, with the blame for poverty lying with the poor themselves.

In contrast, a new paradigm views the condition of poverty as undeserved and unwarranted. As discussed in the first premise, its roots can be traced back to the lack of economic opportunities and social supports (see Sections III and IV). There simply are not enough decent-paying jobs and mechanisms in place (such as affordable health care, housing, or childcare) to adequately support all American households. The condition of poverty represents an economic wrong falling on too many of our fellow citizens. What makes this injustice particularly grievous is the stark contrast between the wealth and abundance of America on the one hand, and its levels of destitution on the other.

Let us employ Adam Smith's thought experiment of what this might look like to an "impartial spectator" (1759). Smith raises the question of what would an impartial spectator make of a particular scenario—in this case the high levels of U.S. poverty within the context of vast material resources and wealth. As the impartial spectator delved into the current situation, he or she would soon learn that at any point in time over one-third of the poor are children and another 10 percent are elderly. Those of working age who encounter poverty have labored most of their lives but are often employed at jobs that do not pay enough to raise their families above the poverty line. Health care and childcare assistance for such families are minimal. For those not working, they may be suffering from a physical disability or illness preventing employment. In fact, one out of six of the poor between the ages of 25 and 64 have some type of disability. The impartial spectator would also see isolated cases of individuals who appear to have brought their poverty upon themselves. He or she would observe that these cases are often used to characterize the entire population who experiences poverty.

On the other hand, the impartial spectator also would see the vast amounts of American prosperity and wealth. The standards of living for families in the upper portions of society surpass all other nations in the world. The impartial spectator would note that such families enjoy many tax benefits and public policies to further strengthen their economic position. He or she would observe that although these individuals work hard, much of this wealth has been inherited from generation to generation. Yet the impartial spectator would rarely hear this dynamic being used to characterize the affluent portion of the population. Rather, hard work and ingenuity have become the key words used to account for their success. She or he would also note that there are scattered cases in which individuals have indeed risen from rags to riches.

The impartial spectator would soon learn that in spite of the material resources of American society, and in spite of the assistance for the well-to-do, the U.S. government does the least of any nation in the industrialized world to help its economically vulnerable escape from poverty. Rather, it resorts to encouraging the poor to engage in moral and responsible behavior, while at the same time cutting back its social safety net and economic supports. By doing so, the argument is made that it is helping the most vulnerable in society to escape poverty.

What would an impartial spectator make of all this? I believe that the answer would be moral outrage at the injustice of the situation. The impartial spectator would be able to see this for what it is—a masquerade that gives to the economically comfortable while taking away from those who have the least, and then justifying the whole process in terms of virtue. The injustice of this situation would be abundantly clear.

A new paradigm acknowledges this. Injustice, rather than blame, becomes the moral compass on which such a perspective is based. Poverty is viewed as a societal injustice and an economic wrong. It is particularly glaring because it is both unnecessary and preventable. If the United States were an extremely impoverished country with a broken economy, widespread poverty would be regrettable but certainly understandable given the economic constraints. Yet this is not the situation we face. The United States has both the means and the resources available to address and substantially reduce its high levels of poverty. Yet we have chosen not to. This inaction is simply unconscionable given that we have the ability to confront such deprivation and human misery.

This type of injustice constitutes a strong impetus for change. It signals that a wrong is being committed that cries out for a remedy. From the Revolutionary War, to the abolitionists, through women's suffrage, to civil rights, all have been fueled by an understanding and a passion to correct specific injustices taking place in particular historical times. The existence of poverty amidst widespread prosperity must be seen in a similar light.

The new paradigm recognizes this and is premised upon the idea that change is essential in addressing the injustices of poverty. This is in sharp contrast with the old paradigm, in which the moral focus is on individual blame. This has had the effect of simply reinforcing the status quo of doing little, resulting in continued rates of elevated poverty. A new paradigm allows us to actively engage and confront poverty, rather than comfortably settling for the status quo of widespread impoverishment.

THE CONDITION OF POVERTY AFFECTS
AND UNDERMINES US ALL

A final building block of a new paradigm is the recognition that poverty impacts and undermines us all. Indeed, the subtitle of my earlier book—*Why American Poverty Affects Us All*—reflects this central theme. In the past we have viewed poverty as primarily affecting those who fill its ranks and occasionally their proximate neighborhoods. The old paradigm has consistently failed to recognize the connections that all Americans have to poverty. This is epitomized by the distinction that we often implicitly make between *them* versus *us*—that is, the poor versus the nonpoor.

The new paradigm breaks down this distinction by demonstrating that virtually all Americans are affected by poverty in one way or another. There are significant economic costs that are incurred by the entire population as a consequence of excessive poverty. Impoverishment produces greater numbers and more severe health problems, inadequately educated children, and higher rates of criminal activity. As a result, we pay more for health care, produce less productive workers, and divert needed resources to the building and maintaining of correctional facilities. In each of these cases, money is being spent on the back end of the problem rather than on the front end, which is assuredly a more expensive approach to take. In fact, one study found that the annual cost of childhood poverty was conservatively estimated at $500 billion per year or 4 percent of GDP (Holzer et al. 2007). To argue that we do not pay a steep price for our widespread poverty is putting our head in the sand.

It has also been demonstrated in some of my prior work that a majority of the American population will encounter poverty directly at some point during their lifetimes. Between the ages of 20 and 75, 59 percent of Americans will experience at least one year below the official poverty line, 76 percent will encounter poverty or near poverty (at the 1.50 level), and 33 percent will experience dire poverty (below .50 of the official poverty line). In addition, two-thirds of Americans will utilize some type of safety net program by the time they reach age 65 (Rank 2004). These numbers drive home the fact that poverty casts a very long shadow across the population. Rather than it being a question of *them*, poverty is clearly a question of *us*.

Yet we are also connected to poverty in a somewhat different fashion as well—its presence undermines us as a people and as a nation. It diminishes us all by tarnishing the integrity of our values. For example, the presence of widespread poverty juxtaposed against immense material prosperity would appear to contradict much of what the Judeo-Christian ethic stands for. The Judeo-Christian ethic emphasizes that the barometer for a just and compassionate society lies in its treatment of the poor and vulnerable. As a nation and as a people we would appear to be badly failing at this test. Similarly, poverty impedes the ability of lower income Americans to enjoy the full blessings of liberty, equality, or justice. The words "liberty and justice for all" take on a hollow meaning when a significant percentage of the population is economically and politically disenfranchised. This undermines every citizen, for it suggests that the American ideals we profess to believe in apply to some more than others. This contradicts the very core of the American promise, diminishing us all.

Just as each of us is affected by poverty, each of us also has a responsibility for ending poverty. The new paradigm suggests that the alleviation of poverty will require a collective commitment from all Americans. This is in sharp contrast with the old paradigm, where the poor are basically left to fend for themselves. The new paradigm recognizes that poverty is an issue of public policy and requires a broad-based commitment. Within the old paradigm, the public's apathy toward the poor has been part of the problem. Within the new paradigm, the public's engagement in alleviating poverty is part of the solution.

CONCLUDING NOTE

In conclusion, a new paradigm asks us to view poverty on a different conceptual level. As discussed earlier, we have traditionally placed both the problem and the solution to poverty within the context of the individual. In contrast, a new paradigm suggests that we understand the condition of poverty within the wider context of an interconnected environment. This handbook has stressed the importance of such a context.

This shift in thinking can be illustrated in how we have begun to think differently about the environment and environmental protections. Until recently, we failed to recognize the harm befalling us all as a result of air, water, and ground pollutants. These had been seen as having little consequence beyond the immediate location of the pollution. However, mounting evidence suggested that this way of thinking about pollution was incorrect and dangerous. We have begun to understand the impact that pollution has within a wider environmental context. Pollutants that occur in one community may very well affect those in other communities down wind or down stream. The use of coal in midwestern power plants results in acid rain in northeastern forests. The burning of fossil fuels or the use of chlorofluorocarbons can have a profound impact upon the global climate, such as global warming or the loss of the atmospheric ozone layer. The physical environment is increasingly being understood as an interconnected system. What occurs in one part of the system may very well affect other parts.

As our awareness of these interconnections has increased, we have begun to realize that we each have a role to play in the solution. The increased popularity of recycling programs illustrates this. The very small individual act of bringing newspapers or aluminum cans to the curbside for a weekly pick up can collectively have a large impact on reducing environmental degradation. At the same time, we have also realized the necessity of regulation and governmental controls to help curb pollution. Leaving the problem solely up to the individual polluters is no longer viable. Structural changes are increasingly needed to help alleviate levels of national and global pollution.

In a similar fashion, we must begin to understand poverty within the context of an interconnected environment. Here, however, our environment consists of the social, economic, and political institutions of society. Poverty must be understood as having profound ripple effects that denigrate and diminish those environments. This understanding also allows us to appreciate the fact that we each have a role to play in the alleviation of poverty. Individual actions over a sustained period of time can result in sizeable changes. Yet, as with our environmental problems, it is vital to recognize the importance that local, state, and federal governments must play in providing the resources, supports, and structure needed for a sustained effort.

Such a shift is now needed in the case of poverty. Widespread poverty amidst prosperity must be seen as unacceptable. The status quo of an exceedingly high risk of poverty during the life course must be recognized as detrimental to us all. This chapter and book has sketched out a rough framework for what a new understanding of this issue might look like. Now it is time to act on this understanding.

NOTES

1. Portions of this chapter have been adapted and updated from *One Nation, Underprivileged: Why American Poverty Affects Us All.*
2. This is much more the case within the conservative version of the old paradigm. The liberal version recognizes to a greater extent that certain opportunities (such as a decent education) must also be made available.
3. This is not to say that numbers and empirical work are unimportant. On the contrary, I view them as highly important. However, my point is that empirical work represents only one aspect of poverty. It is essential to understand and appreciate the human meaning as well and to let that inform one's work. As I have argued before, such an understanding calls for a variety of approaches to studying poverty, including a range of qualitative methodologies.
4. However, one must always exert caution in making these types of one-to-one arguments at the macrolevel. Various factors may be operating in society to raise or lower the overall poverty rates. Simply because two trends are occurring at the same time by no means proves that one is causing the other to occur.
5. There has been much discussion with respect to revising the manner in which poverty is measured in the United States (see Chapter 2 by Timothy Smeeding). Yet these discussions have almost exclusively focused on better ways of measuring low income, not the wider concept of deprivation that has been proposed here.

REFERENCES

Bush, George W. 2002. "President Announces Welfare Reform Agenda." Speech at St. Luke's Catholic Church, February 26, Washington, DC.

Galbraith, John Kenneth. 1986. *A View from the Stands: Of People, Politics, Military Power and the Arts*. Boston: Houghton Mifflin.

Gilder, George. 2012. *Wealth and Poverty*. 2nd ed. New York: Regnery.

Glennerster, Howard. 2002. "United States Poverty Studies and Poverty Measurement: The Past Twenty-Five Years." *Social Service Review* 76:83–107.

Goffman, Erving. 1963. *Stigma: Notes on the Management of Spoiled Identity*. Englewood Cliffs, NJ: Prentice Hall.

Herrnstein, Richard J. and Charles Murray. 1994. *The Bell Curve: Intelligence and Class Structure in American Life*. New York: Free Press.

Holzer, Harry J., Diane Whitmore Schanzenback, Greg J. Duncan, and Jens Ludwig. 2007. "The Economic Costs of Poverty in the United States: Subsequent Effects of Children Growing Up Poor." Institute for Research on Poverty Discussion Paper no. 1327-07, Institute for Research on Poverty, University of Wisconsin, Madison.

Kingdon, John W. 1999. *America the Unusual*. New York: St. Martin's.

Mead, Lawrence. 1986. *Beyond Entitlement: The Social Obligations of Citizenship*. New York: Free Press.

Mead, Lawrence. 1992. *The New Politics of Poverty: The Nonworking Poor in America*. New York: Basic Books.

Rank, Mark Robert. 1994. *Living on the Edge: The Realities of Welfare in America*. New York: Columbia University Press.

Rank, Mark Robert. 2004. *One Nation, Underprivileged: Why American Poverty Affects Us All*. New York: Oxford University Press.

Rank, Mark Robert, Thomas A. Hirschl, and Kirk A. Foster. 2014. *Chasing the American Dream: Understanding What Shapes Our Fortunes*. New York: Oxford University Press.

Sawhill, Isabel V. 2003. "The Behavioral Aspects of Poverty." *Public Interest* 153:79–93.

Schwartz, Joel. 2000. *Fighting Poverty with Virtue: Moral Reform and America's Urban Poor, 1825–2000*. Bloomington: Indiana University Press.

Sen, Amartya. 1999. *Inequality Reexamined*. New York: Russell Sage Foundation.

Smith, Adam. [1759] 1976. *The Theory of Moral Sentiments*. Oxford: Clarendon Press.

Tocqueville, Alexis D. 1983. "Memoir on Pauperism." *Public Interest* 70:102–20.

Toner, Robin. 2002. "Rallies in Capital Protest Bush Welfare Proposals." *New York Times*, March 6, Section A, p. 17.

United National Development Programme. 2012. *Human Development Report 2013*. New York: United Nations.

Index
....

CPSIA information can be obtained
at www.ICGtesting.com
Printed in the USA
BVHW051148260120
570238BV00011B/4